CSG STATE DIRECTORY

Directory III - Administrative Officials 1999

CSG State Directory

Directory III
Administrative Officials
1999

The Council of State Governments
Lexington, Kentucky

Headquarters: (606) 244-8000
FAX: (606) 244-8001
E-mail: info@csg.org
Internet: www.csg.org

To order the print or CD-ROM format of:
Directory I — Elective Officials 1999
Directory II — Legislative Leadership, Committees and Staff 1999
Directory III — Administrative Officials 1999
or mailing lists of state government officials
contact Publication Sales Department: 1-800-800-1910.

ISBN 0-87292-854-3
90000>
9 780872 928541

The Council of State Governments

Promoting State Solutions Regionally and Nationally

The Council of State Governments, the multibranch association of the states and U.S. territories, works with state leaders across the nation and through its regions to put the best ideas and solutions into practice. To this end, The Council of State Governments:

- Builds leadership skills to improve decision-making;
- Advocates multistate problem-solving and partnerships;
- Interprets changing national and international conditions to prepare states for the future; and
- Promotes the sovereignty of the states and their role in the American federal system.

Founded in 1933, CSG is an innovative, nonprofit, nonpartisan organization promoting excellence in state government.

CSG is the premier information resource and institutional voice for the state government community.

Council Officers

Chair: Sen. Kenneth McClintock, P.R.
Chair-Elect: Rep. Tom Ryder, Ill.
Vice Chair: Sen. Manny M. Aragon, N.M.

President: Gov. Tommy Thompson, Wis.
President-Elect: Gov. Paul Patton, Ky.
Vice President: Gov. Dirk Kempthorne, Idaho

Council Offices

Headquarters:
2760 Research Park Drive
P.O. Box 11910
Lexington, KY 40578-1910
(606) 244-8000
FAX: (606) 244-8001
E-mail: info@csg.org
Internet: www.csg.org

Daniel M. Sprague, Executive Director
Bob Silvanik, Deputy Director

Eastern: Alan V. Sokolow, Director
5 World Trade Center, Suite 9241
New York, NY 10048, (212) 912-0128
FAX: (212) 912-0549, E-mail: csg-east@csg.org

Midwestern: Michael H. McCabe, Director
641 E. Butterfield Road, Suite 401
Lombard, IL 60148, (630) 810-0210
FAX: (630) 810-0145, E-mail: csg-midwest@csg.org

Southern: Colleen Cousineau, Director
3355 Lenox Road, Suite 1050
Atlanta, GA 30326, (404) 266-1271
FAX: (404) 266-1273, E-mail: csg-south@csg.org

Western: Kent Briggs, Director
121 Second Street, 4th Floor
San Francisco, CA 94105, (415) 974-6422
FAX: (415) 974-1747, E-mail: csg-west@csg.org
Denver, CO (303) 572-5454, FAX (303) 572-5499

Washington:
Jim Brown, General Counsel & Director
444 N. Capitol Street, NW, Suite 401
Washington, DC 20001, (202) 624-5460
FAX: (202) 624-5452, E-mail: csg-dc@csg.org

Manufactured in the United States of America

D024-9900
ISBN # 0-87292-854-3
Price: $49.99
This information is available on CD-ROM. Call 1-800-800-1910 for more information.

Call the Publication Sales Order Department
The Council of State Governments
1-800-800-1910

The Council of State Governments Regions

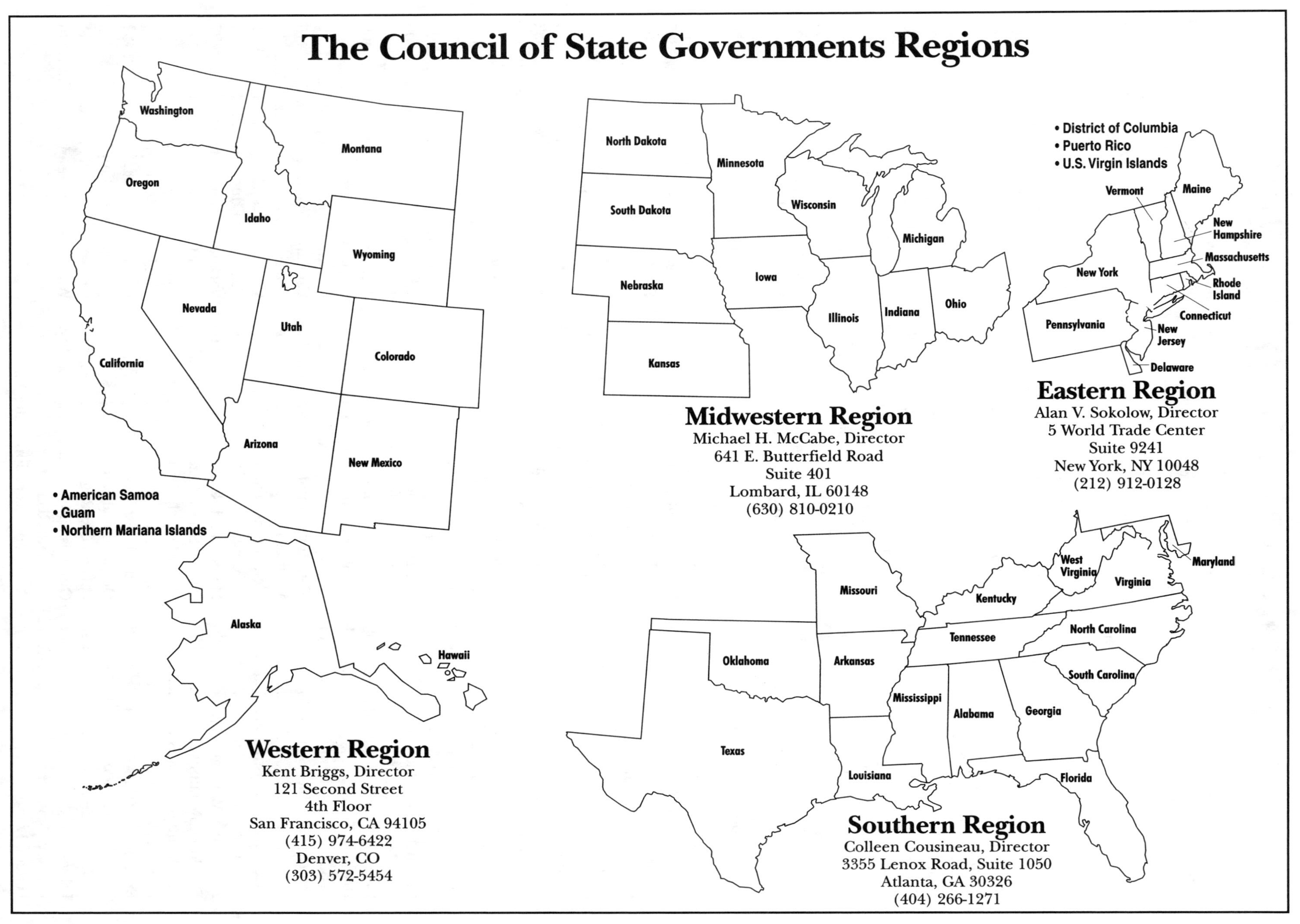

Western Region

Kent Briggs, Director
121 Second Street
4th Floor
San Francisco, CA 94105
(415) 974-6422
Denver, CO
(303) 572-5454

Midwestern Region

Michael H. McCabe, Director
641 E. Butterfield Road
Suite 401
Lombard, IL 60148
(630) 810-0210

Eastern Region

Alan V. Sokolow, Director
5 World Trade Center
Suite 9241
New York, NY 10048
(212) 912-0128

Southern Region

Colleen Cousineau, Director
3355 Lenox Road, Suite 1050
Atlanta, GA 30326
(404) 266-1271

Table of Contents

Overview

This annual directory provides basic information about elected and appointed officials with primary responsibility in more than 150 state government functions. The directory includes names, addresses, telephone, fax and e-mail addresses. The information is organized alphabetically by function (e.g., Labor) and by state and jurisdiction name. Generally, there is one entry per function for each state or jurisdiction. State names and jurisdications are listed whether or not there is a corresponding entry for a given section.

CSG collected the information for the 1999 directory between February and May 1999. California and Idaho's listings are reprints from the 1998 edition. Many of the listings for American Samoa, Colorado, District of Columbia, Iowa, New Jersey, New Mexico, Northern Mariana Islands and Pennsylvania also are from the prior volume. CSG reprinted the listings from its 1998 directory when updated information was not furnished.

The database for this directory is maintained by The Council of State Governments. Any additions or corrections to this directory should be sent to: Editor: CSG State Directories, The Council of State Governments, 2760 Research Park Drive, P.O. Box 11910, Lexington, KY 40578-1910. For verification purposes, all updates require the name, agency affiliation, address and phone number of the person submitting the updates.

Your comments regarding this directory or any other CSG publication are appreciated. Please send comments or inquiries to: Marketing Department, The Council of State Governments, 2760 Research Park Drive, P.O. Box 11910, Lexington, KY 40578-1910 or call the Marketing Department toll-free at (800) 800-1910.

Party Abbreviations

AI	Alaskan Independent
D	Democrat
DFL	Democrat-Farmer Labor
I	Independent
ICM	Independent Citizens Movement
IR	Independent Republican
NPP	New Progressive Party
NP	Nonpartisan
PDP	Popular Democratic Party
PIP	Puerto Rican Independent Party
Reform	Reform
R	Republican

The Council of State Governments
2760 Research Park Drive
P.O. Box 11910
Lexington, KY 40578-1910

Headquarters – (606) 244-8000
Publication Sales Department – (800) 800-1910
Fax – (606) 244-8001
E-mail – info@csg.org
Internet – www.csg.org
State Directory Questions – (606) 244-8000

Adjutant General

The executive or administrative head of the state's military service.

ALABAMA
Willie Alexander
Director
State Military Services
1720 Dickinson Dr.
P.O. Box 3711
Montgomery, AL 36109
Phone: (334) 271-7200
Fax: (334) 213-7511

ALASKA
Phillip Oates
Adjutant General
Dept. of Military & Veteran Affairs
P.O. Box 5800
Ft. Richardson, AK 99505
Phone: (907) 428-6003
Fax: (907) 428-6019

AMERICAN SAMOA

ARIZONA
David P. Rataczak
Adjutant General
Natl. Guard
5636 E. McDowell Rd.
Phoenix, AZ 85008
Phone: (602) 267-2700

ARKANSAS
Don Morrow
Adjutant General
State Military Dept.
Camp Robinson, Box 678
N. Little Rock, AR 72118
Phone: (501) 212-5001
Fax: (501) 212-5009

CALIFORNIA
Tandy Bozeman
Adjutant General
Dept. of Military
9800 Goethe Rd.
Sacramento, CA 95826-9101
Phone: (916) 854-3500

COLORADO
William A. Westerdahl
Adjutant General
Dept. of Military Affairs
6848 S. Revere Pkwy.
Englewood, CO 80112
Phone: (303) 397-3000
Fax: (303) 397-3003

CONNECTICUT
David W. Gay
Adjutant General
Military Dept.
Natl. Guard Armory
360 Broad St.
Hartford, CT 06105
Phone: (860) 524-4953

DELAWARE
Frank D. Vavala
Adjutant General
Natl. Guard
First Regiment Rd.
Wilmington, DE 19808
Phone: (302) 326-7001
Fax: (302) 326-7196
E-mail: vavalaf@de-ngnet.ngb.army.mil

DISTRICT OF COLUMBIA
Warren L. Freeman
Commanding General
Natl. Guard
2001 E. Capitol St.
Washington, DC 20003-1719
Phone: (202) 433-5220

FLORIDA
Ronald O. Harrison
Adjutant General
Dept. of Military Affairs
St. Francis Barracks
P.O. Box 1008
St. Augustine, FL 32085-1008
Phone: (904) 823-0100
Fax: (904) 823-0125
E-mail: harrisonr@fng2sur.army.mil

GEORGIA
William P. Bland, Jr.
Adjutant General
Dept. of Defense
P.O. Box 17965
Atlanta, GA 30316-0965
Phone: (404) 624-6001
Fax: (404) 624-6005

GUAM
Benny M. Paulino
Adjutant General
Natl. Guard
Military Affairs
622 E. Harmon, Industrial Park Rd.
Ft. Juan Muna
Tamuning, GU 96911-4421
Phone: (671) 475-0802
Fax: (671) 477-9317
E-mail: paulinobm@gu-arng.ngb.army.mil

HAWAII
E.V. Richardson
Adjutant General
Dept. of Defense
3949 Diamond Head Rd.
Honolulu, HI 96816
Phone: (808) 733-4246
Fax: (808) 733-4238

IDAHO
John F. Kane
Adjutant General
Military Div.
4040 W. Guard St.
Boise, ID 83705-5004
Phone: (208) 389-5242

ILLINOIS
Richard G. Austin
Adjutant General
Dept. of Military Affairs
Camp Lincoln
1301 N. MacArthur Blvd.
Springfield, IL 62702-2399
Phone: (217) 761-3500
Fax: (217) 761-3736

INDIANA
Robert J. Mitchell
Adjutant General
Military Dept.
2002 S. Holt Rd.
Indianapolis, IN 46241-4839
Phone: (317) 247-3274
Fax: (317) 247-3540

IOWA
Warren G. Lawson
Adjutant General
Natl. Guard
Camp Dodge
7700 NW Beaver Dr.
Johnston, IA 50131-1902
Phone: (515) 252-4211
Fax: (515) 252-4656

KANSAS
Gregory Gardner
Adjutant General
2800 SW Topeka Blvd.
Topeka, KS 66601
Phone: (785) 274-1001

KENTUCKY
John R. Groves, Jr.
Adjutant General
Dept. of Military Affairs
Boone Natl. Guard Ctr.
Frankfort, KY 40601
Phone: (502) 564-8558
Fax: (502) 564-6271

LOUISIANA
Bennett C. Landreneau, Jr.
Adjutant General
Dept. of Military
Jackson Barracks, Bldg. 1
New Orleans, LA 70146-0330
Phone: (504) 278-8211
Fax: (504) 278-6554

MAINE
Earl L. Adams
Commissioner/Adjutant General
Dept. of Defense & Veterans Services
33 State House Station
Augusta, ME 04333-0033
Phone: (207) 626-4225

MARYLAND
James F. Frettard
Adjutant General
Military Dept.
Fifth Regiment Armory
29th Div. St.
Baltimore, MD 21201-2288
Phone: (410) 576-6097
Fax: (410) 576-6079
E-mail: fretterdjf@md-arng.ngb.army.mil

MASSACHUSETTS
Raymond Vezina
Adjutant General
Army
c/o Camp Curtis Guild
Haverhill St.
Reading, MA 01867-1999
Phone: (617) 944-0500
Fax: (617) 727-5574

MICHIGAN
E. Gordon Stump
Adjutant General
Dept. of Military Affairs
2500 S. Washington Ave.
Lansing, MI 48913-5101
Phone: (517) 483-5507
Fax: (517) 482-0356

MINNESOTA
Eugene R. Andreotti
Adjutant General
Dept. of Military Affairs
Veterans Service Bldg.
20 W. 12th St.
St. Paul, MN 55155-2098
Phone: (651) 282-4666
Fax: (651) 282-4541
E-mail: bmelter@mdva.state.mn.us

MISSISSIPPI
James H. Garner
Special Advisor for Military Affairs
Dept. of the Military
P.O. Box 5027
Jackson, MS 39216-5021
Phone: (601) 313-6329
Fax: (601) 313-6251

MISSOURI
John D. Havens
Adjutant General
Natl. Guard
Dept. of Public Safety
2302 Militia Dr.
Jefferson City, MO 65101-1203
Phone: (573) 526-9711
Fax: (573) 526-9929
E-mail: tagmo@mo-arng.ngb.army.mil

MONTANA
John E. Prendergast
Adjutant General
Dept. of Military Affairs
P.O. Box 202101
Helena, MT 59620
Phone: (406) 841-3010
Fax: (406) 841-3335

NEBRASKA
Stan Heng
Adjutant General
Military Dept.
Natl. Guard Ctr.
1300 Military Rd.
Lincoln, NE 68508-1090
Phone: (402) 471-7114
Fax: (402) 471-7171

NEVADA
Tony Clark
Adjutant General
Military Dept.
2525 S. Carson St.
Carson City, NV 89701
Phone: (775) 887-7302
Fax: (775) 887-7369

NEW HAMPSHIRE
John E. Blair
Adjutant General
1 Airport Rd.
Concord, NH 03301-5353
Phone: (603) 271-1200
Fax: (603) 271-2110

NEW JERSEY
Paul J. Glazar
Adjutant General
Dept. of Military & Veterans Affairs
Eggert Crossing Rd.
P.O. Box 340
Trenton, NJ 08625-0340
Phone: (609) 530-6957
Fax: (609) 530-7097

NEW MEXICO
Melvin S. Montano
Adjutant General
Ofc. of Military Affairs
Natl. Guard Bldg.
47 Bataan Blvd.
Santa Fe, NM 87505-4695
Phone: (505) 474-1202
Fax: (505) 474-1289

NEW YORK
John H. Fenimore
Adjutant General
Military & Naval Affairs
330 Old Niskayuna Rd.
Latham, NY 12110-2224
Phone: (518) 786-4501

NORTH CAROLINA
Gerald A. Rudisill
Adjutant General
Div. of the Natl. Guard
Crime Control & Public Safety
4105 Reedy Creek Rd.
Raleigh, NC 27607-6410
Phone: (919) 664-6101
Fax: (919) 664-6400

NORTH DAKOTA
Keith Bjerke
Adjutant General
Natl. Guard
P.O. Box 5511
Bismarck, ND 58506-5511
Phone: (701) 224-5100
Fax: (701) 224-5180
E-mail: bjerkekd@nd-arng.ngb.army.mil

NORTHERN MARIANA ISLANDS

OHIO
John Smith
Adjutant General
2825 W. Granville Rd.
Columbus, OH 43235-2789
Phone: (614) 336-7070
Fax: (614) 336-7074

OKLAHOMA
Stephen Cortright
Adjutant General
Dept. of the Military
3501 Military Cir.
Oklahoma City, OK 73111-4398
Phone: (405) 425-8000
Fax: (405) 425-8524

OREGON
Alex Burgin
Adjutant General
Military Dept.
1776 Militia Way, SE
Salem, OR 97309-5407
Phone: (503) 945-3981
Fax: (503) 945-3987

PENNSYLVANIA
William B. Lynch
Adjutant General
Dept. of Military & Veterans Affairs
Ft. Indiantown Gap
Annville, PA 17003
Phone: (717) 861-8500
Fax: (717) 861-8481
E-mail: lynchwb@pa.arng.ngb.army

PUERTO RICO
Emilio Diaz Colon
Adjutant General
Natl. Guard
P.O. Box 902-3786
San Juan, PR 00902-3786
Phone: (787) 724-1295
Fax: (787) 723-6360

RHODE ISLAND
Reginald Centracchio
Major General
Natl. Guard/Emergency Mgmt. Agency
Command Readiness Ctr.
645 New London Ave.
Cranston, RI 02920
Phone: (401) 457-4102
Fax: (401) 457-4308
E-mail: tagcri-arng.ngb.army.mil

SOUTH CAROLINA
Stan Spears
Adjutant General
1 Natl. Guard Rd.
Columbia, SC 29201-4766
Phone: (803) 806-4217

SOUTH DAKOTA
Phillip Killey
Adjutant General
Dept. of Military & Veterans Affairs
425 E. Capitol Ave.
Pierre, SD 57501
Phone: (605) 773-3269
Fax: (605) 773-5380

TENNESSEE
Dan Wood
Adjutant General
Dept. of Military
3041 Sidco Dr.
Nashville, TN 37204
Phone: (615) 313-3001
Fax: (615) 313-3100

TEXAS
Daniel James, III
Adjutant General
Adjutant Gen's. Dept.
Camp Mabry, Bldg. 8
Austin, TX 78763
Phone: (512) 465-5006
Fax: (512) 465-5578

U.S. VIRGIN ISLANDS
Jean A. Romney
Major General
Natl. Guard
4031 La Grande Princesse, Lot 1B
Christiansted, VI 00820
Phone: (340) 712-7711
Fax: (340) 712-7782

UTAH
James Miller
Adjutant General
Natl. Guard
12953 S. Minuteman Dr.
Draper, UT 84020
Phone: (801) 523-4401
Fax: (801) 523-4677
E-mail: millerj
@ut-arng.ngb.army.mil

VERMONT
Martha Rainville
Adjutant General
Military Dept.
Green Mountain Armory
Colchester, VT 05446
Phone: (802) 654-0124
Fax: (802) 654-0425

VIRGINIA
Claude A. Williams
Adjutant General
Dept. of Military Affairs
VAAG
10th St., Bldg. 316
Blackstone, VA 23824
Phone: (804) 298-6102
Fax: (804) 298-6338

WASHINGTON
Greg Barlow
Adjutant General
Dept. of the Military
M/S: TA-20
Camp Murray
Tacoma, WA 98430-5000
Phone: (253) 512-8000
Fax: (253) 512-8497

WEST VIRGINIA
Allen Tackett
Adjutant General
1707 Coonskin Dr.
Charleston, WV 25311
Phone: (304) 341-6316
Fax: (304) 341-6466

WISCONSIN
Jerome Berard
Adjutant General
Dept. of Military Affairs
2400 Wright St.
P.O. Box 8111
Madison, WI 53708-8111
Phone: (608) 242-3001
Fax: (608) 242-3111

WYOMING
Ed Boenisch
Adjutant General
Dept. of the Military
P.O. Box 1709
Cheyenne, WY 82003
Phone: (307) 772-5234
Fax: (307) 772-5910

Administration

Umbrella agency of administration that coordinates administrative services provided to state agencies.

ALABAMA
Nick D. Bailey
Executive Secretary
Governor's Ofc.
Executive Dept.
State Capitol Bldg.
600 Dexter Ave., Ste. 104-N
Montgomery, AL 36104
Phone: (334) 242-7100
Fax: (334) 242-3004

ALASKA
Robert Poe, Jr.
Commissioner
Dept. of Administration
P.O. Box 110200
Juneau, AK 99811
Phone: (907) 465-2200
Fax: (907) 465-2135

AMERICAN SAMOA
Eliu Paopao
Acting Director
Dept. of Adm. Services
AS Govt.
Pago Pago, AS 96799
Phone: (684) 633-4156
Fax: (684) 633-1841

ARIZONA
J. Elliott Hibbs
Director
Dept. of Administration
Capitol Tower, Rm. 601
1700 W. Washington
Phoenix, AZ 85007
Phone: (602) 542-1500
Fax: (602) 542-2199
E-mail: ehibbs
@gv.state.az.us

ARKANSAS
Richard Weiss
Director
Dept. of Finance & Administration
401 DFA Bldg.
1509 W. 7th St.
Little Rock, AR 72201
Phone: (501) 682-2242
Fax: (501) 682-1086
E-mail: richard.weiss
@dfa.state.ar.us

CALIFORNIA
Steve Olsen
Chief Deputy Director
Dept. of Services
1325 J St., Ste. 1910
Sacramento, CA 95814
Phone: (916) 323-9969

Peter G. Stamison
Director
Dept. of Services
1325 J St., Ste. 1910
Sacramento, CA 95814
Phone: (916) 445-3441

COLORADO
Larry E. Trujillo, Sr.
Executive Director
Support Services
Dept. of Personnel
1525 Sherman St., 2nd Fl.
Denver, CO 80203
Phone: (303) 866-6559
Fax: (303) 866-6569

CONNECTICUT
Barbara Waters
Commissioner
Dept. of Adm. Services
165 Capitol Ave., Rm. 491
Hartford, CT 06106
Phone: (860) 713-5100

DELAWARE
Vincent P. Meconi
Secretary
Dept. of Adm. Services
Townsend Bldg.
P.O. Box 1401
Dover, DE 19903
Phone: (302) 739-3611
Fax: (302) 739-6704
E-mail: vmecon
i@state.de.us

DISTRICT OF COLUMBIA

FLORIDA
Thomas Barry, Jr.
Secretary
Director's Ofc.
Dept. of Transportation
Haydon Burns Bldg.
605 Suwannee St.
Tallahassee, FL 32399-0450
Phone: (850) 414-5205
Fax: (850) 488-5526
E-mail: tom.barry
@dot.state.fl.us

Thomas D. McGurk
Secretary
Director's Ofc.
Dept. of Mgmt. Services
4050 Esplanade Way, Ste. 250
Tallahassee, FL 32399-0950
Phone: (850) 488-2786
Fax: (850) 922-6149
E-mail: mcgurkt
@dms.state.fl.us

GEORGIA
Dotty W. Roach
Commissioner
Dept. of Adm. Services
200 Piedmont Ave., Ste. 1804
Atlanta, GA 30334-5500
Phone: (404) 656-5514
Fax: (404) 651-9595

GUAM
Michael J. Reidy
Director
Dept. of Administration
P.O. Box 884
Hagatna, GU 96932
Phone: (671) 475-1136
Fax: (671) 477-6788

HAWAII
Raymond Sato
Comptroller
Dept. of Accounting & Services
P.O. Box 119
Honolulu, HI 96810
Phone: (808) 586-0400
Fax: (808) 586-0707

IDAHO
Pamela Ahrens
Director
Dept. of Administration
650 W. State St., Rm. 100
Boise, ID 83720
Phone: (208) 334-3382

ILLINOIS
Michael S. Schwartz
Director
Dept. of Central Mgmt. Services
715 Stratton Ofc. Bldg.
401 S. Spring
Springfield, IL 62706
Phone: (217) 782-2141
Fax: (217) 524-1880

INDIANA
Betty Cockrum
Commissioner
Dept. of Administration
IGC-South, Rm. W479
402 W. Washington St.
Indianapolis, IN 46204
Phone: (317) 232-3115
Fax: (317) 233-5022

IOWA
Richard Haines
Director
Dept. of Services
Hoover State Ofc. Bldg.
1305 E. Walnut
Des Moines, IA 50319
Phone: (515) 281-3196
Fax: (515) 242-5974

KANSAS
Daniel Stanley
Secretary
Dept. of Administration
State Capitol, Rm. 263-E
Topeka, KS 66612-1572
Phone: (785) 296-3011
Fax: (785) 296-2702

KENTUCKY
Don Speer
Commissioner
Finance & Administration Cabinet
Dept. of Administration
Capitol Annex, Rm. 362
700 Capitol Ave.
Frankfort, KY 40601
Phone: (502) 564-2317
Fax: (502) 564-4279

LOUISIANA
Mark Drennen
Commissioner
Div. of Administration
P.O. Box 94095
Baton Rouge, LA 70804-9095
Phone: (225) 342-7000
Fax: (225) 342-1057

MAINE
Janet E. Waldron
Commissioner
Dept. of Adm. & Financial Services
78 State House Station
Augusta, ME 04333-0078
Phone: (207) 624-7800

MARYLAND
Peta Richkus
Secretary
Ofc. of the Secretary
Dept. of Services
301 W. Preston St., Rm. 1401
Baltimore, MD 21201
Phone: (410) 767-4960
Fax: (410) 333-5480
E-mail: prichkus@dgs.state.md.us

MASSACHUSETTS
Andrew Natsios
Secretary
Executive Ofc. for Administration & Finance
State House, Rm. 373
Boston, MA 02133
Phone: (617) 727-2040
Fax: (617) 727-2496

MICHIGAN
Janet E. Phipps
Director
Dept. of Mgmt. & Budget
320 S. Walnut
Lansing, MI 48909
Phone: (517) 373-1004
Fax: (517) 373-7268

MINNESOTA
David Fisher
Commissioner
Dept. of Administration
200 Administration Bldg.
50 Sherburne Ave.
St. Paul, MN 55155
Phone: (651) 296-1424
Fax: (651) 297-7909

MISSISSIPPI
Andy Cole
Deputy Director
Dept. of Finance & Administration
1501 Sillers Bldg.
Jackson, MS 39201
Phone: (601) 359-3635
Fax: (601) 359-2470

Edward L. Ranck
Director
Dept. of Finance & Administration
906 Sillers Bldg.
Jackson, MS 39201
Phone: (601) 359-3204
Fax: (601) 359-2405

MISSOURI
Richard A. Hanson
Commissioner
Administration
Ofc. of Administration
State Capitol, Rm. 125
P.O. Box 809
Jefferson City, MO 65102
Phone: (573) 751-3311
Fax: (573) 751-1212
E-mail: hansod@mail.oa.state.mo.us

MONTANA
Lois A. Menzies
Director & Ex Officio State Treasurer
Dept. of Administration
Rm. 155, Mitchell Bldg.
P.O. Box 200101
Helena, MT 59620-0101
Phone: (406) 444-2032
Fax: (406) 444-2812
E-mail: lmenzies@mt.gov

NEBRASKA
Lori McClurg
Director
Dept. of Adm. Services
P.O. Box 94664
Lincoln, NE 68509-4664
Phone: (402) 471-2331
Fax: (402) 471-4157

NEVADA
John P. Comeaux
Director
Dept. of Administration
Blasdel Bldg., Rm. 200
209 E. Musser St.
Carson City, NV 89701
Phone: (775) 684-0222
Fax: (775) 684-0260

NEW HAMPSHIRE
Donald S. Hill
Commissioner
Commissioner's Ofc.
Dept. of Adm. Services
25 Capitol St., Rm. 120
Concord, NH 03301-6312
Phone: (603) 271-3201

NEW JERSEY
George M. Gross
Administrator
Services Administration
Dept. of Treasury
P.O. Box 039
Trenton, NJ 08625-0039
Phone: (609) 292-4330
Fax: (609) 984-8495

NEW MEXICO
Steven Beffort
Secretary
Services Dept.
715 Alta Vista
P.O. Drawer 26110
Santa Fe, NM 87502-0110
Phone: (505) 827-2000
Fax: (505) 827-2041
E-mail: cjackson@state.nm.us

NEW YORK
Joseph Seymour
Commissioner
Ofc. of Services
Corning Tower Bldg., 41st Fl.
Empire State Plz.
Albany, NY 12242
Phone: (518) 474-5991
Fax: (518) 486-9179

NORTH CAROLINA
Katie G. Dorsett
Secretary
Dept. of Administration
116 W. Jones St.
Raleigh, NC 27603
Phone: (919) 733-7232
Fax: (919) 733-9571

NORTH DAKOTA

NORTHERN MARIANA ISLANDS
Jose I. Deleon Guerrero
Special Assistant for Administration
Ofc. of the Governor
Caller Box 10007
Saipan, MP 96950
Phone: (670) 664-2212
Fax: (670) 664-2210

OHIO
Sandra Drabik
Director
Dept. of Adm. Services
30 E. Broad St., 40th Fl.
Columbus, OH 43266
Phone: (614) 466-6511
Fax: (614) 644-8151

OKLAHOMA
Pam Warren
Secretary of Administration
Dept. of Central Services
2401 N. Lincoln Blvd., Ste. 206
Oklahoma City, OK 73105
Phone: (405) 521-2121
Fax: (405) 425-2713

OREGON
Jon Yunker
Director
Dept. of Adm. Services
155 Cottage St., NE
Salem, OR 97310
Phone: (503) 378-3104
Fax: (503) 373-7643
E-mail: jon.yunker@state.or.us

PENNSYLVANIA
Tom Paese
Cabinet Secretary
Ofc. of Administration
Rm. 207, Finance Bldg.
Harrisburg, PA 17120
Phone: (717) 787-9945
Fax: (717) 783-4374
E-mail: tpaese@state.pa.us

PUERTO RICO
Maribel Rodriguez
Director
Central Ofc. of Personnel Administration
P.O. Box 8476
San Juan, PR 00910
Phone: (787) 721-4300
Fax: (787) 722-3390

RHODE ISLAND
Robert L. Carl, Jr.
Director
Dept. of Administration
1 Capitol Hill
Providence, RI 02903
Phone: (401) 222-2280
Fax: (401) 222-6436

SOUTH CAROLINA
Richard W. Kelly
Chief of Staff
Budget & Control Board
Wade Hampton Bldg.
P.O. Box 12444
Columbia, SC 29211
Phone: (803) 734-2320

SOUTH DAKOTA
Tom D. Geraets
Commissioner
Bur. of Administration
500 E. Capitol Ave.
Pierre, SD 57501
Phone: (605) 773-3688
Fax: (605) 773-3887

TENNESSEE
John Ferguson
Commissioner
Finance & Administration
State Capitol, 1st Fl.
600 Charlotte Ave.
Nashville, TN 37243-0001
Phone: (615) 741-2401
Fax: (615) 741-9872

TEXAS
Tom Treadway
Executive Director
Services Comm.
1711 San Jacinto
P.O. Box 13047
Austin, TX 78701-3047
Phone: (512) 463-3446
Fax: (512) 463-7966
E-mail: tomtreadway@gsc.state.tx.us

U.S. VIRGIN ISLANDS
Marc Biggs
Acting Commissioner
Dept. of Property & Procurement
Sub Base, Bldg. 1
St. Thomas, VI 00801
Phone: (340) 774-0828
Fax: (340) 777-9587

UTAH
Raylene Ireland
Executive Director
Dept. of Adm. Services
3120 State Ofc. Bldg.
Salt Lake City, UT 84114
Phone: (801) 538-3010
Fax: (801) 538-3844
E-mail: rireland.asitmain@state.ut.us

VERMONT
Kathleen C. Hoyt
Secretary
Agency of Administration
109 State St.
Montpelier, VT 05609-0201
Phone: (802) 828-3322
Fax: (802) 828-3320
E-mail: khoyt@state.vt.us

VIRGINIA
G. Bryan Slater
Secretary of Administration
Governor's Cabinet
202 N. 9th St., Ste. 633
Richmond, VA 23219
Phone: (804) 786-1201
Fax: (804) 371-0038

WASHINGTON
Marsha Tadano Long
Director
Dept. of Administration
P.O. Box 41000
Olympia, WA 98504-1000
Phone: (360) 902-7300
Fax: (360) 586-5898

WEST VIRGINIA
Joseph F. Markus
Cabinet Secretary
Dept. of Administration
State Capitol, Rm. E119
1900 Kanawha Blvd., E.
Charleston, WV 25305
Phone: (304) 558-4331
Fax: (304) 558-2999

WISCONSIN
Mark Bugher
Secretary
Dept. of Administration
101 E. Wilson, 10th Fl.
P.O. Box 7869
Madison, WI 53707
Phone: (608) 266-1741
Fax: (608) 267-3842

WYOMING
Art Ellis
Director
Dept. of Administration & Info.
Emerson Bldg., Rm. 104
2001 Capitol Ave.
Cheyenne, WY 82002
Phone: (307) 777-7201
Fax: (307) 777-3633

Aeronautics

Issues rules and regulations on aviation safety and prepares plans for the state's airway systems.

ALABAMA
John C. Eagerton
Director
Dept. of Aeronautics
RSA Plz., Ste. 544
770 Washington Ave.
Montgomery, AL 36130-0351
Phone: (334) 242-4480
Fax: (334) 240-3274

ALASKA
Tony Johansen
Regional Director
Central Region
Dept. of Transportation & Public Facilities
P.O. Box 196900
Anchorage, AK 99519-6900
Phone: (907) 266-1440
Fax: (907) 248-1573

AMERICAN SAMOA
Faauaa K. Elisara
Director
Dept. of Port Administration
Pago Pago, AS 96799
Phone: (684) 633-4251
Fax: (684) 633-5281

ARIZONA
Gary Adams
Assistant Director
Aeronautics Div.
Dept. of Transportation
1833 W. Buchanan St.
Phoenix, AZ 85007
Phone: (602) 255-6234

ARKANSAS
John Knight
Director
Dept. of Aeronautics
Regional Airport Terminal
1 Airport Dr., 3rd Fl.
Little Rock, AR 72202
Phone: (501) 376-6781
Fax: (501) 378-0820

CALIFORNIA
Marlin Beckwith
Program Manager
Aeronautics Program
Dept. of Transportation
P.O. Box 942874
Sacramento, CA 94274
Phone: (916) 654-5470
Fax: (809) 722-7867

COLORADO
Travis Vallin
Director
Aeronautics Div.
Dept. of Transportation
56 Inverness Dr., E.
Englewood, CO 80112
Phone: (303) 792-2160
Fax: (303) 792-2180

CONNECTICUT
Robert F. Juliano
Bureau Chief
Bur. of Aviation & Ports
Dept. of Transportation
2800 Berlin Tpke.
P.O. Box 317546
Newington, CT 06131-7546
Phone: (860) 594-2529

DELAWARE
Anthony Amato
Administrator
Aeronautics Administration
Dept. of Transportation
Transportation Administration Bldg.
Dover, DE 19901
Phone: (302) 739-3264
Fax: (302) 739-5711

DISTRICT OF COLUMBIA

FLORIDA

GEORGIA
Jack Joiner
Manager
Aviation Programs
Dept. of Transportation
276 Memorial Dr., SW
Atlanta, GA 30303
Phone: (404) 651-5206

GUAM
Gerald Yingling
Executive Manager
Airport Authority
P.O. Box 8770
Tamuning, GU 96931
Phone: (671) 646-0300
Fax: (671) 646-8823
E-mail: drew@iftech.net

HAWAII
Jerry Matsuda
Airport Administrator
Dept. of Transportation
Honolulu Intl. Airport
Honolulu, HI 96819
Phone: (808) 838-8600
Fax: (808) 838-8750

IDAHO
Bart Welsh
Chief
Bur. of Aeronautics
P.O. Box 7129
Boise, ID 83707
Phone: (208) 334-8775

ILLINOIS
William L. Blake
Director
Div. of Aeronautics
Dept. of Transportation
Capitol Airport
Springfield, IL 62707
Phone: (217) 785-8515
Fax: (217) 785-4533

INDIANA
Larry Goode
Division Chief
Intermodal Transportation Div.
Dept. of Transportation
100 N. Senate Ave., N901
Indianapolis, IN 46204
Phone: (317) 232-1495
Fax: (317) 232-1499

IOWA
Michael Audino
Director
Air & Transit Div.
Dept. of Transportation
100 E. Euclid Ave., # 7
Des Moines, IA 50313
Phone: (515) 237-3321

KANSAS
Michael Armour
Director of Aviation
Div. of Aviation
Dept. of Transportation
Docking State Ofc. Bldg., 7th Fl.
300 SW 10th St.
Topeka, KS 66612-1568
Phone: (785) 296-2553
Fax: (785) 296-3833

KENTUCKY
Jesse Sams
Director
Ofc. of Aeronautics
Transportation Cabinet
125 Holmes St.
Frankfort, KY 40622
Phone: (502) 564-4480
Fax: (502) 564-7953

LOUISIANA
Anthony Culp
Director of Aviation
Dept. of Transportation & Dev.
P.O. Box 94245, Rm. 240
Baton Rouge, LA 70804
Phone: (225) 379-1242
Fax: (225) 379-1961

MAINE
Ron Roy
Director
Aeronautics Div.
Dept. of Transportation
16 State House Station
Augusta, ME 04333
Phone: (207) 287-3185

MARYLAND
Theodore E. Mathison
Executive Director
Aviation Administration
Dept. of Transportation
P.O. Box 8766
BWI Airport, MD 21240-0755
Phone: (410) 859-7060
Fax: (410) 850-4729

MASSACHUSETTS
Sherman W. Saltmarsh, Jr.
Chair
Aeronautics Comm.
10 Park Plz., Rm. 6620
Boston, MA 02116-3966
Phone: (617) 973-8881
Fax: (617) 973-8889

MICHIGAN
William E. Gehman
Director
Bur. of Aeronautics
2700 E. Airport Service Dr.
Lansing, MI 48906
Phone: (517) 335-9943

MINNESOTA
Raymond Rought
Director
Ofc. of Aeronautics
Dept. of Transportation
222 E. Plato Blvd.
St. Paul, MN 55107
Phone: (651) 296-8202
Fax: (651) 297-5643
E-mail: ray.rought
@aero.dot.state.mn.us

MISSISSIPPI
Elton Jay
Director
Aeronautics Comm.
P.O. Box 1850
Jackson, MS 39215
Phone: (601) 359-7850
Fax: (601) 359-7855

MISSOURI
Brian Weiler
Administrator
Aviation Unit
Dept. of Hwys. &
Transportation
Hwy. Bldg.
P.O. Box 270
Jefferson City, MO 65102
Phone: (573) 526-7912
Fax: (573) 526-4709
E-mail: weileb
@mail.modot.state.mo.us

MONTANA
Michael D. Ferguson
Administrator
Aeronautics Div.
Dept. of Transportation
2630 Airport Rd.
Helena, MT 59620-0507
Phone: (406) 444-2506
Fax: (406) 444-2519

NEBRASKA
Kent Penney
Director
Dept. of Aeronautics
Lincoln Municipal Airport
P.O. Box 82088
Lincoln, NE 68501
Phone: (402) 471-2371
Fax: (402) 471-2906

NEVADA

NEW HAMPSHIRE
Jack Ferns
Director
Aeronautics Div.
Dept. of Transportation
65 Airport Rd.
Concord, NH 03301-5298
Phone: (603) 271-2551
Fax: (603) 271-1689

NEW JERSEY
Theodore Matthews
Executive Director
Div. of Aeronautics
Dept. of Transportation
1035 Pkwy. Ave.
P.O. Box 610
Trenton, NJ 08625-0610
Phone: (609) 530-8026
Fax: (609) 530-2900

NEW MEXICO
John D. Rice
Director
Aviation Div.
State Hwy. &
Transportation Dept.
P.O. Box 1149
1550 Pacheco St.
Santa Fe, NM 87505
Phone: (505) 827-1525
Fax: (505) 827-1531

NEW YORK
Joseph Boardman
Commissioner
Dept. of Transportation
State Ofc. Bldg. Campus,
Bldg. 5
Albany, NY 12232
Phone: (518) 457-4422
Fax: (518) 457-5583

NORTH CAROLINA
William H. Williams, Jr.
Director
Div. of Aviation
Dept. of Transportation
P.O. Box 25201
Raleigh, NC 27611
Phone: (919) 571-4904
Fax: (919) 571-4908

NORTH DAKOTA
Gary R. Ness
Director
Aeronautics Comm.
P.O. Box 5020
Bismarck, ND 58502-5020
Phone: (701) 328-9650
Fax: (701) 328-9656
E-mail: gness
@pioneer.state.nd.us

NORTHERN MARIANA ISLANDS
Carlos H. Salas
Executive Director
Commonwealth Ports
Authority
P.O. Box 1055
Saipan, MP 96950
Phone: (670) 644-3500
Fax: (670) 234-5962
E-mail: cpa.csalas
@saipan.com

OHIO
Robert H. Rudolph
Administrator
Ofc. of Aviation
Dept. of Transportation
2829 W. Dublin-Granville
Rd.
Columbus, OH 43235
Phone: (614) 793-5042
Fax: (614) 793-8972

OKLAHOMA
William Miller
Director
Aeronautics Comm.
200 NE 21st St.
Oklahoma City, OK 73105
Phone: (405) 521-2377
Fax: (405) 521-2379
E-mail: b.miller@odot.org

OREGON
Betsy Johnson
Manager
Aeronautics Div.
Dept. of Transportation
3040 25th St., SE
Salem, OR 97310
Phone: (503) 378-8689
Fax: (503) 373-1688

PENNSYLVANIA
Elizabeth Sarge Voras
Special Assistant to the
Secretary
Aviation, Rail & Ports
Dept. of Transportation
Forum Pl., 9th Fl.
555 Walnut St.
Harrisburg, PA 17101-1900
Phone: (717) 783-2026
Fax: (717) 787-5491

PUERTO RICO
Hector Rivera
Executive Director
Port Authority
G.P.O. Box 362829
San Juan, PR 00936-2829
Phone: (787) 729-8806
Fax: (787) 722-7867

RHODE ISLAND
Elaine Roberts
Executive Director
Div. of Airports
Airport Corp.
T.F. Green State Airport
Warwick, RI 02886
Phone: (401) 737-4000
Fax: (401) 732-4953

SOUTH CAROLINA
Ira E. Coward, II
Director
Div. of Aeronautics
Dept. of Commerce
P.O. Box 280068
Columbia, SC 29228
Phone: (803) 896-6261
Fax: (803) 896-6277

SOUTH DAKOTA
Ron Wheeler
Secretary
Dept. of Transportation
700 E. Broadway
Pierre, SD 57501
Phone: (605) 773-3265
Fax: (605) 773-3921

TENNESSEE
Fred Vogt
Director
Div. of Aeronautics
Dept. of Transportation
P.O. Box 17326
Nashville, TN 37217
Phone: (615) 741-3208
Fax: (615) 741-4959

TEXAS
David S. Fulton
Director
Aviation Div.
Dept. of Transportation
125 E. 11th St.
Austin, TX 78701-2483
Phone: (512) 416-4501

U.S. VIRGIN ISLANDS
Gordon Finch
Executive Director
Port Authority
P.O. Box 301707
St. Thomas, VI 00803
Phone: (340) 774-1629
Fax: (340) 774-0025

UTAH
Robert Philip Barrett
Director
Aeronautical Operations
Dept. of Transportation
135 N. 2400 W.
Salt Lake City, UT 84116
Phone: (801) 715-2262
Fax: (801) 715-2276
E-mail: rbarrett
@dot.state.ut.us

VERMONT
Greg Maguire
Director
Div. of Rail, Air & Public
Transportation
Agency of Transportation
Natl. Life Bldg., Drawer 33
Montpelier, VT 05633-5001
Phone: (802) 828-2093
Fax: (802) 828-2829

VIRGINIA
Kenneth F. Wiegand
Director
Dept. of Aviation
5702 Gulfstream Rd.
Richmond Intl. Airport, VA
23250-2422
Phone: (804) 236-3625
Fax: (804) 236-3635

WASHINGTON
Bill Brubaker
Director
Div. of Aviation
8900 E. Marginal Way
Seattle, WA 98108
Phone: (206) 764-4131
Fax: (206) 764-4001

WEST VIRGINIA
Susan Chernenko
Acting Director
Aeronautics Comm.
Bldg. 5, Rm. A109
1900 Kanawha Blvd., E.
Charleston, WV 25305
Phone: (304) 558-0444
Fax: (304) 558-1004

WISCONSIN
Geoffrey Wheeler
Administrator
Div. of State Agency
Services
Dept. of Administration
101 E. Wilson, 6th Fl.
P.O. Box 7867
Madison, WI 53707
Phone: (608) 266-1011
Fax: (608) 267-0600

WYOMING
Richard Spaeth
Administrator
Aeronautics Div.
Transportation Dept.
P.O. Box 1708
Cheyenne, WY 82003
Phone: (307) 777-4880
Fax: (307) 637-7352

Aging

Develops and strengthens services for the aged and conducts or promotes research into their problems.

ALABAMA
Melissa Mauser-Galvin
Executive Director
Comm. of Aging
RSA Plz., Ste. 470
Montgomery, AL 36130
Phone: (334) 242-5743
Fax: (334) 242-5594

ALASKA
Jane Demmert
Executive Director
Comm. on Aging
Dept. of Administration
P.O. Box 110209
Juneau, AK 99811-0209
Phone: (907) 465-3250
Fax: (907) 465-4108

AMERICAN SAMOA
Lualemaga Faoa
Director
Territorial Administration on Aging
AS Govt.
Pago Pago, AS 96799
Phone: (684) 633-1251
Fax: (684) 633-7723

ARIZONA
Malena Albo
Assistant Director
Aging & Adult Administration
Dept. of Economic Security
1789 W. Jefferson
Phoenix, AZ 85007
Phone: (602) 542-4446

ARKANSAS
Herb Sanderson
Deputy Director
Aging & Adult Services
P.O. Box 1437
Little Rock, AR 72203
Phone: (501) 682-2441
Fax: (501) 682-8155

CALIFORNIA
Dixon Arnett
Director
Dept. of Aging
1600 K St.
Sacramento, CA 95814
Phone: (916) 322-5290

COLORADO
Rita Barreras
Director
Aging & Adult Services Div.
Dept. of Human Services
110 16th St., 2nd Fl.
Denver, CO 80202
Phone: (303) 620-4147
Fax: (303) 620-4189

CONNECTICUT
Cynthia Matthews
Executive Director
Comm. on Aging
25 Sigourney St., 12th Fl.
Hartford, CT 06106-5003
Phone: (860) 424-5360

DELAWARE
Eleanor Cain
Director
Div. of Aging & Physically Handicapped
Health & Social Services Dept.
1901 N. DuPont Hwy.
New Castle, DE 19720
Phone: (302) 577-4660
Fax: (302) 577-4793

DISTRICT OF COLUMBIA
E. Veronica Pace
Executive Director
Ofc. of Aging
441 4th St., NW
Washington, DC 20001-2714

FLORIDA
Gema Hernandez
Secretary
Director's Ofc.
Dept. of Elder Affairs
4040 Esplanade Way
Tallahassee, FL 32399-7000
Phone: (850) 414-2000
Fax: (850) 414-2004
E-mail: hernandezg@eldraffairs.org

GEORGIA
Judith Hagabak
Director
Div. of Aging Services
Dept. of Human Resources
2 Peachtree St., NW, Rm. 36-385
Atlanta, GA 30303
Phone: (404) 657-5255
Fax: (404) 657-5285

GUAM
Dennis G. Rodriguez
Director
Dept. of Public Health & Social Services
P.O. Box 2816
Hagatna, GU 96932
Phone: (671) 735-7102
Fax: (671) 734-5910
E-mail: dennis_ r_@NS.GOV.GU

HAWAII
Marilyn Seely
Director
Executive Ofc. on Aging
Ofc. of the Governor
250 S. Hotel St., Ste. 107
Honolulu, HI 96813-2831
Phone: (808) 586-0100
Fax: (808) 586-0185

IDAHO
Arlene Davidson
Director
Ofc. on Aging
Statehouse, Rm. 108
700 W. Jefferson
Boise, ID 83720
Phone: (208) 334-3833

ILLINOIS
Margo E. Schreiber
Director
Dept. on Aging
421 E. Capitol Ave., #100
Springfield, IL 62701-1789
Phone: (217) 785-2870

INDIANA
Debra Simmons Wilson
Director
Div. of Disability, Aging & Rehab.
Family & Social Services Administration
402 W. Washington, Rm. W451
Indianapolis, IN 46204
Phone: (317) 232-1147
Fax: (317) 232-1240

IOWA
Judy Conlin
Executive Director
Dept. of Elder Affairs
Clemens Bldg.
200 10th St.
Des Moines, IA 50309-3609
Phone: (515) 281-5187
Fax: (515) 281-4036
E-mail: judy.conlin@idea.state.ia.us

KANSAS
Thelma Gordon
Secretary
Dept. of Aging
New England Bldg.
503 S. Kansas, #1
Topeka, KS 66603-3404
Phone: (785) 296-4986
Fax: (785) 296-0256

KENTUCKY
Jerry Whitley
Director
Div. of Aging Services
Dept. for Social Services
275 E. Main St., 5 W.
Frankfort, KY 40621
Phone: (502) 564-6930
Fax: (502) 564-4595

LOUISIANA
Paul F. Arceneaux
Executive Director
Ofc. of Elderly Affairs
P.O. Box 80374
Baton Rouge, LA 70898
Phone: (225) 342-7100
Fax: (225) 342-7133

MAINE
Christine Gianopoulos
Director
Bur. of Elderly & Adult Services
Dept. of Human Services
11 State House Station
Augusta, ME 04333
Phone: (207) 624-5335

MARYLAND
Sue F. Ward
Secretary
Ofc. of the Secretary
Dept. of Aging
301 W. Preston St., Rm. 1007
Baltimore, MD 21201
Phone: (410) 767-1102
Fax: (410) 333-7943
E-mail: sfw@mail.ooa.state.md.us

MASSACHUSETTS
Lillian Glickman
Secretary
Executive Ofc. of Elder Affairs
One Ashburton Pl., 5th Fl., Rm. 517
Boston, MA 02108
Phone: (617) 727-7750
Fax: (617) 727-6944

MICHIGAN
Lynn Alexander
Director
Ofc. of Services to the Aging
Dept. of Community Health
611 W. Ottawa St.
Lansing, MI 48909
Phone: (517) 373-7876
Fax: (517) 373-4092

MINNESOTA
James Varpness
Executive Secretary
Board on Aging
Human Services Bldg., 4th Fl.
444 Lafayette Rd.
St. Paul, MN 55155
Phone: (651) 296-2770
Fax: (651) 297-7855

MISSISSIPPI
Eddie Anderson
Director
Council on Aging
Dept. of Human Services
P.O. Box 352
Jackson, MS 39205-0352
Phone: (601) 359-4929
Fax: (601) 359-4370

MISSOURI
Andrea Routh
Director
Div. of Aging
Dept. of Social Services
615 Howerton Ct.
P.O. Box 1337
Jefferson City, MO 65102
Phone: (573) 751-8535
Fax: (573) 751-8687
E-mail: arouth@mail.state.mo.us

MONTANA
Charlie Rehbein
Aging Coordinator
Aging Services Bur.
Dept. of Public Health & Human Services
111 Sanders St., Rm. 210
Helena, MT 59620
Phone: (406) 444-7788
Fax: (406) 444-7743

NEBRASKA
Mark Intermill
Deputy Director
Dept. of Health & Human Services
P.O. Box 95044
Lincoln, NE 68509-5044
Phone: (402) 471-4617
Fax: (402) 471-0820

NEVADA
Carla Sloan
Administrator
Div. for Aging Services
340 N. 11th St., Ste. 203
Las Vegas, NV 89101
Phone: (702) 486-3545
Fax: (702) 486-3572
E-mail: csloan@govmail.state.nv.us

NEW HAMPSHIRE
Catherine Keane
Acting Director
Div. of Elderly & Adult Services
Dept. of Health & Human Services
129 Pleasant St.
Brown Bldg.
Concord, NH 03301
Phone: (603) 271-4394
Fax: (603) 271-4643

NEW JERSEY
Susan Reinhard
Assistant Commissioner
Div. of Senior Affairs
Dept. of Community Affairs
101 S. Broad St.
P.O. Box 807
Trenton, NJ 08625-0807
Phone: (609) 292-3766
Fax: (609) 633-6609

NEW MEXICO
Michelle Lujan Grisham
Director
State Agency on Aging
228 E. Palace Ave.
Santa Fe, NM 87501
Phone: (505) 827-7640
Fax: (505) 827-7649

NEW YORK
Walter G. Hoefer
Director
Ofc. of the Aging
Agency Bldg. 2, 5th Fl.
Empire State Plz.
Albany, NY 12223
Phone: (518) 474-4425
Fax: (518) 474-1398

NORTH CAROLINA
Karen Gottovi
Director
Aging Div.
Dept. of Health & Human Services
693 Palmer Dr.
Raleigh, NC 27603-2001
Phone: (919) 733-3983

NORTH DAKOTA
Linda Wright
Director
Aging Services Div.
Dept. of Human Services
600 S. 2nd St., Ste. 1C
Bismarck, ND 58504-5729
Phone: (701) 328-8910
Fax: (701) 328-8989
E-mail: sowril@state.nd.us

NORTHERN MARIANA ISLANDS
Annie Flores
Director
Aging Ofc.
Community & Cultural Affairs
Caller Box 10007
Saipan, MP 96950
Phone: (670) 233-1320
Fax: (670) 233-1327

OHIO
Joan Lawrence
Director
Comm. on Aging
Dept. of Aging
50 W. Broad St., 9th Fl.
Columbus, OH 43266
Phone: (614) 466-7246
Fax: (614) 466-5741

OKLAHOMA
Howard Hendrick
Director
Human Services
Dept. of Human Services
P.O. Box 25352
Oklahoma City, OK 73125
Phone: (405) 521-3646
Fax: (405) 521-6458

OREGON
Roger Auerbach
Administrator
Senior & Disabled Services Div.
Dept. of Human Resources
500 Summer St., NE, 2nd Fl.
Salem, OR 97310-1015
Phone: (503) 945-5811
Fax: (503) 373-7823
E-mail: roger.auerbach@state.or.us

PENNSYLVANIA
Richard Browdie
Cabinet Secretary
Dept. of Aging
5th Fl., Forum Bldg.
555 Walnut St.
Harrisburg, PA 17101-2301
Phone: (717) 783-1550
Fax: (717) 772-3382
E-mail: browdie@aging.state.pa.us

PUERTO RICO
Ruby Rodriguez-Ramirez
Executive Director
Gericulture Comm.
Cobian Plz., Piso U-M
Ponce de Leon Ave.
Santurce, PR 00912
Phone: (787) 721-5710
Fax: (787) 721-6510

RHODE ISLAND
Barbara Raynor
Director
Dept. of Elderly Affairs
160 Pine St.
Providence, RI 02903
Phone: (401) 222-2894
Fax: (401) 222-1490

SOUTH CAROLINA
Betsy Fuller
Deputy Director
Div. on Aging
Ofc. on Aging
P.O. Box 8206
Columbia, SC 29202-8206
Phone: (803) 898-2500
Fax: (803) 253-4137

SOUTH DAKOTA
Gail Ferris
Administrator
Div. of Adult Services & Aging
Dept. of Social Services
Kneip Bldg.
700 Governors Dr.
Pierre, SD 57501
Phone: (605) 773-3165
Fax: (605) 773-4855

TENNESSEE
James S. Whaley
Executive Director
Comm. on Aging
Andrew Jackson Bldg., 9th Fl.
500 Deaderick St.
Nashville, TN 37243
Phone: (615) 741-2056
Fax: (615) 741-3309

TEXAS
Mary Sapp
Executive Director
Dept. on Aging
P.O. Box 12786
Austin, TX 78711
Phone: (512) 424-6840
Fax: (512) 424-6890

U.S. VIRGIN ISLANDS
Ferrynesia Benjamin
Assistant Commissioner
Dept. of Human Services
20A Strand St. & 5BB Smith St.
Christiansted
St. Croix, VI 00820
Phone: (340) 773-2323
Fax: (340) 777-6121

UTAH
Helen Goddard
Director
Div. of Aging & Adult Services
Dept. of Human Services
120 N. 200 W., Rm. 325
Salt Lake City, UT 84103
Phone: (801) 538-3918
Fax: (801) 538-4395
E-mail: hgoddard.hsadm2@state.ut.us

VERMONT
David W. Yacovone
Commissioner
Agency of Human Services
Dept. of Aging & Disabilities
103 S. Main St.
Waterbury, VT 05671
Phone: (802) 241-2400
Fax: (802) 241-2325
E-mail: dyaco@dad.state.vt.us

VIRGINIA
Ann Y. McGee
Commissioner
Dept. for the Aging
Preston Bldg., Ste. 102
1600 Forest St.
Richmond, VA 23229
Phone: (804) 662-9333
Fax: (804) 662-9354

WASHINGTON
Ralph Smith
Assistant Secretary
Aging & Adult Services Administration
Dept. of Social & Health Services
P.O. Box 45050
Olympia, WA 98504
Phone: (360) 902-7797
Fax: (360) 902-7848

WEST VIRGINIA
Gaylene Miller
Executive Director
Bur. of Senior Services
Holly Grove
1710 Kanawha Blvd., E.
Charleston, WV 25311
Phone: (304) 558-3317
Fax: (304) 558-0004

WISCONSIN
Donna McDowell
Director
Bur. on Aging
Dept. of Health & Social Services
217 S. Hamilton, Ste. 300
P.O. Box 7851
Madison, WI 53707
Phone: (608) 266-1345
Fax: (608) 266-7882

George Potaracke
Executive Director
Board on Aging & Long-Term Care
214 N. Hamilton, 2nd Fl.
Madison, WI 53702
Phone: (608) 266-8944
Fax: (608) 261-6570

WYOMING
Morris Gardner
Administrator
Div. on Aging
Dept. of Health
139 Hathaway Bldg.
2300 Capitol Ave.
Cheyenne, WY 82002
Phone: (307) 777-7986

Agriculture

Enforces agriculture laws and administers agricultural programs in the state.

ALABAMA
Charles Bishop
Commissioner
Agri. & Industries Dept.
1445 Federal Dr.
P.O. Box 3336
Montgomery, AL 36109-0336
Phone: (334) 240-7171
Fax: (334) 240-3414

ALASKA
Rob Wells
Director
Div. of Agri.
Dept. of Natural Resources
Glenn Hwy., Ste. 12
P.O. Box 9491800
Palmer, AK 99645-6736
Phone: (907) 745-7200
Fax: (907) 745-7112

AMERICAN SAMOA
Frank Markstein
Director
Dept. of Agri.
Pago Pago, AS 96799
Phone: (684) 699-9272
Fax: (684) 699-4031

ARIZONA
Sheldon R. Jones
Director
Dept. of Agri.
1688 W. Adams
Phoenix, AZ 85007
Phone: (602) 542-0998
Fax: (602) 542-5420

ARKANSAS
Donald Alexander
Director
Plant Board
1 Natural Resources Dr.
Little Rock, AR 72205
Phone: (501) 225-1598
Fax: (501) 225-3590

CALIFORNIA
Ann Veneman
Secretary
Dept. of Food & Agri.
P.O. Box 942871
Sacramento, CA 94271-0001
Phone: (916) 654-0433

COLORADO
Don Ament
Commissioner
Dept. of Agri.
700 Kipling St., Ste. 4000
Lakewood, CO 80215-5894
Phone: (303) 239-4100
Fax: (303) 239-4176
E-mail: don.ament@ag.state.co.us

CONNECTICUT
Shirley Ferris
Commissioner
Dept. of Agri.
765 Asylum Ave.
Hartford, CT 06105
Phone: (860) 713-2501

DELAWARE
John Tarburton
Secretary
Dept. of Agri.
2320 S. DuPont Hwy.
Dover, DE 19901
Phone: (302) 739-4811
Fax: (302) 697-4463
E-mail: jackt@smtp.dda.state.de.us

DISTRICT OF COLUMBIA

FLORIDA
Bob Crawford
Commissioner
Dept. of Agri. & Consumer Services
State Capitol, PL 10
Tallahassee, FL 32399-0810
Phone: (850) 488-3022
Fax: (850) 488-7585

GEORGIA
Thomas T. Irvin
Commissioner
Dept. of Agri.
Capitol Sq., Rm. 204
Atlanta, GA 30334
Phone: (404) 656-3600
Fax: (404) 651-8206

GUAM
Juan Taijito
Acting Director
Dept. of Agri.
192 Dairy Rd.
Mangilao, GU 96923
Phone: (671) 734-3942
Fax: (671) 734-6569

HAWAII
James J. Nakatani
Chair
Dept. of Agri.
1428 S. King St.
Honolulu, HI 96814
Phone: (808) 973-9550
Fax: (808) 973-9613

IDAHO
Pat Tagasuki
Director
Dept. of Agri.
2270 Old Penitentiary Rd.
Boise, ID 83701
Phone: (208) 334-3240

ILLINOIS
Joe Hampton
Director
Dept. of Agri.
P.O. Box 19281
Springfield, IL 62794
Phone: (217) 785-4789
Fax: (217) 785-4509

INDIANA
Joseph R. Pearson
Assistant Commissioner
Comm. for Agri. & Rural Dev.
ISTA Ctr., Ste. 414
150 W. Market St.
Indianapolis, IN 46204
Phone: (317) 232-8770
Fax: (317) 232-1362

IOWA
Patty Judge
Secretary
Dept. of Agri. & Land Stewardship
Wallace State Ofc. Bldg.
E. 9th and Grand Aves.
Des Moines, IA 50319
Phone: (515) 281-5322
Fax: (515) 281-6236

KANSAS
Allie Devine
Secretary
Dept. of Agri.
901 S. Kansas Ave., 4th Fl.
Topeka, KS 66612-1280
Phone: (785) 296-3556
Fax: (785) 296-8389

KENTUCKY
Billy Ray Smith
Commissioner of Agriculture
Capital Plz. Tower, 7th Fl.
500 Mero St.
Frankfort, KY 40601
Phone: (502) 564-4696
Fax: (502) 564-2133

LOUISIANA
Bob Odom
Commissioner
Dept. of Agri. & Forestry
P.O. Box 631
Baton Rouge, LA 70821-0631
Phone: (225) 922-1234
Fax: (225) 922-1253

MAINE
Robert W. Spear
Commissioner
Dept. of Agri., Food & Rural Resources
28 State House Station
Augusta, ME 04333
Phone: (207) 287-3871

MARYLAND
Henry A. Virts
Secretary
Ofc. of the Secretary
Dept. of Agri.
50 Harry S. Truman Pkwy.
Annapolis, MD 21401
Phone: (410) 841-5880
Fax: (410) 841-5914

MASSACHUSETTS
Jonathan L. Healy
Commissioner
Executive Ofc. of Environmental Affairs
Dept. of Food & Agri.
100 Cambridge St., 21st Fl.
Boston, MA 02202
Phone: (617) 727-3002
Fax: (617) 727-7235
E-mail: jhealy_dfa_boston@state.ma.us

MICHIGAN
Dan Wyant
Director
Dept. of Agri.
P.O. Box 30017
Lansing, MI 48909
Phone: (517) 373-1050
Fax: (517) 335-1423

MINNESOTA
Gene Hugoson
Commissioner
Dept. of Agri.
90 W. Plato Blvd.
St. Paul, MN 55107
Phone: (651) 297-3219
Fax: (651) 297-5522
E-mail: gene.hugoson@state.mn.us

MISSISSIPPI
Lester Spell
Commissioner
Dept. of Agri. & Commerce
121 N. Jefferson
Jackson, MS 39202
Phone: (601) 354-1100
Fax: (601) 354-6290

MISSOURI
John L. Saunders
Director
Dept. of Agri.
1616 Missouri Blvd.
P.O. Box 630
Jefferson City, MO 65102
Phone: (573) 751-3359
Fax: (573) 751-1784
E-mail: jsaunder@mail.state.mo.us

MONTANA
Ralph Peck
Director
Dept. of Agri.
303 N. Roberts, Rm. 220
P.O. Box 200201
Helena, MT 59620-0201
Phone: (406) 444-3144
Fax: (406) 444-5409

NEBRASKA
Merlyn Carlson
Director
Dept. of Agri.
301 Centennial Mall, S.
P.O. Box 94947
Lincoln, NE 68509
Phone: (402) 471-2341
Fax: (402) 471-2759

NEVADA
Paul Iverson
Administrator
Div. of Agri.
Dept. of Business & Industry
350 Capitol Hill Ave.
Reno, NV 89502
Phone: (775) 688-1182
Fax: (775) 688-1178

NEW HAMPSHIRE
Stephen Taylor
Commissioner
Agri., Markets & Food
P.O. Box 2042
Concord, NH 03302-2042
Phone: (603) 271-3700
Fax: (603) 271-1109

NEW JERSEY
Arthur Brown, Jr.
Secretary
Dept. of Agri.
John Fitch Plz.
P.O. Box 330
Trenton, NJ 08625-0330
Phone: (609) 292-3976
Fax: (609) 292-3978

NEW MEXICO
Frank A. DuBois
Secretary
NM State Univ.
Dept. of Agri.
P.O. Box 30005, Dept. 3189
Las Cruces, NM 88003-8005
Phone: (505) 646-3007
Fax: (505) 646-8120
E-mail: pv@nmda.nmsu.edu

NEW YORK
Donald R. Davidsen
Commissioner
Dept. of Agri. & Markets
One Winners Cir.
Albany, NY 12235
Phone: (518) 457-5496
Fax: (518) 457-3087

NORTH CAROLINA
James A. Graham
Commissioner of Agriculture
2 W. Edenton St.
Raleigh, NC 27601
Phone: (919) 733-7125
Fax: (919) 733-1141

NORTH DAKOTA
Roger Johnson
Commissioner
Dept. of Agri.
600 E. Blvd., 6th Fl.
Bismarck, ND 58505-0020
Phone: (701) 328-2231
Fax: (701) 328-4567
E-mail: rojohnso@state.nd.us

NORTHERN MARIANA ISLANDS
Vacant
Director
Div. of Agri. & Quarantine
Dept. of Lands & Natural Resources
Caller Box 10007
Saipan, MP 96950
Phone: (670) 256-3317
Fax: (670) 256-7154

OHIO
Fred L. Dailey
Director
Dept. of Agri.
8995 E. Main St.
Reynoldsburg, OH 43068
Phone: (614) 466-2732
Fax: (614) 728-6226

OKLAHOMA
Dennis Howard
Secretary of Agriculture
Dept. of Agri.
2800 N. Lincoln Blvd.
Oklahoma City, OK 73105
Phone: (405) 521-3864
Fax: (405) 521-4912
E-mail: okagri@icon.net

OREGON
Phil Ward
Director
Dept. of Agri.
635 Capitol St., NE
Salem, OR 97310
Phone: (503) 986-4552
Fax: (503) 986-4747

PENNSYLVANIA
Samuel E. Hayes, Jr.
Cabinet Secretary
Dept. of Agri.
Agri. Bldg., Rm. 211
Harrisburg, PA 17120
Phone: (717) 722-2853
Fax: (717) 783-9709

PUERTO RICO
Miguel Munoz
Secretary
Dept. of Agri.
P.O. Box 10163
Santurce, PR 00908-0163
Phone: (787) 721-2120
Fax: (787) 723-9747

RHODE ISLAND
Stephen M. Volpe
Chief
Div. of Agri. & Marketing
Dept. of Environmental Mgmt.
235 Promenade St.
Providence, RI 02908-5767
Phone: (401) 222-2781

SOUTH CAROLINA
D. Leslie Tindal
Commissioner
Dept. of Agri.
P.O. Box 11280
Columbia, SC 29211
Phone: (803) 734-2210

SOUTH DAKOTA
Darrell D. Cruea
Secretary
Dept. of Agri.
Foss Bldg.
523 E. Capitol Ave.
Pierre, SD 57501-3182
Phone: (605) 773-3375
Fax: (605) 773-5926

TENNESSEE
Dan Wheeler
Commissioner
Dept. of Agri.
Ellington Agri. Ctr.
Nashville, TN 37204
Phone: (615) 837-5100
Fax: (615) 837-5333

TEXAS
Susan Combs
Dept. of Agri.
1700 N. Congress
Austin, TX 78701
Phone: (512) 463-7476
Fax: (512) 463-1104

U.S. VIRGIN ISLANDS
Clement C. Magras
Acting Commissioner of Tourism
Dept. of Tourism
Elainco Bldg.
78-1-2-3 Contant
St. Thomas, VI 00802
Phone: (340) 774-8784
Fax: (340) 777-4390

UTAH
Cary Peterson
Commissioner
Dept. of Agri. & Food
350 N. Redwood Rd.
Salt Lake City, UT 84116
Phone: (801) 538-7101
Fax: (801) 538-7126
E-mail: cpeterso.agmain@state.ut.us

VERMONT
Leon C. Graves
Commissioner
Dept. of Agri.
116 State St.
Montpelier, VT 05602
Phone: (802) 828-2430
Fax: (802) 828-2361
E-mail: lgraves@agr.state.vt.us

VIRGINIA
J. Carlton Courter, III
Commissioner
Dept. of Agri. & Consumer Services
Washington Bldg., Ste. 210
1100 Bank St.
Richmond, VA 23219
Phone: (804) 786-3501
Fax: (804) 371-2945

WASHINGTON
Jim Jesernig
Director
Dept. of Agri.
P.O. Box 42560
Olympia, WA 98504-2560
Phone: (360) 902-1800
Fax: (360) 902-2092

WEST VIRGINIA
Gus R. Douglass
Commissioner of Agriculture
Capitol Bldg., Rm. M28
1900 Kanawha Blvd., E.
Charleston, WV 25305
Phone: (304) 558-3550
Fax: (304) 558-0451
E-mail: douglass@wvlc.wvnet.edu

WISCONSIN
Ben Brancel
Secretary
Dept. of Agri., Trade & Consumer Protection
P.O. Box 8911
Madison, WI 53708
Phone: (608) 224-5012
Fax: (608) 224-5045
E-mail: brancb@wheel.DATCP.state.wi.us

WYOMING
Ron Micheli
Director
Dept. of Agri.
2219 Carey Ave.
Cheyenne, WY 82001
Phone: (307) 777-6569
Fax: (307) 777-6593

Air Quality

Administers the state's clean air laws.

ALABAMA
Ron Gore
Chief
Air Div.
Dept. of Environmental Mgmt.
1751 Cong. Dickinson Dr.
Montgomery, AL 36130-1463
Phone: (334) 271-7861
Fax: (334) 279-3044

ALASKA
Mike Conway
Director
Div. of Air & Water Quality
Dept. of Environmental Conservation
410 Willoughby Ave., Ste. 105
Juneau, AK 99801
Phone: (907) 465-5100
Fax: (907) 465-5274

AMERICAN SAMOA
Togipa Tausaga
Director
Environmental Protection Agency
Ofc. of the Governor
Pago Pago, AS 96799
Phone: (684) 633-7691

ARIZONA
Nancy C. Wrona
Assistant Director
Ofc. of Air Quality
Dept. of Environmental Quality
3033 N. Central Ave.
Phoenix, AZ 85012
Phone: (602) 207-2308
Fax: (602) 207-2218

ARKANSAS
Keith Michaels
Chief
Air Div.
Pollution Control & Ecology
P.O. Box 8913
Little Rock, AR 72219
Phone: (501) 682-0745
Fax: (501) 682-0707

CALIFORNIA
Alan Lloyd
Chair
Air Resources Board
Environmental Protection Agency
P.O. Box 2815
Sacramento, CA 95812
Phone: (916) 322-5840

COLORADO
Doug Lempke
Technical Secretary
Air Quality Comm.
Dept. of Public Health & Environment
4300 Cherry Creek Dr., S.
Denver, CO 80246-1530
Phone: (303) 692-3279
Fax: (303) 782-5493
E-mail: Douglas.Lempke@state.co.us

CONNECTICUT
Carmen DiBattista
Bureau Chief
Air Mgmt.
Dept. of Environmental Protection
79 Elm St.
Hartford, CT 06106
Phone: (860) 424-3026

DELAWARE
Darryl D. Tyler
Program Administrator
Air Quality Mgmt. Section
Dept. of Natural Resources & Environmental Control
P.O. Box 1401
Dover, DE 19903
Phone: (302) 739-4791
Fax: (302) 739-3106

DISTRICT OF COLUMBIA
David Wambsgans
Acting Program Manager
Air Resources
Consumer & Regulatory Affairs
2100 M.L. King, Jr., Ave. SE, #203
Washington, DC 20020
Phone: (202) 404-1180

FLORIDA
David B. Struhs
Secretary
Div. of Air Resources Mgmt.
Dept. of Environmental Protection
3900 Commonwealth Blvd., Douglass Blvd.
2600 Blair Stone Rd., Twin Towers Location
Tallahassee, FL 32399-2400
Phone: (850) 488-4805
Fax: (850) 488-7093
E-mail: struhs_d@epic5.dep.state.fl.us

GEORGIA
Harold Reheis
Director
Environmental Protection Div.
Dept. of Natural Resources
205 Butler St., SW, Ste. 1152
Atlanta, GA 30334
Phone: (404) 656-4713
Fax: (404) 651-5778

GUAM
Jesus T. Salas
Administrator
Environmental Protection Agency
15-6101 Mariner Ave., Tiyan
P.O. Box 22439
Barrigada, GU 96921
Phone: (671) 475-1658
Fax: (671) 477-9402

HAWAII
Wilfred Nagamine
Manager
Clean Air Branch
Environmental Health Administration
P.O. Box 3378
Honolulu, HI 96801-3378
Phone: (808) 586-4200
Fax: (808) 586-4359

IDAHO
Steve Allred
Administrator
Div. of Environmental Quality
Dept. of Health & Welfare
1410 N. Hilton
Boise, ID 83706-1255
Phone: (208) 334-5500

ILLINOIS
Bharat Mathur
Bureau Chief
Div. of Air Pollution Control
Environmental Protection Agency
1340 N. 9th St.
Springfield, IL 62703
Phone: (217) 785-4141

INDIANA
Janet McCabe
Assistant Commissioner
Ofc. of Air Mgmt.
Dept. of Environmental Mgmt.
P.O. Box 6015
Indianapolis, IN 46206
Phone: (317) 232-8222
Fax: (317) 233-5967

IOWA
Peter Hamlin
Chief
Air Quality & Solid Waste Protection
Dept. of Natural Resources
900 E. Grand Ave.
Des Moines, IA 50319
Phone: (515) 281-8852
Fax: (515) 281-8895

KANSAS
Jan Sides
Director
Bur. of Air & Radiation
Dept. of Health & Environment
Forbes Field, Bldg. 740
6700 SE Topeka Blvd.
Topeka, KS 66620
Phone: (785) 296-1593
Fax: (785) 296-1545

KENTUCKY
John Hornback
Director
Div. for Air Quality
Dept. for Environmental Protection
803 Schenkel Ln.
Frankfort, KY 40601
Phone: (502) 573-3382
Fax: (502) 573-3787

LOUISIANA
Gus Von Boudungen
Assistant Secretary
Ofc. of Air Quality
Dept. of Environmental Quality
P.O. Box 82135
Baton Rouge, LA 70884-2135
Phone: (225) 765-0102
Fax: (225) 765-0222

MAINE
James Brooks
Director
Bur. of Air Quality Control
Dept. of Environmental Protection
17 State House Station
Augusta, ME 04333
Phone: (207) 289-2437

MARYLAND
George Aburn
Administrator
Air Quality, Planning & Regulation Dev. Program
Dept. of the Environment
2500 Broening Hwy.
Baltimore, MD 21224
Phone: (410) 631-3245
Fax: (410) 631-3391
E-mail: gaburn@mde.state.md.us

MASSACHUSETTS
Lauren A. Liss
Commissioner
Executive Ofc. of Environmental Affairs
Dept. of Environmental Protection
1 Winter St.
Boston, MA 02108
Phone: (617) 292-5856
Fax: (617) 574-6880

MICHIGAN
Dennis Drake
Chief
Air Quality Div.
Dept. of Environmental Quality
P.O. Box 30260
Lansing, MI 48909
Phone: (517) 373-7069
Fax: (517) 335-6993

MINNESOTA
Mike Sandusky
Director
Div. of Air Quality
Pollution Control Agency
520 Lafayette Rd.
St. Paul, MN 55155
Phone: (651) 296-7331
Fax: (651) 297-7709
E-mail: michael.sandusky@pca.state.mn.us

MISSISSIPPI
Dwight Wylie
Chief
Air Div.
Dept. of Environmental Quality
P.O. Box 10385
Jackson, MS 39289
Phone: (601) 961-5000
Fax: (601) 961-5742

MISSOURI
Roger Randolph
Director
Air Pollution Control Program
Jefferson Bldg., Rm. 125
P.O. Box 176
Jefferson City, MO 65102
Phone: (573) 751-4817
Fax: (573) 751-2706
E-mail: nrrandr@mail.dnr.state.mo.us

MONTANA
Don Vidrine
Bureau Chief
Permitting & Compliance Div.
Dept. of Environmental Quality
P.O. Box 200901
Helena, MT 59620-0901
Phone: (406) 444-3490
Fax: (406) 444-1499

NEBRASKA
Joe Francis
Associate Director
Customer & Technical Assistance Div.
Dept. of Environmental Quality
P.O. Box 98922
Lincoln, NE 68509-8922
Phone: (402) 471-0001
Fax: (402) 471-2909

NEVADA
Jolaine Johnson
Chief
Bur. of Air Quality
Div. of Environmental Protection
333 W. Nye Ln., Rm. 138
Carson City, NV 89706-0851
Phone: (775) 687-4670
Fax: (775) 687-6396

NEW HAMPSHIRE
Kenneth Colburn
Director
Air Resources Div.
Dept. of Environmental Services
64 N. Main St.
Concord, NH 03301-4913
Phone: (603) 271-1370
Fax: (603) 271-1381

NEW JERSEY
John Elston
Administrator
Air Quality Mgmt.
Dept. of Environmental Protection
401 E. State St.
P.O. Box 418
Trenton, NJ 08625-0418
Phone: (609) 292-6710
Fax: (609) 633-6198

NEW MEXICO
Richard Goodyear
Chief
Air Quality Bur.
Dept. of Environment
2048 Galisteo St.
Santa Fe, NM 87505
Phone: (505) 827-1494
Fax: (505) 827-1523

Richard Tavares
Acting Director
Behavioral Health Services Div.
Dept. of Health
1190 St. Francis Dr.
P.O. Box 26110
Santa Fe, NM 87502
Phone: (505) 827-2601
Fax: (505) 827-0097

NEW YORK
James Ralston
Director
Bur. of Air Quality Planning
Dept. of Environmental Conservation
50 Wolf Rd.
Albany, NY 12233
Phone: (518) 457-2823
Fax: (518) 457-0794

NORTH CAROLINA
Alan Klimek
Director
Div. of Air Quality
Div. of Environment Health & Natural Resources
P.O. Box 29535
Raleigh, NC 27626
Phone: (919) 733-3340
Fax: (919) 733-2496

NORTH DAKOTA
Dana K. Mount
Director
Environmental Engineering Div.
Environmental Health Section
P.O. Box 5520
Bismarck, ND 58506-5520
Phone: (701) 328-5150
Fax: (701) 328-5200
E-mail: dmount@state.nd.us

NORTHERN MARIANA ISLANDS
Ignacio Cabrera
Director
Div. of Environmental Quality
Public Works
P.O. Box 1304
Saipan, MP 96950
Phone: (670) 234-1011
Fax: (670) 234-1003

OHIO
Bob Hodanbosi
Deputy Director
Air Pollution Control
Environmental Protection Agency
122 S. Front St.
P.O. Box 1049
Columbus, OH 43215
Phone: (614) 644-2270
Fax: (614) 644-3681

OKLAHOMA
Eddie Terrel
Chief
Air Quality Services
Dept. of Health
1000 NE 10th St.
P.O. Box 53551
Oklahoma City, OK 73152
Phone: (405) 702-6100
Fax: (405) 702-4101

OREGON
Gregory Green
Administrator
Div. of Air Quality
Dept. of Environmental Quality
811 SW 6th Ave.
Portland, OR 97204
Phone: (503) 229-5397
Fax: (503) 229-5675

PENNSYLVANIA
James M. Seif
Cabinet Secretary
Dept. of Environmental Protection
Rachel Carson State Ofc. Bldg., 16th Fl.
400 Market St.
Harrisburg, PA 17120
Phone: (717) 787-2814
Fax: (717) 705-4980
E-mail: seif.james@dep.state.pa.us

PUERTO RICO
Hector Russe
President
Environmental Quality Board
P.O. Box 11488
San Juan, PR 00910-1488
Phone: (787) 767-8056
Fax: (787) 754-8294

RHODE ISLAND
Stephen Majkut
Chief
Air Quality Div.
291 Promenade St.
Providence, RI 02908
Phone: (401) 222-2797

SOUTH CAROLINA
Jim Joy
Chief
Bur. of Air Quality Control
Environmental Quality Control Ofc.
2600 Bull St.
Columbia, SC 29201
Phone: (803) 898-4123

SOUTH DAKOTA
Nettie Myers
Secretary
Dept. of Environment & Natural Resources
Joe Foss Bldg.
523 E. Capitol Ave.
Pierre, SD 57501
Phone: (605) 773-3151
Fax: (605) 773-6035

TENNESSEE
Tracy Carter
Director
Div. of Air Pollution Control
Dept. of Environmental Conservation
401 Church St., 9th Fl.
Nashville, TN 37243-1542
Phone: (615) 532-0554
Fax: (615) 532-0614

TEXAS
Walter C. Bradley
Acting Deputy Director
Ofc. of Air Quality
Natural Resources Conservation Comm.
P.O. Box 13087
Austin, TX 78711-3087
Phone: (512) 239-1000
Fax: (512) 239-1123

U.S. VIRGIN ISLANDS
Leonard Reed
Acting Director
Environmental Protection Div.
Dept. of Planning & Natural Resources
Foster's Plz, 396-1 Anna's Retreat
St. Thomas, VI 00802
Phone: (340) 777-4577
Fax: (340) 774-5416

UTAH
Ursula Trueman
Director
Div. of Air Quality
Dept. of Environmental Quality
150 N. 1950 W.
Salt Lake City, UT 84114
Phone: (801) 536-4015
Fax: (801) 536-4099
E-mail: utrueman@deq.state.ut.us

VERMONT
Richard Valentinetti
Director
Air Quality Div.
Agency of Natural Resources
103 S. Main St.
Waterbury, VT 05671-0402
Phone: (802) 241-3840
Fax: (802) 241-2590
E-mail: dick.valentinetti@anrmail.anr.state.vt.us

VIRGINIA
Dennis H. Treacy
Director
Dept. of Environmental Quality
629 E. Main St.
Richmond, VA 23219
Phone: (804) 698-4020
Fax: (804) 698-4019

WASHINGTON
Mary E. Burg
Program Manager
Air Quality Program
Dept. of Ecology
P.O. Box 47600
Olympia, WA 98504-7600
Phone: (360) 407-6000

WEST VIRGINIA
John Johnston
Chief
Air Pollution Control Comm.
1558 Washington St., E.
Charleston, WV 25311
Phone: (304) 558-2275
Fax: (304) 558-3287

WISCONSIN
Lloyd Eagen
Director
Bur. of Air Mgmt.
Dept. of Natural Resources
101 S. Webster, AM/7
P.O. Box 7921
Madison, WI 53707
Phone: (608) 266-7718
Fax: (608) 267-0560

WYOMING
Dan Olson
Administrator
Air Quality Div.
Dept. of Environmental Quality
Herschler Bldg.
122 W. 25th St.
Cheyenne, WY 82002
Phone: (307) 777-7391
Fax: (307) 777-5616

Alcohol and Drug Abuse

Plans, establishes and administers programs for the prevention, treatment and rehabilitation of alcohol and/or drug and other abusers.

ALABAMA
O'Neill Pollingue
Director
Substance Abuse Services
Mental Health & Retardation Dept.
100 N. Union
Montgomery, AL 36130-1410
Phone: (334) 242-3961
Fax: (334) 242-0759

ALASKA
Loren Jones
Director
Alcoholism & Drug Abuse Div.
Dept. of Health & Social Services
P.O. Box 110607
Juneau, AK 99811-0607
Phone: (907) 465-2071
Fax: (907) 465-2185

AMERICAN SAMOA
Marie F. Ma'o
Director
Dept. of Human & Social Services
AS Govt.
P.O. Box 997534
Pago Pago, AS 96799
Phone: (684) 633-2926
Fax: (684) 633-7449
E-mail: dhss@samoatelco.com

ARIZONA
Aimee Schwartz
Medical Director
Ofc. of Substance Abuse
Behavioral Health Services Div.
2122 E. Highland, Ste. 100
Phoenix, AZ 85016
Phone: (602) 381-8999

ARKANSAS
Joe Hill
Director
Alcohol & Drug Abuse Prevention
Dept. of Health
4815 W. Markham
Little Rock, AR 72205
Phone: (501) 280-4501
Fax: (501) 280-4519

CALIFORNIA
Elaine Bush
Chief Deputy Director
Dept. of Alcohol & Drug Programs
1700 K St.
Sacramento, CA 95814
Phone: (916) 445-0834

Andrew M. Mecca
Director
Dept. of Alcohol & Drug Programs
1700 K St.
Sacramento, CA 95814
Phone: (916) 445-0834

COLORADO
Janet Wood
Director
Alcohol & Drug Abuse Div.
Dept. of Human Services
4055 S. Lowell Blvd.
Denver, CO 80236
Phone: (303) 866-7480
Fax: (303) 866-7481

CONNECTICUT
Joxel Garcia
Commissioner
Dept. of Public Health
410 Capitol Ave., MS#13COM
P.O. Box 340308
Hartford, CT 06134
Phone: (860) 509-7101

DELAWARE
Judith E. Johnston
Acting Director
Div. of Alcoholism, Drug Abuse & Mental Health
Health & Social Services
1901 N. Dupont Hwy., Main Bldg.
New Castle, DE 19720
Phone: (302) 577-4461
Fax: (302) 577-4484

DISTRICT OF COLUMBIA
Deidra Y. Roach
Administrator
Addiction Prevention: Recovery Administration (APRA)
Dept. of Health
1300 1st St., NE
Washington, DC 20002
Phone: (202) 727-0740
Fax: (202) 535-2028

FLORIDA
John Bryant
Assistant Secretary
Mental Health Program Ofc.
Dept. of Children & Family Services
1317 Winewood Blvd., Rm. 102, Bldg. 3
Tallahassee, FL 32399-0700
Phone: (850) 488-8304
Fax: (850) 487-2239

Kathleen Kearney
Secretary
Mental Health Program Ofc.
Dept. of Children & Family Services
1317 Winewood Blvd., Rm. 102, Bldg. 3
Tallahassee, FL 32399-0700
Phone: (850) 487-1111
Fax: (850) 922-2993
E-mail: kathleen_kearney@dcf.state.fl.us

GEORGIA
Beth Howell
Director
Alcoholism & Drug Abuse
Dept. of Human Resources
2 Peachtree St., 4th Fl.
Atlanta, GA 30303
Phone: (404) 657-6413

GUAM
John W. Leon Guerrero
Director
Dept. of Mental Health & Substance Abuse
790 Gov. Carlos G. Camacho Rd.
Tamuning, GU 96911
Phone: (671) 647-5330
Fax: (671) 649-6948

HAWAII
Elaine Wilson
Chief
Alcohol & Drug Abuse Div.
Dept. of Health
601 Kamoklia Blvd., Rm. 360
Kapolei, HI 96707
Phone: (808) 692-7506
Fax: (808) 692-7521

IDAHO
Roy Sargeant
Chief
Mental Health & Substance Abuse Bur.
Dept. of Health & Welfare
450 W. State, 5th Fl.
P.O. Box 83720
Boise, ID 83720-0036
Phone: (208) 334-5528
Fax: (208) 334-6664

ILLINOIS
Nick Gontes
Associate Director
Dept. of Alcoholism & Substance Abuse
622 E. Washington, 3rd Fl.
P.O. Box 19429
Springfield, IL 62794
Phone: (217) 785-9067
Fax: (217) 785-0954

INDIANA
John Viernes
Deputy Director
Ofc. of Public Policy
Family & Social Services Administration
402 W. Washington, Rm. W353
Indianapolis, IN 46204
Phone: (317) 233-4320
Fax: (317) 233-3472

IOWA
Janet Zwick
Director
Div. of Substance Abuse & Health
Dept. of Public Health
Lucas State Ofc. Bldg.
312 E. 12th St.
Des Moines, IA 50319
Phone: (515) 281-4417
Fax: (515) 281-4958

KANSAS
Andrew O'Donovan
Commissioner
Alcohol & Drug Abuse Services
Biddle Bldg., 2nd Fl.
300 SW Oakley
Topeka, KS 66606-1995
Phone: (785) 296-3925
Fax: (785) 296-0494

KENTUCKY
Mike Townsend
Director
Div. of Substance Abuse
Health Services Cabinet
275 E. Main St.
Frankfort, KY 40601
Phone: (502) 564-2880
Fax: (502) 564-7152

LOUISIANA
Jake Hadley
Assistant Secretary
Ofc. of Alcohol & Drug Abuse
P.O. Box 2790
Baton Rouge, LA 70821
Phone: (225) 342-6717
Fax: (225) 342-3931

MAINE
Lynn F. Duby
Director
Ofc. of Substance Abuse
159 State House Station
Augusta, ME 04333-0159
Phone: (207) 287-2595

MARYLAND
Thomas Davis
Director
Alcohol & Drug Abuse Administration
Dept. of Health & Mental Hygiene
201 W. Preston St., 4th Fl.
Baltimore, MD 21201
Phone: (410) 767-6925
Fax: (410) 333-7206

Shane Dennis
Deputy Director
Alcohol & Drug Abuse Administration
Dept. of Health & Mental Hygiene
201 W. Preston St., 4th Fl.
Baltimore, MD 21201
Phone: (410) 767-6872
Fax: (410) 333-7206

MASSACHUSETTS
Howard K. Koh
Commissioner
Dept. of Public Health
250 Washington St.
Boston, MA 02108-4619
Phone: (617) 624-5200
Fax: (617) 624-5206
E-mail: howard.koh@state.ma.us

MICHIGAN
Darnell Jackson
Director
Ofc. of Drug Control Policy
Dept. of Community Health
124 W. Allegan
Lansing, MI 48909
Phone: (517) 373-4700
Fax: (517) 373-2963

MINNESOTA
Carolyn Pollard
Acting Director
Chemical Dependency Program Div.
Dept. of Human Services
444 Lafayette Rd.
St. Paul, MN 55101
Phone: (651) 582-1846
Fax: (651) 582-1865

MISSISSIPPI
Roger McMurtry
Bureau Chief
Div. of Alcohol & Drug Abuse
Dept. of Mental Health
901 Robert E. Lee Bldg.
Jackson, MS 39201
Phone: (601) 359-1288
Fax: (601) 359-6295

MISSOURI
Michael Couty
Director
Div. of Alcohol & Drug Abuse
Dept. of Mental Health
1706 E. Elm St.
P.O. Box 687
Jefferson City, MO 65102
Phone: (573) 751-4942
Fax: (573) 751-7814
E-mail: coutym@mail.dmh.state.mo.us

MONTANA
Dan Anderson
Administrator
Addictive & Mental Disorders Div.
Dept. of Public Health & Human Services
Cogswell Bldg., Rm. C118
1400 Broadway
Helena, MT 59620
Phone: (406) 444-3969
Fax: (406) 444-4435

NEBRASKA
Gordon Tush
Division Director
Alcoholism & Drug Abuse Div.
Dept. of Health & Human Services
Folsom & W. Prospector
P.O. Box 94728
Lincoln, NE 68509
Phone: (402) 479-5579
Fax: (402) 471-0820

NEVADA
Rob Johnston
Chief
Bur. of Alcohol & Drug Abuse
Dept. of Employment, Training & Rehab.
Kinkaid Bldg., Rm. 500
505 E. King St.
Carson City, NV 89701
Phone: (775) 684-4190
Fax: (775) 684-4185

NEW HAMPSHIRE
Paul Gorman
Director
Div. of Behavioral Health
Behavioral Health, Substance Abuse Services
105 Pleasant St.
Concord, NH 03301-3816
Phone: (603) 271-5007
Fax: (603) 271-6116

NEW JERSEY
Terrence O'Connor
Assistant Commissioner
Div. of Addiction Services
Dept. of Health
120 S. Stockton St.
P.O. Box 362
Trenton, NJ 08625
Phone: (609) 292-5760
Fax: (609) 292-3816

NEW MEXICO

NEW YORK
Jean Somers Miller
Commissioner
Ofc. of Alcoholism & Substance Abuse Services
Executive Park, S.
1450 Western Ave.
Albany, NY 12203-3526
Phone: (518) 457-2061
Fax: (518) 457-5474

NORTH CAROLINA
Flo Stein
Chief
Alcohol & Drug Abuse Services
Dept. of Health & Human Services
325 N. Salisbury St., Ste. 1168
Raleigh, NC 27603
Phone: (919) 733-4670
Fax: (919) 733-9455

NORTH DAKOTA
Karen Larson
Director
Substance Abuse Services
Dept. of Human Services
600 S. 2nd St., Ste. 1E
Bismarck, ND 58504-5729
Phone: (701) 328-8920
Fax: (701) 328-8969
E-mail: solark@state.nd.us

NORTHERN MARIANA ISLANDS
Vacant
Special Assistant for Drug & Substance Abuse
Ofc. of the Governor
P.O. Box 10007
Saipan, MP 96950

OHIO
Luceille Fleming
Director
Dept. of Alcohol & Drug Addiction Services
2 Nationwide Plz., 12th Fl.
280 N. High St.
Columbus, OH 43215
Phone: (614) 466-3455
Fax: (614) 728-4936

OKLAHOMA
Dennis Doyle
Deputy Commissioner
Dept. of Mental Health & Substance Abuse Services
P.O. Box 53277
Oklahoma City, OK 73152
Phone: (405) 522-3908
Fax: (405) 522-3650

OREGON
Barbara Cimaglio
Director
Alcohol & Drug Abuse
Dept. of Human Resources
500 Summer St., NE
Salem, OR 97310-1016
Phone: (217) 945-5763
Fax: (217) 373-8467
E-mail: barbara.cimaglio @state.or.us

PENNSYLVANIA
Gary L. Gurian
Acting Secretary
Health Promotion Disease & Substance Abuse Prevention
Dept. of Health
802 Health and Welfare Bldg.
Harrisburg, PA 17108
Phone: (717) 787-6436
Fax: (717) 787-0191
E-mail: ggurian @health.state.pa.us

PUERTO RICO
Jose A. Acevedo
Administrator
Addiction Control Service Administration
P.O. Box 21414
San Juan, PR 00928-1414
Phone: (787) 764-3795
Fax: (787) 765-5895

RHODE ISLAND
Patricia A. Nolan
Director
Dept. of Health
3 Capitol Hill
Providence, RI 02908
Phone: (401) 222-2231
Fax: (401) 222-6548

SOUTH CAROLINA
Rick Wade
Director
Dept. of Alcohol & Other Drug Abuse Services
3700 Forest Dr., Ste. 300
Columbia, SC 29204
Phone: (803) 734-9520
Fax: (803) 734-9663

SOUTH DAKOTA
Gib Sudbeck
Director
Div. of Alcohol & Drug Abuse
Human Resources
500 E. Capitol Ave.
Pierre, SD 57501
Phone: (605) 773-3123
Fax: (605) 773-5483

TENNESSEE
Stephanie W. Perry
Assistant Commissioner
Bur. of Alcohol & Drug Abuse
Dept. of Health
Cordell Hull Bldg., 3rd Fl.
425 5th Ave., N.
Nashville, TN 37247-4401
Phone: (615) 741-1921
Fax: (615) 532-2419

TEXAS
Terry Bleier
Executive Director
Comm. on Alcohol & Drug Abuse
9001 N. I H 35, #105
Austin, TX 78753-5233
Phone: (512) 349-6600
Fax: (512) 837-4123

U.S. VIRGIN ISLANDS

UTAH
Leon Povey
Director
Div. of Substance Abuse
Dept. of Human Services
120 N. 200 W., Rm. 201
Salt Lake City, UT 84103
Phone: (801) 538-3939
Fax: (801) 538-4696
E-mail: lpovey.hsadmin1 @state.ut.us

VERMONT
Thomas E. Perras
Director
Alcohol & Drug Programs
Dept. of Health
P.O. Box 70
Burlington, VT 05402
Phone: (802) 651-1550
Fax: (802) 651-1573
E-mail: tom @adap.adp.state.vt.us

VIRGINIA
Richard E. Kellogg
Commissioner
Dept. of Mental Health, Mental Retardation & Substance Abuse Services
109 Governor St., Rm. 1301-A
Richmond, VA 23219
Phone: (804) 786-5682
Fax: (804) 371-6638

WASHINGTON
Ken Stark
Director
Alcohol & Substance Abuse Bur.
Social & Health Services Dept.
P.O. Box 45330
Olympia, WA 98504-5330
Phone: (360) 438-8200
Fax: (360) 438-8078

WEST VIRGINIA
Dee Dee Severino
Acting Director
Div. of Alcohol & Drug Abuse
Bldg. 6, Rm. 717
1900 Kanawha Blvd., E.
Charleston, WV 25305
Phone: (304) 558-2276

WISCONSIN
Claude Gilmore
Director
Alliance for Drug-Free WI
Dept. of Health & Family Services
1 W. Wilson, 5th Fl.
Madison, WI 53702
Phone: (608) 266-9354
Fax: (608) 264-9832

WYOMING
Jean DeFratis
Manager
Div. of Behavioral Health
Dept. of Health
Hathaway Bldg., Rm. 451
2300 Capitol Ave.
Cheyenne, WY 82002
Phone: (307) 777-6494
Fax: (307) 777-5580

Alcoholic Beverage Control

Administers and enforces the laws governing the manufacturing, distribution and dispensing of alcoholic beverages.

ALABAMA
Randall Smith
Director
Alcoholic Beverage Control Board
2715 Gunter Park Dr., W.
Montgomery, AL 36109
Phone: (334) 271-3840
Fax: (334) 244-1815

ALASKA
Doug Griffin
Director
Alcoholic Beverage Control Board
Dept. of Revenue
550 W. 7th Ave., Ste. 350
Anchorage, AK 99501-3510
Phone: (907) 277-8638
Fax: (907) 272-9412

AMERICAN SAMOA
Magalei Logovii
Chair
Alcoholic Beverage Control Board
Ofc. of the Governor
Pago Pago, AS 96799
Phone: (684) 633-4201
Fax: (684) 633-1148

ARIZONA
Howard G. Adams
Director
Dept. of Liquor Licenses
800 W. Washington, Ste. 500
Phoenix, AZ 85007
Phone: (602) 542-5141
Fax: (602) 542-5707

ARKANSAS
Robert Moore
Director
Alcoholic Beverage Control Administration
100 Main St., Rm. 503
Little Rock, AR 72201
Phone: (501) 682-1105
Fax: (501) 682-2221

CALIFORNIA
Jay R. Stroh
Director
Dept. of Alcoholic Beverage Control
3801 Rosin Ct. #150
Sacramento, CA 95834-1633
Phone: (916) 263-6888

COLORADO
Dave Reitz
Director
Liquor Enforcement Div.
Dept. of Revenue
1881 Pierce St., Rm. 108A
Denver, CO 80214-1495
Phone: (303) 205-2300
Fax: (303) 205-2341

CONNECTICUT
Maria Delaney
Director
Liquor Control Comm.
Dept. of Consumer Protection
165 Capitol Ave., Rm. 556
Hartford, CT 06106
Phone: (860) 566-4175

DELAWARE
Donald J. Bowman
Executive Secretary
Alcoholic Beverage Control Comm.
820 N. French St.
Wilmington, DE 19801
Phone: (302) 577-3200
Fax: (302) 577-3204

DISTRICT OF COLUMBIA
Paul E. Waters
Program Manager
Alcoholic Beverage Control Div.
Consumer & Regulatory Affairs
614 H St., NW, Rm. 505
Washington, DC 20001
Phone: (202) 727-7375

FLORIDA
Cynthia A. Henderson
Secretary
Alcoholic Beverages & Tobacco
Dept. of Business & Professional Regulation
1940 N. Monroe St.
Tallahassee, FL 32399-1020
Phone: (850) 488-0755
Fax: (850) 922-2936
E-mail: chenders@mail.dbpr.state.fl.us

GEORGIA
Chester Bryant
Director
Alcohol & Tobacco Tax Unit
Dept. of Revenue
270 Washington St., SW
Atlanta, GA 30334
Phone: (404) 656-4252

GUAM
Joseph T. Duenas
Director
Dept. of Revenue & Taxation
13-1 Mariner Dr., Tiyan
P.O. Box 23607
GMF, GU 96921
Phone: (671) 475-1817
Fax: (671) 472-2643

HAWAII
Eric Honma
Director
Dept. of Liquor Control
County of Kauai
4280-A Rice St.
Lihue, HI 96766
Phone: (808) 241-6580
Fax: (808) 241-6585

Janice A. Pakele
Director
Dept. of Liquor Control
County of Hawaii
101 Aupuni St., Ste. 230
Hilo, HI 96720
Phone: (808) 961-8218
Fax: (808) 961-8684

Frank Silva
Director
Dept. of Liquor Control
County of Maui
200 S. High St.
Wailuku, HI 96793
Phone: (808) 243-7753
Fax: (808) 243-7870

Wallace Weatherwax
Liquor Control Administrator
Liquor Comm.
City & County of Honolulu
711 Kapiolani Blvd., Ste. 600
Honolulu, HI 96813-5249
Phone: (808) 527-6280
Fax: (808) 591-2700

IDAHO
John Gould
Chief
Alcoholic Beverage Control Div.
Dept. of Law Enforcement
P.O. Box 700
Meridian, ID 83680-0700
Phone: (208) 884-7003

ILLINOIS
Sam Panayotovich
Executive Director
Liquor Control Comm.
100 W. Randolph, Ste. 5-300
Chicago, IL 60601
Phone: (312) 814-3930
Fax: (312) 814-2241

INDIANA
John Hanley
Chair
Alcoholic Beverage Comm.
302 W. Washington St., Rm. E114
Indianapolis, IN 46204
Phone: (317) 232-2448
Fax: (317) 233-6114

IOWA
Jack Nystrom
Administrator
Alcoholic Beverages Div.
Dept. of Commerce
1918 SE Hulsizer
Ankeny, IA 50021
Phone: (515) 281-7407
Fax: (515) 281-7385

KANSAS
Vacant
Director
Alcoholic Beverage Control Div.
Dept. of Revenue
#4 Townsite Plz., Rm. 210
200 SE 6th St.
Topeka, KS 66603-3512
Phone: (785) 296-3946
Fax: (785) 296-0922

KENTUCKY
Richard Johnstone
Commissioner
Alcoholic Beverage Control
1003 Twilight Trail, Ste. A2
Frankfort, KY 40601
Phone: (502) 564-4850
Fax: (502) 564-1442

LOUISIANA
Murphy Painter
Commissioner
Alcohol & Beverage Control
P.O. Box 66404
Baton Rouge, LA 70896
Phone: (225) 925-4041
Fax: (225) 925-3975

MAINE
Eben B. Marsh
Director
Bur. of Alcoholic Beverages & Lottery Operations
Dept. of Adm. & Financial Services
8 State House Station
Augusta, ME 04333
Phone: (207) 287-3721

MARYLAND
Charles W. Ehart
Director
Alcohol & Tobacco Tax Div.
Comptroller of the Treasury
Goldstein Treasury Bldg., Rm. 310
Annapolis, MD 21404-2999
Phone: (410) 260-7311
Fax: (410) 974-3201

MASSACHUSETTS
Walter J. Sullivan, Jr.
Chair
Alcoholic Beverages Control Comm.
100 Cambridge St., Rm. 2204
Boston, MA 02202
Phone: (617) 727-3040
Fax: (617) 727-1258

MICHIGAN
Jackie Stewart
Chair
Liquor Control Comm.
Consumer & Industry Services
7150 Harris Dr.
Lansing, MI 48909
Phone: (517) 322-1353
Fax: (517) 322-5188

MINNESOTA
Thomas Brownell
Director
Alcohol & Gambling Enforcement Div.
Dept. of Public Safety
444 Cedar St., Ste. 133
St. Paul, MN 55101-5133
Phone: (651) 296-6430
Fax: (651) 297-5259

MISSISSIPPI
Ed Buelow
Chair
State Tax Comm.
P.O. Box 22828
Jackson, MS 39225
Phone: (601) 923-7400
Fax: (601) 923-7423

Jimmy Sullivan
Director
Alcoholic Beverage Control Div.
State Tax Comm.
P.O. Box 540
Madison, MS 39130
Phone: (601) 856-1301
Fax: (601) 856-1390

MISSOURI
Hope E. Whitehead
Director
Div. of Liquor Control
Dept. of Public Safety
Truman Bldg., Rm. 860
P.O. Box 837
Jefferson City, MO 65102
Phone: (573) 751-2333
Fax: (573) 526-4540
E-mail: hwitehe@mail.state.mo.us

MONTANA
Diana Koon
License Bureau Chief
Liquor Bur.
Dept. of Revenue
P.O. Box 1712
Helena, MT 59624
Phone: (406) 444-0700
Fax: (406) 444-0750

NEBRASKA
Jack Crowley
Chair
Liquor Control Comm.
301 Centennial Mall, S.
P.O. Box 95046
Lincoln, NE 68509-5046
Phone: (402) 471-2571
Fax: (402) 471-2814

NEVADA

NEW HAMPSHIRE
John Byrne
Chair
Liquor Comm.
P.O. Box 503
Concord, NH 03302-0503
Phone: (603) 271-3132
Fax: (603) 271-1107

NEW JERSEY
John G. Holl
Director
Alcoholic Beverage Control Div.
Dept. of Law & Public Safety
140 E. Front St.
P.O. Box 087
Trenton, NJ 08625-0087
Phone: (609) 984-2830
Fax: (609) 633-6078

NEW MEXICO
Lillian Martinez
Deputy Director
Alcohol & Gaming Div.
Dept. of Regulation & Licensing
P.O. Box 25101
Santa Fe, NM 87504
Phone: (505) 827-7066
Fax: (505) 827-7168

NEW YORK
Edward F. Kelly
Acting Chairperson & Commissioner
Div. of Alcoholic Beverage Control
State Liquor Authority
84 Holland Ave.
Albany, NY 12208
Phone: (518) 473-6559
Fax: (518) 402-4015

NORTH CAROLINA
George F. Bason
Chair
Alcohol Beverage Control Comm.
Dept. of Commerce
3322 Old Garner Rd.
Raleigh, NC 27610
Phone: (919) 779-0700
Fax: (919) 662-1946

NORTH DAKOTA
Laverne Reinbold
Licensing Administrator
Licensing Section
Attorney Gen's. Ofc.
600 E. Blvd., 17th Fl.
Bismarck, ND 58505-0040
Phone: (701) 328-2329
Fax: (701) 328-3535
E-mail: msmail.lreinbol@ranch.state.nd.us

NORTHERN MARIANA ISLANDS
Enrique A. Santos
Administrator
Alcoholic Beverage Control Board
Commerce Dept.
Caller Box 10007
Saipan, MP 96950
Phone: (670) 664-3058
Fax: (670) 664-3067
E-mail: commerce@mtccnmi.com

OHIO
Rae Ann Estep
Superintendent
Div. of Liquor Control
Dept. of Commerce
P.O. Box 4005
Reynoldsburg, OH 43068-9005
Phone: (614) 644-2360
Fax: (614) 644-2480

OKLAHOMA
Ron L. Willis
Director
Alcoholic Beverage Control Board
4545 N. Lincoln Blvd., Ste. 270
Oklahoma City, OK 73105
Phone: (405) 521-3484
Fax: (405) 521-6578

OREGON
Pam Erickson
Administrator
Liquor Control
9079 SE McLoughlin Blvd.
Portland, OR 97222
Phone: (503) 872-5200
Fax: (503) 872-5266
E-mail: pamela.erickson
@state.or.us

PENNSYLVANIA
John Jones
Chair
Liquor Control Board
518 NW Ofc. Bldg.
Harrisburg, PA 17124
Phone: (717) 787-5230
Fax: (717) 772-3714
E-mail: jjones
@lcb.state.pa.us

PUERTO RICO
Julio E. Gonzalez Caban
Director
Bur. of Alcoholic Beverage
Taxes
Dept. of Treasury
P.O. Box 9024140
San Juan, PR 00902-4140
Phone: (787) 721-5245
Fax: (787) 722-6749

RHODE ISLAND
Anthony V. Arico, Jr.
Acting Director
Dept. of Business
Regulation
233 Richmond St.
Providence, RI 02903
Phone: (401) 222-2562
Fax: (401) 222-6098

SOUTH CAROLINA
Patricia L. Stites
Supervisor
Div. of Alcohol Beverage
Control
Dept. of Revenue &
Taxation
301 Gervais St.
Columbia, SC 29201
Phone: (803) 898-5864

SOUTH DAKOTA
James Fry
Director
Div. of Special Taxes
Dept. of Revenue
Anderson Bldg.
445 E. Capitol Ave.
Pierre, SD 57501
Phone: (605) 773-3311
Fax: (605) 773-6729

TENNESSEE
Gregory Harrison
Director
Alcoholic Beverage Comm.
226 Capitol Blvd., Ste. 300
Nashville, TN 37243-0775
Phone: (615) 741-1602
Fax: (615) 741-0847

TEXAS
Doyne Bailey
Administrator
Alcoholic Beverage Comm.
5806 Mesa Dr.
Austin, TX 78731
Phone: (512) 206-3217
Fax: (512) 206-3350

U.S. VIRGIN ISLANDS
Andrew Rutnik
Acting Commissioner
Dept. of Licensing &
Consumer Affairs
Property & Procurement
Bldg.
Sub Base Bldg. 1, Rm. 205
St. Thomas, VI 00802
Phone: (340) 774-3130
Fax: (340) 776-8303

UTAH
Kenneth F. Wynn
Director
Administration
Dept. of Alcoholic
Beverage Control
1625 S. 900 W.
P.O. Box 30408
Salt Lake City, UT 84130-
0408
Phone: (801) 977-6800
Fax: (801) 977-6888
E-mail: kwynn.abcmain
@state.ut.us

VERMONT
Michael J. Hogan
Interim Commissioner
Dept. of Liquor Control
Green Mountain Dr.
Drawer 20
Montpelier, VT 05620-4501
Phone: (802) 828-2345
Fax: (802) 828-2803

VIRGINIA
Clarence W. Roberts
ABC Board Chair
Dept. of Alcoholic
Beverage Control
2901 Hermitage Rd.
Richmond, VA 23220
Phone: (804) 213-4405
Fax: (804) 213-4411

WASHINGTON
Eugene Prince
Chair
Liquor Control Board
P.O. Box 43075
Olympia, WA 98504-3075
Phone: (360) 753-6262
Fax: (360) 664-9689

WEST VIRGINIA
Don Stemple
Commissioner
Alcoholic Beverage Control
322 70th St., SE
Charleston, WV 25304-2900
Phone: (304) 558-2481
Fax: (304) 558-0081

WISCONSIN
Jim Jenkins
Chief
Alcohol & Tobacco
Enforcement
Dept. of Revenue
4610 Univ. Ave.
P.O. Box 8910
Madison, WI 53708
Phone: (608) 266-3969
Fax: (608) 266-1703

WYOMING
Lisa Burgess
Administrator
Dept. of Revenue
1520 E. 5th St.
Cheyenne, WY 82002
Phone: (307) 777-6448
Fax: (307) 777-6255

Archives

Identifies, acquires, preserves and makes available state government records of continuing historical and research value.

ALABAMA
Edwin C. Bridges
Director
Dept. of Archives & History
P.O. Box 300100
Montgomery, AL 36130-0100
Phone: (334) 242-4441
Fax: (334) 240-3125

ALASKA
John Stewart
State Archivist
Dept. of Education
141 Willoughby Ave.
Juneau, AK 99801-1720
Phone: (907) 465-2275
Fax: (907) 465-2465

AMERICAN SAMOA
James Himphill
Archivist
Dept. of Adm. Services
AS Govt.
Pago Pago, AS 96799
Phone: (684) 633-1609
Fax: (684) 633-1010

ARIZONA
Gladys Ann Wells
Director
Library, Archives & Public Records
State Law Library
1700 W. Washington St.
Phoenix, AZ 85007-2812
Phone: (602) 542-4035
Fax: (602) 542-4972

ARKANSAS
John L. Ferguson
State Historian
History Comm.
1 Capitol Mall
Little Rock, AR 72201
Phone: (501) 682-6900

CALIFORNIA
Walter P. Gray, III
State Archivist
State Archives
1020 O St.
Sacramento, CA 95814
Phone: (916) 653-7715

COLORADO
Terry Ketelsen
State Archivist
Info./Archival Services
Info. Technology Services
1313 Sherman St., Rm. 1B-20
Denver, CO 80203
Phone: (303) 866-2055
Fax: (303) 866-2257

CONNECTICUT
Mark Jones
State Archivist
State Library
231 Capitol Ave.
Hartford, CT 06106
Phone: (860) 566-5650
Fax: (860) 566-4460

DELAWARE
Howard P. Lowell
Administrator
State Archives
Dept. of State
Hall of Records
Dover, DE 19901
Phone: (302) 739-5318
Fax: (502) 739-6710

DISTRICT OF COLUMBIA
Clarence Davis
Archivist
Ofc. of the Secretary
1300 Naylor Ct., NW
Washington, DC 20001
Phone: (202) 727-2052
Fax: (202) 727-6076

FLORIDA
Jim Berberich
Chief
Bur. of Archives & Records Mgmt.
Dept. of State
R.A. Gray Bldg.
500 S. Bronough St.
Tallahassee, FL 32399-0250
Phone: (850) 487-2073
Fax: (850) 488-4894

Katherine Harris
Secretary of State
Bur. of Archives & Records Mgmt.
Dept. of State
400 S. Monroe St.
PL 02, The Capitol
Tallahassee, FL 32399-0250
Phone: (850) 488-3680
Fax: (850) 488-4894

GEORGIA
Edward Weldon
Director
Secretary of State
Archives & History Dept.
330 Capitol Ave., SW
Atlanta, GA 30334
Phone: (404) 656-2358
Fax: (404) 657-8427

GUAM
Antonio M. Palomo
Director
Museum
13-6 Seagull Ave., Tiyan
P.O. Box 2950
Hagatna, GU 96932
Phone: (671) 475-4228
Fax: (671) 475-6727

Christine Scott-Smith
Director
Public Library
Nieves M. Flores Library
254 Martyr St.
Hagatna, GU 96910
Phone: (671) 475-4753
Fax: (671) 477-9777
E-mail: csctsmth@kuentos.guam.net

HAWAII
Jolyn G. Tamura
State Archivist
Archives Div.
Dept. of Accounting & Services
Iolani Palace Grounds
Honolulu, HI 96813
Phone: (808) 586-0310
Fax: (808) 586-0330

IDAHO
Sarah H. Theimer
Administrator/Librarian
Library/Archives
State Historical Society
450 N. 4th St.
Boise, ID 83702
Phone: (208) 334-3356

ILLINOIS
John Daly
Director
State Archives & Records Div.
M.C. Norton Bldg., Fl. 2W
Springfield, IL 62756
Phone: (217) 782-3492

INDIANA
F. Gerald Handfield, Jr.
Director
Comm. on Public Records
402 W. Washington, Rm. W472
Indianapolis, IN 46204
Phone: (317) 232-3373
Fax: (317) 233-1713

IOWA
Gordon Hendrickson
State Archivist
Dept. of Cultural Affairs
600 E. Locust
Des Moines, IA 50319
Phone: (515) 281-3007
Fax: (515) 282-0502

KANSAS
Patricia Michaelis
State Archivist
History Ctr.
6425 SW 6th Ave.
Topeka, KS 66615-1099
Phone: (785) 272-8681
Fax: (785) 272-8682

KENTUCKY
Richard N. Belding
State Archivist
Public Libraries Div.
Dept. for Libraries & Archives
P.O. Box 537
Frankfort, KY 40602
Phone: (502) 564-8300
Fax: (502) 564-5773

LOUISIANA
W. Fox McKeithen
Secretary of State
Dept. of State
P.O. Box 94125
Baton Rouge, LA 70804-9125
Phone: (225) 342-4479
Fax: (225) 342-5577

MAINE
James Henderson
State Archivist
84 State House Station
Augusta, ME 04333
Phone: (207) 289-5790

MARYLAND
Edward C. Papenfuse
State Archivist
Hall of Records Comm.
State Archives
350 Rowe Blvd.
Annapolis, MD 21401
Phone: (410) 260-6403
Fax: (410) 974-3895
E-mail: edp@mdarchives.state.md.us

MASSACHUSETTS
John D. Warner, Jr.
Archivist
Ofc. of the Secretary of the Commonwealth
220 Morrissey Blvd.
Boston, MA 02125
Phone: (617) 727-2816
Fax: (617) 288-8429
E-mail: jwarner@sec.state.ma.us

MICHIGAN
David Johnson
State Archivist
Bur. of History
Dept. of State
717 W. Allegan
Lansing, MI 48918
Phone: (517) 373-1408
Fax: (517) 241-1658

MINNESOTA
Robert Horton
Head of State Archives
Historical Society
345 Kellogg Blvd., W.
St. Paul, MN 55102
Phone: (651) 215-5866
Fax: (651) 296-9961
E-mail: robert.horton@mnhs.org

MISSISSIPPI
Elbert R. Hilliard
Director
Dept. of Archives & History
P.O. Box 571
Jackson, MS 39205-0571
Phone: (601) 359-6881
Fax: (601) 359-6975

MISSOURI
Kenneth Winn
State Archivist
Ofc. of Secretary of State
600 W. Main St.
P.O. Box 778
Jefferson City, MO 65102
Phone: (573) 751-4717
Fax: (573) 526-3867
E-mail: kwinn1@mail.more.net

MONTANA
Robert M. Clark
Society Librarian
Library & Archives Program
Historical Society
225 N. Roberts St.
Helena, MT 59620
Phone: (406) 444-4787
Fax: (406) 444-2696

NEBRASKA
Lawrence J. Sommer
Director
State Historical Society
P.O. Box 82554
Lincoln, NE 68501-2554
Phone: (402) 471-4745
Fax: (402) 471-3100

NEVADA
Guy Louis Rocha
Assistant Administrator
Div. of Archives & Records
Dept. of Museums, Library & Arts
100 Stewart St.
Carson City, NV 89701
Phone: (775) 687-8317
Fax: (775) 687-8311
E-mail: glrocha@clan.lib.nv.us

NEW HAMPSHIRE
Frank C. Mevers
Director & State Archivist
Records Mgmt. & Archives
Secretary of State Ofc.
71 S. Fruit St.
Concord, NH 03301-2410
Phone: (603) 271-2236

NEW JERSEY
Karl Niederer
Director
Div. of Archives & Records Mgmt.
Dept. of State
2300 Stuyvesant Ave.
P.O. Box 307
Trenton, NJ 08625-0307
Phone: (609) 530-3200

NEW MEXICO
Elaine Olah
Administrator
State Records Ctr. & Archives
1205 Camino Carlos Rey
Santa Fe, NM 87505
Phone: (505) 476-7900
Fax: (505) 476-7901

NEW YORK
Richard P. Mills
Commissioner
State Education Dept.
89 Washington Ave., Rm. 111
Albany, NY 12234
Phone: (518) 474-6569
Fax: (518) 473-4909

NORTH CAROLINA
Jeffrey Crow
Director
Div. of Archives & History
Dept. of Cultural Resources
109 E. Jones St.
Raleigh, NC 27601
Phone: (919) 733-7305
Fax: (919) 733-8807

NORTH DAKOTA
Gerald G. Newborg
Director
State Archives & Historical Research Library
State Historical Society
612 E. Blvd. Ave.
Bismarck, ND 58505-0830
Phone: (701) 328-2668
Fax: (701) 328-3710
E-mail: gnewborg@state.nd.us

NORTHERN MARIANA ISLANDS
Herbert S. Del Rosario
Archivist
Commonwealth Archives
Northern Marianas College
P.O. Box 1250 CK
Saipan, MP 96950
Phone: (670) 234-7394
Fax: (670) 234-0759

OHIO
Gary C. Ness
Director
Historical Society
1982 Velma Ave.
Columbus, OH 43211
Phone: (614) 297-2350
Fax: (614) 297-2352

OKLAHOMA
Robert L. Clark
Director
Dept. of Libraries
200 NE 18th St.
Oklahoma City, OK 73105
Phone: (405) 521-2502
Fax: (405) 525-7804
E-mail: bclark@ohn.odl.state.ok.us

OREGON
Roy C. Turnbaugh
State Archivist
Archives Div.
Ofc. of Secretary of State
800 Summer St., NE
Salem, OR 97310
Phone: (503) 373-0701
Fax: (503) 373-0953

PENNSYLVANIA
Brent Glass
Executive Director
State Historical & Museum Comm.
P.O. Box 1026
Harrisburg, PA 17108-1026
Phone: (717) 787-2891
Fax: (717) 705-0482
E-mail: bglass@phmc.state.pa.us

PUERTO RICO
Nelly Cruz
Director
Archives
Ponde de Leon, #500
Puerta de Tierra
San Juan, PR 00902
Phone: (787) 722-0331

RHODE ISLAND
Gwendolyn Stearn
State Archivist
Ofc. of Secretary of State
337 Westminster St.
Providence, RI 02903
Phone: (401) 222-2353

SOUTH CAROLINA
Rodger E. Stroup
Director
Dept. of Archives & History
8301 Parkland Rd.
Columbia, SC 29223-4905
Phone: (803) 896-6187
Fax: (803) 896-6186

SOUTH DAKOTA
Richard Popp
State Archivist
State Historical Society
Dept. of Education & Cultural Affairs
Cultural Heritage Ctr.
900 Governors Dr.
Pierre, SD 57501
Phone: (605) 773-3804
Fax: (605) 773-6041

TENNESSEE
Edwin S. Gleaves
State Librarian & Archivist
State Library & Archives
403 7th Ave., N.
Nashville, TN 37243-0312
Phone: (615) 741-2451
Fax: (615) 741-6471

TEXAS
Chris La Plante
State Archivist
State Library & Archives Comm.
P.O. Box 12927
Austin, TX 78711
Phone: (512) 463-5455
Fax: (512) 463-5436

U.S. VIRGIN ISLANDS
E. Marlene Hendricks
Assistant Director
Libraries, Archives & Museums
Dept. of Planning & Natural Resources
23 Dronningens Gade
St. Thomas, VI 00802
Phone: (340) 774-3407
Fax: (340) 775-1887

UTAH
Jeffery O. Johnson
Director of State Archives
Div. of State Archives
Dept. of Adm. Services
Archives Bldg.
Salt Lake City, UT 84114
Phone: (801) 538-3012
Fax: (801) 538-3354
E-mail: jjohnson.asitmain@state.ut.us

VERMONT
D. Gregory Sanford
State Archivist
Ofc. of Secretary of State
Pavilion Ofc. Bldg.
109 State St.
Montpelier, VT 05609
Phone: (802) 828-2369
Fax: (802) 828-2496
E-mail: gsanford@sec.state.vt.us

VIRGINIA
Nolan T. Yelich
State Librarian
State Library
Serials Section
800 E. Broad St.
Richmond, VA 23219
Phone: (804) 692-3535
Fax: (804) 692-3594

WASHINGTON
Vacant
State Archivist
Archives & Record Mgmt. Div.
Ofc. of Secretary of State
P.O. Box 40238
Olympia, WA 98504-0238
Phone: (360) 586-2660
Fax: (360) 664-8814

WEST VIRGINIA
Fredrick Armstrong
Director
Archives & History Div.
Div. of Culture & History
Capitol Complex, Cultural Ctr.
Charleston, WV 25305
Phone: (304) 558-0230
Fax: (304) 558-2779

WISCONSIN
Peter Gottlieb
State Archivist
State Historical Society
816 State St., Rm. 421
Madison, WI 53706
Phone: (608) 264-6480
Fax: (608) 264-6486

WYOMING
Vacant
Division Director
Cultural Resources Div.
Commerce Dept.
Barrett Bldg.
Cheyenne, WY 82002
Phone: (307) 777-7013
Fax: (307) 777-3543

Arts Council

Encourages the study and presentation of the performing and fine arts and promotes participation in and appreciation of the arts.

ALABAMA
Albert Head
Executive Director
Council on Arts & Humanities
1 Dexter Ave.
Montgomery, AL 36130-1800
Phone: (334) 242-4076
Fax: (334) 240-3269

ALASKA
Helen Howarth
Executive Director
State Council on the Arts
411 W. 4th Ave., Ste. 1E
Anchorage, AK 99501
Phone: (907) 269-6610
Fax: (907) 269-6601

AMERICAN SAMOA
Faailoilo Lauvao
Executive Director
Council on Arts, Culture & Humanities
Museum
Pago Pago, AS 96799
Phone: (684) 633-4347
Fax: (684) 633-2059

ARIZONA
Shelley Cohn
Executive Director
Comm. on the Arts
417 W. Roosevelt
Phoenix, AZ 85003
Phone: (602) 255-5882
Fax: (602) 256-0282

ARKANSAS
Jim Mitchell
Director
State Arts Council
323 Ctr. St., Ste. 1500
Little Rock, AR 72201
Phone: (501) 324-9766
Fax: (501) 324-9154

CALIFORNIA
Barbara Pieper
Director
Arts Council
1300 I St., Ste. 930
Sacramento, CA 95814
Phone: (916) 322-6333
Fax: (916) 322-6575

COLORADO
Fran Holden
Director
Council on the Arts
Dept. of Higher Education
750 Pennsylvania St.
Denver, CO 80203-3699
Phone: (303) 894-2617
Fax: (303) 894-2615

CONNECTICUT
John E. Ostrout
Executive Director
Comm. on the Arts
755 Main St.
Hartford, CT 06103
Phone: (860) 566-4770

DELAWARE
Annabelle Kressman
Chair
Arts Council
Carvel State Ofc. Bldg.
820 N. French St.
Wilmington, DE 19801
Phone: (302) 577-8278
Fax: (302) 577-6561

DISTRICT OF COLUMBIA
Anthony Gittens
Executive Director
Comm. on Arts & Humanities
410 8th St., NW, Ste. 500
Washington, DC 20005
Phone: (202) 724-5613

FLORIDA
Peg Richardson
Director
Div. of Cultural Affairs
Dept. of State
1001 DeSoto Park Dr.
Tallahassee, FL 32301
Phone: (850) 487-2980
Fax: (850) 922-5259

GEORGIA
Caroline B. Leake
Executive Director
Council for the Arts
260 14th St., NW, Ste. 401
Atlanta, GA 30318
Phone: (404) 685-2787
Fax: (404) 685-2788

GUAM
Deborah J. Bordallo
Executive Director
Council on the Arts & Humanities
701 & 703 Central Ave.
P.O. Box 2950
Hagatna, GU 96932
Phone: (671) 475-2242
Fax: (671) 472-2781

HAWAII
Holly Richards
Executive Director
Foundation on Culture & the Arts
Dept. of Accounting & Services
44 Merchant St.
Honolulu, HI 96813
Phone: (808) 586-0300
Fax: (808) 586-0308

IDAHO
Frederick J. Herbert
Executive Director
Comm. on the Arts
Ofc. of Secretary of State
304 W. State St.
Boise, ID 83720
Phone: (208) 334-2119

ILLINOIS
Rhonda D. Pierce
Executive Director
State Arts Council
100 W. Randolph, Ste. 10-500
Chicago, IL 60601
Phone: (312) 814-6759
Fax: (312) 814-1471

INDIANA
Dorothy Ilgen
Executive Director
State Arts Comm.
402 W. Washington St., Rm. 72
Indianapolis, IN 46204-2741
Phone: (317) 232-1286
Fax: (317) 232-5595

IOWA
Dan Hunterdan
Director
Dept. of Cultural Affairs
State Historical Bldg.
600 E. Locust
Des Moines, IA 50319
Phone: (515) 281-7471
Fax: (515) 242-6498
E-mail: dan.hunter@dca.state.ia.us

KANSAS
David M. Wilson
Executive Director
Arts Comm.
700 SW Jackson St., Ste. 1004
Topeka, KS 66603
Phone: (785) 296-3335
Fax: (785) 296-4849

KENTUCKY
Gerri Combs
Director
Arts Council
Education & Humanities Cabinet
31 Fountain Pl.
Frankfort, KY 40601
Phone: (502) 564-3757
Fax: (502) 564-2839

LOUISIANA
James Borders
Director
Div. of Arts
Ofc. of Culture, Recreation & Tourism
P.O. Box 44247
Baton Rouge, LA 70804
Phone: (225) 342-8180
Fax: (225) 342-8173

MAINE
Alden C. Wilson
Executive Director
State Arts Comm.
25 State House Station
Augusta, ME 04333
Phone: (207) 287-2724

MARYLAND
James Backas
Executive Director
State Arts Council
Dept. of Business & Economic Dev.
601 N. Howard St.
Baltimore, MD 21201
Phone: (410) 767-6412
Fax: (410) 333-1062

MASSACHUSETTS
Mary Kelley
Executive Director
Cultural Council
120 Boylston St., 2nd Fl.
Boston, MA 02116-4600
Phone: (617) 727-3668
Fax: (617) 727-0044
E-mail: mary@art.state.ma.us

MICHIGAN
Betty Boone
Executive Director
Council for Arts & Cultural Affairs
Consumer & Industry Affairs
1200 6th St.
Detroit, MI 78226-2461
Phone: (313) 256-3731
Fax: (313) 256-3781

MINNESOTA
Robert Booker
Executive Director
State Arts Board
400 Sibley St., Ste. 200
St. Paul, MN 55101-1928
Phone: (651) 215-1600
Fax: (651) 215-1602
E-mail: rbooker@state.mn.us

MISSISSIPPI
Betsy Bradley
Executive Director
Arts Comm.
239 N. Lamar St., Ste. 207
Jackson, MS 39201
Phone: (601) 359-6030
Fax: (601) 359-6008

MISSOURI
Flora Maria Garcia
Executive Director
Arts Council
Dept. of Economic Dev.
111 N. 7th St., Ste. 105
St. Louis, MO 63101-2188
Phone: (314) 340-6845
Fax: (314) 340-7215
E-mail: fgarcia@mail.state.mo.us

MONTANA
Arlynn Fishbaugh
Director
Arts Council
316 N. Park Ave., Rm. 252
Helena, MT 59620-2201
Phone: (406) 444-6430
Fax: (406) 444-6548

NEBRASKA
Jennifer Severin Clark
Executive Director
Arts Council
3838 Davenport St.
Omaha, NE 68131
Phone: (402) 595-2122
Fax: (402) 595-2334

NEVADA
Kathie Bartlett
Chair of the Board
Council of the Arts
Dept. of Museums
602 N. Curry St.
Carson City, NV 89703
Phone: (775) 684-6680
Fax: (775) 684-6688

NEW HAMPSHIRE
Becky Lawrence
Director
Div. of the Arts
Cultural Affairs
40 N. Main St.
Concord, NH 03301-4974
Phone: (603) 271-2789
Fax: (603) 271-3584

NEW JERSEY
Barbara F. Russo
Executive Director
Council on the Arts
Dept. of State
20 W. State St.
P.O. Box 306
Trenton, NJ 08625-0306
Phone: (609) 292-6130
Fax: (609) 989-1440

NEW MEXICO
Margaret Brommelsek
Director
Arts. Div.
Ofc. of Cultural Affairs
228 E. Palace Ave.
Santa Fe, NM 87501
Phone: (505) 827-6490
Fax: (505) 827-7308

NEW YORK
Richard J. Schwartz
Chairperson
Council on Arts
915 Broadway, 8th Fl.
New York, NY 10010
Phone: (212) 387-7003
Fax: (212) 387-7164

NORTH CAROLINA
Mary Regan
Director
Arts Council
Dept. of Cultural Resources
221 E. Lane St.
Raleigh, NC 27601-2807
Phone: (919) 733-2821
Fax: (919) 733-4834

NORTH DAKOTA
Patsy Thompson
Executive Director
Council on the Arts
418 E. Broadway Ave., Ste. 70
Bismarck, ND 58501-4086
Phone: (701) 328-3954
Fax: (701) 328-3963
E-mail: thompson@pioneer.state.nd.us

NORTHERN MARIANA ISLANDS
Robert H. Hunter
Director
Commonwealth Council for Arts & Culture
Community & Cultural Affairs
P.O. Box 553 CHRB
Saipan, MP 96950
Phone: (670) 322-9982
Fax: (670) 322-9028

OHIO
Wayne P. Lawson
Executive Director
Arts Council
727 E. Main St.
Columbus, OH 43205
Phone: (614) 466-2613
Fax: (614) 466-4494

OKLAHOMA
Betty Price
Executive Director
Arts Council
2101 Jim Thorpe Bldg., Rm. 640
2501 N. Lincoln Blvd.
Oklahoma City, OK 73105
Phone: (405) 521-2931
Fax: (405) 521-6418
E-mail: okarts@oklaosf.state.ok.us

OREGON
Christine D'Arcy
Executive Director
Arts Comm.
775 Summer St., NE
Salem, OR 97310
Phone: (503) 986-0088
Fax: (503) 986-0260

PENNSYLVANIA
Philip J. Horn
Executive Director
Council on the Arts
Rm. 216, Finance Bldg.
Harrisburg, PA 17120
Phone: (717) 787-6883
Fax: (717) 783-2538
E-mail: phorn@oa.state.pa.us

PUERTO RICO
Jose Ramon De La Torre
Executive Director
Institute of Puerto Rican Culture
P.O. Box 9024184
San Juan, PR 00902-4184
Phone: (787) 723-2115
Fax: (787) 724-8393

RHODE ISLAND
Randall Rosenbaum
Executive Director
Council on the Arts
95 Cedar St., Ste. 103
Providence, RI 02903
Phone: (401) 222-3880

SOUTH CAROLINA
Suzette Surkamer
Executive Director
Arts Comm.
1800 Gervais St.
Columbia, SC 29201
Phone: (803) 734-8687

SOUTH DAKOTA
Dennis Holub
Executive Director
Arts Council
230 S. Phillips, Ste. 204
Sioux Falls, SD 57102-0720
Phone: (605) 367-5678

TENNESSEE
Bennett Tarleton
Director
Arts Comm.
401 Charlotte Ave.
Nashville, TN 37243-0780
Phone: (615) 741-1701
Fax: (615) 741-8559

TEXAS
John Paul Batiste
Executive Director
Comm. on the Arts
Ernest O. Thompson Bldg., 5th Fl.
920 Colorado
Austin, TX 78701
Phone: (512) 463-5535
Fax: (512) 475-2699

U.S. VIRGIN ISLANDS
John Jowers
Executive Director
Council on the Arts
41 Norre Gade
St. Thomas, VI 00802
Phone: (340) 774-5984
Fax: (340) 774-6206

UTAH
Bonnie H. Stephens
Director
Arts Council
Community & Economic Dev. Dept.
617 E. S. Temple
Salt Lake City, UT 84102-1177
Phone: (801) 236-7555
Fax: (801) 236-7556
E-mail: bstephen@arts.state.ut.us

VERMONT
Alexander L. Aldrich
Executive Director
Council on the Arts
136 State St., Drawer 33
Montpelier, VT 05633-6001
Phone: (802) 828-3293
Fax: (802) 828-3363

VIRGINIA
Peggy J. Baggett
Executive Director
Comm. for the Arts
223 Governor St., 2nd Fl.
Richmond, VA 23219
Phone: (804) 225-3132
Fax: (804) 225-4327

WASHINGTON
Kris Tucker
Executive Director
Arts Comm.
234 E. 8th Ave.
P.O. Box 42675
Olympia, WA 98504
Phone: (360) 753-3860
Fax: (360) 586-5351

WEST VIRGINIA
Lakin Ray Cook
Acting Director
Arts & Humanities Div.
Cultural Ctr.
Charleston, WV 25305
Phone: (304) 348-0240
Fax: (304) 558-2779

WISCONSIN
George Tzougros
Executive Director
Arts Board
Tourism
101 E. Wilson St., 1st Fl.
Madison, WI 53702
Phone: (608) 266-0190
Fax: (608) 267-0380

WYOMING
John Coe
Arts Program Manager
Div. of Cultural Resources
Dept. of Commerce
6101 Yellowstone
Cheyenne, WY 82002
Phone: (307) 777-7742

Attorney General

The chief legal officer of the state who represents the state or its offices in all litigation.

ALABAMA
Bill Pryor (R)
Attorney General
State House
11 S. Union St., Ste. 310
Montgomery, AL 36130-0152
Phone: (334) 242-7300
Fax: (334) 242-7458

ALASKA
Bruce M. Botelho (APPT.)
Attorney General
Diamond Courthouse
P.O. Box 110300
Juneau, AK 99811-0300
Phone: (907) 465-3600
Fax: (907) 465-2075

AMERICAN SAMOA
Albert Mailo Toetagata (APPT.)
Attorney General
Dept. of Legal Affairs
AS Govt.
Pago Pago, AS 96799
Phone: (684) 633-4163
Fax: (684) 633-1838

ARIZONA
Janet Napolitano (D)
Attorney General
Attorney Gen's. Ofc.
Law Bldg.
1275 W. Washington
Phoenix, AZ 85007
Phone: (602) 542-4266
Fax: (602) 542-4085

ARKANSAS
Mark Pryor (D)
Attorney General
200 Tower Bldg.
323 Ctr. St.
Little Rock, AR 72201
Phone: (501) 682-2007
Fax: (501) 682-8084

CALIFORNIA
Bill Lockyer (D)
Attorney General
1300 I St., 11th Fl.
Sacramento, CA 95814
Phone: (916) 324-5437

COLORADO
Ken Salazar (D)
Attorney General
Dept. of Law
1525 Sherman St.
Denver, CO 80203
Phone: (303) 866-3052
Fax: (303) 866-3955

CONNECTICUT
Richard Blumenthal (D)
Attorney General
55 Elm St.
Hartford, CT 06141-0120
Phone: (860) 808-5318
E-mail: attorney.general@po.state.ct.us

DELAWARE
M. Jane Brady (R)
Attorney General
Carvel State Ofc. Bldg.
820 N. French St.
Wilmington, DE 19801
Phone: (302) 577-8338
Fax: (302) 577-2610

DISTRICT OF COLUMBIA
Joanne Robinson
Interim Corporate Counsel
Ofc. of Corp. Counsel
441 4th St., NW, Ste. 1060N
Washington, DC 20001
Phone: (202) 727-6248
Fax: (202) 347-8922

FLORIDA
Robert A. Butterworth (D)
Attorney General
PL 01, The Capitol
Tallahassee, FL 32399-1050
Phone: (850) 487-1963
Fax: (850) 487-2564

GEORGIA
Thurbert E. Baker (D)
Attorney General
40 Capitol Sq., SW
Atlanta, GA 30334-1300
Phone: (404) 656-3300
Fax: (404) 657-8733

GUAM
John F. Tarantino
Acting Attorney General
Dept. of Law
Judicial Ctr. Bldg., Ste. 2-200E
120 W. O'Brien Dr.
Hagatna, GU 96910
Phone: (671) 475-3324
Fax: (671) 475-2493
E-mail: law@ns.gov.gu

HAWAII
Margery S. Bronster (APPT.)
Attorney General
425 Queen St.
Honolulu, HI 96813
Phone: (808) 586-1282
Fax: (808) 586-1239

IDAHO
Alan G. Lance (R)
Attorney General
State House
700 W. Jefferson
Boise, ID 83720-0010
Phone: (208) 334-2400
Fax: (208) 334-2530

ILLINOIS
Jim Ryan (R)
Attorney General
James R. Thompson Ctr.
100 W. Randolph St., 12th Fl.
Chicago, IL 60601
Phone: (312) 814-2503

INDIANA
Jeffrey A. Modisett (D)
Attorney General
Indiana Govt. Ctr., S., 5th Fl.
402 W. Washington St.
Indianapolis, IN 46204
Phone: (317) 232-6201
Fax: (317) 232-7979

IOWA
Tom Miller (D)
Attorney General
Hoover State Ofc. Bldg.
Des Moines, IA 50319
Phone: (515) 281-5164
Fax: (515) 281-4209

KANSAS
Carla J. Stovall (R)
Attorney General
Judicial Bldg.
300 SW 10th St.
Topeka, KS 66612-1597
Phone: (785) 296-2215
Fax: (785) 296-6296

KENTUCKY
Albert Benjamin Chandler, III (D)
Attorney General
Ofc. of the Attorney Gen.
State Capitol, Ste. 118
Frankfort, KY 40601
Phone: (502) 696-5300
Fax: (502) 564-8310

LOUISIANA
Richard P. Ieyoub, Jr. (D)
Attorney General
Dept. of Justice
P.O. Box 94005
Baton Rouge, LA 70804-9005
Phone: (225) 342-7013
Fax: (225) 342-2090

MAINE
Andrew Ketterer (D)
Attorney General
6 State House Station
Augusta, ME 04333
Phone: (207) 626-8800
Fax: (207) 287-3145

MARYLAND
J. Joseph Curran, Jr. (D)
Attorney General
Ofc. of the Attorney Gen.
200 St. Paul Pl., 17th Fl.
Baltimore, MD 21201-2021
Phone: (410) 576-6300
Fax: (410) 576-7003
E-mail: jcurran@oag.state.md.us

MASSACHUSETTS
Thomas Reilly (D)
Attorney General
One Ashburton Pl.
Boston, MA 02108-1698
Phone: (617) 727-2200
Fax: (617) 727-3251

MICHIGAN
Jennifer Granholm (D)
Attorney General
525 W. Ottawa St.
P.O. Box 30212
Lansing, MI 48909-0212
Phone: (517) 373-1110
Fax: (517) 241-1850

MINNESOTA
Mike Hatch (DFL)
Attorney General
State Capitol, Rm. 102
75 Constitution Ave.
St. Paul, MN 55155
Phone: (651) 296-6196
Fax: (651) 297-4193
E-mail: attorney.general@state.mn.us

MISSISSIPPI
Mike Moore (D)
Attorney General
450 High St., 5th Fl., Gartin Bldg.
P.O. Box 220
Jackson, MS 39205-0220
Phone: (601) 359-3692
Fax: (601) 359-3441
E-mail: mmexec@ago.state.ms.us

MISSOURI
Jeremiah W. Nixon (D)
Attorney General
Supreme Ct. Bldg.
207 W. High St.
Jefferson City, MO 65101
Phone: (573) 751-3321
Fax: (573) 751-0774
E-mail: attgenmail@moago.org

MONTANA
Joseph P. Mazurek (D)
Attorney General
Ofc. of the Attorney Gen.
Justice Bldg.
215 N. Sanders
P.O. Box 201401
Helena, MT 59620
Phone: (406) 444-2026
Fax: (406) 444-3549
E-mail: jmazurek@mt.gov

NEBRASKA
Don B. Stenberg (R)
Attorney General
State Capitol
P.O. Box 98920
Lincoln, NE 68509-8920
Phone: (402) 471-2682
Fax: (402) 471-3297

NEVADA
Frankie Sue Del Papa (D)
Attorney General
Old Supreme Ct. Bldg.
100 N. Carson St.
Carson City, NV 89701
Phone: (775) 687-4170
Fax: (775) 687-5798
E-mail: aginfo@govmail.state.nv.us

NEW HAMPSHIRE
Philip T. McLaughlin (APPT.)
Attorney General
State House Annex
25 Capitol St.
Concord, NH 03301-6397
Phone: (603) 271-3658

NEW JERSEY
Peter Verniero (APPT.)
Attorney General
Dept. of Law
Richard J. Hughes Justice Complex
25 Market St., P.O. Box 081
Trenton, NJ 08625-0081
Phone: (609) 292-4925
Fax: (609) 292-3508

NEW MEXICO
Patricia Madrid (D)
Attorney General
P.O. Drawer 1508
Santa Fe, NM 87504-1508
Phone: (505) 827-6000

NEW YORK
Eliot Spitzer (D)
Attorney General
Dept. of Law
The Capitol, 2nd Fl.
Albany, NY 12224
Phone: (518) 474-7330
Fax: (518) 473-9909

NORTH CAROLINA
Michael F. Easley (D)
Attorney General
Dept. of Justice
P.O. Box 629
Raleigh, NC 27602
Phone: (919) 716-6400
Fax: (919) 716-6750

NORTH DAKOTA
Heidi Heitkamp (D)
Attorney General
Attorney Gen's. Ofc.
600 E. Blvd. Ave., 1st Fl.
Bismarck, ND 58505-0040
Phone: (701) 328-2210
Fax: (701) 328-2226
E-mail: ndaghd@pioneer.state.nd.us

NORTHERN MARIANA ISLANDS
Maya B. Kara
Acting Attorney General
Ofc. of the Attorney Gen.
2nd Fl., Administration Bldg., Capitol Hill
Caller Box 10007
Saipan, MP 96950
Phone: (670) 664-2341
Fax: (670) 664-2349
E-mail: attorneygeneral.com.saipan

OHIO
Betty D. Montgomery (R)
Attorney General
30 E. Broad St., 17th Fl.
Columbus, OH 43266-4320
Phone: (614) 466-3376
Fax: (614) 752-5083

OKLAHOMA
W.A. Drew Edmondson (D)
Attorney General
State Capitol Bldg., Rm. 112
2300 N. Lincoln Blvd.
Oklahoma City, OK 73105
Phone: (405) 521-3921
Fax: (405) 521-6246
E-mail: ok@oag.state.ok.us

OREGON
Hardy Myers (D)
Attorney General
Justice Bldg.
Salem, OR 97310
Phone: (503) 378-6002
Fax: (503) 378-4017

PENNSYLVANIA
Michael Fisher (R)
Attorney General
Ofc. of the Attorney Gen.
Strawberry Sq., 16th Fl.
Harrisburg, PA 17120
Phone: (717) 787-3391
Fax: (717) 783-1107

PUERTO RICO
Jose A. Fuentes Agostini
Attorney General
Ofc. of the Attorney Gen.
P.O. Box 9020192
San Juan, PR 00902-0192
Phone: (787) 721-7700
Fax: (787) 724-4770

RHODE ISLAND
Sheldon Whitehouse (D)
Attorney General
150 S. Main St.
Providence, RI 02903
Phone: (401) 274-4400
Fax: (401) 222-1302

SOUTH CAROLINA
Charlie Condon (R)
Attorney General
Rembert C. Dennis Ofc. Bldg.
P.O. Box 11549
Columbia, SC 29211-1549
Phone: (803) 734-3970
Fax: (803) 253-6283
E-mail: INFO@scattorneygeneral.org

SOUTH DAKOTA
Mark Barnett (R)
Attorney General
Ofc. of the Attorney Gen.
500 E. Capitol Ave.
Pierre, SD 57501-5070
Phone: (605) 773-3215
Fax: (605) 773-4106

TENNESSEE
John Knox Walkup (APPT.)
Attorney General
500 Charlotte Ave.
Nashville, TN 37243
Phone: (615) 741-3491
Fax: (615) 741-2009

TEXAS
John Cornyn (R)
Attorney General
Ofc. of the Attorney Gen.
P.O. Box 12548
Austin, TX 78711-2548
Phone: (512) 463-2100
Fax: (512) 463-2063

U.S. VIRGIN ISLANDS
Iver Stirdiron
Attorney General
Dept. of Justice
G.E.R.S. Complex
4813-50C Kronprinsdens Gade
St. Thomas, VI 00802
Phone: (340) 774-5666
Fax: (340) 774-9710

UTAH
Jan Graham (D)
Attorney General
236 State Capitol
Salt Lake City, UT 84114-1326
Phone: (801) 538-1130
Fax: (801) 538-1121
E-mail: jgraham.atcap01@state.ut.us

VERMONT
William Sorrell (D)
Attorney General
109 State St.
Montpelier, VT 05609
Phone: (802) 828-3171
Fax: (802) 828-2154

VIRGINIA
Mark L. Earley (R)
Attorney General
Pocahontas Bldg., 6th Fl.
900 E. Main St.
Richmond, VA 23219
Phone: (804) 786-2071
Fax: (804) 786-1991

WASHINGTON
Christine O. Gregoire (D)
Attorney General
1125 Washington St., SE
P.O. Box 40100
Olympia, WA 98504-0100
Phone: (360) 664-8564
Fax: (360) 664-0228

WEST VIRGINIA
Darrell V. McGraw, Jr. (D)
Attorney General
Ofc. of the Attorney Gen.
Capitol Bldg.
1900 Kanawha Blvd., E.
Charleston, WV 25305
Phone: (304) 558-2021
Fax: (304) 558-0140

WISCONSIN
James E. Doyle (D)
Attorney General
State Capitol, Ste. 114 E.
P.O. Box 7857
Madison, WI 53707-7857
Phone: (608) 266-1221
Fax: (608) 267-2779
E-mail: doyleje@doj.state.wi.us

WYOMING
Gay Woodhouse (APPT.)
Attorney General
Attorney Gen's. Ofc.
State Capitol Bldg.
Cheyenne, WY 82002
Phone: (307) 777-7841
Fax: (307) 777-6869

Banking

Administers laws regulating the operation of banking institutions in the state.

ALABAMA
Norman B. Davis, Jr.
Commissioner
Savings & Loan Board
Dept. of State Banking
401 Adams Ave., Ste. 480
Montgomery, AL 36130-1201
Phone: (334) 242-3452
Fax: (334) 242-3500

ALASKA
Franklin T. Elder
Acting Director
Div. of Banking, Securities & Corps.
Dept. of Commerce & Economic Dev.
P.O. Box 110807
Juneau, AK 99811-0807
Phone: (907) 465-2521
Fax: (907) 465-2549

AMERICAN SAMOA

ARIZONA
Richard C. Houseworth
Superintendent
Dept. of Banking
2910 N. 44th St., Ste. 310
Phoenix, AZ 85018
Phone: (602) 255-4421
Fax: (602) 381-1225

ARKANSAS
Frank White
Commissioner
State Bank Dept.
323 Ctr. St., Ste. 500
Little Rock, AR 72201
Phone: (501) 324-9019
Fax: (501) 324-9028

CALIFORNIA
Conrad Hewitt
Superintendent
Dept. of Financial Institutions
111 Pine St., Ste. 1100
San Francisco, CA 94111
Phone: (415) 263-8507

COLORADO
Richard Fulkerson
Commissioner
Div. of Banking
Dept. of Regulatory Agencies
1560 Broadway, Rm. 1175
Denver, CO 80202
Phone: (303) 894-7575
Fax: (303) 894-7570

CONNECTICUT
John P. Burke
Commissioner
Dept. of Banking
260 Constitution Plz.
Hartford, CT 06103
Phone: (860) 240-8100

DELAWARE
Robert A. Glen
State Bank Commissioner
Dept. of State
P.O. Box 1401
Dover, DE 19903
Phone: (302) 739-4235
Fax: (302) 739-3609

DISTRICT OF COLUMBIA
J. Anthony Romero, III
Interim Superintendent
Ofc. of Banking & Financial Institutions
717 14th St., NW, Ste. 1100
Washington, DC 20005
Phone: (202) 727-1563

FLORIDA
Robert F. Milligan
Comptroller
Dept. of Banking & Finance
The Capitol, PL 09
Tallahassee, FL 32399-0350
Phone: (850) 488-0370
Fax: (850) 488-9818

GEORGIA
Steven D. Bridges
Commissioner
Dept. of Banking & Finance
2990 Brandywine Rd., # 200
Atlanta, GA 30341
Phone: (770) 986-1633
Fax: (770) 986-1655

GUAM
Joseph T. Duenas
Director
Dept. of Revenue & Taxation
13-1 Mariner Dr., Tiyan
P.O. Box 23607
GMF, GU 96921
Phone: (671) 475-1817
Fax: (671) 472-2643

HAWAII
Lynn Y. Wakatsuki
Commissioner
Div. of Financial Institutions
Commerce & Consumer Affairs
1010 Richards St., Rm. 602-A
Honolulu, HI 96813
Phone: (808) 586-2820
Fax: (808) 586-2818

IDAHO
Gavin Gee
Director
Dept. of Finance
700 W. State St.
Boise, ID 83720
Phone: (208) 332-8010

ILLINOIS
William A. Darr
Commissioner
Ofc. of Banks & Real Estate
500 E. Monroe, Ste. 900
Springfield, IL 62701
Phone: (217) 782-1398
Fax: (217) 524-5941

INDIANA
Charles W. Phillips
Director
Dept. of Financial Institutions
Rm. W066
402 W. Washington St.
Indianapolis, IN 46204
Phone: (317) 232-3955
Fax: (317) 232-7655

IOWA
Michael Guttau
Superintendent
Banking Div.
Dept. of Commerce
200 E. Grand Ave., Ste. 300
Des Moines, IA 50309
Phone: (515) 281-4014
Fax: (515) 281-4862

KANSAS
Clyde Graber
Commissioner
Ofc. of the State Bank Commissioner
700 Jack, Ste. 300
Topeka, KS 66603
Phone: (785) 296-2266
Fax: (785) 296-0168

KENTUCKY
Arthur Freeman
Commissioner
Public Protection & Regulation Cabinet
Dept. of Financial Institutions
477 Versailles Rd.
Frankfort, KY 40601
Phone: (502) 573-3390
Fax: (502) 573-8787

LOUISIANA
Doris B. Gunn
Acting Commissioner
Ofc. of Financial Institutions
P.O. Box 94095
Baton Rouge, LA 70804-9095
Phone: (225) 925-4660
Fax: (225) 925-4548

MAINE
H. Donald DeMatteis
Superintendent
Bur. of Banking
Dept. of Professional & Financial Regulation
36 State House Station
Augusta, ME 04333
Phone: (207) 582-8713

MARYLAND
Mary Louise Preis
Commissioner
Div. of Financial Regulation
Dept. of Labor, Licensing & Regulation
500 N. Calvert St., Rm. 402
Baltimore, MD 21202
Phone: (410) 230-6098
Fax: (410) 333-0475
E-mail: mlpreis@dllr.state.md.us

MASSACHUSETTS
Thomas J. Curry
Commissioner of Banks
Div. of Banks
100 Cambridge St., Rm. 2004
Boston, MA 02202
Phone: (617) 727-3145
Fax: (617) 727-7631

MICHIGAN
Pat McQueen
Commissioner
Financial Institutions Bur.
Consumer & Industry Services
P.O. Box 30224
Lansing, MI 48909
Phone: (517) 373-7279
Fax: (517) 335-0908

MINNESOTA
Kevin M. Murphy
Deputy Commissioner
Div. of Financial Examinations
Dept. of Commerce
133 7th St., E.
Minneapolis, MN 55101
Phone: (651) 296-2715
Fax: (651) 296-8591

MISSISSIPPI
Ronny Parham
Commissioner
Banking & Consumer Finances Dept.
550 High St., Ste. 304
Jackson, MS 39202
Phone: (601) 359-1103
Fax: (601) 359-3557

MISSOURI
Earl Manning
Director of Finance
Div. of Finance
Dept. of Economic Dev.
Truman Bldg., Rm. 630
P.O. Box 716
Jefferson City, MO 65102
Phone: (573) 751-2545
Fax: (573) 751-9192
E-mail: emanning@mail.state.mo.us

MONTANA
Donald W. Hutchinson
Commissioner
Div. of Banking & Financial Institutions
Dept. of Commerce
846 Front St.
P.O. Box 200546
Helena, MT 59620-0546
Phone: (406) 444-2091
Fax: (406) 444-4186

NEBRASKA
Sam Baird
Director
Dept. of Banking & Finance
1200 N. St., Atrium #311
P.O. Box 95006
Lincoln, NE 68509
Phone: (402) 471-2171
Fax: (402) 471-3062

NEVADA
L. Scott Walshaw
Commissioner
Div. of Financial Institutions
Dept. of Business & Industry
406 E. 2nd St., Ste. 3
Carson City, NV 89701
Phone: (775) 687-4259
Fax: (775) 687-6909

NEW HAMPSHIRE
A. Roland Roberge
Commissioner
Dept. of Banking
169 Manchester St., Bldg. 3
Concord, NH 03301-5127
Phone: (603) 271-3561
Fax: (603) 271-1090

NEW JERSEY
John Traier
Deputy Commissioner
Banking & Insurance
Ofc. of the Commissioner
Dept. of Banking
P.O. Box 040
Trenton, NJ 08625-0040
Phone: (609) 292-3420
Fax: (609) 777-0107

NEW MEXICO
William J. Verant
Director
Financial Institutions Div.
Dept. of Regulation & Licensing
725 St. Michael's St.
P.O. Box 25101
Santa Fe, NM 87504
Phone: (505) 827-7100
Fax: (505) 984-0617

NEW YORK
Elizabeth McCaul
Acting Superintendent
Dept. of Banking
2 Rector St., 19th Fl.
New York, NY 10006
Phone: (212) 618-6558
Fax: (212) 618-6599

NORTH CAROLINA
Hal Lingerfelt
Commissioner
Banking Comm.
Dept. of Commerce
702 Oberlin Rd., Ste. 400
Raleigh, NC 27605
Phone: (919) 733-3016
Fax: (919) 733-6918

NORTH DAKOTA
Gary Preszler
Commissioner
Dept. of Banking & Financial Institutions
2000 Schafer St., Ste. G
Bismarck, ND 58501-1204
Phone: (701) 328-9933
Fax: (701) 328-9955
E-mail: gpreszle@pioneer.state.nd.us

NORTHERN MARIANA ISLANDS
Oscar Camacho
Director
Economic Dev./Banking & Insurance
Dept. of Commerce
P.O. Box 10007
Saipan, MP 96950
Phone: (670) 664-3023
Fax: (670) 664-3066

OHIO
Scott O'Donnell
Superintendent
Div. of Financial Institutions
Dept. of Commerce
77 S. High St., 21st Fl.
Columbus, OH 43266-0544
Phone: (614) 728-8400
Fax: (614) 644-1631

OKLAHOMA
Mick Thompson
Commissioner
Dept. of Banking
4545 N. Lincoln Blvd., Ste. 164
Oklahoma City, OK 73105-3427
Phone: (405) 521-2782
Fax: (405) 522-2993

OREGON
Dick Nockleby
Administrator
Finance & Corporate Securities
Dept. of Consumer & Business Services
21 Labor & Industries Bldg.
350 Winter St., NW, #410
Salem, OR 97310-1321
Phone: (503) 378-4140
Fax: (503) 947-7862

PENNSYLVANIA
Richard C. Rishel
Cabinet Secretary
Dept. of Banking
Harristown 2, 16th Fl.
Harrisburg, PA 17120
Phone: (717) 787-6991
Fax: (717) 787-8773
E-mail: rrishel@banking.state.pa.us

PUERTO RICO
Joseph O'Neill
Commissioner
Ofc. of Financial Institutions, #600
1492 Ponce de Leon Centro Europa
San Juan, PR 00907-4022
Phone: (787) 723-3131
Fax: (787) 723-4042

RHODE ISLAND
Dennis F. Ziroli
Associate Director & Superintendent of Banking
Banking Div.
Dept. of Business Regulation
233 Richmond St., Ste. 231
Providence, RI 02903-4231
Phone: (401) 222-2405
Fax: (401) 222-5628

SOUTH CAROLINA
Grady L. Patterson, Jr.
State Treasurer
1200 Senate St.
Wade Hampton Bldg., 1st Fl.
Columbia, SC 29201
Phone: (803) 734-2635

SOUTH DAKOTA
Dick Duncan
Director
Div. of Banking & Finance
Dept. of Commerce & Regulation
217 W. Missouri
Pierre, SD 57501
Phone: (605) 773-3421
Fax: (605) 773-5367

TENNESSEE
Bill Houston
Commissioner
Dept. of Financial Institutions
John Sevier Bldg., 4th Fl.
Nashville, TN 37243
Phone: (615) 741-5603
Fax: (615) 741-2883

TEXAS
Catherine A. Ghiglieri
Commissioner
Dept. of Banking
2601 N. Lamar Blvd.
Austin, TX 78705
Phone: (512) 475-1300
Fax: (512) 475-1313

U.S. VIRGIN ISLANDS
Maryleen Thomas
Director
Banking & Insurance Div
#18 Kongens Gade
St. Thomas, VI 00801
Phone: (340) 774-2991
Fax: (340) 774-9458

UTAH
G. Edward Leary
Commissioner
Administration
Dept. of Financial Institutions
324 S. State, Ste. 201
P.O. Box 89
Salt Lake City, UT 84110-0089
Phone: (801) 538-8854
Fax: (801) 538-8894
E-mail: eleary.bdfipost@state.ut.us

VERMONT
Elizabeth R. Costle
Commissioner
Dept. of Banking, Insurance, Securities & Health
Care Administration
89 State St.
Montpelier, VT 05620-3101
Phone: (802) 828-3301
Fax: (802) 828-3306
E-mail: bcostle@state.vt.us

VIRGINIA
Theodore W. Morrison, Jr.
Chair
State Corp. Comm.
Tyler Bldg.
1300 E. Main St.
Richmond, VA 23219
Phone: (804) 371-9608
Fax: (804) 371-9376

WASHINGTON
John Bley
Director
Dept. of Financial Institutions
P.O. Box 41200
Olympia, WA 98504-1201
Phone: (360) 902-8700
Fax: (360) 586-5068

WEST VIRGINIA
Sharon G. Bias
Commissioner
Div. of Banking
Bldg. 3, Rm. 311-A
1800 Washington St., E.
Charleston, WV 25305
Phone: (304) 558-2294
Fax: (304) 558-0442

WISCONSIN
Michael Mach
Administrator
Ofc. of Banking
Dept. of Financial Institutions
345 W. Washington
P.O. Box 7876
Madison, WI 53707-7876
Phone: (608) 266-1621
Fax: (608) 267-1234

WYOMING
Bruce Hendrickson
Commissioner
Banking Board
Herschler Bldg., 3rd Fl., E.
Cheyenne, WY 82002
Phone: (307) 777-7792
Fax: (307) 777-3555

Boating Law Administration

Administers and enforces state boating laws and boating education efforts.

ALABAMA
William B. Garner
Director
Marine Police Div.
Conservation & Natural Resources
64 N. Union St.
Montgomery, AL 36130-1451
Phone: (334) 242-3673
Fax: (334) 242-0336

ALASKA
James Stratton
Director
Div. of Parks & Outdoor Recreation
Dept. of Natural Resources
3601 C St., Ste. 1200
Anchorage, AK 99503-5921
Phone: (907) 269-8700
Fax: (907) 269-8907

AMERICAN SAMOA

ARIZONA
Kim Keith
Boating Law Administrator
Law Enforcement Branch
Wildlife Mgmt. Div.
Game & Fish Dept.
7200 E. Univ.
Mesa, AZ 85207-6502
Phone: (602) 981-9400
Fax: (602) 789-3920

ARKANSAS
Butch Potts
Boating Law Administrator
Boating Safety Section
State Game & Fish Comm.
2 Natural Resources Dr.
Little Rock, AR 72205
Phone: (501) 223-6300
Fax: (501) 223-6425

CALIFORNIA
Charles Raysbrook
Director
Dept. of Boating & Waterways
1629 S St.
Sacramento, CA 95814
Phone: (916) 445-6881
Fax: (916) 327-7250

COLORADO
Rick Storm
Boating Administrator
Div. of Parks & Outdoor Recreation
13787 S. Hwy. 85
Littleton, CO 80125
Phone: (303) 791-1954
Fax: (303) 470-0782

CONNECTICUT
Randolph W. Dill
Boating Law Administrator
Boating Div.
Environmental Protection Dept.
P.O. Box 280
Old Lyme, CT 06371-0280
Phone: (860) 434-8638
Fax: (860) 434-3501

DELAWARE
Rodney L. Harmic
Boating Law Administrator
Dept. of Natural Resources & Environmental Control
P.O. Box 1401
Dover, DE 19903
Phone: (302) 739-3440
Fax: (302) 739-6157

DISTRICT OF COLUMBIA
Langston Clay
Boating Law Administrator
Metropolitan Police Dept.
Harbor Section
550 Water St., SW
Washington, DC 20024
Phone: (202) 727-4582
Fax: (202) 727-3663

FLORIDA
Mickey Watson
Boating Law Administrator
Div. of Law Enforcement
Dept. of Environmental Protection
3900 Commonwealth Blvd., MS600
Tallahassee, FL 32399-3000
Phone: (850) 488-5600
Fax: (850) 487-2642

GEORGIA
Joel M. Brown
Boating Law Administrator
Wildlife Resources Div.
Dept. of Natural Resources
2070 U.S. Hwy. 278, SE
Social Cir., GA 30279
Phone: (770) 918-6408
Fax: (770) 918-6410

GUAM
Bradley A. Hokanson
Boating Law Administrator
Special Programs Section
Police Dept.
233 Central Ave., Tiyan
P.O. Box 23909
GMF, GU 96921
Phone: (671) 475-8447
Fax: (671) 472-9704
E-mail: hokanson@kuentos.guam.net

HAWAII
Howard Gehring
Administrator
Div. of Boating & Ocean Recreation Land & Natural Resources Dept.
333 Queen St., Ste. 300
Honolulu, HI 96813
Phone: (808) 587-1966
Fax: (808) 587-1977

IDAHO
Mark Brandt
Boating Program Supervisor
Statehouse
Dept. of Parks & Recreation
700 W. Jefferson
P.O. Box 83720
Boise, ID 83720
Phone: (208) 334-4199
Fax: (208) 334-3741

ILLINOIS
Larry Closson
Deputy Chief
Ofc. of Law Enforcement
Dept. of Natural Resources
524 S. Second St.
Springfield, IL 62701
Phone: (217) 782-6431
Fax: (217) 785-8405

INDIANA
Samuel Purvis
Boating Law Administrator/Law Enforcement
Dept. of Natural Resources
IGC-South, Rm. W255-D
402 W. Washington
Indianapolis, IN 46204
Phone: (317) 232-4010
Fax: (317) 232-8035

IOWA
Rick McGeough
Bureau Chief
Law Enforcement
Fish & Wildlife Div.
Wallace State Ofc. Bldg.
E. 9th & Grand Aves.
Des Moines, IA 50319-0034
Phone: (515) 281-5919
Fax: (515) 281-6794

J. Sunny Satre
Recreational Safety Coordinator
Fish & Wildlife Div.
Dept. of Natural Resources
Wallace State Ofc. Bldg.
E. 9th & Grand Aves.
Des Moines, IA 50319-0034
Phone: (515) 281-8652
Fax: (515) 281-6794

KANSAS
Cheryl Swayne
Boating Law Administrator
Dept. of Wildlife & Parks
900 SW Jackson St., Ste. 502
Topeka, KS 66612-1233
Phone: (785) 296-2281
Fax: (785) 296-6953

KENTUCKY
David Loveless
Director
Div. of Water Patrol
1 Game Farm Rd.
Frankfort, KY 40601
Phone: (502) 564-3074
Fax: (502) 564-3178

LOUISIANA
Charles Clark
Assistant Chief
Enforcement Div.
Dept. of Wildlife & Fisheries
P.O. Box 98000
Baton Rouge, LA 70898-9000
Phone: (225) 765-2983
Fax: (225) 765-2832

MAINE
Timothy E. Peabody
Chief Warden
Warden Service
Dept. of Inland Fisheries & Wildlife
41 State House Station
Augusta, ME 04333
Phone: (207) 287-2766
Fax: (207) 287-6395

MARYLAND
Bruce A. Gilmore
Director
Licensing & Registration Service
Dept. of Natural Resources
Tawes State Ofc. Bldg.
580 Taylor Ave., Rm. B-1
Annapolis, MD 21401
Phone: (410) 260-8233

MASSACHUSETTS
Richard A. Murray
Director
Div. of Environmental Law Enforcement
175 Portland St.
Boston, MA 02114
Phone: (617) 727-3190
Fax: (617) 727-8551

MICHIGAN
Herbert Burns
Chief
Law Enforcement Div.
Dept. of Natural Resources
P.O. Box 30028
Lansing, MI 48909
Phone: (517) 335-3427
Fax: (517) 373-6816

MINNESOTA
Kim A. Elverum
Boating & Water Safety Coordinator
Dept. of Natural Resources
500 Lafayette Rd.
St. Paul, MN 55155-4046
Phone: (651) 296-0905
Fax: (651) 296-0902
E-mail: kim.elverum@state.mn.us

MISSISSIPPI
Elizabeth Raymond
Boating Law Administrator
Dept. of Wildlife, Fisheries & Parks
P.O. Box 451
Jackson, MS 39205
Phone: (601) 364-2185
Fax: (601) 364-2239

MISSOURI
Larry Whitten
Commissioner
State Water Patrol
Dept. of Public Safety
2728B Plz. Dr.
P.O. Box 1368
Jefferson City, MO 65102
Phone: (573) 751-3333
Fax: (573) 636-8428

MONTANA
Liz Lodman
Boating Law Administrator
Conservation Education Div.
Dept. of Fish, Wildlife & Parks
P.O. Box 200701
Helena, MT 59620
Phone: (406) 444-2615
Fax: (406) 444-4952

NEBRASKA
Herb Angell
Boating Law Administrator
Outdoor Education Div.
Game & Parks Comm.
2200 N. 33rd St.
P.O. Box 30370
Lincoln, NE 68503-0370
Phone: (402) 471-5579
Fax: (402) 471-5528
E-mail: hangell@ngpsun.ngpc.state.ne.us

NEVADA
Fred Messmann
Deputy Chief Game Warden
Dept. of Wildlife
P.O. Box 10678
Reno, NV 89520
Phone: (775) 688-1542
Fax: (775) 688-1551

NEW HAMPSHIRE
David T. Barrett
Director
Div. of Safety Services
Bur. of Marine Patrol
Dept. of Safety
31 Dock Rd.
Gilford, NH 03246-7626
Phone: (603) 293-0091

Thomas McCabe, Jr.
Chief
Div. of Safety Services, Marine Patrol Div.
Safety Dept.
31 Dock Rd.
Gilford, NH 03246-7626
Phone: (603) 293-2037

NEW JERSEY
Charles Liber
Bureau Chief
Bur. of Marine Law Enforcement
State Police Headquarters
P.O. Box 7068
W. Trenton, NJ 08628-0068
Phone: (609) 882-2000
Fax: (609) 539-0718

NEW MEXICO
Ben Hoffacker
Boating Administrator
Park & Recreation Div.
Energy, Minerals & Natural Resources Dept.
P.O. Box 1147
Santa Fe, NM 87505
Phone: (505) 827-7125
Fax: (505) 827-1376

NEW YORK
Nelson Potter
Director
Marine & Recreational Vehicles Bur.
Ofc. of Parks, Recreation & Historic Preservation
Empire State Plz., Bldg. 1
Albany, NY 12238
Phone: (518) 474-0445
Fax: (518) 486-7378

NORTH CAROLINA
Charles Fullwood
Executive Director
Wildlife Resources Comm.
Dept. of Environment & Natural Resources
P.O. Box 27687
Raleigh, NC 27611
Phone: (919) 733-3391
Fax: (919) 733-7083

NORTH DAKOTA
Wilmer Pich
Boat & Water Safety Coordinator
Game & Fish Dept.
100 N. Bismarck Expy.
Bismarck, ND 58501-5095
Phone: (701) 328-6300
Fax: (701) 328-6352
E-mail: wpich@state.nd.us

NORTHERN MARIANA ISLANDS
Raymond Camacho
Officer in Charge
Boating Safety Div.
Public Safety Dept.
Lower Base, Tanapag
Saipan, MP 96950
Phone: (670) 322-4037
Fax: (670) 233-1542

OHIO
Jeff Hoedt
Chief
Watercraft Div.
Dept. of Natural Resources
4435 Fountain Sq. Dr., A-3
Columbus, OH 43224-1300
Phone: (614) 265-6476
Fax: (614) 267-8883

OKLAHOMA
Bob Sanders
Commander
Lake Patrol Div.
Dept. of Public Safety
P.O. Box 11415
Oklahoma City, OK 73136
Phone: (405) 425-2143
Fax: (405) 425-2894

OREGON
Paul Donheffner
Director
State Marine Board
435 Commercial St., NE, Ste. 400
Salem, OR 97310-0650
Phone: (503) 373-1405
Fax: (503) 378-4597

PENNSYLVANIA
Peter A. Colengelo
Executive Director
Fish & Boat Comm.
3532 Walnut St.
P.O. Box 67000
Harrisburg, PA 17106-7000
Phone: (717) 657-4515
Fax: (717) 657-4033
E-mail: pcolengelo@fish.state.pa.us

PUERTO RICO
Jose L. Campos Abella
Commissioner of Navigation
Dept. of Natural Resources
Puerta de Tierra
P.O. Box 9066600
San Juan, PR 00906-6600
Phone: (787) 724-2340
Fax: (787) 724-7335

RHODE ISLAND
Steven Hall
Boating Law Administrator
Dept. of Environmental Mgmt.
83 Park St.
Providence, RI 02903
Phone: (401) 222-6647
Fax: (401) 222-6823

SOUTH CAROLINA
Alvin A. Taylor
Boating Law Administrator
Div. of Law Enforcement & Boating
Dept. of Natural Resources
P.O. Box 12559
Charleston, SC 29422-2559
Phone: (803) 762-5034
Fax: (803) 762-5091

SOUTH DAKOTA
Bill Shattuck
Boating Safety Coordinator
Div. of Wildlife
523 E. Capitol Ave.
Pierre, SD 57501-5182
Phone: (605) 773-4506
Fax: (605) 773-6245

TENNESSEE
Ed Carter
Chief
Boating Div.
Wildlife Resources Agency
P.O. Box 40747
Nashville, TN 37204
Phone: (615) 781-6682
Fax: (615) 781-5268

TEXAS
Steve Hall
Director, Education Services
Law Enforcement Div.
Dept. of Parks & Wildlife
4200 Smith School Rd.
Austin, TX 78744
Phone: (512) 389-4568
Fax: (512) 389-4740

Carlos Vaca
Boating Law Administrator
Law Enforcement Div.
Dept. of Parks & Wildlife
4200 Smith School Rd.
Austin, TX 78744
Phone: (512) 389-4850
Fax: (512) 389-4740

U.S. VIRGIN ISLANDS
Robert A. Danet
Director of Enforcement
Dept. of Planning & Natural Resources
Nisky Ctr., Ste. 231
St. Thomas, VI 00802
Phone: (340) 776-8600
Fax: (340) 776-8608

UTAH
Ted Woolley
Boating Coordinator
Div. of Parks & Recreation
Dept. of Natural Resources
1594 W. N. Temple, Ste. 116
P.O. Box 145610
Salt Lake City, UT 84114-5610
Phone: (801) 538-7341
Fax: (801) 538-7378
E-mail: twooley.nrdpr@state.ut.us

VERMONT
Alan F. Buck
Boating Law Administrator
Marine Div.
State Police
103 S. Main St.
Waterbury, VT 05671-2101
Phone: (802) 244-8778
Fax: (802) 244-1106
E-mail: abuck@dps.state.vt.us

VIRGINIA
William L. Woodfin, Jr.
Director
Dept. of Game & Inland Fisheries
4010 W. Broad St.
Richmond, VA 23230
Phone: (804) 367-9231
Fax: (804) 367-0405

WASHINGTON
James Horan
Boating Law Administrator
State Parks & Recreation Comm.
P.O. Box 42654
Olympia, WA 98504-2654
Phone: (360) 902-8580
Fax: (360) 753-1594

WEST VIRGINIA
James Fields
Chief
Law Enforcement Section
Dept. of Natural Resources
Capitol Complex, Bldg. 3
Charleston, WV 25305
Phone: (304) 558-2783
Fax: (304) 558-1170

WISCONSIN
William G. Engfer
Boating Law Administrator
Dept. of Natural Resources
101 S. Webster St., LE/5
P.O. Box 7921
Madison, WI 53707
Phone: (608) 266-0859
Fax: (608) 266-3696

WYOMING
Russ Pollard
Wildlife Law Enforcement Coordinator
Dept. of Game & Fish
5400 Bishop Blvd.
Cheyenne, WY 82006
Phone: (307) 777-4579
Fax: (307) 777-4650

Budget

Collects and analyzes budget requests and supporting materials and prepares the executive budget document.

ALABAMA
Henry Mabry
State Finance Director
State Capitol Bldg.
600 Dexter Ave., Ste. 105-N
Montgomery, AL 36104
Phone: (334) 242-7160
Fax: (334) 242-4488

ALASKA
Annalee McConnell
Director
Ofc. of Mgmt. & Budget
P.O. Box 110020
Juneau, AK 99811-0020
Phone: (907) 465-4660
Fax: (907) 465-3008

AMERICAN SAMOA
Opa Iosefo K. Iuli
Director
Program Planning & Budget
Pago Pago, AS 96799
Phone: (684) 633-4201
Fax: (684) 633-1148

ARIZONA
Tom Betlach
Director
Ofc. of Strategic Planning & Budgeting
1700 W. Washington, 5th Fl.
Phoenix, AZ 85007
Phone: (602) 542-5381
Fax: (602) 542-0868

ARKANSAS
Mike Stormes
Administrator
Ofc. of Budget
Dept. of Finance & Administration
P.O. Box 3278
Little Rock, AR 72203
Phone: (501) 682-1941
Fax: (501) 682-1086

CALIFORNIA
Craig Brown
Director
Dept. of Finance
State Capitol, 1st Fl.
Sacramento, CA 95814
Phone: (916) 445-4141

COLORADO
Nancy J. McCallin
Executive Director
Ofc. of State Planning & Budgeting
Ofc. of the Governor
State Capitol, Rm. 114
200 E. Colfax Ave.
Denver, CO 80203-1792
Phone: (303) 866-2980
Fax: (303) 866-3044

CONNECTICUT
John Bacewicz
Acting Executive Budget Officer
Budget & Finance Div.
Ofc. of Policy & Mgmt.
450 Capitol Ave., MS 53BUD
Hartford, CT 06134
Phone: (860) 418-6444

DELAWARE
Peter M. Ross
Director
Ofc. of the Budget
P.O. Box 1401
Dover, DE 19901
Phone: (302) 739-4204
Fax: (302) 739-5661
E-mail: pross@state.de.us

DISTRICT OF COLUMBIA
Gordon McDonald
Director
Dept. of Finance & Revenue
441 4th St., NW
Washington, DC 20001

FLORIDA
Donna Arduin
Director
Ofc. of Planning & Budgeting
Executive Ofc. of the Governor
1601 The Capitol
Tallahassee, FL 32399-0001
Phone: (850) 488-7810
Fax: (850) 488-9005
E-mail: arduind@eog.state.fl.us

GEORGIA
Bill Tomlinson
Director
Ofc. of Planning & Budget
270 Washington St., SW, Rm. 8060
Atlanta, GA 30334
Phone: (404) 656-3820
Fax: (404) 656-7198

GUAM
Joseph E. Rivera
Director
Bur. of Budget & Mgmt. Research
P.O. Box 2950
Hagatna, GU 96932
Phone: (671) 475-9429
Fax: (671) 472-2825

HAWAII
Neal Miyahira
Interim Director of Finance
Dept. of Budget & Finance
P.O. Box 150
Honolulu, HI 96810
Phone: (808) 586-1518
Fax: (808) 586-1976

IDAHO
Darrell V. Manning
Administrator
Div. of Financial Mgmt.
Ofc. of the Governor
Statehouse
700 W. Jefferson
Boise, ID 83720
Phone: (208) 334-3900

ILLINOIS
Steve Schnorf
Director
Bur. of the Budget
Ofc. of the Governor
108 State House
Springfield, IL 60706
Phone: (217) 782-4520
Fax: (217) 524-1514

INDIANA
Peggy Boehm
Director
Budget Agency
State House, Rm. 212
Indianapolis, IN 46204
Phone: (317) 232-5612
Fax: (317) 233-3323

IOWA
Randy Bauer
Director
Dept. of Mgmt.
Ofc. of the Governor
State Capitol, Rm. 12
Des Moines, IA 50319
Phone: (515) 281-7811

KANSAS
Duane Goossen
Director
Div. of the Budget
Dept. of Administration
State Capitol, 1st Fl.
300 SW 10th St.
Topeka, KS 66612
Phone: (785) 296-2436
Fax: (785) 296-0231

KENTUCKY
Crit Luallen
State Budget Director
Governor's Ofc.
700 Capitol Ave., Ste. 284
Frankfort, KY 40601
Phone: (502) 564-7300
Fax: (502) 564-6684

LOUISIANA
Steve Winham
Budget Director
Div. of Administration
Ofc. of the Governor
P.O. Box 94095
Baton Rouge, LA 70804
Phone: (225) 342-7005
Fax: (225) 342-7220

MAINE
John R. Nicholas
State Budget Officer
Bur. of the Budget
Dept. of Adm. & Financial Services
58 State House Station
Augusta, ME 04333
Phone: (207) 624-7810

MARYLAND
Frederick W. Puddester
Secretary
Ofc. of the Secretary
Dept. of Budget & Mgmt.
45 Calvert St., 1st Fl.
Annapolis, MD 21401
Phone: (410) 260-7041
Fax: (410) 974-2585
E-mail: fpudd@dbm.state.md.us

MASSACHUSETTS
Thomas Graf
Budget Director
Executive Ofc. for Administration & Finance
State House, Rm. 272
Boston, MA 02133
Phone: (617) 727-2081
Fax: (617) 727-1024

MICHIGAN
Mary A. Lannoye
State Budget Director
Dept. of Mgmt. & Budget
320 S. Walnut
Lansing, MI 48909
Phone: (517) 373-1004
Fax: (517) 373-7268

MINNESOTA
Pam Wheelock
Commissioner
Dept. of Finance
Centennial Ofc. Bldg., 4th Fl.
658 Cedar St.
St. Paul, MN 55155
Phone: (651) 297-7881
Fax: (651) 296-8685

MISSISSIPPI
Deb Collier
Director
Ofc. of Budget & Fund Mgmt.
Dept. of Finance & Administration
P.O. Box 139
Jackson, MS 39205
Phone: (601) 359-5758
Fax: (601) 359-6758

MISSOURI
Mark E. Ward
Director
Div. of Budget & Planning
Ofc. of Administration
State Capitol, Rm. 124
P.O. Box 809
Jefferson City, MO 65102
Phone: (573) 751-3925
Fax: (573) 526-4811
E-mail: wardm@mail.oa.state.mo.us

MONTANA
David Lewis
Director
Ofc. of Budget & Program Planning
State Capitol, Rm. 236
Helena, MT 59620
Phone: (406) 444-3616
Fax: (406) 444-5529

NEBRASKA
Gerry A. Oligmueller
Administrator
Budget Div.
Dept. of Adm. Services
State Capitol, Rm. 1322
P.O. Box 94664
Lincoln, NE 68509-4664
Phone: (402) 471-2526
Fax: (402) 471-4157

NEVADA
John P. Comeaux
Director
Dept. of Administration
Blasdel Bldg., Rm. 200
209 E. Musser St.
Carson City, NV 89701
Phone: (775) 684-0222
Fax: (775) 684-0260

NEW HAMPSHIRE
Donald S. Hill
Commissioner
Commissioner's Ofc.
Dept. of Adm. Services
25 Capitol St., Rm. 120
Concord, NH 03301-6312
Phone: (603) 271-3201

Vacant
Assistant Commissioner & Budget Officer
Budget Ofc.
Adm. Services
25 Capitol St., Rm. 119
Concord, NH 03301-6312
Phone: (603) 271-3204

NEW JERSEY
Elizabeth L. Pugh
Director
Ofc. of Mgmt. & Budget
Dept. of Treasury
P.O. Box 221
Trenton, NJ 08625-0221
Phone: (609) 292-6746
Fax: (609) 633-8179

NEW MEXICO
Paul Minogue
Director
Budget Div.
Dept. of Finance & Administration
180 Bataan Memorial Bldg.
Santa Fe, NM 87501
Phone: (505) 827-3642
Fax: (505) 827-4984

NEW YORK
Robert L. King
Director
Div. of Budget
Executive Dept.
State Capitol
Albany, NY 12224
Phone: (518) 473-3885
Fax: (518) 473-4875

NORTH CAROLINA
Marvin K. Dorman
State Budget Officer
Ofc. of State Budget
116 W. Jones St.
Raleigh, NC 27603-8005
Phone: (919) 733-7061
Fax: (919) 733-0640

NORTH DAKOTA
Rod Backman
Director
Ofc. of Mgmt. & Budget
600 E. Blvd. Ave., 4th Fl.
Bismarck, ND 58505-0400
Phone: (701) 328-2680
Fax: (701) 328-3230
E-mail: rbackman@state.nd.us

Dave Krabbenhoft
Budget Analyst
Ofc. of Mgmt. & Budget
600 E. Blvd. Ave., 4th Fl.
Bismarck, ND 58505-0400
Phone: (701) 328-2680
Fax: (701) 328-3230
E-mail: dkrabben@state.nd.us

NORTHERN MARIANA ISLANDS
Virginia C. Villagomez
Acting Special Assistant for Management & Budget
Ofc. of Mgmt. & Budget
Ofc. of the Governor
P.O. Box 10007
Saipan, MP 96950
Phone: (670) 664-2265
Fax: (670) 664-2272

OHIO
Tom Johnson
Director
Ofc. of Budget & Mgmt.
30 E. Broad St., 34th Fl.
Columbus, OH 43266
Phone: (614) 752-2577
Fax: (614) 466-5400

OKLAHOMA
Tom Daxon
Director
Ofc. of State Finance
122 State Capitol
2300 N. Lincoln Blvd.
Oklahoma City, OK 73105
Phone: (405) 521-2081
Fax: (405) 521-3902

OREGON
Theresa McHugh
Deputy Director
Dept. of Adm. Services
155 Cottage St., NE
Salem, OR 97310
Phone: (503) 378-4691
Fax: (503) 373-7643
E-mail: theresa.r.mchugh@state.or.us

PENNSYLVANIA
Robert Bittenbender
Cabinet Secretary
Ofc. of the Budget
Budget Dept.
Main Capitol Bldg., Rm. 238
Harrisburg, PA 17120
Phone: (717) 787-4472
Fax: (717) 787-4590
E-mail: rbittenbe@gois.state.pa.us

PUERTO RICO
Jorge Aponte Hernandez
Director
Ofc. of Budget & Mgmt.
P.O. Box 9023228
San Juan, PR 00902-3228
Phone: (787) 725-9420
Fax: (787) 724-1374

RHODE ISLAND
Stephen P. McAllister
Executive Director/State Budget Officer
State Budget Ofc.
Dept. of Administration
1 Capitol Hill, 4th Fl.
Providence, RI 02908
Phone: (401) 222-6300
Fax: (401) 222-6410

SOUTH CAROLINA
Les Boles
Director
Ofc. of State Budget
Budget & Control Board
1122 Lady St., 12th Fl.
Columbia, SC 29201
Phone: (803) 734-2280

SOUTH DAKOTA
Curt Everson
Commissioner
Bur. of Finance & Mgmt.
500 E. Capitol Ave., Rm. 216
Pierre, SD 57501
Phone: (605) 773-3411
Fax: (605) 773-4711

TENNESSEE
Jerry Lee
Assistant Commissioner
Budget Div.
Dept. of Finance & Administration
TN Tower, 9th Fl.
Nashville, TN 37243
Phone: (615) 532-9608

TEXAS
Albert Hawkins
Director
Budget & Planning
Ofc. of the Governor
P.O. Box 12428
Austin, TX 78711
Phone: (512) 463-1778
Fax: (512) 463-1880
E-mail: ahawkins@governor.texas.gov

U.S. VIRGIN ISLANDS
Ira Mills
Director
Ofc. of Mgmt. & Budget
#41 Norre Gade
Emancipation Garden Station, 2nd Fl.
St. Thomas, VI 00802
Phone: (340) 774-0750
Fax: (340) 774-0069

UTAH
Lynne Koga
Director
Ofc. of Planning & Budget
Governor's Ofc.
116 State Capitol
Salt Lake City, UT 84114
Phone: (801) 538-1562
Fax: (801) 538-1547
E-mail: lkoga@gov.state.ut.us

VERMONT
Thomas Pelham
Commissioner
Agency of Administration
Dept. of Finance & Mgmt.
109 State St.
Montpelier, VT 05609-0401
Phone: (802) 828-2376
Fax: (802) 828-2428
E-mail: tpelham@fin.state.vt.us

VIRGINIA
Scott D. Pattison
Director
Dept. of Planning & Budget
202 N. 9th St., Rm. 418
Richmond, VA 23219
Phone: (804) 786-5375
Fax: (804) 225-3291

WASHINGTON
Dick Thompson
Director
Ofc. of Financial Mgmt.
300 Insurance Bldg.
P.O. Box 43113
Olympia, WA 98504
Phone: (360) 902-0555
Fax: (360) 664-2832

WEST VIRGINIA
Roger L. Smith
Director
Budget Div.
Dept. of Finance & Administration
State Capitol
1900 Kanawha Blvd., E.
Charleston, WV 25305-0470
Phone: (304) 558-2344
Fax: (304) 558-2999

WISCONSIN
Richard G. Chandler
Director
Div. of Executive Budget & Finance
Dept. of Administration
101 E. Wilson, 10th Fl.
P.O. Box 7864
Madison, WI 53707
Phone: (608) 266-1035
Fax: (608) 267-0372

WYOMING
Art Burgess
Administrator
Budget Div.
2001 Capitol Ave.
Cheyenne, WY 82002
Phone: (307) 777-7203
Fax: (307) 777-3688

Building Codes

Establishes and enforces standards of construction, materials and occupancy for all buildings.

ALABAMA
Stedman B. McCollough
Director
Building Comm.
770 Washington Ave., Ste. 444
Montgomery, AL 36130-1150
Phone: (334) 242-4082
Fax: (334) 242-4182

ALASKA

AMERICAN SAMOA
Toafa Vaiagae
Director
Dept. of Public Works
AS Govt.
Pago Pago, AS 96799
Phone: (684) 633-4141
Fax: (684) 633-5958

ARIZONA
N. Eric Borg
Director
Dept. of Bldg. & Fire Safety
99 E. Virginia, Ste. 100
Phoenix, AZ 85004
Phone: (602) 255-4072
Fax: (602) 255-4962

ARKANSAS
Howard Williams
Administrator
Contractor's Licensing Board
621 E. Capitol
Little Rock, AR 72202
Phone: (501) 372-4661
Fax: (501) 372-2247

CALIFORNIA
Travis Pitts
Deputy Director
Div. of Codes & Standards
Housing & Community Dev. Dept.
P.O. Box 1407
Sacramento, CA 95812
Phone: (916) 445-9471

COLORADO
Lester Field
Program Manager
Div. of Housing Codes
Dept. of Local Affairs
1313 Sherman St., Rm. 518
Denver, CO 80203
Phone: (303) 866-2033
Fax: (303) 866-4077

CONNECTICUT
Christopher Laux
State Building Inspector
Dept. of Public Safety
P.O. Box 2794
Middletown, CT 06457
Phone: (860) 685-8310

DELAWARE

DISTRICT OF COLUMBIA
Lloyd J. Jordan
Director
Environmental Regulation Administration
Dept. of Consumer & Regulatory Affairs
941 N. Capitol St., NE, 9th Fl.
Washington, DC 20002
Phone: (202) 442-8947
Fax: (202) 442-9444

FLORIDA
Rick Dixon
Section Administrator
Codes & Standards Section
2555 Shumard Oak Blvd.
Tallahassee, FL 32399-2100
Phone: (850) 487-1824
Fax: (850) 414-8436

GEORGIA
Steve Black
Executive Director
Bldg. Authority
1 Martin Luther King, Jr. Dr.
Atlanta, GA 30334
Phone: (404) 656-3252

GUAM
Daniel Lizama
Acting Director
Dept. of Public Works
542 N. Marine Dr.
Tamuning, GU 96911
Phone: (671) 646-3131
Fax: (671) 649-9178

HAWAII

IDAHO
Joe Hunter
Administrator
Div. of Bldg. Safety
Self Governing Dept.
277 N. 6th
Boise, ID 83702
Phone: (208) 334-3950
Fax: (208) 334-2683

ILLINOIS
John Varones
Executive Director
Housing Dev. Authority
401 N. Michigan Ave.
Chicago, IL 60611
Phone: (312) 836-5337
Fax: (312) 836-5313

INDIANA
Gerald Dunn
State Building Commissioner
Fire & Bldg. Services
IGC, Rm. W246
402 W. Washington
Indianapolis, IN 46204
Phone: (317) 232-1404
Fax: (317) 232-0146

IOWA
Roy Marshall
State Fire Marshal
Dept. of Public Safety
Wallace State Ofc. Bldg.
E. 9th & Grand Aves.
Des Moines, IA 50319
Phone: (515) 281-8622
Fax: (515) 242-6299

KANSAS
Jim Reardon
Director
Div. of Facilities Mgmt.
Dept. of Administration
900 SW Jackson, Rm 653-S
Topeka, KS 66612-1318
Phone: (785) 296-4142
Fax: (785) 296-3456

KENTUCKY
Charles A. Cotton
Commissioner
Dept. of Housing, Bldgs. & Construction
1047 U.S. 127 S., Bay 1
Frankfort, KY 40601
Phone: (502) 564-8044
Fax: (502) 564-6799

LOUISIANA
Roger Magendie
Director
Facility Planning & Control Ofc.
Div. of Administration
P.O. Box 94095
Baton Rouge, LA 70804
Phone: (225) 342-0820
Fax: (225) 342-7624

MAINE

MARYLAND
James C. Hanna
Director
Codes Administrator
Housing & Community Dev.
100 Community Pl.
Crownsville, MD 21032
Phone: (410) 514-7212

MASSACHUSETTS
Tom Rogers
Chief
Board of Bldg. Regulations & Standards
One Ashburton Pl., Rm. 1301
Boston, MA 02108
Phone: (617) 727-3200
Fax: (617) 227-1754

MICHIGAN
Henry Green
Executive Director
Bur. of Construction Codes
Consumer & Industry Services
P.O. Box 30254
Lansing, MI 48909
Phone: (517) 322-5247

MINNESOTA
Thomas Joachim
State Building Official
Bldg. Codes & Standards Div.
Dept. of Administration
121 E. 7th Pl., Ste. 408
St. Paul, MN 55101
Phone: (651) 296-4639
Fax: (651) 297-1973
E-mail: tom.joachim@state.mn.us

MISSISSIPPI
Jerry Oakes
Director & Chief Architect
Div. of Services
Dept. of Finance & Administration
1501 Walter Sillers Bldg.
550 High St.
Jackson, MS 39201-1198
Phone: (601) 359-3633
Fax: (601) 359-2470

MISSOURI
Randall G. Allen
Director
Div. of Design & Construction
Ofc. of Administration
Truman Bldg., Rm. 730
P.O. Box 809
Jefferson City, MO 65102
Phone: (573) 751-3339
Fax: (573) 751-7277
E-mail: allenr@mail.oa.state.mo.us

MONTANA
James Brown
Division Administrator
Bldg. Codes Bur.
Dept. of Commerce
1218 E. 6th Ave.
Helena, MT 59620-0517
Phone: (406) 444-3933
Fax: (406) 444-4240

NEBRASKA
Ken Fougeron
Administrator
State Bldg. Div.
Dept. of Adm. Services
521 S. 14th, Ste. 500
Lincoln, NE 68508-2707
Phone: (402) 471-3191
Fax: (402) 471-0421

NEVADA

NEW HAMPSHIRE
Donald Bliss
Director
Div. of Fire Safety
Dept. of Safety
10 Hazen Dr.
Concord, NH 03305
Phone: (603) 271-3294
Fax: (603) 271-1091

NEW JERSEY
Robert Brehm
Director
Div. of Bldg. & Construction
Dept. of the Treasury
P.O. Box 235
Trenton, NJ 08646-0235
Phone: (609) 292-4724

NEW MEXICO
Anita Lockwood
Chief
Construction Bur.
Regulation & Licensing Dept.
20555 Pacheo St.
Santa Fe, NM 87505
Phone: (505) 827-7030
Fax: (505) 827-7083

NEW YORK
Joseph Lynch
Commissioner
Div. of Housing & Community Renewal
Hampton Plz.
38-40 State St.
Albany, NY 12207
Phone: (518) 473-8384
Fax: (518) 473-9462

NORTH CAROLINA
Tim Bradley
Senior Deputy Commissioner
Engineering Div.
Dept. of Insurance
410 N. Boylan Ave.
Raleigh, NC 27603
Phone: (919) 733-3901
Fax: (919) 733-9171

NORTH DAKOTA
Rich Gray
Program Manager
ADA & Bldg. Codes
Ofc. of Intergovernmental Assistance
600 E. Blvd. Ave., 14th Fl.
Bismarck, ND 58505-0170
Phone: (701) 328-3698
Fax: (701) 328-2308
E-mail: rgray@state.nd.us

NORTHERN MARIANA ISLANDS
John B. Cepeda
Secretary
Dept. of Public Works
Chalan Laulau
P.O. Box 2950
Saipan, MP 96950
Phone: (670) 235-5827
Fax: (670) 235-5253

OHIO
David Williamson
Superintendent
Div. of Industrial Compliance
Dept. of Commerce
6606 Tussing Rd.
Reynoldsburg, OH 43068
Phone: (614) 644-3130
Fax: (614) 644-2618

OKLAHOMA
Bob Thomas
Administrator
Construction & Properties Div.
Ofc. of Public Affairs
P.O. Box 53448
Oklahoma City, OK 73152-3448
Phone: (405) 522-2111
Fax: (405) 521-6403

OREGON
Joseph A. Brewer, III
Administrator
DCBS Bldg. Codes Agency
1535 Edgewater, NW
Salem, OR 97310
Phone: (503) 378-3176
Fax: (503) 378-2322

PENNSYLVANIA
Charles J. Sludden, Jr.
Director
Occupational & Industrial Safety
Dept. of Labor & Industry
1529 Labor & Industry Bldg.
Harrisburg, PA 17120
Phone: (717) 787-3323
Fax: (717) 787-8363
E-mail: csludden@dli.state.pa.us

PUERTO RICO
Sigfrido Garcia Alfonso
Administrator
Housing Codes
P.O. Box 41179
Minillas Station
Santurce, PR 00940
Phone: (787) 721-8282
Fax: (787) 728-8882

RHODE ISLAND
Joseph Cirillo
Commissioner
Bldg. Codes
Dept. of Administration
1 Capitol Hill
Providence, RI 02903
Phone: (401) 222-1220

SOUTH CAROLINA
Helen Zeigler
Director
Div. of Services
State Budget & Control Board
1201 Main St., Ste. 420
Columbia, SC 29201
Phone: (803) 737-3880

SOUTH DAKOTA
Tom D. Geraets
Commissioner
Bur. of Administration
500 E. Capitol Ave.
Pierre, SD 57501
Phone: (605) 773-3688
Fax: (605) 773-3887

TENNESSEE
Larry Kirk
Assistant Commissioner
Capitol Projects Real Property Mgmt.
Dept. of Finance & Administration
Wm. R. Snodgrass TN Tower, 22nd Fl.
Nashville, TN 37243
Phone: (615) 741-4042
Fax: (615) 741-6191

TEXAS
Tom Treadway
Executive Director
Services Comm.
1711 San Jacinto
P.O. Box 13047
Austin, TX 78701-3047
Phone: (512) 463-3446
Fax: (512) 463-7966
E-mail: tomtreadway@gsc.state.tx.us

U.S. VIRGIN ISLANDS
Dean Plaskett
Commissioner
Dept. of Planning & Natural Resources
Foster's Plz., 396-1 Anna's Retreat
St. Thomas, VI 00802
Phone: (340) 774-3320
Fax: (340) 775-5706

UTAH
Larry Naccarato
Structural Engineer
Div. of Facilities Construction & Mgmt.
Dept. of Adm. Services
4110 State Ofc. Bldg.
Salt Lake City, UT 84114
Phone: (801) 538-3283
Fax: (801) 538-3378
E-mail: lnaccara@dfcm.state.ut.us

VERMONT
Steve Jansen
Commissioner
Dept. of Labor & Industry
Natl. Life Bldg.
Drawer 20
Montpelier, VT 05620-3401
Phone: (802) 828-2288
Fax: (802) 828-2195

VIRGINIA
William C. Shelton
Director
Dept. of Housing & Community Dev.
Jackson Ctr.
501 N. 2nd St.
Richmond, VA 23219
Phone: (804) 371-7081
Fax: (804) 371-7090

WASHINGTON
Patrick Woods
Assistant Director
Specialty Compliance Services
Dept. of Labor & Industries
P.O. Box 44001
Olympia, WA 98504-4001
Phone: (360) 902-6348
Fax: (360) 902-4202

WEST VIRGINIA
Walter Smittle, III
Fire Marshal
1207 Quarrier St., Rm. 202
Charleston, WV 25301
Phone: (304) 558-2191
Fax: (304) 558-2537

WISCONSIN
Richard L. Meyer
Director
Code Dev. & Section Bur. of Program Dev.
Dept. of Commerce
P.O. Box 7969
Madison, WI 53707
Phone: (608) 261-6546
Fax: (608) 266-3080

WYOMING
Bruce Jaspersen
Structural Safety Principal Analyst
Dept. of Fire Prevention & Electrical Safety
Herschler Bldg., Rm. 2E
122 W. 25th St.
Cheyenne, WY 82002
Phone: (307) 777-7960

Campaign Finance Administration

Administers and enforces campaign finance laws.

ALABAMA
Jim Bennett
Secretary of State
State Capitol
600 Dexter Ave.
Montgomery, AL 36130-4650
Phone: (334) 242-7205
Fax: (334) 242-4993
E-mail: alsecst@alaline.net

ALASKA
Karen Boorman
Director
Public Ofcs. Comm.
2221 E. Northern Lights Blvd., Rm. 128
Anchorage, AK 99508-4149
Phone: (907) 276-4176
Fax: (907) 276-7018

AMERICAN SAMOA

ARIZONA
Jane Dee Hull
Governor
State Capitol
1700 W. Washington St., 9th Fl.
Phoenix, AZ 85007
Phone: (602) 542-4331
Fax: (602) 542-7601

ARKANSAS
Sharon Priest
Secretary of State
State Capitol, Rm. 256
Little Rock, AR 72201
Phone: (501) 682-1010
Fax: (501) 682-3510
E-mail: sharonpriest@ccm1.state.ar.us

CALIFORNIA
Jim Hall
Chair
Fair Political Practices Comm.
428 J St., Ste. 600
P.O. Box 807
Sacramento, CA 95804
Phone: (916) 322-5660

COLORADO
Ed Arcuri
Director
Div. of Elections
Dept. of State
1560 Broadway, Rm. 200
Denver, CO 80202
Phone: (303) 894-2680
Fax: (303) 894-7732

CONNECTICUT

DELAWARE
Thomas J. Cook
Commissioner
Dept. of Elections
32 Loockerman St., M101
Dover, DE 19904
Phone: (302) 739-4277
Fax: (302) 739-6794

DISTRICT OF COLUMBIA
Cecily Collier-Montgomery
Director
Board of Elections & Ethics
Ofc. of Campaign Finance
2000 14th St., NW, Rm. 420
Washington, DC 20009
Phone: (202) 939-8710

FLORIDA
Ethel Baxter
Director
Div. of Elections
Dept. of State
The Capitol, Rm. 1801
Tallahassee, FL 32399-0250
Phone: (850) 488-7690
Fax: (850) 488-1768

GEORGIA

GUAM

HAWAII
Robert Watada
Executive Director
Campaign Spending Comm.
235 S. Beretania St., #300
Honolulu, HI 96813-2437
Phone: (808) 586-0285
Fax: (808) 586-0288

IDAHO
Pete T. Cenarrusa
Secretary of State
State Capitol, Rm. 203
Boise, ID 83720
Phone: (208) 334-2300
Fax: (208) 334-2282

ILLINOIS

INDIANA
Laurie Christie
Co-Director
State Election Comm.
302 W. Washington, #E204
Indianapolis, IN 46204
Phone: (317) 232-3939
Fax: (317) 233-6793

Spencer Valentine
Co-Director
State Election Comm.
302 W. Washington, E204
Indianapolis, IN 46204
Phone: (317) 232-3939
Fax: (317) 233-6793

IOWA
Kay Williams
Executive Director
Ethics & Campaign Disclosure Board
514 E. Locust, Ste. 104
Des Moines, IA 50309

KANSAS
Carol Williams
Executive Director
Govt. Ethics Comm.
109 SW 9th, 5th Fl.
Topeka, KS 66612-1287
Phone: (785) 296-4219
Fax: (785) 296-2548

KENTUCKY
Mack Bushart
Director
Registry of Election Finance
140 Walnut St.
Frankfort, KY 40601
Phone: (502) 573-7100
Fax: (502) 573-5622

LOUISIANA
W. Fox McKeithen
Secretary of State
Dept. of State
P.O. Box 94125
Baton Rouge, LA 70804-9125
Phone: (225) 342-4479
Fax: (225) 342-5577

MAINE
Bill Haines
Director
Governmental Ethics & Election Practices Comm.
135 State House Station
Augusta, ME 04333
Phone: (207) 287-6219

MARYLAND
Rebecca M. Wicklund
Director
Div. of Candidacy & Campaign Finance
State Board of Election
P.O. Box 231
Annapolis, MD 21404
Phone: (410) 974-3711
Fax: (410) 974-5415
E-mail: rwicklund@elections.state.md.us

MASSACHUSETTS
Michael J. Sullivan
Director
Ofc. of Campaign & Political Finance
One Ashburton Pl., Rm. 411
Boston, MA 02108
Phone: (617) 727-8352
Fax: (617) 727-6549

MICHIGAN
Candice Miller
Secretary of State
Treasury Bldg., 1st Fl.
430 W. Allegan St.
Lansing, MI 48918
Phone: (517) 373-2510
Fax: (517) 373-0727

MINNESOTA
Jeanne Olson
Executive Director
Campaign Finance & Public Disclosure Board
100 Centennial Ofc. Bldg.
658 Cedar St.
St. Paul, MN 55155
Phone: (651) 296-5148
Fax: (651) 296-1722
E-mail: jeanne.olson@state.mn.us

MISSISSIPPI
Eric Clark
Secretary of State
401 Mississippi St.
P.O. Box 136
Jackson, MS 39205
Phone: (601) 359-1350
Fax: (601) 354-6243

MISSOURI
Joseph Carroll
Director
Campaign Finance Reporting
Ethics Comm.
P.O. Box 1254
Jefferson City, MO 65102
Phone: (573) 751-2020
Fax: (573) 526-4506
E-mail: jcarrol@mail.state.mo.us

MONTANA
Linda Vaughey
Commissioner
Political Practices
1205 8th Ave.
P.O. Box 202401
Helena, MT 59620-2401
Phone: (406) 444-2942
Fax: (406) 444-1643

NEBRASKA
Scott Moore
Secretary of State
State Capitol, Ste. 2300
P.O. Box 94608
Lincoln, NE 68509-4608
Phone: (402) 471-2554
Fax: (402) 471-3237

NEVADA
Dean Heller
Secretary of State
State Capitol Bldg.
101 N. Carson St., Ste. 3
Carson City, NV 89701
Phone: (775) 684-5708
Fax: (775) 684-5725
E-mail: sosmail@govmail.state.nv.us

NEW HAMPSHIRE
William Gardner
Secretary of State
Secretary of State Ofc.
State House, Rm. 204
107 N. Main St.
Concord, NH 03301
Phone: (603) 271-3242
Fax: (603) 271-6316
E-mail: sof.karen.ladd@leg.state.nh.us

NEW JERSEY
Frederick M. Herrmann
Executive Director
Election Law Enforcement Comm.
28 W. State St., 13th Fl.
P.O. Box 185
Trenton, NJ 08625-0185
Phone: (609) 292-8700
Fax: (609) 777-1457

NEW MEXICO
Denise Lamb
Director
Election Bur.
Ofc. of Secretary of State
State Capitol Bldg., Rm. 420
Santa Fe, NM 87503
Phone: (505) 827-3622
Fax: (505) 827-3634
E-mail: deniselamb@state.nm.us

NEW YORK
Thomas R. Wilkey
Executive Director
Board of Elections
Swan St. Bldg., Core 1
Empire State Plz.
Albany, NY 12223-1650
Phone: (518) 474-8100
Fax: (518) 486-4068

NORTH CAROLINA
Elaine F. Marshall
Secretary of State
300 N. Salisbury St., Ste. 301
Raleigh, NC 27603-5909
Phone: (919) 733-4161
Fax: (919) 733-5172
E-mail: emarshall@mail.secstate.state.nc.us

NORTH DAKOTA
Cory Fong
Election Supervisor
Elections
Secretary of State's Ofc.
600 E. Blvd. Ave., 1st Fl.
Bismarck, ND 58505-0500
Phone: (701) 328-2900
Fax: (701) 328-2992
E-mail: cfong@state.nd.us

NORTHERN MARIANA ISLANDS
Gregorio C. Sablan
Executive Director
Board of Elections
P.O. Box 470
Saipan, MP 96950
Phone: (670) 664-8683
Fax: (670) 664-8689

OHIO
J. Kenneth Blackwell
Secretary of State
30 E. Broad St., 14th Fl.
Columbus, OH 43266-0421
Phone: (614) 466-2655
Fax: (614) 644-0649

OKLAHOMA
Marilyn Hughes
Executive Director
Ethics Comm.
State Capitol Bldg., Rm. B-5
2300 N. Lincoln Blvd.
Oklahoma City, OK 73105
Phone: (405) 521-3451
Fax: (405) 521-4905

OREGON
Phil Keisling
Secretary of State
136 State Capitol
Salem, OR 97310
Phone: (503) 986-1500
Fax: (503) 986-1616

PENNSYLVANIA
Mary Heinlen
Director of Campaign Finance
Bur. of Comms., Elections & Legislation
304 N. Ofc. Bldg.
Harrisburg, PA 17120-0029
Phone: (717) 787-5280

PUERTO RICO
Juan R. Meleccio
President
State Election Comm.
P.O. Box 9066525
San Juan, PR 00906-6525
Phone: (787) 723-1006
Fax: (787) 721-7940

RHODE ISLAND
Henry Johnson
Chief of Campaign Finance
Board of Elections
50 Branch Ave.
Providence, RI 02904
Phone: (401) 222-2056

SOUTH CAROLINA

SOUTH DAKOTA
Joyce Hazeltine
Secretary of State
500 E. Capitol Ave., Ste. 204
Pierre, SD 57501
Phone: (605) 773-3537
Fax: (605) 773-6580
E-mail: Patty.Pearson@state.sd.us

TENNESSEE

TEXAS
Tom Harrison
Director
Ethics Comm.
201 E. 14th St., 10th Fl.
Austin, TX 78701
Phone: (512) 463-5800
Fax: (512) 463-5777
E-mail: ethics@state.tx.us

U.S. VIRGIN ISLANDS
John Abramson
Director of Elections
Dept. of Finance
P.O. Box 6038
St. Thomas, VI 00801
Phone: (340) 774-3107
Fax: (340) 776-2391

UTAH
Olene S. Walker
Lieutenant Governor
210 State Capitol
Salt Lake City, UT 84114
Phone: (801) 538-1520
Fax: (801) 538-1557
E-mail: owalker@gov.state.ut.us

VERMONT
Deborah Markowitz
Secretary of State
109 State St.
Montpelier, VT 05609-1101
Phone: (802) 828-2148
Fax: (802) 828-2496

VIRGINIA
Cameron P. Quinn
Secretary
State Board of Elections
202 N. 9th St., Ste. 101
Richmond, VA 23219
Phone: (804) 786-6551
Fax: (804) 371-0194

WASHINGTON
Melissa Warheit
Executive Director
Public Disclosure Comm.
711 Capitol Way, Rm. 403
P.O. Box 40908
Olympia, WA 98504-0908
Phone: (360) 753-1111
Fax: (360) 753-1112

WEST VIRGINIA
Ken Hechler
Secretary of State
Bldg. 1, Ste. 157K
1900 Kanawha Blvd., E.
Charleston, WV 25305
Phone: (304) 558-6000
Fax: (304) 558-0900
E-mail: wvsos
@secretary.state.wv.us

WISCONSIN
Kevin J. Kennedy
Executive Director
State Elections Board
132 E. Wilson, Ste. 200
P.O. Box 2973
Madison, WI 53701-2973
Phone: (608) 266-8005
Fax: (608) 267-0500

WYOMING
Peggy Nighswanger
Director of Elections
Secretary of State's Ofc.
State Capitol
200 W. 24th St.
Cheyenne, WY 82002
Phone: (307) 777-5333

Cash Management

Manages the flow of funds deposited in the state's bank accounts for the payment of immediate obligations.

ALABAMA
Lucy Baxley
State Treasurer
State Capitol, Rm. S106
P.O. Box 302510
Montgomery, AL 36130-2510
Phone: (334) 242-7500
Fax: (334) 242-7592
E-mail: altreas@alaline.com

ALASKA
Michelle Daugherty
Cash Manager
Treasury Div.
Dept. of Revenue
P.O. Box 110405
Juneau, AK 99811
Phone: (907) 465-2360
Fax: (907) 465-2394

AMERICAN SAMOA
Tifi Ale
Treasurer
Dept. of the Treasury
AS Govt.
Pago Pago, AS 96799
Phone: (684) 633-4155
Fax: (684) 633-4100

ARIZONA
Carol Springer
State Treasurer
Treasurer's Ofc.
1700 W. Washington, 1st Fl.
Phoenix, AZ 85007
Phone: (602) 542-1463
Fax: (602) 542-7176

ARKANSAS
Tom Smith
Administrator
Ofc. of Accounting
Dept. of Finance & Administration
403 DFA Bldg.
1509 W. 7th St.
Little Rock, AR 72201
Phone: (501) 682-2583
Fax: (501) 682-1086

CALIFORNIA
Bruce VanHouten
Director
Cash Mgmt. Div.
915 Capitol Mall, Rm. 107
Sacramento, CA 95814
Phone: (916) 653-3601

COLORADO
Nancy J. McCallin
Executive Director
Ofc. of State Planning & Budgeting
Ofc. of the Governor
State Capitol, Rm. 114
200 E. Colfax Ave.
Denver, CO 80203-1792
Phone: (303) 866-2980
Fax: (303) 866-3040

CONNECTICUT
Denise Nappier
State Treasurer
33 Elm St.
Hartford, CT 06106-1773

DELAWARE
Jack Markell
State Treasurer
Thomas Collins Bldg.
P.O. Box 1401
Dover, DE 19904
Phone: (302) 739-3382
Fax: (302) 739-5635

DISTRICT OF COLUMBIA
J. Anthony Romero, III
Interim Superintendent
Ofc. of Banking & Financial Institutions
717 14th St., NW, Ste. 1100
Washington, DC 20005
Phone: (202) 727-1563

FLORIDA
Bill Nelson
State Treasurer & Insurance Commissioner
Dept. of Insurance
PL-11, The Capitol
Tallahassee, FL 32399-0300
Phone: (850) 922-3100
Fax: (850) 488-0699
E-mail: webmaster@doi.state.fl.us

GEORGIA
W. Daniel Ebersole
Treasurer
Ofc. of Treasury & Fiscal Services
1202 W. Tower
200 Piedmont Ave., SE
Atlanta, GA 30334
Phone: (404) 656-2168
Fax: (404) 656-9048

GUAM
Michael J. Reidy
Director
Dept. of Administration
P.O. Box 884
Hagatna, GU 96932
Phone: (671) 475-1101
Fax: (671) 477-6788

HAWAII
Neal Miyahira
Interim Director of Finance
Dept. of Budget & Finance
P.O. Box 150
Honolulu, HI 96810
Phone: (808) 586-1518
Fax: (808) 586-1976

IDAHO
Ron Crane
State Treasurer
102 State Capitol
Boise, ID 83720
Phone: (208) 334-3200
Fax: (208) 334-2543

ILLINOIS
Judy Baar Topinka
State Treasurer
219 State House
Springfield, IL 62706
Phone: (217) 782-2211
Fax: (217) 785-2777

INDIANA
Tim Berry
Treasurer
State House, Rm. 242
200 W. Washington St.
Indianapolis, IN 46204
Phone: (317) 232-6386
Fax: (317) 233-1928

IOWA
Michael L. Fitzgerald
State Treasurer
State Capitol Bldg.
Des Moines, IA 50319
Phone: (515) 281-5368
Fax: (515) 281-6962

KANSAS

KENTUCKY
John Kennedy Hamilton
State Treasurer
Capitol Annex, Rm. 183
Frankfort, KY 40601
Phone: (502) 564-4722
Fax: (502) 564-6545

LOUISIANA
Ken Duncan
State Treasurer
P.O. Box 44154
Baton Rouge, LA 70804-0154
Phone: (225) 342-0010
Fax: (225) 342-5008

MAINE
Dale McCormick
State Treasurer
State Ofc. Bldg., Rm. 318
39 State House Station
Augusta, ME 04333
Phone: (207) 287-2771
Fax: (207) 287-2367
E-mail: dale.mccormick@state.me.us

MARYLAND
Richard N. Dixon
Treasurer
Ofc. of the State Treasurer
State Treasurer's Ofc.
Treasury Bldg., Rm. 109
Annapolis, MD 21401-1991
Phone: (410) 260-7160
Fax: (410) 974-3530
E-mail: rdixon@treasurer.state.md.us

MASSACHUSETTS

MICHIGAN
Mark Murray
Treasurer
Dept. of Treasury
P.O. Box 11097
Lansing, MI 48901
Phone: (517) 373-3223
Fax: (517) 335-1785

MINNESOTA

MISSISSIPPI
Marshall G. Bennett
State Treasurer
Dept. of Treasury
404 Walter Sillers Bldg.
P.O. Box 138
Jackson, MS 39205
Phone: (601) 359-3600
Fax: (601) 359-2001

MISSOURI
Bob Holden
Treasurer
State Capitol, Rm. 229
P.O. Box 210
Jefferson City, MO 65102
Phone: (573) 751-2411
Fax: (573) 751-9443
E-mail: BOB_HOLDEN @mail.sto.state.mo.us

MONTANA
Ray Hofland
Unit Supervisor
Treasury Unit
Dept. of Administration
Sam Mitchell Bldg., Rm. 175
125 Roberts St.
Helena, MT 59620
Phone: (406) 444-2624
Fax: (406) 444-2812

NEBRASKA
David E. Heineman
State Treasurer
State Capitol, Rm. 2003
P.O. Box 94788
Lincoln, NE 68509-4788
Phone: (402) 471-2455
Fax: (402) 471-4390

NEVADA
Brian Krolicki
State Treasurer
101 N. Carson St., Ste. 4
Carson City, NV 89701
Phone: (775) 684-5600
Fax: (775) 684-5623
E-mail: bkkrolicki @treasurer.state.nv.us

NEW HAMPSHIRE
Georgie A. Thomas
State Treasurer
121 State House Annex
Concord, NH 03301
Phone: (603) 271-2621
Fax: (603) 271-3922
E-mail: gthomas@tec.nh.us

NEW JERSEY
Elizabeth L. Pugh
Director
Ofc. of Mgmt. & Budget
Dept. of Treasury
P.O. Box 221
Trenton, NJ 08625-0221
Phone: (609) 292-6746
Fax: (609) 633-8179

NEW MEXICO
Leroy Aragon
Cash Manager
Ofc. of State Treasurer
P.O. Box 608
Santa Fe, NM 87504
Phone: (505) 827-6411
Fax: (505) 827-6395

NEW YORK
H. Carl McCall
Comptroller
A.E. Smith Ofc. Bldg., 6th Fl.
Albany, NY 12236
Phone: (518) 474-3506
Fax: (518) 473-3004

NORTH CAROLINA
Harlan E. Boyles
State Treasurer
Albemarle Bldg.
325 N. Salisbury St.
Raleigh, NC 27603-1385
Phone: (919) 508-5176

NORTH DAKOTA
Sheila Peterson
Director
Fiscal Mgmt.
Ofc. of Mgmt. & Budget
600 E. Blvd. Ave., 4th Fl.
Bismarck, ND 58505-0400
Phone: (701) 328-2680
Fax: (701) 328-3230
E-mail: peterson @state.nd.us

NORTHERN MARIANA ISLANDS
Lucia DLG. Neilsen
Secretary of Finance
Finance & Accounting
Dept. of Finance
P.O. Box 5234 CHRB
Saipan, MP 96950
Phone: (670) 664-1198
Fax: (670) 664-1115

OHIO
Joseph T. Deters
State Treasurer
30 E. Broad St., 9th Fl.
Columbus, OH 43266-0421
Phone: (614) 466-2160
Fax: (614) 644-7313

OKLAHOMA
Vacant
Director
Legislative Service Bur.
State Capitol, Rm. B-30
2300 N. Lincoln Blvd.
Oklahoma City, OK 73105
Phone: (405) 521-4144
Fax: (405) 521-5507

OREGON
Jim Hill
State Treasurer
159 State Capitol
Salem, OR 97310
Phone: (503) 378-4329
Fax: (503) 373-7051

PENNSYLVANIA
Barbara Hafer
State Treasurer
129 Finance Bldg.
Harrisburg, PA 17120
Phone: (717) 787-2465
Fax: (717) 783-9760
E-mail: bhafer @libertynet.org

PUERTO RICO
Jorge Aponte Hernandez
Director
Ofc. of Budget & Mgmt.
P.O. Box 9023228
San Juan, PR 00902-3228
Phone: (787) 725-7019
Fax: (787) 724-1374

RHODE ISLAND
Paul J. Tavares
Treasurer
State House, Rm. 102
Providence, RI 02903
Phone: (401) 222-2397

SOUTH CAROLINA
Grady L. Patterson, Jr.
State Treasurer
1200 Senate St.
Wade Hampton Bldg., 1st Fl.
Columbia, SC 29201
Phone: (803) 734-2635

SOUTH DAKOTA
Richard Butler
State Treasurer
212 State Capitol
500 E. Capitol Ave.
Pierre, SD 57501-5070
Phone: (605) 773-3378
Fax: (605) 773-3115

TENNESSEE
Stephen D. Adams
State Treasurer
State Capitol, 1st Fl.
Nashville, TN 37219
Phone: (615) 741-2956
Fax: (615) 253-1591
E-mail: sadams @mail.state.tn.us

TEXAS
Carole Keeton Rylander
Comptroller
Comptroller of Public Accounts
P.O. Box 13528
Austin, TX 78711-3528
Phone: (512) 463-4000
Fax: (512) 463-4965

U.S. VIRGIN ISLANDS

UTAH
Edward T. Alter
State Treasurer
215 State Capitol
Salt Lake City, UT 84114
Phone: (801) 538-1042
Fax: (801) 538-1465
E-mail: ealter.stmain. @state.ut.us

VERMONT
James H. Douglas
Treasurer
State Administration Bldg., 2nd Fl.
133 State St.
Montpelier, VT 05633-6200
Phone: (802) 828-2301
Fax: (802) 828-2772
E-mail: jdouglas @tre.state.vt.us

VIRGINIA
Mary G. Morris
State Treasurer
Dept. of the Treasury
Monroe Bldg., 3rd Fl.
101 N. 14th St.
Richmond, VA 23219
Phone: (804) 225-2142
Fax: (804) 225-3187

WASHINGTON
Michael J. Murphy
State Treasurer
Legislative Bldg.
P.O. Box 40200
Olympia, WA 98504-0200
Phone: (360) 753-7139
Fax: (360) 586-6147
E-mail: MichaelJ
@TRE.WA.GOV

WEST VIRGINIA
John Perdue
State Treasurer
Bldg. 1, Ste. E145
1900 Kanawha Blvd., E.
Charleston, WV 25305-0860
Phone: (304) 558-5000
Fax: (304) 558-4097
E-mail: www.wvtreasury
.com/countacts.htm

WISCONSIN
Jack C. Voight
State Treasurer
1 S. Pinckney St., Ste. 550
P.O. Box 7871
Madison, WI 53707-7871
Phone: (608) 266-3712
Fax: (608) 266-2647

WYOMING
Cynthia M. Lummis
State Treasurer
State Capitol Bldg.
Cheyenne, WY 82002
Phone: (307) 777-7408
Fax: (307) 777-5411

Chief Justice

The chief justice or judge of the state court of last resort.

ALABAMA
Perry O. Hooper, Sr.
Chief Justice
Supreme Ct.
300 Dexter Ave.
Montgomery, AL 36104-3741
Phone: (334) 242-4599
Fax: (334) 242-4483

ALASKA
Warren W. Matthews
Chief Justice
Supreme Ct.
303 K St.
Anchorage, AK 99501-2084
Phone: (907) 264-0607

AMERICAN SAMOA
Michael Kruse
Chief Justice
High Ct.
Courthouse
Pago Pago, AS 96799
Phone: (684) 633-1410
Fax: (684) 633-1318

ARIZONA
Thomas A. Zlaket
Chief Justice
Supreme Ct.
1501 W. Washington
Phoenix, AZ 85007
Phone: (602) 542-9300
Fax: (602) 542-9480

ARKANSAS
W.H. Arnold
Chief Justice
Justice Bldg.
625 Marshall
Little Rock, AR 72201
Phone: (501) 682-6861
Fax: (501) 682-6877

CALIFORNIA
Ronald M. George
Chief Justice
Supreme Ct.
303 2nd St., S. Tower, 8th Fl.
San Francisco, CA 94107
Phone: (415) 396-9432

COLORADO
Mary J. Mullarkey
Chief Justice
Supreme Ct.
State Judicial Bldg.
2 E. 14th Ave.
Denver, CO 80203
Phone: (303) 861-1111
Fax: (303) 837-3702

CONNECTICUT
Robert J. Callahan
Chief Justice
Supreme Ct.
P.O. Drawer N, Station A
Hartford, CT 06106
Phone: (860) 566-3054

DELAWARE
E. Norman Veasey
Chief Justice
Supreme Ct.
Carvel State Ofc. Bldg.
820 N. French St.
Wilmington, DE 19801
Phone: (302) 739-4155

DISTRICT OF COLUMBIA
Annice M. Wagner
Chief Judge
Ct. of Appeals
500 Indiana Ave., NW
Washington, DC 20001
Phone: (202) 879-2700

FLORIDA
Gerald Kogan
Chief Justice
Supreme Ct.
Supreme Ct. Bldg.
500 S. Duval St.
Tallahassee, FL 32399-1925
Phone: (850) 488-0007

GEORGIA
Robert Benham
Chief Justice
507 State Judicial Bldg.
Atlanta, GA 30334
Phone: (404) 656-3476

GUAM
Benjamin J. Cruz
Supreme Ct.
120 W. O'Brien Dr.
Hagatna, GU 96910
Phone: (671) 475-3510
Fax: (671) 477-4676

HAWAII
Ronald T.Y. Moon
Chief Justice
Supreme Ct.
417 S. King St.
P.O. Box 2560
Honolulu, HI 96813
Phone: (808) 539-4700
Fax: (808) 539-4703

IDAHO
Linda Copple Trout
Chief Justice
Supreme Ct.
451 W. State
Boise, ID 83702
Phone: (208) 334-3464
Fax: (208) 334-2146

ILLINOIS
Charles E. Freeman
Chief Justice
160 N. La Salle St., 20th Fl.
Chicago, IL 60601-3103
Phone: (312) 793-5480

INDIANA
Randall T. Shepard
Chief Justice
Supreme Ct.
State House, Rm. 304
200 W. Washington St.
Indianapolis, IN 46204
Phone: (317) 232-2550
Fax: (317) 233-3990

IOWA
Arthur A. McGiverin
Chief Justice
Supreme Ct.
State Capitol
1007 E. Grand
Des Moines, IA 50319
Phone: (515) 281-5174
Fax: (515) 242-6164

KANSAS
Kay McFarland
Chief Justice
Supreme Ct.
Judicial Ctr.
301 SW 10th Ave., Rm. 374
Topeka, KS 66612-1507
Phone: (785) 296-3229

KENTUCKY
Joseph E. Lambert
Chief Justice
Supreme Court
700 Capitol Ave., Rm. 239
Frankfort, KY 40601
Phone: (502) 564-4162

LOUISIANA
Pascal F. Calogero, Jr.
Chief Justice
Supreme Ct.
Supreme Ct. Bldg.
301 Loyola Ave.
New Orleans, LA 70112
Phone: (504) 568-5707
Fax: (504) 568-2846

MAINE
Daniel E. Wathen
Chief Justice
Judicial Ctr.
65 Stone St.
Augusta, ME 04330-5222
Phone: (207) 287-6950

MARYLAND
Robert M. Bell
Chief Judge
Ct. of Appeals
Judiciary
Ct. of Appeals Bldg.
361 Rowe Blvd.
Annapolis, MD 21401
Phone: (410) 260-1490

MASSACHUSETTS
Herbert P. Wilkins
Chief Justice
Supreme Judicial Ct.
1404 New Ct. House
Boston, MA 02108
Phone: (617) 557-1100
Fax: (617) 248-0771

MICHIGAN
Betty Weaver
Chief Justice
Supreme Ct.
P.O. Box 30052
Lansing, MI 48909
Phone: (517) 373-0120

MINNESOTA
Kathleen A. Blatz
Chief Justice
Supreme Ct.
25 Constitution Ave.
St. Paul, MN 55155
Phone: (651) 296-3380
Fax: (651) 282-5115

MISSISSIPPI
Lenore L. Prather
Chief Justice
Supreme Ct.
Gartin Bldg., 3rd Fl.
P.O. Box 249
Jackson, MS 39205
Phone: (601) 359-3697
Fax: (601) 359-2443

MISSOURI
Duane Benton
Chief Justice
P.O. Box 150
Jefferson City, MO 65102
Phone: (573) 751-4144
Fax: (573) 751-7514
E-mail: duane_benton@osca.state.mo.us

MONTANA
Jean Turnage
Chief Justice
Supreme Ct.
Justice/State Library Bldg., Rm. 414
P.O. Box 203001
Helena, MT 59620
Phone: (406) 444-5490
Fax: (406) 444-5705

NEBRASKA
John Hendry
Chief Justice
Supreme Ct.
State Capitol, Rm. 2413
P.O. Box 98910
Lincoln, NE 68509-8910
Phone: (402) 471-3738

NEVADA
Robert E. Rose
Chief Justice
Supreme Ct. Bldg.
Capitol Complex
201 S. Carson St.
Carson City, NV 89701-4702
Phone: (775) 687-5170
Fax: (775) 687-8627

NEW HAMPSHIRE
David A. Brock
Chief Justice
Supreme Ct.
Supreme Ct. Bldg.
Nobel Dr.
Concord, NH 03301
Phone: (603) 271-2646
Fax: (603) 271-6630

NEW JERSEY
Deborah Poritz
Chief Justice
Supreme Ct.
Hughes Justice Complex
P.O. Box 023
Trenton, NJ 08625-0023
Phone: (609) 292-2448
Fax: (609) 984-6988

NEW MEXICO
Gene E. Franchini
Chief Justice
Supreme Ct.
P.O. Box 848
Santa Fe, NM 87504-0848
Phone: (505) 827-4880
Fax: (505) 827-4837

NEW YORK
Judith S. Kaye
Chief Justice
Ct. of Appeals Hall
20 Eagle St.
Albany, NY 12207
Phone: (518) 455-7700

NORTH CAROLINA
Burley B. Mitchell, Jr.
Chief Justice
Supreme Ct.
2 E. Morgan St.
Raleigh, NC 27601-1400
Phone: (919) 733-3723

NORTH DAKOTA
Gerald VandeWalle
Chief Justice
Supreme Ct.
Judicial Wing, 1st Fl.
600 E. Blvd. Ave.
Bismarck, ND 58505-0530
Phone: (701) 328-2221
Fax: (701) 328-4480
E-mail: vandewalle@sc3.court.state.nd.us

NORTHERN MARIANA ISLANDS
Alexandro C. Castro
Acting Chief Justice
Commonwealth Supreme Ct.
P.O. Box 2165 C.K.
Saipan, MP 96950-2165
Phone: (670) 236-9700
Fax: (670) 236-9701
E-mail: supreme.court@saipan.com

OHIO
Thomas J. Moyer
Chief Justice
Supreme Ct.
30 E. Broad St., 3rd Fl.
Columbus, OH 43266
Phone: (614) 466-3627
Fax: (614) 752-8736

OKLAHOMA
Hardy Summers
Chief Justice
Supreme Ct.
State Capitol, Rm. B-2
2300 N. Lincoln Blvd.
Oklahoma City, OK 73105
Phone: (405) 521-3843
Fax: (405) 528-1607

OREGON
Wallace P. Carson, Jr.
Chief Justice
Supreme Ct.
1163 State St.
Salem, OR 97310
Phone: (503) 986-5700
Fax: (503) 986-5730

PENNSYLVANIA
John P. Flaherty
Chief Justice
Supreme Ct.
11 Stanwix St., Ste. 1020
Pittsburgh, PA 15222-1312
Phone: (412) 565-5525
Fax: (412) 565-7533

PUERTO RICO
Jose A. Andreu-Garcia
Chief Justice
Supreme Ct.
P.O. Box 2392
San Juan, PR 00902-2392
Phone: (787) 724-3535
Fax: (787) 725-4910

RHODE ISLAND
Joseph R. Weisberger
Chief Justice
Supreme Ct.
Frank Licht Judicial Complex
250 Benefit St.
Providence, RI 02903
Phone: (401) 222-3274

SOUTH CAROLINA
Ernest A. Finney, Jr.
Chief Justice
Supreme Ct.
P.O. Box 11330
Columbia, SC 29211
Phone: (803) 734-1080
Fax: (803) 734-0427

SOUTH DAKOTA
Robert A. Miller
Chief Justice
Supreme Ct.
State Capitol
500 E. Capitol Ave.
Pierre, SD 57501
Phone: (605) 773-6254
Fax: (605) 773-6128

TENNESSEE
E. Riley Anderson
Chief Justice
Supreme Ct.
719 Locust St., SW
P.O. Box 444
Knoxville, TN 37901-0444
Phone: (423) 594-6400
Fax: (423) 594-5813

TEXAS
Thomas R. Phillips
Chief Justice
Supreme Ct.
P.O. Box 12248
Austin, TX 78711
Phone: (512) 463-1316

U.S. VIRGIN ISLANDS
Thomas Moore
Chief Justice
5500 Veteran's Dr., Fte. 310
Charlotte Amalie
St. Thomas, VI 00802-6424
Phone: (340) 774-0640
Fax: (340) 774-1293
E-mail: vidc@vid.uscourts.gov

UTAH
Richard C. Howe
Chief Justice
450 S. State St.
Salt Lake City, UT 84114-0210
Phone: (801) 238-7958
Fax: (801) 238-7980
E-mail: jettab@email.utcourts.gov

VERMONT
Jeffrey L. Amestoy
Chief Justice
Supreme Ct.
111 State St.
Montpelier, VT 05609-0701
Phone: (802) 828-3278
Fax: (802) 828-3457

VIRGINIA
Harry L. Carrico
Chief Justice
Supreme Ct.
Supreme Ct. Bldg., 4th Fl.
100 N. 9th St.
Richmond, VA 23219
Phone: (804) 786-2023
Fax: (804) 786-4542

WASHINGTON
Richard P. Guy
Chief Justice
Supreme Ct.
Temple of Justice
P.O. Box 40929
Olympia, WA 98504
Phone: (360) 357-2077

WEST VIRGINIA
Larry Starcher
Chief Justice
Supreme Ct. of Appeals
State Capitol Bldg., Rm. E-317
1900 Kanawha Blvd., E.
Charleston, WV 25305
Phone: (304) 558-2601
Fax: (304) 558-3815

WISCONSIN
Shirley S. Abrahamson
Chief Justice
Supreme Ct.
State Capitol, Rm. 231 E.
Madison, WI 53701
Phone: (608) 266-1885
Fax: (608) 261-8299
E-mail: sabraha@itis.com

WYOMING
Larry L. Lehman
Chief Justice
Supreme Ct.
Supreme Ct. Bldg.
2301 Capitol Ave.
Cheyenne, WY 82002
Phone: (307) 777-7316

Chief of Staff (Governor's) —

ALABAMA
Paul Hamrick
Chief of Staff
State Capitol
600 Dexter Ave.
Montgomery, AL 36130
Phone: (334) 242-7100
Fax: (334) 242-2766

ALASKA
Jim Ayers
Chief of Staff
P.O. Box 110001
Juneau, AK 99811-0001
Phone: (907) 465-3500
Fax: (907) 465-3532

AMERICAN SAMOA
Pati Faiai
Acting Chief of Staff
Ofc. of the Governor
Pago Pago, AS 96799
Phone: (684) 633-4116
Fax: (684) 633-2269

ARIZONA
Rick Collins
Chief of Staff
Governor's Ofc.
1700 W. Washington St.
Phoenix, AZ 85007
Phone: (602) 542-1317
Fax: (602) 542-7601

ARKANSAS
Brenda Turner
Chief of Staff
State Capitol, Rm. 250
Little Rock, AR 72201
Phone: (501) 682-3608
Fax: (501) 682-3597
E-mail: brenda.turner@gov.state.ar.us

CALIFORNIA
George W. Dunn, III
Chief of Staff
State Capitol
Sacramento, CA 95814
Phone: (916) 445-2864

COLORADO
Roy Palmer
Chief of Staff
Ofc. of the Governor
State Capitol, Rm. 136
200 E. Colfax
Denver, CO 80203
Phone: (303) 866-2471
Fax: (303) 866-2003

CONNECTICUT
Peter N. Ellef
Co-Chief of Staff
State Capitol
Hartford, CT 06106
Phone: (860) 566-4840

Sidney J. Holbrook
Co-Chief of Staff
Governor's Ofc.
210 State Capitol Ave.
Hartford, CT 06106
Phone: (860) 566-4840

DELAWARE
Jeff Bullock
Chief of Staff
Carvel State Ofc. Bldg.
820 N. French St.
Wilmington, DE 19801
Phone: (302) 577-3210
Fax: (302) 577-3118

DISTRICT OF COLUMBIA
Marie Drissel
Special Assistant to the Mayor
City Boards & Comms.
Executive Ofc. of the Mayor
441 4th St., NW, Ste. 1050
Washington, DC 20001
Phone: (202) 727-1372
Fax: (202) 727-2359

Abdusalam H. Omer
Chief of Staff
Ofc. of the Mayor
441 4th St., NW, Rm. 1110S
Washington, DC 20001
Phone: (202) 727-2643
Fax: (202) 727-2975

FLORIDA
Sally Bradshaw
Chief of Staff
Executive Ofc. of the Governor
The Capitol, Rm. PL05
Tallahassee, FL 32399
Phone: (850) 488-5603
Fax: (850) 922-4292
E-mail: bradshs@eog.state.fl.us

GEORGIA
Bobby Kahn
Chief of Staff
Ofc. of the Governor
201 State Capitol
Atlanta, GA 30334
Phone: (404) 656-1776

GUAM
Gil A. Shinohara
Assistant to the Governor
Governor's Ofc.
Executive Chamber
P.O. Box 2950
Hagatna, GU 96932
Phone: (671) 472-8931
Fax: (671) 477-4826

HAWAII
Sam Callejo
Chief of Staff
Ofc. of the Governor
State Capitol, 5th Fl.
Honolulu, HI 96813
Phone: (808) 586-0034
Fax: (808) 586-0006

IDAHO
Tana Shillingstad
Chief of Staff
State Capitol
Boise, ID 83720-0034
Phone: (208) 334-2100
E-mail: tshillin@gov.state.id.us

ILLINOIS
Robert Newtson
Chief of Staff
State Capitol, Rm. 207
Springfield, IL 62706
Phone: (217) 782-6830

INDIANA
Thomas New
Chief of Staff
206 State House
Indianapolis, IN 46204
Phone: (317) 232-4567
Fax: (317) 232-3443

IOWA
John Norris
Chief of Staff
Ofc. of the Governor
State Capitol
Des Moines, IA 50319
Phone: (515) 281-0159
Fax: (515) 281-6611
E-mail: john.norris@idom.state.ia.us

KANSAS
Joyce Glasscock
Chief of Staff
State Capitol, 2nd Fl.
Topeka, KS 66612-1590
Phone: (785) 296-3232
Fax: (785) 296-7973

KENTUCKY
Skipper Martin
Chief of Staff
State Capitol
Frankfort, KY 40601
Phone: (502) 564-2611
Fax: (502) 564-2517

LOUISIANA
Stephen Perry
Chief of Staff
State Capitol
P.O. Box 94004
Baton Rouge, LA 70804-9004
Phone: (225) 342-1624
Fax: (225) 342-0002

MAINE
Kathryn J. Rand
Chief of Staff
1 State House Station
Augusta, ME 04333
Phone: (207) 287-3531
Fax: (207) 287-1034

MARYLAND
Major F. Riddick, Jr.
Chief of Staff
Governor's Chief of Staff
Executive Dept.
State House
Annapolis, MD 21401
Phone: (410) 974-3570
E-mail: mriddick@gov.state.md.us

MASSACHUSETTS
Virginia B. Buckingham
Chief of Staff
State House, Rm. 360
Boston, MA 02133
Phone: (617) 727-9173
Fax: (617) 727-9723

MICHIGAN
Sharon Rothwell
Chief of Staff
Ofc. of the Governor
P.O. Box 30013
Lansing, MI 48909
Phone: (517) 335-7863
Fax: (517) 335-6949

MINNESOTA
Steven Bosacker
Chief of Staff
State Capitol, Rm. 130
St. Paul, MN 55155
Phone: (651) 296-3391
Fax: (651) 296-0674

MISSISSIPPI
Mark Garriga
Chief of Staff
P.O. Box 139
Jackson, MS 39205
Phone: (601) 359-3100
Fax: (601) 359-3741
E-mail: mgarriga
@govoff.state.ms.us

MISSOURI
Brad Ketcher
Chief of Staff
P.O. Box 720
State Capitol, Rm. 216
Jefferson City, MO 65101
Phone: (573) 751-3222
Fax: (573) 751-4458
E-mail: ketchb
@mail.gov.state.mo.us

MONTANA
Judy Browning
Chief of Staff
Governor's Ofc.
State Capitol
Helena, MT 59620
Phone: (406) 444-3111
Fax: (406) 444-5529

NEBRASKA
Larry Bare
Director of Governor's Staff
& Legislative Affairs
P.O. Box 94848
Lincoln, NE 68509
Phone: (402) 471-2244
Fax: (402) 471-6031

NEVADA
Pete Ernaut
Chief of Staff
Governor's Ofc.
101 N. Carson St.
Carson City, NV 89701
Phone: (775) 684-5670
Fax: (775) 684-5683
E-mail: pernaut
@govmail.state.nv.us

NEW HAMPSHIRE
Rich Sigel
Chief of Staff
Ofc. of the Governor
Executive Dept.
107 N. Main St.,
Rm. 208-214
Concord, NH 03301-4990
Phone: (603) 271-2121

NEW JERSEY
Michael P. Torpey
Chief of Staff
State House
Governor's Ofc.
P.O. Box 001
Trenton, NJ 08625-0001
Phone: (609) 777-2475
Fax: (609) 292-5181

NEW MEXICO
Lou Gallegos
Chief of Staff
Governor's Ofc.
State Capitol, 4th Fl.
Santa Fe, NM 87503
Phone: (505) 827-3000
Fax: (505) 827-3026

NEW YORK
Bradford J. Race
Secretary to the Governor
Governor's Ofc.
State Capitol
Albany, NY 12224
Phone: (518) 474-8390

NORTH CAROLINA
Franklin Freeman
Chief of Staff
State Capitol
Raleigh, NC 27603
Phone: (919) 733-4240
Fax: (919) 715-3175

NORTH DAKOTA
William G. Goetz
Chief of Staff
Ofc. of the Governor
600 E. Blvd. Ave.
Bismarck, ND 58505-0001
Phone: (701) 328-2200
Fax: (701) 328-2205
E-mail: governor
@state.nd.us

NORTHERN MARIANA ISLANDS
Jose I. Deleon Guerrero
Special Assistant for
Administration
Ofc. of the Governor
Caller Box 10007
Saipan, MP 96950
Phone: (670) 664-2200
Fax: (670) 664-2210

OHIO
Brian K. Hicks
Chief of Staff
77 S. High St., 30th Fl.
Columbus, OH 43266-0601
Phone: (614) 466-3555
Fax: (614) 466-9354

OKLAHOMA
Ken Lackey
Chief of Staff
State Capitol, Ste. 212
Oklahoma City, OK 73105
Phone: (405) 521-2342

OREGON
Bill Wyatt
Chief of Staff
254 State Capitol
Salem, OR 97310
Phone: (503) 373-3111
Fax: (503) 378-4863

PENNSYLVANIA
Mark Holman
Chief of Staff
Rm. 225, Main Capitol
Bldg.
Harrisburg, PA 17120
Phone: (717) 787-2500
Fax: (412) 772-3155
E-mail: mholman
@gois.state.pa.us

PUERTO RICO
Angel Morey
Chief of Staff
La Fortaleza
San Juan, PR 00901
Phone: (787) 721-7000
Fax: (787) 724-4235

RHODE ISLAND
Michael Di Baise
Chief of Staff
State House
Providence, RI 02903
Phone: (401) 222-2080
Fax: (401) 273-5729

SOUTH CAROLINA
Kevin Geddings
Chief of Staff
Governor's Ofc.
P.O. Box 11829
Columbia, SC 29211
Phone: (803) 734-9400

SOUTH DAKOTA
James Soyer
Chief of Staff
Governor's Ofc.
500 E. Capitol Ave.
Pierre, SD 57501
Phone: (605) 773-3212
Fax: (605) 773-5844
E-mail: jim.soyer
@state.sd.us

TENNESSEE
Hardy Mays
Chief of Staff
State Capitol
Nashville, TN 37243-0001
Phone: (615) 741-2001
Fax: (615) 532-9711

TEXAS
Joe Allbaugh
Executive Assistant
Ofc. of the Governor
P.O. Box 12428
Austin, TX 78711
Phone: (512) 463-2000
Fax: (512) 463-1849

U.S. VIRGIN ISLANDS
Juel Molloy
Chief of Staff
Govt. House
Charlotte Amalie
St. Thomas, VI 00802
Phone: (340) 774-0001
Fax: (340) 777-4546

UTAH
Ted Stewart
Chief of Staff
210 State Capitol
Salt Lake City, UT 84114
Phone: (801) 538-1527
Fax: (801) 538-1528
E-mail: tstewart
@gov.state.ut.us

VERMONT
Julie Peterson
Chief of State
Governor's Ofc.
109 State St.
Montpelier, VT 05609
Phone: (802) 828-3333

VIRGINIA
M. Boyd Marcus, Jr.
Chief of Staff to the Governor
State Capitol, 3rd Fl.
Richmond, VA 23219
Phone: (804) 786-2211
Fax: (804) 786-6351

WASHINGTON
Joseph A. Dear
Chief of Staff
Ofc. of the Governor
P.O. Box 40002
Olympia, WA 98504-0002
Phone: (360) 902-4111
Fax: (360) 753-4110

WEST VIRGINIA
James W. Teets
Chief of Staff
Ofc. of the Governor
State Capitol
Charleston, WV 25305
Phone: (304) 558-2000
Fax: (304) 342-7025
E-mail: JTeets@governor.com

WISCONSIN
Bob Wood
Chief of Staff
Governor's Ofc.
P.O. Box 7863
125 S. State Capitol
Madison, WI 53707-7863
Phone: (608) 266-1212
Fax: (608) 267-8983
E-mail: bob.wood@gov.state.wi.us

WYOMING
Rita Meyer
Chief of Staff
Governor's Ofc.
State Capitol
Cheyenne, WY 82002
Phone: (307) 777-7434
Fax: (307) 632-3909

Child Labor

Administers and enforces child labor laws.

ALABAMA
Alice McKinney
Director
Dept. of Industrial Relations
649 Monroe St.
Montgomery, AL 36131
Phone: (334) 242-8990
Fax: (334) 242-3960

ALASKA
Al Dwyer
Director
Div. of Labor Standards & Safety
Dept. of Labor
P.O. Box 107021
Anchorage, AK 99510-7021
Phone: (907) 269-4914
Fax: (907) 465-4915

AMERICAN SAMOA
Sapini Siatu'u
Director
Dept. of Human Resources
AS Govt.
Pago Pago, AS 96799
Phone: (684) 633-4485
Fax: (684) 633-1139

ARIZONA
Larry J. Etchechury
Director
Industrial Comm.
800 W. Washington
Phoenix, AZ 85007
Phone: (602) 542-4411
Fax: (602) 542-3070

ARKANSAS
Sandra King
Labor Standards Administrator
Wage & Hour Div.
Dept. of Labor
10421 W. Markham, Rm. 100
Little Rock, AR 72205
Phone: (501) 682-4505
Fax: (501) 682-4532

CALIFORNIA

COLORADO
Carlos Renteria
Program Administrator
Div. of Labor Standards
Dept. of Labor & Employment
Tower 2, Ste. 375
1515 Arapahoe St.
Denver, CO 80202-2117
Phone: (303) 572-2241

CONNECTICUT
Steven Wheeler
Director
Occupational Safety & Health
Dept. of Labor
38 Wolcott Hill Rd.
Wethersfield, CT 06109
Phone: (860) 566-4550
Fax: (860) 566-6916

DELAWARE
Lisa L. Blunt-Bradley
Secretary
Dept. of Labor
4425 N. Market St., 4th Fl.
Wilmington, DE 19802
Phone: (302) 761-8001
Fax: (302) 761-6621

DISTRICT OF COLUMBIA
Arlene Ackerman
Superintendent of Schools
Public Schools
825 N. Capitol St., NE, Ste. 9026
Washington, DC 20002
Phone: (202) 442-5885

FLORIDA
Mary B. Hooks
Secretary of Labor
Ofc. of Compliance
Labor & Employment Security
Hartman Bldg.
2012 Capital Cir., SE
Tallahassee, FL 32399-2150
Phone: (850) 922-7021
Fax: (850) 922-7119
E-mail: mary_b._hooks@fdles.state.fl.us

GEORGIA
John Clark
Chief of Child Labor
Dept. of Labor
Sussex Pl.
148 Intl. Blvd.
Atlanta, GA 30303
Phone: (404) 656-3623

GUAM
James Underwood
Acting Director
Dept. of Labor
504 E. Sunset Blvd., Tiyan
P.O. Box 9970
Tamuning, GU 96931
Phone: (671) 475-0101
Fax: (671) 477-2988

HAWAII
Alan Asao
Administrator
Child Labor/Wage Claims Branch
Labor & Industrial Relations Dept.
830 Punchbowl St., Rm. 340
Honolulu, HI 96813
Phone: (808) 586-8777
Fax: (808) 586-8766

IDAHO

ILLINOIS
Robert M. Healey
Director
Dept. of Labor
160 N. LaSalle St., 13th Fl.
Chicago, IL 60601
Phone: (312) 793-2800
Fax: (312) 793-5257

INDIANA
Peter Rimsans
Director
Bur. of Child Labor
Dept. of Labor
402 W. Washington St., Rm. W195
Indianapolis, IN 46204
Phone: (317) 232-2683
Fax: (317) 233-3790

IOWA
Olga Duran
Administrative Assistant
Div. of Labor Services
Workforce Dev.
1000 E. Grand Ave.
Des Moines, IA 50319
Phone: (515) 281-3606
Fax: (515) 242-5144

KANSAS

KENTUCKY
Denis Langford
Director
Employee Standards & Mediation
Labor Cabinet
1047 U.S. 127 S., Ste. 4
Frankfort, KY 40601
Phone: (502) 564-2784
Fax: (502) 564-2248

LOUISIANA
Mike Long
Labor Program Manager
Dept. of Labor
P.O. Box 94094
Baton Rouge, LA 70804-9094
Phone: (225) 342-7823
Fax: (225) 342-2717

MAINE
James McGowan
Director
Bur. of Labor Standards
Dept. of Labor
45 State House Station
Augusta, ME 04333
Phone: (207) 624-6400

MARYLAND
John P. O'Connor
Secretary/Commissioner
Labor & Industry
Labor, Licensing & Regulation
1100 N. Eutaw St., Rm. 600
Baltimore, MD 21201
Phone: (410) 767-2999
Fax: (410) 767-2220

MASSACHUSETTS
Ardith A. Wieworka
Director
Ofc. of Child Care Services
One Ashburton Pl., Rm. 1105
Boston, MA 02108-1518
Phone: (617) 626-2011
Fax: (617) 626-2028

MICHIGAN
Michael Dankert
Director
Wage & Hour Div.
Consumer & Industry Services
P.O. Box 30476
Lansing, MI 48909-7976
Phone: (517) 322-5269
Fax: (517) 322-6352

MINNESOTA
Gregory J. Sands
Director
Labor Standards Unit
Dept. of Labor & Industry
443 LaFayette Rd., N.
St. Paul, MN 55155
Phone: (651) 297-3349
Fax: (651) 215-0104
E-mail: greg.sands@state.mn.us

MISSISSIPPI

MISSOURI
Colleen Baker
Director
Div. of Labor Standards
Labor & Industrial Relations Dept.
3315 W. Truman Blvd., Ste. 205
P.O. Box 449
Jefferson City, MO 65102-0449
Phone: (573) 751-3403
Fax: (573) 751-3721
E-mail: cbaker@mail.state.mo.us

MONTANA
John Andrew
Chief
Employment Relations Div.
Labor Standards Bur.
P.O. Box 6518
Helena, MT 59604
Phone: (406) 444-4619
Fax: (406) 444-4140

NEBRASKA
Ray Griffin
Manager
Labor Law Compliance Program
Dept. of Labor
Safety & Labor Standards Div.
1313 Farnam
Omaha, NE 68102
Phone: (402) 595-3095
Fax: (402) 595-3200

NEVADA
Vacant
Deputy Labor Commissioner
Labor Comm.
Dept. of Business & Industry
1445 Hot Springs Rd., Ste. 109
Carson City, NV 89706
Phone: (775) 687-4850
Fax: (775) 687-6409
E-mail: labor@govmail.state.nv.us

NEW HAMPSHIRE
James Casey
Commissioner
Dept. of Labor
95 Pleasant St.
Concord, NH 03301
Phone: (603) 271-3171
Fax: (603) 271-7064

NEW JERSEY
Melvin L. Gelade
Commissioner
Div. of Administration
Dept. of Labor
John Fitch Plz.
P.O. Box 110
Trenton, NJ 08625-0110
Phone: (609) 292-2323
Fax: (609) 633-9271

NEW MEXICO
Rudy J. Maestas
Director
Labor & Industrial Div.
Labor Dept.
1596 Pacheco St.
Santa Fe, NM 87505
Phone: (505) 827-6875
Fax: (505) 827-1664

NEW YORK
James J. McGowan
Commissioner
Dept. of Labor
State Ofc. Bldg. Campus, Bldg. 12
Albany, NY 12240
Phone: (518) 457-2741
Fax: (518) 457-6908

NORTH CAROLINA
Harry Payne
Commissioner
Wage & Hour Div.
Dept. of Labor
4 W. Edenton St.
Raleigh, NC 27601-1092
Phone: (919) 733-2152
Fax: (919) 715-3858

NORTH DAKOTA
Mark Bachmeier
Interim Commissioner
Labor Dept.
600 E. Blvd. Ave., 13th Fl.
Bismarck, ND 58505
Phone: (701) 328-2660
Fax: (701) 328-2031
E-mail: bachmeie@pioneer.state.nd.us

NORTHERN MARIANA ISLANDS
Robert Goldberg
Assistant Attorney General
Div. of Labor
Attorney Gen's. Ofc.
P.O. Box 10007
Saipan, MP 96950
Phone: (670) 664-2341
Fax: (670) 664-2349

OHIO
Bill Vasil
Director
Wage & Hour Div.
Bur. of Employment Services
145 S. Front St.
Columbus, OH 43216-1618
Phone: (614) 644-8684
Fax: (614) 728-8639

OKLAHOMA
Johnny Coleman
Director
Employment Standards Div.
Dept. of Labor
4001 N. Lincoln Blvd.
Oklahoma City, OK 73105
Phone: (405) 528-1500
Fax: (405) 528-5751

OREGON
Christine Hammond
Administrator
Wage & Hour Div.
Bur. of Labor & Industries
800 NE Oregon St., #32
Portland, OR 97232
Phone: (503) 731-4074
Fax: (503) 731-4606

PENNSYLVANIA
Helen Friedman
Director
Bur. of Labor Standards
Dept. of Labor & Industry
Labor & Industry Bldg., Rm. 1305
Harrisburg, PA 17120
Phone: (717) 787-4670
Fax: (412) 787-8826

PUERTO RICO
Aura Gonzalez
Secretary
Dept. of Labor & Human Resources
Prudencio Rivera Martinez
505 Munoz Rivera Ave.
Hato Rey, PR 00918
Phone: (787) 754-2120
Fax: (787) 753-9550

RHODE ISLAND
Lee Arnold
Director
Dept. of Labor & Training
101 Friendship St.
Providence, RI 02903
Phone: (401) 222-3732
Fax: (401) 222-1473

SOUTH CAROLINA
Rita M. McKinney
Director
Dept. of Labor, Licensing & Regulations
110 Centerview Dr.
P.O. Box 11329
Columbia, SC 29210
Phone: (803) 896-4390
Fax: (803) 896-4393

SOUTH DAKOTA
James E. Marsh
Director
Div. of Labor & Mgmt.
Dept. of Labor
Kneip Bldg.
700 Governors Dr.
Pierre, SD 57501
Phone: (605) 773-3681
Fax: (605) 773-4211

TENNESSEE
Jon Moffett
Assistant Commissioner
Labor Standards
Dept. of Labor
Andrew Johnson Tower, 3rd Fl.
Nashville, TN 37243
Phone: (615) 532-1327
Fax: (615) 532-1469

TEXAS
Mike Sheridan
Executive Director
Workforce Comm.
TWC Bldg.
101 E. 15th St.
Austin, TX 78778-0001
Phone: (512) 463-0735
Fax: (512) 475-2321
E-mail: mike.sheridian@twc.state.tx.us

U.S. VIRGIN ISLANDS
Eleuteria Roberts
Acting Commissioner
Dept. of Labor
2203 Church St.
Christiansted
St. Croix, VI 00820
Phone: (340) 773-1994
Fax: (340) 773-0094

UTAH
Joseph Gallegos
Director
Anti-Discrimination & Labor Div.
Labor Comm.
160 E. 300 S., 3rd Fl.
Salt Lake City, UT 84114-6630
Phone: (801) 530-6801
Fax: (801) 530-7609
E-mail: jgallego.icmain@state.ut.us

VERMONT
Steve Jansen
Commissioner
Dept. of Labor & Industry
Natl. Life Bldg.
Drawer 20
Montpelier, VT 05620-3401
Phone: (802) 828-2288
Fax: (802) 828-2195

VIRGINIA
John Mills Barr
Commissioner
Dept. of Labor & Industry
Powers-Taylor Bldg.
13 S. 13th St.
Richmond, VA 23219
Phone: (804) 786-2377
Fax: (804) 371-6524

WASHINGTON
Greg Mowat
Program Manager
Labor & Industries
Employee Standards, Apprenticeships & Crime
Victims Div.
P.O. Box 44510
Olympia, WA 98504
Phone: (360) 902-5316
Fax: (360) 902-5300

WEST VIRGINIA
Steve Allred
Commissioner
Div. of Labor
State Capitol, Bldg. 3
1900 Kanawha Blvd., E.
Charleston, WV 25305
Phone: (304) 558-7890
Fax: (304) 558-3797

WISCONSIN
Sheehan Donoghue
Administrator
Div. of Equal Rights
Dept. of Workforce Dev.
201 E. Washington, Rm. 407
P.O. Box 8928
Madison, WI 53708
Phone: (608) 266-6860
Fax: (608) 267-4592

WYOMING
Charlie Rando
Acting Administrator
Div. of Labor Standards
Dept. of Employment
Herschler Bldg.
122 W. 25th St.
Cheyenne, WY 82002
Phone: (307) 777-7672

Child Support Enforcement

Processes child support cases and implements required provisions of child support enforcement program.

ALABAMA
Carolyn Lapsley
Child Support Enforcement Div.
Dept. of Human Resources
50 N. Ripley St.
Montgomery, AL 36130
Phone: (334) 242-9300
Fax: (334) 242-0606

ALASKA
Barbara Miklos
Director
Child Support Enforcement Div.
Dept. of Revenue
550 W. 7th Ave., Ste. 310
Anchorage, AK 99501-6699
Phone: (907) 269-6800
Fax: (907) 269-6868

AMERICAN SAMOA

ARIZONA
Nancy Mendoza
Assistant Director
Div. of Family Support
Dept. of Economic Security
3443 N. Central, 021A
Phoenix, AZ 85012
Phone: (602) 274-7646

ARKANSAS
Dan McDonald
Administrator
Child Support Enforcement
Dept. of Finance & Administration
P.O. Box 1272
Little Rock, AR 72203
Phone: (501) 682-6169
Fax: (501) 682-6002

CALIFORNIA
Leslie Frye
Chief
Child Support Program Branch
Dept. of Social Services
744 P St., MS 17-29
Sacramento, CA 95814
Phone: (916) 654-1556

COLORADO
Pauline Burton
Director
Child Support Enforcement Div.
Dept. of Human Services
1575 Sherman St., 2nd Fl.
Denver, CO 80203-1714
Phone: (303) 866-5994
Fax: (303) 866-3874

CONNECTICUT
Anthony DiNallo
Chief
Child Support Enforcement Bur.
Dept. of Social Services
25 Sigourney St.
Hartford, CT 06105
Phone: (860) 424-5251

DELAWARE
Karryl Hubbard
Director
Child Support Enforcement Div.
Health & Social Services Dept.
1901 N. DuPont Hwy.
New Castle, DE 19720
Phone: (302) 577-4800
Fax: (302) 577-4863

DISTRICT OF COLUMBIA
Marceline Alexander
Chief
Child Support Enforcement
441 4th St., NW
Washington, DC 20001
Phone: (202) 727-3839
Fax: (202) 727-3588

FLORIDA
Patricia Pillar
Director
Child Support Enforcement Program
Dept. of Revenue
P.O. Box 8030
Tallahassee, FL 32314-8030
Phone: (850) 922-9590
Fax: (850) 488-4401

GEORGIA
Dan Elmore
Director
Ofc. of Child Support Recovery
Dept. of Human Resources
P.O. Box 38450
Atlanta, GA 30334-0450
Phone: (404) 657-3856

GUAM
Kathryn Montague
Deputy Attorney General
Family Div.
Dept. of Law
238 Archbishop F.C. Flores St.
Pacific News Bldg., Ste. 701
Hagatna, GU 96910
Phone: (671) 475-3360
Fax: (671) 475-6118

HAWAII
Michael Meaney
Administrator
Child Support Enforcement
Dept. of the Attorney Gen.
601 Kamokila Blvd., #207
Kapolei, HI 96707
Phone: (808) 692-7000
Fax: (808) 692-7134

IDAHO
Shannon Barnes
Bureau Chief
Child Support Services
Dept. of Health & Welfare
450 W. State St.
P.O. Box 83720
Boise, ID 83720-0036
Phone: (208) 334-6515
Fax: (208) 334-0666

ILLINOIS
Robert Lyons
Administrator
Div. of Child Support
Dept. of Public Aid
201 S. Grand
Springfield, IL 62763
Phone: (217) 524-4602

INDIANA
Joseph B. Mamlin
Director
Child Support Div.
IGC-South, Rm. W360
402 W. Washington
Indianapolis, IN 46204
Phone: (317) 232-4885
Fax: (317) 233-4925

IOWA
Jim Hennessey
Chief
Bur. of Collections
Dept. of Human Services
Hoover State Ofc. Bldg.
1305 E. Walnut
Des Moines, IA 50319
Phone: (515) 281-5767
Fax: (515) 281-4597

KANSAS
James A. Robertson
Administrator
Child Support Enforcement Social & Rehab. Services
Biddle Bldg.
415 SW 8th
Topeka, KS 66603
Phone: (785) 296-3237
Fax: (785) 296-5206

KENTUCKY
Steve Veno
Director
Div. of Child Support Enforcement
Human Resources Cabinet
275 E. Main St.
Frankfort, KY 40621
Phone: (502) 564-2285
Fax: (502) 564-5988

LOUISIANA
Madlyn Bagneris
Secretary
Dept. of Social Services
P.O. Box 3776
Baton Rouge, LA 70821
Phone: (225) 342-0286
Fax: (225) 342-8636

MAINE
Colburn Jackson
Director
Div. of Support Enforcement & Recovery
Dept. of Human Services
11 State House Station
Augusta, ME 04333
Phone: (207) 287-2886

MARYLAND
Joyce Mitchell
Project Director
Child Support Enforcement
Dept. of Human Resources
200 N. Howard St.
Baltimore, MD 21201
Phone: (410) 347-5000

MASSACHUSETTS
Amy Pitter
Deputy Commissioner
Child Support Enforcement
Dept. of Revenue
P.O. Box 9492
Boston, MA 02205
Phone: (617) 626-4000
Fax: (617) 626-4049

MICHIGAN
John D. Ferry, Jr.
State Court Administrator
Supreme Ct.
State Ct. Adm. Ofc.
309 N. Washington Sq.
P.O. Box 30048
Lansing, MI 48909
Phone: (517) 373-0130
Fax: (517) 373-8922

MINNESOTA
Laura Kadwell
Director
Child Support Enforcement Div.
Dept. of Human Services
444 Lafayette Rd.
St. Paul, MN 55155-3846
Phone: (651) 297-8232
Fax: (651) 297-4450
E-mail: laura.kadwell@state.mn.us

MISSISSIPPI
Richard Harris
Director
Div. of Child Support Enforcement
P.O. Box 352
Jackson, MS 39205
Phone: (601) 359-4861
Fax: (601) 359-4415

MISSOURI
Brian Kinkade
Director
Child Support Enforcement Div.
Dept. of Social Services
3418 Knipp Dr., Ste. F
P.O. Box 2320
Jefferson City, MO 65102-2320
Phone: (573) 751-4301
Fax: (573) 751-8450
E-mail: bkinkade@mail.state.mo.us

MONTANA
Mary Ann Wellbank
Administrator
Child Support Enforcement Div.
Dept. of Public Health & Human Services
P.O. Box 202943
Helena, MT 59620
Phone: (406) 442-7278
Fax: (406) 444-1370

NEBRASKA
Daryl Wusk
Administrator
Child Support Enforcement
Dept. of Health & Human Services
P.O. Box 95044
Lincoln, NE 68509
Phone: (402) 479-5510
Fax: (402) 479-5145

NEVADA
Myla Florence
Administrator
Welfare Div.
Dept. of Human Resources
2527 N. Carson St.
Carson City, NV 89706
Phone: (775) 687-4128
Fax: (775) 687-5080

NEW HAMPSHIRE
Kathleen Kerr
Director
Ofc. of Program Support
Health & Human Services
6 Hazen Dr.
Concord, NH 03301-6527
Phone: (603) 271-4335
Fax: (603) 271-4787

NEW JERSEY
David Heins
Director
Div. of Family Dev.
Dept. of Human Services
Quakerbridge Rd.
P.O. Box 716
Trenton, NJ 08625-0716
Phone: (609) 588-2485
Fax: (609) 584-4404

NEW MEXICO
Ben Silva
Director
Child Support Enforcement
Human Services Dept.
P.O. Box 2348
Santa Fe, NM 87504
Phone: (505) 476-7040
Fax: (505) 827-6286

NEW YORK
Robert Doar
Director
Child Support Enforcement Ofc.
Dept. of Social Services
1 Commerce Plz.
P.O. Box 14
Albany, NY 12260
Phone: (518) 474-1078
Fax: (518) 486-3127

NORTH CAROLINA
Michael Adams
Assistant Director
Div. of Social Services
Dept. of Health & Human Services
325 N. Salisbury St.
Raleigh, NC 27603-5905
Phone: (919) 571-4120

NORTH DAKOTA
William Strate
Director
Child Support Enforcement
Dept. of Human Services
1929 N. Washington St.
Bismarck, ND 58501
Phone: (701) 328-3582
Fax: (701) 328-6575
E-mail: dhs@pioneer.state.nd.us

NORTHERN MARIANA ISLANDS
Vacant
Assistant
Attorney Gen's. Ofc.
Ofc. of the Governor
P.O. Box 10007
Saipan, MP 96950
Phone: (670) 664-2340
Fax: (670) 664-2349

OHIO
Barbara Saunders
Deputy Director
Ofc. of Child Support
Dept. of Human Services
50 W. Broad St., 4th Fl.
Columbus, OH 43266
Phone: (614) 752-6561
Fax: (614) 752-9760

OKLAHOMA
Ray Weaver
IV-D Administrator
Child Support Enforcement Div.
2400 N. Lincoln Blvd.
P.O. Box 25352
Oklahoma City, OK 73125
Phone: (405) 521-3646
Fax: (405) 521-6458

OREGON
Cindy Chinnock
Administrator
Support Enforcement Div.
Justice Dept.
1162 Court St., NE
Salem, OR 97310
Phone: (503) 986-6083
Fax: (503) 986-6158

PENNSYLVANIA
John Stuff
Director
Child Support
Enforcement Bur.
Dept. of Public Welfare
P.O. Box 8018
Harrisburg, PA 17105
Phone: (717) 783-8729
Fax: (412) 772-2062

PUERTO RICO
Miguel Verdiales
Administrator
Child Support
P.O. Box 3349
San Juan, PR 00902
Phone: (787) 767-1500
Fax: (787) 282-8324

RHODE ISLAND
Charles Anthony
Chief of Division
Child Support
Enforcement
77 Dorrance St.
Providence, RI 02903
Phone: (401) 464-2421

SOUTH CAROLINA
Elizabeth G. Patterson
Director
Dept. of Social Services
1535 Confederate Ave.,
Extension
Columbia, SC 29202
Phone: (803) 898-7360

SOUTH DAKOTA
Terry Walter
Program Administrator
Div. of Child Support
Enforcement
Dept. of Social Services
Kneip Bldg.
700 Governors Dr.
Pierre, SD 57501
Phone: (605) 773-3641
Fax: (605) 773-4855

TENNESSEE
Natasha Metcalf
Commissioner
Dept. of Human Services
Citizens Plz., 15th Fl.
400 Deaderick St.
Nashville, TN 37248-0001
Phone: (615) 313-4700
Fax: (615) 741-4165

TEXAS
Howard Baldwin
Child Support
Enforcement Div.
Ofc. of the Attorney Gen.
P.O. Box 12548
Austin, TX 78711
Phone: (512) 460-6000

U.S. VIRGIN ISLANDS
Cisselon Nichols
Acting Director
Paternity & Child Support
Justice Dept.
Time Ctr., 2nd Fl.
7 Charlotte Amalie
St. Thomas, VI 00802
Phone: (340) 775-3070
Fax: (340) 775-3808

UTAH
Emma Chacon
Director
Ofc. of Recovery Services
Dept. of Human Services
515 E. 100 S.
Salt Lake City, UT 84102
Phone: (801) 536-8901
Fax: (801) 536-8509
E-mail: echacon.hsorsslc
@state.ut.us

VERMONT
Jeffrey Cohen
Director
Ofc. of Child Support
103 S. Main St.
Waterbury, VT 05671
Phone: (802) 241-2319
Fax: (802) 244-1483
E-mail: jeffc
@wpgate1.ahs.state.vt.us

VIRGINIA
Clarence H. Carter
Commissioner
Dept. of Social Services
Theater Row Bldg.
730 E. Broad St.
Richmond, VA 23219
Phone: (804) 692-1901
Fax: (804) 692-1964

WASHINGTON
Meg Sollenberger
Director
Div. of Child Support
Social & Health Services
Dept.
P.O. Box 45860
Olympia, WA 98504-5860
Phone: (360) 586-3162
Fax: (360) 586-3274

WEST VIRGINIA
Sallie H. Hunt
Commissioner
Bur. for Child Support
Enforcement
Bldg. 6, Rm. 817
1900 Kanawha Blvd., E.
Charleston, WV 25305
Phone: (304) 558-3780
Fax: (304) 558-4092

WISCONSIN
Jean Rogers
Administrator
Div. of Economic Support
Dept. of Workforce Dev.
1 W. Wilson St., Rm. 358
P.O. Box 7935
Madison, WI 53707-7935
Phone: (608) 266-3035
Fax: (608) 261-6376

WYOMING
Shirley Carson
Director
Dept. of Family Services
Hathaway Bldg., 3rd Fl.
2300 Capitol Ave.
Cheyenne, WY 82002
Phone: (307) 777-6948

Children and Youth Services

Implements programs designed to protect children and youth against abuse, neglect and exploitation.

ALABAMA
Jerry Milner
Director
Bur. of Family & Children Services
Dept. of Human Resources
50 N. Ripley St.
Montgomery, AL 36130
Phone: (334) 242-9500
Fax: (334) 242-0939

ALASKA
Theresa Tanonry
Administrator
Div. of Family & Youth Services
Dept. of Health & Social Services
P.O. Box 110630
Juneau, AK 99811-0630
Phone: (907) 465-3191
Fax: (907) 465-3397

AMERICAN SAMOA
Marie F. Ma'o
Director
Dept. of Human & Social Services
AS Govt.
P.O. Box 997534
Pago Pago, AS 96799
Phone: (684) 633-2696
Fax: (684) 633-7449
E-mail: dhss@samoatelco.com

ARIZONA
James Hart
Assistant Director
Children, Youth & Families
Dept. of Economic Security
1789 W. Jefferson, 750A
Phoenix, AZ 85005
Phone: (602) 542-3598

ARKANSAS
Diane O'Connell
Director
Children & Family Services
Dept of Human Services
P.O. Box 1437
Little Rock, AR 72203
Phone: (501) 682-8772
Fax: (501) 682-8666

CALIFORNIA
Marjorie Kelly
Deputy Director
Children & Family Services Div.
Dept. of Social Services
744 P St., MS 17-18
Sacramento, CA 95814
Phone: (916) 657-2614

COLORADO
John Dario
Co-Director
Child Welfare Program
Dept. of Human Services
1575 Sherman St., 2nd Fl.
Denver, CO 80203-1714
Phone: (303) 866-5932
Fax: (303) 866-2214

Karen Studen
Co-Director
Child Welfare Program
Dept. of Human Services
1575 Sherman St., 2nd Fl.
Denver, CO 80203-1714
Phone: (303) 866-5932
Fax: (303) 866-2214

CONNECTICUT
Kristine Ragaglia
Commissioner
Dept. of Children & Families
505 Hudson St.
Hartford, CT 06106-7107
Phone: (860) 550-6300

DELAWARE
Thomas P. Eichler
Secretary
Dept. of Services for Children, Youth & Their Families
1825 Faulkland Rd.
Wilmington, DE 19805
Phone: (302) 633-2500
Fax: (302) 995-8290
E-mail: teichler@dscyf.state.de.us

DISTRICT OF COLUMBIA
Lou Woolard
Acting Administrator
Children & Youth Services
Bldg. L
2700 M.L. King, Jr. Ave., SE
Washington, DC 20032
Phone: (202) 373-7157

FLORIDA
Linda Radigan
Assistant Secretary
Family Safety & Preservation
Dept. of Children & Family Services
1317 Winewood Blvd., Bldg. 8
Tallahassee, FL 32399
Phone: (850) 488-8762
Fax: (850) 487-0688

GEORGIA
Orlando Martinez
Commissioner
Dept. of Juvenile Justice
2 Peachtree St., 5th Fl.
Atlanta, GA 30303
Phone: (404) 657-2410

GUAM
David M. Dell'Isola
Director
Dept. of Youth Affairs
P.O. Box 23672
GMF, GU 96921
Phone: (671) 734-3911
Fax: (671) 734-7536

Dennis G. Rodriguez
Director
Dept. of Public Health & Social Services
P.O. Box 2816
Hagatna, GU 96932
Phone: (671) 735-7102
Fax: (671) 734-5910
E-mail: dennis_r_@NS.GOV.GU

HAWAII
John Walters
Acting Program Administrator
Child Protective Services
Dept. of Human Services
810 Richards St., Ste. 400
Honolulu, HI 96813
Phone: (808) 586-5667
Fax: (808) 586-5700

IDAHO
Vacant
Bureau Chief
Children's Services
Dept. of Health & Welfare
450 W. State St.
P.O. Box 83720
Boise, ID 83720-0036
Phone: (208) 334-5700
Fax: (208) 334-6699

ILLINOIS
Jess McDonald
Director
Dept. of Children & Family Services
406 E. Monroe St.
Springfield, IL 62701
Phone: (217) 785-2509
Fax: (217) 785-1052

INDIANA
James Hmurovich
Director
Div. of Families & Children
Family & Social Services Administration
IGC-South, Rm. W392
Indianapolis, IN 46204
Phone: (317) 232-4705
Fax: (317) 232-4490

IOWA
Mary Nelson
Administrator
Adult, Children & Family Services
Dept. of Human Services
Hoover State Ofc. Bldg.
1305 E. Walnut
Des Moines, IA 50319
Phone: (515) 281-5521
Fax: (515) 281-4597

KANSAS
Joyce Allegrucci
Commissioner
Children & Family Services
Social & Rehab. Services
915 SW Harrison - 5th Fl.,S
Topeka, KS 66612-1570
Phone: (785) 296-4653
Fax: (785) 296-4649

KENTUCKY
Dennis Corrigan
Director
Div. of Family Services
Dept. for Social Services
275 E. Main St.
Frankfort, KY 40601
Phone: (502) 564-6852
Fax: (502) 564-3096

LOUISIANA
Madlyn Bagneris
Secretary
Dept. of Social Services
P.O. Box 3776
Baton Rouge, LA 70821
Phone: (225) 342-0286
Fax: (225) 342-8636

MAINE
Margaret Semple
Director
Child & Family Services
Dept. of Human Services
11 State House Station
Augusta, ME 04333
Phone: (207) 287-5060
Fax: (207) 287-5282

MARYLAND
Kenneth Rumsey
Executive Director
Director's Ofc. - Governor's Ofc. of Children, Youth & Families
Executive Dept.
301 W. Preston St., 15th Fl.
Baltimore, MD 21201
Phone: (410) 767-6225
Fax: (410) 333-5248

Linda S. Thompson
Special Secretary
Governor's Ofc. of Children, Youth & Families
Executive Dept.
301 W. Preston St., 15th Fl.
Baltimore, MD 21201
Phone: (410) 767-4092
Fax: (410) 333-5248

MASSACHUSETTS
Robert P. Gittens
Commissioner
Executive Ofc. of Health & Human Services
Dept. of Youth Services
27-43 Wormwood St., Ste. 400
Boston, MA 02210
Phone: (617) 727-7575
Fax: (617) 951-2409

MICHIGAN
Vacant
Ofc. of Children's Services
Family Independence Agency
235 S. Grand Ave.
Lansing, MI 48909
Phone: (517) 335-6158
Fax: (517) 335-6320

MINNESOTA
Erin Sullivan Sutton
Director
Family & Children Services Div.
Dept. of Human Services
444 Lafayette Rd.
St. Paul, MN 55155
Phone: (651) 296-2487
Fax: (651) 297-1949
E-mail: erin.sullivan-sutton@state.mn.us

MISSISSIPPI
Ronnie McGinnis
Director
Div. of Family & Children's Services
P.O. Box 352
Jackson, MS 39205
Phone: (601) 359-4555
Fax: (601) 359-4477

MISSOURI
Richard Matt
Deputy Director
Children's Services
Div. of Family Services
Dept. of Social Services
615 Howerton Ct., P.O. Box 88
Jefferson City, MO 65103
Phone: (573) 751-2882
Fax: (573) 526-3971
E-mail: mattl@mail.state.mo.us

MONTANA
Chuck Hunter
Administrator
Child & Family Services Div.
Dept. of Public Health & Human Services
1400 Broadway, Rm. C114
Helena, MT 59620
Phone: (406) 444-9740
Fax: (406) 444-5956

NEBRASKA
Chris Hanus Schulenberg
Administrator
Protection & Safety Div.
Dept. of Health & Human Services
P.O. Box 95044
Lincoln, NE 68509
Phone: (402) 471-9308
Fax: (402) 471-0934

NEVADA
Stephen A. Shaw
Administrator
Div. of Child & Family Services
711 E. 5th St.
Carson City, NV 89701-5092
Phone: (775) 684-4400
Fax: (775) 684-4455
E-mail: sshaw@govmail.state.nv.us

NEW HAMPSHIRE
Nancy Rollins
Director
Ofc. of Family Services
Div. of Children, Youth & Families
Health & Human Services
6 Hazen Dr.
Concord, NH 03301-6505
Phone: (603) 271-4714
Fax: (603) 271-4729

NEW JERSEY
John Lewis
Director
Education Ofc.
Human Services Dept.
P.O. Box 710
Trenton, NJ 08625-0710
Phone: (609) 588-3165
Fax: (609) 588-7239

Charles Venti
Director
Youth & Family Services
Dept. of Human Services
Quakerbridge Rd.
P.O. Box 717
Trenton, NJ 08625-0717
Phone: (609) 292-6920
Fax: (609) 584-4404

NEW MEXICO
Soledad Martinez
Health Program Manager
Family Preservation Unit
PERA Bldg., Rm. 254
P.O. Drawer 5160
Santa Fe, NM 87502-5160
Phone: (505) 827-8400
Fax: (505) 827-8480

NEW YORK
John A. Johnson
Commissioner
Ofc. of Children & Family Services
Capitol View Ofc. Park
52 Washington St.
Rensselaer, NY 12144
Phone: (518) 473-8437
Fax: (518) 473-9131

NORTH CAROLINA
Kevin Fitzgerald
Director of Social Services
Dept. of Health & Human Services
325 N. Salisbury St.
Raleigh, NC 27603-5905
Phone: (919) 733-3055
Fax: (919) 715-3581

NORTH DAKOTA
Linda Schell
Director
Children & Family Services
Dept. of Human Services
600 E. Blvd. Ave., 3rd Fl. - Judicial Wing
Bismarck, ND 58505-0250
Phone: (701) 328-2316
Fax: (701) 328-2359
E-mail: soschl@state.nd.us

NORTHERN MARIANA ISLANDS
Eloise A. Furey
Director
Div. of Youth Services
Dept. of Community & Cultural Affairs
P.O. Box 1000 CK
Saipan, MP 96950
Phone: (670) 664-2254
Fax: (670) 664-2560

OHIO
Geno Natalucci-Persischetti
Director
Dept. of Youth Services
65 E. State St.
Columbus, OH 43215
Phone: (614) 466-8783
Fax: (614) 752-9078

OKLAHOMA
Howard Hendrick
Director
Human Services
Dept. of Human Services
P.O. Box 25352
Oklahoma City, OK 73125
Phone: (405) 521-3646
Fax: (405) 521-6458

OREGON
Donna Middleton
Director
Comm. on Children & Families
530 Ctr. St., NE, Ste. 300
Salem, OR 97310
Phone: (503) 373-1283
Fax: (503) 373-8395

PENNSYLVANIA
Jo Ann Lawer
Deputy Secretary
Children, Youth & Families
Dept. of Public Welfare
P.O. Box 2675
Harrisburg, PA 17105
Phone: (717) 787-4756
Fax: (412) 787-0414

PUERTO RICO
Angie Varela
Secretary
Dept. of Social Services
P.O. Box 11398
San Juan, PR 00910
Phone: (787) 722-7400
Fax: (787) 723-1223

RHODE ISLAND
Jay Lindgren
Director
Dept. of Children, Youth & Families
610 Mt. Pleasant Ave.
Providence, RI 02908
Phone: (401) 457-4750
Fax: (401) 457-5363

SOUTH CAROLINA
Wilbert Lewis
Director
Child Protective & Preventative Services
Dept. of Social Services
P.O. Box 1520
Columbia, SC 29202
Phone: (803) 898-7423

SOUTH DAKOTA
Judy Hines
Administrator
Child Protection Services Div.
Dept. of Social Services
Kneip Bldg.
700 Governors Dr.
Pierre, SD 57501
Phone: (605) 773-3227
Fax: (605) 773-6834

TENNESSEE
George Hattaway
Commissioner
Dept. of Children's Services
Cordell Hull Bldg., 7th Fl.
710 James Robertson Pkwy.
Nashville, TN 37243
Phone: (615) 741-9701
Fax: (615) 532-8079

TEXAS
Jim Hine
Executive Director
Dept. of Protective & Regulatory Services
Mail Code E-654
701 W. 51st St.
Austin, TX 78751
Phone: (512) 438-4870

U.S. VIRGIN ISLANDS
Sedonie Halbert
Commissioner
Dept. of Human Services
Knud Hansen Complex, Bldg. A
1303 Hospital Grounds
St. Thomas, VI 00802
Phone: (340) 774-0930
Fax: (340) 774-3466

UTAH
Ken Patterson
Director
Div. of Child & Family Services
Dept. of Human Services
120 N. 200 W., Rm. 225
Salt Lake City, UT 84103
Phone: (801) 538-4099
Fax: (801) 538-3993
E-mail: kpatterson.hsadmin1@state.ut.us

VERMONT
William Young
Director
Dept. of Social & Rehab. Services
103 S. Main St.
Waterbury, VT 05671
Phone: (802) 241-2101
E-mail: wmy@srs.state.vt.us

VIRGINIA
Clarence H. Carter
Commissioner
Dept. of Social Services
Theater Row Bldg.
730 E. Broad St.
Richmond, VA 23219
Phone: (804) 692-1901
Fax: (804) 692-1964

WASHINGTON
Carole Holland
Director
Children's Administration - Program & Policy
Dept. of Social & Health Services
P.O. Box 45710
Olympia, WA 98504-4571
Phone: (360) 902-7910
Fax: (360) 902-7903

WEST VIRGINIA
Patricia Moore-Moss
Director, Office of Maternal & Child Health
Bur. for Public Health
Dept. of Health & Human Resources
1411 Virginia St., E.
Charleston, WV 25301-3013
Phone: (304) 558-5388
Fax: (304) 558-2183

WISCONSIN
Susan Dreyfus
Administrator
Div. of Children & Family Services
Health & Family Services
1 W. Wilson, Rm. 465
P.O. Box 7851
Madison, WI 53707
Phone: (608) 266-3036
Fax: (608) 264-6750

WYOMING
Shirley Carson
Director
Dept. of Family Services
Hathaway Bldg., 3rd Fl.
2300 Capitol Ave.
Cheyenne, WY 82002
Phone: (307) 777-6948

Civil Rights

Overall responsibility for preventing and redressing discrimination in employment, education, housing, public accommodations and credit (because of race, color, sex, age, national origin, religion or disability).

ALABAMA
Eugene Crum
Executive Director
Ctr. for Justice
88 W. South Blvd.
P.O. Box 11218
Montgomery, AL 36111-0218
Phone: (334) 242-0474
Fax: (334) 353-1222

ALASKA
Paula Haley
Executive Director
Human Rights Comm.
Ofc. of the Governor
800 A St., Ste. 204
Anchorage, AK 99501-3669
Phone: (907) 276-7474
Fax: (907) 278-8588

AMERICAN SAMOA

ARIZONA
Gloria Ybarra
Chief Counsel
Civil Rights Div.
Ofc. of the Attorney Gen.
1275 W. Washington
Phoenix, AZ 85007
Phone: (602) 542-5263

ARKANSAS

CALIFORNIA
Nancy C. Gutierrez
Director
Fair Employment & Housing
2014 T St., Ste. 210
Sacramento, CA 95814
Phone: (916) 227-2873

COLORADO
Jack T. Lang Y. Marquez
Director
Civil Rights Div.
Dept. of Regulatory Agencies
1560 Broadway, Rm. 1050
Denver, CO 80202
Phone: (303) 894-2997
Fax: (303) 894-7830

CONNECTICUT
Cynthia Watts-Elder
Director
Comm. on Human Rights & Opportunities
21 Grand St.
Hartford, CT 06106
Phone: (860) 541-3400

DELAWARE
Juana Fuentes
Chair
Human Relations Comm.
Dept. of Community Affairs
820 N. French St., 4th Fl.
Wilimington, DE 19801
Phone: (302) 577-3485
Fax: (302) 577-3486

DISTRICT OF COLUMBIA
Jackie Flowers
Director
Ofc. of Human Rights
441 4th St., NW, Ste. 970
Washington, DC 20001
Phone: (202) 727-3900
Fax: (202) 727-3786

FLORIDA
Carolyn Franklin
Assistant Director
Ofc. of Civil Rights
Labor & Employment Security
Sutton Bldg., Ste. 200
2670 Executive Ctr. Cir., W.
Tallahassee, FL 32399-2157
Phone: (850) 488-5905
Fax: (850) 921-4210

GEORGIA
Joy Berry
Executive Director
Human Relations Comm.
225 Peachtree St., NE, Ste. 1207
Atlanta, GA 30303-1701
Phone: (404) 651-9115
Fax: (404) 656-6046

GUAM
John F. Tarantino
Acting Attorney General
Dept. of Law
Judicial Ctr. Bldg., Ste. 2-200E
120 W. O'Brien Dr.
Hagatna, GU 96910
Phone: (671) 475-3324
Fax: (671) 475-2493
E-mail: law@ns.gov.gu

HAWAII
William D. Hoshijo
Executive Director
Civil Rights Comm.
Labor & Industrial Relations Dept.
830 Punchbowl St., Ste. 420
Honolulu, HI 96813
Phone: (808) 586-8636
Fax: (808) 586-8655

IDAHO
Leslie Goddard
Director
Human Rights Comm.
Ofc. of the Governor
450 W. State St.
Boise, ID 83720
Phone: (208) 334-2873

ILLINOIS
Carlos J. Salazar
Director
Dept. of Human Rights
100 W. Randolph, Ste. 10-100
Chicago, IL 60601
Phone: (312) 814-6245
Fax: (312) 814-1436

INDIANA
Sandra D. Leek
Director
Civil Rights Comm.
100 N. Senate Ave., Rm. E103
Indianapolis, IN 46204
Phone: (317) 232-2600
Fax: (317) 232-6580

IOWA
Diann Wilder-Tomlinson
Director
Civil Rights Comm.
211 E. Maple St., 2nd Fl.
Des Moines, IA 50319
Phone: (515) 281-4121
Fax: (515) 281-5840
E-mail: diann.wilder-tomlinson@civil.state.ia.us

KANSAS
William V. Minner
Executive Director
Human Rights Comm.
Landon State Ofc. Bldg., Ste. 851-8
900 SW Jackson
Topeka, KS 66612
Phone: (785) 296-3206

KENTUCKY
Beverly L. Watts
Executive Director
Comm. on Human Rights
The Heyburn Bldg., 7th Fl.
332 W. Broadway
Louisville, KY 40202
Phone: (502) 595-4024
Fax: (502) 595-4801

LOUISIANA
Leah Raby
Executive Assistant
Comm. on Human Rights
P.O. Box 94094
Baton Rouge, LA 70804
Phone: (225) 342-6969
Fax: (225) 342-2063

MAINE
Patricia Ryan
Executive Director
Human Rights Comm.
51 State House Station
Augusta, ME 04333
Phone: (207) 624-6050

MARYLAND
Henry Ford
Executive Director
Executive Dept.
Comm. on Human Relations
6 St. Paul St., 9th Fl.
Baltimore, MD 21202
Phone: (410) 767-8563
Fax: (410) 333-1841
E-mail: hford@mail.mchr.state.md.us

MASSACHUSETTS
Charles Walker
Chair
Comm. Against Discrimination
One Ashburton Pl., Rm. 601
Boston, MA 02108
Phone: (617) 727-3990
Fax: (617) 720-6053

MICHIGAN
Nanette Lee Reynolds
Director
Dept. of Civil Rights
201 N. Washington, Ste. 700
Lansing, MI 48913
Phone: (517) 335-3164
Fax: (517) 335-6790

MINNESOTA
Janeen Rosas
Commissioner
Dept. of Human Rights
190 E. 5th St., Ste. 700
Minneapolis, MN 55101
Phone: (651) 296-5665
Fax: (651) 296-1736

MISSISSIPPI

MISSOURI
Donna Cavitte
Director, Commission on Human Rights
Comm. on Human Rights
Dept. of Labor & Industrial Relations
3315 W. Truman Blvd.
P.O. Box 1129
Jefferson City, MO 65102-1129
Phone: (573) 751-3325
Fax: (573) 751-2905
E-mail: dcavitte@mail.state.mo.us

MONTANA
Kathy Hilland
Bureau Chief
Human Rights Bur.
Dept. of Labor & Industry
Steamboat Block
616 Helena Ave., Ste. 302
Helena, MT 59624-1728
Phone: (406) 444-4345
Fax: (406) 444-2798

NEBRASKA
Alfonza Whitaker
Executive Director
Equal Opportunity Comm.
301 Centennial Mall, S.
P.O. Box 94934
Lincoln, NE 68509-4934
Phone: (402) 471-2024
Fax: (402) 471-4059

NEVADA
William H. Stewart
Administrator
Equal Rights Comm.
Employment Training & Rehab.
1515 E. Tropicana, Ste. 590
Las Vegas, NV 89119
Phone: (702) 486-7161
Fax: (702) 486-7054

NEW HAMPSHIRE
Katharine Daly
Executive Director
Comm. for Human Rights
2 Chenell Dr.
Concord, NH 03301
Phone: (603) 271-2767
Fax: (603) 271-6339

NEW JERSEY
Rolando Torres, Jr.
Director
Div. on Civil Rights
Dept. of Law & Public Safety
P.O. Box 46001
Newark, NJ 07101
Phone: (973) 648-6262

NEW MEXICO
Jack Martinez
Programs Division Director
Human Rights Div.
Labor Dept.
1596 Pacheco St.
Santa Fe, NM 87505-3979
Phone: (505) 827-6838
Fax: (505) 827-6878

NEW YORK
Edward Mercado
Commissioner
Div. of Human Rights
Executive Dept.
55 W. 125th St., 13th Fl.
New York, NY 10027
Phone: (212) 961-8790
Fax: (212) 961-4119

NORTH CAROLINA
Eddie W. Lawrence
Executive Director
Human Relations Council
217 W. Jones St.
Raleigh, NC 27603
Phone: (919) 733-7996
Fax: (919) 733-7940

NORTH DAKOTA
Mark Bachmeier
Interim Commissioner
Labor Dept.
600 E. Blvd. Ave., 13th Fl.
Bismarck, ND 58505
Phone: (701) 328-2660
Fax: (701) 328-2031
E-mail: bachmeie@pioneer.state.nd.us

NORTHERN MARIANA ISLANDS
Vicente M. Sablan
Chair
Civil Service Comm.
P.O. Box 5150
Saipan, MP 96950
Phone: (670) 322-4363
Fax: (670) 322-3327

OHIO
Melanie Mitchell
Executive Director
Civil Rights Comm.
1111 E. Broad St., #301
Columbus, OH 43205-1303
Phone: (614) 466-6715
Fax: (614) 644-8776

OKLAHOMA
Gracie Monson
Director
Human Rights Comm.
2101 N. Lincoln Blvd., Rm. 481
Oklahoma City, OK 73105
Phone: (405) 521-2360
Fax: (405) 522-3635
E-mail: ohrc2@onenet.net

OREGON
Johnnie Bell
Administrator
Civil Rights Div.
Bur. of Labor & Industries
800 NE Oregon St., # 32
Portland, OR 97232
Phone: (503) 731-4873
Fax: (503) 731-4069

PENNSYLVANIA
Homer C. Floyd
Executive Director
Human Relations Comm.
P.O. Box 3145
Harrisburg, PA 17105
Phone: (717) 787-4410
Fax: (717) 787-0420

PUERTO RICO
Jose Aulet Concepcion
Executive Director
Civil Rights Comm.
P.O. Box 192338
San Juan, PR 00919-2338
Phone: (787) 764-8779
Fax: (787) 765-9360

RHODE ISLAND
Gene L. Booth
Executive Director
Human Rights Comm.
10 Abbott Park Pl.
Providence, RI 02903-3768
Phone: (401) 222-2661
Fax: (401) 222-2616

SOUTH CAROLINA
William C. Ham
Commissioner
Comm. on Human Affairs
P.O. Box 4490
Columbia, SC 29240
Phone: (803) 737-7800

SOUTH DAKOTA
Jeffrey Holden
Director
Div. of Human Rights
Dept. of Commerce & Regulation
118 W. Capitol Ave.
Pierre, SD 57501-2017
Phone: (605) 773-4493
Fax: (605) 773-6893

David Volk
Secretary
Div. of Insurance
Dept. of Commerce & Regulation
118 W. Capitol Ave.
Pierre, SD 57501-2017
Phone: (605) 773-3178
Fax: (605) 773-3018

TENNESSEE
Julius Sloss
Executive Director
Human Rights Comm.
530 Church St., Ste. 400
Nashville, TN 37243
Phone: (615) 741-5825
Fax: (615) 532-2197

TEXAS
William M. Hale
Executive Director
Comm. on Human Rights
6330 Hwy., 290 E., Ste. 250
Austin, TX 78723
Phone: (512) 437-3450
Fax: (512) 437-3478

U.S. VIRGIN ISLANDS
Lunsford Williams
Executive Director
Civil Rights Comm.
P.O. Box 6645
St. Thomas, VI 00804
Phone: (340) 776-2485

UTAH
Joseph Gallegos
Director
Anti-Discrimination & Labor Div.
Labor Comm.
160 E. 300 S., 3rd Fl.
Salt Lake City, UT 84114-6630
Phone: (801) 530-6801
Fax: (801) 530-7609
E-mail: jgallego.icmain@state.ut.us

VERMONT
Harvey Golubock
Executive Director
Human Rights Comm.
135 State St.
Montpelier, VT 05633-6301
Phone: (802) 828-2480
Fax: (802) 828-3522

Wendy Morgan
Chief
Public Protection Div.
Ofc. of the Attorney Gen.
109 State St.
Montpelier, VT 05602
Phone: (802) 828-3171

VIRGINIA
Roxie Raines Kornegay
Director
Council on Human Rights
Washington Bldg., 12th Fl.
1100 Bank St.
Richmond, VA 23219
Phone: (804) 225-2292
Fax: (804) 225-3294

WASHINGTON
Susan Jordan
Executive Director
Human Rights Comm.
711 S. Capitol Way, Ste. 402
P.O. Box 42490
Olympia, WA 98504-2490
Phone: (360) 753-6770
Fax: (360) 586-2282

WEST VIRGINIA
Patricia L. Stinnett
Executive Director
Human Rights Director
E. End Plz.
Morris & Lewis Sts.
Charleston, WV 25301
Phone: (304) 558-2616
Fax: (304) 558-0085

WISCONSIN
Sheehan Donoghue
Administrator
Div. of Equal Rights
Dept. of Workforce Dev.
201 E. Washington, Rm. 407
P.O. Box 8928
Madison, WI 53708
Phone: (608) 266-6860
Fax: (608) 267-4592

WYOMING
Dan Romero
EEO, Grievance & Appeals Coordinator
Personnel Div.
Dept. of Administration & Info.
Emerson Bldg.
2001 Capitol Ave.
Cheyenne, WY 82002
Phone: (307) 777-6730

Clerk of State Court of Last Resort

Individual who keeps records of the state court of last resort.

ALABAMA
Robert Esdale
Clerk
Supreme Ct.
300 Dexter Ave.
Montgomery, AL 36104-3741
Phone: (334) 242-4609
Fax: (334) 242-0588

ALASKA
Marilyn May
Supreme Court Clerk
Supreme Ct.
303 K St.
Anchorage, AK 99501-2084
Phone: (907) 264-0607
Fax: (907) 264-0878

AMERICAN SAMOA
Robert Gorniak
Clerk
High Ct.
Pago Pago, AS 96799
Phone: (684) 633-4131
Fax: (684) 633-1318

ARIZONA
Noel Dessaint
Clerk of the Supreme Court
1501 W. Washington, Rm. 402
Phoenix, AZ 85007
Phone: (602) 542-9396

ARKANSAS
Leslie W. Steen
Clerk
Supreme Ct.
Justice Bldg.
625 Marshall
Little Rock, AR 72201
Phone: (501) 682-6841
Fax: (501) 682-6877

CALIFORNIA
Robert Wandruff
Clerk
Supreme Ct.
S. Tower, 8th Fl.
303 2nd St.
San Francisco, CA 94107
Phone: (415) 396-9888

COLORADO
Mac Danford
Clerk
Supreme Ct.
State Judicial Bldg., # 415
2 E. 14th Ave.
Denver, CO 80203
Phone: (303) 861-1111
Fax: (303) 837-3702

CONNECTICUT
Francis J. Drumm, Jr.
Chief Clerk
Supreme Ct.
Drawer Z, Station A
231 Capitol Ave.
Hartford, CT 06106
Phone: (860) 566-8160
Fax: (860) 566-6731

DELAWARE
Cathy L. Howard
Supreme Court Clerk
55 The Green
Dover, DE 19901
Phone: (302) 739-4155
Fax: (302) 739-3751

DISTRICT OF COLUMBIA
Garland Pinkston, Jr.
Clerk
Ct. of Appeals
500 Indiana Ave., NW, Ste. 6000
Washington, DC 20001
Phone: (202) 879-2725
Fax: (202) 626-8847

FLORIDA
Sid J. White
Clerk
Supreme Ct.
Supreme Ct. Bldg.
500 S. Duval St.
Tallahassee, FL 32399-1925
Phone: (850) 488-0125

GEORGIA
Sherie M. Welch
Clerk
Supreme Ct.
244 Washington St., SW, Rm. 572
Atlanta, GA 30334
Phone: (404) 656-3470

GUAM
Keira K. Quan
Clerk of Court
Supreme Ct.
120 W. O'Brien Dr.
Hagatna, GU 96910
Phone: (671) 475-3124
Fax: (671) 477-4676

HAWAII
Darrell N. Phillips
Chief Clerk
417 S. King St.
Honolulu, HI 96813
Phone: (808) 539-4919
Fax: (808) 539-4928

IDAHO
Frederick C. Lyon
Clerk of the Supreme Court
Ct. of Appeals
P.O. Box 83720
Boise, ID 83720-0101
Phone: (208) 334-2210
Fax: (208) 334-2616

ILLINOIS
Juleann Hornyak
Supreme Court Clerk
Supreme Ct. Bldg.
Springfield, IL 62701
Phone: (217) 782-2035

INDIANA
Brian Bishop
Clerk of Supreme/Appellate Courts
State House, Rm. 217
200 W. Washington St.
Indianapolis, IN 46204
Phone: (317) 232-1930
Fax: (317) 232-8365

IOWA
R.K. Richardson
Clerk
Supreme Ct.
State Capitol
1007 E. Grand Ave.
Des Moines, IA 50319
Phone: (515) 281-5911
Fax: (515) 242-6164

KANSAS
Carol G. Green
Clerk of Appellate Courts
Supreme Ct. Judicial Ctr.
301 SW 10th Ave., Rm. 374
Topeka, KS 66612-1507
Phone: (785) 296-3229
Fax: (785) 296-1028

KENTUCKY
Susan Stokley-Clary
Supreme Court Clerk
700 Capitol Ave., Rm. 209
Frankfort, KY 40601
Phone: (502) 564-4720
Fax: (502) 564-5491

LOUISIANA
John Tarlton Olivier
Clerk
Supreme Ct.
Supreme Ct. Bldg.
301 Loyola Ave.
New Orleans, LA 70112
Phone: (504) 568-5707

MAINE
James P. Chute
Clerk of the Law Court
Supreme Ct.
P.O. Box 368
Portland, ME 04112
Phone: (207) 822-4146

MARYLAND
Alexander L. Cummings
Clerk of Court
Ct. of Appeals Clerk's Ofc.
Judiciary
Ct. of Appeals Bldg.
361 Rowe Blvd.
Annapolis, MD 21401
Phone: (410) 260-1502

MASSACHUSETTS
Maura Doyle
Clerk
1404 New Ct. House
Boston, MA 02108
Phone: (617) 557-1100
Fax: (617) 523-1540

MICHIGAN
Corbin Davis
Clerk
Supreme Ct.
P.O. Box 30052
Lansing, MI 48909
Phone: (517) 373-0120

MINNESOTA
Frederick K. Grittner
Clerk of Appellate Courts
Supreme Ct.
25 Constitution Ave.
St. Paul, MN 55155
Phone: (651) 297-5529
Fax: (651) 297-4149

MISSISSIPPI
Charlotte Williams
Clerk
Supreme Ct.
Gartin Bldg., 3rd Fl.
P.O. Box 249
Jackson, MS 39205
Phone: (601) 359-3697
Fax: (601) 359-2407

MISSOURI
Thomas F. Simon
Supreme Court Clerk
P.O. Box 150
Jefferson City, MO 65102
Phone: (573) 751-4144
Fax: (573) 751-7514
E-mail: thomas_f_simon
@osca.state.mo.us

MONTANA
Ed Smith
Clerk of Supreme Court
Justice Bldg., 215 N.
Sanders
P.O. Box 203003
Helena, MT 59620
Phone: (406) 444-3858
Fax: (406) 444-5705

NEBRASKA
Lanet S. Asmussen
Clerk
Supreme Ct.
P.O. Box 98910
Lincoln, NE 68509-8910
Phone: (402) 471-3731
Fax: (402) 471-3480

NEVADA
Janette M. Bloom
Clerk
Supreme Ct. Bldg.
201 S. Carson St., Ste. 201
Carson City, NV 89701
Phone: (775) 687-5180
Fax: (775) 687-3155

NEW HAMPSHIRE
Howard J. Zibel
Clerk
Supreme Ct.
Supreme Ct. Bldg.
1 Noble Dr.
Concord, NH 03301
Phone: (603) 271-2646

NEW JERSEY
Stephen W. Townsend
Clerk
Supreme Ct.
P.O. Box 970
Trenton, NJ 08625
Phone: (609) 984-7791

NEW MEXICO
Kathleen Jo Gibson
Chief Clerk
Supreme Ct.
P.O. Box 848
Santa Fe, NM 87504-0848
Phone: (505) 827-4860
Fax: (505) 827-4837

NEW YORK
Stuart M. Cohen
Clerk
Ct. of Appeals Hall
20 Eagle St.
Albany, NY 12207
Phone: (518) 455-7700

NORTH CAROLINA
Christie Speir Cameron
Clerk
Justice Bldg.
2 E. Morgan St.
Raleigh, NC 27601-1400
Phone: (919) 733-3723
Fax: (919) 733-0105

NORTH DAKOTA
Penny Miller
Clerk of Court
Supreme Ct.
600 E. Blvd. Ave., 1st Fl. -
Judicial Wing
Bismarck, ND 58505-0530
Phone: (701) 328-2221
Fax: (701) 328-4480
E-mail: pennym
@sc3.court.state.nd.us

NORTHERN MARIANA ISLANDS
Chris Kaipat
Clerk of the Court
Supreme Ct.
P.O. Box 2165
Saipan, MP 96950
Phone: (670) 236-9700
Fax: (670) 236-9701
E-mail: supreme.court
@saipan.com

OHIO
Marcia Mengel
Clerk
Supreme Ct.
30 E. Broad St., 2nd Fl.
Columbus, OH 43215-3414
Phone: (614) 466-3931
Fax: (614) 752-4418

OKLAHOMA
James Patterson
Supreme Court Clerk
State Capitol, Rm. B-2
2300 N. Lincoln Blvd.
Oklahoma City, OK 73105
Phone: (405) 521-2163

OREGON
Kingsley W. Click
Administrator
Supreme Ct. Bldg.
1163 State St.
Salem, OR 97310
Phone: (503) 986-5900
Fax: (503) 986-5503

PENNSYLVANIA
Shirley Bailey
Chief Clerk
Supreme Ct.
434 Main Capitol
P.O. Box 624
Harrisburg, PA 17108
Phone: (717) 787-6181
Fax: (717) 787-1549

Patty Honard
Chief Clerk, Supreme
Court
Supreme Ct.
801 City-County Bldg.
Pittsburgh, PA 15219-2816
Phone: (412) 565-2816
Fax: (412) 565-2149

Patricia Johnson
Chief Clerk
Supreme Ct.
468 City Hall
Philadelphia, PA 19107
Phone: (215) 560-6370
Fax: (215) 560-5972

PUERTO RICO
Francisco R. Agrait-Llado
General Secretary
Supreme Ct.
P.O. Box 2392
San Juan, PR 00902-2392
Phone: (787) 723-6033
Fax: (787) 722-9177

RHODE ISLAND
Brian Burns
Clerk
Supreme Ct.
250 Benefits St.
Providence, RI 02903
Phone: (401) 222-3273
Fax: (401) 222-3599

SOUTH CAROLINA
Daniel E. Shearouse
Clerk
Supreme Ct.
P.O. Box 11330
Columbia, SC 29211
Phone: (803) 734-1080
Fax: (803) 734-1499
E-mail: DSHEAROUSE@
scjd.state.sc.us

SOUTH DAKOTA
Dorothy A. Smith
Clerk
Supreme Ct.
State Capitol
500 E. Capitol Ave.
Pierre, SD 57501
Phone: (605) 773-3511
Fax: (605) 773-6128

TENNESSEE
Cecil Crowson, Jr.
Clerk of the Appellate
Courts
Middle Div.
401 7th Ave., N.
Nashville, TN 37219-1407
Phone: (615) 741-2687

TEXAS
John T. Adams
Chief Deputy Clerk
Supreme Ct.
P.O. Box 12248
Capitol Station
Austin, TX 78711
Phone: (512) 463-1312

U.S. VIRGIN ISLANDS
Orrin Arnold
Clerk
U.S. District Ct.
3013 Estate Golden Rock, Lot #13
Christiansted
St. Thomas, VI 00802-4355
Phone: (340) 773-1130
Fax: (340) 773-1563
E-mail: vidc@vid.uscourts.gov

UTAH
Patricia H. Bartholomew
Clerk of the Court
Supreme Ct.
450 S. State St.
P.O. Box 140210
Salt Lake City, UT 84114-0210
Phone: (801) 238-7974
Fax: (801) 238-7980
E-mail: pathb@email.utcourts.gov

VERMONT
Lee Suskin
Court Administrator
Supreme Ct.
109 State St.
Montpelier, VT 05609-0701
Phone: (802) 828-3278
Fax: (802) 828-3457

VIRGINIA
David B. Beach
Supreme Court Clerk
Supreme Ct.
100 N. 9th St., 5th Fl.
Richmond, VA 23219
Phone: (804) 786-6455
Fax: (804) 786-6249

WASHINGTON
C.J. Merritt
Clerk
Supreme Ct.
Temple of Justice
P.O. Box 40929
Olympia, WA 98504-0929
Phone: (360) 357-2077
Fax: (360) 357-2102

WEST VIRGINIA
Deborah McHenry
Supreme Court Clerk
Supreme Ct. of Appeals
Bldg. 1, Rm. E317
State Capitol Complex
Charleston, WV 25305-0831
Phone: (304) 558-2601
Fax: (304) 558-3815

WISCONSIN
Marilyn L. Graves
Supreme Court Clerk
110 E. Main St., Ste. 215
P.O. Box 1688
Madison, WI 53701-1688
Phone: (608) 266-1880
Fax: (608) 267-0640

WYOMING
Judy Pacheco
Clerk of the Supreme Court
Supreme Ct.
Supreme Ct. Bldg.
2301 Capitol Ave.
Cheyenne, WY 82002
Phone: (307) 777-7316
Fax: (307) 777-6129

Coastal Zone Management –

Plans and implements programs for the orderly development of coastal zones.

ALABAMA
Phillip Hinsley
Coastal Zone Management Manager
Coastal Zone Mgmt. Program
Science, Technology & Energy Div.
401 Adams Ave.
P.O. Box 5690
Montgomery, AL 36130-5690
Phone: (334) 626-0042
Fax: (334) 626-3503

ALASKA
Gabrielle LaRoche
Coordinator
Coastal Program
Div. of Governmental Coordinator
Ofc. of Mgmt. & Budget
P.O. Box 110030
Juneau, AK 99811-0030
Phone: (907) 465-3541
Fax: (907) 465-3075

AMERICAN SAMOA
Aliimau Scanlan, Jr.
Director
Dept. of Commerce
AS Govt.
Pago Pago, AS 96799
Phone: (684) 633-5155
Fax: (684) 633-4195

ARIZONA

ARKANSAS

CALIFORNIA
Peter R. Douglas
Executive Director
Coastal Comm.
Resources Agency
45 Fremont, Ste. 2000
San Francisco, CA 94105
Phone: (415) 904-5200

COLORADO

CONNECTICUT
Arthur J. Rocque
Senior Advisor
Long Island Sound Program Ofc.
Dept. of Environmental Protection
79 Elm St.
Hartford, CT 06106
Phone: (860) 424-3034

DELAWARE
Sarah Cooksey
Administrator
Coastal Zone Mgmt. Program
Dept. of Natural Resources & Environment
89 Kings Hwy.
Dover, DE 19903
Phone: (302) 739-3451
Fax: (302) 739-2048

DISTRICT OF COLUMBIA

FLORIDA
Al Devereaux
Chief
Bur. of Beaches & Coastal Systems
Dept. of Environmental Protection
3900 Commonwealth Blvd., MS 300
Tallahassee, FL 32399-3000
Phone: (850) 487-4469
Fax: (850) 488-5257

GEORGIA
Duane Harris
Director
Coastal Resources Div.
Dept. of Natural Resources
1 Conservation Way
Brunswick, GA 31523-8600
Phone: (912) 264-7218
Fax: (912) 262-3143

GUAM
Michael L. Ham
Administrator
Coastal Mgmt. Program
Bur. of Planning
P.O. Box 2950
Hagatna, GU 96932
Phone: (671) 472-4201
Fax: (671) 477-1812
E-mail: mham@kuentos.guam.net

HAWAII
Douglas Tom
Program Manager
Coastal Zone Mgmt. Program
Ofc. of Planning
P.O. Box 2359
Honolulu, HI 96804
Phone: (808) 587-2875
Fax: (808) 587-2899

IDAHO

ILLINOIS
Joel Park
Chief of Planning
Water Pollution Control Div.
Environmental Protection Agency
2200 Churchill Rd.
Springfield, IL 62702
Phone: (217) 782-3362
Fax: (217) 785-1225

INDIANA
Mike Neyer
Director
Div. of Water
Dept. of Natural Resources
402 W. Washington
Indianapolis, IN 46204
Phone: (317) 232-4158
Fax: (317) 233-4579

IOWA

KANSAS

KENTUCKY

LOUISIANA
Randy Hanchey
Assistant Secretary
Ofc. of Coastal Restoration & Mgmt.
Dept. of Natural Resources
P.O. Box 94396
Baton Rouge, LA 70804
Phone: (225) 342-3583
Fax: (225) 342-1377

MAINE
David Keeley
Director
Coastal Program
State Planning Ofc.
38 State House Station
Augusta, ME 04333
Phone: (207) 287-3261

MARYLAND
David Burke
Director
Chesapeake & Coastal Watershed
Dept. of Natural Resources
Tawes State Ofc. Bldg., Bldg. E2
Annapolis, MD 21401
Phone: (410) 260-8705
Fax: (410) 260-8709

MASSACHUSETTS
Susan Snow-Carter
Acting Director
Coastal Zone Mgmt.
Environmental Affairs
20th Fl., Rm. 2006
100 Cambridge St.
Boston, MA 02202
Phone: (617) 727-9530
Fax: (617) 727-2754

MICHIGAN
Tracy Mehan
Director
Ofc. of the Great Lakes
Dept. of Environmental Quality
P.O. Box 30028
Lansing, MI 48909
Phone: (517) 335-4056
Fax: (517) 335-4242

MINNESOTA
Kent Lokkesmoe
Director
Div. of Waters
Dept. of Natural Resources
500 Lafayette Rd.
St. Paul, MN 55155
Phone: (651) 296-4810
Fax: (651) 296-0445
E-mail: kent.lokkesmoe@dir.state.mn.us

MISSISSIPPI
Glade Woods
Executive Director
Dept. of Marine Resources
1141 Bayview Ave., Ste. 101
Biloxi, MS 39530
Phone: (228) 374-5000
Fax: (228) 374-5005

MISSOURI

MONTANA

NEBRASKA

NEVADA

NEW HAMPSHIRE
Jeffrey Taylor
Director
Ofc. of State Planning, Executive Dept.
Governor's Recycling Program
2 1/2 Beacon St.
Concord, NH 03301-4497
Phone: (603) 271-2155
Fax: (603) 271-1728

NEW JERSEY
Ruth Ehinger
Bureau Chief
Bur. of Coastal Regulation
Dept. of Environmental Protection
501 E. State St.
P.O. Box 401
Trenton, NJ 08625-0401
Phone: (609) 633-2289
Fax: (609) 292-8115

NEW MEXICO

NEW YORK
Alexander F. Treadwell
Secretary of State
Dept. of State
41 State St.
Albany, NY 12231
Phone: (518) 486-9844
Fax: (518) 474-4765

NORTH CAROLINA
Roger Schecter
Director
Coastal Mgmt. Div.
Dept. of Environment, Health & Natural Resources
2728 Capital Blvd.
Raleigh, NC 27604
Phone: (919) 733-2293
Fax: (919) 733-1495

NORTH DAKOTA

NORTHERN MARIANA ISLANDS
Vacant
Director
Coastal Resources Mgmt. Ofc.
Caller Box 10007
Saipan, MP 96950
Phone: (670) 234-6623
Fax: (670) 234-0007

OHIO
Michael Colvin
Chief
Div. of Water
Dept. of Natural Resources
Fountain Sq., Bldg. C
Columbus, OH 43224
Phone: (614) 265-6413

OKLAHOMA

OREGON
Mike Llewelyn
Administrator
Div. of Water Quality
Dept. of Environmental Quality
811 SW 6th Ave..
Portland, OR 97204
Phone: (503) 229-5324
Fax: (503) 229-6124

PENNSYLVANIA
Michael Krempasky
Director
Land & Water Conservation
Dept. of Environmental Resources
Market St. State Ofc. Bldg.
Harrisburg, PA 17101
Phone: (717) 783-9500
Fax: (717) 772-3249

PUERTO RICO
Hector Russe
President
Environmental Quality Board
P.O. Box 11488
San Juan, PR 00910-1488
Phone: (787) 767-8056
Fax: (787) 754-8294

RHODE ISLAND
James Beattie
Chief
Coastal Resources, DEM
9 Hayes St.
Providence, RI 02908
Phone: (401) 222-2476

Grover Fugate
Executive Director
Coastal Resources Mgmt. Council
Oliver Stedman Govt. Ctr.
4808 Tower Hill Rd.
Wakefield, RI 02879-1900
Phone: (401) 222-2476

SOUTH CAROLINA
Chris Brooks
Assistant Deputy Commissioner
Ofc. of Ocean & Coastal Resources Mgmt.
Dept. of Health & Environmental Control
2600 Bull St.
Columbia, SC 29201
Phone: (843) 744-5838
Fax: (843) 744-5847

SOUTH DAKOTA

TENNESSEE

TEXAS
Sally S. Davenport
Director
Coastal Div.
Land Ofc.
1700 N. Congress Ave.
Austin, TX 78701
Phone: (512) 463-5059
Fax: (512) 475-0680
E-mail: Sally.Davenport@glo.state.tx.us

U.S. VIRGIN ISLANDS
Dean Plaskett
Commissioner
Dept. of Planning & Natural Resources
Foster's Plz., 396-1 Anna's Retreat
St. Thomas, VI 00802
Phone: (340) 774-3320
Fax: (340) 775-5706

UTAH

VERMONT

VIRGINIA
Dennis H. Treacy
Director
Dept. of Environmental Quality
629 E. Main St.
Richmond, VA 23219
Phone: (804) 698-4020
Fax: (804) 698-4019

WASHINGTON
Keith Phillips
Manager
Water Resources Program
Dept. of Ecology
P.O. Box 47600
Olympia, WA 98504-7600
Phone: (360) 407-6602
Fax: (360) 407-7162

WEST VIRGINIA

WISCONSIN
Vacant
Chief
Coastal Mgmt. Section
Dept. of Administration
P.O. Box 7868
Madison, WI 53707-7868
Phone: (608) 266-8234
Fax: (608) 267-6931

WYOMING

Commerce

Umbrella agency of commerce responsible for the overall regulation and growth of the state's economy.

ALABAMA
Ken Funderburk
Director
Dev. Ofc.
401 Adams Ave., 6th Fl., Ste. 670
Montgomery, AL 36130
Phone: (334) 242-0400
Fax: (334) 242-5669

ALASKA
Debby Sedwick
Commissioner
Dept. of Commerce & Economic Dev.
P.O. Box 110800
Juneau, AK 99811-0800
Phone: (907) 465-2500
Fax: (907) 465-5442

AMERICAN SAMOA
Aliimau Scanlan, Jr.
Director
Dept. of Commerce
AS Govt.
Pago Pago, AS 96799
Phone: (684) 633-5155
Fax: (684) 633-4195

ARIZONA
Jackie Vieh
Director
Dept. of Commerce
3800 N. Central Ave., Ste. 1500
Phoenix, AZ 85012
Phone: (602) 280-1306
Fax: (602) 280-1302

ARKANSAS
Barbara Pardue
Director
Dept. of Economic Dev.
1 Capitol Mall, Rm. 4C-300
Little Rock, AR 72201
Phone: (501) 682-2052
Fax: (501) 682-7394

CALIFORNIA
Lee Grissom
Secretary
Trade & Commerce Agency
801 K St., Ste. 1700
Sacramento, CA 95814
Phone: (916) 322-3962

COLORADO
David Solin
Director
Economic Dev. Ofc.
Ofc. of the Governor
1625 Broadway, Rm. 1710
Denver, CO 80202
Phone: (303) 892-3840
Fax: (303) 892-3848
E-mail: david.solin@state.co.us

CONNECTICUT
Arthur H. Diedrick
Chair of Development
Dev. Authority
999 West St.
Rocky Hill, CT 06067
Phone: (860) 258-4200

DELAWARE
Edward J. Freel
Secretary of State
The Townsend Bldg.
P.O. Box 898
Dover, DE 19903
Phone: (302) 739-4111
Fax: (302) 739-3811
E-mail: efreel@state.de.us

DISTRICT OF COLUMBIA
Douglas J. Patton
Deputy Mayor for Planning & Economic Development
441 4th St., NW, 11th Fl., Rm. 1140
Washington, DC 20001
Phone: (202) 727-6365
Fax: (202) 727-5776

FLORIDA
Antonio Villamil
Director
Ofc. of Tourism, Trade & Economic Dev.
The Capitol, Rm. 2001
Tallahassee, FL 32399-2000
Phone: (850) 487-2568
Fax: (850) 487-3014
E-mail: villamj@eog.state.fl.us

GEORGIA
Randolph B. Cardoza
Commissioner
Dept. of Industry, Trade & Tourism
285 Peachtree Ctr. Ave., NE, Ste. 1100
Atlanta, GA 30303
Phone: (404) 656-3545

GUAM
Joseph C. Cruz
Director
Dept. of Commerce
102 M St.
Tiyan, GU 96913
Phone: (671) 475-0321
Fax: (671) 477-9013
E-mail: COMMERCE@ns.gov.gu

HAWAII
Kathryn Matayoshi
Director
Dept. of Commerce & Consumer Affairs
P.O. Box 541
Honolulu, HI 96809
Phone: (808) 586-2850
Fax: (808) 586-2856

IDAHO
Thomas Arnold
Director
Dept. of Commerce
700 W. State St.
Boise, ID 83720
Phone: (208) 334-2470

ILLINOIS
Pam McDonough
Director
Dept. of Commerce & Community Affairs
620 E. Adams St., 3rd Fl.
Springfield, IL 62701
Phone: (217) 782-3233
Fax: (217) 524-0864

INDIANA
Thomas McKenna
Executive Director
Dept. of Commerce
1 N. Capitol St., Ste. 700
Indianapolis, IN 46204
Phone: (317) 232-8804
Fax: (317) 232-4146

IOWA
Terri Vaughan
Commissioner
Insurance Div.
Dept. of Commerce
330 Maple St.
Des Moines, IA 50319
Phone: (515) 281-5705
Fax: (515) 281-3059

KANSAS
Gary Sherrer
Lieutenant Governor/Secretary
Dept. of Commerce & Housing
700 SW Harrison, Ste. 1300
Topeka, KS 66603-3712
Phone: (785) 296-3481
Fax: (785) 296-5669

KENTUCKY
Gene Strong
Secretary
Economic Dev. Cabinet
Capital Plz. Tower, 24th Fl.
500 Mero St.
Frankfort, KY 40601
Phone: (502) 564-7670
Fax: (502) 564-1535

LOUISIANA
Kevin Reilly
Secretary
Dept. of Economic Dev.
P.O. Box 94185
Baton Rouge, LA 70804-9185
Phone: (225) 342-5388
Fax: (225) 342-5389

MAINE
Steven H. Levesque
Commissioner
Dept. of Economic & Community Dev.
59 State House Station
Augusta, ME 04333
Phone: (207) 287-2656

MARYLAND
Richard C. Lewin
Secretary
Ofc. of the Secretary
Business & Economic Dev.
217 E. Redwood St., 23rd Fl.
Baltimore, MD 21202
Phone: (410) 767-6300
Fax: (410) 767-8628

MASSACHUSETTS
Carolyn Boviard
Director
Executive Ofc. of Economic Affairs
Dept. of Economic Dev.
One Ashburton Pl., Rm. 2101
Boston, MA 02108
Phone: (617) 727-8380
Fax: (617) 727-4426

MICHIGAN
Kathy Wilbur
Director
Consumer & Industry Services
Law Bldg., 4th Fl.
P.O. Box 30004
Lansing, MI 48909
Phone: (517) 373-7230
Fax: (517) 373-3872

MINNESOTA
David Jennings
Commissioner
Dept. of Commerce
133 E. 7th St.
Minneapolis, MN 55101
Phone: (651) 296-6694
Fax: (651) 297-3238

MISSISSIPPI
James B. Heidel
Executive Director
Dept. of Economic & Community Dev.
P.O. Box 849
Jackson, MS 39205-0849
Phone: (601) 359-3449
Fax: (601) 359-3613

MISSOURI
Joseph L. Driskill
Director
Dept. of Economic Dev.
301 W. High St.
P.O. Box 1157
Jefferson City, MO 65102
Phone: (573) 751-3946
Fax: (573) 751-7258
E-mail: jdriskil@mail.state.mo.us

MONTANA
Peter S. Blouke
Director
Dept. of Commerce
1424 9th Ave.
Helena, MT 59620
Phone: (406) 444-3797
Fax: (406) 444-2903

NEBRASKA
Allan Wenstrand
Director
Dept. of Economic Dev.
301 Centennial Mall, S.
P.O. Box 94666
Lincoln, NE 68509
Phone: (402) 471-3747
Fax: (402) 471-3778

NEVADA
Dan Tom
Director
Dept. of Business & Industry
555 E. Washington Ave., Ste. 4900
Las Vegas, NV 89101
Phone: (702) 486-2750
Fax: (702) 486-2758

NEW HAMPSHIRE
George Bald
Commissioner
Dept. of Resources & Economic Dev.
P.O. Box 1856
Concord, NH 03302
Phone: (603) 271-2411
Fax: (603) 271-2629

NEW JERSEY
Gualberto Medina
Secretary
Dept. of Commerce & Economic Dev.
20 W. State St.
P.O. Box 820
Trenton, NJ 08625-0820
Phone: (609) 292-2444
Fax: (609) 777-4097

NEW MEXICO
John Garcia
Secretary
Dept. of Economic Dev.
P.O. Box 20003
Santa Fe, NM 87504
Phone: (505) 827-0305
Fax: (505) 827-0328

NEW YORK
Charles A. Gargano
Commissioner
Dept. of Economic Dev.
One Commerce Plz., 9th Fl.
Albany, NY 12245
Phone: (518) 474-4100
Fax: (518) 473-9374

NORTH CAROLINA
Rick Carlisle
Secretary
Dept. of Commerce
430 N. Salisbury St.
Raleigh, NC 27603-5900
Phone: (919) 733-4962
Fax: (919) 733-8356

NORTH DAKOTA
Kevin Cramer
Director
Dept. of Economic Dev. & Finance
1833 E. Bismarck Expy.
Bismarck, ND 58504
Phone: (701) 328-5300
Fax: (701) 328-5320
E-mail: kcramer@state.nd.us

NORTHERN MARIANA ISLANDS
Frank B. Villanueva
Secretary of Commerce
Dept. of Commerce
Ofc. of the Governor
Caller Box 10007 CK
Saipan, MP 96950
Phone: (670) 664-3000
Fax: (670) 664-3067

OHIO
Gary Suhadolnik
Director
Dept. of Commerce
Vern Riffe Ctr.
77 S. High St., 23rd Fl.
Columbus, OH 43266
Phone: (614) 644-7047
Fax: (614) 466-5650

OKLAHOMA
Howard Barnett
Director/Secretary of Commerce
Dept. of Commerce
900 N. Stiles Ave.
P.O. Box 26980
Oklahoma City, OK 73105
Phone: (405) 815-6552
Fax: (405) 815-5290

OREGON

PENNSYLVANIA
Sam McCullough
Cabinet Secretary
Dept. of Community & Economic Dev.
Forum Bldg., Rm. 433
Harrisburg, PA 17120
Phone: (717) 783-3003
Fax: (717) 787-6866
E-mail: sam_mccullough@gois.state.pa.us

PUERTO RICO
Carlos Vivoni
Secretary
Dept. of Commerce & Economic Dev.
P.O. Box 9023960
San Juan, PR 00902-3960
Phone: (787) 758-4747
Fax: (787) 765-7709

RHODE ISLAND
John Swen
Director
Economic Dev. Corp.
1 W. Exchange St.
Providence, RI 02903
Phone: (401) 222-2601
Fax: (401) 222-2102

SOUTH CAROLINA
Charles S. Way, Jr.
Secretary of Commerce
Dept. of Commerce
P.O. Box 927
Columbia, SC 29202
Phone: (803) 737-0400
Fax: (803) 737-0418

SOUTH DAKOTA
David Volk
Secretary
Div. of Insurance
Dept. of Commerce & Regulation
118 W. Capitol Ave.
Pierre, SD 57501-2017
Phone: (605) 773-3178
Fax: (605) 773-3018

TENNESSEE
Bill Baxter
Commissioner
Dept. of Economic & Community Dev.
Rachel Jackson Bldg., 8th Fl.
320 6th Ave., N.
Nashville, TN 37243
Phone: (615) 741-1888
Fax: (615) 741-7306

TEXAS
Jeff Moseley
Executive Director
Dept. of Economic Dev.
1700 N. Congress, Ste. 130
Austin, TX 78701
Phone: (512) 936-0101
Fax: (512) 936-0303

U.S. VIRGIN ISLANDS
Clement C. Magras
Acting Commissioner of Tourism
Dept. of Tourism
Elainco Bldg.
78-1-2-3 Contant
St. Thomas, VI 00802
Phone: (340) 774-8784
Fax: (340) 777-4390

UTAH
Douglas Borba
Executive Director
Administration
Dept. of Commerce
160 E. 300 S.
Salt Lake City, UT 84111
Phone: (801) 530-6701
Fax: (801) 530-6001
E-mail: dborba@br.state.ut.us

VERMONT
Molly Lambert
Secretary
Agency of Commerce & Community Affairs
Natl. Life Bldg.
Montpelier, VT 05602
Phone: (802) 828-3211
Fax: (802) 828-3258

VIRGINIA
Barry E. DuVal
Secretary of Commerce & Trade
Governor's Cabinet
202 N. 9th St., Ste. 723
Richmond, VA 23219
Phone: (804) 786-7831
Fax: (804) 371-0250

WASHINGTON
Tim Douglas
Director
Dept. of Trade & Economic Dev.
906 Columbia St., SW
P.O. Box 48300
Olympia, WA 98504-8300
Phone: (360) 753-2200
Fax: (360) 586-3582

WEST VIRGINIA
Robert A. Reintsema
Commissioner
Bur. of Commerce
1900 Kanawha Blvd., E., Bldg. 17
Charleston, WV 25305
Phone: (304) 558-2200
Fax: (304) 558-2956

WISCONSIN
Brenda Blanchard
Secretary
Dept. of Commerce
123 W. Washington
P.O. Box 7970
Madison, WI 53707
Phone: (608) 266-7088
Fax: (608) 266-3447

WYOMING
Vacant
Director
Dept. of Commerce
Barrett Bldg.
Cheyenne, WY 82002
Phone: (307) 777-6303

Community Affairs

Provides a broad range of services designed to assist communities in the delivery of essential public services.

ALABAMA
Dewayne Freeman
Director
Dept. of Economic & Community Affairs
P.O. Box 5690
Montgomery, AL 36103-5690
Phone: (334) 242-5591
Fax: (334) 242-5099

ALASKA
Mike Irwin
Commissioner
Dept. of Community & Regional Affairs
P.O. Box 112100
Juneau, AK 99811-2100
Phone: (907) 465-4700
Fax: (907) 465-2948

AMERICAN SAMOA
John Faumuina, Jr.
Director
Economic Dev. & Planning Ofc.
Dept. of Commerce
Pago Pago, AS 96799
Phone: (684) 633-5155
Fax: (684) 633-4195

ARIZONA
Jackie Vieh
Director
Dept. of Commerce
3800 N. Central Ave., Ste. 1500
Phoenix, AZ 85012
Phone: (602) 280-1306
Fax: (602) 280-1302

ARKANSAS
Kurt Knickrehm
Director
Dept. of Human Services
P.O. Box 1437, Slot 316
Little Rock, AR 72203
Phone: (501) 682-8650
Fax: (501) 682-6836

CALIFORNIA
William Pavao
Acting Deputy Chief
Div. of Community Affairs
Dept. of Housing & Community Dev.
1800 Third St., Ste. 390
Sacramento, CA 95814
Phone: (916) 322-1560

COLORADO
Hal Knott
Director
Div. of Local Govt.
Dept. of Local Affairs
1313 Sherman St., Rm. 521
Denver, CO 80203
Phone: (303) 866-2156
Fax: (303) 866-4819

CONNECTICUT
Marc Ryan
Secretary
Ofc. of Policy & Mgmt.
450 Capitol Ave., MS 54SLP
P.O. Box 341441
Hartford, CT 06134-1441
Phone: (860) 418-6500

DELAWARE

DISTRICT OF COLUMBIA
Carlene Cheatam
Director
Ofc. of the Public Advocate
2000 14th St., NW, Ste. 300
Washington, DC 20009
Phone: (202) 673-4421

FLORIDA
Steven M. Seibert
Secretary
Dept. of Community Affairs
2555 Shumard Oak Blvd.
Tallahassee, FL 32399-2100
Phone: (850) 488-8466
Fax: (850) 921-0781

GEORGIA
Jim Higdon
Commissioner
Dept. of Community Affairs
60 Executive Park, S.
Atlanta, GA 30329
Phone: (404) 679-4940

GUAM
Evelyn G. Ybarra
Special Assistant
Div. of Community Affairs
Governor's Ofc.
P.O. Box 2950
Hagatna, GU 96932
Phone: (671) 472-8931
Fax: (671) 477-4826

HAWAII
Brad Mossman
Deputy Director
Dept. of Business, Economic Dev. & Tourism
P.O. Box 2359
Honolulu, HI 96804
Phone: (808) 586-3035
Fax: (808) 586-2377

IDAHO
Jan Peter Blickenstaff
Administrator
Div. of Community Dev.
Dept. of Commerce
700 W. State St.
Boise, ID 83720
Phone: (208) 334-2470

ILLINOIS
Pam McDonough
Director
Dept. of Commerce & Community Affairs
620 E. Adams St., 3rd Fl.
Springfield, IL 62701
Phone: (217) 782-3233
Fax: (217) 524-0864

INDIANA
Joseph Smith, Sr.
Executive Director
Comm. on Community Service
302 W. Washington St., Rm. E220
Indianapolis, IN 46204
Phone: (317) 233-3295
Fax: (317) 233-5660

IOWA
Lane Palmer
Administrator
Div. of Community & Rural Dev.
Dept. of Economic Dev.
200 E. Grand Ave.
Des Moines, IA 50309
Phone: (515) 242-4807
Fax: (515) 242-4832

KANSAS
Ned Webb
Director
Community Dev. Div.
Dept. of Commerce & Housing
700 SW Harrison, Ste. 1300
Topeka, KS 66603
Phone: (785) 296-3485
Fax: (785) 296-5055

KENTUCKY
Bob Arnold
Commissioner
Dept. of Local Govt.
1024 Capitol Ctr. Dr., Ste. 340
Frankfort, KY 40601
Phone: (502) 573-2382
Fax: (502) 573-2512

LOUISIANA
Pat Robinson
Special Project Director
Economic Dev.
P.O. Box 94185
Baton Rouge, LA 70804
Phone: (225) 342-3000
Fax: (225) 342-5389

MAINE

MARYLAND
Carol Chase
Director
Community Services Administration
Dept. of Human Resources
311 W. Saratoga St.
Baltimore, MD 21201
Phone: (410) 767-7463

MASSACHUSETTS
Jane W. Gumble
Director
Executive Ofc. of Communities & Dev.
Dept. of Housing & Community Dev.
100 Cambridge St., Rm. 1804
Boston, MA 02202
Phone: (617) 727-7765
Fax: (617) 727-5060

MICHIGAN
Jim Donaldson
Director
Economic Dev. Corp.
201 N. Washington Sq.
Lansing, MI 48913
Phone: (517) 335-7989
Fax: (517) 373-0314

MINNESOTA
Gary L. Fields
Deputy Commissioner
Community Dev. Div.
Dept. of Trade & Economic Dev.
121 7th Pl., E.
St. Paul, MN 55101
Phone: (651) 296-4039
Fax: (651) 296-5287
E-mail: gary.fields@state.mn.us

MISSISSIPPI
Alice Lusk
Director
Community Services
Dept. of Economic & Community Dev.
P.O. Box 849
Jackson, MS 39205
Phone: (601) 359-3449
Fax: (601) 359-3613

MISSOURI
Denise Cross
Director
Div. of Family Services
Dept. of Social Services
615 Howerton Ct.
P.O. Box 88
Jefferson City, MO 65103
Phone: (573) 751-4247
Fax: (573) 526-0507
E-mail: dcross@mail.state.mo.us

MONTANA
Newell B. Anderson
Administrator
Local Govt. Assistance Div.
Dept. of Commerce
1424 9th Ave.
Helena, MT 59620
Phone: (406) 444-3757
Fax: (406) 444-4482

NEBRASKA
Jenne Rodriguez
Director
Community & Rural Dev. Div.
Dept. of Economic Dev.
P.O. Box 94666
Lincoln, NE 68509
Phone: (402) 471-4388
Fax: (402) 471-3778

NEVADA
Donny Loux
Chief
Community Based Services
Dept. of Employment, Training & Rehab.
711 S. Stewart St.
Carson City, NV 89701
Phone: (775) 687-4452
Fax: (775) 687-3292

NEW HAMPSHIRE
Jeffrey Taylor
Director
Ofc. of State Planning, Executive Dept.
Governor's Recycling Program
2 1/2 Beacon St.
Concord, NH 03301-4497
Phone: (603) 271-2155
Fax: (603) 271-1728

NEW JERSEY
Jane Kenny
Commissioner
Dept. of Community Affairs
101 S. Broad St.
P.O. Box 800
Trenton, NJ 08625-0800
Phone: (609) 292-6420
Fax: (609) 984-6696

NEW MEXICO
Allan Richardson
Director
Economic Dev. Div.
Dept. of Economic Dev.
P.O. Box 20003
Santa Fe, NM 87504
Phone: (505) 827-0300
Fax: (505) 827-0407
E-mail: alan@edd.state.nm.us

NEW YORK
Alexander F. Treadwell
Secretary of State
Dept. of State
41 State St.
Albany, NY 12231
Phone: (518) 486-9844
Fax: (518) 474-4765

NORTH CAROLINA
Bill McNeil
Director
Community Assistance
Dept. of Commerce
P.O. Box 12600
Raleigh, NC 27605-2600
Phone: (919) 733-2850
Fax: (919) 733-5262

NORTH DAKOTA
Susan Wefald
President
Public Service Comm.
600 E. Blvd. Ave., 12th Fl.
Bismarck, ND 58505-0480
Phone: (701) 328-2400
Fax: (701) 328-2410
E-mail: msmail.sew@oracle.psc.state.nd.us

NORTHERN MARIANA ISLANDS
Thomas A. Tebuteb
Secretary
Dept. of Community & Cultural Affairs
P.O. Box 10007
Saipan, MP 96950
Phone: (670) 664-2571
Fax: (670) 664-2570

OHIO
Jack Riordan
Assistant Director
Div. of Community Dev.
Dept. of Dev.
77 S. High St.
P.O. Box 1001
Columbus, OH 43266-0101
Phone: (614) 466-5863
Fax: (614) 644-1864

OKLAHOMA
Vacant
Chief Operating Officer
Dept. of Commerce
900 N. Stiles Ave.
Oklahoma City, OK 73105
Phone: (405) 815-6552
Fax: (405) 815-5199

Brenda Williams
Division Director
Community Dev.
Dept. of Commerce
900 N. Stiles Ave.
Oklahoma City, OK 73105
Phone: (405) 815-5352
Fax: (405) 815-5344

OREGON
Bob Repine
Director
Dept. of Housing & Community Services
1600 State St.
Salem, OR 97310
Phone: (503) 986-2005
Fax: (503) 986-2020

PENNSYLVANIA
James Buckheit
Acting Director
Bur. of Community Services
Dept. of Education
Harristown 2, 5th Fl.
Harrisburg, PA 17120-0029
Phone: (717) 783-3755
Fax: (717) 783-6617

PUERTO RICO
Jose Otero
Administrator
Ofc. of Municipal Affairs
P.O. Box 70167
San Juan, PR 00936
Phone: (787) 754-8827
Fax: (787) 753-6080

RHODE ISLAND
Armeather Gibbs
Director
Community Relations & Constituent Affairs
Governor's Ofc.
State House, Rm. 112
Providence, RI 02903
Phone: (401) 222-2080
Fax: (401) 273-5301

SOUTH CAROLINA

SOUTH DAKOTA
Ron Wheeler
Commissioner
Governor's Ofc. of Economic Dev.
Capitol Lake Plz.
711 Wells Ave.
Pierre, SD 57501-3369
Phone: (605) 773-5032
Fax: (605) 773-3256

TENNESSEE
Bill Baxter
Commissioner
Dept. of Economic & Community Dev.
Rachel Jackson Bldg., 8th Fl.
320 6th Ave., N.
Nashville, TN 37243
Phone: (615) 741-1888
Fax: (615) 741-7306

TEXAS
Daisy Stiner
Acting Executive Director
Dept. of Housing & Community Affairs
507 Sabine, Ste. 400
Austin, TX 78701
Phone: (512) 475-5000
Fax: (512) 472-8526

U.S. VIRGIN ISLANDS
Louis Hill
Administrator
Ofc. of the Governor
21-22 Kongens Gade
St. Thomas, VI 00802
Phone: (340) 774-0001
Fax: (340) 774-0151

UTAH
David Winder
Executive Director
Administration
Dept. of Community & Economic Dev.
324 S. State St., Ste. 500
Salt Lake City, UT 84111
Phone: (801) 538-8720
Fax: (801) 538-8888
E-mail: dwinder@dced.state.ut.us

VERMONT
Molly Lambert
Secretary
Agency of Commerce & Community Affairs
Natl. Life Bldg.
Montpelier, VT 05602
Phone: (802) 828-3211
Fax: (802) 828-3258

VIRGINIA
William C. Shelton
Director
Dept. of Housing & Community Dev.
Jackson Ctr.
501 N. 2nd St.
Richmond, VA 23219
Phone: (804) 371-7081
Fax: (804) 371-7090

WASHINGTON
Delee Shoemaker
Director of External Affairs
Ofc. of the Governor
P.O. Box 40002
Olympia, WA 98504-0002
Phone: (360) 902-4111
Fax: (360) 753-4110
E-mail: DeLee.Shoemaker@gov.wa.gov

WEST VIRGINIA
Dana Davis
Acting Director
Dev. Ofc.
Bldg. 6, Rm. 525
1900 Kanawha Blvd., E.
Charleston, WV 25305
Phone: (304) 558-2234
Fax: (304) 558-1189

WISCONSIN
Roger Nacker
Acting Administrator
Div. of Economic Dev.
Dept. of Commerce
201 W. Washington, 5th Fl.
Madison, WI 53707
Phone: (608) 266-1386
Fax: (608) 266-5551

WYOMING
John Reardon
Chief Executive Officer
Economic & Community Dev.
Business Council
214 W. 15th St.
Cheyenne, WY 82002
Phone: (307) 777-2800
Fax: (307) 777-5840

Comptroller

The principal accounting and disbursing officer of the state.

ALABAMA
Robert L. Childree
Comptroller
Dept. of Finance
RSA Union, Ste. 220
100 N. Union St.
Montgomery, AL 36130-2602
Phone: (334) 242-7063
Fax: (334) 242-7466

ALASKA
Betty Martin
Comptroller
Treasury Div.
Dept. of Revenue
P.O. Box 110405
Juneau, AK 99811-0405
Phone: (907) 465-2350
Fax: (907) 465-2394

AMERICAN SAMOA
Tifi Ale
Treasurer
Dept. of the Treasury
AS Govt.
Pago Pago, AS 96799
Phone: (684) 633-4155
Fax: (684) 633-4100

ARIZONA
Robert Rocha
State Comptroller
Dept. of Administration
1700 W. Washington, Rm. 290
Phoenix, AZ 85007
Phone: (602) 542-5405
Fax: (602) 542-5749

ARKANSAS
Richard Weiss
Director
Dept. of Finance & Administration
401 DFA Bldg.
1509 W. 7th St.
Little Rock, AR 72201
Phone: (501) 682-2242
Fax: (501) 682-1086
E-mail: richard.weiss@dfa.state.ar.us

CALIFORNIA
Kathleen Connell
Controller
300 Capitol Mall, 18th Fl.
P.O. Box 942850
Sacramento, CA 94250
Phone: (916) 445-2636

COLORADO
Arthur L. Barnhart
State Controller
Ofc. of the State Controller
Support Services
1525 Sherman St., Ste. 250
Denver, CO 80203
Phone: (303) 866-3281
Fax: (303) 866-4233

CONNECTICUT
Nancy Wyman
Comptroller
55 Elm St.
Hartford, CT 06106
Phone: (860) 702-3301

DELAWARE
Clifford B. Edwards
Director
Div. of Accounting
Dept. of Finance
Thomas Collins Bldg.
540 S. DuPont Hwy.
Dover, DE 19903
Phone: (302) 739-5454

DISTRICT OF COLUMBIA
Jennifer Mumford
Comptroller
Ofc. of Deputy Mayor for Finance
444 4th St.
Washington, DC 20001
Phone: (202) 727-2410

FLORIDA
Robert F. Milligan
Comptroller
Dept. of Banking & Finance
The Capitol, PL 09
Tallahassee, FL 32399-0350
Phone: (850) 413-0550
Fax: (850) 488-9818
E-mail: rfm@samplaza.mail.ufl.edu

GEORGIA
John W. Oxendine
Commissioner
Insurance Commissioner's Ofc.
W. Tower, 7th Fl.
2 Martin Luther King, Jr. Dr.
Atlanta, GA 30334
Phone: (404) 656-2117

GUAM
John Denorcey
Comptroller
Dept. of Administration
P.O. Box 884
Hagatna, GU 96932
Phone: (671) 475-1101
Fax: (671) 477-6788

HAWAII
Raymond Sato
Comptroller
Dept. of Accounting & Services
P.O. Box 119
Honolulu, HI 96810
Phone: (808) 586-0400
Fax: (808) 586-0707

IDAHO
J.D. Williams
State Controller
700 W. State St., 5th Fl.
Boise, ID 83720
Phone: (208) 334-3100

ILLINOIS
Daniel W. Hynes
Comptroller
201 State House
301 S. 2nd St.
Springfield, IL 62706
Phone: (217) 782-6000
Fax: (217) 782-7561

INDIANA
Connie Naas
State Auditor
Ofc. of the State Auditor
State House, Rm. 240
Indianapolis, IN 46204
Phone: (317) 232-3300
Fax: (317) 232-6097

IOWA
Robert L. Rafferty
Director
Dept. of Mgmt.
State Capitol, Rm. 12
Des Moines, IA 50319
Phone: (515) 281-5211
Fax: (515) 281-6611

KANSAS
Shirley Moses
Director
Div. of Accounts & Reports
Dept. of Administration
900 Jackson St., Rm. 355
Topeka, KS 66612-1220
Phone: (785) 296-2311
Fax: (785) 296-6841

KENTUCKY
John McCarty
Secretary
Finance & Administration Cabinet
Capitol Annex, Rm. 383
Frankfort, KY 40601
Phone: (502) 564-4240
Fax: (502) 564-6785

LOUISIANA
Mark Drennen
Commissioner
Div. of Administration
P.O. Box 94095
Baton Rouge, LA 70804-9095
Phone: (225) 342-7000
Fax: (225) 342-1057

MAINE
Carol Whitney
Controller
Bur. of Accounts & Control
Dept. of Adm. & Financial Services
14 State House Station
Augusta, ME 04333
Phone: (207) 626-8422

MARYLAND
William Donald Schaefer
Comptroller
Ofc. of the Comptroller
Comptroller of the Treasury
Treasury Bldg., Rm. 121
P.O. Box 466
Annapolis, MD 21404
Phone: (410) 260-7801
Fax: (410) 974-3808
E-mail: wdschaefer@comp.state.md.us

MASSACHUSETTS
Martin Benison
Comptroller
Executive Ofc. for Administration & Finance
One Ashburton Pl., Rm. 909
Boston, MA 02108
Phone: (617) 727-5000
Fax: (617) 727-2163

MICHIGAN
John Linderman
Director
Ofc. of Financial Mgmt.
Dept. of Mgmt. & Budget
P.O. Box 30026
Lansing, MI 48909
Phone: (517) 373-1010

MINNESOTA
Pam Wheelock
Commissioner
Dept. of Finance
Centennial Ofc. Bldg., 4th Fl.
658 Cedar St.
St. Paul, MN 55155
Phone: (651) 297-7881
Fax: (651) 296-8685

MISSISSIPPI
Edward L. Ranck
Director
Dept. of Finance & Administration
906 Sillers Bldg.
Jackson, MS 39201
Phone: (601) 359-3204
Fax: (601) 359-2405

MISSOURI
James Carder
Director
Ofc. of Administration
Div. of Accounting
Truman Bldg., Rm. 579
P.O. Box 809
Jefferson City, MO 65102
Phone: (573) 751-2971
Fax: (573) 751-0159
E-mail: cardej@mail.oa.state.mo.us

MONTANA
Lois A. Menzies
Director & Ex Officio State Treasurer
Dept. of Administration
Rm. 155, Mitchell Bldg.
P.O. Box 200101
Helena, MT 59620-0101
Phone: (406) 444-2032
Fax: (406) 444-2812
E-mail: lmenzies@mt. gov

NEBRASKA
Wes Mohling
Acting Administrator
Accounting Div.
Dept. of Adm. Services
1309 State Capitol
P.O. Box 94664
Lincoln, NE 68509
Phone: (402) 471-2581
Fax: (402) 471-4157

NEVADA

NEW HAMPSHIRE
Thomas E. Martin
Comptroller/Director
Div. of Accounting Services
Dept. of Adm. Services
25 Capitol St., Rm. 413
Concord, NH 03301-6312
Phone: (603) 271-3190
Fax: (603) 271-6666

NEW JERSEY
Elizabeth L. Pugh
Director
Ofc. of Mgmt. & Budget
Dept. of Treasury
P.O. Box 221
Trenton, NJ 08625-0221
Phone: (609) 292-6746
Fax: (609) 633-8179

NEW MEXICO
Michael A. Montoya
State Treasurer
P.O. Box 608
Santa Fe, NM 87504-0608
Phone: (505) 827-6400
Fax: (505) 827-6395

NEW YORK
H. Carl McCall
Comptroller
A.E. Smith Ofc. Bldg., 6th Fl.
Albany, NY 12236
Phone: (518) 474-3506
Fax: (518) 473-3004

NORTH CAROLINA
Ed Renfrow
State Controller
3512 Bush St.
Raleigh, NC 27609-7509
Phone: (919) 981-5406
Fax: (919) 981-5567

NORTH DAKOTA
Rod Backman
Director
Ofc. of Mgmt. & Budget
600 E. Blvd. Ave., 4th Fl.
Bismarck, ND 58505-0400
Phone: (701) 328-2680
Fax: (701) 328-3230
E-mail: rbackman@state.nd.us

Sheila Peterson
Director
Fiscal Mgmt.
Ofc. of Mgmt. & Budget
600 E. Blvd. Ave., 4th Fl.
Bismarck, ND 58505-0400
Phone: (701) 328-2680
Fax: (701) 328-3230
E-mail: peterson@state.nd.us

NORTHERN MARIANA ISLANDS
Lucia DLG. Neilsen
Secretary of Finance
Finance & Accounting
Dept. of Finance
P.O. Box 5234 CHRB
Saipan, MP 96950
Phone: (670) 664-1198
Fax: (670) 664-1115

OHIO
Joseph T. Deters
State Treasurer
30 E. Broad St., 9th Fl.
Columbus, OH 43266-0421
Phone: (614) 466-2160
Fax: (614) 644-7313

OKLAHOMA
Keith Johnson
State Comptroller
Ofc. of State Finance
Div. of Central Accounting
122 State Capitol
2300 N. Lincoln Blvd.
Oklahoma City, OK 73105
Phone: (405) 521-2141
Fax: (405) 521-3902
E-mail: kjohnson@oklaosf.state.us

OREGON
John Radford
State Controller
State Controllers Div.
Dept. of Adm. Services
155 Cottage St., NE
Salem, OR 97310
Phone: (503) 378-3156
Fax: (503) 378-3518

PENNSYLVANIA
Harvey C. Eckert
Deputy Secretary
Ofc. of the Budget
Comptroller Operations
207 Finance Bldg.
Harrisburg, PA 17120
Phone: (717) 787-6496
Fax: (717) 787-3376

PUERTO RICO
Manuel Diaz-Saldana
Comptroller
P.O. Box 366069
San Juan, PR 00936-6069
Phone: (787) 754-3030
Fax: (787) 751-6768

RHODE ISLAND
Lawrence C. Franklin, Jr.
State Controller
Ofc. of Accounts & Control
Dept. of Administration
1 Capitol Hill
Providence, RI 02908-5883
Phone: (401) 222-2271

SOUTH CAROLINA
James A. Lander
Comptroller General
Wade Hampton Ofc. Bldg.
P.O. Box 11228
Columbia, SC 29211
Phone: (803) 734-2121

SOUTH DAKOTA
Vernon L. Larson
State Auditor
Ofc. of State Auditor
State Capitol Bldg.
500 E. Capitol Ave.
Pierre, SD 57501-5070
Phone: (605) 773-3341
Fax: (605) 773-5929

TENNESSEE
Jan Sylvis
Chief of Accounts
Dept. of Finance & Administration
Wm. R. Snodgrass TN Towers, 21st Fl.
Nashville, TN 37243-0293
Phone: (615) 741-2382
Fax: (615) 532-8532

TEXAS
Carole Keeton Rylander
Comptroller
Comptroller of Public Accounts
P.O. Box 13528
Austin, TX 78711-3528
Phone: (512) 463-4000
Fax: (512) 463-4965

U.S. VIRGIN ISLANDS
Bernice Turnbull
Acting Commissioner
Dept. of Finance
76 Kronprindsens Gade
St. Thomas, VI 00802
Phone: (340) 774-4750
Fax: (340) 776-4028

UTAH
Kim Thorne
Director
Div. of Finance
Dept. of Adm. Services
2110 State Ofc. Bldg.
Salt Lake City, UT 84114
Phone: (801) 538-3020
Fax: (801) 538-3244
E-mail: kthorne@fi.state.ut.us

VERMONT
Thomas Pelham
Commissioner
Agency of Administration
Dept. of Finance & Mgmt.
109 State St.
Montpelier, VT 05609-0401
Phone: (802) 828-2376
Fax: (802) 828-2428
E-mail: tpelham@fin.state.vt.us

VIRGINIA
William E. Landsidle
Comptroller
Dept. of Accounts
Monroe Bldg., 2nd Fl.
101 N. 14th St.
Richmond, VA 23219
Phone: (804) 225-2109
Fax: (804) 371-8587

WASHINGTON
Michael J. Murphy
State Treasurer
Legislative Bldg.
P.O. Box 40200
Olympia, WA 98504-0200
Phone: (360) 753-7139
Fax: (360) 586-6147
E-mail: MichaelJ@TRE.WA.GOV

WEST VIRGINIA
Glen B. Gainer, III
State Auditor
State Capitol, Rm. W-100
1900 Kanawha Blvd., E.
Charleston, WV 25305-0470
Phone: (304) 558-2251
Fax: (304) 558-5200
E-mail: www.wvauditor.com

WISCONSIN
William Raftery
Director
Bur. of Financial Operations
Dept. of Administration
101 E. Wilson, 8th Fl.
Madison, WI 53703
Phone: (608) 266-1694
Fax: (608) 266-7734

WYOMING
Max Maxfield
State Auditor
State Capitol, Rm. 114
200 W. 24th St.
Cheyenne, WY 82002
Phone: (307) 777-7831

Consumer Affairs

Investigates and mediates consumer complaints of deceptive and fraudulent business practices.

ALABAMA
Dennis Wright
Chief
Consumer Affairs
Ofc. of the Attorney Gen.
11 S. Union
Montgomery, AL 36130-0156
Phone: (334) 242-7334
Fax: (334) 242-7458

ALASKA
Daveed Schwartz
Chief
Antitrust & Consumer Protection Section
Dept. of Law
1031 W. 4th Ave., Ste. 200
Anchorage, AK 99501-1994
Phone: (907) 269-5100
Fax: (907) 276-3697

AMERICAN SAMOA
Albert Mailo Toetagata
Attorney General
Dept. of Legal Affairs
AS Govt.
Pago Pago, AS 96799
Phone: (684) 633-4163
Fax: (684) 633-1838

ARIZONA
Sydney K. Davis
Chief Counsel
Consumer Protection & Advocacy Div.
Ofc. of the Attorney Gen.
1275 W. Washington
Phoenix, AZ 85007
Phone: (602) 542-3702

ARKANSAS
Sheila McDonald
Deputy Attorney General
Consumer Protection
200 Tower Bldg.
323 Ctr. St., Ste. 200
Little Rock, AR 72201
Phone: (501) 682-2341
Fax: (501) 682-8084

CALIFORNIA
Marilyn Brazell
Director
Dept. of Consumer Affairs
400 R St., Rm. 1060
Sacramento, CA 95814-6213
Phone: (916) 445-4465

COLORADO
Garth Lucero
Deputy Attorney General
Div. of Business Regulation
Dept. of Law
1525 Sherman St., 5th Fl.
Denver, CO 80203
Phone: (303) 866-3613
Fax: (303) 866-5691

CONNECTICUT
James Fleming
Commissioner
Dept. of Consumer Protection
165 Capitol Ave.
Hartford, CT 06106
Phone: (860) 566-4999

DELAWARE
Mary McDonough
Director
Div. of Consumer Affairs
Dept. of Justice
820 N. French St., 4th Fl.
Wilmington, DE 19801
Phone: (302) 577-3250

DISTRICT OF COLUMBIA
Eileen Hemphill
Chief
Ofc. of Consumer Education & Info.
Consumer & Regulatory Affairs
614 H St., NW, Rm. 108
Washington, DC 20001
Phone: (202) 727-7067

Bill Nelson
Acting Chief
Ofc. of Compliance
Consumer & Regulatory Affairs Dept.
614 H St., NW
Washington, DC 20001

FLORIDA
J.R. Kelly
Director
Div. of Consumer Services
Agri. & Consumer Services Dept.
407 S. Calhoun St., Rm. 235
Tallahassee, FL 32399-0800
Phone: (850) 922-2966
Fax: (850) 487-4177

GEORGIA
Barry Reid
Administrator
Ofc. of Consumer Affairs
Plz. Level, E. Tower
2 Martin Luther King, Jr. Dr., SE
Atlanta, GA 30334
Phone: (404) 656-3790

GUAM
Bernie Alvarez
Consumer Advocate
Consumer Protection
Dept. of Law
Attorney Gen.'s Ofc.
120 W. O'Brien Dr., Ste. 2-200
Hagatna, GU 96910
Phone: (671) 475-3324
Fax: (671) 472-2493
E-mail: law@ns.gov.gu

HAWAII
Joann Uchida
Executive Director
Ofc. of Consumer Protection
235 S. Beretania St., Ste. 801
Honolulu, HI 96813-2437
Phone: (808) 586-2636
Fax: (808) 586-2640

IDAHO
Alan G. Lance
Attorney General
State House
700 W. Jefferson
Boise, ID 83720-0010
Phone: (208) 334-2400
Fax: (208) 334-2530

ILLINOIS
Jim Ryan
Attorney General
James R. Thompson Ctr.
100 W. Randolph St., 12th Fl.
Chicago, IL 60601
Phone: (312) 814-2503

INDIANA
Barbara Crawford
Chief Counsel
Div. of Consumer Protection
Ofc. of the Attorney Gen.
219 State House
Indianapolis, IN 46204
Phone: (317) 232-6217
Fax: (317) 233-4393

IOWA
William L. Brauch
Director
Consumer Protection Div.
Ofc. of the Attorney Gen.
Hoover State Ofc. Bldg.
1300 E. Walnut
Des Moines, IA 50319
Phone: (515) 281-5926

KANSAS
C. Steven Rarrick
Deputy Attorney General
Consumer Protection Div.
Judicial Ctr., 2nd Fl.
301 W. 10th
Topeka, KS 66612-1597
Phone: (785) 296-3751
Fax: (785) 296-6296

KENTUCKY
Albert Benjamin Chandler, III
Attorney General
Ofc. of the Attorney Gen.
State Capitol, Ste. 118
Frankfort, KY 40601
Phone: (502) 696-5300
Fax: (502) 564-8310

LOUISIANA
John Sheppard
Director
Public Protection Div.
Dept. of Justice
P.O. Box 94005
Baton Rouge, LA 70804-9005
Phone: (225) 342-7897
Fax: (225) 342-7901

MAINE
William N. Lund
Superintendent
Bur. of Consumer Credit Protection
35 State House Station
Augusta, ME 04333
Phone: (207) 582-8718

MARYLAND
William Leibovici
Counsel
Consumer Protection Div.
Ofc. of the Attorney Gen.
200 St. Paul Pl.
Baltimore, MD 21202
Phone: (410) 576-6557
Fax: (410) 576-6566
E-mail: wleibovici@oag.state.md.us

MASSACHUSETTS
Daniel A. Grabauskas
Director
Executive Ofc. of Consumer Affairs
Dept. of Consumer Affairs & Business Regulation
One Ashburton Pl., Rm. 1411
Boston, MA 02108-1518
Phone: (617) 727-7755
Fax: (617) 727-1399

MICHIGAN
Fredrick H. Hoffecker
Assistant in Charge
Consumer Protection Div.
Ofc. of Attorney Gen.
585 W. Ottawa
Lansing, MI 48909
Phone: (517) 335-0855

MINNESOTA
Eric Swanson
Director of Consumer Policy
Ofc. of the Attorney Gen.
1400 NCL Tower
St. Paul, MN 55101
Phone: (651) 296-7575
Fax: (651) 296-9663

MISSISSIPPI
Leyser Morris
Director
Ofc. of the Attorney Gen.
Consumer Protection Div.
P.O. Box 220
Jackson, MS 39205
Phone: (601) 359-4230
Fax: (601) 359-4231

MISSOURI
Jeremiah W. Nixon
Attorney General
Supreme Ct. Bldg.
207 W. High St.
Jefferson City, MO 65101
Phone: (573) 751-3321
Fax: (573) 751-0774
E-mail: attgenmail@moago.org

MONTANA
Annie Bartos
Chief Legal Counsel
Dept. of Commerce
1424 9th Ave.
Helena, MT 59620
Phone: (406) 444-3553
Fax: (406) 444-2903

NEBRASKA
Paul Potadle
Assistant Attorney General
Consumer Fraud Section
Ofc. of the Attorney Gen.
P.O. Box 98920
Lincoln, NE 68509-4906
Phone: (402) 471-2682
Fax: (402) 471-3297

NEVADA
Patricia Morse Jarman Manning
Commissioner
Consumer Affairs Div.
Dept. of Business & Industry
1850 E. Sahara Ave., Ste. 101
Las Vegas, NV 89104
Phone: (702) 486-7355
Fax: (702) 486-7371

NEW HAMPSHIRE
Walter L. Maroney
Senior Assistant Attorney General
Ofc. of the Attorney Gen.
Dept. of Justice
33 Capitol St.
Concord, NH 03301-6397
Phone: (603) 271-3641
Fax: (603) 271-2110

NEW JERSEY
Mark S. Herr
Director
Div. of Consumer Affairs
P.O. Box 45027
Newark, NJ 07102
Phone: (201) 504-6200
Fax: (201) 648-3538

NEW MEXICO
Frank Weissbarth
Acting Director
Consumer Protection & Economic Crimes
Ofc. of the Attorney Gen.
P.O. Drawer 1508
Santa Fe, NM 87504
Phone: (505) 827-6009
Fax: (505) 827-6685

NEW YORK
Timothy S. Carey
Chair & Executive Director
Consumer Protection Board
5 Empire State Plz., Ste. 2101
Albany, NY 12223-1556
Phone: (518) 474-3514
Fax: (518) 474-2474

NORTH CAROLINA
Michael F. Easley
Attorney General
Dept. of Justice
P.O. Box 629
Raleigh, NC 27602
Phone: (919) 733-7741
Fax: (919) 733-7491

NORTH DAKOTA
Parrell Grossman
Director
Consumer Protection & Antitrust Div.
Attorney Gen's. Ofc.
600 E. Blvd. Ave., 17th Fl.
Bismarck, ND 58505-0040
Phone: (701) 328-3404
Fax: (701) 328-3535
E-mail: msmail.pgrossma@ranch.state.nd.us

NORTHERN MARIANA ISLANDS
Vacant
Assistant Attorney General
Ofc. of the Attorney Gen.
Saipan, MP 96950
Phone: (670) 664-2340
Fax: (670) 664-2349

OHIO
Susan Merryman
Consumers' Counsel
77 S. High St., 15th Fl.
Columbus, OH 43266-0550
Phone: (614) 466-8574
Fax: (614) 466-9475

OKLAHOMA
Dan Hardin
Administrator
Consumer Credit Dept.
4545 N. Lincoln Blvd., #104
Oklahoma City, OK 73105
Phone: (405) 521-3653
Fax: (405) 521-6740

OREGON
Joel Ario
Manager
Insurance Div.
Consumer Protection
350 Winter St., NE, Rm. 440-1
Salem, OR 97310
Phone: (503) 947-7270
Fax: (503) 378-4351

Jan Margosian
Consumer Information Officer
Civil Enforcement Div.
Dept. of Justice
1162 Court St., NE
Salem, OR 97310
Phone: (503) 378-4732
Fax: (503) 378-5017

PENNSYLVANIA
Joseph K. Goldberg
Director
Bur. of Consumer Protection
Ofc. of the Attorney Gen.
Strawberry Sq., 14th Fl.
Harrisburg, PA 17120
Phone: (717) 787-9707
Fax: (717) 787-1190

PUERTO RICO
Jose Antonio Alicea
Secretary
Consumer Affairs Dept.
P.O. Box 41059
San Juan, PR 00940-1059
Phone: (787) 722-7555
Fax: (787) 726-0077

RHODE ISLAND
Sheldon Whitehouse
Attorney General
150 S. Main St.
Providence, RI 02903
Phone: (401) 274-4400
Fax: (401) 272-1302

SOUTH CAROLINA
Philip Porter
Administrator
Dept. of Consumer Affairs
2801 Devine St.
P.O. Box 5757
Columbia, SC 29250-5757
Phone: (803) 734-9452

SOUTH DAKOTA
Tim Bartlett
Director
Div. of Consumer Protection
Ofc. of the Attorney Gen.
State Capitol
500 E. Capitol Ave.
Pierre, SD 57501
Phone: (605) 773-4400
Fax: (605) 773-7163

TENNESSEE
Mark Williams
Director
Div. of Consumer Affairs
500 James Robertson Pkwy., 5th Fl.
Nashville, TN 37243-0600
Phone: (615) 741-4737
Fax: (615) 532-4994

TEXAS
John Cornyn
Attorney General
Ofc. of the Attorney Gen.
P.O. Box 12548
Austin, TX 78711-2548
Phone: (512) 463-2100
Fax: (512) 463-2063

U.S. VIRGIN ISLANDS
Andrew Rutnik
Acting Commissioner
Dept. of Licensing & Consumer Affairs
Property & Procurement Bldg.
Sub Base Bldg. 1, Rm. 205
St. Thomas, VI 00802
Phone: (340) 774-3130
Fax: (340) 776-8303

UTAH
Francine Giani
Director
Div. of Consumer Protection
Dept. of Commerce
160 E. 300 S.
Salt Lake City, UT 84111
Phone: (801) 530-6601
Fax: (801) 530-6001
E-mail: fgiani@br.state.ut.us

VERMONT
Wendy Morgan
Chief
Public Protection Div.
Ofc. of the Attorney Gen.
109 State St.
Montpelier, VT 05602
Phone: (802) 828-3171
Fax: (802) 828-2154

VIRGINIA
J. Carlton Courter, III
Commissioner
Dept. of Agri. & Consumer Services
Washington Bldg., Ste. 210
1100 Bank St.
Richmond, VA 23219
Phone: (804) 786-3501
Fax: (804) 371-2945

WASHINGTON
Kathleen D. Mix
Chief Deputy Attorney General
Ofc. of the Attorney Gen.
P.O. Box 40100
Olympia, WA 98504-0100
Phone: (360) 753-6200
Fax: (360) 664-0228

WEST VIRGINIA
Jill Miles
Deputy Attorney General
Div. of Consumer Protection
Ofc. of the Attorney Gen.
P.O. Box 1789
Charleston, WV 25326-1789
Phone: (304) 558-8986

WISCONSIN
Jerry Hancock
Director
Ofc. of Consumer Protection
Dept. of Justice
123 W. Washington, Rm. 658
P.O. Box 7857
Madison, WI 53707-7857
Phone: (608) 267-8948
Fax: (608) 267-2778

William Oemichen
Administrator
Trade & Consumer Protection Div.
Agri., Trade & Consumer Protection
2811 Agri. Dr.
P.O. Box 8911
Madison, WI 53708
Phone: (608) 224-4970
Fax: (608) 224-4939

WYOMING
Mark Moran
Director
Div. of Consumer Affairs
Ofc. of the Attorney Gen.
State Capitol
200 W. 24th St.
Cheyenne, WY 82002
Phone: (307) 777-6702

Corporate Records

Maintains a variety of corporate filings, records and documents.

ALABAMA
Robina J. Wilson
Corporate Records Supervisor
Corp. Div.
Ofc. of Secretary of State
11 S. Union, Rm. 207
Montgomery, AL 36130
Phone: (334) 242-5974
Fax: (334) 240-3138

ALASKA
Franklin T. Elder
Acting Director
Div. of Banking, Securities & Corps.
Dept. of Commerce & Economic Dev.
P.O. Box 110807
Juneau, AK 99811-0807
Phone: (907) 465-2521
Fax: (907) 465-2549

AMERICAN SAMOA

ARIZONA
Brian McNeil
Executive Secretary
Corp. Comm.
1200 W. Washington
Phoenix, AZ 85007
Phone: (602) 542-3931

ARKANSAS
Sharon Priest
Secretary of State
State Capitol, Rm. 256
Little Rock, AR 72201
Phone: (501) 682-1010
Fax: (501) 682-3510
E-mail: sharonpriest@ccm1.state.ar.us

CALIFORNIA
Tony Peacock
Chief
Corporate Filing Div.
Ofc. of Secretary of State
1500 11th St.
Sacramento, CA 95814
Phone: (916) 653-6564

COLORADO
Keith Whitelaw
Program Administrator
Div. of Commercial Recordings
Dept. of State
1560 Broadway, Ste. 200
Denver, CO 80202
Phone: (303) 894-2251
Fax: (303) 894-2242

CONNECTICUT
Maria Greenslade
Assistant Deputy
Commercial Recording Div.
Ofc. of Secretary of State
30 Trinity St.
Hartford, CT 06106
Phone: (860) 509-6268

DELAWARE
Laura Marvel
Administrator
Corp. Div.
Dept. of State
Townsend Bldg.
Federal & Duke of York Sts.
Dover, DE 19901
Phone: (302) 739-3077
Fax: (302) 739-2238

DISTRICT OF COLUMBIA
Patricia Grays
Program Manager
Corps. Div.
Dept. of Consumer & Regulatory Affairs
614 H St., NW, Rm. 407
Washington, DC 20009
Phone: (202) 442-4430

FLORIDA
Dave Mann
Director
Div. of Corps.
409 E. Gaines St.
Tallahassee, FL 32399
Phone: (850) 487-6000
Fax: (850) 487-6012

GEORGIA
Warren Rary
Director
Business Services & Regulations
Ofc. of Secretary of State
2 Martin Luther King, Jr. Dr., SE, Ste. 306
Atlanta, GA 30334
Phone: (404) 656-6478

GUAM
Joseph T. Duenas
Director
Dept. of Revenue & Taxation
13-1 Mariner Dr., Tiyan
P.O. Box 23607
GMF, GU 96921
Phone: (671) 475-1817
Fax: (671) 472-2643

HAWAII
Kathryn Matayoshi
Director
Dept. of Commerce & Consumer Affairs
P.O. Box 541
Honolulu, HI 96809
Phone: (808) 586-2850
Fax: (808) 586-2856

IDAHO
Sally Clark
Supervisor
Corps. Div.
Ofc. of Secretary of State
Statehouse, Rm. 203
700 W. Jefferson
Boise, ID 83720
Phone: (208) 334-2301

ILLINOIS
Helen Conlee
Administrator
Corp. Div.
Ofc. of the Secretary of State
330 Howlett Bldg.
Springfield, IL 62756
Phone: (217) 782-4909
Fax: (217) 782-4528

INDIANA
Todd Rokita
Director
Corp. Section
Ofc. of Secretary of State
302 W. Washington, Rm. E111
Indianapolis, IN 46204
Phone: (317) 232-6541
Fax: (317) 233-3675

IOWA
Monty Bertelli
Director
Ofc. of Secretary of State
Hoover State Ofc. Bldg., 2nd Fl.
1300 E. Walnut
Des Moines, IA 50319
Phone: (515) 281-5204

KANSAS
Ron Thornburgh
Secretary of State
State Capitol, 2nd Fl.
300 SW 10th St.
Topeka, KS 66612
Phone: (785) 296-4564
Fax: (785) 296-4570

KENTUCKY
John Y. Brown, III
Secretary of State
State Capitol, Ste. 152
Frankfort, KY 40601
Phone: (502) 564-3490
Fax: (502) 564-4075

LOUISIANA
W. Fox McKeithen
Secretary of State
Dept. of State
P.O. Box 94125
Baton Rouge, LA 70804-9125
Phone: (225) 342-4479
Fax: (225) 342-5577

MAINE
Julie Flynn
Director
Corps. & Elections
101 State House Station
Augusta, ME 04333
Phone: (207) 287-4189
Fax: (207) 287-5874

MARYLAND
Ronald W. Wineholt
Director
Ofc. of Director
Dept. of Assessments & Taxation
301 W. Preston St.
Baltimore, MD 21201
Phone: (410) 767-1184
Fax: (410) 333-5873

MASSACHUSETTS
William Galvin
Secretary of the Commonwealth
Rm. 337 - State House
Boston, MA 02133
Phone: (617) 727-9180
Fax: (617) 742-4722

MICHIGAN
Julie Croll
Director
Corps., Securities & Land Dev.
Consumer & Industry Services
P.O. Box 30054
Lansing, MI 48909-7554
Phone: (517) 334-6212
Fax: (517) 334-6223

MINNESOTA
Mary Kiffmeyer
Secretary of State
180 State Ofc. Bldg.
100 Constitution Ave.
St. Paul, MN 55155-1299
Phone: (651) 296-1299
Fax: (651) 296-9073
E-mail: secretary.state@state.mn.us

MISSISSIPPI
Ray Bailey
Assistant Secretary of State
Corps. Div.
Ofc. of Secretary of State
P.O. Box 136
Jackson, MS 39205
Phone: (601) 359-1350
Fax: (601) 359-1607

MISSOURI
Linda Oliver
Director of Corporations
Ofc. of Secretary of State
600 W. Main St.
P.O. Box 778
Jefferson City, MO 65102
Phone: (573) 751-3200
Fax: (573) 751-5841
E-mail: loliver@mail.sos.state.mo.us

MONTANA
Leslee Shell-Beckert
Deputy
Business Services Bur.
Secretary of State
State Capitol, Rm. 225
P.O. Box 202801
Helena, MT 59620-2801
Phone: (406) 444-5372
Fax: (406) 444-3976

NEBRASKA
Julie Von Busch
Office Manager
Corp. Div.
Secretary of State
State Capitol, Rm. 1301
P.O. Box 94608
Lincoln, NE 68509-4608
Phone: (402) 471-4079
Fax: (402) 471-3666

NEVADA
Dean Heller
Secretary of State
State Capitol Bldg.
101 N. Carson St., Ste. 3
Carson City, NV 89701
Phone: (775) 684-5708
Fax: (775) 684-5725
E-mail: sosmail@govmail.state.nv.us

NEW HAMPSHIRE
William Gardner
Secretary of State
Secretary of State Ofc.
State House, Rm. 204
107 N. Main St.
Concord, NH 03301
Phone: (603) 271-3242
Fax: (603) 271-6316
E-mail: sof.karen.ladd@leg.state.nh.us

NEW JERSEY
James Frucione
Director
Div. of Commercial Recordings
Dept. of State
P.O. Box 308
Trenton, NJ 08625-0308
Phone: (609) 530-6400

NEW MEXICO
Orlanda Romero
Acting Chief of Staff
Corps. Bur.
Public Regulation Comm.
P.O. Box 1269
Santa Fe, NM 87504
Phone: (505) 827-4502
Fax: (505) 476-0161

NEW YORK
Alexander F. Treadwell
Secretary of State
Dept. of State
41 State St.
Albany, NY 12231
Phone: (518) 486-9844
Fax: (518) 474-4765

NORTH CAROLINA
Charlene Dawkins
Director
Corps. Div.
Ofc. of Secretary of State
300 N. Salisbury St.
Raleigh, NC 27603-5909
Phone: (919) 733-4201
Fax: (919) 733-5172

NORTH DAKOTA
Clara Jenkins
Director
Central Indexing
Secretary of State's Ofc.
600 E. Blvd. Ave., 1st Fl.
Bismarck, ND 58505-0500
Phone: (701) 328-2900
Fax: (701) 328-2992
E-mail: cjenkins@state.nd.us

NORTHERN MARIANA ISLANDS
Vacant
Registrar of Corporations
Dept. of Commerce
Saipan, MP 96950

OHIO
Sherri Dembinski
Assistant Secretary of State
Ofc. of Secretary of State
30 E. Broad St., 14th Fl.
Columbus, OH 43266
Phone: (614) 466-4980
Fax: (614) 466-3899

OKLAHOMA
Mike Hunter
Secretary of State
State Capitol Bldg., Rm. 101
Oklahoma City, OK 73105
Phone: (405) 521-3721
Fax: (405) 521-3771

OREGON
Jan Sullivan
Director
Ofc. of Secretary of State
Public Service Bldg.
255 Capitol St., NE, Ste. 151
Salem, OR 97310
Phone: (503) 986-2205
Fax: (503) 378-4381

PENNSYLVANIA
Michael Frick
Director
Corp. Bur.
Dept. of State
308 N. Ofc. Bldg.
Harrisburg, PA 17120
Phone: (717) 787-9941
Fax: (717) 787-2244

PUERTO RICO

RHODE ISLAND
Sandra Williams
Director
Corp. Div.
Ofc. of Secretary of State
100 N. Main St.
Providence, RI 02903
Phone: (401) 222-3040

SOUTH CAROLINA
Jim Miles
Secretary of State
Wade Hampton Bldg.
P.O. Box 11350
Columbia, SC 29211
Phone: (803) 734-2170
Fax: (803) 734-2164

SOUTH DAKOTA
Joyce Hazeltine
Secretary of State
500 E. Capitol Ave., Ste. 204
Pierre, SD 57501
Phone: (605) 773-3537
Fax: (605) 773-6580
E-mail: Patty.Pearson@state.sd.us

TENNESSEE
Robert Grunow
Director of Services
Business Services
Ofc. of Secretary of State
James K. Polk Bldg., 18th Fl.
Nashville, TN 37243
Phone: (615) 741-0584
Fax: (615) 741-7310

TEXAS
Lorna Wassdorf
Director
Statutory Filings Div.
Ofc. of Secretary of State
P.O. Box 12697
Austin, TX 78711
Phone: (512) 463-5586
Fax: (512) 463-5709

U.S. VIRGIN ISLANDS
Maryleen Thomas
Director
Banking & Insurance Div.
#18 Kongens Gade
St. Thomas, VI 00801
Phone: (340) 774-2991
Fax: (340) 774-9458

UTAH
Lorena P. Riffo
Director
Div. of Corps.
Dept. of Commerce
160 E. 300 S.
Salt Lake City, UT 84111
Phone: (801) 530-6027
Fax: (801) 530-6438
E-mail: lriffo@br.state.ut.us

VERMONT
Betty Poulin
Director
Corps. Div.
Ofc. of Secretary of State
109 State St.
Montpelier, VT 05609
Phone: (802) 828-2386
E-mail: bpoulin
@heritage.sec.state.vt.us

VIRGINIA
Theodore W. Morrison, Jr.
Chair
State Corp. Comm.
Tyler Bldg.
1300 E. Main St.
Richmond, VA 23219
Phone: (804) 371-9608
Fax: (804) 371-9376

WASHINGTON
Mike Ricchio
Director
Corps., Trademarks &
Limited Partnerships
Ofc. of Secretary of State
P.O. Box 40220
Olympia, WA 98504-0220
Phone: (360) 753-7115
Fax: (360) 664-8781

WEST VIRGINIA
Ken Hechler
Secretary of State
State Capitol, Rm. W-157K
1900 Kanawha Blvd., E.
Charleston, WV 25305
Phone: (304) 558-6000
Fax: (304) 558-0900
E-mail: wvsos
@secretary.state.wv.us

WISCONSIN
David Mancl
Administrator
Div. of Corporate &
Consumer Services
Dept. of Financial
Institutions
345 W. Washington, 3rd Fl.
P.O. Box 7846
Madison, WI 53707-7846
Phone: (608) 261-9555
Fax: (608) 267-6813

WYOMING
Jeanne Sawyer
Director
Corps. Div.
Ofc. of Secretary of State
State Capitol
200 W. 24th St.
Cheyenne, WY 82002
Phone: (307) 777-5334

Corrections

Manages the state's corrections system.

ALABAMA
Michael Haley
Commissioner
Dept. of Corrections
1400 Lloyd St.
Montgomery, AL 36130
Phone: (334) 353-3883
Fax: (334) 353-3891

ALASKA
Margaret Pugh
Commissioner
Dept. of Corrections
240 Main St., Ste. 700
Juneau, AK 99801
Phone: (907) 465-4652
Fax: (907) 465-3390

AMERICAN SAMOA
Te'o Fuavai
Commissioner
Dept. of Public Safety
AS Govt.
Pago Pago, AS 96799
Phone: (684) 633-1111
Fax: (684) 633-5111

ARIZONA
Terry Stewart
Director
Dept. of Corrections
1601 W. Jefferson
Phoenix, AZ 85007
Phone: (602) 542-5497
Fax: (602) 542-2859

ARKANSAS
Larry Norris
Director
Dept. of Correction
P.O. Box 8707
Pine Bluff, AR 71611
Phone: (501) 247-1800
Fax: (501) 247-3700

CALIFORNIA
Robert Presley
Secretary
Youth and Adult Correctional Agency
1100 11th St., Ste. 400
Sacramento, CA 95814
Phone: (916) 323-6001
Fax: (916) 442-2637

COLORADO
John Suthers
Executive Director
Dept. of Corrections
2862 S. Circle Dr., Ste. 400
Colorado Springs, CO 80906
Phone: (303) 579-9580
Fax: (303) 540-4700

CONNECTICUT
John J. Armstrong
Commissioner
Dept. of Corrections
24 Wolcott Hill Rd.
Wethersfield, CT 06109-1152
Phone: (860) 692-7780

DELAWARE
Stanley W. Taylor
Commissioner
Dept. of Corrections
245 McKee Rd.
Dover, DE 19904-2232
Phone: (302) 739-5601
Fax: (302) 653-2892
E-mail: sttaylor@state.de.us

DISTRICT OF COLUMBIA
Odie Washington
Interim Director
Dept. of Corrections
1923 Vermont Ave., NW
Washington, DC 20001
Phone: (202) 673-7316

FLORIDA
Michael W. Moore
Secretary
Dept. of Corrections
2601 Blair Stone Rd.
Tallahassee, FL 32399-2500
Phone: (850) 488-7480
Fax: (850) 922-2848
E-mail: moore.michael@mail.dc.state.fl.us

GEORGIA
Jim Wetherington
Commissioner
Dept. of Corrections
Twin Towers, E., Rm. 770
2 Martin Luther King, Jr. Dr.
Atlanta, GA 30334
Phone: (404) 656-6002

GUAM
Angel Sablan
Acting Director
Dept. of Corrections
P.O. Box 3236
Hagatna, GU 96932
Phone: (671) 734-4668
Fax: (671) 734-4490

HAWAII
Ted Sakai
Director
Ofc. of the Director
Dept. of Public Safety
919 Ala Moana Blvd., 4th Fl.
Honolulu, HI 96814
Phone: (808) 587-1288
Fax: (808) 587-1282

IDAHO
James C. Spalding
Director
Dept. of Corrections
500 S. 10th St.
Boise, ID 83702
Phone: (208) 334-2318

ILLINOIS
Donald N. Snyder
Director
Dept. of Corrections
P.O. Box 19277
Springfield, IL 62794
Phone: (217) 522-2666
Fax: (217) 522-8719

INDIANA
Edward Cohn
Commissioner
Dept. of Corrections
IGC-S., Rm. E334
Indianapolis, IN 46204
Phone: (317) 232-5711
Fax: (317) 232-6798

IOWA
W.L. Kautzky
Director
Dept. of Corrections
Capitol Annex
523 E. 12th St.
Des Moines, IA 50319
Phone: (515) 281-4811
Fax: (515) 281-7345

KANSAS
Charles Simmons
Secretary
Dept. of Corrections
Landon State Ofc. Bldg.
900 SW Jackson, 4th Fl.
Topeka, KS 66612
Phone: (785) 296-3317
Fax: (785) 296-0014

KENTUCKY
Doug Sapp
Commissioner
Dept. of Corrections
State Ofc. Bldg., Rm. 503
Frankfort, KY 40601
Phone: (502) 564-4726
Fax: (502) 564-5037

LOUISIANA
Richard Stalder
Secretary
Dept. of Public Safety & Corrections
P.O. Box 94304
Baton Rouge, LA 70804
Phone: (225) 342-6741
Fax: (225) 342-3095

MAINE
Martin Magnusson
Commissioner
Dept. of Corrections
111 State House Station
Augusta, ME 04333-0111
Phone: (207) 287-4360

MARYLAND
Richard A. Lanham, Sr.
Commissioner
Div. of Corrections
Public Safety & Correctional Services
6776 Reisterstown Rd., Ste. 310
Baltimore, MD 21215-2342
Phone: (410) 764-4184
Fax: (410) 764-4182

MASSACHUSETTS
Michael T. Maloney
Commissioner
Executive Ofc. of Public Safety
Dept. of Corrections
100 Cambridge St., 22nd Fl.
Boston, MA 02202
Phone: (617) 727-3300
Fax: (617) 727-3048

MICHIGAN
Bill Martin
Director
Dept. of Corrections
Grand View Plz. Bldg.
P.O. Box 30003
Lansing, MI 48909
Phone: (517) 373-0720
Fax: (517) 373-3882

MINNESOTA
Sheryl Ramstad Huass
Commissioner
Dept. of Corrections
1450 Energy Park Dr., Ste. 200
St. Paul, MN 55108
Phone: (651) 642-0282
Fax: (651) 642-0414

MISSISSIPPI
James Anderson
Commissioner
Dept. of Corrections
723 N. President St.
Jackson, MS 39202
Phone: (601) 359-5600
Fax: (601) 359-5624

MISSOURI
Dora Schriro
Director
Dept. of Corrections
2729 Plz. Dr.
P.O. Box 236
Jefferson City, MO 65102
Phone: (573) 751-2389
Fax: (573) 751-4099
E-mail: docdir@mail.state.mo.us

MONTANA
Rick Day
Director
Dept. of Corrections
1539 11th Ave., Rm. 210
Helena, MT 59620-1301
Phone: (406) 444-3930
Fax: (406) 444-4920

NEBRASKA
Harold Clarke
Director
Dept. of Correctional Services
Folsom & W. Prospector Pl., Bldg. 15
P.O. Box 94661
Lincoln, NE 68509
Phone: (402) 471-2654
Fax: (402) 479-5623

NEVADA
Bob Bayer
Director
Dept. of Prisons
P.O. Box 7011
Carson City, NV 89702
Phone: (775) 887-3285
Fax: (775) 687-6715

NEW HAMPSHIRE
Henry Risley
Commissioner
Dept. of Corrections
P.O. Box 1806
Concord, NH 03302-1806
Phone: (603) 271-5600
Fax: (603) 271-5643

NEW JERSEY
Jack Terhune
Commissioner
Dept. of Corrections
Whittlesey Rd.
P.O. Box 863
Trenton, NJ 08625-0863
Phone: (609) 292-9860
Fax: (609) 777-0445

NEW MEXICO
Robert J. Perry
Secretary
Dept. of Corrections
P.O. Box 27116
Santa Fe, NM 87502-0116
Phone: (505) 827-8709
Fax: (505) 827-8220

NEW YORK
Glen Goord
Commissioner
Dept. of Correctional Services
State Campus, Bldg. 2
1220 Washington Ave.
Albany, NY 12226-2050
Phone: (518) 457-8134
Fax: (518) 457-0076

NORTH CAROLINA
Joe Hamilton
Secretary
Dept. of Corrections
214 W. Jones St.
Raleigh, NC 27603
Phone: (919) 733-4926
Fax: (919) 733-4790

NORTH DAKOTA
Elaine Little
Director
Dept. of Corrections & Rehab.
P.O. Box 1898
Bismarck, ND 58502-1898
Phone: (701) 328-6390
Fax: (701) 328-6651
E-mail: elittle@state.nd.us

NORTHERN MARIANA ISLANDS
Gregorio Castro
Director
Corrections Div.
Dept. of Public Safety
Ofc. of the Governor
Saipan, MP 96950
Phone: (670) 234-8534
Fax: (670) 664-9065

OHIO
Reginald A. Wilkinson
Director
Dept. of Rehab. & Corrections
1050 Freeway Dr., N.
Columbus, OH 43229
Phone: (614) 752-1164
Fax: (614) 752-1171

OKLAHOMA
James L. Saffle
Director
Dept. of Corrections
3400 Martin Luther King Ave.
P.O. Box 11400
Oklahoma City, OK 73136
Phone: (405) 425-2500
Fax: (405) 425-2578

OREGON
David Cook
Director
Dept. of Corrections
2575 Ctr. St., NE
Salem, OR 97310
Phone: (503) 945-0920
Fax: (503) 373-1173

PENNSYLVANIA
Martin Horn
Cabinet Secretary
Dept. of Corrections
P.O. Box 598
Camp Hill, PA 17011
Phone: (717) 975-4918
Fax: (717) 731-0486
E-mail: mhorn@cor.pa.state.us

PUERTO RICO
Zoe Laboy
Secretary
Dept. of Correction & Rehab.
P.O. Box 40945
Minillas Station
San Juan, PR 00924
Phone: (787) 758-0033
Fax: (787) 754-8290

RHODE ISLAND
George A. Vose, Jr.
Director
Dept. of Corrections
75 Howard Ave.
Cranston, RI 02920
Phone: (401) 462-2611
Fax: (401) 462-2630

SOUTH CAROLINA
William D. Catoe
Director
Dept. of Corrections
4444 Broad River Rd.
P.O. Box 21787
Columbia, SC 29221
Phone: (803) 896-8500

SOUTH DAKOTA
Jeff Bloomberg
Secretary
Dept. of Corrections
Herm Solem Public Safety Ctr.
500 E. Capitol Ave.
Pierre, SD 57501-5070
Phone: (605) 773-3478
Fax: (605) 773-3194

TENNESSEE
Donal Campbell
Commissioner
Dept. of Corrections
Rachel Jackson Bldg., 4th Fl.
320 6th Ave., N.
Nashville, TN 37243
Phone: (615) 741-2071
Fax: (615) 532-8281

TEXAS
Wayne Scott
Executive Director
Dept. of Criminal Justice
P.O. Box 99
Huntsville, TX 77340
Phone: (409) 295-6371
Fax: (409) 294-2123

U.S. VIRGIN ISLANDS
Iver Stirdiron
Attorney General
Dept. of Justice
G.E.R.S. Complex
4813-50C Kronprinsdens Gade
St. Thomas, VI 00802
Phone: (340) 774-5666
Fax: (340) 774-9710

UTAH
H.L. Haun
Executive Director
Administration
Dept. of Corrections
6100 S. 300 E.
Murray, UT 84107
Phone: (801) 265-5513
Fax: (801) 265-5726
E-mail: phaun.crdept@state.ut.us

VERMONT
John Gorczyk
Commissioner
Agency of Human Services
Dept. of Corrections
103 S. Main St.
Waterbury, VT 05671
Phone: (802) 241-2442
Fax: (802) 241-2565
E-mail: johng@doc.state.vt.us

VIRGINIA
Ronald J. Angelone
Director
Dept. of Corrections
6900 Atmore Dr.
Richmond, VA 23225
Phone: (804) 674-3119
Fax: (804) 674-3509

WASHINGTON
Joe Lehman
Secretary
Dept. of Corrections
410 Capitol Ctr. Bldg.
P.O. Box 41100
Olympia, WA 98504
Phone: (360) 753-1573
Fax: (360) 664-4056

WEST VIRGINIA
Paul W. Kirby
Commissioner
Div. of Corrections
112 California Ave.
Charleston, WV 25305
Phone: (304) 558-2036
Fax: (304) 558-5934

WISCONSIN
Jon Litscher
Secretary
Dept. of Corrections
149 E. Wilson St.
P.O. Box 7925
Madison, WI 53707-7925
Phone: (608) 261-6778
Fax: (608) 267-3661
E-mail: jon.litscher@doc.state.wi.us

WYOMING
Judy Uphoff
Director
Dept. of Corrections
700 W. 21st St.
Cheyenne, WY 82002
Phone: (307) 777-7405
Fax: (307) 777-7479

Court Administration

Performs administrative duties for the state court of last resort.

ALABAMA
Frank W. Gregory
Administrator
Adm. Ofc. of the Cts.
300 Dexter Ave.
Montgomery, AL 36104-3741
Phone: (334) 242-0300
Fax: (334) 242-2099

ALASKA
Stephanie J. Cole
Administration Director
Ct. System
303 K St.
Anchorage, AK 99501-2084
Phone: (907) 264-0547
Fax: (907) 276-6985

AMERICAN SAMOA
Otto Thomsen
Court Administrator
High Ct.
Pago Pago, AS 96799
Phone: (684) 633-4131
Fax: (684) 633-1318

ARIZONA
David K. Byers
Director
Supreme Ct.
Adm. Ofc. of the Ct.
1501 W. Washington
Phoenix, AZ 85007
Phone: (602) 542-9301
Fax: (602) 542-9480

ARKANSAS
James D. Gingerich
Director
Adm. Ofc. of the Cts.
Justice Bldg.
625 Marshall
Little Rock, AR 72201
Phone: (501) 682-9400
Fax: (501) 682-9410

CALIFORNIA
William C. Vickrey
Director
Judicial Council
Adm. Ofc. of the Cts.
303 Second St.
San Francisco, CA 94107
Phone: (415) 396-9100
Fax: (415) 396-9362

COLORADO
Steven V. Berson
State Court Administrator
1301 Pennsylvania, Ste. 300
Denver, CO 80203
Phone: (303) 861-1111

CONNECTICUT
Aaron Ment
Chief Court Administrator
Ofc. of Chief Ct. Administrator
Drawer N, Station A
Hartford, CT 06106
Phone: (860) 566-4461

DELAWARE
Lawrence Webster
Director of Administration
Ct. System
820 N. French St., 11th Fl.
Wilmington, DE 19801
Phone: (302) 577-2480
Fax: (302) 577-3139

DISTRICT OF COLUMBIA
Ulysses B. Hammond
Executive Officer
Cts.
500 Indiana Ave., NW, Rm. 1500
Washington, DC 20001
Phone: (202) 879-1700

FLORIDA
Ken Palmer
State Courts Administrator
Supreme Ct.
Supreme Ct. Bldg.
500 S. Duval St.
Tallahassee, FL 32399-1900
Phone: (850) 922-5081
Fax: (850) 488-0156

GEORGIA
George Lange
Director
Adm. Ofc. of the Cts.
244 Washington St., SW, Ste. 550
Atlanta, GA 30334-9007
Phone: (404) 656-5171

GUAM
Anthony P. Sanchez
Administration Director
Superior Ct.
Judicial Ctr.
120 W. O'Brien Dr.
Hagatna, GU 96910
Phone: (671) 475-3544
Fax: (671) 477-3184

HAWAII
Clyde Namuo
Deputy Administrative Director
Cts.
P.O. Box 2560
Honolulu, HI 96804
Phone: (808) 539-4902
Fax: (808) 539-4985

IDAHO
Patricia Tobias
Director
Supreme Cts.
Adm. Ofc. of the Ct.
451 W. State St.
Boise, ID 83720
Phone: (208) 334-2246

ILLINOIS
Joseph A. Schillaci
Director
Adm. Ofc. of the Cts.
222 N. LaSalle St., 13th Fl.
Chicago, IL 60601
Phone: (312) 793-3250

INDIANA

IOWA
William J. O'Brien
State Court Administrator
Judicial Dept.
State Capitol Bldg.
1007 E. Grand Ave.
Des Moines, IA 50319
Phone: (515) 281-5241
Fax: (515) 242-6164

KANSAS
Howard Schwartz
Judicial Administrator
Supreme Ct.
Judicial Ctr.
301 W. 10th
Topeka, KS 66612-1507
Phone: (785) 296-4873

KENTUCKY
Cicely Lambert
Director
Adm. Ofc. of the Cts.
100 Millcreek Pk.
Frankfort, KY 40601
Phone: (502) 573-2350
Fax: (502) 695-1759

LOUISIANA
Hugh M. Collins
Judicial Administrator
Supreme Ct.
155 Poydras, Ste. 1540
New Orleans, LA 70112
Phone: (504) 568-5747
Fax: (504) 568-5687

MAINE
James T. Glessner
Administrator
Adm. Ofc. of the Cts.
Judicial Dept.
P.O. Box 4820
Portland, ME 04112
Phone: (207) 822-0793

MARYLAND
George B. Riggin, Jr.
State Court Administrator
Administration Ofc. of the Cts.
Judiciary
361 Rowe Blvd.
Annapolis, MD 21401
Phone: (410) 260-1405
Fax: (410) 974-5577

MASSACHUSETTS
Barbara Dortch-O'Kara
Chief Administrative Justice
Ofc. of the Chief Adm. Justice
2 Centre Plz., 5th Fl.
Boston, MA 02108
Phone: (617) 742-8575
Fax: (617) 742-0968

MICHIGAN
John D. Ferry, Jr.
State Court Administrator
Supreme Ct.
State Ct. Adm. Ofc.
309 N. Washington Sq.
P.O. Box 30048
Lansing, MI 48909
Phone: (517) 373-0130

MINNESOTA
Sue K. Dosal
Administrator
Ofc. of State Ct. Administrator
135 MN Judicial Ctr.
25 Constitution Ave.
St. Paul, MN 55155-1500
Phone: (651) 296-2474
Fax: (651) 297-5636
E-mail: sue.dosal@courts.state.mn.us

MISSISSIPPI
Rick Patt
Court Administrator
Supreme Ct.
P.O. Box 117
Jackson, MS 39205
Phone: (601) 359-3697
Fax: (601) 359-2443

MISSOURI
Ronald L. Larkin
State Court Administrator
2112 Industrial Dr.
P.O. Box 104480
Jefferson City, MO 65110-4480
Phone: (573) 751-4337
Fax: (573) 751-5540
E-mail: Ronald_Larkin@osca.state.mo.us

MONTANA
Patrick A. Chenovick
Administrator
Court Administration
Judiciary Dept.
Justice/State Library Bldg., Rm. 315
Helena, MT 59620
Phone: (406) 444-2621
Fax: (406) 444-0834

NEBRASKA
Joe C. Steele
Administrator
Ofc. of Ct. Administrator
State Capitol, Rm. 1220
P.O. Box 98910
Lincoln, NE 68509-8910
Phone: (402) 471-2755
Fax: (402) 471-2197

NEVADA
Karen Kavanau
Director
Adm. Ofc. of the Cts.
201 S. Carson St., Ste. 250
Carson City, NV 89701-4702
Phone: (775) 687-5076
Fax: (775) 687-5079

NEW HAMPSHIRE
Donald D. Goodnow
Director
Adm. Ofc. of the Cts.
Supreme Ct. Bldg.
Noble Dr.
Concord, NH 03301
Phone: (603) 271-2521
Fax: (603) 271-3977

NEW JERSEY
James J. Ciancia
Director
Adm. Ofc. of the Cts.
Judiciary Dept.
Hughes Justice Complex
P.O. Box 037
Trenton, NJ 08625-0037
Phone: (609) 984-0275
Fax: (609) 292-3320

NEW MEXICO
John M. Greacen
Director
Adm. Ofc. of the Cts.
237 Don Gaspar, Rm. 25
Santa Fe, NM 87501-2178
Phone: (505) 827-4800
Fax: (505) 827-4824

NEW YORK
Jonathan Lippman
Chief Administrator of the Courts
Ofc. of Cts. Administration
Agency Bldg. 4, 20th Fl.
Empire State Plz.
Albany, NY 12223
Phone: (518) 474-7469
Fax: (518) 473-5514

NORTH CAROLINA
Dallas Cameron
Director
Adm. Ofc. of the Cts.
2 E. Morgan St.
Raleigh, NC 27601-1400
Phone: (919) 733-7107
Fax: (919) 715-5779

NORTH DAKOTA
Keithe E. Nelson
Court Administrator
Adm. Ofc.
Supreme Ct.
600 E. Blvd. Ave., 1st Fl. - Judicial Wing
Bismarck, ND 58505-0530
Phone: (701) 328-4216
Fax: (701) 328-4480
E-mail: keithen@sc3.court.state.nd.us

NORTHERN MARIANA ISLANDS
Margarita M. Palacios
Court Administrator
Commonwealth Superior Ct.
Civil Ctr.
Saipan, MP 96950
Phone: (670) 236-9800
Fax: (670) 236-9701
E-mail: supreme.court@saipan.com

OHIO
Steven C. Hollon
Administrative Director
Supreme Ct.
State Ofc. Tower
30 E. Broad St., 3rd Fl.
Columbus, OH 43266-0419
Phone: (614) 466-2653
Fax: (614) 752-8736

OKLAHOMA
Howard W. Conyers
Administrative Director
Adm. Ofc. of the Cts.
Denver Davison Bldg.
1915 N. Stiles, Ste. 305
Oklahoma City, OK 73105
Phone: (405) 521-2450
Fax: (405) 521-6815

OREGON
Kingsley W. Click
Administrator
Supreme Ct. Bldg.
1163 State St.
Salem, OR 97310
Phone: (503) 986-5900
Fax: (503) 986-5503

PENNSYLVANIA
Nancy Sobolevitch
Administrator
Adm. Ofc. of the Cts.
1515 Market St., Ste. 1414
Philadelphia, PA 19102
Phone: (215) 560-6337
Fax: (215) 560-4585

PUERTO RICO
Mercedes M. Bauermeister
Administrative Director of the Courts
Ofc. of Cts. Administration
P.O. Box 190917
San Juan, PR 00919-0917
Phone: (787) 763-3358
Fax: (787) 250-7448

RHODE ISLAND
Leo Skenyon
Administrator
Adm. Adjudication Ct.
345 Harris Ave.
Providence, RI 02909-1082
Phone: (401) 222-2251

SOUTH CAROLINA
Rosalyn W. Frierson
Director
Ct. Administration
1015 Sumter St., 2nd Fl.
Columbia, SC 29201
Phone: (803) 734-1800

SOUTH DAKOTA
Mike Buenger
Administrator
Supreme Ct.
Unified Judicial System
500 E. Capitol Ave.
Pierre, SD 57501
Phone: (605) 773-3474
Fax: (605) 773-6128

TENNESSEE
Libby Sykes
Acting Director
Supreme Ct.
Adm. Ofc. of the Cts.
Nashville City Ctr., Ste. 600
Nashville, TN 37243
Phone: (615) 741-2687
Fax: (615) 741-6285

TEXAS
Jerry Benedict
Administrative Director
Ofc. of Ct. Administration
205 W. 14th St., Ste. 600
Austin, TX 78701
Phone: (512) 463-1625
Fax: (512) 463-1648

U.S. VIRGIN ISLANDS
Orrin Arnold
Clerk
U.S. District Ct.
2 & 3 King St.
Christiansted
St. Croix, VI 00802
Phone: (340) 773-1130
Fax: (340) 773-1563

UTAH
Daniel J. Becker
Administrator
Adm. Ofc. of the Cts.
P.O. Box 140241
Salt Lake City, UT 84114-0241
Phone: (801) 578-3806
Fax: (801) 578-3843
E-mail: danb@email.utcourts.gov

VERMONT
Lee Suskin
Court Administrator
Supreme Ct.
109 State St.
Montpelier, VT 05609-0701
Phone: (802) 828-3278
Fax: (802) 828-3457

VIRGINIA
Robert N. Baldwin
Executive Secretary
Supreme Ct.
100 N. 9th St., 3rd Fl.
Richmond, VA 23219
Phone: (804) 786-6455
Fax: (804) 786-4542

WASHINGTON
Mary McQueen
Administrator for the Courts
P.O. Box 41170
Olympia, WA 98504-1170
Phone: (360) 753-3365
Fax: (360) 357-2129

WEST VIRGINIA
Ted Philyaw
Court Administrator
Supreme Ct. of Appeals
State Capitol, Rm. E-400
1900 Kanawha Blvd., E.
Charleston, WV 25305
Phone: (304) 558-0145
Fax: (304) 558-1212

WISCONSIN
J. Denis Moran
Director
Supreme Ct.
State Cts.
State Capitol, 213 NE
P.O. Box 1688
Madison, WI 53701
Phone: (608) 266-6828
Fax: (608) 267-0980

WYOMING
Robert L. Duncan
Court Coordinator
Supreme Ct.
Supreme Ct. Bldg.
2301 Capitol Ave.
Cheyenne, WY 82002
Phone: (307) 777-7581

Crime Victims Compensation

Provides compensation to victims of crime.

ALABAMA
J. Philip Land
Director
Crime Victims
Compensation Comm.
100 N. Union St., Ste. 778
Montgomery, AL 36130
Phone: (334) 242-4007
Fax: (334) 353-1401

ALASKA
Susan Browne
Administrator
Violent Crime
Compensation Board
Dept. of Public Safety
P.O. Box 111200
Juneau, AK 99811-1200
Phone: (907) 465-3040
Fax: (907) 465-2379

AMERICAN SAMOA

ARIZONA
Janet Napolitano
Attorney General
Attorney Gen's. Ofc.
Law Bldg.
1275 W. Washington
Phoenix, AZ 85007
Phone: (602) 542-4266
Fax: (602) 542-4085

ARKANSAS
Ginger Bailey
Deputy Director
Outreach Div.
Ofc. of Attorney Gen.
323 Ctr. St., Ste. 200
Little Rock, AR 72201
Phone: (501) 682-2007
Fax: (501) 682-8084

CALIFORNIA
Darlene Ayeres-Johnson
Executive Director
State Board of Control
P.O. Box 48
Sacramento, CA 95812-0648
Phone: (916) 323-3432

COLORADO
Debbie Kasyon
State Victims
Compensation
Coordinator
Div. of Criminal Justice
Dept. of Public Safety
700 Kipling St., #1000
Lakewood, CO 80215
Phone: (303) 239-4402
Fax: (303) 239-4411

CONNECTICUT
Karen Chorney
Acting Director
Ofc. of Victim Services
1155 Silas Deane Hwy.
Wethersfield, CT 06109
Phone: (860) 529-3089

DELAWARE
Ann L. Del Negro
Executive Director
Violent Crimes
Compensation Board
1500 E. Newport Pike,
Ste. 10
Wilmington, DE 19804
Phone: (302) 995-8383
Fax: (302) 995-8387

DISTRICT OF COLUMBIA
Joan Watson
Chief
Crime Victims
Compensation
1200 Upshur St., NW
Washington, DC 20011
Phone: (202) 724-2345

FLORIDA
Mary Vancore
Chief
Bur. of Advocacy & Grants
Mgmt.
Dept. of Legal Affairs
The Capitol, PL01
Tallahassee, FL 32399-1050
Phone: (850) 414-3300
Fax: (850) 487-3013

GEORGIA
David Moskowitz
Director
Crime Victims
Compensation Board
P.O. Box 95603
Atlanta, GA 30347
Phone: (404) 321-4060

GUAM

HAWAII
Paula Ferguson-Brey
Administrator
Criminal Injuries
Compensation
Dept. of Public Safety
333 Queen St., Rm. 404
Honolulu, HI 96813
Phone: (808) 587-1143
Fax: (808) 587-1146

IDAHO
Bill von Tagen
Director
Intergovernmental & Fiscal
Law Div.
Ofc. of Attorney Gen.
700 W. Jefferson, Rm. 210
Boise, ID 83720-0010
Phone: (208) 334-2400
Fax: (208) 334-2530

ILLINOIS
Matthew Finnell
Court Administrator
Ct. of Claims
630 S. College
Springfield, IL 62756
Phone: (217) 782-7101

INDIANA
Kimberly Howell
Program Director
Violent Crime
Compensation Ofc.
Criminal Justice Institute
302 W. Washington St.,
Rm. E203
Indianapolis, IN 46204
Phone: (317) 232-7103
Fax: (317) 232-4979

IOWA
Marti Anderson
Administrator
Crime Victim Assistance
Ofc. of Attorney Gen.
Hoover State Ofc. Bldg.
1300 E. Walnut
Des Moines, IA 50319
Phone: (515) 281-5044

KANSAS
Frank Henderson, Jr.
Executive Director
Crime Victims
Compensation Board
700 SW Jackson, Ste. 400
Topeka, KS 66603
Phone: (785) 296-2359
Fax: (785) 296-0652

KENTUCKY
Jackie Howell
Executive Director
Crime Victims
Compensation Board
Public Protection &
Regulation Cabinet
115 Myrtle Ave.
Frankfort, KY 40601
Phone: (502) 564-2290
Fax: (502) 564-4817

LOUISIANA
Richard P. Ieyoub, Jr.
Attorney General
Dept. of Justice
P.O. Box 94005
Baton Rouge, LA 70804-9005
Phone: (225) 342-7013
Fax: (225) 342-8703

MAINE

MARYLAND
Esther Scaljon
Director
Criminal Injuries
Compensation Board
Public Safety &
Correctional Services
6776 Reisterstown Rd.,
Ste. 312
Baltimore, MD 21215-2341
Phone: (410) 764-4214
Fax: (410) 764-3815

MASSACHUSETTS
Shelagh Lafferty
Executive Director
Ofc. for Victim Assistance
One Ashburton Pl.,
Rm. 1101
Boston, MA 02108
Phone: (617) 727-5200
Fax: (617) 727-6552
E-mail: mova@state.ma.us

MICHIGAN
Michael J. Fullwood
Director
Crime Victims Services
Dept. of Community
Health
P.O. Box 30026
Lansing, MI 48909
Phone: (517) 373-7373

MINNESOTA
Charlie Weaver
Commissioner
Dept. of Public Safety
NCL Tower, Ste. 1000
445 Minnesota St.
Minneapolis, MN 55101
Phone: (651) 296-6642
Fax: (651) 297-5728

MISSISSIPPI
Sandra Morrison
Director
Crime Victims
Compensation
Dept. of Finance &
Administration
P.O. Box 267
Jackson, MS 39205
Phone: (601) 359-6766
Fax: (601) 359-2470

MISSOURI
Sandy Wright
Program Manager
Crime Victims
Compensation
Dept. of Labor & Industrial
Relations
P.O. Box 58
Jefferson City, MO 65102
Phone: (573) 526-3511
Fax: (573) 526-4940
E-mail: swright
@dolir.state.mo.us

MONTANA
Dara Smith
Program Manager
Crime Victims
Compensation Unit
Dept. of Justice
303 N. Roberts
Helena, MT 59620-1408
Phone: (406) 444-6678
Fax: (406) 444-4722

NEBRASKA
Allen Curtis
Executive Director
Comm. on Law
Enforcement &
Criminal Justice
P.O. Box 94946
Lincoln, NE 68509
Phone: (402) 471-2194
Fax: (402) 471-2837

NEVADA
Bryan Nix
Coordinator
Victims of Crime Program
Dept. of Administration
555 E. Washington 3300
Las Vegas, NV 89101
Phone: (702) 486-2525

NEW HAMPSHIRE
Sandra Matheson
Director
Victim Witness Program
Justice Dept.
33 Capitol St.
Concord, NH 03301-6397
Phone: (603) 271-3671
Fax: (603) 271-2110

NEW JERSEY
James O'Brien
Chair
Violent Crimes
Compensation Board
Dept. of Law & Public
Safety
50 Park Pl.
Newark, NJ 07102
Phone: (201) 648-2107
Fax: (201) 648-7031

NEW MEXICO
Larry Tackman
Director
Crime Victims Reparation
Comm.
8100 Mountain Rd., NE,
Ste. 106
Albuquerque, NM 87110
Phone: (505) 841-9432
Fax: (505) 841-9437

NEW YORK
Joan Cusack
Chair
Crime Victims Board
270 Broadway, Rm. 200
New York, NY 10007
Phone: (212) 417-5136
Fax: (212) 417-5262

NORTH CAROLINA
Gary Eichelberger
Director
Victim & Justice Services
Dept. of Crime Control &
Public Safety
512 N. Salisbury St.
Raleigh, NC 27604-1159
Phone: (919) 733-7974
Fax: (919) 715-4209

NORTH DAKOTA
Paul Coughlin
Administrator
Crime Victims
Compensation
Parole & Probation Div.
P.O. Box 5521
Bismarck, ND 58506-5521
Phone: (701) 328-6195
Fax: (701) 328-6651
E-mail: pcoughli
@state.nd.us

NORTHERN MARIANA ISLANDS
Liza Hammermeister
Assistant Attorney General
Ofc. of the Attorney Gen.
Caller Box 10007
Saipan, MP 96950
Phone: (670) 664-2370
Fax: (670) 234-7016
E-mail: cnmiago
@mtccnmi.com

OHIO
Brian Cook
Chief
Crime Victim Services
Ofc. of Attorney Gen.
65 E. State, 8th Fl.
Columbus, OH 43215
Phone: (614) 466-5610
Fax: (614) 752-8736

OKLAHOMA
Suzanne Breedlove
Administrator
Crime Victims
Compensation Board
2200 Classen Blvd.,
Ste. 1800
Oklahoma City, OK 73106
Phone: (405) 557-6704

OREGON
Mary Ellen Johnson
Director
Crime Victims
Compensation Program
Dept. of Justice
1162 Court St., NE
Salem, OR 97310
Phone: (503) 378-5348
Fax: (503) 378-5738

PENNSYLVANIA
Carol Lavery
Director/PCCD
Bur. of Victims Services
Victims Compensation Div.
P.O. Box 1167
Harrisburg, PA 17108-1167
Phone: (717) 783-5153
Fax: (717) 783-7713

PUERTO RICO

RHODE ISLAND
Elaine Rendine
Director
Victim/Witness Assistance
Ofc. of the Attorney Gen.
150 S. Main St.
Providence, RI 02903-2907
Phone: (401) 274-4400

SOUTH CAROLINA
Mia McLoud-Butler
Director
Div. of Victims Assistance
Ofc. of the Governor
Edgar A. Brown Bldg.
1205 Pendleton St.,
Rm. 401
Columbia, SC 29202
Phone: (803) 734-1900
Fax: (803) 734-1708

SOUTH DAKOTA
Ann Holzhauser
Administrator
Crime Victims
Compensation
Dept. of Social Services
Kneip Bldg.
700 Governors Dr.
Pierre, SD 57501
Phone: (605) 773-6317
Fax: (605) 773-6834

TENNESSEE
Stephen D. Adams
State Treasurer
State Capitol
600 Charlotte
Nashville, TN 37243
Phone: (615) 741-2956
Fax: (615) 253-1591
E-mail: sadams@mail.state.tn.us

TEXAS
Richard Nedelkoff
Interim Director
Crime Stoppers
Ofc. of the Governor
P.O. Box 12428
Austin, TX 78711
Phone: (512) 463-1919
Fax: (512) 475-2440

U.S. VIRGIN ISLANDS
Sedonie Halbert
Commissioner
Dept. of Human Services
Knud Hansen Complex, Bldg. A
1303 Hospital Grounds
St. Thomas, VI 00802
Phone: (340) 774-0930
Fax: (340) 774-3466

UTAH
Dan Davis
Director
Crime Victim Reparation
350 E. 500 S., Ste. 200
Salt Lake City, UT 84111
Phone: (801) 238-2367
Fax: (801) 533-4127
E-mail: ddavis@gov.state.ut.us

VERMONT
Lori E. Hayes
Executive Director
Ctr. for Crime Victims
103 S. Main St.
Waterbury, VT 05671-2001
Phone: (802) 828-3374
Fax: (802) 828-3389

VIRGINIA
Joseph B. Benedetti
Director
Dept. of Criminal Justice Services
8th St. Ofc. Bldg., 10th Fl.
805 E. Broad St.
Richmond, VA 23219
Phone: (804) 786-8718
Fax: (804) 786-0588

WASHINGTON
Doug Connell
Assistant Director
Consultation & Compliance Services
Dept. of Labor & Industries
P.O. Box 44000
Olympia, WA 98504
Phone: (360) 902-4209
Fax: (360) 902-4940

WEST VIRGINIA
Darrell V. McGraw, Jr.
Attorney General
Ofc. of the Attorney Gen.
Capitol Bldg.
1900 Kanawha Blvd., E.
Charleston, WV 25305
Phone: (304) 558-2021
Fax: (304) 558-0140

WISCONSIN
Kitty Kocol
Executive Director
Crime Victims Services
Dept. of Justice
123 W. Washington Ave., 8th Fl.
P.O. Box 7951
Madison, WI 53707
Phone: (608) 264-9497
Fax: (608) 264-6368

WYOMING
Sharon Montagnino
Administrator
Crime Victims Compensation
Barrett Bldg., 4th Fl.
Cheyenne, WY 82002
Phone: (307) 777-6271
Fax: (307) 638-7208

Criminal Justice Data

Responsible for storage and retrieval of criminal justice data.

ALABAMA
Larry Wright
Director
Criminal Justice Info. Ctr.
770 Washington Ave., Ste. 350
Montgomery, AL 36130-0660
Phone: (334) 242-4900
Fax: (334) 242-0577

ALASKA
Ken Bischoff
Director
Div. of Adm. Services
Dept. of Public Safety
P.O. Box 111200
Juneau, AK 99811-1200
Phone: (907) 465-4336
Fax: (907) 465-3656

AMERICAN SAMOA
Alalamua Laauli Filoiali'i
Director
Criminal Justice Planning Agency
AS Govt.
Pago Pago, AS 96799
Phone: (684) 633-5221
Fax: (684) 633-7552

ARIZONA
Joe Albo
Director
Dept. of Public Safety
2102 W. Encanto Blvd.
Phoenix, AZ 85005-6638
Phone: (602) 223-2359
Fax: (602) 223-2917

ARKANSAS
David Eberdt
Director
Crime Info. Ctr.
1 Capitol Mall, Rm. 4D-200
Little Rock, AR 72201
Phone: (501) 682-2222
Fax: (501) 682-7444

CALIFORNIA
Gary Maggy
Chief
Criminal Identification
Dept. of Justice
4949 Broadway
Sacramento, CA 95820
Phone: (916) 227-3844

COLORADO
Scott Hromas
Director
Planning & Analysis Div.
Dept. of Corrections
2862 S. Circle
Colorado Springs, CO 80906
Phone: (719) 579-9580
Fax: (719) 226-4755

CONNECTICUT
James M. Thomas
Director of Justice Planning
Ofc. of Policy & Mgmt.
Policy Dev. & Planning Div.
450 Capitol Ave., #52-CPD
P.O. Box 341441
Hartford, CT 06134
Phone: (860) 418-6394
Fax: (860) 418-6496
E-mail: james.thomas@po.state.ct.us

DELAWARE
Thomas J. Quinn
Executive Director
Criminal Justice Planning Comm.
820 N. French St.
Wilmington, DE 19801
Phone: (302) 577-3431

DISTRICT OF COLUMBIA

FLORIDA
Donna Ozzell
Director
Criminal Justice Info.
Dept. of Law Enforcement
P.O. Box 1489
Tallahassee, FL 32302
Phone: (850) 488-3961
Fax: (850) 414-1512

GEORGIA
Martha Gilland
Director
Criminal Justice Coordinating Council
503 Oak Pl., #540
Atlanta, GA 30349
Phone: (404) 559-4949

GUAM
James M. Marques
Chief of Police
Police Dept.
233 Central Ave.
Tiyan, GU 96913
Phone: (671) 475-8505
Fax: (671) 472-4036

HAWAII
Liane M. Moriyama
Administrator
Criminal Justice Data Ctr.
Dept. of Attorney Gen.
465 S. King St., Rm. 101
Honolulu, HI 96813
Phone: (808) 587-3100
Fax: (808) 587-3109

IDAHO
Jerry Brannon
Chief
Bur. of Criminal Identification
Dept. of Law Enforcement
P.O. Box 700
Meridian, ID 83680-0700
Phone: (208) 884-7130

ILLINOIS
Candice Kane
Acting Director
Criminal Justice Info. Authority
120 S. Riverside Plz., #1016
Chicago, IL 60606
Phone: (312) 793-8550
Fax: (312) 793-8422

INDIANA
Fred C. Pryor
Commander
Info. Technology Div.
State Police
N340, 100 N. Senate Ave.
Indianapolis, IN 46204
Phone: (317) 232-8318
Fax: (317) 232-0652

IOWA
Richard G. Moore
Administrator
Criminal & Juvenile Justice Planning Agency
Lucas State Ofc. Bldg., 1st Fl.
321 E. 12th St.
Des Moines, IA 50319
Phone: (515) 282-5816

KANSAS
Barbara S. Tombs
Executive Director
Sentencing Comm.
700 SW Jackson St., Ste. 501
Topeka, KS 66603-3757
Phone: (785) 296-0923
Fax: (785) 296-0927

KENTUCKY
Gary Rose
Commissioner
State Police
Justice Cabinet
919 Versailles Rd.
Frankfort, KY 40601
Phone: (502) 695-6300
Fax: (502) 573-1479

LOUISIANA
Michael A. Ranatza
Director
Comm. on Law Enforcement
Ofc. of the Governor
1885 Wooddale Blvd., Rm. 708
Baton Rouge, LA 70806
Phone: (225) 925-4418
Fax: (225) 925-1998

MAINE
Michael F. Kelley
Commissioner
Dept. of Public Safety
42 State House Station
Augusta, ME 04333
Phone: (207) 624-7068

MARYLAND
William Hicks
Director
Computer Operations
Public Safety & Correctional Services
1201 Reisterstown Rd.
Baltimore, MD 21208
Phone: (410) 653-4569
Fax: (410) 653-4526

MASSACHUSETTS
Kevin Harrington
Executive Director
Criminal Justice Training Council
411 Waverley Oaks Rd., Ste. 325
Waltham, MA 02452
Phone: (617) 727-7827
Fax: (617) 642-6898

MICHIGAN
Mike Robinson
Director
Dept. of State Police
714 S. Harrison Rd.
E. Lansing, MI 48823
Phone: (517) 336-6157

MINNESOTA
Nicholas V. O'Hara
Superintendent
Bur. of Criminal Apprehension
Dept. of Public Safety
1246 Univ. Ave.
St. Paul, MN 55104
Phone: (651) 642-0600
Fax: (651) 642-0633
E-mail: nicholas.o'hara@state.mn.us

MISSISSIPPI
Jim Ingram
Commissioner
Dept. of Public Safety
Hwy. Patrol Bldg., I-55 N.
P.O. Box 958
Jackson, MS 39205
Phone: (601) 987-1490
Fax: (601) 987-1498

MISSOURI
Gerald E. Wethington
Director of Information Systems
State Hwy. Patrol
Dept. of Public Safety
1510 E. Elm
P.O. Box 568
Jefferson City, MO 65102
Phone: (573) 526-6200
Fax: (573) 751-9382
E-mail: gwething@mail.state.mo.us

MONTANA
Ellis E. Kiser
Executive Director
Crime Control Div.
Dept. of Justice
303 N. Roberts, Rm. 463
Helena, MT 59620-1408
Phone: (406) 444-3604
Fax: (406) 444-4722

NEBRASKA
Allen Curtis
Executive Director
Comm. on Law Enforcement & Criminal Justice
P.O. Box 94946
Lincoln, NE 68509
Phone: (402) 471-2194
Fax: (402) 471-2837

NEVADA
Dennis Debacco
Program Manager
Parole & Probation
State Hwy. Patrol
555 Wright Way
Carson City, NV 89711
Phone: (775) 684-4660

NEW HAMPSHIRE
John J. Barthelmes
Director
Div. of State Police
Criminal Records Ofc.
Safety Dept.
10 Hazen Dr.
Concord, NH 03305-0002
Phone: (603) 271-3636
Fax: (603) 271-1153

NEW JERSEY
Paul H. Zoubek
Director
Div. of Criminal Justice
Dept. of Law & Public Safety
P.O. Box 085
Trenton, NJ 08625-0085
Phone: (609) 984-6500

NEW MEXICO
Joe Cantergiani
MIS Bureau Chief
Corrections
P.O. Box 27116
Sante Fe, NM 87502
Phone: (505) 827-8605
Fax: (505) 827-8634

NEW YORK
Katherine N. Lapp
Director of Criminal Justice
Div. of Criminal Justice Services
Executive Park Tower
Stuyvesant Plz.
Albany, NY 12203
Phone: (518) 457-1260
Fax: (518) 457-3089

NORTH CAROLINA
Ron Hawley
Assistant Director
State Bur. of Investigation
Dept. of Justice
407 N. Blount St.
Raleigh, NC 27601-1073
Phone: (919) 733-3171
Fax: (919) 715-2692

NORTH DAKOTA
Bill Broer
Director
Bur. of Criminal Investigation
Attorney Gen's. Ofc.
P.O. Box 1054
Bismarck, ND 58502-1054
Phone: (701) 328-5500
Fax: (701) 328-5510
E-mail: msmail.bbroer@ranch.state.nd.us

NORTHERN MARIANA ISLANDS
Harry C. Blanco
Executive Director
Criminal Justice Planning Agency
Dept. of Public Safety
P.O. Box 1133 CK
Saipan, MP 96950
Phone: (670) 664-4557
Fax: (670) 322-1066
E-mail: harry.cjpa@saipan.com

OHIO
Ted Alnay
Superintendent
Criminal Identification & Investigation Section
P.O. Box 365
London, OH 43140
Phone: (614) 466-8204
Fax: (614) 852-4453

OKLAHOMA
Paul O'Connell
Director
Criminal Justice Resources Ctr.
Dept. of Corrections
5500 N. Western Ave., Ste. 245
Oklahoma City, OK 73118
Phone: (405) 858-7025
Fax: (405) 858-7040

OREGON
David Yardell
Manager
Law Enforcement Data System
State Police
400 Public Services Bldg.
955 Ctr. St., NE, 5th Fl.
Salem, OR 97310
Phone: (503) 378-3054
Fax: (503) 363-8249

PENNSYLVANIA
Paul Evanko
Commissioner
State Police
1800 Elmerton Ave.
Harrisburg, PA 17110
Phone: (717) 783-5558
Fax: (717) 787-2948

PUERTO RICO
David Gonzalez
Director
Statistics
Dept. of Justice
P.O. Box 192
San Juan, PR 00902
Phone: (787) 721-2900
Fax: (787) 725-6144

RHODE ISLAND
Joseph Smith
Executive Director
Governor's Justice Comm.
Administration Bldg.
1 Capitol Hill, 4th Fl.
Providence, RI 02908
Phone: (401) 222-2620

SOUTH CAROLINA
Nita Danenburg
Director
Criminal Justice Info. Communications Systems
Dept. of Law Enforcement
P.O. Box 21398
Columbia, SC 29221
Phone: (803) 896-7051

SOUTH DAKOTA
Doug Lake
Director
Div. of Criminal Investigation
Ofc. of the Attorney Gen.
500 E. Capitol Ave.
Pierre, SD 57501-5070
Phone: (605) 773-3332
Fax: (605) 773-4629

TENNESSEE

TEXAS
Tony Fabelo
Executive Director
Criminal Justice Policy Council
P.O. Box 13332
Austin, TX 78711-3332
Phone: (512) 463-1810
Fax: (512) 475-4843

U.S. VIRGIN ISLANDS
Franz A. Christian, Sr.
Acting Commissioner
Police Dept.
8172 Sub Base
St. Thomas, VI 00802
Phone: (340) 774-6400
Fax: (340) 776-3317

UTAH
Stuart Smith
Bureau Chief
Criminal Identification Bur.
Dept. of Public Safety
4501 S. 2700 W., 2nd Fl.
Salt Lake City, UT 84119
Phone: (801) 965-4570
Fax: (801) 965-4749
E-mail: ssmith1.psmain@state.ut.us

VERMONT
Gregory R. Schlueter
Director
Criminal Info. Ctr.
Dept. of Public Safety
P.O. Box 189
Waterbury, VT 05676
Phone: (802) 244-8727
Fax: (802) 244-1106

VIRGINIA
Joseph B. Benedetti
Director
Dept. of Criminal Justice Services
8th St. Ofc. Bldg., 10th Fl.
805 E. Broad St.
Richmond, VA 23219
Phone: (804) 786-8718
Fax: (804) 786-0588

WASHINGTON
John Broome
Division Commander
Criminal Records Div.
State Patrol
P.O. Box 42622
Tumwater, WA 98501
Phone: (360) 705-5352
Fax: (360) 664-0654

WEST VIRGINIA
Gary L. Edgell
Superintendent
Public Safety Div.
725 Jefferson Rd.
S. Charleston, WV 25309-1698
Phone: (304) 746-2111
Fax: (304) 746-2230

WISCONSIN
Michael Roberts
Director
Crime Information Bur.
Dept. of Justice
123 W. Washington Ave.
Madison, WI 53703
Phone: (608) 266-7314
Fax: (608) 267-2223

WYOMING
Tom Pagel
Director
Criminal Investigation Div.
Ofc. of the Attorney Gen.
316 W. 22nd
Cheyenne, WY 82002
Phone: (307) 777-7181

Criminal Justice Planning—

Plans improvements to crime prevention, crime control and criminal justice in the state.

ALABAMA
Doug Miller
Chief
Law Enforcement/Traffic Safety Div.
Dept. of Economic & Community Affairs
P.O. Box 5690
Montgomery, AL 36130
Phone: (334) 242-5843
Fax: (334) 242-0712

ALASKA
Diane Schenker
Criminal Justice Planner
Dept. of Public Safety
5700 E. Tudor Rd.
Anchorage, AK 99507-1225
Phone: (907) 269-5092
Fax: (907) 269-5617

AMERICAN SAMOA
Alalamua Laauli Filoiali'i
Director
Criminal Justice Planning Agency
AS Govt.
Pago Pago, AS 96799
Phone: (684) 633-5221
Fax: (684) 633-7552

ARIZONA
Rex M. Holgerson
Director
Criminal Justice Comm.
3737 N. 7th St., Ste. 260
Phoenix, AZ 85007
Phone: (602) 230-0252

ARKANSAS
Tom Mars
Director
State Police
#1 State Police Plz.
Little Rock, AR 72209
Phone: (501) 618-8200
Fax: (501) 618-8222

CALIFORNIA
Ray Johnson
Executive Director
Criminal Justice Planning Ofc.
1130 K St., Ste. 300
Sacramento, CA 95814
Phone: (916) 324-9140

COLORADO
William Woodward
Director
Div. of Criminal Justice
Dept. of Public Safety
700 Kipling St., Ste. 3000
Denver, CO 80215
Phone: (303) 239-4442
Fax: (303) 239-4491

CONNECTICUT
Ann Moore
Undersecretary
Policy Dev. & Planning Div.
Ofc. of Policy & Mgmt.
P.O. Box 341441
Hartford, CT 06134-1441
Phone: (860) 418-6484

DELAWARE
Thomas J. Quinn
Executive Director
Criminal Justice Planning Comm.
820 N. French St.
Wilmington, DE 19801
Phone: (302) 577-3431

DISTRICT OF COLUMBIA

FLORIDA
Leon Lowry
Director
Criminal Justice Standards/Training
Dept. of Law Enforcement
P.O. Box 1489
Tallahassee, FL 32302
Phone: (850) 487-0491
Fax: (850) 922-5971

GEORGIA
Martha Gilland
Director
Criminal Justice Coordinating Council
503 Oak Pl., #540
Atlanta, GA 30349
Phone: (404) 559-4949

GUAM
Clifford A. Guzman
Director
Bur. of Planning
P.O. Box 2950
Hagatna, GU 96932
Phone: (671) 472-4201
Fax: (671) 477-1812

HAWAII
Laraine Koga
Administrator
Crime Prevention & Justice Assistance Div.
Dept. of Attorney Gen.
425 Queen St.
Honolulu, HI 96813-2903
Phone: (808) 586-1150
Fax: (808) 586-1373

IDAHO

ILLINOIS
Sam Nolen
Director
State Police
103 State Armory
Springfield, IL 62706
Phone: (217) 782-7263
Fax: (217) 785-2821

INDIANA
Catherine O'Connor
Director
Criminal Justice Institute
302 W. Washington St., Rm. E209
Indianapolis, IN 46204
Phone: (317) 232-1233
Fax: (317) 232-4979

IOWA
Richard G. Moore
Administrator
Criminal & Juvenile Justice Planning Agency
Lucas State Ofc. Bldg., 1st Fl.
321 E. 12th St.
Des Moines, IA 50319
Phone: (515) 282-5816

KANSAS
David Debenham
Deputy Attorney General
Criminal Litigation Div.
Judicial Ctr., 2nd Fl.
301 W. 10th St.
Topeka, KS 66612-1597
Phone: (785) 296-2215
Fax: (785) 296-6296

KENTUCKY
Robert F. Stephens
Secretary
Justice Cabinet
Bush Bldg.
403 Wapping
Frankfort, KY 40601
Phone: (502) 564-7554
Fax: (502) 564-4840

LOUISIANA
Michael A. Ranatza
Director
Comm. on Law Enforcement
Ofc. of the Governor
1885 Wooddale Blvd., Rm. 708
Baton Rouge, LA 70806
Phone: (225) 925-4418
Fax: (225) 925-1998

MAINE
Michael F. Kelley
Commissioner
Dept. of Public Safety
42 State House Station
Augusta, ME 04333
Phone: (207) 624-7068

MARYLAND
Michael A. Sarbanes
Executive Director
Governor's Ofc. of Crime Control & Prevention
Executive Dept.
300 E. Joppa Rd., Ste. 1105
Baltimore, MD 21286-3016
Phone: (410) 321-3521
Fax: (410) 321-3116

MASSACHUSETTS
Jane Perlov
Secretary
Executive Ofc. of Public Safety
100 Cambridge St., Rm. 2100
Boston, MA 02202
Phone: (617) 727-6300
Fax: (617) 727-5356

MICHIGAN
Mike Robinson
Director
Dept. of State Police
714 S. Harrison Rd.
E. Lansing, MI 48823
Phone: (517) 336-6157

MINNESOTA
Charlie Weaver
Commissioner
Dept. of Public Safety
NCL Tower, Ste. 1000
445 Minnesota St.
Minneapolis, MN 55101
Phone: (651) 296-6642
Fax: (651) 297-5728

MISSISSIPPI
Ron Sennett
Executive Director
Div. of Public Safety Planning
Dept. of Public Safety
P.O. Box 23039
Jackson, MS 39225-3039
Phone: (601) 359-7880
Fax: (601) 359-7832

MISSOURI
Gary B. Kempker
Director
Dept. of Public Safety
Truman Bldg., Rm. 870
P.O. Box 749
Jefferson City, MO 65102
Phone: (573) 751-4905
Fax: (573) 751-5399
E-mail: gary@dps.state.mo.us

MONTANA
Ellis E. Kiser
Executive Director
Crime Control Div.
Dept. of Justice
303 N. Roberts, Rm. 463
Helena, MT 59620-1408
Phone: (406) 444-3604
Fax: (406) 444-4722

NEBRASKA
Allen Curtis
Executive Director
Comm. on Law Enforcement & Criminal Justice
P.O. Box 94946
Lincoln, NE 68509
Phone: (402) 471-2194
Fax: (402) 471-2837

NEVADA
Bob Bayer
Director
Dept. of Prisons
P.O. Box 7011
Carson City, NV 89702
Phone: (775) 887-3285
Fax: (775) 687-6715

NEW HAMPSHIRE
Mark C. Thompson
Law Office Administrator
Ofc. of the Attorney Gen.
Justice Dept.
33 Capitol St.
Concord, NH 03301-6397
Phone: (603) 271-3658
Fax: (603) 271-2110

NEW JERSEY
Paul H. Zoubek
Director
Div. of Criminal Justice
Dept. of Law & Public Safety
P.O. Box 085
Trenton, NJ 08625-0085
Phone: (609) 984-6500

NEW MEXICO
Robert J. Perry
Secretary
Dept. of Corrections
P.O. Box 27116
Santa Fe, NM 87502-0116
Phone: (505) 827-8709
Fax: (505) 827-8220

NEW YORK
Katherine N. Lapp
Director of Criminal Justice
Div. of Criminal Justice Services
Executive Park Tower
Stuyvesant Plz.
Albany, NY 12203
Phone: (518) 457-1260
Fax: (518) 457-3089

NORTH CAROLINA
Rob Lubitz
Director
Governor's Crime Comm.
Dept. of Crime Control & Public Safety
1201 Front St., #200
Raleigh, NC 27609-7533
Phone: (919) 733-4564
Fax: (919) 733-4625

NORTH DAKOTA
Bill Broer
Director
Bur. of Criminal Investigation
Attorney Gen's. Ofc.
P.O. Box 1054
Bismarck, ND 58502-1054
Phone: (701) 328-5500
Fax: (701) 328-5510
E-mail: msmail.bbroer@ranch.state.nd.us

NORTHERN MARIANA ISLANDS
Harry C. Blanco
Executive Director
Criminal Justice Planning Agency
Dept. of Public Safety
P.O. Box 1133 CK
Saipan, MP 96950
Phone: (670) 664-4557
Fax: (670) 322-1066
E-mail: harry.cjpa@saipan.com

OHIO
John Bender
Director
Governor's Ofc. of Criminal Justice Services
400 E. Town St., Ste. 300
Columbus, OH 43215
Phone: (614) 466-7782
Fax: (614) 466-0308

OKLAHOMA

OREGON
Beverlee Venell
Director
Criminal Justice Services Div.
State Police
400 Public Service Bldg.
Salem, OR 97310
Phone: (503) 378-3720
Fax: (503) 378-6993

PENNSYLVANIA
Michael Fisher
Attorney General
Ofc. of the Attorney Gen.
Strawberry Sq., 16th Fl.
Harrisburg, PA 17120
Phone: (717) 787-3391
Fax: (717) 783-1107

PUERTO RICO
Jose A. Fuentes Agostini
Attorney General
Ofc. of the Attorney Gen.
P.O. Box 9020192
San Juan, PR 00902-0192
Phone: (787) 721-7700
Fax: (787) 724-4770

RHODE ISLAND
Joseph Smith
Executive Director
Governor's Justice Comm.
Administration Bldg.
1 Capitol Hill, 4th Fl.
Providence, RI 02908
Phone: (401) 222-2620

SOUTH CAROLINA
B. Boykin Rose
Director
Dept. of Public Safety
5400 Broad River Rd.
Columbia, SC 29212-3540
Phone: (803) 896-7839

SOUTH DAKOTA
Doug Lake
Director
Div. of Criminal Investigation
Ofc. of the Attorney Gen.
500 E. Capitol Ave.
Pierre, SD 57501-5070
Phone: (605) 773-3332
Fax: (605) 773-4629

TENNESSEE

TEXAS
Richard Nedelkoff
Director
Criminal Justice Div.
Ofc. of the Governor
P.O. Box 12428
Austin, TX 78711
Phone: (512) 463-1919
Fax: (512) 475-2440

U.S. VIRGIN ISLANDS
Franz A. Christian, Sr.
Acting Commissioner
Police Dept.
8172 Sub Base
St. Thomas, VI 00802
Phone: (340) 774-6400
Fax: (340) 776-3317

UTAH
Camille Anthony
Executive Director
Comm. on Criminal & Juvenile Justice
State Capitol, Rm. 101
Salt Lake City, UT 84114
Phone: (801) 538-1056
Fax: (801) 538-1024
E-mail: canthony@gov.state.ut.us

VERMONT
James Walton
Commissioner
Dept. of Public Safety
103 S. Main St.
Waterbury, VT 05671-2101
Phone: (802) 244-8718
Fax: (802) 244-1106
E-mail: jwalton@dps.state.vt.us

VIRGINIA
Joseph B. Benedetti
Director
Dept. of Criminal Justice Services
8th St. Ofc. Bldg., 10th Fl.
805 E. Broad St.
Richmond, VA 23219
Phone: (804) 786-8718
Fax: (804) 786-0588

WASHINGTON
Annette Sandberg
Chief
State Patrol
Administration Bldg.
P.O. Box 42601
Olympia, WA 98504-2601
Phone: (360) 753-6540
Fax: (360) 664-0663

WEST VIRGINIA
James Albert
Director
Criminal Justice & Hwy. Safety
Ofc. of Community & Individual Dev.
1204 Kanawha Blvd., E.
Charleston, WV 25301
Phone: (304) 558-8814

WISCONSIN
Jerry Baumbach
Executive Director
Ofc. of Justice Assistance
Dept. of Administration
131 W. Wilson, Ste. 202
Madison, WI 53702
Phone: (608) 266-3323
Fax: (608) 266-6676

WYOMING

Debt Management

Responsible for structuring debt issues.

ALABAMA
Henry Mabry
State Finance Director
State Capitol Bldg.
600 Dexter Ave., Ste. 105-N
Montgomery, AL 36104
Phone: (334) 242-7160
Fax: (334) 242-4488

ALASKA
Deven Mitchell
Acting Debt Manager
Treasury Div.
Dept. of Revenue
P.O. Box 114405
Juneau, AK 99811
Phone: (907) 465-2750
Fax: (907) 465-2394

AMERICAN SAMOA
Tifi Ale
Treasurer
Dept. of the Treasury
AS Govt.
Pago Pago, AS 96799
Phone: (684) 633-4155
Fax: (684) 633-4100

ARIZONA
Carol Springer
State Treasurer
Treasurer's Ofc.
1700 W. Washington, 1st Fl.
Phoenix, AZ 85007
Phone: (602) 542-1463
Fax: (602) 542-7176

ARKANSAS
Rush Deacon
Director
Dev. Finance Authority
100 Main St., Ste. 200
P.O. Box 8023
Little Rock, AR 72203-8023
Phone: (501) 682-5900
Fax: (501) 682-5939

CALIFORNIA
Bruce VanHouten
Director
Cash Mgmt. Div.
915 Capitol Mall, Rm. 107
Sacramento, CA 95814
Phone: (916) 653-3601

COLORADO
Larry E. Trujillo, Sr.
Executive Director
Support Services
Dept. of Personnel
1525 Sherman St., 2nd Fl.
Denver, CO 80203
Phone: (303) 866-6559
Fax: (303) 866-6569

CONNECTICUT

DELAWARE
Jack Markell
State Treasurer
Thomas Collins Bldg.
P.O. Box 1401
Dover, DE 19904
Phone: (302) 739-3382
Fax: (302) 739-5635

DISTRICT OF COLUMBIA
Thomas F. Huestis
Treasurer
Ofc. of Finance & Treasury
Ofc. of the Chief Financial Officer
1 Judiciary Sq.
441 4th St., NW, Ste. 360
Washington, DC 20001
Phone: (202) 727-6055
Fax: (202) 727-6049

FLORIDA
J. Ben Watkins, III
Director
State Board of Administration
Manager of Board Programs
P.O. Box 13300
Tallahassee, FL 32317-3300
Phone: (850) 488-4782
Fax: (850) 413-1315

GEORGIA
W. Daniel Ebersole
Treasurer
Ofc. of Treasury & Fiscal Services
1202 W. Tower
200 Piedmont Ave., SE
Atlanta, GA 30334
Phone: (404) 656-2168
Fax: (404) 656-9048

GUAM
Edward G. Untalan
Administrator
Economic Dev. Authority
ITC Bldg., Ste. 511
590 S. Marine Dr.
Tamuning, GU 96911
Phone: (671) 647-4332
Fax: (671) 649-4146

HAWAII
Neal Miyahira
Interim Director of Finance
Dept. of Budget & Finance
P.O. Box 150
Honolulu, HI 96810
Phone: (808) 586-1518
Fax: (808) 586-1976

IDAHO
Ron Crane
State Treasurer
102 State Capitol
Boise, ID 83720
Phone: (208) 334-3200
Fax: (208) 334-2543

ILLINOIS
Mike Colsch
Deputy Director
Bur. of the Budget
Ofc. of the Governor
108 State House
Springfield, IL 60706
Phone: (217) 782-4520
Fax: (217) 524-1514

INDIANA
Diana Hamilton
Director of Public Finance
Dev. Finance Authority
1 N. Capitol, Ste. 320
Indianapolis, IN 46204
Phone: (317) 233-4332
Fax: (317) 232-6786

IOWA
Michael L. Fitzgerald
State Treasurer
State Capitol Bldg.
Des Moines, IA 50319
Phone: (515) 281-5366
Fax: (515) 281-6962

KANSAS
Tim Shallenburger
State Treasurer
Landon State Ofc. Bldg.
900 SW Jackson St., Rm. 201-N
Topeka, KS 66612-1235
Phone: (785) 296-3171
Fax: (785) 296-7950

KENTUCKY
Gordon Mullis
Executive Director
Ofc. of Financial Mgmt. & Economic Analysis
Capitol Annex
700 Capitol Ave.
Frankfort, KY 40601
Phone: (502) 564-2924
Fax: (502) 564-7416

LOUISIANA
Ken Duncan
State Treasurer
P.O. Box 44154
Baton Rouge, LA 70804-0154
Phone: (225) 342-0010
Fax: (225) 342-5008

MAINE

MARYLAND
Richard N. Dixon
Treasurer
Ofc. of the State Treasurer
State Treasurer's Ofc.
Treasury Bldg., Rm. 109
Annapolis, MD 21401-1991
Phone: (410) 260-7160
Fax: (410) 974-3530
E-mail: rdixon@treasurer.state.md.us

MASSACHUSETTS
Shannon O'Brien
State Treasurer
Rm. 227 - State House
Boston, MA 02133
Phone: (617) 367-6900
Fax: (617) 248-0372

MICHIGAN
Mark Murray
Treasurer
Dept. of Treasury
P.O. Box 11097
Lansing, MI 48901
Phone: (517) 373-3223
Fax: (517) 335-1785

MINNESOTA

MISSISSIPPI
Margie Fanning
Director
Investments Div.
Dept. of Treasury
P.O. Box 138
Jackson, MS 39205
Phone: (601) 359-3600
Fax: (601) 359-2001

MISSOURI
Richard A. Hanson
Commissioner
Administration
Ofc. of Administration
State Capitol, Rm. 125
P.O. Box 809
Jefferson City, MO 65102
Phone: (573) 751-3311
Fax: (573) 751-1212
E-mail: hansod
@mail.oa.state.mo.us

MONTANA
Lois A. Menzies
Director & Ex Officio State Treasurer
Dept. of Administration
Rm. 155, Mitchell Bldg.
P.O. Box 200101
Helena, MT 59620-0101
Phone: (406) 444-2032
Fax: (406) 444-2812
E-mail: lmenzies@mt.gov

NEBRASKA

NEVADA
Brian Krolicki
State Treasurer
101 N. Carson St., Ste. 4
Carson City, NV 89701
Phone: (775) 684-5600
Fax: (775) 684-5623
E-mail: bkkrolicki
@treasurer.state.nv.us

NEW HAMPSHIRE
Georgie A. Thomas
State Treasurer
121 State House Annex
Concord, NH 03301
Phone: (603) 271-2621
Fax: (603) 271-3922
E-mail: gthomas@tec.nh.us

NEW JERSEY

NEW MEXICO
Victor Vigil
Director
Debt Mgmt.
Ofc. of State Treasurer
130 S. Capitol
Santa Fe, NM 87501
Phone: (505) 827-6400
Fax: (505) 827-6395

NEW YORK
H. Carl McCall
Comptroller
A.E. Smith Ofc. Bldg., 6th Fl.
Albany, NY 12236
Phone: (518) 474-3506
Fax: (518) 473-3004

NORTH CAROLINA
Harlan E. Boyles
State Treasurer
Albemarle Bldg.
325 N. Salisbury St.
Raleigh, NC 27603-1385
Phone: (919) 508-5176

NORTH DAKOTA
Rod Backman
Director
Ofc. of Mgmt. & Budget
600 E. Blvd. Ave., 4th Fl.
Bismarck, ND 58505-0400
Phone: (701) 328-2680
Fax: (701) 328-3230
E-mail: rbackman
@state.nd.us

NORTHERN MARIANA ISLANDS
Lucia DLG. Neilsen
Secretary of Finance
Finance & Accounting
Dept. of Finance
P.O. Box 5234 CHRB
Saipan, MP 96950
Phone: (670) 664-1198
Fax: (670) 664-1115

OHIO
Herb Kruse
Debt Coordinator
Ofc. of Budget & Mgmt.
30 E. Broad St., 34th Fl.
Columbus, OH 43266-0411
Phone: (614) 466-0691
Fax: (614) 466-3813

OKLAHOMA
Jim Josephs
State Bond Advisor
State Bond Advisor's Ofc.
301 NW 63rd, Ste. 225
Oklahoma City, OK 73116
Phone: (405) 521-6198
Fax: (405) 848-3314
E-mail: jjoseph
@oklaosf.state.ok.us

OREGON
Chuck Smith
Director
Debt Mgmt. Div.
State Treasury
100 L & I Bldg.
350 Winter St., NE
Salem, OR 97310-0840
Phone: (503) 378-4930
Fax: (503) 378-2870

PENNSYLVANIA
Arthur Heilman
Director
Bur. of Revenue, Cash Flow & Debt
Ofc. of the Budget
Bell Tower, 7th Fl.
303 Walnut St.
Harrisburg, PA 17120-0029
Phone: (717) 783-3086
Fax: (717) 787-1743

PUERTO RICO

RHODE ISLAND
Paul J. Tavares
Treasurer
State House, Rm. 102
Providence, RI 02903
Phone: (401) 222-2397

SOUTH CAROLINA
Grady L. Patterson, Jr.
State Treasurer
1200 Senate St.
Wade Hampton Bldg., 1st Fl.
Columbia, SC 29201
Phone: (803) 734-2635

SOUTH DAKOTA
Richard Butler
State Treasurer
212 State Capitol
500 E. Capitol Ave.
Pierre, SD 57501-5070
Phone: (605) 773-5070
Fax: (605) 773-3115

TENNESSEE
John Morgan
Comptroller of the Treasury
State Capitol, 1st Fl.
600 Charlotte
Nashville, TN 37243
Phone: (615) 741-2501
Fax: (615) 741-7328

TEXAS
Kimberly K. Edwards
Executive Director
Public Finance Authority
P.O. Box 12906
Austin, TX 78711-2047
Phone: (512) 463-5544
Fax: (512) 463-5501

U.S. VIRGIN ISLANDS

UTAH
Edward T. Alter
State Treasurer
215 State Capitol
Salt Lake City, UT 84114
Phone: (801) 538-1042
Fax: (801) 538-1465
E-mail: ealter.stmain
@state.ut.us

VERMONT
James H. Douglas
Treasurer
State Administration Bldg., 2nd Fl.
133 State St.
Montpelier, VT 05633-6200
Phone: (802) 828-2301
Fax: (802) 828-2772
E-mail: jdouglas
@tre.state.vt.us

VIRGINIA
Mary G. Morris
State Treasurer
Dept. of the Treasury
Monroe Bldg., 3rd Fl.
101 N. 14th St.
Richmond, VA 23219
Phone: (804) 225-2142
Fax: (804) 225-3187

WASHINGTON
Michael J. Murphy
State Treasurer
Legislative Bldg.
P.O. Box 40200
Olympia, WA 98504-0200
Phone: (360) 753-7139
Fax: (360) 586-6147
E-mail: MichaelJ
@TRE.WA.GOV

WEST VIRGINIA
Craig Slaughter
Executive Director
Investment Mgmt. Board
One Cantley Dr., Ste. 3
Charleston, WV 25314
Phone: (304) 558-5000
Fax: (304) 344-9284

WISCONSIN
Jack C. Voight
State Treasurer
1 S. Pinckney St., Ste. 550
P.O. Box 7871
Madison, WI 53707-7871
Phone: (608) 266-3712
Fax: (608) 266-2647
E-mail: Treasury
@mail.state.wi.us

WYOMING
Cynthia M. Lummis
State Treasurer
State Capitol Bldg.
Cheyenne, WY 82002
Phone: (307) 777-7408
Fax: (307) 777-5411

Developmentally Disabled—

Oversees the care, treatment and future service needs of the developmentally disabled.

ALABAMA
Myra Jones
Interim Executive Director
Developmental Disabilities Planning Council
Dept. of Mental Health & Mental Retardation
100 N. Union St., Ste. 498
Montgomery, AL 36130
Phone: (334) 242-3973
Fax: (334) 242-0797

ALASKA
Karl Brimner
Director
Div. of Mental Health & Developmental Disabilities
Dept. of Health & Social Services
P.O. Box 110620
Juneau, AK 99811-0620
Phone: (907) 465-3370
Fax: (907) 465-2668

AMERICAN SAMOA

ARIZONA
Roger Deshaies
Assistant Director
Developmental Disabilities Div.
Dept. of Economic Security
1789 W. Jefferson
Phoenix, AZ 85007
Phone: (602) 542-6853

ARKANSAS
Mike McCreight
Director
Developmental Disabilities Services
Human Services
Donaghey Plz. S., 5th Fl.
Little Rock, AR 72201
Phone: (501) 682-8662
Fax: (501) 682-8380

CALIFORNIA
Clifford Allenby
Director
Dept. of Developmental Services
1600 9th St., Rm. 240
Sacramento, CA 95814
Phone: (916) 654-1897

COLORADO
Charlie Allinson
Director
Developmental Disabilities Div.
Dept. of Human Services
3824 W. Princeton Cir.
Denver, CO 80236
Phone: (303) 866-7454
Fax: (303) 866-7470

CONNECTICUT

DELAWARE
Roseanne Griff-Cabelli
Part H Coordinator
Div. of Mgmt. Services
Dept. of Health & Social Services
1901 N. Dupont Hwy., Main Bldg.
New Castle, DE 19720
Phone: (302) 577-5647
Fax: (302) 577-4083

DISTRICT OF COLUMBIA
Arlene Robinson
Commissioner
Mental Health & Mental Retardation Services
Dept. of Human Services
Superior Courthouse
500 Indiana Ave., NW, 4475, 4th Fl.
Washington, DC 20001-2131
Phone: (202) 879-1040

FLORIDA
Charles Kimber
Assistant Secretary
Developmental Services
Dept. of Children & Family Services
1317 Winewood Blvd., Bldg. 3
Tallahassee, FL 32399-0700
Phone: (850) 488-4257
Fax: (850) 922-6456

GEORGIA
Eric Jacobson
Executive Director
Governor's Council on Developmentally Disabled
2 Peachtree St., 3rd Fl.
Atlanta, GA 30303
Phone: (404) 657-2126

GUAM
Joseph Artero-Cameron
Director
Dept. of Integrated Services for Individuals with Disabilities
1313 Central Ave.
Tiyan, GU 96913
Phone: (671) 478-4646
Fax: (671) 477-2892

Tomas J. Paulino
Executive Director
Developmental Disabilities Council
104 E. St., Tiyan
Barrigada, GU 96913
Phone: (671) 475-9127
Fax: (671) 475-9128
E-mail: lada@netpci.com

HAWAII
Stanley Yee
Chief
Developmentally Disabled Div.
Dept. of Health
P.O. Box 3378
Honolulu, HI 96801-3378
Phone: (808) 586-4583
Fax: (808) 586-7409

IDAHO
Paul Swatsenbarg
Chief
Developmental Disabilities Div.
Dept. of Health & Welfare
450 W. State St.
P.O. Box 83720
Boise, ID 83720-0036
Phone: (208) 334-5512
Fax: (208) 334-6664

ILLINOIS
Carl Suter
Director
Dept. of Rehab. Services
623 E. Adams St.
Springfield, IL 62794
Phone: (217) 785-0218
Fax: (217) 785-5753

INDIANA
Debra Simmons Wilson
Director
Div. of Disability, Aging & Rehab.
Family & Social Services Administration
402 W. Washington, Rm. W451
Indianapolis, IN 46204
Phone: (317) 232-1147
Fax: (317) 232-1240

IOWA
Harold Templeman
Administrator
Mental Health & Developmental Disabilities Div.
Hoover State Ofc. Bldg.
1300 E. Walnut
Des Moines, IA 50319
Phone: (515) 281-5126
Fax: (515) 281-4597

KANSAS
Sharon Brown
Director
Disability Determination Services
915 Harrison, 10th Fl.
Topeka, KS 66612-1596
Phone: (785) 267-4400
Fax: (785) 296-2545

KENTUCKY
Robin Hearn
Director
Disability Determination
Dept. for Health Services
102 Athletic Dr.
Frankfort, KY 40601
Phone: (502) 564-5028
Fax: (502) 564-5035

LOUISIANA
Sandee Winchell
Acting Executive Director
Developmental Disabilities Council
P.O. Box 3455
Baton Rouge, LA 70821-3455
Phone: (225) 342-6804
Fax: (225) 342-1970

MAINE
John G. Shattuck
Director
Bur. of Rehab.
Dept. of Human Services
11 State House Station
Augusta, ME 04333
Phone: (207) 624-5300

MARYLAND
Beatrice Rodgers
Director
Ofc. for Individuals with Disabilities
Executive Dept.
300 W. Lexington St.
Box 10
Baltimore, MD 21201-3435
Phone: (410) 333-3098
Fax: (410) 333-6674

MASSACHUSETTS
Daniel Shannon
Director
Developmental Disabilities
Executive Ofc. of Administration & Finance
174 Portland St., Ste. 5
Boston, MA 02114-1714
Phone: (617) 727-4178
Fax: (617) 727-1174

MICHIGAN
James K. Haveman, Jr.
Director
Dept. of Community Health
Louis Cass Bldg.
320 S. Walnut
Lansing, MI 48913
Phone: (517) 373-3500
Fax: (517) 335-3090

MINNESOTA
Shirley Patterson
Director
Community Supports for Minnesotans with Disabilities
Dept. of Human Services
444 Lafayette Rd.
St. Paul, MN 55155
Phone: (651) 296-9139
Fax: (651) 282-9922
E-mail: shirley.patterson@state.mn.us

MISSISSIPPI
Ed Butler
Executive Director
Developmental Disabilities Planning Council
Dept. of Mental Health
1101 Robert E. Lee Bldg.
Jackson, MS 39201
Phone: (601) 359-1288
Fax: (601) 359-6295

MISSOURI
John Solomon
Director
Div. of Mental Retardation & Developmental Disabilities
Dept. of Mental Health
P.O. Box 687
Jefferson City, MO 65102
Phone: (573) 751-8676
Fax: (573) 751-9207
E-mail: solomj@mail.dmh.state.mo.us

MONTANA
Joe Mathews
Administrator
Disability Services Div.
Dept. of Public Health & Human Services
P.O. Box 4210
Helena, MT 59604
Phone: (406) 444-2591
Fax: (406) 444-3632

NEBRASKA
Cathy Anderson
SE Area Administrator & Developmental Disabilities Administrator
Dept. of Health & Human Services
P.O. Box 94728
Lincoln, NE 68509
Phone: (402) 479-5110
Fax: (402) 479-5162

NEVADA
Carlos Brandenburg
Administrator
Mental Hygiene & Retardation
Dept. of Human Resources
Kinkaid Bldg., Rm. 602
505 E. King St.
Carson City, NV 89701-3790
Phone: (775) 684-5943
Fax: (775) 684-5966

NEW HAMPSHIRE
Alan Robichaud
Executive Director
Developmental Disabilities Council
Health & Human Services
10 Ferry St., #315
Concord, NH 03301-5081
Phone: (603) 271-3236
Fax: (603) 271-1156

NEW JERSEY
Krystal Odell
Director
Div. of Developmental Disability
Dept. of Human Services
50 E. State St.
P.O. Box 726
Trenton, NJ 08625
Phone: (609) 292-7260
Fax: (609) 292-6610

NEW MEXICO
Ramona Flores-Lopez
Director
Long Term Services Div.
Dept. of Health
P.O. Box 26110
Santa Fe, NM 87502
Phone: (505) 827-2574
Fax: (505) 827-2455

NEW YORK
Thomas A. Maul
Commissioner
Dept. of Mental Retardation & Developmental Disabilities
44 Holland Ave.
Albany, NY 12229
Phone: (518) 473-1997
Fax: (518) 473-1271

NORTH CAROLINA
Holly Riddle
Executive Director
Council on Developmentally Disabled
Dept. of Health & Human Services
1001 Navaho Dr., #GL103
Raleigh, NC 27609-7318
Phone: (919) 850-2833
Fax: (919) 850-2895

NORTH DAKOTA
Gene Hysjulien
Director
Developmental Disabilities
Dept. of Human Services
600 S. 2nd St., Ste. 1-B
Bismarck, ND 58504-5729
Phone: (701) 328-8930
Fax: (701) 328-8969
E-mail: sohysg@state.nd.us

NORTHERN MARIANA ISLANDS
Thomas J. Camacho
Executive Director
Developmental Disabilities Planning Ofc.
Ofc. of the Governor
P.O. Box 2565
Saipan, MP 96950
Phone: (670) 323-3014
Fax: (670) 322-4168
E-mail: dd.council@saipan.com

OHIO
Kenneth W. Ritchey
Director
Dept. of Mental Retardation & Developmental Disabilities
30 E. Broad St., 12th Fl.
Columbus, OH 43266-0415
Phone: (614) 466-5214
Fax: (614) 644-5013

OKLAHOMA
Jim Nicholson
Director
Developmental Disabilities Services Div.
P.O. Box 25352
Oklahoma City, OK 73125
Phone: (405) 521-6267
Fax: (405) 522-3037

OREGON
James D. Toews
Assistant Administrator
Developmental Disabilities Services
Mental Health & Developmental Disabilities Services Div.
2575 Bittern St., NE
Salem, OR 97310
Phone: (503) 945-9819
Fax: (503) 373-7274

PENNSYLVANIA

PUERTO RICO
David Cruz
Developmentally Disabled Procurator
Ofc. of the Procurator
P.O. Box 41309
San Juan, PR 00940-1309
Phone: (787) 721-4299
Fax: (787) 721-2455

Angie Varela
Secretary
Dept. of Social Services
P.O. Box 11398
San Juan, PR 00910
Phone: (787) 722-7400
Fax: (787) 723-1223

RHODE ISLAND
Christine Ferguson
Director
Dept. of Human Services
600 New London Ave.
Cranston, RI 02920
Phone: (401) 462-2121
Fax: (401) 462-3677

SOUTH CAROLINA
Charles Lang
Deputy Director
Div. of Human Services
Ofc. of the Governor
1205 Pendleton St., Rm. 372
Columbia, SC 29201
Phone: (803) 734-0465

SOUTH DAKOTA
Kim Malsam-Rysdom
Director
Div. of Developmental Disabilities
Dept. of Human Services
Hillsview Plz.
500 E. Capitol Ave.
Pierre, SD 57501
Phone: (605) 773-3438
Fax: (605) 773-5483

TENNESSEE
Carl Brown
Assistant Commissioner
Div. of Rehab. Services
Dept. of Human Services
Citizen's Plz. Bldg., 15th Fl.
400 Deaderick St.
Nashville, TN 37248-6000
Phone: (615) 313-4714
Fax: (615) 741-4165

TEXAS
Pat Pound
Executive Director
Cmte. on People with Disabilities
Ofc. of the Governor
P.O. Box 12428
Austin, TX 78711
Phone: (512) 463-5739
Fax: (512) 463-5745

U.S. VIRGIN ISLANDS
Sedonie Halbert
Commissioner
Dept. of Human Services
Knud Hansen Complex, Bldg. A
1303 Hospital Grounds
St. Thomas, VI 00802
Phone: (340) 774-0930
Fax: (340) 774-3466

UTAH
Joseph Gordon
Superintendent
State Dev. Ctr.
895 N. 900 E.
American Fork, UT 84003
Phone: (801) 763-4091
Fax: (801) 763-4024
E-mail: jgordon.hsusdc@state.ut.us

VERMONT
Charles Moseley
Director
Div. of Mental Retardation
Agency of Human Services
103 S. Main St.
Waterbury, VT 05671-1601
Phone: (802) 241-2648
Fax: (802) 241-3052
E-mail: charles@dmh.state.vt.us

VIRGINIA
Richard E. Kellogg
Commissioner
Dept. of Mental Health, Mental Retardation & Substance Abuse Services
109 Governor St., Rm. 1301-A
Richmond, VA 23219
Phone: (804) 786-5682
Fax: (804) 371-6638

WASHINGTON
Timothy Brown
Director
Developmental Disabilities Services
Dept. of Social & Health Services
P.O. Box 45310
Olympia, WA 98504-5310
Phone: (360) 902-8484
Fax: (360) 902-8482

WEST VIRGINIA
Donna Heuneman
Director
Developmental Disabilities Planning
110 Stockton St.
Charleston, WV 25312-2521
Phone: (304) 558-0416
Fax: (304) 558-0941

WISCONSIN
Thomas Alt
Administrator
Care & Treatment Facilities
Dept. of Health & Human Services
1 W. Wilson, Rm. 850
P.O. Box 7850
Madison, WI 53703
Phone: (608) 266-8740
Fax: (608) 266-2579

WYOMING
Robert T. Clabby, II
Administrator
Div. of Developmental Disabilities
Dept. of Health
Herschler Bldg., 1st Fl.
122 W. 25th St.
Cheyenne, WY 82002
Phone: (307) 777-6047

Drinking Water

Responsible for public drinking water supplies in the state.

ALABAMA
Charles Horn
Chief
Water Supply Branch
Water Div.
1751 Cong. Dickinson Dr.
P.O. Box 301463
Montgomery, AL 36130-1463
Phone: (334) 271-7773
Fax: (334) 279-3051

ALASKA
James Weise
Program Manager
Div. of Environmental Quality, Drinking Water & Wastewater Section
Dept. of Environmental Conservation
555 Cordova St.
Anchorage, AK 99501
Phone: (907) 269-7647
Fax: (907) 269-7655

AMERICAN SAMOA
Abe U. Malae
Executive Director
Power Authority
AS Govt.
Pago Pago, AS 96799
Phone: (684) 644-5251
Fax: (684) 644-5005

ARIZONA
Peggy Guichard-Watters
Program Manager
Compliance Section, Water Quality
Dept. of Environmental Quality
3033 N. Central
Phoenix, AZ 85012
Phone: (602) 207-2305

ARKANSAS
Harold Seifert
Director
Engineering Div.
Dept. of Health
4815 W. Markham St.
Little Rock, AR 72205-3867
Phone: (501) 661-2623
Fax: (501) 661-2032

CALIFORNIA
David P. Spath
Chief
Div. of Drinking Water & Environment
Dept. of Health Services
P.O. Box 942732, MS 396
Sacramento, CA 94234-7320
Phone: (916) 322-2308

COLORADO
David Holm
Director
Water Quality Control Div.
Dept. of Public Health & Environment
4300 Cherry Creek Dr., S.
Denver, CO 80246-1530
Phone: (303) 692-3500
Fax: (303) 782-0390

CONNECTICUT
Gerald R. Iwan
Chief
Water Supply
Dept. of Health Services
450 Capitol Ave., MS# 51WAT
P.O. Box 340308
Hartford, CT 06134-0308
Phone: (860) 509-7333

DELAWARE
Gerald L. Esposito
Director
Div. of Water Resources
Dept. of Natural Resources & Environmental Control
89 Kings Hwy.
Dover, DE 19901
Phone: (302) 739-4860
Fax: (302) 739-3491

DISTRICT OF COLUMBIA
Jerry Johnson
General Manager
Water & Sewer Authority
5000 Overlook Ave., SW
Washington, DC 20032
Phone: (202) 767-7651

FLORIDA
Mimi Drew
Director
Div. of Water Facilities
Dept. of Environmental Protection
2600 Blairstone Rd.
Tallahassee, FL 32399-2400
Phone: (850) 487-1855
Fax: (850) 487-3618

GEORGIA
Nolton Johnson
Branch Chief
Water Protection Branch
Dept. of Natural Resources
Twin Towers, E., #1362
205 Butler St., Ste. 1058
Atlanta, GA 30334
Phone: (404) 656-4713

GUAM
Richard Quintanilla
General Manager
Waterworks Authority
126 Lower E. Sunset Blvd., Tiyan
P.O. Box 3010
Hagatna, GU 96932
Phone: (671) 479-7823
Fax: (671) 649-0158

HAWAII
Gary Gill
Deputy Director
Environmental Health Administration
Dept. of Health
1250 Punchbowl St.
Honolulu, HI 96813
Phone: (808) 586-4424
Fax: (808) 586-4444

IDAHO
Lance Nielsen
Program Manager
Drinking Water Program
1410 N. Hilton St.
Boise, ID 83706-1255
Phone: (208) 373-0502

ILLINOIS
Roger Selburg
Manager
Div. of Public Water Supply
Environmental Protection Agency
1340 N. 9th St.
Springfield, IL 62703
Phone: (217) 785-8653

INDIANA
Matt Rueff
Assistant Commissioner
Ofc. of Water Mgmt.
Dept. of Environmental Mgmt.
P.O. Box 6015
Indianapolis, IN 46206-6015
Phone: (317) 232-8476
Fax: (317) 232-8406

IOWA
Dennis Alt
Supervisor
Water Supply Section
Surface & Groundwater Protection
Wallace State Ofc. Bldg.
E. 9th & Grand Aves.
Des Moines, IA 50319-0034
Phone: (515) 281-8998

KANSAS
Karl Mueldener
Director
Bur. of Water
Dept. of Health & Environment
Forbes Field Bldg. 283
6700 SW Topeka Blvd.
Topeka, KS 66619
Phone: (785) 296-5500
Fax: (785) 296-5509

KENTUCKY
Keith Phillips
Director
Div. of Water
Natural Resources & Environmental Protection Cabinet
14 Reilly Rd.
Frankfort, KY 40601
Phone: (502) 564-3410
Fax: (502) 564-4245

LOUISIANA
Bobby Savoie
Director
Environmental Health Services
Ofc. of Public Health
6867 Bluebonnet
Baton Rouge, LA 70810
Phone: (225) 763-3590
Fax: (225) 763-5552

MAINE
Clough Toppan
Director
Div. of Health Engineering
Dept. of Human Services
11 State House Station
Augusta, ME 04333
Phone: (207) 287-5338

MARYLAND
Saeid Kasraei
Program Administrator
Public Drinking Water Program
Dept. of the Environment
2500 Broening Hwy.
Baltimore, MD 21224
Phone: (410) 631-3702
Fax: (410) 631-3157
E-mail: skasraei@mde.state.md.us

MASSACHUSETTS
David Terry
Program Director
Drinking Water Program
Dept. of Environmental Protection
1 Winter St., 6th Fl.
Boston, MA 02108
Phone: (617) 292-5770
Fax: (617) 292-5696

MICHIGAN
Flint Watt
Chief
Drinking Water & Radiological Protection Div.
Dept. of Environmental Quality
P.O. Box 30630
Lansing, MI 48909-8130
Phone: (517) 335-9216
Fax: (517) 335-8298

MINNESOTA
Gary L. Englund
Program Manager
Drinking Water Protection
Health Dept.
121 E. 7th Pl.
P.O. Box 64975
St. Paul, MN 55164-0975
Phone: (651) 215-0746
Fax: (651) 215-0775
E-mail: gary.englund@health.state.mn.us

MISSISSIPPI
David Mitchell
Chief
Water Supply Div.
Dept. of Health
P.O. Box 1700
Jackson, MS 39215
Phone: (601) 960-7518
Fax: (601) 354-6115

MISSOURI
Jerry L. Lane
Director
Public Drinking Water Program
Dept. of Natural Resources
Jefferson Bldg., Rm. 315
P.O. Box 176
Jefferson City, MO 65102
Phone: (573) 751-5331
Fax: (573) 751-3110
E-mail: nrlanej@mail.dnr.state.mo.us

MONTANA
Jon Dillard
Chief
Community Services Bur.
Dept. of Environmental Quality
P.O. Box 200901
Helena, MT 59620-0901
Phone: (406) 444-4400
Fax: (406) 444-4386

NEBRASKA
Jack L. Daniel
Health Section Administrator
Health & Human Services, Regulation & Licensure
P.O. Box 95007
Lincoln, NE 68509
Phone: (402) 471-0510
Fax: (402) 471-6436

NEVADA

NEW HAMPSHIRE
Harry Stewart
Director
Water Div.
Environmental Services
P.O. Box 95
Concord, NH 03302-0095
Phone: (603) 271-3503
Fax: (603) 271-2867

NEW JERSEY
Thomas G. Baxter
Executive Director
Water Supply Authority
Dept. of Environmental Protection
P.O. Box 5196
Clinton, NJ 08809-0196
Phone: (908) 638-6121
Fax: (908) 638-6679

NEW MEXICO
Robert Gallegos
Bureau Chief
Drinking Water Bur.
Dept. of Environment
525 Camino de las Marquez
P.O. Box 26110
Santa Fe, NM 87502
Phone: (505) 827-2778
Fax: (505) 827-7545
E-mail: robertgallegos@nmenv.state.nm.us

NEW YORK
Michael Burke
Director
Bur. of Public Water Supply Protection
Dept. of Health
2 Univ. Pl., Rm. 410
Albany, NY 12203
Phone: (518) 458-6731
Fax: (518) 458-6732

NORTH CAROLINA
Linda Sewall
Director
Environmental Health
Dept. of Environment & Natural Resources
2728 Capitol Blvd.
Raleigh, NC 27604
Phone: (919) 733-2321
Fax: (919) 715-3242

NORTH DAKOTA
Jack Long
Professional Engineer/Director
Municipal Facilities
Environmental Health Section
P.O. Box 5520
Bismarck, ND 58506-5520
Phone: (701) 328-5211
Fax: (701) 328-5200
E-mail: jlong@state.nd.us

NORTHERN MARIANA ISLANDS
Timothy P. Villagomez
Executive Director
Commonwealth Utilities Corp.
Ofc. of the Governor
Lower Base
P.O. Box 1220
Saipan, MP 96950
Phone: (670) 235-7025
Fax: (670) 235-6152

OHIO
Kirk Leifheit
Acting Chief
Div. of Drinking & Ground Waters
Environmental Protection Agency
122 S. Front St.
P.O. Box 1049
Columbus, OH 43216
Phone: (614) 644-2752
Fax: (614) 644-2909

OKLAHOMA
John Craig
Chief
Water Quality Services
Environmental Health Services
1000 NE 10th St.
Oklahoma City, OK 73117
Phone: (405) 702-6100
Fax: (405) 702-8101

OREGON
David Leland
Manager
Div. of Health
Drinking Water Administration
800 NE Oregon St.
Portland, OR 97232
Phone: (503) 731-4010
Fax: (503) 731-4077

PENNSYLVANIA
Glenn E. Maurer
Director
Bur. of Water Quality Protection
Dept. of Environmental Resources
400 Market St., 11th Fl.
Harrisburg, PA 17105
Phone: (717) 787-2666
Fax: (717) 772-5156

PUERTO RICO
Carmen Feliciano
Secretary
Dept. of Health
P.O. Box 70184
San Juan, PR 00936-0184
Phone: (787) 274-7601
Fax: (787) 250-6547

RHODE ISLAND
June Swallow
Chief
Water Supply
Dept. of Health
3 Capitol Hill
Providence, RI 02908
Phone: (401) 222-6867

SOUTH CAROLINA
Alton C. Boozer
Chief
Bur. of Water
Dept. of Health & Environmental Control
2600 Bull St.
Columbia, SC 29201
Phone: (803) 898-4300

SOUTH DAKOTA
Darron Busch
Administrator
Div. of Land & Water Quality
Dept. of Environment & Natural Resources
523 E. Capitol Ave.
Pierre, SD 57501
Phone: (605) 773-3754
Fax: (605) 773-5286

TENNESSEE
W. David Draughon, Jr.
Director
Div. of Water Supply
Dept. of Environment & Conservation
401 Church St.
Nashville, TN 37247
Phone: (615) 532-0191
Fax: (615) 532-0503

TEXAS
Ken Peterson
Deputy Director
Water Resource Mgmt.
Natural Resources Conservation
12100 Park 35 Cir.
Austin, TX 78711-3087
Phone: (512) 239-4300
Fax: (512) 239-4303

U.S. VIRGIN ISLANDS
Raymond George
Executive Director
Water & Power Authority
P.O. Box 1400
St. Thomas, VI 00804
Phone: (340) 774-3552
Fax: (340) 774-3422

UTAH
Kevin Brown
Director
Div. of Drinking Water
Dept. of Environmental Quality
150 N. 1950 W.
Salt Lake City, UT 84114-4830
Phone: (801) 536-4208
Fax: (801) 536-4211
E-mail: kbrown@deq.state.ut.us

VERMONT
Jay Rutherford
Director
Groundwater Mgmt. Section
Water Supply Div.
103 S. Main St.
Waterbury, VT 05671-0403
Phone: (802) 241-3434
Fax: (802) 241-3284

VIRGINIA
E. Anne Peterson
Acting Commissioner
Dept. of Health
Main St. Station, Rm. 214
1500 E. Main St.
Richmond, VA 23219
Phone: (804) 786-3561
Fax: (804) 786-4616

WASHINGTON
Gregg Gruenfelder
Director
Div. of Drinking Water
Dept. of Health
P.O. Box 47822
Olympia, WA 98504-7822
Phone: (360) 236-3100
Fax: (360) 236-2252

WEST VIRGINIA
Donald A. Kuntz
Director
Environmental Engineering Div.
Ofc. of Environmental Health Services
1800 Washington St., E.
Charleston, WV 25305
Phone: (304) 558-2981
Fax: (304) 558-1291

WISCONSIN
Ron Kazmierczach
Acting Director
Drinking Water & Ground Water
Dept. of Natural Resources
101 S. Webster St., DG/12
P.O. Box 7921
Madison, WI 53703
Phone: (608) 267-7651
Fax: (608) 267-7650

WYOMING
Howard Hutchings
Director
Environmental Health
Dept. of Health & Social Services
Hathaway Bldg., Rm. 482
2300 Capitol Ave.
Cheyenne, WY 82002
Phone: (307) 777-6017

Economic Development

Responsible for efforts designed to encourage industry to locate, develop and expand in the state.

ALABAMA
Dewayne Freeman
Director
Dept. of Economic & Community Affairs
P.O. Box 5690
Montgomery, AL 36103-5690
Phone: (334) 242-5591
Fax: (334) 242-5099

ALASKA
Greg Wolf
Director
Div. of Trade & Dev.
Dept. of Commerce & Economic Dev.
3601 C St., Ste. 700
Anchorage, AK 99503
Phone: (907) 269-8110
Fax: (907) 465-8125

AMERICAN SAMOA
Aliimau Scanlan, Jr.
Director
Dept. of Commerce
AS Govt.
Pago Pago, AS 96799
Phone: (684) 633-5155
Fax: (684) 633-4195

ARIZONA
Jackie Vieh
Director
Dept. of Commerce
3800 N. Central Ave., Ste. 1500
Phoenix, AZ 85012
Phone: (602) 280-1306
Fax: (602) 280-1302

ARKANSAS
Barbara Pardue
Director
Dept. of Economic Dev.
1 Capitol Mall, Rm. 4C-300
Little Rock, AR 72201
Phone: (501) 682-2052
Fax: (501) 682-7394

CALIFORNIA
Lee Grissom
Secretary
Trade & Commerce Agency
801 K St., Ste. 1700
Sacramento, CA 95814
Phone: (916) 322-3962

COLORADO
David Solin
Director
Economic Dev. Ofc.
Ofc. of the Governor
1625 Broadway, Rm. 1710
Denver, CO 80202
Phone: (303) 892-3840
Fax: (303) 892-3848
E-mail: david.solin@state.co.us

CONNECTICUT
James Abromaitis
Commissioner
Dept. of Economic & Community Dev.
505 Hudson St.
Hartford, CT 06106
Phone: (860) 270-8009

DELAWARE
Darrell J. Minott
Director
Economic Dev. Ofc.
99 Kings Hwy.
Dover, DE 19901-7305
Phone: (302) 739-4271
Fax: (302) 739-5749

DISTRICT OF COLUMBIA
Douglas J. Patton
Deputy Mayor for Planning & Economic Development
441 4th St., NW, 11th Fl., Rm. 1140
Washington, DC 20001
Phone: (202) 727-6365
Fax: (202) 727-5776

FLORIDA
John Anderson
President
Enterprise Florida
390 N. Orange Ave., Ste. 1300
Orlando, FL 32303
Phone: (407) 316-4600
Fax: (407) 425-1921

GEORGIA

GUAM
Edward G. Untalan
Administrator
Economic Dev. Authority
ITC Bldg., Ste. 511
590 S. Marine Dr.
Tamuning, GU 96911
Phone: (671) 647-4332
Fax: (671) 649-4146

HAWAII
Seiji Naya
Director
Dept. of Business, Economic Dev. & Tourism
250 S. Hotel St., 5th Fl.
Honolulu, HI 96813
Phone: (808) 586-2355
Fax: (808) 586-2377

IDAHO
Jay E. Engstrom
Administrator
Div. of Economic Dev.
Dept. of Commerce
P.O. Box 83720
Boise, ID 83720-0093
Phone: (208) 334-2470

ILLINOIS
Pam McDonough
Director
Dept. of Commerce & Community Affairs
620 E. Adams St., 3rd Fl.
Springfield, IL 62701
Phone: (217) 782-3233
Fax: (217) 524-0864

INDIANA
Bob Murphy
Director
Business Dev. & Marketing Group
Dept. of Commerce
1 N. Capitol, Ste. 700
Indianapolis, IN 46204
Phone: (317) 232-0159
Fax: (317) 232-4146

IOWA
Dave Lyons
Director
Dept. of Economic Dev.
200 E. Grand Ave.
Des Moines, IA 50309
Phone: (515) 242-4814
Fax: (515) 242-4832

KANSAS
Steve Kelly
Director
Business Dev. Div.
Dept. of Commerce & Housing
700 SW Harrison, Ste. 1300
Topeka, KS 66603-3712
Phone: (785) 296-5298
Fax: (785) 296-5055

Charles Ransom
President
Kansas, Inc.
632 SW Van Buren St., Ste. 100
Topeka, KS 66603
Phone: (785) 296-1460

Gary Sherrer
Lieutenant Governor/ Secretary
Dept. of Commerce & Housing
700 SW Harrison, Ste. 1300
Topeka, KS 66603-3712
Phone: (785) 296-3480
Fax: (785) 296-5669

KENTUCKY
Gene Strong
Secretary
Economic Dev. Cabinet
Capital Plz. Tower, 24th Fl.
500 Mero St.
Frankfort, KY 40601
Phone: (502) 564-7670
Fax: (502) 564-1535

LOUISIANA
Kevin Reilly
Secretary
Dept. of Economic Dev.
P.O. Box 94185
Baton Rouge, LA 70804-9185
Phone: (225) 342-5388
Fax: (225) 342-5389

MAINE
Steven H. Levesque
Commissioner
Dept. of Economic & Community Dev.
59 State House Station
Augusta, ME 04333
Phone: (207) 287-2656

MARYLAND
Richard C. Lewin
Secretary
Ofc. of the Secretary
Business & Economic Dev.
217 E. Redwood St.,
23rd Fl.
Baltimore, MD 21202
Phone: (410) 767-6300
Fax: (410) 767-8628

MASSACHUSETTS
Carolyn Boviard
Director
Executive Ofc. of
Economic Affairs
Dept. of Economic Dev.
One Ashburton Pl.,
Rm. 2101
Boston, MA 02108
Phone: (617) 727-8380
Fax: (617) 727-4426

MICHIGAN
Greg Burkart
Director
Economic Dev. Corp.
Industry & Investment
Relations
201 N. Washington Sq.
Lansing, MI 48913
Phone: (517) 335-7989
Fax: (517) 373-0314

MINNESOTA
Gerald Carlson
Commissioner
Dept. of Trade & Economic
Dev.
500 Metro Sq.
121 7th Pl., E.
Minneapolis, MN 55101
Phone: (651) 296-9706
Fax: (651) 296-4772

MISSISSIPPI
James B. Heidel
Executive Director
Dept. of Economic &
Community Dev.
P.O. Box 849
Jackson, MS 39205-0849
Phone: (601) 359-3449
Fax: (601) 359-3613

MISSOURI
Joseph L. Driskill
Director
Dept. of Economic Dev.
301 W. High St.
P.O. Box 1157
Jefferson City, MO 65102
Phone: (573) 751-3946
Fax: (573) 751-7258
E-mail: jdriskil
@mail.state.mo.us

MONTANA
Andy Poole
Deputy Director
Dept. of Commerce
1424 9th Ave.
Helena, MT 59620
Phone: (406) 444-3797
Fax: (406) 444-2903

NEBRASKA
Allan Wenstrand
Director
Dept. of Economic Dev.
301 Centennial Mall, S.
P.O. Box 94666
Lincoln, NE 68509
Phone: (402) 471-3747
Fax: (402) 471-3778

NEVADA
Robert E. Shriver
Executive Director
Comm. on Economic Dev.
5151 S. Carson St.
Carson City, NV 89701
Phone: (775) 687-4325
Fax: (775) 687-4450

NEW HAMPSHIRE
Stuart Arnett
Director
Economic Dev.
Resources & Economic
Dev. Dept.
P.O. Box 1856
Concord, NH 03302
Phone: (603) 271-2341
Fax: (603) 271-6784

NEW JERSEY
Gualberto Medina
Secretary
Dept. of Commerce &
Economic Dev.
20 W. State St.
P.O. Box 820
Trenton, NJ 08625-0820
Phone: (609) 292-2444
Fax: (609) 777-4097

NEW MEXICO
John Garcia
Secretary
Dept. of Economic Dev.
P.O. Box 20003
Santa Fe, NM 87504
Phone: (505) 827-0305
Fax: (505) 827-0328

NEW YORK
Charles A. Gargano
Commissioner
Dept. of Economic Dev.
One Commerce Plz.,
9th Fl.
Albany, NY 12245
Phone: (518) 474-4100
Fax: (518) 473-9374

NORTH CAROLINA
Doug Byrd
Acting Director
Business/Industry Dev.
Dept. of Commerce
301 N. Wilmington St.
Raleigh, NC 27626
Phone: (919) 733-4151
Fax: (919) 733-9265

NORTH DAKOTA
Kevin Cramer
Director
Dept. of Economic Dev. &
Finance
1833 E. Bismarck Expy.
Bismarck, ND 58504
Phone: (701) 328-5300
Fax: (701) 328-5320
E-mail: kcramer
@state.nd.us

NORTHERN MARIANA ISLANDS
Oscar Camacho
Director
Economic Dev./Banking &
Insurance
Dept. of Commerce
P.O. Box 10007
Saipan, MP 96950
Phone: (670) 664-3023
Fax: (670) 664-3066
E-mail: commerce
@mtccnmi.com

OHIO
Lee Johnson
Director
Dept. of Dev.
77 S. High St., 29th Fl.
Columbus, OH 43266-0101
Phone: (614) 466-0990
Fax: (614) 644-0745

OKLAHOMA
Vacant
Chief Operating Officer
Dept. of Commerce
900 N. Stiles Ave.
Oklahoma City, OK 73105
Phone: (405) 815-6552
Fax: (405) 815-5199

OREGON
Bill Scott
Director
Dept. of Economic Dev.
775 Summer St., NE
Salem, OR 97310
Phone: (503) 986-0110
Fax: (503) 986-0256

PENNSYLVANIA
Sam McCullough
Cabinet Secretary
Dept. of Community &
Economic Dev.
Forum Bldg., Rm. 433
Harrisburg, PA 17120
Phone: (717) 783-3003
Fax: (717) 787-6866
E-mail: sam_mccullough
@gois.state.pa.us

PUERTO RICO
Xavier Romeo
Administrator
Industrial Dev. Co.
P.O. Box 362350
San Juan, PR 00936
Phone: (787) 758-4747
Fax: (787) 753-6874

RHODE ISLAND
John Swen
Director
Economic Dev. Corp.
1 W. Exchange St.
Providence, RI 02903
Phone: (401) 222-2601
Fax: (401) 222-2102

SOUTH CAROLINA
Charles S. Way, Jr.
Secretary of Commerce
Dept. of Commerce
P.O. Box 927
Columbia, SC 29202
Phone: (803) 737-0400
Fax: (803) 737-0418

SOUTH DAKOTA
Ron Wheeler
Commissioner
Governor's Ofc. of
Economic Dev.
Capitol Lake Plz.
711 Wells Ave.
Pierre, SD 57501-3369
Phone: (605) 773-5032
Fax: (605) 773-3256

TENNESSEE
Bill Baxter
Commissioner
Dept. of Economic &
Community Dev.
Rachel Jackson Bldg.,
8th Fl.
320 6th Ave., N.
Nashville, TN 37243
Phone: (615) 741-1888
Fax: (615) 741-7306

TEXAS
Jeff Moseley
Executive Director
Dept. of Economic Dev.
1700 N. Congress, Ste. 130
Austin, TX 78701
Phone: (512) 936-0101
Fax: (512) 936-0303

U.S. VIRGIN ISLANDS
Clement C. Magras
Acting Commissioner of
Tourism
Dept. of Tourism
Elainco Bldg.
78-1-2-3 Contant
St. Thomas, VI 00802
Phone: (340) 774-8784
Fax: (340) 777-4390

UTAH
Richard J. Mayfield
Director
Div. of Business &
Economic Dev.
Dept. of Community &
Economic Dev.
324 S. State St., Ste. 500
Salt Lake City, UT 84111
Phone: (801) 538-8820
Fax: (801) 538-8889
E-mail: rmayfiel
@dced.state.ut.us

VERMONT
Robert Miller
Commissioner
Dept. of Economic Dev.
Natl. Life Bldg.
Montpelier, VT 05602
Phone: (802) 828-3211
Fax: (802) 828-3258

VIRGINIA
Mark R. Kilduff
Executive Director
Economic Dev. Partnership
W. Tower, 19th Fl.
901 E. Byrd St.
Richmond, VA 23219
Phone: (804) 371-8108
Fax: (804) 371-8112

WASHINGTON
Tim Douglas
Director
Dept. of Trade & Economic
Dev.
906 Columbia St., SW
P.O. Box 48300
Olympia, WA 98504-8300
Phone: (360) 753-2200
Fax: (360) 586-3582

WEST VIRGINIA
Dana Davis
Acting Director
Dev. Ofc.
Bldg. 6, Rm. 525
1900 Kanawha Blvd., E.
Charleston, WV 25305
Phone: (304) 558-2234
Fax: (304) 558-1189

WISCONSIN
Roger Nacker
Acting Director
Bur. of Business Expense &
Recruitment
Dept. of Commerce
201 W. Washington, 5th Fl.
P.O. Box 7970
Madison, WI 53707
Phone: (608) 266-1386
Fax: (608) 266-5551

WYOMING
John Reardon
Chief Executive Officer
Economic & Community
Dev.
Business Council
214 W. 15th St.
Cheyenne, WY 82002
Phone: (307) 777-2800
Fax: (307) 777-5840

Education (Chief State School Officer)

Overall responsibility for public elementary and secondary school systems.

ALABAMA
Ed Richardson
Superintendent
Dept. of Education
50 N. Ripley St.
Montgomery, AL 36130-2101
Phone: (334) 242-9700
Fax: (334) 242-9708

ALASKA
Rick Cross
Acting Commissioner
Dept. of Education
801 W. 10th St., Ste. 200
Juneau, AK 99801
Phone: (907) 465-2800
Fax: (907) 465-4156

AMERICAN SAMOA
Sili K. Sataua
Director
Dept. of Education
AS Govt.
Pago Pago, AS 96799
Phone: (684) 633-5237
Fax: (684) 633-4240

ARIZONA
Lisa Graham Keegan
Superintendent of Public Instruction
Dept. of Education
1535 W. Jefferson
Phoenix, AZ 85007
Phone: (602) 542-6417
Fax: (602) 542-5440

ARKANSAS
Ray Simon
Director
Dept. of Education
Capitol Mall, Bldg. 4
Little Rock, AR 72201-1071
Phone: (501) 682-4205
Fax: (501) 682-4466

CALIFORNIA
Delaine Eastin
State Superintendent of Public Instruction
Dept. of Education
721 Capitol Mall, Rm. 524
Sacramento, CA 95814-4702
Phone: (916) 657-4766

COLORADO
William J. Moloney
Commissioner
Dept. of Education
201 E. Colfax
Denver, CO 80203-1715
Phone: (303) 866-6646
Fax: (303) 830-0793

CONNECTICUT
Theodore Sergi
Commissioner
Dept. of Education
165 Capitol Ave.
Hartford, CT 06106
Phone: (860) 566-5061

DELAWARE
Iris T. Metts
Secretary of Education
Dept. of Public Instruction
Townsend Bldg.
Dover, DE 19901
Phone: (302) 739-4601
Fax: (302) 739-4654

DISTRICT OF COLUMBIA
Arlene Ackerman
Superintendent of Schools
Public Schools
825 N. Capitol St., NE, Ste. 9026
Washington, DC 20002
Phone: (202) 442-5885

FLORIDA
Tom Gallagher
Commissioner
Dept. of Education
The Capitol
Tallahassee, FL 32399
Phone: (850) 487-1785
Fax: (850) 488-1492

GEORGIA
Linda Schrenko
Superintendent of Schools
Dept. of Education
2066 Twin Towers, E.
205 Butler St., SW
Atlanta, GA 30334
Phone: (404) 656-2800

GUAM
Michael J. Reidy
Director
Dept. of Administration
P.O. Box 884
Hagatna, GU 96932
Phone: (671) 475-0462
Fax: (671) 472-5003

HAWAII
Paul LeMahieu
Superintendent
Dept. of Education
1390 Miller St.
Honolulu, HI 96813
Phone: (808) 586-3310
Fax: (808) 586-3234

IDAHO
Anne C. Fox
Superintendent of Public Instruction
Dept. of Education
650 W. State St.
Boise, ID 83720
Phone: (208) 334-3300

ILLINOIS
Glenn W. McGee
Superintendent
State Board of Education
100 N. 1st St.
Springfield, IL 62777
Phone: (217) 782-2221
Fax: (217) 785-3972

INDIANA
Suellen Reed
Superintendent of Public Instruction
Dept. of Education
State House, Rm. 227
Indianapolis, IN 46204
Phone: (317) 232-6665
Fax: (317) 232-8004

IOWA
Ted Stilwill
Director
Dept. of Education
Grimes State Ofc. Bldg.
E. 14th & Grand Aves.
Des Moines, IA 50319
Phone: (515) 281-5294
Fax: (515) 242-5988

KANSAS
Andy Tompkins
Commissioner
State Board of Education
120 E. 10th St.
Topeka, KS 66612-1182
Phone: (785) 296-3201
Fax: (785) 296-7933

KENTUCKY
Wilmer S. Cody
Commissioner
Dept. of Education
Capitol Plz. Tower, 1st Fl.
500 Mero St.
Frankfort, KY 40601
Phone: (502) 564-3141
Fax: (502) 564-5680

LOUISIANA
Cecil Picard
Superintendent
Dept. of Education
P.O. Box 94064
Baton Rouge, LA 70804
Phone: (225) 342-3602
Fax: (225) 342-7316

MAINE
J. Duke Albanese
Commissioner
Dept. of Education
23 State House Station
Augusta, ME 04333-0023
Phone: (207) 287-5802

MARYLAND
Nancy S. Grasmick
State Superintendent
Ofc. of the State Superintendent
Dept. of Education
200 W. Baltimore St.
Baltimore, MD 21201
Phone: (410) 767-0462
Fax: (410) 333-6033

MASSACHUSETTS
Michael J. Sentance
Advisor on Education
Executive Ofc. of Education
One Ashburton Pl., Rm. 1401
Boston, MA 02108
Phone: (617) 727-9323
Fax: (617) 727-5570

MICHIGAN
Arthur Ellis
Superintendent
Dept. of Education
Ottawa Bldg., S., 5th Fl.
P.O. Box 30008
Lansing, MI 48909
Phone: (517) 373-3354
Fax: (517) 335-4565

MINNESOTA
Christine Jax
Commissioner
Dept. of Children, Families & Learning
550 Cedar St., 7th Fl.
Minneapolis, MN 55101
Phone: (651) 582-8204
Fax: (651) 582-8724

MISSISSIPPI
Richard Thompson
State Superintendent
Dept. of Education
P.O. Box 771
Jackson, MS 39205
Phone: (601) 359-3513
Fax: (601) 359-3242

MISSOURI
Robert E. Bartman
Commissioner
Dept. of Elementary & Secondary Education
Jefferson Bldg., 6th Fl.
P.O. Box 480
Jefferson City, MO 65102
Phone: (573) 751-4446
Fax: (573) 751-1179
E-mail: rbartman@mail.dese.state.mo.us

MONTANA
Nancy Keenan
Superintendent of Public Instruction
P.O. Box 202501
Helena, MT 59620
Phone: (406) 444-7362
Fax: (406) 444-3696

NEBRASKA
Doug D. Christensen
Commissioner
Dept. of Education
301 Centennial Mall, S.
P.O. Box 94987
Lincoln, NE 68509-4987
Phone: (402) 471-5020
Fax: (402) 471-0117

NEVADA
Mary Peterson
Superintendent
Dept. of Education
700 E. 5th St.
Carson City, NV 89701
Phone: (775) 687-9200
Fax: (775) 687-9202

NEW HAMPSHIRE
Elizabeth Twomey
Commissioner
Dept. of Education
101 Pleasant St.
Concord, NH 03301-3860
Phone: (603) 271-3144
Fax: (603) 271-1953

NEW JERSEY
David C. Hespe
Commissioner
Ofc. of the Commissioner
Dept. of Education
225 E. State St.
P.O. Box 080
Trenton, NJ 08625
Phone: (609) 984-9579

NEW MEXICO
Michael J. Davis
Superintendent of Public Instruction
Dept. of Education
Education Bldg.
300 Don Gaspar
Santa Fe, NM 87501
Phone: (505) 827-6516
E-mail: mdavis@sde.state.nm.us

NEW YORK
Richard P. Mills
Commissioner
State Education Dept.
89 Washington Ave., Rm. 111
Albany, NY 12234
Phone: (518) 474-6569
Fax: (518) 473-4909

NORTH CAROLINA
Mike Ward
Superintendent
Public Instruction
301 N. Wilmington St.
Raleigh, NC 27601-2825
Phone: (919) 715-1299
Fax: (919) 715-1278

NORTH DAKOTA
Wayne G. Sanstead
State Superintendent
Dept. of Public Instruction
600 E. Blvd. Ave., 11th Fl.
Bismarck, ND 58505-0440
Phone: (701) 328-2260
Fax: (701) 328-2461
E-mail: wsanstea@mail.dpi.state.nd.us

NORTHERN MARIANA ISLANDS
Rita H. Inos
Commissioner of Education
Public School System
Ofc. of the Governor
Saipan, MP 96950
Phone: (670) 664-3720
Fax: (670) 664-3798

OHIO
Susan Tave Zelman
Superintendent
Dept. of Education
65 S. Front St., Rm. 1005
Columbus, OH 43266-0308
Phone: (614) 466-7578
Fax: (614) 728-9703

OKLAHOMA
Sandy Garrett
Superintendent of Public Instruction
Dept. of Education
2500 N. Lincoln Blvd.
Oklahoma City, OK 73105
Phone: (405) 521-3301
Fax: (405) 521-6205

OREGON
Stan Bunn
Superintendent of Public Instruction
Dept. of Education
255 Capitol St., NE
Salem, OR 97310
Phone: (503) 378-3573
Fax: (503) 378-4772

PENNSYLVANIA
Eugene Welch Hickok, Jr.
Secretary
Dept. of Education
Harristown 2, 10th Fl.
Harrisburg, PA 17120
Phone: (717) 787-5820
Fax: (717) 787-7222

PUERTO RICO
Victor Fajardo
Secretary
Dept. of Education
P.O. Box 190759
San Juan, PR 00919-0759
Phone: (787) 759-2000
Fax: (787) 250-0275

RHODE ISLAND
Peter McWalters
Commissioner
Dept. of Elementary & Secondary Education
255 Westminster St.
Providence, RI 02903-3400
Phone: (401) 222-2031

SOUTH CAROLINA
Inez Tenenbaum
Superintendent
Dept. of Education
Rutledge Bldg., Rm. 1006
1429 Senate St.
Columbia, SC 29201
Phone: (803) 734-8492

SOUTH DAKOTA
Ray Christensen
Secretary
Dept. of Education & Cultural Affairs
700 Governors Dr.
Pierre, SD 57501
Phone: (605) 773-5669
Fax: (605) 773-6139

TENNESSEE
Jane Walters
Commissioner
Dept. of Education
710 James Robertson Pkwy.
Nashville, TN 37243
Phone: (615) 741-2731
Fax: (615) 532-4791

TEXAS
Michael Moses
Commissioner of Education
Education Agency
1701 N. Congress Ave.
Austin, TX 78701
Phone: (512) 463-8985
Fax: (512) 463-9008

U.S. VIRGIN ISLANDS
Ruby Simmonds
Acting Commissioner
Dept. of Education
44-46 Kongens Gade
St. Thomas, VI 00802
Phone: (340) 774-0100
Fax: (340) 774-4679

UTAH
Steven O. Laing
State Superintendent
Ofc. of Education
250 E. 500 S.
Salt Lake City, UT 84111
Phone: (801) 538-7510
Fax: (801) 538-7521

VERMONT
Marc Hull
Commissioner
Dept. of Education
120 State St.
Montpelier, VT 05620
Phone: (802) 828-3135
Fax: (802) 828-3140

VIRGINIA
Paul D. Stapleton
Superintendent of Public Instruction
Dept. of Education
Monroe Bldg., 25th Fl.
101 N. 14th St.
Richmond, VA 23219
Phone: (804) 225-2023
Fax: (804) 371-2099

WASHINGTON
Terry Bergeson
Superintendent of Public Instruction
Old Capitol Bldg.
P.O. Box 47200
Olympia, WA 98504-7200
Phone: (360) 753-6738
Fax: (360) 753-6712

WEST VIRGINIA
David Ice
Cabinet Secretary
Ofc. of the Secretary
Dept. of Education and the Arts
Bldg. 5, Rm. 205
1900 Kanawha Blvd., E.
Charleston, WV 25305
Phone: (304) 558-2440
Fax: (304) 558-1311

Hank Marockie
Superintendent
Dept. of Education
1800 Washington St., E., Bldg. 6
Charleston, WV 25305
Phone: (304) 558-2681
Fax: (304) 558-0048

WISCONSIN
John Benson
Superintendent
Dept. of Public Instruction
125 S. Webster St.
P.O. Box 7841
Madison, WI 53707
Phone: (608) 266-1771
Fax: (608) 267-1052

WYOMING
Judy Catchpole
Superintendent of Public Instruction
Dept. of Education
Hathaway Bldg., 2nd Fl.
2300 Capitol Ave.
Cheyenne, WY 82002-0050
Phone: (307) 777-7675

Elections Administration

Administers state election laws and supervises the printing and distribution of ballots.

ALABAMA
Vicki Balogh
Director
Elections Div.
Ofc. of Secretary of State
600 Dexter Ave., Ste. E-204
Montgomery, AL 36130-4650
Phone: (334) 242-7210
Fax: (334) 242-2444

ALASKA
Sandra Stout
Director
Div. of Elections
Ofc. of Governor
P.O. Box 110017
Juneau, AK 99811-0017
Phone: (907) 465-4611
Fax: (907) 465-3203

AMERICAN SAMOA
Soliai T. Fuimaono
Chief Election Officer
Elections Comm. Ofc.
P.O. Box 3790
Pago Pago, AS 96799
Phone: (684) 633-4962
Fax: (684) 633-7116

ARIZONA
Betsy Bayless
Secretary of State
State Capitol, 7th Fl.
1700 W. Washington St.
Phoenix, AZ 85007-2808
Phone: (602) 542-3012
Fax: (602) 542-1575

ARKANSAS
Jeanette Heinbockel
Supervisor of Elections
State Capitol, Rm. 026
Little Rock, AR 72201
Phone: (501) 682-3451
Fax: (501) 682-3408

Sharon Priest
Secretary of State
State Capitol, Rm. 256
Little Rock, AR 72201
Phone: (501) 682-1010
Fax: (501) 682-3510
E-mail: sharonpriest@ccm1.state.ar.us

CALIFORNIA
John Mott-Smith
Chief of Elections Division
Ofc. of Secretary of State
1500 11th St., 5th Fl.
Sacramento, CA 95814
Phone: (916) 657-2166
Fax: (916) 653-3214

Robert Steele
Chief
Political Reform Div.
Ofc. of the Secretary of State
1500 11th St., Rm. 495
Sacramento, CA 95814
Phone: (916) 653-5943

COLORADO
Bill Compton
Elections Officer
Elections Div.
Dept. of State
1560 Broadway, Ste. 200
Denver, CO 80202
Phone: (303) 894-2680
Fax: (303) 894-7732

CONNECTICUT
Thomas Ferguson
Director
Elections Div.
Ofc. of Secretary of State
30 Trinity St.
Hartford, CT 06106
Phone: (860) 509-6100

DELAWARE
Thomas J. Cook
Commissioner
Dept. of Elections
32 Loockerman St., M101
Dover, DE 19904
Phone: (302) 739-4277
Fax: (302) 739-6794

DISTRICT OF COLUMBIA
Alice P. Miller
Executive Director
Board of Elections & Ethics
441 4th St., NW, Ste. 250
Washington, DC 20001
Phone: (202) 727-2525
Fax: (202) 347-2648

FLORIDA
Ethel Baxter
Director
Div. of Elections
Dept. of State
The Capitol, Rm. 1801
Tallahassee, FL 32399-0250
Phone: (850) 488-7690
Fax: (850) 488-1768

GEORGIA
Linda Beazley
Director
Elections Div.
Secretary of State's Ofc.
1104 W. Tower
2 Martin Luther King, Jr. Dr., SE
Atlanta, GA 30334-1505
Phone: (404) 656-2871
Fax: (404) 651-9531

GUAM
Elizabeth M. Blaz
Acting Executive Director
Election Comm.
P.O. Box BG
Hagatna, GU 96932
Phone: (671) 477-9791
Fax: (671) 477-1895

HAWAII
Dwayne Yoshina
Chief Election Officer
Ofc. of Elections
802 Lehua Ave.
Pearl City, HI 96782
Phone: (808) 453-8683
Fax: (808) 453-6006

IDAHO
Ben T. Ysursa
Chief Deputy Secretary of State
Elections Div.
Secretary of State Ofc.
P.O. Box 83720
Boise, ID 83720
Phone: (208) 334-2300

ILLINOIS
Ronald D. Michaelson
Executive Director
State Board of Elections
1020 S. Spring St.
Springfield, IL 62708-4187
Phone: (217) 782-4141
Fax: (217) 782-5959

INDIANA
Laurie Christie
Co-Director
State Election Comm.
302 W. Washington, #E204
Indianapolis, IN 46204
Phone: (317) 232-3939
Fax: (317) 233-6793

Spencer Valentine
Co-Director
State Election Comm.
302 W. Washington, E204
Indianapolis, IN 46204
Phone: (317) 232-3939
Fax: (317) 233-6793

IOWA
Chet Culver
Secretary of State
State House
Des Moines, IA 50319
Phone: (515) 281-5204
Fax: (515) 242-5952
E-mail: sos@sos.state.ia.us

Sandy Steinbach
Director of Elections
Hoover Bldg., 2nd Fl.
1305 E. Walnut
Des Moines, IA 50319
Phone: (515) 281-5823
Fax: (515) 242-5953

KANSAS
Brad Bryant
Deputy Assistant for Elections
Capitol Bldg., 2nd Fl.
300 SW 10th Ave.
Topeka, KS 66612-1594
Phone: (785) 296-4559
Fax: (785) 296-4570

Ron Thornburgh
Secretary of State
State Capitol, 2nd Fl.
300 SW 10th St.
Topeka, KS 66612
Phone: (785) 296-4575
Fax: (785) 296-4570

KENTUCKY
Mack Bushart
Director
Registry of Election Finance
140 Walnut St.
Frankfort, KY 40601
Phone: (502) 573-7100
Fax: (502) 573-5622

LOUISIANA
Jerry M. Fowler
Commissioner
Dept. of Elections & Registration
P.O. Box 14179
Baton Rouge, LA 70898
Phone: (225) 925-7885
Fax: (225) 925-1841

MAINE
Julie Flynn
Director
Corps. & Elections
101 State House Station
Augusta, ME 04333
Phone: (207) 287-4189
Fax: (207) 287-5874

MARYLAND
Linda H. Lamone
Administrator
Administrator's Ofc.
State Board of Election
P.O. Box 231
Annapolis, MD 21401-0231
Phone: (410) 974-3711
Fax: (410) 974-2019
E-mail: llamone@elections.state.md.us

MASSACHUSETTS
John Cloonan
Director
Elections Div.
Ofc. of Secretary of the Commonwealth
One Ashburton Pl., Rm. 1705
Boston, MA 02108
Phone: (617) 727-2828
Fax: (617) 742-3238

MICHIGAN
Candice Miller
Secretary of State
Treasury Bldg., 1st Fl.
430 W. Allegan St.
Lansing, MI 48918
Phone: (517) 373-2510
Fax: (517) 373-0727

Christopher M. Thomas
Director
Bur. of Elections
Ofc. of the Secretary of State
Mutual Bldg., 4th Fl.
208 N. Capitol Ave.
Lansing, MI 48918
Phone: (517) 373-2540
Fax: (517) 373-0941

MINNESOTA
Mary Kiffmeyer
Secretary of State
180 State Ofc. Bldg.
100 Constitution Ave.
St. Paul, MN 55155-1299
Phone: (651) 296-1299
Fax: (651) 296-9073
E-mail: secretary.state@state.mn.us

Joseph Mansky
Director
Ofc. of Secretary of State
Election Div.
180 State Ofc. Bldg.
100 Constitution Ave.
St. Paul, MN 55155-1299
Phone: (651) 215-1440
Fax: (651) 296-9073
E-mail: elections@sos.state.mn.us

MISSISSIPPI
Phil Carter
Assistant Secretary of State for Elections & Counsel
P.O. Box 136
Jackson, MS 39205
Phone: (601) 359-6359
Fax: (304) 359-5019

MISSOURI
Debbie Cheshire
Director
Div. of Elections
Ofc. of Secretary of State
600 W. Main St.
P.O. Box 778
Jefferson City, MO 65102
Phone: (573) 751-4875
Fax: (573) 526-3242
E-mail: dchesir@mail.sos.state.mo.us

MONTANA
Joe Kerwin
Deputy
Elections & Legislative Bur.
Secretary of State's Ofc.
State Capitol, Rm. 225
Helena, MT 59620
Phone: (406) 444-4732
Fax: (406) 444-3976

NEBRASKA
Neal Erickson
Assistant Secretary of State for Elections
Election Div.
Secretary of State
P.O. Box 94608
Lincoln, NE 68509-4608
Phone: (402) 471-2554
Fax: (402) 471-3237

NEVADA
Pamela Bissell Crowell
Deputy Secretary of State for Elections
Ofc. of the Secretary of State
101 N. Carson St., Ste. 3
Carson City, NV 89701
Phone: (775) 684-5705
Fax: (775) 684-5718

Dean Heller
Secretary of State
State Capitol Bldg.
101 N. Carson St., Ste. 3
Carson City, NV 89701
Phone: (775) 684-5708
Fax: (775) 687-5725
E-mail: sosmail@govmail.state.nv.us

Donald J. Reis
Chief Deputy Secretary of State
Ofc. of Secretary of State
101 N. Carson St., Ste. 3
Carson City, NV 89701
Phone: (775) 684-5708
Fax: (775) 684-5725

NEW HAMPSHIRE
William Gardner
Secretary of State
Secretary of State Ofc.
State House, Rm. 204
107 N. Main St.
Concord, NH 03301
Phone: (603) 271-3242
Fax: (603) 271-6316
E-mail: sof.karen.ladd@leg.state.nh.us

NEW JERSEY
Inez M. Killian
Director
Election Div.
Dept. of State
P.O. Box 304
Trenton, NJ 08625-0304
Phone: (609) 292-8337

NEW MEXICO
Denise Lamb
Director
Election Bur.
Ofc. of Secretary of State
State Capitol Bldg., Rm. 420
Santa Fe, NM 87503
Phone: (505) 827-3622
Fax: (505) 827-3634
E-mail: deniselamb@state.nm.us

NEW YORK
Thomas R. Wilkey
Executive Director
Board of Elections
Swan St. Bldg., Core 1
Empire State Plz.
Albany, NY 12223-1650
Phone: (518) 474-8100
Fax: (518) 486-4068

NORTH CAROLINA
Gary O. Bartlett
Executive Secretary
State Board of Elections
133 Fayetteville St. Mall, Ste. 100
Raleigh, NC 27601-1392
Phone: (919) 733-7173
Fax: (919) 715-0135

NORTH DAKOTA
Cory Fong
Election Supervisor
Elections
Secretary of State's Ofc.
600 E. Blvd. Ave., 1st Fl.
Bismarck, ND 58505-0500
Phone: (701) 328-4146
Fax: (701) 328-2992
E-mail: cfong@state.nd.us

NORTHERN MARIANA ISLANDS
Gregorio C. Sablan
Executive Director
Board of Elections
P.O. Box 470
Saipan, MP 96950
Phone: (670) 664-8683
Fax: (670) 664-8682

OHIO
Dana Walch
Director
Ofc. of the Secretary of State
Borden Bldg.
Columbus, OH 43266-0418
Phone: (614) 466-2585

OKLAHOMA
Lance Ward
Secretary of the Senate
State Capitol, Rm. 3-B
2300 N. Lincoln Blvd.
Oklahoma City, OK 73105
Phone: (405) 521-2391

OREGON
Colleen Sealock
Director
Elections & Public Records
Ofc. of Secretary of State
141 State Capitol
900 Court St., NE
Salem, OR 97310
Phone: (503) 986-1518
Fax: (503) 373-7414

PENNSYLVANIA
Dick Filling
Commissioner
Bur. of Comms., Elections & Legislation
Dept. of State
301 N. Ofc. Bldg.
Harrisburg, PA 17120
Phone: (717) 787-5280
Fax: (717) 783-2244

PUERTO RICO
Juan R. Meleccio
President
State Election Comm.
P.O. Box 9066525
San Juan, PR 00906-6525
Phone: (787) 723-1006
Fax: (787) 721-7940

RHODE ISLAND
Roger N. Begin
Chair
Board of Elections
50 Branch Ave.
Providence, RI 02904
Phone: (401) 222-2345

SOUTH CAROLINA
James Hendrix
Executive Director
State Election Comm.
2221 Devine St., Ste. 105
P.O. Box 5987
Columbia, SC 29250
Phone: (803) 734-9060

SOUTH DAKOTA
Chris Nelson
Supervisor of Elections
500 E. Capitol Ave.
Pierre, SD 57501-5077
Phone: (605) 773-3536
Fax: (605) 773-6580

TENNESSEE
Brook Thompson
Coordinator of Elections
Div. of Elections
Dept. of States
James K. Polk Bldg., Ste. 1700
505 Deaderick St.
Nashville, TN 37219
Phone: (615) 741-7956
Fax: (615) 741-1278

TEXAS
Elton Bomer
Secretary of State
Ofc. of the Secretary of State
P.O. Box 12697
Austin, TX 78711-2697
Phone: (512) 475-2810
Fax: (512) 475-2761

Ann McGeehan
Deputy Assistant
Ofc. of the Secretary of State
P.O. Box 12697
Austin, TX 78711
Phone: (512) 463-5650
Fax: (512) 475-2811

U.S. VIRGIN ISLANDS
John Abramson
Supervisor
Ofc. of the Supervisor
Board of Elections
P.O. Box 6038
St. Thomas, VI 00801
Phone: (340) 774-3107
Fax: (340) 776-2391

UTAH
Ann M. Peterson
Director
Elections
Governor's Ofc.
115 State Capitol
Salt Lake City, UT 84114
Phone: (801) 538-1522
Fax: (801) 538-1133
E-mail: ampeters@gov.state.ut.us

VERMONT
Deborah Markowitz
Secretary of State
109 State St.
Montpelier, VT 05609-1101
Phone: (802) 828-2148
Fax: (802) 828-2496

Ellen Tofferi
Director of Elections
Ofc. of Secretary of State
109 State St.
Montpelier, VT 05609-1101
Phone: (802) 828-2304
Fax: (802) 828-2496

VIRGINIA
Cameron P. Quinn
Secretary
State Board of Elections
202 N. 9th St., Ste. 101
Richmond, VA 23219
Phone: (804) 786-6551
Fax: (804) 371-0194

WASHINGTON
Gary McIntosh
Director
Elections Div.
Ofc. of Secretary of State
Legislative Bldg.
P.O. Box 40220
Olympia, WA 98504-0229
Phone: (360) 753-7121
Fax: (360) 586-5629

WEST VIRGINIA
Ken Hechler
Secretary of State
Bldg. 1, Ste. 157K
1900 Kanawha Blvd., E.
Charleston, WV 25305
Phone: (304) 558-6000
Fax: (304) 558-0900
E-mail: wvsos@secretary.state.wv.us

WISCONSIN
Kevin J. Kennedy
Executive Director
State Elections Board
132 E. Wilson, Ste. 200
P.O. Box 2973
Madison, WI 53701-2973
Phone: (608) 266-8005
Fax: (608) 267-0500

WYOMING
Peggy Nighswanger
Elections Officer
Secretary of State's Ofc.
State Capitol
200 W. 24th St.
Cheyenne, WY 82002-0020
Phone: (307) 777-5333
Fax: (307) 777-6217

Emergency Management—

Prepares, maintains and/or implements state disaster plans and coordinates emergency activities.

ALABAMA
Willie Alexander
Director
Emergency Mgmt. Agency
P.O. Drawer 2160
Clanton, AL 35045
Phone: (334) 271-7200
Fax: (334) 271-7511

ALASKA
David Liebersbach
Director
Div. of Emergency Mgmt. Services
Dept. of Military & Veteran Affairs
P.O. Box 5750
Ft. Richardson, AK 99505
Phone: (907) 428-7039
Fax: (907) 428-7009

AMERICAN SAMOA
Te'o Fuavai
Commissioner
Dept. of Public Safety
AS Govt.
Pago Pago, AS 96799
Phone: (684) 633-1111
Fax: (684) 633-5111

ARIZONA
Michael Austin
Director
Div. of Emergency Services
5636 E. McDowell Rd.
Phoenix, AZ 85008
Phone: (602) 231-6245
Fax: (602) 231-6356

ARKANSAS
W.R. Harper
Director
Ofc. of Emergency Services
P.O. Box 758
Conway, AR 72033
Phone: (501) 730-9750
Fax: (501) 730-9778

CALIFORNIA
Richard Andrews
Director
Ofc. of Emergency Services
2800 Meadowview Rd.
Sacramento, CA 95832
Phone: (916) 262-1816
Fax: (916) 262-1677

COLORADO
Tommy Grier, Jr.
Director
Ofc. of Emergency Mgmt.
Dept. of Local Affairs
15075 S. Golden Rd.
Golden, CO 80401
Phone: (303) 273-1622
Fax: (303) 273-1795

CONNECTICUT
Robert Plant
Director
Ofc. of Emergency Mgmt.
360 Broad St.
Hartford, CT 06105
Phone: (860) 566-3180
Fax: (860) 247-0664

DELAWARE
Sean P. Mulhern
Director
Div. of Emergency Planning & Operations
P.O. Box 527
Delaware City, DE 19706
Phone: (302) 326-6000
Fax: (302) 326-6045

DISTRICT OF COLUMBIA
Samuel Jordan
Director
Emergency Mgmt. Services
2000 14th St., NW, 8th Fl.
Washington, DC 20009
Phone: (202) 727-6161
Fax: (202) 673-2290

FLORIDA
Joseph F. Myers
Director
Div. of Emergency Mgmt.
Dept. of Community Affairs
2555 Shumard Oak Blvd.
Tallahassee, FL 32399-2100
Phone: (850) 413-9969
Fax: (850) 488-1016

GEORGIA
Gary W. McConnell
Director
Emergency Mgmt. Agency
P.O. Box 18055
Atlanta, GA 30316
Phone: (404) 635-7002
Fax: (404) 635-7205

GUAM
Robert F. Kelley
Acting Director
Div. of Civil Defense
Emergency Services Ctr.
P.O. Box 2877
Hagatna, GU 96932
Phone: (671) 475-9600
Fax: (671) 477-3727

HAWAII
Roy C. Price, Sr.
Vice Director
State Civil Defense
Dept. of Defense
3949 Diamond Head Rd.
Honolulu, HI 96816
Phone: (808) 733-4300
Fax: (808) 733-4287

IDAHO
John J. Cline
Director
Bur. of Disaster Services
Military Div.
4040 Guard St., Bldg. 600
Boise, ID 83705-5004
Phone: (208) 334-3460
Fax: (208) 334-2322

ILLINOIS
Michael Chamness
Director
Emergency Mgmt. Agency
110 E. Adams St.
Springfield, IL 62701
Phone: (217) 782-2700
Fax: (217) 785-6043

INDIANA
Patrick Ralston
Director
State Emergency Mgmt. Agency
IGC-South, Rm. 208
302 W. Washington St.
Indianapolis, IN 46204
Phone: (317) 232-3980
Fax: (317) 232-3895

IOWA
Ellen Gordon
Administrator
Emergency Mgmt. Div.
Dept. of Public Defense
Hoover State Ofc. Bldg.
1300 E. Walnut
Des Moines, IA 50319
Phone: (515) 281-3231
Fax: (515) 281-7539

KANSAS
Lloyd E. Krase
Deputy Director
Div. of Emergency Mgmt.
Dept. of Adjutant Gen.
2800 SW Topeka Blvd.
Topeka, KS 66601-0300
Phone: (785) 274-1400
Fax: (785) 274-1426

KENTUCKY
Ron Padgett
Director
Disaster & Emergency Services
Dept. of Military Affairs
100 Minuteman Pkwy.
Frankfort, KY 40601
Phone: (502) 564-8682
Fax: (502) 564-8614

LOUISIANA
Mike Brown
Assistant Director
Ofc. of Emergency Preparedness
P.O. Box 44217
Baton Rouge, LA 70804
Phone: (225) 342-5470
Fax: (225) 342-5471

MAINE
John W. Libby
Director
Emergency Mgmt. Agency
72 State House Station
Augusta, ME 04333-0072
Phone: (207) 626-4202
Fax: (207) 626-4495

MARYLAND
David A. McMillion
Director
Ofc. of the Director
Emergency Mgmt. Agency
2 Sudbrook Ln., E.
Baltimore, MD 21208
Phone: (410) 486-4422
Fax: (410) 486-1867
E-mail: dmcmillion@mema.state.md.us

MASSACHUSETTS
Peter G. LaPorte
Director
Emergency Mgmt. Agency
Executive Ofc. of Public Safety
400 Worcester Rd.
P.O. Box 1496
Framingham, MA 01701
Phone: (508) 820-2000
Fax: (508) 820-2030

MICHIGAN
Robert Tarrant
Commanding Officer
Emergency Mgmt. Div.
State Police
300 S. Washington Sq., Ste. 300
Lansing, MI 48913
Phone: (517) 334-5103
Fax: (517) 482-7914

MINNESOTA
Kevin Leuer
Director
Div. of Emergency Mgmt.
Dept. of Public Safety
444 Cedar St., Ste. 223
Minneapolis, MN 55101-6223
Phone: (651) 296-0450
Fax: (651) 296-0459

MISSISSIPPI
James E. Maher
Director
Emergency Mgmt. Agency
Fondren Station
P.O. Box 4501
Jackson, MS 39296
Phone: (601) 352-9100
Fax: (601) 352-8314

MISSOURI
Jerry Uhlmann
Director
State Emergency Mgmt. Agency
Dept. of Public Safety
2302 Militia Dr.
P.O. Box 116
Jefferson City, MO 65102
Phone: (573) 526-9101
Fax: (573) 634-7966
E-mail: juhlmann@mail.state.mo.us

MONTANA
Jim Greene
Administrator
Disaster & Emergency Services Div.
Dept. of Military Affairs
1100 N. Last Chance Gulch
Helena, MT 59604-4789
Phone: (406) 841-3953
Fax: (406) 841-3965

NEBRASKA
B.G. Francis Laden
Acting Assistant Director
Emergency Mgmt. Agency
Natl. Guard Ctr.
1300 Military Rd.
Lincoln, NE 68508
Phone: (402) 471-7410
Fax: (402) 471-7171

NEVADA
Frank Siracusa
Chief
Emergency Mgmt. Div.
Dept. of Motor Vehicles & Public Safety
2525 S. Carson St.
Carson City, NV 89711
Phone: (775) 687-4240
Fax: (775) 687-6788

NEW HAMPSHIRE
Woodbury Fogg
Director
Dept. of Emergency Mgmt.
107 Pleasant St.
Concord, NH 03301-3809
Phone: (603) 271-2231
Fax: (603) 225-7341

NEW JERSEY
Tom Davies
Section Supervisor
Ofc. of Emergency Mgmt.
P.O. Box 7068
W. Trenton, NJ 08628-0068
Phone: (609) 538-6050
Fax: (609) 538-0345

NEW MEXICO
Ray Denison
Director
Div. of Technical Emergency Support
Dept. of Public Safety
P.O. Box 1628
Santa Fe, NM 87504
Phone: (505) 827-3376
Fax: (505) 827-3434

NEW YORK
Edward F. Jacoby
Director
State Emergency Mgmt. Ofc.
Public Security Bldg. 22, State Campus
Albany, NY 12226
Phone: (518) 457-2222
Fax: (518) 457-8924

NORTH CAROLINA
Eric L. Tolbert
Director
Div. of Emergency Mgmt.
Dept. of Crime Control & Public Safety
116 W. Jones St.
Raleigh, NC 27603-1335
Phone: (919) 733-3825
Fax: (919) 733-5406

NORTH DAKOTA
Douglas C. Friez
Division Director
Div. of Emergency Mgmt.
P.O. Box 5511
Bismarck, ND 58506-5511
Phone: (701) 328-3300
Fax: (701) 328-8181
E-mail: dfriez@state.nd.us

NORTHERN MARIANA ISLANDS
Gregorio A. Guerrero
Director
Emergency Mgmt. Ofc.
P.O. Box 10007
Saipan, MP 96950
Phone: (670) 322-9529
Fax: (670) 322-3598

OHIO
James R. Williams
Deputy Director
Emergency Mgmt. Agency
Dept. of Adjutant Gen.
2855 W. Dublin Granville Rd.
Columbus, OH 43235-2206
Phone: (614) 889-7150
Fax: (614) 889-7183

OKLAHOMA
Albert Ashwood
Director
Dept. of Civil Emergency Mgmt.
Will Rogers-Sequayah Bldgs.
P.O. Box 53365
Oklahoma City, OK 73152
Phone: (405) 521-2481
Fax: (405) 521-4053

OREGON
Myra Thompson Lee
Director
Ofc. of Emergency Mgmt.
595 Cottage St., NE
Salem, OR 97310
Phone: (503) 378-2911
Fax: (503) 588-1378

PENNSYLVANIA
Charles F. Wynne
Director
Emergency Mgmt. Agency
Transportation & Safety Bldg., Rm. B-153
2605 Interstate Dr.
Harrisburg, PA 17110
Phone: (717) 783-8016
Fax: (717) 783-7396

PUERTO RICO
Epifano Jimenez
Director
State Civil Defense Agency
P.O. Box 9066597
San Juan, PR 00906-6597
Phone: (787) 724-0124
Fax: (787) 725-4244

RHODE ISLAND
Reginald Centracchio
Major General
Natl. Guard/Emergency Mgmt. Agency
Command Readiness Ctr.
645 New London Ave.
Cranston, RI 02920
Phone: (401) 421-7333
Fax: (401) 751-0827
E-mail: tagcri-arng.ngb.army.mil

SOUTH CAROLINA
Stan M. McKinney
Director
Div. of Emergency Preparedness
Ofc. of Adjutant Gen.
1429 Senate St.
Columbia, SC 29201
Phone: (803) 734-8020
Fax: (803) 735-8062

SOUTH DAKOTA
John Berheim
Director
Div. of Emergency Mgmt.
425 E. Capitol Ave.
Pierre, SD 57501
Phone: (605) 773-3233
Fax: (605) 773-3580

TENNESSEE
John White
Director
Emergency Mgmt. Agency
Dept. of Military
3041 Sidco Dr.
Nashville, TN 37204
Phone: (615) 741-0001
Fax: (615) 242-9635

TEXAS
Tom Millwee
State Coordinator
Div. of Emergency Mgmt.
Dept. of Public Safety
P.O. Box 4087
Austin, TX 78773
Phone: (512) 424-2443
Fax: (512) 424-2444

U.S. VIRGIN ISLANDS
Gene Walker
State Director
VITEMA
2-C Contant, AQ Bldg.
St. Thomas, VI 00802
Phone: (340) 774-2244
Fax: (340) 774-1491

UTAH
Earl R. Morris
Director
Div. of Comprehensive Emergency Mgmt.
Dept. of Public Safety
1110 State Ofc. Bldg.
Salt Lake City, UT 84114
Phone: (801) 538-3400
Fax: (801) 538-3770
E-mail: emorris.psmain@state.ut.us

VERMONT
Edward Von Turkovich
Director
Emergency Mgmt. Div.
Dept. of Public Safety
103 S. Main St.
Waterbury, VT 05671
Phone: (802) 244-8721
Fax: (802) 244-8655

VIRGINIA
Michael M. Cline
State Coordinator
Dept. of Emergency Services
10501 Trade Ct.
Richmond, VA 23236
Phone: (804) 897-6500
Fax: (804) 897-6506

WASHINGTON
Glen Woodbury
Director
Emergency Mgmt. Military Dept.
Military Dept.
P.O. Box 40955
Olympia, WA 98504-0955
Phone: (360) 459-9191
Fax: (360) 923-4591

WEST VIRGINIA
John W. Pack, Jr.
Director
Ofc. of Emergency Services
Bldg. 1, Rm. EB-80
1900 Kanawha Blvd., E.
Charleston, WV 25305
Phone: (304) 558-5380
Fax: (304) 344-4538

WISCONSIN
Steven D. Sell
Administrator
Div. of Emergency Govt.
2400 Wright St.
P.O. Box 7865
Madison, WI 53707-7865
Phone: (608) 242-3232
Fax: (608) 242-3247

WYOMING
Robert J. Bezek
Coordinator
Emergency Mgmt. Agency
5500 Bishop Blvd.
Cheyenne, WY 82009-3320
Phone: (307) 777-4900
Fax: (307) 635-6017

Emergency Medical Services

Administers comprehensive and allied programs to reduce unnecessary mortality and disability from emergency medical conditions.

ALABAMA
Steven Kenndy
Interim Director
Emergency Medical Services Div.
Dept. of Public Health
434 Monroe St.
Montgomery, AL 36130
Phone: (334) 206-5283
Fax: (334) 206-5263

ALASKA
Mark S. Johnson
Chief
Emergency Medical Services
Dept. of Health & Social Services
P.O. Box 110616
Juneau, AK 99811-0616
Phone: (907) 465-3027
Fax: (907) 465-4101

AMERICAN SAMOA
Fuapopo Avegalio
EMS Coordinator
Emergency Medical Services
LBJ Tropical Medical Ctr.
AS Govt.
Pago Pago, AS 96799
Phone: (684) 633-4590
Fax: (684) 633-1869

ARIZONA
Garth Gemar
Medical Director
Emergency Medical Services Div.
1651 E. Morten, Ste. 120
Phoenix, AZ 85020
Phone: (602) 861-0809

ARKANSAS
David Moskowitz
Director
Emergency Medical Services
Dept. of Health
4815 W. Markham St.
Little Rock, AR 72205-3867
Phone: (501) 661-2262
Fax: (501) 280-4901

CALIFORNIA
Richard Watson
Interim Director
Emergency Medical Services Authority
1930 9th St.
Sacramento, CA 95814
Phone: (916) 322-4336
Fax: (916) 324-2875

COLORADO
Jillian Jacobellis
Director
Emergency Medical Services & Prevention Div.
Dept. of Public Health & Environment
4300 Cherry Creek Dr., S.
Denver, CO 80246-1530
Phone: (303) 692-2500
Fax: (303) 782-0095

CONNECTICUT
Deborah Haliscak
Public Health Services Provider
Ofc. of Emergency Medical Services
P.O. Box 340308
Hartford, CT 06134
Phone: (860) 509-7975

DELAWARE
William Stevenson
Director
Emergency Medical Services Ofc.
Blue Hen Corporate Ctr.
655 Bay Rd., Ste. 4H
Dover, DE 19901
Phone: (302) 739-4710
Fax: (302) 739-2352

DISTRICT OF COLUMBIA
Wayne Moore
Medical Director
Emergency Medical Services Ofc.
1018 13th St., NW, 3rd Fl.
Washington, DC 20005
Phone: (202) 673-3360

FLORIDA
Dino Villani
Clearinghouse
Emergency Medical Services
Bldg. D
2002 Old St. Augustine Rd.
Tallahassee, FL 32301-4881
Phone: (850) 487-1911
Fax: (850) 487-2911

GEORGIA
Kathleen E. Toomey
Director
Div. of Public Health
Dept. of Human Resources
2 Peachtree St., Rm. 7-300
Atlanta, GA 30303
Phone: (404) 657-2700

GUAM
Dennis G. Rodriguez
Director
Dept. of Public Health & Social Services
P.O. Box 2816
Hagatna, GU 96932
Phone: (671) 735-7102
Fax: (671) 734-5910
E-mail: dennis_r_@NS.GOV.GU

HAWAII
Donna Maiava
Chief
Emergency Medical Service System
Dept. of Health
3627 Kiluaea Ave., Rm. 102
Honolulu, HI 96816
Phone: (808) 733-9210
Fax: (808) 733-8332

IDAHO
Dia Gainor
Chief
Emergency Medical Services Bur.
Dept. of Health & Welfare
3092 Elder St.
P.O. Box 83720
Boise, ID 83720-0036
Phone: (208) 334-4000
Fax: (208) 334-4015

ILLINOIS
Leslee Stein-Spencer
Chief
Div. of Emergency Medical Services
Dept. of Public Health
525 W. Jefferson St., 3rd Fl.
Springfield, IL 62761
Phone: (217) 785-2080

INDIANA
Patrick Ralston
Director
State Emergency Mgmt. Agency
IGC-South, Rm. 208
302 W. Washington St.
Indianapolis, IN 46204
Phone: (317) 232-3980
Fax: (317) 232-3895

IOWA
Steve Mercer
Program Administrator
Emergency Medical Services Section
Dept. of Public Health
Lucas State Ofc. Bldg.
321 E. 12th St.
Des Moines, IA 50319-0075
Phone: (515) 281-4951

KANSAS
Bob McDaneld
Administrator
Emergency Medical Services Board
109 SW 6th St.
Topeka, KS 66603-3826
Phone: (785) 296-7296
Fax: (785) 296-6212

KENTUCKY
Robert Calhoun
Branch Manager
Emergency Medical Services Branch
Dept. for Health Services
275 E. Main St.
Frankfort, KY 40621
Phone: (502) 564-8965
Fax: (502) 564-6533

LOUISIANA
Nancy Bourgeois
Director
Bur. of Emergency Medical Services
1201 Capitol Access Rd.
P.O. Box 94215
Baton Rouge, LA 70804
Phone: (225) 342-4881
Fax: (225) 342-4876

MAINE
John R. Bradshaw, Jr.
Director of Emergency Medical Services
Emergency Medical Services
Public Safety
42 State House Station
Augusta, ME 04333
Phone: (207) 624-7068

MARYLAND
Robert R. Bass
Executive Director
Ofc. of the Executive Director
Institute for Emergency Medical Services Systems
653 W. Pratt St.
Baltimore, MD 21201
Phone: (410) 706-5074
Fax: (410) 706-4768

MASSACHUSETTS
Louise Goyette
Director
Ofc. of Emergency Medical Services
Dept. of Public Health
470 Atlantic Ave., 2nd Fl.
Boston, MA 02210-2208
Phone: (617) 753-8300
Fax: (617) 753-8350

MICHIGAN
John Hubinger
Division Chief
Div. of Emergency Medical Services
Dept. of Community Health
525 W. Ottawa
P.O. Box 30664
Lansing, MI 48933
Phone: (517) 241-3018
Fax: (517) 241-2895

MINNESOTA
Mary Hedges
Executive Director
Emergency Medical Services Regulating Board
2829 Univ. Ave., SE, Ste. 310
Minneapolis, MN 55414
Phone: (651) 627-6000
Fax: (651) 627-5442

MISSISSIPPI
Wade N. Spruill, Jr.
Director
Emergency Medical Services
Dept. of Health
P.O. Box 1700
Jackson, MS 39215-1700
Phone: (601) 987-3882
Fax: (601) 987-3880

MISSOURI
Carey Smith
Director
Bur. of Emergency Medical Services
Dept. of Health
920 Wildwood Dr.
P.O. Box 570
Jefferson City, MO 65102-0570
Phone: (573) 751-6356
Fax: (573) 526-4102

MONTANA
Drew Dawson
Section Supervisor
Emergency Medical Services & Injury Prevention
Dept. of Public Health & Human Services Section
1400 Broadway, Rm. C204
Helena, MT 59620
Phone: (406) 444-3895
Fax: (406) 444-1814

NEBRASKA
Richard P. Nelson
Director
Dept. of Health & Human Services, Regulation & Licensure
P.O. Box 95007
Lincoln, NE 68509-5007
Phone: (402) 471-3979
Fax: (402) 471-0820

NEVADA

NEW HAMPSHIRE
Dianne Luby
Director
Ofc. of Health Mgmt.
Health & Human Services
6 Hazen Dr.
Concord, NH 03301-6527
Phone: (603) 271-4501
Fax: (603) 271-4827

NEW JERSEY
Gerard Muench
Director
Emergency & Medical Services
Dept. of Health
50 E. State St., 6th Fl.
P.O. Box 360
Trenton, NJ 08625
Phone: (609) 633-7777
Fax: (609) 633-7954

NEW MEXICO
Barak Wolff
Director
Injury Prevention EMS
Dept. of Health
P.O. Box 26110
Sante Fe, NM 87502
Phone: (505) 476-7000
Fax: (505) 476-7010

NEW YORK
Dennis P. Whalen
Executive Deputy Commissioner
Dept. of Health
Corning Tower Bldg., Rm. 1408
Empire State Plz.
Albany, NY 12237
Phone: (518) 474-0458
Fax: (518) 474-5450

NORTH CAROLINA
Bob Bailey
Chief
Emergency Medical Services
Dept. of Health & Human Services
701 Barbour Dr.
Raleigh, NC 27603-2008
Phone: (919) 733-2285
Fax: (919) 733-7021

NORTH DAKOTA
Timothy Wiedrich
Director
Emergency Health Services
Health Resources Section
600 E. Blvd. Ave., 2nd Fl. - Judicial Wing
Bismarck, ND 58505-0200
Phone: (701) 328-2388
Fax: (701) 328-4727
E-mail: twiedric@state.nd.us

NORTHERN MARIANA ISLANDS
Joseph Kevin P. Villagomez
Secretary of Public Health
Commonwealth Health Ctr.
Dept. of Public Health
P.O. Box 409
Saipan, MP 96950
Phone: (670) 234-8950
Fax: (670) 234-8931

OHIO
Linda Ishler
Executive Administrator
Public Safety Services
Emergency Medical Services Agency
1970 W. Broad St.
Columbus, OH 43223-1102
Phone: (614) 466-9447
Fax: (614) 466-9461

OKLAHOMA
Eddie Manley
Director
Emergency Medical Services
1000 NE 10th St.
Oklahoma City, OK 73117-1299
Phone: (405) 271-4027
Fax: (405) 271-3431

OREGON
Gregg Lander
Manager
Emergency Medical Services
Health Div.
Portland State Ofc. Bldg.
800 NE Oregon, #21
Portland, OR 97232
Phone: (503) 731-4011
Fax: (503) 731-4077

PENNSYLVANIA
Margret E. Trimble
Director
Emergency Medical Services
Dept. of Health
Health & Welfare Bldg., Rm. 1033
Harrisburg, PA 17108
Phone: (717) 787-8741
Fax: (717) 772-0910

PUERTO RICO

RHODE ISLAND
Peter Leary
Chief
Emergency Medical Services Div.
Dept. of Health
3 Capitol Hill
Providence, RI 02903
Phone: (401) 222-2401

SOUTH CAROLINA
Joe Fanning
Director
Emergency Medical Services Div.
Dept. of Health & Environmental Control
2600 Bull St.
Columbia, SC 29201
Phone: (803) 737-7204
Fax: (803) 737-7212

SOUTH DAKOTA
Robert Sines
Director
Emergency Medical Services, Div. of Health Services
Dept. of Health
600 E. Capitol Ave.
Pierre, SD 57501
Phone: (605) 773-4928
Fax: (605) 773-5509

TENNESSEE
Joseph B. Phillips
Director
Emergency Medical Services
Cordell Hull Bldg., 1st Fl.
Nashville, TN 37247-0701
Phone: (615) 741-2584
Fax: (615) 741-4217

TEXAS
Gene Weatherall
Emergency Medical Services Div.
Dept. of Health
1100 W. 49th St.
Austin, TX 78756
Phone: (512) 458-7111
Fax: (512) 834-6736

U.S. VIRGIN ISLANDS
Alexander Williams
District Director
Emergency Medical Services
Dept. of Health
St. Thomas Hospital
St. Thomas, VI 00802
Phone: (340) 776-8311
Fax: (340) 777-4001

UTAH
Jan M. Buttrey
Director
Emergency Medical Services Bur.
Dept. of Health-EMS
P.O. Box 142851
Salt Lake City, UT 84114-2851
Phone: (801) 538-6718
Fax: (801) 538-6808
E-Mail: jbuttrey@doh.state.ut.us

VERMONT
Dan Manz
Director
Emergency Medical Services Div.
Dept. of Health
108 Cherry St.
P.O. Box 70
Burlington, VT 05402
Phone: (802) 863-7310
Fax: (802) 863-7577

VIRGINIA
E. Anne Peterson
Acting Commissioner
Dept. of Health
Main St. Station, Rm. 214
1500 E. Main St.
Richmond, VA 23219
Phone: (804) 786-3561
Fax: (804) 786-4616

WASHINGTON
Janet Griffith
Program Director
Emergency Medical Services
Dept. of Health
2725 Harrison Ave., NW, Unit 500
P.O. Box 47853
Olympia, WA 98504
Phone: (360) 705-6745
Fax: (360) 705-6706

WEST VIRGINIA
Mark E. King
Director
Emergency Medical Service Ofc.
1411 Virginia St., E.
Charleston, WV 25305
Phone: (304) 558-3956
Fax: (304) 558-1437

WISCONSIN
Jon Morgan
Bureau Director
Emergency Medical Services & Injury Prevention
Div. of Public Health
1414 E. Washington, Rm. 227
Madison, WI 53703-3044
Phone: (608) 266-1568
Fax: (608) 261-6392

WYOMING
Jim Murray
Program Manager
Emergency Medical Services
Health & Medical Services Div.
Hathaway Bldg., Rm. 527
2300 Capitol Ave.
Cheyenne, WY 82002
Phone: (307) 777-6020

Employee Relations

Handles state employee grievances and appeals.

ALABAMA
Thomas Flowers
Director
State Personnel Dept.
64 N. Union St.
Montgomery, AL 36130-4100
Phone: (334) 242-3389
Fax: (334) 353-3320

ALASKA
Vacant
Director
Div. of Personnel
Dept. of Administration
P.O. Box 110201
Juneau, AK 99811-0201
Phone: (907) 465-4404
Fax: (907) 465-2269

AMERICAN SAMOA
Sapini Siatu'u
Director
Dept. of Human Resources
AS Govt.
Pago Pago, AS 96799
Phone: (684) 633-4485
Fax: (684) 633-1139

ARIZONA
James Matthews
Human Resources Director
Personnel Div.
Dept. of Administration
1831 W. Jefferson
Phoenix, AZ 85007
Phone: (602) 542-5482
Fax: (602) 542-2796

ARKANSAS
Artee Williams
State Personnel Administrator
Ofc. of Personnel Mgmt.
Dept. of Finance & Administration
201 DFA Bldg.
1509 W. 7th St.
Little Rock, AR 72201
Phone: (501) 682-1823
Fax: (501) 682-5094

CALIFORNIA
David J. Tirapelle
Director
Dept. of Personnel Administration
1515 S St., N. Bldg., Ste. 400
Sacramento, CA 95814
Phone: (916) 322-5193

COLORADO
Larry E. Trujillo, Sr.
Executive Director
Support Services
Dept. of Personnel
1525 Sherman St., 2nd Fl.
Denver, CO 80203
Phone: (303) 866-6559
Fax: (303) 866-6569

CONNECTICUT
Barbara Waters
Commissioner
Dept. of Adm. Services
165 Capitol Ave., Rm. 491
Hartford, CT 06106
Phone: (860) 713-5100

DELAWARE
Harriet Smith-Windsor
Director
Ofc. of Personnel
Townsend Bldg.
P.O. Box 1401
Dover, DE 19903
Phone: (302) 739-4195
Fax: (302) 739-3000
E-mail: hnsmith@state.de.us

DISTRICT OF COLUMBIA
Judy D. Banks
Director
Ofc. of Personnel
441 4th St., NW, Ste. 300, S.
Washington, DC 20001
Phone: (202) 727-6406
Fax: (202) 727-6827

FLORIDA
Sharon Larson
Director
Human Resource Mgmt.
Dept. of Mgmt. Services
4050 Esplanade Way, Bldg. 4040, Ste. 360
Tallahassee, FL 32399-0950
Phone: (850) 922-5449
Fax: (850) 921-4117

GEORGIA
Diane Schlachter
Director
Training & Organizational Dev.
Merit System
529A Church St.
Decatur, GA 30030-2515
Phone: (404) 371-7371

GUAM
Eloy P. Hara
Executive Director
Civil Service Comm.
490 Chalan Palasyo, Agana Heights
P.O. Box 3156
Hagatna, GU 96932
Phone: (671) 475-1300
Fax: (671) 477-3301

HAWAII
Ann Morimoto
Division Chief
Labor Relations Div.
Dept. of Human Resources Dev.
235 S. Beretania St., 14th Fl., Rm. 1402
Honolulu, HI 96813
Phone: (808) 587-0918
Fax: (808) 587-0930

IDAHO
Richard Hutchison
Director
Personnel Comm.
700 W. State St.
Boise, ID 83720
Phone: (208) 334-3345
Fax: (208) 334-3182

ILLINOIS
Michael S. Schwartz
Director
Dept. of Central Mgmt. Services
715 Stratton Ofc. Bldg.
401 S. Spring
Springfield, IL 62706
Phone: (217) 782-2141
Fax: (217) 524-1880

INDIANA
William T. Johnson
Deputy Director
Employee/Labor Relations
Personnel Dept.
IGC-South, Rm. W161
Indianapolis, IN 46204
Phone: (317) 232-3036
Fax: (317) 232-1197

IOWA
Mollie Anderson
Director
Dept. of Personnel
Grimes State Ofc. Bldg.
E. 14th & Grand Aves.
Des Moines, IA 50319
Phone: (515) 281-3351
Fax: (515) 242-6450
E-mail: mollie.anderson@idop.state.ia.us

KANSAS
Roger Aeschliman
Deputy Secretary
Div. of Staff Services
Dept. of Human Resources
410 SW Topeka Blvd.
Topeka, KS 66603-3182
Phone: (785) 296-0821

KENTUCKY
Carol Palmore
Secretary
Personnel Cabinet
200 Fairoaks, Ste. 516
Frankfort, KY 40601
Phone: (502) 564-4460
Fax: (502) 564-7603

LOUISIANA
Allan H. Reynolds
Civil Service Director
Personnel Mgmt. Div.
Dept. of Civil Service
P.O. Box 94111
Baton Rouge, LA 70804-9111
Phone: (225) 342-8272
Fax: (225) 342-6074

MAINE
Kenneth A. Walo
Director
Bur. of Employee Relations
Dept. of Adm. & Financial Services
79 State House Station
Augusta, ME 04333
Phone: (207) 287-4447

MARYLAND
Frederick E. Ramsey
Director
Employee Relations Div.
Dept. of Budget & Mgmt.
301 W. Preston St., Rm. 608
Baltimore, MD 21202
Phone: (410) 767-1012
Fax: (410) 333-7603
E-mail: framsey@dbm.state.md.us

MASSACHUSETTS
John Jesensky
Director
Ofc. of Employee Relations
Executive Ofc. for Administration & Finance
One Ashburton Pl., Rm. 301
Boston, MA 02108
Phone: (617) 727-5403
Fax: (617) 727-3252

MICHIGAN
John Palmer
Director
Employment Service Agency
Economic Dev. Corp.
105 W. Allegan, 3rd Fl.
Lansing, MI 48933
Phone: (313) 241-2751

Janine Winters
Director
Ofc. of State Employer
Dept. of Mgmt. & Budget
P.O. Box 30026
Lansing, MI 48909
Phone: (517) 373-1554

MINNESOTA
Karen L. Carpenter
Commissioner
Dept. of Employee Relations
200 Centennial Ofc. Bldg.
658 Cedar St.
St. Paul, MN 55101-1603
Phone: (651) 296-2914
Fax: (651) 296-1990
E-mail: karen.carpenter@state.mn.us

MISSISSIPPI
J.K. Stringer, Jr.
Director
State Personnel Board
301 N. Lamar St., Ste. 201
Jackson, MS 39201
Phone: (601) 359-2702
Fax: (601) 359-2729

MISSOURI
Julia A. Hawkins
Chair
Personnel Advisory Board
Ofc. of Administration
Truman Bldg., Rm. 430
P.O. Box 388
Jefferson City, MO 65102
Phone: (573) 751-4576
Fax: (573) 751-1622
E-mail: whites@mail.oa.state.mo.us

MONTANA
Jerry Keck
Administrator
Employment Relations Div.
Dept. of Labor & Industry
P.O. Box 8011
Helena, MT 59604-8011
Phone: (406) 444-1555
Fax: (406) 444-4140

NEBRASKA
William Wood
Labor Relations Administrator
Div. of Employee Relations
Dept. of Adm. Services
P.O. Box 95061
Lincoln, NE 68509-5061
Phone: (402) 471-4106
Fax: (402) 471-3394

NEVADA
Jeanne Greene
Acting Director
Dept. of Personnel
209 E. Musser St., Rm. 300
Carson City, NV 89710-4204
Phone: (775) 684-0131
Fax: (775) 684-0124

NEW HAMPSHIRE
Parker A. Denaco
Executive Director
Public Employees Labor Relations Board
GAA Plz., Bldg. #1
153 Manchester St.
Concord, NH 03301-5122
Phone: (603) 271-2587

NEW JERSEY
Millicent A. Wasell
Chair
Public Employment Relations Comm.
P.O. Box 428
Trenton, NJ 08625-0428
Phone: (609) 292-6780
Fax: (609) 777-0087

NEW MEXICO
Rex Robberson
Director
State Personnel Ofc.
2600 Cerillos
Santa Fe, NM 87505-0127
Phone: (505) 476-7805
Fax: (505) 476-7806

NEW YORK
Linda Angello
Director
Governor's Ofc. of Employee Relations
Agency Bldg. 2, 12th Fl.
Empire State Plz.
Albany, NY 12223
Phone: (518) 474-6988
Fax: (518) 486-7304

NORTH CAROLINA
Ronald G. Penny
Director
Ofc. of State Personnel
Dept. of Administration
116 W. Jones St.
Raleigh, NC 27603-8003
Phone: (919) 733-7108
Fax: (919) 733-0653

NORTH DAKOTA
Dan LeRoy
Director
Central Personnel Div.
600 E. Blvd. Ave., 14th Fl.
Bismarck, ND 58505-0120
Phone: (701) 328-3290
Fax: (701) 328-1475
E-mail: dleroy@state.nd.us

NORTHERN MARIANA ISLANDS
Eugene A. Santos
Board Chair
Civil Service Comm.
Personnel Mgmt. Ofc.
Ofc. of the Governor
P.O. Box 5150 CHRB
Saipan, MP 96950
Phone: (670) 322-4363
Fax: (670) 322-3327
E-mail: csc@saipan.com

OHIO
Roger W. Tracy
Chair
Personnel Board of Review
65 E. State St., 12th Fl.
Columbus, OH 43266-0319
Phone: (614) 466-7046
Fax: (614) 466-6539

OKLAHOMA
James L. Howard
Executive Director
Merit Projection Comm.
310 NE 28th, Ste. 201
Oklahoma City, OK 73105
Phone: (405) 525-9144
Fax: (405) 528-6245

OREGON
Dan Kennedy
Administrator
Human Resources Services Div.
Dept. of Adm. Services
155 Cottage St., NE
Salem, OR 97310
Phone: (503) 378-3020
Fax: (503) 378-7684

PENNSYLVANIA
Christ J. Zervanos
Director
Bur. of Labor Relations
Ofc. of Administration
404 Finance Bldg.
Harrisburg, PA 17105
Phone: (717) 787-5837
Fax: (717) 783-0430

PUERTO RICO
Samuel De La Rosa
Director
Bur. of Employment Security
Labor & Human Resources Dept.
505 Munoz Rivera Ave.
Hato Rey, PR 00918
Phone: (787) 753-5454
Fax: (787) 753-9550

RHODE ISLAND
John Turano
Labor Relations Administrator
Dept. of Administration
1 Capitol Hill
Providence, RI 02908
Phone: (401) 222-2154

SOUTH CAROLINA
Donna Traywick
Director
Ofc. of Human Resources
Budget & Control Board
1201 Main St., Ste. 1000
Columbia, SC 29201
Phone: (803) 737-0900
Fax: (803) 737-0968

SOUTH DAKOTA
Sandy Zinter
Commissioner
Bur. of Personnel
500 E. Capitol Ave.
Pierre, SD 57501
Phone: (605) 773-3148
Fax: (605) 773-4344

TENNESSEE
Patsy McGee
Director
Employee Relations
Dept. of Personnel
James K. Polk Bldg., 2nd Fl.
Nashville, TN 37243
Phone: (615) 741-1646
Fax: (615) 532-0728

TEXAS
William M. Hale
Executive Director
Comm. on Human Rights
6330 Hwy., 290 E., Ste. 250
Austin, TX 78723
Phone: (512) 437-3450
Fax: (512) 437-3478

U.S. VIRGIN ISLANDS
Karen Andrews
Chief Negotiator
Ofc. of Collective Bargaining
Ofc. of the Governor
#8 GD Lyttons Fancy
St. Thomas, VI 00802
Phone: (340) 774-6450
Fax: (340) 777-4622

UTAH
Robert N. White
Administrator
Career Service Review Board
1120 State Ofc. Bldg.
Salt Lake City, UT 84114-1201
Phone: (801) 538-3047
Fax: (801) 538-3139
E-mail: rwhite.pedhrm@state.ut.us

VERMONT
Thomas D. Ball
Director of Employee Relations
Dept. of Personnel
110 State St.
Montpelier, VT 05602
Phone: (802) 828-3642
Fax: (802) 828-3409

VIRGINIA
Neil A.G. McPhie
Director
Dept. of Employee Relations Counselors
Exchange Pl., Ste. 305
1313 E. Main St.
Richmond, VA 23219-3600
Phone: (804) 786-7994
Fax: (804) 786-0100

WASHINGTON
Dennis Karras
Director
Dept. of Personnel
521 Capitol Way, S.
P.O. Box 47500
Olympia, WA 98504
Phone: (360) 753-5368
Fax: (360) 586-4694

WEST VIRGINIA
Edison L. Casto
Director of Personnel
Div. of Personnel
State Capitol, Bldg. 6, Rm. B-416
1900 Kanawha Blvd., E.
Charleston, WV 25305-0139
Phone: (304) 558-3950
Fax: (304) 558-1587

WISCONSIN
Peter D. Fox
Secretary
Dept. of Employment Relations
345 W. Washington Ave.
P.O. Box 7855
Madison, WI 53707-7855
Phone: (608) 266-9820
Fax: (605) 267-1020

WYOMING
Mike Miller
Administrator
Personnel Div.
Dept. of Administration & Info.
2001 Capitol Ave.
Cheyenne, WY 82002-0060
Phone: (307) 777-6713

Employment Services

Provides job counseling, testing and placement services in the state.

ALABAMA
Sylvia Williams
Chief
Employment Services Div.
Dept. of Industrial Relations
649 Monroe St.
Montgomery, AL 36130-3301
Phone: (334) 242-8003
Fax: (334) 242-8012

ALASKA
Rebecca Gamez
Director
Div. of Employment Security
Dept. of Labor
P.O. Box 25509
Juneau, AK 99802
Phone: (907) 465-2711
Fax: (907) 465-4537

AMERICAN SAMOA
Sapini Siatu'u
Director
Dept. of Human Resources
AS Govt.
Pago Pago, AS 96799
Phone: (684) 633-4485
Fax: (684) 633-1139

ARIZONA
Bill F. Hernandez
Assistant Director
Employment & Rehab. Services
Dept. of Economic Security
1789 W. Washington St.
Phoenix, AZ 85007
Phone: (602) 542-4910

ARKANSAS
Ed Rolle
Director
Employment Security Dept.
#2 Capitol Mall, Rm. 506
Little Rock, AR 72201
Phone: (501) 682-2121
Fax: (501) 682-3223

CALIFORNIA
Ray Remy
Director
Dept. of Employment Dev.
800 Capitol Mall, Rm. 5000
Sacramento, CA 95814
Phone: (916) 654-8210

COLORADO
Vickie Armstrong
Executive Director
Dept. of Labor & Employment
1515 Arapahoe St.
Tower 2, Ste. 400
Denver, CO 80202
Phone: (303) 620-4700
Fax: (303) 620-4714

CONNECTICUT
Jean E. Zurbrigen
Deputy Commissioner/ Executive Director
Employment Security Div.
Dept. of Labor
38 Wolcott Hill Rd.
Wethersfield, CT 06109
Phone: (860) 263-6785

DELAWARE
Lisa L. Blunt-Bradley
Secretary
Dept. of Labor
4425 N. Market St., 4th Fl.
Wilmington, DE 19802
Phone: (302) 761-8001
Fax: (302) 761-6621

DISTRICT OF COLUMBIA
Gregory Irish
Director
Dept. of Employment Services
500 C St., NW, Rm. 600
Washington, DC 20001
Phone: (202) 724-7101

FLORIDA
Kathleen McLeskey
Director
Div. of Jobs & Benefits
Dept. of Labor & Employment Services
Atkins Bldg., Ste. 300
1320 Executive Ctr. Dr.
Tallahassee, FL 32399-0667
Phone: (850) 488-7228
Fax: (850) 487-1753

GEORGIA
Helen Parker
Assistant Commissioner
Employment Services Div.
Dept. of Labor
148 Intl. Blvd., Rm. 400
Atlanta, GA 30303
Phone: (404) 656-6380

GUAM
Dennis G. Rodriguez
Director
Dept. of Public Health & Social Services
P.O. Box 2816
Hagatna, GU 96932
Phone: (671) 735-7102
Fax: (671) 734-5910
E-mail: dennis_r_@NS.GOV.GU

James Underwood
Acting Director
Dept. of Labor
504 E. Sunset Blvd., Tiyan
P.O. Box 9970
Tamuning, GU 96931
Phone: (671) 475-0101
Fax: (671) 477-2988

HAWAII
Elaine Young
Administrator
Workforce Dev. Div.
Dept. of Labor & Industrial Relations
830 Punchbowl St., Rm. 329
Honolulu, HI 96814
Phone: (808) 586-8812
Fax: (808) 586-8822

IDAHO
Roger Madsen
Director
Dept. of Labor
317 Main St.
Boise, ID 83702
Phone: (208) 334-6100
Fax: (208) 334-6430

ILLINOIS
Linda Renee Baker
Director
Dept. of Employment Security
401 S. State St., 6th Fl.
Chicago, IL 60605
Phone: (312) 793-5700
Fax: (312) 793-9834

INDIANA
Craig E. Hartzer
Commissioner
Dept. of Workforce Dev.
10 N. Senate, Rm. SE-302
Indianapolis, IN 46204
Phone: (317) 233-5661
Fax: (317) 232-1815

IOWA
Richard Running
Director
Workforce Dev.
1000 E. Grand Ave.
Des Moines, IA 50319
Phone: (515) 281-5365
Fax: (515) 281-4698

KANSAS
Rick Beyer
Secretary
Dept. of Human Resources
401 SW Topeka Blvd.
Topeka, KS 66603
Phone: (785) 296-7474
Fax: (785) 296-0179

KENTUCKY
David Cooke
Director
Application Counseling & Exams
Personnel Cabinet
200 Fairoaks
Frankfort, KY 40601
Phone: (502) 564-6920
Fax: (502) 564-5826

LOUISIANA
Linda Duscoe
Acting Director
Employment Services Div.
Dept. of Labor
P.O. Box 94094
Baton Rouge, LA 70804-9094
Phone: (225) 342-3016
Fax: (225) 342-5208

MAINE

MARYLAND
Steven D. Serra
Director
Recruitment & Examination
Dept. of Budget & Mgmt.
300 W. Preston St., Rm. 307
Baltimore, MD 21201
Phone: (410) 767-4917
Fax: (410) 333-7674
E-mail: sserra@dbm.state.md.us

MASSACHUSETTS
John A. King
Deputy Director
Div. of Employment & Training
Dept. of Labor & Workforce Dev.
19 Staniford St., 3rd Fl.
Boston, MA 02114
Phone: (617) 626-6600
Fax: (617) 727-0315

MICHIGAN
Jack F. Wheatley
Acting Director
Unemployment Agency
7310 Woodward Ave., Rm. 510
Detroit, MI 48202
Phone: (313) 876-5901
Fax: (313) 876-5587

MINNESOTA
John Weidenbach
Assistant Commissioner
Job Services & Re-employment Insurance Div.
Dept. of Economic Security
390 N. Robert St.
St. Paul, MN 55101
Phone: (651) 296-1692
Fax: (651) 296-0994

MISSISSIPPI
Tom Lord
Director
Employment Security Comm.
1520 W. Capitol
P.O. Box 1699
Jackson, MS 39215-1699
Phone: (601) 961-7500
Fax: (601) 961-7405

MISSOURI
Catherine B. Leapheart
Director
Div. of Employment Security
Dept. of Labor & Industrial Relations
P.O. Box 59
Jefferson City, MO 65104-0059
Phone: (573) 751-3976
Fax: (573) 751-4945
E-mail: cleapheart@dolir.state.mo.us

MONTANA
Wendy Keating
Administrator
Job Services Div.
Dept. of Labor & Industry
Walt Sullivan Bldg., 1327 Lockey
P.O. Box 1728
Helena, MT 59624
Phone: (406) 444-2648
Fax: (406) 444-3037

NEBRASKA
Linda Kirk
Director
Job Training Div.
Dept. of Labor
550 S. 16th St.
Lincoln, NE 68509
Phone: (402) 471-9903
Fax: (402) 471-2318

NEVADA
Stanley Jones
Administrator
Div. of Employment Security
Employment, Training & Rehab. Dept.
500 E. 3rd St.
Carson City, NV 89713
Phone: (775) 684-3909
Fax: (775) 684-3910

NEW HAMPSHIRE
John J. Ratoff
Commissioner
Dept. of Employment Security
32 S. Main St.
Concord, NH 03301-4857
Phone: (603) 224-3311
Fax: (603) 228-4145

NEW JERSEY
Connie O. Hughes
Director
Workforce NJ
Dept. of Labor
John Fitch Plz.
P.O. Box 055
Trenton, NJ 08625-0055
Phone: (609) 984-2244
Fax: (609) 777-0483

NEW MEXICO
Clint Harden
Secretary
Dept. of Labor
P.O. Box 1928
Albuquerque, NM 87103
Phone: (505) 841-8409
Fax: (505) 841-8491

NEW YORK
James J. McGowan
Commissioner
Dept. of Labor
State Ofc. Bldg. Campus, Bldg. 12
Albany, NY 12240
Phone: (518) 457-2741
Fax: (518) 457-6908

NORTH CAROLINA
J. Parker Chesson
Chair
Employment Security Comm.
Dept. of Commerce
700 Wade Ave.
Raleigh, NC 27605
Phone: (919) 733-7546
Fax: (919) 733-1129

NORTH DAKOTA
Jennifer Gladden
Executive Director
Job Service
P.O. Box 5507
Bismarck, ND 58506-5507
Phone: (701) 328-2836
Fax: (701) 328-4000
E-mail: jgladden@state.nd.us

NORTHERN MARIANA ISLANDS
Jose B. Cruz
Director
Employment Services
Dept. of Labor & Immigration
P.O. Box 10007
Saipan, MP 96950
Phone: (670) 664-2086
Fax: (670) 664-3175

OHIO
Jim Mermis
Administrator
Bur. of Employment Services
145 S. Front St.
Columbus, OH 43215
Phone: (614) 466-8032
Fax: (614) 466-5025

OKLAHOMA
Jon Brock
Executive Director
Employment Security Comm.
2401 N. Lincoln Blvd.
Oklahoma City, OK 73105
Phone: (405) 557-7200
Fax: (405) 557-7256

Oscar Jackson
Administrator & Cabinet Secretary of Human Resources
Ofc. of Personnel Mgmt.
2101 N. Lincoln Blvd.
Oklahoma City, OK 73105
Phone: (405) 521-6301
Fax: (405) 524-6942
E-mail: oscar.jackson@oklaosf.state.ok.us

OREGON
Virlena Crosley
Director
Employment Dept.
875 Union St., NE
Salem, OR 97311
Phone: (503) 947-1477
Fax: (503) 947-1472

PENNSYLVANIA
Alan Williamson
Deputy Secretary
Employment Security & Job Training
Dept. of Labor & Industry
Labor & Industry Bldg., Rm. 1700
Harrisburg, PA 17120
Phone: (717) 787-3907
Fax: (717) 787-8826

PUERTO RICO
Ednidia Padilla
Director
Bur. of Employment Security
Dept. of Labor & Human Resources
505 Munoz Rivera Ave.
Hato Rey, PR 00918
Phone: (787) 754-5375
Fax: (787) 763-2227

RHODE ISLAND
Lee Arnold
Director
Dept. of Labor & Training
101 Friendship St.
Providence, RI 02903
Phone: (401) 222-3732
Fax: (401) 222-1473

SOUTH CAROLINA
Joel T. Cassidy
Executive Director
Employment Security Comm.
P.O. Box 995
Columbia, SC 29202
Phone: (803) 737-2617

SOUTH DAKOTA
Lloyd Schipper
Deputy Secretary
Div. of Job Services
Dept. of Labor
700 Governors Dr.
Pierre, SD 57501
Phone: (605) 773-3372
Fax: (605) 773-6680

TENNESSEE
Hazel Albert
Commissioner
Dept. of Employment Security
Davy Crockett Tower, 12th Fl.
500 James Robertson Pkwy.
Nashville, TN 37245-0001
Phone: (615) 741-2131
Fax: (615) 741-2741

TEXAS
Mike Sheridan
Executive Director
Workforce Comm.
TWC Bldg.
101 E. 15th St.
Austin, TX 78778-0001
Phone: (512) 463-0735
Fax: (512) 475-2321
E-mail: mike.sheridan@twc.state.tx.us

U.S. VIRGIN ISLANDS
Eleuteria Roberts
Acting Commissioner
Dept. of Labor
2203 Church St.
Christiansted
St. Croix, VI 00820
Phone: (340) 773-1994
Fax: (340) 773-0094

UTAH
Robert C. Gross
Executive Director
Ofc. of the Executive Director
Dept. of Workforce Services
140 E. 300 S.
Salt Lake City, UT 84111
Phone: (801) 526-9207
Fax: (801) 526-9211
E-mail: rgross.wsadmpo@state.ut.us

VERMONT
Steven Gold
Commissioner
Dept. of Employment & Training Administration
5 Green Mountain Dr.
Montpelier, VT 05601-0488
Phone: (802) 828-4000
Fax: (802) 828-4022

VIRGINIA
Thomas J. Towberman
Commissioner
Employment Comm.
703 E. Main St.
Richmond, VA 23219
Phone: (804) 786-3001
Fax: (804) 225-3923

WASHINGTON
Gary Gallwas
Assistant Commissioner
Employment & Training Div.
Dept. of Employment Security
P.O. Box 9046, MS 6000
Olympia, WA 98507-9046
Phone: (360) 438-4611
Fax: (360) 438-3224

WEST VIRGINIA
William Vieweg
Commissioner
Bur. of Unemployment Programs
Bldg. 4, Rm. 610
112 California Ave.
Charleston, WV 25332
Phone: (304) 558-2630

WISCONSIN
Eric Baker
Deputy Administrator
Div. of Workforce Excellence
Dept. of Workforce Dev.
201 E. Washington, Rm. 201X
Madison, WI 53703
Phone: (608) 266-0327
Fax: (608) 267-2392

WYOMING
Patricia Smith
Program Consultant
Employment Resources Div.
P.O. Box 2760
Casper, WY 82602
Phone: (307) 235-3611
Fax: (307) 235-3293

Energy

Develops and administers programs relating to energy conservation, alternative energy research and development, and energy information.

ALABAMA
Terry Adams
Division Director
Science, Technology & Energy Div.
Economic & Community Affairs Dept.
401 Adams Ave.
P.O. Box 5690
Montgomery, AL 36103
Phone: (334) 242-5292
Fax: (334) 242-0552

ALASKA
Percy Frisby
Director
Div. of Energy
Dept. of Community & Regional Affairs
333 W. 4th Ave., Ste. 220
Anchorage, AK 99519-2341
Phone: (907) 269-4640
Fax: (907) 269-4645

AMERICAN SAMOA
Reupena Tagaloa
Director
Territorial Energy Ofc.
AS Govt.
Pago Pago, AS 96799
Phone: (684) 699-1101
Fax: (684) 699-2835

ARIZONA
Amanda Ormond
Director
Energy Dev. & Utilization
Dept. of Commerce
3800 N. Central Ave., Ste. 1200
Phoenix, AZ 85012
Phone: (602) 280-1402
Fax: (602) 280-1445

ARKANSAS
Alan McVey
Deputy Director
Dept. of Economic Dev.
1 Capitol Mall, Rm. 4C-300
Little Rock, AR 72201
Phone: (501) 682-7350
Fax: (501) 682-7394

CALIFORNIA
Bill Keese
Chair
Energy Comm.
1516 9th St.
Sacramento, CA 95814
Phone: (916) 654-5000

COLORADO
Rick Grice
Director
Ofc. of Energy Conservation
Ofc. of the Governor
1675 Broadway, Ste. 1300
Denver, CO 80212
Phone: (303) 620-4237
Fax: (303) 620-4288

CONNECTICUT
Ann Moore
Undersecretary
Policy Dev. & Planning Div.
Ofc. of Policy & Mgmt.
P.O. Box 341441
Hartford, CT 06134-1441
Phone: (806) 418-6484

DELAWARE
Charles Smisson
Energy Program Administrator
Energy Ofc.
Dept. of Adm. Services
P.O. Box 1401
Dover, DE 19903
Phone: (302) 739-5644

DISTRICT OF COLUMBIA
Charles J. Clinton
Director
Energy Ofc.
2000 14th St., NW, Ste. 300, E.
Washington, DC 20009
Phone: (202) 673-6736

FLORIDA
Jim Tait
Director
Energy Ofc.
Dept. of Community Affairs
2555 Shumard Oak Blvd.
Tallahassee, FL 32399-2100
Phone: (850) 488-2475
Fax: (850) 488-7688

GEORGIA
Paul Burks
Executive Director
Enviroment Facilities Authority
100 Peachtree NW, Ste. 2090
Atlanta, GA 30303-1911
Phone: (404) 656-0938

GUAM
Fred P. Camacho
Director
Energy Ofc.
1504 E. Sunset Blvd.
Tiyan, GU 96913
Phone: (671) 477-0538
Fax: (671) 477-0589
E-mail: guamenergy@kuentos.guam.net

HAWAII
Maurice Kaya
Division Head
Energy, Resources & Technology Div.
Business, Economic Dev. & Tourism
P.O. Box 2359
Honolulu, HI 96804
Phone: (808) 587-3807
Fax: (808) 586-2536

IDAHO
Bob Hoppie
Administrator
Energy Div.
Dept. of Water Resources
1301 N. Orchard St.
Boise, ID 83720
Phone: (208) 327-7910

ILLINOIS
Pam McDonough
Director
Dept. of Commerce & Community Affairs
620 E. Adams St., 3rd Fl.
Springfield, IL 62701
Phone: (217) 782-3233
Fax: (217) 524-0864

INDIANA
Cheryl DeVol
Director
Div. of Energy Policy
Dept. of Commerce
1 N. Capitol, Ste. 700
Indianapolis, IN 46204
Phone: (317) 232-8939
Fax: (317) 232-8995

IOWA
Larry L. Bean
Administrator
Energy & Geological Resource Div.
Dept. of Natural Resources
Wallace State Ofc. Bldg.
E. 9th & Grand Aves.
Des Moines, IA 50319
Phone: (515) 281-4308

KANSAS
Jim Ploger
Manager
Energy Programs
Corps. Comm.
1500 SW Arrowhead Rd.
Topeka, KS 66604-4027
Phone: (785) 271-3349
Fax: (785) 271-3268

KENTUCKY
John M. Stapleton
Director
Energy Div.
Natural Resources Dept.
663 Teton Trail
Frankfort, KY 40601
Phone: (502) 564-7192
Fax: (502) 564-7484

LOUISIANA
Philip Asprodites
Commissioner of Conservation
Dept. of Natural Resources
P.O. Box 94275
Baton Rouge, LA 70804
Phone: (225) 342-5540
Fax: (225) 342-2584

MAINE
Evan Richert
Director
State Planning Ofc.
38 State House Station
Augusta, ME 04333
Phone: (207) 287-6077

MARYLAND
Frederick H. Hoover, Jr.
Director
Energy Administration
Executive Dept.
45 Calvert St., 4th Fl.
Annapolis, MD 21401
Phone: (410) 260-7511
Fax: (410) 974-2250

MASSACHUSETTS
David O'Connor
Commissioner
Div. of Energy Resources
100 Cambridge St., Rm. 1500
Boston, MA 02202
Phone: (617) 727-4732
Fax: (617) 727-0030

MICHIGAN

MINNESOTA
Linda S. Taylor
Assistant Commissioner
Energy Div.
Dept. of Public Service
121 7th Pl., E., #200
Minneapolis, MN 55101
Phone: (651) 296-6711
Fax: (651) 297-7891
E-mail: ltaylor@dpsu.state.mn.us

MISSISSIPPI
Chester Smith
Director
Div. of Energy
Dept. of Economic & Community Dev.
P.O. Box 850
Jackson, MS 39205-0850
Phone: (601) 359-6600
Fax: (601) 359-6642

MISSOURI
Anita Randolph
Director
Div. of Energy
Dept. of Natural Resources
1500 Southridge Dr.
P.O. Box 176
Jefferson City, MO 65102
Phone: (573) 751-4000
Fax: (573) 751-6860
E-mail: nrranda@mail.dnr.state.mo.us

MONTANA
Tim Fox
Acting Administrator
Planning, Prevention & Assistance
Dept. of Environmental Quality
Metcalf Bldg.
1520 E. 6th Ave.
Helena, MT 59620
Phone: (406) 444-6697
Fax: (406) 444-6836

NEBRASKA
Larry Pearce
Acting Director
Energy Ofc.
P.O. Box 95085
Lincoln, NE 68509
Phone: (402) 471-2867
Fax: (402) 471-3064

NEVADA
DeeAnn Parsons
Administrator
Energy Ofc.
Dept. of Business & Industry
1050 E. Williams St., Ste. 435
Carson City, NV 89710
Phone: (775) 687-4910
Fax: (775) 687-4914
E-mail: dparson@govmail.state.nv.us

NEW HAMPSHIRE
Deborah Schachter
Director
Governor's Ofc. of Energy & Community Services
Executive Dept.
57 Regional Dr.
Concord, NH 03301-4497
Phone: (603) 271-2611
Fax: (603) 271-2615

NEW JERSEY
Herbert H. Tate, Jr.
Commissioner
Board of Public Utilities
Div. of Energy
2 Gateway Ctr., 9th Fl.
Newark, NJ 07102
Phone: (973) 648-2503
Fax: (973) 648-4195

NEW MEXICO
Jennifer Salisbury
Cabinet Secretary
Energy & Conservation Mgmt. Div.
Dept. of Energy, Minerals & Natural Resources
2040 S. Pacheco St.
Santa Fe, NM 87505
Phone: (505) 827-5950
Fax: (505) 827-1150
E-mail: jsalisbury@emnrds.state.nm.us

NEW YORK
F. William Valentino
President
Energy & Research & Dev. Authority
Corporate Plz., W.
286 Washington Ave. Extension
Albany, NY 12203
Phone: (518) 862-1090
Fax: (518) 862-1091

NORTH CAROLINA
T.C. Adams
Director
Div. of Energy
Dept. of Commerce
1830-A Tillery Pl.
Raleigh, NC 27604
Phone: (919) 733-2230
Fax: (919) 733-2953

NORTH DAKOTA
James Luptak
Director
Energy Dev. Impact Ofc.
Land Dept.
P.O. Box 5523
Bismarck, ND 58506-5523
Phone: (701) 328-2800
Fax: (701) 328-3650
E-mail: jim@poldy.land.state.us

NORTHERN MARIANA ISLANDS
Juan Camacho
Administrator
Div. of Energy
Public Works
P.O. Box 340
Saipan, MP 96950
Phone: (670) 322-9229
Fax: (670) 322-9237

OHIO
Jeff Westhoven
Deputy Director
Ofc. of Energy Services
Dept. of Adm. Services
4200 Surface Rd.
Columbus, OH 43228-1395
Phone: (614) 466-6776
Fax: (614) 728-2400

OKLAHOMA
Mike Smith
Secretary of Energy
Dept. of Energy
1140 NW 63rd St., Ste. 416
Oklahoma City, OK 73116
Phone: (405) 840-9228
Fax: (405) 840-2638

OREGON
John Savage
Director
Dept. of Energy
625 Marion St., NE
Salem, OR 97310
Phone: (503) 378-4131
Fax: (503) 373-7806

PENNSYLVANIA
Frederick Carlson
Director of Policy
Ofc. of Policy & Communications
Dept. of Conservation & Natural Resources
Rachel Carson State Ofc. Bldg.
P.O. Box 8767
Harrisburg, PA 17105-8767
Phone: (717) 772-9087
Fax: (717) 772-9106

PUERTO RICO
Carlos La Santa Melendez
Coordinator of Energy Program
Dept. of Consumer Affairs
Minillas Station
P.O. Box 41059
Santurce, PR 00940
Phone: (787) 722-7555

RHODE ISLAND
William Ferguson
Director
Energy Ofc.
1 Capitol Hill
Providence, RI 02903

SOUTH CAROLINA
Tony Kester
Director
Div. of Finance & Administration
Ofc. of the Governor
1205 Pendleton St.
Columbia, SC 29201
Phone: (803) 734-0565

SOUTH DAKOTA
Abbie Rathbun
Administrator
Energy Assistance
Dept. of Social Services
206 W. Missouri Ave.
Pierre, SD 57501
Phone: (605) 773-3668
Fax: (605) 773-6657

TENNESSEE
Cynthia Oliphant
Director
Div. of Energy
Dept. of Economic & Community Dev.
Rachel Jackson Bldg., 6th Fl.
320 6th Ave., N.
Nashville, TN 37243
Phone: (615) 741-2994
Fax: (615) 741-5070

TEXAS
Tobin Harvey
Director
Services Comm.
P.O. Box 13047
Austin, TX 78711-3047
Phone: (512) 463-1931
Fax: (512) 475-2569

U.S. VIRGIN ISLANDS
Victor Somme, III
Director
Energy Ofc.
No. 200 Strand St.
Frederiksted
St. Croix, VI 00840
Phone: (340) 772-2616
Fax: (340) 772-0063

UTAH
Michael Glenn
Director
Ofc. of Energy Services
Dept. of Community & Economic Dev.
324 S. State St., Ste. 500
Salt Lake City, UT 84111
Phone: (801) 538-8654
Fax: (801) 538-8660
E-mail: mglenn@dced.state.ut.us

VERMONT
Richard Sedano
Commissioner
Dept. of Public Service
120 State St.
Montpelier, VT 05620
Phone: (802) 828-2321
Fax: (802) 828-2342

VIRGINIA
O. Gene Dishner
Director
Dept. of Mines, Minerals & Energy
202 N. 9th St., 8th Fl.
Richmond, VA 23219
Phone: (804) 692-3200
Fax: (804) 692-3237

WASHINGTON

WEST VIRGINIA
Michael P. Miano
Director
Bur. of Environment
Div. of Environmental Protection
10 McJunkin Rd.
Nitro, WV 25143-2506
Phone: (304) 759-0515
Fax: (304) 759-0526

WISCONSIN
Nathaniel E. Robinson
Administrator
Energy & Intergovernmental Relations
Dept. of Administration
101 E. Wilson, 6th Fl.
P.O. Box 7868
Madison, WI 53707
Phone: (608) 266-8234
Fax: (608) 267-6931

WYOMING
John Nunley, III
Director of Energy
Business Council
214 W. 15th St.
Cheyenne, WY 82002
Phone: (307) 777-2800

Environmental Protection—

Oversees the overall quality of the environment by coordinating and managing the state's pollution control programs and planning, permit granting and regulation of standards.

ALABAMA
James W. Warr
Director
Dept. of Environmental Mgmt.
1400 Coliseum Blvd.
P.O. Box 301463
Montgomery, AL 36130-1463
Phone: (334) 271-7710
Fax: (334) 279-3043

ALASKA
Michele Brown
Commissioner
Dept. of Environmental Conservation
410 Willoughby Ave., Ste. 105
Juneau, AK 99801
Phone: (907) 465-5050
Fax: (907) 465-5070

AMERICAN SAMOA
Togipa Tausaga
Director
Environmental Protection Agency
Ofc. of the Governor
Pago Pago, AS 96799
Phone: (684) 633-7691

ARIZONA
Jacqueline Schafer
Director
Dept. of Environmental Quality
3033 N. Central Ave.
Phoenix, AZ 85012
Phone: (602) 207-2203
Fax: (602) 207-2218

ARKANSAS
Randall Mathis
Director
Dept. of Environmental Quality
P.O. Box 8913
Little Rock, AR 72219
Phone: (501) 682-0744
Fax: (501) 682-0798

CALIFORNIA
Winston H. Hickox
Secretary
Environmental Protection Agency
555 Capitol Mall, Ste. 525
Sacramento, CA 95814
Phone: (916) 445-3846

COLORADO
Patrick Teegarden
Acting Director
Ofc. of Environment
Dept. of Public Health & Environment
4300 Cherry Creek Dr., S.
Denver, CO 80246-1530
Phone: (303) 692-2000
Fax: (303) 782-0095

CONNECTICUT
Arthur J. Rocque
Commissioner
Div. of Environmental Qualiy
Dept. of Environmental Protection
P.O. Box 483
Westbrook, CT 06498-0483
Phone: (860) 424-3001

DELAWARE
Nicholas A. DiPasquale
Secretary
Dept. of Natural Resources & Environmental Control
P.O. Box 1401
Dover, DE 19903
Phone: (302) 739-4403
Fax: (302) 739-6242
E-mail: ndipasquale@state.de.us

DISTRICT OF COLUMBIA
Jerry Galloway
Secretary
Intl. Jt. Comm.
U.S. Section
1250 23rd St., NW, Ste. 100
Washington, DC 20440
Phone: (202) 736-9000

Lloyd J. Jordan
Director
Environmental Regulation Administration
Dept. of Consumer & Regulatory Affairs
941 N. Capitol St., NE, 9th Fl.
Washington, DC 20002
Phone: (202) 442-8947

FLORIDA
Virginia Wetherell
Secretary
Dept. of Environmental Protection
3900 Commonwealth Blvd., MS-10
Tallahassee, FL 32399-3000
Phone: (850) 488-4805
Fax: (850) 921-4303

GEORGIA
Harold Reheis
Director
Environmental Protection Div.
Dept. of Natural Resources
205 Butler St., SW, Ste. 1152
Atlanta, GA 30334
Phone: (404) 656-4713
Fax: (404) 651-5778

GUAM
Jesus T. Salas
Administrator
Environmental Protection Agency
15-6101 Mariner Ave., Tiyan
P.O. Box 22439
Barrigada, GU 96921
Phone: (671) 475-1658
Fax: (671) 477-9402

HAWAII
Gary Gill
Deputy Director
Environmental Health Administration
Dept. of Health
1250 Punchbowl St.
Honolulu, HI 96813
Phone: (808) 586-4424
Fax: (808) 586-4444

IDAHO
Steve Allred
Administrator
Div. of Environmental Quality
Dept. of Health & Welfare
1410 N. Hilton
Boise, ID 83706-1255
Phone: (208) 334-5500
Fax: (208) 334-0417

ILLINOIS
Thomas V. Skinner
Director
Environmental Protection Agency
P.O. Box 19276
Springfield, IL 62794
Phone: (217) 782-9540
Fax: (217) 782-9039

INDIANA
Lori Kaplan
Commissioner
Dept. of Environmental Mgmt.
100 N. Senate Ave., N1301
Indianapolis, IN 46204
Phone: (317) 232-8611
Fax: (317) 233-6647

IOWA
Allan Stokes
Director
Environmental Protection Div.
Dept. of Natural Resources
Wallace State Ofc. Bldg.
E. 9th & Grand Aves.
Des Moines, IA 50319
Phone: (515) 281-6284

KANSAS
Ronald Hammerschmidt
Director
Div. of the Environment
Dept. of Health & Environment
Forbes Field Bldg.
6700 SW Topeka Blvd.
Topeka, KS 66619
Phone: (785) 296-1535

KENTUCKY
Robert Logan
Commissioner
Dept. for Environmental Protection
Frankfort Ofc. Park
14 Reilly Rd.
Frankfort, KY 40601
Phone: (502) 564-2150
Fax: (502) 564-4245

LOUISIANA
John Dale Givens
Secretary
Dept. of Environmental Quality
P.O. Box 82263
Baton Rouge, LA 70804
Phone: (225) 765-0741
Fax: (225) 765-0746

MAINE
Brooke Barnes
Acting Commisioner
Dept. of Environmental Protection
17 State House Station
Augusta, ME 04333
Phone: (207) 287-2812

MARYLAND
Jane T. Nishida
Secretary
Ofc. of the Secretary
Dept. of Environment
Bldg. 30A, 2nd Fl.
2500 Broening Hwy.
Baltimore, MD 21224-6612
Phone: (410) 631-3084
Fax: (410) 631-3888
E-mail: jnishida@mde.state.md.us

MASSACHUSETTS
Lauren A. Liss
Commissioner
Executive Ofc. of Environmental Affairs
Dept. of Environmental Protection
1 Winter St.
Boston, MA 02108
Phone: (617) 292-5856
Fax: (617) 574-6880

MICHIGAN
Russell Harding
Director
Dept. of Environmental Quality
P.O. Box 30473
Lansing, MI 48909-7973
Phone: (517) 373-7917

MINNESOTA
Michael Sullivan
Executive Director
Environmental Quality Board
Strategic & Long Range Planning
658 Cedar St., Ste. 300
St. Paul, MN 55155
Phone: (651) 296-2603
Fax: (651) 296-3698
E-mail: michael.sullivan@mnplan.state.mn.us

MISSISSIPPI
J.I. Palmer, Jr.
Executive Director
Dept. of Environmental Quality
P.O. Box 20305
Jackson, MS 39289
Phone: (601) 961-5000
Fax: (601) 354-6965

MISSOURI
John Young
Director
Div. of Environmental Quality
Dept. of Natural Resources
Jefferson Bldg., 12th Fl.
P.O. Box 176
Jefferson City, MO 65102
Phone: (573) 751-0763
Fax: (573) 751-9277
E-mail: nryounj@mail.dnr.state.mo.us

MONTANA
Mark Simonich
Director
Dept. of Environmental Quality
1520 E. 6th Ave.
Helena, MT 59620
Phone: (406) 444-2544
Fax: (406) 444-4386

NEBRASKA
Mike Linder
Director
Dept. of Environmental Quality
1200 N St., Ste. #400
Lincoln, NE 68509
Phone: (402) 471-2186
Fax: (402) 471-2909

NEVADA
Allen Biaggi
Administrator
Div. of Environmental Protection
333 W. Nye Ln., Rm. 138
Carson City, NV 89706
Phone: (775) 687-4670
Fax: (775) 687-5856

NEW HAMPSHIRE
Robert W. Varney
Commissioner
Dept. of Environmental Services
P.O. Box 95
Concord, NH 03302-0095
Phone: (603) 271-3503
Fax: (603) 271-2867

NEW JERSEY
Robert C. Shinn, Jr.
Commissioner
Dept. of Environmental Protection
401 E. State St.
P.O. Box 402
Trenton, NJ 08625-0402
Phone: (609) 292-2885
Fax: (609) 292-7695

NEW MEXICO
Peter Maggiore
Director
Solid Waste Bur.
Dept. of Environment
P.O. Box 26110
Santa Fe, NM 87502
Phone: (505) 827-2855
Fax: (505) 827-2836

NEW YORK
John Cahill
Commissioner
Dept. of Environmental Conservation
50 Wolf Rd.
Albany, NY 12233-1010
Phone: (518) 457-1162
Fax: (518) 457-7744

NORTH CAROLINA
Bill Holman
Assistant Secretary
Environmental Protection
Dept. of Environment & Natural Resources
P.O. Box 27687
Raleigh, NC 27604
Phone: (919) 715-4140
Fax: (919) 715-3060

NORTH DAKOTA
Francis J. Schwindt
Chief
Environmental Health Section
Dept. of Health
P.O. Box 5520
Bismarck, ND 58506-5520
Phone: (701) 328-5150
Fax: (701) 328-5200
E-mail: fschwind@state.nd.us

NORTHERN MARIANA ISLANDS
Ignacio Cabrera
Director
Div. of Environmental Quality
Public Works
P.O. Box 1304
Saipan, MP 96950
Phone: (670) 234-1011
Fax: (670) 234-1003

OHIO
Chris Jones
Director
Environmental Protection Agency
P.O. Box 1049
Columbus, OH 43216-1049
Phone: (614) 644-2782
Fax: (614) 644-3184

OKLAHOMA
Mark S. Coleman
Executive Director
Dept. of Environmental Quality
707 N. Robinson
Oklahoma City, OK 73102
Phone: (405) 702-7100
Fax: (405) 702-7101

OREGON
Langdon Marsh
Director
Dept. of Environmental Quality
811 SW 6th Ave.
Portland, OR 97204
Phone: (503) 229-5300
Fax: (503) 229-6124

PENNSYLVANIA
Terry Fabian
Deputy Secretary
DER-Field Operations
P.O. Box 2063
Harrisburg, PA 17105-2063
Phone: (717) 787-5028
Fax: (717) 772-3314

PUERTO RICO
Hector Russe
President
Environmental Quality Board
P.O. Box 11488
San Juan, PR 00910-1488
Phone: (787) 767-8056
Fax: (787) 754-8294

RHODE ISLAND
Jan Reitsma
Director
Dept. of Environmental Mgmt.
235 Promenade St.
Providence, RI 02908
Phone: (401) 222-2771
Fax: (401) 222-6802

SOUTH CAROLINA
R. Lewis Shaw
Deputy Commissioner
Environmental Quality Control Ofc.
Dept. of Health & Environmental Control
2600 Bull St.
Columbia, SC 29201
Phone: (803) 898-3900

SOUTH DAKOTA
Nettie Myers
Secretary
Dept. of Environment & Natural Resources
Joe Foss Bldg.
523 E. Capitol Ave.
Pierre, SD 57501
Phone: (605) 773-3151
Fax: (605) 773-6035

TENNESSEE

TEXAS
Jeffrey Saitas
Executive Director
Natural Resource Conservation Comm.
12100 Park 35 Cir., Bldg. A
P.O. Box 13087, MC 109
Austin, TX 78711-3087
Phone: (512) 239-3900
Fax: (512) 239-3939

U.S. VIRGIN ISLANDS
Dean Plaskett
Commissioner
Dept. of Planning & Natural Resources
Foster's Plz., 396-1 Anna's Retreat
St. Thomas, VI 00802
Phone: (340) 774-3320
Fax: (340) 775-5706

UTAH
Dianne R. Nielson
Executive Director
Ofc. of the Executive Director
Dept. of Environmental Quality
168 N. 1950 W.
P.O. Box 144810
Salt Lake City, UT 84114-4810
Phone: (801) 536-4402
Fax: (801) 536-0061
E-mail: dnielso@deq.state.ut.us

VERMONT

VIRGINIA
Dennis H. Treacy
Director
Dept. of Environmental Quality
629 E. Main St.
Richmond, VA 23219
Phone: (804) 698-4020
Fax: (804) 698-4019

WASHINGTON
Tom Fitzsimmons
Director
Dept. of Ecology
P.O. Box 47600
Olympia, WA 98504-7600
Phone: (360) 407-6000
Fax: (360) 407-6989

WEST VIRGINIA
Michael P. Miano
Director
Bur. of Environment
Div. of Environmental Protection
10 McJunkin Rd.
Nitro, WV 25143-2506
Phone: (304) 759-0515
Fax: (304) 759-0526

WISCONSIN
Susan L. Sylvester
Administrator
Div. of Water
Dept. of Natural Resources
P.O. Box 7921
Madison, WI 53707
Phone: (608) 266-1099
Fax: (608) 266-6983

WYOMING
Dennis Hemmer
Director
Dept. of Environmental Quality
122 W. 25th St.
Cheyenne, WY 82002
Phone: (307) 777-7192

Equal Employment Opportunity

Enforces laws promoting equal employment opportunity in the state.

ALABAMA

ALASKA
Thelma Buchholdt
Executive Director
Ofc. of Equal Employment Opportunity
3601 C St., Ste. 250
Anchorage, AK 99503
Phone: (907) 269-7495
Fax: (907) 269-7497

AMERICAN SAMOA
Sapini Siatu'u
Director
Dept. of Human Resources
AS Govt.
Pago Pago, AS 96799
Phone: (684) 633-4485
Fax: (684) 633-1139

ARIZONA
Ruben Alvarez
Director
Governor's Ofc. of Equal Opportunity
1700 W. Washington, Rm. 104
Phoenix, AZ 85007
Phone: (602) 542-3711
Fax: (602) 542-3712

ARKANSAS
Richard Weiss
Director
Dept. of Finance & Administration
401 DFA Bldg.
1509 W. 7th St.
Little Rock, AR 72201
Phone: (501) 682-2242
Fax: (501) 682-1086
E-mail: richard.weiss@dfa.state.ar.us

CALIFORNIA
Nancy C. Gutierrez
Director
Fair Employment & Housing
2014 T St., Ste. 210
Sacramento, CA 95814
Phone: (916) 227-2873

COLORADO
Jack T. Lang Y. Marquez
Director
Civil Rights Div.
Dept. of Regulatory Agencies
1560 Broadway, Rm. 1050
Denver, CO 80202
Phone: (303) 894-2997
Fax: (303) 894-7830

CONNECTICUT
Cynthia Watts-Elder
Director
Comm. on Human Rights & Opportunities
21 Grand St.
Hartford, CT 06106
Phone: (860) 541-3400

DELAWARE
Gregory T. Chambers
Program Administrator
EEO/AA Program
State Personnel Ofc.
820 N. French St.
Wilmington, DE 19801
Phone: (302) 577-3950

DISTRICT OF COLUMBIA
Jackie Flowers
Director
Ofc. of Human Rights
441 4th St., NW, Ste. 970
Washington, DC 20001
Phone: (202) 727-3900
Fax: (202) 727-3786

FLORIDA
Ron McElrath
Executive Director
Human Relations Comm.
Dept. of Administration
Bldg. F, Ste. 240-F
325 John Knox Rd.
Tallahassee, FL 32303-4149
Phone: (850) 488-7082
Fax: (850) 488-5291

GEORGIA
Mustafa A. Aziz
Administrator
Comm. on Equal Opportunity
410 Intl. Tower, Peachtree Ctr.
229 Peachtree St., NE
Atlanta, GA 30303-1605
Phone: (404) 656-1736
Fax: (404) 656-4399

GUAM
James Underwood
Acting Director
Dept. of Labor
504 E. Sunset Blvd., Tiyan
P.O. Box 9970
Tamuning, GU 96931
Phone: (671) 475-0101
Fax: (671) 477-2988

HAWAII
William D. Hoshijo
Executive Director
Civil Rights Comm.
Labor & Industrial Relations Dept.
830 Punchbowl St., Ste. 420
Honolulu, HI 96813
Phone: (808) 586-8636
Fax: (808) 586-8655

IDAHO
Leslie Goddard
Director
Human Rights Comm.
Ofc. of the Governor
450 W. State St.
Boise, ID 83720
Phone: (208) 334-2873

ILLINOIS
Carlos J. Salazar
Director
Dept. of Human Rights

100 W. Randolph,

Ste. 10-100

Chicago, IL 60601
Phone: (312) 814-6284
Fax: (312) 814-1436

INDIANA
James Ladd
Division Director
AA/EEO/ADA Div.
Dept. of Personnel
IGC-South, Rm. W161
402 W. Washington
Indianapolis, IN 46204
Phone: (317) 233-4687
Fax: (317) 232-3089

IOWA
Don Grove
Director
Civil Rights Comm.
211 E. Maple St., 2nd Fl.
Des Moines, IA 50319
Phone: (515) 281-4121
Fax: (515) 242-5840

KANSAS
Rick Beyer
Secretary
Dept. of Human Resources
401 SW Topeka Blvd.
Topeka, KS 66603
Phone: (785) 296-7474
Fax: (785) 296-0179

KENTUCKY
Beverly L. Watts
Executive Director
Comm. on Human Rights
The Heyburn Bldg., 7th Fl.

332 W. Broadway
Louisville, KY 40202
Phone: (502) 595-4024
Fax: (502) 595-4801

LOUISIANA
Liz Hayes-Roberson
Director of Compliance Programs
Dept. of Labor
P.O. Box 94094
Baton Rouge, LA 70804-9094
Phone: (225) 342-3075
Fax: (225) 342-7961

MAINE
Patricia Ryan
Executive Director
Human Rights Comm.
51 State House Station
Augusta, ME 04333
Phone: (207) 624-6050

MARYLAND
Henry Ford
Executive Director
Executive Dept.
Comm. on Human Relations
6 St. Paul St., 9th Fl.
Baltimore, MD 21202
Phone: (410) 767-8563
Fax: (410) 333-1841
E-mail: hford@mail.mchr.state.md.us

MASSACHUSETTS
Mark Bolling
Director
Ofc. of Affirmative Action
One Ashburton Pl., Rm. 213
Boston, MA 02108
Phone: (617) 727-7441
Fax: (617) 727-0568

MICHIGAN
Nanette Lee Reynolds
Director
Dept. of Civil Rights
201 N. Washington, Ste. 700
Lansing, MI 48913
Phone: (517) 335-3164
Fax: (517) 373-3103

MINNESOTA
Janeen Rosas
Commissioner
Dept. of Human Rights
190 E. 5th St., Ste. 700
Minneapolis, MN 55101
Phone: (651) 296-5665
Fax: (651) 296-1736

MISSISSIPPI
Tom Lord
Director
Employment Security Comm.
1520 W. Capitol
P.O. Box 1699
Jackson, MS 39215-1699
Phone: (601) 961-7500
Fax: (601) 961-7405

J.K. Stringer, Jr.
Director
State Personnel Board
301 N. Lamar St., Ste. 201
Jackson, MS 39201
Phone: (601) 359-2702
Fax: (601) 359-2729

MISSOURI
Donna Cavitte
Director, Commission on Human Rights
Comm. on Human Rights
Dept. of Labor & Industrial Relations
3315 W. Truman Blvd.
P.O. Box 1129
Jefferson City, MO 65102-1129
Phone: (573) 751-3325
Fax: (573) 751-2905
E-mail: dcavitte@mail.state.mo.us

MONTANA
Kathy Hilland
Bureau Chief
Human Rights Bur.
Dept. of Labor & Industry
Steamboat Block
616 Helena Ave., Ste. 302
Helena, MT 59624-1728
Phone: (406) 444-4345
Fax: (406) 444-2798

NEBRASKA
Alfonza Whitaker
Executive Director
Equal Opportunity Comm.
301 Centennial Mall, S.
P.O. Box 94934
Lincoln, NE 68509-4934
Phone: (402) 471-2024
Fax: (402) 471-4059

NEVADA
William H. Stewart
Administrator
Equal Rights Comm.
Employment Training & Rehab.
1515 E. Tropicana, Ste. 590
Las Vegas, NV 89119
Phone: (702) 486-7161
Fax: (702) 486-7054

NEW HAMPSHIRE
Katharine Daly
Executive Director
Comm. for Human Rights
2 Chenell Dr.
Concord, NH 03301
Phone: (603) 271-2767
Fax: (603) 271-6339

NEW JERSEY
Valerie Holman
Director
EEO-Affirmative Action Div.
Dept. of Personnel
P.O. Box 315
Trenton, NJ 08625-0315
Phone: (609) 777-0919
Fax: (609) 292-9335

NEW MEXICO
Richard Galaz
Director
Human Rights Div.
Labor Dept.
1596 Pacheco St.
Santa Fe, NM 87505
Phone: (505) 827-6838
Fax: (505) 827-6878

NEW YORK
George C. Sinnott
Commissioner & President
Dept. of Civil Service
State Campus, Bldg. 1, 2nd Fl.
Albany, NY 12239
Phone: (518) 457-3701
Fax: (518) 457-7547

NORTH CAROLINA
Nellie Riley
Director
Equal Opportunity Services
Ofc. of State Personnel
116 W. Jones St.
Raleigh, NC 27603
Phone: (919) 733-0205
Fax: (919) 733-0653

NORTH DAKOTA
Mark Bachmeier
Interim Commissioner
Labor Dept.
600 E. Blvd. Ave., 13th Fl.
Bismarck, ND 58505
Phone: (701) 328-2660
Fax: (701) 328-2031
E-mail: bachmeie@pioneer.state.nd.us

NORTHERN MARIANA ISLANDS
Jesus Matagolai
Chief
Employment & Employee Relations
Personnel Mgmt.
P.O. Box 5153 CHRB
Saipan, MP 96950
Phone: (670) 233-1272
Fax: (670) 234-1013

OHIO
Merelyn Bates-Mims
Coordinator
Dept. of Adm. Services
30 E. Broad St., 18th Fl.
Columbus, OH 43215
Phone: (614) 466-8380
Fax: (614) 728-5628

OKLAHOMA
Janice Wadkins
Assistant Administrator of Employment Services
Ofc. of Personnel Mgmt.
2101 N. Lincoln Blvd.
Oklahoma City, OK 73105
Phone: (405) 521-2177

OREGON
Johnnie Bell
Administrator
Civil Rights Div.
Bur. of Labor & Industries
800 NE Oregon St., # 32
Portland, OR 97232
Phone: (503) 731-4873
Fax: (503) 731-4069

PENNSYLVANIA
Denise Motley-Brownlee
Director
Bur. of Affirmative Action/Contract Compliance

508-B Finance Bldg.
Harrisburg, PA 17120
Phone: (717) 783-1130
Fax: (717) 772-3302

PUERTO RICO
Carmen Ana Lugo
Director
Fair Employment
Dept. of Labor & Human Resources
505 Munoz Rivera Ave.
Hato Rey, PR 00918
Phone: (787) 754-2105

RHODE ISLAND
Vincent Igliozzi
Administrator
Equal Opportunity Ofc.
Dept. of Administration
1 Capitol Hill
Providence, RI 02903
Phone: (401) 222-3090

SOUTH CAROLINA
Joel T. Cassidy
Executive Director
Employment Security Comm.
P.O. Box 995
Columbia, SC 29202
Phone: (803) 737-2617

SOUTH DAKOTA
Sandy Zinter
Commissioner
Bur. of Personnel
500 E. Capitol Ave.
Pierre, SD 57501
Phone: (605) 773-3148
Fax: (605) 773-4344

TENNESSEE
Evelyn Gaines
Affirmative Action Officer
Equal Employment Opportunity
Dept. of Employment Security
500 James Robertson Pkwy.
Nashville, TN 37243
Phone: (615) 741-5292
Fax: (615) 741-3203

TEXAS
William M. Hale
Executive Director
Comm. on Human Rights
6330 Hwy., 290 E., Ste. 250
Austin, TX 78723
Phone: (512) 437-3450
Fax: (512) 437-3478

U.S. VIRGIN ISLANDS
Eleuteria Roberts
Acting Commissioner
Dept. of Labor
2203 Church St.
Christiansted
St. Croix, VI 00820
Phone: (340) 773-1994
Fax: (340) 773-0094

UTAH
Joseph Gallegos
Director
Anti-Discrimination & Labor Div.
Labor Comm.
160 E. 300 S., 3rd Fl.
Salt Lake City, UT 84114-6630
Phone: (801) 530-6801
Fax: (801) 530-7609
E-mail: jgallego.icmain@state.ut.us

VERMONT
David Tucker
Director
State Economic Opportunity Ofc.
Agency of Human Services
103 S. Main St.
Waterbury, VT 05671
Phone: (802) 241-2450

VIRGINIA
Sara Redding Wilson
Director
Dept. of Personnel & Training
Monroe Bldg., 12th Fl.
101 N. 14th St.
Richmond, VA 23219
Phone: (804) 225-2237
Fax: (804) 371-7401

WASHINGTON
Roy Standifer
Administrator
Affirmative Action Program
Dept. of Personnel
P.O. Box 47500
Olympia, WA 98504-7500
Phone: (360) 753-5368
Fax: (360) 586-4694

WEST VIRGINIA
Debra J. Hart
Director
Ofc. of the Governor
1900 Kanawha Blvd., E., Bldg. 1
Charleston, WV 25305
Phone: (304) 558-0400
Fax: (304) 558-3861

WISCONSIN
Sheehan Donoghue
Administrator
Div. of Equal Rights
Dept. of Workforce Dev.
201 E. Washington, Rm. 407
P.O. Box 8928
Madison, WI 53708
Phone: (608) 266-6860
Fax: (608) 267-4592

WYOMING
Dan Romero
EEO, Grievance & Appeals Coordinator
Personnel Div.
Dept. of Administration & Info.
Emerson Bldg.
2001 Capitol Ave.
Cheyenne, WY 82002
Phone: (307) 777-6730

Ethics

Administers and enforces the state ethics laws applying to public officials.

ALABAMA
James Sumner
Director
Ethics Comm.
RSA Union, Ste. 104
100 N. Union St.
Montgomery, AL 36104
Phone: (334) 242-2997
Fax: (334) 242-0248

ALASKA
Karen Boorman
Director
Public Ofcs. Comm.
2221 E. Northern Lights Blvd., Rm. 128
Anchorage, AK 99508-4149
Phone: (907) 276-4176
Fax: (907) 276-7018

Neil Slotuik
Assistant Attorney General
Dept. of Law
P.O. Box 110300
Juneau, AK 99811
Phone: (907) 465-3600
Fax: (907) 465-2539

AMERICAN SAMOA

ARIZONA
Janet Napolitano
Attorney General
Attorney Gen's. Ofc.
Law Bldg.
1275 W. Washington
Phoenix, AZ 85007
Phone: (602) 542-4266
Fax: (602) 542-4085

ARKANSAS
Bob Brooks
Director
State Ethics Comm.
910 W. 2nd St., Ste. 100
Little Rock, AR 72201
Phone: (501) 324-9600
Fax: (501) 324-9606

CALIFORNIA
Jim Hall
Chair
Fair Political Practices Comm.
428 J St., Ste. 600
P.O. Box 807
Sacramento, CA 95804
Phone: (916) 322-5660

COLORADO
Troy Eid
Chief Counsel
Ofc. of the Governor
136 State Capitol
200 E. Colfax
Denver, CO 80203
Phone: (303) 866-6390
Fax: (303) 866-2003

Timothy Tymkovich
Chair
Board of Ethics
1675 Broadway
Denver, CO 80203
Phone: (303) 866-6390

CONNECTICUT
Alan S. Plofsky
Executive Director
State Ethics Comm.
18-20 Trinity St.
Hartford, CT 06106
Phone: (860) 566-4472

DELAWARE
Janet Wright
Commission Counsel
Public Integrity Comm.
Townsend Bldg.
Federal & Duke of York Sts.
Dover, DE 19901
Phone: (302) 739-2397

DISTRICT OF COLUMBIA
Joanne Robinson
Acting Corporation Counsel
Ofc. of Corporate Counsel
441 4th St., NW, Ste. 1060
Washington, DC 20001
Phone: (202) 727-6248
Fax: (202) 347-8922

FLORIDA
Kathy Chinoy
Chair
Comm. on Ethics
2822 Remington Green Cir., Ste. 101
Tallahassee, FL 32308
Phone: (850) 488-7864
Fax: (850) 488-3077

GEORGIA
C. Theodore Lee
Executive Secretary
State Ethics Comm.
8440 Courthouse Sq., E., #C
Douglasville, GA 30134-1794
Phone: (770) 920-4385
Fax: (770) 920-4395

GUAM
John F. Tarantino
Acting Attorney General
Dept. of Law
Judicial Ctr. Bldg., Ste. 2-200E
120 W. O'Brien Dr.
Hagatna, GU 96910
Phone: (671) 475-3324
Fax: (671) 472-2493
E-mail: law@ns.gov.gu

HAWAII
Daniel J. Mollway
Executive Director
State Ethics Comm.
Pacific Tower, Ste. 970
1001 Bishop St., Ste. 970
Honolulu, HI 96813
Phone: (808) 587-0460
Fax: (808) 587-0470

IDAHO
Alan G. Lance
Attorney General
State House
700 W. Jefferson
Boise, ID 83720-0010
Phone: (208) 334-2400
Fax: (208) 334-2530

ILLINOIS

INDIANA
David Maidenberg
Director
State Ethics Comm.
402 W. Washington St., Rm. W189
Indianapolis, IN 46204
Phone: (317) 232-3850
Fax: (317) 232-0707

IOWA
Kay Williams
Executive Director
Ethics & Campaign Disclosure Board
514 E. Locust, Ste. 104
Des Moines, IA 50309
Phone: (515) 281-6841

KANSAS
Carol Williams
Executive Director
Govt. Ethics Comm.
109 SW 9th, 5th Fl.
Topeka, KS 66612-1287
Phone: (785) 296-4219
Fax: (785) 296-2548

KENTUCKY
Jill LeMaster
Executive Director
Executive Branch Ethics Comm.
Capitol Annex, Rm. 273
700 Capitol Ave.
Frankfort, KY 40601
Phone: (502) 564-7954
Fax: (502) 564-2686

LOUISIANA
Grey Sexton
Executive Secretary
Board of Ethics
8401 United Plz. Blvd., Ste. 200
Baton Rouge, LA 70809-7017
Phone: (225) 922-1400
Fax: (225) 922-1414

MAINE
Bill Haines
Director
Governmental Ethics & Election Practices Comm.
135 State House Station
Augusta, ME 04333
Phone: (207) 287-6219

MARYLAND
John E. O'Donnell
Executive Director
State Ethics Comm.
Ofc. of Executive Dir.
300 E. Joppa Rd., Ste. 301
Towson, MD 21286
Phone: (410) 321-3636
Fax: (410) 321-4060

MASSACHUSETTS
Stephanie S. Lovell
Executive Director
State Ethics Comm.
One Ashburton Pl., Rm. 619
Boston, MA 02108
Phone: (617) 727-0060
Fax: (617) 723-5851

MICHIGAN
Ted Benca
Executive Secretary
State Board of Ethics
Dept. of Civil Service
P.O. Box 30002
Lansing, MI 48909
Phone: (517) 373-2754

MINNESOTA
Jeanne Olson
Executive Director
Campaign Finance & Public Disclosure Board
100 Centennial Ofc. Bldg.
658 Cedar St.
St. Paul, MN 55155
Phone: (651) 296-5148
Fax: (651) 296-1722
E-mail: jeanne.olson@state.mn.us

MISSISSIPPI
Ronald Crowe
Executive Director
Ethics Comm.
P.O. Box 22746
Jackson, MS 39225-3476
Phone: (601) 359-1285
Fax: (601) 354-6253

MISSOURI
Michael C. Reid
Director of Compliance
Div. of Compliance
Ethics Comm.
P.O. Box 1254
Jefferson City, MO 65102
Phone: (800) 392-8660
Fax: (573) 526-4506
E-mail: mreid01@mail.state.mo.us

MONTANA
Linda Vaughey
Commissioner
Political Practices
1205 8th Ave.
P.O. Box 202401
Helena, MT 59620-2401
Phone: (406) 444-2942
Fax: (406) 444-1643

NEBRASKA
Tim Dempsey
Executive Director
Accountability & Disclosure Comm.
P.O. Box 95086
Lincoln, NE 68509
Phone: (402) 471-2522
Fax: (402) 471-6599

NEVADA
Mary Boetsch
Chair
Comm. on Ethics
755 N. Roop St., Rm. 212
Carson City, NV 89701
Phone: (775) 687-5469
Fax: (775) 687-1279

NEW HAMPSHIRE
Vacant
Associate Attorney General
Ofc. of the Attorney Gen.
Dept. of Justice
33 Capitol St.
Concord, NH 03301-6397
Phone: (603) 271-3671
Fax: (603) 271-2110

NEW JERSEY
Rita L. Strmensky
Executive Director
Executive Comm. on Ethical Standards
P.O. Box 085
Trenton, NJ 08625-0085
Phone: (609) 292-1892
Fax: (609) 633-9252

NEW MEXICO
Rebecca Vigil-Giron
Secretary of State
State Capitol Bldg., Rm. 420
Santa Fe, NM 87503
Phone: (505) 827-3600
Fax: (505) 827-3634

NEW YORK
Barbara Smith
Acting Executive Director & Counsel
State Ethics Comm.
39 Columbia St., 4th Fl.
Albany, NY 12207
Phone: (518) 432-8250
Fax: (518) 432-8255

NORTH CAROLINA
George F. Bason
Chair
Board of Ethics
116 W. Jones St.
Raleigh, NC 27603-8003
Phone: (919) 733-5103
Fax: (919) 733-2785

NORTH DAKOTA
Robert Harms
Legal Counsel
Ofc. of the Governor
600 E. Blvd. Ave.
Bismarck, ND 58505-0001
Phone: (701) 328-2200
Fax: (701) 328-2205
E-mail: governor@state.nd.us

NORTHERN MARIANA ISLANDS
Leo Lawrence LaMotte
Public Auditor
P.O. Box 1399 CTC
Saipan, MP 96950
Phone: (670) 234-6481
Fax: (670) 234-7812
E-mail: opa@mtccnmi.com

OHIO
David Freel
Executive Director
Ethics Comm.
8 E. Long St., 10th Fl.
Columbus, OH 43215
Phone: (614) 466-7090
Fax: (614) 466-8368

OKLAHOMA
Marilyn Hughes
Executive Director
Ethics Comm.
State Capitol Bldg., Rm. B-5
2300 N. Lincoln Blvd.
Oklahoma City, OK 73105
Phone: (405) 521-3451
Fax: (405) 521-4905

OREGON
L. Patrick Hearn
Executive Director
Govt. Standards & Practices Comm.
100 High St., SE, Ste. 220
Salem, OR 97310
Phone: (503) 378-5105
Fax: (503) 373-1456

PENNSYLVANIA
Daneen E. Reese
Chair
State Ethics Comm.
P.O. Box 11470
Harrisburg, PA 17108-1470
Phone: (717) 783-1610
Fax: (717) 787-0806

PUERTO RICO
Hiram Morales
Executive Director
Ofc. of Govt. Ethics
P.O. Box 194629
San Juan, PR 00919-4629
Phone: (787) 766-4401
Fax: (787) 754-0977

RHODE ISLAND
Martin Healey
Executive Director
State Ethics Comm.
40 Fountain St.
Providence, RI 02903-1844
Phone: (401) 222-3790

SOUTH CAROLINA
Gary R. Baker
Executive Director
State Ethics Comm.
P.O. Box 11926
Columbia, SC 29211
Phone: (803) 253-4192

SOUTH DAKOTA
Patty Pearson
Special Projects Director
Ofc. of the Secretary of State
500 E. Capitol Ave., Ste. 204
Pierre, SD 57501
Phone: (605) 773-3537
Fax: (605) 773-6580

TENNESSEE
Peggy Nance Williams
Executive Director
Registry of Election Finance
Ofc. of Secretary of State
404 James Robertson Pkwy., 16th Fl.
Nashville, TN 37243
Phone: (615) 741-7959
Fax: (615) 532-8905

TEXAS
Tom Harrison
Executive Director
Ethics Comm.
201 E. 14th St., 10th Fl.
Austin, TX 78701
Phone: (512) 463-5800
Fax: (512) 463-5777
E-mail: ethics@state.tx.us

U.S. VIRGIN ISLANDS
Pamela Tepper
Acting Solicitor General
Dept. of Justice
GERS Bldg., 2nd Fl.
St. Thomas, VI 00802
Phone: (340) 774-5666
Fax: (340) 774-9710

UTAH
Jan Graham
Attorney General
236 State Capitol
Salt Lake City, UT 84114-1326
Phone: (801) 538-1130
Fax: (801) 538-1121
E-mail: jgraham.atcap01@state.ut.us

VERMONT
Janet Ancel
Legal Counsel
Ofc. of the Governor
109 State St.
Montpelier, VT 05609
Phone: (802) 828-3333
Fax: (802) 828-3339

VIRGINIA
David E. Anderson
Counselor to the Governor & Director of Policy
Governor's Cabinet
State Capitol, 3rd Fl.
Richmond, VA 23219
Phone: (804) 786-2211
Fax: (804) 786-3985

WASHINGTON
Melissa Warheit
Executive Director
Public Disclosure Comm.
711 Capitol Way, Rm. 403
P.O. Box 40908
Olympia, WA 98504-0908
Phone: (360) 753-1111
Fax: (360) 753-1112

WEST VIRGINIA
Richard Alker
Executive Director
State Ethics Comm.
1207 Quarrier St.
Charleston, WV 25301
Phone: (304) 558-0664
Fax: (304) 558-2169

WISCONSIN
R. Roth Judd
Executive Director
Ethics Board
44 E. Mifflin St., Ste. 601
Madison, WI 53703-2800
Phone: (608) 266-8123
Fax: (608) 264-9309

WYOMING
Richard H. Miller
Director
Legislative Services Ofc.
State Capitol, Rm. 213
200 W. 24th St.
Cheyenne, WY 82002
Phone: (307) 777-7881

Facilities Management

Maintains, constructs, designs, renovates and delivers basic services to state-owned facilities.

ALABAMA
Curtis Hayes
Chief of Services
Services Div.
Dept. of Finance
425 S. Union St.
Montgomery, AL 36130-2605
Phone: (334) 242-2773
Fax: (334) 240-3402

ALASKA
Rod Wilson
Staff Architect
Div. of Engineering & Operations
Dept. of Transportation & Public Facilities
3132 Channel Dr.
Juneau, AK 99801-7898
Phone: (907) 465-6962
Fax: (907) 465-2460

AMERICAN SAMOA
Eliu Paopao
Acting Director
Dept. of Adm. Services
AS Govt.
Pago Pago, AS 96799
Phone: (684) 633-4156
Fax: (684) 633-1841

ARIZONA
Robert Teel
Assistant Director
Services Div.
Dept. of Administration
15 S. 15th Ave., Ste. 101
Phoenix, AZ 85007-3223
Phone: (602) 542-0697
Fax: (602) 542-3858

ARKANSAS
Robert L. Laman
Director
State Bldg. Services
1515 W. 7th St., Ste. 700
Little Rock, AR 72201
Phone: (501) 682-5558
Fax: (501) 682-5589
E-mail: rlaman@asbs.state.ar.us

CALIFORNIA
Rosamond Bolden
Chief
Ofc. of Bldgs. & Grounds
Dept. of Services
1304 O St.
Sacramento, CA 95814
Phone: (916) 327-6224
Fax: (916) 327-2831

COLORADO
Nanci Kadlecek
Director
Purchasing Div.
Support Services/Dept. of Personnel
225 E. 16th Ave., Rm. 900
Denver, CO 80203-1613
Phone: (303) 866-6191
Fax: (303) 894-7445

CONNECTICUT
Richard M. Cianci
Deputy Commissioner
Facilities Mgmt.
Dept. of Public Works
165 Capitol Ave., Rm. G-39
Hartford, CT 06106
Phone: (860) 566-2815
Fax: (860) 566-7658

DELAWARE
Paul Ignudo
Director
Div. of Facilities Mgmt.
O'Neill Bldg.
P.O. Box 1401
Dover, DE 19903
Phone: (302) 739-3041
Fax: (302) 739-6148

DISTRICT OF COLUMBIA
Kenneth R. Kimbrough
Chief Property Management Officer
Ofc. of Property Mgmt.
441 4th St., NW, Ste.721
Washington, DC 20001
Phone: (202) 724-4400
Fax: (202) 727-9877

FLORIDA
Phil Maher
Director
Div. of Facilities Mgmt.
Dept. of Mgmt. Services
Bldg. 4030, Ste. 380
4050 Esplanade Way
Tallahassee, FL 32399-0950
Phone: (850) 488-2074
Fax: (850) 922-5844

GEORGIA
Steve Black
Executive Director
Bldg. Authority
1 Martin Luther King, Jr. Dr.
Atlanta, GA 30334
Phone: (404) 656-3252

GUAM
Daniel Lizama
Acting Director
Dept. of Public Works
542 N. Marine Dr.
Tamuning, GU 96911
Phone: (671) 646-3131
Fax: (671) 649-9178

Michael J. Reidy
Director
Dept. of Administration
P.O. Box 884
Hagatna, GU 96932
Phone: (671) 475-1101
Fax: (671) 477-6788

HAWAII
James Richardson
Division Chief
Central Services
729-B Kakoi St.
Honolulu, HI 96819
Phone: (808) 831-6730
Fax: (808) 831-6750

IDAHO
Larry Osgood
Administrator
Div. of Public Works
Dept. of Administration
502 N. 4th
Boise, ID 83720
Phone: (208) 334-3453
Fax: (208) 334-4031
E-mail: losgood@adm.state.id.us

ILLINOIS
Patricia Bergmann
Manager
Real Estate Div.
Bur. of Property Mgmt.
721 Stratton Ofc. Bldg.
401 S. Spring
Springfield, IL 62706
Phone: (217) 782-9117
Fax: (217) 524-8919

INDIANA

IOWA
Lee Hammer
Director
Facilities Mgmt.
Dept. of Transportation
800 Lincoln Way
Ames, IA 50010
Phone: (515) 239-1327
Fax: (515) 239-1964

KANSAS
Thaine Hoffman
Director
Div. of Architectural Services
Dept. of Administration
1020 S. Kansas Ave.
Topeka, KS 66612-1300
Phone: (785) 296-8899
Fax: (785) 233-9398

KENTUCKY
Armond Russ
Commissioner
Dept. of Facilities Mgmt.
Capitol Annex, Rm. 76
Frankfort, KY 40601
Phone: (502) 564-2623
Fax: (502) 564-2933

LOUISIANA
Roger Magendie
Director
Facility Planning & Control Ofc.
Div. of Administration
P.O. Box 94095
Baton Rouge, LA 70804
Phone: (225) 342-0820
Fax: (225) 342-7624

MAINE
Elaine Clark
Director
Bur. of Services
Dept. of Adm. & Financial Services
77 State House Station
Augusta, ME 04333
Phone: (207) 287-4000

MARYLAND
Gerald P. Walls
Assistant Secretary
Asst. Secretariat of Facilities Operation & Maintenance
Dept. of Services
29 St. Johns St.
Annapolis, MD 21401
Phone: (410) 974-2887
Fax: (410) 974-2555
E-mail: gwalls@dgs.state.md.us

MASSACHUSETTS
Stephen J. Hines
Acting Commissioner
Capitol Asset Mgmt.
One Ashburton Pl., Rm. 1505
Boston, MA 02108
Phone: (617) 727-4050
Fax: (617) 727-5363

MICHIGAN
Duane Berger
Director
Ofc. of Property Mgmt.
Dept. of Mgmt. & Budget
P.O. Box 30026
Lansing, MI 48909
Phone: (517) 241-2960

MINNESOTA
A. Thomas Ulness
Assistant Commissioner
Facilities Mgmt. Bur.
Dept. of Administration
200 Administration Bldg.
50 Sherburne Ave.
St. Paul, MN 55155
Phone: (651) 296-6852
Fax: (651) 297-7909
E-mail: tom.ulness@state.mn.us

MISSISSIPPI
Jerry Oakes
Director & Chief Architect
Div. of Services
Dept. of Finance & Administration
1501 Walter Sillers Bldg.
550 High St.
Jackson, MS 39201-1198
Phone: (601) 359-3633
Fax: (601) 359-2470

MISSOURI
Arvid West, Jr.
Director
Div. of Facilities Mgmt.
Ofc. of Administration
301 W. High St., Rm. 590
Jefferson City, MO 65102
Phone: (573) 751-1034
Fax: (573) 751-1466
E-mail: westa1@mail.oa.state.mo.us

MONTANA
Bill Bayless
Administrator
Services Div.
Dept. of Administration
Capitol Annex Bldg.
P.O. Box 200110
Helena, MT 59620-0110
Phone: (406) 444-3060
Fax: (406) 444-3039

NEBRASKA
Ken Fougeron
Administrator
State Bldg. Div.
Dept. of Adm. Services
521 S. 14th, Ste. 500
Lincoln, NE 68508-2707
Phone: (402) 471-3191
Fax: (402) 471-0421

NEVADA
Mike Meizel
Administrator
Bldg. & Grounds Div.
Dept. of Administration
406 E. 2nd St.
Carson City, NV 89701
Phone: (775) 687-4030
Fax: (775) 687-7633

NEW HAMPSHIRE
Michael P. Connor
Administrator
Bur. of Services
Adm. Services
25 Capitol St., Rm. 408
Concord, NH 03301
Phone: (603) 271-3148
Fax: (603) 271-1115

NEW JERSEY
Robert Rusciano
Deputy Administrator
Services Div.
Dept. of Treasury
P.O. Box 229
Trenton, NJ 08625-0229
Phone: (609) 292-5229

NEW MEXICO

NEW YORK
Joseph Seymour
Commissioner
Ofc. of Services
Corning Tower Bldg., 41st Fl.
Empire State Plz.
Albany, NY 12242
Phone: (518) 474-5991
Fax: (518) 486-9179

NORTH CAROLINA
Tony Jordan, Jr.
Director
Facilities Mgmt.
Dept. of Administration
431 N. Salisbury St.
Raleigh, NC 27603-1361
Phone: (919) 733-3514

NORTH DAKOTA
Curt Zimmerman
Director
Facility Mgmt.
Ofc. of Mgmt. & Budget
600 E. Blvd. Ave., 4th Fl.
Bismarck, ND 58505-0400
Phone: (701) 328-2471
Fax: (701) 328-3230
E-mail: czimmerm@state.nd.us

NORTHERN MARIANA ISLANDS
John B. Cepeda
Secretary
Dept. of Public Works
Chalan Laulau
P.O. Box 2950
Saipan, MP 96950
Phone: (670) 235-5827
Fax: (670) 235-5253

OHIO
Les Hughes
Deputy Director
Services Div.
Dept. of Adm. Services
4200 Surface Rd.
Columbus, OH 43228-5578
Phone: (614) 466-5578
Fax: (614) 644-1040

OKLAHOMA
Paula J. Falkenstein
Chief Administrator
Construction & Properties Div.
Dept. of Central Services
Will Rogers Ofc. Bldg.
2401 Lincoln, Ste. 206
Oklahoma City, OK 73152-3218
Phone: (405) 521-2111
Fax: (405) 521-6403

OREGON
C. David White
Administrator
Facilities Div.
Dept. of Adm. Services
1225 Ferry St., SE
Salem, OR 97310
Phone: (503) 378-4138
Fax: (503) 378-7210
E-mail: c.david.white@state.or.us

PENNSYLVANIA
Thomas E. Stanback
Director
Bur. of Bldgs. & Grounds
Dept. of Services
403 N. Ofc. Bldg.
Harrisburg, PA 17120
Phone: (717) 787-3893
Fax: (717) 772-2037

PUERTO RICO
Maria T. Mujica
Administrator
Services Administration
P.O. Box 7428
San Juan, PR 00916
Phone: (787) 724-1064
Fax: (787) 722-7965

RHODE ISLAND
William Tacelli
Buildings & Grounds Coordinator
Div. of Central Services
Dept. of Administration
1 Capitol Hill
Providence, RI 02908-5853
Phone: (401) 222-6238

SOUTH CAROLINA
William J. Clement
Assistant Director
Dept. of Services
1201 Main St., Ste. 420
Columbia, SC 29201
Phone: (803) 734-3528

SOUTH DAKOTA
Tom D. Geraets
Commissioner
Bur. of Administration
500 E. Capitol Ave.
Pierre, SD 57501
Phone: (605) 773-3688
Fax: (605) 773-3887

TENNESSEE
Larry Kirk
Assistant Commissioner
Facilities Mgmt.
Dept. of Finance & Administration
Wm. R. Snodgrass TN Tower, 22nd Fl.
Nashville, TN 37243
Phone: (615) 741-4042
Fax: (615) 741-2335

TEXAS
Tom Treadway
Executive Director
Services Comm.
1711 San Jacinto
P.O. Box 13047
Austin, TX 78701-3047
Phone: (512) 463-3446
Fax: (512) 463-7966
E-mail: tomtreadway@gsc.state.tx.us

U.S. VIRGIN ISLANDS
Harold G. Thompson
Acting Commissioner
Dept. of Public Works
No. 8 Sub Base
St. Thomas, VI 00802
Phone: (340) 776-4844
Fax: (340) 776-8990

UTAH
Richard Byfield
Director
Div. of Facilities, Construction & Mgmt.
Dept. of Adm. Services
4110 State Ofc. Bldg.
Salt Lake City, UT 84114
Phone: (801) 538-3261
Fax: (801) 538-3267
E-mail: rbyfield@dfcm.state.ut.us

VERMONT
Thomas W. Torti
Commissioner
Dept. of State Bldgs.
2 Governor Aiken Ave.
Drawer 33
Montpelier, VT 05633-5802
Phone: (802) 828-3314
Fax: (802) 828-3533
E-mail: ttorti@state.vt.us

VIRGINIA
Donald C. Williams
Director
Dept. of Services
202 N. 9th St., Ste. 209
Richmond, VA 23219
Phone: (804) 786-3311
Fax: (804) 371-8305

WASHINGTON
Bill Moore
Assistant Director
Div. of Capitol Facilities
Dept. of Administration
P.O. Box 41019
Olympia, WA 98504-1019
Phone: (360) 753-5686
Fax: (360) 586-5954

WEST VIRGINIA
Raymond V. Prozzillo
Director
Services Div.
Bldg. 1, Rm. MB60
1900 Kanawha Blvd., E.
Charleston, WV 25305
Phone: (304) 558-3517
Fax: (304) 558-2334

WISCONSIN
Bob Brandherm
Administrator
Div. Facilities Dev.
Dept. of Administration
101 E. Wilson, 7th Fl.
P.O. Box 7866
Madison, WI 53707
Phone: (608) 266-1031
Fax: (608) 267-2710

WYOMING
Mike Abel
Administrator
Services Div.
Woodson Bldg.
801 W. 20th
Cheyenne, WY 82002
Phone: (307) 777-7767
Fax: (307) 638-4898

Federal Liaison

The individual, typically based in Washington, D.C., who serves as the chief representative of state government in the nation's capital and works to promote state-federal relations.

ALABAMA

ALASKA
John Katz
Special Counsel
State & Federal Relations
AK Ofc. of the Governor
Hall of the States, Ste. 336
444 N. Capitol St., NW
Washington, DC 20001
Phone: (202) 624-5858
Fax: (202) 624-5857

AMERICAN SAMOA
Jan Lipsen
Washington Office Representative AS
1000 16th St,. NW, Ste. 400
Washington, DC 20007
Phone: (202) 785-0550

ARIZONA
Leslie Johnson
Deputy Counsel/Special Assistant
AZ Strategic Affairs
Ofc. of the Governor
1700 W. Washington
Phoenix, AZ 85007
Phone: (602) 542-1428

ARKANSAS

CALIFORNIA
Olivia Morgan
Director
CA Ofc. of the Governor
Hall of the States, Ste. 134
444 N. Capitol St., NW
Washington, DC 20001
Phone: (202) 624-5270
Fax: (202) 624-5280

COLORADO
Rick O'Donnell
Director
Policy & Initiatives Div.
Governor's Ofc.
136 State Capitol
Denver, CO 80203
Phone: (303) 866-2471
Fax: (303) 866-2003

CONNECTICUT
Ruth Ravitz
Director
CT Washington Ofc.
Hall of the States
444 N. Capitol St., NW, Ste. 317
Washington, DC 20001
Phone: (202) 347-4535
Fax: (202) 347-7151

DELAWARE
J. Jonathan Jones
Director
DE Washington Ofc.
Hall of the States, Ste. 230
444 N. Capitol St., NW
Washington, DC 20001
Phone: (202) 624-7724
Fax: (202) 624-5495

DISTRICT OF COLUMBIA
Warren Graves
Director
DC Ofc. of Intergovernmental Relations
441 4th St., NW, Rm. 1010-S
Washington, DC 20001
Phone: (202) 727-6265
Fax: (202) 727-6895

James Wareck
Deputy Director for Federal Affairs
Exec. Ofc. of the Mayor
DC Ofc. of Intergovernmental Affairs
441 4th St., NW, Ste. 1010
Washington, DC 20001
Phone: (202) 727-6265
Fax: (202) 727-6895

FLORIDA
Charlie Salem
Director
State Federal Relations
FL Executive Ofc. of the Governor
Hall of the States, Ste. 349
444 N. Capitol St., NW
Washington, DC 20001
Phone: (202) 624-5885
Fax: (202) 624-5886

GEORGIA
Dotti Crews
Director
Intergovernmental Relations
Ofc. of the Governor
245 State Capitol
Atlanta, GA 30334
Phone: (404) 651-7768
Fax: (404) 656-5947

GUAM
Joshua Tnorio
Special Assistant
GU Ofc. of the Governor
Hall of the States, Ste. 532
444 N. Capitol St., NW
Washington, DC 20001
Phone: (202) 624-3670

HAWAII
Kerrie Doerr
Special Assistant
HI Washington Ofc.
700 13th St., NW, Ste. 400
Washington, DC 20005-5917
Phone: (202) 879-0369
Fax: (202) 347-0785

IDAHO
Tana Shillingstad
Chief of Staff
State Capitol
Boise, ID 83720-0034
Phone: (208) 334-2100
E-mail: tshillin@gov.state.id.us

ILLINOIS
Bernie Robinson
Director
IL Washington Ofc.
Hall of the States, Ste. 240
444 N. Capitol St., NW
Washington, DC 20001
Phone: (202) 624-7760
Fax: (202) 724-0689

INDIANA
Jeff Viohl
Executive Assistant
IN Federal Relations
444 N. Capitol St., NW, Ste. 428
Washington, DC 20001-1512
Phone: (202) 624-1474
Fax: (202) 624-1475

IOWA
Philip C. Smith
Director
IA Ofc. for State/Federal Relations
Hall of the States, Ste. 359
444 N. Capitol St., NW
Washington, DC 20001
Phone: (202) 624-5442
Fax: (202) 624-8189

KANSAS

KENTUCKY
Kevin Goldsmith
Director of Intergovernmental Affairs
Governor's Ofc.
700 Capitol Ave., Ste. 105
Frankfort, KY 40601
Phone: (502) 564-2611
Fax: (502) 564-2517

LOUISIANA

MAINE
Susan Bell
Legislative Policy Analyst
1 State House Station, Rm. 236
Augusta, ME 04333-0001
Phone: (207) 287-3531

MARYLAND
Elizabeth Pyke
Director of Federal Relations
MD Ofc. of the Governor - Washington
Executive Dept.
444 N. Capital St., NW, Ste. 311
Washington, DC 20001
Phone: (202) 624-1430
Fax: (202) 783-3061

MASSACHUSETTS
Charles Steele
Director
Federal Relations
MA Washington Ofc.
Hall of the States, Ste. 400
444 N. Capitol St., NW
Washington, DC 20001
Phone: (202) 624-7713
Fax: (202) 624-7714

MICHIGAN
LeAnne Wilson
Director
MI Governor's Washington Ofc.
Hall of the States, Ste. 411
444 N. Capitol St., NW
Washington, DC 20001
Phone: (202) 624-5840
Fax: (202) 624-5841

MINNESOTA
Vacant
Deputy Director
MN State Ofc.
Hall of the States
400 N. Capitol St., NW, Ste. 365
Washington, DC 20001
Phone: (202) 624-5308
Fax: (202) 624-5425

MISSISSIPPI

MISSOURI
Susan Harris
Director
MO Washington Ofc.
Hall of the States, Ste. 376
400 N. Capitol St., NW
Washington, DC 20001
Phone: (202) 624-7720
Fax: (202) 624-5855
E-mail: harris@sso.org

MONTANA

NEBRASKA
David I. Maurstad
Lieutenant Governor
State Capitol, Rm. 3215
P.O. Box 94863
Lincoln, NE 68509-4863
Phone: (402) 471-2256
Fax: (402) 471-6031

NEVADA
Victoria Soberinsky
Deputy Chief of Staff
Ofc. of the Governor
101 N. Carson St.
Carson City, NV 89701
Phone: (775) 684-5670
Fax: (775) 684-5683

NEW HAMPSHIRE
Rich Sigel
Chief of Staff
Ofc. of the Governor
Executive Dept.
107 N. Main St., Rm. 208-214
Concord, NH 03301-4990
Phone: (603) 271-2121

NEW JERSEY
Marguerite H. Sullivan
Director
NJ Governor's Washington Ofc.
Hall of the States, Ste. 201
444 N. Capitol St., NW
Washington, DC 20001
Phone: (202) 638-0631
Fax: (202) 638-2296

NEW MEXICO
Dave Miller
Legislative Liaison
Ofc. of the Governor
State Capitol, Rm. 400
416 Don Gaspar
Santa Fe, NM 87503
Phone: (505) 827-3000
Fax: (505) 827-3026

NEW YORK
James A. Mazzarella
Director
NYS Ofc. of Federal Affairs
444 N. Capitol St., NW
Hall of the States, Ste. 301
Washington, DC 20001
Phone: (202) 434-7100
Fax: (202) 434-7110

NORTH CAROLINA
Vacant
Director
NC Washington Ofc.
Hall of the States, Ste. 332
444 N. Capitol St., NW
Washington, DC 20001
Phone: (202) 624-5830
Fax: (202) 624-5836

NORTH DAKOTA

NORTHERN MARIANA ISLANDS
Juan N. Babauta
Resident Representative to the U.S.
Commonwealth of the Northern Mariana Islands
2121 R St., NW
Washington, DC 20008
Phone: (202) 673-5869
Fax: (202) 673-5873

OHIO
Mike McGarey
Director
OH Ofc. of the Governor
Hall of the States, Ste. 546
444 N. Capitol St., NW
Washington, DC 20001
Phone: (202) 624-5844
Fax: (202) 624-5847

OKLAHOMA
Mike Hunter
Secretary of State
State Capitol Bldg., Rm. 101
Oklahoma City, OK 73105
Phone: (405) 521-3721
Fax: (405) 521-3771

OREGON

PENNSYLVANIA
Rebecca Halkias
Director
PA Governor's Ofc.
Hall of the States, Ste. 700
444 N. Capitol St., NW
Washington, DC 20001
Phone: (202) 624-7828
Fax: (202) 624-7831

PUERTO RICO
Alcides Ortiz
Director
PR Federal Affairs Ofc.
1100 17th St., NW, Ste. 800
Washington, DC 20036
Phone: (202) 778-0710
Fax: (202) 778-0721

RHODE ISLAND
Geri Guardino
Deputy Chief of Staff
Governor's Ofc.
State House
Providence, RI 02903
Phone: (401) 222-2080
Fax: (401) 273-5729

SOUTH CAROLINA
Michael Tecklenburg
Director
SC Washington Ofc.
Hall of the States, Ste. 203
444 N. Capitol St.
Washington, DC 20001
Phone: (202) 624-7784
Fax: (202) 624-7800

SOUTH DAKOTA
James Soyer
Chief of Staff
Governor's Ofc.
500 E. Capitol Ave.
Pierre, SD 57501
Phone: (605) 773-3212
Fax: (605) 773-5844
E-mail: jim.soyer@state.sd.us

TENNESSEE

TEXAS
Laurie Rich
Executive Director
TX Ofc. of Federal Relations
122 C St., NW, Ste. 200
Washington, DC 20001
Phone: (202) 638-3927
Fax: (202) 628-1943

U.S. VIRGIN ISLANDS
Carlyle Corbin
Special Assistant to the Governor for External Affairs
VI Ofc. of the Governor
444 N. Capitol St., NW, Ste. 298
Washington, DC 20006
Phone: (202) 624-3591
Fax: (202) 624-3594
E-mail: c.corbinmon@worldnet.att.net

UTAH
Joanne Neumann
Administrative Assistant
UT Ofc. of the Governor
Hall of the States, Ste. 388
400 N. Capitol St., NW
Washington, DC 20001
Phone: (202) 624-7704
Fax: (202) 624-7707
E-mail: jneumann@gov.state.ut.us

VERMONT
Vacant
Deputy Chief of State
Ofc. of the Governor
Pavillion Ofc. Bldg.
109 State St.
Montpelier, VT 05609
Phone: (802) 828-3333
Fax: (802) 828-3339

VIRGINIA
Michael T. McSherry
Director
VA Liaison Ofc.
Hall of the States, Ste. 214
444 N. Capitol St., NW
Washington, DC 20001
Phone: (202) 783-1769
Fax: (202) 783-7687
E-mail: dmcclung@sso.org

WASHINGTON
Jan Shinpoch
Director
WA State Washington Ofc.
Hall of the States, Ste. 617
444 N. Capitol St., NW
Washington, DC 20001
Phone: (202) 624-3680
Fax: (202) 624-3682

WEST VIRGINIA
Phyllis Cole
Senior Executive Assistant
Ofc. of the Governor
State Capitol
1900 Kanawha Blvd., E.
Charleston, WV 25305
Phone: (304) 558-3702
Fax: (304) 342-7025

WISCONSIN
Schuyler Babb
Director
WI Ofc. of Federal/State
Relations
Hall of the States
444 N. Capitol St., NW,
Ste. 613
Washington, DC 20001
Phone: (202) 624-5870
Fax: (202) 624-5871

WYOMING

Finance

Responsible for multiple financial functions (budget, payroll, accounting, revenue estimation).

ALABAMA
Henry Mabry
State Finance Director
State Capitol Bldg.
600 Dexter Ave., Ste. 105-N
Montgomery, AL 36104
Phone: (334) 242-7160
Fax: (334) 242-4488

ALASKA
David Essary
Director
Div. of Finance
Dept. of Administration
P.O. Box 110204
Juneau, AK 99811-0204
Phone: (907) 465-2240
Fax: (907) 465-2169

AMERICAN SAMOA
Tifi Ale
Treasurer
Dept. of the Treasury
AS Govt.
Pago Pago, AS 96799
Phone: (684) 633-4155
Fax: (684) 633-4100

ARIZONA
Lee Baron
Assistant Director
Finance Div.
Dept. of Administration
1700 W. Washington, Rm. 308
Phoenix, AZ 85007
Phone: (602) 542-9997

ARKANSAS
Richard Weiss
Director
Dept. of Finance & Administration
401 DFA Bldg.
1509 W. 7th St.
Little Rock, AR 72201
Phone: (501) 682-2242
Fax: (501) 682-1086
E-mail: richard.weiss@dfa.state.ar.us

CALIFORNIA
Craig Brown
Director
Dept. of Finance
State Capitol, 1st Fl.
Sacramento, CA 95814
Phone: (916) 445-4141

COLORADO
Arthur L. Barnhart
State Controller
Ofc. of the State Controller
Support Services
1525 Sherman St., Ste. 250
Denver, CO 80203
Phone: (303) 866-3281
Fax: (303) 866-4233

CONNECTICUT
Marc Ryan
Senior Economic Advisor to the Governor
Ofc. of Policy Mgmt.
P.O. Box 341441
Hartford, CT 06134
Phone: (860) 566-4840

DELAWARE
John Carney, Jr.
Secretary
Dept. of Finance
820 French St.
Wilmington, DE 19801
Phone: (302) 577-2074
Fax: (302) 577-3106
E-mail: jcarney@state.de.us

DISTRICT OF COLUMBIA
Valerie Holt
Interim Chief Financial Officer
Ofc. of the Chief Financial Officer
441 4th St., NW, Ste. 1150
Washington, DC 20001
Phone: (202) 727-2476
Fax: (202) 737-5258

FLORIDA
Don Saxon
Director
Div. of Finance
Dept. of Banking & Finance
101 E. Gaines St.
Tallahassee, FL 32399-0350
Phone: (850) 488-9805
Fax: (850) 681-2428

GEORGIA
W. Daniel Ebersole
Treasurer
Ofc. of Treasury & Fiscal Services
1202 W. Tower
200 Piedmont Ave., SE
Atlanta, GA 30334
Phone: (404) 656-2168
Fax: (404) 656-9048

GUAM
Michael J. Reidy
Director
Dept. of Administration
P.O. Box 884
Hagatna, GU 96932
Phone: (671) 475-1136
Fax: (671) 477-6788

HAWAII
Earl I. Anzai
Director of Finance
Dept. of Budget & Finance
P.O. Box 150
Honolulu, HI 96810
Phone: (808) 586-1518
Fax: (808) 586-1976

IDAHO
Darrell V. Manning
Administrator
Div. of Financial Mgmt.
Ofc. of the Governor
Statehouse
700 W. Jefferson
Boise, ID 83720
Phone: (208) 334-3900

ILLINOIS
Steve Schnorf
Director
Bur. of the Budget
Ofc. of the Governor
108 State House
Springfield, IL 60706
Phone: (217) 782-4520
Fax: (217) 524-1514

INDIANA
Peggy Boehm
Director
Budget Agency
State House, Rm. 212
Indianapolis, IN 46204
Phone: (317) 232-5612
Fax: (317) 233-3323

IOWA
Gerald D. Bair
Director
Dept. of Revenue & Finance
Hoover State Ofc. Bldg.
1300 E. Walnut
Des Moines, IA 50319
Phone: (515) 281-3204
Fax: (515) 242-6040

Robert L. Rafferty
Director
Dept. of Mgmt.
State Capitol, Rm. 12
Des Moines, IA 50319
Phone: (515) 281-5211

KANSAS

KENTUCKY
John McCarty
Secretary
Finance & Administration Cabinet
Capitol Annex., Rm. 383
Frankfort, KY 40601
Phone: (502) 564-4240
Fax: (502) 564-6785

LOUISIANA
Mark Drennen
Commissioner
Div. of Administration
P.O. Box 94095
Baton Rouge, LA 70804-9095
Phone: (225) 342-7000
Fax: (225) 342-1057

MAINE
Janet E. Waldron
Commissioner
Dept. of Adm. & Financial Services
78 State House Station
Augusta, ME 04333-0078
Phone: (207) 624-7800

MARYLAND
Frederick W. Puddester
Secretary
Ofc. of the Secretary
Dept. of Budget & Mgmt.
45 Calvert St., 1st Fl.
Annapolis, MD 21401
Phone: (410) 260-7041
Fax: (410) 974-2585
E-mail: fpudd@dbm.state.md.us

MASSACHUSETTS
Andrew Natsios
Secretary
Executive Ofc. for Administration & Finance
State House, Rm. 373
Boston, MA 02133
Phone: (617) 727-2040
Fax: (617) 727-2496

MICHIGAN
Mary A. Lannoye
State Budget Director
Dept. of Mgmt. & Budget
320 S. Walnut
Lansing, MI 48909
Phone: (517) 373-1004
Fax: (517) 373-7268

MINNESOTA
Pam Wheelock
Commissioner
Dept. of Finance
Centennial Ofc. Bldg., 4th Fl.
658 Cedar St.
St. Paul, MN 55155
Phone: (651) 297-7881
Fax: (651) 296-8685

MISSISSIPPI
Edward L. Ranck
Director
Dept. of Finance & Administration
906 Sillers Bldg.
Jackson, MS 39201
Phone: (601) 359-3204
Fax: (601) 359-2405

MISSOURI
Richard A. Hanson
Commissioner
Administration
Ofc. of Administration
State Capitol, Rm. 125
P.O. Box 809
Jefferson City, MO 65102
Phone: (573) 751-3311
Fax: (573) 751-1212
E-mail: hansod@mail.oa.state.mo.us

MONTANA
David Lewis
Director
Ofc. of Budget & Program Planning
State Capitol, Rm. 236
Helena, MT 59620
Phone: (406) 444-3616
Fax: (406) 444-5529

Lois A. Menzies
Director & Ex Officio State Treasurer
Dept. of Administration
Rm. 155, Mitchell Bldg.
P.O. Box 200101
Helena, MT 59620-0101
Phone: (406) 444-2032
Fax: (406) 444-2812
E-mail: lmenzies@mt.gov

NEBRASKA
Mary Jane Egr
State Tax Commissioner
Dept. of Revenue
P.O. Box 94818
Lincoln, NE 68509
Phone: (402) 471-2971
Fax: (402) 471-5608

Gerry A. Oligmueller
Administrator
Budget Div.
Dept. of Adm. Services
State Capitol, Rm. 1322
P.O. Box 94664
Lincoln, NE 68509-4664
Phone: (402) 471-2526
Fax: (402) 471-4157

Kate Witek
Auditor of Public Accounts
State Capitol, Ste. 2303
Lincoln, NE 68509
Phone: (402) 471-2111
Fax: (402) 471-3301

NEVADA

NEW HAMPSHIRE
Donald S. Hill
Commissioner
Commissioner's Ofc.
Dept. of Adm. Services
25 Capitol St., Rm. 120
Concord, NH 03301-6312
Phone: (603) 271-3201

NEW JERSEY
Elizabeth L. Pugh
Director
Ofc. of Mgmt. & Budget
Dept. of Treasury
P.O. Box 221
Trenton, NJ 08625-0221
Phone: (609) 292-6746
Fax: (609) 633-6179

NEW MEXICO
David Harris
Secretary
Finance & Administration
180 Bataan Memorial Bldg.
Santa Fe, NM 87501
Phone: (505) 827-4985
Fax: (505) 827-4984

NEW YORK
H. Carl McCall
Comptroller
A.E. Smith Ofc. Bldg., 6th Fl.
Albany, NY 12236
Phone: (518) 474-3506
Fax: (518) 473-3004

NORTH CAROLINA
Marvin K. Dorman
State Budget Officer
Ofc. of State Budget
116 W. Jones St.
Raleigh, NC 27603-8005
Phone: (919) 733-7061
Fax: (919) 733-0640

NORTH DAKOTA
Rod Backman
Director
Ofc. of Mgmt. & Budget
600 E. Blvd. Ave., 4th Fl.
Bismarck, ND 58505-0400
Phone: (701) 328-2680
Fax: (701) 328-3230
E-mail: rbackman@state.nd.us

Sheila Peterson
Director
Fiscal Mgmt.
Ofc. of Mgmt. & Budget
600 E. Blvd. Ave., 4th Fl.
Bismarck, ND 58505-0400
Phone: (701) 328-2680
Fax: (701) 328-3230
E-mail: peterson@state.nd.us

NORTHERN MARIANA ISLANDS
Lucia DLG. Neilsen
Secretary of Finance
Finance & Accounting
Dept. of Finance
P.O. Box 5234 CHRB
Saipan, MP 96950
Phone: (670) 664-1198
Fax: (670) 664-1115

OHIO
Tom Johnson
Director
Ofc. of Budget & Mgmt.
30 E. Broad St., 34th Fl.
Columbus, OH 43266
Phone: (614) 752-2577
Fax: (614) 466-5400

OKLAHOMA
Tom Daxon
Director
Ofc. of State Finance
122 State Capitol
2300 N. Lincoln Blvd.
Oklahoma City, OK 73105
Phone: (405) 521-2081
Fax: (405) 521-3902

OREGON
Theresa McHugh
Deputy Director
Dept. of Adm. Services
155 Cottage St., NE
Salem, OR 97310
Phone: (503) 378-4691
Fax: (503) 373-7643
E-mail: theresa.r.mchugh@state.or.us

PENNSYLVANIA
Robert Bittenbender
Cabinet Secretary
Ofc. of the Budget
Budget Dept.
Main Capitol Bldg., Rm. 238
Harrisburg, PA 17120
Phone: (717) 787-4472
Fax: (717) 787-4590
E-mail: rbittenb@gois.state.pa.us

PUERTO RICO
Jorge Aponte Hernandez
Director
Ofc. of Budget & Mgmt.
P.O. Box 9023228
San Juan, PR 00902-3228
Phone: (787) 725-9420
Fax: (787) 724-1374

RHODE ISLAND
Stephen P. McAllister
Executive Director/State Budget Officer
State Budget Ofc.
Dept. of Administration
1 Capitol Hill, 4th Fl.
Providence, RI 02908
Phone: (401) 222-6300
Fax: (401) 222-6410

SOUTH CAROLINA
L. Fred Carter
Executive Director
Budget & Control Board
P.O. Box 12444
Columbia, SC 29211
Phone: (803) 734-2320

SOUTH DAKOTA
Curt Everson
Commissioner
Bur. of Finance & Mgmt.
500 E. Capitol Ave.,
Rm. 216
Pierre, SD 57501
Phone: (605) 773-3411
Fax: (605) 773-4711

TENNESSEE
John Ferguson
Commissioner
Finance & Administration
State Capitol, 1st Fl.
600 Charlotte Ave.
Nashville, TN 37243-0001
Phone: (615) 741-2401
Fax: (615) 741-9872

TEXAS
Carole Keeton Rylander
Comptroller
Comptroller of Public
Accounts
P.O. Box 13528
Austin, TX 78711-3528
Phone: (512) 463-4000
Fax: (512) 463-4965

U.S. VIRGIN ISLANDS
Bernice Turnbull
Acting Commissioner
Dept. of Finance
76 Kronprindsens Gade
St. Thomas, VI 00802
Phone: (340) 774-4750
Fax: (340) 776-4028

UTAH
Kim Thorne
Director
Div. of Finance
Dept. of Adm. Services
2110 State Ofc. Bldg.
Salt Lake City, UT 84114
Phone: (801) 538-3020
Fax: (801) 538-3244
E-mail: kthorne
@fi.state.ut.us

VERMONT
Thomas Pelham
Commissioner
Agency of Administration
Dept. of Finance & Mgmt.
109 State St.
Montpelier, VT 05609-0401
Phone: (802) 828-2376
Fax: (802) 828-2428
E-mail: tpelham
@fin.state.vt.us

VIRGINIA
Ronald L. Tillett
Secretary of Finance
Governor's Cabinet
9th St. Ofc. Bldg., Ste. 636
202 N. 9th St.
Richmond, VA 23219
Phone: (804) 786-1148
Fax: (804) 692-0676

WASHINGTON
Dick Thompson
Director
Ofc. of Financial Mgmt.
300 Insurance Bldg.
P.O. Box 43113
Olympia, WA 98504
Phone: (360) 902-0555
Fax: (360) 664-2832

WEST VIRGINIA
Joseph F. Markus
Cabinet Secretary
Dept. of Administration
State Capitol, Rm. E119
1900 Kanawha Blvd., E.
Charleston, WV 25305
Phone: (304) 558-4331
Fax: (304) 558-2999

WISCONSIN
Jennifer Reinert
Administrator
DOA/Div. of Technical
Mgmt.
101 E. Wilson St., 8th Fl.
Madison, WI 53702
Phone: (608) 266-1651
Fax: (608) 267-0626

WYOMING
Max Maxfield
State Auditor
State Capitol, Rm. 114
200 W. 24th St.
Cheyenne, WY 82002
Phone: (307) 777-7831

Fire Marshal

Inspects businesses and public places for fire hazards.

ALABAMA
John Robinson
State Fire Marshal
Insurance Dept.
201 Monroe St., Ste. 1780
Montgomery, AL 36104
Phone: (334) 241-4166
Fax: (334) 241-4158

ALASKA
Craig P. Goodrich
State Fire Marshal
Div. of Fire Prevention
Dept. of Public Safety
5700 E. Tudor Rd.
Anchorage, AK 99507-1225
Phone: (907) 269-5491
Fax: (907) 338-4375

AMERICAN SAMOA
Te'o Fuavai
Commissioner
Dept. of Public Safety
AS Govt.
Pago Pago, AS 96799
Phone: (684) 633-1111
Fax: (684) 633-5111

ARIZONA
Duane D. Pell
State Fire Marshal
Dept. of Bldg. & Fire Safety
99 E. Virginia, Ste. 100
Phoenix, AZ 85007
Phone: (602) 255-4964

ARKANSAS
Ray Carnahan
Commander
Ofc. of Fire Marshal
State Police
1 State Police Plz.
Little Rock, AR 72209
Phone: (501) 618-8600
Fax: (501) 618-8621

CALIFORNIA
Ronny J. Coleman
State Fire Marshal
P.O. Box 944246
Sacramento, CA 94244-2460
Phone: (916) 262-1883

COLORADO
Paul Cooke
Director
Fire Safety Div.
Dept. of Public Safety
700 Kipling St.
Lakewood, CO 80215
Phone: (303) 239-4463
Fax: (303) 239-4405

CONNECTICUT
Vacant
Deputy Fire Marshal
Bur. of State Fire Marshal
Dept. of Public Safety
1111 Country Club Rd.
P.O. Box 2794
Middletown, CT 06457
Phone: (860) 685-8380

DELAWARE
Daniel R. Kiley
State Fire Marshal
Fire Service Ctr.
1537 Chestnut Grove Rd.
Dover, DE 19904-9610
Phone: (302) 739-4393
Fax: (302) 739-3696

DISTRICT OF COLUMBIA
Donald Edwards
Fire Chief
Fire Dept.
1923 Vermont Ave., NW
Washington, DC 20001
Phone: (202) 673-3320
Fax: (202) 462-0807

FLORIDA
Charles D. Clark
Director
Div. of State Fire Marshal
200 E. Gaines St.
Tallahassee, FL 32399-0340
Phone: (850) 413-3603
Fax: (850) 922-1235

GEORGIA
L.C. Cole
State Fire Marshal
Dept. of Insurance
W. Tower, 7th Fl.
2 Martin Luther King, Jr. Dr.
Atlanta, GA 30334
Phone: (404) 656-2064

GUAM
Gil P. Reyes
Chief
Fire Dept.
1301-1 Central Ave., Tiyan
P.O. Box 2950
Hagatna, GU 96932
Phone: (671) 472-3304
Fax: (671) 472-3360

HAWAII

IDAHO
Don McCoy
State Fire Marshal
Dept. of Insurance
700 W. State St.
Boise, ID 83720
Phone: (208) 334-4370

ILLINOIS
Thomas Armstead
State Fire Marshal
1035 Stevenson Dr.
Springfield, IL 62703-4259
Phone: (217) 785-4143
Fax: (217) 782-1062

INDIANA
M. Tracy Boatwright
State Fire Marshal
Dept. of Fire & Bldg. Services
402 W. Washington St., Rm. E241
Indianapolis, IN 46204
Phone: (317) 232-2226
Fax: (317) 233-0307

IOWA
Roy Marshall
State Fire Marshal
Dept. of Public Safety
Wallace State Ofc. Bldg.
E. 9th & Grand Aves.
Des Moines, IA 50319
Phone: (515) 281-8622

KANSAS
Gale Hagg
Fire Marshal
700 SW Jackson, Ste. 600
Topeka, KS 66603-3714
Phone: (785) 296-3401
Fax: (785) 296-0151

KENTUCKY
Dave Manley
Fire Marshal
Div. of Fire Prevention
Public Protection & Regulation Cabinet
1047 U.S. 127 S.
Frankfort, KY 40601
Phone: (502) 564-3626
Fax: (502) 564-6799

LOUISIANA
Vincent J. Bella
Fire Marshal
Dept. of Public Safety
P.O. Box 94304
Baton Rouge, LA 70804
Phone: (225) 925-4911
Fax: (225) 925-4414

MAINE
John C. Dean
Fire Marshal
Dept. of Public Safety
52 State House Station
Augusta, ME 04333
Phone: (207) 287-3473

MARYLAND
Rocco J. Gabriele
Fire Marshal
Ofc. of the State Fire Marshal
Dept. of Public Safety & Correctional Services
300 E. Joppa Rd., Ste. 1002
Baltimore, MD 21286-3020
Phone: (410) 339-4200
Fax: (410) 339-4215

MASSACHUSETTS
Stephen Coan
State Fire Marshal
Dept. of Fire Services
Executive Ofc. of Public Safety
State Rd. St.
P.O. Box 1025
Stow, MA 01775
Fax: (617) 556-2600

MICHIGAN
Anthony Sanfillipo
Director
Ofc. of Fire Safety
Consumer & Industry Services
7150 Harris Dr.
Lansing, MI 48913
Phone: (517) 322-1924

MINNESOTA
Thomas R. Brace
State Fire Marshal
444 Cedar St., Ste. 145
St. Paul, MN 55101-5145
Phone: (651) 215-0503
Fax: (651) 215-0541
E-mail: thomas.brace@state.mn.us

MISSISSIPPI
Millard Mackey
Chief
Fire Div.
Insurance Dept.
P.O. Box 22542
Jackson, MS 39205
Phone: (601) 354-6900
Fax: (601) 354-6899

MISSOURI
Bill Farr
State Fire Marshal
Div. of Fire Safety
Dept. of Public Safety
1709 Industrial Dr.
P.O. Box 844
Jefferson City, MO 65102
Phone: (573) 751-2930
Fax: (573) 751-1744
E-mail: bfarr@mail.state.mo.us

MONTANA
Terry L. Phillips
State Fire Marshal
Fire Prevention & Investigation Bur.
Dept. of Justice
1310 E. Lockey
P.O. Box 201415
Helena, MT 59620-1415
Phone: (406) 444-2050
Fax: (406) 444-9155

NEBRASKA
Ken Winters
Fire Marshal
246 S. 14th St.
Lincoln, NE 68508
Phone: (402) 471-2027
Fax: (402) 471-3118

NEVADA
Marvin Carr
Fire Marshal
Fire Marshal Ofc.
Dept. of Motor Vehicles
107 Jacobsen Way
Carson City, NV 89711
Phone: (775) 687-4290
Fax: (775) 687-5122

NEW HAMPSHIRE
Donald Bliss
Director
Div. of Fire Safety
Dept. of Safety
10 Hazen Dr.
Concord, NH 03305
Phone: (603) 271-3294
Fax: (603) 271-1091

NEW JERSEY
William H. Cane
Director
Fire Safety Comm.
Dept. of Community Affairs
101 S. Broad St., CN809
Trenton, NJ 08625-0809
Phone: (609) 292-9446

NEW MEXICO
George Chavez
State Fire Marshal
Public Regulation Comm.
P.O. Box 1269
Santa Fe, NM 87504-1269
Phone: (505) 827-3721
Fax: (505) 476-0161
E-mail: GChavez@scc.state.nm.us

NEW YORK
James A. Burns
State Fire Administrator
Ofc. of Fire Prevention & Control
Dept. of State
41 State St.
Albany, NY 12207
Phone: (518) 474-6746
Fax: (515) 474-3240

NORTH CAROLINA
Jim Long
State Fire Marshal
State Fire Comm.
Dept. of Insurance
430 N. Salisbury St.
Raleigh, NC 27603-1212
Phone: (919) 733-2142
Fax: (919) 733-9076

NORTH DAKOTA
Dan Boium
Fire Marshal
Attorney Gen's. Ofc.
P.O. Box 1054
Bismarck, ND 58502-1054
Phone: (701) 328-5555
Fax: (701) 328-5510
E-mail: msmail.ndag@ranch.state.nd.us

NORTHERN MARIANA ISLANDS
Jose T. Ada
Director
Fire Div.
Dept. of Public Safety
Susupe, Civic Ctr.
Saipan, MP 96950
Phone: (670) 234-6222
Fax: (670) 234-8581

OHIO
Robert Rielage
State Fire Marshal
Dept. of Commerce
8895 E. Main St.
Reynoldsburg, OH 43068
Phone: (614) 752-8200
Fax: (614) 752-7213

OKLAHOMA
Tom Wilson
Fire Marshal
Fire Marshal Agency
4545 Lincoln Blvd.
Oklahoma City, OK 73105
Phone: (405) 522-5005
Fax: (405) 524-9810

OREGON
Robert T. Panuccio
State Fire Marshal
State Police
4760 Portland Rd., NE
Salem, OR 97305-1760
Phone: (503) 378-3473
Fax: (503) 373-1825

PENNSYLVANIA
David L. Smith
State Fire Commissioner
P.O. Box 3321
Harrisburg, PA 17105-3321
Phone: (717) 651-2201
Fax: (717) 651-2210
E-mail: dsmith@pema.state.pa.us

PUERTO RICO
Jose Rosa Carrasquillo
Director
Fire Services
P.O. Box 13325
San Juan, PR 00908-3325
Phone: (787) 725-3444
Fax: (787) 725-3788

RHODE ISLAND
Irving Owens
State Fire Marshal
24 Conway Ave.
Quonset/Davisville Industrial Park
N. Kingstown, RI 02852
Phone: (401) 294-0861

SOUTH CAROLINA
Lewis Lee
State Fire Marshal
Div. of State Fire Marshal
141 Monticello Trail
Columbia, SC 29203
Phone: (803) 896-9800

SOUTH DAKOTA
Dan Carlson
Fire Marshal
Div. of Fire Safety
Dept. of Commerce & Regulation
118 W. Capitol Ave.
Pierre, SD 57501
Phone: (605) 773-3562
Fax: (605) 773-3018

TENNESSEE
Stuart Crine
Assistant Commissioner
Div. of Fire Prevention
500 James Robertson Pkwy., 3rd Fl.
Nashville, TN 37243
Phone: (615) 741-2981
Fax: (615) 741-1583

TEXAS
Gary L. Warren
Executive Director
Comm. on Fire Protection
12675 Research Blvd.
Austin, TX 78759
Phone: (512) 918-7100
Fax: (512) 918-7107

U.S. VIRGIN ISLANDS
Pedro Encarnicion
Director
Fire Service
Universal Plz.
8A E. Thomas
St. Thomas, VI 00802
Phone: (340) 774-7610
Fax: (340) 774-4718

UTAH
Gary Wise
State Fire Marshal
Dept. of Public Safety
5272 S. College Dr.,
Ste. 302
Murray, UT 84123
Phone: (801) 284-6358
Fax: (801) 284-6351
E-mail: gwise.psudi
@state.ut.us

VERMONT
Steve Jansen
Commissioner
Dept. of Labor & Industry
Natl. Life Bldg.
Drawer 20
Montpelier, VT 05620-3401
Phone: (802) 828-2288
Fax: (802) 828-2195

VIRGINIA
Ed Altizer
Fire Marshal
Dept. of Housing &
Community Dev.
Jackson Ctr.
501 N. 2nd St.
Richmond, VA 23219
Phone: (804) 371-7153
Fax: (804) 371-7092

WASHINGTON
Mary L. Corso
State Fire Marshal
Fire Protection Bur.
State Patrol
P.O. Box 42600
Olympia, WA 98504-2600
Phone: (360) 753-0404
Fax: (360) 753-0395

WEST VIRGINIA
Walter Smittle, III
Fire Marshal
1207 Quarrier St., Rm. 202
Charleston, WV 25301
Phone: (304) 558-2191
Fax: (304) 558-2537

WISCONSIN
Carolyn Kelly
State Fire Marshal
Div. of Criminal
Investigation
Dept. of Justice
123 W. Washington, 7th Fl.
P.O. Box 7857
Madison, WI 53707
Phone: (608) 266-1671
Fax: (608) 267-2777

WYOMING
Jim Noel
State Fire Marshal
Fire Prevention & Electrical
Safety
Herschler Bldg., 1st Fl., W.
122 W. 25th St.
Cheyenne, WY 82002
Phone: (307) 777-7288

Fish and Wildlife

Protects and manages fish and wildlife resources and enforces the state's fish and game laws.

ALABAMA
Corky Pugh
Assistant Director
Div. of Game & Fish
Conservation & Natural Resources
64 N. Union St., Rm. 567
Montgomery, AL 36130
Phone: (334) 242-3465

ALASKA
Frank Rue
Commissioner
Dept. of Fish & Game
P.O. Box 25526
Juneau, AK 99802-5526
Phone: (907) 465-6141
Fax: (907) 465-2332

AMERICAN SAMOA
Ufagafa Ray Tulafono
Director
Dept. of Marine & Wildlife Resources
Pago Pago, AS 96799
Phone: (684) 633-4456
Fax: (684) 633-5944

ARIZONA
Duane L. Shroufe
Director
Dept. of Game & Fish
2221 W. Greenway Rd.
Phoenix, AZ 85023
Phone: (602) 542-3278

ARKANSAS
Steve N. Wilson
Director
Game & Fish Comm.
2 Natural Resources Dr.
Little Rock, AR 72205
Phone: (501) 223-6305
Fax: (501) 223-6448

CALIFORNIA
Jacqueline Schafer
Director
Dept. of Fish & Game
1416 9th St., 12th Fl.
Sacramento, CA 95814
Phone: (916) 653-7667

COLORADO
John Mumma
Director
Div. of Wildlife
Dept. of Natural Resources
6060 Broadway
Denver, CO 80216
Phone: (303) 297-1192
Fax: (303) 866-5417

CONNECTICUT
Ernest Beckwith, Jr.
Director
Fisheries Div.
79 Elm St.
Hartford, CT 06106
Phone: (860) 424-3474

Dale May
Director
Wildlife Div.
79 Elm St.
Hartford, CT 06106
Phone: (860) 424-3011

DELAWARE
Andrew T. Manus
Director
Dept. of Natural Resources & Environmental Control
89 Kings Hwy.
Dover, DE 19901
Phone: (302) 739-4506
Fax: (302) 739-6242

DISTRICT OF COLUMBIA
Ira Palmer
Director
Fisheries & Wildlife
Environmental Health Administration
2100 M.L. King, Jr. Ave., Ste. 203
Washington, DC 20020
Phone: (202) 645-6601
Fax: (202) 645-6622

FLORIDA
Allan Egbert
Executive Director
Game & Fresh Water Fish Comm.
620 S. Meridian St.
Tallahassee, FL 32399-1600
Phone: (850) 488-2975
Fax: (850) 488-6988

GEORGIA
David Waller
Director
Wildlife Resources Div.
Dept. of Natural Resources
2070 U.S. Hwy. 278, SE
Social Cir., GA 30279
Phone: (770) 918-6400

GUAM
Juan Taijito
Acting Director
Dept. of Agri.
192 Dairy Rd.
Mangilao, GU 96923
Phone: (671) 734-3942
Fax: (671) 734-6569

HAWAII
William Devick
Acting Administrator
Div. of Aquatic Resources
Dept. of Land & Natural Resources
1151 Punchbowl St., Rm. 330
Honolulu, HI 96813
Phone: (808) 587-0100
Fax: (808) 587-0115

IDAHO
Steve Mealey
Director
Dept. of Fish & Game
600 W. Walnut
Boise, ID 83707
Phone: (208) 334-3700

ILLINOIS
Brent Manning
Director
Dept. of Natural Resources
Lincoln Towers Plz., Rm. 425
524 S. 2nd St.
Springfield, IL 62706
Phone: (217) 782-6302
Fax: (217) 785-9236

INDIANA
Gary Doxtater
Division Director
Fish & Wildlife Div.
402 W. Washington St., Rm. W-273
Indianapolis, IN 46204
Phone: (317) 232-4080
Fax: (317) 232-8150

IOWA
Allen Farris
Administrator
Fish & Wildlife Div.
Dept. of Natural Resources
Wallace State Ofc. Bldg.
E. 9th & Grand Aves.
Des Moines, IA 50319
Phone: (515) 281-5154

KANSAS
Roger Wolfe
Supervisor
Fisheries/Wildlife Div.
Dept. of Wildlife & Parks
3300 SW 29th St.
Topeka, KS 66614
Phone: (785) 273-6740
Fax: (785) 273-6757
E-mail: rogerw@wp.state.ks.us

KENTUCKY
Tom Bennett
Commissioner
Fish & Wildlife
1 Game Farm Rd.
Frankfort, KY 40601
Phone: (502) 564-3400
Fax: (502) 564-6508

LOUISIANA
James Jenkins, Jr.
Secretary
Dept. of Wildlife & Fisheries
P.O. Box 98000
Baton Rouge, LA 70898
Phone: (225) 765-2800
Fax: (225) 765-2607

MAINE
Lee Perry
Commissioner
Dept. of Inland Fisheries/Wildlife
41 State House Station
Augusta, ME 04333
Phone: (207) 287-5202

MARYLAND
Robert A. Bachman
Director
Fisheries Service
Dept. of Natural Resources
Tawes State Ofc. Bldg., B-2
Annapolis, MD 21401-2397
Phone: (410) 260-8251

Michael Slattery
Director
Wildlife Administration
Dept. of Natural Resrcs
Tawes State Ofc. Bldg., E-1
Annapolis, MD 21401
Phone: (410) 260-8540
Fax: (410) 260-8595

MASSACHUSETTS
David M. Peters
Commissioner
Dept. of Fisheries & Wildlife
100 Cambridge St., Rm. 1902, 19th Fl.
Boston, MA 02202
Phone: (617) 727-1614
Fax: (617) 727-7235

MICHIGAN
Kelley Smith
Chief
Fisheries Div.
Dept. of Natural Resources
P.O. Box 30028
Lansing, MI 48909
Phone: (517) 373-1263

Vacant
Chief
Wildlife Div.
Dept. of Natural Resources
P.O. Box 30028
Lansing, MI 48909
Phone: (517) 373-9311

MINNESOTA
Roger Holmes
Director
Div. of Fish & Wildlife
Dept. of Natural Resources
500 Lafayette Rd.
St. Paul, MN 55155
Phone: (651) 297-1308
Fax: (651) 297-7272
E-mail: roger.holmes@dnr.state.mn.us

MISSISSIPPI
Sam Polles
Director
Parks & Recreation
Dept. of Wildlife, Fisheries & Parks
P.O. Box 451
Jackson, MS 39205
Phone: (601) 362-9212
Fax: (601) 364-2147

MISSOURI
Ronald Glover
Administrator
Div. of Protection
Dept. of Conservation
2901 W. Truman Blvd.
P.O. Box 180
Jefferson City, MO 65102
Phone: (573) 751-4115
Fax: (573) 751-8971
E-mail: glover@mail.conservation.state.mo.us

Norm Stucky
Administrator
Div. of Fisheries
Dept. of Conservation
2901 W. Truman Blvd.
P.O. Box 180
Jefferson City, MO 65102
Phone: (573) 751-4115
Fax: (573) 526-4047
E-mail: stuckn@mail.conservation.state.mo.us

Ollie Torgerson
Administrator
Div. of Wildlife
Dept. of Conservation
2901 W. Truman Blvd.
P.O. Box 180
Jefferson City, MO 65102
Phone: (573) 751-4115
Fax: (573) 526-4663
E-mail: torgeo@mail.conservation.state.mo.us

MONTANA
Pat Graham
Director
Dept. of Fish, Wildlife & Parks
1420 E. 6th Ave.
Helena, MT 59620-0701
Phone: (406) 444-3186
Fax: (406) 444-4952

Larry Peterman
Administrator
Fisheries Div.
Dept. of Fish, Wildlife & Parks
1420 E. 6th Ave.
Helena, MT 59620-0701
Phone: (406) 444-2449
Fax: (406) 444-4952

NEBRASKA
Rex Amack
Division Administrator
Fisheries Div.
Game & Parks Comm.
P.O. Box 30370
Lincoln, NE 68503
Phone: (402) 471-5515
Fax: (402) 471-5528

James Douglas
Division Administrator
Wildlife Div.
Game & Parks Comm.
P.O. Box 30370
Lincoln, NE 68503
Phone: (402) 471-5411
Fax: (402) 471-5528

NEVADA
Terry Crawforth
Administrator
Div. of Wildlife
Conservation & Natural Resources Dept.
1100 Valley Rd.
P.O. Box 10678
Reno, NV 89520
Phone: (775) 688-1590
Fax: (775) 688-1595

NEW HAMPSHIRE
Wayne E. Vetter
Executive Director
Fish & Game Dept.
2 Hazen Dr.
Concord, NH 03301-6500
Phone: (603) 271-3421
Fax: (603) 271-1438

NEW JERSEY
Robert McDowell
Director
Fish, Game & Wildlife Div.
Dept. of Environmental Protection
501 E. State St.
P.O. Box 400
Trenton, NJ 08625-0400
Phone: (609) 292-9410
Fax: (609) 984-1414

NEW MEXICO
Gerald A. Maracchini
Director
Dept. of Game & Fish
P.O. Box 25112
Santa Fe, NM 87504
Phone: (505) 827-7899
Fax: (505) 827-7915
E-mail: j_maracchini@gmfsh.state.nm.us

NEW YORK
Jerry Barnhart
Director
Div. of Fish & Wildlife & Marine Resources
Dept. of Environmental Conservation
50 Wolf Rd.
Albany, NY 12233
Phone: (518) 457-5690
Fax: (518) 457-0341

NORTH CAROLINA
Charles Fullwood
Executive Director
Wildlife Resources Comm.
Dept. of Environment & Natural Resources
P.O. Box 27687
Raleigh, NC 27611
Phone: (919) 733-3391
Fax: (919) 733-7083

NORTH DAKOTA
Dean Hildebrand
Director
Game & Fish Dept.
100 N. Bismarck Expy.
Bismarck, ND 58501-5095
Phone: (701) 328-6300
Fax: (701) 328-6352
E-mail: dhildebr@state.nd.us

NORTHERN MARIANA ISLANDS
Arnold I. Palacios
Chief
Fish & Wildlife Div.
Dept. of Natural Resources
Caller Box 10007
Saipan, MP 96950
Phone: (670) 322-9627
Fax: (670) 322-9629

OHIO
Michael J. Budzik
Chief
Div. of Wildlife
Dept. of Natural Resources
1840 Belcher Dr., Bldg. G-3
Columbus, OH 43224
Phone: (614) 265-6304
Fax: (614) 262-1143

OKLAHOMA
Greg Duffy
Director
Dept. of Wildlife Conservation
1801 N. Lincoln Blvd.
Oklahoma City, OK 73105
Phone: (405) 521-3851
Fax: (405) 521-6535

OREGON
Jim Greer
Director
Dept. of Fish & Wildlife
P.O. Box 59
Portland, OR 97207
Phone: (503) 872-5272
Fax: (503) 872-5276

PENNSYLVANIA
Peter A. Colangelo
Executive Director
Fish Comm.
P.O. Box 67000
Harrisburg, PA 17106
Phone: (717) 657-4518
Fax: (717) 657-4549

Donald C. Madl
Executive Director
Game Comm.
2001 Elmerton Ave.
Harrisburg, PA 17110
Phone: (717) 787-3633
Fax: (717) 772-0502

PUERTO RICO
Daniel Pagan
Secretary
Dept. of Natural Resources
P.O. Box 5887
San Juan, PR 00906
Phone: (787) 723-3090
Fax: (787) 723-4255

RHODE ISLAND
Jan Reitsma
Director
Dept. of Environmental Mgmt.
235 Promenade St.
Providence, RI 02908
Phone: (401) 222-2771
Fax: (401) 222-6802

SOUTH CAROLINA
Paul Sandifer
Director
Div. of Wildlife & Marine Resources
Dept. of Natural Resources
P.O. Box 167
Columbia, SC 29203
Phone: (803) 734-3888

SOUTH DAKOTA
Doug Hansen
Director
Wildlife Div.
Dept. of Game, Fish & Parks
523 E. Capitol Ave.
Pierre, SD 57501
Phone: (605) 773-3381
Fax: (605) 773-6245

TENNESSEE
Gary Myers
Executive Director
Wildlife Resources Agency
P.O. Box 40747
Nashville, TN 37204
Phone: (615) 781-6552
Fax: (615) 781-6551

TEXAS
Andrew S. Sansom
Executive Director
Dept. of Parks & Wildlife
4200 Smith School Rd.
Austin, TX 78744
Phone: (512) 389-4802
Fax: (512) 389-4814

U.S. VIRGIN ISLANDS
Dean Plaskett
Commissioner
Dept. of Planning & Natural Resources
Foster's Plz., 396-1 Anna's Retreat
St. Thomas, VI 00802
Phone: (340) 774-3320
Fax: (340) 775-5706

UTAH
John Kimball
Director
Div. of Wildlife Resources
Dept. of Natural Resources
1594 W. N. Temple, Ste. 2110
Salt Lake City, UT 84114
Phone: (801) 538-4702
Fax: (801) 538-4709
E-mail: jkimball.nrdwr@state.ut.us

VERMONT
Ron Regan
Commissioner
Agency of Natural Resources
Dept. of Fish & Wildlife
103 S. Main St.
Waterbury, VT 05676
Phone: (802) 241-3700
Fax: (802) 241-3295

VIRGINIA
William L. Woodfin, Jr.
Director
Dept. of Game & Inland Fisheries
4010 W. Broad St.
Richmond, VA 23230
Phone: (804) 367-9231
Fax: (804) 367-0405

WASHINGTON
Jeff Koenings
Director
Dept. of Fish & Wildlife
600 Capitol Way, N.
Olympia, WA 98501-1091
Phone: (360) 902-2200
Fax: (360) 902-2947

WEST VIRGINIA
Robert L. Miles
Chief
Div. of Wildlife Resources
Dept. of Natural Resources
Capitol Complex, Bldg. 3
1900 Kanawha Blvd., E.
Charleston, WV 25305
Phone: (304) 558-2771
Fax: (304) 558-3147

WISCONSIN
Tom Hauge
Director
Bur. of Wildlife Mgmt.
Div. of Resource Mgmt.
P.O. Box 7921
Madison, WI 53707
Phone: (608) 266-2193
Fax: (608) 267-7857

Michael Staggs
Director
Bur. of Fish Mgmt.
Dept. of Natural Resources
101 S. Webster, FH/4
P.O. Box 7921
Madison, WI 53707
Phone: (608) 267-0796
Fax: (608) 267-7857

WYOMING
John Baughman
Director
Game & Fish Comm.
5400 Bishop Blvd.
Cheyenne, WY 82006
Phone: (307) 777-4501

Fleet Management

Manages the state's central fleet of vehicles that are made available to other state agencies.

ALABAMA
Curtis Hays
Director
Ofc. of Fleet Mgmt.
Dept. of Finance
386 S. Ripley St.
Montgomery, AL 36130
Phone: (334) 242-4043
Fax: (334) 240-3297

ALASKA

AMERICAN SAMOA
Vacant
Director
Dept. of Public Works
AS Govt.
Pago Pago, AS 96799
Phone: (684) 633-4141
Fax: (684) 633-5958

ARIZONA
Bill Hernandez
General Manager
Mgmt. Services Div.
Dept. of Administration
1700 W. Washington, Rm. 250
Phoenix, AZ 85007
Phone: (602) 542-5675

ARKANSAS
Ron Lester
Information Systems Manager
Ofc. of Adm. Services
Dept. of Finance & Admin.
P.O. Box 2485
Little Rock, AR 72203
Phone: (501) 324-9058
Fax: (501) 324-9070

CALIFORNIA
Timothy Bow
Chief
Ofc. of Fleet Administration
Dept. of Services
802 Q St.
Sacramento, CA 95814-6422
Phone: (916) 327-2007

COLORADO
Rick Malinowski
Director
Central Services Div.
Support Services
Dept. of Personnel
225 E. 16th Ave., Rm. 800
Denver, CO 80203
Phone: (303) 866-3970
Fax: (303) 894-2375

CONNECTICUT
Stephen Dygus
Director
Ofc. of Fleet Operations
Dept. of Adm. Services
190 Huyshope Ave.
Hartford, CT 06106
Phone: (860) 566-5940

DELAWARE
Terry Barton
Fleet Administrator
Dept. of Adm. Services
820 Silver Lake Blvd., Ste. 100
Dover, DE 19904
Phone: (302) 739-3039
Fax: (302) 739-5450

DISTRICT OF COLUMBIA
Ronald Flowers
Administrator
Fleet Mgmt. Administration
Dept. of Public Works
1725 15th St., NE
Washington, DC 20002
Phone: (202) 576-6799
Fax: (202) 576-7715

FLORIDA
Harrison Rivers
Director
Div. of Motor Pool
Dept. of Mgmt. Services
3266 Capitol Cir., SW
Tallahassee, FL 32310
Phone: (850) 488-4099
Fax: (850) 488-3760

GEORGIA
Dotty W. Roach
Commissioner
Dept. of Adm. Services
200 Piedmont Ave., Ste. 1804
Atlanta, GA 30334-5500
Phone: (404) 656-5514
Fax: (404) 651-9595

GUAM
Daniel Lizama
Acting Director
Dept. of Public Works
542 N. Marine Dr.
Tamuning, GU 96911
Phone: (671) 646-3131
Fax: (671) 649-9178

HAWAII
Harold Sonomura
Division Head
Automotive Mgmt. Div.
Accounting & Services
869-A Punchbowl St.
Honolulu, HI 96813
Phone: (808) 586-0343
Fax: (808) 586-0354

IDAHO
Pamela Ahrens
Director
Dept. of Administration
650 W. State St., Rm. 100
Boise, ID 83720
Phone: (208) 334-3382

ILLINOIS
Barbara Bonansinga
Manager
Div. of Vehicles
Dept. of Central Mgmt. Services
200 E. Ash St.
Springfield, IL 62706
Phone: (217) 782-2535

INDIANA
Brian Renner
Superintendent
State Motor Pool
29 N. Tibbs Ave.
Indianapolis, IN 46222
Phone: (317) 232-1380
Fax: (317) 233-4881

IOWA
Dale Schroeder
State Vehicle Dispatcher
Vehicle Dispatcher Div.
Dept. of Services
301 E. 7th St.
Des Moines, IA 50319
Phone: (515) 281-7702

KANSAS
Orion Jordan
Director
Central Motor Pool
Dept. of Administration
400 SW Van Buren
Topeka, KS 66603-3332
Phone: (785) 296-2245
Fax: (785) 296-8100

KENTUCKY
Joe Heady
Director
Div. of Transportation Services
Transportation Cabinet
369 Warsaw St.
Frankfort, KY 40622
Phone: (502) 564-2260
Fax: (502) 564-9708

LOUISIANA
Irene Babin
Director
Property Assistance Agency
Div. of Administration
P.O. Box 94095
Baton Rouge, LA 70804-9095
Phone: (225) 342-6890
Fax: (225) 342-6891

MAINE
William S. Pratt
Fleet Manager
Vehicle Rental Agency
Central Fleet Mgmt.
9 State House Station
Augusta, ME 04333
Phone: (207) 287-3521

MARYLAND
Larry Williams
Fleet & Travel Program Administrator
State Fleet & Travel Mgmt.
Dept. of Budget & Mgmt.
45 Calvert St.
Annapolis, MD 21401
Phone: (410) 260-7195
Fax: (410) 974-3274
E-mail: larryw@dbm.state.md.us

MASSACHUSETTS
Herb Faulconer
Fleet Administrator
Motor Vehicle Mgmt. Bur.
Executive Ofc. of Administration & Finance
One Ashburton Pl., Rm. 1017
Boston, MA 02108
Phone: (617) 727-8844
Fax: (617) 727-1812

MICHIGAN
Gayle Pratt
Director
Motor Transport Div.
P.O. Box 30026
Lansing, MI 48909
Phone: (517) 322-5001
Fax: (517) 322-1423

MINNESOTA
Dan Oehmke
Director
Travel Mgmt. Div.
Dept. of Administration
296 Chester St.
St. Paul, MN 55107
Phone: (651) 296-9998
Fax: (651) 296-3911
E-mail: dan.oehmke@state.mn.us

MISSISSIPPI
Don Buffum
Director
Bur. of Purchasing
Ofc. of Purchasing & Travel
1504 Sillers Bldg.
Jackson, MS 39201
Phone: (601) 359-3409
Fax: (601) 359-2470

MISSOURI
Stan Perovich
Director
Div. of Services
Ofc. of Administration
Truman Bldg., Rm. 760
P.O. Box 809
Jefferson City, MO 65102
Phone: (573) 751-4656
Fax: (573) 751-7819
E-mail: perovs@mai.oa.state.mo.us

MONTANA
John Blacker
Maintenance Administrator
Maintenance Div.
Dept. of Transportation
2701 Prospect Ave.
Helena, MT 59620-1001
Phone: (406) 444-6158
Fax: (406) 444-7684

NEBRASKA
Dennis Johnk
Administrator
Transportation Services Bur.
Dept. of Adm. Services
P.O. Box 95025
Lincoln, NE 68509
Phone: (402) 471-2897
Fax: (402) 471-2999

NEVADA
Clay Thomas
Assistant Chief
Motor Carrier Bur.
Dept. of Motor Vehicles
555 Wright Way
Carson City, NV 89711
Phone: (775) 684-4711
Fax: (775) 684-4619
E-mail: cthomas@govmail.state.nv.us

NEW HAMPSHIRE

NEW JERSEY
Bud Montague
Fleet Manager
Central Motor Pool
P.O. Box 233
Trenton, NJ 08625-0233
Phone: (609) 984-7277
Fax: (609) 633-0839

NEW MEXICO
James E. Russell
Director
Transportation Motor Pool
Dept. of Services
P.O. Box 26110
Sante Fe, NM 87502
Phone: (505) 827-1955
Fax: (505) 827-2041

NEW YORK
Joseph Seymour
Commissioner
Ofc. of Services
Corning Tower Bldg., 41st Fl.
Empire State Plz.
Albany, NY 12242
Phone: (518) 474-5991
Fax: (518) 486-9179

NORTH CAROLINA
John T. Massey, Jr.
Director
Div. of Motor Fleet Mgmt.
Dept. of Administration
1915 Blue Ridge Rd.
Raleigh, NC 27607-6403
Phone: (919) 733-6540
Fax: (919) 733-2432

NORTH DAKOTA
Paul Feyereisen
Manager
State Fleet Services
Dept. of Transportation
608 E. Blvd. Ave.
Bismarck, ND 58505-0700
Phone: (701) 328-1434
Fax: (701) 328-4623
E-mail: pfeyerei@state.nd.us

NORTHERN MARIANA ISLANDS
Jose I. Deleon Guerrero
Special Assistant for Administration
Ofc. of the Governor
Caller Box 10007
Saipan, MP 96950
Phone: (670) 664-2212
Fax: (670) 664-2210
E-mail: gov.tasaa@saipan.com

OHIO
Leilani Napier
Fleet Administrator
Div. of Adm. Services
Dept. of Adm. Services
4200 Surface Rd.
Columbus, OH 43228-1313
Phone: (614) 466-6607
Fax: (614) 752-8883

OKLAHOMA
Steve Dwyer
Director
Div. of Fleet Mgmt.
Dept. of Central Services
3301-A N. Santa Fe
Oklahoma City, OK 73118
Phone: (405) 521-2206

OREGON
Rob Cameron
Motor Fleet Manager
Fleet Administration
Dept. of Adm. Services
1100 Airport Rd., SE
Salem, OR 97310
Phone: (503) 378-3367
Fax: (503) 378-5813

PENNSYLVANIA
James W. Martin
Director
Fleet Mgmt.
2221 Forester St.
Harrisburg, PA 17105
Phone: (717) 787-3162
Fax: (717) 787-0276

PUERTO RICO
Maria T. Mujica
Administrator
Services Administration
P.O. Box 7428
San Juan, PR 00916
Phone: (787) 724-1064
Fax: (787) 722-7965

RHODE ISLAND
Robert L. Carl, Jr.
Director
Dept. of Administration
1 Capitol Hill
Providence, RI 02903
Phone: (401) 222-2280
Fax: (401) 222-6436

SOUTH CAROLINA
Gerald W. Calk
Budget & Control Board
State Fleet Mgmt.
1022 Senate St.
Columbia, SC 29201
Phone: (803) 737-1502
Fax: (803) 737-1160

SOUTH DAKOTA
Eileen Crom
Assistant State Administrator
Fleet & Travel Mgmt.
Bur. of Administration
500 E. Capitol Ave.
Pierre, SD 57501
Phone: (605) 773-3162
Fax: (605) 773-3502

TENNESSEE
Bobby Parton
Director
Div. of Motor Vehicle Mgmt.
Dept. of Services
2200 Charlotte Ave.
Nashville, TN 37243
Phone: (615) 741-1637
Fax: (615) 741-2161

TEXAS
James A. Green, Jr.
Vehicle Fleet Manager
Adm. Services
Services Comm.
P.O. Box 13047
Capitol Station
Austin, TX 78711-3047
Phone: (512) 463-3035

U.S. VIRGIN ISLANDS
Ian Williams
Director
Div. of Transportation
Dept. of Property & Procurement
Sub Base, Bldg. 1
St. Thomas, VI 00802
Phone: (340) 774-0388
Fax: (340) 774-1163

UTAH
Steven Saltzgiver
Director
Div. of Fleet Operations
Dept. of Adm. Services
4120 State Ofc. Bldg.
Salt Lake City, UT 84114
Phone: (801) 538-3452
Fax: (801) 538-1773
E-mail: ssaltzgi@fo.state.ut.us

VERMONT
George S. Combes
Superintendent
Central Garage Div.
Agency of Transportation
133 State St.
Montpelier, VT 05633
Phone: (802) 828-2564
Fax: (802) 828-3576

VIRGINIA
William Colavita
State Fleet Manager
Dept. of Transportation
1401 E. Broad St.
Richmond, VA 23219
Phone: (804) 367-6886
Fax: (804) 367-8987

WASHINGTON
Linda Bremmer
Assistant Director
Div. of Transportation Services
Dept. of Administration
P.O. Box 41032
Auburn, WA 98504-1032
Phone: (360) 438-8247
Fax: (360) 438-8239

WEST VIRGINIA
Ken Miller
Coordinator of Travel & Fleet Management
Travel Mgmt. Ofc.
Dept. of Administration
212 California Ave.
Charleston, WV 25305
Phone: (304) 558-3259
Fax: (304) 558-2137

WISCONSIN
Jeff Knight
Director
Bur. of Transportation
Dept. of Administration
101 E. Wilson, 6th Fl.
P.O. Box 7867
Madison, WI 53703
Phone: (608) 267-7693
Fax: (608) 267-0600

WYOMING
Bernie Kerschner
Vehicle Fleet Supervisor
ANI/Central Services
723 W. 19th St.
Cheyenne, WY 82002
Phone: (307) 777-6857

Food Protection

Protects the state's food supply, from the production and processing of food through its marketing and distribution.

ALABAMA
John Block
Director
Agri. Chemistry & Plant Industry Div.
Dept. of Agri.
P.O. Box 3336
Montgomery, AL 36109-0336
Phone: (334) 240-7171
Fax: (334) 240-3103

ALASKA
Janice Adair
Director
Div. of Environmental Health
Dept. of Environmental Conservation
555 Gordova St.
Anchorage, AK 99501
Phone: (907) 269-7644
Fax: (907) 269-7654

AMERICAN SAMOA
Iotamo Saleapaga
Director
Dept. of Health
Pago Pago, AS 96799
Phone: (684) 633-4590

ARIZONA
Lee Bland
Assistant Director
Disease Control Services Div.
Dept. of Health Services
3815 N. Black Canyon Hwy.
Phoenix, AZ 85015
Phone: (602) 230-5808

ARKANSAS
Sandra Lancaster
Administrator
Div. of Sanitarian Services
Food & Dairy Section
4815 W. Markham St.
Little Rock, AR 72205
Phone: (501) 661-2171
Fax: (501) 661-2152

CALIFORNIA
Ann Veneman
Secretary
Dept. of Food & Agri.
P.O. Box 942871
Sacramento, CA 94271-0001
Phone: (916) 654-0433

COLORADO
Tom Messenger
Director
Consumer Protection Div.
Dept. of Public Health & Environment
4300 Cherry Creek Dr., S.
Denver, CO 80246-1530
Phone: (303) 692-3620
Fax: (303) 753-6809

CONNECTICUT
John McGuire
Director
Food Div. & Standards
Dept. of Consumer Protection
165 Capitol Ave.
Hartford, CT 06106
Phone: (860) 566-3388

DELAWARE
David C. Rodeheaver
Director
Div. of Public Health/ DHSS
Health Systems Protection
Jesse Cooper Bldg.
Dover, DE 19901
Phone: (302) 739-4731
Fax: (302) 577-4510

DISTRICT OF COLUMBIA
Sidney Hall
Chief
Food Protection Branch
Dept. of Consumer & Regulatory Affairs
614 H St., NW, Rm. 616
Washington, DC 20001
Phone: (202) 727-7250

FLORIDA
Dan S. Smyly
Director
Div. of Food Safety
Dept. of Agri. & Consumer Services
3125 Conner Blvd., MS C-18
Tallahassee, FL 32399-1650
Phone: (850) 488-0295
Fax: (850) 488-7946

GEORGIA
Jim Drinnon
Acting Director
Environmental Health Section
Dept. of Human Resources
2 Peachtree St.
Atlanta, GA 30303
Phone: (404) 657-2733

GUAM
Dennis G. Rodriguez
Director
Dept. of Public Health & Social Services
P.O. Box 2816
Hagatna, GU 96932
Phone: (671) 735-7102
Fax: (671) 734-5910
E-mail: dennis_r_@NS.GOV.GU

HAWAII
Gary Gill
Deputy Director
Environmental Health Administration
Dept. of Health
1250 Punchbowl St.
Honolulu, HI 96813
Phone: (808) 586-4424
Fax: (808) 586-4444

IDAHO
Don Brothers
Supervisor
Bur. of Environmental Health & Safety
Food Protection Program
P.O. Box 83720
Boise, ID 83720-0036
Phone: (208) 334-5938

ILLINOIS
John Lumpkin
Director
Dept. of Public Health
535 W. Jefferson St.
Springfield, IL 62761
Phone: (217) 782-4977
Fax: (217) 782-3987

INDIANA
Howard Cundiff
Director
Consumer Protection
State Board of Health
2 N. Meridian
Indianapolis, IN 46204
Phone: (317) 233-7182
Fax: (317) 233-7334

IOWA
Robert Haxton
Program Manager
Inspections Div.
Dept. of Inspections & Appeals
Lucas State Ofc. Bldg.
321 E. 12th St.
Des Moines, IA 50319
Phone: (515) 281-6539

KANSAS
Stephen N. Paige
Director
Food & Drug Section
Dept. of Health & Environment
109 SW 9th St., Ste. 604
Topeka, KS 66612-1274
Phone: (785) 296-5600
Fax: (785) 296-6522

KENTUCKY
Sarah Castanis
Assistant Director
Div. of Food Distribution
Dept. of Agri.
100 Fairoaks
Frankfort, KY 40601
Phone: (502) 564-4387
Fax: (502) 564-3773

LOUISIANA
Jimmy Guidry
Assistant Secretary
Ofc. of Public Health
Dept. of Health & Hospitals
P.O. Box 3214, Bin #4
Baton Rouge, LA 70821-0629
Phone: (225) 342-8092
Fax: (225) 342-8098

MAINE
Robert W. Spear
Commissioner
Dept. of Agri., Food & Rural Resources
28 State House Station
Augusta, ME 04333
Phone: (207) 287-3871

MARYLAND
Alan Taylor
Director
Food Protection & Consumer Health Services
Dept. of Health & Mental Hygiene
6 St. Paul St., Ste. 1301
Baltimore, MD 21201
Phone: (410) 767-8440
Fax: (410) 333-8931
E-mail: alan@dhmh.state.md.us

MASSACHUSETTS
Richard Waskiewicz
Director
Food Protection Program
Dept. of Public Health
305 S. St.
Jamaica Plain, MA 02130
Phone: (617) 727-2670
Fax: (617) 524-8062

MICHIGAN
Kathy Fedder
Director
Food Div.
Dept. of Agri.
Ottawa Bldg., 4th Fl.
P.O. Box 30017
Lansing, MI 48909
Phone: (517) 373-1060

MINNESOTA
Fred Mitchell
Director
Dairy & Food Inspection Div.
Dept. of Agri.
90 W. Plato Blvd.
St. Paul, MN 55107
Phone: (651) 296-2629
Fax: (651) 297-5637
E-mail: m.fred.mitchell@state.mn.us

MISSISSIPPI
Lydia Strayer
Director
Div. of Sanitation
Dept. of Health
P.O. Box 1700
Jackson, MS 39215
Phone: (601) 960-7690
Fax: (601) 354-6120

MISSOURI
Russell Lilly
Environmental Public Health Specialist V
Section for Environmental Public Health
Dept. of Health
P.O. Box 570
930 Wildwood Dr.
Jefferson City, MO 65102
Phone: (573) 751-6095
Fax: (573) 526-7377
E-mail: lillyr@mail.health.state.mo.us

MONTANA
Mitzi Schwab
Section Supervisor
Food & Consumer Safety Section
Dept. of Public Health & Human Services
1400 Broadway, Rm. C317B
Helena, MT 59620
Phone: (406) 444-2408
Fax: (406) 444-4135

NEBRASKA
George Hanssen
Food Division Manager
Bur. of Dairies & Foods
Dept. of Agri.
P.O. Box 94947
Lincoln, NE 68509-4947
Phone: (402) 471-2536
Fax: (402) 471-2759

NEVADA
Sharon Ezell
Deputy Administrator
Health Div.
Dept. of Human Resources
505 E. King St., Rm. 201
Carson City, NV 89701-4797
Phone: (775) 684-4200
Fax: (775) 684-4211
E-mail: sezell@govmail.statenv.us

NEW HAMPSHIRE
Kathleen Kerr
Director
Ofc. of Program Support
Health & Human Services
6 Hazen Dr.
Concord, NH 03301-6527
Phone: (603) 271-4335
Fax: (603) 271-4859

NEW JERSEY
Dhun B. Patel
Director
Div. of Dairy & Commodity Regulation
Dept. of Agri.
John Fitch Plz.
P.O. Box 330
Trenton, NJ 08625-0330
Phone: (609) 292-5575
Fax: (609) 984-2508

NEW MEXICO
Frank Du Bois
Secretary
NM State Univ.
Dept. of Agri.
P.O. Box 30005, Dept. 3189
Las Cruces, NM 88003-8005
Phone: (505) 646-3007
Fax: (505) 646-8120

NEW YORK
Donald R. Davidsen
Commissioner
Dept. of Agri. & Markets
One Winners Cir.
Albany, NY 12235
Phone: (518) 457-5496
Fax: (518) 457-3087

NORTH CAROLINA
Robert W. Gordon
Director
Food & Drug Protection
Dept. of Agri.
4000 Reedy Creek Rd.
Raleigh, NC 27607-6468
Phone: (919) 733-7366
Fax: (919) 733-6801

NORTH DAKOTA
Kenan Bullinger
Director
Food & Lodging
Preventive Health Section
600 E. Blvd. Ave., 2nd Fl. - Judicial Wing
Bismarck, ND 58505-0200
Phone: (701) 328-1292
Fax: (701) 328-1412
E-mail: kbulling@state.nd.us

NORTHERN MARIANA ISLANDS
Josephine T. Sablan-Hall
Director
Public Health Services Div.
Dept. of Public Health & Environment
P.O. Box 409 CK
Saipan, MP 96950
Phone: (670) 234-9344
Fax: (670) 233-0214
E-mail: publichealth.paradise@saipan.com

OHIO
Roland Stewart
Chief
Div. of Food Safety
Dept. of Agri.
8995 E. Main St.
Reynoldsburg, OH 43068
Phone: (614) 728-6250
Fax: (614) 644-0720

OKLAHOMA
Mike Bailey
Director
Food Protection Services
OK City County Dept. of Health
921 NE 23rd St.
Oklahoma City, OK 73105
Phone: (405) 425-4347

OREGON
Ronald McKay
Administrator
Food Safety Div.
Dept. of Agri.
635 Capitol St., NE
Salem, OR 97310
Phone: (503) 986-4727
Fax: (503) 986-4729

PENNSYLVANIA
Leroy Corbin
Director
Bur. of Food Safety & Laboratory Services
Dept. of Agri.
112 Agri. Bldg.
Harrisburg, PA 17120-0029
Phone: (717) 787-4315
Fax: (717) 772-2780

PUERTO RICO

RHODE ISLAND
Ernest Julian
Chief
Food Protection & Sanitation
Dept. of Health
3 Capitol Hill
Providence, RI 02908
Phone: (401) 222-2758

SOUTH CAROLINA
Robert L. Dickinson
Director
Div. of Food Protection
Dept. of Health & Environmental Control
2600 Bull St.
Columbia, SC 29201
Phone: (803) 935-7958

SOUTH DAKOTA
Doneen Hollingsworth
Secretary
Dept. of Health
600 E. Capitol Ave.
Pierre, SD 57501
Phone: (605) 773-3361
Fax: (605) 773-5683

TENNESSEE
Jimmy Hopper
Director
Quality Standards
Dept. of Agri.
Ellington Agri. Ctr.
Nashville, TN 37204
Phone: (615) 837-5150
Fax: (615) 837-5335

TEXAS
Susan Tennyson
Acting Bureau Director
Div. of Food & Drugs
Dept. of Health
1100 W. 49th St.
Austin, TX 78756
Phone: (512) 719-0222
Fax: (512) 719-0202

U.S. VIRGIN ISLANDS
Wilbur Callender
Commissioner
Dept. of Health
No. 48 Sugar Estate
St. Thomas, VI 00802
Phone: (340) 774-0117
Fax: (340) 777-4001

UTAH
Kyle R. Stephens
Director
Div. of Regulatory Services
Dept. of Agri. & Food
350 N. Redwood Rd.
Salt Lake City, UT 84116
Phone: (801) 538-7150
Fax: (801) 538-7126
E-mail: kstephen.agmain@state.ut.us

VERMONT
Alfred Burns
Sanitatian Supervisor
Div. of Environmental Health
Dept. of Health
108 Cherry St.
P.O. Box 70
Burlington, VT 05402
Phone: (802) 863-7220
Fax: (802) 863-7483

VIRGINIA
J. Carlton Courter, III
Commissioner
Dept. of Agri. & Consumer Services
Washington Bldg., Ste. 210
1100 Bank St.
Richmond, VA 23219
Phone: (804) 786-3501
Fax: (804) 371-2945

WASHINGTON
Candace Jacobs
Assistant Director
Food Safety & Animal Health Div.
Dept. of Agri.
P.O. Box 42560
Olympia, WA 98502-2560
Phone: (360) 902-1875
Fax: (360) 902-2087

WEST VIRGINIA
Joseph P. Schock
Director
Environmental Health Services Ofc.
Div. of Health
815 Quarrier St.
Charleston, WV 25305-2616
Phone: (304) 558-2981
Fax: (304) 558-0691

WISCONSIN
Steve Steinhoff
Administrator
Div. of Food Safety
Agri., Trade & Consumer Protection
2811 Agri. Dr.
P.O. Box 8911
Madison, WI 53708
Phone: (608) 224-4700
Fax: (608) 224-4710

WYOMING
John Misock
Manager
Consumer Health Services
Dept. of Agri.
2219 Carey Ave.
Cheyenne, WY 82002
Phone: (307) 777-6587

Forestry

Manages and protects the state's forest resources.

ALABAMA
Timothy Boyce
State Forester
State Forestry Comm.
513 Madison Ave.
Montgomery, AL 36130-2550
Phone: (334) 240-9304
Fax: (334) 240-9390

ALASKA
Jeff Jahnke
Director & State Forester
Div. of Forestry
Dept. of Natural Resources
400 Willoughby Ave., 3rd Fl.
Juneau, AK 99801-1724
Phone: (907) 465-3379
Fax: (907) 586-3113

AMERICAN SAMOA

ARIZONA
Michael Hart
Director
Forestry Div.
State Land Dept.
1616 W. Adams
Phoenix, AZ 85007
Phone: (602) 542-4627

ARKANSAS
John Shannon
State Forester
Forestry Comm.
3821 W. Roosevelt Rd.
Little Rock, AR 72204-6395
Phone: (501) 664-2531
Fax: (501) 664-5906

CALIFORNIA
Richard A. Wilson
Director
Dept. of Forestry & Fire Protection
P.O. Box 944246
Sacramento, CA 94244
Phone: (916) 653-7772

COLORADO
James E. Hubbard
State Forester
Forest Service
CO State Univ.
203 Forestry Bldg.
Fort Collins, CO 80523
Phone: (970) 491-6303
Fax: (970) 491-7736

CONNECTICUT
Donald H. Smith, Jr.
State Forester
Forestry Div.
Dept. of Environmental Protection
79 Elm St.
Hartford, CT 06106
Phone: (860) 424-2485

DELAWARE
E. Austin Short, III
State Forest Administrator
Dept. of Agri.
2320 S. DuPont Hwy.
Dover, DE 19901
Phone: (302) 739-4811
Fax: (302) 697-6287

DISTRICT OF COLUMBIA
Sandra Hill
Manager
Tree Maintenance Div.
Dept. of Public Works
2750 S. Capitol St., SE
Washington, DC 20032
Phone: (202) 727-5321
Fax: (202) 724-1406

FLORIDA
Earl Peterson
Director
Div. of Forestry
Dept. of Agri. & Consumer Services
3125 Conner Blvd.
Tallahassee, FL 32399-1650
Phone: (850) 488-4274
Fax: (850) 488-0863

GEORGIA
J. Fred Allen
Director
Forestry Comm.
P.O. Box 819
Macon, GA 31298-4599
Phone: (912) 751-3480

GUAM
Juan Taijito
Acting Director
Dept. of Agri.
192 Dairy Rd.
Mangilao, GU 96923
Phone: (671) 734-3942
Fax: (671) 734-6569

HAWAII
Michael Buck
Administrator
Forestry & Wildlife Div.
Dept. of Land & Natural Resources
1151 Punchbowl St., #325
Honolulu, HI 96813
Phone: (808) 587-0166
Fax: (808) 587-0160

IDAHO
Winston Wiggins
Assistant Director
Forestry & Fire
Dept. of Lands
1215 W. 8th St.
Boise, ID 83720
Phone: (208) 334-0200

ILLINOIS
Stewart Pequignot
Chief
Forest Resources Div.
Dept. of Natural Resources
524 S. 2nd St.
Springfield, IL 62701-1787
Phone: (217) 782-2361

INDIANA
Burnell Fischer
State Forester
Forestry Div.
Dept. of Natural Resources
IGC-South, Rm. W296
Indianapolis, IN 46204
Phone: (317) 232-4105
Fax: (317) 233-3863

IOWA
William Farris
State Forester
Forest & Forestry Div.
Dept. of Natural Resources
Wallace State Ofc. Bldg.
E. 9th & Grand Aves.
Des Moines, IA 50319
Phone: (515) 281-8656

KANSAS
Raymond G. Aslin
State Forester
Forestry Service
2610 Claflin Rd.
Manhattan, KS 66502-2798
Phone: (785) 532-3300
Fax: (785) 532-3305
E-mail: raslin@oz.oznet.ksu.edu

KENTUCKY
Mark Matuszewski
Director
Div. of Forestry
627 Comanche Trail
Frankfort, KY 40601
Phone: (502) 564-4496
Fax: (502) 564-6553

LOUISIANA
Paul D. Frey
Assistant Commissioner
Ofc. of Forestry
Dept. of Agri.
P.O. Box 1628
Baton Rouge, LA 70821
Phone: (225) 925-4500
Fax: (225) 922-1356

MAINE
Donald Mansius
Acting Director
Bur. of Forestry
Dept. of Conservation
22 State House Station
Augusta, ME 04333
Phone: (207) 287-2791

MARYLAND
James Mallow
Director, Forest Service
Forest, Wildlife & Heritage Services
Dept. of Natural Resources
Tawes State Ofc. Bldg.
Annapolis, MD 21401
Phone: (410) 260-8531
Fax: (410) 260-8596

MASSACHUSETTS
Lauren A. Liss
Commissioner
Executive Ofc. of Environmental Affairs
Dept. of Environmental Protection
1 Winter St.
Boston, MA 02108
Phone: (617) 292-5856
Fax: (617) 574-6880

MICHIGAN
John Robertson
Chief, State Forester
Forest Mgmt. Div.
Dept. of Natural Resources
P.O. Box 30028
Lansing, MI 48909
Phone: (517) 373-1275

MINNESOTA
Gerald Rose
Director
Forestry Div.
Dept. of Natural Resources
500 Lafayette Rd.
St. Paul, MN 55155
Phone: (651) 296-4484
Fax: (651) 296-5954
E-mail: jerry.rose
@dnr.state.mn.us

MISSISSIPPI
James L. Sledge
State Forester
Forestry Comm.
301 N. Lamar, Ste. 300
Jackson, MS 39201
Phone: (601) 359-1386
Fax: (601) 359-1349

MISSOURI
Marvin Brown
Administrator
Div. of Forestry
Dept. of Conservation
2901 W. Truman Blvd.
P.O. Box 180
Jefferson City, MO 65102
Phone: (573) 751-4115
Fax: (573) 526-6670
E-mail: brownm
@mail.conservation.
state.mo.us

MONTANA
Don Artley
Administrator
Forestry Div.
Dept. of Natural Resources
& Conservation
2705 Spurgin Rd.
Missoula, MT 59804
Phone: (406) 542-4300
Fax: (406) 542-4217

NEBRASKA
Gary Hergenrader
State Forester
Forestry, Fisheries &
Wildlife
Univ. of NE
101 Plant Industry Bldg.
Lincoln, NE 68583-0814
Phone: (402) 472-2944
Fax: (402) 472-2964

NEVADA
Roy Trenoweth
State Forester
Div. of Forestry
Dept. of Conservation &
Natural Resources
1201 Johnson St., #D
Carson City, NV 89706
Phone: (775) 684-2500
Fax: (775) 687-4244
E-mail: forester
@govmail.state.nv.us

NEW HAMPSHIRE
Philip Bryce
Director
Forest & Lands Div.
Dept. of Resources &
Economic Dev.
P.O. Box 1856
Concord, NH 03302-1856
Phone: (603) 271-2214
Fax: (603) 271-2629

NEW JERSEY
Gregory A. Marshall
Director
Div. of Parks & Forestry
Dept. of Environmental
Protection
501 E. State St.
P.O. Box 404
Trenton, NJ 08625-0404
Phone: (609) 292-2733
Fax: (609) 984-0503

NEW MEXICO
Toby Martinez
Director
Forestry & Resource
Conservation
Energy, Minerals & Natural
Resources Dept.
P.O. Box 1948
Santa Fe, NM 87504
Phone: (505) 827-7861
Fax: (505) 827-3903

NEW YORK
John Cahill
Commissioner
Dept. of Environmental
Conservation
50 Wolf Rd.
Albany, NY 12233-1010
Phone: (518) 457-1162
Fax: (518) 457-7744

NORTH CAROLINA
Stan Adams
Director
Forest Resources
Dept. of Environment &
Natural Resources
P.O. Box 27687
Raleigh, NC 27611
Phone: (919) 733-2162
Fax: (919) 715-4350

NORTH DAKOTA
Larry Kotchman
State Forester
Forest Service
307 1st St., E.
Bottineau, ND 58318-1100
Phone: (701) 228-5490
Fax: (701) 228-5448
E-mail: forest
@pioneer.state.nd.us

NORTHERN MARIANA ISLANDS
Vacant
Director
Div. of Agri. & Quarantine
Caller Box 10007
Saipan, MP 96950
Phone: (670) 256-3317
Fax: (670) 256-7154

OHIO
Ron Abraham
Chief
Div. of Forestry
Dept. of Natural Resources
Fountain Sq., Bldg. H-1
Columbus, OH 43224
Phone: (614) 265-6690
Fax: (614) 447-9231

OKLAHOMA
Roger L. Davis
Director
Div. of Forestry
Dept. of Agri.
2800 N. Lincoln Blvd.
Oklahoma City, OK 73105
Phone: (405) 521-3864
Fax: (405) 521-4912

OREGON
James E. Brown
State Forester
Dept. of Forestry
2600 State St.
Salem, OR 97310
Phone: (503) 945-7211
Fax: (503) 945-7212

PENNSYLVANIA
James R. Grace
Director
Bur. of Forestry
Dept. of Environmental
Protection
P.O. Box 8552
Harrisburg, PA 17105-8552
Phone: (717) 787-2703
Fax: (717) 783-5109

PUERTO RICO
Daniel Pagan
Secretary
Dept. of Natural Resources
P.O. Box 5887
San Juan, PR 00906
Phone: (787) 723-3090
Fax: (787) 723-4255

RHODE ISLAND
Jan Reitsma
Director
Dept. of Environmental
Mgmt.
235 Promenade St.
Providence, RI 02908
Phone: (401) 222-2771
Fax: (401) 222-6802

SOUTH CAROLINA
J. Hugh Ryan
State Forester
Forestry Comm.
P.O. Box 21707
Columbia, SC 29221
Phone: (803) 896-8800
Fax: (803) 798-8097

SOUTH DAKOTA
Ron Cody
Director
Resource, Conservation &
Forestry
Dept. of Agri.
523 E. Capitol Ave.
Pierre, SD 57501
Phone: (605) 773-3623
Fax: (605) 773-4003

TENNESSEE
Ken Arney
State Forester
Div. of Forestry
Dept. of Agri.
Ellington Agri. Ctr.
Nashville, TN 37204
Phone: (615) 837-5520
Fax: (615) 837-5003

TEXAS
James B. Hull
Director/State Forester
Forest Service
TX A&M Univ.
301 Tarrow, Ste. 364
College Station, TX 77840-7896
Phone: (409) 845-2601
Fax: (409) 862-2463
E-mail: Jim-Hull@tamu.edu

U.S. VIRGIN ISLANDS

UTAH
Art DuFault
State Forester/Director
Div. of Forestry, Fire & State Lands
Dept. of Natural Resources
1594 W. N. Temple, Ste. 3520
Salt Lake City, UT 84114-5703
Phone: (801) 538-5530
Fax: (801) 533-4111
E-mail: adufault.nrslf@state.ut.us

VERMONT
Conrad Motyka
Commissioner
Dept. of Forests, Parks & Recreation
103 S. Main St.
Waterbury, VT 05676
Phone: (802) 241-3670
Fax: (802) 244-1481

VIRGINIA
James W. Garner
State Forester
Dept. of Forestry
P.O. Box 3758
Charlottesville, VA 22903
Phone: (804) 977-6555
Fax: (804) 296-2369

WASHINGTON
John Edwards
Division Manager
Forest Practices Div.
Dept. of Natural Resources
P.O. Box 47012
Olympia, WA 98504-7012
Phone: (360) 902-1730
Fax: (360) 902-1784

WEST VIRGINIA
Charles Randy Dye
Director
Div. of Forestry
1900 Kanawha Blvd., E.
Charleston, WV 25305
Phone: (304) 558-2788
Fax: (304) 558-0143

WISCONSIN
Gene Fransisco
Director
Bur. of Forestry
Dept. of Natural Resources
101 S. Webster, 4th Fl.
P.O. Box 7921
Madison, WI 53703
Phone: (608) 267-7494
Fax: (608) 266-8576

WYOMING
Tom Ostermann
State Forester
State Forestry Div.
1100 W. 22nd St.
Cheyenne, WY 82002
Phone: (307) 777-7586
Fax: (307) 637-8726
E-mail: wyjo36@wydsprod.state.wy.us

Gaming Officials

Head of the entity that administers and regulates state gaming laws.

ALABAMA

ALASKA
Jeff Prather
Director
Charitable Gaming Audit & Examination
Dept. of Revenue
P.O. Box 110440
Juneau, AK 99811-0440
Phone: (907) 465-2229
Fax: (907) 465-3098

AMERICAN SAMOA

ARIZONA
Stephan Hart
Director
Dept. of Gaming
202 E. Earll Dr., #200
Phoenix, AZ 85012
Phone: (602) 604-1801
Fax: (602) 255-3883

ARKANSAS

CALIFORNIA
Bill Lockyer
1300 I St., 11th Fl.
Sacramento, CA 95814
Phone: (916) 324-5437

COLORADO
George Turner
Director
Gaming Div.
Dept. of Revenue
1881 Pierce St.
Denver, CO 80214
Phone: (303) 205-1300

CONNECTICUT
Thomas Rotunda
Executive Director
Div. of Special Revenue
Dept. of Revenue Services
555 Russell Rd.
Newington, CT 06111
Phone: (860) 594-0501
Fax: (860) 594-0696

DELAWARE
Wayne Lemons
Director
State Lottery
Dept. of Finance
1575 McKee Rd., #102
Dover, DE 19904-1903
Phone: (302) 739-5291
Fax: (302) 739-6706

DISTRICT OF COLUMBIA

FLORIDA
Debra Miller
Director
Div. of Pari-Mutuel Wagering
Dept. of Business & Professional Regulation
1940 N. Monroe St.
Tallahassee, FL 32399-1035
Phone: (850) 488-9130
Fax: (850) 488-0550

GEORGIA
Milton E. Nix, Jr.
Director
Bur. of Investigation
P.O. Box 370808
Decatur, GA 30037
Phone: (404) 244-2501

GUAM
Joseph T. Duenas
Director
Dept. of Revenue & Taxation
13-1 Mariner Dr., Tiyan
P.O. Box 23607
GMF, GU 96921
Phone: (671) 475-1817
Fax: (671) 472-2643

HAWAII

IDAHO
Dennis Jackson
Director
State Lottery
1199 Shoreline Ln., Ste. 100
Boise, ID 83702
Phone: (208) 334-2600

ILLINOIS
Michael Belletire
Administrator
Gaming Board
160 N. LaSalle, Ste. 300S
Chicago, IL 60601-3103
Phone: (312) 814-4707
Fax: (312) 814-4692

INDIANA
Jack Thar
Executive Director
Gaming Comm.
115 W. Washington St., #950 S. Tower
Indianapolis, IN 46204-3407
Phone: (317) 233-0044
Fax: (317) 233-0047

IOWA
Jack Ketterer
Administrator
Racing & Gaming Comm.
Dept. of Inspections & Appeals
Lucas State Ofc. Bldg.
321 E. 12th St.
Des Moines, IA 50319
Phone: (515) 281-7352

KANSAS
Tracy Diel
Executive Director
State Gaming Comm.
700 SW Jackson, Ste. 200
Topeka, KS 66612
Phone: (785) 368-6202
Fax: (785) 291-3798

Gregory P. Ziemak
Director
Lottery
128 N. Kansas Ave.
Topeka, KS 66603-3638
Phone: (785) 296-5700
Fax: (785) 296-5712

KENTUCKY
Sarah Jackson
Director
Charitable Gamings
Justice Cabinet
403 Wapping St.
Frankfort, KY 40601
Phone: (502) 564-5528
Fax: (502) 564-6625

LOUISIANA
Hillary Crain
Chair
Gaming Control Board
9100 Bluebonnet Ctr., Ste. 500
Baton Rouge, LA 70809
Phone: (225) 295-8450
Fax: (225) 295-8479

MAINE
Michael F. Kelley
Commissioner
Dept. of Public Safety
42 State House Station
Augusta, ME 04333
Phone: (207) 624-7068

MARYLAND
Bruce H. Hoffman
Executive Director
Stadium Authority
Executive Dept.
333 W. Camden St., Ste. 500
Baltimore, MD 21201
Phone: (410) 333-1560
Fax: (410) 333-1888

MASSACHUSETTS
Edward Lashman
Acting Executive Director
State Lottery Comm.
60 Columbian St.
Braintree, MA 02184
Phone: (781) 849-5500
Fax: (781) 849-5509

MICHIGAN
Dan Wyant
Acting Racing Commissioner
Dept. of Agri.
37650 Professional Ctr. Dr.
Livonia, MI 48154-1114
Phone: (734) 462-2400
Fax: (734) 462-2429

MINNESOTA
Harold W. Baltzer
Director
Gambling Control
1711 W. County Rd., B, Ste. 300S
Roseville, MN 55113
Phone: (651) 639-4000
Fax: (651) 639-4032

MISSISSIPPI
Bill Gresham
Chair
Gaming Comm.
202 E. Pearl
P.O. Box 23577
Jackson, MS 39202
Phone: (601) 351-2800
Fax: (601) 351-2810

Chuck Patton
Executive Director
Gaming Comm.
P.O. Box 23577
Jackson, MS 39202
Phone: (601) 351-2800
Fax: (601) 351-2810

MISSOURI
C.E. Fisher
Acting Executive Director
Gaming Comm.
3417 Knipp Dr.
Jefferson City, MO 65109
Phone: (573) 526-4080
Fax: (573) 526-4084
E-mail: mfisher@mail.state.mo.us

MONTANA
Jim Oppedahl
Administrator
Gambling Control Div.
Dept. of Justice
2550 Prospect Ave.
Helena, MT 59620
Phone: (406) 444-1971
Fax: (406) 444-9157

NEBRASKA
James Bogatz
Charitable Gaming Div.
Dept. of Revenue
P.O. Box 94818
Lincoln, NE 68509-4818
Phone: (402) 471-5942

NEVADA
Steve DuCharme
Chair
State Gaming Control Board
1919 E. College Pkwy.
Carson City, NV 89706
Phone: (775) 687-6500
Fax: (775) 687-5817

NEW HAMPSHIRE
Rick Wisler
Executive Director
Sweepstakes Comm.
P.O. Box 1208
Concord, NH 03302-1208
Phone: (603) 271-3391
Fax: (603) 271-1160

NEW JERSEY
John Peter Suarez
Director
Div. of Gaming Enforcement
Dept. of Law & Public Safety
140 E. Front St.
P.O. Box 047
Trenton, NJ 08625-0047
Phone: (609) 292-9394
Fax: (609) 633-7355

NEW MEXICO
Lillian Martinez
Deputy Director
Alcohol & Gaming Div.
Dept. of Regulation & Licensing
P.O. Box 25101
Santa Fe, NM 87504
Phone: (505) 827-7066
Fax: (505) 827-7168

NEW YORK
Michael J. Hoblock, Jr.
Chair
State Racing & Wagering Board
1 Watervliet Ave. Ext., Ste. 2
Albany, NY 12206-1668
Phone: (518) 453-8460
Fax: (518) 453-8490

NORTH CAROLINA
Charles Fullwood
Executive Director
Wildlife Resources Comm.
Dept. of Environment & Natural Resources
P.O. Box 27687
Raleigh, NC 27611
Phone: (919) 733-3391
Fax: (919) 733-7083

NORTH DAKOTA
Keith Lauer
Director
Gaming Div.
Attorney Gen's. Ofc.
600 E. Blvd. Ave,, 17th Fl.
Bismarck, ND 58505-0040
Phone: (701) 328-4848
Fax: (701) 328-3535
E-mail: msmail.klauer@ranch.state.nd.us

NORTHERN MARIANA ISLANDS
Lucia DLG. Neilsen
Secretary of Finance
Finance & Accounting
Dept. of Finance
P.O. Box 5234 CHRB
Saipan, MP 96950
Phone: (670) 664-1198
Fax: (670) 664-1115

OHIO
Clifford A. Nelson, II
Executive Director
State Racing Comm.
77 S. High St., 18th Fl.
Columbus, OH 43266-0416
Phone: (614) 466-2757
Fax: (614) 466-1900

OKLAHOMA

OREGON
Robert Miller
Director
Gaming Enforcement Div.
State Police
400 Public Service Bldg.
Salem, OR 97310
Phone: (503) 378-3720

PENNSYLVANIA
Donald C. Madl
Executive Director
Game Comm.
2001 Elmerton Ave.
Harrisburg, PA 17110
Phone: (717) 787-3633
Fax: (717) 772-0502

PUERTO RICO
James McCurdy
Director
Gambling Div.
Dept. of Gaming
P.O. Box 4435
San Juan, PR 00902-4435
Phone: (787) 721-2635

RHODE ISLAND

SOUTH CAROLINA

SOUTH DAKOTA
Larry Eliason
Executive Secretary
Div. of Gaming
Dept. of Commerce & Regulation
118 E. Missouri
Pierre, SD 57501
Phone: (605) 773-6050
Fax: (605) 773-3018

TENNESSEE

TEXAS

U.S. VIRGIN ISLANDS
Eileen Peterson
Chair
Casino Control Comm.
#5 Orange Grove
Christiansted
St. Croix, VI 00820
Phone: (340) 773-3616
Fax: (340) 773-3136

UTAH

VERMONT
Alan R. Yandow
Director
Lottery Comm.
379 S. Barre Rd.
P.O. Box 420
S. Barre, VT 05670-0420
Phone: (802) 479-5686
Fax: (802) 479-4294

VIRGINIA
Jerry W. Rowe
Executive Secretary
Charitable Gaming Comm.
Monroe Bldg., 17th Fl.
101 N. 14th St.
Richmond, VA 23219
Phone: (804) 786-0238
Fax: (804) 786-1079

WASHINGTON
Ben Bishop
Director
State Gambling Comm.
P.O. Box 42400
Olympia, WA 98504-2400
Phone: (360) 438-7640
Fax: (360) 438-7503

WEST VIRGINIA
Robin Capehart
Cabinet Secretary
Dept. of Tax & Revenue
Bldg. 1, Rm. WW-300
1900 Kanawha Blvd., E.
Charleston, WV 25305
Phone: (304) 558-0211
Fax: (304) 558-2324

WISCONSIN
Scott Scepaniak
Division Administrator
Gaming Board
Dept. of Administration
2005 W. Beltline Hwy., Ste. 201
P.O. Box 8979
Madison, WI 53708-8979
Phone: (608) 270-2555
Fax: (608) 270-2564

WYOMING
Frank Lamb
Executive Director
Pari-Mutuel Comm.
6101 Yellowstone
Cheyenne, WY 82002
Phone: (307) 777-5928

General Services

Responsible for a variety of centralized services within state government.

ALABAMA
Curtis Hayes
Chief of Services
Services Div.
Dept. of Finance
425 S. Union St.
Montgomery, AL 36130-2605
Phone: (334) 242-2773
Fax: (334) 240-3402

ALASKA
Marsha Hubbard
Director
Div. of Services & Supply
Dept. of Administration
P.O. Box 110210
Juneau, AK 99811
Phone: (907) 465-2250
Fax: (907) 465-2205

AMERICAN SAMOA
Lolo Moliga
Chief Procurement Officer
Ofc. of Procurement
AS Govt.
Pago Pago, AS 96799
Phone: (684) 699-1170
Fax: (684) 699-2387

ARIZONA
Robert Teel
Assistant Director
Services Div.
Dept. of Administration
15 S. 15th Ave., Ste. 101
Phoenix, AZ 85007-3223
Phone: (602) 542-0697
Fax: (602) 542-3858

ARKANSAS
Tim Leathers
Deputy Director
Dept. of Finance & Administration
401 DFA Bldg.
1509 W. 7th St.
Little Rock, AR 72201
Phone: (501) 682-2242
Fax: (501) 682-1086

CALIFORNIA
Peter G. Stamison
Director
Dept. of Services
1325 J St., Ste. 1910
Sacramento, CA 95814
Phone: (916) 445-3441

COLORADO
Larry E. Trujillo, Sr.
Executive Director
Support Services
Dept. of Personnel
1525 Sherman St., 2nd Fl.
Denver, CO 80203
Phone: (303) 866-6559
Fax: (303) 866-6569

CONNECTICUT
Roy Dion
Director
Div. of Printing & Mailing Services
Dept. of Adm. Services
165 Capitol Ave., Rm. 491
Hartford, CT 06106
Phone: (860) 713-5100

DELAWARE
Vincent P. Meconi
Secretary
Dept. of Adm. Services
Townsend Bldg.
P.O. Box 1401
Dover, DE 19903
Phone: (302) 739-3611
Fax: (302) 739-6704
E-mail: vmeconi@state.de.us

DISTRICT OF COLUMBIA

FLORIDA
Thomas D. McGurk
Secretary
Director's Ofc.
Dept. of Mgmt. Services
4050 Esplanade Way, Ste. 250
Tallahassee, FL 32399-0950
Phone: (850) 488-2786
Fax: (850) 922-6149
E-mail: mcgurkt@dms.state.fl.us

GEORGIA
Debra White
Director
Interagency Support Services
Dept. of Adm. Services
W. Tower, Floyd Bldg.
200 Piedmont Ave., SE
Atlanta, GA 30334
Phone: (404) 656-5753

GUAM
Lorenzo C. Aflague
Chief Procurement Officer
Services Administration
P.O. Box FG
Hagatna, GU 96932
Phone: (671) 477-1725
Fax: (671) 472-7538

HAWAII
Lloyd Unebasami
Administrator
State Procurement Ofc.
Accounting & Services
1151 Punchbowl St., Rm. 230A
Honolulu, HI 96813
Phone: (808) 587-4700
Fax: (808) 587-4703

IDAHO

ILLINOIS
Michael S. Schwartz
Director
Dept. of Central Mgmt. Services
715 Stratton Ofc. Bldg.
401 S. Spring
Springfield, IL 62706
Phone: (217) 782-2141
Fax: (217) 524-1880

INDIANA
Betty Cockrum
Commissioner
Dept. of Administration
IGC-South, Rm. W479
402 W. Washington St.
Indianapolis, IN 46204
Phone: (317) 232-3115
Fax: (317) 233-5022

IOWA
Richard Haines
Director
Dept. of Services
Hoover State Ofc. Bldg.
1305 E. Walnut
Des Moines, IA 50319
Phone: (515) 281-3196
Fax: (515) 242-5974

KANSAS
Daniel Stanley
Secretary
Dept. of Administration
State Capitol, Rm. 263-E
Topeka, KS 66612-1572
Phone: (785) 296-3011
Fax: (785) 296-2702

KENTUCKY
Don Speer
Commissioner
Finance & Administration Cabinet
Dept. of Administration
Capitol Annex, Rm. 362
700 Capitol Ave.
Frankfort, KY 40601
Phone: (502) 564-2317
Fax: (502) 564-4279

LOUISIANA
Mark Drennen
Commissioner
Div. of Administration
P.O. Box 94095
Baton Rouge, LA 70804-9095
Phone: (225) 342-7000
Fax: (225) 342-1057

MAINE
Elaine Clark
Director
Bur. of Services
Dept. of Adm. & Financial Services
77 State House Station
Augusta, ME 04333
Phone: (207) 287-4000

MARYLAND
Peta Richkus
Secretary
Ofc. of the Secretary
Dept. of Services
301 W. Preston St., Rm. 1401
Baltimore, MD 21201
Phone: (410) 767-4960
Fax: (410) 333-5480
E-mail: prichkus@dgs.state.md.us

MASSACHUSETTS
Andrew Natsios
Secretary
Executive Ofc. for Administration & Finance
State House, Rm. 373
Boston, MA 02133
Phone: (617) 727-2040
Fax: (617) 727-2496

MICHIGAN
Duane Berger
Director
Ofc. of Support Services
Dept. of Mgmt. & Budget
P.O. Box 30026
Lansing, MI 48909
Phone: (517) 335-1988

MINNESOTA
David Fisher
Commissioner
Dept. of Administration
200 Administration Bldg.
50 Sherburne Ave.
St. Paul, MN 55155
Phone: (651) 296-1424
Fax: (651) 297-7909

MISSISSIPPI
Andy Cole
Deputy Director
Dept. of Finance & Administration
1501 Sillers Bldg.
Jackson, MS 39201
Phone: (601) 359-3635
Fax: (601) 359-2470

MISSOURI
Stan Perovich
Director
Div. of Services
Ofc. of Administration
Truman Bldg., Rm. 760
P.O. Box 809
Jefferson City, MO 65102
Phone: (573) 751-4656
Fax: (573) 751-7819
E-mail: perovs@mai.oa.state.mo.us

MONTANA
Bill Bayless
Administrator
Services Div.
Dept. of Administration
Capitol Annex Bldg.
P.O. Box 200110
Helena, MT 59620-0110
Phone: (406) 444-3060
Fax: (406) 444-3039

NEBRASKA
Doni Peterson
Acting Administrator
Material Div.
Dept. of Adm. Services
301 Centennial Mall, S.
P.O. Box 94847
Lincoln, NE 68509
Phone: (402) 471-2401

NEVADA
John P. Comeaux
Director
Dept. of Administration
Blasdel Bldg., Rm. 200
209 E. Musser St.
Carson City, NV 89701
Phone: (775) 684-0222
Fax: (775) 684-0260

NEW HAMPSHIRE
Donald S. Hill
Commissioner
Commissioner's Ofc.
Dept. of Adm. Services
25 Capitol St., Rm. 120
Concord, NH 03301-6312
Phone: (603) 271-3201

NEW JERSEY
Lana Sims
Director
Services Administration
Dept. of Treasury
P.O. Box 039
Trenton, NJ 08625-0039
Phone: (609) 292-4886
Fax: (609) 984-2575

NEW MEXICO
Steven Beffort
Secretary
Services Dept.
715 Alta Vista
P.O. Drawer 26110
Santa Fe, NM 87502-0110
Phone: (505) 827-2000
Fax: (505) 827-2041

NEW YORK
Joseph Seymour
Commissioner
Ofc. of Services
Corning Tower Bldg., 41st Fl.
Empire State Plz.
Albany, NY 12242
Phone: (518) 474-5991
Fax: (518) 486-9179

NORTH CAROLINA
Katie G. Dorsett
Secretary
Dept. of Administration
116 W. Jones St.
Raleigh, NC 27603
Phone: (919) 733-7232
Fax: (919) 733-9571

NORTH DAKOTA
Rod Backman
Director
Ofc. of Mgmt. & Budget
600 E. Blvd. Ave., 4th Fl.
Bismarck, ND 58505-0400
Phone: (701) 328-2680
Fax: (701) 328-3230
E-mail: rbackman@state.nd.us

NORTHERN MARIANA ISLANDS
Jose I. Deleon Guerrero
Special Assistant for Administration
Ofc. of the Governor
Caller Box 10007
Saipan, MP 96950
Phone: (670) 664-2212
Fax: (670) 664-2210
E-mail: gov.tasaa@saipan.com

OHIO
George Kaitsa
Deputy Director
Services Div., Ofc. of Direct Services
Dept. of Adm. Services
4200 Surface Rd.
Columbus, OH 43228-1395
Phone: (614) 466-5579
Fax: (614) 466-1040

OKLAHOMA
Pam Warren
Secretary of Administration
Dept. of Central Services
2401 N. Lincoln Blvd., Ste. 206
Oklahoma City, OK 73105
Phone: (405) 521-2121
Fax: (405) 425-2713

OREGON
Jon Yunker
Director
Dept. of Adm. Services
155 Cottage St., NE
Salem, OR 97310
Phone: (503) 378-3104
Fax: (503) 373-7643
E-mail: jon.yunker@state.or.us

PENNSYLVANIA
Gary E. Crowell
Secretary
Dept. of General Services
N. Ofc. Bldg., Rm. 515
Harrisburg, PA 17120
Phone: (717) 787-5996
Fax: (717) 772-2026

PUERTO RICO
Maria T. Mujica
Administrator
Services Administration
P.O. Box 7428
San Juan, PR 00916
Phone: (787) 724-1064
Fax: (787) 722-7965

RHODE ISLAND
Robert L. Carl, Jr.
Director
Dept. of Administration
1 Capitol Hill
Providence, RI 02903
Phone: (401) 222-2280
Fax: (401) 222-6436

SOUTH CAROLINA
Voigt Shealy
State Procurement Officer
Materials Mgmt. Div.
Dept. of Services
1201 Main St., Ste. 600
Columbia, SC 29201
Phone: (803) 737-0600

SOUTH DAKOTA
Tom D. Geraets
Commissioner
Bur. of Administration
500 E. Capitol Ave.
Pierre, SD 57501
Phone: (605) 773-3688
Fax: (605) 773-3887

TENNESSEE
Larry Haynes
Commissioner
Dept. of Services
Wm. R. Snodgrass
TN Towers, 24th Fl.
Nashville, TN 37243-0530
Phone: (615) 741-9263
Fax: (615) 532-8594

TEXAS
Tom Treadway
Executive Director
Services Comm.
1711 San Jacinto
P.O. Box 13047
Austin, TX 78701-3047
Phone: (512) 463-3446
Fax: (512) 463-7966
E-mail: tomtreadway
@gsc.state.tx.us

U.S. VIRGIN ISLANDS
Marc Biggs
Acting Commissioner
Dept. of Property &
Procurement
Sub Base, Bldg. 1
St. Thomas, VI 00801
Phone: (340) 774-0828
Fax: (340) 777-9587

UTAH
Douglas Richins
Director
Div. of Purchasing &
Services
Dept. of Adm. Services
3150 State Ofc. Bldg.
P.O. Box 141061
Salt Lake City, UT 84114-
1061
Phone: (801) 538-3143
Fax: (801) 538-3882
E-mail: drichins.pamain
@state.ut.us

VERMONT
Thomas W. Torti
Commissioner
Dept. of State Bldgs.
2 Governor Aiken Ave.
Drawer 33
Montpelier, VT 05633-5802
Phone: (802) 828-3331
Fax: (802) 828-2327

VIRGINIA
Donald C. Williams
Director
Dept. of Services
202 N. 9th St., Ste. 209
Richmond, VA 23219
Phone: (804) 786-3311
Fax: (804) 371-8305

WASHINGTON
Marsha Tadano Long
Director
Dept. of Administration
P.O. Box 41000
Olympia, WA 98504-1000
Phone: (360) 902-7300
Fax: (360) 586-5898

WEST VIRGINIA
Raymond V. Prozzillo
Director
Services Div.
Bldg. 1, Rm. MB60
1900 Kanawha Blvd., E.
Charleston, WV 25305
Phone: (304) 558-3517
Fax: (304) 558-2334

WISCONSIN
Mark Bugher
Secretary
Dept. of Administration
101 E. Wilson, 10th Fl.
P.O. Box 7869
Madison, WI 53707
Phone: (608) 266-1741
Fax: (608) 267-3842

WYOMING
Art Ellis
Director
Dept. of Administration &
Info.
Emerson Bldg., Rm. 104
2001 Capitol Ave.
Cheyenne, WY 82002
Phone: (307) 777-7201

Geographic Information Systems

Coordinates geographic information systems within state government.

ALABAMA

ALASKA
Richard McMahon
Chief
Land Records Info.
Dept. of Natural Resources
3601 C St., Ste. 916
Anchorage, AK 99503-5936
Phone: (907) 269-8836
Fax: (907) 563-1497

AMERICAN SAMOA

ARIZONA
Gary Irish
GIS Program Manager
Land Resources Info. System
State Land Dept.
1616 W. Adams
Phoenix, AZ 85007
Phone: (602) 542-4061
Fax: (602) 542-2600

ARKANSAS
Michael Hipp
Director
Dept. of Info. Systems
P.O. Box 3155
Little Rock, AR 72203
Phone: (501) 682-2701
Fax: (501) 682-4310

CALIFORNIA
Randy Moory
Branch Manager
Teale Data Ctr.
P.O. Box 13436
Sacramento, CA 95813
Phone: (916) 263-1886

COLORADO

CONNECTICUT
Edward C. Parker
Bureau Chief
Bur. of Natural Resources
Dept. of Environmental Protection
79 Elm St.
Hartford, CT 06106
Phone: (860) 424-3010

DELAWARE
Rich Collins
Manager
Planning & Data Administration
Ofc. of Info. Services
801 Silver Lake Blvd.
Dover, DE 19904
Phone: (302) 739-9621
Fax: (302) 739-6251

DISTRICT OF COLUMBIA

FLORIDA
P.J. Ponder
Administrator
State Technology
Mgmt. Services
4050 Esplanade Way, Bldg. 4030, Ste. 315
Tallahassee, FL 32399-0950
Phone: (850) 488-4494
Fax: (850) 922-5929

GEORGIA
William McLemore
State Geologist
Environmental Protection Div.
Dept. of Natural Resources
19 Martin Luther King, Jr. Dr., Rm. 400
Atlanta, GA 30334
Phone: (404) 656-3214

GUAM
Carl J.C. Aguon
Director
Dept. of Land Mgmt.
1 Stop Bldg.
P.O. Box 2950
Anigua-Agana, GU 96932
Phone: (671) 475-5252
Fax: (671) 477-0883

HAWAII
Craig Tasaka
Planning Program Manager
Ofc. of Planning
235 S. Beretania St., 6th Fl.
Honolulu, HI 96813
Phone: (808) 587-2894
Fax: (808) 587-2899

IDAHO
Dave Gruenhager
Analyst
GIS Section
Bur. of Technical Services
Dept. of Lands
1215 W. State St.
Boise, ID 83720
Phone: (208) 334-0277

ILLINOIS

INDIANA

IOWA

KANSAS
Bill Harrison
Assistant Director
Technical Info. Services
Geology Survey
1930 Constant Ave., Campus W.
Lawrence, KS 66047
Phone: (785) 864-3965
Fax: (785) 864-4317

KENTUCKY
Susan Lambert
Director
Ofc. of Geographic Info. Systems
1024 Capital Plz. Dr., Ste. 305
Frankfort, KY 40601
Phone: (502) 573-1460
Fax: (502) 573-1458

LOUISIANA
Katherine Vaughn
Deputy Secretary
Ofc. of Coastal Restoration & Mgmt.
Dept. of Natural Resources
P.O. Box 94396
Baton Rouge, LA 70804
Phone: (225) 342-1375
Fax: (225) 342-4313

MAINE
Dan Walters
Director
Ofc. of Geographic Info. System
Dept. of Adm. & Financial Services
22 State House Station
Augusta, ME 04333
Phone: (207) 287-3897

MARYLAND
Emery T. Cleaves
Director
Geological Survey
Dept. of Natural Resources
2300 St. Paul St.
Baltimore, MD 21218
Phone: (410) 554-5503
Fax: (410) 554-5502

MASSACHUSETTS
Robert Durand
Secretary
Executive Ofc. of Environmental Affairs
Geographic Info. Systems
20 Somerset St., 3rd Fl.
Boston, MA 02108
Phone: (617) 727-9800
Fax: (617) 227-7045

MICHIGAN
Vacant
Resource Manager
Land & Water Mgmt. Div.
Dept. of Natural Resources
P.O. Box 30028
Lansing, MI 48909
Phone: (517) 373-8000

MINNESOTA
Henry May
Chief Information Officer
MIS Bur.
500 Lafayette Rd.
St. Paul, MN 55155
Phone: (651) 297-4945
Fax: (651) 297-4946
E-mail: henry.may
@dnr.state.mn.us

MISSISSIPPI
Paul Davis
MARIS Director
Research & Dev. Ctr.
3825 Ridgewood Rd.
Jackson, MS 39211
Phone: (601) 982-6354
Fax: (601) 987-5587

MISSOURI
Tim Haithcoat
Program Director
Geographic Resource Ctr.
Univ. of MO-Columbia
18 Stuart Hall
Columbia, MO 65211
Phone: (573) 882-1404
Fax: (573) 884-4239
E-mail: haithcoatt
@missouri.edu

MONTANA
Jim Stimson
Director
Natural Resource Info. System
State Library
1515 E. 6th Ave.
Helena, MT 59620
Phone: (406) 444-5355
Fax: (406) 444-0581

NEBRASKA
Mark Kuzila
Director
Conservation & Survey Div.
Univ. of NE
113 Nebraska Hall
Lincoln, NE 68588
Phone: (402) 472-3471
Fax: (402) 472-4608

NEVADA
John Price
State Geologist
Bur. of Mines & Geology
Univ. of NV
307 Scrugham Engineering Mines
Mail Stop 178
Reno, NV 89557-0088
Phone: (775) 784-6691
Fax: (775) 784-1709
E-mail: jprice
@nbmg.nur.edu

NEW HAMPSHIRE
Robert W. Varney
Commissioner
Dept. of Environmental Services
P.O. Box 95
Concord, NH 03302-0095
Phone: (603) 271-3503
Fax: (603) 271-2867

NEW JERSEY
Hank Garie
Chief of Staff
Dept. of Environmental Protection
401 E. State St.
P.O. Box 428
Trenton, NJ 08625-0428
Phone: (609) 984-2243

NEW MEXICO
E. Foster McDowell
Deputy Director
Info. Systems Services
P.O. Drawer 26110
Sante Fe, NM 87502
Phone: (505) 827-2001
Fax: (505) 827-2041

NEW YORK

NORTH CAROLINA
Charles H. Gardner
Director
Div. of Land Resources
Dept. of Environment & Natural Resources
512 N. Salisbury St.
Raleigh, NC 27604-1148
Phone: (919) 733-3833
Fax: (919) 715-8801

NORTH DAKOTA

NORTHERN MARIANA ISLANDS
Edward M. Guerrero
Secretary of Public Works
Ofc. of the Secretary
Dept. of Public Works
P.O. Box 2950
Saipan, MP 96950
Phone: (670) 235-5827
Fax: (670) 235-5253

Bruce Lloyd
Public Information Officer
Ofc. of the Governor
Saipan, MP 96950
Phone: (670) 322-5191
Fax: (670) 322-5192

OHIO
Stuart R. Davis
Executive Director
Geographically Referenced Info. Program
Dept. of Adm. Services
1320 Arthur E. Adams Dr.
Columbus, OH 43221-3595
Phone: (614) 466-4747
Fax: (614) 644-2133

OKLAHOMA
Brian Griffin
Secretary of the Environment
Water Resources Board
3800 N. Classen Blvd.
Oklahoma City, OK 73118
Phone: (405) 530-8995

OREGON
Theresa Valentine
Manager
GIS Program
Dept. of Adm. Services
155 Cottage St., NE
Salem, OR 97310
Phone: (503) 378-4163
Fax: (503) 986-3242

PENNSYLVANIA
William A. Gast
Chair
Bur. of Watershed Conservation
Div. of Water Use Planning
Rachel Carson State Ofc. Bldg., 10th Fl.
P.O. Box 8555
Harrisburg, PA 17105-8555
Phone: (717) 787-5267

PUERTO RICO
Norma Burgos Andujar
Secretary of State
Department of State
P.O. Box 3271
San Juan, PR 00902-3271
Phone: (787) 723-4334
Fax: (787) 725-7303

RHODE ISLAND
John Stachelhaus
GIS Coordinator
Div. of Planning
Dept. of Administration
1 Capitol Hill
Providence, RI 02908
Phone: (401) 222-6483

SOUTH CAROLINA
Alfred H. Vang
Deputy Director
Land Resources & Conservation Districts Div.
Dept. of Natural Resources
2221 Devine St., Ste. 222
Columbia, SC 29205
Phone: (803) 734-9113
Fax: (803) 734-9200

SOUTH DAKOTA
Kevin Dahlstad
Director
Engineering Resource Ctr.
SD State Univ.
Box 2220, Harding Hall
Brookings, SD 57007-0199
Phone: (605) 688-4184
Fax: (605) 688-5880

TENNESSEE
Clifton Whitehead
Chief Planner
Div. of Federal Aid
Wildlife Resources Agency
P.O. Box 40747, Melrose Station
Nashville, TN 37204
Phone: (615) 781-6599
Fax: (615) 741-4606

TEXAS
Carolyn Purcell
Executive Director
Dept. of Info. Resources
300 W. 15th St., Ste. 1300
Austin, TX 78701
Phone: (512) 475-4720
Fax: (512) 475-4759

U.S. VIRGIN ISLANDS
Dean Plaskett
Commissioner
Dept. of Planning & Natural Resources
Foster's Plz., 396-1 Anna's Retreat
St. Thomas, VI 00802
Phone: (340) 774-3320
Fax: (340) 775-5706

UTAH
Dennis Goreham
Manager, AGRC
Info. Tech. Services
Adm. Services
5130 State Ofc. Bldg.
Salt Lake City, UT 84114
Phone: (801) 538-3163
Fax: (801) 538-3550
E-mail: dgoreham.asitmain@state.ut.us

VERMONT
Carol Miller
Director
Ofc. of Geographic Info. Service
Univ. of VT
206 Morrill Hall
Burlington, VT 05405
Phone: (802) 656-4277
Fax: (802) 656-0776

VIRGINIA
N. Jerry Simonoff
Director
Council on Info. Mgmt.
Richmond Plz. Bldg., Ste. 135
110 S. 7th St.
Richmond, VA 23219
Phone: (804) 225-3622
Fax: (804) 371-2795

WASHINGTON
Al Bloomberg
Manager
Info. Technology Div.
Dept. of Natural Resources
P.O. Box 47020
Olympia, WA 98504-7020
Phone: (360) 902-1500
Fax: (360) 902-1790

WEST VIRGINIA
Mike Slater
Director
Info. Services & Communications
Bldg. 6, Rm. 110
1900 Kanawha Blvd., E.
Charleston, WV 25305
Phone: (304) 558-8918

WISCONSIN

WYOMING
Rick Memmel
Software Specialist
Computer Technology Div.
Dept. of Administration & Info.
Emerson Bldg.
2001 Capitol Ave.
Cheyenne, WY 82002
Phone: (307) 777-4231

Geological Survey

Conducts research on the state's terrain, mineral resources and possible geological hazards such as earthquakes, faults, etc.

ALABAMA
Donald F. Oltz
State Geologist & Administrator
State Geological Survey
Oil & Gas Board
P.O. Box O
Tuscaloosa, AL 35486-9780
Phone: (205) 349-2852
Fax: (205) 349-2861

ALASKA
Milt Wiltse
Director
Geological & Geophysical Survey Div.
Dept. of Natural Resources
794 Univ. Ave., Ste. 200
Fairbanks, AK 99707
Phone: (907) 451-5001
Fax: (907) 451-5050

AMERICAN SAMOA

ARIZONA
Larry D. Fellows
Director & State Geologist
Geological Survey
416 W. Congress St., #100
Tucson, AZ 85701-1315
Phone: (520) 770-3500
Fax: (520) 770-3505

ARKANSAS
William Bush
State Geologist
Geological Comm.
3815 W. Roosevelt Rd.
Little Rock, AR 72204
Phone: (501) 663-9714
Fax: (501) 671-1450

CALIFORNIA
James F. Davis
State Geologist
Div. of Mines & Geology
Dept. of Conservation
801 K St., 12th Fl.
Sacramento, CA 95814-3533
Phone: (916) 445-1923

COLORADO
Vicki Cowart
Director & State Geologist
Dept. of Natural Resources
1313 Sherman St., Rm. 715
Denver, CO 80203
Phone: (303) 866-2611
Fax: (303) 866-2461

CONNECTICUT
Edward C. Parker
Bureau Chief
Bur. of Natural Resources
Dept. of Environmental Protection
79 Elm St.
Hartford, CT 06106
Phone: (860) 424-3010

DELAWARE
Robert R. Jordan
State Geologist
Geological Survey
Univ. of DE
101 Penny Hall
Newark, DE 19711
Phone: (302) 451-2833

DISTRICT OF COLUMBIA

FLORIDA
Walter Schmidt
State Geologist & Chief
Div. of Adm. & Technical Services
Dept. of Environmental Protection
903 W. Tennessee St.
Tallahassee, FL 32304-7700
Phone: (850) 488-4191
Fax: (850) 488-8086

GEORGIA
William McLemore
State Geologist
Environmental Protection Div.
Dept. of Natural Resources
19 Martin Luther King, Jr. Dr., Rm. 400
Atlanta, GA 30334
Phone: (404) 656-3214

GUAM
Jose T. Nededog
President
College of Science
Univ. of GU
303 Univ. Dr., UOG Station
Mangilao, GU 96923
Phone: (671) 735-2990
Fax: (671) 734-2296
E-mail: nedcode1@uog9.uog.edu

HAWAII
Klaus Keil
Director
Institute of Geophysics & Planetology
Univ. of HI
Institute of Geophysics, Rm. 131
2525 Correa Rd.
Honolulu, HI 96822
Phone: (808) 956-8761
Fax: (808) 956-3188

IDAHO
Earl Bennett
State Geologist
Geological Survey
Morrill Hall, 3rd Fl.
Univ. of ID
Moscow, ID 83844-3014
Phone: (208) 885-7991

ILLINOIS
William W. Shilts
Chief
State Geological Survey
Natural Resources Bldg.
615 E. Peabody Dr.
Champaign, IL 61820-6964
Phone: (217) 333-4747
Fax: (217) 244-7004

INDIANA
John Steinmetz
State Geologist
Geological Survey
611 N. Walnut Grove
Bloomington, IN 47405
Phone: (812) 855-7785
Fax: (812) 855-2862

IOWA
Donald L. Koch
Chief
Geological Survey Bur.
123 N. Capitol St.
Iowa City, IA 52240
Phone: (319) 335-1575

KANSAS
Lee Gerhard
Director
Geology Survey
Univ. of KS
1930 Constant Ave., Campus W.
Lawrence, KS 66047
Phone: (785) 864-3965
Fax: (785) 864-5317

KENTUCKY
Donald C. Haney
State Geologist
Univ. of KY
Geological Survey
228 Mining & Mineral Research Bldg.
Lexington, KY 40506-0107
Phone: (606) 257-5500
Fax: (606) 257-1147

LOUISIANA
Chacko John
Acting State Geologist
Dept. of Natural Resources
P.O. Box G
Baton Rouge, LA 70893
Phone: (225) 388-8385
Fax: (225) 388-5328

MAINE
Robert Marvinney
State Geologist
Geological Survey
Dept. of Conservation
22 State House Station
Augusta, ME 04333
Phone: (207) 287-2801

MARYLAND
Emery T. Cleaves
Director
Geological Survey
Dept. of Natural Resources
2300 St. Paul St.
Baltimore, MD 21218
Phone: (410) 554-5503
Fax: (410) 554-5502

MASSACHUSETTS

MICHIGAN
Harold Fitch
Chief & State Geologist
Geological Survey
Dept. of Natural Resources
735 E. Hazel St.
Lansing, MI 48917
Phone: (517) 334-6907

MINNESOTA
David Southwick
Director & Professor
Univ. of MN
Geological Survey
2642 Univ. Ave., W.
St. Paul, MN 55114-1057
Phone: (651) 627-4780
Fax: (651) 627-4778
E-mail: south002
@maroon_tc.umn.edu

MISSISSIPPI
Cragin Knox
Director
Ofc. of Geology
Dept. of Environmental
Quality
P.O. Box 20307
Jackson, MS 39289
Phone: (601) 961-5502
Fax: (601) 961-5521

MISSOURI
James Williams
State Geologist
Div. of Geology & Land
Survey
Dept. of Natural Resources
111 Fairgrounds Rd.
P.O. Box 250
Rolla, MO 65401
Phone: (573) 368-2100
Fax: (573) 368-2111
E-mail: nrwillj
@mail.dnr.state.mo.us

MONTANA
John C. Steinmetz
Director
Bur. of Mines & Geology
Univ. of MT
Butte College of
Technology
25 Basin Creek Rd.
Butte, MT 59701
Phone: (406) 496-4181
Fax: (406) 496-3710

NEBRASKA
Mark Kuzila
Director
Conservation & Survey Div.
Univ. of NE
113 Nebraska Hall
Lincoln, NE 68588
Phone: (402) 472-3471
Fax: (402) 472-4608

NEVADA
John Price
State Geologist
Bur. of Mines & Geology
Univ. of NV
307 Scrugham Engineering
Mines
Mail Stop 178
Reno, NV 89557-0088
Phone: (775) 784-6691
Fax: (775) 784-1709
E-mail: jprice
@nbmg.nur.edu

NEW HAMPSHIRE
Eugene L. Boudette
State Geologist
Water Div.
Environmental Services
P.O. Box 95
Concord, NH 03302-0095
Phone: (603) 271-3406
Fax: (603) 271-2867

NEW JERSEY
Haig Kasabach
State Geologist
Environmental Protection
Dept.
29 Arctic Pkwy.
P.O. Box 427
Trenton, NJ 08625-0427
Phone: (609) 292-1185
Fax: (609) 633-1004

NEW MEXICO
Charles E. Chapin
Director
Bur. of Mines & Mineral
Resources
Institute of Mining &
Technology
801 Leroy Pl.
Socorro, NM 87801-4796
Phone: (505) 835-5302
Fax: (505) 835-6333
E-mail: bureau
@gis.nmt.edu

NEW YORK
Robert Fakundiny
State Geologist
Ofc. of Cultural Education
Dept. of Education
Cultural Education Ctr.,
Rm. 3140
Empire State Plz.
Albany, NY 12234
Phone: (518) 474-5816
Fax: (518) 486-3696

NORTH CAROLINA
Jeffrey C. Reid
Chief
Geological Survey
Div. of Land Resources
P.O. Box 27687
Raleigh, NC 27611
Phone: (919) 733-2423
Fax: (919) 733-2876

NORTH DAKOTA
John Bluemle
State Geologist
Geological Survey
Industrial Comm.
600 E. Blvd. Ave.
Bismarck, ND 58505-0840
Phone: (701) 328-8000
Fax: (701) 328-8010
E-mail: bluemle
@rival.ndgs.state.nd.us

**NORTHERN MARIANA
ISLANDS**
Eugene A. Santos
Acting Secretary
Ofc. of the Secretary
Lands & Natural Resources
Caller Box 10007
Saipan, MP 96950
Phone: (670) 322-9830
Fax: (670) 322-2633

OHIO
Thomas M. Berg
State Geologist & Chief
Geological Survey
4383 Fountain Sq.,
Bldg. B-2
Columbus, OH 43224-1362
Phone: (604) 265-6988
Fax: (604) 268-3669

OKLAHOMA
Charles Mankin
Director
Geological Survey
Sarkey's Energy Ctr.
100 E. Boyd, Rm. N-131
Norman, OK 73019
Phone: (405) 325-3031
Fax: (405) 325-7069

OREGON
Donald A. Hull
State Geologist
Dept. of Geology & Mineral
Industries
800 NE Oregon St., #27,
Ste. 965
Portland, OR 97232
Phone: (503) 731-4100
Fax: (503) 731-4066

PENNSYLVANIA
Donald M. Hoskins
State Geologist
Topographic & Geological
Survey
Dept. of Environmental
Resources
P.O. Box 8453
Harrisburg, PA 17105-8453
Phone: (717) 787-2169
Fax: (717) 783-7267

PUERTO RICO
Daniel Pagan
Secretary
Dept. of Natural Resources
P.O. Box 5887
San Juan, PR 00906
Phone: (787) 723-3090
Fax: (787) 723-4255

RHODE ISLAND
J. Allen Cain
State Geologist
Univ. of RI
Dept. of Geology
Green Hall, Rm. 103
Kingston, RI 02881
Phone: (401) 792-2184

SOUTH CAROLINA
Charles Clendenin
State Geologist
Geological Survey
Dept. of Natural Resources
5 Geology Rd.
Columbia, SC 29210
Phone: (803) 896-7708

SOUTH DAKOTA
Derric Iles
State Geologist
Div. of Geological Survey
Univ. of SD
415 E. Clark St.
Vermillion, SD 57069
Phone: (605) 677-5227
Fax: (605) 677-5895

TENNESSEE
Ronald P. Zurawski
Director
Div. of Geology
Dept. of Environment &
Conservation
L & C Tower, 13th Fl.
Nashville, TN 37243-0445
Phone: (615) 532-1500
Fax: (615) 532-1517

TEXAS
Null Tyler
Director
Bur. of Economic Geology
Univ. of TX
Research Ctr.
Pickel Bldg. 130
Austin, TX 78713-8924
Phone: (512) 471-1534
Fax: (512) 471-0140

U.S. VIRGIN ISLANDS
Dean Plaskett
Commissioner
Dept. of Planning & Natural Resources
Foster's Plz., 396-1 Anna's Retreat
St. Thomas, VI 00802
Phone: (340) 774-3320
Fax: (340) 775-5706

UTAH
M. Lee Allison
Director
Geological Survey
Dept. of Natural Resources
1594 W. N. Temple, Ste. 3110
Salt Lake City, UT 84114-6100
Phone: (801) 537-3301
Fax: (801) 537-3400
E-mail: lallison.nrugs@state.ut.us

VERMONT
Larry Becker
State Geologist
Agency of Natural Resources
103 S. Main St.
Waterbury, VT 05671-0401
Phone: (802) 241-3496
Fax: (802) 241-3281

VIRGINIA
O. Gene Dishner
Director
Dept. of Mines, Minerals & Energy
202 N. 9th St., 8th Fl.
Richmond, VA 23219
Phone: (804) 692-3200
Fax: (804) 692-3237

WASHINGTON
Ray Lasmanis
State Geologist
Div. of Geology & Earth Resources
Dept. of Natural Resources
P.O. Box 47007
Olympia, WA 98504-7007
Phone: (360) 902-1450
Fax: (360) 902-1785

WEST VIRGINIA
Larry Woodfork
State Geologist
Geological & Economic Survey
P.O. Box 879
Morgantown, WV 26507
Phone: (304) 557-3170
Fax: (304) 594-2575

WISCONSIN
James M. Robertson
Director & State Geologist
Geological & Natural History Survey
Univ. of WI Extension
3817 Mineral Point Rd.
Madison, WI 53705
Phone: (608) 262-1705
Fax: (608) 262-8086

WYOMING
Lance Cook
State Geologist
Geological Survey Staff
Univ. Station
P.O. Box 3008
Laramie, WY 82071
Phone: (307) 766-2286

Governor

ALABAMA
Don Siegelman (D)
Governor
Ofc. of the Governor
State Capitol, N104
600 Dexter Ave.
Montgomery, AL 36130-2751
Phone: (334) 242-7100
Fax: (334) 353-1054

ALASKA
Tony Knowles (D)
Governor
State Capitol
P.O. Box 110001
Juneau, AK 99811-0001
Phone: (907) 465-3500
Fax: (907) 465-3532

AMERICAN SAMOA
Tauese P.F. Sunia (D)
Governor
Ofc. of the Governor
Pago Pago, AS 96799
Phone: (684) 633-4116
Fax: (684) 633-2269

ARIZONA
Jane Dee Hull (R)
Governor
State Capitol
1700 W. Washington St., 9th Fl.
Phoenix, AZ 85007
Phone: (602) 542-4331
Fax: (602) 542-7601

ARKANSAS
Mike Huckabee (R)
Governor
State Capitol, Rm. 250
Little Rock, AR 72201
Phone: (501) 682-2345
Fax: (501) 682-1382

CALIFORNIA
Gray Davis (D)
Governor
State Capitol, 1st Fl.
Sacramento, CA 95814
Phone: (916) 445-2841

COLORADO
Bill Owens (R)
Governor
136 State Capitol Bldg.
Denver, CO 80203-1792
Phone: (303) 866-2471
Fax: (303) 866-2003

CONNECTICUT
John G. Rowland (R)
Governor
State Capitol
210 Capitol Ave.
Hartford, CT 06106
Phone: (860) 566-4840
Fax: (860) 524-7395
E-mail: governor.rowland@po.state.ct.us

DELAWARE
Thomas R. Carper (D)
Governor
Carvel State Ofc. Bldg., 12th Fl.
820 N. French St.
Wilmington, DE 19801
Phone: (302) 577-3210
Fax: (302) 577-3118

DISTRICT OF COLUMBIA
Anthony Williams (D)
Mayor
441 4th St. NW, 11th Fl.
Washington, DC 20001
Phone: (202) 727-2980

FLORIDA
Jeb Bush (R)
Governor
PL 05, The Capitol
Tallahassee, FL 32399-0001
Phone: (850) 488-2272
Fax: (850) 487-0801
E-mail: bushj@eog.state.fl.us

GEORGIA
Roy E. Barnes (D)
Governor
203 State Capitol
Atlanta, GA 30334
Phone: (404) 656-1776
Fax: (404) 657-7332

GUAM
Carl T.C. Gutierrez (D)
Governor
Executive Chamber
P.O. Box 2950
Hagatna, GU 96932
Phone: (671) 472-8931
Fax: (671) 477-4826
E-mail: governor@ns.gov.gu

HAWAII
Benjamin J. Cayetano (D)
Governor
State Capitol, 5th Fl.
Honolulu, HI 96813
Phone: (808) 586-0034
Fax: (808) 586-0006
E-mail: gov@gov.state.hi.us

IDAHO
Dirk Kempthorne (R)
Governor
State Capitol
700 W. Jefferson
Boise, ID 83720-0034
Phone: (208) 334-2100
Fax: (208) 334-2175

ILLINOIS
George H. Ryan, Sr. (R)
Governor
207 State House
Springfield, IL 62706
Phone: (217) 782-6830

INDIANA
Frank O'Bannon (D)
Governor
State House, Rm. 206
200 W. Washington St.
Indianapolis, IN 46204
Phone: (317) 232-4567
Fax: (317) 232-3443

IOWA
Tom Vilsack (D)
Governor
State Capitol Bldg.
Des Moines, IA 50319-0001
Phone: (515) 281-5211
Fax: (515) 281-6611

KANSAS
Bill Graves (R)
Governor
State Capitol, 2nd Fl.
Topeka, KS 66612-1590
Phone: (785) 296-3232
Fax: (785) 296-7973

KENTUCKY
Paul E. Patton (D)
Governor
Ofc. of the Governor
State Capitol
700 Capitol Ave.
Frankfort, KY 40601
Phone: (502) 564-2611
Fax: (502) 564-2517

LOUISIANA
Mike Foster, Jr. (R)
Governor
P.O. Box 94004
Baton Rouge, LA 70804-9004
Phone: (225) 342-7015
Fax: (225) 342-7099
E-mail: lagov@linknet.net

MAINE
Angus S. King, Jr. (I)
Governor
Ofc. of the Governor
1 State House Station
Augusta, ME 04333-0001
Phone: (207) 287-3531
Fax: (207) 287-1034
E-mail: governor@state.me.us

MARYLAND
Parris N. Glendening (D)
Governor
Executive Dept.
State House
100 State Cir.
Annapolis, MD 21401-1925
Phone: (410) 974-3901
Fax: (410) 974-3275
E-mail: pglendening@goc.state.md.us

MASSACHUSETTS
Argeo Paul Cellucci (R)
Governor
Executive Ofc.
Rm. 360 - State House
Boston, MA 02133
Phone: (617) 727-9173
Fax: (617) 523-7984
E-mail: govoff@state.ma.us

MICHIGAN
John Engler (R)
Governor
P.O. Box 30013
Lansing, MI 48909
Phone: (517) 373-3400
Fax: (517) 335-6863

MINNESOTA
Jesse Ventura (Reform)
Governor
State Capitol, Rm. 130
75 Constitution Ave.
St. Paul, MN 55155
Phone: (651) 296-3391
Fax: (651) 296-2089
E-mail: jesse.ventura@state.mn.us

MISSISSIPPI
Kirk Fordice (R)
Governor
P.O. Box 139
Jackson, MS 39205
Phone: (601) 359-3150
Fax: (601) 359-3741
E-mail: governor@govoff.state.ms.us

MISSOURI
Mel Carnahan (D)
Governor
State Capitol, Rm. 216
P.O. Box 720
Jefferson City, MO 65102-0720
Phone: (573) 751-3222
Fax: (573) 751-1495
E-mail: constit@mail.state.mo.us

MONTANA
Marc Racicot (R)
Governor
State Capitol Bldg., Rm. 204
P.O. Box 200801
1301 E. 6th Ave.
Helena, MT 59620-0801
Phone: (406) 444-3111
Fax: (406) 444-5529

NEBRASKA
Mike Johanns (R)
Governor
State Capitol, 2nd Fl.
P.O. Box 94848
Lincoln, NE 68509-4848
Phone: (402) 471-2244
Fax: (402) 471-6031

NEVADA
Kenny Guinn (R)
Governor
Executive Chambers
101 N. Carson St.
Carson City, NV 89710
Phone: (775) 684-5670
Fax: (775) 684-5683

NEW HAMPSHIRE
Jeanne Shaheen (D)
Governor
Ofc. of the Governor
State House
107 N. Main St., Rm. 208
Concord, NH 03301-4990
Phone: (603) 271-2121
Fax: (603) 271-2130

NEW JERSEY
Christine T. Whitman (R)
Governor
Ofc. of the Governor
State House
P.O. Box 001
Trenton, NJ 08625-0001
Phone: (609) 292-6000
Fax: (609) 984-6886

NEW MEXICO
Gary E. Johnson (R)
Governor
400 State Capitol
Santa Fe, NM 87503
Phone: (505) 827-3000
Fax: (505) 827-3026
E-mail: gov.@gov.state.nm.us

NEW YORK
George E. Pataki (R)
Governor
Executive Chamber
State Capitol
Albany, NY 12224
Phone: (518) 474-8390

NORTH CAROLINA
James B. Hunt, Jr. (D)
Governor
State Capitol
116 W. Jones St.
Raleigh, NC 27603-8001
Phone: (919) 733-4240
Fax: (919) 715-3175

NORTH DAKOTA
Edward T. Schafer (R)
Governor
Ofc. of the Governor
600 E. Blvd. Ave.
Bismarck, ND 58505-0001
Phone: (701) 328-2200
Fax: (701) 328-2205
E-mail: governor@state.nd.us

NORTHERN MARIANA ISLANDS
Pedro P. Tenorio (R)
Governor
Ofc. of the Governor
Caller Box 10007 CK
Saipan, MP 96950
Phone: (670) 664-2200
Fax: (670) 664-2211
E-mail: governor.cnmi@saipan.com

OHIO
Bob Taft (R)
Governor
77 S. High St., 30th Fl.
Columbus, OH 43266-0601
Phone: (614) 466-3555
Fax: (614) 466-9354

OKLAHOMA
Frank Keating (R)
Governor
State Capitol Bldg, Rm. 212
Oklahoma City, OK 73105
Phone: (405) 521-2342
Fax: (405) 521-3353

OREGON
John A. Kitzhaber (D)
Governor
254 State Capitol
Salem, OR 97310
Phone: (503) 378-3111
Fax: (503) 378-4863

PENNSYLVANIA
Tom Ridge (R)
Governor
225 Main Capitol Bldg., Rm. 225
Harrisburg, PA 17120
Phone: (717) 787-2500
Fax: (717) 772-8284

PUERTO RICO
Pedro Rosselló (D and NPP)
Governor
La Fortaleza
P.O. Box 82
San Juan, PR 00901
Phone: (787) 721-7000
Fax: (787) 729-0900

RHODE ISLAND
Lincoln C. Almond (R)
Governor
222 State House
Providence, RI 02903
Phone: (401) 222-2080
Fax: (401) 861-5894

SOUTH CAROLINA
Jim Hodges (D)
Governor
State House
P.O. Box 11829
Columbia, SC 29211
Phone: (803) 734-9400
Fax: (803) 734-9413
E-mail: GOVERNOR@govoepp.state.sc.us

SOUTH DAKOTA
William J. Janklow (R)
Governor
State Capitol
500 E. Capitol Ave.
Pierre, SD 57501
Phone: (605) 773-3212
Fax: (605) 773-4711

TENNESSEE
Don Sundquist (R)
Governor
State Capitol Bldg.
600 Charlotte Ave.
Nashville, TN 37243-0001
Phone: (615) 741-2001
Fax: (615) 741-1416

TEXAS
George W. Bush (R)
Governor
Ofc. of the Governor
P.O. Box 12428
Austin, TX 78711-2428
Phone: (512) 463-2000
Fax: (512) 463-1849

U.S. VIRGIN ISLANDS
Charles W. Turnbull (D)
Governor
Govt. House
21-22 Kongens Gade
St. Thomas, VI 00802
Phone: (340) 774-9133
Fax: (340) 774-1361

UTAH
Michael O. Leavitt (R)
Governor
210 State Capitol
Salt Lake City, UT 84114
Phone: (801) 538-1500
Fax: (801) 538-1528
E-mail: governor_leavitt@gov.state.ut.us

VERMONT
Howard Dean (D)
Governor
Pavilion Ofc. Bldg.
109 State St.
Montpelier, VT 05609
Phone: (802) 828-3333
Fax: (802) 828-3339

VIRGINIA
James S. Gilmore, III (R)
Governor
Commonwealth of Virginia
State Capitol, 3rd Fl.
Richmond, VA 23219
Phone: (804) 786-2211
Fax: (804) 371-6351

WASHINGTON
Gary Locke (D)
Governor
Legislative Bldg.
P.O. Box 40002
Olympia, WA 98504-0002
Phone: (360) 902-4111
Fax: (360) 753-4110

WEST VIRGINIA
Cecil H. Underwood (R)
Governor
State Capitol Complex
Charleston, WV 25305-0370
Phone: (304) 558-2000
Fax: (304) 342-7025
E-mail: governor
@mail.governor.com

WISCONSIN
Tommy G. Thompson (R)
Governor
State Capitol
P.O. Box 7863
Madison, WI 53707-7863
Phone: (608) 266-1212
Fax: (608) 267-8983
E-mail: wisgov
@mail.state.wi.us

WYOMING
Jim Geringer (R)
Governor
State Capitol Bldg.,
Rm. 124
Cheyenne, WY 82002
Phone: (307) 777-7434
Fax: (307) 632-3909
E-mail: governor
@missc.state.wy.us

Groundwater Management –

Manages the state's groundwater resources.

ALABAMA
Charles Horn
Chief
Water Quality Branch
Water Div.
Dept. of Environmental Mgmt.
1751 Cong. Dickinson Dr.
Montgomery, AL 36130-1463
Phone: (334) 271-7826
Fax: (334) 279-3051

ALASKA
Bob Loeffler
Director
Div. of Mining & Water Mgmt.
Dept. of Natural Resources
3601 C St., Ste. 800
Anchorage, AK 99503
Phone: (907) 269-8624
Fax: (907) 562-1384

AMERICAN SAMOA
Abe U. Malae
Executive Director
Power Authority
AS Govt.
Pago Pago, AS 96799
Phone: (684) 644-5251
Fax: (684) 644-5005

ARIZONA
Rita P. Pearson
Director
Dept. of Water Resources
500 N. 3rd St.
Phoenix, AZ 85004-3903
Phone: (602) 417-2410
Fax: (602) 417-2415

ARKANSAS
Chuck Bennett
Chief
Water Div.
Dept. of Environmental Quality
P.O. Box 8913
Little Rock, AR 72219
Phone: (501) 682-0656
Fax: (501) 682-0707

CALIFORNIA
Raymond D. Hart
Deputy Director
Dept. of Water Resources
1020 9th St., 3rd Fl.
Sacramento, CA 95814
Phone: (916) 327-1632

COLORADO
Hal D. Simpson
State Engineer
Div. of Water Resources
Dept. of Natural Resources
1313 Sherman St., Rm. 818
Denver, CO 80203
Phone: (303) 866-3581
Fax: (303) 866-3589

CONNECTICUT
Robert Smith
Chief
Bur. of Water Mgmt.
Water Compliance Unit
Dept. of Environmental Protection
79 Elm St.
Hartford, CT 06106
Phone: (860) 424-3704

DELAWARE
Rodney Wyatt
Program Manager II
Groundwater Mgmt. Branch
Natural Resources & Environmental Dept.
P.O. Box 1401
Dover, DE 19903
Phone: (302) 739-4860
Fax: (302) 739-3491

DISTRICT OF COLUMBIA
Jerry Johnson
General Manager
Water & Sewer Authority
5000 Overlook Ave., SW
Washington, DC 20032
Phone: (202) 767-7651

FLORIDA
Mimi Drew
Director
Div. of Water Facilities
Dept. of Environmental Protection
2600 Blairstone Rd.
Tallahassee, FL 32399-2400
Phone: (850) 488-1855
Fax: (850) 921-4303

GEORGIA
William McLemore
State Geologist
Environmental Protection Div.
Dept. of Natural Resources
19 Martin Luther King, Jr. Dr., Rm. 400
Atlanta, GA 30334
Phone: (404) 656-3214

GUAM
Richard Quintanilla
General Manager
Waterworks Authority
126 Lower E. Sunset Blvd., Tiyan
P.O. Box 3010
Hagatna, GU 96932
Phone: (671) 479-7823
Fax: (671) 649-0158

HAWAII
Edwin Sakoda
Acting Deputy Director
Div. of Water Resource Mgmt.
Land & Natural Resources Dept.
1151 Punchbowl St.
Honolulu, HI 96813
Phone: (808) 587-0214
Fax: (808) 587-0219

IDAHO
Donna Rodman
Bureau Chief
Watershed Mgmt.
1410 N. Hilton
Boise, ID 83706
Phone: (208) 373-0460

ILLINOIS
Thomas V. Skinner
Director
Environmental Protection Agency
P.O. Box 19276
Springfield, IL 62794
Phone: (217) 782-9540
Fax: (217) 782-9039

INDIANA
Mike Neyer
Director
Div. of Water
Dept. of Natural Resources
402 W. Washington
Indianapolis, IN 46204
Phone: (317) 232-4160
Fax: (317) 233-4579

IOWA
Darrell McAllister
Chief
Surface & Groundwater Protection
Environmental Protection Div.
Wallace State Ofc. Bldg.
E. 9th & Grand Aves.
Des Moines, IA 50319
Phone: (515) 281-8869

KANSAS
Karl Mueldener
Director
Bur. of Water
Dept. of Health & Environment
Forbes Field Bldg. 283
6700 SW Topeka Blvd.
Topeka, KS 66619
Phone: (785) 296-5500
Fax: (785) 296-5509

KENTUCKY

LOUISIANA
Linda Korn Levy
Assistant Secretary
Ofc. of Water Resources
Dept. of Environmental Quality
P.O. Box 82215
Baton Rouge, LA 70884
Phone: (225) 765-0634
Fax: (225) 765-0635

MAINE
Martha Kirkpatrick
Director
Land & Water Quality Control
Dept. of Environmental Protection
17 State House Station
Augusta, ME 04333
Phone: (207) 287-3901

MARYLAND
Jane Gottfredson
Division Chief
Groundwater Permits Program
Dept. of the Environment
2500 Broening Hwy.
Baltimore, MD 21224-6612
Phone: (410) 631-3778
Fax: (410) 631-3163

MASSACHUSETTS
Mike Repaz
Director
Regulatory Branch
Water Pollution Control Div.
20 Riverside Dr.
Lakeville, MA 02347
Phone: (508) 946-2867
Fax: (508) 947-6557

MICHIGAN
Jim Sygo
Chief
Waste Mgmt. Div.
Dept. of Environmental Quality
P.O. Box 30028
Lansing, MI 48909
Phone: (517) 373-2730

MINNESOTA
Brian Rongitsch
Supervisor
Natural Resources
Dept. of Natural Resources - Ground Water Unit
500 Lafayette Rd.
St. Paul, MN 55155-4032
Phone: (651) 296-0434
Fax: (651) 296-0445
E-mail: brian.rongitsch@dnr.state.mn.us

MISSISSIPPI
Bill Barnett
Chief
Groundwater Div.
Ofc. of Pollution Control
P.O. Box 10385
Jackson, MS 39289
Phone: (601) 961-5119
Fax: (601) 354-6965

MISSOURI
Steve McIntosh
Director
Water Resources Program
Div. of Geology & Land Survey/Dept. of Natural Resources
111 Fairgrounds Rd.
P.O. Box 176
Jefferson City, MO 65102
Phone: (573) 751-2867
Fax: (573) 751-8475
E-mail: nrmcins@mail.dnr.state.mo.us

MONTANA
Bonnie Lovelace
Chief
Water Protection Bur.
Dept.of Environmental Quality
Metcalf Bldg., 1520 E. 6th Ave.
Helena, MT 59620
Phone: (406) 444-4969
Fax: (406) 444-1499

NEBRASKA
Dennis Heitmann
Supervisor
Ground Water Section
Dept. of Environmental Quality
P.O. Box 98922
Lincoln, NE 68509
Phone: (402) 471-0096
Fax: (402) 471-2909

NEVADA
Allen Biaggi
Administrator
Air, Mining & Water Section
Div. of Environmental Protection
333 W. Nye Ln., Rm. 138
Carson City, NV 89706
Phone: (775) 687-4670
Fax: (775) 687-5856

NEW HAMPSHIRE
Harry Stewart
Director
Water Div.
Environmental Services
P.O. Box 95
Concord, NH 03302-0095
Phone: (603) 271-3503
Fax: (603) 271-2867

NEW JERSEY
James Mumman
Administrator
Water Monitoring Mgmt.
401 E. State St.
P.O. Box 409
Trenton, NJ 08625-0409
Phone: (609) 292-1623
Fax: (609) 292-7340

NEW MEXICO
Marcy Leavitt
Bur. Chief
Groundwater Bur.
Dept. of Environment
P.O. Box 26110
Santa Fe, NM 87502
Phone: (505) 827-2919
Fax: (505) 827-2836

NEW YORK
John Cahill
Commissioner
Dept. of Environmental Conservation
50 Wolf Rd.
Albany, NY 12233-1010
Phone: (518) 457-1162
Fax: (518) 457-7744

NORTH CAROLINA
Arthur Mouberry
Section Chief
Groundwater Section
Div. of Water Quality
P.O. Box 27687
Raleigh, NC 276011
Phone: (919) 733-3221
Fax: (919) 733-2496

NORTH DAKOTA
Dennis Fewless
Director
Water Quality
Environmental Health Section
P.O. Box 5520
Bismarck, ND 58506-5520
Phone: (701) 328-5210
Fax: (701) 328-5200
E-mail: dfewless@state.nd.us

NORTHERN MARIANA ISLANDS
Timothy P. Villagomez
Executive Director
Commonwealth Utilities Corp.
Ofc. of the Governor
Lower Base
P.O. Box 1220
Saipan, MP 96950
Phone: (670) 322-5088
Fax: (670) 322-4323
E-mail: cuc.edp@mtccnmi.com

OHIO
Kirk Leifheit
Acting Chief
Div. of Drinking & Ground Waters
Environmental Protection Agency
122 S. Front St.
P.O. Box 1049
Columbus, OH 43216
Phone: (614) 644-2752
Fax: (614) 644-2909

OKLAHOMA
Duane Smith
Executive Director
Water Resources Board
3800 N. Classen Blvd.
Oklahoma City, OK 73118
Phone: (405) 530-8800
Fax: (405) 530-8900

OREGON
Amy Patton
Manager
Groundwater Section
Dept. of Environmental Quality
811 SW 6th Ave.
Portland, OR 97204
Phone: (503) 229-5875
Fax: (503) 229-6124

PENNSYLVANIA
Glenn E. Maurer
Director
Bur. of Water Quality Protection
Dept. of Environmental Resources
400 Market St., 11th Fl.
Harrisburg, PA 17105
Phone: (717) 787-2666
Fax: (717) 722-5156

PUERTO RICO
Daniel Pagan
Secretary
Dept. of Natural Resources
P.O. Box 5887
San Juan, PR 00906
Phone: (787) 723-3090
Fax: (787) 723-4255

RHODE ISLAND
Edward Szymanski
Deputy Bureau Chief
Dept. of Environmental Mgmt.
235 Promenade St.
Providence, RI 02908
Phone: (401) 222-2234

SOUTH CAROLINA
Rod W. Cherry
Director
Div. of Hydrology
Water Resources Comm.
1201 Main St., Ste. 1100
Columbia, SC 29201
Phone: (803) 737-0800

SOUTH DAKOTA
Bill Markley
Director
Div. of Environmental Regulation
Dept. of Environment & Natural Resources
523 E. Capitol Ave.
Pierre, SD 57501
Phone: (605) 773-3296
Fax: (605) 773-6035

TENNESSEE
Kent D. Taylor
Director
Div. of Groundwater Protection
Dept. of Environment & Conservation
L & C Tower, 10th Fl.
Nashville, TN 37243
Phone: (615) 532-0761
Fax: (615) 532-0778

TEXAS
Ken Peterson
Deputy Director
Ofc. of Waste Mgmt.
Natural Resources Conservation Comm.
P. O. Box 13087
Austin, TX 78711-3087
Phone: (512) 239-4300
Fax: (512) 239-4303

U.S. VIRGIN ISLANDS
Dean Plaskett
Commissioner
Dept. of Planning & Natural Resources
Foster's Plz., 396-1 Anna's Retreat
St. Thomas, VI 00802
Phone: (340) 774-3320
Fax: (340) 775-5706

UTAH
Don Ostler
Director
Div. of Water Quality
Dept. of Environmental Quality
288 N. 1460 W.
Salt Lake City, UT 84114-4870
Phone: (801) 538-6047
Fax: (801) 538-6016
E-mail: dostler@deq.state.ut.us

VERMONT
Jay Rutherford
Director
Groundwater Mgmt. Section
Water Supply Div.
103 S. Main St.
Waterbury, VT 05671-0403
Phone: (802) 241-3434
Fax: (802) 241-3284

VIRGINIA
Dennis H. Treacy
Director
Dept. of Environmental Quality
629 E. Main St.
Richmond, VA 23219
Phone: (804) 698-4020
Fax: (804) 698-4019

WASHINGTON
Megan White
Program Manager
Water Quality Program
Dept. of Ecology
P.O. Box 47600
Olympia, WA 98504-7600
Phone: (360) 407-6405
Fax: (360) 407-6426

WEST VIRGINIA
Mark A. Scott
Chief
Ofc. of Water Resources
Dept. of Environmental Protection
1201 Greenbrier St.
Charleston, WV 25311
Phone: (304) 558-2107
Fax: (304) 558-5905

WISCONSIN
Michael Lemcke
Chief
Groundwater Mgmt. Section
Bur. of Water Resource Mgmt.
Dept. of Natural Resources
P.O. Box 7921
Madison, WI 53707-7921
Phone: (608) 266-2104
Fax: (608) 267-7650

WYOMING
Richard G. Stockdale
Administrator
Ground Water Div.
Ofc. of State Engineer
Herschler Bldg.
122 W. 25th St.
Cheyenne, WY 82002
Phone: (307) 777-6160

Hazardous Waste Management

Develops and maintains a comprehensive hazardous waste management program in the state.

ALABAMA
Gerald Hardy
Chief
Compliance Branch, Land Div.
Dept. of Environmental Mgmt.
1751 Cong. Dickinson Dr.
Montgomery, AL 36130
Phone: (334) 271-7732
Fax: (334) 279-3050

ALASKA
Heather Stockard
Chief
Solid & Hazardous Waste Mgmt. Section
410 Willoughby Ave., Ste. 105
Juneau, AK 99801-1795
Phone: (907) 465-5150
Fax: (907) 465-5164

AMERICAN SAMOA
Togipa Tausaga
Director
Environmental Protection Agency
Ofc. of the Governor
Pago Pago, AS 96799
Phone: (684) 633-7691

ARIZONA
Tim Hudson
Section Manager
Hazardous Waste Section
Dept. of Environmental Quality
3033 N. Central Ave.
Phoenix, AZ 85012
Phone: (602) 207-2381

ARKANSAS
Mike Bates
Chief
Hazardous Waste Div.
Dept. of Environmental Quality
P.O. Box 8913
Little Rock, AR 72219
Phone: (501) 682-0833
Fax: (501) 682-0880

CALIFORNIA
Jesse Huff
Director
Toxic Substance Control
400 P St., 4th Fl.
P.O. Box 806
Sacramento, CA 95812-0806
Phone: (916) 323-9723

COLORADO
Howard Roitman
Director
Hazardous Materials & Waste Mgmt.
Dept. of Public Health & Environment
4300 Cherry Creek Dr., S.
Denver, CO 80246-1530
Phone: (303) 692-3300
Fax: (303) 759-5355

CONNECTICUT
Richard Barlow
Director
Bur. of Waste Mgmt.
Dept. of Environmental Protection
79 Elm St.
Hartford, CT 06106
Phone: (860) 424-3021

DELAWARE
Nancy C. Marker
Program Manager II
Waste Mgmt. Section
Natural Resources & Environmental Control
89 Kings Hwy.
Dover, DE 19901
Phone: (302) 739-3689
Fax: (302) 739-5060

DISTRICT OF COLUMBIA
Leslie Hotaling
Administrator
Solid Waste Mgmt. Administration
Dept. of Public Works
2750 S. Capitol St., SE
Washington, DC 20003
Phone: (202) 767-8512

FLORIDA
John Rudell
Director
Div. of Waste Mgmt.
Dept. of Environmental Protection
2600 Blairstone Rd.
Tallahassee, FL 32399-2400
Phone: (850) 487-3299
Fax: (850) 922-4939

GEORGIA
Harold Reheis
Director
Environmental Protection Div.
Dept. of Natural Resources
205 Butler St., SW, Ste. 1152
Atlanta, GA 30334
Phone: (404) 656-4713
Fax: (404) 651-5778

GUAM
Jesus T. Salas
Administrator
Environmental Protection Agency
15-6101 Mariner Ave., Tiyan
P.O. Box 22439
Barrigada, GU 96921
Phone: (671) 475-1658
Fax: (671) 477-9402

HAWAII
Steven Chang
Branch Chief
Solid & Hazardous Waste Branch
Dept. of Health
919 Ala Moana Blvd., Ste. 212
Honolulu, HI 96813
Phone: (808) 586-4225
Fax: (808) 586-7509

IDAHO
Orville Green
Assistant Administrator
Permits & Enforcement
Div. of Environmental Quality
1410 N. Hilton
Boise, ID 83706-1255
Phone: (208) 373-0440
Fax: (208) 373-0417

ILLINOIS
George Vander Velde
Director
Waste Mgmt. & Research Ctr.
One E. Hazelwood Dr.
Champaign, IL 61820
Phone: (217) 333-8940

INDIANA
Bruce Palin
Acting Assistant Commissioner
IDEM
100 N. Senate Ave., Rm. 1154
Indianapolis, IN 46204
Phone: (317) 232-3210
Fax: (317) 232-3403

IOWA
Peter Hamlin
Chief
Air Quality & Solid Waste Protection
Dept. of Natural Resources
900 E. Grand Ave.
Des Moines, IA 50319
Phone: (515) 281-8852

KANSAS
William Bider
Director
Bur. of Waste Mgmt., KDHE
Forbes Field Bldg. 740
6700 SW Topeka Blvd.
Topeka, KS 66620-0001
Phone: (785) 296-1600
Fax: (785) 296-1592

KENTUCKY
Michael Welch
Branch Manager
Hazardous Waste Branch
Div. of Waste Mgmt.
14 Reilly Rd.
Frankfort, KY 40601
Phone: (502) 564-6716
Fax: (502) 564-4049

LOUISIANA
James Brent
Assistant Secretary
Ofc. of Waste Services
Dept. of Environmental Quality
P.O. Box 82178
Baton Rouge, LA 70884-2178
Phone: (225) 765-0355
Fax: (225) 765-0617

MAINE
Vacant
Director
Oil & Hazardous Materials Bur.
Dept. of Environmental Protection
17 State House Station
Augusta, ME 04333
Phone: (207) 287-2651

MARYLAND
Richard Collins
Director
Waste Mgmt. Administration
Dept. of the Environment
2500 Broening Hwy.
Baltimore, MD 21224
Phone: (410) 631-3304
Fax: (410) 631-3321

MASSACHUSETTS
Steven DeGabriel
Director
Business Compliance Div.
Dept. of Environmental Protection
1 Winter St., 3rd Fl.
Boston, MA 02108
Phone: (617) 556-1120
Fax: (617) 292-5778

MICHIGAN
Kenneth Burda
Chief
Hazardous Waste Program Section
Dept. of Natural Resources
P.O. Box 30028
Lansing, MI 48909
Phone: (517) 373-2730

MINNESOTA
Timothy K. Scherkenbach
Manager
Hazardous Waste Div.
Pollution Control Agency
520 Lafayette Rd.
St. Paul, MN 55155-4194
Phone: (651) 297-8502
Fax: (651) 297-8676
E-mail: tim.scherkenbach@pca.state.mn.us

MISSISSIPPI
Sam Mabry
Administrator
Hazardous Waste Div.
Dept. of Environmental Quality
P.O. Box 10385
Jackson, MS 39289
Phone: (601) 961-5062
Fax: (601) 354-6965

MISSOURI
Cindy Kemper
Director
Hazardous Waste Program
Dept. of Natural Resources
1738 E. Elm St.
Jefferson City, MO 65102
Phone: (573) 751-3176
Fax: (573) 751-7869
E-mail: nrkempc@mail.dnr.state.mo.us

MONTANA
Don Vidrine
Bureau Chief
Air & Waste Mgmt. Bur.
Dept. of Environmental Quality
1520 E. 6th Ave.
Helena, MT 59620
Phone: (406) 444-3490
Fax: (406) 444-1499

NEBRASKA
Dave Haldeman
Supervisor
Integrated Waste Mgmt. Section
Dept. of Environmental Quality
P.O. Box 98922
Lincoln, NE 68509
Phone: (402) 471-4210
Fax: (402) 471-2909

NEVADA
David Emme
Chief
Bur. of Waste Mgmt.
Dept. of Environmental Protection
Capitol Complex
333 W. Nye Ln., Rm. 138
Carson City, NV 89706
Phone: (775) 687-4670
Fax: (775) 687-5856

NEW HAMPSHIRE
Philip J. O'Brien
Director
Waste Mgmt.
Environmental Services
6 Hazen Dr.
Concord, NH 03301-6509
Phone: (603) 271-2900
Fax: (603) 271-2867

NEW JERSEY
Susan Boyle
Director
Div. of Responsible Party Sites Remediation
Environmental Protection Dept.
401 E. State St.
P.O. Box 028
Trenton, NJ 08625-0028
Phone: (609) 633-1408
Fax: (609) 633-1454

NEW MEXICO
Benito Garcia
Bureau Chief
Hazardous Waste Bur.
Dept. of Environment
P.O. Box 26110
Santa Fe, NM 87502
Phone: (505) 827-1557
Fax: (505) 827-2836

NEW YORK
John Cahill
Commissioner
Dept. of Environmental Conservation
50 Wolf Rd.
Albany, NY 12233-1010
Phone: (518) 457-1162
Fax: (518) 457-7744

NORTH CAROLINA
Bill Meyer
Director
Hazardous Waste Section
Div. of Solid Waste Mgmt.
401 Oberlin Rd., Ste. 150
Raleigh, NC 27605
Phone: (919) 733-0692

NORTH DAKOTA
Neil Knatterud
Director
Waste Mgmt.
Environmental Health Section
P.O. Box 5520
Bismarck, ND 58506-5520
Phone: (701) 328-5166
Fax: (701) 328-5200
E-mail: nknatter@state.nd.us

NORTHERN MARIANA ISLANDS
Juan I. Castro
Director
Environmental Quality
Public Works
P.O. Box 1304
Saipan, MP 96950
Phone: (670) 234-1011
Fax: (670) 234-1003
E-mail: john.castro@saipan.com

OHIO
Mike Savage
Division Chief
Hazardous Waste Mgmt.
P.O. Box 1049
Columbus, OH 43216
Phone: (614) 644-2917
Fax: (614) 728-1245

OKLAHOMA
H.A. Caves
Director
Solid Waste Mgmt. Services
Environmental Health Services
P.O. Box 1677
Oklahoma City, OK 73101
Phone: (405) 702-5158

OREGON
Anne Price
Manager
Hazardous Waste Policy & Program Dev.
Dept. of Environmental Quality
811 SW 6th Ave.
Portland, OR 97204
Phone: (503) 229-6585
Fax: (503) 229-6977

PENNSYLVANIA
Leon Kuchinski
Chief
Bur. of Land Recycling & Waste Mgmt.
Div. of Hazardous Waste Mgmt./Dept. of Environmental Protection
P.O. Box 8471
Harrisburg, PA 17105-8471
Phone: (717) 787-6239
Fax: (717) 787-0884

PUERTO RICO
Hector Russe
President
Environmental Quality Board
P.O. Box 11488
San Juan, PR 00910-1488
Phone: (787) 767-8056
Fax: (787) 754-8294

RHODE ISLAND
Ronald Gagnon
Director
Ofc. of Technical & Customer Assistance
Dept. of Environmental Mgmt.
235 Promenade St., Rm. 250
Providence, RI 02908
Phone: (401) 222-2797

SOUTH CAROLINA
Hartsill Truesdale
Chief
Bur. of Solid & Hazardous Waste Mgmt.
Dept. of Health & Environmental Control
2600 Bull St.
Columbia, SC 29201
Phone: (803) 896-4000

SOUTH DAKOTA
Vonnie Kallemeyn
Senior Scientist
Environmental Program
Div. of Environmental Regulation Waste Mgmt. Program
523 E. Capitol Ave.
Pierre, SD 57501
Phone: (605) 773-3151
Fax: (605) 773-6035

TENNESSEE
Tom Tiesler
Director
Hazardous Waste Mgmt. Section
Dept. of Environment & Conservation
401 Church St., 5th Fl.
Nashville, TN 37243
Phone: (615) 532-0780
Fax: (615) 532-0886

TEXAS
Leigh Ing
Deputy Director
Ofc. of Waste Mgmt.
Natural Resources Conservation Comm.
P.O. Box 13087
Austin, TX 78711-3087
Phone: (512) 239-2206
Fax: (512) 239-5151

U.S. VIRGIN ISLANDS
Leonard Reed
Acting Director
Environmental Protection Div.
Dept. of Planning & Natural Resources
Foster's Plz., 396-1 Anna's Retreat
St. Thomas, VI 00802
Phone: (340) 777-4577
Fax: (340) 774-5416

UTAH
Dennis R. Downs
Director
Div. of Solid & Hazardous Waste
Dept. of Environmental Quality
288 N. 1460 W.
Salt Lake City, UT 84116
Phone: (801) 538-6775
Fax: (801) 538-6715
E-mail: ddowns@deq.state.ut.us

VERMONT
P. Howard Flanders
Director
Hazardous Materials Mgmt. Div.
Agency of Natural Resources
103 S. Main St.
Waterbury, VT 05671-0404
Phone: (802) 241-3888
Fax: (802) 241-3296

VIRGINIA
Dennis H. Treacy
Director
Dept. of Environmental Quality
629 E. Main St.
Richmond, VA 23219
Phone: (804) 698-4020
Fax: (804) 698-4019

WASHINGTON
Greg Sorlie
Program Manager
Hazardous Waste & Toxic Reduction
Dept. of Ecology
P.O. Box 47600
Olympia, WA 98504-7600
Phone: (360) 407-7150
Fax: (360) 407-6989

WEST VIRGINIA
Max Robertson
Chief
Ofc. of Waste Mgmt.
1356 Hansford St.
Charleston, WV 25301
Phone: (304) 558-5929
Fax: (304) 558-0256

WISCONSIN
Kevin Kessler
Chief
Policy Section
Bur. of Waste Mgmt.
101 S. Webster, 3rd Fl.
P.O. Box 7921
Madison, WI 53707
Phone: (608) 266-7055
Fax: (608) 267-2768

WYOMING
David Finley
Administrator
Solid & Hazardous Waste Div.
Dept. of Environmental Quality
Herschler Bldg.
122 W. 25th St.
Cheyenne, WY 82002
Phone: (307) 777-7753

Health

Enforces public health laws and administers health programs and services in the state.

ALABAMA
Don Williamson
State Health Officer
State Public Health Dept.
201 Monroe St., Ste. 1552
Montgomery, AL 36104
Phone: (334) 206-5200
Fax: (334) 206-2008

ALASKA
Peter Nakamura
Director
Div. of Public Health
Dept. of Health & Social Services
P.O. Box 110610
Juneau, AK 99811-0610
Phone: (907) 465-3090
Fax: (907) 586-1877

AMERICAN SAMOA
Iotamo Saleapaga
Director
Dept. of Health
Pago Pago, AS 96799
Phone: (684) 633-1222
Fax: (684) 633-1869

ARIZONA
James Allen
Director
Dept. of Health Services
1740 W. Adams St.
Phoenix, AZ 85007
Phone: (602) 542-1025
Fax: (602) 542-0883

ARKANSAS
Faye Boozman
Director
Dept. of Health
4815 W. Markham St.
Little Rock, AR 72205
Phone: (501) 661-2111
Fax: (501) 671-1450

CALIFORNIA
S. Kimberly Belshe
Director
Dept. of Health Services
714 P St., Rm. 1253
Sacramento, CA 95814
Phone: (916) 657-1425

COLORADO
Jane E. Norton
Executive Director
Dept. of Public Health & Environment
4300 Cherry Creek Dr., S.
Denver, CO 80246-1530
Phone: (303) 692-2100
Fax: (303) 782-0095

CONNECTICUT
Joxel Garcia
Commissioner
Dept. of Public Health
410 Capitol Ave., MS#13COM
P.O. Box 340308
Hartford, CT 06134
Phone: (860) 509-7101

DELAWARE
Ulder J. Tillman
Director
Div. of Public Health
P.O. Box 637
Dover, DE 19903
Phone: (302) 739-4701
Fax: (302) 739-6659

DISTRICT OF COLUMBIA
Marlene Kelly
Interim Director
Comm. of Public Health
Dept. of Human Services
825 N. Capitol St., NE
Washington, DC 20002
Phone: (202) 442-5999

FLORIDA
Jim Howell
Secretary
Dept. of Health
1317 Winewood Blvd.
Tallahassee, FL 32399-0700
Phone: (850) 487-2945
Fax: (850) 487-3729

GEORGIA
Kathleen E. Toomey
Director
Div. of Public Health
Dept. of Human Resources
2 Peachtree St., Rm. 7-300
Atlanta, GA 30303
Phone: (404) 657-2700

GUAM
Dennis G. Rodriguez
Director
Dept. of Public Health & Social Services
P.O. Box 2816
Hagatna, GU 96932
Phone: (671) 735-7102
Fax: (671) 734-5910
E-mail: dennis_r_@NS.GOV.GU

HAWAII
Bruce Anderson
Director
Dept. of Health
1250 Punchbowl St.
Honolulu, HI 96813
Phone: (808) 586-4410
Fax: (808) 586-4444

IDAHO
Linda Caballero
Director
Dept. of Health & Welfare
450 W. State St., 10th Fl.
P.O. Box 83720
Boise, ID 83720-0036
Phone: (208) 334-5500

ILLINOIS
John Lumpkin
Director
Dept. of Public Health
535 W. Jefferson St.
Springfield, IL 62761
Phone: (217) 782-4977
Fax: (217) 782-3987

INDIANA
Richard Feldman
Commissioner
State Board of Health
2 N. Meridian St.
Indianapolis, IN 46204
Phone: (317) 233-7400
Fax: (317) 233-7387

IOWA
Christopher Atchison
Director
Dept. of Public Health
Lucas State Ofc. Bldg.
321 E. 12th St.
Des Moines, IA 50319
Phone: (515) 281-5605
Fax: (515) 281-4958

KANSAS
Vacant
Secretary
Dept. of Health & Environment
Landon State Ofc. Bldg., 6th Fl.
Topeka, KS 66612-1290
Phone: (785) 296-1500
Fax: (785) 296-1231

KENTUCKY
Rice C. Leach
Commissioner
Health Services Cabinet
Dept. for Public Health
275 E. Main St.
Frankfort, KY 40601
Phone: (502) 564-3970
Fax: (502) 564-6533

LOUISIANA
David Hood
Secretary
Ofc. of Health & Hospitals
P.O. Box 629
Baton Rouge, LA 70821-0629
Phone: (225) 342-9503
Fax: (225) 342-5568

MAINE
Kevin Concannon
Commissioner
Dept. of Human Services
11 State House Station
Augusta, ME 04333
Phone: (207) 287-2736

MARYLAND
Georges C. Benjamin
Secretary
Ofc. of the Secretary
Dept. of Health & Mental Hygiene
201 W. Preston St., 5th Fl.
Baltimore, MD 21201
Phone: (410) 767-6505
Fax: (410) 767-6489

MASSACHUSETTS
Howard K. Koh
Commissioner
Dept. of Public Health
250 Washington St.
Boston, MA 02108-4619
Phone: (617) 624-5200
Fax: (617) 624-5206
E-mail: howard.koh@state.ma.us

MICHIGAN
James K. Haveman, Jr.
Director
Dept. of Community Health
Louis Cass Bldg.
320 S. Walnut
Lansing, MI 48913
Phone: (517) 335-0267
Fax: (517) 335-3090

MINNESOTA
Jan Malcolm
Commissioner
Dept. of Health
85 E. 7th Pl., Ste. 400
Minneapolis, MN 55101
Phone: (651) 296-8401
Fax: (651) 215-5801

MISSISSIPPI
Ed Thompson
State Health Officer
Dept. of Health
2423 N. State St.
P.O. Box 1700
Jackson, MS 39216
Phone: (601) 960-7400
Fax: (601) 960-7931

MISSOURI
Maureen Dempsey
Director
Dept. of Health
920 Wildwood
P.O. Box 570
Jefferson City, MO 65102
Phone: (573) 751-6400
Fax: (573) 751-6041
E-mail: depmsm@mail.health.state.mo.us

MONTANA
Laurie Ekanger
Director
Dept. of Public Health & Human Services
111 Sanders St.
P.O. Box 4210
Helena, MT 59620
Phone: (406) 444-5622
Fax: (406) 444-1970

NEBRASKA

NEVADA
Yvonne Sylva
Administrator
Health Div.
Dept. of Human Resources
505 E. King St., Rm. 201
Carson City, NV 89701-4797
Phone: (775) 684-4200
Fax: (775) 684-4211

NEW HAMPSHIRE
Dianne Luby
Director
Ofc. of Health Mgmt.
Health & Human Services
6 Hazen Dr.
Concord, NH 03301-6527
Phone: (603) 271-4501
Fax: (603) 271-4827

NEW JERSEY
Christine Grant
Commissioner
Dept. of Health & Senior Services
John Fitch Plz.
P.O. Box 413
Trenton, NJ 08625-0413
Phone: (609) 292-7837
Fax: (609) 292-0053

NEW MEXICO
Alex Valdez
Secretary
Dept. of Health
P.O. Box 26110
Sante Fe, NM 87502-6110
Phone: (505) 827-2613
Fax: (505) 827-2530

NEW YORK
Dennis P. Whalen
Executive Deputy Commissioner
Dept. of Health
Corning Tower Bldg., Rm. 1408
Empire State Plz.
Albany, NY 12237
Phone: (518) 473-0458
Fax: (518) 473-5450

NORTH CAROLINA
Andrew McBride
State Health Director
Dept. of Health & Human Services
101 Blair Dr.
Raleigh, NC 27603
Phone: (919) 715-4125
Fax: (919) 733-0513

NORTH DAKOTA
Murray G. Sagsveen
State Health Officer
Dept. of Health
600 E. Blvd. Ave., 2nd Fl. - Judicial Wing
Bismarck, ND 58505-0200
Phone: (701) 328-2372
Fax: (701) 328-4727
E-mail: sagsveen@state.nd.us

NORTHERN MARIANA ISLANDS
Isamu Abraham
Secretary
Ofc. of the Secretary
Public Health
P.O. Box 409 CK
Saipan, MP 96950
Phone: (670) 234-6225
Fax: (670) 234-8930

OHIO
James Baird
Director
Dept. of Health
246 N. High St.
P.O. Box 118
Columbus, OH 43266-0118
Phone: (614) 466-2253
Fax: (614) 644-0085

OKLAHOMA
Jerry Nida
Commissioner
Dept. of Health
1000 NE 10th
Oklahoma City, OK 73117-1299
Phone: (405) 271-4200

OREGON
Elinor C. Hall
Administrator
Health Div.
Dept. of Human Resources
800 NE Oregon St., # 21
Portland, OR 97232
Phone: (503) 731-4000
Fax: (503) 731-4078

PENNSYLVANIA
Dan Hoffman
Secretary
Dept. of Health
Health & Welfare Bldg., Rm. 802
Harrisburg, PA 17120
Phone: (717) 787-6436
Fax: (717) 787-0191

PUERTO RICO
Carmen Feliciano
Secretary
Dept. of Health
P.O. Box 70184
San Juan, PR 00936-0184
Phone: (787) 274-7601
Fax: (787) 250-6547

RHODE ISLAND
Patricia A. Nolan
Director
Dept. of Health
3 Capitol Hill
Providence, RI 02908
Phone: (401) 222-2231
Fax: (401) 222-6548

SOUTH CAROLINA
Doug Bryant
Commissioner
Dept. of Health & Environmental Control
2600 Bull St.
Columbia, SC 29201
Phone: (803) 898-3300

SOUTH DAKOTA
Doneen Hollingsworth
Secretary
Dept. of Health
600 E. Capitol Ave.
Pierre, SD 57501
Phone: (605) 773-3361
Fax: (605) 773-5683

TENNESSEE
Fredia Wadley
Chief Health Officer
Dept. of Health
TN Towers, 9th Fl.
Nashville, TN 37247
Phone: (615) 741-3111
Fax: (615) 741-9879

TEXAS
William R. Archer, III
Commissioner
Dept. of Health
1100 W. 49th St.
Austin, TX 78756
Phone: (512) 458-7375
Fax: (512) 458-7477
E-mail: William.Arch@TDH.state.tx.us

U.S. VIRGIN ISLANDS
Wilbur Callender
Commissioner
Dept. of Health
No. 48 Sugar Estate
St. Thomas, VI 00802
Phone: (340) 774-0117
Fax: (340) 777-4001

UTAH
Rod Betit
Executive Director
Dept. of Health
P.O. Box 142802
Salt Lake City, UT 84114-2802
Phone: (801) 538-6111
Fax: (801) 538-6306
E-mail: rbetit@doh.state.ut.us

Michael Deily
Director
Div. of Health Care Financing
Dept. of Health
P.O. Box 142901
Salt Lake City, UT 84114-2901
Phone: (801) 538-6406
Fax: (801) 538-6478
E-mail: mdeily@doh.state.ut.us

VERMONT
Jan Carney
Commissioner
Dept. of Health
108 Cherry St.
P.O. Box 70
Burlington, VT 05402
Phone: (802) 863-7280
Fax: (802) 863-7425

VIRGINIA
E. Anne Peterson
Acting Commissioner
Dept. of Health
Main St. Station, Rm. 214
1500 E. Main St.
Richmond, VA 23219
Phone: (804) 786-3561
Fax: (804) 786-4616

WASHINGTON
Mary Selecky
Secretary
Dept. of Health
P.O. Box 47890
Olympia, WA 98504-7890
Phone: (360) 586-5846
Fax: (360) 586-7424

WEST VIRGINIA
Joan Ohl
Secretary
Dept. of Health & Human Resources
Capitol Complex, Bldg. 3, Rm. 206
1900 Kanawha Blvd., E.
Charleston, WV 25305
Phone: (304) 558-0684
Fax: (304) 558-1130

WISCONSIN
John Chapin
Administrator
Div. of Health
Dept. of Health & Family Services
1 W. Wilson St., Rm. 218
P.O. Box 309
Madison, WI 53701-0309
Phone: (608) 266-1511
Fax: (608) 267-2832

WYOMING
Garry McKee
Director
Dept. of Health
Hathaway Bldg.
2300 Capitol Ave.
Cheyenne, WY 82002
Phone: (307) 777-7656

Higher Education

Serves as coordinating and planning agency for state-supported post-secondary education.

ALABAMA
Henry J. Hector
Executive Director
Comm. on Higher Education
100 N. Union St.
Montgomery, AL 36130-2000
Phone: (334) 242-2123
Fax: (334) 242-0268

ALASKA
Diane Barrans
Executive Director
Post-secondary Education Comm.
Dept. of Education
3030 Vintage Blvd.
Juneau, AK 99801-7109
Phone: (907) 465-6740
Fax: (907) 465-3293

AMERICAN SAMOA
Salu Hunkin
President
AS Community College
Pago Pago, AS 96799
Phone: (684) 699-9155
Fax: (684) 699-2062

ARIZONA
Verna L. Allen
Executive Director
Comm. for Post-secondary Education
2020 N. Central Ave., Ste. 275
Phoenix, AZ 85004-4503
Phone: (602) 229-2595
Fax: (602) 229-2599

ARKANSAS
Lu Hardin
Director
Dept. of Higher Education
114 E. Capitol
Little Rock, AR 72201
Phone: (501) 371-2000
Fax: (501) 371-2003

CALIFORNIA
Warren H. Fox
Executive Director
Post-secondary Education Comm.
1303 J St., Ste. 500
Sacramento, CA 95814-2932
Phone: (916) 445-1000
Fax: (916) 327-4417

COLORADO
Tim Foster
Executive Director
Comm. on Higher Education
1300 Broadway, 2nd Fl.
Denver, CO 80203
Phone: (303) 866-2723
Fax: (303) 860-9750
E-mail: Tim_Foster@cche.state.co.us

CONNECTICUT
Andrew DeRocco
Commissioner
Board of Higher Education
61 Woodland St.
Hartford, CT 06105
Phone: (860) 947-1801

DELAWARE
Marilyn B. Quinn
Executive Director
Higher Education Comm.
820 N. French St., 4th Fl.
Wilmington, DE 19801
Phone: (302) 577-3240
Fax: (302) 577-3862

DISTRICT OF COLUMBIA
Michelle Hogans
Chair
Board of Trustees
Univ. of DC
4200 Connecticut Ave., NW
Washington, DC 20008
Phone: (202) 282-2070

Julius F. Nimmons, Jr.
Interim President
Univ. of DC
4200 Connecticut Ave., NW
Washington, DC 20008
Phone: (202) 274-5100
Fax: (202) 274-5304

FLORIDA
Adam Herbert
Chancellor
Board of Regents
Dept. of Education
1514 FL Education Ctr.
Tallahassee, FL 32399
Phone: (850) 488-4234
Fax: (850) 922-6565

GEORGIA
Stephen R. Portch
Chancellor
Board of Regents of the Univ. System
270 Washington St., SW, Rm. 7025
Atlanta, GA 30334
Phone: (404) 656-2202

GUAM
Jose T. Nededog
President
College of Science
Univ. of GU
303 Univ. Dr., UOG Station
Mangilao, GU 96923
Phone: (671) 735-2990
Fax: (671) 734-2296
E-mail: nedcode1@uog9.ugo.edu

HAWAII
Kenneth P. Mortimer
President
Univ. of HI
2444 Dole St.
Honolulu, HI 96822
Phone: (808) 956-8207
Fax: (808) 956-5286

IDAHO
Gregory Fitch
Executive Director
State Board of Education
650 W. State St., Rm. 307
Boise, ID 83720
Phone: (208) 334-2270

ILLINOIS
Phil Rock
Executive Director
Board of Higher Education
350 N. LaSalle, Ste. 900
Chicago, IL 60610
Phone: (312) 464-3500
Fax: (312) 464-3525

INDIANA
Stanley G. Jones
Commissioner
Higher Education Comm.
101 W. Ohio St., #550
Indianapolis, IN 46204-1971
Phone: (317) 464-4400
Fax: (317) 464-4410

IOWA
Ted Stilwill
Director
Dept. of Education
Grimes State Ofc. Bldg.
E. 14th & Grand Aves.
Des Moines, IA 50319
Phone: (515) 281-5294
Fax: (515) 242-5988

Frank J. Stork
Executive Director
Board of Regents
Old Historical Bldg.
E. 12th and Grand Aves.
Des Moines, IA 50319
Phone: (515) 281-3934

KANSAS
Kim A. Wilcox
Interim Executive Director
Board of Regents
700 SW Harrison, Ste. 1410
Topeka, KS 66603
Phone: (785) 296-3421
Fax: (785) 296-0983

KENTUCKY
Gordon Davies
President
Council on Post Secondary Education
1024 Capitol Ctr. Dr., Ste. 300
Frankfort, KY 40601
Phone: (503) 573-1550
Fax: (502) 573-1535

LOUISIANA
E. Joseph Savoie
Commissioner of Higher Education
Board of Regents
150 3rd St., Ste. 129
Baton Rouge, LA 70801-1389
Phone: (225) 342-4253
Fax: (225) 342-6926

MAINE
James E. Rier, Jr.
Chair
State Board of Education
Dept. of Education
23 State House Station
Augusta, ME 04333
Phone: (207) 289-2321

MARYLAND
Patricia S. Florestano
Secretary of Higher Education
Ofc. of the Secretary
Higher Education Comm.
16 Francis St.
Annapolis, MD 21401
Phone: (410) 974-2971
Fax: (410) 974-3513
E-mail: pflorest@mhec.state.md.us

MASSACHUSETTS
Stanley Koplik
Chancellor
Board of Higher Education
One Ashburton Pl., Rm. 1401
Boston, MA 02108
Phone: (617) 727-7785

MICHIGAN
James Folkening
Director
Ofc. of Higher Education Services
Dept. of Education
P.O. Box 30008
Lansing, MI 48909
Phone: (517) 373-3820

MINNESOTA
Morrie Anderson
Acting Chancellor
State Colleges & Univ.
700 World Trade Ctr.
30 E. 7th St.
St. Paul, MN 55101
Phone: (651) 296-7971
Fax: (651) 297-3312
E-mail: morrie.anderson@so.mnscu.edu

MISSISSIPPI
Thomas D. Layzell
Commissioner
Institutions of Higher Learning
3825 Ridgewood Rd.
Jackson, MS 39211-6611
Phone: (601) 982-6611
Fax: (601) 987-4172

MISSOURI
Kala M. Stroup
Commissioner
Dept. of Higher Education
3515 Amazonas Dr.
Jefferson City, MO 65109
Phone: (573) 751-2361
Fax: (573) 751-6635
E-mail: stroup?cbhe400@admin.mocbhc.gov

MONTANA
Richard A. Crofts
Commissioner
Comm. of Higher Education
Univ. System
2500 Broadway
Helena, MT 59620
Phone: (406) 444-6570
Fax: (406) 444-1469

NEBRASKA
David R. Powers
Executive Director
Coordinating Comm. for Post-secondary Education
P.O. Box 95005
Lincoln, NE 68509-5005
Phone: (402) 471-2847
Fax: (402) 471-2886

NEVADA
Richard S. Jarvis
Chancellor
Univ. & Community College System
2601 Enterprise Rd.
Reno, NV 89512
Phone: (775) 784-4905
Fax: (775) 784-1127

NEW HAMPSHIRE
James A. Busselle
Executive Director
Post-secondary Education Comm.
2 Industrial Park Dr.
Concord, NH 03301-8512
Phone: (603) 271-2555
Fax: (603) 271-2696

NEW JERSEY
James Sultan
Executive Director
Comm. on Higher Education
P.O. Box 542
Trenton, NJ 08625-0542
Phone: (609) 292-4310
Fax: (609) 292-7225

NEW MEXICO
Bruce Hamlet
Executive Director
Comm. on Higher Education
1068 Cerrillos Rd.
Santa Fe, NM 87501
Phone: (505) 827-7383
Fax: (505) 827-7392

NEW YORK
Richard P. Mills
Commissioner
State Education Dept.
89 Washington Ave., Rm. 111
Albany, NY 12234
Phone: (518) 474-6569
Fax: (518) 473-4909

NORTH CAROLINA
Molly Corbett Broad
President
Administration
Univ. of NC
P.O. Box 2688
Chapel Hill, NC 27515-2688
Phone: (919) 962-1000
Fax: (919) 962-7139

NORTH DAKOTA
Larry Isaak
Chancellor
Univ. System
600 E. Blvd. Ave., 10th Fl.
Bismarck, ND 58505-0230
Phone: (701) 328-2960
Fax: (701) 328-2961
E-mail: larry_isaak@ndus.nodak.edu

NORTHERN MARIANA ISLANDS
Agnes McPhetres
President
Northern Marianas College
P.O. Box 1250
Saipan, MP 96950
Phone: (670) 234-5499
Fax: (670) 234-1270

OHIO
Rod Chu
Chancellor
Board of Regents
30 E. Broad St., 36th Fl.
Columbus, OH 43266-0417
Phone: (614) 466-0887
Fax: (614) 466-5866

OKLAHOMA
Hans Brisch
Chancellor
State Regents for Higher Education
State Capitol Complex
500 Education Bldg.
Oklahoma City, OK 73105
Phone: (405) 524-9100
Fax: (405) 524-9230

OREGON
Joseph W. Cox
Chancellor
Board of Higher Education
P.O. Box 3175
Eugene, OR 97403
Phone: (541) 346-5700
Fax: (541) 346-5764

PENNSYLVANIA
Michael Poliakoff
Commissioner for Higher Education
Dept. of Education
333 Market St., 12th Fl.
Harrisburg, PA 17120
Phone: (717) 787-5041
Fax: (717) 783-0583

PUERTO RICO
Norman I. Maldonado
President
Univ. of PR
P.O. Box 364984
San Juan, PR 00936-4984
Phone: (787) 250-0000
Fax: (787) 759-6917

RHODE ISLAND
Stephen T. Hulbert
Commissioner of Higher Education
301 Promenade St.
Providence, RI 02903-5748
Phone: (401) 222-6560
Fax: (401) 222-2545

SOUTH CAROLINA
Rayburn Barton
Commissioner
Comm. on Higher Education
1333 Main St., Ste. 300
Columbia, SC 29201
Phone: (803) 737-2276

SOUTH DAKOTA
Tad Perry
Executive Director
Board of Regents
213 E. Capitol Ave.
Pierre, SD 57501
Phone: (605) 773-3455
Fax: (605) 773-5320

TENNESSEE
Richard G. Rhoda
Executive Director
Higher Education Comm.
Pkwy. Towers, Ste. 1900
404 James Robertson Pkwy.
Nashville, TN 37243
Phone: (615) 741-3605
Fax: (615) 741-6230

TEXAS
Don Brown
Commissioner
Higher Education
Coordinating Board
7745 Chevy Chase Dr.,
Rm. 5.260
Austin, TX 78752
Phone: (512) 483-6101
Fax: (512) 483-6169

U.S. VIRGIN ISLANDS
Evadney Varlack-Testamark
Executive Director
Board of Education
P.O. Box 11900
St. Thomas, VI 00802
Phone: (340) 774-4546
Fax: (340) 774-3384

UTAH
Cecelia Foxley
Commissioner
Board of Regents
3 Triad Ctr., Ste. 550
Salt Lake City, UT 84180-1205
Phone: (801) 321-7103
Fax: (801) 321-7199
E-mail: cfoxley@utahsbr.edu

VERMONT
Charles Bunting
Chancellor
State Colleges of VT
103 S. Main St.
Waterbury, VT 05676
Phone: (802) 241-2520
Fax: (802) 241-3369

VIRGINIA
William B. Allen
Director
State Council of Higher
Education
101 N. 14th St., 9th Fl.
Richmond, VA 23219
Phone: (804) 255-2600
Fax: (804) 371-7911

WASHINGTON
Marcus S. Gaspard
Executive Director
Higher Education
Coordinating Board
P.O. Box 43430
Olympia, WA 98504-3430
Phone: (360) 753-7800
Fax: (360) 753-7808

WEST VIRGINIA
David Ice
Cabinet Secretary
Ofc. of the Secretary
Dept. of Education and the
Arts
Bldg. 5, Rm. 205
1900 Kanawha Blvd., E.
Charleston, WV 25305
Phone: (304) 558-2440
Fax: (304) 558-1311

Charles Manning
University System
Chancellor
Board of Trustees for
Higher Education
Dept. of Education & the
Arts
1018 Kanawha Blvd., E.
Charleston, WV 25301
Phone: (304) 558-0264
Fax: (304) 558-1011

Clifford M. Trump
Chancellor
State College System
Dept. of Education
1018 Kanawha Blvd., E.
Charleston, WV 25301
Phone: (304) 558-0699
Fax: (304) 558-1011

WISCONSIN

WYOMING
Thomas Henry
Executive Director
Community College Comm.
2020 Carey Ave., 8th Fl.
Cheyenne, WY 82002
Phone: (307) 777-7763
Fax: (307) 777-6567

Highway Safety

Develops and administers a statewide traffic safety program.

ALABAMA
Doug Miller
Chief
Law Enforcement/Traffic Safety Div.
Dept. of Economic & Community Affairs
P.O. Box 5690
Montgomery, AL 36130
Phone: (334) 242-5843
Fax: (334) 242-0712

ALASKA
Mary Moran
Administrator
Hwy. Safety Planning Agency
Dept. of Public Safety
P.O. Box 111200
Juneau, AK 99811
Phone: (907) 465-4371
Fax: (907) 463-5860

AMERICAN SAMOA
Te'o Fuavai
Commissioner
Dept. of Public Safety
AS Govt.
Pago Pago, AS 96799
Phone: (684) 633-1111
Fax: (684) 633-5111

ARIZONA
Joe Albo
Director
Dept. of Public Safety
2102 W. Encanto Blvd.
Phoenix, AZ 85005-6638
Phone: (602) 223-2359
Fax: (602) 223-2917

Alberto Gutier
Director
Governor's Ofc. of Hwy. Safety
3030 N. Central Ave., Ste. 1550
Phoenix, AZ 85012
Phone: (602) 255-3216
Fax: (602) 255-1265

ARKANSAS
Dan Flowers
Director
Dept. of Hwys. & Transportation
P.O. Box 2261
Little Rock, AR 72203
Phone: (501) 569-2211
Fax: (501) 569-2400

CALIFORNIA
Martha Glass
Chief
Div. of Hwys.
Dept. of Transportation
1120 N St., Rm. 440
Sacramento, CA 95814
Phone: (916) 654-6228

COLORADO
John Conger
Director
Ofc. of Transportation Safety
Dept. of Transportation
4201 E. Arkansas Ave., W. Annex
Denver, CO 80222
Phone: (303) 757-9468
Fax: (303) 757-9439

CONNECTICUT
Thomas Perrone
Info. Systems
Dept. of Transportation
2710 Berlin Tpke.
Newington, CT 06131
Phone: (860) 594-2204

DELAWARE
Trisha Roberts
Director
Ofc. of Hwy. Safety
303 Transportation Cir.
Dover, DE 19903
Phone: (302) 739-4475
Fax: (302) 739-5995

DISTRICT OF COLUMBIA
Arthuro V. Lawson
Acting Director
Dept. of Public Works
2000 14th St., NW, 6th Fl.
Washington, DC 20009
Phone: (202) 939-8000
Fax: (202) 939-8191

FLORIDA
Fred O. Dickinson, III
Executive Director
Dept. of Hwy. Safety & Motor Vehicles
Neil Kirkman Bldg., Rm. B443
2900 Apalachee Pky.
Tallahassee, FL 32399-0500
Phone: (850) 487-3132
Fax: (850) 922-6274

GEORGIA
Tim Jones
Director
Governor's Ofc. of Hwy. Safety
1 Park Tower
34 Peachtree St., Ste. 1600
Atlanta, GA 30303
Phone: (404) 656-6996

GUAM
Daniel Lizama
Acting Director
Dept. of Public Works
542 N. Marine Dr.
Tamuning, GU 96911
Phone: (671) 646-3131
Fax: (671) 649-9178

HAWAII
Lawrence K. Hao
Administrator
Motor Vehicle Safety Ofc.
Dept. of Transportation
601 Kamokila Blvd.
Kapolei, HI 96707
Phone: (808) 692-7650
Fax: (808) 692-7665

IDAHO
Marie Bishop
Manager
Hwy. Safety
Dept. of Transportation
P.O. Box 7129
Boise, ID 83707
Phone: (208) 334-8101

ILLINOIS
Roger Sweet
Director
Div. of Traffic Safety
Dept. of Transportation
3215 Executive Park Dr.
Springfield, IL 62794
Phone: (217) 782-4972

INDIANA
Jerry McCory
Director
Governor's Council on Dangerous & Impaired Driving
150 W. Market St., Ste. 330
Indianapolis, IN 46204
Phone: (317) 232-1295
Fax: (317) 233-5150

IOWA
J. Michael Laski
Director
Governor's Traffic Safety Bur.
Dept. of Public Safety
Wallace State Ofc. Bldg.
E. 9th & Grand Aves.
Des Moines, IA 50319
Phone: (515) 281-3907
Fax: (515) 281-6190

KANSAS
Rosalie Thornburgh
Chief
Bur. of Traffic Safety
217 SE 4th, 3rd Fl.
Topeka, KS 66603
Phone: (785) 296-3756
Fax: (785) 291-3010

KENTUCKY
Gary Rose
Commissioner
State Police
Justice Cabinet
919 Versailles Rd.
Frankfort, KY 40601
Phone: (502) 695-6300
Fax: (502) 573-1479

LOUISIANA
James Champagne
Executive Director
Hwy. Safety Comm.
Public Safety & Corrections Dept.
P.O. Box 66614
Baton Rouge, LA 70896
Phone: (225) 925-6991
Fax: (225) 922-0083

MAINE
Richard E. Perkins
Director
Bur. of Highway Safety
164 State House Station
Augusta, ME 04333-0164
Phone: (207) 624-8756

MARYLAND
Thomas Hicks
Director
Ofc. of Traffic & Safety
Dept. of Transportation
7491 Connelley Dr.
Hanover, MD 21076
Phone: (410) 787-5815
E-mail: thicks@sha.state.md.us

MASSACHUSETTS
Nancy J. Luther
Director
Hwy. Safety Bur.
Executive Ofc. of Public Safety
21st Fl., Rm. 2104
100 Cambridge St.
Boston, MA 02202
Phone: (617) 727-5074
Fax: (617) 727-5077

MICHIGAN
Betty J. Mercer
Executive Director
Ofc. of Hwy. Safety Planning
4000 Collins Rd.
P.O. Box 30633
Lansing, MI 48909-8133
Phone: (517) 336-6477

MINNESOTA
Eugene E. Ofstead
Assistant Commissioner
Transportation Research & Investment Mgmt.
Transportation Bldg., 4th Fl.
395 John Ireland Blvd.
St. Paul, MN 55155
Phone: (651) 296-1344
Fax: (651) 282-2656
E-mail: gene.ofstead@dot.state.mn.us

MISSISSIPPI
Ron Sennett
Executive Director
Div. of Public Safety Planning
Dept. of Public Safety
P.O. Box 23039
Jackson, MS 39225-3039
Phone: (601) 359-7880
Fax: (601) 359-7832

MISSOURI
Joyce S. Marshall
Director
Div. of Hwy. Safety
Dept. of Public Safety
1719 Southridge Dr.
P.O. Box 104808
Jefferson City, MO 65110
Phone: (573) 751-4161
Fax: (573) 634-5977
E-mail: jmarshal@mdhs.state.mo.us

MONTANA
Albert E. Goke
Chief
Traffic Safety Bur.
Transportation Planning Div.
Dept. of Transportation
2701 Prospect Ave.
Helena, MT 59620
Phone: (406) 444-7301
Fax: (406) 444-7671

NEBRASKA
Derald Kohles
Administrator
Hwy. Safety & Ofc. Services
Dept. of Rds.
1500 Nebraska Hwy. 2
Lincoln, NE 68509-4759
Phone: (402) 479-4645
Fax: (402) 479-4325

NEVADA
John Drew
Acting Director
Dept. of Motor Vehicles & Public Safety
555 Wright Way
Carson City, NV 89711
Phone: (775) 684-4549
Fax: (775) 684-4692

NEW HAMPSHIRE
Peter Thomson
Coordinator
Hwy. Safety Agency
117 Manchester St.
Concord, NH 03301-5101
Phone: (603) 271-2131
Fax: (603) 271-3790

NEW JERSEY
Peter J. O'Hagan
Director
Div. of Hwy. Traffic Safety
Dept. of Law & Public Safety
P.O. Box 048
Trenton, NJ 08625-0048
Phone: (609) 633-9300
Fax: (609) 633-9020

NEW MEXICO
Darren White
Secretary
Dept. of Public Safety
P.O. Box 1628
Santa Fe, NM 87504-1628
Phone: (505) 827-3370
Fax: (505) 827-3434

NEW YORK
Richard E. Jackson, Jr.
Commissioner
Dept. of Motor Vehicles
Swan St. Bldg., 5th Fl.
Empire State Plz.
Albany, NY 12228
Phone: (518) 473-9324
Fax: (518) 474-9578

NORTH CAROLINA
Joe M. Parker
Director
Governor's Hwy. Safety Program
Dept. of Transportation
215 E. Ln.
Raleigh, NC 27603
Phone: (919) 733-3083
Fax: (919) 733-0604

NORTH DAKOTA
Marsha Lembke
Director
Driver's License & Traffic Safety
Dept. of Transportation
608 E. Blvd. Ave.
Bismarck, ND 58505-0700
Phone: (701) 328-2601
Fax: (701) 328-2435
E-mail: mlembke@state.nd.us

NORTHERN MARIANA ISLANDS
Claudio K. Norita
Director
Hwy. Safety
Dept. of Public Safety
Ofc. of the Governor
Saipan, MP 96950
Phone: (670) 234-6021
Fax: (670) 234-8531
E-mail: cnmi.dps.ohsfp@saipan.com

OHIO
Maureen O'Connor
Director
Dept. of Public Safety
1970 W. Broad St.
Columbus, OH 43223-1102
Phone: (614) 466-3383
Fax: (614) 466-0433

OKLAHOMA
Joe McDonald
Director
Hwy. Safety Ofc.
Dept. of Public Safety
3223 N. Lincoln Blvd.
Oklahoma City, OK 73105
Phone: (405) 521-3314
Fax: (405) 524-4906

OREGON
Troy Costales
Manager
Transportation Safety
Dept. of Transportation
555 13th St., NE
Salem, OR 97310
Phone: (503) 986-4192
Fax: (503) 986-4189

PENNSYLVANIA
Betty Serian
Deputy Secretary
Safety Administration
Dept. of Transportation
1200 Transportation & Safety Bldg.
1101 S. Front St., 4th Fl.
Harrisburg, PA 17104
Phone: (717) 787-3928
Fax: (717) 705-1046

PUERTO RICO
Magaly Melendez
Executive Director
Traffic Safety Comm.
P.O. Box 41289
Minillas Station
Santurce, PR 00940
Phone: (787) 721-4142
Fax: (787) 727-0486

RHODE ISLAND
Edward Walsh
Coordinator
Div. of Hwy. Safety
Dept. of Transportation
345 Harris Ave.
Providence, RI 02909
Phone: (401) 222-3024

SOUTH CAROLINA
Burke Fitzpatrick
Administrator
Ofc. of Safety Grant Services
Dept. of Public Safety
5410 Broad River Rd.
Columbia, SC 29210
Phone: (803) 896-7844

SOUTH DAKOTA
David Volk
Secretary
Div. of Insurance
Dept. of Commerce & Regulation
118 W. Capitol Ave.
Pierre, SD 57501-2017
Phone: (605) 773-3178
Fax: (605) 773-3018

TENNESSEE
Mike Greene
Commissioner
Dept. of Safety
1150 Foster Ave.
Nashville, TN 37249
Phone: (615) 251-5165
Fax: (615) 251-2091

TEXAS
Tom Newbern
Director
Traffic Operations Div.
Dept. of Transportation
118 E. Riverside
Austin, TX 78704
Phone: (512) 416-3200
Fax: (512) 416-3214

U.S. VIRGIN ISLANDS
Franz A. Christian, Sr.
Acting Commissioner
Police Dept.
8172 Sub Base
St. Thomas, VI 00802
Phone: (340) 774-6400
Fax: (340) 776-3317

UTAH
K. Craig Allred
Director
Hwy. Safety Ofc.
Dept. of Public Safety
5263 S. 300 W., Ste. 202
Murray, UT 84107-5307
Phone: (801) 293-2481
Fax: (801) 293-2498
E-mail: callred.pshs@state.ut.us

VERMONT
Jeanne Johnson
Coordinator
Governor's Hwy. Safety Program
Public Safety
103 S. Main St.
Waterbury, VT 05671-2501
Phone: (802) 244-1317
Fax: (802) 244-1106

VIRGINIA
Vince Burgess
Transportation Safety Administrator
Transportation Safety
Dept. of Motor Vehicles
P.O. Box 27412
Richmond, VA 23269
Phone: (804) 367-8140
Fax: (804) 367-6631

WASHINGTON
John Moffat
Director
Traffic Safety Comm.
1000 S. Cherry St.
P.O. Box 40944
Olympia, WA 98504
Phone: (360) 753-6197
Fax: (360) 586-6489

WEST VIRGINIA
William Wilshire
Division Director
Traffic Engineering
Div. of Hwys.
State Capitol, Bldg. 5, Rm. 550
1900 Kanawha Blvd., E.
Charleston, WV 25305
Phone: (304) 558-3722
Fax: (304) 558-1209

WISCONSIN

WYOMING
Gene Roccabruna
Director
Hwy. Safety Div.
Dept. of Transportation
5300 Bishop Blvd.
Cheyenne, WY 82002
Phone: (307) 777-4198

Highways

Responsible for planning, developing, designing, constructing and maintaining the state's highways.

ALABAMA
G.M. Roberts
Director
Hwy. Dept.
Dept. of Transportation
1409 Coliseum Blvd.
Montgomery, AL 36130
Phone: (334) 242-6311
Fax: (334) 262-8041

ALASKA
Thomas Brigham
Director
Div. of Statewide Planning
Dept. of Transportation & Public Facilities
3132 Channel Dr.
Juneau, AK 99801-7898
Phone: (907) 465-4070
Fax: (907) 465-6984

AMERICAN SAMOA

ARIZONA
Thomas G. Schmitt
State Engineer
Hwys. Div.
Dept. of Transportation
206 S. 17th Ave., Rm. 133
Phoenix, AZ 85007
Phone: (602) 255-7391

ARKANSAS
Dan Flowers
Director
Dept. of Hwys. & Transportation
P.O. Box 2261
Little Rock, AR 72203
Phone: (501) 569-2211
Fax: (501) 569-2400

CALIFORNIA
Martha Glass
Chief
Div. of Hwys.
Dept. of Transportation
1120 N St., Rm. 440
Sacramento, CA 95814
Phone: (916) 654-6228

COLORADO
Tom Norton
Executive Director
Dept. of Transportation
4201 E. Arkansas Ave.
Denver, CO 80222
Phone: (303) 757-9201
Fax: (303) 757-9657

CONNECTICUT
Harry P. Harris
Deputy Commissioner
Engineering & Hwy. Operations
Dept. of Transportation
2800 Berlin Tpke.
P.O. Box 317546
Newington, CT 06131-7546
Phone: (860) 594-2800

DELAWARE
Anne P. Canby
Secretary
Dept. of Transportation
P.O. Box 778
Dover, DE 19903
Phone: (302) 739-4303
Fax: (302) 739-5736
E-mail: acanby@smtp.dot.state.de.us

DISTRICT OF COLUMBIA
Gary Burch
Chief Transportation Engineer
Div. of Transportation
2000 14th St., NW
Washington, DC 20009
Phone: (202) 939-8060

FLORIDA
Thomas Barry, Jr.
Secretary
Director's Ofc.
Dept. of Transportation
Haydon Burns Bldg.
605 Suwannee St.
Tallahassee, FL 32399-0450
Phone: (850) 414-5205
Fax: (850) 488-5526
E-mail: tom.barry@dot.state.fl.us

GEORGIA
Wayne Shackelford
Commissioner
Dept. of Transportation
2 Capitol Sq.
Atlanta, GA 30334
Phone: (404) 656-5206

GUAM
Daniel Lizama
Acting Director
Dept. of Public Works
542 N. Marine Dr.
Tamuning, GU 96911
Phone: (671) 646-3131
Fax: (671) 649-9178

HAWAII
Pericles Manthos
Administrator
Hwys. Div.
Dept. of Transportation
869 Punchbowl St.
Honolulu, HI 96813
Phone: (808) 587-2220
Fax: (808) 587-2219

IDAHO
Dwight Bower
Director
Dept. of Transportation
P.O. Box 7129
Boise, ID 83707
Phone: (208) 334-8800

ILLINOIS
James C. Slifer
Director
Div. of Hwys.
Dept. of Transportation
2300 S. Dirksen Pkwy., Rm. 300
Springfield, IL 62764
Phone: (217) 782-2151

INDIANA
Curtis A. Wiley
Commissioner
Dept. of Transportation
IGC-North, Rm. N755
Indianapolis, IN 46204
Phone: (317) 232-5525
Fax: (317) 232-0238

IOWA
Tom Cackler
Director
Hwy. Div.
Dept. of Transportation
800 Lincoln Way
Ames, IA 50010
Phone: (515) 239-1124

KANSAS
E. Dean Carlson
Secretary
Dept. of Transportation
Docking State Ofc. Bldg.
915 Harrison, 7th Fl.
Topeka, KS 66612-1568
Phone: (785) 296-3566
Fax: (785) 296-1095

KENTUCKY
Mac Yowell
State Highway Engineer
Transportation Cabinet
501 High St.
State Ofc. Bldg., 10th Fl.
Frankfort, KY 40601
Phone: (502) 564-3730
Fax: (502) 564-2277

LOUISIANA
Kam Movassaghi
Secretary
Dept. of Transportation & Dev.
P.O. Box 94245
Baton Rouge, LA 70804
Phone: (225) 379-1201
Fax: (225) 379-1851

MAINE
John Melrose
Commissioner
Dept. of Transportation
16 State House Station
Augusta, ME 04333
Phone: (207) 287-2551

MARYLAND
Parker F. Williams
Administrator
State Highway Administration
Dept. of Transportation
707 N. Calvert St.
Baltimore, MD 21202
Phone: (410) 545-0400
E-mail: pwilliams@sha.state.md.us

MASSACHUSETTS
Matthew Amorello
Commissioner
Hwy. Dept.
10 Park Plz., Rm. 3510
Boston, MA 02116
Phone: (617) 973-7800
Fax: (617) 973-8040

MICHIGAN
James R. De Sana
Director
Dept. of Transportation
425 W. Ottawa
Lansing, MI 48909
Phone: (517) 373-2114
Fax: (517) 373-5457

MINNESOTA
Patrick C. Hughes
Assistant Commissioner
Operations Div.
Dept. of Transportation
Transportation Bldg., 4th Fl.
395 John Ireland Blvd.
St. Paul, MN 55155
Phone: (651) 296-3156
Fax: (651) 296-6135

MISSISSIPPI
Kenneth Warren
Director
Dept. of Transportation
P.O. Box 1850
Jackson, MS 39215-1850
Phone: (601) 359-7001
Fax: (601) 359-7050

MISSOURI
Henry Hungerbeeler
Director
Dept. of Transportation
Support Ctr.
P.O. Box 270
Jefferson City, MO 65102
Phone: (573) 751-4622
Fax: (573) 526-5419
E-mail: hungeh@mail.modot.state.mo.us

MONTANA
Marvin Dye
Director
Dept. of Transportation
2701 Prospect Ave.
Helena, MT 59620
Phone: (406) 444-6201
Fax: (406) 444-7643

NEBRASKA
John Craig
Director
Dept. of Rds.
P.O. Box 94759
Lincoln, NE 68509
Phone: (402) 479-4615
Fax: (402) 479-4325

NEVADA
Tom Stephens
Director
Dept. of Transportation
1263 S. Stewart St., Rm. 201
Carson City, NV 89712
Phone: (775) 888-7440
Fax: (775) 888-7201

NEW HAMPSHIRE
Leon S. Kenison
Commissioner
Dept. of Transportation
P.O. Box 483
Concord, NH 03302-0483
Phone: (603) 271-3734
Fax: (603) 271-3914

NEW JERSEY
James Weinstein
Commissioner of Transportation
Dept. of Transportation
1035 Pkwy. Ave.
P.O. Box 600
Trenton, NJ 08625-0600
Phone: (609) 530-3536
Fax: (609) 530-3894

NEW MEXICO
Pete Rahn
Secretary
Dept. of Hwys. & Transportation
P.O. Box 1149
Santa Fe, NM 87504
Phone: (505) 827-5110
Fax: (505) 827-5469

NEW YORK
Joseph Boardman
Commissioner
Dept. of Transportation
State Ofc. Bldg. Campus, Bldg. 5
Albany, NY 12232
Phone: (518) 457-4422
Fax: (518) 457-5583

NORTH CAROLINA
Len Sanderson
Highway Administrator
Dept. of Transportation
1 S. Wilmington St.
Raleigh, NC 27601-1494
Phone: (919) 733-7384
Fax: (919) 733-9428

NORTH DAKOTA
Marshall W. Moore
Director
Dept. of Transportation
608 E. Blvd. Ave.
Bismarck, ND 58505-0700
Phone: (701) 328-2500
Fax: (701) 328-1420
E-mail: mmoore@state.nd.us

NORTHERN MARIANA ISLANDS
Edward M. Deleon Guerrero
Secretary
Dept. of Public Works
Lower Base
P.O. Box 2950
Saipan, MP 96950
Phone: (670) 235-5827
Fax: (670) 235-5253

OHIO
Gordon Proctor
Director
Dept. of Transportation
1980 W. Broad St.
Columbus, OH 43223
Phone: (614) 466-7170
Fax: (614) 644-8662

OKLAHOMA
Neal McCaleb
Director
Dept. of Transportation
200 NE 21st St.
Oklahoma City, OK 73105
Phone: (405) 521-2631
Fax: (405) 521-2093

OREGON
Grace Crunican
Director
Dept. of Transportation
135 Transportation Bldg.
355 Capitol St.
Salem, OR 97310
Phone: (503) 986-3200
Fax: (503) 986-4264

PENNSYLVANIA
Mike M. Ryan
Deputy Secretary
Hwy. Administration
Dept. of Transportation
Forum Pl., 9th Fl.
555 Walnut St.
Harrisburg, PA 17101-1900
Phone: (717) 787-5574
Fax: (717) 787-5491

PUERTO RICO
Sergio Gonzales
Executive Director
Hwys. Authority & Transportation
P.O. Box 42007
San Juan, PR 00940-2007
Phone: (787) 721-8787
Fax: (787) 727-5456

RHODE ISLAND
William Ankner
Director
Dept. of Transportation
Two Capitol Hill
Providence, RI 02908
Phone: (401) 222-2481
Fax: (401) 222-6038

SOUTH CAROLINA
Elizabeth S. Mabry
Executive Director
Dept. of Transportation
955 Park St.
P.O. Box 191
Columbia, SC 29202
Phone: (803) 737-1302

SOUTH DAKOTA
Jim Jenssen
Director
Planning & Engineering
Dept. of Transportation
700 E. Broadway
Pierre, SD 57501-2586
Phone: (605) 773-3267
Fax: (605) 773-3921

TENNESSEE
Bruce Saltsman
Commissioner
Dept. of Transportation
James K. Polk Bldg., Ste. 700
Nashville, TN 37243
Phone: (615) 741-2848
Fax: (615) 741-2508

TEXAS
Charles Heald
Executive Director
Dept. of Transportation
D.C. Greer Bldg., 2nd Fl.
125 E. 11th St.
Austin, TX 78701
Phone: (512) 305-9501
Fax: (512) 305-3050

U.S. VIRGIN ISLANDS
Aloy Nielsen
Director
Hwy. Engineering
Dept. of Public Works
Sub Base # 8
St. Thomas, VI 00802
Phone: (340) 776-4844
Fax: (340) 774-5869

UTAH
Thomas R. Warne
Executive Director
Administration
Dept. of Transportation
4501 S. 2700 W.
Salt Lake City, UT 84119-5998
Phone: (801) 965-4113
Fax: (801) 965-4338
E-mail: twarne@dot.state.ut.us

VERMONT
Glenn Gershaneck
Secretary
Agency of Transportation
133 State St.
Montpelier, VT 05633-5001
Phone: (802) 828-2657
Fax: (802) 828-3522

VIRGINIA
David R. Gehr
Commissioner
Dept. of Transportation
1401 E. Broad St.
Richmond, VA 23219
Phone: (804) 786-2701
Fax: (804) 786-2940

WASHINGTON
Sid Morrison
Secretary
Dept. of Transportation
P.O. Box 47316
Olympia, WA 98504-7316
Phone: (360) 705-7000
Fax: (360) 705-6808

WEST VIRGINIA
Samuel H. Beverage
Commissioner
Div. of Hwys.
Bldg. 5, Rm. A109
1900 Kanawaha Blvd., E.
Charleston, WV 25305
Phone: (304) 558-0444
Fax: (304) 558-1004

WISCONSIN
Frederic Ross
Administrator
Div. of Hwys. & Transportation Service
Dept. of Transportation
4802 Sheboygan Ave., Rm. 951
P.O. Box 7916
Madison, WI 53707
Fax: (608) 266-7818

WYOMING
Gene Roccabruna
Director
Hwy. Safety Div.
Dept. of Transportation
5300 Bishop Blvd.
Cheyenne, WY 82002
Phone: (307) 777-4198

Historic Preservation

Surveys, restores and preserves structures and/ or sites of historical or architectural significance in the state.

ALABAMA
Lee Warner
Executive Director
Historical Comm.
468 S. Perry St.
Montgomery, AL 36130
Phone: (334) 242-3184
Fax: (334) 240-3477

ALASKA
Judy Bittner
Historical Comm.
Dept. of Natural Resources
3601 C St., Ste. 1278
Anchorage, AK 99503-5921
Phone: (907) 762-2626
Fax: (907) 762-2622

AMERICAN SAMOA
John Enright
Chair
Historic Preservation Cmte.
AS Govt.
Pago Pago, AS 96799
Phone: (684) 633-9513

ARIZONA
James W. Garrison
State Historic Preservation Officer
Historic Preservation Div.
State Parks Board
1300 W. Washington
Phoenix, AZ 85007
Phone: (602) 542-4009

ARKANSAS
Cathy Slater
Director
Historic Preservation
1500 Tower Bldg.
323 Ctr. St.
Little Rock, AR 72201
Phone: (501) 324-9150
Fax: (501) 324-9184

CALIFORNIA
Cherilyn Widell
Historic Preservation Officer
State Historic Preservation
Dept. of Parks & Recreation
P.O. Box 942896
Sacramento, CA 94296
Phone: (916) 653-6624

COLORADO
Georgianna Contiguglia
President & State Historic Preservation Officer
State Historical Society
Dept. of Higher Education
1300 Broadway
Denver, CO 80203
Phone: (303) 866-3355
Fax: (303) 866-4464

CONNECTICUT
John W. Shannahan
Director
Historical Comm.
59 S. Prospect St.
Hartford, CT 06106
Phone: (860) 566-3005

DELAWARE
Daniel R. Griffith
Director
Historical & Cultural Affairs
Hall of Records
P.O. Box 1401
Dover, DE 19903
Phone: (302) 739-5313
Fax: (302) 739-5660

DISTRICT OF COLUMBIA
Stephen J. Raiche
Chief
Historic Preservation Div.
Dept. of Consumer & Regulatory Affairs
614 8th St., NW, Ste. 312
Washington, DC 20001
Phone: (202) 727-7360
Fax: (202) 727-8040

FLORIDA
George W. Percy
Director
Div. of Historical Resources
Dept. of State
R.A. Gray Bldg.
500 S. Bronough St.
Tallahassee, FL 32399-0250
Phone: (850) 488-1480
Fax: (850) 488-3353

GEORGIA
Mark R. Edwards
Director
Historic Preservation Div.
Dept. of Natural Resources
500 The Healey Bldg.
57 Forsyth St., NW
Atlanta, GA 30303
Phone: (404) 656-2840
Fax: (404) 651-8739

GUAM
Austin J. Shelton
Director
Dept. of Parks & Recreation
13-8 Seagull Ave.
Hagatna, GU 96932
Phone: (671) 475-6296
Fax: (671) 472-9626

HAWAII
Timothy Johns
Chair
Dept. of Land & Natural Resources
1151 Punchbowl St.
Honolulu, HI 96813
Phone: (808) 587-0400
Fax: (808) 587-0390

IDAHO
Steve Guerber
Interim Director
Historical Society
1109 Main St., Ste. 250
Boise, ID 83702-5642
Phone: (208) 334-2682

ILLINOIS
Susan Mogerman
Director
Historic Preservation Agency
313 S. 6th St.
Springfield, IL 62701
Phone: (217) 785-7930
Fax: (217) 785-7937

INDIANA
Jon Smith
Director
Historic Preservation & Archaeology
Dept. of Natural Resources
IGC S., Rm. W274
Indianapolis, IN 46204
Phone: (317) 232-1646
Fax: (317) 232-0693

IOWA
Tom Morain
Administrator
State Historical Society
Dept. of Cultural Affairs
Historical Bldg.
600 E. Locust
Des Moines, IA 50319
Phone: (515) 281-8837
Fax: (515) 242-6498

KANSAS
Ramon Powers
Executive Director
State Historical Society
6425 SW 6th Ave.
Topeka, KS 66615-1099
Phone: (785) 272-8681
Fax: (785) 272-8682

KENTUCKY
Kevin Gaffagnino
Director
Historical Society
Old Capitol Annex
P.O. Box H
Frankfort, KY 40601
Phone: (502) 564-3016
Fax: (502) 564-4701

LOUISIANA
Jonathan Fricker
Director
Culture, Recreation & Tourism
P.O. Box 44247
Baton Rouge, LA 70804
Phone: (225) 342-8160
Fax: (225) 342-8173

MAINE
Earle Shettleworth, Jr.
Executive Director
Historic Preservation Comm.
65 State House Station
Augusta, ME 04333
Phone: (207) 287-2132

MARYLAND
J. Rodney Little
Director
Historical & Cultural Programs
Dept. of Housing & Community Dev.
100 Community Pl.
Crownsville, MD 21032
Phone: (410) 514-7601
Fax: (410) 987-4071

MASSACHUSETTS
Judith B. McDonough
Executive Director
Historical Comm.
Archives Bldg.
220 William T. Morrissey Blvd.
Boston, MA 02125-3314
Phone: (617) 727-8470
Fax: (617) 727-5128

MICHIGAN
Sandra Clark
Director
Bur. of History
Dept. of State
717 W. Allegan
Lansing, MI 48918
Phone: (517) 373-6362

MINNESOTA
Nina Archabal
Director
Historical Society
345 Kellogg Blvd., W.
St. Paul, MN 55102-1906
Phone: (651) 296-2747
Fax: (651) 282-2374
E-mail: mnshpo@mnhs.org

MISSISSIPPI
Elbert R. Hilliard
Director
Dept. of Archives & History
P.O. Box 571
Jackson, MS 39205-0571
Phone: (601) 359-6881
Fax: (601) 359-6975

MISSOURI
Claire F. Blackwell
Director
Historic Preservation Program
Dept. of Natural Resources
Lohman Bldg.,
100 Jefferson St.
P.O. Box 176
Jefferson City, MO 65102
Phone: (573) 751-7858
Fax: (573) 526-2852
E-mail: nrblacc @mail.dnr.state.mo.us

MONTANA
Paul Putz
Preservation Officer
Preservation Reference Services
Historical Society
1410 8th Ave.
Helena, MT 59620
Phone: (406) 444-7717
Fax: (406) 444-6575

NEBRASKA
Lawrence J. Sommer
Director
State Historical Society
P.O. Box 82554
Lincoln, NE 68501-2554
Phone: (402) 471-4745
Fax: (402) 471-3100

NEVADA
Ronald M. James
State Historic Preservation Officer
Historic Preservation
Museums, Library & Arts
100 N. Stewart St.
Carson City, NV 89701
Phone: (775) 687-6360
Fax: (775) 687-3442
E-mail: rmjames @clan.lib.nv.us

NEW HAMPSHIRE
Van McLeod
Commissioner
Historical Resources
Dept. of Cultural Affairs
19 Pillsbury St.
Concord, NH 03301-3570
Phone: (603) 271-3483
Fax: (603) 271-3433

NEW JERSEY
James F. Hall
Assistant Commissioner
Natural & Historic Resources
Dept. of Environmental Protection
501 E. State St.
P.O. Box 404
Trenton, NJ 08625-0404
Phone: (609) 292-3541
Fax: (609) 984-0836

NEW MEXICO
Lynne Sebastian
Historic Preservation Officer
Historic Preservation Div.
Cultural Affairs Ofc.
228 E. Palace Ave.
Santa Fe, NM 87501
Phone: (505) 827-6320
Fax: (505) 827-7308

NEW YORK
Bernadette Castro
Commissioner
Ofc. of Parks, Recreation & Historic Preservation
Agency Bldg. 1, 20th Fl.
Empire State Plz.
Albany, NY 12238
Phone: (518) 474-0443
Fax: (518) 474-1365

NORTH CAROLINA
David Brook
Administrator
Archaeology & Historic Preservation
Dept. of Cultural Resources
507 N. Blount St.
Raleigh, NC 27604-1190
Phone: (919) 733-4763
Fax: (919) 733-8653

NORTH DAKOTA
Merl Paaverud
Director
Archaeology & Historic Preservation
State Historical Society
612 E. Blvd. Ave.
Bismarck, ND 58505
Phone: (701) 328-2672
Fax: (701) 328-3710
E-mail: mpaaveru @state.nd.us

NORTHERN MARIANA ISLANDS
Joseph P. Guerrero
Director
Historic Preservation Ofc.
Community & Cultural Affairs
Ofc. of the Governor
Saipan, MP 96950
Phone: (617) 664-2120
Fax: (670) 664-2139
E-mail: cnmihpo @itccnmi.com

OHIO
Amos Loveday
Director
Historical Society
1982 Velma Ave.
Columbus, OH 43211
Phone: (614) 297-2300
Fax: (614) 297-2352

OKLAHOMA
J. Blake Wade
Director
Historical Society
Historical Bldg.
2100 N. Lincoln Blvd.
Oklahoma City, OK 73105
Phone: (405) 521-2491
Fax: (405) 521-2492

OREGON
Chet Orloff
Executive Director
Historical Society
1220 SW Park Ave.
Portland, OR 97205
Phone: (503) 222-1741
Fax: (503) 221-2035

PENNSYLVANIA
Brenda Barrett
Director
Bur. of Historic Preservation
Historical & Museum Comm.
P.O. Box 1026
Harrisburg, PA 17108
Phone: (717) 783-5321
Fax: (717) 772-0920

PUERTO RICO
Lilliane Lopez
Executive Director
Historic Preservation Ofc.
P.O. Box 82
La Fortaleza
San Juan, PR 00901
Phone: (787) 721-3737
Fax: (787) 723-0957

RHODE ISLAND
Edward F. Sanderson
Executive Director
Historical Preservation & Heritage Comm.
150 Benefit St.
Providence, RI 02903
Phone: (401) 222-2678

SOUTH CAROLINA
Mary Edmonds
Deputy State Preservation Officer
Dept. of Archives & History
P.O. Box 11669
Columbia, SC 29211
Phone: (803) 896-6168

SOUTH DAKOTA
Mary B. Edelen
Director
State Historical Society
Cultural Heritage Ctr.
900 Governors Dr.
Pierre, SD 57501
Phone: (605) 773-3458
Fax: (605) 773-6041

TENNESSEE
Herbert Harper
Executive Director
Historical Comm.
Dept. of Environment & Conservation
2941 Lebanon Rd.
Nashville, TN 37243
Phone: (615) 532-1550
Fax: (615) 532-1549

TEXAS
Curtis Tunnell
Executive Director
Historical Comm.
P.O. Box 12276
Austin, TX 78711
Phone: (512) 463-6100
Fax: (512) 475-4872
E-mail: thcnueces@thc.state.tx.us

U.S. VIRGIN ISLANDS
Eric Christian
Assistant Director
Historic Preservation Div.
Dept. of Planning & Natural Resources
Foster's Plz., 396-1 Anna's Retreat
St. Thomas, VI 00802
Phone: (340) 776-8605
Fax: (340) 776-7236

UTAH
Max Evans
Director
Div. of State History
Dept. of Community & Economic Dev.
300 Rio Grande
Salt Lake City, UT 84101
Phone: (801) 533-3551
Fax: (801) 533-3503
E-mail: mevans@history.state.ut.us

VERMONT
Eric Gilbertson
Director
Div. for Historic Preservation
Agency of Commerce & Community Affairs
109 State St.
Montpelier, VT 05609
Phone: (802) 828-3211
Fax: (802) 828-3206

VIRGINIA
H. Alexander Wise, Jr.
Director
Dept. of Historic Resources
2801 Kensington Ave.
Richmond, VA 23221
Phone: (804) 367-2323
Fax: (804) 367-2391

WASHINGTON
David Hansen
Acting State Historic Preservation Officer
Archaeology & History Preservation
Dept. of Community Dev.
P.O. Box 48343
Olympia, WA 98504-8343
Phone: (360) 407-0752
Fax: (360) 586-3582

WEST VIRGINIA
Susan Pierce
Deputy Historic Preservation Officer
Div. of Culture & History
Cultural Ctr.
1900 Kanawha Blvd., E.
Charleston, WV 25305
Phone: (304) 558-0220
Fax: (304) 558-2779

WISCONSIN
Alicia L. Goehring
Administrator
Historic Preservation Div.
State Historical Society
816 State St., Rm. 300
Madison, WI 53706
Phone: (608) 264-6500
Fax: (608) 264-6504

WYOMING
John Keck
State Historic Preservation Officer
Div. of Parks & Cultural Resources
Dept. of Commerce
6101 Yellowstone
Cheyenne, WY 82002
Phone: (307) 777-6696

Horse Racing

Licenses and regulates horse racing in the state.

ALABAMA

ALASKA

AMERICAN SAMOA

ARIZONA
James H. Higginbottom
Director
Dept. of Racing
3877 N. 7th St., Ste. 201
Phoenix, AZ 85014-5072
Phone: (602) 277-1704
Fax: (602) 277-1165

ARKANSAS
Carole Kessler
Manager
State Racing Comm.
Finance & Administration Dept.
101 E. Capitol, Ste. 114
Little Rock, AR 72203
Phone: (501) 682-1467
Fax: (501) 682-5273

CALIFORNIA
Ralph Scurfield
Chair
Horse Racing Board
1010 Hurley Way, Rm. 190
Sacramento, CA 95825
Phone: (916) 446-7211

COLORADO
Larry Huls
Director
Div. of Racing Events
Dept. of Revenue
1881 Pierce St.
Lakewood, CO 80214
Phone: (303) 205-2990
Fax: (303) 205-2950

CONNECTICUT
Thomas Rotunda
Executive Director
Div. of Special Revenue
Dept. of Revenue Services
555 Russell Rd.
Newington, CT 06111
Phone: (860) 594-0501
Fax: (860) 594-0696

DELAWARE
John Wayne
State Racing Commissioner
State Harness Racing Comm.
Dept. of Agri.
2320 S. DuPont Hwy.
Dover, DE 19901
Phone: (302) 739-4811
Fax: (302) 571-1253

Patricia Yossick
Administrative Assistant
Div. of Resource Mgmt.
Dept. of Agri.
2320 S. DuPont Hwy.
Dover, DE 19901
Phone: (302) 739-4811
Fax: (302) 697-6287

DISTRICT OF COLUMBIA

FLORIDA
Debra Miller
Director
Div. of Pari-Mutuel Wagering
Dept. of Business & Professional Regulation
1940 N. Monroe St.
Tallahassee, FL 32399-1035
Phone: (850) 488-9130
Fax: (850) 488-0550

GEORGIA

GUAM

HAWAII

IDAHO
Jack Baker
Executive Director
State Racing Comm.
Dept. of Law Enforcement
P.O. Box 700
Meridian, ID 83680-0700
Phone: (208) 884-7080

ILLINOIS
Jack Kubik
Executive Director
State Racing Board
100 W. Randolph, Ste. 11-100
Chicago, IL 60601
Phone: (312) 814-2600
Fax: (312) 814-5062

INDIANA
Joe Gorajec
Executive Director
Horse Racing Comm.
150 W. Market St., # 412
Indianapolis, IN 46204-2810
Phone: (317) 233-3121
Fax: (317) 233-4470

IOWA
Jack Ketterer
Administrator
Racing & Gaming Comm.
Dept. of Inspections & Appeals
Lucas State Ofc. Bldg.
321 E. 12th St.
Des Moines, IA 50319
Phone: (515) 281-7352

KANSAS
Tracy Diel
Executive Director
State Gaming Comm.
700 SW Jackson, Ste. 200
Topeka, KS 66612
Phone: (785) 368-6202
Fax: (785) 291-3798

Myron Scafe
Executive Director
Kansas Racing Comm.
3400 Van Buren
Topeka, KS 66611-2228
Phone: (785) 296-5800
Fax: (785) 296-0900

KENTUCKY
Smitty Taylor
Chair
State Racing Comm.
4063 Iron Works Pike
Lexington, KY 40511-8462
Phone: (606) 246-2040
Fax: (606) 246-2039

LOUISIANA
Paul Burgess
Executive Director
State Racing Comm.
Dept. of Commerce
320 N. Carrollton., Ste. 2B
New Orleans, LA 70119
Phone: (504) 483-4000
Fax: (504) 483-4898

MAINE
Henry Jackson
Director
Harness Racing Comm.
Dept. of Agri., Food & Rural Resources
28 State House Station
Augusta, ME 04333
Phone: (207) 287-3871

MARYLAND
Kenneth A. Schertle
Executive Director
Racing Comm.
Dept. of Labor, Licensing & Regulation
501 St. Paul Pl.
Baltimore, MD 21202-2272
Phone: (410) 230-6330
Fax: (410) 333-8308

MASSACHUSETTS
Robert Hutchinson
Chair
State Racing Comm.
One Ashburton Pl., Rm. 1313
Boston, MA 02108
Phone: (617) 727-2581
Fax: (617) 227-6062

MICHIGAN
Dan Wyant
Acting Racing Commissioner
Dept. of Agri.
37650 Professional Ctr. Dr.
Livonia, MI 48154-1114
Phone: (734) 462-2400
Fax: (734) 462-2429

MINNESOTA
Richard Krueger
Executive Director
Racing Comm.
P.O. Box 630
Shakopee, MN 55379-0630
Phone: (651) 496-7950
Fax: (651) 496-7954
E-mail: richard.krueger@state.mn.us

MISSISSIPPI

MISSOURI
Kevin Mullally
Deputy Director
Gaming Comm.
3417 Knipp Dr.
Jefferson City, MO 65109
Phone: (573) 526-4083
Fax: (573) 526-1999
E-mail: kmullall
@mail.state.mo.us

MONTANA
Sam Murfitt
Executive Secretary
Board of Horse Racing
Dept. of Commerce
1424 9th Ave.
Helena, MT 59620
Phone: (406) 444-4287
Fax: (406) 444-4305

NEBRASKA
Dennis Oelschlager
Executive Secretary
Racing Comm.
P.O. Box 95014
Lincoln, NE 68509-5014
Phone: (402) 471-2577
Fax: (402) 471-2339

NEVADA
Steve DuCharme
Chair
State Gaming Control
Board
1919 E. College Pkwy.
Carson City, NV 89706
Phone: (775) 687-6500
Fax: (775) 687-5817

NEW HAMPSHIRE
Paul Kelley
Director
Pari-Mutuel Comm.
Carrigain Commons
244 N. Main St.
Concord, NH 03301-5041
Phone: (603) 271-2158
Fax: (603) 271-3381

NEW JERSEY
Frank Zanzuccki
Executive Director
Racing Comm.
Dept. of Law & Public
Safety
140 E. Front St.
P.O. Box 088
Trenton, NJ 08625-0088
Phone: (609) 292-0613
Fax: (609) 599-1785

NEW MEXICO
Julian Luna
Executive Director
State Racing Comm.
300 San Mateo, NE,
Ste. 110
Albuquerque, NM 87108
Phone: (505) 841-6400
Fax: (505) 841-6413

NEW YORK
Michael J. Hoblock, Jr.
Chair
State Racing & Wagering
Board
1 Watervliet Ave. Ext., Ste. 2
Albany, NY 12206-1668
Phone: (518) 453-8460
Fax: (518) 453-8490

NORTH CAROLINA

NORTH DAKOTA
Roger Reule
Racing Commissioner
Racing Comm.
Attorney Gen's. Ofc.
900 E. Blvd. Ave.
Bismarck, ND 58505-0041
Phone: (701) 328-4633
Fax: (701) 328-4300
E-mail: msmail.rreule
@ranch.state.nd.us

NORTHERN MARIANA ISLANDS

OHIO
Clifford A. Nelson, II
Executive Director
State Racing Comm.
77 S. High St., 18th Fl.
Columbus, OH 43266-0416
Phone: (614) 466-2757
Fax: (614) 466-1900

OKLAHOMA
Gordon Hare
Executive Director
Horse Racing Comm.
2614 Villa Prom
Oklahoma City, OK 73107
Phone: (405) 943-6472
Fax: (405) 943-6474

OREGON
Steven W. Barham
Executive Secretary
Racing Comm.
800 NE Oregon St., #11,
Ste. 405
Portland, OR 97232-2109
Phone: (503) 731-4052
Fax: (503) 731-4053

PENNSYLVANIA
Ben H. Nolt, Jr.
Executive Director
Horse Racing Comm.
Dept. of Agri.
Agri. Bldg., Rm. 304
Harrisburg, PA 17110
Phone: (717) 787-1942
Fax: (717) 787-2271

PUERTO RICO
Juan A. Alves Rueda
Administrator
Horse Racing
Administration
P.O. Box 29156
San Juan, PR 00929
Phone: (787) 768-2005
Fax: (787) 762-1105

RHODE ISLAND
Mario R. Forte
Chief of Hearings &
Investigations
Div. of Racing & Athletics
Dept. of Business
Regulation
Richmond St.
Providence, RI 02903
Phone: (401) 222-6541

SOUTH CAROLINA

SOUTH DAKOTA
Larry Eliason
Executive Secretary
Div. of Gaming
Dept. of Commerce &
Regulation
118 E. Missouri
Pierre, SD 57501
Phone: (605) 773-6050
Fax: (605) 773-3018

TENNESSEE

TEXAS
Paula C. Flowerday
Executive Director
Racing Comm.
P.O. Box 12080
Austin, TX 78711
Phone: (512) 833-6699
Fax: (512) 833-6907

U.S. VIRGIN ISLANDS
Trevor James
Chair
Horse Racing Comm.
P.O. Box 774
Frederiksted
St. Croix, VI 00840
Phone: (340) 773-0160
Fax: (340) 773-3150

UTAH

VERMONT
Harlan Sylvester
Chair
Racing Comm.
128 Merchants Row
Rutland, VT 05701
Phone: (802) 786-5050
Fax: (802) 786-5051

VIRGINIA
Donald R. Price
Executive Secretary
Racing Comm.
10700 Horsemen's Rd.
New Kent, VA 23124
Phone: (804) 966-4200
Fax: (804) 966-8906

WASHINGTON
Bruce Batson
Executive Secretary
Horse Racing Comm.
7912 Martin Way, Ste. D
P.O. Box 40906
Olympia, WA 98504-0906
Phone: (360) 459-6462
Fax: (360) 459-6461

WEST VIRGINIA
Robert Burke
Chair
Racing Comm.
106 Dee Dr.
Charleston, WV 25311
Phone: (304) 558-2150
Fax: (304) 558-6319

WISCONSIN
Scott Scepaniak
Division Administrator
Gaming Board
Dept. of Administration
2005 W. Beltline Hwy.,
Ste. 201
P.O. Box 8979
Madison, WI 53708-8979
Phone: (608) 270-2555
Fax: (608) 270-2564

WYOMING
Frank Lamb
Executive Director
Pari-Mutuel Comm.
6101 Yellowstone
Cheyenne, WY 82002
Phone: (307) 777-5928

Housing Finance

Administers the state's housing assistance programs, provides low- and moderate-income housing by financing low-interest loans.

ALABAMA
Robert Strickland
Director
State Housing Finance Authority
P.O. Box 230909
Montgomery, AL 36123-0909
Phone: (334) 244-9200
Fax: (334) 244-9214

ALASKA
Dan Fauske
Executive Director
State Housing Finance Corp.
P.O. Box 101020
Anchorage, AK 99510
Phone: (907) 561-1900
Fax: (907) 561-0364

AMERICAN SAMOA
Meloma Afuola
President
Dev. Bank
Pago Pago, AS 96799
Phone: (684) 633-4031
Fax: (684) 633-1163

ARIZONA
Steve Capobres
Director
Financial Services & Housing Dev.
Dept. of Commerce
3800 N. Central
Phoenix, AZ 85012
Phone: (602) 280-1365

ARKANSAS
Rush Deacon
Director
Dev. Finance Authority
100 Main St., Ste. 200
P.O. Box 8023
Little Rock, AR 72203-8023
Phone: (501) 682-5900
Fax: (501) 682-5939

CALIFORNIA
Theresa Parker
Executive Director
Housing Finance Agency
1121 L St., 7th Fl.
Sacramento, CA 95814
Phone: (916) 322-3991

COLORADO
Tom Hart
Director
Div. of Housing
Dept. of Local Affairs
1313 Sherman St., Rm. 518
Denver, CO 80203
Phone: (303) 866-2033
Fax: (303) 866-4077

CONNECTICUT
Gary E. King
President/Executive Director
Housing Finance Authority
999 West St.
Rocky Hill, CT 06067
Phone: (860) 721-9501

DELAWARE
Susan W. Frank
Director
State Housing Authority
18 The Green
Dover, DE 19901
Phone: (302) 739-4263
Fax: (302) 739-6122

DISTRICT OF COLUMBIA
Richard Monteith
Director
Dept. of Housing & Community Dev.
801 N. Capital St., NE, 6th Fl.
Washington, DC 20002
Phone: (202) 442-7200
Fax: (202) 442-7090

FLORIDA
Susan Leigh
Executive Director
Housing Finance Agency
Dept. of Community Affairs
227 N. Bronough St., Ste. 5000
Tallahassee, FL 32301
Phone: (850) 488-4197
Fax: (850) 488-9809

GEORGIA
David Pinson
Division Director
Housing Finance
Dept. of Community Affairs
60 Executive Park S., NE
Atlanta, GA 30329-2231
Phone: (404) 679-0607

GUAM
James G. Sablan
President
Housing Corp.
6-5000 E. Sunset Blvd., Tiyan
P.O. Box 3457
Hagatna, GU 96932
Phone: (671) 475-4927
Fax: (671) 477-7409

HAWAII
Donald Lau
Executive Director
Housing Finance & Dev. Corp.
Dept. of Budget & Finance
677 Queen St., Ste. 300
Honolulu, HI 96813
Phone: (808) 587-0680
Fax: (808) 587-3416

IDAHO
Gerald M. Hunter
Executive Director
Housing & Finance Assoc.
P.O. Box 7899
Boise, ID 83707-1899

ILLINOIS
John Varones
Executive Director
Housing Dev. Authority
401 N. Michigan Ave.
Chicago, IL 60611
Phone: (312) 836-5337
Fax: (312) 836-5313

INDIANA
Robert Welch
Executive Director
Housing Finance Authority
115 W. Washington St., Ste. 1350, S.
Indianapolis, IN 46204
Phone: (317) 232-7788
Fax: (317) 232-7778

IOWA
Ted Chapler
Executive Director
State Finance Authority
Dept. of Economic Dev.
200 E. Grand Ave., Ste. 222
Des Moines, IA 50309
Phone: (515) 242-4490

KANSAS
Randy Speaker
Director
Housing Div.
Dept. of Commerce & Housing
700 SW Harrison, Ste. 1300
Topeka, KS 66603-3712
Phone: (785) 296-5865
Fax: (785) 296-8985

KENTUCKY
Lynn Luallen
Executive Director
Housing Corp.
1231 Louisville Rd.
Frankfort, KY 40601
Phone: (502) 564-7057
Fax: (502) 564-5708

LOUISIANA
V. Jean Butler
President
Housing Finance Agency
200 Lafayette St., Ste. 300
Baton Rouge, LA 70801-1203
Phone: (225) 342-1320
Fax: (225) 342-1310

MAINE
David Lakari
Director
State Housing Authority
89 State House Station
Augusta, ME 04333
Phone: (207) 626-4600

MARYLAND
Roy Westlund
Deputy Director
Finance
Dept. of Housing & Community Dev.
100 Community Pl.
Crownsville, MD 21032
Phone: (410) 514-7411

MASSACHUSETTS
Steve Pierce
Executive Director
Housing Finance Agency
1 Beacon St.
Boston, MA 02108
Phone: (617) 854-1000
Fax: (617) 854-1029

MICHIGAN
Jim Logue
Director
State Housing Dev. Authority
Consumer & Industry Services
401 S. Washington Sq.
Lansing, MI 48909
Phone: (517) 373-6022

MINNESOTA
Katherine Hadley
Commissioner
Housing Finance Agency
400 Sibley St., Ste. 300
St. Paul, MN 55101-1998
Phone: (651) 296-3738
Fax: (651) 296-8139
E-mail: kit.hadley@state.mn.us

MISSISSIPPI
Diane Bolen
Executive Director
Home Corp.
P.O. Box 23369
Jackson, MS 39225-3369
Phone: (601) 354-6062
Fax: (601) 354-7076

MISSOURI
Richard Grose
Director
Housing Dev. Comm.
Dept. of Economic Dev.
3435 Broadway
Kansas City, MO 64111-2415
Phone: (816) 759-6600
Fax: (816) 759-6608
E-mail: rgrose@mhdc.com

MONTANA
Maureen Rude
Administrator
Housing Div.
Dept. of Commerce
836 Front St.
Helena, MT 59620
Phone: (406) 444-3040
Fax: (406) 444-4688

NEBRASKA
Lara Huskey
Housing Coordinator
Dept. of Economic Dev.
P.O. Box 94666
Lincoln, NE 68509
Phone: (402) 471-3759
Fax: (402) 471-3778

NEVADA
Charles L. Horsey, III
Administrator
Housing Div.
Dept. of Business & Industry
1802 N. Carson St., Ste. 154
Carson City, NV 89701
Phone: (775) 885-4258
Fax: (775) 687-4040
E-mail: nhd@govmail.state.nv.us

NEW HAMPSHIRE
Claira P. Monier
Executive Director
Housing Finance Authority
32 Constitution Dr.
Bedford, NH 03110
Phone: (800) 439-7247
Fax: (603) 472-8501

NEW JERSEY
Deborah DeSantis
Assistant Executive Director
Housing & Mortgage Finance Agency
P.O. Box 18550
Trenton, NJ 08650-2085
Phone: (609) 278-7400
Fax: (609) 278-1754

NEW MEXICO
James Stretz
Executive Director
Mortage Finance Authority
344 4th St., SW
Albuquerque, NM 87102
Phone: (505) 843-6880
Fax: (505) 243-3289

NEW YORK
Stephen Hunt
Executive Director
State Housing Finance Agency
641 Lexington Ave.
New York, NY 10022
Phone: (212) 688-4000
Fax: (212) 872-0301

NORTH CAROLINA
Robert Kucab
Director
Housing Finance Agency
3801 Lake Boone Trail
Raleigh, NC 27607
Phone: (919) 781-6115
Fax: (919) 571-4960

NORTH DAKOTA
Pat Fricke
Executive Director
Housing Finance Agency
P.O. Box 1535
Bismarck, ND 58502-1535
Phone: (701) 328-8080
Fax: (701) 328-8090
E-mail: ndhfa@btigate.com

NORTHERN MARIANA ISLANDS
Marylou A. Sirote
Corporate Director
Housing Corp.
P.O. Box 514
Saipan, MP 96950
Phone: (670) 234-7689
Fax: (670) 234-9021

OHIO
Richard Everhart
Executive Director
Housing Finance Agency
Dept. of Dev.
77 S. High St., 26th Fl.
Columbus, OH 43266-0101
Phone: (614) 466-7970
Fax: (614) 644-5393

OKLAHOMA
Dennis Shockley
Executive Director
Housing Finance Agency
1140 NW 63rd St., Ste. 200
Oklahoma City, OK 73116
Phone: (405) 848-1144
Fax: (405) 840-1109

OREGON
Bob Repine
Director
Dept. of Housing & Community Services
1600 State St.
Salem, OR 97310
Phone: (503) 986-2005
Fax: (503) 986-2020

PENNSYLVANIA
William C. Bostic
Executive Director
Housing Finance Agency
P.O. Box 8029
Harrisburg, PA 17105-8029
Phone: (717) 780-3911
Fax: (717) 780-3905

PUERTO RICO
Mildred Goyco
President
Housing Finance Bank
Housing Dept.
P.O. Box 345
Hato Rey, PR 00919
Phone: (787) 765-2537

RHODE ISLAND
Richard H. Godfrey, Jr.
Executive Director
Housing & Mortgage Finance
44 Washington St.
Providence, RI 02903-1721
Phone: (401) 751-5566

SOUTH CAROLINA
David M. Leopard
Executive Director
State Housing Authority
P.O. Box 2326
Columbia, SC 29202-2326
Phone: (803) 734-2277

SOUTH DAKOTA
Darlys J. Baum
Executive Director
Housing Dev. Authority
P.O. Box 1237
Pierre, SD 57501-1237
Phone: (605) 773-3181
Fax: (605) 773-5154

TENNESSEE
Jeff Reynolds
Director
Housing Dev. Agency
404 James Robertson Pkwy., Rm. 1114
Nashville, TN 37243-0900
Phone: (615) 741-2473
Fax: (615) 741-9634

TEXAS
Daisy Stiner
Acting Executive Director
Dept. of Housing & Community Affairs
507 Sabine, Ste. 400
Austin, TX 78701
Phone: (512) 475-5000
Fax: (512) 472-8526

U.S. VIRGIN ISLANDS
Claude Richards, Jr.
Acting Executive Director
Housing Finance Authority
P.O. Box 308760
St. Thomas, VI 00803
Phone: (340) 774-4481
Fax: (340) 775-7913

UTAH
William H. Erickson
Executive Director
Housing Finance Agency
554 S. 300 E.
Salt Lake City, UT 84111
Phone: (801) 521-6950
Fax: (801) 359-1701
E-mail: wericksо@uhfa.state.ut.us

VERMONT
Allan Hunt
Executive Director
Housing Finance Agency
1 Burlington Sq.
P.O. Box 408
Burlington, VT 05402
Phone: (802) 864-5743
Fax: (802) 864-5746

VIRGINIA
John Ritchie, Jr.
Executive Director
Housing Dev. Authority
601 S. Belvidere St.
Richmond, VA 23220-6504
Phone: (804) 343-5701
Fax: (804) 783-6704

WASHINGTON
Kim Herman
Executive Director
Housing Finance Comm.
1000 2nd Ave., Ste. 2700
Seattle, WA 98104-1046
Phone: (206) 464-7139
Fax: (206) 464-7222

WEST VIRGINIA
Joe Hatfield
Executive Director
Housing Dev. Fund
814 Virginia St., E.
Charleston, WV 25301
Phone: (304) 345-6475
Fax: (304) 345-4828

WISCONSIN
J. Frederick Ruf
Executive Director
Housing & Economic Dev. Authority
201 W. Washington Ave., Ste. 700
P.O. Box 1728
Madison, WI 53703
Phone: (608) 266-7884
Fax: (608) 267-1099

WYOMING
George Auxlund
Executive Director
Community Dev. Authority
123 S. Durbin
Casper, WY 82602
Phone: (307) 265-0603

Human Resources

Umbrella human resources agency that has overall responsibility for the administration of public assistance, medical care and other human services.

ALABAMA
Tony Petelos
Commissioner
Dept. of Human Resources
50 N. Ripley St.
Montgomery, AL 36130-4000
Phone: (334) 242-1310
Fax: (334) 242-0198

ALASKA
James Nordlund
Director
Div. of Public Assistance
Dept. of Health & Social Services
P.O. Box 110640
Juneau, AK 99811-0640
Phone: (907) 465-3347
Fax: (907) 465-5154

AMERICAN SAMOA
Sapini Siatu'u
Director
Dept. of Human Resources
AS Govt.
Pago Pago, AS 96799
Phone: (684) 633-4485
Fax: (684) 633-1139

ARIZONA
Phyllis Beidess
Director
Health Care Cost Containment System
801 E. Jefferson
Phoenix, AZ 85034
Phone: (602) 417-4680
Fax: (602) 252-6536

John Clayton
Director Designate
Dept. of Economic Security
1717 W. Jefferson
Phoenix, AZ 85007
Phone: (602) 542-5678
Fax: (602) 542-5339

ARKANSAS
Kurt Knickrehm
Director
Dept. of Human Services
P.O. Box 1437, Slot 316
Little Rock, AR 72203
Phone: (501) 682-8650
Fax: (501) 682-6836

CALIFORNIA
Sandra R. Smoley
Secretary
Health & Welfare Agency
1600 9th St., Rm. 460
Sacramento, CA 95814
Phone: (916) 445-6951

COLORADO
Marva Livingston Hammons
Executive Director
Dept. of Human Services
1575 Sherman St., 8th Fl.
Denver, CO 80203-1714
Phone: (303) 866-5096
Fax: (303) 866-4740

CONNECTICUT
Pat Wilson-Coker
Commissioner
Dept. of Social Services
25 Sigourney St.
Hartford, CT 06106
Phone: (860) 424-5008

DELAWARE
Elaine Archangelo
Director
Div. of Social Services
P.O. Box 906
New Castle, DE 19720
Phone: (302) 421-6734
Fax: (302) 577-4405

DISTRICT OF COLUMBIA
Jearline F. Williams
Director
Dept. of Human Services
2700 M.L. King, Jr. Ave., SE
Washington, DC 20032
Phone: (202) 279-6002
Fax: (202) 279-6014

FLORIDA
Douglas M. Cook
Executive Director
Agency for Health Care Administration
2727 Mahan Dr., Bldg. 3, Ste. 3116
Tallahassee, FL 32308
Phone: (850) 922-5527
Fax: (850) 488-0043

GEORGIA
Tommy Olmstead
Commissioner
Dept. of Human Resources
2 Peachtree St., NW, Rm. 29-250
Atlanta, GA 30334
Phone: (404) 656-5680

GUAM
Dennis G. Rodriguez
Director
Dept. of Public Health & Social Services
P.O. Box 2816
Hagatna, GU 96932
Phone: (671) 735-7102
Fax: (671) 734-5910
E-mail: dennis_r_@NS.GOV.GU

HAWAII
Susan Chandler
Director
Dept. of Human Services
1390 Miller St.
Honolulu, HI 96813
Phone: (808) 586-4997
Fax: (808) 586-4890

IDAHO
Linda Caballero
Director
Dept. of Health & Welfare
450 W. State St., 10th Fl.
P.O. Box 83720
Boise, ID 83720
Phone: (208) 334-5500

ILLINOIS
Howard A. Peters, III
Secretary
Dept. of Human Services
100 S. Grand Ave., E.
Springfield, IL 62762
Phone: (217) 557-1606

INDIANA
Peter Sybinsky
Secretary
Family & Social Services Administration
402 W. Washington St., W461
Indianapolis, IN 46204
Phone: (317) 233-4690
Fax: (317) 233-4693

IOWA
Charles Palmer
Director
Dept. of Human Services
Hoover State Ofc. Bldg.
1300 E. Walnut
Des Moines, IA 50319
Phone: (515) 281-5452
Fax: (515) 281-4597

KANSAS
Rochelle Chronister
Secretary
Dept. of Social & Rehabilitative Services
Docking State Ofc. Bldg.
915 Harrison, Rm. 603N
Topeka, KS 66612
Phone: (785) 296-3271
Fax: (785) 296-4685

KENTUCKY
Viola Miller
Secretary
Families & Children Cabinet
275 E. Main St.
Frankfort, KY 40621
Phone: (502) 564-7130
Fax: (502) 564-3866

John Morse
Secretary
Health Services Cabinet
275 E. Main St.
Frankfort, KY 40621
Phone: (502) 564-7130
Fax: (502) 564-3866

LOUISIANA
David Hood
Secretary
Ofc. of Health & Hospitals
P.O. Box 629
Baton Rouge, LA 70821-0629
Phone: (225) 342-9503
Fax: (225) 342-5568

MAINE
Kevin Concannon
Commissioner
Dept. of Human Services
11 State House Station
Augusta, ME 04333
Phone: (207) 287-2736

MARYLAND
Lynda G. Fox
Secretary
Ofc. of the Secretary
Dept. of Human Resources
Saratoga Ctr.
311 W. Saratoga St.
Baltimore, MD 21201
Phone: (410) 767-7109
Fax: (410) 333-0099

MASSACHUSETTS
William D. O'Leary
Secretary
Executive Ofc. of Health & Human Services
One Ashburton Pl., Rm. 1109
Boston, MA 02108
Phone: (617) 727-7600
Fax: (617) 727-1396

MICHIGAN
Douglas Howard
Director
Family Independence Agency
P.O. Box 30037
Lansing, MI 48909
Phone: (517) 373-2000
Fax: (517) 373-8471

MINNESOTA
Michael O'Keefe
Commissioner
Dept. of Human Services
444 Lafayette Rd., 2nd Fl.
St. Paul, MN 55155
Phone: (651) 296-2701
Fax: (651) 296-5868

MISSISSIPPI
Don Taylor
Executive Director
Dept. of Human Services
P.O. Box 352
Jackson, MS 39205
Phone: (601) 354-4500
Fax: (601) 359-4477

MISSOURI
Gary Stangler
Director
Dept. of Social Services
221 W. High, Rm. 240
P.O. Box 1527
Jefferson City, MO 65102
Phone: (573) 751-4815
Fax: (573) 751-3203
E-mail: gstangle@mail.state.mo.us

MONTANA
Laurie Ekanger
Director
Dept. of Public Health & Human Services
111 Sanders St.
P.O. Box 4210
Helena, MT 59620
Phone: (406) 444-5622
Fax: (406) 444-1970

NEBRASKA
Ron Ross
Director
Dept. of Health & Human Services
P.O. Box 95044
Lincoln, NE 68509
Phone: (402) 471-2306
Fax: (402) 471-0820

NEVADA
Charlotte Crawford
Director
Dept. of Human Resources
Kinkaid Bldg., Rm. 600
505 E. King St.
Carson City, NV 89701
Phone: (775) 684-4000
Fax: (775) 684-4010
E-mail: charlott@govmail.state.nv.us

NEW HAMPSHIRE
Dianne Luby
Director
Ofc. of Health Mgmt.
Health & Human Services
6 Hazen Dr.
Concord, NH 03301-6527
Phone: (603) 271-4501
Fax: (603) 271-4827

NEW JERSEY
Michele K. Guhl
Commissioner
Div. of Mgmt. & Budget
Dept. of Human Services
222 S. Warren St.
P.O. Box 717
Trenton, NJ 08625-0717
Phone: (609) 292-3717
Fax: (609) 292-3824

NEW MEXICO
Alex Valdez
Secretary
Dept. of Human Services
P.O. Box 2348
Santa Fe, NM 87504
Phone: (505) 827-7750
Fax: (505) 827-6286

NEW YORK
Brian Wing
Commissioner
Ofc. of Temporary & Disability Assistance
40 N. Pearl St., 16th Fl.
Albany, NY 12243
Phone: (518) 473-8772
Fax: (518) 486-6255

NORTH CAROLINA
David Bruton
Secretary
Dept. of Human Resources
Adams Bldg.
101 Blair Dr.
Raleigh, NC 27626-0526
Phone: (919) 733-4534
Fax: (919) 715-4645

NORTH DAKOTA
Carol K. Olson
Executive Director
Dept. of Human Services
600 E. Blvd. Ave., 3rd Fl. - Judicial Wing
Bismarck, ND 58505-0250
Phone: (701) 328-2310
Fax: (701) 328-2359
E-mail: socols@state.nd.us

NORTHERN MARIANA ISLANDS
Isamu Abraham
Secretary
Health Services
Commonwealth Health Ctr.
P.O. Box 409
Saipan, MP 96950
Phone: (670) 234-6225
Fax: (670) 234-8930

Thomas A. Tebuteb
Secretary
Dept. of Community & Cultural Affairs
P.O. Box 10007
Saipan, MP 96950
Phone: (670) 664-2571
Fax: (670) 664-2570

OHIO
Jacqui Sensky
Director
Dept. of Human Services
30 E. Broad St., 32nd Fl.
Columbus, OH 43266-0423
Phone: (614) 466-6282
Fax: (614) 466-2815

OKLAHOMA
Howard Hendrick
Director
Human Services
Dept. of Human Services
P.O. Box 25352
Oklahoma City, OK 73125
Phone: (405) 521-3646
Fax: (405) 521-6458

OREGON
Gary Weeks
Director
Dept. of Human Resources
500 Summer St., NE, 4th Fl.
Salem, OR 97310-1012
Phone: (503) 945-5944
Fax: (503) 378-2897

PENNSYLVANIA
Feather Houstoun
Secretary
Dept. of Public Welfare
Health & Welfare Bldg., Rm. 333
Harrisburg, PA 17120
Phone: (717) 787-2600
Fax: (717) 772-2062

PUERTO RICO
Angie Varela
Secretary
Dept. of Social Services
P.O. Box 11398
San Juan, PR 00910
Phone: (787) 722-7400
Fax: (787) 723-1223

RHODE ISLAND
Christine Ferguson
Director
Dept. of Human Services
600 New London Ave.
Cranston, RI 02920
Phone: (401) 462-2121
Fax: (401) 462-3677

SOUTH CAROLINA
Elizabeth G. Patterson
Director
Dept. of Social Services
1535 Confederate Ave., Extension
Columbia, SC 29202
Phone: (803) 898-7360

Donna Traywick
Director
Ofc. of Human Resources
Budget & Control Board
1201 Main St., Ste. 1000
Columbia, SC 29201
Phone: (803) 737-0900
Fax: (803) 737-0968

SOUTH DAKOTA
John Jones
Secretary
Dept. of Human Services
Hillsview Plz.
500 E. Capitol Ave.
Pierre, SD 57501
Phone: (605) 773-5990
Fax: (605) 773-5483

TENNESSEE
Natasha Metcalf
Commissioner
Dept. of Human Services
Citizens Plz., 15th Fl.
400 Deaderick St.
Nashville, TN 37248-0001
Phone: (615) 313-4700
Fax: (615) 741-4165

TEXAS
Don A. Gilbert
Commissioner
Health & Human Services Comm.
P.O. Box 13247
Austin, TX 78711
Phone: (512) 424-6502
Fax: (512) 424-6587

U.S. VIRGIN ISLANDS
Sedonie Halbert
Commissioner
Dept. of Human Services
Knud Hansen Complex, Bldg. A
1303 Hospital Grounds
St. Thomas, VI 00802
Phone: (340) 774-0930
Fax: (340) 774-3466

UTAH
Robert C. Gross
Executive Director
Ofc. of the Executive Director
Dept. of Workforce Services
140 E. 300 S.
Salt Lake City, UT 84111
Phone: (801) 526-9207
Fax: (801) 526-9211
E-mail: rgross.wsadmpo@state.ut.us

VERMONT
Cornelius Hogan
Secretary
Agency of Human Services
103 S. Main St.
Waterbury, VT 05671
Phone: (802) 241-2220
Fax: (802) 241-2979

VIRGINIA
Claude A. Allen
Secretary of Health & Human Resources
Governor's Cabinet
202 N. 9th St., Ste. 622
Richmond, VA 23219
Phone: (804) 786-7765
Fax: (804) 371-6984

WASHINGTON
Lyle Quasim
Secretary
Dept. of Social & Health Services
P.O. Box 45010
Olympia, WA 98504-5010
Phone: (360) 902-8400
Fax: (360) 902-7848

WEST VIRGINIA
Joan Ohl
Secretary
Dept. of Health & Human Resources
Capitol Complex, Bldg. 3, Rm. 206
1900 Kanawha Blvd., E.
Charleston, WV 25305
Phone: (304) 558-0684
Fax: (304) 558-1130

WISCONSIN

WYOMING

Information Systems

Provides statewide computer services or coordinates the operation of various data processing systems within state government.

ALABAMA
Eugene J. Akers
Director
Data Systems Mgmt. Div.
Dept. of Finance
64 N. Union St.
Montgomery, AL 36130
Phone: (334) 242-0900
Fax: (334) 242-3228

ALASKA
Mark Badger
Director
Div. of Info. Services
Dept. of Administration
P.O. Box 110206
Juneau, AK 99811-0206
Phone: (907) 465-2220
Fax: (907) 465-3450

AMERICAN SAMOA
Tifi Ale
Treasurer
Dept. of the Treasury
AS Govt.
Pago Pago, AS 96799
Phone: (684) 633-4155
Fax: (684) 633-4100

ARIZONA
Bill Parker
Assistant Director
Info. Services Div.
Dept. of Administration
1616 W. Adams St.
Phoenix, AZ 85007
Phone: (602) 542-2250
Fax: (602) 542-4272

ARKANSAS
Michael Hipp
Director
Dept. of Info. Systems
P.O. Box 3155
Little Rock, AR 72203
Phone: (501) 682-2701
Fax: (501) 682-4310

CALIFORNIA
John Thomas Flynn
Chief Information Officer
801 K St., #2100
Sacramento, CA 95814-3701
Phone: (916) 657-0318

COLORADO
Len Meyer
Interim Chief Information Officer
Info. Technology Services
Support Services/Dept. of Personnel
1525 Sherman, Rm. 100
Denver, CO 80203
Phone: (303) 239-4313
Fax: (303) 866-2168

CONNECTICUT
Greg Regan
Chief Information Officer & Technical Services
Dept. of Info. Technology
340 Capitol Ave.
Hartford, CT 06106
Phone: (860) 566-7093

DELAWARE
John J. Nold
Director
Ofc. of Info. Systems
801 Silver Lake Blvd.
Dover, DE 19904-2407
Phone: (302) 739-9629
Fax: (302) 739-6251
E-mail: nold@ois.state.de.us

DISTRICT OF COLUMBIA
Suzanne Peck
Chief Technology Officer
Info. Resources Mgmt. Administration
Dept. of Administration Services
441 4th St., NW, Rm. 750
Washington, DC 20001
Phone: (202) 727-2277

FLORIDA
Linda Nelson
Acting Director
Div. of Info. Services
Dept. of Mgmt. Services
Bldg. 4030, Ste. 180
4050 Esplanade Way
Tallahassee, FL 32399
Phone: (850) 487-2914
Fax: (850) 487-2329

GEORGIA
Bob Simpson
Director
Info. Technology
Dept. of Adm. Services
200 Piedmont Ave.
Atlanta, GA 30334
Phone: (404) 656-3992

GUAM
Michael J. Reidy
Director
Dept. of Administration
P.O. Box 884
Hagatna, GU 96932
Phone: (671) 475-1101
Fax: (671) 477-6788

HAWAII
Lester Nakamura
Division Head
Info. & Communication Services
Dept. of Accounting & Services
1151 Punchbowl St., Basement
Honolulu, HI 96813
Phone: (808) 586-1910
Fax: (808) 586-1922

IDAHO
Pamela Ahrens
Director
Dept. of Administration
650 W. State St., Rm. 100
Boise, ID 83720
Phone: (208) 334-3382

ILLINOIS
Michael S. Schwartz
Director
Dept. of Central Mgmt. Services
715 Stratton Ofc. Bldg.
401 S. Spring
Springfield, IL 62706
Phone: (217) 782-2141
Fax: (217) 524-1880

INDIANA
Laura Larimer
Director
Info. Services Div.
Dept. of Administration
100 N. Senate, #N551
Indianapolis, IN 46204
Phone: (317) 232-6750
Fax: (317) 232-0748

IOWA
Jim Youngblood
Director
Info. Technology Services
Dept. of Services
Hoover Bldg., Level B
1300 E. Walnut
Des Moines, IA 50319
Phone: (515) 281-5503
Fax: (515) 281-6137

KANSAS
Don Heiman
Director
Info. Systems & Communications
Dept. of Administration
Landon Ofc. Bldg., Rm 751-S
Topeka, KS 66612-1275
Phone: (785) 296-3343
Fax: (785) 296-1168

KENTUCKY
Steve Dooley
Commissioner
Dept. of Info. Systems
101 Cold Harbor
Frankfort, KY 40601
Phone: (502) 564-7777
Fax: (502) 564-6856
E-mail: sdooley@state.ky.us

Doug Robinson
Executive Director
Info. Resources Mgmt.
Finance & Administration
1024 Capital Ctr. Dr.
Frankfort, KY 40601
Phone: (502) 573-5476
Fax: (502) 573-1458
E-mail: drobinson@mail.state.ky.us

LOUISIANA
Allen Doescher
Assistant Commissioner
Technical Services & Communications
Div. of Administration
P.O. Box 94095
Baton Rouge, LA 70804-9095
Phone: (225) 342-7085
Fax: (225) 342-1057

MAINE
Bob Mayer
Chief Information Officer
Info. Services
Adm. & Financial Services
145 State House Station
Augusta, ME 04333
Phone: (207) 624-7840

MARYLAND
Preston Dillard
Director
Ofc. of Info. Technology/
Telecoms. Div.
Dept. of Budget & Mgmt.
301 W. Preston St.,
Rm. 1304
Baltimore, MD 21201
Phone: (410) 767-4647
Fax: (410) 333-7285
E-mail: pdillard
@dbm.state.md.us

MASSACHUSETTS
David Lewis
Acting Director
Mgmt. Info. Systems
Executive Ofc. for
Administration &
Finance
One Ashburton Pl., Rm. 801
Boston, MA 02108
Phone: (617) 973-0975
Fax: (617) 727-3766

MICHIGAN
Gary Swinden
Director
Ofc. of Mgmt. & Info.
Services
320 S. Walnut
P.O. Box 30026
Lansing, MI 48909
Phone: (517) 373-8816

MINNESOTA
Doug Schneider
Assistant Commissioner
Dept. of Administration
500 Centennial Ofc. Bldg.
658 Cedar St.
St. Paul, MN 55155
Phone: (651) 297-5610
Fax: (651) 297-5368
E-mail: doug.schneider
@state.mn.us

MISSISSIPPI
David Litchliter
Executive Director
Dept. of Info. Technology
Services
301 N. Lamar St., Ste. 508
Jackson, MS 39201
Phone: (601) 359-1395
Fax: (601) 345-6016

MISSOURI
Michael Benzen
Chief Information Officer
Ofc. of Info. Technology
P.O. Box 809
Jefferson Bldg., Rm. 1315
Jefferson City, MO 65102
Phone: (573) 526-7741
Fax: (573) 526-7747
E-mail: benzem
@mail.oit.state.mo.us

MONTANA
Tony Herbert
Administrator
Info. Services Div.
Dept. of Administration
Mitchell Bldg., Rm. 229
125 Roberts
Helena, MT 59620
Phone: (406) 444-2700
Fax: (406) 444-2701

NEBRASKA
Thomas Conroy
Administrator
Central Data Processing
501 S. 14th St.
Lincoln, NE 68508
Phone: (402) 471-2065
Fax: (402) 471-4864

NEVADA
Marlene Lockard
Director
Dept. of Info. Technology
Kinkaid Bldg., Rm. 403
505 E. King St.
Carson City, NV 89701
Phone: (775) 684-5801
Fax: (775) 684-5846
E-mail:
mlockard@doit.state.nv.us

NEW HAMPSHIRE
Donald S. Hill
Commissioner
Commissioner's Ofc.
Dept. of Adm. Services
25 Capitol St., Rm. 120
Concord, NH 03301-6312
Phone: (603) 271-3201

NEW JERSEY
Adel Ebeid
Chief Technology Officer
Ofc. of Telecoms. & Info.
Systems
300 Riverview Plz., 1st Fl.
P.O. Box 212
Trenton, NJ 08625-0212
Phone: (609) 633-8128

NEW MEXICO
Jim Hall
Chief Information Officer
Info. Technology Mgmt.
Governor's Ofc.
State Capitol Bldg.,
Rm. 400
Santa Fe, NM 87503
Phone: (505) 476-0400
E-mail: jim.hall
@state.nm.us

NEW YORK
Joseph Seymour
Commissioner
Ofc. of Services
Corning Tower Bldg.,
41st Fl.
Empire State Plz.
Albany, NY 12242
Phone: (518) 474-5991
Fax: (518) 486-9179

NORTH CAROLINA
Dennis McCarty
IT Legislative Analyst
Manager
Info. Systems Div.
Assembly
Legislative Ofc. Bldg.,
Ste. 400
300 N. Salisbury St.
Raleigh, NC 27602-5925
Phone: (919) 733-6834
Fax: (919) 715-7586

NORTH DAKOTA
James Heck
Director
Info. Services Div.
600 E. Blvd. Ave.
Bismarck, ND 58505-0100
Phone: (701) 328-3190
Fax: (701) 328-3000
E-mail: jheck@state.nd.us

NORTHERN MARIANA ISLANDS
Lawrence J. Laveque
Director
Electronic & Data
Processing
Dept. of Finance
P.O. Box 5234, CHRB
Saipan, MP 96950
Phone: (670) 644-1400
Fax: (670) 664-1415

OHIO
Ronald Vidmar
Deputy Director
Computer Services Div.
Dept. of Adm. Services
30 E. Broad St., 39th Fl.
Columbus, OH 43215
Phone: (614) 466-5860
Fax: (614) 644-9152

OKLAHOMA
Buddy Kidd
Director
Data Processing &
Planning Div.
Dept. of Transportation
200 NE 21st St.
Oklahoma City, OK 73105
Phone: (405) 521-2528

Bill Shafer
Director
Info. Services Div. Mgmt.
Ofc. of State Finance
State Capitol Bldg.,
Rm. 122
2300 N. Lincoln Blvd.
Oklahoma City, OK 73105
Phone: (405) 521-2804

OREGON
Don Mazziotti
Chief Information Officer
Info. Resources Mgmt. Div.
Dept. of Adm. Services
155 Cottage St., NE
Salem, OR 97310
Phone: (503) 378-3161
Fax: (503) 378-5200

PENNSYLVANIA
Larry Olson
Deputy Secretary for
Information Technology
Ofc. of Administration
Finance Bldg., Rm. 209
Harrisburg, PA 17120
Phone: (717) 787-5440
Fax: (717) 787-4523

PUERTO RICO
Maria T. Mujica
Administrator
Services Administration
P.O. Box 7428
San Juan, PR 00916
Phone: (787) 724-1064
Fax: (787) 722-7965

RHODE ISLAND
Richard Pierson
Acting Information Processing Officer
Div. of Info. Processing
Dept. of Administration
1 Capitol Hill
Providence, RI 02908-5898
Phone: (401) 222-2276

SOUTH CAROLINA
Ted Lightle
Director
Div. of Info. Resource Mgmt.
Budget & Control Bd.
1201 Main St., Ste. 1500
Columbia, SC 29201
Phone: (803) 737-0077

SOUTH DAKOTA
Otto Doll
Commissioner
Bur. of Telecom. & Info.
Kneip Bldg.
700 Governors Dr.
Pierre, SD 57501
Phone: (605) 773-3416
Fax: (605) 773-3741

TENNESSEE
Bradley Dugger
Chief of Information Systems
Ofc. for Info. Resources
Dept. of Finance & Administration
Wm. R. Snodgrass TN Towers, 16th Fl.
312 8th Ave., N.
Nashville, TN 37243-0288
Phone: (615) 741-2569
Fax: (615) 532-0471

TEXAS
Carolyn Purcell
Executive Director
Dept. of Info. Resources
300 W. 15th St., Ste. 1300
Austin, TX 78701
Phone: (512) 475-4720
Fax: (512) 475-4759

U.S. VIRGIN ISLANDS
Ira Mills
Director
Ofc. of Mgmt. & Budget
#41 Norre Gade
Emancipation Garden Station, 2nd Fl.
St. Thomas, VI 00802
Phone: (340) 774-0750
Fax: (340) 774-0069

UTAH
Leon Miller
Director
Div. of Info. Technology Services
Dept. of Adm. Services
6000 State Ofc. Bldg.
Salt Lake City, UT 84114-1172
Phone: (801) 538-3476
Fax: (801) 538-3321
E-mail: lmiller.asitmain@state.ut.us

VERMONT
Patricia Urban
Chief Information Officer
Administration
109 State St.
Montpelier, VT 05609
Phone: (802) 828-3322
Fax: (802) 828-3320

VIRGINIA
Michael F. Thomas
Director
Dept. of Info. Technology
Richmond Plz. Bldg., 3rd Fl.
110 S. 7th St.
Richmond, VA 23219
Phone: (804) 371-5500
Fax: (804) 371-5273

WASHINGTON
Steve Kolodney
Director
Dept. of Info. Services
P.O. Box 42445
Olympia, WA 98504-2445
Phone: (360) 902-3560
Fax: (360) 664-0733

WEST VIRGINIA
Mike Slater
Director
Info. Services & Communications
Bldg. 6, Rm. 110
1900 Kanawha Blvd., E.
Charleston, WV 25305
Phone: (304) 558-8918

WISCONSIN
Jim Schmolesky
Director
Ofc. of Computer Services
Dept. of Administration
101 E. Wilson St., 9th Fl.
P.O. Box 7864
Madison, WI 53703
Phone: (608) 266-7627
Fax: (608) 264-9500

WYOMING
David Bliss
Interim Administrator
Computer Technology Div.
Administration & Fiscal Control Dept.
Emerson Bldg.
2001 Capitol Ave.
Cheyenne, WY 82002
Phone: (307) 777-5000

Inspector General

Investigates and prosecutes fraud, waste and abuse.

ALABAMA

ALASKA
Eric Johnson
Chief Assistant Attorney General
Ofc. of Special Prosecution & Appeals
Dept. of Law
310 K St.
Anchorage, AK 99501
Phone: (907) 269-6250
Fax: (907) 269-6270

AMERICAN SAMOA

ARIZONA
Douglas Norton
Auditor General
Auditor Gen's. Ofc.
2910 N. 44th St., Ste. 410
Phoenix, AZ 85018
Phone: (602) 553-0333
Fax: (602) 553-0051

ARKANSAS

CALIFORNIA

COLORADO

CONNECTICUT

DELAWARE
R. Thomas Wagner, Jr.
State Auditor
Auditor of Accounts
P.O. Box 1401
Dover, DE 19903-1401
Phone: (302) 739-4241
Fax: (302) 739-6707
E-mail: rwagner@legis.state.de.us

DISTRICT OF COLUMBIA
Charles Maddox
Inspector General
Ofc. of the Inspector Gen.
717 14th St., NW, 5th Fl.
Washington, DC 20005
Phone: (202) 727-2540
Fax: (202) 727-9846

FLORIDA
Marvin Doyle
Inspector General
Executive Ofc. of the Governor
The Capitol, Rm. 2107
Tallahassee, FL 32399-0001
Phone: (850) 922-4637
Fax: (850) 921-0817

GEORGIA

GUAM
Robert G.P. Cruz
Public Auditor
Ofc. of the Public Auditor
1208 E. Sunset Blvd., Tiyan
GMF, GU 96921
Phone: (671) 475-0393
Fax: (671) 472-7951

HAWAII

IDAHO
Russ Reneau
Chief Investigator
Criminal Div.
Ofc. of the Attorney Gen.
Statehouse
700 W. Jefferson
Boise, ID 83720
Phone: (208) 334-2400

ILLINOIS
Sam Nolen
Director
State Police
103 State Armory
Springfield, IL 62706
Phone: (217) 782-7263
Fax: (217) 785-2821

INDIANA

IOWA
Kim Schmett
Director
Dept. of Inspections & Appeals
Lucas State Ofc. Bldg.
321 E. 12th St.
Des Moines, IA 50319
Phone: (515) 281-5457
Fax: (515) 242-5022

KANSAS
Carla J. Stovall
Attorney General
Judicial Bldg.
300 SW 10th St.
Topeka, KS 66612-1597
Phone: (785) 296-2215
Fax: (785) 296-6296

KENTUCKY
Timothy Veno
Inspector General
Cabinet for Human Resources
275 E. Main St.
Frankfort, KY 40621
Phone: (502) 564-2888
Fax: (502) 564-6546

LOUISIANA
Bill Lynch
Inspector General
Div. of Administration
P.O. Box 94095
Baton Rouge, LA 70804
Phone: (225) 342-4262
Fax: (225) 342-1947

MAINE
Stephen L. Wessler
Chief Attorney
Public Protection Unit
Dept. of the Attorney Gen.
6 State House Station
Augusta, ME 04333
Phone: (207) 626-8844

MARYLAND
Vacant
Inspector General
Dept. of Human Resources
311 W. Saratoga St.
Baltimore, MD 21201
Phone: (410) 767-7424

MASSACHUSETTS
Robert A. Cerasoli
Inspector General
One Ashburton Pl., Rm. 1311
Boston, MA 02108
Phone: (617) 727-9140
Fax: (617) 723-3540

MICHIGAN
Thomas L. Casey
Solicitor General
Law Bldg., 7th Fl.
P.O. Box 30212
Lansing, MI 48909
Phone: (517) 373-1124

MINNESOTA
Allan Gilbert
Deputy Attorney General
Ofc. of the Attorney Gen.
102 State Capitol
75 Constitution Ave.
St. Paul, MN 55155
Phone: (651) 296-7519
Fax: (651) 297-4193

John Stanoch
Deputy Attorney General
Ofc. of the Attorney Gen.
102 State Capitol
75 Constitution Ave.
St. Paul, MN 55155
Phone: (651) 296-2351
Fax: (651) 297-4193

MISSISSIPPI

MISSOURI
Jeremiah W. Nixon
Attorney General
Supreme Ct. Bldg.
207 W. High St.
Jefferson City, MO 65101
Phone: (573) 751-3321
Fax: (573) 751-0774
E-mail: attgenmail@moago.org

MONTANA
Scott Seacat
Legislative Auditor
Legislative Audit Div.
State Capitol, Rm. 135
1301 E. 6th Ave.
Helena, MT 59620
Phone: (406) 444-3122
Fax: (406) 444-9784

NEBRASKA
Don B. Stenberg
Attorney General
State Capitol
P.O. Box 98920
Lincoln, NE 68509-8920
Phone: (402) 471-2682
Fax: (402) 471-3297

NEVADA
Bob Pike
Chief Investigator
Investigation Div.
Ofc. of the Attorney Gen.
100 N. Carson St.
Carson City, NV 89701
Phone: (775) 687-3543
Fax: (775) 687-5798

NEW HAMPSHIRE
Philip T. McLaughlin
Attorney General
State House Annex
25 Capitol St.
Concord, NH 03301-6397
Phone: (603) 271-3658
Fax: (603) 271-2110

NEW JERSEY
Peter Verniero
Attorney General
Dept. of Law
Richard J. Hughes Justice Complex
25 Market St., P.O. Box 081
Trenton, NJ 08625-0081
Phone: (609) 292-4925
Fax: (609) 292-3508

NEW MEXICO
Frank D. Katz
Deputy Attorney General
Ofc. of the Attorney Gen.
P.O. Drawer 1508
Santa Fe, NM 87504
Phone: (505) 827-6000
Fax: (505) 827-5826

NEW YORK
Roslynn Mauskopf
State Inspector General
State Capitol, Rm. 254
Albany, NY 12224
Phone: (518) 474-1010
Fax: (518) 486-3745

NORTH CAROLINA
Ralph Campbell
State Auditor
Dept. of State Auditor
300 N. Salisbury St., Rm. 201
Raleigh, NC 27603
Phone: (919) 733-3217
Fax: (919) 733-8443

NORTH DAKOTA
Parrell Grossman
Director
Consumer Protection & Antitrust Div.
Attorney Gen's. Ofc.
600 E. Blvd. Ave., 17th Fl.
Bismarck, ND 58505-0040
Phone: (701) 328-3404
Fax: (701) 328-3535
E-mail: msmail.pgrossma@ranch.state.nd.us

NORTHERN MARIANA ISLANDS
Leo L. LeMotte
Public Auditor
P.O. Box 1399
Saipan, MP 96950
Phone: (670) 234-6481
Fax: (670) 234-7812
E-mail: opa@mtccnmi.com

OHIO
Thomas Charles
Inspector General
30 E. Broad St., Ste. 1820
Columbus, OH 43266-0820
Phone: (614) 644-9110
Fax: (614) 644-9504
E-mail: oig_watchdog@ohio.gov

OKLAHOMA
Dan Fitzgerald
Division Administrator
Ofc. of Inspector Gen.
Dept. of Human Services
2409 N. Kelly, #406
Oklahoma City, OK 73111
Phone: (402) 522-5880

OREGON
Pete Shepherd
Attorney in Charge
Financial Fraud
Dept. of Justice
1162 Court St., NE
Salem, OR 97310
Phone: (503) 378-4732
Fax: (503) 378-5017

PENNSYLVANIA
Nicolette Parisi
Inspector General
Ofc. of Administration
333 Market St., 9th Fl.
Harrisburg, PA 17126
Phone: (717) 787-6835
Fax: (717) 772-5135

PUERTO RICO
Manuel Diaz-Saldana
Comptroller
P.O. Box 366069
San Juan, PR 00936-6069
Phone: (787) 754-3030
Fax: (787) 751-6768

RHODE ISLAND
Ernest Almonte
Auditor General
Ofc. of the Auditor Gen.
1145 Main St.
Pawtucket, RI 02860-4807
Phone: (401) 222-2435

SOUTH CAROLINA
Thomas L. Wagner, Jr.
State Auditor
Ofc. of the State Auditor
1401 Main St., Ste. 1200
Columbia, SC 29201
Phone: (803) 253-4160
Fax: (803) 343-0723

SOUTH DAKOTA
Curt Everson
Commissioner
Bur. of Finance & Mgmt.
500 E. Capitol Ave., Rm. 216
Pierre, SD 57501
Phone: (605) 773-3411
Fax: (605) 773-4711

TENNESSEE

TEXAS
Paul Elliott
Chief of Consumer Protection
Attorney Gen's. Ofc.
Consumer Protection Div.
P.O. Box 12548
Austin, TX 78711-2548
Phone: (512) 463-2185
Fax: (512) 473-8301

U.S. VIRGIN ISLANDS
Steven G. van Beverhoudt
Inspector General
Bur. of Audit & Control
75 Kronprindsens Gade
St. Thomas, VI 00802
Phone: (340) 774-3388
Fax: (340) 774-6431

UTAH
Mike Hanks
Administrator
Law Enforcement Bur.
Dept. of Corrections
6100 S. 300 E.
Salt Lake City, UT 84107
Phone: (801) 265-5669
Fax: (801) 265-5726
E-mail: mhanks.crdept@state.ut.us

VERMONT

VIRGINIA
Merritt L. Cogswell
State Internal Auditor
Dept. of the State Internal Auditor
Monroe Bldg., 4th Fl.
101 N. 14th St.
Richmond, VA 23219
Phone: (804) 225-3106
Fax: (804) 371-0165

WASHINGTON
Christine O. Gregoire
Attorney General
1125 Washington St., SE
P.O. Box 40100
Olympia, WA 98504-0100
Phone: (360) 753-6200
Fax: (360) 664-0228

WEST VIRGINIA
Darrell V. McGraw, Jr.
Attorney General
Ofc. of the Attorney Gen.
Capitol Bldg.
1900 Kanawha Blvd., E.
Charleston, WV 25305
Phone: (304) 558-2021
Fax: (304) 558-0140

WISCONSIN
James E. Doyle
Attorney General
State Capitol, Ste. 114 E.
P.O. Box 7857
Madison, WI 53707-7857
Phone: (608) 266-1221
Fax: (608) 267-2779

WYOMING
Gay Woodhouse
Attorney General
Inspector Gen's. Ofc.
State Capitol Bldg.
Cheyenne, WY 82002
Phone: (307) 777-7841
Fax: (307) 777-6869

Insurance

Licenses and regulates insurance agents and insurance and title companies in the state.

ALABAMA
D. David Parsons
Commissioner
Insurance Dept.
201 Monroe St., Ste. 1700
Montgomery, AL 36130
Phone: (334) 269-3550
Fax: (334) 241-4192

ALASKA
Marianne Burke
Director
Div. of Insurance
Dept. of Commerce & Economic Dev.
P.O. Box 110805
Juneau, AK 99811-0805
Phone: (907) 465-2515
Fax: (907) 465-3422

AMERICAN SAMOA
Vacant
Insurance Commissioner
Ofc. of the Insurance Commissioner
Governor's Ofc.
AS Govt.
Pago Pago, AS 96799
Phone: (684) 633-4116
Fax: (684) 633-2269

ARIZONA
Charles Cohen
Director
Dept. of Insurance
2910 N. 44th St., #201
Phoenix, AZ 85018
Phone: (602) 912-8456
Fax: (602) 912-8412

ARKANSAS
Mike Pickens
Commissioner
Dept. of Insurance
1200 W. 3rd
Little Rock, AR 72201
Phone: (501) 371-2600
Fax: (501) 371-2629

CALIFORNIA
Charles W. Quackenbush
Insurance Commissioner
300 Capitol Mall, Ste. 1500
Sacramento, CA 95814
Phone: (916) 445-5544

COLORADO
William J. Kirven, III
Commissioner
Div. of Insurance
Dept. of Regulatory Agencies
1560 Broadway, Ste. 850
Denver, CO 80202
Phone: (303) 894-7499
Fax: (303) 894-7455

CONNECTICUT
George Reider
Commissioner
Dept. of Insurance
P.O. Box 816
Hartford, CT 06142-0816
Phone: (860) 297-3802

DELAWARE
Donna Lee Williams
Commissioner
Dept. of Insurance
Rodney Bldg.
841 Silver Lake Blvd.
Dover, DE 19901-1507
Phone: (302) 739-4251
Fax: (302) 739-5280

DISTRICT OF COLUMBIA
Reginald Berry
Acting Commissioner
Insurance Administration
Dept. of Consumer & Regulatory Affairs
613 G St., NW, Rm. 600
Washington, DC 20001
Phone: (202) 727-8000

FLORIDA
Bill Nelson
State Treasurer & Insurance Commissioner
Dept. of Insurance
PL-11, The Capitol
Tallahassee, FL 32399-0300
Phone: (850) 922-3100
Fax: (850) 488-6581
E-mail: webmaster@doi.state.fl.us

GEORGIA
John W. Oxendine
Commissioner
Insurance Commissioner's Ofc.
W. Tower, 7th Fl.
2 Martin Luther King, Jr. Dr.
Atlanta, GA 30334
Phone: (404) 656-2117

GUAM
Joseph T. Duenas
Director
Dept. of Revenue & Taxation
13-1 Mariner Dr., Tiyan
P.O. Box 23607
GMF, GU 96921
Phone: (671) 475-1817
Fax: (671) 472-2643

HAWAII
Wayne Metcalf
Insurance Commissioner
Div. of Insurance
Commerce & Consumer Affairs Dept.
1010 Richards St.
Honolulu, HI 96813
Phone: (808) 586-2799
Fax: (808) 586-2806

IDAHO
Mary Hartung
Director
Dept. of Insurance
700 W. State St., 3rd Fl.
Boise, ID 83720-7015
Phone: (208) 334-2255

ILLINOIS
Nathaniel S. Shapo
Acting Director
Dept. of Insurance
320 W. Washington, 4th Fl.
Springfield, IL 62767
Phone: (217) 782-4515
Fax: (217) 524-6500

INDIANA
Sally McCarty
Commissioner
Dept. of Insurance
311 W. Washington St., Ste. 300
Indianapolis, IN 46204
Phone: (317) 232-3520
Fax: (317) 232-5251

IOWA
Terri Vaughan
Commissioner
Insurance Div.
Dept. of Commerce
330 Maple St.
Des Moines, IA 50319
Phone: (515) 281-5705

KANSAS
Kathleen Sebelius
Commissioner
Insurance Dept.
420 SW 9th St.
Topeka, KS 66612-1678
Phone: (785) 296-3071
Fax: (785) 296-2283

KENTUCKY
George Nichols, III
Commissioner
Public Protection & Regulation Cabinet
Dept. of Insurance
215 W. Main St.
Frankfort, KY 40601
Phone: (502) 564-6027
Fax: (502) 564-6090

LOUISIANA
Jim Brown
Commissioner
Dept. of Insurance
P.O. Box 94214
Baton Rouge, LA 70804-9214
Phone: (225) 342-5423
Fax: (225) 342-3078

MAINE
S. Catherine Longley
Commissioner
Professional & Financial Regulation
35 State House Station
Augusta, ME 04333-0035
Phone: (207) 624-8500

MARYLAND
Steve B. Larsen
Insurance Commissioner
Ofc. of the Commissioner
Insurance Administrator
525 St. Paul Pl.
Baltimore, MD 21202-2272
Phone: (410) 468-2090
Fax: (410) 468-2020

MASSACHUSETTS
Linda Ruthardt
Commissioner
Div. of Insurance
Executive Ofc. of Consumer Affairs
470 Atlantic Ave.
Boston, MA 02210-2223
Phone: (617) 521-7301
Fax: (617) 521-7770

MICHIGAN
Frank Fitzgerald
Commissioner of Insurance
Consumer & Industry Services
P.O. Box 30220
Lansing, MI 48909
Phone: (517) 335-3167

MINNESOTA
David Jennings
Commissioner
Dept. of Commerce
133 E. 7th St.
Minneapolis, MN 55101
Phone: (651) 296-6694
Fax: (651) 297-3238

MISSISSIPPI
George Dale
Commissioner
Dept. of Insurance
1804 Sillers Bldg.
P.O. Box 79
Jackson, MS 39201
Phone: (601) 359-3569
Fax: (601) 359-2474

MISSOURI
Keith Wenzel
Director
Dept. of Insurance
301 W. High St.
P.O. Box 690
Jefferson City, MO 65102
Phone: (573) 751-1927
Fax: (573) 751-1165
E-mail: kwenzel@mail.state.mo.us

MONTANA
Mark O'Keefe
Commissioner of Insurance
State Auditor
P.O. Box 4009
Helena, MT 59604
Phone: (406) 444-2040
Fax: (406) 444-3497

NEBRASKA
Tim Wagner
Director
Dept. of Insurance
Terminal Bldg., Ste. 400
941 O St.
Lincoln, NE 68508
Phone: (402) 471-2201
Fax: (402) 471-4610

NEVADA
Alice Molasky-Arman
Commissioner
Div. of Insurance
Dept. of Business & Industry
1665 Hot Springs Rd., Ste. 152
Carson City, NV 89706
Phone: (775) 687-7668
Fax: (775) 687-3937
E-mail: icommish@govmail.state.nv.us

NEW HAMPSHIRE
Charles Blossom
Commissioner
Insurance Dept.
169 Manchester St.
Concord, NH 03301-5151
Phone: (603) 271-2261
Fax: (603) 271-1406

NEW JERSEY
Jaynee LaVecchia
Commissioner
Banking & Insurance
Dept. of Insurance
P.O. Box 325
Trenton, NJ 08625-0325
Phone: (609) 633-7667
Fax: (609) 633-7620

NEW MEXICO
Mike Batte
Acting Superintendent
Insurance Div.
Public Regulation Comm.
P.O. Drawer 1269
Santa Fe, NM 87504
Phone: (505) 827-4299
Fax: (505) 476-0161

NEW YORK
Neil D. Levin
Superintendent
Insurance Dept.
25 Beaver St., 3rd Fl.
New York, NY 10004
Phone: (212) 480-2289
Fax: (212) 480-2310

NORTH CAROLINA
James E. Long
Commissioner of Insurance
430 N. Salisbury St.
Raleigh, NC 27603-5908
Phone: (919) 733-2142
Fax: (919) 733-6495

NORTH DAKOTA
Glenn Pomeroy
Commissioner
Insurance Dept.
600 E. Blvd. Ave., 5th Fl.
Bismarck, ND 58505-0320
Phone: (701) 328-2440
Fax: (701) 328-4880
E-mail: gpomeroy@state.nd.us

NORTHERN MARIANA ISLANDS
Oscar Camacho
Director
Ofc. of the Governor
Dept. of Commerce
Saipan, MP 96950
Phone: (670) 664-3000
Fax: (670) 664-3067
E-mail: commerce@mtccnmi.com

OHIO
Lee Covington
Director
Dept. of Insurance
2100 Stella Ct.
Columbus, OH 43266-0566
Phone: (614) 644-2651
Fax: (614) 644-3743

OKLAHOMA
Carroll Fisher
Insurance Commissioner
Dept. of Insurance
3814 N. Santa Fe
Oklahoma City, OK 73118
Phone: (405) 521-2668

OREGON
Nancy Ellison
Administrator
Insurance Div.
Dept. of Consumer & Business Services
21 Labor & Industries Bldg.
350 Winter St., NE
Salem, OR 97310
Phone: (503) 947-7980
Fax: (503) 378-4351

PENNSYLVANIA
Diane Koken
Commissioner
Dept. of Insurance
Strawberry Sq., 13th Fl.
Harrisburg, PA 17120
Phone: (717) 787-5173
Fax: (717) 772-1969

PUERTO RICO
Juan Antonio Garcia
Commissioner
Insurance Comm.
P.O. Box 8330
Santurce, PR 00910
Phone: (787) 722-8686
Fax: (787) 722-4400

RHODE ISLAND
Charles Kwolek
Superintendent of Insurance & Associate Director
Dept. of Business Regulation
233 Richmond St., Ste. 233
Providence, RI 02903
Phone: (401) 222-2246

SOUTH CAROLINA
Ernst N. Csiszar
Director of Insurance
Dept. of Insurance
1612 Marion St.
Columbia, SC 29201
Phone: (803) 737-6212

SOUTH DAKOTA
David Volk
Secretary
Div. of Insurance
Dept. of Commerce & Regulation
118 W. Capitol Ave.
Pierre, SD 57501-2017
Phone: (605) 773-3178
Fax: (605) 773-3018

TENNESSEE
Doug Sizemore
Commissioner
Dept. of Commerce & Insurance
500 James Robertson Pkwy.
Nashville, TN 37243-0565
Phone: (615) 741-2241
Fax: (615) 532-6934

TEXAS
Jose Montemayor
Commissioner
Dept. of Insurance
333 Guadalupe, Tower I, 13th Fl.
Austin, TX 78701
Phone: (512) 463-6468
Fax: (512) 475-2005

U.S. VIRGIN ISLANDS
Gerard Luz James, II
Lieutenant Governor
Insurance Div.
#18 Kongens Gade
St. Thomas, VI 00801
Phone: (340) 774-2991
Fax: (340) 774-6953

UTAH
Merwin U. Stewart
Insurance Commissioner
State Insurance Dept.
3110 State Ofc. Bldg.
Salt Lake City, UT 84114
Phone: (801) 538-3804
Fax: (801) 538-3829
E-mail: mstewart.idmain@state.ut.us

VERMONT
Elizabeth R. Costle
Commissioner
Dept. of Banking, Insurance, Securities & Health
Care Administration
89 State St.
Montpelier, VT 05620-3101
Phone: (802) 828-3301
Fax: (802) 828-3306
E-mail: bcostle@state.vt.us

VIRGINIA
Theodore W. Morrison, Jr.
Chair
State Corp. Comm.
Tyler Bldg.
1300 E. Main St.
Richmond, VA 23219
Phone: (804) 371-9608
Fax: (804) 371-9376

WASHINGTON
Deborah Senn
Commissioner
Ofc. of the Insurance Commissioner
Insurance Bldg.
P.O. Box 40255
Olympia, WA 98504-0255
Phone: (360) 753-7300
Fax: (360) 586-3535

WEST VIRGINIA
Hanley Clark
Commissioner
Insurance Comm.
2019 Washington St., E.
P.O. Box 50540
Charleston, WV 25305
Phone: (304) 558-3354
Fax: (304) 558-0412

WISCONSIN
Connie O'Connell
Commissioner
Ofc. of Commissioner of Insurance
121 E. Wilson St.
Madison, WI 53702
Phone: (608) 266-7543
Fax: (608) 261-8579
E-mail: coconnel@mail.state.wi.us

WYOMING
John P. McBride
Commissioner
Dept. of Insurance
Herschler Bldg.
122 W. 25th St.
Cheyenne, WY 82002
Phone: (307) 777-6896

International Trade

Promotes state exports, attracts overseas investments in the state and directs trade and investment missions.

ALABAMA

ALASKA
Priscilla Wohl
Trade Program Manager
Div. of Trade & Dev.
Dept. of Commerce & Economic Dev.
3601 C St., Ste. 700
Anchorage, AK 99503-5934
Phone: (907) 269-8110
Fax: (907) 269-8125

AMERICAN SAMOA
John Faumuina, Jr.
Director
Economic Dev. & Planning Ofc.
Dept. of Commerce
Pago Pago, AS 96799
Phone: (684) 633-5155
Fax: (684) 633-4195

ARIZONA
Carol Sanger
Assistant Deputy Director
Dept. of Commerce
3800 N. Central Ave., Ste. 1500
Phoenix, AZ 85012
Phone: (602) 280-1370

ARKANSAS
Alan McVey
Deputy Director
Intl. Marketing Div.
Dept. of Economic Dev.
1 Capitol Mall, Rm. 4C-300
Little Rock, AR 72201
Phone: (501) 682-7690
Fax: (501) 324-9856

CALIFORNIA
Lee Grissom
Secretary
Trade & Commerce Agency
801 K St., Ste. 1700
Sacramento, CA 95814
Phone: (916) 322-3962

COLORADO
Marc Holtzman
Director
Intl. Trade Ofc.
Ofc. of the Governor
1625 Broadway, Ste. 900
Denver, CO 80202
Phone: (303) 892-3850
Fax: (303) 892-3820

CONNECTICUT
Rita Zangari
Deputy Commissioner
Intl. Trade Div.
Dept. of Economic & Community Dev.
505 Hudson St.
Hartford, CT 06106
Phone: (860) 270-8020
Fax: (860) 270-8008

DELAWARE
Darrell J. Minott
Director
Economic Dev. Ofc.
99 Kings Hwy.
Dover, DE 19901-7305
Phone: (302) 739-4271
Fax: (302) 739-5749

DISTRICT OF COLUMBIA
Bill Byrd
Executive Director
Ofc. of Intl. Business
717 14th St., NW, Ste. 1100
Washington, DC 20005-3206
Phone: (202) 727-1576

FLORIDA
John Anderson
President
Enterprise FL
390 N. Orange Ave., Ste. 1300
Orlando, FL 32303
Phone: (407) 316-4600
Fax: (407) 425-1921

GEORGIA
Randolph B. Cardoza
Commissioner
Dept. of Industry, Trade & Tourism
285 Peachtree Ctr. Ave., NE, Ste. 1100
Atlanta, GA 30303
Phone: (404) 656-3545

GUAM
Joseph C. Cruz
Director
Dept. of Commerce
102 M St.
Tiyan, GU 96913
Phone: (671) 475-0321
Fax: (671) 477-9013
E-mail: COMMERCE@ns.gov.gu

HAWAII
Seiji Naya
Director
Dept. of Business, Economic Dev. & Tourism
250 S. Hotel St., 5th Fl.
Honolulu, HI 96813
Phone: (808) 586-2355
Fax: (808) 586-2377

IDAHO

ILLINOIS
Pam McDonough
Director
Dept. of Commerce & Community Affairs
620 E. Adams St., 3rd Fl.
Springfield, IL 62701
Phone: (217) 782-3233
Fax: (217) 524-0864

INDIANA
Carlos Barbera
Director
Intl. Trade Div.
Dept. of Commerce
1 N. Capitol, Ste. 700
Indianapolis, IN 46204
Phone: (317) 232-4949
Fax: (317) 233-1680

IOWA
Mike Doyle
Division Administrator
Bur. of Intl. Marketing
Dept. of Economic Dev.
200 E. Grand Ave.
Des Moines, IA 50309
Phone: (515) 242-4729

KANSAS
Michael Farmer
Director
Trade Dev. Div.
Dept. of Commerce & Housing
700 SW Harrison, Ste. 1300
Topeka, KS 66612
Phone: (785) 296-4027
Fax: (785) 296-5055

KENTUCKY
Hugh Haydon
Commissioner
Community Dev.
Capitol Plz. Tower, 23rd Fl.
500 Mero St.
Frankfort, KY 40601
Phone: (502) 564-7140
Fax: (502) 564-3256

LOUISIANA
Larry Collins
Director of International Trade
Ofc. of Intl. Trade
Dept. of Economic Dev.
P.O. Box 94185
Baton Rouge, LA 70804
Phone: (225) 342-4320
Fax: (225) 342-5389

MAINE
Perry Newman
Executive Director
Intl. Trade Ctr.
511 Congress St.
Portland, ME 04101-3428
Phone: (207) 541-7400
Fax: (207) 541-7420

MARYLAND
James Hughes
Director
Ofc. of Intl. Business
Dept. of Business & Economic Dev.
217 E. Redwood St., 13th Fl.
Baltimore, MD 21202
Phone: (410) 767-0684
Fax: (410) 333-4302

MASSACHUSETTS
Kathleen Molony
Executive Director
Ofc. of Intl. Trade & Investment
10 Park Plz., Ste. 4510
Boston, MA 02116-3933
Phone: (617) 367-1830
Fax: (617) 227-3488

MICHIGAN
Greg Burkart
Director
Economic Dev. Corp.
201 N. Washington Sq.
Lansing, MI 48913
Phone: (517) 335-7989
Fax: (517) 373-0314

MINNESOTA
Noor Doja
Executive Director
Trade Ofc.
1000 World Trade Ctr.
30 E. 7th St.
St. Paul, MN 55101
Phone: (651) 297-4658
Fax: (651) 296-3555
E-mail: noor.doja@state.mn.us

MISSISSIPPI
Jay Moon
Deputy Director
Intl. Div.
Dept. of Economic & Community Dev.
P.O. Box 849
Jackson, MS 39205
Phone: (601) 359-3448
Fax: (601) 354-6646

MISSOURI
Chris Gutierrez
Director
Ofc. of Intl. Marketing
Community & Economic Dev.
Truman Bldg., Rm. 720
P.O. Box 118
Jefferson City, MO 65102
Phone: (573) 751-4855
Fax: (573) 526-1567
E-mail: cgutierr@mail.state.mo.us

MONTANA
Mark Bisom
Program Manager
Trade Div.
Dept. of Commerce
1424 9th Ave.
Helena, MT 59620
Phone: (406) 444-4380
Fax: (406) 444-2903

NEBRASKA
Susan Rouch
Director
Intl. Ofc.
Dept. of Economic Dev.
301 Centennial Mall, S.
P.O. Box 94666
Lincoln, NE 68509-4666
Phone: (402) 471-4668
Fax: (402) 471-3778

NEVADA
Robert E. Shriver
Executive Director
Comm. on Economic Dev.
5151 S. Carson St.
Carson City, NV 89701
Phone: (775) 687-4325
Fax: (775) 687-4450

NEW HAMPSHIRE
Dawn Wivell
Director
Intl. Commerce
Dept. of Resources & Economic Dev.
601 Spaulding Tpke., Ste. 29
Portsmouth, NH 03801
Phone: (603) 334-6074
Fax: (603) 334-6110

NEW JERSEY
Edward Burton
Director
Div. of Intl. Trade
Dept. of Commerce & Dev.
28 W. State St., 8th Fl.
P.O. Box 836
Trenton, NJ 08625-0836
Phone: (609) 633-3606
Fax: (609) 633-3675

NEW MEXICO
Roberto Castillo
Director
Intl. Trade Div.
Dept. of Economic Dev.
P.O. Box 20003
Santa Fe, NM 87503
Phone: (505) 827-0309
Fax: (505) 827-0263
E-mail: Robertoc@edd.state.nm.us

NEW YORK
Charles A. Gargano
Commissioner
Dept. of Economic Dev.
One Commerce Plz., 9th Fl.
Albany, NY 12245
Phone: (518) 474-4100
Fax: (518) 473-9374

NORTH CAROLINA
Mac Epps
Director
Intl. Trade Div.
Dept. of Commerce
P.O. Box 29571
Raleigh, NC 27603
Phone: (919) 733-7193
Fax: (919) 733-0110

NORTH DAKOTA
Kevin Cramer
Director
Dept. of Economic Dev. & Finance
1833 E. Bismarck Expy.
Bismarck, ND 58504
Phone: (701) 328-5300
Fax: (701) 328-5320
E-mail: kcramer@state.nd.us

NORTHERN MARIANA ISLANDS
Pedro Q. Dela Cruz
Secretary
Ofc. of the Governor
Dept. of Commerce
Caller Box 10007 CK
Saipan, MP 96950
Phone: (670) 664-3000
Fax: (670) 664-3067
E-mail: commerce@mtccnmi.com

OHIO
James E.P. Sisto
Deputy Director
Div. of Intl. Trade
Dept. of Dev.
P.O. Box 1001
Columbus, OH 43266
Phone: (614) 466-5017
Fax: (614) 463-1540

OKLAHOMA
Kevin Chambers
Director
Intl. Trade Div.
Dept. of Economic Dev.
900 N. Stiles Ave.
P.O. Box 26980
Oklahoma City, OK 73126-0980
Phone: (405) 815-6552
Fax: (405) 815-5199

OREGON
Warren Banks
Manager
Economic Dev. Dept.
1 World Trade Ctr.
121 SW Salmon, Ste. 300
Portland, OR 97204
Phone: (503) 229-5625
Fax: (503) 222-5050

PENNSYLVANIA
Roger Cranville
Director
Ofc. of Intl. Dev.
Dept. of Commerce
449 Forum Bldg.
Harrisburg, PA 17120
Phone: (717) 787-7190
Fax: (717) 234-4560

PUERTO RICO
Lissette Diaz de Rivera
Director
Dept. of Commerce
P.O. Box S-4275
San Juan, PR 00905
Phone: (787) 724-1451

RHODE ISLAND
John Swen
Director
Economic Dev. Corp.
1 W. Exchange St.
Providence, RI 02903
Phone: (401) 222-2601
Fax: (401) 222-2102

SOUTH CAROLINA
Will Lacey
Manager
Existing Industry & Trade Dev. Ofc.
Dept. of Commerce
P.O. Box 927
Columbia, SC 29202
Phone: (803) 737-0400

SOUTH DAKOTA
Ron Wheeler
Commissioner
Governor's Ofc. of Economic Dev.
Capitol Lake Plz.
711 Wells Ave.
Pierre, SD 57501-3369
Phone: (605) 773-5032
Fax: (605) 773-3256

TENNESSEE
G.C. Hixson
Director of Marketing
Intl. Marketing
Dept. of Economic & Community Dev.
320 6th Ave., N., 8th Fl.
Nashville, TN 37243
Phone: (615) 741-2549
Fax: (615) 741-5829

TEXAS
Jeff Moseley
Executive Director
Dept. of Economic Dev.
1700 N. Congress, Ste. 130
Austin, TX 78701
Phone: (512) 936-0101
Fax: (512) 936-0303

U.S. VIRGIN ISLANDS

UTAH
Richard J. Mayfield
Director
Div. of Business & Economic Dev.
Dept. of Community & Economic Dev.
324 S. State St., Ste. 500
Salt Lake City, UT 84111
Phone: (801) 538-8820
Fax: (801) 538-8889
E-mail: rmayfiel@dced.state.ut.us

VERMONT
Tom Myers
Director
Intl. Business
Dept. of Economic Dev.
109 State St.
Montpelier, VT 05609
Phone: (802) 828-3637
Fax: (802) 828-3258

VIRGINIA
Mark R. Kilduff
Executive Director
Economic Dev. Partnership
W. Tower, 19th Fl.
901 E. Byrd St.
Richmond, VA 23219
Phone: (804) 371-8108
Fax: (804) 371-8112

WASHINGTON
Paul Isaki
Special Trade Representative
CTED
2001 6th Ave., Ste. 2600
Seattle, WA 98121
Phone: (360) 464-7143
Fax: (360) 464-7222

WEST VIRGINIA
Dana Davis
Acting Director
Dev. Ofc.
Bldg. 6, Rm. 525
1900 Kanawha Blvd., E.
Charleston, WV 25305
Phone: (304) 558-2234
Fax: (304) 558-1189

WISCONSIN
Mary Regel
Division Administrator
Div. of Intl. Trade
Dept. of Commerce
123 W. Washington Ave.
P.O. Box 7970
Madison, WI 53707
Phone: (608) 267-9227
Fax: (608) 266-5551

WYOMING
John Reardon
Chief Executive Officer
Economic & Community Dev.
Business Council
214 W. 15th St.
Cheyenne, WY 82002
Phone: (307) 777-2800
Fax: (307) 777-5840

Job Training

Administers job training and services for the unemployed, underemployed and economically disadvantaged in the state.

ALABAMA
Steven Walkley
Director
Job Training Div.
Economic & Community Affairs Dept.
P.O. Box 5690
Montgomery, AL 36130
Phone: (334) 242-8672
Fax: (334) 242-5099

ALASKA
Mike Andrews
Director
Human Resource Investment Council
Ofc. of the Governor
3601 C St., Ste. 380
Anchorage, AK 99501
Phone: (907) 269-7485
Fax: (907) 269-7489

AMERICAN SAMOA
Sapini Siatu'u
Director
Dept. of Human Resources
AS Govt.
Pago Pago, AS 96799
Phone: (684) 633-4485
Fax: (684) 633-1139

ARIZONA
Bill F. Hernandez
Assistant Director
Employment & Rehab. Services
Dept. of Economic Security
1789 W. Washington St.
Phoenix, AZ 85007
Phone: (602) 542-4910

ARKANSAS
Ed Rolle
Director
Employment Security Dept.
#2 Capitol Mall, Rm. 506
Little Rock, AR 72201
Phone: (501) 682-2121
Fax: (501) 682-3713

CALIFORNIA
Ray Remy
Director
Dept. of Employment Dev.
800 Capitol Mall, Rm. 5000
Sacramento, CA 95814
Phone: (916) 654-8210
Fax: (916) 657-5294

COLORADO
Judith Richendifer
Director
Employment Programs
Dept. of Labor & Employment
1515 Arapahoe St.
Tower 2, Ste. 400
Denver, CO 80202
Phone: (303) 620-4200
Fax: (303) 620-4257

CONNECTICUT
Wallace Barnes
Chair
Job Training Partnership Act Administration
Dept. of Labor
1875 Perkins St.
Bristol, CT 06010
Phone: (860) 263-6590

DELAWARE
Michael M. Benefield, Jr.
Director
Div. of Employment & Training
Dept. of Labor
P.O. Box 9828
Wilmington, DE 19808-0828
Phone: (302) 761-8110
Fax: (302) 761-6617

DISTRICT OF COLUMBIA
Gregory Irish
Director
Dept. of Employment Services
500 C St., NW, Rm. 600
Washington, DC 20001
Phone: (202) 724-7101
Fax: (202) 724-7112

FLORIDA
Kathleen McLeskey
Director
Div. of Jobs & Benefits
Dept. of Labor & Employment Services
Atkins Bldg., Ste. 300
1320 Executive Ctr. Dr.
Tallahassee, FL 32399-0667
Phone: (850) 488-7228
Fax: (850) 487-1753

GEORGIA
Ronald Russell
Job Training Director
Dept. of Labor
Sussex Pl. Bldg., Rm. 560
148 International Blvd.
Atlanta, GA 30303
Phone: (404) 656-5810

GUAM
Juanita Mafnas
Agency for Human Resources Dev.
108 B St., E. Sunset Blvd.
P.O. Box CQ
Hagatna, GU 96932
Phone: (671) 475-0750
Fax: (671) 477-5022

HAWAII
Lorraine Akiba
Director
Dept. of Labor & Industrial Relations
830 Punchbowl St., Rm. 321
Honolulu, HI 96813
Phone: (808) 586-8844
Fax: (808) 586-9099

IDAHO
Cheryl Brush
Chief
Workforce Systems Bur.
Dept. of Labor
317 Main St.
Boise, ID 83702
Phone: (208) 334-6303
Fax: (208) 334-6430

ILLINOIS
Pam McDonough
Director
Dept. of Commerce & Community Affairs
620 E. Adams St., 3rd Fl.
Springfield, IL 62701
Phone: (217) 782-3233
Fax: (217) 524-0864

INDIANA
Craig E. Hartzer
Commissioner
Dept. of Workforce Dev.
10 N. Senate, Rm. SE-302
Indianapolis, IN 46204
Phone: (317) 233-5661
Fax: (317) 232-1815

IOWA
Jeff Nall
Administrator
Div. of Job Training
Dept. of Economic Dev.
200 E. Grand Ave.
Des Moines, IA 50309
Phone: (515) 281-4219

KANSAS
Heather M. Whitley
Director
Div. of Employment & Training
Dept. of Human Resources
512 SW 6th Ave.
Topeka, KS 66603
Phone: (785) 296-7874
Fax: (785) 296-5112

KENTUCKY
Marsha Whittet
Commissioner
Cabinet for Human Resources
Dept. for Employment Services
275 W. Main St.
Frankfort, KY 40621
Phone: (502) 564-5331
Fax: (502) 564-7452

LOUISIANA
Garey Forster
Secretary
Dept. of Labor
P.O. Box 94094
Baton Rouge, LA 70804
Phone: (225) 342-3111
Fax: (225) 342-3778

MAINE
Val Landry
Commissioner
Dept. of Labor
54 State House Station
Augusta, ME 04333
Phone: (207) 287-3788

MARYLAND
Gary Moore
Executive Director
Div. of Employment & Training
Labor, Licensing & Regulation
1100 N. Eutaw St., Rm. 600
Baltimore, MD 21201
Phone: (410) 767-2800
Fax: (410) 767-2010

MASSACHUSETTS
John A. King
Deputy Director
Div. of Employment & Training
Dept. of Labor & Workforce Dev.
19 Staniford St., 3rd Fl.
Boston, MA 02114
Phone: (617) 626-6600
Fax: (617) 727-0315

MICHIGAN
Douglas Stites
Acting Director
Dept. of Career Dev.
201 N. Washington
Lansing, MI 48913
Phone: (517) 373-4871

MINNESOTA
Earl Wilson
Commissioner
Dept. of Economic Security
390 N. Robert St.
St. Paul, MN 55105
Phone: (651) 297-4336
Fax: (651) 296-0994

MISSISSIPPI
Jean Denson
Director
Employment & Training Div.
Dept. of Economic & Community Dev.
301 W. Pearl St.
Jackson, MS 39203
Phone: (601) 949-2000
Fax: (601) 949-2291

MISSOURI
Mike Pulliam
Acting Director
Div. of Job Dev. & Training
Dept. of Economic Dev.
2023 St. Mary's Blvd.
P.O. Box 1087
Jefferson City, MO 65102-1087
Phone: (573) 751-4750
Fax: (573) 751-6765
E-mail: mpulliam@mail.state.mo.us

MONTANA
Wendy Keating
Administrator
Job Services Div.
Dept. of Labor & Industry
Walt Sullivan Bldg., 1327 Lockey
P.O. Box 1728
Helena, MT 59624
Phone: (406) 444-2648
Fax: (406) 444-3037

NEBRASKA
Dennis Lacquement
Director
Job Training of Greater NE
Dept. of Labor
1010 N. St., Ste. A
Lincoln, NE 68508
Phone: (402) 471-3181
Fax: (402) 471-3482

NEVADA
Valerie Hopkins
Acting Administrator
State Job Training Ofc.
Dept. of Employment Training & Rehab.
505 E. King St., Rm. 504
Carson City, NV 89701-4798
Phone: (775) 684-4210
Fax: (775) 684-4187

NEW HAMPSHIRE
John Hamilton
Executive Director
Job Training Council
64 Old Suncook Rd.
Concord, NH 03301
Phone: (603) 228-9500
Fax: (603) 228-8557

NEW JERSEY
Mark B. Boyd
Deputy Commissioner
Div. of Administration
Labor Dept.
P.O. Box 055
Trenton, NJ 08625
Phone: (609) 292-5005

Connie O. Hughes
Director
Employment Security & Job Training
Dept. of Labor
John Fitch Plz.
P.O. Box 058
Trenton, NJ 08625-0058
Phone: (609) 984-2593

NEW MEXICO
Jack Martinez
Programs Division Director
Human Rights Div.
Labor Dept.
1596 Pacheco St.
Santa Fe, NM 87505-3979
Phone: (505) 827-6838
Fax: (505) 827-6878

NEW YORK
James J. McGowan
Commissioner
Dept. of Labor
State Ofc. Bldg. Campus, Bldg. 12
Albany, NY 12240
Phone: (518) 457-2741
Fax: (518) 457-6908

NORTH CAROLINA
Allen Alexander
Director
Employment & Training
Commerce Dept.
441 N. Harrington
Raleigh, NC 27603
Phone: (919) 733-6383
Fax: (919) 733-6923

NORTH DAKOTA
James Hirsch
Director
Job Training
Job Service
P.O. Box 5507
Bismarck, ND 58506-5507
Phone: (701) 328-2825
Fax: (701) 328-4000
E-mail: jhirsch@state.nd.us

NORTHERN MARIANA ISLANDS
Felix Nogis
Director
Job Training Partnership Administration
Dept. of Labor
Saipan, MP 96950
Phone: (670) 664-1700
Fax: (670) 322-7333

OHIO
Evelyn Bissonett
Director
Power OH
Bur. of Employment Services
145 S. Front St., 4th Fl.
Columbus, OH 43215
Phone: (614) 466-3817
Fax: (614) 752-6582

OKLAHOMA
Jon Brock
Executive Director
Employment Security Comm.
2401 N. Lincoln Blvd.
Oklahoma City, OK 73105
Phone: (405) 557-7200
Fax: (405) 557-7256

OREGON
Roger Bassett
Commissioner
Job Training Partnership Administration
255 Capitol St., NE, Rm. 399
Salem, OR 97310
Phone: (503) 373-1995
Fax: (503) 378-3365

PENNSYLVANIA
Alan Williamson
Deputy Secretary
Employment Security & Job Training
Dept. of Labor & Industry
Labor & Industry Bldg., Rm. 1700
Harrisburg, PA 17120
Phone: (717) 787-3907
Fax: (717) 787-8826

PUERTO RICO
Aura Gonzalez
Secretary
Dept. of Labor & Human Resources
Prudencio Rivera Martinez
505 Munoz Rivera Ave.
Hato Rey, PR 00918
Phone: (787) 754-2120
Fax: (787) 753-9550

RHODE ISLAND
Lee Arnold
Director
Dept. of Labor & Training
101 Friendship St.
Providence, RI 02903
Phone: (401) 222-3732
Fax: (401) 222-1473

SOUTH CAROLINA
Joel T. Cassidy
Executive Director
Employment Security Comm.
P.O. Box 995
Columbia, SC 29202
Phone: (843) 737-2617

SOUTH DAKOTA
Lloyd Schipper
Deputy Secretary
Div. of Job Services
Dept. of Labor
700 Governors Dr.
Pierre, SD 57501
Phone: (605) 773-3372
Fax: (605) 773-6680

TENNESSEE
Maria Peroulas Draper
Deputy Commissioner
Dept. of Labor
710 James Robertson Pkwy., 2nd Fl.
Nashville, TN 37243
Phone: (615) 741-1906
Fax: (615) 741-3003

TEXAS
Mike Sheridan
Executive Director
Workforce Comm.
TWC Bldg.
101 E. 15th St.
Austin, TX 78778-0001
Phone: (512) 463-0735
Fax: (512) 475-2321
E-mail: mikesheridian@twc.state.tx.us

U.S. VIRGIN ISLANDS
Eleuteria Roberts
Acting Commissioner
Dept. of Labor
2203 Church St.
Christiansted
St. Croix, VI 00820
Phone: (340) 773-1994
Fax: (340) 773-0094

UTAH
Helen Thatcher
Director
Div. of Employment Dev.
Dept. of Workforce Services
1385 S. State
Salt Lake City, UT 84115
Phone: (801) 468-0177
Fax: (801) 468-0160
E-mail: hthatch.wsadmpo@state.ut.us

VERMONT
Robert Ware
Director
Jobs & Training Div.
Dept. of Employment & Training
P.O. Box 488
Montpelier, VT 05601-0488
Phone: (802) 828-4151
Fax: (802) 828-4022

VIRGINIA
Clarence H. Carter
Commissioner
Dept. of Social Services
Theater Row Bldg.
730 E. Broad St.
Richmond, VA 23219
Phone: (804) 692-1901
Fax: (804) 692-1964

WASHINGTON
Gary Gallwas
Assistant Commissioner
Employment & Training Div.
Dept. of Employment Security
P.O. Box 9046, MS 6000
Olympia, WA 98507-9046
Phone: (360) 438-4611
Fax: (360) 438-3224

WEST VIRGINIA
Quetta Muzzle
Director
Job Training Program Div.
Bldg. 4, Rm. 610
612 California Ave.
Charleston, WV 25305
Phone: (304) 558-5920
Fax: (304) 558-0675

WISCONSIN
Eric Baker
Administrator
Jobs, Employment, & Training Services
Dept. of Workforce Dev.
201 E. Washington, Rm. 201
P.O. Box 7946
Madison, WI 53703
Phone: (608) 266-0327
Fax: (608) 267-2392

WYOMING
Matt Johnson
Liaison
Job Training Program
Dept. of Employment
P.O. Box 2760
Casper, WY 82602
Phone: (307) 235-3601

Judicial Conduct Organizations

Oversees the investigation and hearings of judges charged with misconduct.

ALABAMA
Margaret S. Childers
Director
Judicial Inquiry Comm.
800 S. McDonough St., Ste. 201
Montgomery, AL 36130
Phone: (334) 242-4089
Fax: (334) 240-3327

ALASKA
Marla Greenstein
Executive Director
Comm. on Judicial Conduct
310 K St., Ste. 301
Anchorage, AK 99501
Phone: (907) 272-1033
Fax: (907) 272-9309

AMERICAN SAMOA

ARIZONA
E. Keith Stott
Executive Director
Comm. on Judicial Conduct
1501 W. Washington, #229
Phoenix, AZ 85007
Phone: (602) 542-5200

ARKANSAS
Jim Badami
Executive Director
Judicial Discipline & Disability Comm.
323 Ctr. St., Ste. 1060
Little Rock, AR 72201
Phone: (501) 682-1050
Fax: (501) 682-1049

CALIFORNIA
William C. Vickrey
Director
Judicial Council
Administration Ofc. of the Cts.
303 Second St.
San Francisco, CA 94107
Phone: (415) 396-9100
Fax: (415) 396-9362

COLORADO

CONNECTICUT

DELAWARE
Cathy L. Howard
Supreme Court Clerk
55 The Green
Dover, DE 19901
Phone: (302) 739-4155
Fax: (302) 739-3751

DISTRICT OF COLUMBIA

FLORIDA
Brook S. Kennerly
Executive Director
Judicial Qualifications Comm.
The Historic Capitol, Ste. 102
Tallahassee, FL 32399-6000
Phone: (850) 488-1581
Fax: (850) 922-6781

GEORGIA
Earle B. May, Jr.
Director
Judicial Qualifications Comm.
77 E. Crossville Rd., Ste. 206
Roswell, GA 30075-3085
Phone: (770) 587-5208
Fax: (770) 587-5422

GUAM
Benjamin J. Cruz
Chief Justice
Judicial Council
Supreme Ct.
120 W. O'Brien Dr.
Hagatna, GU 96910
Phone: (671) 475-3510
Fax: (671) 477-4676

HAWAII
Gerald Sekiya
Chair
Comm. on Judicial Conduct
The Judiciary/Supreme Ct.
P.O. Box 2560
Honolulu, HI 96804-2560
Phone: (808) 539-4790
Fax: (808) 539-4838

IDAHO
Robert G. Hamlin
Executive Director
Judicial Council
P.O. Box 16488
Boise, ID 83715-6488
Phone: (208) 344-8474

ILLINOIS
Kathy Twine
Executive Director
Judicial Inquiry Board
100 W. Randolph St., Ste. 14-500
Chicago, IL 60601
Phone: (312) 814-5554

INDIANA
Meg W. Babcock
Counsel
Comm. on Judicial Qualifications
115 W. Washington St., Ste. 1080
Indianapolis, IN 46204-3417
Phone: (317) 232-4706
Fax: (317) 233-6586

IOWA
William J. O'Brien
State Court Administrator
Judicial Dept.
State Capitol Bldg.
1007 E. Grand Ave.
Des Moines, IA 50319
Phone: (515) 281-5241
Fax: (515) 242-6164

KANSAS
Carol G. Green
Clerk of Appellate Courts
Supreme Ct. Judicial Ctr.
301 SW 10th Ave., Rm. 374
Topeka, KS 66612-1507
Phone: (785) 296-3229
Fax: (785) 296-1028

KENTUCKY
James D. Lawson
Secretary
Judicial Retirement & Removal Comm.
P.O. Box 21868
Lexington, KY 40522
Phone: (606) 233-4128

LOUISIANA
Pascal F. Calogero, Jr.
Chief Justice
Supreme Ct.
Supreme Ct. Bldg.
301 Loyola Ave.
New Orleans, LA 70112
Phone: (504) 568-5707

MAINE
Merle Loper
Executive Secretary
Cmte. on Judicial Responsibility & Disability
P.O. Box 8058
Portland, ME 04104
Phone: (207) 780-4364

MARYLAND
Bedford T. Bentley
Secretary
State Board of Law Examiners
Robert F. Sweeny District Ct. Bldg., 3rd Fl.
251 Rowe Blvd.
Annapolis, MD 21401
Phone: (410) 260-1960

MASSACHUSETTS
Barbara Morgan Fauth
Executive Director
Comm. on Judicial Conduct
14 Beacon St.
Boston, MA 02108
Phone: (617) 725-8050
Fax: (617) 248-9938

MICHIGAN
Allan Sobel
Executive Director & General Counsel
Judicial Tenure Comm.
211 W. Fort St.
Detroit, MI 48226
Phone: (313) 256-9104

MINNESOTA
De Paul Willette
Executive Secretary
Board on Judicial Standards
2025 Centre Point Blvd., Ste. 420
Mendota Heights, MN 55120
Phone: (651) 296-3999
Fax: (651) 452-3433

MISSISSIPPI
Luther T. Brantley, III
Executive Director
Comm. on Judicial Performance
P.O. Box 22527
Jackson, MS 39225-2527
Phone: (601) 359-1273
Fax: (601) 354-6277

MISSOURI
James M. Smith
Administrator & Counselor
Comm. on Retirement, Removal & Discipline of Judges
2190 S. Mason Rd., Ste. 201
St. Louis, MO 63131-1637
Phone: (314) 966-1007
Fax: (314) 966-0076
E-mail: jsmith@osca.state.mo.us

MONTANA
Sharon Parrish
Administrative Secretary
Court Administration
Judiciary
215 N. Sanders
P.O. Box 203002
Helena, MT 59620
Phone: (406) 444-2608
Fax: (406) 444-3274

NEBRASKA
Joseph C. Steele
State Court Administrator
Comm. on Judicial Qualifications
State Capitol, Rm. 1220
P.O. Box 98910
Lincoln, NE 68509
Phone: (402) 471-3730

NEVADA
Leonard Gang
Executive Director & General Counsel
Comm. on Judicial Discipline
P.O. Box 48
Carson City, NV 89702
Phone: (775) 687-4017
Fax: (775) 687-3607

NEW HAMPSHIRE
William R. Johnson
Chair
Cmte. for Judicial Conduct
Supreme Ct.
P.O. Box 1476
Concord, NH 03302-1476
Phone: (603) 271-2646

NEW JERSEY
Patrick J. Monahan, Jr.
Chief
Professional Services
Judiciary
Hughes Justice Complex
P.O. Box 037
Trenton, NJ 08625-0037
Phone: (609) 292-2552
Fax: (609) 292-6848

NEW MEXICO
Douglas W. Turner
Chair
Judicial Standards Comm.
P.O. Box 1012
Albuquerque, NM 87103-1012
Phone: (505) 841-9438
Fax: (505) 841-9431

NEW YORK
Gerald Stern
Administrator
State Comm. on Judicial Conduct
801 2nd Ave.
New York, NY 10017
Phone: (212) 949-8860
Fax: (212) 949-8864

NORTH CAROLINA
John B. Lewis, Jr.
Chair
Judicial Standards Comm.
P.O. Box 1122
Raleigh, NC 27602
Phone: (919) 733-2690

NORTH DAKOTA
Vivian E. Berg
Secretary
Disciplinary Board
Supreme Ct.
600 E. Blvd. Ave., 1st Fl. - Judicial Wing
Bismarck, ND 58505-0530
Phone: (701) 328-2221
Fax: (701) 328-4480

NORTHERN MARIANA ISLANDS

OHIO
Jonathon W. Marshall
Director & Secretary to Board
Board of Comms. on Grievances & Discipline
Supreme Ct.
41 S. High St., Ste. 3370
Columbus, OH 43215
Phone: (614) 644-5800
Fax: (614) 644-5804

OKLAHOMA
Howard Conyers
Director
Council on Judicial Complaints
1915 N. Stiles, Ste. 305
Oklahoma City, OK 73105
Phone: (405) 521-2450

OREGON
Pamela Knowles
Executive Director
Judicial Fitness Comm.
2835 NE Broadway St.
Portland, OR 97232-1762
Phone: (503) 284-4636
Fax: (503) 284-4668

PENNSYLVANIA
Robert Curran
Chairman
Judicial Conduct Board
225 Market St.
Harrisburg, PA 17101-2126
Phone: (717) 234-7911

PUERTO RICO

RHODE ISLAND
Alice Bridget Gibney
Chair
Comm. on Judicial Tenure & Discipline
Superior Ct.
250 Benefit St.
Providence, RI 02903
Phone: (401) 222-1188

SOUTH CAROLINA
Sally Speth
Director
Judicial Standards Comm.
Judicial Dept.
1015 Sumter St.
Columbia, SC 29201-3739
Phone: (803) 734-1965

SOUTH DAKOTA
Thomas Welk
Chair
Judicial Qualifications Comm.
P.O. Box 5015
Sioux Falls, SD 57117
Phone: (605) 336-2424
Fax: (605) 334-0618

TENNESSEE
Joe G. Riley, Jr.
Presiding Judge
Ct. of the Judiciary
111 Lake St.
Ridgely, TN 38080
Phone: (901) 264-5671
Fax: (901) 264-9433

TEXAS
Robert Flowers
Executive Director
State Comm. on Judicial Conduct
P.O. Box 12265
Austin, TX 78711
Phone: (512) 463-5533

U.S. VIRGIN ISLANDS
Thomas Moore
Chief Justice
District Ct.
District Ct. Bldg.
St. Thomas, VI 00802
Phone: (340) 774-0640
Fax: (340) 774-1293
E-mail: vidc@vid.uscourts.gov

UTAH
Steven Stewart
Executive Director
Judicial Conduct Comm.
645 S. 200 E., Ste. 104
Salt Lake City, UT 84111
Phone: (801) 533-3200
Fax: (801) 533-3208

VERMONT
David Gibson
Chair
Judicial Conduct Board
P.O. Box 796
White River Junction, VT 05001
Phone: (802) 295-5631

VIRGINIA
Donald H. Kent
Counsel
Judicial Inquiry & Review Comm.
Supreme Ct. Bldg., Ste. 661
100 N. 9th St.
Richmond, VA 23219
Phone: (804) 786-6636
Fax: (804) 371-0650

WASHINGTON
David Akana
Executive Director
Comm. on Judicial Conduct
P.O. Box 1817
Olympia, WA 98507-1817
Phone: (360) 753-4585
Fax: (360) 586-2918

WEST VIRGINIA
Betty L. Lambert
Executive Secretary
Judicial Investigation Comm.
Bldg. 1, Rm. E400
1900 Kanawha Blvd., E.
Charleston, WV 25304
Phone: (304) 558-0169
Fax: (304) 558-0831

WISCONSIN

WYOMING
Maxwell E. Osborn
Chair
Comm. on Judicial Conduct & Ethics
P.O. Box 1585
Cheyenne, WY 82003
Phone: (307) 777-7581

Juvenile Rehabilitation

Administers rehabilitative facilities and programs for delinquent youth committed by the courts.

ALABAMA
John Rickicki
Director
Dept. of Youth Affairs
P.O. Box 66
Mt. Meigs, AL 36057
Phone: (334) 215-8100
Fax: (334) 215-1453

ALASKA
George Buhite
Youth Corrections Administrator
Div. of Family & Youth Services
Dept of Health & Social Services
P.O. Box 110630
Juneau, AK 99811-0630
Phone: (907) 465-3170
Fax: (907) 465-3397

AMERICAN SAMOA
Te'o Fuavai
Commissioner
Dept. of Public Safety
AS Govt.
Pago Pago, AS 96799
Phone: (684) 633-1111
Fax: (684) 633-5111

ARIZONA
David Gaspar
Director
Dept. of Juvenile Corrections
1624 W. Adams St.
Phoenix, AZ 85007
Phone: (602) 542-3987
Fax: (602) 542-5156

ARKANSAS
Russell Rigsby
Director
Div. of Youth Services
Dept. of Human Services
P.O. Box 1437, Slot 450
Little Rock, AR 72203
Phone: (501) 682-8654
Fax: (501) 682-1339

CALIFORNIA
Francisco J. Alarcon
Director
Dept. of Youth Authority
4241 Williamsborough Dr., Ste. 201
Sacramento, CA 95823
Phone: (916) 262-1467

COLORADO
Jerry Adamek
Director
Div. of Youth Corrections
Dept. of Human Services
4255 S. Knox Ct.
Denver, CO 80236
Phone: (303) 866-7345
Fax: (303) 866-7344

CONNECTICUT
Joseph D. D'Alesio
Executive Director of Operations
Superior Court
231 Capitol Ave.
Hartford, CT 06106
Phone: (860) 722-5897

DELAWARE
Cherise Brewington-Carr
Director
Youth Rehab. Services Div.
Children, Youth & Families
1825 Faulkland Rd.
Wilmington, DE 19805
Phone: (302) 633-2620
Fax: (302) 633-2697

DISTRICT OF COLUMBIA

FLORIDA
Calvin Ross
Secretary
Dept. of Juvenile Justice
Knight Bldg.
2737 Centerview Dr.
Tallahassee, FL 32399-3100
Phone: (850) 921-0904
Fax: (850) 921-4159

GEORGIA
Orlando Martinez
Commissioner
Dept. of Juvenile Justice
2 Peachtree St., 5th Fl.
Atlanta, GA 30303
Phone: (404) 657-2410

GUAM
David M. Dell'Isola
Director
Dept. of Youth Affairs
P.O. Box 23672
GMF, GU 96921
Phone: (671) 734-3911
Fax: (671) 734-7536

HAWAII
Bert Matsuoka
Executive Director
Ofc. of Youth Services
Dept. of Human Services
820 Mililani St., Ste. 817
Honolulu, HI 96813-2938
Phone: (808) 587-5706
Fax: (808) 587-5734

IDAHO
Brent Reinke
Director
Dept. of Juvenile Corrections
400 N. 10th, 2nd Fl.
Boise, ID 83702
Phone: (208) 334-5102

ILLINOIS
Donald N. Snyder
Director
Dept. of Corrections
P.O. Box 19277
Springfield, IL 62794
Phone: (217) 522-2666
Fax: (217) 522-8719

INDIANA
Pam Cline
Director
Juvenile Services
Dept. of Corrections
402 W. Washington St., Rm. W341-A
Indianapolis, IN 46204
Phone: (317) 232-1746
Fax: (317) 233-4948

IOWA
Mary Nelson
Administrator
Adult, Children & Family Services
Dept. of Human Services
Hoover State Ofc. Bldg.
1305 E. Walnut
Des Moines, IA 50319
Phone: (515) 281-5521

KANSAS
Albert Murray
Commissioner
Juvenile Justice Authority
714 SW Jackson, Ste. 300
Topeka, KS 66603
Phone: (785) 296-4213
Fax: (785) 296-1412

KENTUCKY
Donna Harmon
Commissioner
Cabinet for Families & Children
Dept. for Social Services
275 E. Main St.
Frankfort, KY 40621
Phone: (502) 564-4650
Fax: (502) 564-5002

LOUISIANA
George White
Deputy Assistant Secretary
Ofc. of Juvenile Services
P.O. Box 94304
Baton Rouge, LA 70804-9304
Phone: (225) 342-6001
Fax: (225) 342-4441

MAINE
Lars Olsen
Superintendent
Youth Ctr.
Dept. of Corrections
675 Westbrook St.
S. Portland, ME 04106
Phone: (207) 822-0000

MARYLAND
Gilberto de Jesus
Secretary
Ofc. of the Secretary
Dept. of Juvenile Justice
120 W. Fayette St.
Baltimore, MD 21201
Phone: (410) 230-3100
Fax: (410) 333-4199

MASSACHUSETTS
Robert P. Gittens
Commissioner
Executive Ofc. of Health & Human Services
Dept. of Youth Services
27-43 Wormwood St., Ste. 400
Boston, MA 02210
Phone: (617) 727-7575
Fax: (617) 951-2409

MICHIGAN
Jim Beougher
Director
Bur. of Child & Family Services
Family Independence Agency
235 S. Grand Ave.
Lansing, MI 48909
Phone: (517) 335-6158

MINNESOTA
William D. Ellis
Project Manager
Juvenile Services & Legislative Relations Div.
Dept. of Corrections
1450 Energy Park Dr., #200
St. Paul, MN 55108-5227
Phone: (651) 642-0274
Fax: (651) 642-0417
E-mail: wellis@smtpco.doc.state.mn.us

MISSISSIPPI
Don Taylor
Executive Director
Dept. of Human Services
P.O. Box 352
Jackson, MS 39205
Phone: (601) 354-4500
Fax: (601) 359-4477

MISSOURI
Mark Steward
Director
Div. of Youth Services
Dept. of Social Services
Broadway Bldg., Rm. 540
P.O. Box 447
Jefferson City, MO 65102
Phone: (573) 751-3324
Fax: (573) 751-4494

MONTANA
Mike Ferriter
Administrator
Community Corrections Div.
Dept. of Corrections
1539 11th Ave.
Helena, MT 59620
Phone: (406) 444-4913
Fax: (406) 444-4920

NEBRASKA
Mark Martin
Acting Director
Youth Rehab. & Treatment Ctrs.
Dept. of Health & Human Services
P.O. Box 95044
Lincoln, NE 68509
Phone: (402) 471-8403
Fax: (402) 471-9034

NEVADA
Stephen A. Shaw
Administrator
Div. of Child & Family Services
711 E. 5th St.
Carson City, NV 89701-5092
Phone: (775) 684-4400
Fax: (775) 684-4455
E-mail: sshaw@govmail.state.nv.us

NEW HAMPSHIRE
Peter R. Favreau
Commissioner
Youth Dev. Ctr.
Youth Dev. Services
1056 N. River Rd.
Manchester, NH 03104-1958
Phone: (603) 625-5471
Fax: (603) 624-0512

NEW JERSEY
Frank Gripp
Director
Bur. of Community Programs
Dept. of Corrections
Whittlesey Rd.
P.O. Box 863
Trenton, NJ 08625-0863
Phone: (609) 292-4640
Fax: (609) 633-2065

NEW MEXICO
Doug Mitchell
Director
Juvenile Justice Div.
Dept. of Children, Youth & Families
P.O. Drawer 5160
Sante Fe, NM 87502
Phone: (505) 827-7629
Fax: (505) 827-4053

NEW YORK
John A. Johnson
Commissioner
Ofc. of Children & Family Services
Capital View Ofc. Park
52 Washington St.
Rensselaer, NY 12144
Phone: (518) 473-8437
Fax: (518) 473-9131

NORTH CAROLINA
George L. Sweat
Director
Ofc. of Juvenile Justice
Governor's Ofc.
410 S. Salisbury St.
Raleigh, NC 27601
Phone: (919) 733-3388
Fax: (919) 733-1045

NORTH DAKOTA
Al Lick
Director
Div. of Juvenile Services
Dept. of Corrections & Rehab.
P.O. Box 1898
Bismarck, ND 58502-1898
Phone: (701) 328-6390
Fax: (701) 328-6651
E-mail: alick@state.nd.us

NORTHERN MARIANA ISLANDS
Eloise A. Furey
Director
Div. of Youth Services
Dept. of Community & Cultural Affairs
P.O. Box 1000 CK
Saipan, MP 96950
Phone: (670) 664-2254
Fax: (670) 664-2560

OHIO
Linda Bess
Deputy Director
Ofc. of Prevention, Protection & Self Sufficiency
Dept. of Human Services
65 E. State St., 9th Fl.
Columbus, OH 43215
Phone: (614) 466-1213
Fax: (614) 466-9247

OKLAHOMA
Jerry Regier
Director
Ofc. of Juvenile Affairs
P.O. Box 268812
Oklahoma City, OK 73126-8812
Phone: (405) 530-2800

OREGON
Rick Hill
Director
Youth Authority
530 Ctr. St., NE, Ste. 200
Salem, OR 97310-3740
Phone: (503) 373-7205
Fax: (503) 373-7622

Donna Middleton
Director
Comm. on Children & Families
530 Ctr. St., NE, Ste. 300
Salem, OR 97310
Phone: (503) 373-1283
Fax: (503) 378-8395

PENNSYLVANIA
JoAnn Lower
Deputy Secretary
Children, Youth & Families
Dept. of Public Welfare
P.O. Box 2675
Harrisburg, PA 17105
Phone: (717) 787-4756
Fax: (717) 787-0414

PUERTO RICO
Aura Gonzalez
Secretary
Dept. of Labor & Human Resources
Prudencio Rivera Martinez
505 Munoz Rivera Ave.
Hato Rey, PR 00918
Phone: (787) 754-2120
Fax: (787) 753-9550

RHODE ISLAND
Jay Lindgren
Director
Dept. of Children, Youth & Families
610 Mt. Pleasant Ave.
Providence, RI 02908
Phone: (401) 457-4750
Fax: (401) 457-5363

SOUTH CAROLINA
Gina Wood
Director
Dept. of Juvenile Justice
P.O. Box 21069
Columbia, SC 29221-1069
Phone: (803) 896-9359

SOUTH DAKOTA
Judy Hines
Administrator
Child Protection Services Div.
Dept. of Social Services
Kneip Bldg.
700 Governors Dr.
Pierre, SD 57501
Phone: (605) 773-3227
Fax: (605) 773-6834

TENNESSEE
George Hattaway
Commissioner
Dept. of Children's Services
Cordell Hull Bldg., 7th Fl.
710 James Robertson Pkwy.
Nashville, TN 37243
Phone: (615) 741-9701
Fax: (615) 532-8079

TEXAS
Steve Robinson
Executive Director
Youth Comm.
P.O. Box 4260
Austin, TX 78765-4260
Phone: (512) 424-6001
Fax: (512) 424-6010

U.S. VIRGIN ISLANDS
Sedonie Halbert
Commissioner
Dept. of Human Services
Knud Hansen Complex, Bldg. A
1303 Hospital Grounds
St. Thomas, VI 00802
Phone: (340) 774-0930
Fax: (340) 774-3466

UTAH
Gary Dalton
Director
Div. of Youth Corrections
Dept. of Human Services
120 N. 200 W., Rm. 422
Salt Lake City, UT 84103
Phone: (801) 538-4323
Fax: (801) 538-4334
E-mail: gdalton.hsadmin1@state.ut.us

VERMONT
William Young
Director
Dept. of Social & Rehab. Services
103 S. Main St.
Waterbury, VT 05671
Phone: (802) 241-2101

VIRGINIA
Gerald O. Glenn
Director
Dept. of Juvenile Justice
700 Centre, 4th Fl.
7th & Franklin Sts.
Richmond, VA 23219
Phone: (804) 371-0700
Fax: (804) 371-0725

WASHINGTON
Sid Sidorowicz
Assistant Secretary
Juvenile Rehab. Div.
Social & Health Services Dept.
P.O. Box 45045
Olympia, WA 98504
Phone: (360) 902-7804
Fax: (360) 902-7848

WEST VIRGINIA
Susan Salmons
Director
Youth Services
Dept. of Health & Human Resources
3135 16th St.
Huntington, WV 25705
Phone: (304) 528-5800
Fax: (304) 528-5512

WISCONSIN
Eurial Jordan
Secretary
Dept. of Corrections
149 E. Wilson
Madison, WI 53703
Phone: (608) 267-9507
Fax: (608) 267-3661

WYOMING
Shirley Carson
Director
Dept. of Family Services
Hathaway Bldg., 3rd Fl.
2300 Capitol Ave.
Cheyenne, WY 82002
Phone: (307) 777-7561
Fax: (307) 777-7747

Labor

Overall responsibility for administering and enforcing the state's labor laws.

ALABAMA
Barney Weeks
Commissioner
Dept. of Labor
RSA Union, Ste. 620
100 N. Union St.
Montgomery, AL 36130
Phone: (334) 242-3460
Fax: (334) 240-3417

ALASKA
Ed Flanagan
Commissioner
Dept. of Labor
P.O. Box 21149
Juneau, AK 99802
Phone: (907) 465-2700
Fax: (907) 465-2784

AMERICAN SAMOA
Sapini Siatu'u
Director
Dept. of Human Resources
AS Govt.
Pago Pago, AS 96799
Phone: (684) 633-4485
Fax: (684) 633-1139

ARIZONA
Larry J. Etchechury
Director
Industrial Comm.
800 W. Washington
Phoenix, AZ 85007
Phone: (602) 542-4411
Fax: (602) 542-3070

ARKANSAS
James Salkeld
Director
Dept. of Labor
10421 W. Markham, Ste. 100
Little Rock, AR 72205
Phone: (501) 682-4500
Fax: (501) 682-4532

CALIFORNIA
John Duncan
Director
Dept. of Industrial Relations
45 Fremont St., Ste. 3270
San Francisco, CA 94105
Phone: (415) 972-8835
Fax: (415) 972-8848

COLORADO
Vickie Armstrong
Executive Director
Dept. of Labor & Employment
1515 Arapahoe St.
Tower 2, Ste. 400
Denver, CO 80202
Phone: (303) 620-4700
Fax: (303) 620-4714

CONNECTICUT
James Butler
Commissioner
Dept. of Labor
200 Folly Brook Blvd.
Weathersfield, CT 06109
Phone: (860) 263-6505

DELAWARE
Lisa L. Blunt-Bradley
Secretary
Dept. of Labor
4425 N. Market St., 4th Fl.
Wilmington, DE 19802
Phone: (302) 761-8001
Fax: (302) 761-6621

DISTRICT OF COLUMBIA
Gregory Irish
Director
Dept. of Employment Services
500 C St., NW, Rm. 600
Washington, DC 20001
Phone: (202) 724-7101
Fax: (202) 724-7112

FLORIDA
Doug Jamerson
Secretary
Labor & Employment Security
Hartman Bldg., Ste. 303
2012 Capitol Cir., SE
Tallahassee, FL 32399-2152
Phone: (850) 922-7021
Fax: (850) 922-7119

GEORGIA
Michael Thurmond
Commissioner
Dept. of Labor
Sussex Pl. Bldg.
148 Intl. Blvd., Rm. 600
Atlanta, GA 30303
Phone: (404) 656-3011

GUAM
James Underwood
Acting Director
Dept. of Labor
504 E. Sunset Blvd., Tiyan
P.O. Box 9970
Tamuning, GU 96931
Phone: (671) 475-0101
Fax: (671) 477-2988

HAWAII
Lorraine Akiba
Director
Dept. of Labor & Industrial Relations
830 Punchbowl St., Rm. 321
Honolulu, HI 96813
Phone: (808) 586-8844
Fax: (808) 586-9099

IDAHO
Roger Madsen
Director
Dept. of Labor
317 Main St.
Boise, ID 83702
Phone: (208) 334-6100
Fax: (208) 334-6430

ILLINOIS
Robert M. Healey
Director
Dept. of Labor
160 N. LaSalle St., 13th Fl.
Chicago, IL 60601
Phone: (312) 793-2800
Fax: (312) 793-5257

INDIANA
Timothy Joyce
Commissioner
Dept. of Labor
402 W. Washington, Rm. W195
Indianapolis, IN 46204
Phone: (317) 232-2378
Fax: (317) 233-3790

IOWA
Byron Orton
Commissioner
Labor Div.
Workforce Dev.
1000 E. Grand Ave.
Des Moines, IA 50319
Phone: (515) 281-8067
Fax: (515) 242-5144

KANSAS
Vacant
Secretary
Legal Div. Employment Standards
Dept. of Human Resources
401 SW Topeka Blvd.
Topeka, KS 66603-3182
Phone: (785) 296-4902
Fax: (785) 296-0196

KENTUCKY
Joe Norsworthy
Secretary
Labor Cabinet
1047 U.S. 127 S.
Frankfort, KY 40601
Phone: (502) 564-3070
Fax: (502) 564-5387

LOUISIANA
Garey Forster
Secretary
Dept. of Labor
P.O. Box 94094
Baton Rouge, LA 70804
Phone: (225) 342-3111
Fax: (225) 342-3778

MAINE
Val Landry
Commissioner
Dept. of Labor
54 State House Station
Augusta, ME 04333
Phone: (207) 287-3788

MARYLAND
John P. O'Connor
Secretary/Commissioner
Labor & Industry
Labor, Licensing & Regulation
1100 N. Eutaw St., Rm. 600
Baltimore, MD 21201
Phone: (410) 767-2999
Fax: (410) 767-2220

MASSACHUSETTS
Angelo Buonopane
Director
Dept. of Labor & Workforce Dev.
One Ashburton Pl., Rm. 1402
Boston, MA 02108
Phone: (617) 727-6573
Fax: (617) 727-1090

MICHIGAN
Kal Smith
Deputy Director
Consumer & Industry Services
P.O. Box 30015
Lansing, MI 30015
Phone: (517) 373-9600
Fax: (517) 373-3728

MINNESOTA
Gretchen Maglich
Commissioner
Dept. of Labor & Industry
443 Lafayette Rd.
St. Paul, MN 55101
Phone: (651) 296-7958
Fax: (651) 282-5405
E-mail: gretchen.maglich@state.mn.us

MISSISSIPPI

MISSOURI
Karla McLucas
Director
Dept. of Labor & Industrial Relations
3315 W. Truman Blvd.
P.O. Box 504
Jefferson City, MO 65102
Phone: (573) 751-4091
Fax: (573) 526-4135
E-mail: kmclucas@dolir.state.mo.us

MONTANA
Pat Haffey
Commissioner
Dept. of Labor & Industry
P.O. Box 1728
Helena, MT 59624
Phone: (406) 444-3555
Fax: (406) 444-1394

NEBRASKA
Fernando Lecuona, III
Commissioner
Dept. of Labor
P.O. Box 94600
Lincoln, NE 68509
Phone: (402) 471-9000
Fax: (402) 471-2318

NEVADA
Carol Jackson
Director
Dept. of Employment, Training & Rehab.
1830 E. Sahara Ave., Ste. 201
Las Vegas, NV 89104
Phone: (702) 486-7923
Fax: (702) 486-7924
E-mail: cjackson@govmail.state.nv.us

NEW HAMPSHIRE
James Casey
Commissioner
Dept. of Labor
95 Pleasant St.
Concord, NH 03301
Phone: (603) 271-3176
Fax: (603) 271-7064

NEW JERSEY
Melvin L. Gelade
Commissioner
Dept. of Labor
John Fitch Plz.
P.O. Box 110
Trenton, NJ 08625-0110
Phone: (609) 292-3717
Fax: (609) 292-3824

NEW MEXICO
Clint Harden
Secretary
Dept. of Labor
P.O. Box 1928
Albuquerque, NM 87103
Phone: (505) 841-8409
Fax: (505) 841-8491

NEW YORK
James J. McGowan
Commissioner
Dept. of Labor
State Ofc. Bldg. Campus, Bldg. 12
Albany, NY 12240
Phone: (518) 457-2741
Fax: (518) 457-6908

NORTH CAROLINA
Harry E. Payne, Jr.
Commissioner
Dept. of Labor
4 W. Edenton St.
Raleigh, NC 27601-1092
Phone: (919) 733-7166
Fax: (919) 733-6197

NORTH DAKOTA
Mark Bachmeier
Interim Commissioner
Labor Dept.
600 E. Blvd. Ave., 13th Fl.
Bismarck, ND 58505
Phone: (701) 328-2660
Fax: (701) 328-2031
E-mail: bachmeie@pioneer.state.nd.us

NORTHERN MARIANA ISLANDS
Patrick A. Guerrero
Director
Dept. of Labor
P.O. Box 10007
Saipan, MP 96950
Phone: (670) 664-2000
Fax: (670) 664-2020

OHIO
David Williamson
Superintendent
Div. of Industrial Compliance
Dept. of Commerce
6606 Tussing Rd.
Reynoldsburg, OH 43068
Phone: (614) 644-2223
Fax: (614) 644-3505

OKLAHOMA
Brenda Reneau
Commissioner of Labor
Dept. of Labor
4001 N. Lincoln Blvd.
Oklahoma City, OK 73105
Phone: (405) 528-1500
Fax: (405) 528-5751

OREGON
Jack Roberts
Commissioner
Bur. of Labor & Industries
800 NE Oregon St., #32
Portland, OR 97232
Phone: (503) 731-4070
Fax: (503) 731-4103

PENNSYLVANIA
Johnny J. Butler
Secretary
Dept. of Labor & Industry
Labor & Industry Bldg., Rm. 1700
Harrisburg, PA 17120
Phone: (717) 787-3756
Fax: (717) 787-8826

PUERTO RICO
Aura Gonzalez
Secretary
Dept. of Labor & Human Resources
Prudencio Rivera Martinez
505 Munoz Rivera Ave.
Hato Rey, PR 00918
Phone: (787) 754-2120
Fax: (787) 753-9550

RHODE ISLAND
Lee Arnold
Director
Dept. of Labor & Training
101 Friendship St.
Providence, RI 02903
Phone: (401) 222-3732
Fax: (401) 222-1473

SOUTH CAROLINA
Rita M. McKinney
Director
Dept. of Labor, Licensing & Regulations
110 Centerview Dr.
P.O. Box 11329
Columbia, SC 29210
Phone: (803) 896-4390
Fax: (803) 896-4393

SOUTH DAKOTA
Craig Johnson
Secretary
Dept. of Labor
700 Governors Dr.
Pierre, SD 57501
Phone: (605) 773-3101
Fax: (605) 773-4211

TENNESSEE
Michael Magill
Commissioner
Dept. of Labor
Andrew Johnson Tower, 2nd Fl.
Nashville, TN 37243
Phone: (615) 741-2582
Fax: (615) 741-5078

TEXAS
Mike Sheridan
Executive Director
Workforce Comm.
TWC Bldg.
101 E. 15th St.
Austin, TX 78778-0001
Phone: (512) 463-0735
Fax: (512) 475-2321
E-mail: mikesheridian
@twc.state.tx.us

U.S. VIRGIN ISLANDS
Eleuteria Roberts
Acting Commissioner
Dept. of Labor
2203 Church St.
Christiansted
St. Croix, VI 00820
Phone: (340) 773-1994
Fax: (340) 773-0094

UTAH
Richard Lee Ellertson
Commissioner
Div. of Administration
Labor Comm.
160 E. 300 S., 3rd Fl.
P.O. Box 146600
Salt Lake City, UT 84114-6600
Phone: (801) 530-6880
Fax: (801) 530-6390
E-mail: rellerts.icmain
@state.ut.us

VERMONT
Steve Jansen
Commissioner
Dept. of Labor & Industry
Natl. Life Bldg.
Drawer 20
Montpelier, VT 05620-3401
Phone: (802) 828-2288
Fax: (802) 828-2195

VIRGINIA
John Mills Barr
Commissioner
Dept. of Labor & Industry
Powers-Taylor Bldg.
13 S. 13th St.
Richmond, VA 23219
Phone: (804) 786-2377
Fax: (804) 371-6524

WASHINGTON
Gary Moore
Director
Dept. of Labor & Industries
P.O. Box 44001
Olympia, WA 98504
Phone: (360) 902-5800
Fax: (360) 902-4202

WEST VIRGINIA
Steve Allred
Commissioner
Div. of Labor
State Capitol, Bldg. 3
1900 Kanawha Blvd., E.
Charleston, WV 25305
Phone: (304) 558-7890
Fax: (304) 558-3797

WISCONSIN
Linda Stewart
Secretary
Dept. of Workforce Dev.
201 E. Washington Ave.
P.O. Box 7946
Madison, WI 53707
Phone: (608) 266-7552
Fax: (608) 266-1784

WYOMING
Charlie Rando
Acting Administrator
Div. of Labor Standards
Dept. of Employment
Herschler Bldg.
122 W. 25th St.
Cheyenne, WY 82002
Phone: (307) 777-7672

Labor (Arbitration & Mediation)

Promotes voluntary and peaceful settlement of labor disputes.

ALABAMA
Barney Weeks
Commissioner
Dept. of Labor
RSA Union, Ste. 620
100 N. Union St.
Montgomery, AL 36130
Phone: (334) 242-3460
Fax: (334) 240-3417

ALASKA
Vacant
Director
Div. of Personnel
Dept. of Administration
P.O. Box 110201
Juneau, AK 99811-0201
Phone: (907) 465-4430

AMERICAN SAMOA
Sapini Siatu'u
Director
Dept. of Human Resources
AS Govt.
Pago Pago, AS 96799
Phone: (684) 633-4485
Fax: (684) 633-1139

ARIZONA

ARKANSAS
Edward L. House
Mediator
Mediation & Conciliation Div.
Dept. of Labor
10421 W. Markham St., Ste. 100
Little Rock, AR 72205
Phone: (501) 682-4511
Fax: (501) 682-4508

CALIFORNIA
John Duncan
Director
Dept. of Industrial Relations
45 Fremont St., Ste 3270
San Francisco, CA 94105
Phone: (415) 972-8835
Fax: (415) 972-8848

COLORADO
Vickie Armstrong
Executive Director
Dept. of Labor & Employment
1515 Arapahoe St.
Tower 2, Ste. 400
Denver, CO 80202
Phone: (303) 620-4700
Fax: (303) 620-4714

CONNECTICUT
Laurie Cain
Deputy Chair
Mediation & Arbitration Board
Dept. of Labor
38 Wolcott Hill Rd.
Wethersfield, CT 06109
Phone: (860) 566-7533

DELAWARE
Lisa L. Blunt-Bradley
Secretary
Dept. of Labor
4425 N. Market St., 4th Fl.
Wilmington, DE 19802
Phone: (302) 761-8001
Fax: (302) 761-6621

DISTRICT OF COLUMBIA
James Odell Baxter, II
Interim Director
Ofc. of Labor
441 4th St, NW, 2nd Fl.
Washington, DC 20001
Phone: (202) 724-4953
Fax: (202) 727-6887

FLORIDA
Barbara Griffin
Assistant Director
Div. of Jobs & Benefits
Dept. of Labor & Employment Services
1320 Executive Ctr. Dr.
Tallahassee, FL 32399-0667
Phone: (850) 488-7228
Fax: (850) 487-1753

GEORGIA
Michael Thurmond
Commissioner
Dept. of Labor
Sussex Pl. Bldg.
148 Intl. Blvd., Rm. 600
Atlanta, GA 30303
Phone: (404) 656-3011

GUAM
James Underwood
Acting Director
Dept. of Labor
504 E. Sunset Blvd., Tiyan
P.O. Box 9970
Tamuning, GU 96931
Phone: (671) 475-0101
Fax: (671) 477-2988

HAWAII
Bert Tomasu
Chair
State Labor Relations Board
Dept. of Labor & Industrial Relations
830 Punchbowl St., Rm. 434
Honolulu, HI 96813
Phone: (808) 586-8610
Fax: (808) 586-8613

IDAHO
Suzanne Sherlock
Mediator
Adjudication Div.
State Industrial Comm.
P.O. Box 83720
Boise, ID 83720-0041
Phone: (208) 334-6002
Fax: (208) 334-2321

ILLINOIS
Robert M. Healey
Director
Dept. of Labor
160 N. LaSalle St., 13th Fl.
Chicago, IL 60601
Phone: (312) 793-2800
Fax: (312) 793-5257

INDIANA
Timothy Joyce
Commissioner
Dept. of Labor
402 W. Washington, Rm. W195
Indianapolis, IN 46204
Phone: (317) 232-2378
Fax: (317) 233-3790

IOWA
Richard R. Ramsey
Chair
Public Employment Relations Board
515 E. Locust, Ste. 202
Des Moines, IA 50309
Phone: (515) 281-4414

KANSAS
Vacant
Secretary
Legal Div. Employment Standards
Dept. of Human Resources
401 SW Topeka Blvd.
Topeka, KS 66603-3182
Phone: (785) 296-4902
Fax: (785) 296-0196

KENTUCKY
Gary Moberly
Executive Director
Labor-Mgmt. Relations
Labor Cabinet
1047 U.S. Hwy. 127 S., Ste. 4
Frankfort, KY 40601
Phone: (502) 564-3070
Fax: (502) 564-1682

LOUISIANA

MAINE
Mark Ayotte
Executive Director
Labor Relations Board
Dept. of Labor
90 State House Station
Augusta, ME 04333
Phone: (207) 287-2015

MARYLAND

MASSACHUSETTS
Robert Dumont
Chair
Dept. of Labor & Workforce Dev.
100 Cambridge St., 16th Fl.
Boston, MA 02202
Phone: (617) 727-3505
Fax: (617) 727-4402

MICHIGAN
John Palmer
Director
Employment Service Agency
Economic Dev. Corp.
105 W. Allegan, 3rd Fl.
Lansing, MI 48933
Phone: (313) 256-3501
Fax: (313) 256-3090

MINNESOTA
Lance Teachworth
Commissioner
Bur. of Mediation Services
1380 Energy Ln., Ste. 2
St. Paul, MN 55108-5253
Phone: (651) 649-5433
Fax: (651) 643-3013
E-mail: lteachworth@state.mn.us

MISSISSIPPI

MISSOURI
John Birch
Chair
State Board of Mediation
Dept. of Labor & Industrial Relations
P.O. Box 591
Jefferson City, MO 65102-0591
Phone: (573) 751-3614
Fax: (573) 751-0215
E-mail: jbirch@dolir.state.mo.us

MONTANA
Jerry Keck
Administrator
Employment Relations Div.
Dept. of Labor & Industry
P.O. Box 8011
Helena, MT 59604-8011
Phone: (406) 444-1555
Fax: (406) 444-4140

NEBRASKA
William Wood
Labor Relations Administrator
Div. of Employee Relations
Dept. of Adm. Services
P.O. Box 95061
Lincoln, NE 68509-5061
Phone: (402) 471-4106
Fax: (402) 471-3394

NEVADA
Shari L. Thomas
Commissioner
Local Govt., Employee Mgmt. & Relations Board
2501 E. Sahara, Ste. 203
Las Vegas, NV 89104
Phone: (702) 486-4504
Fax: (702) 486-4355

NEW HAMPSHIRE
James Casey
Commissioner
Dept. of Labor
95 Pleasant St.
Concord, NH 03301
Phone: (603) 271-3176
Fax: (603) 271-7064

NEW JERSEY
Vivien Shapiro
Executive Director
Div. of Planning & Research
P.O. Box 388
Trenton, NJ 08625
Phone: (609) 292-2643

NEW MEXICO
Rudy J. Maestas
Director
Labor & Industrial Div.
Labor Dept.
1596 Pacheco St.
Santa Fe, NM 87505
Phone: (505) 827-6875
Fax: (505) 827-1664

NEW YORK
Michael R. Cuevas
Chair
Public Employee Relations Board
80 Wolf Rd., 5th Fl.
Albany, NY 12205
Phone: (518) 457-2578
Fax: (518) 457-0965

NORTH CAROLINA
Ardis Watkins
Director
Employment Mediation Bur.
Dept. of Labor
4 W. Edenton St.
Raleigh, NC 27601
Phone: (919) 715-3843
Fax: (919) 733-6197

NORTH DAKOTA
Mark Bachmeier
Interim Commissioner
Labor Dept.
600 E. Blvd. Ave., 13th Fl.
Bismarck, ND 58505
Phone: (701) 328-2660
Fax: (701) 328-2031
E-mail: bachmeie@pioneer.state.nd.us

NORTHERN MARIANA ISLANDS
Patrick A. Guerrero
Director
Dept. of Labor
P.O. Box 10007
Saipan, MP 96950
Phone: (670) 664-2000
Fax: (670) 664-2020

OHIO
Sue Pohler
Chair
State Employment Relations Board
65 E. State St., 12th Fl.
Columbus, OH 43266-0336
Phone: (614) 644-8573
Fax: (614) 466-3074

OKLAHOMA
Brenda Reneau
Commissioner of Labor
Dept. of Labor
4001 N. Lincoln Blvd.
Oklahoma City, OK 73105
Phone: (405) 528-1500
Fax: (405) 528-5751

OREGON
David Stiteler
Chair
Employment Relations Board
528 Cottage St., NE
Salem, OR 97310
Phone: (503) 378-3807
Fax: (503) 373-0021

PENNSYLVANIA
Mark A. Lamont
Director
Bur. of Mediation
Dept. of Labor & Industry
Labor & Industry Bldg., Rm. 1610
Harrisburg, PA 17120
Phone: (717) 787-2803
Fax: (717) 783-5225

PUERTO RICO
Samuel De La Rosa
Director
Bur. of Employment Security
Labor & Human Resources Dept.
505 Munoz Rivera Ave.
Hato Rey, PR 00918
Phone: (787) 753-5454
Fax: (787) 753-9550

RHODE ISLAND
Lee Arnold
Director
Dept. of Labor & Training
101 Friendship St.
Providence, RI 02903
Phone: (401) 222-3732
Fax: (401) 222-1473

SOUTH CAROLINA
Rita M. McKinney
Director
Dept. of Labor, Licensing & Regulations
110 Centerview Dr.
P.O. Box 11329
Columbia, SC 29210
Phone: (803) 896-4390
Fax: (803) 896-4393

SOUTH DAKOTA
James E. Marsh
Director
Div. of Labor & Mgmt.
Dept. of Labor
Kneip Bldg.
700 Governors Dr.
Pierre, SD 57501
Phone: (605) 773-3681
Fax: (605) 773-4211

TENNESSEE
Jon Moffett
Assistant Commissioner
Labor Standards
Dept. of Labor
710 James Robertson Pkwy.
Nashville, TN 37243
Phone: (615) 532-1327
Fax: (615) 532-1469

TEXAS
Mike Sheridan
Executive Director
Workforce Comm.
TWC Bldg.
101 E. 15th St.
Austin, TX 78778-0001
Phone: (512) 463-0735
Fax: (512) 475-2321
E-mail: mikesheridan@twc.state.tx.us

U.S. VIRGIN ISLANDS
Karen Andrews
Chief Negotiator
Ofc. of Collective Bargaining
Ofc. of the Governor
#8 GD Lyttons Fancy
St. Thomas, VI 00802
Phone: (340) 774-6450
Fax: (340) 777-4622

UTAH
Joseph Gallegos
Director
Anti-Discrimination & Labor Div.
Labor Comm.
160 E. 300 S., 3rd Fl.
Salt Lake City, UT 84114-6630
Phone: (801) 530-6801
Fax: (801) 530-7609
E-mail: jgallego.icmain@state.ut.us

VERMONT
Tim Noonan
Executive Director
Labor Relations Board
13 Baldwin St.
Montpelier, VT 05602
Phone: (802) 828-2700

VIRGINIA
John Mills Barr
Commissioner
Dept. of Labor & Industry
Powers-Taylor Bldg.
13 S. 13th St.
Richmond, VA 23219
Phone: (804) 786-2377
Fax: (804) 371-6524

WASHINGTON
Steve Puz
Assistant Attorney General
Ofc. of the Attorney Gen.
P.O. Box 40121
Olympia, WA 98504-0100
Phone: (360) 459-6563
Fax: (360) 438-7485

WEST VIRGINIA
Steve Allred
Commissioner
Div. of Labor
State Capitol, Bldg. 3
1900 Kanawha Blvd., E.
Charleston, WV 25305
Phone: (304) 558-7890
Fax: (304) 558-3797

WISCONSIN
James Meier
Chair
Employment Relations Comm.
18 S. Thornton Ave.
P.O. Box 7870
Madison, WI 53707
Phone: (608) 266-1381
Fax: (608) 266-6930

WYOMING
Charlie Rando
Acting Administrator
Div. of Labor Standards
Dept. of Employment
Herschler Bldg.
122 W. 25th St.
Cheyenne, WY 82002
Phone: (307) 777-7672

Latino Affairs

Represents and examines the concerns of Latin Americans.

ALABAMA

ALASKA

AMERICAN SAMOA

ARIZONA
Ruben Alvarez
Director
Governor's Ofc. of Equal Opportunity
1700 W. Washington, Rm. 104
Phoenix, AZ 85007
Phone: (602) 542-3711
Fax: (602) 542-3712

ARKANSAS

CALIFORNIA
Suzanna Tashiro
Director
Ofc. of Community Relations
18952 MacArthur Blvd.
Irvine, CA 92715
Phone: (714) 553-3566

COLORADO

CONNECTICUT
Fernando Betancourt
Executive Director
Comm. on Latino & Puerto Rican Affairs
18-20 Trinity St.
Hartford, CT 06106
Phone: (860) 240-8330

DELAWARE
Jaime Rivera
Chair
Council on Hispanic Affairs
Dept. of Health & Human Services
Administration Campus
1901 N. DuPont Hwy., Main Bldg.
New Castle, DE 19720
Phone: (302) 577-4502
Fax: (302) 577-4510

DISTRICT OF COLUMBIA
Frank Yurrita
Interim Director
Ofc. of Latino Affairs
2000 14th St., NW, 2nd Fl.
Washington, DC 20009-4473
Phone: (202) 671-2825
Fax: (202) 673-4557

FLORIDA
Mariela Fraser
Executive Director
State Comm. on Hispanic Affairs
Ofc. of the Governor
Tallahassee, FL 32399
Phone: (850) 488-2272

GEORGIA

GUAM

HAWAII

IDAHO
Dan Ramirez
Executive Director
Comm. on Hispanic Affairs
5460 Franklin Rd., #B
Boise, ID 83705-1080
Phone: (208) 334-3776

ILLINOIS
Joe Munoz
Special Assistant to the Governor for Hispanic Affairs
Ofc. of the Governor
100 W. Randolph, 16th Fl.
Chicago, IL 60601
Phone: (312) 814-2166
Fax: (312) 814-5512

INDIANA

IOWA
Sylvia Tijerina
Administrator
Div. of Latino Affairs
Dept. of Human Rights
Lucas State Ofc. Bldg.
321 E. 12th St.
Des Moines, IA 50319
Phone: (515) 281-4080

KANSAS
Tina De La Rosa
Executive Director
Advisory Comm. on Hispanic Affairs
Dept. of Human Resources
1430 SW Topeka Blvd.
Topeka, KS 66612-2201
Phone: (785) 296-3465
Fax: (785) 296-8118

KENTUCKY

LOUISIANA

MAINE

MARYLAND
Luis Ortega
Director
Governor's Comm. on Hispanic Affairs
Dept. of Human Resources
311 W. Saratoga St.
Baltimore, MD 21201
Phone: (410) 767-7857
Fax: (410) 333-0392

MASSACHUSETTS
Antonia Jimenez
Governor's Comm. on Hispanic Affairs
Administration & Finance
State House, Rm. 373
Boston, MA 02133
Phone: (617) 727-2040
Fax: (617) 727-5570

MICHIGAN
Marylou Mason
Director
Comm. on Spanish-Speaking Affairs
Dept. of Civil Rights
611 W. Ottawa
Lansing, MI 48933
Phone: (517) 373-8339

MINNESOTA
Edwina Cogarcia
Executive Director
Council on the Affairs of Chicano/Latino People
555 Park St., Ste. 408
St. Paul, MN 55103
Phone: (651) 296-9587

MISSISSIPPI

MISSOURI

MONTANA
Kathy Hilland
Bureau Chief
Human Rights Bur.
Dept. of Labor & Industry
Steamboat Block
616 Helena Ave., Ste. 302
Helena, MT 59624-1728
Phone: (406) 444-4345
Fax: (406) 444-2798

NEBRASKA
Cecilia Olivarez Huerta
Executive Director
Mexican-American Comm.
P.O. Box 94965
Lincoln, NE 68509-4965
Phone: (402) 471-2791
Fax: (402) 471-4381

NEVADA

NEW HAMPSHIRE

NEW JERSEY
Alicia Diaz
Director
Ctr. for Hispanic Policy
Dept. of Community Affairs
101 S. Broad St.
P.O. Box 800
Trenton, NJ 08625-0800
Phone: (609) 984-3223
Fax: (609) 984-6696

NEW MEXICO
J. Eugene Mahta
Director
Hispanic Cultural Div.
Cultural Affairs Ofc.
600 Central, SW, Ste. 201
Albuquerque, NM 87102
Phone: (505) 246-2439
Fax: (505) 246-2613

NEW YORK
Debbie Del Pino
Assistant to the Governor for Hispanic Affairs
Executive Chamber
633 3rd Ave., 38th & 39th Fls.
New York, NY 10017
Phone: (212) 681-4561
Fax: (212) 681-7666

NORTH CAROLINA
Nolo Martinez
Director
Hispanic/Latino Affairs
116 W. Jones St.
Raleigh, NC 27603
Phone: (919) 715-3521
Fax: (919) 733-2120

NORTH DAKOTA

NORTHERN MARIANA ISLANDS

OHIO
Linda Garcia
Executive Director
Comm. on Hispanic/Latino Affairs
77 S. High St., 18th Fl.
Columbus, OH 43215
Phone: (614) 466-8333
Fax: (614) 995-0896

OKLAHOMA
Rafael Elias
Chair
Latin American-Hispanic Advisory Cmte.
Dept. of Personnel Mgmt.
2101 N. Lincoln Blvd.
Oklahoma City, OK 73105
Phone: (405) 521-2177

OREGON
Christopher Williams
Executive Director
Comm. on Hispanic Affairs
c/o State Police
255 Capitol St., NE, 4th Fl.
Salem, OR 97310
Phone: (503) 378-3725
Fax: (503) 378-8282

PENNSYLVANIA
Maritza Robert
Executive Director
Governor's Advisory Comm. on Latino Affairs
544 Forum Bldg.
Harrisburg, PA 17120
Phone: (800) 233-1407
Fax: (717) 705-0791

PUERTO RICO

RHODE ISLAND

SOUTH CAROLINA
William C. Ham
Commissioner
Comm. on Human Affairs
P.O. Box 4490
Columbia, SC 29240
Phone: (803) 737-7800

SOUTH DAKOTA

TENNESSEE

TEXAS

U.S. VIRGIN ISLANDS

UTAH
Leticia Medina
Director
Ethnic Ofcs. - Hispanic Affairs
Dept. of Community & Economic Dev.
324 S. State, Ste. 500
Salt Lake City, UT 84111
Phone: (801) 538-8634
Fax: (801) 538-8678
E-mail: lmedina@dced.state.ut.us

VERMONT
Harvey Golubock
Executive Director
Human Rights Comm.
135 State St.
Montpelier, VT 05633-6301
Phone: (802) 828-2480
Fax: (802) 828-3522

VIRGINIA
Roxie Raines Kornegay
Director
Council on Human Rights
Washington Bldg., 12th Fl.
1100 Bank St.
Richmond, VA 23219
Phone: (804) 225-2292
Fax: (804) 225-3294

WASHINGTON
Manuel Romero
Executive Director
State Comm. on Hispanic Affairs
P.O. Box 40924
Olympia, WA 98504
Phone: (360) 753-3159
Fax: (360) 753-0199

WEST VIRGINIA

WISCONSIN

WYOMING

Law Enforcement

Conducts state-level criminal investigations.

ALABAMA
Michael B. Sullivan
Director
Dept. of Public Safety
500 Dexter Ave.
Montgomery, AL 36130
Phone: (334) 242-4394
Fax: (334) 353-1400

ALASKA
Ronald L. Otte
Commissioner
Dept. of Public Safety
P.O. Box 111200
Juneau, AK 99811-1200
Phone: (907) 465-4322
Fax: (907) 465-4362

AMERICAN SAMOA
Te'o Fuavai
Commissioner
Dept. of Public Safety
AS Govt.
Pago Pago, AS 96799
Phone: (684) 633-1111
Fax: (684) 633-5111

ARIZONA
Joe Albo
Director
Dept. of Public Safety
2102 W. Encanto Blvd.
Phoenix, AZ 85005-6638
Phone: (602) 223-2359
Fax: (602) 223-2917

ARKANSAS
Tom Mars
Director
State Police
#1 State Police Plz.
Little Rock, AR 72209
Phone: (501) 618-8600
Fax: (501) 618-8222

CALIFORNIA
Bill Lockyer
Attorney General
1300 I St., 11th Fl.
Sacramento, CA 95814
Phone: (916) 324-5437

COLORADO
Carl W. Whiteside
Director
Bur. of Investigation
Dept. of Public Safety
690 Kipling St.
Lakewood, CO 80215
Phone: (303) 239-4201
Fax: (303) 235-0568

CONNECTICUT
John M. Bailey
Chief State's Attorney
Div. of Criminal Justice
300 Corporate Pl.
Rocky Hill, CT 06067
Phone: (860) 258-5800

DELAWARE
Alan D. Ellingsworth
Superintendent
State Police
State Police Headquarters
1441 N. DuPont Hwy.
Dover, DE 19901
Phone: (302) 739-5911
Fax: (302) 739-5966

DISTRICT OF COLUMBIA
Charles H. Ramsey
Chief
Metropolitan Police Dept.
300 Indiana Ave., NW, Rm. 5080
Washington, DC 20001
Phone: (202) 727-4218
Fax: (202) 727-9524

FLORIDA
Tim Moore
Commissioner
Dept. of Law Enforcement
P.O. Box 1489
Tallahassee, FL 32302
Phone: (850) 488-8771
Fax: (850) 488-2189

GEORGIA
Milton E. Nix, Jr.
Director
Bur. of Investigation
P.O. Box 370808
Decatur, GA 30037
Phone: (404) 244-2501

GUAM
James M. Marques
Chief of Police
Police Dept.
233 Central Ave.
Tiyan, GU 96913
Phone: (671) 475-8509
Fax: (671) 472-4036

HAWAII
Margery S. Bronster
Attorney General
425 Queen St.
Honolulu, HI 96813
Phone: (808) 586-1500
Fax: (808) 586-1239

IDAHO
Robert Sobba
Director
Alcohol Beverage Control Div.
Dept. of Law Enforcement
P.O. Box 700
Meridian, ID 83680
Phone: (208) 884-7003

ILLINOIS
Sam Nolen
Director
State Police
103 State Armory
Springfield, IL 62706
Phone: (217) 782-7263
Fax: (217) 785-2821

INDIANA
Melvin Carraway
Superintendent
State Police
IGC-North, 3rd Fl.
100 N. Senate Ave.
Indianapolis, IN 46204
Phone: (317) 232-8241
Fax: (317) 232-5682

IOWA
Darwin Chapman
Director
Div. of Criminal Investigation
Dept. of Public Safety
Wallace State Ofc. Bldg.
E. 9th & Grand Aves.
Des Moines, IA 50319
Phone: (515) 281-6203

KANSAS
Larry Welch
Director
Bur. of Investigation
1620 SW Tyler
Topeka, KS 66612-1837
Phone: (785) 296-8200
Fax: (785) 296-6781

KENTUCKY
Gary Rose
Commissioner
State Police
Justice Cabinet
919 Versailles Rd.
Frankfort, KY 40601
Phone: (502) 695-6300
Fax: (502) 573-1479

LOUISIANA
Jannitta Antoine
Deputy Secretary
Dept. of Public Safety & Corrections
P.O. Box 94304
Baton Rouge, LA 70804-9304
Phone: (225) 342-6744
Fax: (225) 342-3095

MAINE
Andrew Ketterer
Attorney General
6 State House Station
Augusta, ME 04333
Phone: (207) 626-8800
Fax: (207) 287-3145

MARYLAND
David B. Mitchell
Superintendent
Ofc. of the Superintendent
Dept. of State Police
1201 Reisterstown Rd.
Baltimore, MD 21208-3899
Phone: (410) 653-4219
Fax: (410) 653-9651

MASSACHUSETTS
Reed Hillman
Commissioner/Superintendent
Div. of State Police
Dept. of Public Safety
470 Worcester Rd.
Framingham, MA 01701
Phone: (508) 820-2350
Fax: (617) 727-6874

MICHIGAN
Mike Robinson
Director
Dept. of State Police
714 S. Harrison Rd.
E. Lansing, MI 48823
Phone: (517) 336-6157
Fax: (517) 336-6255

MINNESOTA
Nicholas V. O'Hara
Superintendent
Bur. of Criminal Apprehension
Dept. of Public Safety
1246 Univ. Ave.
St. Paul, MN 55104
Phone: (612) 642-0600
Fax: (612) 642-0633
E-mail: nicholas.o'hara@state.mn.us

MISSISSIPPI
Jim Ingram
Commissioner
Dept. of Public Safety
Hwy. Patrol Bldg., I-55 N.
P.O. Box 958
Jackson, MS 39205
Phone: (601) 987-1490
Fax: (601) 987-1498

MISSOURI
Gary B. Kempker
Director
Dept. of Public Safety
Truman Bldg., Rm. 870
P.O. Box 749
Jefferson City, MO 65102
Phone: (573) 751-4905
Fax: (573) 751-5399
E-mail: gary@dps.state.mo.us

MONTANA
Joseph P. Mazurek
Attorney General
Ofc. of the Attorney Gen.
Justice Bldg.
215 N. Sanders
P.O. Box 201401
Helena, MT 59620
Phone: (406) 444-2026
Fax: (406) 444-3549

NEBRASKA
Tom Nesbitt
Superintendent
State Patrol
P.O. Box 94907
Lincoln, NE 68509
Phone: (402) 471-4545
Fax: (402) 479-4002

NEVADA
Rick Cypher
Acting Chief
Div. of Investigations
Dept. of Motor Vehicles & Public Safety
555 Wright Way
Carson City, NV 89711
Phone: (775) 687-4412
Fax: (775) 687-4405

NEW HAMPSHIRE
John J. Barthelmes
Director
Div. of State Police
Criminal Records Ofc.
Safety Dept.
10 Hazen Dr.
Concord, NH 03305-0002
Phone: (603) 271-3636
Fax: (603) 271-1153

NEW JERSEY
Peter Verniero
Attorney General
Dept. of Law
Richard J. Hughes Justice Complex
25 Market St., P.O. Box 081
Trenton, NJ 08625-0081
Phone: (609) 292-4925
Fax: (609) 292-3508

NEW MEXICO
Frank Taylor
Chief
State Police
P.O. Box 1628
Santa Fe, NM 87504
Phone: (505) 827-9002
Fax: (505) 827-3395

NEW YORK
James McMahon
Superintendent
Div. of State Police
Public Security, Bldg. 22
1220 Washington Ave.
Albany, NY 12226-2252
Phone: (518) 457-6721
Fax: (518) 485-7505

NORTH CAROLINA
Jim Coman
Director
State Bur. of Investigation
Dept. of Justice
3320 Garner Rd.
Raleigh, NC 27610-5698
Phone: (919) 662-4500
Fax: (919) 662-4523

NORTH DAKOTA
Bill Broer
Director
Bur. of Criminal Investigation
Attorney Gen's. Ofc.
P.O. Box 1054
Bismarck, ND 58502-1054
Phone: (701) 328-5500
Fax: (701) 328-5510
E-mail: msmail.bbroer@ranch.state.nd.us

NORTHERN MARIANA ISLANDS
Jose M. Castro
Director
Dept. of Public Safety
Caller Box 10007
Saipan, MP 96950
Phone: (670) 235-4441
Fax: (670) 234-8531
E-mail: commish@mtccnmi.com

OHIO
Michael Quinn
Chief
Ofc. of Criminal Investigation
Dept. of Public Safety, State Hwy. Patrol
1970 W. Broad St.
Columbus, OH 43223-1102
Phone: (614) 466-3375
Fax: (614) 644-0652

OKLAHOMA
Bob Ricks
Secretary of Safety & Security
Dept. of Public Safety
3600 N. Martin Luther King, Jr. Dr.
Oklahoma City, OK 73136
Phone: (405) 425-2424
Fax: (405) 425-7709

OREGON
LeRon Howland
Superintendent
State Police
400 Public Services Bldg.
255 Capitol St., NE
Salem, OR 97310
Phone: (503) 378-3720
Fax: (503) 378-8282

PENNSYLVANIA
Paul Evanko
Commissioner
State Police
1800 Elmerton Ave.
Harrisburg, PA 17110
Phone: (717) 783-5558
Fax: (717) 787-2948

PUERTO RICO
Jose A. Fuentes Agostini
Attorney General
Ofc. of the Attorney Gen.
P.O. Box 9020192
San Juan, PR 00902-0192
Phone: (787) 721-7700
Fax: (787) 724-4770

RHODE ISLAND
Edmund Culhane
Superintendent
Dept. of State Police
311 Danielson Pike
N. Scituate, RI 02857
Phone: (401) 444-1111

SOUTH CAROLINA
Robert Stewart
Chief
Law Enforcement Div.
Broad River Rd.
P.O. Box 21398
Columbia, SC 29221
Phone: (803) 896-7136

SOUTH DAKOTA
Doug Lake
Director
Div. of Criminal Investigation
Ofc. of the Attorney Gen.
500 E. Capitol Ave.
Pierre, SD 57501-5070
Phone: (605) 773-3332
Fax: (605) 773-4629

TENNESSEE
Larry Wallace
Director
Bur. of Investigation
1148 Foster Ave.
Nashville, TN 37210-4406
Phone: (615) 741-0430

TEXAS
Dudley Thomas
Director
Dept. of Public Safety
5805 N. Lamar Blvd.
Austin, TX 78752
Phone: (512) 424-2000
Fax: (512) 483-5708

U.S. VIRGIN ISLANDS
Franz A. Christian, Sr.
Acting Commissioner
Police Dept.
8172 Sub Base
St. Thomas, VI 00802
Phone: (340) 774-6400
Fax: (340) 776-3317

UTAH
Herb Katz
Director
Div. of Criminal
Investigations &
Technical Services
Dept. of Public Safety
4501 S. 2700 W.
Salt Lake City, UT 84119
Phone: (801) 965-4489
Fax: (801) 965-4716

VERMONT
Nicholas Ruggiero
Commissioner
Div. of State Police
Dept. of Criminal
Investigations
103 S. Main St.
Waterbury, VT 05671-2101
Phone: (802) 244-8781
Fax: (802) 244-1106

VIRGINIA
M. Wayne Huggins
Superintendent
Dept. of State Police
7700 Midlothian Tpke.
Richmond, VA 23235
Phone: (804) 674-2087
Fax: (804) 674-2132

WASHINGTON
Annette Sandberg
Chief
State Patrol
Administration Bldg.
P.O. Box 42601
Olympia, WA 98504-2601
Phone: (360) 753-6540
Fax: (360) 664-0663

WEST VIRGINIA
Gary L. Edgell
Superintendent
Public Safety Div.
725 Jefferson Rd.
S. Charleston, WV 25309-1698
Phone: (304) 746-2111
Fax: (304) 746-2230

WISCONSIN
James Warren
Administrator
Div. of Criminal
Investigation
Dept. of Justice
123 W. Washington, 7th Fl.
P.O. Box 7857
Madison, WI 53707
Phone: (608) 266-1671
Fax: (608) 267-2777

WYOMING
Tom Pagel
Director
Criminal Investigation Div.
Ofc. of the Attorney Gen.
316 W. 22nd
Cheyenne, WY 82002
Phone: (307) 777-7181

Law Library

Legal resource for the state court of last resort.

ALABAMA
Timothy A. Lewis
Director
Supreme Ct. Law Library
300 Dexter Ave.
Montgomery, AL 36104-3741
Phone: (334) 242-4347
Fax: (334) 242-4484

ALASKA
Cynthia Fellows
State Law Librarian
State Ct. Libraries
303 K St.
Anchorage, AK 99501-2084
Phone: (907) 264-0580
Fax: (907) 264-0733

AMERICAN SAMOA

ARIZONA
Gladys Ann Wells
Director
Library, Archives & Public Records
State Law Library
1700 W. Washington St.
Phoenix, AZ 85007-2812
Phone: (602) 542-4035
Fax: (602) 542-4972

ARKANSAS
Tim Holthoff
Law Librarian
Supreme Ct.
Justice Bldg.
1 Capitol Mall
Little Rock, AR 72201
Phone: (501) 682-2147
Fax: (501) 682-6877

CALIFORNIA
Karen Toran
Law Librarian
Supreme Ct.
303 Second St., S. Tower
San Francisco, CA 94107
Phone: (415) 396-9439

COLORADO
Martha Campbell
Librarian
Supreme Ct. Library
State Judicial Bldg., #B112
2 E. 14th Ave.
Denver, CO 80203
Phone: (303) 861-1111

CONNECTICUT
Diane Pizzo
Serials Librarian
State Library
Collection Mgmt. Unit
231 Capitol Ave.
Hartford, CT 06106
Phone: (860) 566-4601

DELAWARE
Mary Tylecki Dickson
Librarian
Law Library
Sussex County Superior Ct.
P.O. Box 717
Georgetown, DE 19947
Phone: (302) 856-5483
Fax: (302) 856-5891

Aurora Gardner
Law Librarian
State Law Library in Kent County
38 The Green
Dover, DE 19901
Phone: (302) 739-5467
Fax: (302) 739-6721

Rene Yucht
Librarian
New Castle County Law Library
Daniel Hermann Courthouse
1020 N. King St.
Wilmington, DE 19801
Phone: (302) 577-2437
Fax: (302) 577-2813

DISTRICT OF COLUMBIA
Harriet E. Rotter
Librarian
Ct. of Appeals
500 Indiana Ave., NW, Rm. 6085
Washington, DC 20001
Phone: (202) 879-2767
Fax: (202) 626-8840

FLORIDA
Joan Cannon
Head Librarian
Supreme Ct.
Supreme Ct. Bldg.
500 S. Duval St.
Tallahassee, FL 32399-1926
Phone: (850) 488-1531
Fax: (850) 922-5219

GEORGIA
Martha Lappe
State Law Librarian
Dept. of Law
244 Washington St., Rm. 68
Atlanta, GA 30334
Phone: (404) 656-3468

GUAM
Tom Sterling
President, BOT
Law Library
141 San Ramon Rd.
Hagatna, GU 96910
Phone: (671) 472-8062
Fax: (671) 472-1246

HAWAII
Ann Koto
Law Librarian
Supreme Ct. Law Library
The Judiciary/Supreme Ct.
417 S. King St., Rm. 119
Honolulu, HI 96813
Phone: (808) 539-4964
Fax: (808) 539-4974
E-mail: hisclla@pixi.com

IDAHO
Beth Peterson
State Law Library
451 W. State St.
Boise, ID 83720-0051
Phone: (208) 334-2477
Fax: (208) 334-4019
E-mail: bpeterso@jsc.state.id.us

ILLINOIS
Brenda Larison
Director
Supreme Ct. Library
Supreme Ct. Bldg.
Springfield, IL 62706
Phone: (217) 782-2424
Fax: (217) 782-5287
E-mail: blarison@pop.state.il.us

INDIANA
Rebecca Bethel
Law Librarian
Supreme Ct. Law Library
State House, Rm. 316
Indianapolis, IN 46204
Phone: (317) 232-2557
Fax: (317) 232-8372

IOWA
Linda Robertson
Law Librarian
State Law Library
State Capitol Bldg.
1007 E. Grand Ave.
Des Moines, IA 50319
Phone: (515) 281-5124
Fax: (515) 281-5405

KANSAS
Fred Knecht
Law Librarian
Supreme Ct. Law Library
Judical Ctr.
301 W. 10th St.
Topeka, KS 66612-1598
Phone: (785) 296-3257
Fax: (785) 296-1863

KENTUCKY
Sallie M. Howard
State Law Librarian
State Law Library
700 Capitol Ave.
Frankfort, KY 40601-3489
Phone: (502) 564-5041
Fax: (502) 564-4187
E-mail: showard@mail.state.ky.us

LOUISIANA
Carol Billings
Librarian
State Law Library
301 Loyola Ave., Rm. 100
New Orleans, LA 70112
Phone: (504) 568-5705
Fax: (504) 568-5069

MAINE
Lynn E. Randall
State Law Librarian
Law & Legislative Reference Library
43 State House Station
Augusta, ME 04333-0043
Phone: (207) 287-1600
Fax: (207) 287-6467
E-mail: lynn.randall@state.me.us

MARYLAND
Michael S. Miller
Director
State Law Library
Judiciary
361 Rowe Blvd.
Annapolis, MD 21401
Phone: (410) 260-1430

MASSACHUSETTS
Stephen A. Fulchino
State Librarian
State House Library
State House, Rm. 341
24 Beacon St.
Boston, MA 02133
Phone: (617) 727-2592
Fax: (617) 727-5819

MICHIGAN
Susan Adamczak
Administrator
Law Library Div.
Library of MI
525 W. Ottawa St.
P.O. Box 30007
Lansing, MI 48909
Phone: (517) 373-0630
Fax: (517) 373-3915
E-mail: sadamcza
@libofmich.lib.mi.us

MINNESOTA
Marvin R. Anderson
State Law Librarian
State Law Library
25 Constitution Ave.
St. Paul, MN 55155
Phone: (651) 297-2084
Fax: (651) 296-6740
E-mail: marvin.anderson
@courts.state.mn.us

MISSISSIPPI
Mary Miller
State Librarian
Law Library
P.O. Box 1040
Jackson, MS 39215
Phone: (601) 359-3672
Fax: (601) 359-2912

MISSOURI
Tyronne Allen
Librarian
Supreme Ct. Library
Supreme Ct. Bldg.
Jefferson City, MO 65101
Phone: (573) 751-2636
Fax: (573) 751-2573
E-mail: tallen
@mail.state.mo.us

MONTANA
Judith Meadows
State Law Librarian
State Law Library
P.O. Box 203004
Helena, MT 59620
Phone: (406) 444-3660
Fax: (406) 444-3603

NEBRASKA
Marie Wiechman
Librarian
State Library
State Capitol, 3rd Fl.
P.O. Box 98931
Lincoln, NE 68509
Phone: (402) 471-3189
Fax: (402) 471-2197

NEVADA
Susan Southwick
Law Librarian
Supreme Ct. Library
Supreme Ct. Bldg.
201 S. Carson St., #100
Carson City, NV 89701
Phone: (775) 687-5140
Fax: (775) 687-8762

NEW HAMPSHIRE
Christine Swan
Law Librarian
State Law Library
Supreme Ct. Bldg.
Noble Dr.
Concord, NH 03301-6160
Phone: (603) 271-3777

NEW JERSEY

NEW MEXICO
Thaddeus Bejnar
Director
Supreme Ct. Law Library
237 Don Gaspar Ave.
Santa Fe, NM 87501
Phone: (505) 827-4854
Fax: (505) 827-4824

NEW YORK
Ruth A. Fraley
Division Director
Div. of Legal Resources & Records Mgmt.
Agency Bldg. 4, Ste. 2001
Empire State Plz.
Albany, NY 12223
Phone: (518) 473-1196
Fax: (518) 473-6860

NORTH CAROLINA
Louise Stafford
Librarian
Supreme Ct. Library
Justice Bldg., Rm. 500
2 E. Morgan St.
Raleigh, NC 27601-1400
Phone: (919) 733-3425
E-mail: lhs@aol.state.nc.us

NORTH DAKOTA
Ted Smith
Law Librarian
Supreme Ct. Law Library
Supreme Ct.
600 E. Blvd. Ave., 2nd Fl. - Judicial Wing
Bismarck, ND 58505-0530
Phone: (701) 328-4594
Fax: (701) 328-4480
E-mail: teds
@sc3.court.state.nd.us

NORTHERN MARIANA ISLANDS
Margarita M. Palacios
Court Administrator
Supreme Ct.
P.O. Box 2165
Saipan, MP 96950
Phone: (670) 236-9800
Fax: (670) 236-9701
E-mail: supreme.court
@saipan.com

OHIO
Paul S. Fu
Librarian Director
Supreme Ct. Law Library
30 E. Broad St., 4th Fl.
Columbus, OH 43266-0419
Phone: (614) 466-2044
Fax: (614) 466-1559

OKLAHOMA
Marilyn Jacobs
Library Administrator
Law Reference Div.
Jan Eric Cartwright Memorial Library
200 NE 18th St.
Oklahoma City, OK 73105
Phone: (405) 521-2502

OREGON
Joe Stephens
Law Librarian
Supreme Ct. Library
Supreme Ct. Bldg.
1163 State St.
Salem, OR 97310
Phone: (503) 986-5644
Fax: (503) 986-5560

PENNSYLVANIA
Alice Lubrecht
Director
State Library Bur.
Dept. of Education
203 Forum Bldg.
P.O. Box 1601
Harrisburg, PA 17105-1601
Phone: (717) 783-5968
Fax: (717) 772-8268
E-mail: ali
@unix1.stlib.state.pa.us

PUERTO RICO
Ivette Torres
Director
Supreme Ct. Library
P.O. Box 2392
San Juan, PR 00903
Phone: (787) 723-3863

RHODE ISLAND
Kendall Svengalis
State Law Librarian
State Law Library
Providence County Courthouse
250 Benefit St.
Providence, RI 02903
Phone: (401) 222-3275
Fax: (401) 222-3865
E-mail: ksven@ids.net

SOUTH CAROLINA
Janet Myer
Librarian
Supreme Ct. Library
Supreme Ct. Bldg.
1231 Gervais St.
Columbia, SC 29201
Phone: (803) 734-1080
Fax: (803) 734-0519

SOUTH DAKOTA
Sheri Anderson
Chief of Legal Research
Supreme Ct.
500 State Capitol, 1st Fl.
Pierre, SD 57501
Phone: (605) 773-3474
Fax: (605) 773-6128

TENNESSEE
Donna Wair
Librarian
State Law Library
Supreme Ct. Bldg.
Nashville, TN 37243
Phone: (615) 741-2016

TEXAS
Kay Schlueter
Director
State Law Library
P.O. Box 12367
Austin, TX 78711
Phone: (512) 463-1722
Fax: (512) 463-1728

U.S. VIRGIN ISLANDS
Thomas Moore
Chief Justice
District Ct.
District Ct. Bldg.
St. Thomas, VI 00802
Phone: (340) 774-0640
Fax: (340) 774-1293
E-mail: vidc@vid.uscourts.gov

UTAH
Nancy Cheng
Law Librarian
Supreme Ct. Law Library
450 S. State St.
Salt Lake City, UT 84114-0220
Phone: (801) 238-7979
Fax: (801) 238-7993
E-mail: nancyc@email.utcourts.gov

VERMONT
Sybil B. McShane
Librarian
Reference & Law Info. Services Unit
Dept. of Libraries
109 State St.
Montpelier, VT 05609
Phone: (802) 828-3268
Fax: (802) 828-2199

VIRGINIA
Robert N. Baldwin
Executive Secretary
Supreme Ct.
100 N. 9th St., 3rd Fl.
Richmond, VA 23219
Phone: (804) 786-6455
Fax: (804) 786-4542

WASHINGTON
Deborah Norwood
State Law Librarian
Temple of Justice
P.O. Box 40751
Olympia, WA 98504
Phone: (360) 357-2145
Fax: (360) 357-2099
E-mail: smpt.debby.norwood@courts.wa.gov

WEST VIRGINIA
Marjorie Price
Supreme Court Law Librarian
State Law Library
Supreme Ct. of Appeals
State Capitol, Rm. E-404
1900 Kanawha Blvd., E.
Charleston, WV 25305
Phone: (304) 558-2607
Fax: (304) 558-3673

WISCONSIN
Marcia J. Koslov
State Law Librarian
State Law Library
310 E. State Capitol
P.O. Box 7881
Madison, WI 53707-7881
Phone: (608) 266-1600
Fax: (608) 267-2319
E-mail: mkoslov@wsll.state.wi.us

WYOMING
Kathy Carlson
State Law Librarian
Law Library
Supreme Ct.
Supreme Ct. Bldg.
2301 Capitol Ave.
Cheyenne, WY 82002
Phone: (307) 777-7509
Fax: (307) 777-7240

Licensing (Occupational and Professional)

Licenses and regulates the function of various professions in the state. Since there are hundreds of autonomous boards in the states, it is the centralized agencies that are represented in this listing.

ALABAMA

ALASKA
Catherine Reardon
Director
Div. of Occupational Licensing
Dept. of Commerce & Economic Dev.
P.O. Box 110806
Juneau, AK 99811-0806
Phone: (907) 465-2538
Fax: (907) 465-2974

AMERICAN SAMOA
John Faumuina, Jr.
Director
Economic Dev. & Planning Ofc.
Dept. of Commerce
Pago Pago, AS 96799
Phone: (684) 633-5155
Fax: (684) 633-4195

ARIZONA

ARKANSAS

CALIFORNIA
Marilyn Brazell
Director
Dept. of Consumer Affairs
400 R St., Rm. 1060
Sacramento, CA 95814-6213
Phone: (916) 445-4465

COLORADO
Michael Cooke
Executive Director
Dept. of Regulatory Agencies
1560 Broadway, Rm. 1550
Denver, CO 80202
Phone: (303) 894-7850
Fax: (303) 894-7885

CONNECTICUT
James Fleming
Commissioner
Dept. of Consumer Protection
165 Capitol Ave.
Hartford, CT 06106
Phone: (860) 566-4999

DELAWARE
Carol Ellis
Director
Div. of Professional Regulation
Dept. of Adm. Services
Cannon Bldg., Ste. 203
861 Silver Lake Blvd.
Dover, DE 19904-2467
Phone: (302) 739-4522
Fax: (302) 739-2711

DISTRICT OF COLUMBIA
R. James Fagelson
Administrator
Occupational & Professional Licensure Administration
Dept. of Consumer & Regulatory Affairs
614 H St., NW, Rm. 903
Washington, DC 20001
Phone: (202) 727-7480

FLORIDA
John Russi
Director
Div. of Licensing
Dept. of State
P.O. Box 6687
Tallahassee, FL 32314-6687
Phone: (850) 488-6982
Fax: (850) 488-2789

GEORGIA
William G. Miller, Jr.
Joint Secretary
Examining Boards
Ofc. of Secretary of State
166 Pryor St., SW
Atlanta, GA 30303
Phone: (404) 656-3900

GUAM
Joseph T. Duenas
Director
Dept. of Revenue & Taxation
13-1 Mariner Dr., Tiyan
P.O. Box 23607
GMF, GU 96921
Phone: (671) 475-1817
Fax: (671) 472-2643

HAWAII
Kathryn Matayoshi
Director
Dept. of Commerce & Consumer Affairs
P.O. Box 541
Honolulu, HI 96809
Phone: (808) 586-2850
Fax: (808) 586-2856

IDAHO
Carmen Westberg
Chief
Occupational Licenses
1109 Main St., Ste. 220
Boise, ID 83702-5642
Phone: (208) 334-3233

ILLINOIS
Leonard Sherman
Director
Dept. of Professional Regulation
320 W. Washington St., 3rd Fl.
Springfield, IL 62786
Phone: (217) 785-0822
Fax: (217) 782-7645

INDIANA
Laura Langford
Executive Director
Health Professions Bur.
402 W. Washington St., Rm. E041
Indianapolis, IN 46204
Phone: (317) 232-2960
Fax: (317) 233-4236

Gerald Quigley
Executive Director
Professional Licensing Agency
302 W. Washington St., Rm. E034
Indianapolis, IN 46204
Phone: (317) 232-3997
Fax: (317) 232-2312

IOWA
Roger Halvorson
Administrator
Professional Licensing & Registration Div.
Dept. of Commerce
1918 SE Hulsizer
Ankeny, IA 50021
Phone: (515) 281-5596
Fax: (515) 281-7411

KANSAS
Betty Rose
Executive Director
Board of Technical Professions
Landon State Ofc. Bldg., Ste. 507
900 SW Jackson
Topeka, KS 66612-1257
Phone: (785) 296-3053
Fax: (785) 296-8054

KENTUCKY
Nancy Black
Director
Occupations & Professions Div.
Dept. of Administration
P.O. Box 456
Frankfort, KY 40602
Phone: (502) 564-3296
Fax: (502) 564-4818

LOUISIANA
Lilly McCallister
Manager
Ofc. of Licensing & Regulation
Health & Human Resources Dept.
P.O. Box 3767
Baton Rouge, LA 70821
Phone: (225) 342-0138
Fax: (225) 342-5292

MAINE
Anne Head
Director
Ofc. of Licensing & Registration
Dept. of Professional & Financial Regulation
35 State House Station
Augusta, ME 04330
Phone: (207) 624-8603

MARYLAND
Charles P. Kelly
Director
Div. of Occupational & Professional Licensing
Dept. of Labor, Licensing & Regulation
500 N. Calvert St., Rm. 301
Baltimore, MD 21201
Phone: (410) 230-6220

MASSACHUSETTS
William Wood
Director
Div. of Registration
Executive Ofc. of Consumer Affairs
100 Cambridge St., Rm. 1520
Boston, MA 02202
Phone: (617) 727-3074
Fax: (617) 727-2197

MICHIGAN
Kathy Wilber
Director
Consumer & Industry Services
P.O. Box 30018
Lansing, MI 48909
Phone: (517) 373-1253

MINNESOTA
Gary LaVasseur
Deputy Commissioner
Enforcement & Licensing
Dept. of Commerce
133 E. 7th St.
St. Paul, MN 55101
Phone: (651) 296-3528
Fax: (651) 296-4328
E-mail: gary.lavasseur@state.mn.us

MISSISSIPPI

MISSOURI
Randall J. Singer
Director
Div. of Professional Registration
Dept. of Economic Dev.
3605 Missouri Blvd.
P.O. Box 1335
Jefferson City, MO 65102
Phone: (573) 751-1081
Fax: (573) 751-4176
E-mail: rsinger@mail.state.mo.us

MONTANA
Steve Meloy
Bureau Chief
Professional & Occupational Licensing Bur.
Dept. of Commerce
111 N. Jackson, Lower Level
Helena, MT 59620
Phone: (406) 444-3737
Fax: (406) 444-1667

NEBRASKA
Helen Meeks
Health Division Director
Dept. of Health & Human Services, Regulation & Licensure
P.O. Box 95007
Lincoln, NE 68509-5007
Phone: (402) 471-4923
Fax: (402) 471-0820

NEVADA

NEW HAMPSHIRE

NEW JERSEY
Mark S. Herr
Director
Div. of Consumer Affairs
P.O. Box 45027
Newark, NJ 07102
Phone: (201) 504-6200
Fax: (201) 648-3538

NEW MEXICO
Robin Otten
Director
Dept. of Regulation & Licensing
20555 Pacheo St.
Santa Fe, NM 87505
Phone: (505) 827-7002
Fax: (505) 827-7083

NEW YORK
Richard P. Mills
Commissioner
State Education Dept.
89 Washington Ave., Rm. 111
Albany, NY 12234
Phone: (518) 474-6569
Fax: (518) 473-4909

Frank Munoz
Executive Director
Ofc. of Professional Responsibility
Dept. of State Education
Cultural Education Ctr., Rm. 3021
Albany, NY 12230
Phone: (518) 486-1765
Fax: (518) 474-3863

Alexander F. Treadwell
Secretary of State
Dept. of State
41 State St.
Albany, NY 12231
Phone: (518) 486-9844
Fax: (518) 474-4765

NORTH CAROLINA

NORTH DAKOTA
Alvin A. Jaeger
Secretary of State
Secretary of State's Ofc.
600 E. Blvd. Ave., 1st Fl.
Bismarck, ND 58505-0500
Phone: (701) 328-2900
Fax: (701) 328-2992
E-mail: ajaeger@state.nd.us

NORTHERN MARIANA ISLANDS
Florence S. Bocago
Administrator
Board of Professional Licensing
Capitol Hill
Saipan, MP 96950
Phone: (670) 234-5897
Fax: (670) 234-6040

OHIO
Lynne Hengle
Director
Div. Real Estate & Professional Licensing
Dept. of Commerce
77 S. High St., 20th Fl.
Columbus, OH 43266
Phone: (614) 466-3411
Fax: (614) 644-0584

OKLAHOMA

OREGON

PENNSYLVANIA
Dorothy Childress
Commissioner
Professional & Occupational Affairs
Dept. of State
124 Pine St.
Harrisburg, PA 17101
Phone: (717) 783-7194
Fax: (717) 783-0510

PUERTO RICO
Luis A. Isaac Sanchez
Director
Examiners Board
Dept. of State
P.O. Box 9023271
San Juan, PR 00902-3271
Phone: (787) 722-2122

RHODE ISLAND
Russell J. Spaight
Administrator
Div. of Professional Regulation
Dept. of Health
3 Capitol Hill, Rm. 104
Providence, RI 02908-5097
Phone: (401) 222-2827

SOUTH CAROLINA
Rita M. McKinney
Director
Dept. of Labor, Licensing & Regulations
110 Centerview Dr.
P.O. Box 11329
Columbia, SC 29210
Phone: (803) 896-4390
Fax: (803) 896-4393

SOUTH DAKOTA
Coral Assam
Director
Professional & Occupational Licensing, Commerce & Regulation Dept.
118 W. Capitol Ave.
Pierre, SD 57501
Phone: (605) 773-3178
Fax: (605) 773-6631

TENNESSEE
Stephanie Chivers
Assistant Commissioner
Regulatory Boards
Dept. of Commerce & Insurance
Davy Crockett Tower
500 James Robertson Pkwy.
Nashville, TN 37243-0572
Phone: (615) 741-3449
Fax: (615) 741-6470

TEXAS
Racelle A. Martin
Executive Director
Dept. of Licensing & Regulation
P.O. Box 12157
Austin, TX 78711
Phone: (512) 463-3173
Fax: (512) 475-2874

U.S. VIRGIN ISLANDS
Andrew Rutnik
Acting Commissioner
Dept. of Licensing & Consumer Affairs
Property & Procurement Bldg.
Sub Base Bldg.1, Rm. 205
St. Thomas, VI 00802
Phone: (340) 774-3130
Fax: (340) 776-8303

UTAH
Diane J. Blake
Acting Director
Div. of Occupational & Professional Licensing
Commerce Dept.
160 E. 300 S.
Salt Lake City, UT 84111
Phone: (801) 530-6179
Fax: (801) 530-6511
E-mail: dblake@br.state.ut.us

VERMONT
Thomas J. Lehner
Director
Ofc. of Professional Regulation
Ofc. of the Secretary of State
26 Terrace St.
Montpelier, VT 05609-1101
Phone: (802) 828-2458
Fax: (802) 828-2496

VIRGINIA
John E. Kotvas, Jr.
Director
Dept. of Professional & Occupational Regulation
3600 W. Broad St.
Richmond, VA 23230
Phone: (804) 367-8519
Fax: (804) 367-9537

WASHINGTON
Fred Stephens
Director
Dept. of Licensing
Hwys. & Licensing Bldg.
1125 Washington St.
Olympia, WA 98504
Phone: (360) 902-3600
Fax: (360) 902-4042

WEST VIRGINIA

WISCONSIN
Marlene A. Cummings
Secretary
Regulation & Licensing Dept.
1400 E. Washington
P.O. Box 8935
Madison, WI 53708-8935
Phone: (608) 266-8609
Fax: (608) 267-0644

WYOMING
Gary Stephenson
Director
Adm. Div.
Dept. of Commerce
6101 Yellowstone
Cheyenne, WY 82002
Phone: (307) 777-6300

Lieutenant Governor

The statewide elected official who is next in line of succession to the governorship. (In Maine, New Hampshire, New Jersey, Tennessee and West Virginia, the presidents (or speakers) of the Senate are next in line of succession to the governorship. In Tennessee, the speaker of the Senate bears the statutory title of lieutenant governor. In Arizona, Oregon and Wyoming, the secretary of state is next in line of succession to the governorship.)

ALABAMA
Steven Windom (R)
Lieutenant Governor
State Capitol, Ste. 725
600 Dexter St.
Montgomery, AL 36130
Phone: (334) 242-7900
Fax: (334) 242-4666

ALASKA
Fran Ulmer (D)
Lieutenant Governor
State Capitol
P.O. Box 110015
Juneau, AK 99811-0015
Phone: (907) 465-3520
Fax: (907) 465-5400

AMERICAN SAMOA
Togiola T. Tulafono (D)
Lieutenant Governor
Ofc. of the Lieutenant Governor
AS Govt.
Executive Ofc. Bldg., 3rd Fl.
Pago Pago, AS 96799
Phone: (684) 633-4116
Fax: (684) 633-2269

ARIZONA

ARKANSAS
Winthrop Rockefeller (R)
Lieutenant Governor
State Capitol Bldg., Rm. 270
Little Rock, AR 72201
Phone: (501) 682-2144
Fax: (501) 682-2894

CALIFORNIA
Cruz M. Bustamante (D)
State Capitol, Rm. 1114
Sacramento, CA 95814
Phone: (916) 445-8994

COLORADO
Joe Rogers (R)
Lieutenant Governor
130 State Capitol
Denver, CO 80203-1792
Phone: (303) 866-2087
Fax: (303) 866-3044

CONNECTICUT
M. Jodi Rell (R)
Lieutenant Governor
State Capitol, Rm. 304
300 Capitol Ave.
Hartford, CT 06106
Phone: (860) 524-7384
Fax: (860) 524-7304
E-mail: jodi.rell@po.state.ct.us

DELAWARE
Ruth Ann Minner (D)
Lieutenant Governor
Tatnall Bldg., 3rd Fl.
William Penn St.
P.O. Box 1401
Dover, DE 19903
Phone: (302) 739-4151
Fax: (302) 739-6965

DISTRICT OF COLUMBIA

FLORIDA
Frank Brogan (R)
Lieutenant Governor
PL 05, The Capitol
Tallahassee, FL 32399-0001
Phone: (850) 488-4711
Fax: (850) 921-6114

GEORGIA
Mark Taylor (D)
Lieutenant Governor
240 State Capitol
Atlanta, GA 30334
Phone: (404) 656-5030
Fax: (404) 656-6739

GUAM
Madeleine Bordallo (D)
Lieutenant Governor
Executive Chambers
P.O. Box 2950
Hagatna, GU 96932
Phone: (671) 472-8931
Fax: (671) 477-4826

HAWAII
Mazie Hirono (D)
Lieutenant Governor
Ofc. of the Governor
State Capitol
P.O. Box 3226
Honolulu, HI 96801
Phone: (808) 586-0255
Fax: (808) 586-0231

IDAHO
C.L. Butch Otter (R)
Lieutenant Governor
State House, Rm. 225
Boise, ID 83720
Phone: (208) 334-2200
Fax: (208) 334-3259

ILLINOIS
Corinne G. Wood (R)
Lieutenant Governor
214 State House
Springfield, IL 62706
Phone: (217) 782-7884
Fax: (217) 524-6262

INDIANA
Joe Kernan (D)
Lieutenant Governor
State House, Rm. 333
200 W. Washington St.
Indianapolis, IN 46204
Phone: (317) 232-4545
Fax: (317) 232-4788

IOWA
Sally Pederson (D)
Lieutenant Governor
State Capitol, Rm. 9
Des Moines, IA 50319
Phone: (515) 281-3421
Fax: (515) 281-6611

KANSAS
Gary Sherrer (R)
Lieutenant Governor
State House, 2nd Fl.
Topeka, KS 66612-1504
Phone: (785) 296-2213
Fax: (785) 296-5669

KENTUCKY
Stephen Henry (D)
Lieutenant Governor
Ofc. of the Lieutenant Governor
State Capitol, Rm. 100
Frankfort, KY 40601
Phone: (502) 564-2611
Fax: (502) 564-2517

LOUISIANA
Kathleen Babineaux Blanco (D)
Lieutenant Governor
Pentagon Ct. Barracks
900 N. 3rd St.
P.O. Box 44243
Baton Rouge, LA 70804
Phone: (225) 342-7009
Fax: (225) 342-1949
E-mail: kblanco@crt.state.la.us

MAINE

MARYLAND
Kathleen Kennedy Townsend (D)
Lieutenant Governor
Executive Dept.
State House
100 State Cir.
Annapolis, MD 21401
Phone: (410) 974-2804
Fax: (410) 974-5882
E-mail: ktownsend@goc.state.md.us

MASSACHUSETTS
Jane M. Swift (R)
Lieutenant Governor
Executive Ofc.
Rm. 360, State House
Boston, MA 02133
Phone: (617) 727-3600
Fax: (617) 727-9725

MICHIGAN
Dick Posthumus (R)
Lieutenant Governor
5215 Capitol Bldg.
P.O. Box 30026
Lansing, MI 48909
Phone: (517) 373-6800
Fax: (517) 335-6763

MINNESOTA
Mae Schunk (Reform)
Lieutenant Governor
State Capitol, Rm. 130
75 Constitution Ave.
St. Paul, MN 55155
Phone: (651) 296-3391
Fax: (651) 296-0674
E-mail: ltgov@state.mn.us

MISSISSIPPI
Ronnie Musgrove (D)
Lieutenant Governor
New Capitol, Rm. 315
P.O. Box 1018
Jackson, MS 39215-1018
Phone: (601) 359-3200
Fax: (601) 359-3935
E-mail: lt.gov
@mail.senate.state.ms.us

MISSOURI
Roger B. Wilson (D)
Lieutenant Governor
State Capitol, Rm. 121
Jefferson City, MO 65101
Phone: (573) 751-4727
Fax: (573) 751-9422
E-mail: wilson
@mail.state.mo.us

MONTANA
Judy Martz (R)
Lieutenant Governor
State Capitol Bldg.,
Rm. 207
P.O. Box 201901
Helena, MT 59620-1901
Phone: (406) 444-3111
Fax: (406) 444-4648

NEBRASKA
David I. Maurstad (R)
Lieutenant Governor
State Capitol, Rm. 3215
P.O. Box 94863
Lincoln, NE 68509-4863
Phone: (402) 471-2256
Fax: (402) 471-6031

NEVADA
Lorraine Hunt (R)
Lieutenant Governor
State Capitol Bldg.
101 N. Carson St., Ste. 2
Carson City, NV 89701
Phone: (775) 684-5637
Fax: (775) 684-5782

NEW HAMPSHIRE

NEW JERSEY

NEW MEXICO
Walter D. Bradley (R)
Lieutenant Governor
417 State Capitol
Santa Fe, NM 87503
Phone: (505) 827-3050
Fax: (505) 827-3057

NEW YORK
Mary Donohue (R)
Lieutenant Governor
Executive Chamber
State Capitol
Albany, NY 12224
Phone: (518) 474-4623
Fax: (518) 474-8581

NORTH CAROLINA
Dennis A. Wicker (D)
Lieutenant Governor
State Capitol
116 W. Jones St.
Raleigh, NC 27603-8006
Phone: (919) 733-7350
Fax: (919) 733-6595

NORTH DAKOTA
Rosemarie Myrdal (R)
Lieutenant Governor
Ofc. of the Governor
600 E. Blvd. Ave.
Bismarck, ND 58505-0001
Phone: (701) 328-2200
Fax: (701) 328-2205
E-mail: governor
@state.nd.us

NORTHERN MARIANA ISLANDS
Jesus Sablan (R)
Lieutenant Governor
Ofc. of the Governor
Caller Box 10007
Saipan, MP 96950
Phone: (670) 664-2300
Fax: (670) 664-2311

OHIO
Maureen O'Connor (R)
Lieutenant Governor
Vern Riffe Ctr.
77 S. High St., 30th Fl.
Columbus, OH 43215-0602
Phone: (614) 466-3396
Fax: (614) 644-0575

OKLAHOMA
Mary Fallin (R)
Lieutenant Governor
State Capitol, Rm. 211
Oklahoma City, OK 73105
Phone: (405) 521-2161
Fax: (405) 525-2702

OREGON

PENNSYLVANIA
Mark S. Schweiker (R)
Lieutenant Governor
200 Main Capitol Bldg.,
Rm. 200
Harrisburg, PA 17120
Phone: (717) 787-3300
Fax: (717) 783-0150

PUERTO RICO

RHODE ISLAND
Charles J. Fogarty (D)
Lieutenant Governor
318 State House
Providence, RI 02903
Phone: (401) 222-6655

SOUTH CAROLINA
Bob Peeler (R)
Lieutenant Governor
State House
P.O. Box 142
Columbia, SC 29202
Phone: (803) 734-2080
Fax: (803) 734-2082
E-mail: BOB
@ltgov.state.sc.us

SOUTH DAKOTA
Carole Hillard (R)
Lieutenant Governor
State Capitol
500 E. Capitol Ave.
Pierre, SD 57501
Phone: (605) 773-3661
Fax: (605) 773-4711

TENNESSEE
John S. Wilder (D)
Lieutenant Governor
1 Legislative Plz.
600 Charlotte Ave.
Nashville, TN 37243
Phone: (615) 741-2368
Fax: (615) 741-9349

TEXAS
Rick Perry (R)
Lieutenant Governor
Senate
State Capitol
P.O. Box 12068
Austin, TX 78711-2068
Phone: (512) 463-0001
Fax: (512) 463-0039

U.S. VIRGIN ISLANDS
Gerard Luz James, II (D)
Lieutenant Governor
#18 Kongens Gade
St. Thomas, VI 00801
Phone: (340) 774-2991
Fax: (340) 774-6953

UTAH
Olene S. Walker (R)
Lieutenant Governor
210 State Capitol
Salt Lake City, UT 84114
Phone: (801) 538-1520
Fax: (801) 538-1557
E-mail: owalker
@gov.state.ut.us

VERMONT
Douglas A. Racine (D)
Lieutenant Governor
State House
Montpelier, VT 05633
Phone: (802) 828-2226
Fax: (802) 828-3198

VIRGINIA
John H. Hager (R)
Lieutenant Governor
Ofc. of the Lieutenant
Governor
Pocahontas Bldg., 14th Fl.
900 E. Main St.
Richmond, VA 23219
Phone: (804) 786-2078
Fax: (804) 786-7514

WASHINGTON
Brad Owen (D)
Lieutenant Governor
Legislative Bldg.
P.O. Box 40482
Olympia, WA 98504-0220
Phone: (360) 786-7700
Fax: (360) 786-7520

WEST VIRGINIA

WISCONSIN
Scott McCallum (R)
Lieutenant Governor
22 E. State Capitol
Madison, WI 53702
Phone: (608) 266-3516
Fax: (608) 267-3571
E-mail: ltgov
@mail.state.wi.us

WYOMING

Lobby Law Administration—

Administers registration and reporting requirements for lobbyists.

ALABAMA
Jim Bennett
Secretary of State
State Capitol
600 Dexter Ave.
Montgomery, AL 36130-4650
Phone: (334) 242-7205
Fax: (334) 242-4993
E-mail: alsecst@alaline.net

ALASKA
Karen Boorman
Director
Public Ofcs. Comm.
2221 E. Northern Lights Blvd., Rm. 128
Anchorage, AK 99508-4149
Phone: (907) 276-4176
Fax: (907) 276-7018

AMERICAN SAMOA

ARIZONA
Betsy Bayless
Secretary of State
State Capitol, 7th Fl.
1700 W. Washington St.
Phoenix, AZ 85007-2808
Phone: (602) 542-3012
Fax: (602) 542-1575

ARKANSAS
Sharon Priest
Secretary of State
State Capitol, Rm. 256
Little Rock, AR 72201
Phone: (501) 682-1010
Fax: (501) 682-3510
E-mail: sharonpriest@ccm1.state.ar.us

CALIFORNIA
Robert Steele
Chief
Political Reform Div.
Ofc. of the Secretary of State
1500 11th St., Rm. 495
Sacramento, CA 95814
Phone: (916) 653-5943

COLORADO
Victoria Buckley
Secretary of State
Dept. of State
1560 Broadway, Rm. 200
Denver, CO 80202
Phone: (303) 894-2200
Fax: (303) 894-2242

CONNECTICUT
Alan S. Plofsky
Executive Director
State Ethics Comm.
18-20 Trinity St.
Hartford, CT 06106
Phone: (860) 566-4472

DELAWARE
Janet Wright
Commission Counsel
Public Integrity Comm.
Townsend Bldg.
Federal & Duke of York Sts.
Dover, DE 19901
Phone: (302) 739-2397

DISTRICT OF COLUMBIA
Cecily Collier-Montgomery
Director
Board of Elections & Ethics
Ofc. of Campaign Finance
2000 14th St., NW, Rm. 420
Washington, DC 20009
Phone: (202) 939-8710

FLORIDA
Mildred Bunton
Director
Div. of Legislative Info. Services
Pepper Bldg., Rm. 704
Tallahassee, FL 32399-1400

Bonnie J. Williams
Executive Director
Comm. on Ethics
P.O. Drawer 15709
Tallahassee, FL 32317-5709
Phone: (904) 488-7864
Fax: (904) 488-3077

GEORGIA
C. Theodore Lee
Executive Secretary
State Ethics Comm.
8440 Courthouse Sq., E., #C
Douglasville, GA 30134-1794
Phone: (770) 920-4385
Fax: (770) 920-4395

GUAM

HAWAII
Daniel J. Mollway
Executive Director
State Ethics Comm.
Pacific Tower, Ste. 970
1001 Bishop St., Ste. 970
Honolulu, HI 96813
Phone: (808) 587-0460
Fax: (808) 587-0470

IDAHO
Ben T. Ysursa
Chief Deputy Secretary of State
Elections Div.
Secretary of State Ofc.
P.O. Box 83720
Boise, ID 83720
Phone: (208) 334-2852
Fax: (208) 334-2282

ILLINOIS
Sherri A. Montgomery
Director
Index Dept.
Ofc. of Secretary of State
111 E. Monroe
Springfield, IL 62756
Phone: (217) 782-0643
Fax: (217) 524-0930

INDIANA
Gerald L. Bepko
Chair
Lobby Registration Comm.
115 W. Washington St., Ste. 1375S
Indianapolis, IN 46204-3420
Phone: (317) 232-9860
Fax: (317) 233-0077

IOWA
Liz A. Isaacson
Chief Clerk of the House
State Capitol, 2nd Fl.
Des Moines, IA 50319
Phone: (515) 281-5381
Fax: (515) 281-8758

Mike Marshall
Secretary of the Senate
State Capitol
Des Moines, IA 50319
Phone: (515) 281-5307

KANSAS
Ron Thornburgh
Secretary of State
State Capitol, 2nd Fl.
300 SW 10th St.
Topeka, KS 66612
Phone: (785) 296-4575
Fax: (785) 296-4570

KENTUCKY
Albert Benjamin Chandler, III
Attorney General
Ofc. of the Attorney Gen.
State Capitol, Ste. 118
Frankfort, KY 40601
Phone: (502) 696-5300
Fax: (502) 564-8310

LOUISIANA
Alfred W. Speer
Clerk of the House
P.O. Box 44281
Baton Rouge, LA 70804
Phone: (225) 342-7259
Fax: (225) 342-5045

MAINE
Bill Haines
Director
Governmental Ethics & Election Practices Comm.
135 State House Station
Augusta, ME 04333
Phone: (207) 287-6219

MARYLAND
John E. O'Donnell
Executive Director
State Ethics Comm.
Ofc. of Executive Dir.
300 E. Joppa Rd., Ste. 301
Towson, MD 21286
Phone: (410) 321-3636
Fax: (410) 321-4060

MASSACHUSETTS
Carolyn Kelly MacWilliam
Supervisor
Public Records
Ofc. of the Secretary of the Commonwealth
One Ashburton Pl., Rm. 1719
Boston, MA 02108
Phone: (617) 727-2832
Fax: (617) 727-5914

MICHIGAN
Candice Miller
Secretary of State
Treasury Bldg., 1st Fl.
430 W. Allegan St.
Lansing, MI 48918
Phone: (517) 373-2510
Fax: (517) 373-0727

MINNESOTA
Jeanne Olson
Executive Director
Campaign Finance & Public Disclosure Board
100 Centennial Ofc. Bldg.
658 Cedar St.
St. Paul, MN 55155
Phone: (651) 296-5148
Fax: (651) 296-1722
E-mail: jeanne.olson@state.mn.us

MISSISSIPPI
Eric Clark
Secretary of State
401 Mississippi St.
P.O. Box 136
Jackson, MS 39205
Phone: (601) 359-1350
Fax: (601) 354-6243

MISSOURI
Michael C. Reid
Director of Compliance
Div. of Compliance
Ethics Comm.
P.O. Box 1254
Jefferson City, MO 65102
Phone: (800) 392-8660
Fax: (573) 526-4506
E-mail: mreid01@mail.state.mo.us

MONTANA
Linda Vaughey
Commissioner
Political Practices
1205 8th Ave.
P.O. Box 202401
Helena, MT 59620-2401
Phone: (406) 444-2942
Fax: (406) 444-1643

NEBRASKA
Tim Dempsey
Executive Director
Accountability & Disclosure Comm.
P.O. Box 95086
Lincoln, NE 68509
Phone: (402) 471-2522
Fax: (402) 471-6599

NEVADA
Lorne J. Malkiewich
Director
Legislative Counsel Bur.
401 S. Carson St.
Carson City, NV 89701
Phone: (775) 687-6800
Fax: (775) 687-5962

NEW HAMPSHIRE
William Gardner
Secretary of State
Secretary of State Ofc.
State House, Rm. 204
107 N. Main St.
Concord, NH 03301
Phone: (603) 271-3242
Fax: (603) 271-6316
E-mail: sof.karen.ladd@leg.state.nh.us

NEW JERSEY
Frederick M. Herrmann
Executive Director
Election Law Enforcement Comm.
28 W. State St., 13th Fl.
P.O. Box 185
Trenton, NJ 08625-0185
Phone: (609) 292-8700
Fax: (609) 777-1457

NEW MEXICO
Rebecca Vigil-Giron
Secretary of State
State Capitol Bldg., Rm. 420
Santa Fe, NM 87503
Phone: (505) 827-3600
Fax: (505) 827-3634

NEW YORK
David M. Grandeau
Executive Director
Temporary Comm. on Lobbying
2 Empire State Plz., Rm. 1701
Albany, NY 12223
Phone: (518) 474-7126
Fax: (518) 473-6492

NORTH CAROLINA
Mary Kelly
Lobbyist Registrar
Lobbyist Registration Adm. Div.
Secretary of State
Legislative Ofc. Bldg.
300 N. Salisbury St.
Raleigh, NC 27603-5909
Phone: (919) 733-5181
Fax: (919) 733-9146

NORTH DAKOTA
Alvin A. Jaeger
Secretary of State
Secretary of State's Ofc.
600 E. Blvd. Ave., 1st Fl.
Bismarck, ND 58505-0500
Phone: (701) 328-2900
Fax: (701) 328-2992
E-mail: ajaeger@state.nd.us

NORTHERN MARIANA ISLANDS
Juan M. Diaz
Executive Director
Board of Elections
P.O. Box 470
Saipan, MP 96950
Phone: (670) 234-6481
Fax: (670) 233-6880

Leo Lawrence LaMotte
Public Auditor
P.O. Box 1399 CTC
Saipan, MP 96950
Phone: (670) 234-6481
Fax: (670) 234-7812
E-mail: opa@mtccnmi.com

OHIO
William L. Hills
Executive Director
Jt. Cmte. on Agency Rules Review
Vern Riffe Ctr.
77 S. High St., Ground Level
Columbus, OH 43266-0603
Phone: (614) 466-4086
Fax: (614) 752-8803

OKLAHOMA
Marilyn Hughes
Executive Director
Ethics Comm.
State Capitol Bldg., Rm. B-5
2300 N. Lincoln Blvd.
Oklahoma City, OK 73105
Phone: (405) 521-3451
Fax: (405) 521-4905

OREGON
L. Patrick Hearn
Executive Director
Govt. Standards & Practices Comm.
100 High St., SE, Ste. 220
Salem, OR 97310
Phone: (503) 378-5105
Fax: (503) 373-1456

PENNSYLVANIA
Mark Corrigan
Secretary of the Senate
462 Main Capitol Bldg.
Harrisburg, PA 17120
Phone: (717) 787-5920
Fax: (717) 772-2344

PUERTO RICO
Scott E. Thomas
Director
Corp. Div.
Dept. of State
P.O. Box 3271
San Juan, PR 00904
Phone: (787) 722-2121

RHODE ISLAND
James R. Langevin
Secretary of State
220 State House
Providence, RI 02903
Phone: (401) 222-2357
Fax: (401) 222-1356

SOUTH CAROLINA
Jim Miles
Secretary of State
Wade Hampton Bldg.
P.O. Box 11350
Columbia, SC 29211
Phone: (803) 734-2170
Fax: (803) 734-2164

SOUTH DAKOTA
Joyce Hazeltine
Secretary of State
500 E. Capitol Ave., Ste. 204
Pierre, SD 57501
Phone: (605) 773-3537
Fax: (605) 773-6580
E-mail: patty.pearson@state.sd.us

TENNESSEE
Peggy Nance Williams
Executive Director
Registry of Election Finance
Ofc. of Secretary of State
404 James Robertson Pkwy., 16th Fl.
Nashville, TN 37243
Phone: (615) 741-7959
Fax: (615) 532-8905

TEXAS
Kristin Newkirk
Director
Div. of Disclosure Filings
Ethics Comm.
P.O. Box 12070
Austin, TX 78711
Phone: (512) 463-5800
Fax: (512) 463-5777

U.S. VIRGIN ISLANDS
Iver Stirdiron
Attorney General
Dept. of Justice
G.E.R.S. Complex
4813-50C Kronprinsdens Gade
St. Thomas, VI 00802
Phone: (340) 774-5666
Fax: (340) 774-9710

UTAH
Olene S. Walker
Lieutenant Governor
210 State Capitol
Salt Lake City, UT 84114
Phone: (801) 538-1520
Fax: (801) 538-1557
E-mail: owalker@gov.state.ut.us

VERMONT
Deborah Markowitz
Secretary of State
109 State St.
Montpelier, VT 05609-1101
Phone: (802) 828-2148
Fax: (802) 828-2496

VIRGINIA
Anne P. Petera
Secretary of the Commonwealth
Governor's Cabinet
Old Finance Bldg., 1st Fl.
Capitol Sq.
Richmond, VA 23219
Phone: (804) 786-2441
Fax: (804) 371-0017

WASHINGTON
Melissa Warheit
Executive Director
Public Disclosure Comm.
711 Capitol Way, Rm. 403
P.O. Box 40908
Olympia, WA 98504-0908
Phone: (360) 753-1111
Fax: (360) 753-1112

WEST VIRGINIA
Richard Alker
Executive Director
State Ethics Comm.
1207 Quarrier St.
Charleston, WV 25301
Phone: (304) 558-0664
Fax: (304) 558-2169

WISCONSIN

WYOMING
Richard H. Miller
Director
Legislative Services Ofc.
State Capitol, Rm. 213
200 W. 24th St.
Cheyenne, WY 82002
Phone: (307) 777-7881

Local Government Relations

Coordinates federal and state programs affecting local government, and informs state officials about local government needs.

ALABAMA
Dewayne Freeman
Director
Dept. of Economic & Community Affairs
P.O. Box 5690
Montgomery, AL 36103-5690
Phone: (334) 242-5591
Fax: (334) 242-5099

ALASKA
Pat Poland
Director
Div. of Municipal & Regional Assistance
Community & Regional Affairs
333 W. 4th Ave., Ste. 220
Anchorage, AK 99501
Phone: (907) 269-4500
Fax: (907) 269-4539

AMERICAN SAMOA

ARIZONA
Jackie Vieh
Director
Dept. of Commerce
3800 N. Central Ave., Ste. 1500
Phoenix, AZ 85012
Phone: (602) 280-1306
Fax: (602) 280-1302

ARKANSAS

CALIFORNIA
Mac Strobl
Director
Ofc. of Planning & Resource
1400 10th St.
Sacramento, CA 95814
Phone: (916) 323-5446

COLORADO
Bob Brooks
Executive Director
Dept. of Local Affairs
1313 Sherman St., Rm. 323
Denver, CO 80203
Phone: (303) 866-2771
Fax: (303) 866-2251

CONNECTICUT
Marc Ryan
Secretary
Ofc. of Policy & Mgmt.
450 Capitol Ave., MS 54SLP
P.O. Box 341441
Hartford, CT 06134-1441
Phone: (860) 418-6500

DELAWARE

DISTRICT OF COLUMBIA
Warren Graves
Director
Ofc. of Intergovernmental Relations
441 4th St., NW, Rm. 1010-S
Washington, DC 20001
Phone: (202) 727-6265
Fax: (202) 727-6895

Ronald L. Magnus
Deputy Director-Regional/National Affairs
Exec. Ofc. of the Mayor
Ofc. of Intergovernmental Relations
441 4th St., NW, Ste. 1010
Washington, DC 20001
Phone: (202) 727-6265
Fax: (202) 727-6895
E-mail: rmagnus-eom@dcgov.org

FLORIDA
Steve Phieffer
Acting Director
Resource Planning & Mgmt. Div.
Dept. of Community Affairs
2555 Shumard Oak Blvd.
Tallahassee, FL 32399-2100
Phone: (850) 488-2356
Fax: (850) 921-0781

GEORGIA
Jim Higdon
Commissioner
Dept. of Community Affairs
60 Executive Park, S.
Atlanta, GA 30329
Phone: (404) 679-4940

GUAM
Madeleine Bordallo
Lieutenant Governor
Federal Programs/State Clearing House
Ofc. of the Governor
Executive Chambers, Adelup
Hagatna, GU 96932
Phone: (671) 472-8931
Fax: (671) 477-4826

HAWAII

IDAHO

ILLINOIS
Pam McDonough
Director
Dept. of Commerce & Community Affairs
620 E. Adams St., 3rd Fl.
Springfield, IL 62701
Phone: (217) 782-3233
Fax: (217) 524-0864

INDIANA
Robert Kovach
Executive Assistant
Ofc. of the Governor
206 State House
Indianapolis, IN 46204
Phone: (317) 233-3747
Fax: (317) 232-3443

IOWA

KANSAS
Dan Hermes
Director
Governmental Affairs
Ofc. of the Governor
State Capitol, 2nd Fl.
300 SW 10th St.
Topeka, KS 66612-1590
Phone: (785) 296-3232
Fax: (785) 296-7973

KENTUCKY
Bob Arnold
Commissioner
Dept. of Local Govt.
1024 Capitol Ctr. Dr., Ste. 340
Frankfort, KY 40601
Phone: (502) 573-2382
Fax: (502) 573-2512

LOUISIANA
Lynda Imes
Director of Municipal Affairs
Ofc. of the Governor
P.O. Box 94004
Baton Rouge, LA 70804-9004
Phone: (225) 342-6201
Fax: (225) 342-1488

MAINE

MARYLAND

MASSACHUSETTS
Jane W. Gumble
Director
Executive Ofc. of Communities & Dev.
Dept. of Housing & Community Dev.
100 Cambridge St., Rm. 1804
Boston, MA 02202
Phone: (617) 727-7765
Fax: (617) 727-5060

MICHIGAN
Mark Hilpert
Director
Bur. of Local Govt.
Dept. of Treasury
430 W. Allegan St.
Lansing, MI 48922
Phone: (517) 373-3305

MINNESOTA
Andrew Koebrick
Librarian
Planning Library
Centennial Ofc. Bldg., 3rd Fl.
658 Cedar St.
St. Paul, MN 55155
Phone: (651) 297-2325
Fax: (651) 297-2820
E-mail: ann.schluter@mn.plan.state.us

MISSISSIPPI

MISSOURI
Lois Pohl
Director,
Intergovernmental Relations
Div. of Services
Ofc. of Administration
Jefferson Bldg., Rm. 915
P.O. Box 809
Jefferson City, MO 65102
Phone: (573) 751-4834
Fax: (573) 522-4395
E-mail: pohll@mail.oa.state.mo.us

MONTANA
Newell B. Anderson
Administrator
Local Govt. Assistance Div.
Dept. of Commerce
1424 9th Ave.
Helena, MT 59620
Phone: (406) 444-3757
Fax: (406) 444-4482

NEBRASKA

NEVADA

NEW HAMPSHIRE
Jeffrey Taylor
Director
Ofc. of State Planning, Executive Dept.
Governor's Recycling Program
2 1/2 Beacon St.
Concord, NH 03301-4497
Phone: (603) 271-2155
Fax: (603) 271-1728

NEW JERSEY
Ulrich Steinberg
Director
Div. of Local Govt. Services
Dept. of Community Affairs
101 S. Broad St.
P.O. Box 803
Trenton, NJ 08625-0803
Phone: (609) 292-6613

NEW MEXICO
Walter D. Bradley
Lieutenant Governor
417 State Capitol
Santa Fe, NM 87503
Phone: (505) 827-3050
Fax: (505) 827-3057

NEW YORK
Alexander F. Treadwell
Secretary of State
Dept. of State
41 State St.
Albany, NY 12231
Phone: (518) 486-9844
Fax: (518) 474-4765

NORTH CAROLINA
Ann Lichner
Director
Intergovernmental Relations
Ofc. of the Governor
116 W. Jones St.
Raleigh, NC 27603
Phone: (919) 733-5201
Fax: (919) 733-2120

NORTH DAKOTA

NORTHERN MARIANA ISLANDS
Herman T. Guerrero
Executive Assistant to the Governor
Ofc. of the Governor
Caller Box 10007
Saipan, MP 96950
Phone: (670) 664-2282
Fax: (670) 664-2390
E-mail: gov.eag@saipan.com

OHIO
Scott Sigel
State & Local Govt. Comm.
Ofc. of Governor
Vern Riffe Ctr.
77 S. High St., 7th Fl.
Columbus, OH 43215-0602
Phone: (614) 466-2108
Fax: (614) 466-9150

OKLAHOMA
Craig J. Smith
Director
Intergovernmental Affairs
440 S. Houston St., Ste. 304
Tulsa, OK 74127
Phone: (405) 581-2801
Fax: (405) 581-2835

OREGON
Olivia Clark
Director
Intergovernmental Relations
Ofc. of the Governor
160 State Capitol
900 Court St., NE
Salem, OR 97310
Phone: (503) 378-5726
Fax: (503) 378-6827

PENNSYLVANIA
Kim Coon
Director
Bur. of Local Govt. Services
Dept. of Community & Economic Dev.
Forum Bldg., Rm. 325
Harrisburg, PA 17120
Phone: (717) 787-7160

PUERTO RICO

RHODE ISLAND
Anthony Phillips
Federal Liaison
Municipal Affairs
Governor's Ofc.
State House, Rm. 143
Providence, RI 02903
Phone: (401) 222-2080
Fax: (401) 861-5894

SOUTH CAROLINA

SOUTH DAKOTA
James Soyer
Chief of Staff
Governor's Ofc.
500 E. Capitol Ave.
Pierre, SD 57501
Phone: (605) 773-3212
Fax: (605) 773-5844
E-mail: jim.soyer@state.sd.us

TENNESSEE

TEXAS
Daisy Stiner
Acting Executive Director
Dept. of Housing & Community Affairs
507 Sabine, Ste. 400
Austin, TX 78701
Phone: (512) 475-5000
Fax: (512) 472-8526

U.S. VIRGIN ISLANDS
Ira Mills
Director
Ofc. of Mgmt. & Budget
#41 Norre Gade
Emancipation Garden Station, 2nd Fl.
St. Thomas, VI 00802
Phone: (340) 774-0750
Fax: (340) 774-0069

UTAH
Olene S. Walker
Lieutenant Governor
210 State Capitol
Salt Lake City, UT 84114
Phone: (801) 538-1520
Fax: (801) 538-1557
E-mail: owalker@gov.state.ut.us

VERMONT
Gregory G. Brown
Commissioner
Agency of Commerce & Community Affairs
Housing & Community Affairs Dept.
109 State St.
Montpelier, VT 05602
Phone: (802) 828-3211
Fax: (802) 828-2928

VIRGINIA
Micha H. Wilkinson
Executive Director
Comm. on Local Govt.
Pocahontas Bldg., Ste. 103
900 E. Main St.
Richmond, VA 23219
Phone: (804) 786-6508
Fax: (804) 371-7999

WASHINGTON
Helen P. Howell
Director of Intergovernmental Affairs
Ofc. of the Governor
P.O. Box 40002
Olympia, WA 98504-8300
Phone: (360) 902-4111
Fax: (360) 902-4110
E-mail: Helen.Howell@gov.wa.gov

WEST VIRGINIA
Phyllis Cole
Senior Executive Assistant
Ofc. of the Governor
State Capitol
1900 Kanawha Blvd., E.
Charleston, WV 25305
Phone: (304) 558-3702
Fax: (304) 342-7025

WISCONSIN
Bruce Fox
Administrator
Div. of Community Dev.
Dept. of Commerce
201 W. Washington, 6th Fl.
Madison, WI 53707
Phone: (608) 266-9467
Fax: (608) 266-5551

WYOMING
Margaret Spearman
Policy Advisor
State Capitol Bldg.
200 W. 24th St.
Cheyenne, WY 82002
Phone: (307) 777-7434
Fax: (307) 632-3909

Lottery

Administers the state lottery system.

ALABAMA

ALASKA

AMERICAN SAMOA

ARIZONA
Jeffery Gonsher
Director
State Lottery
4740 E. Univ. Dr.
Phoenix, AZ 85034
Phone: (602) 921-4514
Fax: (602) 921-4488

ARKANSAS

CALIFORNIA
William Popejoy
Interim Director
Lottery Comm.
600 N. 10th St.
Sacramento, CA 95814
Phone: (916) 324-2025

COLORADO
Mark Zamarippa
Director
Lottery Div.
Dept. of Revenue
201 W. 8th St., Rm. 600
Pueblo, CO 81003
Phone: (719) 546-2400

CONNECTICUT
Thomas Rotunda
Executive Director
Div. of Special Revenue
Dept. of Revenue Services
555 Russell Rd.
Newington, CT 06111
Phone: (860) 594-0501
Fax: (860) 594-0696

DELAWARE
Wayne Lemons
Director
State Lottery
Dept. of Finance
1575 McKee Rd., #102
Dover, DE 19904-1903
Phone: (302) 739-5291
Fax: (302) 739-6706

DISTRICT OF COLUMBIA
Anthony S. Cooper
Executive Director
Lottery & Charitable Games Control Board
2101 M.L. King, Jr., Ave., SE
Washington, DC 20020
Phone: (202) 433-8011

FLORIDA
Marcia Mann
Secretary
Dept. of the Lottery
250 Marriott Dr.
Tallahassee, FL 32399-4000
Phone: (850) 487-7728
Fax: (850) 487-7709

GEORGIA
Rebecca Paul
President/Chief Executive Officer
Lottery Corp.
250 Williams St.
Atlanta, GA 30303
Phone: (404) 215-5000

GUAM

HAWAII

IDAHO
Dennis Jackson
Director
State Lottery
1199 Shoreline Ln., Ste. 100
Boise, ID 83702
Phone: (208) 334-2600

ILLINOIS
Lori Montana
Director
State Lottery
201 E. Madison
Springfield, IL 62702
Phone: (217) 524-5259
Fax: (217) 524-5235

INDIANA
James Maguire
Executive Director
Lottery Comm.
201 S. Captiol, Ste. 1100
Indianapolis, IN 46225
Phone: (317) 264-4800
Fax: (317) 264-4908

IOWA
Edward J. Stanek, II
Lottery Comm.
2015 Grand Ave.
Des Moines, IA 50312
Phone: (515) 281-7900
Fax: (515) 281-7882

KANSAS
Gregory P. Ziemak
Executive Director
Lottery
128 N. Kansas Ave.
Topeka, KS 66603-3638
Phone: (785) 296-5700
Fax: (785) 296-5712

KENTUCKY
Arthur L. Gleason, Jr.
President & Chief Executive Officer
State Lottery Corp.
1011 W. Main St.
Louisville, KY 40202-2623
Phone: (502) 473-2200

LOUISIANA
Randy Davis
President
State Lottery Corp.
11200 Industriplex Blvd., Ste. 190
Baton Rouge, LA 70879
Phone: (225) 297-2002
Fax: (225) 297-2005

MAINE
Eben B. Marsh
Director
Bur. of Alcoholic Beverages & Lottery Operations
Dept. of Adm. & Financial Services
8 State House Station
Augusta, ME 04333
Phone: (207) 287-3721

MARYLAND
Buddy Roogow
Director
Ofc. of the Director
State Lottery Agency
6776 Reisterstown Rd.
Baltimore, MD 21215
Phone: (410) 764-6370
E-mail: broogow@msmail.awii.com

MASSACHUSETTS
Edward Lashman
Acting Executive Director
State Lottery Comm.
60 Columbian St.
Braintree, MA 02184
Phone: (781) 849-5500
Fax: (781) 849-5509

MICHIGAN
Don Gilmer
Commissioner
State Lottery
Treasury
101 E. Hillsdale
Lansing, MI 48909
Phone: (517) 335-5608

MINNESOTA
George Andersen
Director
State Lottery
2645 Long Lake Rd.
Roseville, MN 55113-2533
Phone: (651) 635-8101
Fax: (651) 297-7496
E-mail: andege@winternet.com

MISSISSIPPI

MISSOURI
James Scroggins
Administrative Director
Lottery
1823 Southridge Dr.
P.O. Box 1603
Jefferson City, MO 65102-1603
Phone: (573) 751-4050
Fax: (573) 751-5188
E-mail: scrogj@exec.molot.com

MONTANA
Gerald J. LaChere
Director
Lottery
Dept. of Commerce
2525 N. Montana
Helena, MT 59601
Phone: (406) 444-5825
Fax: (406) 444-5830

NEBRASKA
James E. Quinn
Lottery Director
Lottery Div.
Dept. of Revenue
P.O. Box 98901
Lincoln, NE 68509
Phone: (402) 471-6101
Fax: (402) 471-6108

NEVADA

NEW HAMPSHIRE
Rick Wisler
Executive Director
Sweepstakes Comm.
P.O. Box 1208
Concord, NH 03302-1208
Phone: (603) 271-3391
Fax: (603) 271-1160

NEW JERSEY
Virginia Haines
Executive Director
Div. of State Lottery
Dept. of the Treasury
Brunswick Ave.
P.O. Box 041
Trenton, NJ 08625-0041
Phone: (609) 599-5900
Fax: (609) 599-5935

NEW MEXICO
David Miller
Chief Executive Director
State Lottery
P.O. Box 93130
Albuquerque, NM 87199-3130
Phone: (505) 342-7611
Fax: (505) 342-7510

NEW YORK
Jeff Perlee
Director
Div. of Lottery
1 Broadway Ctr.
P.O. Box 7500
Schenectady, NY 12301
Phone: (518) 388-3400
Fax: (518) 388-3403

NORTH CAROLINA

NORTH DAKOTA

NORTHERN MARIANA ISLANDS
Lucia DLG. Neilsen
Secretary of Finance
Finance & Accounting
Dept. of Finance
P.O. Box 5234 CHRB
Saipan, MP 96950
Phone: (670) 664-1198
Fax: (670) 664-1115

OHIO
Mitchell Brown
Director
Lottery Comm.
615 W. Superior Ave.
Cleveland, OH 44113
Phone: (604) 787-4333
Fax: (604) 787-3313

OKLAHOMA

OREGON
Chris Lyons
Director
State Lottery
500 Airport Rd., SE
Salem, OR 97301
Phone: (503) 540-1017
Fax: (503) 540-1001

PENNSYLVANIA
Dan Cook
Director
Bur. of Lotteries
Dept. of Revenue
2850 Tpke. Industrial Dr.
Middletown, PA 17057
Phone: (717) 986-4759
Fax: (717) 783-8824

PUERTO RICO
Luis Tovet
Director
Lottery Administration
New San Juan Ctr.
Chardon Ave.
Hato Rey, PR 00919
Phone: (787) 759-8686

RHODE ISLAND
Gerald Aubin
Executive Director
State Lottery
1425 Pontiac Ave.
Cranston, RI 02920
Phone: (401) 463-6500

SOUTH CAROLINA

SOUTH DAKOTA
Rodger Leonard
Executive Director
State Lottery
St. Charles Bldg., Ste. 200
207 E. Capitol Ave.
Pierre, SD 57501
Phone: (605) 773-5770
Fax: (605) 773-5786

TENNESSEE

TEXAS
Linda Cloud
Executive Director
Lottery Comm.
P.O. Box 16630
Austin, TX 78761-6630
Phone: (512) 344-5000
Fax: (512) 478-3682

U.S. VIRGIN ISLANDS
George Golden
Acting Executive Director
8A Ross Estate, Barbel Plz.
St. Thomas, VI 00802
Phone: (340) 774-2502
Fax: (340) 776-4730

UTAH

VERMONT
Alan R. Yandow
Director
Lottery Comm.
379 S. Barre Rd.
P.O. Box 420
S. Barre, VT 05670-0420
Phone: (802) 479-5686
Fax: (802) 479-4294

VIRGINIA
Penelope W. Kyle
Director
State Lottery Dept.
900 E. Main St., 13th Fl.
Richmond, VA 23219
Phone: (804) 692-7000
Fax: (804) 692-7102

WASHINGTON
Merritt Long
Director
State Lottery
814 4th Ave.
P.O. Box 43000
Olympia, WA 98504-3000
Phone: (360) 753-1412
Fax: (360) 753-2602

WEST VIRGINIA
John Musgrave
Director
State Lottery Comm.
P.O. Box 2067
Charleston, WV 25327-2067
Phone: (304) 558-0500
Fax: (304) 558-3321

WISCONSIN
Don Walsh
Administrator
Lottery Div.
Gaming Comm.
1802 W. Beltline Hwy.
P.O. Box 8941
Madison, WI 53713
Phone: (608) 261-8800
Fax: (608) 264-6644

WYOMING

Mass Transportation

Develops the state's mass transportation policies.

ALABAMA
G.M. Roberts
Director
Hwy. Dept.
Dept. of Transportation
1409 Coliseum Blvd.
Montgomery, AL 36130
Phone: (334) 242-6311
Fax: (334) 262-8041

ALASKA
Joseph L. Perkins
Commissioner
Dept. of Transportation & Public Facilities
3132 Channel Dr.
Juneau, AK 99801-7898
Phone: (907) 465-3900
Fax: (907) 586-8365

AMERICAN SAMOA
Fa'aua'a Kataferu
Director
Dept. of Port Admin.
Pago Pago, AS 96799
Phone: (684) 633-4116

ARIZONA
Jay Klagge
Assistant Director
Transportation Planning Div.
Dept. of Transportation
206 S. 17th Ave.
Phoenix, AZ 85007
Phone: (602) 255-6872

ARKANSAS
Dan Flowers
Director
Dept. of Hwys. & Transportation
P.O. Box 2261
Little Rock, AR 72203
Phone: (501) 569-2211
Fax: (501) 569-2400

CALIFORNIA
Allan Hendrix
Deputy Director
Transportation Planning
Dept. of Transportation
1120 N St.
Sacramento, CA 95814
Phone: (916) 654-5368

COLORADO
Tom Norton
Executive Director
Dept. of Transportation
4201 E. Arkansas Ave.
Denver, CO 80222
Phone: (303) 757-9201
Fax: (303) 757-9657

CONNECTICUT
James Sullivan
Commissioner
Dept. of Transportation
2800 Berlin Tpke.
Newington, CT 06111
Phone: (860) 594-3000

DELAWARE
Anne P. Canby
Secretary
Dept. of Transportation
P.O. Box 778
Dover, DE 19903
Phone: (302) 739-4303
Fax: (302) 739-5736
E-mail: acanby@smtp.dot.state.de.us

DISTRICT OF COLUMBIA
Alex Eckman
Administrator
Ofc. of Mass Transit
Dept. of Public Works
2000 14th St., NW, 6th Fl.
Washington, DC 20009
Phone: (202) 939-8050

FLORIDA
Marion Hart
State Public Transportation Administrator
Ofc. of Public Transportation
Dept. of Transportation
605 Suwannee St., MS 57
Tallahassee, FL 32399-0450
Phone: (850) 414-4500
Fax: (850) 488-5526

GEORGIA
Wayne Shackelford
Commissioner
Dept. of Transportation
2 Capitol Sq.
Atlanta, GA 30334
Phone: (404) 656-5206

GUAM
Tony Martinez
Acting General Manager
Mass Transit Authority
236 E. O'Brien Dr.
P.O. Box 2950
Hagatna, GU 96932
Phone: (671) 475-4682
Fax: (671) 477-4600

HAWAII
Kazu Hayashida
Director
Dept. of Transportation
869 Punchbowl St.
Honolulu, HI 96813
Phone: (808) 587-2150
Fax: (808) 587-2167

IDAHO
Dwight Bower
Director
Dept. of Transportation
P.O. Box 7129
Boise, ID 83707
Phone: (208) 334-8800

ILLINOIS
Stephen E. Schindel
Director
Div. of Public Transportation
Dept. of Transportation
310 S. Michigan, Rm. 1608
Chicago, IL 60604
Phone: (312) 793-2111

INDIANA
Clemenc Ligocki
Chief
Transportation Planning
Dept. of Transportation
100 N. Senate Ave., N901
Indianapolis, IN 46204-2208
Phone: (317) 232-2380
Fax: (317) 232-1499

IOWA
Darrel Rensink
Director
Dept. of Transportation
800 Lincoln Way
Ames, IA 50010
Phone: (515) 239-1111
Fax: (515) 239-1639

KANSAS

KENTUCKY
James C. Codell, III
Secretary
Transportation Cabinet
State Ofc. Bldg., 10th Fl.
Frankfort, KY 40601
Phone: (502) 564-4890
Fax: (502) 564-4809

LOUISIANA
Carol Cranshaw
Public Transportation Administrator
Div. of Public Transportation
Dept. of Transportation & Dev.
P.O Box 94245, Rm. 400
Baton Rouge, LA 70804-9245
Phone: (225) 379-1436
Fax: (225) 379-1848

MAINE
John Melrose
Commissioner
Dept. of Transportation
16 State House Station
Augusta, ME 04333
Phone: (207) 287-2551

MARYLAND
Ronald L. Freeland
Administrator
Mass Transit Administration
Dept. of Transportation
William Donald Schaefer Tower
6 St. Paul St.
Baltimore, MD 21202-1614
Phone: (410) 767-3943
Fax: (410) 333-3279

MASSACHUSETTS
Kevin Sullivan
Secretary
Executive Ofc. of Transportation & Construction
10 Park Plz., Rm. 3170
Boston, MA 02116
Phone: (617) 973-8080
Fax: (617) 973-8445

MICHIGAN
Phil Kazmierski
Deputy Director
Bur. of Urban & Public Transportation
Dept. of Transportation
P.O. Box 30050
Lansing, MI 48909
Phone: (517) 373-2282

MINNESOTA
Jeff Hamiel
Executive Director
Metropolitan Airports Comm.
6040 28th Ave., S.
Minneapolis, MN 55450
Phone: (612) 726-8100
Fax: (612) 726-5296

Elwyn Tinklenberg
Commissioner
Dept. of Transportation
Transportation Bldg., 4th Fl.
395 John Ireland Blvd.
St. Paul, MN 55155
Phone: (651) 297-2930
Fax: (651) 296-3587

MISSISSIPPI
Chester Smith
Director
Div. of Energy
Dept. of Economic & Community Dev.
P.O. Box 850
Jackson, MS 39205-0850
Phone: (601) 359-6600
Fax: (601) 359-6642

MISSOURI
Phil Richeson
Administrator of Transit
Multimodal Operations Div.
Dept. of Transportation
P.O. Box 720
Support Ctr.
Jefferson City, MO 65102
Phone: (573) 751-2523
Fax: (573) 526-4709
E-mail: richep@mail.modot.state.mo.us

MONTANA
Patricia Saindon
Administrator
Transportation Planning Div.
Dept. of Transportation
2701 Prospect Ave.
Helena, MT 59620
Phone: (406) 444-3423
Fax: (406) 444-7671

NEBRASKA
Tom Wais
Deputy Director
Planning Div.
Dept. of Rds.
P.O. Box 94759
Lincoln, NE 68509-4759
Phone: (402) 479-4671
Fax: (402) 479-4325

NEVADA
Tom Stephens
Director
Dept. of Transportation
1263 S. Stewart St., Rm. 201
Carson City, NV 89712
Phone: (775) 888-7440
Fax: (775) 888-7201

NEW HAMPSHIRE
Chris Morgan
Administrator
Rail & Transit Bur.
Transportation Dept.
P.O. Box 483
Concord, NH 03302-0483
Phone: (603) 271-2468
Fax: (603) 271-6767

NEW JERSEY
James Weinstein
Commissioner of Transportation
Dept. of Transportation
1035 Pkwy. Ave.
P.O. Box 600
Trenton, NJ 08625-0600
Phone: (609) 530-3536
Fax: (609) 530-3894

NEW MEXICO
Harold Fenner
Director
Transportation Programs Div.
State Hwy. Dept.
P.O. Box 1149
Santa Fe, NM 87504
Phone: (505) 827-0410
Fax: (505) 827-0431

NEW YORK
Joseph Boardman
Commissioner
Dept. of Transportation
State Ofc. Bldg. Campus, Bldg. 5
Albany, NY 12232
Phone: (518) 457-4422
Fax: (518) 457-5583

NORTH CAROLINA
David King
Deputy Secretary for Transportation
Dept. of Transportation
1 S. Wilmington St.
Raleigh, NC 27601-1494
Phone: (919) 733-2520
Fax: (919) 733-9150

NORTH DAKOTA
Don Laschkewitsch
Transportation Senior Manager
Transportation Program & Planning
Dept. of Transportation
608 E. Blvd. Ave.
Bismarck, ND 58505-0700
Phone: (701) 328-2673
Fax: (701) 328-1404
E-mail: dlaschke@state.nd.us

NORTHERN MARIANA ISLANDS
Edward M. Deleon Guerrero
Secretary
Dept. of Public Works
Lower Base
P.O. Box 2950
Saipan, MP 96950
Phone: (670) 235-5827
Fax: (670) 235-5253

OHIO
Patricia A. Moore
Administrator
Public Transportation
Dept. of Transportation
1980 W. Broad St., 2nd Fl.
Columbus, OH 43223
Phone: (614) 466-8957
Fax: (614) 466-0822

OKLAHOMA
Ken LaRue
Manager for Transit Programs
Dept. of Transportation
200 NE 21st St.
Oklahoma City, OK 73105
Phone: (405) 521-2584
Fax: (405) 521-2533

OREGON
Martin Loring
Manager
Public Transit Section
Dept. of Transportation
Mill Creek Bldg.
555 13th St., NE, Ste. 3
Salem, OR 97301-4179
Phone: (503) 986-3413
Fax: (503) 986-4189

PENNSYLVANIA
Joseph Daversa
Director
Bur. of Public Transportation & Goods
1215 Transportation & Safety Bldg.
Harrisburg, PA 17120
Phone: (717) 787-3921
Fax: (717) 772-2985

PUERTO RICO
Jorge Rivera
President
Metropolitan Bus Authority
P.O. Box 195349
San Juan, PR 00919
Phone: (787) 767-7979
Fax: (787) 751-0527

RHODE ISLAND
Beverly Scott
General Manager
Public Transit Authority
265 Melrose St.
Providence, RI 02907
Phone: (401) 781-9400

SOUTH CAROLINA
Elizabeth S. Mabry
Executive Director
Dept. of Transportation
955 Park St.
Columbia, SC 29202
Phone: (803) 737-1302

SOUTH DAKOTA
Ron Wheeler
Secretary
Dept. of Transportation
700 E. Broadway
Pierre, SD 57501
Phone: (605) 773-3265
Fax: (605) 773-3921

TENNESSEE
Ben Smith
Director
Public Transportation
Dept. of Transportation
James Polk Bldg., 4th Fl.
505 Deaderick St.
Nashville, TN 37243-0325
Phone: (615) 741-2781
Fax: (615) 253-1482

TEXAS
Alvin R. Luedecke, Jr.
Director
State Transportation
Planning & Program
Div.
Dept. of Transportation
(TPP)
P.O. Box 149217
Austin, TX 78714-9217
Phone: (512) 486-5000
Fax: (512) 486-5007

U.S. VIRGIN ISLANDS
Harold G. Thompson
Acting Commissioner
Dept. of Public Works
No. 8 Sub Base
St. Thomas, VI 00802
Phone: (340) 776-4844
Fax: (340) 776-8990

UTAH
Linda Toy-Hull
Director
Div. of Program Dev.
Dept. of Transportation
4501 S. 2700 W.
Salt Lake City, UT 84119
Phone: (801) 965-4082
Fax: (801) 965-4551
E-mail: lhull
@dot.state.ut.us

VERMONT
Greg Maguire
Director
Div. of Air & Public
Transportation
Agency of Transportation
Natl. Life Bldg., Drawer 33
Montpelier, VT 05633-5001
Phone: (802) 828-2093
Fax: (802) 828-2829

VIRGINIA
David R. Gehr
Commissioner
Dept. of Transportation
1401 E. Broad St.
Richmond, VA 23219
Phone: (804) 786-2701
Fax: (804) 786-2940

WASHINGTON
James P. Toohey
Assistant Secretary
Planning & Programming
Service Ctr.
State Dept. of
Transportation
Transportation Bldg.,
Rm. 1A23
P.O. Box 47370
Olympia, WA 98504-7370
Phone: (360) 705-7929
Fax: (360) 705-6853

WEST VIRGINIA
Susan L. O'Connell
Director
Div. of Public Transit
Dept. of Transportation
Bldg. 5, Rm. 716
1900 Kanawha Blvd., E.
Charleston, WV 25305-0432
Phone: (304) 558-0428
Fax: (304) 558-0174

WISCONSIN

WYOMING
Gene Roccabruna
Director
Hwy. Safety Div.
Dept. of Transportation
5300 Bishop Blvd.
Cheyenne, WY 82002
Phone: (307) 777-4198

Medicaid

Administers the medical assistance program that finances medical care for income assistance recipients and other eligible medically needy persons.

ALABAMA
Willis Dale Walley
Commissioner
Medicaid Agency
501 Dexter Ave.
P.O. Box 5624
Montgomery, AL 36103
Phone: (334) 242-5600
Fax: (334) 242-5097

ALASKA
Bob Labbe
Director
Div. of Medical Assistance
P.O. Box 110660
Juneau, AK 99811-0660
Phone: (907) 465-3355
Fax: (907) 465-2204

AMERICAN SAMOA
Joseph Pereira
Chairman
Governing Body
Hospital Authority
LBJ Tropical Medical Ctr.
AS Govt.
Pago Pago, AS 96799
Phone: (684) 633-1222
Fax: (684) 633-1869

ARIZONA
Phyllis Beidess
Director
Health Care Cost Containment System
801 E. Jefferson
Phoenix, AZ 85034
Phone: (602) 417-4680
Fax: (602) 252-6536

ARKANSAS
Ray Hanley
Deputy Director
Div. of Medical Services
Dept. of Human Services
P.O. Box 1437, Slot 316
Little Rock, AR 72203
Phone: (501) 682-8291
Fax: (501) 682-8367

CALIFORNIA
Virgil J. Toney
Chief
Medi-Cal Operations Div.
Dept. of Health Services
P.O. Box 942732
Sacramento, CA 95814
Phone: (916) 657-1282
Fax: (916) 657-2955

COLORADO
Richard C. Allen
Director
Ofc. of Medical Assistance
Health Care Policy & Financing
1575 Sherman St., 4th Fl.
Denver, CO 80203
Phone: (303) 866-2859

CONNECTICUT
David Parella
Director
Health Care Financing
Dept. of Social Services
25 Sigourney St., 8th Fl.
Hartford, CT 06106-5003
Phone: (860) 424-5167

DELAWARE
Philip P. Soule
Director
Div. of Social Services
Medicaid Unit
DHSS Main Campus
1901 N. DuPont Hwy.
New Castle, DE 19720
Phone: (302) 577-4353
Fax: (302) 577-4899

DISTRICT OF COLUMBIA
Paul Offner
Deputy Director
Health Care Finance
Dept. of Human Services
2100 M.L. King, Jr. Ave., SE
Washington, DC 20020
Phone: (202) 727-0735

FLORIDA
Richard Lutz
Director
Bur. of Medicaid
Agency for Health Care Administration
2727 Mahan Dr.
Tallahassee, FL 32308
Phone: (850) 488-3560
Fax: (850) 488-2520

GEORGIA
William Taylor
Commissioner
Dept. of Medical Assistance
2 Peachtree St., Ste. 4043
Atlanta, GA 30303
Phone: (404) 656-4507

GUAM
Dennis G. Rodriguez
Director
Dept. of Public Health & Social Services
P.O. Box 2816
Hagatna, GU 96932
Phone: (671) 735-7102
Fax: (671) 734-5910
E-mail: dennis_r_@NS.GOV.GU

HAWAII
Susan Chandler
Director
Dept. of Human Services
1390 Miller St.
Honolulu, HI 96813
Phone: (808) 586-4997
Fax: (808) 586-4890

IDAHO
Dee Anne Moore
Administrator
Div. of Medicaid
Dept. of Health & Welfare
P.O. Box 83720
Boise, ID 83720-0036
Phone: (208) 334-5747
Fax: (208) 364-1811

ILLINOIS
Ann Patla
Director
Dept. of Public Aid
201 S. Grand Ave., E.
Springfield, IL 62762
Phone: (217) 782-7320
Fax: (217) 524-0835

INDIANA
Kathy Gifford
Assistant Secretary
Medicaid Policy & Planning
Family & Social Services Administration
IGC-S., Rm. W382
Indianapolis, IN 46204
Phone: (317) 233-4455
Fax: (317) 232-7382

IOWA
Donald L. Herman
Chief
Medical Services Div.
Dept. of Human Services
Hoover State Ofc. Bldg.
1300 E. Walnut
Des Moines, IA 50319
Phone: (515) 281-8621

KANSAS
Ann Koci
Commissioner
Adult & Medical Services
Social & Rehab. Services
Docking Bldg., Rm. 628S
915 Harrison
Topeka, KS 66612-1570
Phone: (785) 296-3981
Fax: (785) 296-4813

KENTUCKY
John Morse
Secretary
Health Services Cabinet
275 E. Main St.
Frankfort, KY 40621
Phone: (502) 564-7130
Fax: (502) 564-3866

LOUISIANA
Tom Collins
Director
Bur. of Health Services Financing
Dept. of Health & Hospitals
P.O. Box 91030
Baton Rouge, LA 70821
Phone: (225) 342-3891
Fax: (225) 342-9508

MAINE
Francis Finnegan
Director
Bur. of Medical Services
Dept. of Human Services
11 State House Station
Augusta, ME 04333
Phone: (207) 287-2546

MARYLAND
Craig Smalls
Division Chief
Div. of Medicaid Info. Systems
Dept. of Health & Mental Hygiene
201 W. Preston St., Rm. SS6
Baltimore, MD 21201
Phone: (410) 767-5408

MASSACHUSETTS
Claire McIntire
Commissioner
Executive Ofc. of Health & Human Services
Dept. of Transitional Assistance
600 Washington St., 6th Fl.
Boston, MA 02111
Phone: (617) 348-8400
Fax: (617) 348-8575

MICHIGAN
Robert M. Smedes
Director
Medical Services Administration
Dept. of Community Health
P.O. Box 30037
Lansing, MI 48909
Phone: (517) 335-5001

MINNESOTA
Mary Kennedy
Medicaid Director & Assistant Commissioner for Health Care
Health Care
Dept. of Human Services
444 Lafayette Rd.
St. Paul, MN 55155-3852
Phone: (651) 282-9921
Fax: (651) 297-3230
E-mail: mary.kennedy@state.mn.us

MISSISSIPPI
Helen Weatherbee
Director
Div. of Medicaid
Ofc. of the Governor
239 N. Lamar St., Ste. 801
Jackson, MS 39215-1399
Phone: (601) 359-6050
Fax: (601) 359-6048

MISSOURI
Gregory A. Vadner
Director
Div. of Medical Services
Dept. of Social Services
615 Howerton Ct.
P.O. Box 6500
Jefferson City, MO 65102-6500
Phone: (573) 751-3425
Fax: (573) 751-6564
E-mail: victor9@aol.com

MONTANA
Nancy Ellery
Administrator
Health Policy & Services Div.
Dept. of Public Health & Human Services
1400 Broadway, Rm. A206
Helena, MT 59620
Phone: (406) 444-4141
Fax: (406) 444-1861

NEBRASKA
Ric Compton
Medicaid Administrator
Dept. of Health & Human Services, Finance & Support
P.O. Box 95026
Lincoln, NE 68509
Phone: (402) 471-8241
Fax: (402) 471-9449

NEVADA
April Townley
Deputy Administrator
Medicaid Div.
Dept. of Human Resources
2527 N. Carson St.
Carson City, NV 89706
Phone: (775) 687-4867
Fax: (775) 687-8724

NEW HAMPSHIRE
Dianne Luby
Director
Ofc. of Health Mgmt.
Health & Human Services
6 Hazen Dr.
Concord, NH 03301-6527
Phone: (603) 271-4501
Fax: (603) 271-4827

NEW JERSEY
Margaret Murray
Commissioner
Medical Assistance Health Services
Dept. of Human Services
222 S. Warren St.
P.O. Box 700
Trenton, NJ 08625-0700
Phone: (609) 292-5646

NEW MEXICO
Charles Milligan
Chief
Medical Assistance Div.
Dept. of Human Services
P.O. Box 2348
Santa Fe, NM 87504
Phone: (505) 827-3100
Fax: (505) 827-6286

NEW YORK
Brian Wing
Commissioner
Ofc. of Temporary & Disability Assistance
40 N. Pearl St., 16th Fl.
Albany, NY 12243
Phone: (518) 473-8772
Fax: (518) 486-6255

NORTH CAROLINA
Paul Perruzzi
Director
Div. of Medical Assistance
Dept. of Health & Human Services
Kirby Bldg.
1985 Umstead Dr.
Raleigh, NC 27603-2001
Phone: (919) 857-4011
Fax: (919) 733-6608

NORTH DAKOTA
David J. Zentner
Director
Medical Services
Dept. of Human Services
600 E. Blvd. Ave., 3rd Fl. - Judicial Wing
Bismarck, ND 58505-0250
Phone: (701) 328-2321
Fax: (701) 328-2359
E-mail: sozend@state.nd.us

NORTHERN MARIANA ISLANDS
Galo P. Zudela
Administrator
Medicaid Div.
Dept. of Public Health & Environmental Services
P.O. Box 409
Saipan, MP 96950
Phone: (670) 234-8950
Fax: (670) 234-8930

OHIO
Barbara C. Edwards
Director
Ofc. of Medicaid
Dept. of Human Services
30 E. Broad St., 31st Fl.
Columbus, OH 43215
Phone: (614) 466-0140
Fax: (614) 752-3986

OKLAHOMA
Howard Hendrick
Director
Human Services
Dept. of Human Services
P.O. Box 25352
Oklahoma City, OK 73125
Phone: (405) 521-3646
Fax: (405) 521-6458

OREGON
Hersh Crawford
Director
Ofc. of Medical Assistance Program
Dept. of Human Resources
500 Summer St., NE
Salem, OR 97310-1014
Phone: (503) 945-5767
Fax: (503) 373-7689

PENNSYLVANIA
Darlene C. Collins
Deputy Secretary
Medical Assistance
Dept. of Public Welfare
P.O. Box 2675
Harrisburg, PA 17105-2675
Phone: (717) 787-1870
Fax: (717) 787-0191

PUERTO RICO
Carmen Feliciano
Secretary
Dept. of Health
P.O. Box 70184
San Juan, PR 00936-0184
Phone: (787) 274-7601
Fax: (787) 250-6547

RHODE ISLAND
Robert J. Palumbo
Associate Director
Medical Services
Dept. of Mental Health & Rehab.
600 New London Ave.
Cranston, RI 02920
Phone: (401) 462-3575

SOUTH CAROLINA
Sam Griswold
Director
Dept. of Health & Human Services
P.O. Box 8206
Columbia, SC 29202
Phone: (803) 253-6100

SOUTH DAKOTA
David Christensen
Director
Div. of Medical Services
Dept. of Social Services
700 Governors Dr.
Pierre, SD 57501
Phone: (605) 773-3495
Fax: (605) 773-4855

TENNESSEE

TEXAS
Linda Wertz
Deputy Commissioner
State Medicaid Director
Health & Human Services Comm.
P.O. Box 13247
Austin, TX 78711
Phone: (512) 424-6517
Fax: (512) 424-6585

U.S. VIRGIN ISLANDS
Phyllis Wallace
Deputy Commissioner of Administrative Services & Management
Dept. of Health
St. Croix Hospital
St. Croix, VI 00820
Phone: (340) 773-6551
Fax: (340) 773-1376

UTAH
Allan Elkins
Director
Medicare/Medicaid Program
Dept. of Health
288 N. 1460 W.
Salt Lake City, UT 84116
Phone: (801) 538-6595
Fax: (801) 538-7053
E-mail: aelkins@doh.state.ut.us

VERMONT
Paul Wallace-Brodeur
Director
Medicaid Services Div.
Dept. of Social Welfare
103 S. Main St.
Waterbury, VT 05671-1201
Phone: (802) 241-2880
Fax: (802) 241-2830

VIRGINIA
Dennis G. Smith
Director
Dept. of Medical Assistance Services
600 E. Broad St., Ste. 1300
Richmond, VA 23219
Phone: (804) 786-8099
Fax: (804) 786-4981

WASHINGTON
Tom Bedell
Assistant Secretary
Div. of Medical Assistance
Dept. of Social & Health Services
P.O. Box 45080
Olympia, WA 98504-5080
Phone: (360) 902-7807
Fax: (360) 902-7855

WEST VIRGINIA
Joan Ohl
Secretary
Dept. of Health & Human Resources
Capitol Complex, Bldg. 3, Rm. 206
1900 Kanawha Blvd., E.
Charleston, WV 25305
Phone: (304) 558-0684
Fax: (304) 558-1130

WISCONSIN
Peggy Bartels
Administrator
Div. of Healthcare Financing
Dept. of Health
1 W. Wilson St., Rm. 250
Madison, WI 53701
Phone: (608) 266-1511
Fax: (608) 266-1096

WYOMING
James Shepard
Administrator
Health Care Financing
Dept. of Health
6101 Yellowstone Rd.
Cheyenne, WY 82002
Phone: (307) 777-7531
Fax: (307) 777-6964
E-mail: jshepa@missc.state.wy.us

Mental Health and Mental Retardation

Administers the mental health services of the state and/or plans and coordinates programs for the mentally retarded.

ALABAMA
Kathy Sawyer
Commissioner
Dept. of Mental Health & Mental Retardation
100 N. Union St., Rm. 518
P.O. Box 301410
Montgomery, AL 36130
Phone: (334) 242-3107
Fax: (334) 242-0684

ALASKA
Karl Brimner
Director
Div. of Mental Health & Developmental Disabilities
Dept. of Health & Social Services
P.O. Box 110620
Juneau, AK 99811-0620
Phone: (907) 465-3370
Fax: (907) 465-2668

AMERICAN SAMOA
Marie F. Mao
Director
Dept. of Human & Social Services
AS Govt.
Pago Pago, AS 96799
Phone: (684) 633-2609
Fax: (684) 633-7449
E-mail: dhss@samoatelco.com

ARIZONA
Roger Deshaies
Assistant Director
Developmental Disabilities Div.
Dept. of Economic Security
1789 W. Jefferson
Phoenix, AZ 85007
Phone: (602) 542-6853

ARKANSAS
John Selig
Director
Div. of Mental Health
Dept. of Human Services
4313 W. Markham
Little Rock, AR 72205
Phone: (501) 686-9165
Fax: (501) 686-9182

CALIFORNIA
Stephen Mayberg
Director
Dept. of Mental Health
1600 9th St.
Sacramento, CA 95814
Phone: (916) 654-2309

COLORADO
Tom Barrett
Director
Mental Health Services
Dept. of Human Services
3824 W. Princeton Cir.
Denver, CO 80236
Phone: (303) 866-7400
Fax: (303) 866-7428

CONNECTICUT
Joxel Garcia
Commissioner
Dept. of Public Health
410 Capitol Ave., MS#13COM
P.O. Box 340308
Hartford, CT 06134
Phone: (860) 509-7101

Albert Solnit
Commissioner
Dept. of Mental Health & Addiction Services
410 Capitol Ave., 4th Fl., MS #14COM
P.O. Box 341431
Hartford, CT 06106
Phone: (860) 418-6969

DELAWARE
Judith E. Johnston
Acting Director
Div. of Alcoholism, Drug Abuse & Mental Health
Health & Social Services
1901 N. Dupont Hwy., Main Bldg.
New Castle, DE 19720
Phone: (302) 577-4461
Fax: (302) 577-4484

Marianne Smith
Director
Div. of Mental Retardation
Dept. of Health & Social Services
Jesse Cooper Bldg.
Dover, DE 19901
Phone: (302) 739-4452
Fax: (302) 739-3008

DISTRICT OF COLUMBIA
Arlene Robinson
Commissioner
Mental Health & Mental Retardation Services
Dept. of Human Services
Superior Courthouse
500 Indiana Ave., NW, 4475, 4th Fl.
Washington, DC 20001-2131
Phone: (202) 879-1040

FLORIDA
John Bryant
Assistant Secretary
Mental Health Program Ofc.
Dept. of Children & Family Services
1317 Winewood Blvd., Rm. 102, Bldg. 3
Tallahassee, FL 32399-0700
Phone: (850) 488-8304
Fax: (850) 487-2239

Kenneth DeCerchio
Assistant Secretary
Substance Abuse & Mental Health
Dept. of Children & Family Services
1317 Winewood Blvd., Rm. 101T
Tallahassee, FL 32399-0700
Phone: (850) 488-8304
Fax: (850) 414-7474

GEORGIA
Eddie Roland
Director
Dept. of Mental Health, Mental Retardation &
Substance Abuse
2 Peachtree St., 4th Fl.
Atlanta, GA 30303
Phone: (404) 657-2260

GUAM
John W. Leon Guerrero
Director
Dept. of Mental Health & Substance Abuse
790 Gov. Carlos G. Camacho Rd.
Tamuning, GU 96911
Phone: (671) 647-5330
Fax: (671) 649-6948

HAWAII
Michael Tamanaha
Chief
Waimano Training School & Hospital
Dept. of Health
2201 Waimano Home Rd.
Pearl City, HI 96782
Phone: (808) 453-6255
Fax: (808) 453-6217

IDAHO
Roy Sargeant
Chief
Mental Health & Substance Abuse Bur.
Dept. of Health & Welfare
450 W. State, 5th Fl.
P.O. Box 83720
Boise, ID 83720-0036
Phone: (208) 334-5528
Fax: (208) 334-6664

ILLINOIS
Howard A. Peters, III
Secretary
Dept. of Mental Health & Developmental Disabilities
100 S. Grand Ave., E.
Springfield, IL 62706
Phone: (217) 557-1606

INDIANA
Janet Corson
Director
Div. of Mental Health & Addictions
402 W. Washington St., Rm. W353
Indianapolis, IN 46204
Phone: (317) 232-7845
Fax: (317) 233-3472

IOWA
Sally Titus Cunningham
Deputy Director
Dept. of Human Services
Hoover State Ofc. Bldg.
1300 E. Walnut
Des Moines, IA 50319
Phone: (515) 281-6360
Fax: (515) 281-4597

KANSAS
Connie Hubbell
Commissioner
Mental Health & Developmental Disabilities
Social & Rehab. Services
915 SW Harrison
Topeka, KS 66612
Phone: (785) 296-3773
Fax: (785) 296-6142

KENTUCKY
Elizabeth Rehm Wachtel
Commissioner
Mental Health & Retardation Services Dept.
275 E. Main St.
Frankfort, KY 40621
Phone: (502) 564-4527
Fax: (502) 564-5478

LOUISIANA
Richard Lippincott
Assistant Secretary
Ofc. of Mental Health
Dept. of Health & Hospitals
P.O. Box 629
Baton Rouge, LA 70821
Phone: (225) 342-9238
Fax: (225) 342-5066

MAINE
Melodie Peet
Commissioner
Dept. of Mental Health & Mental Retardation
40 State House Station
Augusta, ME 04333
Phone: (207) 287-4223

MARYLAND
Diane Coughlin
Director
Developmental Disabilities Administration
201 W. Preston St., 4th Fl.
Baltimore, MD 21201
Phone: (410) 767-5600
Fax: (410) 767-5850

Oscar L. Morgan
Director
Mental Hygiene Administration
Health & Mental Hygiene Dept.
201 W. Preston St.
Baltimore, MD 21201
Phone: (410) 767-6655
Fax: (410) 333-5402

MASSACHUSETTS
Gerald Morrissey
Commissioner
Dept. of Mental Retardation
160 N. Washington St.
Boston, MA 02114
Phone: (617) 727-5608
Fax: (617) 727-9868

Marylou Sutters
Commissioner
Executive Ofc. of Human Services
Dept. of Mental Health
25 Staniford St.
Boston, MA 02114
Phone: (617) 727-5500
Fax: (617) 727-5500

MICHIGAN
James K. Haveman, Jr.
Director
Dept. of Community Health
Louis Cass Bldg.
320 S. Walnut
Lansing, MI 48913
Phone: (517) 373-3500
Fax: (517) 335-3090

MINNESOTA
Elaine Timmer
Assistant Commissioner
Continuing Care
Dept. of Human Services
444 Lafayette Rd.
St. Paul, MN 55155-3826
Phone: (651) 582-1801
Fax: (651) 582-1804
E-mail: elaine.timmer@state.mn.us

MISSISSIPPI
Randy Hendrix
Director
Dept. of Mental Health
1101 Robert E. Lee Bldg.
239 N. Lamar St.
Jackson, MS 39201
Phone: (601) 359-1288
Fax: (601) 359-6295

Roger McMurtry
Bureau Chief
Div. of Alcohol & Drug Abuse
Dept. of Mental Health
901 Robert E. Lee Bldg.
Jackson, MS 39201
Phone: (601) 359-1288
Fax: (601) 359-6295

MISSOURI
John Solomon
Director
Div. of Mental Retardation & Developmental Disabilities
Dept. of Mental Health
P.O. Box 687
Jefferson City, MO 65102
Phone: (573) 751-8676
Fax: (573) 751-9207
E-mail: solomj@mail.dmh.state.mo.us

MONTANA
Dan Anderson
Administrator
Addictive & Mental Disorders Div.
Dept. of Public Health & Human Services
Cogswell Bldg., Rm. C118
1400 Broadway
Helena, MT 59620
Phone: (406) 444-3969
Fax: (406) 444-4435

Joe A. Mathews
Administrator
Disability Services Div.
Dept. of Public Health & Human Services
111 Sanders St.
Helena, MT 59620
Phone: (406) 444-2591
Fax: (406) 444-3632

NEBRASKA
Dennis Mohatt
Deputy Director
Individual & Community Service
Dept. of Health & Human Services
P.O. Box 95044
Lincoln, NE 68509
Phone: (402) 471-9106
Fax: (402) 471-0820

Jim Wiley
Deputy Director
Health & Well Being
Dept. of Health & Human Services
P.O. Box 95044
Lincoln, NE 68509
Phone: (402) 471-8419
Fax: (402) 479-0820

NEVADA
Carlos Brandenburg
Administrator
Mental Hygiene & Retardation
Dept. of Human Resources
Kinkaid Bldg., Rm. 602
505 E. King St.
Carson City, NV 89701-3790
Phone: (775) 684-5943
Fax: (775) 684-5966

NEW HAMPSHIRE
Paul Gorman
Director
Community Supports & Long Term Care
Health & Human Services
105 Pleasant St.
Concord, NH 03301-3861
Phone: (603) 271-5007
Fax: (603) 271-5058

NEW JERSEY
Alan Kaufman
Director
Mental Health Services
Dept. of Human Services
Capitol Ctr., 3rd Fl.
P.O. Box 727
Trenton, NJ 08625-0727
Phone: (609) 777-0700
Fax: (609) 777-0662

NEW MEXICO
Ramona Flores-Lopez
Director
Long Term Services Div.
Dept. of Health
P.O. Box 26110
Santa Fe, NM 87502
Phone: (505) 827-2574
Fax: (505) 827-2455

Richard Tavares
Acting Director
Behavioral Health Services Div.
Dept. of Health
1190 St. Francis Dr.
P.O. Box 26110
Santa Fe, NM 87502
Phone: (505) 827-2601
Fax: (505) 827-0097

NEW YORK
James L. Stone
Commissioner
Ofc. of Mental Health
44 Holland Ave.
Albany, NY 12229
Phone: (518) 474-4403
Fax: (518) 474-2149

NORTH CAROLINA
John F. Baggett
Director
Mental Health, Retardation & Substance Abuse
Dept. of Human Resources
325 N. Salisbury St.
Raleigh, NC 27603
Phone: (919) 733-7011
Fax: (919) 733-9455

NORTH DAKOTA
Karen Larson
Director
Mental Health Services
Dept. of Human Services
600 S. 2nd St., Ste. 1-D
Bismarck, ND 58504-5729
Phone: (701) 328-8940
Fax: (701) 328-8969
E-mail: solark@state.nd.us

NORTHERN MARIANA ISLANDS
Isamu Abraham
Secretary
Health Services
Commonwealth Health Ctr.
P.O. Box 409
Saipan, MP 96950
Phone: (670) 234-6225
Fax: (670) 234-8930

OHIO
Michael Hogan
Director
Dept. of Mental Health
30 E. Broad St., 12th Fl.
Columbus, OH 43266-0415
Phone: (614) 644-7596
Fax: (614) 644-5013

OKLAHOMA
Sharron Boehler
Commissioner
Dept. of Mental Health & Substance Abuse Services
1200 NE 13th St.
Oklahoma City, OK 73117
Phone: (405) 522-3877
Fax: (405) 522-3650
E-mail: SBoehler@dmhsas.state.ok.us

OREGON
Barry Kast
Administrator
Mental Health & Developmental Disabilities Services Div.
2575 Bittern St., NE
Salem, OR 97310
Phone: (503) 945-9712
Fax: (503) 378-3796

PENNSYLVANIA
Charles G. Curie
Deputy Secretary
Mental Health
Dept. of Public Welfare
Health & Welfare Bldg., Rm. 502
Harrisburg, PA 17120
Phone: (717) 787-6443
Fax: (717) 787-0191

Nancy R. Thaler
Deputy Secretary
Mental Retardation
Dept. of Public Welfare
Health & Welfare Bldg., Rm. 512
Harrisburg, PA 17120
Phone: (717) 787-3700
Fax: (717) 787-0191

PUERTO RICO
Jose A. Acevedo
Assistant Secretary
Mental Health Care
Dept. of Mental Health
P.O. Box 9342
Santurce, PR 00908
Phone: (787) 763-7575
Fax: (787) 765-5895

RHODE ISLAND
A. Kathryn Power
Director
Dept. of Mental Health, Retardation & Hospitals
600 New London Ave.
Cranston, RI 02920
Phone: (401) 462-3201

SOUTH CAROLINA
Stan Butkus
Director
Dept. of Disabilities & Special Needs
P.O. Box 4706
Columbia, SC 29240
Phone: (803) 898-9769

SOUTH DAKOTA
John Jones
Secretary
Dept. of Human Services
Hillsview Plz.
500 E. Capitol Ave.
Pierre, SD 57501
Phone: (605) 773-5990
Fax: (605) 773-5483

Betty Oldenkamp
Director
Div. of Mental Health
Dept. of Human Services
500 E. Capitol Ave.
Pierre, SD 57501
Phone: (605) 773-5991
Fax: (605) 773-5483

TENNESSEE
Elizabeth Rukeyser
Acting Commissioner
Dept. of Mental Health
Cordell Hull Bldg., 3rd Fl.
Nashville, TN 37243
Phone: (615) 532-6503
Fax: (615) 532-6514

TEXAS
Karen Hale
Commissioner
Dept. of Mental Health & Mental Retardation
909 W. 45th St.
Austin, TX 78756
Phone: (512) 206-4588
Fax: (512) 206-4560

U.S. VIRGIN ISLANDS
Carlos Ortiz
Director of Mental Health
Dept. of Health
Barbel Plz., S., 2nd Fl.
St. Thomas, VI 00802
Phone: (340) 774-4888
Fax: (340) 774-4701

UTAH
Meredith Alden
Director
Div. of Mental Health
Dept. of Human Services
120 N. 200 W., 4th Fl.
Salt Lake City, UT 84103
Phone: (801) 538-4270
Fax: (801) 538-9892
E-mail: malden.hsadmin1@state.ut.us

VERMONT
Rodney Copeland
Commissioner
Mental Health & Retardation
Agency of Human Services
103 S. Main St.
Waterbury, VT 05671-1601
Phone: (802) 241-2610
Fax: (802) 241-3052

VIRGINIA
Richard E. Kellogg
Commissioner
Dept. of Mental Health, Mental Retardation & Substance Abuse Services
109 Governor St., Rm. 1301-A
Richmond, VA 23219
Phone: (804) 786-5682
Fax: (804) 371-6638

WASHINGTON
Ed Hidano
Assistant Secretary
Health & Rehab. Services
Dept. of Social & Health Services
P.O. Box 45060
Olympia, WA 98504-5060
Phone: (360) 902-7799
Fax: (360) 902-7848

WEST VIRGINIA
Joan Ohl
Secretary
Dept. of Health & Human Resources
Capitol Complex, Bldg. 3, Rm. 206
1900 Kanawha Blvd., E.
Charleston, WV 25305
Phone: (304) 558-0684
Fax: (304) 558-1130

WISCONSIN
Beverly Doherty
Director
Bur. of Developmental Disabilities
Dept. of Health & Family Services
1 W. Wilson, Rm. 418
P.O. Box 7851
Madison, WI 53703
Phone: (608) 266-0805
Fax: (608) 261-6752

WYOMING
Pablo Hernandez
Administrator
Div. of Behavioral Health
Dept. of Health
117 Hathaway Bldg.
2300 Capitol Ave.
Cheyenne, WY 82002
Phone: (307) 777-7116

Mined Land Reclamation —

Responsible for ensuring the reclamation of mined lands.

ALABAMA
Bill Guyette
Director
Abandoned Mine Land Reclamation
Dept. of Industrial Relations
649 Monroe St.
Montgomery, AL 36130-3301
Phone: (334) 242-8265
Fax: (334) 242-8403

ALASKA
Bob Loeffler
Director
Div. of Mining & Water Mgmt.
Dept. of Natural Resources
3601 C St., Ste. 800
Anchorage, AK 99503
Phone: (907) 269-8624
Fax: (907) 563-1853

AMERICAN SAMOA

ARIZONA
Michael Anable
State Land Commissioner
Dept. of State Land
1616 W. Adams St.
Phoenix, AZ 85007
Phone: (602) 542-4621
Fax: (602) 542-2590

ARKANSAS
Floyd Durham
Chief
Mining & Reclamation Div.
Dept. of Environmental Quality
P.O. Box 8913
Little Rock, AR 72219
Phone: (501) 682-0807
Fax: (501) 682-0880

CALIFORNIA
Dennis O'Bryant
Assistant Director
Ofc. of Mine Reclamation
Dept. of Conservation
801 K St., 12th Fl.
Sacramento, CA 95814-3533
Phone: (916) 323-9198

COLORADO
Michael B. Long
Director
Div. of Minerals & Geology
Dept. of Natural Resources
1313 Sherman St., Rm. 215
Denver, CO 80203
Phone: (303) 866-3567
Fax: (303) 832-8106

CONNECTICUT

DELAWARE

DISTRICT OF COLUMBIA

FLORIDA
Joseph Bakker
Bureau Chief
Mine Reclamation Bur.
Dept. of Environmental Protection
2051 E. Dirac Dr., MS 715
Tallahassee, FL 32310-3760
Phone: (850) 488-8217
Fax: (850) 488-1254

GEORGIA

GUAM
Juan Taijito
Acting Director
Dept. of Agri.
192 Dairy Rd.
Mangilao, GU 96923
Phone: (671) 734-3942
Fax: (671) 734-6569

HAWAII
Timothy Johns
Chair
Dept. of Land & Natural Resources
1151 Punchbowl St.
Honolulu, HI 96813
Phone: (808) 587-0400
Fax: (808) 587-0390

IDAHO
Scott Nichols
Reclamationist
Dept. of Lands
1215 W. State St.
Boise, ID 83720-7000
Phone: (208) 334-0261

ILLINOIS
Dick Mottershaw
Director
Ofc. of Mines & Minerals
Dept. of Natural Resources
524 S. 2nd St.
Springfield, IL 62701
Phone: (217) 782-6791
Fax: (217) 524-4819

Frank Pisani
Supervisor
Abandoned Mined Lands Reclamation
Dept. of Natural Resources
928 S. Spring
Springfield, IL 62704
Phone: (217) 782-0588
Fax: (217) 524-6674

INDIANA
Paul Ehret
Deputy Director
Bur. of Mine Reclamation
Dept. of Natural Resources
IGC-South, Rm. W256
Indianapolis, IN 46204
Phone: (317) 232-4020
Fax: (317) 233-6811

IOWA
James B. Gulliford
Administrator
Div. of Soil Conservation
Dept. of Agri. & Land
Wallace State Ofc. Bldg.
E. 9th & Grand Aves.
Des Moines, IA 50319
Phone: (515) 281-6146

KANSAS
Murray Balk
Chief
Surface Mining Section
Dept. of Health & Environment
4033 Parkview Dr.
Frontenac, KS 66763-2302
Phone: (316) 231-8540
Fax: (316) 231-0753

KENTUCKY
James E. Bickford
Secretary
Natural Resources & Environmental Protection Cabinet
Capital Plz. Tower
Frankfort, KY 40601
Phone: (502) 564-3350
Fax: (502) 564-3354

LOUISIANA
Tony Duplechin
Geology Supervisor
Regulatory & Land Mining Programs
Dept. of Natural Resources
P.O. Box 94275
Baton Rouge, LA 70804
Phone: (225) 342-5528
Fax: (225) 342-3094

MAINE
Henry Berry
Physical Geologist
Geological Survey
Dept. of Conservation
22 State House Station
Augusta, ME 04333
Phone: (207) 287-2801

MARYLAND
C. Edmond Larrimore
Acting Environmental Resources Administrator
Mining Program
Dept. of the Environment
2500 Broening Hwy.
Dundalk, MD 21224
Phone: (410) 631-8055

MASSACHUSETTS

MICHIGAN
Rodger Whitener
Resource Specialist
Geological Survey Div.
P.O. Box 30256
Lansing, MI 48909
Phone: (517) 334-6907

MINNESOTA
Arlo Knoll
Manager
Mined Land Reclamation
Minerals Div.
1525 3rd Ave., E.
Hibbing, MN 55746
Phone: (218) 262-6767
Fax: (218) 262-7328
E-mail: arlo.knoll@dnr.state.mn.us

MISSISSIPPI
Ken McCarley
Director
Mining & Reclamation Div.
Ofc. of Geology
P.O. Box 20307
Jackson, MS 39289-1307
Phone: (601) 961-5515
Fax: (601) 354-6965

MISSOURI
Larry Coen
Director
Land Reclamation Program
Div. of Environmental Quality
1738 E. Elm St.
P.O. Box 176
Jefferson City, MO 65102
Phone: (573) 751-4041
Fax: (573) 751-0534
E-mail: nrcoenl@mail.dnr.state.mo.us

MONTANA
Vic Andersen
Chief
Mine Waste Clean Up Bur.
Dept. of Environmental Quality
P.O. Box 200901
Helena, MT 59620
Phone: (406) 444-1420
Fax: (406) 444-0443

NEBRASKA
Mike Linder
Director
Dept. of Environmental Quality
1200 N St., Ste. #400
Lincoln, NE 68509
Phone: (402) 471-2186
Fax: (402) 471-2909

NEVADA
Leo Drozdoff
Chief
Bur. of Mining Regulation & Reclamation
Div. of Environmental Protection
333 W. Nye Ln., Rm. 138
Carson City, NV 89706
Phone: (775) 687-4670
Fax: (775) 684-5259

NEW HAMPSHIRE
Eugene L. Boudette
State Geologist
Water Div.
Environmental Services
P.O. Box 95
Concord, NH 03302-0095
Phone: (603) 271-3406
Fax: (603) 271-2867

Philip Bryce
Director
Forests & Lands
Resources & Economic Dev.
P.O. Box 1856
Concord, NH 03301-1856
Phone: (603) 271-2214
Fax: (603) 271-2629

NEW JERSEY

NEW MEXICO
Doug Bland
Acting Director
Mining & Minerals Div.
Dept. of Energy, Minerals & Natural Resources
2040 S. Pacheco
Santa Fe, NM 87505
Phone: (505) 827-5970
Fax: (505) 827-1150

NEW YORK
John Cahill
Commissioner
Dept. of Environmental Conservation
50 Wolf Rd.
Albany, NY 12233-1010
Phone: (518) 457-1162
Fax: (518) 457-7744

NORTH CAROLINA
F. Mell Neuils
Section Chief
Land Quality Section
Div. of Land Resources
512 N. Salisbury St.
Raleigh, NC 27604
Phone: (919) 733-4574
Fax: (919) 733-2876

NORTH DAKOTA
James R. Deutsch
Director
Reclamation
Public Service Comm.
600 E. Blvd. Ave., 12th Fl.
Bismarck, ND 58505-0480
Phone: (701) 328-4096
Fax: (701) 328-2410
E-mail: msmail.jrd@oracle.psc.state.nd.us

NORTHERN MARIANA ISLANDS
Eugene A. Santos
Secretary
Dept. of Lands & Natural Resources
P.O. Box 10007
Saipan, MP 96950
Phone: (670) 322-9830
Fax: (670) 322-2633

OHIO
Russ Scholl
Acting Chief
Div. of Mines & Reclamation
Dept. of Natural Resources
1855 Fountain Sq., Bldg. H-3
Columbus, OH 43224-1387
Phone: (614) 265-6675
Fax: (614) 262-6546

OKLAHOMA
Mary Ann Pritchard
Director
Dept. of Mines
4040 N. Lincoln Blvd., Ste. 107
Oklahoma City, OK 73105
Phone: (405) 521-3859
Fax: (405) 427-9646

OREGON
Gary W. Lynch
Supervisor
Ofc. of Reclamation of Surface Mined Land
Dept. of Geology & Mining
1536 Queen Ave., SE
Albany, OR 97321-6687
Phone: (541) 967-2039
Fax: (541) 967-2075

PENNSYLVANIA
Rogrick A. Fletcher
Director
Bur. of Mining & Reclamation
Dept. of Environmental Resources
Rachel Carson Blvd., 8th Fl.
P.O. Box 8461
Harrisburg, PA 17105
Phone: (717) 787-5103
Fax: (717) 783-4675

PUERTO RICO
Daniel Pagan
Secretary
Dept. of Natural Resources
P.O. Box 5887
San Juan, PR 00906
Phone: (787) 723-3090
Fax: (787) 723-4255

RHODE ISLAND

SOUTH CAROLINA
Patrick T. Walker
Director
Div. of Mining & Reclamation
Bur. of Solid and Hazardous Waste Mgmt.
2600 Bull St.
Columbia, SC 29201
Phone: (803) 896-4000

SOUTH DAKOTA
Robert Townsend
Administrator
Ofc. of Minerals & Mining
523 E. Capitol Ave.
Pierre, SD 57501
Phone: (605) 773-4201
Fax: (605) 773-5286

TENNESSEE
Tim Eagle
Program Manager
Div. of Land Reclamation
Dept. of Environment & Conservation
2700 Middlebrook Pike, Ste. 230
Knoxville, TN 37921
Phone: (423) 594-6203
Fax: (423) 594-6105

TEXAS
Melvin Hodgkiss
Director, Surface Mining & Reclamation
Surface Mining Div.
Railroad Comm.
P.O. Box 12967
Austin, TX 78711
Phone: (512) 463-6901

U.S. VIRGIN ISLANDS

UTAH
Lowell P. Braxton
Director
Div. of Oil, Gas & Mining
Dept. of Natural Resources
1594 W. N. Temple, #1210
Salt Lake City, UT 84114-5801
Phone: (801) 538-5370
Fax: (801) 359-3940
E-mail: lbraxton.nrogm@state.ut.us

VERMONT
John Kassell
Secretary
Agency of Natural Resources
103 S. Main St.
Waterbury, VT 05671-0301
Phone: (802) 241-3600
Fax: (802) 241-3281

VIRGINIA
O. Gene Dishner
Director
Dept. of Mines, Minerals & Energy
202 N. 9th St., 8th Fl.
Richmond, VA 23219
Phone: (804) 692-3200
Fax: (804) 692-3237

WASHINGTON
Ray Lasmanis
State Geologist
Div. of Geology & Earth Resources
Dept. of Natural Resources
P.O. Box 47007
Olympia, WA 98504-7007
Phone: (360) 902-1450
Fax: (360) 902-1785

WEST VIRGINIA
John Ailes
Chief
Ofc. of Mining & Reclamation
Div. of Environmental Protection
10 McJunkin Rd.
Nitro, WV 25143-2506
Phone: (304) 759-0510

WISCONSIN
Larry Lynch
Mining Team Leader
Bur. of Waste Mgmt.
Dept. of Natural Resources
101 S. Webster, 3rd Fl.
P.O. Box 7921
Madison, WI 53703
Phone: (608) 267-7553
Fax: (608) 267-2768

WYOMING
Stan Barnard
Administrator
Div. of Abandoned Mine Lands
Dept. of Environmental Quality
Herschler Bldg., 3rd Fl., W.
122 W. 25th St.
Cheyenne, WY 82002
Phone: (307) 777-6145

Mining Safety

Responsible for ensuring the safety of miners.

ALABAMA
Jerry Scharf
Director
Mine Safety Section
Dept. of Industrial Relations
11 W. Oxmoor Rd.
Birmingham, AL 35209
Phone: (205) 254-1275
Fax: (205) 254-1278

ALASKA

AMERICAN SAMOA

ARIZONA
Douglas Martin
State Mine Inspector
1700 W. Washington, #403
Phoenix, AZ 85007-2805
Phone: (602) 542-5971
Fax: (602) 542-5335

ARKANSAS
James Salkeld
Director
Dept. of Labor
10421 W. Markham, Ste. 100
Little Rock, AR 72205
Phone: (501) 682-4500
Fax: (501) 682-4532

CALIFORNIA
John Howard
Chief
Div. of Occupational Safety & Health
455 Golden Gate Ave., Ste. 5202
San Francisco, CA 94102
Phone: (415) 972-8500

COLORADO
Bill York-Feirn
Supervisor, Mine Safety & Training Programs
Div. of Minerals & Geology
1313 Sherman St., Rm. 215
Denver, CO 80203
Phone: (303) 866-3567
Fax: (303) 832-8106

CONNECTICUT

DELAWARE

DISTRICT OF COLUMBIA

FLORIDA
Joseph Bakker
Bureau Chief
Mine Reclamation Bur.
Dept. of Environmental Protection
2051 E. Dirac Dr., MS 715
Tallahassee, FL 32310-3760
Phone: (850) 488-8217
Fax: (850) 488-1254

GEORGIA

GUAM

HAWAII

IDAHO
Mike Poulin
Industrial Safety Supervisor
Bur. of Logging & Industrial Safety
Div. of Bldg. Safety
277 N. 6th
Boise, ID 83702
Phone: (208) 334-2129
Fax: (208) 334-2683

ILLINOIS
Brent Manning
Director
Dept. of Natural Resources
Lincoln Towers Plz., Rm. 425
524 S. 2nd St.
Springfield, IL 62706
Phone: (217) 782-6302
Fax: (217) 785-9236

INDIANA
Joe Batson
Director
Bur. of Mines & Mine Safety
Dept. of Labor
1615 Willow St.
Vincennes, IN 47591
Phone: (812) 882-7242
Fax: (812) 882-7537

IOWA

KANSAS

KENTUCKY
John Franklin
Commissioner
Dept. of Mines & Minerals
P.O. Box 14080
Lexington, KY 40512
Phone: (606) 246-2026
Fax: (606) 246-2038

LOUISIANA
Philip Asprodites
Commissioner of Conservation
Dept. of Natural Resources
P.O. Box 94275
Baton Rouge, LA 70804
Phone: (225) 342-5540
Fax: (225) 342-2584

MAINE
James McGowan
Director
Bur. of Labor Standards
Dept. of Labor
45 State House Station
Augusta, ME 04333
Phone: (207) 624-6400

MARYLAND

MASSACHUSETTS

MICHIGAN
Douglas R. Earle
Director
Bur. of Safety & Regulation
Consumer & Industry Services
7150 Harris Dr.
P.O. Box 30015
Lansing, MI 48909
Phone: (517) 322-1814

MINNESOTA
Allen Garber
Commissioner
Dept. of Natural Resources
500 Lafayette Rd.
St. Paul, MN 55155
Phone: (651) 296-2549
Fax: (651) 296-4799

MISSISSIPPI

MISSOURI
Colleen Baker
Director
Div. of Labor Standards
Labor & Industrial Relations
3315 W. Truman Blvd., Ste. 205
P.O. Box 449
Jefferson City, MO 65102-0449
Phone: (573) 751-3403
Fax: (573) 751-3721
E-mail: cbaker@dlirapp.dolir.state.mo.us

MONTANA
John Maloney
Bureau Chief
Safety Bur.
Dept. of Labor & Industry
1805 Prospect
P.O. Box 1728
Helena, MT 59624
Phone: (406) 444-1605
Fax: (406) 444-4140

NEBRASKA
Darrell Jensen
Director
Safety Ctr.
Univ. of NE Kearney
W. Ctr.
Kearney, NE 68849
Phone: (308) 865-8256
Fax: (308) 865-8257

NEVADA
Roger Bremner
Administrator
Div. of Industrial Relations
400 W. King St., 4th Fl., Ste. 400
Carson City, NV 89703
Phone: (775) 687-3032
Fax: (775) 687-6305

NEW HAMPSHIRE
Eugene L. Boudette
State Geologist
Water Div.
Environmental Services
P.O. Box 95
Concord, NH 03302-0095
Phone: (603) 271-3406
Fax: (603) 271-2867

NEW JERSEY
Leonard Katz
Assistant Commissioner
Labor Standards & Safety Enforcement
John Fitch Plz.
P.O. Box 385
Trenton, NJ 08625
Phone: (609) 777-0249
Fax: (609) 695-1314

NEW MEXICO
Doug Bland
Acting Director
Mining & Minerals Div.
Dept. of Energy, Minerals & Natural Resources
2040 S. Pacheco
Santa Fe, NM 87505
Phone: (505) 827-5970
Fax: (505) 827-1150

Gilbert Miera
State Mine Inspector
Bur. of Mine Inspection
NM Tech
801 Leroy Pl.
Socorro, NM 87801
Phone: (505) 835-5460
Fax: (505) 835-5430
E-mail: bmi@nmt.edu

NEW YORK
James J. McGowan
Commissioner
Dept. of Labor
State Ofc. Bldg. Campus, Bldg. 12
Albany, NY 12240
Phone: (518) 457-2741
Fax: (518) 457-6908

NORTH CAROLINA
Charles H. Gardner
Director
Div. of Land Resources
Dept. of Environment & Natural Resources
512 N. Salisbury St.
Raleigh, NC 27604-1148
Phone: (919) 733-3833
Fax: (919) 715-8801

NORTH DAKOTA
Wally Kalmbach
Director
Loss Prevention
Worker's Compensation Bur.
500 E. Front Ave.
Bismarck, ND 58504-5685
Phone: (701) 328-3886
Fax: (701) 328-3820
E-mail: msmail.wkalmbac @ranch.state.nd.us

NORTHERN MARIANA ISLANDS
Eugene A. Santos
Board Chair
Civil Service Comm.
Personnel Mgmt. Ofc.
Ofc. of the Governor
P.O. Box 5150 CHRB
Saipan, MP 96950
Phone: (670) 322-4363
Fax: (670) 322-3327
E-mail: csc@saipan.com

OHIO
Russ Scholl
Acting Chief
Div. of Mines & Reclamation
Dept. of Natural Resources
1855 Fountain Sq., Bldg. H-3
Columbus, OH 43224-1387
Phone: (614) 265-6675
Fax: (614) 262-6546

OKLAHOMA
John Hassell
Water Quality Director
Conservation Comm.
413 NW 12th St.
Oklahoma City, OK 73103
Phone: (405) 979-2200
Fax: (405) 979-2211

Mike Kastl
Director of Abandoned Mine Reclamation
Conservation Comm.
2800 N. Lincoln Blvd., Ste. 160
Oklahoma City, OK 73105
Phone: (405) 521-2384
Fax: (405) 521-6686

Dan Sebert
Director of District Operations
Conservation Comm.
2800 N. Lincoln Blvd., Ste. 160
Oklahoma City, OK 73105
Phone: (405) 521-2384
Fax: (405) 521-6686

Mike Thralls
Executive Director of Abandoned Mine Reclamation
Conservation Comm.
2800 N. Lincoln Blvd., Ste. 160
Oklahoma City, OK 73105
Phone: (405) 521-2384
Fax: (405) 521-6686

OREGON
John Widows
Supervisor
US-DOL Mine Safety & Health Administration
1813 14th Ave., SE
Albany, OR 97321
Phone: (541) 924-8495
Fax: (541) 924-8499

PENNSYLVANIA
Richard E. Stickler
Director
Bur. of Deep Mine Reclamation
Dept. of Environmental Protection
100 New Salem Rd.
Uniontown, PA 15401
Phone: (724) 439-7469

PUERTO RICO

RHODE ISLAND
Lee Arnold
Director
Dept. of Labor & Training
101 Friendship St.
Providence, RI 02903
Phone: (401) 222-3732
Fax: (401) 222-1473

SOUTH CAROLINA
Rita M. McKinney
Director
Dept. of Labor, Licensing & Regulations
110 Centerview Dr.
P.O. Box 11329
Columbia, SC 29210
Phone: (803) 896-4390
Fax: (803) 896-4393

SOUTH DAKOTA

TENNESSEE
Charles Green
Director
Mine Safety & Training
Dept. of Labor
P.O. Box 124
Caryville, TN 37714
Phone: (423) 566-9709
Fax: (423) 566-9711

TEXAS
Melvin Hodgkiss
Director, Surface Mining & Reclamation
Surface Mining Div.
Railroad Comm.
P.O. Box 12967
Austin, TX 78711
Phone: (512) 463-6901

U.S. VIRGIN ISLANDS

UTAH
D. Wayne Hedberg
Permit Supervisor
Div. of Oil, Gas & Mining
Dept. of Natural Resources
1594 W. N. Temple, #1210
P.O. Box 145801
Salt Lake City, UT 84114-5801
Phone: (801) 538-5286
Fax: (801) 359-3940
E-mail: whedberg.nrogm @state.ut.us

VERMONT
John Kassell
Secretary
Agency of Natural Resources
103 S. Main St.
Waterbury, VT 05671-0301
Phone: (802) 241-3600
Fax: (802) 241-3281

VIRGINIA
O. Gene Dishner
Director
Dept. of Mines, Minerals & Energy
202 N. 9th St., 8th Fl.
Richmond, VA 23219
Phone: (804) 692-3200
Fax: (804) 692-3237

WASHINGTON
Ray Lasmanis
State Geologist
Div. of Geology & Earth Resources
Dept. of Natural Resources
P.O. Box 47007
Olympia, WA 98504-7007
Phone: (360) 902-1450
Fax: (360) 902-1785

WEST VIRGINIA
Ronald L. Harris
Director
Miners' Health, Safety & Training
Dept. of Energy
1615 Washington St., E.
Charleston, WV 25311
Phone: (304) 558-1425
Fax: (304) 558-1282

WISCONSIN
Joe Hertel
Director
Bur. of Technical Services
Dept. of Workforce Dev.
201 E. Washington
P.O. Box 7969
Madison, WI 53707
Phone: (608) 266-5649
Fax: (608) 267-0592

WYOMING
Donald G. Stauffenberg
State Inspector of Mines
Board of Mines
Dept. of Employment
P.O. Box 1094
Rock Springs, WY 82902
Phone: (307) 856-3470

Motor Vehicle Administration

Issues and maintains all records related to motor vehicle registrations, operators' licenses and certificates of titles in the state.

ALABAMA
Terry Lane
Chief
Motor Vehicles Div.
Dept. of Revenue
64 N. Union St.
P.O. Box 327640
Montgomery, AL 36130-4400
Phone: (334) 242-9000
Fax: (334) 242-0312

Michael B. Sullivan
Chief
Driver License Div.
Dept. of Public Safety
500 Dexter Ave.
Montgomery, AL 36102
Phone: (334) 242-4703
Fax: (334) 353-1400

ALASKA
Kerry Hennings
Acting Director
Div. of Motor Vehicles
Dept. of Administration
3300 Fairbanks St.
Anchorage, AK 99503
Phone: (907) 269-3771
Fax: (907) 269-3774

AMERICAN SAMOA
Te'o Fuavai
Commissioner
Dept. of Public Safety
AS Govt.
Pago Pago, AS 96799
Phone: (684) 633-1111
Fax: (684) 633-5111

ARIZONA
Russell K. Pearce
Assistant Director
Motor Vehicles Div.
Dept. of Transportation
1801 W. Jefferson
Phoenix, AZ 85007
Phone: (602) 255-8152

ARKANSAS
Fred Porter
Administrator
Ofc. of Motor Vehicles
Dept. of Finance & Administration
P.O. Box 1272
Little Rock, AR 72203
Phone: (501) 682-4630

CALIFORNIA
Dorothy L. Hunter
Division Chief
Headquarters Operation
Dept. of Motor Vehicles
P.O. Box 932328
Sacramento, CA 94232-3280
Phone: (916) 657-7061

COLORADO
Dee Hartman
Director
Motor Vehicle Div.
Dept. of Revenue
1881 Pierce St.
Lakewood, CO 80214
Phone: (303) 205-5652

CONNECTICUT
Jose Salinas
Commissioner
Dept. of Motor Vehicles
60 State St.
Wethersfield, CT 06109
Phone: (860) 263-5015

DELAWARE
Michael Shahan
Director
Div. of Motor Vehicles
Dept. of Public Safety
P.O. Box 698
Dover, DE 19903
Phone: (302) 739-4421
Fax: (302) 739-3152

DISTRICT OF COLUMBIA
Henry Lightfoot
Interim Director
Transportation Systems Administration
Dept. of Public Works
65 K St., NE
Washington, DC 20002
Phone: (202) 727-1737

FLORIDA
Charles Brantley
Director
Motor Vehicles Div.
Hwy. Safety & Motor Vehicles
Neil Kirkman Bldg.
2900 Apalachee Pkwy.
Tallahassee, FL 32399-0500
Phone: (850) 488-4597
Fax: (850) 488-0149

GEORGIA
Milton Dufford
Deputy Commissioner
Motor Vehicle Div.
270 Washington St., SW, Rm. 104
Atlanta, GA 30303
Phone: (404) 656-4156

GUAM
Joseph T. Duenas
Director
Dept. of Revenue & Taxation
13-1 Mariner Dr., Tiyan
P.O. Box 23607
GMF, GU 96921
Phone: (671) 475-1817
Fax: (671) 472-2643

HAWAII

IDAHO
Morris Detmar
Chief
Motor Vehicle Bur.
Dept. of Transportation
P.O. Box 7129
Boise, ID 83707-1129
Phone: (208) 334-8606

ILLINOIS
Sherri A. Montgomery
Director
Index Dept.
Ofc. of Secretary of State
111 E. Monroe
Springfield, IL 62756
Phone: (217) 782-0643
Fax: (217) 524-0930

INDIANA
Gary A. Gibson
Commissioner
Bur. of Motor Vehicles
IGC-North, Rm. 440, 100 N. Senate Ave.
Indianapolis, IN 46204
Phone: (317) 233-2349
Fax: (317) 233-3135

IOWA
Shirley Andre
Director
Motor Vehicle Div.
Dept. of Transportation
P.O. Box 10382
Des Moines, IA 50306
Phone: (515) 237-3202

KANSAS
Sheila Walker
Director
Div. of Motor Vehicles
Dept. of Revenue
Docking State Ofc. Bldg., Rm. 162-S
915 Harrison
Topeka, KS 66612
Phone: (785) 296-3601
Fax: (785) 296-3852

KENTUCKY
Ed Logsdon
Commissioner
Transportation Cabinet
Dept. of Vehicle Regulation
State Ofc. Bldg., Rm. 308
501 High St.
Frankfort, KY 40601
Phone: (502) 564-7000
Fax: (502) 564-4603

LOUISIANA
Kay Covington
Assistant Secretary
Ofc. of Motor Vehicles
Public Safety & Corrections Dept.
P.O. Box 64886
Baton Rouge, LA 70896
Phone: (225) 925-6335
Fax: (225) 925-1838

MAINE
Gregory Hanscom
Deputy Secretary of State
Div. of Motor Vehicles
Dept. of State
29 State House Station
Augusta, ME 04333
Phone: (207) 287-2761

MARYLAND
Anne Ferro
Administrator
Motor Vehicle Administration
Dept. of Transportation
6601 Ritchie Hwy., NE, Rm. 120
Glen Burnie, MD 21062
Phone: (410) 768-7274

MASSACHUSETTS
Richard Lyons
Registrar
Registry of Motor Vehicles
1135 Tremont St.
Boston, MA 02120
Phone: (617) 351-2700
Fax: (617) 351-9971

MICHIGAN
Heidi Weber Reed
Director
Bur. of Driver & Vehicle Records
Dept. of State
7064 Crowner Dr.
Lansing, MI 48918
Phone: (517) 322-1528

MINNESOTA
Katherine Burke Moore
Director
Driver & Vehicle Services Div.
Dept. of Public Safety
445 Minnesota St., Ste. 195
St. Paul, MN 55101-5195
Phone: (651) 296-4544
Fax: (651) 296-3141
E-mail: kathy.burke.moore@state.mn.us

MISSISSIPPI
Eagle Day
Executive Director
Motor Vehicle Comm.
1755 Lelia Dr., Ste. 200
P.O. Box 16873
Jackson, MS 39236
Phone: (601) 987-3995
Fax: (601) 987-3997

MISSOURI
Raymond Hune
Director
Div. of Motor Vehicle & Driver Licenses
Dept. of Revenue
P.O. Box 629
Jefferson City, MO 65105
Phone: (573) 751-4429
Fax: (573) 526-4774
E-mail: Raymond_Hune@mail.dor.state.mo.us

MONTANA
Dean G. Roberts
Administrator
Motor Vehicle Div.
Dept. of Justice
303 N. Roberts
Helena, MT 59620
Phone: (406) 444-1773
Fax: (406) 444-1631

NEBRASKA
Ed Wimes
Director
Dept. of Motor Vehicles
P.O. Box 94789
Lincoln, NE 68509
Phone: (402) 471-2281
Fax: (402) 471-9594

NEVADA
John Drew
Acting Director
Dept. of Motor Vehicles & Public Safety
555 Wright Way
Carson City, NV 89711
Phone: (775) 684-4368
Fax: (775) 684-4692

NEW HAMPSHIRE
Virginia Beecher
Director
Div. of Motor Vehicles
Dept. of Safety
10 Hazen Dr.
Concord, NH 03305-0002
Phone: (603) 271-2484

NEW JERSEY
C. Richard Kamin
Director
Div. of Motor Vehicle Services
Dept. of Law & Public Safety
P.O. Box 160
Trenton, NJ 08666-0160
Phone: (609) 292-7500
Fax: (609) 292-4570

NEW MEXICO
Gorden E. Eden, Jr.
Director
Motor Vehicle Div.
Dept. of Taxation & Revenue
P.O. Box 1028
Santa Fe, NM 87504-1028
Phone: (505) 827-2294
Fax: (505) 827-2397

NEW YORK
Richard E Jackson, Jr.
Commissioner
Dept. of Motor Vehicles
Swan St. Bldg., 5th Fl.
Empire State Plz.
Albany, NY 12228
Phone: (518) 473-9324
Fax: (518) 474-9578

NORTH CAROLINA
Janice Faulkner
Commissioner
Div. of Motor Vehicles
Dept. of Transportation
1100 New Bern Ave.
Raleigh, NC 27697-0001
Phone: (919) 733-2403
Fax: (919) 733-0126

NORTH DAKOTA
Keith Magnusson
Director
Driver/Vehicle Services
Dept. of Transportation
608 E. Blvd. Ave.
Bismarck, ND 58505-0700
Phone: (701) 328-2581
Fax: (701) 328-1420
E-mail: kmagnuss@state.nd.us

NORTHERN MARIANA ISLANDS
Antonio G. Adriano
Chief
Motor Vehicle Div.
Public Safety Dept.
Saipan, MP 96950
Phone: (670) 234-6921
Fax: (670) 234-8531

OHIO
Frank Caltrider
Registrar
Bur. of Motor Vehicles
Dept. of Public Safety
1970 W. Broad St.
Columbus, OH 43223-1102
Phone: (614) 752-7500
Fax: (614) 752-7973

OKLAHOMA
Charles W. Eckenrode
Executive Director
Motor Vehicle Div.
Tax Comm.
4334 NW Expy., Ste. 183
Oklahoma City, OK 73116
Phone: (405) 521-2375
Fax: (405) 521-6096

OREGON
Jan Curry
Administrator
Motor Vehicles Div.
Dept. of Transportation
1905 Lana Ave., NE
Salem, OR 97314
Phone: (503) 945-5100
Fax: (503) 945-5254

PENNSYLVANIA
Larry White
Director
Bur. of Motor Vehicles
Dept. of Transportation
1101 S. Front St., 4th Fl.
Harrisburg, PA 17104
Phone: (717) 787-2304
Fax: (717) 705-2400

PUERTO RICO
Carlos Pesquera
Secretary
Hwys. Authority & Transportation
P.O. Box 42007
Santurce, PR 00940-2007
Phone: (787) 723-1390
Fax: (787) 728-8963

RHODE ISLAND
Thomas Harrington
Registrar
Div. of Motor Vehicles
286 Main St.
Pawtucket, RI 02860
Phone: (401) 222-2970

SOUTH CAROLINA
Glenn Beckham
Director
Div. of Motor Vehicles
Dept. of Public Safety
5410 Broad River Rd.
Columbia, SC 29210
Phone: (803) 737-1654

SOUTH DAKOTA
Deb Hillmer
Division Director
Div. of Motor Vehicles
Dept. of Revenue
Commerce Bldg.
118 W. Capitol Ave.
Pierre, SD 57501
Phone: (605) 773-5747
Fax: (605) 773-5129

TENNESSEE
Martha Irwin
Director
Title & Registration Div.
Dept. of Safety
1283 Airways Plz.
Nashville, TN 37243
Phone: (615) 401-6849
Fax: (615) 401-6782

TEXAS
Brett Bray
Director
Motor Vehicle Div.
Dept. of Transportation
200 E. Riverside Dr.,
Bldg. 150
Austin, TX 78704
Phone: (512) 416-4910
Fax: (512) 416-4890

U.S. VIRGIN ISLANDS
Franz A. Christian, Sr.
Acting Commissioner
Police Dept.
8172 Sub Base
St. Thomas, VI 00802
Phone: (340) 774-6400
Fax: (340) 776-3317

UTAH
Dennis Ritz
Acting Director
Processing Div.
Tax Comm.
210 N. 1950 W.
Salt Lake City, UT 84134
Phone: (801) 297-3500
Fax: (801) 297-3502
E-mail: dritz@tax.state.ut.us

VERMONT
Patricia McDonald
Commissioner
Agency of Transportation
Dept. of Motor Vehicles
133 State St.
Montpelier, VT 05602
Phone: (802) 828-2011
Fax: (802) 828-2170

VIRGINIA
Richard D. Holcomb
Commissioner
Dept. of Motor Vehicles
2300 W. Broad St.
Richmond, VA 23220
Phone: (804) 367-6606
Fax: (804) 367-6631

WASHINGTON
Nancy Kelly
Acting Assistant Director
Vehicle Services
Dept. of Licensing
P.O. Box 48020
Olympia, WA 98507-8020
Phone: (360) 902-3818
Fax: (360) 586-6703

WEST VIRGINIA
Joe E. Miller
Commissioner
Div. of Motor Vehicles
Dept. of Transportation
Bldg. 3, Rm. 337
1900 Kanawha Blvd., E.
Charleston, WV 25305
Phone: (304) 558-2723
Fax: (304) 558-1987

WISCONSIN
Roger Cross
Administrator
Div. of Motor Vehicles
Dept. of Transportation
4802 Sheboygan Ave.,
Rm. 225
P.O. Box 7949
Madison, WI 53707
Phone: (608) 266-2233
Fax: (606) 267-6974

WYOMING
Ray Martin
Director
Field Services
Dept. of Revenue &
Taxation
Herschler Bldg.
122 W. 25th St.
Cheyenne, WY 82002
Phone: (307) 777-5216

Native American Affairs

Acts as a liaison between state and tribal officials and advances the concerns of American Indians.

ALABAMA
Darla Graves
Executive Director
Indian Affairs Comm.
One Ct. Sq., Ste. 106
Montgomery, AL 36104
Phone: (334) 242-2831
Fax: (334) 240-3408

ALASKA
Vacant
Special Assistant
Ofc. of the Governor
P.O. Box 110001
Juneau, AK 99811
Phone: (907) 465-3500
Fax: (907) 465-3532

AMERICAN SAMOA

ARIZONA
Ron S. Lee
Executive Director
Comm. of Indian Affairs
1400 W. Washington, Ste. 300
Phoenix, AZ 85007
Phone: (602) 542-3123
Fax: (602) 542-3223

ARKANSAS

CALIFORNIA
Larry Myers
Executive Secretary
Native American Heritage Comm.
915 Capitol Mall, Rm. 288
Sacramento, CA 95814
Phone: (916) 322-7791

COLORADO
Karen D. Rogers
Commissioner
Indian Affairs Comm.
Ofc. of the Governor
130 State Capitol
Denver, CO 80203
Phone: (303) 866-3027
Fax: (303) 866-5469

CONNECTICUT
Edward Serabia
Indian Affairs Coordinator
Indian Affairs Council
165 Capitol Ave., Rm. 245
Hartford, CT 06106
Phone: (860) 566-5191

DELAWARE

DISTRICT OF COLUMBIA

FLORIDA
Joe Quetone
Executive Director
Governor's Council on Indian Affairs
Ofc. of the Governor
1341 Cross Creek Way, Ste. A
Tallahassee, FL 32301-3680
Phone: (850) 488-0730
Fax: (850) 488-5875

GEORGIA
David Crass
Archeological Unit Director
Historic Preservation
Dept. of Natural Resources
500 The Healey Bldg.
57 Forsythe St., NW
Atlanta, GA 30303
Phone: (404) 656-9344
Fax: (404) 657-1040

Chip Morgan
Archaeologist
Historic Preservation
Dept. of Natural Resources
500 The Healey Bldg.
57 Forsythe St., NW
Atlanta, GA 30303
Phone: (404) 656-2840
Fax: (404) 657-1040

GUAM

HAWAII

IDAHO

ILLINOIS
Terry Scrogum
Senior Advisor for Cultural Affairs
Ofc. of the Governor
2 1/2 State House
301 S. 2nd St.
Springfield, IL 62706
Phone: (217) 524-1395
Fax: (217) 524-1678

INDIANA
Michael Wesaw
Chair
Native American Council
Historic Preservation & Archives
Dept. of Natural Resources
IGC-South, Rm. W274
Indianapolis, IN 46204
Phone: (317) 232-1646
Fax: (317) 232-0693

IOWA

KANSAS
Natalie Haag
Counsel to the Governor
Ofc. of the Governor
State Capitol, 2nd Fl.
300 SW 10th St.
Topeka, KS 66612
Phone: (785) 296-3232
Fax: (785) 296-2158

KENTUCKY
Joan Taylor
Administrative Assistant
Ofc. of the Governor
Capitol Bldg., Rm. 157
700 Capitol Ave.
Frankfort, KY 40601
Phone: (502) 564-2611
Fax: (502) 564-2517

LOUISIANA
Joey Strickland
Executive Director
Indian Affairs
Ofc. of the Governor
P.O. Box 94095
Baton Rouge, LA 70804-9095
Phone: (225) 922-0500
Fax: (225) 922-0511

MAINE
Diana Scully
Executive Director
Indian Tribal-State Comm.
P.O. Box 87
Hallowell, ME 04347
Phone: (207) 622-4815

MARYLAND

MASSACHUSETTS
John Peters, Jr.
Executive Director
Indian Affairs Comm.
1 Congress St., 10th Fl.
Boston, MA 02114
Phone: (617) 727-6394
Fax: (617) 727-5060

MICHIGAN
Donna Budnick
Director
Indian Affairs Comm.
Civil Rights Comm.
611 W. Ottawa
Lansing, MI 48909
Phone: (517) 373-0654

MINNESOTA
Joseph Day
Executive Director
American Indian Affairs
1819 Bemidji Ave.
Bemidji, MN 56601
Phone: (218) 755-3825
Fax: (218) 755-3739
E-mail: miac@mail.paulbunyan.net

MISSISSIPPI

MISSOURI

MONTANA
Wyman J. McDonald
Coordinator
Ofc. of Indian Affairs
P.O. Box 200503
Helena, MT 59620
Phone: (406) 444-3702
Fax: (406) 444-1350

NEBRASKA
Judi Morgan
Executive Director
Comm. on Indian Affairs
P.O. Box 94981
Lincoln, NE 68509
Phone: (402) 471-3475
Fax: (402) 471-3392

NEVADA
Gerald Allen
Executive Director
Indian Comm.
4600 Kietzke Ln., A101
Reno, NV 89502
Phone: (775) 688-1347
Fax: (775) 688-1708

NEW HAMPSHIRE

NEW JERSEY

NEW MEXICO
Regis Pecos
Executive Director
Ofc. of Indian Affairs
228 E. Palace Ave.
Santa Fe, NM 87501
Phone: (505) 827-6440
Fax: (505) 827-6445

NEW YORK
Judith Hard
Deputy Counsel
Ofc. of Counsel
Executive Chamber
State Capitol
Albany, NY 12224
Phone: (518) 474-8390
Fax: (518) 474-1513

NORTH CAROLINA
Gregory A. Richardson
Director
Comm. of Indian Affairs
Dept. of Administration
217 W. Jones St.
Raleigh, NC 27603
Phone: (919) 733-5998
Fax: (919) 733-1207

NORTH DAKOTA
Cynthia Mala
Executive Director
Indian Affairs Comm.
600 E. Blvd. Ave., 1st Fl. - Judicial Wing
Bismarck, ND 58505-0300
Phone: (701) 328-2428
Fax: (701) 328-3000
E-mail: cmala@state.nd.us

NORTHERN MARIANA ISLANDS

OHIO

OKLAHOMA
Barbara Warner
Executive Director
Indian Affairs Comm.
4545 N. Lincoln Blvd., Ste. 282
Oklahoma, OK 73105
Phone: (405) 521-3828
Fax: (405) 522-4427
E-mail: bwarner@oklaosf.state.ok.us

OREGON
Karen Quigley
Executive Director
Legislative Comm. on Indian Services
454 State Capitol
900 Court St., NE
Salem, OR 97310
Phone: (503) 986-1067
Fax: (503) 986-1071

PENNSYLVANIA

PUERTO RICO

RHODE ISLAND

SOUTH CAROLINA
William C. Ham
Commissioner
Comm. on Human Affairs
P.O. Box 4490
Columbia, SC 29240
Phone: (803) 737-7800

SOUTH DAKOTA
Webster Two Hawk
Commissioner
Ofc. of Indian Affairs
711 E. Wells Ave.
Pierre, SD 57501
Phone: (605) 773-3415
Fax: (605) 773-6592

TENNESSEE
Toye Heape
Executive Director
Comm. on Indian Affairs
Dept. of Environment & Conservation
401 Church St.
L & C Tower, 7th Fl.
Nashville, TN 37243
Phone: (615) 532-0745
Fax: (615) 532-0732

TEXAS

U.S. VIRGIN ISLANDS

UTAH
Forrest Cuch
Director
Div. of Indian Affairs
Dept. of Community & Economic Dev.
324 S. State St., Ste. 103
Salt Lake City, UT 84111
Phone: (801) 538-8808
Fax: (801) 538-8803
E-mail: fscuch@dced.state.ut.us

VERMONT
Janet Ancel
Legal Counsel
Ofc. of the Governor
109 State St.
Montpelier, VT 05609
Phone: (802) 828-3333
Fax: (802) 828-3339

VIRGINIA
Thomasina Jordan
Chair
Council on Indians
3008 Russell Rd.
Alexandria, VA 22305
Phone: (703) 683-5555
Fax: (703) 519-9191

WASHINGTON
Jennifer Scott
Assistant Director
Gov.'s Ofc. of Indian Affairs
P.O. Box 40909
Olympia, WA 98504-0909
Phone: (360) 753-2411
Fax: (360) 586-3653

WEST VIRGINIA

WISCONSIN
Stewart Simonson
Chief Legal Counsel
Ofc. of the Governor
125 S. State Capitol
Madison, WI 53707-7863
Phone: (608) 266-6672
Fax: (608) 267-8983

WYOMING
Joe Hiller
Policy Analyst
Governor's Ofc.
State Capitol Bldg., Rm. 124
200 W. 24th St.
Cheyenne, WY 82002
Phone: (307) 777-7434

Natural Resources

Formulates and coordinates policies to protect, develop, utilize, restore and enhance the state's natural resources.

ALABAMA
Riley Boykin Smith
Commissioner
Dept. of Conservation & Natural Resources
64 N. Union St., Ste. 468
Montgomery, AL 36130
Phone: (334) 242-3486
Fax: (334) 242-3489

ALASKA
John T. Shively
Commissioner
Dept. of Natural Resources
400 Willoughby Ave.
Juneau, AK 99801-1724
Phone: (907) 465-2400
Fax: (907) 465-3886

AMERICAN SAMOA
Ufagafa Ray Tulafono
Director
Dept. of Marine & Wildlife Resources
Pago Pago, AS 96799
Phone: (684) 633-4456
Fax: (684) 633-5944

ARIZONA
Robert E. Yount
Director
Natural Resources Div.
Dept. of State Land
1616 W. Adams
Phoenix, AZ 85007
Phone: (602) 542-4625

ARKANSAS
Gregg Patterson
Chief
Environmental Preservation Div.
Dept. of Environmental Quality
8001 Natl. Dr.
Little Rock, AR 72201
Phone: (501) 682-0023

CALIFORNIA
Douglas Wheeler
Secretary
Resources Agency
1416 9th St., Rm. 1311
Sacramento, CA 95814
Phone: (916) 653-5656

COLORADO
Greg E. Walcher
Director
Dept. of Natural Resources
1313 Sherman St., Ste. 718
Denver, CO 80203-2239
Phone: (303) 866-3311
Fax: (303) 866-2115

CONNECTICUT
Edward C. Parker
Bureau Chief
Bur. of Natural Resources
Dept. of Environmental Protection
79 Elm St.
Hartford, CT 06106
Phone: (860) 424-3010

DELAWARE
Nicholas A. DiPasquale
Secretary
Dept. of Natural Resources & Environmental Control
P.O. Box 1401
Dover, DE 19903
Phone: (302) 739-4403
Fax: (302) 739-6242
E-mail: ndipasquale@state.de.us

DISTRICT OF COLUMBIA
Lloyd J. Jordan
Director
Environmental Regulation Administration
Dept. of Consumer & Regulatory Affairs
941 N. Capitol St., NE, 9th Fl.
Washington, DC 20002
Phone: (202) 442-8947

FLORIDA
Virginia Wetherell
Secretary
Dept. of Environmental Protection
3900 Commonwealth Blvd., MS-10
Tallahassee, FL 32399-3000
Phone: (850) 488-4805
Fax: (850) 921-4303

GEORGIA
Lonice Barrett
Commissioner
Dept. of Natural Resources
Floyd Towers, E.
205 Butler St., SW
Atlanta, GA 30334
Phone: (404) 656-3500

GUAM
Juan Taijito
Acting Director
Dept. of Agri.
192 Dairy Rd.
Mangilao, GU 96923
Phone: (671) 734-3942
Fax: (671) 734-6569

HAWAII
Timothy Johns
Chair
Dept. of Land & Natural Resources
1151 Punchbowl St.
Honolulu, HI 96813
Phone: (808) 587-0400
Fax: (808) 587-0390

IDAHO

ILLINOIS
Brent Manning
Director
Dept. of Natural Resources
Lincoln Towers Plz., Rm. 425
524 S. 2nd St.
Springfield, IL 62706
Phone: (217) 782-6302
Fax: (217) 785-9236

INDIANA
Larry Macklin
Executive Director
Dept. of Natural Resources
IGC-South, Rm. W256
402 W. Washington St.
Indianapolis, IN 46204
Phone: (317) 232-4020
Fax: (317) 233-6811

IOWA
Larry Wilson
Director
Dept. of Natural Resources
Wallace State Ofc. Bldg.
E. 9th & Grand Aves.
Des Moines, IA 50319
Phone: (515) 281-5385
Fax: (515) 281-8895

KANSAS
Steve Williams
Secretary
Dept. of Wildlife & Parks
Landon State Ofc. Bldg.
900 SW Jackson, Ste. 502
Topeka, KS 66612
Phone: (785) 296-2281
Fax: (785) 296-6953

KENTUCKY
William Martin
Commissioner
Div. Natural Areas
Dept. of Natural Resources
Case 105, Eastern Ky. Univ.
Richmond, KY 40475-3140
Phone: (502) 564-2184
Fax: (502) 564-6193

LOUISIANA
Jack Caldwell
Secretary
Dept. of Natural Resources
P.O. Box 94396
Baton Rouge, LA 70804-9396
Phone: (225) 342-4503
Fax: (225) 342-5861

MAINE
Ronald Lovaglio
Commissioner
Dept. of Conservation
22 State House Station
Augusta, ME 04333
Phone: (207) 287-4903

MARYLAND
John R. Griffin
Secretary
Ofc. of the Secretary
Dept. of Natural Resources
Tawes State Ofc. Bldg.
580 Taylor Ave.
Annapolis, MD 21401
Phone: (410) 260-8101
Fax: (410) 260-8111

MASSACHUSETTS
Lauren A. Liss
Commissioner
Executive Ofc. of Environmental Affairs
Dept. of Environmental Protection
1 Winter St.
Boston, MA 02108
Phone: (617) 292-5856
Fax: (617) 574-6880

MICHIGAN
K. Cool
Director
Dept. of Natural Resources
P.O. Box 30028
Lansing, MI 48909
Phone: (517) 373-2329

MINNESOTA
Allen Garber
Commissioner
Dept. of Natural Resources
500 Lafayette Rd.
St. Paul, MN 55155
Phone: (651) 296-2549
Fax: (651) 296-4799

MISSISSIPPI
J.I. Palmer, Jr.
Executive Director
Dept. of Environmental Quality
P.O. Box 20305
Jackson, MS 39289
Phone: (601) 961-5000
Fax: (601) 354-6965

MISSOURI
Steve Mahfood
Director
Dept. of Natural Resources
Jefferson Bldg., 12th Fl.
P.O. Box 176
Jefferson City, MO 65102
Phone: (573) 751-4422
Fax: (573) 751-7627
E-mail: nrmahfs@mail.dnr.state.mo.us

MONTANA
Bud Clinch
Director
Dept. of Natural Resources & Conservation
1625 11th Ave.
P.O. Box 201601
Helena, MT 59620
Phone: (406) 444-2074
Fax: (406) 444-2684

NEBRASKA
Dayle E. Williamson
Director
Natural Resources Comm.
301 Centennial Mall, S.
P.O. Box 94876
Lincoln, NE 68509-4876
Phone: (402) 471-2081
Fax: (402) 471-3132

NEVADA
Peter G. Morros
Director
Dept. of Conservation & Natural Resources
123 W. Nye Ln., Rm. 230
Carson City, NV 89706
Phone: (775) 687-4360
Fax: (775) 687-6122

NEW HAMPSHIRE
George Bald
Commissioner
Dept. of Resources & Economic Dev.
P.O. Box 1856
Concord, NH 03302
Phone: (603) 271-2411
Fax: (603) 271-2629

NEW JERSEY
Robert C. Shinn, Jr.
Commissioner
Dept. of Environmental Protection
401 E. State St.
P.O. Box 402
Trenton, NJ 08625-0402
Phone: (609) 292-2885
Fax: (609) 292-7695

NEW MEXICO
Jennifer Salisbury
Cabinet Secretary
Energy & Conservation Mgmt. Div.
Dept. of Energy, Minerals & Natural Resources
2040 S. Pacheco St.
Santa Fe, NM 87505
Phone: (505) 827-5950
Fax: (505) 827-1150
E-mail: jsalisbury@emnrds.state.nm.us

NEW YORK
John Cahill
Commissioner
Dept. of Environmental Conservation
50 Wolf Rd.
Albany, NY 12233-1010
Phone: (518) 457-1162
Fax: (518) 457-7744

NORTH CAROLINA
Wayne McDevitt
Secretary
Dept. of Environment & Natural Resources
512 N. Salisbury St.
Raleigh, NC 27604-1148
Phone: (919) 715-4101
Fax: (919) 733-4299

NORTH DAKOTA
Michael McKenna
Chief
Natural Resources Div.
Game & Fish Dept.
100 N. Bismarck Expy.
Bismarck, ND 58501-5095
Phone: (701) 328-6332
Fax: (701) 328-6352
E-mail: mmckenna@state.nd.us

NORTHERN MARIANA ISLANDS
Eugene A. Santos
Secretary
Dept. of Lands & Natural Resources
P.O. Box 10007
Saipan, MP 96950
Phone: (670) 322-9830
Fax: (670) 322-2633

OHIO
Sam Speck
Director
Dept. of Natural Resources
Fountain Sq.
1930 Belcher Dr., Bldg. D-3
Columbus, OH 43224-1387
Phone: (614) 265-6875
Fax: (614) 261-9601

OKLAHOMA
Jane Jayroe
Executive Director
Dept. of Tourism & Recreation
15 N. Robinson, Ste. 100
Oklahoma City, OK 73102
Phone: (405) 521-2413
Fax: (405) 236-0569
E-mail: jcraven@otrd.state.ok.us

OREGON
Paula Burgess
Natural Resources Advisor
Ofc. of Natural Resources
160 State Capitol
900 Court St., NE
Salem, OR 97310
Phone: (503) 378-3548
Fax: (503) 378-6827

PENNSYLVANIA
James M. Seif
Cabinet Secretary
Dept. of Environmental Protection
Rachel Carson State Ofc. Bldg., 16th Fl.
400 Market St.
Harrisburg, PA 17120
Phone: (717) 787-2814
Fax: (717) 705-4980
E-mail: seif.james@dep.state.pa.us

PUERTO RICO
Daniel Pagan
Secretary
Dept. of Natural Resources
P.O. Box 5887
San Juan, PR 00906
Phone: (787) 723-3090
Fax: (787) 723-4255

RHODE ISLAND
Jan Reitsma
Director
Dept. of Environmental Mgmt.
235 Promenade St.
Providence, RI 02908
Phone: (401) 222-2771
Fax: (401) 222-6802

SOUTH CAROLINA
Paul Sandifer
Director
Dept. of Natural Resources
P.O. Box 167
Columbia, SC 29202
Phone: (803) 734-4007

SOUTH DAKOTA
Nettie Myers
Secretary
Dept. of Environment & Natural Resources
Joe Foss Bldg.
523 E. Capitol Ave.
Pierre, SD 57501
Phone: (605) 773-3151
Fax: (605) 773-6035

TENNESSEE
Milton Hamilton
Commissioner
Dept. of Environment & Conservation
L & C Tower, 21st Fl.
Nashville, TN 37243
Phone: (615) 532-0104
Fax: (615) 532-0120

TEXAS
Ralph Marquez
Commissioner
Natural Resource Conservation Comm.
12100 Park 35 Cir., Bldg. A
P.O. Box 13087, MC 100
Austin, TX 78711-3087
Phone: (512) 239-5500
Fax: (512) 239-5533

U.S. VIRGIN ISLANDS
Dean Plaskett
Commissioner
Dept. of Planning & Natural Resources
Foster's Plz., 396-1 Anna's Retreat
St. Thomas, VI 00802
Phone: (340) 774-3320
Fax: (340) 775-5706

UTAH
Kathleen Clarke
Executive Director
Div. of Administration
Dept. of Natural Resources
1594 W. N. Temple, Ste. 3710
P.O. Box 145610
Salt Lake City, UT 84114-5610
Phone: (801) 538-7200
Fax: (801) 538-7315
E-mail: kclarke.nradm@state.ut.us

VERMONT
John Kassell
Secretary
Agency of Natural Resources
103 S. Main St.
Waterbury, VT 05671-0301
Phone: (802) 241-3600
Fax: (802) 241-3281

VIRGINIA
John Paul Woodley, Jr.
Secretary of Natural Resources
Governor's Cabinet
202 N. 9th St., Ste. 733
Richmond, VA 23219
Phone: (804) 786-0044
Fax: (804) 371-8333

WASHINGTON
Jennifer Belcher
Commissioner of Public Lands
Dept. of Natural Resources
P.O. Box 47001
Olympia, WA 98504-7001
Phone: (360) 902-1000
Fax: (360) 902-1775

WEST VIRGINIA
John B. Rader
Director
Div. of Natural Resources
Commerce, Labor & Environmental Resources
Capitol Complex, Bldg. 3
Charleston, WV 25305
Phone: (304) 558-3754
Fax: (304) 558-2768

WISCONSIN
George Meyer
Secretary
Dept. of Natural Resources
101 S. Webster, 5th Fl.
P.O. Box 7921
Madison, WI 53703
Phone: (608) 266-2121
Fax: (608) 267-3579

WYOMING
Mike Besson
Director
Water Dev. Comm.
Herschler Bldg., 4th Fl., W. Wing
122 W. 25th St.
Cheyenne, WY 82002
Phone: (307) 777-7626

Occupational Safety

Enforces safety standards for the protection of employees in places of employment.

ALABAMA
Barney Weeks
Commissioner
Dept. of Labor
RSA Union, Ste. 620
100 N. Union St.
Montgomery, AL 36130
Phone: (334) 242-3460
Fax: (334) 240-3417

ALASKA
Al Dwyer
Director
Div. of Labor Standards & Safety
Dept. of Labor
P.O. Box 107021
Anchorage, AK 99510-7021
Phone: (907) 269-4914
Fax: (907) 465-4915

AMERICAN SAMOA

ARIZONA
Larry J. Etchechury
Director
Industrial Comm.
800 W. Washington
Phoenix, AZ 85007
Phone: (602) 542-4411
Fax: (602) 542-3070

ARKANSAS
James Salkeld
Director
Dept. of Labor
10421 W. Markham, Ste. 100
Little Rock, AR 72205
Phone: (501) 682-4500
Fax: (501) 682-4532

CALIFORNIA
John Howard
Chief
Div. of Occupational Safety & Health
455 Golden Gate Ave., Ste. 5202
San Francisco, CA 94102
Phone: (415) 972-8500

COLORADO
Jack Ehnes
Manager
Risk Mgmt. Div.
Dept. of Human Resources - GSS
1313 Sherman St., Rm. 114
Denver, CO 80203
Phone: (303) 866-3848
Fax: (303) 894-2409

CONNECTICUT
Steven Wheeler
Director
Occupational Safety & Health
Dept. of Labor
38 Wolcott Hill Rd.
Wethersfield, CT 06109
Phone: (860) 566-4550
Fax: (860) 566-6916

DELAWARE
Karen Peterson
Director
Div. of Industrial Affairs
Dept. of Labor
4425 N. Market St., 3rd Fl.
Wilmington, DE 19802
Phone: (302) 761-8176
Fax: (302) 761-6601

DISTRICT OF COLUMBIA
John Cates
Acting Associate Director
Occupational Safety & Health Ofc.
Dept. of Employment Services
950 Upshur St., NW
Washington, DC 20011
Phone: (202) 576-6339

FLORIDA
Altha Manning
Director
Adm. Services
Labor & Employment Security
2012 Capital Cir., SE
Ste. 310, Hartman Bldg.
Tallahassee, FL 32399-2161
Phone: (850) 488-1188
Fax: (850) 922-3883

GEORGIA
Earl Everett
Director
Safety Engineering
223 Courtland St., Rm. 301
Atlanta, GA 30303
Phone: (404) 656-2966

GUAM
James Underwood
Acting Director
Dept. of Labor
504 E. Sunset Blvd., Tiyan
P.O. Box 9970
Tamuning, GU 96931
Phone: (671) 475-0101
Fax: (671) 477-2988

HAWAII
Jennifer Shishido
Administrator
Occupational Safety & Health Div.
Dept. of Labor & Industrial Relations
830 Punchbowl St., Rm. 423
Honolulu, HI 96813
Phone: (808) 586-9116
Fax: (808) 586-9104

IDAHO

ILLINOIS
Al Juskeras
Manager
Dept. of Labor
1 W. Old State Capitol Plz.
Springfield, IL 62706
Phone: (217) 782-9386
Fax: (217) 782-0596

INDIANA
Timothy Joyce
Commissioner
Dept. of Labor
402 W. Washington, Rm. W195
Indianapolis, IN 46204
Phone: (317) 232-2378
Fax: (317) 233-3790

IOWA
Mary L. Bryant
Administrator
Occupational Safety & Health
Dept. of Employment Services
1000 E. Grand Ave.
Des Moines, IA 50319
Phone: (515) 281-3606

KANSAS

KENTUCKY
Joe Norsworthy
Secretary
Labor Cabinet
1047 U.S. 127 S.
Frankfort, KY 40601
Phone: (502) 564-3070
Fax: (502) 564-5387

LOUISIANA
Willis E. Callihan
Safety & Health Manager
Dept. of Labor
P.O. Box 94094
Baton Rouge, LA 70804-9094
Phone: (225) 342-7556
Fax: (225) 342-6756

Seth E. Keener, Jr.
State Risk Director
P.O. Box 94095
Baton Rouge, LA 70804-9095
Phone: (225) 342-8500
Fax: (225) 342-8418

MAINE
James McGowan
Director
Bur. of Labor Standards
Dept. of Labor
45 State House Station
Augusta, ME 04333
Phone: (207) 624-6400

MARYLAND
Keith Goddard
Assistant Commissioner
Occupational Safety & Health
Labor, Licensing & Regulation Dept.
1100 N. Eutah St., Rm. 613
Baltimore, MD 21201
Phone: (410) 767-2196
Fax: (410) 767-2003

MASSACHUSETTS
Robert J. Prezioso
Deputy Director
Div. of Occupational Safety
Dept. of Labor & Workforce Dev.
100 Cambridge St., Rm. 1107
Boston, MA 02202
Phone: (617) 727-3452
Fax: (617) 727-8022

MICHIGAN
Douglas R. Earle
Director
Bur. of Safety & Regulation
Consumer & Industry Services
7150 Harris Dr.
P.O. Box 30015
Lansing, MI 48909
Phone: (517) 322-1814

MINNESOTA
Darrell Anderson
Administrative Director, OSHA Management Team
Occupational Safety & Health Div.
Labor & Industry
443 Lafayette Rd.
St. Paul, MN 55155
Phone: (651) 296-2116
Fax: (651) 297-2527
E-mail: darrell.anderson@state.mn.us

MISSISSIPPI
Kelly Tucker
Director
MS State Univ.
Ctr. for Safety & Health
2906 N. State St., Ste. 201
Jackson, MS 39216
Phone: (601) 987-3981
Fax: (601) 987-3890

MISSOURI
Colleen Baker
Director
Div. of Labor Standards
Labor & Industrial Relations Dept.
3315 W. Truman Blvd., Ste. 205
P.O. Box 449
Jefferson City, MO 65102-0449
Phone: (573) 751-3403
Fax: (573) 751-3721
E-mail: cbaker@mail.state.mo.us

MONTANA
John Maloney
Bureau Chief
Safety Bur.
Dept. of Labor & Industry
1805 Prospect
P.O. Box 1728
Helena, MT 59624
Phone: (406) 444-1605
Fax: (406) 444-4140

NEBRASKA
Gary Hirsh
Director
Labor & Safety Standards Div.
Dept. of Labor
P.O. Box 95024
Lincoln, NE 68509
Phone: (402) 471-4712
Fax: (402) 471-5039

NEVADA
Roger Bremner
Administrator
Div. of Industrial Relations
400 W. King St., 4th Fl., Ste. 400
Carson City, NV 89703
Phone: (775) 687-3032
Fax: (775) 687-6305

NEW HAMPSHIRE
James Casey
Commissioner
Dept. of Labor
95 Pleasant St.
Concord, NH 03301
Phone: (603) 271-3176
Fax: (603) 271-7064

NEW JERSEY
Leonard Katz
Assistant Commissioner
Labor Standards & Safety Enforcement
John Fitch Plz.
P.O. Box 385
Trenton, NJ 08625
Phone: (609) 777-0249
Fax: (609) 695-1314

NEW MEXICO
Sam A. Rogers
Bureau Chief
Occupational Safety & Health Bur.
Environmental Dept.
P.O. Box 26110
Santa Fe, NM 87502
Phone: (505) 827-4230
Fax: (505) 827-4422

NEW YORK
James J. McGowan
Commissioner
Dept. of Labor
State Ofc. Bldg. Campus, Bldg. 12
Albany, NY 12240
Phone: (518) 457-2741
Fax: (518) 457-6908

NORTH CAROLINA
Harry E. Payne, Jr.
Commissioner
Dept. of Labor
4 W. Edenton St.
Raleigh, NC 27601-1092
Phone: (919) 733-7166
Fax: (919) 733-6197

NORTH DAKOTA
Wally Kalmbach
Director
Loss Prevention
Worker's Compensation Bur.
500 E. Front Ave.
Bismarck, ND 58504-5685
Phone: (701) 328-3886
Fax: (701) 328-3820
E-mail: msmail.wkalmbac@ranch.state.nd.us

NORTHERN MARIANA ISLANDS
Patrick A. Guerrero
Director
Dept. of Labor
P.O. Box 10007
Saipan, MP 96950
Phone: (670) 664-2000
Fax: (670) 664-2020

OHIO
Owen Wagner
Director
Occupational Safety & Health
145 S. Front St.
Columbus, OH 43215
Phone: (614) 644-2246
Fax: (614) 644-3133

OKLAHOMA
Tom Monroe
Director
Safety Standards Div.
Dept. of Labor
4001 N. Lincoln
Oklahoma City, OK 73105
Phone: (405) 528-1500
Fax: (405) 528-5751
E-mail: tmonroe@oklaosf.state.ok.us

OREGON
Pete DeLuca
Administrator
Occupational Safety & Health Administration
430 Labor & Industries Bldg.
350 Winter St., NE
Salem, OR 97310
Phone: (503) 378-3272
Fax: (503) 378-5729

PENNSYLVANIA
Charles J. Sludden, Jr.
Director
Occupational & Industrial Safety
Dept. of Labor & Industry
1529 Labor & Industry Bldg.
Harrisburg, PA 17120
Phone: (717) 787-3323
Fax: (717) 787-8363

PUERTO RICO
Aura Gonzalez
Secretary
Dept. of Labor & Human Resources
Prudencio Rivera Martinez
505 Munoz Rivera Ave.
Hato Rey, PR 00918
Phone: (787) 754-2120
Fax: (787) 753-9550

RHODE ISLAND
Robert Lynch
Administrator
Occupational Safety & Health
Dept. of Labor & Training
610 Manton Ave.
Providence, RI 02909
Phone: (410) 457-1826

SOUTH CAROLINA
Rita M. McKinney
Director
Dept. of Labor, Licensing & Regulations
110 Centerview Dr.
P.O. Box 11329
Columbia, SC 29210
Phone: (803) 896-4390
Fax: (803) 896-4393

SOUTH DAKOTA
James E. Marsh
Director
Div. of Labor & Mgmt.
Dept. of Labor
Kneip Bldg.
700 Governors Dr.
Pierre, SD 57501
Phone: (605) 773-3681
Fax: (605) 773-4211

TENNESSEE
John Winkler
Acting Director
Compliance Div.
Dept. of Labor
710 James Robertson Pkwy., 3rd Fl.
Nashville, TN 37243-0659
Phone: (615) 741-2793
Fax: (615) 741-3325

TEXAS
William R. Archer, III
Commissioner
Dept. of Health
1100 W. 49th St.
Austin, TX 78756
Phone: (512) 458-7375
Fax: (512) 458-7477

U.S. VIRGIN ISLANDS
Eleuteria Roberts
Acting Commissioner
Dept. of Labor
2203 Church St.
Christiansted
St. Croix, VI 00820
Phone: (340) 773-1994
Fax: (340) 773-0094

UTAH
Jay W. Bagley
Administrator
Occupational Safety & Health Div.
Labor Comm.
160 E. 300 S.
Salt Lake City, UT 84111
Phone: (801) 530-6898
Fax: (801) 530-7606
E-mail: jbagley.icmain@state.ut.us

VERMONT
Robert McLeod
Manager
Div. of Occupational Safety & Health Administration
Dept. of Labor & Industry
N. Bldg., Natl. Life
Montpelier, VT 05620
Phone: (802) 828-2765
Fax: (802) 828-2748

VIRGINIA
John Mills Barr
Commissioner
Dept. of Labor & Industry
Powers-Taylor Bldg.
13 S. 13th St.
Richmond, VA 23219
Phone: (804) 786-2377
Fax: (804) 371-6524

WASHINGTON
Michael Silverstein
Assistant Director
WISHA
Dept. of Labor & Industries
P.O. Box 44600
Olympia, WA 98504-4600
Phone: (360) 902-5495
Fax: (360) 902-5529

WEST VIRGINIA
Steve Allred
Commissioner
Div. of Labor
State Capitol, Bldg. 3
1900 Kanawha Blvd., E.
Charleston, WV 25305
Phone: (304) 558-7890
Fax: (304) 558-3797

WISCONSIN
Michael Corry
Administrator
Div. of Safety & Bldgs.
Dept. of Commerce
201 E. Washington, 4th Fl.
P.O. Box 2599
Madison, WI 53701-2599
Phone: (608) 266-3151
Fax: (608) 266-9946

WYOMING
Steve Foster
Administrator
Occupational Safety & Health Administration
Dept. of Employment
Herschler Bldg.
122 W. 25th St.
Cheyenne, WY 82002
Phone: (307) 777-7700

Oil and Gas Regulation

Regulates the drilling, operation, maintenance and abandonment of oil and gas wells in the state.

ALABAMA
Donald F. Oltz
State Geologist & Administrator
State Geological Survey
Oil & Gas Board
P.O. Box O
Tuscaloosa, AL 35486-9780
Phone: (205) 349-2852
Fax: (205) 349-2861

ALASKA
Ken Boyd
Director
Div. of Oil & Gas
Dept. of Natural Resources
3601 C St., Ste. 1380
Anchorage, AK 99503-5948
Phone: (907) 269-8800
Fax: (907) 562-3852

AMERICAN SAMOA
Michael Sakaio
U.S. Coast Guard
Executive Ofc. Bldg.
Pago Pago, AS 96799

ARIZONA
Larry D. Fellows
Director & State Geologist
Geological Survey
416 W. Congress St., #100
Tucson, AZ 85701-1315
Phone: (520) 770-3500
Fax: (520) 770-3505

ARKANSAS
William E. Wright
Director
Oil & Gas Comm.
P.O. Box 1472
El Dorado, AR 71731-1472
Phone: (501) 862-4965
Fax: (501) 862-8823

CALIFORNIA
William F. Guerard
Supervisor
Div. of Oil & Gas
Dept. of Conservation
801 K St., 20th Fl.
Sacramento, CA 95814
Phone: (916) 323-1777

COLORADO
Richard T. Greibling
Director
Oil & Gas Conservation Comm.
Dept. of Natural Resources
1120 Lincoln St., Ste. 800
Denver, CO 80203-2136
Phone: (303) 894-2100
Fax: (303) 894-2109

CONNECTICUT
Donald W. Downes
Chair
Dept. of Public Utility Control
1 Central Park Plz.
New Britain, CT 06051
Phone: (860) 827-2801

DELAWARE
Nicholas A. DiPasquale
Secretary
Dept. of Natural Resources & Environmental Control
P.O. Box 1401
Dover, DE 19903
Phone: (302) 739-4403
Fax: (302) 739-6242
E-mail: ndipasquale@state.de.us

DISTRICT OF COLUMBIA

FLORIDA
Mickey Watson
Director
Div. of Law Enforcement
Dept. of Environmental Protection
3900 Commonwealth Blvd., MS600
Tallahassee, FL 32399
Phone: (850) 488-5600
Fax: (850) 488-2642

GEORGIA
William McLemore
State Geologist
Environmental Protection Div.
Dept. of Natural Resources
19 Martin Luther King, Jr. Dr., Rm. 400
Atlanta, GA 30334
Phone: (404) 656-3214

GUAM
Daniel Lizama
Acting Director
Dept. of Public Works
542 N. Marine Dr.
Tamuning, GU 96911
Phone: (671) 646-3131
Fax: (671) 649-9178

HAWAII

IDAHO

ILLINOIS
Larry Bengal
Supervisor
Div. of Oil & Gas
Dept. of Natural Resources
300 W. Jefferson, Ste. 300
Springfield, IL 62791-0137
Phone: (217) 782-1689
Fax: (217) 524-4819

INDIANA
James Slutz
Director
Oil & Gas Div.
Dept. of Natural Resources
IGC-S., Rm. W293
Indianapolis, IN 46204
Phone: (317) 232-4055
Fax: (317) 232-1550

IOWA
Allan T. Thoms
Chair
State Utilities Board
Dept. of Commerce
Lucas State Ofc. Bldg.
321 E. 12th St.
Des Moines, IA 50319
Phone: (515) 281-5167

KANSAS
M.L. Korphage
Director
Oil & Gas Conservation Corps. Comm.
130 S. Market, Rm. 2078
Wichita, KS 67202-3802
Phone: (785) 271-3232
Fax: (785) 271-3268

KENTUCKY
John Franklin
Commissioner
Dept. of Mines & Minerals
P.O. Box 14080
Lexington, KY 40512
Phone: (606) 246-2026
Fax: (606) 246-2038

LOUISIANA
Philip Asprodites
Commissioner of Conservation
Dept. of Natural Resources
P.O. Box 94275
Baton Rouge, LA 70804
Phone: (225) 342-5540
Fax: (225) 342-2584

MAINE
Vacant
Director
Oil & Hazardous Materials Bur.
Dept. of Environmental Protection
17 State House Station
Augusta, ME 04333
Phone: (207) 287-2651

MARYLAND
Herb Meade
Acting Program Administrator
Oil Control Program
Dept. of the Environment
2500 Broening Hwy.
Baltimore, MD 21224
Phone: (410) 631-3386
Fax: (410) 631-3092

MASSACHUSETTS

MICHIGAN
Harold Fitch
Chief & State Geologist
Geological Survey
Dept. of Natural Resources
735 E. Hazel St.
Lansing, MI 48917
Phone: (517) 334-6907

MINNESOTA
William C. Brice
Director
Minerals Div.
Dept. of Natural Resources
500 Lafayette Rd.
St. Paul, MN 55155
Phone: (651) 296-9553
Fax: (651) 296-5939
E-mail: bill.brice
@dnr.state.mn.us

MISSISSIPPI
Walter Boone
Executive Director
State Oil & Gas Board
500 Grey Mont Ave., Ste. 5
Jackson, MS 39202
Phone: (601) 354-7142
Fax: (601) 354-6873

MISSOURI
Evan Kifer
Geologist
Underground Injection
Control & Wellhead
Protection Unit
Dept. of Natural Resources
111 Fairgrounds Rd.
P.O. Box 250
Rolla, MO 65401
Phone: (573) 368-2168
Fax: (573) 368-2111
E-mail: nrkifee
@mail.dnr.state.mo.us

MONTANA
Terri Perrigo
Administrative Officer
Oil & Gas Conservation
Div.
Dept. of Natural Resources
& Conservation
1625 11th Ave.
Helena, MT 59620
Phone: (406) 444-6675
Fax: (406) 444-6721

NEBRASKA
William H. Sydow
Director
Oil & Gas Conservation
Comm.
P.O. Box 399
Sidney, NE 69162
Phone: (308) 254-6919
Fax: (308) 254-6922

NEVADA
Alan Coyner
Administrator
Div. of Minerals
400 W. King St., Ste. 106
Carson City, NV 89703-4212
Phone: (775) 687-5050
Fax: (775) 687-3957
E-mail: rafields
@govmail.state.nv.us

NEW HAMPSHIRE
Eugene L. Boudette
State Geologist
Water Div.
Environmental Services
P.O. Box 95
Concord, NH 03302-0095
Phone: (603) 271-3406
Fax: (603) 271-2867

NEW JERSEY
James P. Jiuliano
Director
Service Evaluation
Board of Public Utilities
2 Gateway Ctr.
Newark, NJ 07102
Phone: (201) 648-6948
Fax: (201) 648-2242

NEW MEXICO
Lori Wrotenbery
Director
Oil Conservation Div.
Dept. of Energy, Minerals &
Natural Resources
2040 S. Pacheco St.
Santa Fe, NM 87505
Phone: (505) 827-7132
Fax: (505) 827-8177

NEW YORK
John Cahill
Commissioner
Dept. of Environmental
Conservation
50 Wolf Rd.
Albany, NY 12233-1010
Phone: (518) 457-1162
Fax: (518) 457-7744

NORTH CAROLINA
Charles H. Gardner
Director
Div. of Land Resources
Dept. of Environment &
Natural Resources
512 N. Salisbury St.
Raleigh, NC 27604-1148
Phone: (919) 733-3833
Fax: (919) 715-8801

NORTH DAKOTA
Wes Norton
Director
Oil & Gas Div.
Industrial Comm.
600 E. Blvd. Ave.
Bismarck, ND 58505-0840
Phone: (701) 328-8020
Fax: (701) 328-8022

NORTHERN MARIANA ISLANDS
Eugene A. Santos
Secretary
Dept. of Lands & Natural
Resources
P.O. Box 10007
Saipan, MP 96950
Phone: (670) 322-9830
Fax: (670) 322-2633

OHIO
Tom Tugend
Chief
Div. of OIl & Gas
Dept. of Natural Resources
Fountain Sq., Bldg. B-3
Columbus, OH 43224
Phone: (614) 265-6893
Fax: (614) 268-4316

OKLAHOMA
Mike Battles
Director
Oil & Gas Conservation
Div.
Corp. Comm.
Jim Thorpe Bldg.
2101 N. Lincoln Blvd.
Oklahoma City, OK 73105
Phone: (405) 521-2302
Fax: (405) 521-3099
E-mail: m.battles
@occmail.occ.state.ok.us

OREGON
Donald A. Hull
State Geologist
Dept. of Geology & Mineral
Industries
800 NE Oregon St., #27,
Ste. 965
Portland, OR 97232
Phone: (503) 731-4100
Fax: (503) 731-4066

PENNSYLVANIA
James Erb
Director
Bur. of Oil & Gas
Regulation
Dept. of Environmental
Resources
Rachel Carson State Ofc.
Bldg.
400 Market St., 5th Fl.
Harrisburg, PA 17120
Phone: (717) 783-9645
Fax: (717) 772-2291

PUERTO RICO

RHODE ISLAND
Thomas Ahearn
Administrator
Div. of Public Utilities &
Carriers
100 Orange St.
Providence, RI 02903
Phone: (401) 222-3500

SOUTH CAROLINA
Rod W. Cherry
Director
Div. of Hydrology
Water Resources Comm.
1201 Main St., Ste. 1100
Columbia, SC 29201
Phone: (803) 737-0800

SOUTH DAKOTA
Curt Johnson
Commissioner
School & Public Lands
Capitol Bldg., 1st Fl.
500 E. Capitol Ave.
Pierre, SD 57501
Phone: (605) 773-3303
Fax: (605) 773-5520

TENNESSEE
Mike Burton
Oil & Gas Board
Dept. of Environment
L & C Tower, 13th Fl.
401 Church St.
Nashville, TN 37243
Phone: (615) 532-0166
Fax: (615) 532-1517

TEXAS
David Schieck
Director
Oil & Gas Div.
Railroad Comm.
Capitol Station
P.O. Box 12967
Austin, TX 78711
Phone: (512) 463-6810
Fax: (512) 463-6780

U.S. VIRGIN ISLANDS

UTAH
Lowell P. Braxton
Director
Div. of Oil, Gas & Mining
Dept. of Natural Resources
1594 W. N. Temple, #1210
Salt Lake City, UT 84114-5801
Phone: (801) 538-5370
Fax: (801) 359-3940
E-mail: lbraxton.nrogm@state.ut.us

VERMONT
John Kassell
Secretary
Agency of Natural Resources
103 S. Main St.
Waterbury, VT 05671-0301
Phone: (802) 241-3600
Fax: (802) 241-3281

VIRGINIA
O. Gene Dishner
Director
Dept. of Mines, Minerals & Energy
202 N. 9th St., 8th Fl.
Richmond, VA 23219
Phone: (804) 692-3200
Fax: (804) 692-3237

WASHINGTON
Joy Keniston-Longrie
Manager
Resource Planning & Asset Mgmt.
Dept. of Natural Resources
P.O. Box 47014
Olympia, WA 98504-7014
Phone: (360) 902-1600
Fax: (360) 902-1789

WEST VIRGINIA
Theodore Streit
Director
Oil & Gas Div.
Div. of Environmental Protection
10 McJunkin Rd.
Nitro, WV 25143
Phone: (304) 759-0516
Fax: (304) 759-0526

WISCONSIN
John Alberts
Administrator
Div. of Environmental & Regulatory Services
Dept. of Commerce
P.O. Box 7839
Madison, WI 53707
Phone: (608) 267-3753
Fax: (608) 267-1381

WYOMING
Donald Likwartz
Director
Oil & Gas Compact Comm.
P.O. Box 2640
Casper, WY 82602
Phone: (307) 234-7147

Ombudsman

Investigates citizens' complaints about the administrative acts of any state agency.

ALABAMA
Josh Hayes
Executive Assistant
Constituent Affairs Ofc.
Governor's Ofc.
600 Dexter Ave.
Montgomery, AL 36130
Phone: (334) 242-7140
Fax: (334) 353-0004

ALASKA
Maria Moya
Acting Ombudsman
P.O. Box 113000
Juneau, AK 99811
Phone: (907) 465-4970
Fax: (907) 465-3330

AMERICAN SAMOA

ARIZONA
Patrick Shannahan
Ombudsman for the State
Ofc. of the Ombudsman-Citizen's Aide
3737 N. 7th St., Ste. 209
Phoenix, AZ 85014
Phone: (602) 277-7292

ARKANSAS
DeWayne Hayes
Director of Constituent Services
Ofc. of the Governor
State Capitol, Ste. 120
Little Rock, AR 72201
Phone: (501) 682-3633
Fax: (501) 682-3596

CALIFORNIA
Kurt R. Sjoberg
State Auditor
Bur. of State Audits
555 Capitol Mall, Ste. 300
Sacramento, CA 95814-4503
Phone: (916) 445-0255
Fax: (916) 327-0019

COLORADO
Leslie Plomondon
Director
Advocacy Ofc.
Ofc. of the Governor
127 State Capitol Bldg.
Denver, CO 80203
Phone: (303) 866-6336
Fax: (303) 866-6326

CONNECTICUT
Julie Cammarata
Director
Ofc. of Constituent Services
Ofc. of the Governor
210 Capitol Ave.
Hartford, CT 06106
Phone: (860) 566-4840
Fax: (860) 524-7396

DELAWARE

DISTRICT OF COLUMBIA

FLORIDA
Richard Doran
Deputy Attorney General
Legal Services
Dept. of Legal Affairs
The Capitol, PL01
Tallahassee, FL 32399-1050
Phone: (850) 414-3300
Fax: (850) 487-2564

GEORGIA
Becky A. Kurtz
State Long Term Care Ombudsman
Div. of Aging Services
Dept. of Human Resources
2 Peachtree St., NW, Ste. 36-233
Atlanta, GA 30303-3176
Phone: (404) 657-5327
Fax: (404) 657-5285

GUAM
Vacant
Suruhanu
Ofc. of the Suruhanu
Legislature
Ada Commercial & Professional Ctr.
Ste. 107-F
Hagatna, GU 96910
Phone: (671) 477-9803
Fax: (671) 472-7980

HAWAII
Robin K. Matsunaga
Ombudsman
Ofc. of the Ombudsman
465 S. King St., 4th Fl.
Honolulu, HI 96813
Phone: (808) 587-0770
Fax: (808) 587-0773

IDAHO
Tana Shillingstad
Chief of Staff
Ofc. of the Governor
State House
700 W. Jefferson
Boise, ID 83720
Phone: (208) 334-2100
Fax: (208) 334-2175
E-mail: tshillin@gov.state.id.us

ILLINOIS
Gail Crossland
Director
Governor's Ofc. of Citizen's Assistance
222 S. College
Springfield, IL 62706
Phone: (217) 782-0244
Fax: (217) 524-4049

INDIANA

IOWA
William C. Angrick, II
Citizens' Aide/Ombudsman
215 E. 7th St.
Des Moines, IA 50319
Phone: (515) 281-3592
Fax: (515) 242-6007

KANSAS
Jennifer Bergen
Constituent Services
Ofc. of the Governor
State Capitol, 2nd Fl.
300 SW 10th St.
Topeka, KS 66612
Phone: (785) 296-3232
Fax: (785) 296-7973

KENTUCKY
Charles Lambert
Ombudsman
Cabinet for Human Resources
275 E. Main St.
Frankfort, KY 40621
Phone: (502) 564-5497
Fax: (502) 564-9523

LOUISIANA
Linda Sadden
State Ombudsman
Ofc. of Elderly Affairs
Governor's Ofc.
P.O. Box 80374
Baton Rouge, LA 70898
Phone: (225) 342-7100
Fax: (225) 342-7144

MAINE

MARYLAND
Terry Curtis
Director
Ofc. of the Governor - Baltimore
Executive Dept.
6 St. Paul St., Ste. 2202
Baltimore, MD 21202
Phone: (410) 767-4800
Fax: (410) 767-8248

MASSACHUSETTS
Barbara Burke
Director
Governor's Ofc. of External Relations
State House, Rm. 111
24 Beacon St.
Boston, MA 02133
Phone: (617) 727-6250
Fax: (617) 727-9725

MICHIGAN

MINNESOTA

MISSISSIPPI

MISSOURI
Roger B. Wilson
Lieutenant Governor
Ofc. of the Governor
Capitol Bldg., Rm. 121
Jefferson City, MO 65101
Phone: (573) 751-4727
Fax: (573) 751-9422
E-mail: wilson@mail.state.mo.us

MONTANA
Myrna Omholt-Mason
Citizens' Advocate
Ofc. of the Governor
State Capitol
1301 E. 6th Ave.
Helena, MT 59620
Phone: (406) 444-3468
Fax: (406) 444-5529

NEBRASKA
Marshall Lux
State Ombudsman
State Capitol, 8th Fl.
P.O. Box 94712
Lincoln, NE 68509-4712
Phone: (402) 471-2035
Fax: (402) 471-4277

NEVADA
Fred Schmidt
Chief Deputy Attorney General
Bur. of Consumer Protection
1000 E. William St., Ste. 200
Carson City, NV 89701
Phone: (775) 687-6300
Fax: (775) 687-6304

NEW HAMPSHIRE
Ted Wash
Director
Ofc. of the Governor
State House, Rm. 124
Concord, NH 03301
Phone: (603) 271-2260
Fax: (603) 271-6998

NEW JERSEY
Noel McGuire
Director
Ofc. of the Governor
Ofc. of Constituent Relations
P.O. Box 001
Trenton, NJ 08625-0001
Phone: (609) 777-2510
Fax: (609) 292-3454

NEW MEXICO
Sue Taylor
Ombudsman
Ofc. of the Governor
State Capitol, Rm. 417
Santa Fe, NM 87503
Phone: (505) 827-3050
Fax: (505) 827-3057

NEW YORK
Alexander F. Treadwell
Secretary of State
Dept. of State
41 State St.
Albany, NY 12231
Phone: (518) 486-9844
Fax: (518) 474-4765

NORTH CAROLINA
Linda Povlich
Director of Citizen & Community Services
Ofc. of the Governor
116 W. Jones St.
Raleigh, NC 27603-8001
Phone: (919) 715-0963
Fax: (919) 733-2120

NORTH DAKOTA
Mark Zimmerman
Director
Constituent Services
Ofc. of the Governor
600 E. Blvd. Ave.
Bismarck, ND 58505-0001
Phone: (701) 328-2200
Fax: (701) 328-2205
E-mail: governor@state.nd.us

NORTHERN MARIANA ISLANDS
Leo Lawrence LaMotte
Public Auditor
Ofc. of the Governor
P.O. Box 1399
Saipan, MP 96950
Phone: (670) 234-6481
Fax: (670) 234-7812
E-mail: opa@mtccnmi.com

OHIO
Thomas Charles
Inspector General
30 E. Broad St., Ste. 1820
Columbus, OH 43266-0820
Phone: (614) 644-9110
Fax: (614) 644-9504
E-mail: oig_watchdog@ohio.gov

OKLAHOMA

OREGON
Annabelle Jaramillo
Governor's Representative
Ofc. of the Governor
160 State Capitol
900 Court St., NE
Salem, OR 97310
Phone: (503) 378-5116
Fax: (503) 378-6827

PENNSYLVANIA

PUERTO RICO
Carlos Lopez
Ombudsman
P.O. Box 41088
Santurce, PR 00940
Phone: (787) 724-7373

RHODE ISLAND
Armeather Gibbs
Director
Community Relations & Constituent Affairs
Governor's Ofc.
State House, Rm. 112
Providence, RI 02903
Phone: (401) 222-2080
Fax: (401) 273-5301

SOUTH CAROLINA
Evelyn Williams
State Ombudsman
Ofc. of the Governor
1205 Pendleton St.
Columbia, SC 29201
Phone: (803) 734-0457
Fax: (803) 734-0546

SOUTH DAKOTA
Susan Stoneback
Special Assistant to the Governor
Constituent Services
Ofc. of the Governor
500 E. Capitol Ave.
Pierre, SD 57501
Phone: (605) 773-3212
Fax: (605) 773-4711

TENNESSEE

TEXAS
Sara Pfeifer
Director, Citizens' Assistance
Correspondence & Constituent Services
Ofc. of the Governor
P.O. Box 12428
Austin, TX 78711
Phone: (512) 463-1782
Fax: (512) 463-7397

U.S. VIRGIN ISLANDS
Julien Harley
St. John Administrator
Govt. House
P.O. Box 488
Cruz Bay
St. John, VI 00830
Phone: (340) 776-6484
Fax: (340) 776-6992

Louis Hill
St. Thomas/Water Island Administrator
Govt. House
21-22 Kongens Gade
St. Thomas, VI 00802
Phone: (340) 774-0943
Fax: (340) 774-0151

Rupert Ross
St. Croix Administrator
Govt. House
1105 Kings St.
Christiansted
St. Croix, VI 00820
Phone: (340) 773-1404
Fax: (340) 773-7978

UTAH
Linda Kedra
Director
Constituent Services
Governor's Ofc.
210 State Capitol
Salt Lake City, UT 84114
Phone: (801) 538-1680
Fax: (801) 538-1528
E-mail: lkedra@gov.state.ut.us

VERMONT
Joan Bagalio
Public Information Officer
Governor's Info. & Referral Ofc.
109 State St.
Montpelier, VT 05609
Phone: (802) 828-3333
Fax: (802) 828-3339

VIRGINIA
Carol Comstock
Director
Constituent Services
Ofc. of the Governor
State Capitol
Richmond, VA 23219
Phone: (804) 786-2211
Fax: (804) 371-6351

WASHINGTON
Linda Long
Deputy State Auditor
P.O. Box 40021
Olympia, WA 98504-0021
Phone: (360) 902-0360
Fax: (360) 753-0646

WEST VIRGINIA

WISCONSIN

WYOMING
Carolyn Teter
Deputy Chief of Staff
Ofc. of the Governor
State Capitol
Cheyenne, WY 82002
Phone: (307) 777-7434
Fax: (307) 632-3909
E-mail: cteter
@missc.state.wy.us

Parks and Recreation

Manages the state's parks, historical sites and recreational areas.

ALABAMA
Don Cooley
Director
Div. of Parks
Conservation & Natural Resources
64 N. Union St., Rm. 718
Montgomery, AL 36130
Phone: (334) 242-3334
Fax: (334) 353-8629

ALASKA
James Stratton
Director
Div. of Parks & Outdoor Recreation
Dept. of Natural Resources
3601 C St., Ste. 1200
Anchorage, AK 99503-5921
Phone: (907) 269-8700
Fax: (907) 269-8907

AMERICAN SAMOA
Laau Seui
Director
Dept. of Parks & Recreation
Pago Pago, AS 96799
Phone: (684) 699-9513
Fax: (684) 699-4427

ARIZONA
Ken Travous
Executive Director
State Parks
1300 W. Washington
Phoenix, AZ 85007
Phone: (602) 542-4174
Fax: (602) 542-4188

ARKANSAS
Richard Davies
Executive Director
Dept. of Parks & Tourism
1 Capitol Mall
Little Rock, AR 72201
Phone: (501) 682-2535
Fax: (501) 682-1364

CALIFORNIA
Patricia Megason
Director
Dept. of Parks & Recreation
P.O. Box 942896
Sacramento, CA 94296-0001
Phone: (916) 653-8380

COLORADO
Laurie Mathews
Director
Parks & Outdoor Recreation
Dept. of Natural Resources
1313 Sherman St., Rm. 618
Denver, CO 80203
Phone: (303) 866-3437

CONNECTICUT
Richard Clifford
Bureau Chief
Parks & Forest Bur.
Dept. of Environmental Protection
79 Elm St.
Hartford, CT 06106
Phone: (860) 424-3014

DELAWARE
Charles A. Salkin
Director
Div. of Parks & Recreation
Dept. of Natural Resources & Environmental Control
89 Kings Hwy.
Dover, DE 19901
Phone: (302) 739-4401
Fax: (302) 739-3817

DISTRICT OF COLUMBIA
Betty Jo Gaines
Director
Dept. of Recreation & Parks
3149 16th St., NW, 2nd Fl.
Washington, DC 20010
Phone: (202) 673-7665

FLORIDA
Fran P. Mainella
Director
Div. of Recreation & Parks
Dept. of Environmental Protection
3900 Commonwealth Blvd., MS 500
Tallahassee, FL 32399-3000
Phone: (850) 488-6131
Fax: (850) 488-8442

GEORGIA
Burt Weerts
Director
Parks, Recreation & Historic Sites
Dept. of Natural Resources
205 Butler St., SW, Ste. 1352
Atlanta, GA 30334
Phone: (404) 656-2770

GUAM
Austin J. Shelton
Director
Dept. of Parks & Recreation
13-8 Seagull Ave.
Hagatna, GU 96932
Phone: (671) 475-6296
Fax: (671) 472-9626

HAWAII
Ralston Nagata
Administrator
Div. of State Parks
Dept. of Land & Natural Resources
1151 Punchbowl St., Rm. 310
Honolulu, HI 96813
Phone: (808) 587-0290
Fax: (808) 587-0311

IDAHO
Yvonne Ferrell
Director
Dept. of Parks & Recreation
5657 Warm Springs Ave.
Boise, ID 83712-8752
Phone: (208) 327-7444

ILLINOIS
Brent Manning
Director
Dept. of Natural Resources
Lincoln Towers Plz., Rm. 425
524 S. 2nd St.
Springfield, IL 62706
Phone: (217) 782-6302
Fax: (217) 785-9236

INDIANA
Gerald J. Pagac
Director
Div. of State Parks & Reservoirs
Dept. of Natural Resources
402 W. Washington, Rm. W298
Indianapolis, IN 46204
Phone: (317) 232-4124
Fax: (317) 232-4132

IOWA
Michael E. Carrier
Administrator
Parks, Recreation & Preserves
Dept. of Natural Resources
Wallace State Ofc. Bldg.
E. 9th & Grand Aves.
Des Moines, IA 50319
Phone: (515) 281-5886

KANSAS
Steve Williams
Secretary
Dept. of Wildlife & Parks
Landon State Ofc. Bldg., Ste. 502
900 SW Jackson, Ste. 502
Topeka, KS 66612-1220
Phone: (785) 296-2281
Fax: (785) 296-6953

KENTUCKY
Kenny Rapier
Commissioner
Tourism Cabinet
Parks Dept.
Capital Plz. Tower
500 Mero St.
Frankfort, KY 40601
Phone: (502) 564-2172
Fax: (502) 564-6100

LOUISIANA
Dwight Landreneau
Assistant Secretary
Ofc. of State Parks
Culture, Recreation & Tourism Dept.
P.O. Box 44426
Baton Rouge, LA 70804-4426
Phone: (225) 342-8110
Fax: (225) 342-8107

MAINE
Herbert Hartman
Acting Director
Bur. of Parks & Recreation
Dept. of Conservation
19 State House Station
Augusta, ME 04333
Phone: (207) 287-3821

MARYLAND
Tom Haines
Associate Director
State Forests & Parks
Dept. of Natural Resources
Tawes State Ofc. Bldg.
580 Taylor Ave., E-3
Annapolis, MD 21401
Phone: (410) 260-8186
Fax: (410) 260-8191

MASSACHUSETTS
Todd Frederick
Director
Div. of Forests & Parks
Dept. of Environmental Mgmt.
100 Cambridge St.
Boston, MA 02202
Phone: (617) 727-3180
Fax: (617) 727-9402

MICHIGAN
Rodney Stokes
Chief
Parks & Div.
Dept. of Natural Resources
P.O. Box 30028
Lansing, MI 48909
Phone: (517) 373-1270

MINNESOTA
Bill Morrissey
Director
Div. of Parks & Recreation
Dept. of Natural Resources
500 Lafayette Rd.
St. Paul, MN 55155-4039
Phone: (651) 296-2270
Fax: (651) 297-1157
E-mail: bill.morrissey@dnr.state.mn.us

MISSISSIPPI
Sam Polles
Director
Parks & Recreation
Dept. of Wildlife, Fisheries & Parks
P.O. Box 451
Jackson, MS 39205
Phone: (601) 362-9212
Fax: (601) 364-2147

Bob Tyler
Department Director
Dept. of Wildlife, Fisheries & Parks
P.O. Box 541
Jackson, MS 39205
Phone: (601) 362-9212
Fax: (601) 354-2147

MISSOURI
Douglas K. Eiken
Director
Div. of State Parks
Dept. of Natural Resources
101 Adams St.
P.O. Box 176
Jefferson City, MO 65102
Phone: (573) 751-9392
Fax: (573) 751-8656
E-mail: nreiked@mail.dnr.state.mo.us

MONTANA
Arnold Olsen
Administrator
Parks Div.
Dept. of Fish, Wildlife & Parks
1420 E. 6th Ave.
Helena, MT 59620
Phone: (406) 444-3750
Fax: (406) 444-4952

NEBRASKA
Rex Amack
Director
Game & Parks Comm.
2200 N. 33rd St.
P.O. Box 30370
Lincoln, NE 68503-0370
Phone: (402) 471-0641
Fax: (402) 471-5528

NEVADA

NEW HAMPSHIRE
Richard McLeod
Director
Div. of Parks & Recreation
Dept. of Resources & Economic Dev.
P.O. Box 1856
Concord, NH 03302-1856
Phone: (603) 271-3556
Fax: (603) 271-2629

NEW JERSEY
Gregory A. Marshall
Director
Div. of Parks & Forestry
Dept. of Environmental Protection
501 E. State St.
P.O. Box 404
Trenton, NJ 08625-0404
Phone: (609) 292-2733
Fax: (609) 984-0503

NEW MEXICO
Tom Trujillo
Director
Park & Recreation Div.
Dept. of Energy, Minerals & Natural Resources
P.O. Box 1147
Santa Fe, NM 87505
Phone: (505) 827-5975
Fax: (505) 827-1376

NEW YORK
Bernadette Castro
Commissioner
Ofc. of Parks, Recreation & Historic Preservation
Agency Bldg. 1, 20th Fl.
Empire State Plz.
Albany, NY 12238
Phone: (518) 474-0443
Fax: (518) 474-1365

NORTH CAROLINA
Philip K. McKnelly
Director
Parks & Recreation Div.
Dept. of Environment & Natural Resources
512 N. Salisbury St.
Raleigh, NC 27604-1148
Phone: (919) 733-4181
Fax: (919) 715-3085

NORTH DAKOTA
Doug Prchal
Director
Parks & Recreation Dept.
1835 E. Bismarck Expy.
Bismarck, ND 58504-6708
Phone: (701) 328-5357
Fax: (701) 328-5363
E-mail: dprchal@pioneer.state.nd.us

NORTHERN MARIANA ISLANDS
Anthony T. Benavente
Director
Parks & Recreation
Dept. of Lands & Natural Resources
P.O. Box 10007
Saipan, MP 96950
Phone: (670) 234-7405
Fax: (670) 234-6480

OHIO
Dan West
Chief
Div. of Parks & Recreation
Dept. of Natural Resources
1952 Belcher Dr., Bldg. C-3
Columbus, OH 43224
Phone: (614) 265-6511
Fax: (614) 261-8407

OKLAHOMA
Jane Jayroe
Executive Director
Dept. of Tourism & Recreation
15 N. Robinson, Ste. 100
Oklahoma City, OK 73102
Phone: (405) 521-2413
Fax: (405) 236-0569
E-mail: jcraven@otrd.state.ok.us

OREGON
Robert Meinen
Director
Dept. of Parks & Recreation
1115 Commercial St., NE
Salem, OR 97310-1001
Phone: (503) 378-5019
Fax: (503) 378-6447

PENNSYLVANIA
Roger Fickes
Director
Bur. of State Parks
Dept. of Environmental Resources
Rachel Carson Ofc. Bldg., 8th Fl.
Harrisburg, PA 17101
Phone: (717) 787-6640
Fax: (717) 787-8817

PUERTO RICO
Eric Labrador
Secretary
Public Recreation & Parks Administration
P.O. Box 3207
San Juan, PR 00904
Phone: (787) 721-2800
Fax: (787) 722-3382

RHODE ISLAND
Larry Mouradjian
Chief
Div. of Parks & Recreation
Dept. of Environmental Mgmt.
2321 Hartford
Johnston, RI 02919
Phone: (401) 222-2632

SOUTH CAROLINA
Buddy Jennings
Director
Parks, Recreation & Tourism
1205 Pendleton St., Ste. 248
Columbia, SC 29201
Phone: (803) 734-0166

SOUTH DAKOTA
Doug Hofer
Director
Div. of Parks & Recreation
Dept. of Game, Fish & Parks
Joe Foss Bldg.
523 E. Capitol Ave.
Pierre, SD 57501
Phone: (605) 773-3391
Fax: (605) 773-6245

TENNESSEE
Walter Butler
Assistant Commissioner
State Parks
Dept. of Environment & Conservation
401 Church St.
Nashville, TN 37243
Phone: (615) 532-0025
Fax: (615) 532-0046

TEXAS
Andrew S. Sansom
Executive Director
Dept. of Parks & Wildlife
4200 Smith School Rd.
Austin, TX 78744
Phone: (512) 389-4802
Fax: (512) 389-4814

U.S. VIRGIN ISLANDS
Ira Hobson
Commissioner
Dept. of Housing, Parks & Recreation
Property & Procurement, Bldg. #1
Sub Base, 2nd Fl., Rm. 206
St. Thomas, VI 00802
Phone: (340) 774-0255
Fax: (340) 774-4600

UTAH
Courtland Nelson
Director
Div. of State Parks & Recreation
Dept. of Natural Resources
P.O. Box 145610
Salt Lake City, UT 84114-5610
Phone: (801) 538-7362
Fax: (801) 538-7378
E-mail: cnelson.nrdpr@state.ut.us

VERMONT
Conrad Motyka
Commissioner
Dept. of Forests, Parks & Recreation
103 S. Main St.
Waterbury, VT 05676
Phone: (802) 241-3670
Fax: (802) 244-1481

VIRGINIA
David G. Brickley
Director
Dept. of Conservation & Recreation
203 Governor St., Ste. 302
Richmond, VA 23219
Phone: (804) 786-2289
Fax: (804) 786-6141

WASHINGTON
Cleve Pinnix
Director
State Parks & Recreation Comm.
7150 Cleanwater Ln.
P.O. Box 42650
Olympia, WA 98504-2650
Phone: (360) 902-8500
Fax: (360) 664-2106

WEST VIRGINIA
Robert A. Reintsema
Commissioner
Div. of Tourism & Parks
2101 Washington St., E.
Charleston, WV 25305
Phone: (304) 558-2200
Fax: (304) 558-2956

WISCONSIN
Sue Black
Director
Bur. of Parks & Recreation
Dept. of Natural Resources
P.O. Box 7921
Madison, WI 53707-7921
Phone: (608) 266-2181
Fax: (608) 267-7474

WYOMING
Gary Thorson
Director of State Parks & Historic Sites
Div. of Parks & Cultural Resources
Dept. of Commerce
6101 Yellowstone
Cheyenne, WY 82002
Phone: (307) 777-6324

Parole and Probation (Adult)

Determines whether paroles should be granted or revoked and supervises adult parolees and probationers.

ALABAMA
Donald Parker
Executive Director
Board of Pardons & Parole
500 Monroe St.
Montgomery, AL 36130
Phone: (334) 242-8700
Fax: (334) 242-1800

ALASKA
Larry Jones
Executive Director
Parole Board
Dept. of Corrections
P.O. Box 112000
Juneau, AK 99811-2000
Phone: (907) 465-3384
Fax: (907) 465-3110

AMERICAN SAMOA
Albert Mailo Toetagata
Attorney General
Dept. of Legal Affairs
AS Govt.
Pago Pago, AS 96799
Phone: (684) 633-4163
Fax: (684) 633-1838

ARIZONA
Edward Leyva
Chair
Board of Executive Clemency
1645 W. Jefferson, Ste. 326
Phoenix, AZ 85007
Phone: (602) 542-5656
Fax: (602) 542-5680

ARKANSAS
Leroy Brownlee
Chair
Post Prison Transfer Board
P.O. Box 34085
Little Rock, AR 72203
Phone: (501) 682-3850
Fax: (501) 682-3860

CALIFORNIA
Jim Nielsen
Chair
Board of Prison Terms
428 J St., Ste. 600
Sacramento, CA 95814-2329
Phone: (916) 322-6366

COLORADO
Tom Coogan
Director
Div. of Adult Parole Supervision
Dept. of Corrections
1600 W. 24th St.
Lakewood, CO 80215
Phone: (303) 238-5967
Fax: (303) 238-0176

CONNECTICUT
Robert J. Bosco
Director
Dept. of Adult Probation
2275 Silas Deane Hwy.
Rocky Hill, CT 06067
Phone: (860) 563-1332

DELAWARE
Marlene Lichtenstadter
Chair
Board of Parole
Carvel State Ofc. Bldg.
820 N. French St.
Wilmington, DE 19801
Phone: (302) 577-3452

DISTRICT OF COLUMBIA
Margaret Quick
Chair
Board of Parole
633 Indiana Ave., NW, 8th Fl.
Washington, DC 20005
Phone: (202) 220-5450
Fax: (202) 220-5466

FLORIDA
Edward M. Spooner
Chair
Parole Comm.
2601 Blairstone Rd., Bldg. C, 3rd Fl.
Tallahassee, FL 32399
Phone: (850) 922-0000
Fax: (850) 414-2627

GEORGIA
Walter S. Ray
Chair
Board of Pardons & Paroles
2 Martin Luther King Jr. Dr., SE
Atlanta, GA 30334
Phone: (404) 656-2808

GUAM
Angel Sablan
Acting Director
Dept. of Corrections
P.O. Box 3236
Hagatna, GU 96932
Phone: (671) 734-4668
Fax: (671) 734-4490

HAWAII
Alfred Beaver
Chair
Paroling Authority
Dept. of Public Safety
1177 Alakea St., #GRDFL
Honolulu, HI 96813-2800
Phone: (808) 587-1290
Fax: (808) 587-1314

IDAHO
Olivia Craven
Executive Director
Comm. for Pardons & Parole
280 N. 8th St., Ste. 140
P.O. Box 83720
Boise, ID 83720-1807
Phone: (208) 334-2520

ILLINOIS
James K. Williams
Chair
Prisoner Review Board
319 E. Madison, Ste. A
Springfield, IL 62701
Phone: (217) 782-7273
Fax: (217) 524-0012

INDIANA
Raymond Justak
Chair
Parole Board
Dept. of Corrections
IGC-S., Rm. E321
302 W. Washington St.
Indianapolis, IN 46204
Phone: (317) 232-5737
Fax: (317) 232-5738

IOWA
Jeanette Bucklew
Deputy Director
Community Based Corrections
Dept. of Corrections
Capitol Annex
523 E. 12th St.
Des Moines, IA 50319
Phone: (515) 281-4806

KANSAS
Marilyn Scafe
Chair
Parole Board
900 SW Jackson, Rm. 452-S
Topeka, KS 66612-1220
Phone: (785) 296-3469
Fax: (785) 296-7949

KENTUCKY
Linda Frank
Chair
State Parole Board
Dept. of Corrections
State Ofc. Bldg., 5th Fl.
Frankfort, KY 40601
Phone: (502) 564-3620
Fax: (502) 564-8995

LOUISIANA
Fred Clark
Chair
Board of Parole
Public Safety & Corrections
P.O. Box 94304
Baton Rouge, LA 70804-9304
Phone: (225) 342-6622
Fax: (225) 342-3701

MAINE

MARYLAND
W. Roland Knapp
Director
Div. of Parole & Probation
Dept. of Public Safety & Correctional Services
6776 Reisterstown Rd., Ste. 305
Baltimore, MD 21215
Phone: (410) 764-4276
Fax: (410) 764-4091

MASSACHUSETTS
Sheila Hubbard
Chair
Parole Board
Executive Ofc. of Public Safety
27/43 Wormwood St., Ste. 300
Boston, MA 02210-1606
Phone: (617) 727-3271
Fax: (617) 727-5047

MICHIGAN
Steve Marske
Chair
Parole Board
Dept. of Corrections
P.O. Box 30003
Lansing, MI 48909
Phone: (517) 373-0270

MINNESOTA
Sheryl Ramstad Huass
Commissioner
Dept. of Corrections
1450 Energy Park Dr., Ste. 200
St. Paul, MN 55108
Phone: (651) 642-0282
Fax: (651) 642-0414

MISSISSIPPI
Walley Naylor
Chair
State Parole Board
Parole Board
201 W. Capitol, Ste. 800
Jackson, MS 39201
Phone: (601) 354-7716
Fax: (601) 354-7725

MISSOURI
Cranston Mitchell
Chair
Board of Probation & Parole
Dept. of Corrections
1511 Christy Dr.
Jefferson City, MO 65101
Phone: (573) 751-8488
Fax: (573) 751-8501

MONTANA
Ron Alsbury
Region 11 Supervisor
Probation & Parole Regional Ofc.
Dept. of Corrections
P.O. Box 201301
Helena, MT 59620
Phone: (406) 444-2482
Fax: (406) 444-9737

NEBRASKA
Linda Krutz
Chair
State Parole Board
P.O. Box 94754
Lincoln, NE 68509
Phone: (402) 471-2156
Fax: (402) 471-2453

NEVADA
Carlos Concha
Chief
Dept. of Parole & Probation
1445 Hot Springs Rd., #104
Carson City, NV 89706
Phone: (775) 687-5040
Fax: (775) 687-5402

NEW HAMPSHIRE
John Eckert
Executive Assistant
Parole Board
281 N. State St.
Concord, NH 03301-3250
Phone: (603) 271-2569

NEW JERSEY
Mary Disabato
Chair
State Parole Board
P.O. Box 862
Trenton, NJ 08625-0862
Phone: (609) 292-4257

Jack Terhune
Chair
State Parole Board
P.O. Box 863
Trenton, NJ 08625-0863
Phone: (609) 292-9860

NEW MEXICO
Kevin H. Dooley
Director
Probation & Parole Div.
Dept. of Corrections
P.O. Box 27116
Santa Fe, NM 87502
Phone: (505) 827-8830
Fax: (505) 827-8220

NEW YORK
Brion D. Travis
Chair
Board of Parole
97 Central Ave.
Albany, NY 12206
Phone: (518) 473-9548
Fax: (518) 473-6037

NORTH CAROLINA
Robert Guy
Director
Div. of Community Corrections
Dept. of Corrections
2020 Yonkers Rd.
Raleigh, NC 27604-2258
Phone: (919) 716-3100
Fax: (919) 716-3996

NORTH DAKOTA
Warren Emmer
Director
Parole & Probation Div.
Dept. of Corrections & Rehab.
P.O. Box 5521
Bismarck, ND 58506-5521
Phone: (701) 328-6193
Fax: (701) 328-6651
E-mail: wemmer @state.nd.us

NORTHERN MARIANA ISLANDS
Jesus C. Bermudes
Parole Officer
Board of Parole
Ofc. of the Governor
Saipan, MP 96950
Phone: (670) 234-4841
Fax: (670) 235-4840

OHIO
Jill D. Goldhart
Deputy Director
Parole & Community Services
Dept. of Rehab. & Corrections
1050 Freeway Dr., N.
Columbus, OH 43229
Phone: (614) 752-1235
Fax: (614) 752-1251

OKLAHOMA
Terry Jenks
Executive Director
Pardon & Parole Board
4040 N. Lincoln Blvd., Ste. 219
Oklahoma City, OK 73105
Phone: (405) 427-8601
Fax: (405) 427-6648

OREGON
Diane Rea
Chair
Board of Parole & Post-Prison Supervision
2575 Ctr. St., NE
Salem, OR 97310
Phone: (503) 945-9009
Fax: (503) 373-7558

PENNSYLVANIA
William F. Ward
Chair
Board of Probations & Parole
1101 S. Front St., #5000
Harrisburg, PA 17104-2537
Phone: (717) 787-5100
Fax: (717) 783-7713

PUERTO RICO
Enrique Garcia
President
Parole Board
P.O. Box 40945
Minillas Station
San Juan, PR 00940
Phone: (787) 759-7127

RHODE ISLAND
Lisa Farrell
Chair
Parole Board
Dept. of Corrections
1 Ctr. Pl.
Providence, RI 02903-1614
Phone: (401) 222-3262

SOUTH CAROLINA
Stephen K. Benjamin
Director
Probation, Parole & Pardon Services
2221 Devine St., #600
P.O. Box 50666
Columbia, SC 29250
Phone: (803) 734-9278

SOUTH DAKOTA
Kris Petersen
Executive Director
State Penitentiary
Ofc. of Correctional Service
P.O. Box 5911
Sioux Falls, SD 57117
Phone: (605) 367-5040
Fax: (605) 367-5025

TENNESSEE
Charles M. Traughber
Chair
Board of Paroles
404 James Robertson Pkwy.
Nashville, TN 37243
Phone: (615) 741-1673

TEXAS
Victor Rodriguez
Chair
Board of Pardons & Paroles
Dept. of Criminal Justice
P.O. Box 13084
Austin, TX 78711
Phone: (512) 463-1679
Fax: (512) 475-1702

U.S. VIRGIN ISLANDS
Verne A. Hodge
Presiding Judge
Territorial Ct.
P.O. Box 70
St. Thomas, VI 00804
Phone: (340) 774-6680
Fax: (340) 777-8187

Chesley Roebuck
Chair
Parole Board
5086 Estate Solitude
Christiansted
St. Thomas, VI 00802
Phone: (340) 778-2036
Fax: (340) 778-1637

UTAH
Kirk M. Torgensen
Director
Field Operations
Dept. of Corrections
155 E. 6100 S.
Murray, UT 84107
Phone: (801) 264-4308
Fax: (801) 264-4311
E-mail: ktorgens.crmurray@state.ut.us

VERMONT
Linda Shambo
Director
Parole Board
103 S. Main St.
Waterbury, VT 05671
Phone: (802) 241-2294
Fax: (802) 241-2565

Richard Turner
Director of Probation
Agency of Human Services
Dept. of Corrections
103 S. Main St.
Waterbury, VT 05671-1001
Phone: (802) 241-2265

VIRGINIA
John R. Alderman
Chair
Parole Board
6900 Atmore Dr.
Richmond, VA 23225
Phone: (804) 674-3081
Fax: (804) 674-3284

WASHINGTON
Kathryn S. Bail
Chair
Indeterminate Sentence Review Board
4317 6th Ave., SE
P.O. Box 40907
Lacey, WA 98504-0907
Phone: (360) 493-9266
Fax: (360) 493-9287

WEST VIRGINIA
Sandra Ilderton
Chair
Board of Parole
Bldg. 4, Rm. 3
112 California Ave.
Charleston, WV 25305
Phone: (304) 558-6366
Fax: (304) 558-5934

WISCONSIN
Bill Groshans
Administrator
Div. of Community Corrections
Dept. of Probation & Parole
149 E. Wilson, 2nd Fl.
Madison, WI 53703
Phone: (608) 266-7740
Fax: (608) 267-1739

WYOMING
Steve Lindly
Director
Probation & Parole
Corrections
700 W. 21st St.
Cheyenne, WY 82002
Phone: (307) 777-7208

Personnel

Formulates, implements and enforces personnel management policies and procedures for the state.

ALABAMA
Thomas Flowers
Director
State Personnel Dept.
64 N. Union St.
Montgomery, AL 36130-4100
Phone: (334) 242-3389
Fax: (334) 353-3320

ALASKA
Vacant
Director
Div. of Personnel
Dept. of Administration
P.O. Box 110201
Juneau, AK 99811-0201
Phone: (907) 465-4430
Fax: (907) 465-2576

AMERICAN SAMOA
Sapini Siatu'u
Director
Dept. of Human Resources
AS Govt.
Pago Pago, AS 96799
Phone: (684) 633-4485
Fax: (684) 633-1139

ARIZONA
James Matthews
Human Resources Director
Personnel Div.
Dept. of Administration
1831 W. Jefferson
Phoenix, AZ 85007
Phone: (602) 542-5482
Fax: (602) 542-2796

ARKANSAS
Artee Williams
State Personnel Administrator
Ofc. of Personnel Mgmt.
Dept. of Finance & Administration
201 DFA Bldg.
1509 W. 7th St.
Little Rock, AR 72201
Phone: (501) 682-1823
Fax: (501) 682-5094

CALIFORNIA
David J. Tirapelle
Director
Dept. of Personnel Administration
1515 S St., N. Bldg., Ste. 400
Sacramento, CA 95814
Phone: (916) 322-5193

COLORADO
Larry E. Trujillo, Sr.
Executive Director
Support Services
Dept. of Personnel
1525 Sherman St., 2nd Fl.
Denver, CO 80203
Phone: (303) 866-6559
Fax: (303) 866-6569

CONNECTICUT
Keith Anderson
Liaison
Labor Relations
Dept. of Adm. Services
1 Hartford Sq., W.
Hartford, CT 06106
Phone: (860) 713-5059

DELAWARE
Harriet Smith-Windsor
Director
Ofc. of Personnel
Townsend Bldg.
P.O. Box 1401
Dover, DE 19903
Phone: (302) 739-4195
Fax: (302) 739-3000
E-mail: hnsmith@state.de.us

DISTRICT OF COLUMBIA
Judy D. Banks
Director
Ofc. of Personnel
441 4th St., NW, Ste. 300, S.
Washington, DC 20001
Phone: (202) 727-6406
Fax: (202) 727-6827

FLORIDA
Sharon Larson
Director
Human Resource Mgmt.
Dept. of Mgmt. Services
4050 Esplanade Way, Bldg. 4040, Ste. 360
Tallahassee, FL 32399-0950
Phone: (850) 922-5449
Fax: (850) 921-4117

GEORGIA
Dana R. Russell
Commissioner
State Merit System
W. Tower, Ste. 502
200 Piedmont Ave. SE
Atlanta, GA 30334-5100
Phone: (404) 656-2705

GUAM
Michael J. Reidy
Director
Dept. of Administration
P.O. Box 884
Hagatna, GU 96932
Phone: (671) 475-1101
Fax: (671) 477-6788

HAWAII
Michael McCartney
Director
Dept. of Human Resources Dev.
235 S. Beretania St., 14th Fl.
Honolulu, HI 96813
Phone: (808) 587-1100
Fax: (808) 587-1106

Paul Shigenaga
Administrative Director
Public Utilities Comm.
Kekuanaoa Bldg., Rm. 103
465 S. King St.
Honolulu, HI 96813
Phone: (808) 586-2028
Fax: (808) 586-2066

IDAHO
Richard Hutchison
Director
Personnel Comm.
700 W. State St.
Boise, ID 83720

ILLINOIS
Diane Hurrelbrink
Manager
Bur. of Personnel Agency Services
Dept. of Central Mgmt. Services
503 Stratton Ofc. Bldg.
401 S. Spring
Springfield, IL 62706
Phone: (217) 782-3379
Fax: (217) 524-0836

INDIANA
D. Sue Roberson
Director
State Personnel Dept.
IGC-S., Rm. W161
402 W. Washington St.
Indianapolis, IN 46204
Phone: (317) 232-3059
Fax: (317) 232-1979

IOWA
Linda Hanson
Director
Dept. of Personnel
Grimes State Ofc. Bldg.
E. 14th & Grand Aves.
Des Moines, IA 50319
Phone: (515) 281-3351
Fax: (515) 242-6450

KANSAS
William B. McGlasson
Director
Div. of Personnel Services
Dept. of Administration
Landon State Ofc. Bldg., Rm. 951-S
900 SW Jackson
Topeka, KS 66612-1251
Phone: (785) 296-4278
Fax: (785) 296-0756

KENTUCKY
Carol Palmore
Secretary
Personnel Cabinet
200 Fairoaks, Ste. 516
Frankfort, KY 40601
Phone: (502) 564-4460
Fax: (502) 564-7603

LOUISIANA
Allan H. Reynolds
Civil Service Director
Personnel Mgmt. Div.
Dept. of Civil Service
P.O. Box 94111
Baton Rouge, LA 70804-9111
Phone: (225) 342-8272
Fax: (225) 342-6074

MAINE
Donald Wills
Director
Bur. of Human Resources
Dept. of Adm. & Financial Services
4 State House Station
Augusta, ME 04333
Phone: (207) 287-3761

MARYLAND
Andrea Fulton
Executive Director
Ofc. of Personnel Services & Benefits
Dept. of Budget & Mgmt.
301 W. Preston St., Rm. 609
Baltimore, MD 21201
Phone: (410) 767-4715
Fax: (410) 333-5262
E-mail: afulton@dbm.state.md.us

MASSACHUSETTS
James Hartnett, Jr.
Chief Personnel Administrator
Div. of Human Resources
One Ashburton Pl., Rm. 213
Boston, MA 02108
Phone: (617) 727-1556
Fax: (617) 727-1175

MICHIGAN
John Lopez
State Personnel Director
Civil Service
400 S. Pine
Lansing, MI 48909
Phone: (517) 373-3020
Fax: (517) 373-3103

MINNESOTA
Karen L. Carpenter
Commissioner
Dept. of Employee Relations
200 Centennial Ofc. Bldg.
658 Cedar St.
St. Paul, MN 55101-1603
Phone: (651) 296-3095
Fax: (651) 296-1990
E-mail: karen.carpenter.@state.mn.us

MISSISSIPPI
J.K. Stringer, Jr.
Director
State Personnel Board
301 N. Lamar St., Ste. 201
Jackson, MS 39201
Phone: (601) 359-2702
Fax: (601) 359-2729

MISSOURI
Lee Capps
Director
Div. of Personnel
Ofc. of Administration
Truman Bldg., Rm. 430
P.O. Box 388
Jefferson City, MO 65102
Phone: (573) 751-3053
Fax: (573) 751-8641
E-mail: cappsl@mail.oa.state.mo.us

MONTANA
John McEwen
Administrator
State Personnel Div.
Dept. of Administration
P.O. Box 200127
Helena, MT 59620
Phone: (406) 444-3871
Fax: (406) 444-2812

NEBRASKA
Sherri Wines
Acting Director
Div. of Personnel
Dept. of Adm. Services
P.O. Box 94905
Lincoln, NE 68509
Phone: (402) 471-2075
Fax: (402) 471-3754

NEVADA
Jeanne Greene
Acting Director
Dept. of Personnel
209 E. Musser St., Rm. 300
Carson City, NV 89710-4204
Phone: (775) 684-0131
Fax: (775) 684-0124

NEW HAMPSHIRE
Virginia Lamberton
Director
Div. of Personnel
Adm. Services
25 Capitol St., Rm. 1
Concord, NH 03301-6395
Phone: (603) 271-3261

NEW JERSEY
Janice Mitchell Mintz
Acting Commissioner
Dept. of Personnel
P.O. Box 317
Trenton, NJ 08625-0317
Phone: (609) 292-4144
Fax: (609) 984-3631
E-mail: csbmint@dop.state.nj.us

NEW MEXICO
Rex Robberson
Director
State Personnel Ofc.
2600 Cerillos
Santa Fe, NM 87505-0127
Phone: (505) 476-7805
Fax: (505) 476-7806

NEW YORK
George C. Sinnott
Commissioner & President
Dept. of Civil Service
State Campus, Bldg. 1, 2nd Fl.
Albany, NY 12239
Phone: (518) 457-3701
Fax: (518) 457-7547

NORTH CAROLINA
Ronald G. Penny
Director
Ofc. of State Personnel
Dept. of Administration
116 W. Jones St.
Raleigh, NC 27603-8003
Phone: (919) 733-7108
Fax: (919) 733-0653

NORTH DAKOTA
Dan LeRoy
Director
Central Personnel Div.
600 E. Blvd. Ave., 14th Fl.
Bismarck, ND 58505-0120
Phone: (701) 328-3290
Fax: (701) 328-1475
E-mail: dleroy@state.nd.us

NORTHERN MARIANA ISLANDS
Luis S. Camacho
Director of Personnel
Personnel Mgmt. Ofc.
Ofc. of the Governor
Saipan, MP 96950
Phone: (670) 234-6958
Fax: (670) 234-1013

OHIO
Steve Gulyaffy
Deputy Director
Human Resources Div.
Dept. of Adm. Services
30 E. Broad St., 28th Fl.
Columbus, OH 43215
Phone: (614) 466-3455
Fax: (614) 728-2785

OKLAHOMA
Oscar Jackson
Administrator & Cabinet Secretary of Human Resources
Ofc. of Personnel Mgmt.
2101 N. Lincoln Blvd.
Oklahoma City, OK 73105
Phone: (405) 521-6301
Fax: (405) 524-6942
E-mail: oscar.jackson@oklaosf.state.ok.us

OREGON
Dan Kennedy
Administrator
Human Resources Services Div.
Dept. of Adm. Services
155 Cottage St., NE
Salem, OR 97310
Phone: (503) 378-3020
Fax: (503) 373-7684

PENNSYLVANIA
Charles T. Sciotto
Deputy Secretary
Employee Relations
Ofc. of Administration
517 Finance Bldg.
Harrisburg, PA 17120
Phone: (717) 787-5545
Fax: (717) 783-4429

PUERTO RICO
Maribel Rodriguez
Director
Central Ofc. of Personnel Administration
P.O. Box 8476
San Juan, PR 00910
Phone: (787) 721-4300
Fax: (787) 722-3390

RHODE ISLAND
Anthony A. Bucci
Personnel Administrator
Ofc. of Personnel Administration
Dept. of Administration
1 Capitol Hill
Providence, RI 02908-5860
Phone: (401) 222-2160

SOUTH CAROLINA
Donna Traywick
Director
Ofc. of Human Resources
Budget & Control Board
1201 Main St., Ste. 1000
Columbia, SC 29201
Phone: (803) 734-0900
Fax: (803) 734-0968

SOUTH DAKOTA
Sandy Zinter
Commissioner
Bur. of Personnel
500 E. Capitol Ave.
Pierre, SD 57501
Phone: (605) 773-3148
Fax: (605) 773-4344

TENNESSEE
Eleanor Yoakum
Commissioner
Dept. of Personnel
James K. Polk Bldg., 2nd Fl.
Nashville, TN 37243-0635
Phone: (615) 741-2958
Fax: (615) 532-0728

TEXAS
Kelli Dan
State Classification Director
State Auditor's Ofc.
206 E. 9th St., Ste. 1900
Austin, TX 78711
Phone: (512) 479-4700
Fax: (512) 479-4884

U.S. VIRGIN ISLANDS
Joanne Barry
Director
Div. of Personnel
GERS Complex, 3rd Fl.
48B-50C Konprindsens Gade
St. Thomas, VI 00802
Phone: (340) 774-8588
Fax: (340) 774-6916

UTAH
Karen Suzuki-Okabe
Executive Director
Administration Div.
Dept. of Human Resources Mgmt.
2120 State Ofc. Bldg.
Salt Lake City, UT 84114-1531
Phone: (801) 538-3080
Fax: (801) 538-3081
E-mail: kokabe.pedhrm@state.ut.us

VERMONT
Eileen Boland
Commissioner
Dept. of Personnel
110 State St.
Montpelier, VT 05602
Phone: (802) 828-3491
Fax: (802) 828-3409

VIRGINIA
Sara Redding Wilson
Director
Dept. of Personnel & Training
Monroe Bldg., 12th Fl.
101 N. 14th St.
Richmond, VA 23219
Phone: (804) 225-2237
Fax: (804) 371-7401

WASHINGTON
Dennis Karras
Director
Dept. of Personnel
521 Capitol Way, S.
P.O. Box 47500
Olympia, WA 98504
Phone: (360) 753-5368
Fax: (360) 586-4694

WEST VIRGINIA
Edison Casto
Director
Div. of Personnel
Bldg. 5, Rm. 416
1900 Kanawha Blvd., E.
Charleston, WV 25305-0291
Phone: (304) 558-3950
Fax: (304) 558-1587

WISCONSIN
Peter D. Fox
Secretary
Dept. of Employment Relations
345 W. Washington Ave.
P.O. Box 7855
Madison, WI 53707-7855
Phone: (608) 266-9820
Fax: (608) 267-1020

WYOMING
Darrell Dykeman
Administrator
Personnel Div.
Dept. of Administration & Info.
2001 Capitol Ave.
Cheyenne, WY 82002-0060
Phone: (307) 777-6713

Planning

Formulates long-range, comprehensive plans for the orderly and coordinated growth of the state.

ALABAMA
Dewayne Freeman
Director
Dept. of Economic & Community Affairs
P.O. Box 5690
Montgomery, AL 36103-5690
Phone: (334) 242-8672
Fax: (334) 242-5099

ALASKA

AMERICAN SAMOA
John Faumuina, Jr.
Director
Economic Dev. & Planning Ofc.
Dept. of Commerce
Pago Pago, AS 96799
Phone: (684) 633-5155
Fax: (684) 633-4195

ARIZONA
Tom Betlach
Director
Ofc. of Strategic Planning & Budgeting
1700 W. Washington, 5th Fl.
Phoenix, AZ 85007
Phone: (602) 542-5381
Fax: (602) 542-0868

ARKANSAS

CALIFORNIA
Paul F. Miner
Director
Ofc. of Planning & Research
1400 10th St.
Sacramento, CA 95814
Phone: (916) 322-2318

COLORADO
Nancy J. McCallin
Executive Director
Ofc. of State Planning & Budgeting
Ofc. of the Governor
State Capitol, Rm. 114
200 E. Colfax Ave.
Denver, CO 80203-1792
Phone: (303) 866-2980
Fax: (303) 866-3044

CONNECTICUT
Ann Moore
Undersecretary
Policy Dev. & Planning Div.
Ofc. of Policy & Mgmt.
P.O. Box 341441
Hartford, CT 06134-1441
Phone: (860) 418-6484

DELAWARE
David S. Hugg, III
Director
State Planning Ofc.
Tatnall Bldg.
William Penn St.
Dover, DE 19901
Phone: (302) 739-3090
Fax: (302) 739-2775

DISTRICT OF COLUMBIA
John Fondersmith
Interim Director
Ofc. of Planning
801 N. Capitol St., NE, #5211
Washington, DC 20004
Phone: (202) 442-7600

FLORIDA
Robert B. Bradley
Director
Ofc. of Planning & Budgeting
Executive Ofc. of the Governor
The Capitol, Rm. 1601
Tallahassee, FL 32399-0001
Phone: (850) 488-7810
Fax: (850) 488-9005

GEORGIA
Bill Tomlinson
Director
Ofc. of Planning & Budget
270 Washington St., SW, Rm. 8060
Atlanta, GA 30334
Phone: (404) 656-3820
Fax: (404) 656-7198

GUAM
Clifford A. Guzman
Director
Bur. of Planning
P.O. Box 2950
Hagatna, GU 96932
Phone: (671) 472-4201
Fax: (671) 477-1812

HAWAII

IDAHO
Thomas Arnold
Director
Dept. of Commerce
700 W. State St.
Boise, ID 83720
Phone: (208) 334-2470

ILLINOIS

INDIANA

IOWA
Dave Lyons
Director
Dept. of Economic Dev.
200 E. Grand Ave.
Des Moines, IA 50309
Phone: (515) 242-4814
Fax: (515) 242-4832

KANSAS
Charles Ransom
President
Kansas, Inc.
632 SW Van Buren St., Ste. 100
Topeka, KS 66603
Phone: (785) 296-1460

KENTUCKY
Crit Luallen
State Budget Director
Governor's Ofc.
700 Capitol Ave., Ste. 284
Frankfort, KY 40601
Phone: (502)564-7300
Fax: (502) 564-6684

LOUISIANA
Joan M. Wharton
Director
Ofc. of State Planning
P.O. Box 94095
Baton Rouge, LA 70804
Phone: (225) 342-7410
Fax: (225) 342-7220

MAINE
Evan Richert
Director
State Planning Ofc.
38 State House Station
Augusta, ME 04333
Phone: (207) 287-6077

MARYLAND
Ronald M. Kreitner
Director
Ofc. of the Director
Ofc. of Planning
301 W. Preston St.
Baltimore, MD 21201
Phone: (410) 767-4510
Fax: (410) 767-4480

MASSACHUSETTS
Carolyn Boviard
Director
Executive Ofc. of Economic Affairs
Dept. of Economic Dev.
One Ashburton Pl., Rm. 2101
Boston, MA 02108
Phone: (617) 727-8380
Fax: (617) 727-4426

MICHIGAN

MINNESOTA
Andrew Koebrick
Librarian
Planning Library
Centennial Ofc. Bldg., 3rd Fl.
658 Cedar St.
St. Paul, MN 55155
Phone: (651) 297-2325
Fax: (651) 297-2820
E-mail: ann.schluter@mn.plan.state.us

MISSISSIPPI
Deb Collier
Director
Ofc. of Budget & Fund Mgmt.
Dept. of Finance & Administration
P.O. Box 139
Jackson, MS 39205
Phone: (601) 359-5758
Fax: (601) 359-6758

MISSOURI
Mark E. Ward
Deputy Commissioner
Div. of Budget & Planning
Ofc. of Administration
State Capitol, Rm. 124
P.O. Box 809
Jefferson City, MO 65102
Phone: (573) 751-3925
Fax: (573) 526-4811
E-mail: wardm@mail.oa.state.mo.us

MONTANA
David Lewis
Director
Ofc. of Budget & Program Planning
State Capitol, Rm. 236
Helena, MT 59620
Phone: (406) 444-3616
Fax: (406) 444-5529

NEBRASKA
Lori McClurg
Director
Dept. of Adm. Services
P.O. Box 94664
Lincoln, NE 68509-4664
Phone: (402) 471-2331
Fax: (402) 471-4157

NEVADA
John P. Comeaux
Director
Dept. of Administration
Blasdel Bldg., Rm. 200
209 E. Musser St.
Carson City, NV 89701
Phone: (775) 684-0222
Fax: (775) 684-0260

NEW HAMPSHIRE
Jeffrey Taylor
Director
Ofc. of State Planning, Executive Dept.
Governor's Recycling Program
2 1/2 Beacon St.
Concord, NH 03301-4497
Phone: (603) 271-2155
Fax: (603) 271-1728

NEW JERSEY
Herbert Simmens
Director
Ofc. of State Planning
Dept. of the Treasury
P.O. Box 204
Trenton, NJ 08625-0204
Phone: (609) 292-7156

NEW MEXICO

NEW YORK
Charles A. Gargano
Commissioner
Dept. of Economic Dev.
One Commerce Plz., 9th Fl.
Albany, NY 12245
Phone: (518) 474-4100
Fax: (518) 473-9374

NORTH CAROLINA
Sheron K. Morgan
State Planning Officer
Ofc. of State Planning
116 W. Jones St.
Raleigh, NC 27603
Phone: (919) 733-4131
Fax: (919) 715-3562

NORTH DAKOTA

NORTHERN MARIANA ISLANDS
Mike Malone
Special Assistant
Ofc. of the Governor
Caller Box 10007
Saipan, MP 96950-8907
Phone: (670) 664-2200
Fax: (670) 664-2211

OHIO
Tom Johnson
Director
Ofc. of Budget & Mgmt.
30 E. Broad St., 34th Fl.
Columbus, OH 43266
Phone: (614) 752-2577
Fax: (614) 466-5400

OKLAHOMA

OREGON
Richard Benner
Director
Dept. of Land Conservation & Dev.
1175 Court St., NE
Salem, OR 97310
Phone: (503) 373-0050
Fax: (503) 362-6705

PENNSYLVANIA
Charles Zogby
Director
Governor's Policy Ofc.
Ofc. of the Governor
Main Capitol Bldg., Rm. 238
Harrisburg, PA 17120
Phone: (717) 772-9005
Fax: (717) 787-4590

PUERTO RICO
Norma Burgos Andujar
Secretary of State
Department of State
P.O. Box 3271
San Juan, PR 00902-3271
Phone: (787) 723-4334
Fax: (787) 725-7303

RHODE ISLAND
John O'Brien
Acting Chief
Statewide Planning Program
1 Capitol Hill
Providence, RI 02908
Phone: (401) 222-5772
Fax: (401) 222-2083

SOUTH CAROLINA
Phyllis M. Mayes
Assistant Executive Director
Budget and Control Board
P.O. Box 12444
Columbia, SC 29201
Phone: (803) 737-1390
Fax: (803) 734-2117

SOUTH DAKOTA
Curt Everson
Commissioner
Bur. of Finance & Mgmt.
500 E. Capitol Ave., Rm. 216
Pierre, SD 57501
Phone: (605) 773-3411
Fax: (605) 773-4711

TENNESSEE

TEXAS
Albert Hawkins
Director
Budget & Planning
Ofc. of the Governor
P.O. Box 12428
Austin, TX 78711
Phone: (512) 463-1778
Fax: (512) 463-1880
E-mail: ahawkins@governor.texas.gov

U.S. VIRGIN ISLANDS
Vacant
Assistant Commissioner
Div. of Planning
Dept. of Planning & Natural Resources
Foster's Plz., 396-1 Anna's Retreat
St. Thomas, VI 00802
Phone: (340) 774-3320
Fax: (340) 775-5706

UTAH
Lynne Koga
Director
Ofc. of Planning & Budget
Governor's Ofc.
116 State Capitol
Salt Lake City, UT 84114
Phone: (801) 538-1562
Fax: (801) 538-1547
E-mail: lkoga@gov.state.ut.us

VERMONT

VIRGINIA
Scott D. Pattison
Director
Dept. of Planning & Budget
202 N. 9th St., Rm. 418
Richmond, VA 23219
Phone: (804) 786-5375
Fax: (804) 225-3291

WASHINGTON
Dick Thompson
Director
Ofc. of Financial Mgmt.
300 Insurance Bldg.
P.O. Box 43113
Olympia, WA 98504
Phone: (360) 902-0555
Fax: (360) 664-2832

WEST VIRGINIA
Joseph F. Markus
Cabinet Secretary
Dept. of Administration
State Capitol, Rm. E119
1900 Kanawha Blvd., E.
Charleston, WV 25305
Phone: (304) 558-4331
Fax: (304) 558-2999

WISCONSIN
Richard G. Chandler
Director
Div. of Executive Budget & Finance
Dept. of Administration
101 E. Wilson, 10th Fl.
P.O. Box 7864
Madison, WI 53707
Phone: (608) 266-1035
Fax: (608) 267-0372

WYOMING
Margaret Spearman
Policy Advisor
State Capitol Bldg.
200 W. 24th St.
Cheyenne, WY 82002
Phone: (307) 777-7434
Fax: (307) 632-3909

Post Audit

Audits the accounts of state offices to determine whether financial transactions have been made in conformity with state laws.

ALABAMA
Ronald L. Jones
Chief Examiner
Dept. of Examiners of Public Accounts
50 N. Ripley St., Rm. 3201
Montgomery, AL 36130-2251
Phone: (334) 242-9200
Fax: (334) 242-1775

ALASKA
Pat Davidson
Legislative Auditor
Div. of Legislative Audit
P.O. Box 11300
Juneau, AK 99811-3300
Phone: (907) 465-3830
Fax: (907) 465-2347

AMERICAN SAMOA
Wendell Harwell
Audit Review Officer
Ofc. of the Governor
Pago Pago, AS 96799
Phone: (684) 633-5191

ARIZONA
Douglas Norton
Auditor General
Auditor Gen's. Ofc.
2910 N. 44th St., Ste. 410
Phoenix, AZ 85018
Phone: (602) 553-0333
Fax: (602) 553-0051

ARKANSAS
Charles L. Robinson
Legislative Auditor
Div. of Legislative Audit
State Capitol Bldg., Rm. 172
Little Rock, AR 72201
Phone: (501) 682-1931
Fax: (501) 376-8723

CALIFORNIA
Kurt R. Sjoberg
State Auditor
Bur. of State Audits
555 Capitol Mall, Ste. 300
Sacramento, CA 95814-4503
Phone: (916) 445-0255
Fax: (916) 327-0019

COLORADO
Dave Barba
State Auditor
Ofc. of State Auditor
200 E. 14th Ave., 2nd Fl.
Denver, CO 80203
Phone: (303) 866-2051
Fax: (303) 866-2060

CONNECTICUT
Robert Jaekle
Auditor of Public Accounts
State Capitol, Rm. 114
300 Capitol Ave.
Hartford, CT 06106-1591
Phone: (860) 566-2119

Kevin Johnston
Auditor of Public Accounts
State Capitol, Rm. 116
300 Capitol Ave.
Hartford, CT 06106-1591
Phone: (860) 566-5572

DELAWARE
R. Thomas Wagner, Jr.
State Auditor
Auditor of Accounts
P.O. Box 1401
Dover, DE 19903-1401
Phone: (302) 739-4241
Fax: (302) 739-6707
E-mail: rwagner@legis.state.de.us

DISTRICT OF COLUMBIA
Deborah Nichols
Auditor
717 14th St., NW, Ste. 900
Washington, DC 20005
Phone: (202) 727-3600

FLORIDA
Charles L. Lester
Auditor General
Legislature
P.O. Box 1735
Tallahassee, FL 32302
Phone: (850) 488-5534
Fax: (850) 488-9175

GEORGIA
Claude Vickers
State Auditor
Dept. of Audits & Accounts
254 Washington St., Rm. 214
Atlanta, GA 30334
Phone: (404) 656-2174

GUAM
Robert G.P. Cruz
Public Auditor
Ofc. of the Public Auditor
1208 E. Sunset Blvd., Tiyan
GMF, GU 96921
Phone: (671) 475-0393
Fax: (671) 472-7951

HAWAII
Marion M. Higa
State Auditor
Ofc. of the Auditor
465 S. King St., Rm. 500
Honolulu, HI 96813
Phone: (808) 587-0800
Fax: (808) 587-0830

James Yamamura
Division Head
Div. of Audit
Accounting & General Services Dept.
1151 Punchbowl St.
Honolulu, HI 96813
Phone: (808) 586-0360
Fax: (808) 586-0738

IDAHO
J.D. Williams
State Controller
700 W. State St., 5th Fl.
Boise, ID 83720
Phone: (208) 334-3100

ILLINOIS
William G. Holland
Auditor General
740 E. Ash, Iles Park Plz.
Springfield, IL 62703
Phone: (217) 782-6046
Fax: (217) 785-8222

INDIANA
Charles Johnson, III
State Examiner
IGC-S., Rm. E418
302 W. Washington St.
Indianapolis, IN 46204-2281
Phone: (317) 232-2524
Fax: (317) 232-4711

IOWA
Richard D. Johnson
State Auditor
State Capitol
1007 E. Grand Ave.
Des Moines, IA 50319
Phone: (515) 281-5835
Fax: (515) 242-6134

KANSAS
Barbara J. Hinton
Legislative Post Auditor
Legislative Div. of Post Audit
800 SW Jackson St., Ste. 1200
Topeka, KS 66612-1216
Phone: (785) 296-3792
Fax: (785) 296-4482
E-mail: BarbH@PostAudit#1.ksleg.state.ks.us

KENTUCKY
Edward B. Hatchett, Jr.
Auditor of Public Accounts
Capitol Annex, Rm. 144
Frankfort, KY 40601-3448
Phone: (502) 564-5841
Fax: (502) 564-2912

LOUISIANA
Daniel G. Kyle
Legislative Auditor
Ofc. of Legislative Auditor
P.O. Box 94397
Baton Rouge, LA 70804
Phone: (225) 342-7237

MAINE
Gail M. Chase
State Auditor
State Ofc. Bldg.
66 State House Station
Augusta, ME 04333-0066
Phone: (207) 287-2201

MARYLAND
Bruce A. Myers
Legislative Auditor
Ofc. of Legislative Audits
Assembly
301 W. Preston St., Rm. 1202
Baltimore, MD 21201
Phone: (410) 767-1400
Fax: (410) 333-5210

MASSACHUSETTS
A. Joseph DeNucci
Auditor of Commonwealth
State House, Rm. 229
Boston, MA 02133
Phone: (617) 727-2075
Fax: (617) 727-5891

MICHIGAN
Thomas McTavish
Auditor General
201 N. Washington Sq.
Lansing, MI 48913
Phone: (517) 334-8050

MINNESOTA
Judith H. Dutcher
State Auditor
525 Park St., # 400
St. Paul, MN 55103
Phone: (651) 296-2551
Fax: (651) 296-4755

James R. Nobles
Legislative Auditor
Centennial Bldg., 1st Fl.
658 Cedar St.
St. Paul, MN 55155
Phone: (651) 296-4710
Fax: (651) 296-4712
E-mail: jim.nobles@state.mn.us

MISSISSIPPI
Phil Bryant
State Auditor
P.O. Box 956
Jackson, MS 39205-0956
Phone: (601) 364-2888
Fax: (601) 364-2828

MISSOURI
Claire McCaskill
State Auditor
P.O. Box 869
State Capitol, Rm. 224
Jefferson City, MO 65102
Phone: (573) 751-4824
Fax: (573) 751-6539
E-mail: claire@mail.auditor.state.mo.us

MONTANA
Scott Seacat
Legislative Auditor
Legislative Audit Div.
State Capitol, Rm. 135
1301 E. 6th Ave.
Helena, MT 59620
Phone: (406) 444-3122
Fax: (406) 444-9784

NEBRASKA
Kate Witek
Auditor of Public Accounts
State Capitol, Ste. 2303
Lincoln, NE 68509
Phone: (402) 471-2111
Fax: (402) 471-3301

NEVADA
William Gary Crews
Legislative Auditor
Legislative Audit
Legislative Counsel Bur.
401 S. Carson St.
Carson City, NV 89701-4747
Phone: (775) 687-6815
Fax: (775) 687-3948
E-mail: crews@lcb.state.nv.us

NEW HAMPSHIRE
Thomas E. Martin
Comptroller/Director
Div. of Accounting Services
Dept. of Adm. Services
25 Capitol St., Rm. 413
Concord, NH 03301-6312
Phone: (603) 271-3190
Fax: (603) 271-6666

NEW JERSEY
Elizabeth L. Pugh
Director
Ofc. of Mgmt. & Budget
Dept. of Treasury
P.O. Box 221
Trenton, NJ 08625-0221
Phone: (609) 292-6746
Fax: (609) 633-8179

NEW MEXICO
Domingo P. Martinez
State Auditor
2113 Warner St.
Santa Fe, NM 87505-5499
Phone: (505) 827-3500
Fax: (505) 827-3512

NEW YORK
H. Carl McCall
Comptroller
A.E. Smith Ofc. Bldg., 6th Fl.
Albany, NY 12236
Phone: (518) 474-3506
Fax: (518) 473-3004

NORTH CAROLINA
Ralph Campbell
State Auditor
Dept. of State Auditor
300 N. Salisbury St., Rm. 201
Raleigh, NC 27603
Phone: (919) 733-3217
Fax: (919) 733-8443

NORTH DAKOTA
Chester E. Nelson, Jr.
Legislative Budget Analyst/Auditor
Legislative Council
600 E. Blvd. Ave, 2nd Fl.
Bismarck, ND 58505-0360
Phone: (701) 328-2916
Fax: (701) 328-3615
E-mail: cnelson@state.nd.us

Robert R. Peterson
State Auditor
State Auditor's Ofc.
600 E. Blvd. Ave., 3rd Fl.
Bismarck, ND 58505-0060
Phone: (701) 328-2241
Fax: (701) 328-1406
E-mail: rpeterso@state.nd.us

NORTHERN MARIANA ISLANDS
Leo Lawrence LaMotte
Public Auditor
P.O. Box 1399 CTC
Saipan, MP 96950
Phone: (670) 234-6481
Fax: (670) 234-7812
E-mail: opa@mtccnmi.com

OHIO
James Petro
State Auditor
88 E. Broad St., 5th Fl.
Columbus, OH 43266-0040
Phone: (614) 466-4971
Fax: (614) 466-6228

OKLAHOMA
Clifton Scott
State Auditor & Inspector
100 State Capitol
2300 N. Lincoln Blvd.
Oklahoma City, OK 73105
Phone: (405) 521-3495
Fax: (405) 521-3426

OREGON
John Lattimer
Director of Audits
Public Service Bldg.
255 Capitol St., NE,| Ste. 500
Salem, OR 97310
Phone: (503) 986-2255
Fax: (503) 373-6767

PENNSYLVANIA
Robert Casey, Jr.
Auditor General
229 Finance Bldg.
Harrisburg, PA 17120
Phone: (717) 787-2543
Fax: (717) 783-4407

PUERTO RICO
Manuel Diaz-Saldana
Comptroller
P.O. Box 366069
San Juan, PR 00936-6069
Phone: (787) 754-3030
Fax: (787) 751-6768

RHODE ISLAND
Christine M. Albuquerque
Chief of General Audit Section
Ofc. of Accounts & Control
Dept. of Administration
1 Capitol Hill
Providence, RI 02908-5883
Phone: (401) 222-2271

Ernest Almonte
Auditor General
Ofc. of the Auditor Gen.
1145 Main St.
Pawtucket, RI 02860-4807
Phone: (401) 222-2435

SOUTH CAROLINA
Thomas L. Wagner, Jr.
State Auditor
Ofc. of the State Auditor
1401 Main St., Ste. 1200
Columbia, SC 29201
Phone: (803) 253-4160
Fax: (803) 343-0723

SOUTH DAKOTA
Maurice C. Christiansen
Auditor General
Dept. of Legislative Audit
435 S. Chapelle
c/o 500 E. Capitol
Pierre, SD 57501
Phone: (605) 773-3595
Fax: (605) 773-6454

TENNESSEE
John Morgan
Comptroller of the Treasury
State Capitol, 1st Fl.
600 Charlotte
Nashville, TN 37243
Phone: (615) 741-2501
Fax: (615) 741-7328

TEXAS
Lawrence F. Alwin
State Auditor
Ofc. of State Auditor
206 E. 9th St., Ste. 1900
Austin, TX 78711
Phone: (512) 479-4700
Fax: (512) 479-4884

U.S. VIRGIN ISLANDS
Steven G. van Beverhoudt
Inspector General
Bur. of Audit & Control
75 Kronprindsens Gade
St. Thomas, VI 00802
Phone: (340) 774-3388
Fax: (340) 774-6431

UTAH
Auston Johnson
State Auditor
211 State Capitol
Salt Lake City, UT 84114
Phone: (801) 538-1360
Fax: (801) 538-1383
E-mail: ajohnson.saaudit@state.ut.us

VERMONT
Edward S. Flanagan
Auditor of Accounts
132 State St.
Montpelier, VT 05602
Phone: (802) 828-2281
Fax: (802) 802-2198

VIRGINIA
Walter J. Kucharski
Auditor of Public Accounts
Ofc. of the Auditor of Public Accounts
Monroe Bldg., 8th Fl.
101 N. 14th St.
Richmond, VA 23218
Phone: (804) 225-3350
Fax: (804) 225-3357

WASHINGTON
Brian Sonntag
State Auditor
P.O. Box 40021
Olympia, WA 98504-0021
Phone: (360) 902-0370
Fax: (360) 753-0646

WEST VIRGINIA
Thedford Shanklin
Director
Post Audit Div.
Legislative Auditor's Ofc.
Bldg. 5, Rm. 751-A
1900 Kanawha Blvd., E.
Charleston, WV 25305
Phone: (304) 558-2040
Fax: (304) 558-2182

WISCONSIN
Janice L. Mueller
State Auditor
Legislative Audit Bur.
131 W. Wilson St., Rm. 402
Madison, WI 53703-3233
Phone: (608) 266-2818
Fax: (608) 267-0410

WYOMING
Max Maxfield
State Auditor
State Capitol, Rm. 114
200 W. 24th St.
Cheyenne, WY 82002
Phone: (307) 777-7831

Pre-Audit

Approves or determines the legality of a proposed expenditure before payment is made.

ALABAMA
Robert L. Childree
Comptroller
Dept. of Finance
RSA Union, Ste. 220
100 N. Union St.
Montgomery, AL 36130-2602
Phone: (334) 242-7063
Fax: (334) 242-7466

ALASKA

AMERICAN SAMOA
Tifi Ale
Treasurer
Dept. of the Treasury
AS Govt.
Pago Pago, AS 96799
Phone: (684) 633-4155
Fax: (684) 633-4100

ARIZONA
Robert Rocha
State Comptroller
Dept. of Administration
1700 W. Washington, Rm. 290
Phoenix, AZ 85007
Phone: (602) 542-5405
Fax: (602) 542-5749

ARKANSAS
Wally Bates
Manager
Pre-Audit Div.
Dept. of Finance & Administration
P.O. Box 3278
Little Rock, AR 72203
Phone: (501) 682-2242

CALIFORNIA
Kathleen Connell
Controller
300 Capitol Mall, 18th Fl.
P.O. Box 942850
Sacramento, CA 94250
Phone: (916) 445-2636

COLORADO
Arthur L. Barnhart
State Controller
Ofc. of the State Controller
Support Services
1525 Sherman St., Ste. 250
Denver, CO 80203
Phone: (303) 866-3281
Fax: (303) 866-4233

CONNECTICUT
Nancy Wyman
Comptroller
55 Elm St.
Hartford, CT 06106
Phone: (860) 702-3301

DELAWARE
R. Thomas Wagner, Jr.
State Auditor
Auditor of Accounts
P.O. Box 1401
Dover, DE 19903-1401
Phone: (302) 739-4241
Fax: (302) 739-6707
E-mail: rwagner@legis.state.de.us

DISTRICT OF COLUMBIA
Valerie Holt
Interim Chief Financial Officer
Ofc. of the Chief Financial Officer
441 4th St., NW, Ste. 1150
Washington, DC 20001
Phone: (202) 727-2476

Jennifer Mumford
Comptroller
Ofc. of Deputy Mayor for Finance
444 4th St.
Washington, DC 20001
Phone: (202) 727-2410

FLORIDA
Larry H. Fuchs
Executive Director
Dept. of Revenue
Carlton Bldg., Rm. 104
5050 W. Tennessee St.
Tallahassee, FL 32399-0100
Phone: (850) 488-5050
Fax: (850) 488-0024

GEORGIA
Claude Vickers
State Auditor
Dept. of Audits & Accounts
254 Washington St., Rm. 214
Atlanta, GA 30334
Phone: (404) 656-2174

GUAM
Joseph E. Rivera
Director
Bur. of Budget & Mgmt. Research
P.O. Box 2950
Hagatna, GU 96932
Phone: (671) 475-9411
Fax: (671) 472-2825

HAWAII
Wayne Horie
Accounting Division Head
Dept. of Accounting & Services
1151 Punchbowl St., Rm. 320
Honolulu, HI 96813
Phone: (808) 586-0600
Fax: (808) 586-0739

IDAHO
J.D. Williams
State Controller
700 W. State St., 5th Fl.
Boise, ID 83720
Phone: (208) 334-3100
Fax: (208) 334-2671

ILLINOIS
Daniel W. Hynes
Comptroller
201 State House
301 S. 2nd St.
Springfield, IL 62706
Phone: (217) 782-6000
Fax: (217) 782-7561

INDIANA
Connie Naas
State Auditor
Ofc. of the State Auditor
State House, Rm. 240
Indianapolis, IN 46204
Phone: (317) 232-3300
Fax: (317) 232-6097

IOWA
Gerald D. Bair
Director
Dept. of Revenue & Finance
Hoover State Ofc. Bldg.
1300 E. Walnut
Des Moines, IA 50319
Phone: (515) 281-3204
Fax: (515) 242-6040

KANSAS
JoAnn Remp
Team Leader, Audit Services
Div. of Accounts & Reports
Dept. of Administration
900 SW Jackson St., Rm. 351-S
Topeka, KS 66612-1248
Phone: (785) 296-3521
Fax: (785) 296-6841

Jerry Serk
Central Account Service Manager
Div. of Accounts & Reports
Dept. of Administration
900 SW Jackson St., Rm. 351-S
Topeka, KS 66612-1248
Phone: (785) 296-3521
Fax: (785) 296-6841

KENTUCKY
John McCarty
Secretary
Finance & Administration Cabinet
Capitol Annex., Rm. 383
Frankfort, KY 40601
Phone: (502) 564-4240
Fax: (502) 564-6785

LOUISIANA
Gene Knecht
Director
Ofc. of Finance & Support
Div. of Administration
P.O. Box 94095
Baton Rouge, LA 70804-9095
Phone: (225) 342-0700
Fax: (225) 342-2606

MAINE
Carol Whitney
Controller
Bur. of Accounts & Control
Dept. of Adm. & Financial Services
14 State House Station
Augusta, ME 04333
Phone: (207) 626-8422

MARYLAND
Patricia Mekeal
Manager
Pre-Audits
Comptroller of the Treasury
Goldstein Treasury Bldg., Rm. 203-E
80 Calvert St.
Annapolis, MD 21404
Phone: (410) 260-7569
E-mail: pmekeal @comp.state.md.us

MASSACHUSETTS
Martin Benison
Comptroller
Executive Ofc. for Administration & Finance
One Ashburton Pl., Rm. 909
Boston, MA 02108
Phone: (617) 727-5000
Fax: (617) 727-2163

MICHIGAN

MINNESOTA
Vacant
Assistant Commissioner
Accounting Services Div.
Dept. of Finance
400 Centennial Bldg.
658 Cedar St.
St. Paul, MN 55155
Phone: (651) 297-2429
Fax: (651) 296-8685

MISSISSIPPI

MISSOURI
James Carder
Director
Ofc. of Administration
Div. of Accounting
Truman Bldg., Rm. 579
P.O. Box 809
Jefferson City, MO 65102
Phone: (573) 751-2971
Fax: (573) 751-0159
E-mail: cardej @mail.oa.state.mo.us

MONTANA

NEBRASKA
Gary Pavel
Administrator
Accounting Div.
Dept. of Adm. Services
1309 State Capitol
P.O. Box 94664
Lincoln, NE 68509
Phone: (402) 471-2581
Fax: (402) 471-4157

NEVADA
John P. Comeaux
Director
Dept. of Administration
Blasdel Bldg., Rm. 200
209 E. Musser St.
Carson City, NV 89701
Phone: (775) 684-0222
Fax: (775) 684-0260

NEW HAMPSHIRE
Thomas E. Martin
Comptroller/Director
Div. of Accounting Services
Dept. of Adm. Services
25 Capitol St., Rm. 413
Concord, NH 03301-6312
Phone: (603) 271-3190
Fax: (603) 271-6666

NEW JERSEY
Elizabeth L. Pugh
Director
Ofc. of Mgmt. & Budget
Dept. of Treasury
P.O. Box 221
Trenton, NJ 08625-0221
Phone: (609) 292-6746
Fax: (609) 633-8179

NEW MEXICO
Anthony I. Armijo
Director/Controller
Financial Control Div.
Dept. of Finance & Administration
180 Bataan Memorial Bldg.
407 Gallastio
Santa Fe, NM 87501
Phone: (505) 827-3689
Fax: (505) 827-4984

NEW YORK
H. Carl McCall
Comptroller
A.E. Smith Ofc. Bldg., 6th Fl.
Albany, NY 12236
Phone: (518) 474-3506
Fax: (518) 473-3004

NORTH CAROLINA
Ralph Campbell
State Auditor
Dept. of State Auditor
300 N. Salisbury St., Rm. 201
Raleigh, NC 27603
Phone: (919) 733-3217
Fax: (919) 733-8443

NORTH DAKOTA
Sheila Peterson
Director
Fiscal Mgmt.
Ofc. of Mgmt. & Budget
600 E. Blvd. Ave., 4th Fl.
Bismarck, ND 58505-0400
Phone: (701) 328-2680
Fax: (701) 328-3230
E-mail: peterson @state.nd.us

NORTHERN MARIANA ISLANDS
Lucia DLG. Neilsen
Secretary of Finance
Finance & Accounting
Dept. of Finance
P.O. Box 5234 CHRB
Saipan, MP 96950
Phone: (670) 664-1198
Fax: (670) 664-1115

OHIO
James Petro
State Auditor
88 E. Broad St., 5th Fl.
Columbus, OH 43266-0040
Phone: (614) 466-4971
Fax: (614) 466-6228

OKLAHOMA
Keith Johnson
State Comptroller
Ofc. of State Finance
Div. of Central Accounting
122 State Capitol
2300 N. Lincoln Blvd.
Oklahoma City, OK 73105
Phone: (405) 521-2141
Fax: (405) 521-3902
E-mail: kjohnson @oklaosf.state.us

OREGON

PENNSYLVANIA
Barbara Hafer
State Treasurer
129 Finance Bldg.
Harrisburg, PA 17120
Phone: (717) 787-2465
Fax: (717) 783-9760

PUERTO RICO

RHODE ISLAND
Lawrence C. Franklin, Jr.
State Controller
Ofc. of Accounts & Control
Dept. of Administration
1 Capitol Hill
Providence, RI 02908-5883
Phone: (401) 222-2271

SOUTH CAROLINA
James A. Lander
Comptroller General
Wade Hampton Ofc. Bldg.
P.O. Box 11228
Columbia, SC 29211
Phone: (803) 734-2121

SOUTH DAKOTA
Vernon L. Larson
State Auditor
Ofc. of State Auditor
State Capitol Bldg.
500 E. Capitol Ave.
Pierre, SD 57501-5070
Phone: (605) 773-3341
Fax: (605) 773-5929

TENNESSEE
Jan Sylvis
Chief of Accounts
Dept. of Finance & Administration
Wm. R. Snodgrass TN Towers, 21st Fl.
Nashville, TN 37243-0293
Phone: (615) 741-2382
Fax: (615) 532-8532

TEXAS
Carole Keeton Rylander
Comptroller
Comptroller of Public Accounts
P.O. Box 13528
Austin, TX 78711-3528
Phone: (512) 463-4000
Fax: (512) 463-4965

U.S. VIRGIN ISLANDS
Bernice Turnbull
Acting Commissioner
Dept. of Finance
76 Kronprindsens Gade
St. Thomas, VI 00802
Phone: (340) 774-4750
Fax: (340) 776-4028

UTAH
Kim Thorne
Director
Div. of Finance
Dept. of Adm. Services
2110 State Ofc. Bldg.
Salt Lake City, UT 84114
Phone: (801) 538-3020
Fax: (801) 538-3244
E-mail: kthorne
@fi.state.ut.us

VERMONT
Thomas Pelham
Commissioner
Agency of Administration
Dept. of Finance & Mgmt.
109 State St.
Montpelier, VT 05609-0401
Phone: (802) 828-2376
Fax: (802) 828-2428
E-mail: tpelham
@fin.state.vt.us

VIRGINIA
William E. Landsidle
Comptroller
Dept. of Accounts
Monroe Bldg., 2nd Fl.
101 N. 14th St.
Richmond, VA 23219
Phone: (804) 225-2109
Fax: (804) 371-8587

WASHINGTON
Michael J. Murphy
State Treasurer
Legislative Bldg.
P.O. Box 40200
Olympia, WA 98504-0200
Phone: (360) 753-7139
Fax: (360) 586-6147
E-mail: MichaelJ
@TRE.WA.GOV

WEST VIRGINIA
Joseph F. Markus
Cabinet Secretary
Dept. of Administration
State Capitol, Rm. E119
1900 Kanawha Blvd., E.
Charleston, WV 25305
Phone: (304) 558-4331
Fax: (304) 558-2999

WISCONSIN
Jim Behrend
Chief
Audit Section
Dept. of Administration
State Controllers Ofc.
P.O. Box 7844
Madison, WI 53707-7844
Phone: (608) 266-1694
Fax: (608) 266-7734

WYOMING
Max Maxfield
State Auditor
State Capitol, Rm. 114
200 W. 24th St.
Cheyenne, WY 82002
Phone: (307) 777-7831

Press Secretary (Governor's)

Individual who handles communications with the public, press conferences and news releases for the Governor.

ALABAMA
Kristin Carvell
Director of Communications
State Capitol
Montgomery, AL 36130
Phone: (334) 242-7150
Fax: (334) 242-4407

ALASKA
Bob King
Press Secretary
P.O. Box 110001
Juneau, AK 99811-0001
Phone: (907) 465-3500
Fax: (907) 465-3533
E-Mail: bob_king@gov.state.ak.us

AMERICAN SAMOA
Rob Shaffer
Public Information Officer
Ofc. of the Governor
Executive Ofc. Bldg.
Pago Pago, AS 96799
Phone: (684) 633-4116
Fax: (684) 633-2269

ARIZONA
Francie Noyes
Deputy Chief of Staff/ Director of Communications
Governor's Ofc.
1700 W. Washington
Phoenix, AZ 85007
Phone: (602) 542-1342
Fax: (602) 542-7601

ARKANSAS
Rex Nelson
Director of Policy & Communications
State Capitol, Rm. 250
Little Rock, AR 72201
Phone: (501) 682-2345
Fax: (501) 682-3597

CALIFORNIA
Sean Walsh
Press Secretary
State Capitol
Sacramento, CA 95814
Phone: (916) 445-4571

COLORADO
Dick Wadhams
Press Secretary
127 State Capitol
Denver, CO 80203
Phone: (303) 866-6324
Fax: (303) 866-6326

CONNECTICUT
Dean Pagani
Director of Communications
State Capitol
Hartford, CT 06106
Phone: (860) 524-7308

DELAWARE
Sheri Woodruff
Governor's Press Secretary
Carvel State Ofc. Bldg.
820 N. French St.
Wilmington, DE 19801
Phone: (302) 577-8711
Fax: (302) 577-3118
E-Mail: swoodruff@state.de.us

DISTRICT OF COLUMBIA
Peggy Armstrong
Press Secretary
Executive Ofc. of the Mayor
441 4th St., NW, Ste. 1160
Washington, DC 20001
Phone: (202) 727-6224
Fax: (202) 727-9561

FLORIDA
April Herrle
Communications Director
State Capitol, Rm. 206
Tallahassee, FL 32399
Phone: (850) 488-5394
Fax: (850) 488-4042

GEORGIA
Howard Mead
Director of Communications
Ofc. of the Governor
100 State Capitol
Atlanta, GA 30334
Phone: (404) 651-7774

GUAM
Ginger M. Cruz
Director of Communications
Executive Chamber
P.O. Box 2950
Hagatna, GU 96932
Phone: (671) 472-8931

HAWAII
Kathleen Racuya-Markrich
Press Secretary
State Capitol
Honolulu, HI 96813
Phone: (808) 586-0034
Fax: (808) 586-0006

IDAHO
Lindsay Nothern
Communications Director
State Capitol
Boise, ID 83720-1000
Phone: (208) 334-2249

ILLINOIS
Dave Urbanek
Press Secretary
Ofc. of the Governor
205 State House
302 S. 2nd St.
Springfield, IL 62706
Phone: (217) 782-7355
Fax: (217) 524-1676

INDIANA
Phil Bremen
Press Secretary
Ofc. of the Governor
State House, Rm. 206
Indianapolis, IN 46204
Phone: (317) 232-4578
Fax: (317) 233-3378

IOWA
Eric Woolson
Press Secretary
State Capitol
Des Moines, IA 50319
Phone: (515) 281-3150
Fax: (515) 281-6611

KANSAS
Mike Matson
Communications Director
State Capitol, 2nd Fl.
Topeka, KS 66612-1590
Phone: (785) 291-3206

KENTUCKY
Melissa Forsythe
Communications Director
State Capitol
Frankfort, KY 40601
Phone: (502) 564-2611
Fax: (502) 564-8154
E-Mail: mforsythe@mail.state.ky.us

LOUISIANA
Marsanne Golsby
Press Secretary
State Capitol
P.O. Box 94004
Baton Rouge, LA 70804
Phone: (225) 342-9037
Fax: (225) 342-6003

MAINE
Dennis Bailey
Director of Communications
1 State House Station
Augusta, ME 04333
Phone: (207) 287-3531
Fax: (207) 287-1034

MARYLAND
Ray Feldmann
Press Secretary
Communications Ofc.
Executive Dept.
State House
Annapolis, MD 21401
Phone: (410) 974-2316
Fax: (410) 974-2542
E-Mail: rfeldmann@gov.state.md.us

MASSACHUSETTS
Ilene Hoffer
Press Secretary
Press Ofc. of the Governor
State House, Rm. 265
Boston, MA 02133
Phone: (617) 727-2759
Fax: (617) 727-9416

MICHIGAN
John Truscott
Director of Communications
P.O. Box 30013
Lansing, MI 48909
Phone: (517) 335-6397

MINNESOTA
John Wodele
Communications Director
130 State Capitol
St. Paul, MN 55155
Phone: (651) 296-0001
Fax: (651) 296-0056
E-Mail: john.wodele@state.mn.us

MISSISSIPPI
Robbie Wilbur
Press Secretary
P.O. Box 139
Jackson, MS 39205
Phone: (601) 359-3111
Fax: (601) 359-2347
E-Mail: rwilbur@govoff.state.ms.us

MISSOURI
Chris Sifford
Director of Communications
Ofc. of the Governor
State Capitol
P.O. Box 720
Jefferson City, MO 65102-0720
Phone: (573) 751-4108
Fax: (573) 751-4458
E-Mail: siffoc@mail.gov.state.mo.us

MONTANA
Andrew Malcolm
Communications Director
Governor's Ofc.
State Capitol
Helena, MT 59620
Phone: (406) 444-3111
Fax: (406) 444-5529

NEBRASKA
Chris Peterson
Director of Media Relations
P.O. Box 94848
Lincoln, NE 68509
Phone: (402) 471-2244
Fax: (402) 471-6031

NEVADA
Jack Finn
Press Secretary
Ofc. of the Governor
101 N. Carson St.
Carson City, NV 89701
Phone: (775) 684-5670
Fax: (775) 684-5684

NEW HAMPSHIRE
Brian Murphy
Press Secretary
Ofc. of the Governor
Executive Dept.
107 N. Main St., Rm. 208-214
Concord, NH 03301
Phone: (603) 271-2121

NEW JERSEY
Peter J. McDonough
Press Secretary
Governor's Ofc.
State House
P.O. Box 001
Trenton, NJ 08625-0001
Phone: (609) 777-2598

NEW MEXICO
Diane Kinderwater
Press Secretary
Ofc. of the Governor
State Capitol Bldg., Rm. 400
Santa Fe, NM 87503
Phone: (505) 827-3000
Fax: (505) 827-3026
E-Mail: kinderwd@gov.state.nm.us

NEW YORK
Zenia Mucha
Director of Communications
State Capitol
Albany, NY 12224
Phone: (518) 474-8418

NORTH CAROLINA
Sean Walsh
Director
Press Ofc.
Ofc. of the Governor
State Capitol
16 W. Jones St.
Raleigh, NC 27601-2905
Phone: (919) 733-5612
Fax: (919) 733-5166

NORTH DAKOTA
Julie Liffrig
Communications Director
Ofc. of the Governor
600 E. Blvd. Ave.
Bismarck, ND 58505-0001
Phone: (701) 328-2200
Fax: (701) 328-2205
E-Mail: governor@state.nd.us

NORTHERN MARIANA ISLANDS
Mark Broadhurst
Public Information & Protocol Officer
Caller Box 10007
Saipan, MP 96950
Phone: (670) 664-2276
E-Mail: gov.pio@saipan.com

OHIO
Scott Milburn
Press Secretary
77 S. High St., 30th Fl.
Columbus, OH 43266-0601
Phone: (614) 644-0957
Fax: (614) 644-0951

OKLAHOMA
Dan Mahoney
Director of Communications
State Capitol, Ste. 212
Oklahoma City, OK 73105
Phone: (405) 523-4219
Fax: (405) 521-3317

OREGON
Bob Applegate
Communications Director
State Capitol
Salem, OR 97310-4789
Phone: (503) 378-6496
Fax: (503) 378-8970

PENNSYLVANIA
Tim Reeves
Director of Communications
Press Ofc.
Main Capitol Bldg., Rm. 308
Harrisburg, PA 17120
Phone: (717) 783-1116

PUERTO RICO
Pedro Rosario Urdaz
Press Secretary
La Fortaleza
San Juan, PR 00901
Phone: (787) 721-7000
Fax: (787) 723-8191

RHODE ISLAND
Lisa Pelosi
Communications Director
Ofc. of the Governor
State House
Providence, RI 02903
Phone: (401) 222-2080
Fax: (401) 861-5894

SOUTH CAROLINA
Nina Brook
Press Secretary
P.O. Box 11829
Columbia, SC 29211
Phone: (803) 734-9400

SOUTH DAKOTA
Bob Mercer
Press Secretary
Governor's Ofc.
500 E. Capitol Ave.
Pierre, SD 57501
Phone: (605) 773-3212
Fax: (605) 773-6115

TENNESSEE
Beth Fortune
Press Secretary
State Capitol, Rm. G-9
Nashville, TN 37243-0001
Phone: (615) 741-3763
Fax: (615) 741-1416

TEXAS
Linda Edwards
Director, Communications
Ofc. of the Governor
P.O. Box 12428
Austin, TX 78711
Phone: (512) 463-1826
Fax: (512) 463-1849

U.S. VIRGIN ISLANDS
James O'Brayan
Senior Public Relations Officer
Govt. House
Charlotte Amalie
St. Thomas, VI 00802
Phone: (340) 774-0294
Fax: (340) 774-4988

UTAH
Vicki Varela
Deputy for Communications
Governor's Ofc.
210 State Capitol
Salt Lake City, UT 84114
Phone: (801) 538-1000
Fax: (801) 538-1528
E-Mail: vvarela@gov.state.ut.us

VERMONT
Susan Allen
Press Secretary
109 State St.
Montpelier, VT 05609
Phone: (802) 828-3333
Fax: (802) 828-3339

VIRGINIA
Mark Miner
Press Secretary
State Capitol
Richmond, VA 23219
Phone: (804) 692-3110
Fax: (804) 692-0121

WASHINGTON
Keith Love
Communications Director
Ofc. of the Governor
Legislative Bldg.
P.O. Box 40002
Olympia, WA 98504
Phone: (360) 902-4111
Fax: (360) 753-4110

WEST VIRGINIA
Rod Blackstone
Press Secretary
Ofc. of the Governor
1900 Kanawha Blvd., E.
Charleston, WV 25305
Phone: (304) 558-2000
Fax: (304) 558-2722

WISCONSIN
Darrin Schmitz
Press Secretary
State Capitol
P.O. Box 7863
Madison, WI 53707
Phone: (608) 266-1212
Fax: (608) 266-3970

WYOMING
Eric Curry
Press Secretary
Governor's Ofc.
State Capitol, Rm. 124
Cheyenne, WY 82002
Phone: (307) 777-7437
Fax: (307) 631-3909
E-Mail: ecurry
@missc.state.wy.us

Printing

Central state entity responsible for fulfilling the printing needs of state government.

ALABAMA
Gerald W. Wilson
Director
Div. of Printing & Publishing
Dept. of Finance
660 Chisholm St.
Montgomery, AL 36130-2606
Phone: (334) 242-2808
Fax: (334) 265-7974

ALASKA
Marsha Hubbard
Director
Div. of Services & Supply
Dept. of Administration
P.O. Box 110210
Juneau, AK 99811
Phone: (907) 465-2250
Fax: (907) 465-2189

AMERICAN SAMOA
Eliu Paopao
Acting Director
Dept. of Adm. Services
AS Govt.
Pago Pago, AS 96799
Phone: (684) 633-4156
Fax: (684) 633-1841

ARIZONA
Tim Boncoskey
Assistant Director
Mgmt. Services Div.
Dept. of Administration
1700 W. Washington, Rm. 250
Phoenix, AZ 85007
Phone: (602) 542-0495

ARKANSAS
Edward Erxleben
Administrator
Ofc. of State Purchasing
Dept. of Finance & Administration
P.O. Box 2940
Little Rock, AR 72203
Phone: (501) 324-9312
Fax: (501) 324-9311

CALIFORNIA
Celeste M. Cron
State Printer
Ofc. of State Printing
344 N. 7th St.
Sacramento, CA 95814
Phone: (916) 445-9110

COLORADO
Marc Wilkerson
Printing Plant Supervisor
Print Shop
Central Services Div.
1001 E. 62nd Ave.
Denver, CO 80216
Phone: (303) 287-8057
Fax: (303) 287-1926

CONNECTICUT
Roy Dion
Director
Div. of Printing & Mailing Services
Dept. of Adm. Services
165 Capitol Ave., Rm. 491
Hartford, CT 06106
Phone: (860) 713-5100

DELAWARE
Patrick T. Coates, Sr.
Director
Div. of Support Operations
820 Silver Lake Blvd., #100
Dover, DE 19904-2464
Phone: (302) 739-5371
Fax: (302) 739-3492

DISTRICT OF COLUMBIA
Freeman M. Murray
Chief
Printing Div.
Dept. of Adm. Services
809 Channing Pl., NE
Washington, DC 20018
Phone: (202) 576-6692

FLORIDA
George C. Banks
Director
Div. of Purchasing
Dept. of Mgmt. Services
4050 Esplanade Way
Tallahassee, FL 32399-0950
Phone: (850) 488-7303
Fax: (850) 921-5979

GEORGIA
Dotty W. Roach
Commissioner
Dept. of Adm. Services
200 Piedmont Ave., Ste. 1804
Atlanta, GA 30334-5500
Phone: (404) 656-5514
Fax: (404) 651-9595

GUAM

HAWAII
Marilyn McAuley
Corrections Industries Administrator
State Corrections Industries
Dept. of Public Safety
99-902 Moanalua Rd.
Aiea, HI 96701
Phone: (808) 486-2600
Fax: (808) 488-4999

IDAHO
Bobbi Eckerle
Chief
Records Mgmt. & Printing Services
5569 Kendall Ctr.
Boise, ID 83720
Phone: (208) 327-7471

ILLINOIS
Nicholas Whitlow
Superintendent
Div. of Contract Printing
Dept. of Central Mgmt. Services
1920 S. 10 1/2 St.
Springfield, IL 62703-3293
Phone: (217) 782-4561
Fax: (217) 785-1229

INDIANA
F. Gerald Handfield, Jr.
Director
Comm. on Public Records
402 W. Washington, Rm. W472
Indianapolis, IN 46204
Phone: (317) 232-3373
Fax: (317) 233-1713

IOWA
Bill Bruce
Administrator
Micrographics & Imaging
Dept. of Services
Grimes State Ofc. Bldg.
Des Moines, IA 50319
Phone: (515) 281-5231
Fax: (515) 242-6307

KANSAS
Richard Gonzales
Director
Div. of Printing
Dept. of Administration
201 NW MacVicar
Topeka, KS 66606-2499
Phone: (785) 296-3631

KENTUCKY
Pam Burns
Director
Finance & Administration Cabinet
Div. of Printing
300 Myrtle Ave.
Frankfort, KY 40601
Phone: (502) 564-2670
Fax: (502) 564-3610

LOUISIANA
Irene Babin
Director
Property Assistance Agency
Div. of Administration
P.O. Box 94095
Baton Rouge, LA 70804-9095
Phone: (225) 342-6890
Fax: (225) 342-6891

MAINE
Richard Thompson
Director
Div. of Public Printing
9 State House Station
Augusta, ME 04333
Phone: (207) 287-3521

MARYLAND
Robert F. Cheeks
Assistant Secretary
Ofc. of Procurement & Logistics
Dept. of Services
301 W. Preston St., Rm. 1400
Baltimore, MD 21201
Phone: (410) 767-4440
Fax: (410) 333-5730

MASSACHUSETTS
Ed Goba
Manager
Central Reproduction Ofc.
One Ashburton Pl.
Boston, MA 02108
Phone: (617) 727-7500

MICHIGAN
Mark Armbrustmacher
Manager
Reproduction Services Section
Ofc. Services Div.
7461 Crowner Dr.
Lansing, MI 48913
Phone: (517) 322-1889

MINNESOTA
Mary Mikes
Director
Communications Media Div.
Dept. of Administration
117 Univ. Ave., Rm. 128A
St. Paul, MN 55155
Phone: (651) 297-3979
Fax: (651) 215-5733
E-mail: mary.mikes@state.mn.us

MISSISSIPPI

MISSOURI
Gary Judd
Printing Services Manager
State Printing Ctr.
Div. of Services
Ofc. of Administration
2733 Merchants Dr.
Jefferson City, MO 65109
Phone: (573) 751-3307
Fax: (573) 526-7900
E-mail: juddg@mail.oa.state.mo.us

MONTANA
Gary Wolf
Bureau Chief
Publications & Graphics Bur.
Dept. of Administration
920 Front St.
Helena, MT 59620
Phone: (406) 444-3881
Fax: (406) 443-2212

NEBRASKA
Doni Peterson
Acting Administrator
Material Div.
Dept. of Adm. Services
301 Centennial Mall, S.
P.O. Box 94847
Lincoln, NE 68509
Phone: (402) 471-8295

NEVADA
Donald L. Bailey, Sr.
State Printer
Printing Div.
Dept. of Administration
301 S. Stewart St.
Carson City, NV 89701
Phone: (775) 687-4860
Fax: (775) 687-6951

NEW HAMPSHIRE
James Dufour
Administrator
Bur. of Graphic Services
Adm. Services
12 Hills Ave.
Concord, NH 03301-4842
Phone: (603) 271-3205
Fax: (603) 271-1949

NEW JERSEY
George Davis
Procurement Supervisor
Purchase Bur.
Div. of Purchasing Property
33 W. State St.
P.O. Box 230
Trenton, NJ 08625-0230
Phone: (609) 984-6234
Fax: (609) 292-0490

NEW MEXICO
Millie Miller
State Printer
State Printing Service Dept.
2641 Siringo Rd.
Santa Fe, NM 87505
Phone: (505) 827-6277
Fax: (505) 827-6276

NEW YORK
Brian Moody
Director
Central Printing & Copy Ctr.
Ofc. of Service
Bldg. 18
1220 Washington Ave.
Albany, NY 12226
Phone: (518) 457-6593
Fax: (518) 457-3081

NORTH CAROLINA

NORTH DAKOTA
Jim Kapp
Printing Manager
Central Duplicating Services
600 E. Blvd. Ave., Basement - Judicial Wing
Bismarck, ND 58505-0420
Phone: (701) 328-2772
Fax: (701) 328-1615
E-mail: csd@state.nd.us

NORTHERN MARIANA ISLANDS

OHIO
Joe Tucker
Administrator
Services Div., Ofc. of State Printing
Dept. of Adm. Services
4200 Surface Rd.
Columbus, OH 43228-1395
Phone: (614) 466-8334
Fax: (614) 644-5799

OKLAHOMA
Gerlinde Williams
Administrator
Central Printing Div.
2120 NE 36th St.
Oklahoma City, OK 73111
Phone: (405) 425-2714
Fax: (405) 425-2717
E-mail: Gerlinde_Williams@dcs.state.ok.us

OREGON
Mike Freese
State Printer
Printing Plant
Dept. of Adm. Services
550 Airport Rd., SE
Salem, OR 97310
Phone: (503) 378-3397
Fax: (503) 373-7789

PENNSYLVANIA
Donald Gibas
Director
Bur. of Public & Paperwork Mgmt.
Dept. of General Services
1825 Stanley Dr.
Harrisburg, PA 17103
Phone: (717) 787-3707
Fax: (717) 787-6379

PUERTO RICO
Maria T. Mujica
Administrator
Services Administration
P.O. Box 7428
San Juan, PR 00916
Phone: (787) 724-1064
Fax: (787) 722-7965

RHODE ISLAND

SOUTH CAROLINA
Bunyan M. Cave
State Printing Officer
Info. Technology Mgmt. Ofc.
Div. of Services
1201 Main St., Ste. 600
Columbia, SC 29201
Phone: (803) 737-0629

SOUTH DAKOTA
Gloria Schultz
Director
Div. of Central Duplicating
Dept. of Administration
500 E. Capitol Ave.
Pierre, SD 57501
Phone: (605) 773-3614
Fax: (605) 773-3837

TENNESSEE
Leroy Richmond
Director of Printing
Dept. of Services
Andrew Jackson Bldg.
Nashville, TN 37243-0450
Phone: (615) 741-1726
Fax: (615) 532-2311

TEXAS
Frank Mays
Director
Support Services
Services Comm.
1711 San Jacinto
Austin, TX 78701
Phone: (512) 463-3208
Fax: (512) 474-5830

U.S. VIRGIN ISLANDS
Lawrence Ottley
Director of Printing
Dept. of Property & Procurement
Sub Base Bldg. 1
St. Thomas, VI 00802
Phone: (340) 774-0828
Fax: (340) 774-9704

UTAH
Mark Shaw
Director
Legislative Printing Ofc.
419 State Capitol
Salt Lake City, UT 84114-0107
Phone: (801) 538-1103
Fax: (801) 538-1728
E-mail: mshaw@le.state.ut.us

VERMONT

VIRGINIA
Donald C. Williams
Director
Dept. of Services
202 N. 9th St., Ste. 209
Richmond, VA 23219
Phone: (804) 786-3311
Fax: (804) 371-8305

WASHINGTON
George Morton
Public Printer
Dept. of Printing
P.O. Box 47100
Olympia, WA 98504-0002
Phone: (360) 753-6820
Fax: (360) 586-8444

WEST VIRGINIA
Scott Padon
Assistant Director
Operations Section
Div. of Purchasing
212 California Ave.
Charleston, WV 25305
Phone: (304) 558-3259
Fax: (304) 558-2137

WISCONSIN
Andrea Konik
Assistant Bureau Director
Div. of Integrated Documented Services
Dept. of Administration
202 S. Thornton
P.O. Box 7840
Madison, WI 53703
Phone: (608) 266-9327
Fax: (608) 267-6933

WYOMING
Jeff Stuart
Manager
Copy Masters
Dept. of Administration & Info.
706 W. 18th St.
Cheyenne, WY 82002
Phone: (307) 777-7527
Fax: (307) 777-7658

Public Broadcasting

Controls and supervises the use of television airwaves, assigned for non-commercial, educational use.

ALABAMA
Judy Stone
Executive Director
Educational Television Comm.
2112 11th Ave., S., Ste. 400
Birmingham, AL 35205-2884
Phone: (205) 328-8756
Fax: (205) 251-2192

ALASKA
Mark Badger
Chief Technical Officer
Public Broadcasting Comm.
Dept. of Administration
P.O. Box 110223
Juneau, AK 99811-0223
Phone: (907) 465-2200
Fax: (907) 465-3450

AMERICAN SAMOA
Vaoita M. Savali
Director
Ofc. of Public Info.
Pago Pago, AS 96799
Phone: (684) 633-4191
Fax: (684) 633-1044

ARIZONA

ARKANSAS
Susan Howarth
Director
Educational Television Comm.
Dept. of Education
350 S. Donaghey St.
Conway, AR 72032
Phone: (501) 682-2386
Fax: (501) 682-4122

CALIFORNIA

COLORADO
Art Ellis
Assistant Commissioner
Educational Telecoms.
Ofc. of Educational Services/Dept. of Education
201 E. Colfax Ave., Rm. 206
Denver, CO 80203
Phone: (303) 866-6859

CONNECTICUT
Joan S. Briggaman
Assistant Superintendent
Instruction and Professional Dev.
165 Capitol Ave.
Hartford, CT 06106
Phone: (860) 566-8113

DELAWARE

DISTRICT OF COLUMBIA
James Brown
Executive Director
Ofc. of Cable Television
2217 14th St., NW
Washington, DC 20009
Phone: (202) 727-0424

FLORIDA
Eric C. Smith
Director
Ofc. of Telecoms.
Dept. of Education
325 W. Gaines St., Ste. 154
Tallahassee, FL 32399-0400
Phone: (850) 488-0940
Fax: (850) 487-8505

GEORGIA
Werner Rogers
Executive Director
Public Telecom. Comm.
260 14th St., NW
Atlanta, GA 30318-5360
Phone: (404) 685-2400

GUAM
Geraldine Underwood
General Manager
Educational Telecoms. Corp.
P.O. Box 21449
GMF, GU 96921
Phone: (671) 734-2207
Fax: (671) 734-5483
E-mail: kgtfl2@ite.net

HAWAII
Sheldon Robbs
Executive Director
Public Broadcasting Authority
Commerce & Consumer Affairs Dept.
2350 Dole St.
Honolulu, HI 96822
Phone: (808) 973-1999
Fax: (808) 973-1090

IDAHO
Peter Morrill
General Manager
Educational Public Broadcasting
State Board of Education
1910 Univ. Dr.
Boise, ID 83725
Phone: (208) 385-3727

ILLINOIS
Glenn W. McGee
Superintendent
State Board of Education
100 N. 1st St.
Springfield, IL 62777
Phone: (217) 782-2221
Fax: (217) 785-3972

INDIANA

IOWA
David Bolender
Director
State Public Television
P.O. Box 6450
Johnston, IA 50131
Phone: (515) 242-3150
Fax: (515) 242-4113

KANSAS
Bill Reed
Chair
Public Broadcasting Council
900 SW Jackson, Ste. 751
Topeka, KS 66612-1275
Phone: (785) 296-3463
Fax: (785) 296-1168

KENTUCKY
Virginia G. Fox
Executive Director
Educational Television Authority
600 Cooper Dr.
Lexington, KY 40502
Phone: (606) 233-3000
Fax: (606) 258-7399

LOUISIANA
Beth Courtney
Executive Director
Educational Television Authority
7733 Perkins Rd.
Baton Rouge, LA 70810
Phone: (225) 767-5660
Fax: (225) 767-4288

MAINE

MARYLAND
Robert J. Shuman
President/CEO
Executive Direction & Control
Public Broadcasting Comm.
11767 Owings Mills Blvd.
Owings Mills, MD 21117
Phone: (410) 581-4141
Fax: (410) 581-0980

MASSACHUSETTS

MICHIGAN

MINNESOTA
Larry Freund
Financial Management Director
Commissioner's Ofc.
Dept. of Administration
50 Sherburne Ave., 2nd Fl.
St. Paul, MN 55155
Phone: (651) 296-5857
Fax: (651) 297-7909
E-mail: larry.freund@state.mn.us

MISSISSIPPI
Larry Miller
Executive Director
Educational Television
3825 Ridgewood Rd.
Jackson, MS 39211-6463
Phone: (601) 982-6565
Fax: (601) 982-6311

MISSOURI

MONTANA
Carl Hotvedt
Chief
Telecoms. Operations Bur.
Dept. of Administration
Mitchell Bldg., Rm. 21
125 Roberts
Helena, MT 59620
Phone: (406) 444-1780
Fax: (406) 444-5545

NEBRASKA
Larue Wunderlich
Chair
Educational Telecom.
1800 N. 33rd St.
P.O. Box 83111
Lincoln, NE 68501
Phone: (402) 472-3611
Fax: (402) 472-1785

NEVADA

NEW HAMPSHIRE

NEW JERSEY
Elizabeth Christopherson
Executive Director
Public Broadcasting Authority
Dept. of Commerce & Economic Dev.
25 S. Stockton St.
P.O. Box 777
Trenton, NJ 08625-0777
Phone: (609) 777-5000
Fax: (609) 633-2912

NEW MEXICO
Jon H. Cooper
Chair
Comm. of Public Broadcasting
c/o KNME, 1130 Univ. Blvd., NE
Albuquerque, NM 87102
Phone: (505) 277-2121
Fax: (505) 277-2191

NEW YORK
Richard P. Mills
Commissioner
State Education Dept.
89 Washington Ave., Rm. 111
Albany, NY 12234
Phone: (518) 474-6569
Fax: (518) 473-4909

NORTH CAROLINA
Tom Howe
General Director
Public Television
P.O. Box 14900
Research Triangle Park, NC 27709-4900
Phone: (919) 549-7000
Fax: (919) 549-7201

NORTH DAKOTA
Joe Linnertz
Staff Director
TelecoCouncil
Dept. of Public Instruction
600 E. Blvd. Ave., 11th Fl.
Bismarck, ND 58505-0440
Phone: (701) 328-2278
Fax: (701) 328-2461
E-mail: jlinnert@mail.dpi.state.nd.us

NORTHERN MARIANA ISLANDS
Timothy P. Villagomez
Executive Director
Commonwealth Utilities Corp.
Ofc. of the Governor
Lower Base
P.O. Box 1220
Saipan, MP 96950
Phone: (670) 322-5088
Fax: (670) 322-4323
E-mail: cuc.edp@mtccnmi.com

OHIO
Dave L. Fornshell
Executive Director
Educational Telecom. Network Comm.
2470 N. Star Rd.
Columbus, OH 43221
Phone: (614) 644-1714
Fax: (614) 644-3112

OKLAHOMA
Mac Wall
Executive Director
Educational Television Authority
7403 N. Kelly
Oklahoma City, OK 73111
Phone: (405) 848-8501
Fax: (405) 841-9216

OREGON

PENNSYLVANIA
H. Sheldon Parker, Jr.
General Manager
Public Television Network Comm.
24 Northeast Dr.
Hershey, PA 17033
Phone: (717) 533-6010
Fax: (717) 533-4326

PUERTO RICO
Jorge Inserni
General Administrator
Corp. for Public Broadcasting
P.O. Box 909
Hato Rey, PR 00919
Phone: (787) 766-0272
Fax: (787) 753-9846

RHODE ISLAND
Susan L. Farmer
General Manager
WSBE-TV Channel 36
Dept. of Education
50 Park Ln.
Providence, RI 02907-3124
Phone: (401) 222-3636

SOUTH CAROLINA
Paul Amos
President
Educational Television Network
1101 George Rogers Blvd.
Columbia, SC 29201
Phone: (803) 737-3240

SOUTH DAKOTA
Julie Andersen
Director
Public Broadcasting
Cherry & Dakota St.
P.O. Box 5000
Vermillion, SD 57069-5000
Phone: (605) 677-6419
Fax: (605) 677-5010

TENNESSEE

TEXAS
Anita Givens
Senior Director, Instructional Technology
Div. of Education Technology
State Education Agency
1701 N. Congress Ave.
Austin, TX 78701
Phone: (512) 463-9400

U.S. VIRGIN ISLANDS
Lorrie Elskoe
General Manager
Public Television Systems Board
P.O. Box 7879
St. Thomas, VI 00801
Phone: (340) 774-6255
Fax: (340) 774-7092

UTAH
Cecelia Foxley
Commissioner
Board of Regents
3 Triad Ctr., Ste. 550
Salt Lake City, UT 84180-1205
Phone: (801) 321-7103
Fax: (801) 321-7199
E-mail: cfoxley@utahshr.edu

VERMONT
John King
Station Manager
State Educational Television
Univ. of VT
88 Ethan Allen Ave.
Colchester, VT 05446
Phone: (802) 655-4800

VIRGINIA
G. Bryan Slater
Secretary of Administration
Governor's Cabinet
202 N. 9th St., Ste. 633
Richmond, VA 23219
Phone: (804) 786-1201
Fax: (804) 371-0038

WASHINGTON
Gayle Pauley
Learning Resources Supervisor
Superintendent of Public Instruction
Old Capitol Bldg.
P.O. Box 47200
Olympia, WA 98504-7200
Phone: (360) 753-6723
Fax: (360) 586-2728

WEST VIRGINIA
Rita Ray
Executive Director
Educational Broadcasting Authority
600 Capitol St.
Charleston, WV 25301
Phone: (304) 558-3400
Fax: (304) 558-1561

WISCONSIN
Thomas L. Fletemeyer
Executive Director
Television Network Programs & Operations
Educational Communications Board
3319 W. Beltline Hwy.
Madison, WI 53713
Phone: (608) 264-9600
Fax: (608) 264-9664

WYOMING
Tom Engbretson
Administrator
Div. of Telecom.
Dept. of Administration & Info.
Emerson Bldg.
2001 Capitol Ave.
Cheyenne, WY 82002
Phone: (307) 777-6410

Public Defender

Represents indigent criminal defendants who desire to appeal their convictions to the state's intermediate appellate court or court of last resort.

ALABAMA

ALASKA
Barbara Brink
Director
Public Defender Agency
Dept. of Administration
900 W. 5th Ave., Ste. 200
Anchorage, AK 99501-2090
Phone: (907) 264-4400
Fax: (907) 269-5476

AMERICAN SAMOA
Reginald Gates
Public Defender
Ofc. of Public Defender
Pago Pago, AS 96799
Phone: (684) 633-1286
Fax: (684) 633-4745

ARIZONA

ARKANSAS
Didi Sallings
Director
Public Defender Comm.
101 E. Capitol, Ste. 201
Little Rock, AR 72201
Phone: (501) 682-9070
Fax: (501) 682-9073

CALIFORNIA
Fern M. Laethem
State Public Defender
801 K St., Ste. 1000
Sacramento, CA 95814
Phone: (916) 322-2676

COLORADO
David F. Vela
State Public Defender
Judicial Dept.
110 16th St., Rm. 1300
Denver, CO 80202
Phone: (303) 620-4888
Fax: (303) 620-4931

CONNECTICUT
Gerard Smyth
Chief Public Defender
Ofc. of Chief Public Defender
1 Hartford Sq., W.
Hartford, CT 06106
Phone: (860) 509-6429

DELAWARE
Lawrence Sullivan
Public Defender
Carvel State Ofc. Bldg.
820 N. French St.
Wilmington, DE 19801
Phone: (302) 577-3230
Fax: (302) 577-3995

DISTRICT OF COLUMBIA
Jo Ann Wallace
Director
Public Defender Service
451 Indiana Ave., NW, Rm. 219
Washington, DC 20001
Phone: (202) 628-1200

FLORIDA
Sheldon Gusky
Executive Director
Public Defender Ofc.
311 S. Calhoun St., Ste. 204
Tallahassee, FL 32301
Phone: (850) 488-6850
Fax: (850) 488-4720

GEORGIA
Thurbert E. Baker
Attorney General
40 Capitol Sq., SW
Atlanta, GA 30334-1300
Phone: (404) 656-3300
Fax: (404) 657-8733

GUAM
Harold F. Parker
Director
Public Defender Services Corp.
200 Judicial Ctr. Annex
110 W. O'Brien Dr.
Hagatna, GU 96910
Phone: (671) 475-3100
Fax: (671) 477-5844

HAWAII
Richard Pollack
Public Defender
Ofc. of Public Defender
Dept. of Budget & Finance
1130 N. Nimitz Hwy., # A 135
Honolulu, HI 96817
Phone: (808) 586-2200
Fax: (808) 586-2222

IDAHO

ILLINOIS
Ted Gottfried
State Appellate Defender
400 S. 9th St., # 201
Springfield, IL 62701-1908
Phone: (217) 782-7203

INDIANA
Susan K. Carpenter
Public Defender
Ofc. of Public Defender
1 N. Capitol Ave., Ste. 800
Indianapolis, IN 46204-2026
Phone: (317) 232-2475
Fax: (317) 232-2307

IOWA
William Wegman
Appellate Defender
Dept. of Inspections & Appeals
Lucas State Ofc. Bldg.
321 E. 12th St.
Des Moines, IA 50319
Phone: (515) 281-8841

KANSAS
Patricia A. Scalia
Executive Director
Board of Indigent's Defense Services
701 SW Jackson St., 3rd Fl.
Topeka, KS 66603-3713
Phone: (785) 296-4505
Fax: (785) 296-7418

KENTUCKY
Erwin Lewis
Public Advocate
Ofc. for Public Advocacy
Public Protection & Regulation Cabinet
Fair Oaks Ln., Ste. 302
Frankfort, KY 40601
Phone: (502) 564-8006

LOUISIANA
Richard P. Ieyoub, Jr.
Attorney General
Dept. of Justice
P.O. Box 94005
Baton Rouge, LA 70804-9005
Phone: (225) 342-7013
Fax: (225) 342-8703

MAINE

MARYLAND
Stephen E. Harris
Public Defender
Public Defender System
William Donald Schaefer Tower
6 St. Paul St., Ste. 1400
Baltimore, MD 21202
Phone: (410) 767-8479
Fax: (410) 333-8496

MASSACHUSETTS
William Leahy
Chief Counsel
Cmte. for Public Counsel Services
470 Atlantic Ave., Ste. 700
Boston, MA 02210
Phone: (617) 482-6212
Fax: (617) 988-8495

MICHIGAN
James Neuhard
State Appellate Defender
Supreme Ct.
3300 Panapscot Bldg.
645 Griswald
Detroit, MI 48226
Phone: (313) 256-9833

MINNESOTA
John Stuart
State Public Defender
2829 Univ. Ave., SE
Minneapolis, MN 55414
Phone: (612) 627-6980
Fax: (612) 627-7979
E-mail: john.stuart@pubdef.state.mn.us

MISSISSIPPI

MISSOURI
J. Marty Robinson
Director
Ofc. of State Public Defender
231 E. Capitol
Jefferson City, MO 65101
Phone: (573) 526-5210
Fax: (573) 526-5213

MONTANA
William Hooks
Attorney
Appellate Defenders Ofc.
Dept. of Administration
P.O. Box 200145
Helena, MT 59620
Phone: (406) 444-4122
Fax: (406) 442-9593

NEBRASKA

NEVADA
Steven G. McGuire
State Public Defender
511 E. Robison St., Ste. 1
Carson City, NV 89701
Phone: (775) 687-4880
Fax: (775) 687-4993

NEW HAMPSHIRE
Michael Skibbie
Executive Director
Public Defender Program
117 N. State St.
Concord, NH 03301
Phone: (603) 224-1236
Fax: (603) 226-4299

NEW JERSEY
Susan L. Reisner
Public Defender
Ofc. of the Public Defender
25 Market St., 2nd Fl., N.
P.O. Box 850
Trenton, NJ 08625
Phone: (609) 292-7087
Fax: (609) 599-9114

NEW MEXICO
Phyllis H. Subin
Chief Public Defender
Public Defender Dept.
301 N. Guadalupe St., Ste. 101
Santa Fe, NM 87501-1852
Phone: (505) 827-3931
Fax: (505) 827-3999

NEW YORK
Eliot Spitzer
Attorney General
Dept. of Law
The Capitol, 2nd Fl.
Albany, NY 12224
Phone: (518) 474-7330
Fax: (518) 473-9909

NORTH CAROLINA
Malcolm Ray Hunter, Jr.
Appellate Defender
Ofc. of Appellate Defender
Judicial Branch
123 W. Main St., #600
Durham, NC 27713-2287
Phone: (919) 560-3334
Fax: (919) 560-3288

NORTH DAKOTA

NORTHERN MARIANA ISLANDS
Daniel DeRienzo
Public Defender
Ofc. of the Public Defender
Caller Box 10007
Saipan, MP 96950
Phone: (670) 234-6215
Fax: (670) 234-1009

OHIO
David H. Bodiker
Public Defender
Public Defender Comm.
8 E. Long St.
Columbus, OH 43215
Phone: (614) 466-5394
Fax: (614) 644-9972

OKLAHOMA
James D. Bednar
Executive Director
Appellate Public Defender System
P.O. Box 926
Norman, OK 73070
Phone: (405) 329-4222
Fax: (405) 325-7567

OREGON
David Groom
Public Defender
1320 Capitol St., NE, #200
Salem, OR 97303-6469
Phone: (503) 378-3349
Fax: (503) 375-9701

PENNSYLVANIA

PUERTO RICO

RHODE ISLAND
Stephen Nugent
Public Defender
Ofc. of Public Defender
100 N. Main St., 4th Fl.
Providence, RI 02903
Phone: (401) 222-3492
Fax: (401) 222-3289

SOUTH CAROLINA
Daniel T. Stacey
Chief Attorney
Ofc. of Appellate Defense
1122 Lady St., Ste. 940
Columbia, SC 29201
Phone: (803) 734-1330

SOUTH DAKOTA

TENNESSEE

TEXAS

U.S. VIRGIN ISLANDS
Thurston McKelvin
Federal Public Defender
P.O. Box 3450
Christiansted
St. Croix, VI 00820
Phone: (340) 773-3585
Fax: (340) 773-3742

UTAH

VERMONT
Robert Appel
Defender General
State Ofc. Bldg.
141 Main St.
Montpelier, VT 05620-3301
Phone: (802) 828-3168
Fax: (802) 828-3163

VIRGINIA
Overton P. Pollard
Executive Director
Public Defender Comm.
701 E. Franklin St., # 1416
Richmond, VA 23219
Phone: (804) 225-3297
Fax: (804) 371-8326

WASHINGTON

WEST VIRGINIA
John A. Rogers
Executive Director
Public Defender Services
Public Legal Services Council
1900 Kanawha Blvd., E.
Charleston, WV 25305
Phone: (304) 348-3905
Fax: (304) 558-1098

WISCONSIN
Nicholas Chiarkas
Public Defender
315 N. Henry, 2nd Fl.
Madison, WI 53707
Phone: (608) 266-0087
Fax: (608) 267-0584

WYOMING
Sylvia Hackl
State Public Defender
Ofc. of State Public Defender
2020 Carey Ave., 3rd Fl.
Cheyenne, WY 82002
Phone: (307) 777-6498

Public Lands

Manages state-owned lands.

ALABAMA
James H. Griggs
Director
Div. of Lands
Conservation & Natural Resources
64 N. Union St., Rm. 702
Montgomery, AL 36130-1454
Phone: (334) 242-3484
Fax: (334) 242-0999

ALASKA
John T. Shively
Commissioner
Dept. of Natural Resources
400 Willoughby Ave.
Juneau, AK 99801-1724
Phone: (907) 465-2400
Fax: (907) 465-3886

AMERICAN SAMOA
Sotoa Savali
Secretary
Ofc. of Samoan Affairs
AS Govt.
Pago Pago, AS 96799

ARIZONA
Michael Anable
State Land Commissioner
Dept. of State Land
1616 W. Adams St.
Phoenix, AZ 85007
Phone: (602) 542-4621
Fax: (602) 542-2590

ARKANSAS
Charlie Daniels
State Land Commissioner
State Capitol, Rm. 109
1 Capitol Mall
Little Rock, AR 72201
Phone: (501) 324-9222
Fax: (501) 324-9422

CALIFORNIA
Robert Hight
Executive Officer
State Lands Comm.
100 Howe Ave.
Sacramento, CA 95825-8202
Phone: (916) 574-1800

COLORADO
Max Vezzani
Director
State Board of Land Commissioners
Dept. of Natural Resources
1313 Sherman St., Rm. 620
Denver, CO 80203
Phone: (303) 866-3454
Fax: (303) 866-3152

CONNECTICUT
Charles Reed
Director
Land Acquisition & Mgmt.
Dept. of Environmental Protection
79 Elm St.
Hartford, CT 06106
Phone: (860) 424-3016

DELAWARE
Charles A. Salkin
Director
Div. of Parks & Recreation
Dept. of Natural Resources & Environmental Control
89 Kings Hwy.
Dover, DE 19901
Phone: (302) 739-4401
Fax: (302) 739-3817

DISTRICT OF COLUMBIA
Kenneth Burnette
Acting Administrator
Real Property Administration
441 4th St., NW, Ste. 750
Washington, DC 20001
Phone: (202) 727-9775

FLORIDA
Pete Mallison
Director
Div. of State Lands
Dept. of Environmental Protection
3900 Commonwealth Blvd., MS 100
Tallahassee, FL 32399-3000
Phone: (850) 488-2725
Fax: (850) 922-6009

GEORGIA
Lonice Barrett
Commissioner
Dept. of Natural Resources
Floyd Towers, E.
205 Butler St., SW
Atlanta, GA 30334
Phone: (404) 656-3500

GUAM
Carl J.C. Aguon
Director
Dept. of Land Mgmt.
1 Stop Bldg.
P.O. Box 2950
Anigua-Agana, GU 96932
Phone: (671) 475-5252
Fax: (671) 477-0883

HAWAII
Timothy Johns
Chair
Dept. of Land & Natural Resources
1151 Punchbowl St.
Honolulu, HI 96813
Phone: (808) 587-0400
Fax: (808) 587-0390

IDAHO
Stan Hamilton
Director
Dept. of Lands
1215 State St.
Boise, ID 83720
Phone: (208) 334-0200

ILLINOIS
Brent Manning
Director
Dept. of Natural Resources
Lincoln Towers Plz., Rm. 425
524 S. 2nd St.
Springfield, IL 62706
Phone: (217) 782-6302
Fax: (217) 785-9236

INDIANA
John T. Costello
Deputy Director
Dept. of Natural Resources
IGC-S., Rm. W256
Indianapolis, IN 46204
Phone: (317) 232-4020
Fax: (317) 233-6811

IOWA
John Beamer
Bureau Chief
Land Acquisition & Land Mgmt.
Dept. of Natural Resources
Wallace State Ofc. Bldg.
E. 9th & Grand Aves.
Des Moines, IA 50319
Phone: (515) 281-5634

KANSAS
John Bond
Public Service Administrator III
Public Land Section
Dept. of Wildlife & Parks
3300 SW 29th St.
Topeka, KS 66614
Phone: (785) 273-6740
Fax: (785) 273-6757
E-mail: johnb@wp.state.ks.us

KENTUCKY
Armond Russ
Commissioner
Finance & Administration Cabinet
Dept. of Facilities Mgmt.
76 Capitol Annex
700 Capitol Ave.
Frankfort, KY 40601
Phone: (502) 564-2623
Fax: (502) 564-2933

LOUISIANA
Jack Caldwell
Secretary
Dept. of Natural Resources
P.O. Box 94396
Baton Rouge, LA 70804-9396
Phone: (225) 342-4503
Fax: (225) 342-5861

MAINE
Thomas Morrison
Acting Director
Bur. of Public Lands
Dept. of Conservation
22 State House Station
Augusta, ME 04333
Phone: (207) 287-3061

MARYLAND
Michael Nelson
Director
Land & Water
Conservation Service
Dept. of Natural Resources
Tawes State Ofc. Bldg., E-4
580 Taylor Ave.
Annapolis, MD 21401
Phone: (410) 260-8401
Fax: (410) 260-8404

MASSACHUSETTS
Stephen J. Hines
Acting Commissioner
Capitol Asset Mgmt.
One Ashburton Pl.,
Rm. 1505
Boston, MA 02108
Phone: (617) 727-4050
Fax: (617) 727-5363

MICHIGAN
Rodney Stokes
Chief
Real Estate Div.
Dept. of Natural Resources
P.O. Box 30028
Lansing, MI 48909
Phone: (517) 373-1246

MINNESOTA
Beverly Kroiss
Director
Real Estate Mgmt. Div.
Dept. of Administration
50 Sherburne Ave.,
Rm. 309
St. Paul, MN 55155
Phone: (651) 296-1896
Fax: (651) 215-6245
E-mail: bev.kroiss
@state.mn.us

MISSISSIPPI
Jim Nelson
Assistant Secretary of State
Ofc. of the Secretary of
State
Dept. of Public Lands
P.O. Box 136
Jackson, MS 39205
Phone: (601) 359-6374
Fax: (601) 359-1461

MISSOURI
Douglas K. Eiken
Director
Div. of State Parks
Dept. of Natural Resources
101 Adams St.
P.O. Box 176
Jefferson City, MO 65102
Phone: (573) 751-9392
Fax: (573) 526-7716
E-mail: nreiked
@mail.dnr.state.mo.us

MONTANA
Bud Clinch
Director
Dept. of Natural Resources
& Conservation
1625 11th Ave.
P.O. Box 201601
Helena, MT 59620
Phone: (406) 444-2074
Fax: (406) 444-2684

NEBRASKA
Rex Amack
Director
Game & Parks Comm.
2200 N. 33rd St.
P.O. Box 30370
Lincoln, NE 68503-0370
Phone: (402) 471-0641
Fax: (402) 471-5528

Richard R. LeBlanc
Executive Secretary
Educational Lands & Funds
Board
555 N. Cotner Blvd.
Lincoln, NE 68505
Phone: (402) 471-2014
Fax: (402) 471-3599

NEVADA
Pamela B. Wilcox
Administrator
Div. of State Lands
333 W. Nye Ln., Rm. 118
Carson City, NV 89706
Phone: (775) 687-4363
Fax: (775) 687-3783

NEW HAMPSHIRE
Philip Bryce
Director
Forest & Lands Div.
Dept. of Resources &
Economic Dev.
P.O. Box 1856
Concord, NH 03302-1856
Phone: (603) 271-2214
Fax: (603) 271-2629

NEW JERSEY
Vacant
Chief
Ofc. of Real Property
Mgmt.
Dept. of Treasury
50 W. State St., 2nd Fl.
P.O. Box 229
Trenton, NJ 08625-0229
Phone: (609) 292-9694
Fax: (609) 292-3521

NEW MEXICO
Ray Powell
Commissioner of Public
Lands
P.O. Box 1148
Santa Fe, NM 87504-1148
Phone: (505) 827-5760
Fax: (505) 827-5766

NEW YORK
John Cahill
Commissioner
Dept. of Environmental
Conservation
50 Wolf Rd.
Albany, NY 12233-1010
Phone: (518) 457-1162
Fax: (518) 457-7744

NORTH CAROLINA
Joe Henderson
Director
Ofc. of State Property
Dept. of Administration
116 W. Jones St.
Raleigh, NC 27603-8003
Phone: (919) 733-4346
Fax: (919) 733-1431

NORTH DAKOTA
Bob Olheiser
Commissioner
Land Dept.
P. O. Box 5523
Bismarck, ND 58506-5523
Phone: (701) 328-2800
Fax: (701) 328-3650
E-mail: rjo@poldy.land.
state.nd.us

NORTHERN MARIANA ISLANDS
Bertha P. Camacho
Director
Public Land Corp.
P.O. Box 380
Saipan, MP 96950
Phone: (670) 322-6914
Fax: (670) 322-4336

OHIO
Wayne Warren
Chief
Real Estate Land Mgmt.
Dept. of Natural Resources
Fountain Sq., Bldg. C-2
Columbus, OH 43224
Phone: (614) 265-6397
Fax: (614) 267-4764

OKLAHOMA
Ernest Hellwege
Secretary
Land Ofc. Comm.
P.O. Box 26910
Oklahoma City, OK 73126
Phone: (405) 271-1000
Fax: (405) 271-2500

OREGON
Paul Cleary
Director
Div. of State Lands
775 Summer St., NE
Salem, OR 97310
Phone: (503) 378-3805
Fax: (503) 378-4844

PENNSYLVANIA
Roger Fickes
Director
Bur. of State Parks
Dept. of Environmental
Resources
Rachel Carson Ofc. Bldg.,
8th Fl.
Harrisburg, PA 17101
Phone: (717) 787-6640
Fax: (717) 787-8817

PUERTO RICO
Jose Figueroa
Executive Director
Land Authority
P.O. Box 363767
San Juan, PR 00036-3767
Phone: (787) 723-9090
Fax: (787) 725-4004

RHODE ISLAND
Jan Reitsma
Director
Dept. of Environmental
Mgmt.
235 Promenade St.
Providence, RI 02908
Phone: (401) 222-2771
Fax: (401) 222-6802

SOUTH CAROLINA
Alton T. Loftis
Director of Property Management
Div. of Services
Budget & Control Board
1201 Main St.
Columbia, SC 29201
Phone: (803) 737-0790

SOUTH DAKOTA
Curt Johnson
Commissioner
School & Public Lands
Capitol Bldg., 1st Fl.
500 E. Capitol Ave.
Pierre, SD 57501
Phone: (605) 773-3303
Fax: (605) 773-5520

TENNESSEE
Milton Hamilton
Commissioner
Dept. of Environment & Conservation
401 Church St.
Nashville, TN 37243
Phone: (615) 532-0104
Fax: (615) 532-0120

TEXAS
David Dewhurst
Commissioner
Land Ofc.
835 Stephen F. Austin Bldg.
Austin, TX 78701
Phone: (512) 463-5256
Fax: (512) 475-1558

U.S. VIRGIN ISLANDS
Marc Biggs
Acting Commissioner
Dept. of Property & Procurement
Sub Base, Bldg. 1
St. Thomas, VI 00801
Phone: (340) 774-0828
Fax: (340) 777-9587

Gordon Finch
Executive Director
Port Authority
P.O. Box 301707
St. Thomas, VI 00803
Phone: (340) 774-1629
Fax: (340) 774-0025

Dean Plaskett
Commissioner
Dept. of Planning & Natural Resources
Foster's Plz., 396-1 Anna's Retreat
St. Thomas, VI 00802
Phone: (340) 774-3320
Fax: (340) 775-5706

UTAH
Art DuFault
State Forester/Director
Div. of Forestry, Fire & State Lands
Dept. of Natural Resources
1594 W. N. Temple, Ste. 3520
Salt Lake City, UT 84114-5703
Phone: (801) 538-5530
Fax: (801) 533-4111
E-mail: adufault.nrslf@state.ut.us

VERMONT
John Kassell
Secretary
Agency of Natural Resources
103 S. Main St.
Waterbury, VT 05671-0301
Phone: (802) 244-7347
Fax: (802) 241-3281

VIRGINIA
Donald C. Williams
Director
Dept. of Services
202 N. 9th St., Ste. 209
Richmond, VA 23219
Phone: (804) 786-3311
Fax: (804) 371-8305

WASHINGTON
Jennifer Belcher
Commissioner of Public Lands
Dept. of Natural Resources
P.O. Box 47001
Olympia, WA 98504-7001
Phone: (360) 902-1000
Fax: (360) 902-1775

WEST VIRGINIA
James H. Jones
Administrator
Real Estate Mgmt.
Dept. of Natural Resources
Bldg. 3, Rm. 669
1900 Kanawha Blvd., E.
Charleston, WV 25305
Phone: (304) 558-3225
Fax: (304) 558-3680

WISCONSIN
Daniel Wisniewski
Secretary
Board of Commissioners of Public Lands
Trust Lands & Investments
P.O. Box 8943
Madison, WI 53708
Phone: (608) 266-1370
Fax: (608) 267-2787

WYOMING
Steve Reynolds
Commissioner
Public Lands
Herschler Bldg.
122 W. 25th St.
Cheyenne, WY 82002
Phone: (307) 777-6523

Public Library Development

Oversees the development of public libraries in the state and administers state and federal programs related to such libraries.

ALABAMA
Lamar Veatch
Director
Public Library Service
6030 Monticello Dr.
Montgomery, AL 36130
Phone: (334) 213-3900
Fax: (334) 213-3993

ALASKA
Karen R. Crane
Director
State Libraries & Archives
Dept. of Education
P.O. Box 110571
Juneau, AK 99811-0571
Phone: (907) 465-2910
Fax: (907) 465-2151

AMERICAN SAMOA
Laloulu E. Tagoilelagi
Director
Dept. of Education
AS Govt.
Pago Pago, AS 96799
Phone: (684) 633-5237
Fax: (684) 633-4240

ARIZONA
Tony Miele
Library Extension Div.
Dept. of Library, Archives & Public Records
1700 W. Washington
Phoenix, AZ 85007
Phone: (602) 542-5841

ARKANSAS
John A. Murphy, Jr.
State Librarian
State Library
Dept. of Education
1 Capitol Mall
Little Rock, AR 72201
Phone: (501) 682-1526
Fax: (501) 682-1529

CALIFORNIA
Kevin Starr
State Librarian
State Info. Reference Ctr.
State Library
900 N St.
Sacramento, CA 95814-4800
Phone: (916) 654-0261
Fax: (916) 654-0241

COLORADO
Nancy Bolt
Assistant Commissioner
State Library & Adult Education Ofc.
Dept. of Education
201 E. Colfax Ave.
Denver, CO 80203
Phone: (303) 866-6900
Fax: (303) 866-6940

CONNECTICUT
Sharon Brettschneider
Director
Library Dev. Div.
State Library
231 Capitol Ave.
Hartford, CT 06106-1548
Phone: (860) 566-5607

DELAWARE
Tom W. Sloan
State Librarian
Div. of Libraries
Dept. of Community Affairs
43 S. DuPont Hwy.
Dover, DE 19901
Phone: (302) 739-4748
Fax: (302) 739-6787

DISTRICT OF COLUMBIA
Mary E. Raphael
Director
Public Library
901 G St., NW, Ste. 400
Washington, DC 20001
Phone: (202) 727-1101
Fax: (202) 727-1129

FLORIDA
Barratt Wilkins
Director
Div. of Library & Info. Services
Dept. of State
R.A. Gray Bldg.
500 S. Bronough St.
Tallahassee, FL 32399-0250
Phone: (850) 487-2651
Fax: (850) 488-2746
E-mail: bwilkins@mail.dos.state.fl.us

GEORGIA
Bill Gambill
Associate State School Superintendent
Ofc. of State Schools & Special Services
205 Butler St., SW
Atlanta, GA 30334
Phone: (404) 656-2591

GUAM
Christine Scott-Smith
Director
Public Library
Nieves M. Flores Library
254 Martyr St.
Hagatna, GU 96910
Phone: (671) 475-4753
Fax: (671) 477-9777
E-mail: csctsmth@kuentos.guam.net

HAWAII
Virginia Lowell
State Librarian
State Public Library System
Dept. of Education
465 S. King St., Rm. B-1
Honolulu, HI 96813
Phone: (808) 586-3704
Fax: (808) 586-3715

IDAHO
Ann Joslin
Associate Director of Library Development
State Library
325 W. State St.
Boise, ID 83702
Phone: (208) 334-2153

ILLINOIS
Jean E. Wilkins
Director
State Library
300 S. 2nd St.
Springfield, IL 62701
Phone: (217) 782-2994

INDIANA
C. Ray Ewick
Director
State Library
140 N. Senate Ave.
Indianapolis, IN 46204
Phone: (317) 232-3692
Fax: (317) 232-0002

IOWA
Sharman B. Smith
State Librarian
State Library Div.
Dept. of Education
E. 12th & Grand Aves.
Des Moines, IA 50319
Phone: (515) 281-4105

KANSAS
Duane F. Johnson
State Librarian
State Library
State Capitol Bldg., 3rd Fl.
300 SW 10th St.
Topeka, KS 66612
Phone: (785) 296-3296
Fax: (785) 296-6650

KENTUCKY
James A. Nelson
State Librarian & Commissioner
Education & Humanities Cabinet
Dept. of Library & Archives
300 Coffee Tree Rd.
P.O. Box 537
Frankfort, KY 40602
Phone: (502) 564-8300
Fax: (502) 564-5773

LOUISIANA
Thomas F. Jaques
State Librarian
Ofc. of State Library
Dept. of Culture, Recreation & Tourism
P.O. Box 131
Baton Rouge, LA 70821
Phone: (225) 342-4923
Fax: (225) 342-3547

MAINE
J. Gary Nichols
State Librarian
Bur. of Library Services
64 State House Station
Augusta, ME 04333
Phone: (207) 287-5600

MARYLAND
J. Maurice Travillian
Assistant State Superintendent
Div. of Library Dev. & Services
State Dept. of Education
200 W. Baltimore St.
Baltimore, MD 21201
Phone: (410) 767-0434
Fax: (410) 333-2507

MASSACHUSETTS
Keith Fields
Director
Board of Library Commissioners
648 Beacon St.
Boston, MA 02215
Phone: (617) 267-9400
Fax: (617) 421-9833

MICHIGAN
George Needham
State Librarian
State Library
P.O. Box 30007
Lansing, MI 48909
Phone: (517) 373-1580
Fax: (517) 373-4480

MINNESOTA
Joyce Swonger
Director
Ofc. of Library Dev. & Services
Dept. of Children Families
1500 Hwy. 36, W.
St. Paul, MN 55113-4266
Phone: (651) 582-8722
Fax: (651) 582-8897
E-mail: joyce.swonger@state.mn.us

MISSISSIPPI
John Pritchard
Executive Director
Library Comm.
P.O. Box 10700
Jackson, MS 39289-0700
Phone: (601) 961-4111
Fax: (601) 354-6713

MISSOURI
Sara Ann Parker
State Librarian
State Library
600 W. Main
P.O. Box 387
Jefferson City, MO 65102-0387
Phone: (573) 751-2751
Fax: (573) 751-3612
E-mail: sparker@mail.sos.state.mo.us

MONTANA
Karen Strege
State Librarian
State Library
1515 E. 6th Ave.
Helena, MT 59620
Phone: (406) 444-3115
Fax: (406) 444-5431

NEBRASKA
Rod Wagner
Director
State Library Comm.
1200 N St., Ste. 120
Lincoln, NE 68508-2023
Phone: (402) 471-4001
Fax: (402) 471-2083

NEVADA
Dale Erquiaga
Director
Museums, Library & Arts Dept.
100 N. Stewart St.
Carson City, NV 89701
Phone: (775) 687-8315
Fax: (775) 687-8311

NEW HAMPSHIRE
Michael York
State Librarian
State Library
Dept. of Cultural Affairs
20 Park St.
Concord, NH 03301
Phone: (603) 271-2081
Fax: (603) 271-6826

NEW JERSEY

NEW MEXICO
Ben Wakashige
State Librarian
State Library
1209 Camino Carlos Rey
Santa Fe, NM 87505-9860
Phone: (505) 476-9762
Fax: (505) 476-9701

NEW YORK
Richard P. Mills
Commissioner
State Education Dept.
89 Washington Ave., Rm. 111
Albany, NY 12234
Phone: (518) 474-6569
Fax: (518) 473-4909

NORTH CAROLINA
Sandra Cooper
Director
State Library
Dept. of Cultural Resources
109 E. Jones St.
Raleigh, NC 27601-2807
Phone: (919) 733-2570
Fax: (919) 733-8748

NORTH DAKOTA
Mike Jaugstetter
State Librarian
State Library
Liberty Memorial Bldg.
604 E. Blvd. Ave.
Bismarck, ND 58505-0800
Phone: (701) 328-2492
Fax: (701) 328-2040
E-mail: mjaugste@state.nd.us

NORTHERN MARIANA ISLANDS
Paul Steere
Director
Josten-Kiyu Public Library
P.O. Box 1092
Saipan, MP 96950
Phone: (670) 234-7322
Fax: (670) 235-7550
E-mail: jklibrary@saipan.com

OHIO
Michael Lucas
State Librarian
State Library
65 S. Front St., Rm. 1206
Columbus, OH 43266-0334
Phone: (614) 644-6843
Fax: (614) 466-3584

OKLAHOMA
Robert L. Clark
Director
Dept. of Libraries
200 NE 18th St.
Oklahoma City, OK 73105
Phone: (405) 521-2502
Fax: (405) 525-7804
E-mail: bclark@ohn.odl.state.ok.us

OREGON
Jim Scheppke
State Librarian
State Library
State Library Bldg.
Salem, OR 97310
Phone: (503) 378-4367
Fax: (503) 588-7119

PENNSYLVANIA
Barbara Cole
Acting Director
Library Dev. Ofc.
Dept. of Education
217 Forum Bldg.
Harrisburg, PA 17120-0029
Phone: (717) 783-5722
Fax: (717) 783-5723

PUERTO RICO
Lidia Santiago
Director
Public Library Div.
Dept. of Education
P.O. Box 759
Hato Rey, PR 00919
Phone: (787) 753-9191

RHODE ISLAND
Barbara Weaver
Director
State Library Services
Dept. of Administration
State Library
1 Capitol Hill
Providence, RI 02908
Phone: (401) 222-2726

SOUTH CAROLINA
James B. Johnson
Director
State Library
P.O. Box 11469
Columbia, SC 29211
Phone: (803) 734-8666

SOUTH DAKOTA
Dennis Holub
Acting State Librarian
State Library
State Library Bldg.
800 Governors Dr.
Pierre, SD 57501
Phone: (605) 773-3131
Fax: (605) 773-6962

TENNESSEE
Edwin S. Gleaves
State Librarian & Archivist
State Library & Archives
403 7th Ave., N.
Nashville, TN 37243-0312
Phone: (615) 741-7996
Fax: (615) 741-6471

TEXAS
Jeanette Larson
Library
Library Dev. Div.
Library & Archives Comm.
P.O. Box 12927
Austin, TX 78711
Phone: (512) 463-5456
Fax: (512) 463-5436

U.S. VIRGIN ISLANDS
E. Marlene Hendricks
Assistant Director
Libraries, Archives & Museums
Dept. of Planning & Natural Resources
23 Dronningens Gade
St. Thomas, VI 00802
Phone: (340) 774-3407
Fax: (340) 775-1887

UTAH
Amy Owen
Director
State Library
Dept. of Community & Economic Dev.
250 N. 1950 W., Ste. A
Salt Lake City, UT 84116-7901
Phone: (801) 715-6770
Fax: (801) 715-6767
E-mail: aowen@library.state.ut.us

VERMONT
Sybil McShane
State Librarian
Dept. of Libraries
109 State St.
Montpelier, VT 05609
Phone: (802) 828-3265
Fax: (802) 828-2199

VIRGINIA
Nolan T. Yelich
State Librarian
State Library
Serials Section
800 E. Broad St.
Richmond, VA 23219
Phone: (804) 692-3535
Fax: (804) 692-3594

WASHINGTON
Nancy L. Zussy
State Librarian
State Library
P.O. Box 42460
Olympia, WA 98504-2460
Phone: (360) 753-2915
Fax: (360) 586-7575

WEST VIRGINIA
David M. Price
Director
Library Comm.
Cultural Ctr.
1900 Kanawha Blvd., E.
Charleston, WV 25305
Phone: (304) 558-2041
Fax: (304) 558-2044

WISCONSIN
Larry Nix
Director
Bur. for Library Dev.
Dept. of Public Instruction
125 S. Webster
P.O. Box 7841
Madison, WI 53707
Phone: (608) 266-2205
Fax: (608) 267-1052

WYOMING
Vacant
State Librarian
State Library
Dept. of Administration & Info.
Supreme Ct. & Library Bldg.
2301 Capitol Ave.
Cheyenne, WY 82002-0600
Phone: (307) 777-7281

Public Utility Regulation

Supervises and regulates the electric, gas, telephone and water utilities in the state.

ALABAMA
Jim Sullivan
President
Public Service Comm.
P.O. Box 991
Montgomery, AL 36101-0991
Phone: (334) 242-5207
Fax: (334) 242-0921

ALASKA
Bob Lohr
Executive Director
Public Utilities Comm.
1016 W. 6th Ave.
Anchorage, AK 99501-1963
Phone: (907) 276-6222
Fax: (907) 276-0160

AMERICAN SAMOA

ARIZONA
Brian McNeil
Executive Secretary
Corp. Comm.
1200 W. Washington
Phoenix, AZ 85007
Phone: (602) 542-3931

ARKANSAS
Jim Von Gremp
Chair
Public Service Comm.
P.O. Box 400
Little Rock, AR 72203
Phone: (501) 682-1453
Fax: (501) 682-5731

CALIFORNIA
Gregory Conlon
President
Public Utilities Comm.
505 Van Ness Ave., Rm. 5218
San Francisco, CA 94102
Phone: (415) 703-2440

COLORADO
Bruce Smith
Director
Public Utilities Comm.
Dept. of Regulatory Agencies
1580 Logan St., Rm. 203
Denver, CO 80203
Phone: (303) 894-2000
Fax: (303) 894-2065

CONNECTICUT
Donald W. Downes
Chair
Dept. of Public Utility Control
1 Central Park Plz.
New Britain, CT 06051
Phone: (860) 827-2801

DELAWARE
Bruce Burcat
Director
Public Service Comm.
861 Silver Lake Blvd., Ste. 100
Dover, DE 19904-2467
Phone: (302) 739-4247
Fax: (302) 739-4849

DISTRICT OF COLUMBIA
Marlene Johnson
Chair
Public Service Comm.
450 5th St., NW, 8th Fl.
Washington, DC 20001
Phone: (202) 626-5100

FLORIDA
William D. Talbott
Executive Director
Public Service Comm.
2540 Shumard Oak Blvd.
Tallahassee, FL 32399-0850
Phone: (850) 413-6344
Fax: (850) 488-4491

GEORGIA
Bob Durden
Chair
Public Service Comm.
47 Trinity Ave., SW, Ste. 511
Atlanta, GA 30334
Phone: (404) 656-4512

GUAM
Terrence Brooks
Chair
Public Utilities Comm.
P.O. Box 862
Hagatna, GU 96932
Phone: (671) 472-8868
Fax: (671) 477-2511

HAWAII
Dennis Yamada
Chair
Public Utilities Comm.
Dept. of Budget & Finance
465 S. King St., Rm. 103
Honolulu, HI 96813
Phone: (808) 586-2028
Fax: (808) 586-2066

IDAHO
Dennis S. Hansen
President
Public Utilities Comm.
472 W. Washington St.
Boise, ID 83702-5983
Phone: (208) 334-0300

ILLINOIS
Charles Fisher
Executive Director
Commerce Comm.
P.O. Box 19280
Springfield, IL 62794-9280
Phone: (217) 785-7456
Fax: (217) 524-6859

INDIANA
William D. McCarty
Chair
State Utility Regulatory Comm.
302 W. Washington, Rm. E306
Indianapolis, IN 46204
Phone: (317) 232-2705
Fax: (317) 232-6758

IOWA
Allan T. Thoms
Chair
State Utilities Board
Dept. of Commerce
Lucas State Ofc. Bldg.
321 E. 12th St.
Des Moines, IA 50319
Phone: (515) 281-5167

KANSAS
John Wine
Chairman
Kansas Corp. Comm.
1500 SW Arrowhead Rd.
Topeka, KS 66604
Phone: (785) 271-3100

KENTUCKY
B.J. Helton
Chair
Public Services Comm.
730 Schenkel Ln.
P.O. Box 615
Frankfort, KY 40601
Phone: (502) 564-3940
Fax: (502) 564-7279

LOUISIANA
Lawrence St. Blanc
Executive Secretary
Public Service Comm.
P.O. Box 91154
Baton Rouge, LA 70821
Phone: (225) 342-4427
Fax: (225) 342-4087

MAINE
Thomas Welch
Chair
Public Utilities Comm.
18 State House Station
Augusta, ME 04333
Phone: (207) 287-3831

MARYLAND
Glenn F. Ivey
Chair
Public Service Comm.
6 St. Paul St., 16th Fl.
Baltimore, MD 21202-6806
Phone: (410) 767-8072

MASSACHUSETTS
Janet Gail Besser
Chair
Executive Ofc. of Consumer Affairs
Dept. of Public Utilities
100 Cambridge St., Rm. 1210
Boston, MA 02202
Phone: (617) 305-3500
Fax: (617) 723-8812

MICHIGAN
John G. Strand
Chair
Public Service Comm.
Consumer & Industry Services
6545 Mercantile Way
Lansing, MI 48909
Phone: (517) 334-6370

MINNESOTA
Edward A. Garvey
Chair
Public Utilities Comm.
121 7th Pl., E., Ste. 350
St. Paul, MN 55101-2147
Phone: (651) 296-2243
Fax: (651) 297-7073

MISSISSIPPI
Bobby Waites
Executive Director
Public Service Comm.
1738 Sillers Bldg.
550 High St.
Jackson, MS 39215
Phone: (601) 961-5493
Fax: (601) 961-5804

MISSOURI
Sheila Lumpe
Chair
Public Service Comm.
Dept. of Economic Dev.
Truman Bldg., Rm. 530
P.O. Box 360
Jefferson City, MO 65102
Phone: (573) 751-3234
Fax: (573) 751-9285
E-mail: slumpe@mail.state.mo.us

MONTANA
Dave Fisher
Chair
Public Service Comm.
Dept. of Public Service Regulation
Vista Bldg., 1701 Prospect Ave.
Helena, MT 59620
Phone: (406) 444-6199
Fax: (406) 444-7618

NEBRASKA
Robert R. Logsdon
Executive Director
Public Service Comm.
P.O. Box 94927
Lincoln, NE 68509-4927
Phone: (402) 471-3101
Fax: (402) 471-0254

NEVADA
Judy Sheldrew
Chair
Public Utilities Comm.
1150 E. William St.
Carson City, NV 89701
Phone: (775) 687-6007
Fax: (775) 687-6110

NEW HAMPSHIRE
Douglass L. Patch
Chair
Public Utilities Comm.
8 Old Suncook St.
Concord, NH 03301-7319
Phone: (603) 271-2431
Fax: (603) 271-3878

NEW JERSEY
Herbert H. Tate, Jr.
Commissioner
Board of Public Utilities
Div. of Energy
2 Gateway Ctr., 9th Fl.
Newark, NJ 07102
Phone: (973) 648-2503
Fax: (973) 648-4195

NEW MEXICO
Lynda Lovejoy
Chair
Public Regulation Comm.
P.O. Box 1269
Santa Fe, NM 87504
Phone: (505) 827-6940
Fax: (505) 827-6973

NEW YORK
Maureen Helmer
Chair
Dept. of Public Service
Agency Bldg. 3, 20th Fl.
Empire State Plz.
Albany, NY 12223
Phone: (518) 474-2523
Fax: (518) 473-2838

NORTH CAROLINA
Jo Anne Sanford
Chair
Utilities Comm.
Dept. of Commerce
430 N. Salisbury St.
Raleigh, NC 27603-5900
Phone: (919) 733-4249
Fax: (919) 733-7300

NORTH DAKOTA
Susan Wefald
President
Public Service Comm.
600 E. Blvd. Ave., 12th Fl.
Bismarck, ND 58505-0480
Phone: (701) 328-2400
Fax: (701) 328-2410
E-mail: msmail.sew@oracle.psc.state.nd.us

NORTHERN MARIANA ISLANDS
Timothy P. Villagomez
Executive Director
Commonwealth Utilities Corp.
P.O. Box 1220
Saipan, MP 96950
Phone: (670) 322-6020
Fax: (670) 322-4323
E-mail: cucedp@mtccnmi.com

OHIO
Alan Schriber
Chair
Public Utilities Comm.
180 E. Broad St.
Columbus, OH 43266-0573
Phone: (614) 466-3204
Fax: (614) 466-7366

OKLAHOMA
Bob Anthony
Commissioner
Corp. Comm.
Jim Thorpe Bldg.
2101 N. Lincoln Blvd.
Oklahoma City, OK 73105
Phone: (405) 521-2261

Ed Apple
Commissioner
Corp. Comm.
Jim Thorpe Bldg.
2101 N. Lincoln Blvd.
Oklahoma City, OK 73105
Phone: (405) 521-2264

Denise A. Bode
Commissioner
Corp. Comm.
Jim Thorpe Bldg.
2101 N. Lincoln Blvd.
Oklahoma City, OK 73105
Phone: (405) 521-2267

Ernest Johnson
Director
Public Utility Div.
Corp. Comm.
Jim Thorpe Bldg.
2101 N. Lincoln Blvd.
Oklahoma City, OK 73105
Phone: (405) 521-3908

OREGON
Ron Eachus
Chair
Public Utility Comm.
550 Capitol St., NE
Salem, OR 97310-1380
Phone: (503) 378-6611
Fax: (503) 378-5505

PENNSYLVANIA
John M. Quain
Chairman
Public Utility Comm.
104 N. Ofc. Bldg.
Harrisburg, PA 17120
Phone: (717) 787-1925
Fax: (717) 787-5813

PUERTO RICO
Perfecto Ocasio
Executive Director
Aqueduct & Sewer Authority
Barrio Obrero Station
P.O. Box 7066
Santurce, PR 00916
Phone: (787) 758-5757

RHODE ISLAND
Thomas Ahearn
Administrator
Div. of Public Utilities & Carriers
100 Orange St.
Providence, RI 02903
Phone: (401) 222-3500

SOUTH CAROLINA
Gary E. Walsh
Executive Director
Public Service Comm.
P.O. Drawer 11649
Columbia, SC 29211
Phone: (803) 737-5133

SOUTH DAKOTA
Jim Burg
Chair
Public Utilities Comm.
State Capitol, 1st Fl.
500 E. Capitol Ave.
Pierre, SD 57501
Phone: (605) 773-3201
Fax: (605) 773-3809

TENNESSEE
Melvin Malone
Director
Public Service Comm.
Dept. of Regulatory Authority
460 James Robertson Pkwy.
Nashville, TN 37243
Phone: (615) 741-3668
Fax: (615) 741-5015

TEXAS
John Laakso
Director
Public Utility Comm.
P.O. Box 13326
Austin, TX 78711
Phone: (512) 936-7000
Fax: (512) 936-7003

U.S. VIRGIN ISLANDS
Keithby Joseph
Executive Director
Public Services Comm.
P.O. Box 40
St. Thomas, VI 00801
Phone: (340) 776-1291
Fax: (340) 774-4971

UTAH
Ric Campbell
Director
Public Utilities
Dept. of Commerce
160 E. 300 S.
Salt Lake City, UT 84111
Phone: (801) 530-6675
Fax: (801) 530-6650
E-mail: rcampbel@br.state.ut.us

VERMONT
Michael Dworkin
Chair
Public Service Board
120 State St.
Montpelier, VT 05620-2701
Phone: (802) 828-2358
Fax: (802) 828-3351

VIRGINIA
Theodore W. Morrison, Jr.
Chair
State Corp. Comm.
Tyler Bldg.
1300 E. Main St.
Richmond, VA 23219
Phone: (804) 371-9608
Fax: (804) 371-9376

WASHINGTON
Marilyn Showalter
Chair
Utilities & Transportation Comm.
1300 S. Evergreen Park Dr., SW
P.O. Box 47250
Olympia, WA 98504-7250
Phone: (360) 753-6423
Fax: (360) 586-1150

WEST VIRGINIA
Charlotte Lane
Chair
Public Service Comm.
201 Brook St.
Charleston, WV 25301
Phone: (304) 340-0306
Fax: (304) 340-0325

WISCONSIN
Ave Bie
Chair
Public Service Comm.
610 N. Whitney Way
P.O. Box 7854
Madison, WI 53707
Phone: (608) 266-5481
Fax: (608) 266-3957

WYOMING
Steve Ellenbecker
Chair
Public Service Comm.
Hansen Bldg.
Cheyenne, WY 82002
Phone: (307) 777-7427

Public Works

Umbrella agency responsible for supervision of public works divisions such as aeronautics, highways and water resources.

ALABAMA

ALASKA
Joseph L. Perkins
Commissioner
Dept. of Transportation & Public Facilities
3132 Channel Dr.
Juneau, AK 99801-7898
Phone: (907) 465-3900
Fax: (907) 586-8365

AMERICAN SAMOA
Vacant
Director
Dept. of Public Works
AS Govt.
Pago Pago, AS 96799
Phone: (684) 633-4141
Fax: (684) 633-5958

ARIZONA

ARKANSAS

CALIFORNIA
James W. Van Loben Sels
Director
Dept. of Transportation
1120 N St., Ste. 1100
Sacramento, CA 95814
Phone: (916) 654-5267

COLORADO

CONNECTICUT
Ted Anson
Commissioner
State Ofc. Bldg.
Dept. of Public Works
165 Capitol Ave.
Hartford, CT 06106
Phone: (860) 566-3360

DELAWARE

DISTRICT OF COLUMBIA
Arthuro V. Lawson
Acting Director
Dept. of Public Works
2000 14th St., NW, 6th Fl.
Washington, DC 20009
Phone: (202) 939-8000

FLORIDA
Thomas Barry, Jr.
Secretary
Director's Ofc.
Dept. of Transportation
Haydon Burns Bldg.
605 Suwannee St.
Tallahassee, FL 32399-0450
Phone: (850) 414-5205
Fax: (850) 488-5526
E-mail: tom.barry@dot.state.fl.us

Virginia Wetherell
Secretary
Dept. of Environmental Protection
3900 Commonwealth Blvd., MS-10
Tallahassee, FL 32399-3000
Phone: (850) 488-4805
Fax: (850) 921-4303

GEORGIA

GUAM
Daniel Lizama
Acting Director
Dept. of Public Works
542 N. Marine Dr.
Tamuning, GU 96911
Phone: (671) 646-3131
Fax: (671) 649-9178

HAWAII

IDAHO
Larry Osgood
Administrator
Div. of Public Works
Dept. of Administration
502 N. 4th
Boise, ID 83720
Phone: (208) 334-3453
Fax: (208) 334-4031
E-mail: losgood@adm.state.id.us

ILLINOIS
Kirk Brown
Secretary
Dept. of Transportation
Harry R. Hanley Bldg., Rm. 300
2300 S. Dirksen Pkwy.
Springfield, IL 62764
Phone: (217) 782-5597
Fax: (217) 782-6828

INDIANA
Sheila Snider
Director
Public Works Div.
Dept. of Administration
IGC-S., Rm. W467
Indianapolis, IN 46204
Phone: (317) 232-3001
Fax: (317) 233-4613

IOWA
Darrel Rensink
Director
Dept. of Transportation
800 Lincoln Way
Ames, IA 50010
Phone: (515) 239-1111
Fax: (515) 239-1639

Larry Wilson
Director
Dept. of Natural Resources
Wallace State Ofc. Bldg.
E. 9th & Grand Aves.
Des Moines, IA 50319
Phone: (515) 281-5385
Fax: (515) 281-8895

KANSAS

KENTUCKY
James C. Codell, III
Secretary
Transportation Cabinet
State Ofc. Bldg., 10th Fl.
Frankfort, KY 40601
Phone: (502) 564-4890
Fax: (502) 564-4809

LOUISIANA
Lawrence St. Blanc
Executive Secretary
Public Service Comm.
P.O. Box 91154
Baton Rouge, LA 70821
Phone: (225) 342-4427
Fax: (225) 342-4087

MAINE

MARYLAND
Sandra K. Reynold
Executive Secretary
Ofc. of the Secretary
Board of Public Works
Goldstein Treasury Bldg., Rm. 213
Annapolis, MD 21401-1991
Phone: (410) 260-7335
Fax: (410) 974-5240
E-mail: sreynold@comp.state.md.us

MASSACHUSETTS
Matthew Amorello
Commissioner
Hwy. Dept.
10 Park Plz., Rm. 3510
Boston, MA 02116
Phone: (617) 973-7800
Fax: (617) 973-8040

MICHIGAN
James R. De Sana
Director
Dept. of Transportation
425 W. Ottawa
Lansing, MI 48909
Phone: (517) 373-2114

MINNESOTA
Elwyn Tinklenberg
Commissioner
Dept. of Transportation
Transportation Bldg., 4th Fl.
395 John Ireland Blvd.
St. Paul, MN 55155
Phone: (651) 297-2930
Fax: (651) 296-3587

MISSISSIPPI

MISSOURI

MONTANA

NEBRASKA
Robert R. Logsdon
Executive Director
Public Service Comm.
P.O. Box 94927
Lincoln, NE 68509-4927
Phone: (402) 471-3101
Fax: (402) 471-0254

NEVADA
Eric Raecke
Manager
Public Works Board
Dept. of Administration
505 E. King St.
Kinkead Bldg., Rm. 301
Carson City, NV 89701
Phone: (775) 684-4141
Fax: (775) 684-4142

NEW HAMPSHIRE
Leon S. Kenison
Commissioner
Dept. of Transportation
P.O. Box 483
Concord, NH 03302-0483
Phone: (603) 271-3734
Fax: (603) 271-3515

NEW JERSEY

NEW MEXICO
Pete Rahn
Secretary
Dept. of Hwys. & Transportation
P.O. Box 1149
Santa Fe, NM 87504
Phone: (505) 827-5110
Fax: (505) 827-5469

Tom C. Turney
State Engineer
101 Bataan Memorial Bldg.
P.O. Box 25102
Santa Fe, NM 87504-5102
Phone: (505) 827-6091
Fax: (505) 827-6188

NEW YORK
Joseph Boardman
Commissioner
Dept. of Transportation
State Ofc. Bldg. Campus, Bldg. 5
Albany, NY 12232
Phone: (518) 457-4422
Fax: (518) 457-5583

NORTH CAROLINA

NORTH DAKOTA
Marshall W. Moore
Director
Dept. of Transportation
608 E. Blvd. Ave.
Bismarck, ND 58505-0700
Phone: (701) 328-2500
Fax: (701) 328-1420
E-mail: mmoore@state.nd.us

NORTHERN MARIANA ISLANDS
Edward M. Deleon Guerrero
Secretary
Dept. of Public Works
Lower Base
P.O. Box 2950
Saipan, MP 96950
Phone: (670) 235-5827
Fax: (670) 235-5253

OHIO

OKLAHOMA
Neal McCaleb
Director
Dept. of Transportation
200 NE 21st St.
Oklahoma City, OK 73105
Phone: (405) 521-2631
Fax: (405) 521-2093

OREGON

PENNSYLVANIA
Merle Ryan
Deputy Secretary for Public Works
Div. of Public Works
Dept. of Services
18th & Herr Sts., Rm. 100
Harrisburg, PA 17125
Phone: (717) 787-7095
Fax: (717) 783-3473

PUERTO RICO

RHODE ISLAND
William Ankner
Director
Dept. of Transportation
Two Capitol Hill
Providence, RI 02908
Phone: (401) 222-2481
Fax: (401) 222-6038

SOUTH CAROLINA
Elizabeth S. Mabry
Executive Director
Dept. of Transportation
955 Park St.
P.O. Box 191
Columbia, SC 29202
Phone: (803) 737-1302

SOUTH DAKOTA
Ron Wheeler
Secretary
Dept. of Transportation
700 E. Broadway
Pierre, SD 57501
Phone: (605) 773-3265
Fax: (605) 773-3921

TENNESSEE
Bruce Saltsman
Commissioner
Dept. of Transportation
James K. Polk Bldg., Ste. 700
Nashville, TN 37243
Phone: (615) 741-2848
Fax: (615) 741-2508

TEXAS

U.S. VIRGIN ISLANDS
Harold G. Thompson
Acting Commissioner
Dept. of Public Works
No. 8 Sub Base
St. Thomas, VI 00802
Phone: (340) 776-4844
Fax: (340) 776-8990

UTAH

VERMONT
Glenn Gershaneck
Secretary
Agency of Transportation
133 State St.
Montpelier, VT 05633-5001
Phone: (802) 828-2657
Fax: (802) 828-3522

VIRGINIA

WASHINGTON
Sid Morrison
Secretary
Dept. of Transportation
P.O. Box 47316
Olympia, WA 98504-7316
Phone: (360) 705-7000
Fax: (360) 705-6808

WEST VIRGINIA
Samuel H. Beverage
Commissioner
Div. of Hwys.
Bldg. 5, Rm. A109
1900 Kanawaha Blvd., E.
Charleston, WV 25305
Phone: (304) 558-0444
Fax: (304) 558-1004

WISCONSIN

WYOMING
Gene Roccabruna
Director
Hwy. Safety Div.
Dept. of Transportation
5300 Bishop Blvd.
Cheyenne, WY 82002
Phone: (307) 777-4484
Fax: (307) 777-4289

Purchasing

Central screening and acquisition point for supplies, equipment and/or services for state agencies.

ALABAMA
Bill Newton
Director
Div. of Purchasing
Dept. of Finance
100 N. Union St., Ste. 192
P.O. Box 302620
Montgomery, AL 36104
Phone: (334) 242-7250
Fax: (334) 242-4419

ALASKA
Marsha Hubbard
Director
Div. of Services & Supply
Dept. of Administration
P.O. Box 110210
Juneau, AK 99811
Phone: (907) 465-2250
Fax: (907) 465-2189

AMERICAN SAMOA
Pat Trevola
Director
Ofc. of Procurement
AS Govt.
Pago Pago, AS 96799
Phone: (684) 633-1205

ARIZONA
Jerry Brink
State Procurement Administrator
Finance Div.
Dept. of Administration
15 S. 15th Ave., Rm. 103
Phoenix, AZ 85007
Phone: (602) 542-5511
Fax: (602) 542-5508

ARKANSAS
Edward Erxleben
Administrator
Ofc. of State Purchasing
Dept. of Finance & Administration
P.O. Box 2940
Little Rock, AR 72203
Phone: (501) 324-9312
Fax: (501) 324-9311

CALIFORNIA
Peter G. Stamison
Director
Dept. of Services
1823 14th St.
Sacramento, CA 95814
Phone: (916) 323-8289

COLORADO
Nanci Kadlecek
Director
Purchasing Div.
Support Services/Dept. of Personnel
225 E. 16th Ave., Rm. 900
Denver, CO 80203-1613
Phone: (303) 866-6191
Fax: (303) 894-7445

CONNECTICUT
James Passier
Manager
Procurement Services
Dept. of Administration Services
165 Capitol Ave.
Hartford, CT 06106
Phone: (860) 713-5086

DELAWARE
Blaine Herrick
Director
Div. of Purchasing
Governor Bacon Health Ctr.
Delaware City, DE 19706
Phone: (302) 834-4550

DISTRICT OF COLUMBIA
Richard Fite
Chief Procurement Officer
Ofc. of Contracts & Procurement
441 4th St., NW, Ste. 800
Washington, DC 20001
Phone: (202) 727-0252

FLORIDA
George C. Banks
Director
Div. of Purchasing
Dept. of Mgmt. Services
4050 Esplanade Way
Tallahassee, FL 32399-0950
Phone: (850) 488-7303
Fax: (850) 921-5979

GEORGIA
Hugh Farley
Director of State Purchasing
Statewide Business Services
Dept. of Adm. Services
W. Tower, Floyd Bldg.
200 Piedmont Ave., SE
Atlanta, GA 30334-5514
Phone: (404) 656-3240

GUAM
Michael J. Reidy
Director
Dept. of Administration
P.O. Box 884
Hagatna, GU 96932
Phone: (671) 475-1101
Fax: (671) 477-6788

HAWAII
Lloyd Unebasami
Administrator
State Procurement Ofc.
Accounting & Services
1151 Punchbowl St., Rm. 230A
Honolulu, HI 96813
Phone: (808) 587-4700
Fax: (808) 587-4703

IDAHO
Jan Cox
Administrator
Div. of Purchasing
Dept. of Administration
650 W. State St.
Boise, ID 83720
Phone: (208) 327-7465

ILLINOIS
Ted Curtis
Manager
Procurement Services Div.
Central Mgmt. Services
801 Stratton Bldg.
401 S. Spring
Springfield, IL 62706
Phone: (217) 785-3868
Fax: (217) 782-5187

INDIANA
Amy McFadden
Director
Div. of Procurement
Dept. of Administration
402 W. Washington, Rm. W468
Indianapolis, IN 46204
Phone: (317) 232-3032
Fax: (317) 233-7312

IOWA
David Ancell
Administrator
Purchasing Div.
Dept. of Services
Hoover State Ofc. Bldg.
Des Moines, IA 50319
Phone: (515) 281-8384
Fax: (515) 242-5974

KANSAS
John Houlihan
Director
Div. of Purchases
Dept. of Administration
Landon State Ofc. Bldg., 1st Fl.
Topeka, KS 66612-1286
Phone: (785) 296-2376
Fax: (785) 296-7240

KENTUCKY
Don Speer
Commissioner
Finance & Administration Cabinet
Dept. of Administration
Capitol Annex, Rm. 362
700 Capitol Ave.
Frankfort, KY 40601
Phone: (502) 564-2317
Fax: (502) 564-4279

LOUISIANA
Denise Lea
Director
Ofc. of State Purchasing
Div. of Administration
P.O. Box 94095
Baton Rouge, LA 70804-9095
Phone: (225) 342-8062
Fax: (225) 342-8688

MAINE
Richard Thompson
Director
Div. of Public Printing
9 State House Station
Augusta, ME 04333
Phone: (207) 287-3521

MARYLAND
George E. Miller
Chief
Purchasing/Commodities Procurement
Dept. of Services
301 W. Preston St., Rm. M-4
Baltimore, MD 21201
Phone: (410) 767-4617
Fax: (410) 333-5482

MASSACHUSETTS
Philmore Anderson, III
Purchasing Agent
Operational Services Div.
One Ashburton Pl., Rm. 1017
Boston, MA 02108
Phone: (617) 727-7500
Fax: (617) 727-4527

MICHIGAN
David F. Ancell
Director
Ofc. of Purchasing
Dept. of Mgmt. & Budget
Mason Bldg., 2nd Fl.
P.O. Box 30026
Lansing, MI 48909
Phone: (517) 373-0300

MINNESOTA
Kent Allin
Director
Div. of Materials Mgmt.
112 Administration Bldg.
50 Sherburne Ave.
St. Paul, MN 55155
Phone: (651) 296-1442
Fax: (651) 297-3996

MISSISSIPPI
Don Buffum
Director
Bur. of Purchasing
Ofc. of Purchasing & Travel
1504 Sillers Bldg.
Jackson, MS 39201
Phone: (601) 359-3409
Fax: (601) 359-2470

MISSOURI
Joyce Murphy
Director
Div. of Purchasing & Materials Mgmt.
Ofc. of Administration
Truman Bldg., Rm. 580
P.O. Box 809
Jefferson City, MO 65102
Phone: (573) 751-3273
Fax: (573) 751-7276
E-mail: murphj@mail.oa.state.mo.us

MONTANA
Sheryl Motl
Bureau Chief
Purchasing Bur.
Dept. of Administration
P.O. Box 200135
Helena, MT 59620
Phone: (406) 444-3315
Fax: (406) 444-2529

NEBRASKA
Doni Peterson
Acting Administrator
Material Div.
Dept. of Adm. Services
301 Centennial Mall, S.
P.O. Box 94847
Lincoln, NE 68509
Phone: (402) 471-8295

NEVADA
William Moell
Administrator
Purchasing Div.
Dept. of Administration
209 E. Musser St., #304
Carson City, NV 89701
Phone: (775) 684-0170
Fax: (775) 684-0188

NEW HAMPSHIRE
Wayne R. Myer
Administrator
Bur. of Purchasing & Property
Adm. Services
25 Capitol St., Rm. 102
Concord, NH 03301-6398
Phone: (603) 271-2201
Fax: (603) 271-2700

NEW JERSEY
Lana Sims
Director
Services Administration
Dept. of Treasury
P.O. Box 039
Trenton, NJ 08625-0039
Phone: (609) 292-4886
Fax: (609) 984-2575

NEW MEXICO
Louis Higgins
Director
Purchasing Div.
Dept. of Services
P.O. Box 26110
Sante Fe, NM 87502
Phone: (505) 827-0472
Fax: (505) 827-2041

NEW YORK
Joseph Seymour
Commissioner
Ofc. of Services
Corning Tower Bldg., 41st Fl.
Empire State Plz.
Albany, NY 12242
Phone: (518) 474-5991
Fax: (518) 486-9179

NORTH CAROLINA
J. Arthur Leaston
State Purchasing Officer
Div. of Purchase & Contract
Dept. of Administration
116 W. Jones St.
Raleigh, NC 27603-8002
Phone: (919) 733-3581
Fax: (919) 733-4782

NORTH DAKOTA
Sheila Peterson
Director
Fiscal Mgmt.
Ofc. of Mgmt. & Budget
600 E. Blvd. Ave., 4th Fl.
Bismarck, ND 58505-0400
Phone: (701) 328-2680
Fax: (701) 328-3230
E-mail: peterson@state.nd.us

NORTHERN MARIANA ISLANDS
Edward B. Palacios
Director
Procurement & Supply Div.
Dept. of Finance
Lower Base
Saipan, MP 96950
Phone: (670) 664-1500
Fax: (670) 664-1515
E-mail: gov.p$s@saipan.com

OHIO
George Kaitsa
Deputy Director
Services Div., Ofc. of Direct Services
Dept. of Adm. Services
4200 Surface Rd.
Columbus, OH 43228-1395
Phone: (614) 466-5579
Fax: (614) 466-1040

OKLAHOMA
Pam Warren
Secretary of Administration
Dept. of Central Services
2401 N. Lincoln Blvd., Ste. 206
Oklahoma City, OK 73105
Phone: (405) 521-2121
Fax: (405) 425-2713

OREGON
Dugan Petty
State Purchasing Manager
Transportation, Purchasing & Print Services Div.
Dept. of Adm. Services
1225 Ferry St., SE
Salem, OR 97310
Phone: (503) 378-3529
Fax: (503) 373-1626

PENNSYLVANIA
Joseph W. Nugent
Director
Bur. of Purchases
Dept. of Services
414 N. Ofc. Bldg.
Harrisburg, PA 17125
Phone: (717) 787-4718
Fax: (717) 783-6241

PUERTO RICO
Maria T. Mujica
Administrator
Services Administration
P.O. Box 7428
San Juan, PR 00916
Phone: (787) 724-1064
Fax: (787) 722-7965

RHODE ISLAND
Peter S. Corr
Purchasing Officer
Dept. of Administration
1 Capitol Hill
Providence, RI 02903
Phone: (401) 222-2321

SOUTH CAROLINA
Voigt Shealy
State Procurement Officer
Materials Mgmt. Div.
Dept. of Services
1201 Main St., Ste. 600
Columbia, SC 29201
Phone: (803) 737-0600

SOUTH DAKOTA
Jeff Holcomb
Director
Purchasing Div.
Bur. of Administration
523 E. Capitol Ave.
Pierre, SD 57501
Phone: (605) 773-3420
Fax: (605) 773-4840

TENNESSEE
Elsie C. Smith
Assistant Commissioner
Purchasing Mgmt.
Dept. of Services
Wm. R. Snodgrass
TN Tower, 24th Fl.
312 8th Ave., N.
Nashville, TN 37243-0532
Phone: (615) 741-5922
Fax: (615) 741-8408

TEXAS
Paul Schlimper
Director
Central Procurement Div.
Services Comm.
Capitol Station
P.O. Box 13047
Austin, TX 78711-3047
Phone: (512) 463-3444

U.S. VIRGIN ISLANDS
Marc Biggs
Acting Commissioner
Dept. of Property &
Procurement
Sub Base, Bldg. 1
St. Thomas, VI 00801
Phone: (340) 774-0828
Fax: (340) 777-9587

UTAH
Douglas Richins
Director
Div. of Purchasing &
Services
Dept. of Adm. Services
3150 State Ofc. Bldg.
P.O. Box 141061
Salt Lake City, UT 84114-
1061
Phone: (801) 538-3143
Fax: (801) 538-3882
E-mail: drichins.pamain
@state.ut.us

VERMONT
Peter E. Noyes
Director
Div. of Purchasing
Dept. of Services
133 State St.
Montpelier, VT 05633-7501
Phone: (802) 828-2211
Fax: (802) 828-2222

VIRGINIA
Donald C. Williams
Director
Dept. of Services
202 N. 9th St., Ste. 209
Richmond, VA 23219
Phone: (804) 786-3311
Fax: (804) 371-8305

WASHINGTON
Pat Kohler
Assistant Director
Ofc. of State Procurement
Dept. of Administration
P.O. Box 41017
Olympia, WA 98504-1017
Phone: (360) 902-7404
Fax: (360) 586-4944

WEST VIRGINIA
David Tincher
Director
Purchasing Div.
Dept. of Administration
Bldg. 1, Rm. E-110
1900 Kanawha Blvd., E.
Charleston, WV 25305
Phone: (304) 558-2648
Fax: (304) 558-3970

WISCONSIN
Jan Hamik
Director
Bur. of Procurement
Dept. of Administration
101 E. Wilson, 6th Fl.
P.O. Box 7867
Madison, WI 53703
Phone: (608) 266-2605
Fax: (608) 267-0600

WYOMING
Mac Landen
Manager
Procurement Services Div.
Dept. of Administration &
Info.
Emerson Bldg.
2001 Capitol Ave.
Cheyenne, WY 82002
Phone: (307) 777-6707

Railroads

Responsible for railroad programming and planning.

ALABAMA
Robert Jilla
Professional Civil Engineer
Bur. of Multimodal Transportation
Dept. of Transportation
1409 Coliseum Blvd.
Montgomery, AL 36130-3050
Phone: (334) 242-6086
Fax: (334) 262-7658

Bob Kratzer
Civil Engineer
Bur. of Multimodal Transportation
Dept. of Transportation
1409 Coliseum Blvd.
Montgomery, AL 36130
Phone: (334) 242-6429
Fax: (334) 262-7658

ALASKA
Bill Sheffield
President/Chief Executive Officer
State Railroad Corp.
P.O. Box 107500
Anchorage, AK 99510
Phone: (907) 265-2403
Fax: (907) 258-1456

AMERICAN SAMOA

ARIZONA
Jay Klagge
Assistant Director
Transportation Planning Div.
Dept. of Transportation
206 S. 17th Ave.
Phoenix, AZ 85007
Phone: (602) 255-6872

ARKANSAS
Dan Flowers
Director
Dept. of Hwys. & Transportation
P.O. Box 2261
Little Rock, AR 72203
Phone: (501) 569-2211
Fax: (501) 569-2400

CALIFORNIA
Kenneth E. Bosanko
Deputy Secretary
Rail & Transit
980 9th St., Ste. 2450
Sacramento, CA 95814
Phone: (916) 327-2892
Fax: (916) 323-5440

COLORADO
Jennifer Finch
Director
Div. of Transportation Dev.
Dept. of Transportation
4201 E. Arkansas Ave.
Denver, CO 80222
Phone: (303) 757-9525

CONNECTICUT
Harry P. Harris
Bureau Chief
Ofc. of Rail Operations
Bur. of Public Transportation
2800 Berlin Tpke.
Newington, CT 06111
Phone: (860) 594-2900

DELAWARE
David W. Campbell
Chief, Rail Services
Ofc. of Rail Services
400 S. Madison St.
Wilmington, DE 19801-5114
Phone: (302) 577-3278
Fax: (302) 577-6066

DISTRICT OF COLUMBIA

FLORIDA
Marion Hart
State Public Transportation Administrator
Ofc. of Public Transportation
Dept. of Transportation
605 Suwannee St., MS 57
Tallahassee, FL 32399-0450
Phone: (850) 414-4500
Fax: (850) 488-5526

Ysela Llort
State Transportation Planner
Ofc. of State Transportation Planner
Dept. of Transportation
605 Suwannee St., MS 57
Tallahassee, FL 32399-0450
Phone: (850) 414-5235
Fax: (850) 488-5526

GEORGIA
Luke Cousins
Administrator
Ofc. of Intermodal Programs
Dept. of Transportation
276 Memorial Dr.
Atlanta, GA 30303
Phone: (404) 651-9201

GUAM

HAWAII

IDAHO
Ron Kerr
Senior Transportation Planner
Transportation Planning & Programming
Dept. of Transportation
P.O. Box 7129
Boise, ID 83707-1129
Phone: (208) 334-8210

ILLINOIS
Merrill Travis
Chief
Bur. of Railroads
Dept. of Transportation
2300 S. Dirksen Pkwy., Rm. 302
Springfield, IL 62764
Phone: (217) 782-2835

INDIANA
Ron Thomas
Railroad Manager
Intermodel Transportation Div.
Div. of Transportation
100 N. Senate Ave., N901
Indianapolis, IN 46204
Phone: (317) 232-1491
Fax: (317) 232-1499

IOWA
Les Holland
Director
Rail & Water Div.
Dept. of Transportation
800 Lincoln Way
Ames, IA 50010
Phone: (515) 239-1646

KANSAS
John Maddox
Manager
Rail Affairs Unit
Dept. of Transportation
Thacher Bldg.
217 SE 4th St.
Topeka, KS 66603
Phone: (785) 296-4286
Fax: (785) 296-2274
E-Mail: johnr@dtthpo.wpo.state.ks.us

KENTUCKY
Jerry Ross
Director
Multimodal Program
Dept. of Hwys.
State Ofc. Bldg. Annex., 3rd Fl.
Frankfort, KY 40601
Phone: (502) 564-7433
Fax: (502) 564-4422

LOUISIANA
Brian Parsons
Rail Program Manager
Div. of Public Transportation
Dept. of Transportation & Dev.
P.O. Box 94245
Baton Rouge, LA 70804-9245
Phone: (225) 379-1928
Fax: (225) 379-1848

MAINE

MARYLAND
Ronald L. Freeland
Administrator
Mass Transit Administration
Dept. of Transportation
William Donald Schaefer Tower
6 St. Paul St.
Baltimore, MD 21202-1614
Phone: (410) 767-3943
Fax: (410) 333-3279

MASSACHUSETTS
Kevin Sullivan
Secretary
Executive Ofc. of Transportation & Construction
10 Park Plz., Rm. 3170
Boston, MA 02116
Phone: (617) 973-8080
Fax: (617) 973-8445

MICHIGAN
Phil Kazmierski
Deputy Director
Bur. of Urban & Public Transportation
Dept. of Transportation
P.O. Box 30050
Lansing, MI 48909
Phone: (517) 373-2282

MINNESOTA
Al Vogel
Director
Ofc. of Freight, Railroads & Waterways
Dept. of Transportation
Transportation Bldg., 4th Fl.
395 John Ireland Blvd.
St. Paul, MN 55155
Phone: (651) 296-1613
Fax: (651) 296-1887
E-Mail: al.vogel@dot.state.mn.us

MISSISSIPPI
Mike Merry
Manager of Railroad Activities
Rails Div.
Dept. of Transportation
P.O. Box 1850
Jackson, MS 39215-1850
Phone: (601) 359-6639
Fax: (601) 359-7110

MISSOURI
Jack Hynes
Administrator of Railroads & Water
Multimodal Operations Div.
Dept. of Transportation
Support Ctr.
P.O. Box 270
Jefferson City, MO 65102
Phone: (573) 751-7476
Fax: (573) 526-4709
E-Mail: hynesj@mail.modot.state.mo.us

MONTANA
Patricia Saindon
Administrator
Transportation Planning Div.
Dept. of Transportation
2701 Prospect Ave.
Helena, MT 59620
Phone: (406) 444-3423
Fax: (406) 444-7671

NEBRASKA
Tom Wais
Deputy Director
Planning Div.
Dept. of Rds.
P.O. Box 94759
Lincoln, NE 68509-4759
Phone: (402) 479-4671
Fax: (402) 479-4325

NEVADA
Thomas Fronapfel
Assistant Director
Planning Div.
Dept. of Transportation
1263 S. Stewart St., Rm. 203
Carson City, NV 89712
Phone: (775) 888-7240
Fax: (775) 687-7203

NEW HAMPSHIRE
Chris Morgan
Administrator
Rail & Transit Bur.
Transportation Dept.
P.O. Box 483
Concord, NH 03302-0483
Phone: (603) 271-2468
Fax: (603) 271-6767

NEW JERSEY
James Weinstein
Commissioner of Transportation
Dept. of Transportation
1035 Pkwy. Ave.
P.O. Box 600
Trenton, NJ 08625-0600
Phone: (609) 530-3536
Fax: (609) 530-3894

NEW MEXICO
Fred Friedman
Chief
Rail Bur.
Hwy. & Transportation Dept.
P.O. Box 1149
Santa Fe, NM 87504-1149
Phone: (505) 827-3233
Fax: (505) 827-5469

NEW YORK
Joseph Boardman
Commissioner
Dept. of Transportation
State Ofc. Bldg. Campus, Bldg. 5
Albany, NY 12232
Phone: (518) 457-4422
Fax: (518) 457-5583

NORTH CAROLINA
David King
Deputy Secretary for Transportation
Dept. of Transportation
1 S. Wilmington St.
Raleigh, NC 27601-1494
Phone: (919) 733-2520
Fax: (919) 733-9150

NORTH DAKOTA
Don Laschkewitsch
Transportation Senior Manager
Transportation Program & Planning
Dept. of Transportation
608 E. Blvd. Ave.
Bismarck, ND 58505-0700
Phone: (701) 328-2673
Fax: (701) 328-1404
E-Mail: dlaschke@state.nd.us

NORTHERN MARIANA ISLANDS

OHIO
Tom O'Leary
Executive Director
Rail Dev. Comm.
Dept. of Transportation
50 W. Broad St., 15th Fl.
Columbus, OH 43215
Phone: (614) 644-0310

OKLAHOMA
Joe Kyle
Planning Engineer
Dept. of Transportation
200 NE 21st St.
Oklahoma City, OK 73105
Phone: (405) 521-4203

OREGON
Claudia Howells
Manager
Rail Section
Dept. of Transportation
555 13th St., NE
Salem, OR 97310
Phone: (503) 986-4125
Fax: (503) 986-4174

PENNSYLVANIA
John E. Brown
Director
Bur. of Rail Freights, Ports & Waterways
Dept. of Transportation
Forum Pl., 8th Fl.
555 Walnut St.
Harrisburg, PA 17101-1900
Phone: (717) 783-8539
Fax: (717) 772-5782

PUERTO RICO

RHODE ISLAND
William Ankner
Director
Dept. of Transportation
Two Capitol Hill
Providence, RI 02908
Phone: (401) 222-2481
Fax: (401) 222-6038

SOUTH CAROLINA
Robert W. Parhan
Director
Public Railways
Dept. of Commerce
P.O. Box 279
Charleston, SC 29402-0279
Phone: (803) 727-2067

SOUTH DAKOTA
Ron Wheeler
Secretary
Dept. of Transportation
700 E. Broadway
Pierre, SD 57501
Phone: (605) 773-3265
Fax: (605) 773-3921

TENNESSEE

TEXAS
Jerry Martin
Director
Rail Div.
Railroad Comm.
Capitol Station
P.O. Box 12967
Austin, TX 78711
Phone: (512) 463-7001
Fax: (512) 463-7153

U.S. VIRGIN ISLANDS

UTAH
Linda Toy-Hull
Director
Div. of Program Dev.
Dept. of Transportation
4501 S. 2700 W.
Salt Lake City, UT 84119
Phone: (801) 965-4082
Fax: (801) 965-4551
E-Mail: lhull
@dot.state.ut.us

VERMONT
Greg Maguire
Director
Rail, Air & Public
Transportation
Agency of Transportation
Natl. Life Bldg., Drawer 33
Montpelier, VT 05633-5001
Phone: (802) 828-2093
Fax: (802) 828-2829

VIRGINIA
Leo J. Bevon
Director
Dept. of Rail & Public
Transportation
1401 E. Broad St.
Richmond, VA 23219
Phone: (804) 786-1051
Fax: (804) 786-7286

WASHINGTON
Ken Uznanski
Manager, Rail Branch
Planning Research &
Public Transportation
Dept. of Transportation
P.O. Box 47387
Olympia, WA 98504-7387
Phone: (360) 705-7901
Fax: (360) 705-6821

WEST VIRGINIA
John Hedrick
Executive Director
State Railroad Authority
120 Water Plant Dr.
Moorefield, WV 26836
Phone: (304) 538-2305
Fax: (304) 538-7474

WISCONSIN
Rodney Kreunen
Commissioner
Ofc. of the Railroads
610 N. Whitney Way
Madison, WI 53702
Phone: (608) 266-3182
Fax: (608) 261-8220

WYOMING
John Lane
Statewide Planning
Engineer
Dept. of Transportation
5300 Bishop Blvd.
Cheyenne, WY 82002
Phone: (307) 777-4180

Records Management

Oversees and coordinates programs to ensure the efficiency, scheduling, storage and reproduction of state government records.

ALABAMA
Tracey Berezansky
Assistant Director
Govt. Records
Dept. of Archives & History
P.O. Box 300100
Montgomery, AL 36130-0100
Phone: (334) 242-4452
Fax: (334) 240-3125

ALASKA
John Stewart
State Archivist
Libraries, Archives & Museums
Dept. of Education
141 Willoughby Ave.
Juneau, AK 99801-1720
Phone: (907) 465-2275
Fax: (907) 465-2465

AMERICAN SAMOA
Eliu Paopao
Acting Director
Dept. of Adm. Services
AS Govt.
Pago Pago, AS 96799
Phone: (684) 633-4156
Fax: (684) 633-1841

ARIZONA
Martin Richelsoph
Records Management Officer
Dept. of Library, Archives & Public Records
1919 W. Jefferson
Phoenix, AZ 85007
Phone: (602) 542-3741

ARKANSAS
John L. Ferguson
State Historian
History Comm.
1 Capitol Mall
Little Rock, AR 72201
Phone: (501) 682-6900

CALIFORNIA
Olive Findleton
Presiding Chief
Ofc. of Info. Services
Dept. of Services
1500 5th St., Ste. 116
Sacramento, CA 95814-5404
Phone: (916) 445-2294

COLORADO
Terry Ketelsen
State Archivist
Info./Archival Services
Info. Technology Services
1313 Sherman St., Rm. 1B-20
Denver, CO 80203
Phone: (303) 866-2055
Fax: (303) 866-2257

CONNECTICUT

DELAWARE
Howard P. Lowell
Administrator
State Archives
Dept. of State
Hall of Records
Dover, DE 19901
Phone: (302) 739-5318
Fax: (302) 739-6710

DISTRICT OF COLUMBIA
Clarence Davis
Public Records Administrator
Ofc. of the Secretary
1300 Naylor Ct., NW
Washington, DC 20001
Phone: (202) 727-2052
Fax: (202) 727-6076

FLORIDA
Jim Berberich
Chief
Bur. of Archives & Records Mgmt.
Dept. of State
R.A. Gray Bldg.
500 S. Bronough St.
Tallahassee, FL 32399-0250
Phone: (805) 487-2073
Fax: (850) 488-4894

GEORGIA
Edward Weldon
Director
Secretary of State
Archives & History Dept.
330 Capitol Ave., SW
Atlanta, GA 30334
Phone: (404) 656-2358
Fax: (404) 657-8427

GUAM
Michael J. Reidy
Director
Dept. of Administration
P.O. Box 884
Hagatna, GU 96932
Phone: (671) 475-1101
Fax: (671) 477-6788

HAWAII
Jolyn G. Tamura
State Archivist
Archives Div.
Dept. of Accounting & Services
Iolani Palace Grounds
Honolulu, HI 96813
Phone: (808) 586-0310
Fax: (808) 586-0330

IDAHO
Michelle Stone
Records Management Supervisor
Central Records Mgmt. Unit
Dept. of Administration
5327 Kendall
Boise, ID 83706
Phone: (208) 327-7060

ILLINOIS
John Daly
Director
State Archives & Records Div.
M.C. Norton Bldg., Fl. 2W
Springfield, IL 62756
Phone: (217) 782-3492

INDIANA
F. Gerald Handfield, Jr.
Director
Comm. on Public Records
402 W. Washington, Rm. W472
Indianapolis, IN 46204
Phone: (317) 232-3373
Fax: (317) 233-1713

IOWA
Gordon Hendrickson
State Archivist
Dept. of Cultural Affairs
Historical Bldg.
600 E. Locust
Des Moines, IA 50319
Phone: (515) 281-3007
Fax: (515) 282-0502

KANSAS

KENTUCKY
James A. Nelson
State Librarian & Commissioner
Education & Humanities Cabinet
Dept. of Library & Archives
300 Coffee Tree Rd.
P.O. Box 537
Frankfort, KY 40602
Phone: (502) 564-8300
Fax: (502) 564-5773

LOUISIANA
Donald J. Lemieux
Director
State Archives
State Archives Bldg.
3851 Essen Ln.
Baton Rouge, LA 70804-9125
Phone: (225) 922-1200
Fax: (225) 922-0433

MAINE

MARYLAND
Paul Lamberson
State Records Administrator
Records Mgmt. & Info. Services
State Records Mgmt. Ctr.
7275 Waterloo Rd.
P.O. Box 275
Jessup, MD 20794
Phone: (410) 799-1379
Fax: (410) 799-8532

MASSACHUSETTS
John D. Warner, Jr.
Archivist
Ofc. of the Secretary of the Commonwealth
220 Morrissey Blvd.
Boston, MA 02125
Phone: (617) 727-2816
Fax: (617) 288-8429
E-mail: jwarner@sec.state.ma.us

MICHIGAN
Jim Kinsella
State Records Manager
Records & Mgmt. Services
Dept. of Mgmt. & Budget
P.O. Box 30026
Lansing, MI 48909
Phone: (517) 335-9130

MINNESOTA
Vacant
Records Management
Info. Policy Analysis Div.
Dept of Administration
305A Centennial Ofc. Bldg.
658 Cedar St.
St. Paul, MN 55155
Phone: (651) 296-6879
Fax: (651) 296-5800

MISSISSIPPI
Elbert R. Hilliard
Director
Dept. of Archives & History
P.O. Box 571
Jackson, MS 39205-0571
Phone: (601) 359-6881
Fax: (601) 359-6975

MISSOURI

MONTANA
Ed Eaton
State Records Manager
Records Mgmt. Bur.
Secretary of State
1320 Bozeman St.
Helena, MT 59620
Phone: (406) 444-9000

NEBRASKA
William P. Ptacek
Director
Records Mgmt. Div.
Secretary of State's Ofc.
P.O. Box 94921
Lincoln, NE 68509
Phone: (402) 471-2559
Fax: (402) 471-2406

NEVADA
Guy Louis Rocha
Assistant Administrator
Div. of Archives & Records
Dept. of Museums, Library & Arts
100 Stewart St.
Carson City, NV 89701
Phone: (775) 687-8317
Fax: (775) 687-8311
E-mail: glrocha@clan.lib.nv.us

NEW HAMPSHIRE
Frank C. Mevers
Director & State Archivist
Records Mgmt. & Archives
Secretary of State Ofc.
71 S. Fruit St.
Concord, NH 03301-2410
Phone: (603) 271-2236

NEW JERSEY
Karl Niederer
Director
Div. of Archives & Records Mgmt.
Dept. of State
2300 Stuyvesant Ave.
P.O. Box 307
Trenton, NJ 08625-0307
Phone: (609) 530-3200

NEW MEXICO
Elaine Olah
Administrator
State Records Ctr. & Archives
1205 Camino Carlos Rey
Santa Fe, NM 87505
Phone: (505) 476-7900
Fax: (505) 476-7901

NEW YORK
Richard P. Mills
Commissioner
State Education Dept.
89 Washington Ave., Rm. 111
Albany, NY 12234
Phone: (518) 474-6569
Fax: (518) 473-4909

NORTH CAROLINA
Jeffrey Crow
Director
Div. of Archives & History
Dept. of Cultural Resources
109 E. Jones St.
Raleigh, NC 27601
Phone: (919) 733-7305
Fax: (919) 733-8807

NORTH DAKOTA
Gerald G. Newborg
Director
State Archives & Historical Research Library
State Historical Society
612 E. Blvd. Ave.
Bismarck, ND 58505-0830
Phone: (701) 328-2668
Fax: (701) 328-3710
E-mail: gnewborg@state.nd.us

NORTHERN MARIANA ISLANDS
Jose I. Deleon Guerrero
Special Assistant for Administration
Ofc. of the Governor
Caller Box 10007
Saipan, MP 96950
Phone: (670) 664-2212
Fax: (670) 664-2210
E-mail: gov.tasaa@saipan.com

OHIO
David R. Larson
State Records Administrator
Info. Mgmt. Section
Dept. of Administration Services
4200 Surface Rd.
Columbus, OH 43228-1395
Phone: (614) 466-3064

OKLAHOMA
Richard Engle
Chair
Archives & Records Comm.
Dept. of Libraries
200 NE 18th St.
Oklahoma City, OK 73105
Phone: (405) 522-3583

OREGON
Roy C. Turnbaugh
State Archivist
Archives Div.
Ofc. of Secretary of State
800 Summer St., NE
Salem, OR 97310
Phone: (503) 373-0701
Fax: (503) 373-0953

PENNSYLVANIA
Donald Gibas
Director
Bur. of Public & Paperwork Mgmt.
Dept. of General Services
1825 Stanley Dr.
Harrisburg, PA 17103
Phone: (717) 787-3707
Fax: (717) 787-6379

PUERTO RICO
Nelly Cruz
Director
Archives
Ponde de Leon, #500
Puerta de Tierra
San Juan, PR 00902
Phone: (787) 722-0331

RHODE ISLAND
Gwendolyn Stearn
State Archivist
Ofc. of Secretary of State
337 Westminster St.
Providence, RI 02903
Phone: (401) 222-2353

SOUTH CAROLINA
Rodger E. Stroup
Director
Dept. of Archives & History
8301 Parkland Rd.
Columbia, SC 29223-4905
Phone: (803) 896-6187
Fax: (803) 896-6186

SOUTH DAKOTA
Susan Pietrus
Director
Records Mgmt. Program
Bur. of Administration
State Capitol
500 E. Capitol Ave.
Pierre, SD 57501
Phone: (605) 773-3589
Fax: (605) 773-5955

TENNESSEE
Chester Hughes
Director
Records Mgmt. Div.
843 Cowan St.
Nashville, TN 37243-0555
Phone: (615) 741-1718
Fax: (615) 741-5327

TEXAS
Robert S. Martin
Director & Librarian
Records Mgmt. Div.
State Archives Comm.
P.O. Box 12927
Austin, TX 78711-2927
Phone: (512) 463-5460
Fax: (512) 463-5436

U.S. VIRGIN ISLANDS
E. Marlene Hendricks
Assistant Director
Libraries, Archives & Museums
Dept. of Planning & Natural Resources
23 Dronningens Gade
St. Thomas, VI 00802
Phone: (340) 774-3407
Fax: (340) 775-1887

UTAH
Jeffery O. Johnson
Director of State Archives
Div. of State Archives
Dept. of Adm. Services
Archives Bldg.
Salt Lake City, UT 84114
Phone: (801) 538-3012
Fax: (801) 538-3354
E-mail: jjohnson.asitmain@state.ut.us

VERMONT
A. John Yacavone
Director
Central Services & Public Record
Services Ctr.
R.R. 2
Middlesex, VT 05633-7601
Phone: (802) 828-3700
Fax: (802) 828-3710

VIRGINIA
Nolan T. Yelich
State Librarian
State Library
Serials Section
800 E. Broad St.
Richmond, VA 23219
Phone: (804) 692-3536
Fax: (804) 692-3594

WASHINGTON
Vacant
State Archivist
Archives & Record Mgmt. Div.
Ofc. of Secretary of State
P.O. Box 40238
Olympia, WA 98504-0238
Phone: (360) 586-2660
Fax: (360) 664-8814

WEST VIRGINIA
Mike Slater
Director
Info. Services & Communications
Bldg. 6, Rm. 110
1900 Kanawha Blvd., E.
Charleston, WV 25305
Phone: (304) 558-8918

WISCONSIN
Steven B. Hirsch
Chief
Records Mgmt. Section
Dept. of Administration
4622 Univ. Ave., 10-A
Madison, WI 53702
Phone: (608) 266-2995
Fax: (608) 266-5050

WYOMING
Tony Adams
Records Manager
Div. of Parks & Cultural Resources
Dept. of Commerce
6101 Yellowstone
Cheyenne, WY 82002
Phone: (307) 777-7035
Fax: (307) 777-7044

Recycling

Responsible for promoting and implementing state oversight of municipal solid waste recycling, source reduction and recycling within state government and industry.

ALABAMA

ALASKA
Heather Stockard
Program Manager
Solid Waste Program
Dept. of Environmental Conservation
410 Willoughby Ave., Ste. 105
Juneau, AK 99801-1795
Phone: (907) 465-5150
Fax: (907) 465-5164

AMERICAN SAMOA
Togipa Tausaga
Director
Environmental Protection Agency
Ofc. of the Governor
Pago Pago, AS 96799
Phone: (684) 633-7691

ARIZONA
Tammy Shreeve
Recycling Coordinator
Dept. of Environmental Quality
3033 N. Central Ave.
Phoenix, AZ 85012
Phone: (602) 207-4171

ARKANSAS
Dennis Burks
Chief
Solid Waste Div.
Dept. of Environmental Quality
P.O. Box 8913
Little Rock, AR 72219
Phone: (501) 682-0600
Fax: (501) 682-0611

CALIFORNIA
Jane Irwin
Director
Recycling Div.
Dept. of Conservation
801 K St., MS20-58
Sacramento, CA 95814
Phone: (916) 323-3836

Dan Pennington
Chair
Integrated Waste Mgmt. Board
8800 California Ctr. Dr.
Sacramento, CA 95826-3268
Phone: (916) 255-2151

COLORADO
Howard Roitman
Director
Hazardous Materials & Waste Mgmt.
Dept. of Public Health & Environment
4300 Cherry Creek Dr., S.
Denver, CO 80246-1530
Phone: (303) 692-3300
Fax: (303) 759-5355

CONNECTICUT
Richard Barlow
Chief
Bur. of Waste Mgmt.
Dept. of Environmental Protection
79 Elm St., 1st Fl.
Hartford, CT 06106
Phone: (860) 424-3004

DELAWARE
N.C. Vasuki
General Manager
Solid Waste Authority
1128 S. Bradford St.
P.O. Box 455
Dover, DE 19903
Phone: (302) 739-5361
Fax: (302) 739-4287

DISTRICT OF COLUMBIA
Arthuro V. Lawson
Acting Director
Dept. of Public Works
2000 14th St., NW, 6th Fl.
Washington, DC 20009
Phone: (202) 939-8000

FLORIDA
William W. Hinkley
Chief
Solid & Hazardous Waste
Dept. of Environmental Protection
2600 Blairstone Rd.
Tallahassee, FL 32399-2400
Phone: (850) 488-0300
Fax: (850) 921-8061

GEORGIA
Nancy Negris
Coordinator of Special Projects
Bldg. Authority
1 Martin Luther King, Jr. Dr.
Atlanta, GA 30334
Phone: (404) 656-3252

GUAM
Daniel Lizama
Acting Director
Dept. of Public Works
542 N. Marine Dr.
Tamuning, GU 96911
Phone: (671) 646-3131
Fax: (671) 649-9178

HAWAII

IDAHO

ILLINOIS
Thomas V. Skinner
Director
Environmental Protection Agency
P.O. Box 19276
Springfield, IL 62794
Phone: (217) 782-9540
Fax: (217) 782-9039

INDIANA
Paula Smith
Acting Assistant Commissioner
Pollution Prevention & Technical Assistance
Dept. of Environmental Mgmt.
P.O. Box 6015
Indianapolis, IN 46206-6015
Phone: (317) 232-8172
Fax: (317) 233-5627

IOWA
Roya Stanley
Administrator
Waste Mgmt. Authority
Wallace State Ofc. Bldg.
E. 9th & Grand Aves.
Des Moines, IA 50319
Phone: (515) 281-8489

KANSAS

KENTUCKY
Joy Morgan
Branch Manager
Resource Conservation Section
Div. of Waste Mgmt.
14 Reilly Rd.
Frankfort, KY 40601
Phone: (502) 564-6716
Fax: (502) 564-4049

LOUISIANA
Karen Fisher Brasher
Program Manager
Recycling Section
Ofc. of Solid & Hazardous Waste
P.O. Box 82178
Baton Rouge, LA 70884
Phone: (225) 765-0249
Fax: (225) 765-0299

MAINE
George McDonald
Director
State Planning Ofc.
38 State House Station
Augusta, ME 04333
Phone: (207) 287-6077

MARYLAND
Lauri Scozzafava
Chief
Recycling Services Div.
Dept. of the Environment
2500 Broening Hwy.
Baltimore, MD 21224-6612
Phone: (410) 631-3315
Fax: (410) 631-3321

MASSACHUSETTS
Greg Cooper
Director
Div. of Solid Waste Mgmt.
Dept. of Environmental Protection
1 Winter St., 9th Fl.
Boston, MA 02108
Phone: (617) 292-5988
Fax: (617) 292-5778

MICHIGAN
Larry Hartwig
Chief
Environmental Services Branch
Dept. of Environmental Quality
Environmental Assistance Div.
P.O. Box 30457
Lansing, MI 48909-7957
Phone: (517) 335-1310
Fax: (517) 335-4729

MINNESOTA
John Ikeda
Environmental Specialist
Policy & Planning
Pollution Control Agency
520 Lafayette Rd.
St. Paul, MN 55155
Phone: (651) 296-7294
Fax: (651) 296-9707
E-mail: john.ikeda@pca.state.mn.us

MISSISSIPPI
Tom Whitten
Director
Waste Reduction & Minimization
Ofc. of Pollution Control
P.O. Box 10385
Jackson, MS 39289
Phone: (601) 961-5241
Fax: (601) 354-6612

MISSOURI
Dennis Hansen
Chief of Planning Unit
Solid Waste Mgmt. Program
Dept. of Natural Resources
1738 E. Elm
P.O. Box 176
Jefferson City, MO 65102
Phone: (573) 751-5401
Fax: (573) 526-3902
E-mail: nrhansd@mail.dnr.state.mo.us

MONTANA

NEBRASKA
Rich Tatum
State Recycling Coordinator
Material Div.
Dept. of Adm. Services
P.O. Box 94847
Lincoln, NE 68509
Phone: (402) 471-2431
Fax: (402) 471-2089

NEVADA
Frank Siracusa
Chief
Emergency Mgmt. Div.
Dept. of Motor Vehicles & Public Safety
2525 S. Carson St.
Carson City, NV 89711
Phone: (775) 687-7372
Fax: (775) 687-6788

NEW HAMPSHIRE
Jeffrey Taylor
Director
Ofc. of State Planning, Executive Dept.
Governor's Recycling Program
2 1/2 Beacon St.
Concord, NH 03301-4497
Phone: (603) 271-2155
Fax: (603) 271-1728

NEW JERSEY
Frank Coolick
Assistant Director
Regulation Element
Dept. of Environmental Protection
401 E. State St.
P.O. Box 421
Trenton, NJ 08625-0421
Phone: (609) 633-1418
Fax: (609) 777-0769

NEW MEXICO
Peter Maggiore
Director
Solid Waste Bur.
Dept. of Environment
P.O. Box 26110
Santa Fe, NM 87502
Phone: (505) 827-2855
Fax: (505) 827-2836

NEW YORK
William C. Colden
Bureau Director
Waste Reduction & Recycling
50 Wolf Rd.
Albany, NY 12233
Phone: (518) 457-7337
Fax: (518) 457-1283

NORTH CAROLINA
Heather Sanders
State Agency Recycling Coordinator
Pollution Prevention & Environment Assistance
Dept. of Environment & Natural Resources
P.O. Box 29569
Raleigh, NC 27626-9569
Phone: (919) 715-6500
Fax: (919) 715-6794

NORTH DAKOTA
Neil Knatterud
Director
Waste Mgmt.
Environmental Health Section
P.O. Box 5520
Bismarck, ND 58506-5520
Phone: (701) 328-5166
Fax: (701) 328-5200
E-mail: nknatter@state.nd.us

NORTHERN MARIANA ISLANDS
Edward M. Deleon Guerrero
Director
Dept. of Public Works
Lower Base
P.O. Box 2950
Saipan, MP 96950
Phone: (670) 235-5827
Fax: (670) 235-5253

OHIO
Mike Canfield
Chief
Litter Prevention & Recycling Ofc.
Dept. of Natural Resources
Fountain Sq., Bldg. F-2
Columbus, OH 43224
Phone: (614) 265-6365
Fax: (614) 265-9387

OKLAHOMA
Bryce Hulsey
Environmental Technician
Solid Waste Mgmt. Services
Dept. of Envirl Health Services
P.O. Box 1677
Oklahoma City, OK 73101-1677
Phone: (405) 702-5170
Fax: (405) 702-5101
E-mail: bryce.hulsey@deqmail.state.ok.us

OREGON
Elin Sigurdson
State Recycling Coordinator
Facilities Div.
Dept. of Adm. Services
1225 Ferry St., SE
Salem, OR 97310
Phone: (503) 378-2168
Fax: (503) 373-7210

PENNSYLVANIA
James P. Snyder
Director
Bur. of Land Recycling & Waste Mgmt.
Dept. of Environmental Protection
Rachel Carson State Ofc. Bldg., 14th Fl.
400 Market St.
Harrisburg, PA 17105
Phone: (717) 787-9870
Fax: (717) 787-1904

PUERTO RICO
Roxanna Longoria
Executive Director
Solid Waste Mgmt. Authority
P.O. Box 40285
San Juan, PR 00940
Phone: (787) 765-7575
Fax: (787) 753-2220

RHODE ISLAND
Sherry Giarusso-Mulhearn
Director
Resource Recovery Agency
Shun Pike
Johnston, RI 02919

SOUTH CAROLINA
Hartsill Truesdale
Chief
Bur. of Solid & Hazardous Waste Mgmt.
Dept. of Health & Environmental Control
2600 Bull St.
Columbia, SC 29201
Phone: (803) 896-4000

SOUTH DAKOTA
Greg Buntrock
Recycling Coordinator
Div. of Environmental Services
Dept. of Environment & Natural Resources
523 E. Capitol Ave.
Pierre, SD 57501
Phone: (605) 773-3153
Fax: (605) 773-6035

TENNESSEE
Milton Hamilton
Commissioner
Dept. of Environment & Conservation
L & C Tower, 21st Fl.
Nashville, TN 37243
Phone: (615) 532-0104
Fax: (615) 532-0120

TEXAS
Ralph Marquez
Commissioner
Natural Resource Conservation Comm.
12100 Park 35 Cir., Bldg. A
P.O. Box 13087, MC 100
Austin, TX 78711-3087
Phone: (512) 239-5500
Fax: (512) 239-5533

U.S. VIRGIN ISLANDS
Harold G. Thompson
Acting Commissioner
Dept. of Public Works
No. 8 Sub Base
St. Thomas, VI 00802
Phone: (340) 776-4844
Fax: (340) 776-8990

UTAH
Sonja Wallace
Pollution Prevention Coordinator
Ofc. of Planning & Public Affairs
Dept. of Environmental Quality
168 N. 1950 W.
Salt Lake City, UT 84114-4810
Phone: (801) 536-4477
Fax: (801) 536-0061
E-mail: swallace@deq.state.ut.us

VERMONT
Andrea Cohen
Chief
Recycling & Conservation Section
Div. of Solid Waste Mgmt.
103 S. Main St.
Waterbury, VT 05671-0407
Phone: (802) 241-2368
Fax: (802) 241-3273

VIRGINIA
Dennis H. Treacy
Director
Dept. of Environmental Quality
629 E. Main St.
Richmond, VA 23219
Phone: (804) 698-4020
Fax: (804) 698-4019

WASHINGTON
Cullen Stephenson
Program Manager
Solid Waste
Dept. of Ecology
P.O. Box 47600
Olympia, WA 98504-7600
Phone: (360) 407-6103
Fax: (360) 407-6102

WEST VIRGINIA
Charles Jordan
Director
Solid Waste Mgmt. Board
1615 Washington St., E.
Charleston, WV 25311-2126
Phone: (304) 558-0844
Fax: (304) 558-0899

WISCONSIN
Catherine Cooper
Coordinator
Waste Reduction & Recycling
Dept. of Natural Resources
101 S. Webster, 3rd Fl.
P.O. Box 7921
Madison, WI 53707
Phone: (608) 267-7566
Fax: (608) 267-2768

WYOMING
Dianna Gentry-Hogle
State Recycling Coordinator
250 Lincoln St.
Lander, WY 82520
Phone: (307) 332-6924
Fax: (307) 332-7726

Reporters of Judicial Decisions

Responsible for the publication and dissemination of appellate judicial decisions in their jurisdiction.

ALABAMA
George Earl Smith
Court Reporter
Appellate Cts.
Judicial Bldg.
300 Dexter Ave.
Montgomery, AL 36104-3741
Phone: (334) 242-4621
Fax: (334) 242-4483

ALASKA
Marilyn May
Clerk
Judiciary Reports
Supreme Ct.
303 K St.
Anchorage, AK 99501-2084
Phone: (907) 264-0608
Fax: (907) 264-0878

AMERICAN SAMOA

ARIZONA
Noel Dessaint
Clerk of the Supreme Court
1501 W. Washington, Rm. 402
Phoenix, AZ 85007
Phone: (602) 542-9396

ARKANSAS
W.H. Arnold
Chief Justice
Justice Bldg.
625 Marshall
Little Rock, AR 72201
Phone: (501) 682-6861
Fax: (501) 682-6877

John Jennings
Chief Judge
Ct. of Appeals
Justice Bldg.
325 Marshall
Little Rock, AR 72201
Phone: (501) 682-7461
Fax: (501) 682-6877

CALIFORNIA
Edward Jessen
Reporter of Decisions
Supreme Ct. of California
303 Second St., S. Tower, 8th Fl.
San Francisco, CA 94107
Phone: (415) 396-9555

COLORADO
Leo H. Smith
Court Reporter
Ct. of Appeals
2 E. 14th Ave.
Denver, CO 80203
Phone: (303) 837-3738
Fax: (303) 837-3702

CONNECTICUT
Emily Lebovitz
Reporter of Judicial Decisions
Supreme Ct.
Drawer N, Station A
Hartford, CT 06106
Phone: (860) 566-5877
Fax: (860) 566-6521

DELAWARE
Stephen Teller
Court Administrator
Supreme Ct.
P.O. Box 1997
Wilmington, DE 19899
Phone: (302) 577-8425
Fax: (302) 577-3702

DISTRICT OF COLUMBIA
Garland Pinkston, Jr.
Clerk
Ct. of Appeals
500 Indiana Ave., NW, Ste. 6000
Washington, DC 20001
Phone: (202) 879-2725
Fax: (202) 626-8847

FLORIDA
Jim Logue
Reporter of Judicial Decisions
Supreme Ct.
500 S. Duval St.
Tallahassee, FL 32399
Phone: (850) 488-0007

GEORGIA
William Scott Henwood
Reporter of Judicial Decisions
Supreme Ct. & Ct. of Appeals
568 State Ofc. Annex
244 Washington St., SW
Atlanta, GA 30334
Phone: (404) 656-3460
Fax: (404) 656-2253

GUAM

HAWAII
Darrell N. Phillips
Chief Clerk
Ofc. of the Chief Clerk
Supreme Ct.
417 S. King St.
Honolulu, HI 96813
Phone: (808) 539-4919
Fax: (808) 539-4928

IDAHO
Frederick C. Lyon
Supreme Court Clerk
Supreme Ct. Bldg.
P.O. Box 83720
Boise, ID 83720
Phone: (208) 334-2210

ILLINOIS
Brian Ervin
Reporter of Decision
P.O. Box 3456
Bloomington, IL 61702-3456
Phone: (309) 827-8513

INDIANA
Brian Bishop
Clerk of Supreme/Appellate Courts
State House, Rm. 217
200 W. Washington St.
Indianapolis, IN 46204
Phone: (317) 232-1930
Fax: (317) 232-8365

IOWA
Kate Wheeler
Secretary to the Chief Justice of Supreme Court
Supreme Ct.
State Capitol Bldg.
Des Moines, IA 50319
Phone: (515) 281-5175

KANSAS
Richard D. Ross
Supreme Ct. and Ct. of Appeals
Judicial Ctr.
301 W. 10th St., Rm. 354
Topeka, KS 66612-1507
Phone: (913) 296-3214
Fax: (913) 296-7076

KENTUCKY
Susan Stokley Clary
Court Administrator
Supreme Ct.
700 Capitol Bldg., 2nd Fl.
Frankfort, KY 40601
Phone: (502) 564-4176
Fax: (502) 564-2665

LOUISIANA
Bo Wolcott
Court Reporter
Supreme Ct.
301 Loyola Ave., Rm. 200
New Orleans, LA 70112
Phone: (504) 568-5707
Fax: (504) 568-2846

MAINE
James P. Chute
Clerk of the Law Court
Supreme Ct.
P.O. Box 368
Portland, ME 04112
Phone: (207) 822-4146

MARYLAND
Alexander L. Cummings
Clerk of Court
Ct. of Appeals Clerk's Ofc.
Judiciary
Ct. of Appeals Bldg.
361 Rowe Blvd.
Annapolis, MD 21401
Phone: (410) 260-1502

MASSACHUSETTS
Charles Clifford Allen, III
Reporter of Decisions
Supreme Judicial Ct.
1407 New Ct. House
Boston, MA 02108
Phone: (617) 557-1196

MICHIGAN
William F. Haggerty
Court Reporter
Supreme Ct.
P.O. Box 30052
Lansing, MI 48909
Phone: (617) 557-1196

MINNESOTA
Janet Chapdelaine
Opinion Clerk
Supreme Ct. & Ct. of Appeals
305 MN Judicial Ctr.
25 Constitution Ave.
St. Paul, MN 55155
Phone: (651) 296-8579
Fax: (651) 297-4149
E-mail: janet.chapdelaine@state.mn.us

MISSISSIPPI

MISSOURI
Cynthia L. Turley
Deputy Clerk in the Court En Banc
Supreme Ct.
Supreme Ct. Bldg.
P.O. Box 150
Jefferson City, MO 65102
Phone: (573) 751-4144
Fax: (573) 751-7514
E-mail: cindy_turley@osca.state.mo.us

MONTANA
Shauna Thomas
State Reporter
P.O. Box 749
Helena, MT 59624
Phone: (406) 449-8889

NEBRASKA
Peggy J. Polacek
Reporter of Decisions
Reporter's Ofc.
Supreme Ct.
State Capitol, Rm. 1214
Lincoln, NE 68509
Phone: (402) 471-3010

NEVADA
Janette M. Bloom
Clerk
Supreme Ct. Bldg.
201 S. Carson St., Ste. 201
Carson City, NV 89701
Phone: (775) 687-5180
Fax: (775) 687-3155

NEW HAMPSHIRE
Howard J. Zibel
Clerk of Court
Supreme Ct.
Noble Dr.
Concord, NH 03301
Phone: (603) 271-2646
Fax: (603) 271-6630

NEW JERSEY
Stephen W. Townsend
Clerk
Supreme Ct.
P.O. Box 970
Trenton, NJ 08625
Phone: (609) 292-4837

NEW MEXICO
Kathleen Jo Gibson
Chief Clerk
Supreme Ct.
P.O. Box 848
Santa Fe, NM 87504-0848
Phone: (505) 827-4860
Fax: (505) 827-4837

NEW YORK
Gary D. Spivey
State Reporter
Law Reporting Bur.
1 Commerce Plz., 17th Fl.
Albany, NY 12210
Phone: (518) 474-8211
Fax: (518) 474-6869

NORTH CAROLINA
Ralph A. White, Jr.
Court Reporter
Supreme Ct.
P.O. Box 2170
Raleigh, NC 27601
Phone: (919) 733-3710
Fax: (919) 715-0669

NORTH DAKOTA
Penny Miller
Clerk of Court
Supreme Ct.
600 E. Blvd. Ave., 1st Fl. - Judicial Wing
Bismarck, ND 58505-0530
Phone: (701) 328-2221
Fax: (701) 328-4480
E-mail: pennym@sc3.court.state.nd.us

NORTHERN MARIANA ISLANDS
Dennis Yamase
Executive Director
Law Revision Comm.
Commonwealth of the Northern Mariana Islands
P.O. Box 2165
Saipan, MP 96950
Phone: (670) 235-5890

OHIO
Walter Kobalka
Reporter of Decisions
Supreme Ct.
30 E. Broad St., 2nd Fl.
Columbus, OH 43266-0419
Phone: (614) 466-4961

OKLAHOMA
James Patterson
Supreme Court Clerk
State Capitol, Rm. B-2
2300 N. Lincoln Blvd.
Oklahoma City, OK 73105
Phone: (405) 521-2163

OREGON
Mary Bauman
Publications Editor
Supreme Ct. Bldg.
1163 State St.
Salem, OR 97310
Phone: (503) 986-5567
Fax: (503) 986-5560

PENNSYLVANIA
Bunny Baum
Director of Judicial Services
Administration Ofc. of Cts.
Supreme Ct.
1515 Market St., Ste. 1414
Philadelphia, PA 19102-2077
Phone: (215) 560-6325

PUERTO RICO
Lourdes Diaz-Antonmattei
Court Reporter
Supreme Ct.
P.O. Box 2392
San Juan, PR 00902-2392
Phone: (787) 723-4466
Fax: (787) 725-4910

RHODE ISLAND
Albert Cippolla
Court Reporter
Supreme Ct.
250 Benefit St.
Providence, RI 02903
Phone: (401) 222-3073

SOUTH CAROLINA
Thomas M. Neal, III
Court Reporter
Supreme Ct.
P.O. Box 11330
Columbia, SC 29211
Phone: (803) 734-1080

SOUTH DAKOTA

TENNESSEE

TEXAS
John T. Adams
Chief Deputy Clerk
Supreme Ct.
P.O. Box 12248
Capitol Station
Austin, TX 78711
Phone: (512) 463-1312

U.S. VIRGIN ISLANDS

UTAH
Hollie Hayes
Legal Secretary
Ct. of Appeals
P.O. Box 140230
Salt Lake City, UT 84114-0230
Phone: (801) 578-3950
Fax: (801) 578-3999
E-mail: hollieh@email.utcourts.gov

Kathy Vass
Legal Secretary
Ct. of Appeals
P.O. Box 140230
Salt Lake City, UT 84114-0230
Phone: (801) 578-3950
Fax: (801) 578-3999
E-mail: kathyv@email.utcourts.gov

VERMONT
Helen E. Wagner
Director, Judicial Operations
Ct. Administration Ofc.
111 State St.
Montpelier, VT 05609
Phone: (802) 828-3278

VIRGINIA
Kent Sinclair
Reporter of Decisions
Supreme Ct.
P.O. Box 5104
Charlottesville, VA 22905
Phone: (804) 924-4689
Fax: (804) 293-7564

WASHINGTON
Deborah Norwood
Reporter of Decisions
Temple of Justice
P.O. Box 40929
Olympia, WA 98504-0929
Phone: (360) 357-2145
Fax: (360) 357-2099
E-mail: smpt.debby.norwood
@courts.wa.gov

WEST VIRGINIA
Darrell V. McGraw, Jr.
Attorney General
Ofc. of the Attorney Gen.
Capitol Bldg.
1900 Kanawha Blvd., E.
Charleston, WV 25305
Phone: (304) 558-2021
Fax: (304) 558-0140

WISCONSIN
Marilyn L. Graves
Supreme Court Clerk
110 E. Main St., Ste. 215
P.O. Box 1688
Madison, WI 53701-1688
Phone: (608) 266-1880
Fax: (608) 267-0640

WYOMING
Judy Pacheco
Clerk of the Supreme
Court
Supreme Ct.
Supreme Ct. Bldg.
2301 Capitol Ave.
Cheyenne, WY 82002
Phone: (307) 777-7316

Retirement (State Employees)

Administers the retirement program for state employees other than teachers.

ALABAMA
David G. Bronner
Secretary/Treasurer
Retirement Systems
135 S. Union St.
Montgomery, AL 36130-2150
Phone: (334) 832-4140
Fax: (334) 240-3268

ALASKA
Guy Bell
Director
Div. of Retirement & Benefits
Dept. of Administration
P.O. Box 110203
Juneau, AK 99811-0203
Phone: (907) 465-4460
Fax: (907) 465-3086

AMERICAN SAMOA
George Odom
Retirement Officer
Dept. of Human Resources
Pago Pago, AS 96799
Phone: (684) 633-5456
Fax: (684) 633-1460

ARIZONA
Leroy Gilbertson
Director
Retirement System
P.O. Box 33910
Phoenix, AZ 85067-3910
Phone: (602) 240-2031
Fax: (602) 264-6113

ARKANSAS
Bill Van Cleve
Director
Public Employees Retirement System
124 W. Capitol Ave.
Little Rock, AR 72201
Phone: (501) 682-7800
Fax: (501) 682-5731

CALIFORNIA
Jim Burton
Chief Executive Officer
Public Employment Retirement System
400 P St.
Sacramento, CA 95814
Phone: (916) 326-3829

COLORADO
Robert J. Scott
Executive Director
Public Employees Retirement Association
1300 Logan St.
Denver, CO 80203
Phone: (303) 832-9550
Fax: (303) 863-3811

CONNECTICUT
Steven Weinberger
Director
Retirement Div.
Ofc. of the Comptroller
55 Elm St.
Hartford, CT 06106
Phone: (860) 702-3481

DELAWARE
David Craik
Director of Pension Office
Ofc. of the State Treasurer
Thomas Collins Bldg.
P.O. Box 1401
Dover, DE 19901
Phone: (302) 739-4208
Fax: (302) 739-6129

DISTRICT OF COLUMBIA
Valerie Holt
Interim Chief Financial Officer
Ofc. of the Chief Financial Officer
441 4th St., NW, Ste. 1150
Washington, DC 20001
Phone: (202) 727-2476

FLORIDA
Andrew J. McMullian, III
Director
Div. of Retirement
Cedars Executive Ctr., Bldg. C
2639 N. Monroe St.
Tallahassee, FL 32399-1560
Phone: (850) 488-5540
Fax: (850) 921-0371

GEORGIA
Rudolph Johnson
Director
Employees' Retirement System
2 Northside 75, Ste. 300
Atlanta, GA 30318
Phone: (404) 352-6400

GUAM
John A. Rios
Director
Retirement Fund
424 Rte. 8
Maite, GU 96927
Phone: (671) 475-8900
Fax: (671) 475-8922

HAWAII
David Shimabukuro
Administrator
Employees' Retirement System
Dept. of Budget & Finance
201 Merchant St., #1400
Honolulu, HI 96813
Phone: (808) 586-1700
Fax: (808) 586-1677

IDAHO
Alan H. Winkle
Director
Public Employee Retirement
820 Washington St.
Boise, ID 83720
Phone: (208) 334-3365

ILLINOIS
Michael L. Mory
Executive Secretary
State Retirement Systems
2101 S. Veteran Park Way
P.O. Box 19255
Springfield, IL 62794-9255
Phone: (217) 785-7444
Fax: (217) 785-7019

INDIANA
William Butler
Director
Public Employees Retirement Fund
143 W. Market St., Ste. 602
Indianapolis, IN 46204
Phone: (317) 233-4162
Fax: (317) 232-1614

IOWA
Greg Cusack
Chief Retirement Benefits Officer
Public Employee Retirement Systems
Dept. of Personnel
600 E. Court Ave.
Des Moines, IA 50306
Phone: (515) 281-0020

KANSAS
Meredith Williams
Executive Secretary
Public Employees Retirement System
611 S. Kansas Ave., #100
Topeka, KS 66603-3803
Phone: (785) 296-6666
Fax: (785) 296-2422

KENTUCKY
Pamela Johnson
General Manager
Retirement Systems
1260 Louisville Rd.
Frankfort, KY 40601
Phone: (502) 564-4646
Fax: (502) 564-5656

LOUISIANA
James Wood
Executive Director
State Employees
Retirement System
P.O. Box 44213
Baton Rouge, LA 70804-4213
Phone: (225) 922-0600
Fax: (225) 922-0614

MAINE
Kay R.H. Evans
Executive Director
State Retirement System
46 State House Station
Augusta, ME 04333
Phone: (207) 287-3461

MARYLAND
Peter Vaughn
Executive Director
Retirement & Pension Systems
State Retirement Agency
301 W. Preston St., Rm. 706
Baltimore, MD 21201
Phone: (410) 767-4051
Fax: (410) 333-7557

MASSACHUSETTS
Robert Stalnaker
Executive Director
Public Employee Retirement Administration Comm.
5 Middlesex Ave., 3rd Fl.
Somerville, MA 02145
Phone: (617) 666-4446
Fax: (617) 628-4002

MICHIGAN
Chris De Rose
Director
Ofc. of Retirement
Dept. of Mgmt. & Budget
P.O. Box 30171
Lansing, MI 48909
Phone: (517) 322-6235

MINNESOTA
David Bergstrom
Executive Director
State Retirement System
175 W. Lafayette Frontage Rd.
St. Paul, MN 55107-1425
Phone: (651) 296-1510
Fax: (651) 297-5238
E-mail: dave.bergstrom@state.mn.us

MISSISSIPPI
Frank Ready
Executive Director
Public Employees
Retirement System
429 Mississippi St.
Jackson, MS 39201-1005
Phone: (601) 359-3589
Fax: (601) 359-2285

MISSOURI
Gary Findlay
Executive Director
State Employees'
Retirement System
907 Wildwood Dr.
Jefferson City, MO 65102
Phone: (573) 632-6100
Fax: (573) 632-6101
E-mail: garyf@mosers.org

MONTANA
Mike O'Connor
Administrator
Public Employee
Retirement Div.
Dept. of Administration
1712 9th Ave.
Helena, MT 59620
Phone: (406) 444-3154
Fax: (406) 444-5428

NEBRASKA
Anna Sullivan
Director
Public Employees
Retirement Systems
P.O. Box 94816
Lincoln, NE 68509
Phone: (402) 471-2053
Fax: (402) 471-9493

NEVADA
George Pyne
Executive Officer
Public Employee
Retirement System
693 W. Nye Ln.
Carson City, NV 89703
Phone: (775) 687-4200
Fax: (775) 687-5131

NEW HAMPSHIRE
Harry M. Descoteau
Executive Secretary
Retirement Dept.
4 Chenell Dr.
Concord, NH 03301-8509
Phone: (603) 271-3351

NEW JERSEY
Margaret M. McMahon
Director
Div. of Pensions & Benefits
Dept. of Treasury
P.O. Box 295
Trenton, NJ 08625-0295
Phone: (609) 292-3678
Fax: (609) 393-4606

NEW MEXICO
Alice Herter
Executive Director
Public Employees
Retirement Board
PERA Bldg.
P.O. Box 2123
Santa Fe, NM 87504
Phone: (505) 827-4700
Fax: (505) 827-4670

NEW YORK
H. Carl McCall
Comptroller
A.E. Smith Ofc. Bldg., 6th Fl.
Albany, NY 12236
Phone: (518) 474-3506
Fax: (518) 473-3004

NORTH CAROLINA
Jack Pruitt
Director of Retirement
Retirement
Ofc. of Treasurer
325 N. Salisbury St.
Raleigh, NC 27603-1388
Phone: (919) 508-5377
Fax: (919) 508-5350

NORTH DAKOTA
Sparb Collins
Executive Director
Public Employees
Retirement System
P.O. Box 1214
Bismarck, ND 58502-1214
Phone: (701) 328-3900
Fax: (701) 328-3920
E-mail: scollins@state.nd.us

NORTHERN MARIANA ISLANDS
Edward H. Manglona
Administrator
Retirement Fund
P.O. Box 1247
Saipan, MP 96950
Phone: (670) 234-7228
Fax: (670) 234-9624
E-mail: nmi.retirement@saipan.com

OHIO
Richard E. Schumacher
Executive Director
Public Employees
Retirement System
277 E. Town St.
Columbus, OH 43215
Phone: (614) 466-2822
Fax: (614) 466-5837

OKLAHOMA
Steve Edmonds
Director
Public Employees
Retirement System
6601 N. Broadway Extension, Ste. 129
Oklahoma City, OK 73116
Phone: (405) 858-6737
Fax: (405) 848-5967

OREGON
Fred McDonnal
Director
Public Employees
Retirement System
P.O. Box 23700
Tigard, OR 97281-3700
Phone: (503) 603-7575
Fax: (503) 598-1218

PENNSYLVANIA
John Brosius
Executive Director
State Employees'
Retirement
30 N. 3rd St.
Harrisburg, PA 17108-1147
Phone: (717) 787-6780
Fax: (717) 783-7300

PUERTO RICO
Andres Barbeito
Administrator
Personnel Retirement Div.
P.O. Box 42003
San Juan, PR 00940-2003
Phone: (787) 754-4600
Fax: (787) 250-7251

RHODE ISLAND
Joann Flaminio
Executive Director
Employee Retirement System
40 Fountain St., 1st Fl.
Providence, RI 02903
Phone: (401) 222-2203
Fax: (401) 222-2430

SOUTH CAROLINA
Robert C. Toomey
Director
Retirement System
State Budget & Control Board
202 Arbor Lake Dr.
Columbia, SC 29223
Phone: (803) 737-6934

SOUTH DAKOTA
Al Asher
Administrator
State Retirement System
P.O. Box 1098
Pierre, SD 57501-1098
Phone: (605) 773-3731
Fax: (605) 773-3947

TENNESSEE
Ed Hennessee
Director
Div. of Retirement
Dept. of Treasury
Andrew Jackson Bldg., 10th Fl.
Nashville, TN 37219
Phone: (615) 741-7063
Fax: (615) 734-6464

TEXAS
Sheila Beckett
Executive Director
Employees Retirement System
P.O. Box 13207
Austin, TX 78711-3207
Phone: (512) 867-7176
Fax: (512) 867-3334

U.S. VIRGIN ISLANDS
Lawrence Bryan
Administrator
Govt. Employee Retirement System
GERS Bldg.
Charlotte Amalie
St. Thomas, VI 00802
Phone: (340) 776-7703
Fax: (340) 776-4499

UTAH
Dee Williams
Executive Director
State Retirement Ofc.
Retirement Systems
540 E. 200 S.
Salt Lake City, UT 84102-2099
Phone: (801) 366-7301
Fax: (801) 366-7734

VERMONT
Cynthia Webster
Director of Retirement Services
Retirement Div.
Ofc. of the Treasurer
133 State St.
Montpelier, VT 05633-6901
Phone: (802) 828-2305
Fax: (802) 828-2772

VIRGINIA
William H. Leighty
Director
Retirement System
1200 E. Main St.
Richmond, VA 23219
Phone: (804) 649-8059
Fax: (804) 371-0613

WASHINGTON
John Charles
Director
Dept. of Retirement Systems
1025 E. Union St.
P.O. Box 48380
Olympia, WA 98504-8380
Phone: (360) 709-4700
Fax: (360) 664-3618

WEST VIRGINIA
Betty S. Ireland
Executive Secretary
Consolidated Public Retirement Board
Bldg. 5, Ste. 1000
Capitol Complex
Charleston, WV 25305-0720
Phone: (304) 558-3570

WISCONSIN
Eric Stanchfield
Secretary
Dept. of Employee Trust Funds
P.O. Box 7931
Madison, WI 53707-7931
Phone: (608) 261-8161
Fax: (608) 267-0633

WYOMING
Jerry Fox
Director
Retirement System Board
Herschler Bldg.
122 W. 25th St.
Cheyenne, WY 82002
Phone: (307) 777-7691

Retirement (Teachers)

Administers the retirement program of the state's public school teachers.

ALABAMA
David G. Bronner
Secretary/Treasurer
Retirement Systems
135 S. Union St.
Montgomery, AL 36130-2150
Phone: (334) 832-4140
Fax: (334) 240-3268

ALASKA
Guy Bell
Director
Div. of Retirement & Benefits
Dept. of Administration
P.O. Box 110203
Juneau, AK 99811-0203
Phone: (907) 465-4460
Fax: (907) 465-3086

AMERICAN SAMOA

ARIZONA
Leroy Gilbertson
Director
Retirement System
P.O. Box 33910
Phoenix, AZ 85067-3910
Phone: (602) 240-2031
Fax: (602) 240-6113

ARKANSAS
Bill Shirron
Executive Director
Teachers Retirement System
1400 W. 3rd St.
Little Rock, AR 72201
Phone: (501) 682-1517
Fax: (501) 682-2663

CALIFORNIA
James D. Mosman
Chief Executive Officer
Teachers Retirement System
7667 Folsom Blvd., Ste. 300
Sacramento, CA 95851
Phone: (916) 229-3870

COLORADO
Robert J. Scott
Executive Director
Public Employees Retirement Association
1300 Logan St.
Denver, CO 80203
Phone: (303) 832-9550
Fax: (303) 863-3811

CONNECTICUT
Bill Sudol
Administrator
Teachers' Retirement Board
165 Capitol Ave., Rm. 202
Hartford, CT 06106
Phone: (860) 241-8402

DELAWARE
David Craik
Director of Pension Office
Ofc. of the State Treasurer
Thomas Collins Bldg.
P.O. Box 1401
Dover, DE 19901
Phone: (302) 739-4208
Fax: (302) 739-6129

DISTRICT OF COLUMBIA
Jorge Morales
Executive Director
Retirement Board
1400 L St., NW, Ste. 300
Washington, DC 20005
Phone: (202) 535-1271

FLORIDA
Andrew J. McMullian, III
Director
Div. of Retirement
Cedars Executive Ctr., Bldg. C
2639 N. Monroe St.
Tallahassee, FL 32399-1560
Phone: (850) 488-5540
Fax: (850) 921-0371

GEORGIA
Gerald S. Gilbert
Executive Director
Teachers' Retirement System
2 Northside 75, Ste. 400
Atlanta, GA 30318
Phone: (404) 352-6500

GUAM
John A. Rios
Director
Retirement Fund
424 Rte. 8
Maite, GU 96927
Phone: (671) 475-8900
Fax: (671) 475-8922

HAWAII
David Shimabukuro
Administrator
Employees' Retirement System
Dept. of Budget & Finance
201 Merchant St., #1400
Honolulu, HI 96813
Phone: (808) 586-1700
Fax: (808) 586-1677

IDAHO
Alan H. Winkle
Director
Public Employee Retirement
820 Washington St.
Boise, ID 83720
Phone: (208) 334-3365

ILLINOIS
Keith Bozarth
Executive Director
Teachers' Retirement System
2815 W. Washington St.
Springfield, IL 62794
Phone: (217) 753-0315
Fax: (217) 753-0967

INDIANA
Mary Pettersen
Executive Secretary
Teachers' Retirement Fund
150 W. Market St., Ste. 300
Indianapolis, IN 46204-2809
Phone: (317) 232-3869
Fax: (317) 232-3882

IOWA
Greg Cusack
Chief Retirement Benefits Officer
Public Employee Retirement Systems
Dept. of Personnel
600 E. Court Ave.
Des Moines, IA 50306
Phone: (515) 281-0020

KANSAS
Meredith Williams
Executive Secretary
Public Employees Retirement System
611 S. Kansas Ave., #100
Topeka, KS 66603-3803
Phone: (785) 296-6666
Fax: (785) 296-2422

KENTUCKY
Pat N. Miller
Executive Secretary
Teachers' Retirement System
479 Versailles Rd.
Frankfort, KY 40601
Phone: (502) 573-5120
Fax: (502) 573-6695

LOUISIANA
James P. Hadley, Jr.
Director
Teachers Retirement System
P.O. Box 94123
Baton Rouge, LA 70804-9123
Phone: (225) 925-6454
Fax: (225) 925-3944

MAINE
Kay R.H. Evans
Executive Director
State Retirement System
46 State House Station
Augusta, ME 04333
Phone: (207) 287-3461

MARYLAND
Arthur N. Caple, Jr.
Executive Director
Supplemental Retirement Plans
Teachers & State Employees
6 St. Paul St., Ste. 200
Baltimore, MD 21202-1608
Phone: (410) 767-8731
Fax: (410) 767-8739

MASSACHUSETTS
Thomas Lussier
Executive Director
Teachers' Retirement Board
Executive Ofc. of Administration & Finance
69 Canal St., 3rd Fl.
Boston, MA 02144
Phone: (617) 727-3661
Fax: (617) 727-6797

MICHIGAN
Chris De Rose
Director
Ofc. of Retirement
Dept. of Mgmt. & Budget
P.O. Box 30171
Lansing, MI 48909
Phone: (517) 322-6235

MINNESOTA
Gary Austin
Executive Director
Teachers Retirement Association
Galary Bldg., Ste. 500
17 W. Exchange St.
St. Paul, MN 55102
Phone: (651) 296-2409
Fax: (651) 297-5999

MISSISSIPPI
Frank Ready
Executive Director
Public Employees Retirement System
429 Mississippi St.
Jackson, MS 39201-1005
Phone: (601) 359-3589
Fax: (601) 359-2285

MISSOURI
Joel Walters
Executive Director
Public School Retirement System
701 W. Main
P.O. Box 268
Jefferson City, MO 65102
Phone: (573) 634-5290
Fax: (573) 634-5375
E-mail: jwolters@psrsmo.org

MONTANA
Dave L. Senn
Administrator
Teacher's Retirement Div.
Dept. of Administration
1500 6th Ave.
Helena, MT 59601
Phone: (406) 444-3134
Fax: (406) 444-2641

NEBRASKA
Anna Sullivan
Director
Public Employees Retirement Systems
P.O. Box 94816
Lincoln, NE 68509
Phone: (402) 471-2053
Fax: (402) 471-9493

NEVADA
George Pyne
Executive Officer
Public Employee Retirement System
693 W. Nye Ln.
Carson City, NV 89703
Phone: (775) 687-4200
Fax: (775) 687-5131

NEW HAMPSHIRE
Harry M. Descoteau
Executive Secretary
Retirement Dept.
4 Chenell Dr.
Concord, NH 03301-8509
Phone: (603) 271-3351

NEW JERSEY
Margaret M. McMahon
Director
Div. of Pensions & Benefits
Dept. of Treasury
P.O. Box 295
Trenton, NJ 08625-0295
Phone: (609) 292-3678
Fax: (609) 393-4606

NEW MEXICO
Danny Joe Lyle
Director
Educational Retirement Board
P.O. Box 26129
Santa Fe, NM 87502-6129
Phone: (505) 827-8030
Fax: (505) 827-1855

NEW YORK
George M. Philip
Executive Director
Teachers' Retirement System
10 Corp. Woods Dr.
Albany, NY 12211
Phone: (518) 447-2700
Fax: (518) 447-2695

NORTH CAROLINA
Jack Pruitt
Director of Retirement
Retirement
Ofc. of Treasurer
325 N. Salisbury St.
Raleigh, NC 27603-1388
Phone: (919) 508-5377
Fax: (919) 508-5350

NORTH DAKOTA
Scott Engmann
Executive Director
Retirement & Investment Ofc.
P.O. Box 7100
Bismarck, ND 58507-7100
Phone: (701) 328-9889
Fax: (701) 328-9897
E-mail: sengmann@state.nd.us

NORTHERN MARIANA ISLANDS
Edward H. Manglona
Administrator
Retirement Fund
P.O. Box 1247
Saipan, MP 96950
Phone: (670) 234-7228
Fax: (670) 234-9624
E-mail: nmi.retirement@saipan.com

OHIO

OKLAHOMA
Tom Beavers
Executive Secretary
Teachers Retirement System
2801 N. Lincoln
Oklahoma City, OK 73150
Phone: (405) 521-2387
Fax: (405) 521-4718

OREGON
Judy Hart
Manager
Membership & Employee Relations
Public Employees Retirement System
P.O. Box 23700
Tigard, OR 97281
Phone: (503) 603-7734
Fax: (503) 598-1218

PENNSYLVANIA
James Perry
Executive Director
School Employees' Retirement
5 N. 5th St., Rm. 317
Harrisburg, PA 17108
Phone: (717) 787-6780
Fax: (717) 783-7300

PUERTO RICO
Sonia Babilonia
President
Teachers Retirement System
P.O. Box 1879
Hato Rey, PR 00919
Phone: (787) 764-8611

RHODE ISLAND
Joann Flaminio
Executive Director
Employee Retirement System
40 Fountain St., 1st Fl.
Providence, RI 02903
Phone: (401) 222-2203
Fax: (401) 222-2430

SOUTH CAROLINA
Robert C. Toomey
Director
Retirement System
State Budget & Control Board
202 Arbor Lake Dr.
Columbia, SC 29223
Phone: (803) 737-6934

SOUTH DAKOTA
Al Asher
Administrator
State Retirement System
P.O. Box 1098
Pierre, SD 57501-1098
Phone: (605) 773-3731
Fax: (605) 773-3947

TENNESSEE
Ed Hennessee
Director
Div. of Retirement
Dept. of Treasury
Andrew Jackson Bldg., 10th Fl.
Nashville, TN 37219
Phone: (615) 741-7063
Fax: (615) 734-6464

TEXAS
Charles L. Dunlap
Executive Director
Teacher Retirement System
1000 Red River
Austin, TX 78701
Phone: (512) 397-6401
Fax: (512) 370-0585

U.S. VIRGIN ISLANDS
Lawrence Bryan
Administrator
Govt. Employee Retirement System
GERS Bldg.
Charlotte Amalie
St. Thomas, VI 00802
Phone: (340) 776-7703
Fax: (340) 776-4499

UTAH
Dee Williams
Executive Director
State Retirement Ofc.
Retirement Systems
540 E. 200 S.
Salt Lake City, UT 84102-2099
Phone: (801) 366-7301
Fax: (801) 366-7734

VERMONT
Cynthia Webster
Director of Retirement Services
Retirement Div.
Ofc. of the Treasurer
133 State St.
Montpelier, VT 05633-6901
Phone: (802) 828-2305
Fax: (802) 828-2772

VIRGINIA
William H. Leighty
Director
Retirement System
1200 E. Main St.
Richmond, VA 23219
Phone: (804) 649-8059
Fax: (804) 371-0613

WASHINGTON
John Charles
Director
Dept. of Retirement Systems
1025 E. Union St.
P.O. Box 48380
Olympia, WA 98504-8380
Phone: (360) 709-4700
Fax: (360) 664-3618

WEST VIRGINIA
Betty S. Ireland
Executive Secretary
Consolidated Public Retirement Board
Bldg. 5, Ste. 1000
Capitol Complex
Charleston, WV 25305-0720
Phone: (304) 558-3570

WISCONSIN
Eric Stanchfield
Secretary
Dept. of Employee Trust Funds
P.O. Box 7931
Madison, WI 53707-7931
Phone: (608) 261-8161
Fax: (608) 267-0633

WYOMING
Jerry Fox
Director
Retirement System Board
Herschler Bldg.
122 W. 25th St.
Cheyenne, WY 82002
Phone: (307) 777-7691

Revenue

Administers state tax laws and the collection and processing of state taxes.

ALABAMA
James P. Hayes, Jr.
Commissioner
Dept. of Revenue
50 Ripley St., 4th Fl.
Montgomery, AL 36130
Phone: (334) 242-1175
Fax: (334) 242-0550

ALASKA
Wilson Condon
Commissioner
Dept. of Revenue
P.O. Box 110400
Juneau, AK 99811-0400
Phone: (907) 465-2300
Fax: (907) 465-2389

AMERICAN SAMOA
Tifi Ale
Treasurer
Dept. of the Treasury
AS Govt.
Pago Pago, AS 96799
Phone: (684) 633-4155
Fax: (684) 633-4100

ARIZONA
Mark W. Killian
Director
Administration Services Div.
Dept. of Revenue
1600 W. Monroe
Phoenix, AZ 85007
Phone: (602) 542-3572
Fax: (602) 542-4772

ARKANSAS
John Theis
Deputy Commissioner
Policy & Legal Revenue Div.
Dept. of Finance & Administration
P.O. Box 1272
Little Rock, AR 72203
Phone: (501) 682-7000
Fax: (501) 682-7900

CALIFORNIA
Gerald Goldberg
Executive Officer
Franchise Tax Board
P.O. Box 1468
Sacramento, CA 95812-1468
Phone: (916) 845-4543

COLORADO
Fred Fisher
Executive Director
Dept. of Revenue
1375 Sherman St., Rm. 404
Denver, CO 80261
Phone: (303) 866-3091
Fax: (303) 866-2400

CONNECTICUT
Gene Gavin
Commissioner
Dept. of Revenue Services
25 Sigourney St.
Hartford, CT 06106
Phone: (860) 297-4900

DELAWARE
William Remington
Director
Div. of Revenue
Dept. of Finance
820 N. French St.
Wilmington, DE 19801
Phone: (302) 577-3315
Fax: (302) 577-3689

DISTRICT OF COLUMBIA
Gordon McDonald
Director
Dept. of Finance & Revenue
441 4th St., NW
Washington, DC 20001

FLORIDA
Larry H. Fuchs
Executive Director
Dept. of Revenue
Carlton Bldg., Rm. 104
5050 W. Tennessee St.
Tallahassee, FL 32399-0100
Phone: (850) 488-5050
Fax: (850) 488-0024

GEORGIA
T. Jerry Jackson
Commissioner
Dept. of Revenue
270 Washington St., SW, Ste. 410
Atlanta, GA 30334
Phone: (404) 656-4015

GUAM
Joseph T. Duenas
Director
Dept. of Revenue & Taxation
13-1 Mariner Dr., Tiyan
P.O. Box 23607
GMF, GU 96921
Phone: (671) 475-1817
Fax: (671) 472-2643

HAWAII
Ray Kamikawa
Director
Dept. of Taxation
830 Punchbowl St., Ste. 221
Honolulu, HI 96813
Phone: (808) 587-1510
Fax: (808) 587-1560

IDAHO
R. Michael Southcombe
Chair
State Tax Comm.
P.O. Box 36
Boise, ID 83702-0036
Phone: (208) 334-7500

ILLINOIS
Glen L. Bower
Director of Revenue
Dept. of Revenue
101 W. Jefferson St., #6-500
Springfield, IL 62702-5145
Phone: (217) 785-7570

INDIANA
Kenneth Miller
Commissioner
Commissioner's Ofc.
Dept. of Revenue
100 N. Senate Ave., Rm. N248
IGC-N.
Indianapolis, IN 46204
Phone: (317) 232-8039
Fax: (317) 232-2103

IOWA
Gerald D. Bair
Director
Dept. of Revenue & Finance
Hoover State Ofc. Bldg.
1300 E. Walnut
Des Moines, IA 50319
Phone: (515) 281-3204
Fax: (515) 242-6040

KANSAS
Karla Pierce
Secretary
Dept. of Revenue
Docking State Ofc. Bldg., 2nd Fl.
915 Harrison
Topeka, KS 66612
Phone: (785) 296-3042
Fax: (785) 296-7928

KENTUCKY
Sarah J. Schaaf
Secretary
Revenue Cabinet
200 Fairoaks
Frankfort, KY 40601
Phone: (502) 564-3226
Fax: (502) 564-3875

LOUISIANA
John N. Kennedy
Secretary
Dept. of Revenue & Taxation
P.O. Box 201
Baton Rouge, LA 70821
Phone: (225) 925-7680
Fax: (225) 925-6797

MAINE
Anthony J. Neves
State Tax Assessor
Revenue Services
24 State House Station
Augusta, ME 04333-0024
Phone: (207) 287-2076

MARYLAND
James M. Arnie
Director
Revenue Administration Div.
Comptroller of the Treasury
Revenue Administration Ctr.
Annapolis, MD 21401
Phone: (410) 260-7445
Fax: (410) 974-3456
E-mail: jarnie@comp.state.md.us

MASSACHUSETTS
Frederick Laskey
Commissioner
Executive Ofc. for Administration & Finance
Dept. of Revenue
100 Cambridge St., Rm. 806
Boston, MA 02202
Phone: (617) 626-2201
Fax: (617) 626-2299

MICHIGAN
B.D. Copping
Commissioner of Revenue
Bur. of Revenue
Dept. of Treasury
Treasury Bldg.
Lansing, MI 48922
Phone: (517) 373-3196

MINNESOTA
Matt Smith
Commissioner
Dept. of Revenue
600 N. Robert St.
St Paul, MN 55146
Phone: (651) 296-3403
Fax: (651) 296-5309

MISSISSIPPI
Ed Buelow
Chair
State Tax Comm.
P.O. Box 22828
Jackson, MS 39225
Phone: (601) 923-7400
Fax: (601) 923-7423

MISSOURI
Quentin Wilson
Director
Dept. of Revenue
Truman Bldg., Rm. 670
P.O. Box 311
Jefferson City, MO 65105
Phone: (573) 751-4450
Fax: (573) 751-7150
E-mail: qwilson@mail.dor.state.mo.us

MONTANA
Mary Bryson
Director
Dept. of Revenue
Sam Mitchell Bldg., Rm. 455
125 Roberts
Helena, MT 59620
Phone: (406) 444-2460
Fax: (406) 444-3696

NEBRASKA
Mary Jane Egr
State Tax Commissioner
Dept. of Revenue
P.O. Box 94818
Lincoln, NE 68509
Phone: (402) 471-2971
Fax: (402) 471-5608

NEVADA
Dave Pursell
Executive Director
Dept. of Taxation
1550 E. College Pkwy., Ste. 115
Carson City, NV 89706
Phone: (775) 687-4839
Fax: (775) 687-5981

NEW HAMPSHIRE
Stanley R. Arnold
Commissioner
Dept. of Revenue Administration
P.O. Box 457
Concord, NH 03302-0457
Phone: (603) 271-2191
Fax: (603) 271-6121

NEW JERSEY
Robert K. Thompson
Director
Div. of Taxation
Dept. of the Treasury
50 Barrack St.
P.O. Box 269
Trenton, NJ 08646
Phone: (609) 292-5185

NEW MEXICO
John Chavez
Secretary
Dept. of Taxation & Revenue
P.O. Box 630
Santa Fe, NM 87504-0630
Phone: (505) 827-0341
Fax: (505) 827-0331
E-mail: jchavez@state.nm.us

NEW YORK
Michael H. Urbach
Commissioner
Dept. of Taxation & Finance
State Campus, Bldg. 9, Rm. 205
Albany, NY 12227
Phone: (518) 457-2244
Fax: (518) 457-7427

NORTH CAROLINA
Muriel K. Offerman
Secretary
Dept. of Revenue
501 N. Wilmington St.
Raleigh, NC 27640
Phone: (919) 733-7211
Fax: (919) 733-0023

NORTH DAKOTA
Rick Clayburgh
Commissioner
Tax Dept.
600 E. Blvd. Ave., 7th Fl.
Bismarck, ND 58505-0599
Phone: (701) 328-2770
Fax: (701) 328-3700
E-mail: rclaybur@state.nd.us

NORTHERN MARIANA ISLANDS
Rufin S. Inos
Director
Revenue & Taxation Div.
Dept. of Finance & Accounting
P.O. Box 5234 CHRB
Saipan, MP 96950
Phone: (670) 664-1020
Fax: (670) 664-1050

OHIO
Thomas M. Zaino
Commissioner
Dept. of Taxation
30 E. Broad St., 22nd Fl.
Columbus, OH 43215-0030
Phone: (614) 466-2166
Fax: (614) 466-6401

OKLAHOMA
Bob Anderson
Chair
Tax Comm.
2501 N. Lincoln Blvd.
Oklahoma City, OK 73194
Phone: (405) 521-3115
Fax: (405) 522-0074

OREGON
Elizabeth Harchenko
Director
Dept. of Revenue
955 Ctr. St., NE
Salem, OR 97310
Phone: (503) 945-8215
Fax: (503) 945-8888

PENNSYLVANIA
Robert A. Judge, Sr.
Secretary
Dept. of Revenue
Strawberry Sq., 11th Fl.
Harrisburg, PA 17120
Phone: (717) 783-3680
Fax: (717) 787-3990

PUERTO RICO
Ruben Guzman
Director
Income Tax Bur.
Dept. of Treasury
P.O. Box S-4515
San Juan, PR 00904
Phone: (787) 721-2020
Fax: (787) 722-6854

RHODE ISLAND
Gary Clark
Tax Administrator
Div. of Taxation
1 Capitol Hill
Providence, RI 02903
Phone: (401) 222-3050

SOUTH CAROLINA
Elizabeth A. Carpentier
Administrator
Dept. of Revenue & Taxation
301 Gervais St.
Columbia, SC 29201
Phone: (803) 898-5040

SOUTH DAKOTA
Gary Viken
Secretary
Dept. of Revenue
Anderson Bldg.
445 E. Capitol Ave.
Pierre, SD 57501
Phone: (605) 773-5131
Fax: (605) 773-5129

TENNESSEE
Ruth Johnson
Commissioner
Dept. of Revenue
1200 Andrew Jackson Bldg.
Nashville, TN 37219
Phone: (615) 741-2461
Fax: (615) 532-2285

TEXAS
Carole Keeton Rylander
Comptroller
Comptroller of Public
Accounts
P.O. Box 13528
Austin, TX 78711-3528
Phone: (512) 463-4000
Fax: (512) 463-4965

U.S. VIRGIN ISLANDS
Claudette Farrington
Acting Director
Bur. of Internal Revenue
9601 Estate Thomas
St. Thomas, VI 00802
Phone: (340) 774-5865
Fax: (340) 714-9345

UTAH
Rodney G. Marrelli
Executive Director
Administration Div.
State Tax Comm.
210 N. 1950 W.
Salt Lake City, UT 84134
Phone: (801) 297-3845
Fax: (801) 297-3891
E-mail: rmarrelli
@tax.state.ut.us

VERMONT
Sean Campbell
Commissioner
Agency of Administration
Dept. of Taxes
109 State St.
Montpelier, VT 05602
Phone: (802) 828-2505

VIRGINIA
Danny M. Payne
Tax Commissioner
Dept. of Taxation
2220 W. Broad St.
Richmond, VA 23220
Phone: (804) 367-8005
Fax: (804) 367-0971

WASHINGTON
Fred Kiga
Director
Dept. of Revenue
Administration Bldg.
P.O. Box 47454
Olympia, WA 98504-7454
Phone: (360) 753-5574
Fax: (360) 586-5543

WEST VIRGINIA
Robin Capehart
Cabinet Secretary
Dept. of Tax & Revenue
Bldg. 1, Rm. WW-300
1900 Kanawha Blvd., E.
Charleston, WV 25305
Phone: (304) 558-0211
Fax: (304) 558-2324

WISCONSIN
Kate Zeuske
Secretary
Dept. of Revenue
P.O. Box 8933
Madison, WI 53708-8933
Phone: (608) 266-6466
Fax: (608) 266-5718

WYOMING
Johnnie Burton
Director
Dept. of Revenue
Herschler Bldg.
122 W. 25th St.
Cheyenne, WY 82002
Phone: (307) 777-5287
Fax: (307) 777-7722

Savings and Loan

Administers laws regulating the operation of savings and loan associations in the state.

ALABAMA
Norman B. Davis, Jr.
Commissioner
Savings & Loan Board
Dept. of State Banking
401 Adams Ave., Ste. 480
Montgomery, AL 36130-1201
Phone: (334) 242-3452
Fax: (334) 242-3500

ALASKA
Franklin T. Elder
Acting Director
Div. of Banking, Securities & Corps.
Dept. of Commerce & Economic Dev.
P.O. Box 110807
Juneau, AK 99811-0807
Phone: (907) 465-2521
Fax: (907) 465-2549

AMERICAN SAMOA

ARIZONA
Richard C. Houseworth
Superintendent
Dept. of Banking
2910 N. 44th St., Ste. 310
Phoenix, AZ 85018
Phone: (602) 255-4421
Fax: (602) 381-1225

ARKANSAS
Mac Dodson
Commissioner
Dept. of Securities
Heritage W. Bldg., Ste. 300
Little Rock, AR 72201
Phone: (501) 324-9260
Fax: (501) 324-9268

CALIFORNIA
Keith Paul Bishop
Commissioner
Dept. of Savings & Loan
300 S. Spring St., Ste. 16502
Los Angeles, CA 90012
Phone: (213) 897-8242

COLORADO
David L. Paul
Commissioner
Div. of Financial Services
Dept. of Regulatory Agencies
1560 Broadway, Rm. 1520
Denver, CO 80202
Phone: (303) 894-2336

CONNECTICUT
John P. Burke
Commissioner
Dept. of Banking
260 Constitution Plz.
Hartford, CT 06103
Phone: (860) 240-8100

DELAWARE
Robert A. Glen
State Bank Commissioner
Dept. of State
P.O. Box 1401
Dover, DE 19903
Phone: (302) 739-4235
Fax: (302) 739-3609

DISTRICT OF COLUMBIA
J. Anthony Romero, III
Interim Superintendent
Ofc. of Banking & Financial Institutions
717 14th St., NW, Ste. 1100
Washington, DC 20005
Phone: (202) 727-1563

FLORIDA
John Alcorn
Financial Administrator
Div. of Banking
Dept. of Banking & Finance
Fletcher Bldg., Ste. 636
101 E. Gaines St.
Tallahassee, FL 32399-0350
Phone: (850) 488-9570
Fax: (850) 488-7060

GEORGIA
Steven D. Bridges
Commissioner
Dept. of Banking & Finance
2990 Brandywine Rd., # 200
Atlanta, GA 30341
Phone: (770) 986-1633
Fax: (770) 986-1655

GUAM
Rashid M. Habib
Chair
Banking Board
378 Chalan San Antonio
Tamuning, GU 96911
Phone: (671) 647-5107
Fax: (671) 472-2643

HAWAII
Lynn Y. Wakatsuki
Commissioner
Div. of Financial Institutions
Commerce & Consumer Affairs
1010 Richards St., Rm. 602-A
Honolulu, HI 96813
Phone: (808) 586-2820
Fax: (808) 586-2818

IDAHO
Gavin Gee
Director
Dept. of Finance
700 W. State St.
Boise, ID 83720
Phone: (208) 332-8010

ILLINOIS
William A. Darr
Commissioner
Ofc. of Banks & Real Estate
500 E. Monroe, Ste. 900
Springfield, IL 62701
Phone: (217) 782-1398
Fax: (217) 524-5941

Jack Schaffer
Commissioner
Savings & Residential Finance
500 E. Monroe, # 800
Springfield, IL 62701-1509
Phone: (217) 782-1398
Fax: (217) 782-6170

INDIANA
Charles W. Phillips
Director
Dept. of Financial Institutions
Rm. W066
402 W. Washington St.
Indianapolis, IN 46204
Phone: (317) 232-3955
Fax: (317) 232-7655

IOWA
Michael Guttau
Superintendent
Banking Div.
Dept. of Commerce
200 E. Grand Ave., Ste. 300
Des Moines, IA 50309
Phone: (515) 281-4014
Fax: (515) 281-4862

Terri Vaughan
Commissioner
Insurance Div.
Dept. of Commerce
330 Maple St.
Des Moines, IA 50319
Phone: (515) 281-5705

KANSAS
Clyde Graber
Commissioner
Ofc. of the State Bank Commissioner
700 Jack, Ste. 300
Topeka, KS 66603
Phone: (785) 296-2266
Fax: (785) 296-0168

KENTUCKY
Arthur Freeman
Commissioner
Public Protection & Regulation Cabinet
Dept. of Financial Institutions
477 Versailles Rd.
Frankfort, KY 40601
Phone: (502) 573-3390
Fax: (502) 573-8787

LOUISIANA
Sidney E. Seymour
Chief Examiner
Ofc. of Financial Institutions
Dept. of Economic Dev.
P.O. Box 94095
Baton Rouge, LA 70804-9095
Phone: (225) 925-4660
Fax: (225) 925-4548

MAINE
H. Donald DeMatteis
Superintendent
Bur. of Banking
Dept. of Professional & Financial Regulation
36 State House Station
Augusta, ME 04333
Phone: (207) 582-8713

MARYLAND
Mary Louise Preis
Commissioner
Div. of Financial Regulation
Dept. of Labor, Licensing & Regulation
500 N. Calvert St., Rm. 402
Baltimore, MD 21202
Phone: (410) 230-6098
E-mail: mlpreis@dllr.state.md.us

MASSACHUSETTS
Thomas J. Curry
Commissioner of Banks
Div. of Banks
100 Cambridge St., Rm. 2004
Boston, MA 02202
Phone: (617) 727-3145
Fax: (617) 727-7631

MICHIGAN
Ronald Rubach
Director
Enforcement Div.
Corp., Security & Land Dev. Bur.
P.O. Box 30224
Lansing, MI 48909
Phone: (517) 334-6209

MINNESOTA
Allyn R. Long
Assistant Deputy Commissioner
Div. of Financial Examinations
Dept. of Commerce
133 7th St., E.
St. Paul, MN 55101
Phone: (651) 296-2715
Fax: (651) 296-8591
E-mail: al.long@state.mn.us

MISSISSIPPI
Ronny Parham
Commissioner
Banking & Consumer Finances Dept.
550 High St., Ste. 304
Jackson, MS 39202
Phone: (601) 359-1103
Fax: (601) 359-3557

MISSOURI
Eric McClure
Acting Commissioner
Div. of Finance
Dept. of Economic Dev.
Truman Bldg., Rm. 630
P.O. Box 716
Jefferson City, MO 65102
Phone: (573) 751-2545
Fax: (573) 751-9192
E-mail: emcclure@mail.state.mo.us

MONTANA
Donald W. Hutchinson
Commissioner
Div. of Banking & Financial Institutions
Dept. of Commerce
846 Front St.
P.O. Box 200546
Helena, MT 59620-0546
Phone: (406) 444-2091
Fax: (406) 444-4186

NEBRASKA
Sam Baird
Director
Dept. of Banking & Finance
1200 N. St., Atrium #311
P.O. Box 95006
Lincoln, NE 68509
Phone: (402) 471-2171
Fax: (402) 471-3062

NEVADA
L. Scott Walshaw
Commissioner
Div. of Financial Institutions
Dept. of Business & Industry
406 E. 2nd St., Ste. 3
Carson City, NV 89701
Phone: (775) 687-4259
Fax: (775) 687-6909

NEW HAMPSHIRE
A. Roland Roberge
Commissioner
Dept. of Banking
169 Manchester St., Bldg. 3
Concord, NH 03301-5127
Phone: (603) 271-3561
Fax: (603) 271-1090

NEW JERSEY
John Traier
Deputy Commissioner
Banking & Insurance
Ofc. of the Commissioner
Dept. of Banking
P.O. Box 040
Trenton, NJ 08625-0040
Phone: (609) 292-3420
Fax: (609) 777-0107

NEW MEXICO
William J. Verant
Director
Financial Institutions Div.
Dept. of Regulation & Licensing
725 St. Michael's St.
P.O. Box 25101
Santa Fe, NM 87504
Phone: (505) 827-7100
Fax: (505) 984-0617

NEW YORK
Elizabeth McCaul
Acting Superintendent
Dept. of Banking
2 Rector St., 19th Fl.
New York, NY 10006
Phone: (212) 618-6558
Fax: (212) 618-6599

NORTH CAROLINA
Stephen Eubanks
Administrator
Savings Institutions Div.
Dept. of Commerce
1110 Navaho Dr., Ste. 301
Raleigh, NC 27609
Phone: (919) 850-2888
Fax: (919) 850-2853

NORTH DAKOTA
Gary Preszler
Commissioner
Dept. of Banking & Financial Institutions
2000 Schafer St., Ste. G
Bismarck, ND 58501-1204
Phone: (701) 328-9933
Fax: (701) 328-9955
E-mail: gpreszle@pioneer.state.nd.us

NORTHERN MARIANA ISLANDS
Oscar Camacho
Director
Economic Dev./Banking & Insurance
Dept. of Commerce
P.O. Box 10007
Saipan, MP 96950
Phone: (670) 664-3023
Fax: (670) 664-3066
E-mail: commerce@mtccnmi.com

OHIO
Scott O'Donnell
Superintendent
Div. of Financial Institutions
Dept. of Commerce
77 S. High St., 21st Fl.
Columbus, OH 43266-0544
Phone: (614) 728-8400
Fax: (614) 644-1631

OKLAHOMA
Mick Thompson
Commissioner
Dept. of Banking
4545 N. Lincoln Blvd., Ste. 164
Oklahoma City, OK 73105-3427
Phone: (405) 521-2782
Fax: (405) 522-2993

OREGON
Dick Nockleby
Administrator
Finance & Corporate Securities
Dept. of Consumer & Business Services
21 Labor & Industries Bldg.
350 Winter St., NW, #410
Salem, OR 97310-1321
Phone: (503) 378-4140
Fax: (503) 947-7862

PENNSYLVANIA
Richard C. Rishel
Cabinet Secretary
Dept. of Banking
Harristown 2, 16th Fl.
Harrisburg, PA 17120
Phone: (717) 787-6991
Fax: (717) 787-8773
E-mail: rrishel@banking.state.pa.us

PUERTO RICO
Pablo Crespo Claudio
Director
Employees' Association
P.O. Box 364508
San Juan, PR 00936-4508
Phone: (787) 753-2100
Fax: (787) 763-8918

RHODE ISLAND
Dennis F. Ziroli
Associate Director & Superintendent of Banking
Banking Div.
Dept. of Business Regulation
233 Richmond St., Ste. 231
Providence, RI 02903-4231
Phone: (401) 222-2405
Fax: (401) 222-5628

SOUTH CAROLINA
Grady L. Patterson, Jr.
State Treasurer
1200 Senate St.
Wade Hampton Bldg., 1st Fl.
Columbia, SC 29201
Phone: (803) 734-2635

SOUTH DAKOTA
Dick Duncan
Director
Div. of Banking & Finance
Dept. of Commerce & Regulation
217 W. Missouri
Pierre, SD 57501
Phone: (605) 773-3421
Fax: (605) 773-5367

TENNESSEE
Roger Thomas
Assistant Commissioner
Compliance Div.
Financial Institutions Dept.
John Sevier Bldg., Ste. 502
Nashville, TN 37243
Phone: (615) 741-3186
Fax: (615) 741-2883

TEXAS
James L. Pledger
Commissioner
Savings & Loan Dept.
2601 N. Lamar Blvd., Ste. 201
Austin, TX 78705
Phone: (512) 475-1350
Fax: (512) 475-1360

U.S. VIRGIN ISLANDS
Maryleen Thomas
Director
Banking & Insurance Div
#18 Kongens Gade
St. Thomas, VI 00801
Phone: (340) 774-2991
Fax: (340) 774-9458

UTAH
G. Edward Leary
Commissioner
Administration
Dept. of Financial Institutions
324 S. State, Ste. 201
P.O. Box 89
Salt Lake City, UT 84110-0089
Phone: (801) 538-8854
Fax: (801) 538-8894
E-mail: eleary.bdfipost@state.ut.us

VERMONT
Elizabeth R. Costle
Commissioner
Dept. of Banking, Insurance, Securities & Health Care Administration
89 State St.
Montpelier, VT 05620-3101
Phone: (802) 828-3301
Fax: (802) 828-3306
E-mail: bcostle@state.vt.us

VIRGINIA
Theodore W. Morrison, Jr.
Chair
State Corp. Comm.
Tyler Bldg.
1300 E. Main St.
Richmond, VA 23219
Phone: (804) 371-9608
Fax: (804) 371-9376

WASHINGTON
G.R. Zachary
Director
Div. of Savings & Loan Associations
Dept. of Financial Institutions
P.O. Box 41200
Olympia, WA 98504
Phone: (360) 902-8704
Fax: (360) 753-6070

WEST VIRGINIA
Sharon G. Bias
Commissioner
Div. of Banking
Bldg. 3, Rm. 311-A
1800 Washington St., E.
Charleston, WV 25305
Phone: (304) 558-2294

WISCONSIN

WYOMING
Mike Geesey
Director
Banking Div.
Audit Dept.
Herschler Bldg., 3rd Fl., E.
Cheyenne, WY 82002
Phone: (307) 777-7792
Fax: (307) 777-5608

Secretary of State

Statewide official who oversees a variety of electoral, registration, publication and legislative duties for the state.

ALABAMA
Jim Bennett (R)
Secretary of State
State Capitol
600 Dexter Ave.
Montgomery, AL 36130-4650
Phone: (334) 242-7205
Fax: (334) 242-4993
E-mail: alsecst@alaline.net

ALASKA
Fran Ulmer (D)
Lieutenant Governor
State Capitol
P.O. Box 110015
Juneau, AK 99811-0015
Phone: (907) 465-3520
Fax: (907) 465-5400

AMERICAN SAMOA

ARIZONA
Betsy Bayless (R)
Secretary of State
State Capitol, 7th Fl.
1700 W. Washington St.
Phoenix, AZ 85007-2808
Phone: (602) 542-3012
Fax: (602) 542-1575

ARKANSAS
Sharon Priest (D)
Secretary of State
State Capitol, Rm. 256
Little Rock, AR 72201
Phone: (501) 682-1010
Fax: (501) 682-3510
E-mail: sharonpriest@ccm1.state.ar.us

CALIFORNIA
Bill Jones (R)
Secretary of State
1500 11th St.
Sacramento, CA 95814
Phone: (916) 653-7244
Fax: (916) 653-4620
E-mail: BJones@ss.ca.gov

COLORADO
Victoria Buckley (R)
Secretary of State
Dept. of State
1560 Broadway, Rm. 200
Denver, CO 80202
Phone: (303) 894-2200
Fax: (303) 894-2242

CONNECTICUT
Susan Bysiewicz (D)
Secretary of State
State Capitol, Rm. 104
300 Capitol Ave.
Hartford, CT 06106
Phone: (860) 509-6200
Fax: (860) 566-6318
E-mail: susan.bysiewicz@po.state.ct.us

DELAWARE
Edward J. Freel (APPT.)
Secretary of State
The Townsend Bldg.
P.O. Box 898
Dover, DE 19903
Phone: (302) 739-4111
Fax: (302) 739-3811
E-mail: efreel@state.de.us

DISTRICT OF COLUMBIA
Beverly D. Rivers (APPT.)
Secretary of the District
Executive Ofc. of the Mayor
441 4th St., NW, Ste. 1130
Washington, DC 20001
Phone: (202) 727-6306
Fax: (202) 727-3582

FLORIDA
Katherine Harris (R)
Secretary of State
PL 02, The Capitol
Tallahassee, FL 32399-0250
Phone: (850) 414-5500
Fax: (850) 487-2214
E-mail: secretary@mail.dos.state.fl.us

GEORGIA
Cathy Cox (D)
Secretary of State
214 State Capitol
Atlanta, GA 30334
Phone: (404) 656-2881
Fax: (404) 657-5804
E-mail: sosweb@sos.state.ga.us

GUAM

HAWAII

IDAHO
Pete T. Cenarrusa (R)
Secretary of State
State Capitol, Rm. 203
Boise, ID 83720
Phone: (208) 334-2300
Fax: (208) 334-2282
E-mail: admin@idsos.state.id.us

ILLINOIS
Jesse White (D)
Secretary of State
213 State House
Springfield, IL 62756
Phone: (217) 782-2201
Fax: (217) 785-0358

INDIANA
Sue Anne Gilroy (R)
Secretary of State
State House, Rm. 201
200 W. Washington St.
Indianapolis, IN 46204
Phone: (317) 232-6531
Fax: (317) 233-3283
E-mail: sos@ai.org

IOWA
Chet Culver (D)
Secretary of State
State House
Des Moines, IA 50319
Phone: (515) 281-5204
Fax: (515) 242-5952
E-mail: sos@sos.state.ia.us

KANSAS
Ron Thornburgh (R)
Secretary of State
State Capitol, 2nd Fl.
300 SW 10th St.
Topeka, KS 66612
Phone: (785) 296-4564
Fax: (785) 296-4570
E-mail: RonT@ssmail.wpo.state.ks.us

KENTUCKY
John Y. Brown, III (D)
Secretary of State
State Capitol, Ste. 152
Frankfort, KY 40601
Phone: (502) 564-3490
Fax: (502) 564-4075
E-mail: jbrown@mail.sos.state.ky.us

LOUISIANA
W. Fox McKeithen (R)
Secretary of State
Dept. of State
P.O. Box 94125
Baton Rouge, LA 70804-9125
Phone: (225) 342-4479
Fax: (225) 342-5577
E-mail: webmaster@sec.state.la.us

MAINE
Dan Gwadosky (D)
Secretary of State
148 State House Station
Augusta, ME 04333-0148
Phone: (207) 626-8400
Fax: (207) 287-8598
E-mail: sosoffice@state.me.us

MARYLAND
John T. Willis (APPT.)
Secretary of State
Ofc. of the Secretary of State
Executive Dept.
16 Francis St.
Annapolis, MD 21401
Phone: (410) 974-5521
Fax: (410) 974-5190
E-mail: cbonsuk@sos.state.md.us

MASSACHUSETTS
William Galvin (D)
Secretary of the Commonwealth
Rm. 337 - State House
Boston, MA 02133
Phone: (617) 727-9180
Fax: (617) 742-4722
E-mail: cis@sec.state.ma.us

MICHIGAN
Candice Miller (R)
Secretary of State
Treasury Bldg., 1st Fl.
430 W. Allegan St.
Lansing, MI 48918
Phone: (517) 373-2510
Fax: (517) 373-0727

MINNESOTA
Mary Kiffmeyer (R)
Secretary of State
180 State Ofc. Bldg.
100 Constitution Ave.
St. Paul, MN 55155-1299
Phone: (651) 296-1299
Fax: (651) 296-9073
E-mail: secretary.state
@state.mn.us

MISSISSIPPI
Eric Clark (D)
Secretary of State
401 Mississippi St.
P.O. Box 136
Jackson, MS 39205
Phone: (601) 359-1350
Fax: (601) 359-6700
E-mail: cjones
@sos.state.ms.us

MISSOURI
Rebecca Cook (D)
Secretary of State
State Capitol, Rm. 208
P.O. Box 778
Jefferson City, MO 65102
Phone: (573) 751-4936
Fax: (573) 526-4903
E-mail: sosmain
@mail.sos.state.mo.us

MONTANA
Mike Cooney (D)
Secretary of State
State Capitol Bldg.,
Rm. 225
P.O. Box 202801
Helena, MT 59620-2801
Phone: (406) 444-2034
Fax: (406) 444-3976
E-mail: mcooney@mt.gov

NEBRASKA
Scott Moore (R)
Secretary of State
State Capitol, Ste. 2300
P.O. Box 94608
Lincoln, NE 68509-4608
Phone: (402) 471-2554
Fax: (402) 471-3237
E-mail: sosadmin
@sos.state.ne.us

NEVADA
Dean Heller (R)
Secretary of State
State Capitol Bldg.
101 N. Carson St., Ste. 3
Carson City, NV 89701
Phone: (775) 684-5708
Fax: (775) 684-5725
E-mail: sosmail
@govmail.state.nv.us

NEW HAMPSHIRE
William Gardner
(elected by the
Legislature)
Secretary of State
Secretary of State Ofc.
State House, Rm. 204
107 N. Main St.
Concord, NH 03301
Phone: (603) 271-3242
Fax: (603) 271-6316
E-mail: sof.karen.ladd
@leg.state.nh.us

NEW JERSEY
DeForest B. Soaries, Jr.
(APPT.)
Secretary of State
State House
P.O. Box 300
Trenton, NJ 08625-0300
Phone: (609) 777-2535

NEW MEXICO
Rebecca Vigil-Giron (D)
Secretary of State
State Capitol Bldg.,
Rm. 420
Santa Fe, NM 87503
Phone: (505) 827-3600
Fax: (505) 827-3634

NEW YORK
Alexander F. Treadwell
(APPT.)
Secretary of State
Dept. of State
41 State St.
Albany, NY 12231
Phone: (518) 486-9844
Fax: (518) 474-4765
E-mail: info@dos.state.ny.us

NORTH CAROLINA
Elaine F. Marshall (D)
Secretary of State
300 N. Salisbury St.,
Ste. 301
Raleigh, NC 27603-5909
Phone: (919) 733-4161
Fax: (919) 733-5172
E-mail: emarshall
@mail.secstate.state.nc.us

NORTH DAKOTA
Alvin A. Jaeger (R)
Secretary of State
Secretary of State's Ofc.
600 E. Blvd. Ave., 1st Fl.
Bismarck, ND 58505-0500
Phone: (701) 328-2900
Fax: (701) 328-2992
E-mail: ajaeger@state.nd.us

NORTHERN MARIANA ISLANDS

OHIO
J. Kenneth Blackwell (R)
Secretary of State
30 E. Broad St., 14th Fl.
Columbus, OH 43266-0421
Phone: (614) 466-4980
Fax: (614) 644-2892

OKLAHOMA
Mike Hunter
Secretary of State
State Capitol Bldg.,
Rm. 101
Oklahoma City, OK 73105
Phone: (405) 521-3721
Fax: (405) 521-3771

OREGON
Phil Keisling (D)
Secretary of State
136 State Capitol
Salem, OR 97310
Phone: (503) 986-1500
Fax: (503) 986-1616

PENNSYLVANIA
Kim Pizzingrilli (APPT.)
Acting Secretary of State
Dept. of State
302 N. Capitol Bldg.
Harrisburg, PA 17120
Phone: (717) 787-7630
Fax: (401) 787-1734
E-mail: state
@pop3.dos.state.pa.us

PUERTO RICO
Norma Burgos Andujar
(NPP)
Secretary of State
Department of State
P.O. Box 3271
San Juan, PR 00902-3271
Phone: (787) 723-4334
Fax: (787) 725-7303

RHODE ISLAND
James R. Langevin (D)
Secretary of State
220 State House
Providence, RI 02903
Phone: (401) 222-2357
Fax: (401) 222-1356

SOUTH CAROLINA
Jim Miles (R)
Secretary of State
Wade Hampton Bldg.
P.O. Box 11350
Columbia, SC 29211
Phone: (803) 734-2170
Fax: (803) 734-2164

SOUTH DAKOTA
Joyce Hazeltine (R)
Secretary of State
500 E. Capitol Ave.,
Ste. 204
Pierre, SD 57501
Phone: (605) 773-3537
Fax: (605) 773-6580
E-mail: patty.pearson
@state.sd.us

TENNESSEE
Riley Darnell (D)
(elected by the
Legislature)
Secretary of State
State Capitol, 1st Fl.
600 Charlotte Ave.
Nashville, TN 37243-0305
Phone: (615) 741-2819
Fax: (615) 741-5962
E-mail: rdarnell
@mail.state.tn.us

TEXAS
Elton Bomer (APPT.)
Secretary of State
Ofc. of the Secretary of
State
P.O. Box 12697
Austin, TX 78711-2697
Phone: (512) 475-2810
Fax: (512) 475-2761

U.S. VIRGIN ISLANDS

UTAH

VERMONT
Deborah Markowitz (D)
Secretary of State
109 State St.
Montpelier, VT 05609-1101
Phone: (802) 828-2148
Fax: (802) 828-2496

VIRGINIA
Anne P. Petera (APPT.)
Secretary of the
Commonwealth
Governor's Cabinet
Old Finance Bldg., 1st Fl.
Capitol Sq.
Richmond, VA 23219
Phone: (804) 786-2441
Fax: (804) 371-0017

WASHINGTON
Ralph Munro (R)
Secretary of State
Legislative Bldg., 2nd Fl.
P.O. Box 40220
Olympia, WA 98504-0220
Phone: (360) 902-4151
Fax: (360) 586-5629
E-mail: mail
@secstate.wa.gov

WEST VIRGINIA
Ken Hechler (D)
Secretary of State
Bldg. 1, Ste. 157K
1900 Kanawha Blvd., E.
Charleston, WV 25305
Phone: (304) 558-6000
Fax: (304) 558-0900
E-mail: wvsos
@secretary.state.wv.us

WISCONSIN
Douglas J. La Follette (D)
Secretary of State
30 W. Mifflin St., 10th Fl.
Madison, WI 53707
Phone: (608) 266-8888
Fax: (608) 266-3159
E-mail: statesec
@mail.state.wi.us

WYOMING
Joe Meyer (R)
Secretary of State
Securities Div.
State Capitol Bldg.
Cheyenne, WY 82002
Phone: (307) 777-5333
Fax: (307) 777-6217
E-mail: secofstate
@missc.state.wy.us

Securities

Regulates the sale of securities and registers securities prior to public sale.

ALABAMA
Joseph Borg
Director
Securities Comm.
770 Washington St., Ste. 570
Montgomery, AL 36130-4700
Phone: (334) 242-2984
Fax: (334) 242-0240

ALASKA
Franklin T. Elder
Acting Director
Div. of Banking, Securities & Corps.
Dept. of Commerce & Economic Dev.
P.O. Box 110807
Juneau, AK 99811-0807
Phone: (907) 465-2521
Fax: (907) 465-2549

AMERICAN SAMOA

ARIZONA
Michael G. Burton
Director
Securities Div.
Corp. Comm.
1200 W. Washington
Phoenix, AZ 85007
Phone: (602) 542-4242

ARKANSAS
Mac Dodson
Commissioner
Dept. of Securities
Heritage W. Bldg., Ste. 300
Little Rock, AR 72201
Phone: (501) 324-9260
Fax: (501) 324-9268

CALIFORNIA
Blake Fowler
Staff Development
Trade & Commerce Agency
801 K St., Ste. 1700
Sacramento, CA 85814
Phone: (916) 323-8022

COLORADO
Philip Feigin
Commissioner
Securities Div.
Dept. of Regulatory Agencies
1580 Lincoln, Rm. 420
Denver, CO 80203
Phone: (303) 894-2320
Fax: (303) 861-2126

CONNECTICUT
Ralph Lambiase
Director
Securities & Business Investments
Dept. of Banking
260 Constitution Plz.
Hartford, CT 06103
Phone: (860) 240-8231

DELAWARE
Charles F. Walker
Securities Commissioner
Louis L. Redding City/ County Bldg.
820 N. French St.
Wilmington, DE 19801
Phone: (302) 577-8424
Fax: (302) 655-0576

DISTRICT OF COLUMBIA
Barbara Jumper
Chief Financial Officer
Financial Mgmt.
441 4th St., NW, Ste. 1150
Washington, DC 20001
Phone: (202) 727-2476

FLORIDA
Don Saxon
Director
Div. of Finance
Dept. of Banking & Finance
101 E. Gaines St.
Tallahassee, FL 32399-0350
Phone: (850) 488-9805
Fax: (850) 681-2428

GEORGIA
Warren Rary
Director
Business Services & Regulations
Ofc. of Secretary of State
2 Martin Luther King, Jr. Dr., SE, Ste. 306
Atlanta, GA 30334
Phone: (404) 656-6478

GUAM
Joseph T. Duenas
Director
Dept. of Revenue & Taxation
13-1 Mariner Dr., Tiyan
P.O. Box 23607
GMF, GU 96921
Phone: (671) 475-1817
Fax: (671) 472-2643

HAWAII
Lynn Y. Wakatsuki
Commissioner
Div. of Financial Institutions
Commerce & Consumer Affairs
1010 Richards St., Rm. 602-A
Honolulu, HI 96813
Phone: (808) 586-2820
Fax: (808) 586-2818

IDAHO
Gavin Gee
Director
Dept. of Finance
700 W. State St.
Boise, ID 83720
Phone: (208) 332-8010

ILLINOIS
Sherri A. Montgomery
Director
Index Dept.
Ofc. of Secretary of State
111 E. Monroe
Springfield, IL 62756
Phone: (217) 782-0643
Fax: (217) 785-0943

INDIANA
Brad Skolnik
Commissioner
Securities Div.
302 W. Washington, Rm. E111
Indianapolis, IN 46204
Phone: (317) 232-6690
Fax: (317) 233-3675

IOWA
Craig Goettsch
Superintendent
Securities Div.
Dept. of Commerce
Lucas State Ofc. Bldg.
321 E. 12th St.
Des Moines, IA 50319
Phone: (515) 281-4441

KANSAS
David Brant
Securities Commissioner
618 S. Kansas Ave., 2nd Fl.
Topeka, KS 66603-3804
Phone: (785) 296-3307
Fax: (785) 296-6872

KENTUCKY
Arthur Freeman
Commissioner
Public Protection & Regulation Cabinet
Dept. of Financial Institutions
477 Versailles Rd.
Frankfort, KY 40601
Phone: (502) 573-3390
Fax: (502) 573-8787

LOUISIANA
Ken Duncan
State Treasurer
P.O. Box 44154
Baton Rouge, LA 70804-0154
Phone: (225) 342-0010
Fax: (225) 342-5008

MAINE
H. Donald DeMatteis
Superintendent
Bur. of Banking
Dept. of Professional & Financial Regulation
36 State House Station
Augusta, ME 04333
Phone: (207) 582-8713

MARYLAND
Melanie Senter Lubin
Commissioner
Div. of Securities
Ofc. of Attorney Gen.
200 St. Paul St.
Baltimore, MD 21202
Phone: (410) 576-6365
Fax: (410) 576-6532

MASSACHUSETTS
Diane Young-Spitzer
Associate Director
Securities Div.
Ofc. of Secretary of Commonwealth
One Ashburton Pl., Rm. 1701
Boston, MA 02108
Phone: (617) 727-7190
Fax: (617) 248-0177

MICHIGAN
Julie Croll
Director
Corps., Securities & Land Dev.
Consumer & Industry Services
P.O. Box 30054
Lansing, MI 48909-7554
Phone: (517) 334-6212

MINNESOTA
Patrick Nelson
Deputy Commissioner
Registration & Analysis Div.
Dept. of Commerce
133 7th St., E.
St. Paul, MN 55101
Phone: (651) 296-6325
Fax: (651) 296-9434
E-mail: patrick.nelson@state.mn.us

MISSISSIPPI
Leslie Scott
Assistant Secretary of State
Securities Div.
P.O. Box 136
Jackson, MS 39205-0136
Phone: (601) 359-6368
Fax: (601) 359-2894

MISSOURI
Douglas F. Wilburn
Commissioner of Securities
Ofc. of Secretary of State
600 W. Main
P.O. Box 1276
Jefferson City, MO 65102
Phone: (573) 751-4704
Fax: (573) 526-3124
E-mail: dwilburn@mail.sos.state.mo.us

MONTANA
Mark O'Keefe
Commissioner of Insurance
State Auditor
P.O. Box 4009
Helena, MT 59604
Phone: (406) 444-2040
Fax: (406) 444-3497

NEBRASKA
Sam Baird
Director
Dept. of Banking & Finance
1200 N. St., Atrium #311
P.O. Box 95006
Lincoln, NE 68509
Phone: (402) 471-2171
Fax: (402) 471-3062

NEVADA
Donald Reis
Deputy Secretary of State
Securities Div.
555 E. Washington Ave., Ste. 5200
Las Vegas, NV 89101
Phone: (702) 486-2440
Fax: (702) 486-2452

NEW HAMPSHIRE
Peter Hildreth
Director
Securities Regulation
Secretary of State
25 Capitol St., Rm. 324
Concord, NH 03301-6312
Phone: (603) 271-1463

NEW JERSEY
Mark S. Herr
Director
Div. of Consumer Affairs
P.O. Box 45027
Newark, NJ 07102
Phone: (201) 504-6200
Fax: (201) 648-3538

NEW MEXICO
Michael Vargon
Deputy Director
Securities Div.
Dept. of Regulations & Licensing
20555 Pacheo St.
Santa Fe, NM 87505
Phone: (505) 827-7140
Fax: (505) 827-7083

NEW YORK

NORTH CAROLINA
Elaine F. Marshall
Secretary of State
300 N. Salisbury St., Ste. 301
Raleigh, NC 27603-5909
Phone: (919) 733-4161
Fax: (919) 733-5172
E-mail: emarshall@mail.secstate.state.nc.us

NORTH DAKOTA
Syver Vinje
Commissioner
Securities Comm.
600 E. Blvd. Ave., 5th Fl.
Bismarck, ND 58505-0510
Phone: (701) 328-2910
Fax: (701) 255-3113
E-mail: svinje@pioneer.state.nd.us

NORTHERN MARIANA ISLANDS
Pedro Q. Dela Cruz
Secretary
Ofc. of the Governor
Dept. of Commerce
Caller Box 10007 CK
Saipan, MP 96950
Phone: (670) 664-3000
Fax: (670) 664-3067
E-mail: commerce@mtccnmi.com

OHIO
Tom Geyer
Commissioner
Div. of Securities
Dept. of Commerce
77 S. High St., 22nd Fl.
Columbus, OH 43215
Phone: (614) 644-7381
Fax: (614) 466-3316

OKLAHOMA
Irving L. Faught
Administrator
Dept. of Securities
120 N. Robinson Ave., #860
Oklahoma City, OK 73102-7405
Phone: (405) 280-7700
Fax: (405) 280-7742

OREGON
Dick Nockleby
Administrator
Finance & Corporate Securities
Dept. of Consumer & Business Services
21 Labor & Industries Bldg.
350 Winter St., NW, #410
Salem, OR 97310-1321
Phone: (503) 378-4140
Fax: (503) 947-7862

PENNSYLVANIA
Robert Lam
Chairman
Securities Comm.
1010 N. 7th St.
Harrisburg, PA 17102-1410
Phone: (717) 787-8061
Fax: (717) 783-5122

PUERTO RICO
Juan Antonio Garcia
Commissioner
Insurance Comm.
P.O. Box 8330
Santurce, PR 00910
Phone: (787) 722-8686
Fax: (787) 722-4400

RHODE ISLAND
Maria D'Alessandro Piccirilli
Associate Director & Superintendent of Securities
Securities Div.
Dept. of Business Regulation
233 Richmond St.
Providence, RI 02903
Phone: (401) 222-3048

SOUTH CAROLINA
David N. Jonson
Deputy Attorney General
Ofc. of the Attorney Gen.
Securities Div.
P.O. Box 11549
Columbia, SC 29211-1549
Phone: (803) 734-9916

SOUTH DAKOTA
Deborah Bollinger
Director
Div. of Securities
Dept. of Commerce & Regulation
118 W. Capitol Ave.
Pierre, SD 57501
Phone: (605) 773-4823
Fax: (605) 773-5953

TENNESSEE
Daphne Smith
Assistant Commissioner
Securities Div.
Dept. of Commerce & Insurance
500 James Robertson Pkwy.
Nashville, TN 37243
Phone: (615) 741-2947
Fax: (615) 532-8375

TEXAS
Denise Voigt Crawford
Commissioner
State Securities Board
P.O. Box 13167
Austin, TX 78711-3167
Phone: (512) 305-8300
Fax: (512) 305-8310

U.S. VIRGIN ISLANDS
Maryleen Thomas
Director
Banking & Insurance Div.
#18 Kongens Gade
St. Thomas, VI 00801
Phone: (340) 774-2991
Fax: (340) 774-9458

UTAH
Tony Taggart
Director
Securities Div.
Dept. of Commerce
160 E. 300 S.
Salt Lake City, UT 84111
Phone: (801) 530-6606
Fax: (801) 530-6980
E-mail: ttaggart@br.state.ut.us

VERMONT
Elizabeth R. Costle
Commissioner
Dept. of Banking, Insurance, Securities & Health
Care Administration
89 State St.
Montpelier, VT 05620-3101
Phone: (802) 828-3301
Fax: (802) 828-3306
E-mail: bcostle@state.vt.us

VIRGINIA
Theodore W. Morrison, Jr.
Chair
State Corp. Comm.
Tyler Bldg.
1300 E. Main St.
Richmond, VA 23219
Phone: (804) 371-9608
Fax: (804) 371-9376

WASHINGTON
Debra Bortner
Administrator
Securities Div.
Dept. of Financial Institutions
P.O. Box 9033
Olympia, WA 98507-9033
Phone: (360) 902-8700
Fax: (360) 586-5068

WEST VIRGINIA
Glen B. Gainer
State Auditor
Securities Div.
Ofc. of State Auditor
State Capitol, Bldg. 1, Rm. W100
1900 Kanawha Blvd., E.
Charleston, WV 25305
Phone: (304) 558-2257
Fax: (304) 558-5200

WISCONSIN
Patricia D. Struck
Administrator
Div. of Securities
Dept. of Financial Institutions
345 W. Washington Ave.
P.O. Box 1768
Madison, WI 53701
Phone: (608) 266-3431
Fax: (608) 256-1259

WYOMING
Joe Meyer
Secretary of State
Securities Div.
State Capitol Bldg.
Cheyenne, WY 82002
Phone: (307) 777-5333
Fax: (307) 777-6217
E-mail: secofstate@misc.state.wy.us

Small and Minority Business Assistance

Provides assistance and information on financing and government procurement opportunities to small and minority business ventures.

ALABAMA
Bea Price Forniss
Director
Minority Business
Ofc. of Minority Business
P.O. Box 5690
Montgomery, AL 36130
Phone: (334) 242-2220
Fax: (334) 242-4203

Ken Funderburk
Director
Dev. Ofc.
401 Adams Ave., 6th Fl., Ste. 670
Montgomery, AL 36130
Phone: (334) 242-0400
Fax: (334) 242-5669

ALASKA
Martin Richard
Director
Div. of Investments
Commerce & Economic Dev. Dept.
P.O. Box 34159
Juneau, AK 99803-4159
Phone: (907) 465-2510
Fax: (907) 465-2103

AMERICAN SAMOA
John Faumuina, Jr.
Director
Economic Dev. & Planning Ofc.
Dept. of Commerce
Pago Pago, AS 96799
Phone: (684) 633-5155
Fax: (684) 633-4195

ARIZONA
Jan Stash
Director
Minority/Women Services
Dept. of Commerce
3800 N. Central Ave., Ste. 1500
Phoenix, AZ 85012
Phone: (602) 280-1476

ARKANSAS
Orville Abrams
Team Leader
Advocacy in Business Services
Dept. of Economic Dev.
1 Capitol Mall, Rm. 4C-300
Little Rock, AR 72201
Phone: (501) 682-1060
Fax: (501) 682-7341

CALIFORNIA
Denise Arend
Executive Director
Ofc. of Small Business
Trade & Commerce Agency
801 K St., Ste. 1700
Sacramento, CA 85814
Phone: (916) 322-3596

COLORADO
Mary Madison
State Director
Small Business Dev. Ctrs.
Ofc. of Economic Dev.
1625 Broadway, Ste. 1710
Denver, CO 80202
Phone: (303) 892-3840
Fax: (303) 892-3848

CONNECTICUT
Meg Yetishefsky
Minority and Small Contractors Set Aside Program
Dept. of Economic & Community Dev.
505 Hudson St.
Hartford, CT 06106
Phone: (860) 270-8000

DELAWARE
Darrell J. Minott
Director
Economic Dev. Ofc.
99 Kings Hwy.
Dover, DE 19901-7305
Phone: (302) 739-4271
Fax: (302) 739-5749

DISTRICT OF COLUMBIA
Jackie Flowers
Executive Director
Ofc. of Business & Economic Dev.
717 14th St., NW, 7th Fl.
Washington, DC 20005
Phone: (202) 727-6600

FLORIDA
Karen Johnson-Street
Vice President
Minority Business Dev. & Urban Initiative
Enterprise FL, Inc.
2801 Ponce De Leon Blvd., Ste. 700
Coral Gables, FL 33134
Phone: (305) 569-2654
Fax: (305) 569-2657

GEORGIA
Calandria Lee
Coordinator
Small & Minority Business
Dept. of Adm. Services
200 Piedmont Ave., Ste. 1302
Atlanta, GA 30334
Phone: (404) 656-6315

GUAM
Joseph T. Duenas
Director
Dept. of Revenue & Taxation
13-1 Mariner Dr., Tiyan
P.O. Box 23607
GMF, GU 96921
Phone: (671) 475-1817
Fax: (671) 472-2643

HAWAII
Seiji Naya
Director
Dept. of Business, Economic Dev. & Tourism
250 S. Hotel St., 5th Fl.
Honolulu, HI 96813
Phone: (808) 586-2355
Fax: (808) 586-2377

IDAHO
Thomas Arnold
Director
Dept. of Commerce
700 W. State St.
Boise, ID 83720
Phone: (208) 334-2470

ILLINOIS
Terri Schierholz
Assistant Director
Business Dev.
Commerce & Community Affairs
100 W. Randolph, Ste. 3-400
Chicago, IL 60601
Phone: (312) 814-2811

INDIANA
Elena Looper
Deputy Commissioner
Minority Business Dev.
Dept. of Administration
IGC-S., Rm. W474
Indianapolis, IN 46204
Phone: (317) 232-3073
Fax: (317) 233-6921

IOWA
Mike Miller
Chief
Business Finance Bur.
200 E. Grand Ave.
Des Moines, IA 50309
Phone: (515) 242-4827

KANSAS
Antonio Augusto
Director
Minority & Women Business Dev.
Dept. of Commerce & Housing
700 SW Harrison Ave., Ste. 1300
Topeka, KS 66603-3712
Phone: (785) 296-5298
Fax: (785) 296-3490

KENTUCKY
Floyd C. Taylor
Director
Small & Minority Business Dev.
Cabinet for Economic Dev.
Capital Plz. Tower
Frankfort, KY 40601
Phone: (502) 564-4252
Fax: (502) 564-9758

LOUISIANA
Henry J. Stamper
Executive Director
Minority & Women Enterprise
Dept. of Economic Dev.
P.O. Box 94185
Baton Rouge, LA 70804-9185
Phone: (225) 342-5373
Fax: (225) 342-5926

MAINE
Steven H. Levesque
Commissioner
Dept. of Economic & Community Dev.
59 State House Station
Augusta, ME 04333
Phone: (207) 287-2656

MARYLAND
Robert C. Brennan
Assistant Secretary
Financing Programs
Dept. of Business & Economic Dev.
217 E. Redwood St., 22nd Fl.
Baltimore, MD 21202
Phone: (410) 767-3213
Fax: (410) 333-6931

MASSACHUSETTS
JoAnn Thompson
Executive Director
State Ofc. of Minority & Women
Business Assistance
100 Cambridge St., 13th Fl.
Boston, MA 02202
Phone: (617) 727-8692
Fax: (617) 727-5915

MICHIGAN
Greg Wallace
Director of Operations
Minority Business Enterprise Div.
Economic Dev. Corp.
210 N. Washington Sq., 1st Fl.
Lansing, MI 48913
Phone: (517) 373-3099

MINNESOTA
Charles Schaffer
Director
Small Business Assistance
Dept. of Trade & Economic Dev.
500 Metro Sq.
121 Seventh Pl., E.
St. Paul, MN 55101-2146
Phone: (651) 296-0617
Fax: (651) 296-1290

MISSISSIPPI
Walter C. Scott
Director
Ofc. of Minority Business
Dept. of Economic & Community Dev.
1200 Siller Bldg.
550 High St.
Jackson, MS 39201
Phone: (601) 359-3449
Fax: (601) 359-3832

MISSOURI
Dora Serrano
Manager
Minority Business Dev. Section
Dept. of Economic Dev.
Truman Bldg., Rm. 720
P.O. Box 118
Jefferson City, MO 65102
Phone: (573) 751-3237
Fax: (573) 751-6899
E-mail: dserrano@mail.state.mo.us

MONTANA
Andy Poole
Deputy Director
Dept. of Commerce
1424 9th Ave.
Helena, MT 59620
Phone: (406) 444-3797
Fax: (406) 444-2903

NEBRASKA
Allan Wenstrand
Director
Dept. of Economic Dev.
301 Centennial Mall, S.
P.O. Box 94666
Lincoln, NE 68509
Phone: (402) 471-3747
Fax: (402) 471-3778

NEVADA
Dan Tom
Director
Dept. of Business & Industry
555 E. Washington Ave., Ste. 4900
Las Vegas, NV 89101
Phone: (702) 486-2750
Fax: (702) 486-2758

NEW HAMPSHIRE
Jack Donovan
Executive Director
Business Finance Authority
14 Dixon Ave., Ste. 101
Concord, NH 03301-4954
Phone: (603) 271-2391
Fax: (603) 271-2396

NEW JERSEY
David Byrd
Director
Small Business
Dept. of Commerce & Economic Dev.
20 W. State St.
P.O. Box 820
Trenton, NJ 08625-0820
Phone: (609) 292-8177
Fax: (609) 292-0082

NEW MEXICO
Louis Higgins
Director
Purchasing Div.
Dept. of Services
P.O. Box 26110
Sante Fe, NM 87502
Phone: (505) 827-0472
Fax: (505) 827-2041

NEW YORK
Michelle Marquez-Melecio
Executive Director
Div. of Minority & Women's Business Dev.
Dept. of Economic Dev.
1 Commerce Plz.
Albany, NY 12245
Phone: (518) 474-0375
Fax: (518) 473-0665

NORTH CAROLINA
Scott Daugherty
Executive Director
Small Business Technology & Dev. Ctr.
333 Fayettville St. Mall, Ste. 1150
Raleigh, NC 27601
Phone: (919) 715-7272
Fax: (919) 715-7777

NORTH DAKOTA
Kevin Cramer
Director
Dept. of Economic Dev. & Finance
1833 E. Bismarck Expy.
Bismarck, ND 58504
Phone: (701) 328-5300
Fax: (701) 328-5320
E-mail: kcramer@state.nd.us

NORTHERN MARIANA ISLANDS
James H. Ripple
Executive Director
Commonwealth Dev. Authority
P.O. Box 2149
Saipan, MP 96950
Phone: (670) 234-7145
Fax: (670) 234-7144
E-mail: cda@itecnmi.com

OHIO
Karen Conrad
Manager
Ofc. of Small Business
Dept. of Dev.
P.O. Box 1001
Columbus, OH 43266-0101
Phone: (614) 466-2718
Fax: (614) 466-0829

Brenda Sinclair
Manager
Minority Business Dev. Ofc.
Dept. of Dev.
77 S. High St.
Columbus, OH 43266
Phone: (614) 466-5700
Fax: (614) 466-4172

OKLAHOMA
Howard Barnett
Director/Secretary of Commerce
Dept. of Commerce
900 N. Stiles Ave.
P.O. Box 26980
Oklahoma City, OK 73105
Phone: (405) 815-6552
Fax: (405) 815-5290

OREGON
Cheri Tebeau-Harrell
Certification Manager
Ofc. of Minority, Women & Emerging Small Business
Dept. of Consumer & Business Services
350 Winter St., NE
Salem, OR 97310
Phone: (503) 947-7948
Fax: (503) 378-3134

PENNSYLVANIA
Linda Goldstein
Director
Ofc. of Small Business
Dept. of Commerce
Forum Bldg., Rm. 400
Harrisburg, PA 17120
Phone: (717) 783-8950
Fax: (717) 234-4560

PUERTO RICO

RHODE ISLAND
Charles Newton
Director
Minority Business Enterprise Program
Dept. of Administration
1 Capitol Hill
Providence, RI 02903
Phone: (401) 222-6253
Fax: (401) 222-6391

SOUTH CAROLINA
Shirley Mack
Acting Director
Small & Minority Business Assistance
Ofc. of the Governor
1205 Pendleton St., Rm. 329
Columbia, SC 29201
Phone: (803) 734-0657
Fax: (803) 734-2498

SOUTH DAKOTA
Ron Wheeler
Commissioner
Governor's Ofc. of Economic Dev.
Capitol Lake Plz.
711 Wells Ave.
Pierre, SD 57501-3369
Phone: (605) 773-5032
Fax: (605) 773-3256

TENNESSEE
Kelly Durham
Director
Ofc. of Minority Business
Economic & Community Dev. Dept.
320 6th Ave., N.
Nashville, TN 37243
Phone: (615) 741-2626
Fax: (615) 532-8715

TEXAS
Tom Treadway
Executive Director
Services Comm.
1711 San Jacinto
P.O. Box 13047
Austin, TX 78701-3047
Phone: (512) 463-3446
Fax: (512) 463-7966
E-mail: tomtreadway@gsc.state.tx.us

U.S. VIRGIN ISLANDS
William Quetel
Director
Small Business Dev. Authority
1050 Norre Gade, #5
St. Thomas, VI 00802
Phone: (340) 714-1700
Fax: (340) 774-8106

UTAH
Johnny Bryan
Director of Procurement
Div. of Business & Economic Dev.
Dept. of Community & Economic Dev.
324 S. State, Ste. 500
Salt Lake City, UT 84111
Phone: (801) 538-8790
Fax: (801) 538-8825
E-mail: jbryan@dced.state.ut.us

VERMONT
David Tucker
Director
State Economic Opportunity Ofc.
Agency of Human Services
103 S. Main St.
Waterbury, VT 05671
Phone: (802) 241-2450

VIRGINIA
Linda Byrd-Harden
Director
Dept. of Minority Business Enterprise
202 N. 9th St., 11th Fl.
Richmond, VA 23219
Phone: (804) 786-5560
Fax: (804) 371-7359

WASHINGTON
James A. Medina
Director
Ofc. of Minority & Women's Business
406 S. Water
P.O. Box 41160
Olympia, WA 98504-1160
Phone: (360) 753-9679
Fax: (360) 586-7079

WEST VIRGINIA
Hazel Kroesser-Palmer
Director
Small Business Dev. Ctr.
Dev. Ofc.
950 Kanawha Blvd., E.
Charleston, WV 25301
Phone: (304) 348-2960
Fax: (304) 558-0127

WISCONSIN
Oscar Herrarra
Director
Bur. of Minority Business Dev.
Dept. of Commerce
P.O. Box 7970
Madison, WI 53707
Phone: (608) 266-8380
Fax: (608) 267-2829

H.H. Rothwell
Director
Bur. of Business & Industry Services
Dept. of Commerce
P.O. Box 7970
Madison, WI 53707-7970
Phone: (608) 267-9550
Fax: (608) 267-0436

WYOMING
John Reardon
Chief Executive Officer
Economic & Community Dev.
Business Council
214 W. 15th St.
Cheyenne, WY 82002
Phone: (307) 777-2800
Fax: (307) 777-5840

Social Services

Responsible for the delivery of services to children, the blind, disabled and elderly.

ALABAMA
Tony Petelos
Commissioner
Dept. of Human Resources
50 N. Ripley St.
Montgomery, AL 36130-4000
Phone: (334) 242-1310
Fax: (334) 242-0198

ALASKA
Karen Perdue
Commissioner
Dept. of Health & Social Services
P.O. Box 110601
Juneau, AK 99811-0601
Phone: (907) 465-3030
Fax: (907) 465-3068

AMERICAN SAMOA
Marie F. Mao
Director
Dept. of Human & Social Services
AS Govt.
Pago Pago, AS 96799
Phone: (684) 633-2609
Fax: (684) 633-7449
E-mail: dhss@samoatelco.com

ARIZONA
John Clayton
Director Designate
Dept. of Economic Security
1717 W. Jefferson
Phoenix, AZ 85007
Phone: (602) 542-5678
Fax: (602) 542-5339

ARKANSAS
Kurt Knickrehm
Director
Dept. of Human Services
P.O. Box 1437, Slot 316
Little Rock, AR 72203
Phone: (501) 682-8650
Fax: (501) 682-6836

CALIFORNIA
Eloise Anderson
Director
Dept. of Social Services
744 P St., MS 17-11
Sacramento, CA 95814
Phone: (916) 657-2598

COLORADO
Karen Beye
Managing Director
Dept. of Human Services
1575 Sherman St., 8th Fl.
Denver, CO 80203-1714
Phone: (303) 866-3063
Fax: (303) 866-4214

CONNECTICUT
Pat Wilson-Coker
Commissioner
Dept. of Social Services
25 Sigourney St.
Hartford, CT 06106
Phone: (860) 424-5008

DELAWARE
Gregg Sylvester
Secretary
Dept. of Health & Social Services
1901 N. DuPont Hwy.
New Castle, DE 19720
Phone: (302) 577-4500
Fax: (302) 577-4510

DISTRICT OF COLUMBIA
Adrian Buckner
Acting Commissioner
Comm. on Social Services
Dept. of Human Services
609 H St., NE, 5th Fl.
Washington, DC 20002
Phone: (202) 727-5930

FLORIDA
Edward A. Feaver
Secretary
Dept. of Children & Family Services
1317 Winewood Blvd.
Tallahassee, FL 32399-0700
Phone: (850) 487-1111
Fax: (850) 922-2993

GEORGIA
Peggy Peters
Director
Family & Children Services
Dept. of Human Resources
2 Peachtree St., Rm. 16-200
Atlanta, GA 30303
Phone: (404) 657-7660

GUAM
Dennis G. Rodriguez
Director
Dept. of Public Health & Social Services
P.O. Box 2816
Hagatna, GU 96932
Phone: (671) 735-7102
Fax: (671) 734-5910
E-mail: dennis_r_@NS.GOV.GU

HAWAII
Susan Chandler
Director
Dept. of Human Services
1390 Miller St.
Honolulu, HI 96813
Phone: (808) 586-4997
Fax: (808) 586-4890

IDAHO
Roseanne Hardin
Administrator
Family & Community Services
Dept. of Health & Welfare
450 W. State St., 3rd Fl.
P.O. Box 83720
Boise, ID 83720-0036
Phone: (208) 334-5700
Fax: (208) 334-6699

ILLINOIS
Jess McDonald
Director
Dept. of Children & Family Services
406 E. Monroe St.
Springfield, IL 62701
Phone: (217) 785-0863
Fax: (217) 785-1052

INDIANA
Peter Sybinsky
Secretary
Family & Social Services Administration
402 W. Washington St., W461
Indianapolis, IN 46204
Phone: (317) 233-4690
Fax: (317) 233-4693

IOWA
Sally Titus Cunningham
Deputy Director
Dept. of Human Services
Hoover State Ofc. Bldg.
1300 E. Walnut
Des Moines, IA 50319
Phone: (515) 281-6360

KANSAS
Rochelle Chronister
Secretary
Dept. of Social & Rehabilitative Services
Docking State Ofc. Bldg.
915 Harrison, Rm. 603N
Topeka, KS 66612
Phone: (785) 296-3959

KENTUCKY
Donna Harmon
Commissioner
Cabinet for Families & Children
Dept. for Social Services
275 E. Main St.
Frankfort, KY 40621
Phone: (502) 564-4650
Fax: (502) 564-5002

LOUISIANA
Madlyn Bagneris
Secretary
Dept. of Social Services
P.O. Box 3776
Baton Rouge, LA 70821
Phone: (225) 342-0286
Fax: (225) 342-8636

MAINE
Kevin Concannon
Commissioner
Dept. of Human Services
11 State House Station
Augusta, ME 04333
Phone: (207) 287-2736

MARYLAND
Linda Ellard
Executive Director
Social Services Administration
Dept. of Human Resources
311 W. Saratoga St.
Baltimore, MD 21201
Phone: (410) 767-7216
Fax: (410) 333-0099

MASSACHUSETTS
Jeffrey Locke
Acting Commissioner
Dept. of Social Services
24 Farnsworth St.
Boston, MA 02110
Phone: (617) 727-0900
Fax: (617) 261-7435

MICHIGAN
Douglas Howard
Director
Family Independence Agency
P.O. Box 30037
Lansing, MI 48909
Phone: (517) 373-2000
Fax: (517) 373-8471

MINNESOTA
Judith Wong
Assistant Commissioner
Children's Initiative
Dept. of Human Services
444 Lafayette Rd.
St. Paul, MN 55155
Phone: (651) 296-2754
Fax: (651) 297-1949
E-mail: judith.m.wong@state.mn.us

MISSISSIPPI

MISSOURI
Gary Stangler
Director
Dept. of Social Services
221 W. High, Rm. 240
P.O. Box 1527
Jefferson City, MO 65102
Phone: (573) 751-4815
Fax: (573) 751-3203
E-mail: gstangle@mail.state.mo.us

MONTANA
Laurie Ekanger
Director
Dept. of Public Health & Human Services
111 Sanders St.
P.O. Box 4210
Helena, MT 59620
Phone: (406) 444-5622
Fax: (406) 444-1970

NEBRASKA
Ron Ross
Director
Dept. of Health & Human Services
P.O. Box 95044
Lincoln, NE 68509
Phone: (402) 471-2306
Fax: (402) 471-0820

NEVADA
Charlotte Crawford
Director
Dept. of Human Resources
Kinkaid Bldg., Rm. 600
505 E. King St.
Carson City, NV 89701
Phone: (775) 687-4000
Fax: (775) 684-4010
E-mail: charlott@govmail.state.nv.us

NEW HAMPSHIRE
Richard A. Chevrefils
Assistant Commissioner
Ofc. of Family Services
Health & Human Services
6 Hazen Dr.
Concord, NH 03301-6505
Phone: (603) 271-4321
Fax: (603) 271-4727

NEW JERSEY
Michele K. Guhl
Commissioner
Div. of Mgmt. & Budget
Dept. of Human Services
222 S. Warren St.
P.O. Box 717
Trenton, NJ 08625-0717
Phone: (609) 292-3717
Fax: (609) 292-3824

NEW MEXICO
Deborah Hartz
Secretary
Social Services Div.
Dept. of Children, Youth & Families
PERA Bldg.
P.O. Box 5160
Sante Fe, NM 87502
Phone: (505) 827-7602
Fax: (505) 827-4053

NEW YORK
Brian Wing
Commissioner
Ofc. of Temporary & Disability Assistance
40 N. Pearl St., 16th Fl.
Albany, NY 12243
Phone: (518) 473-8772
Fax: (518) 486-6255

NORTH CAROLINA
Kevin Fitzgerald
Director of Social Services
Dept. of Health & Human Services
325 N. Salisbury St.
Raleigh, NC 27603-5905
Phone: (919) 733-3055
Fax: (919) 715-3581

NORTH DAKOTA
Carol Olson
Executive Director
Dept. of Human Services
600 E. Blvd. Ave., 3rd Fl. - Judicial Wing
Bismarck, ND 58505-0250
Phone: (701) 328-2310
Fax: (701) 328-2359
E-mail: socols@state.nd.us

NORTHERN MARIANA ISLANDS
Thomas A. Tebuteb
Secretary
Ofc. of the Secretary
Community & Cultural Affairs
P.O. Box 10007
Saipan, MP 96950
Phone: (670) 664-2571
Fax: (670) 664-2570

OHIO
Jacqui Sensky
Director
Dept. of Human Services
30 E. Broad St., 32nd Fl.
Columbus, OH 43266-0423
Phone: (614) 466-6282
Fax: (614) 466-2815

OKLAHOMA
Howard Hendrick
Director
Human Services
Dept. of Human Services
P.O. Box 25352
Oklahoma City, OK 73125
Phone: (405) 522-3877
Fax: (405) 521-6450

OREGON
Gary Weeks
Director
Dept. of Human Resources
500 Summer St., NE, 4th Fl.
Salem, OR 97310-1012
Phone: (503) 945-5944
Fax: (503) 378-2897

PENNSYLVANIA
William Gannon
Deputy Secretary
Dept. of Public Welfare
Health & Welfare Bldg., Rm. 533
Harrisburg, PA 17105
Phone: (717) 787-3438
Fax: (717) 783-4511

PUERTO RICO
Angie Varela
Secretary
Dept. of Social Services
P.O. Box 11398
San Juan, PR 00910
Phone: (787) 722-7400
Fax: (787) 723-1223

RHODE ISLAND
Christine Ferguson
Director
Dept. of Human Services
600 New London Ave.
Cranston, RI 02920
Phone: (401) 462-2121
Fax: (401) 462-3677

SOUTH CAROLINA
Elizabeth G. Patterson
Director
Dept. of Social Services
1535 Confederate Ave., Extension
Columbia, SC 29202
Phone: (803) 898-7360

SOUTH DAKOTA
James Ellenbecker
Secretary
Dept. of Social Services
700 Governors Dr.
Pierre, SD 57501
Phone: (605) 773-3165
Fax: (605) 773-4855

TENNESSEE
Ed Lake
Assistant Commissioner
Community & Field Services
Dept. of Human Services
400 Deaderick St., 15th Fl.
Nashville, TN 37248-0004
Phone: (615) 313-4710
Fax: (615) 741-4165

TEXAS
Don A. Gilbert
Commissioner
Health & Human Services Comm.
P.O. Box 13247
Austin, TX 78711
Phone: (512) 424-6502
Fax: (512) 424-6587

U.S. VIRGIN ISLANDS
Sedonie Halbert
Commissioner
Dept. of Human Services
Knud Hansen Complex, Bldg. A
1303 Hospital Grounds
St. Thomas, VI 00802
Phone: (340) 774-0930
Fax: (340) 774-3466

UTAH
Robin Arnold-Williams
Executive Director
Dept. of Human Service
120 N. 200 W.
Salt Lake City, UT 84145-0500
Phone: (801) 538-4001
Fax: (801) 538-4016
E-mail: rarnold.hsadmin1@state.ut.us

VERMONT
William Young
Director
Dept. of Social & Rehab. Services
103 S. Main St.
Waterbury, VT 05671
Phone: (802) 241-2101

VIRGINIA
Clarence H. Carter
Commissioner
Dept. of Social Services
Theater Row Bldg.
730 E. Broad St.
Richmond, VA 23219
Phone: (804) 692-1901
Fax: (804) 692-1964

WASHINGTON
Lyle Quasim
Secretary
Dept. of Social & Health Services
P.O. Box 45010
Olympia, WA 98504-5010
Phone: (360) 902-8400
Fax: (360) 902-7848

WEST VIRGINIA
Joan Ohl
Secretary
Dept. of Health & Human Resources
Capitol Complex, Bldg. 3, Rm. 206
1900 Kanawha Blvd., E.
Charleston, WV 25305
Phone: (304) 558-0684
Fax: (304) 558-1130

WISCONSIN
Joseph Leean
Secretary
Dept. of Health & Family Services
1 W. Wilson St., Rm. 650
P.O. Box 7850
Madison, WI 53703
Phone: (608) 266-3681
Fax: (608) 266-7882

WYOMING
Shirley Carson
Director
Dept. of Family Services
Hathaway Bldg., 3rd Fl.
2300 Capitol Ave.
Cheyenne, WY 82002
Phone: (307) 777-6948

Soil Conservation

Coordinates programs to conserve and protect the state's soil.

ALABAMA
Stephen M. Cauthen
Executive Secretary
Soil & Water Conservation Comm.
P.O. Box 304800
Montgomery, AL 36130-4800
Phone: (334) 242-2620
Fax: (334) 240-3332

ALASKA
Art Weiner
Executive Director
Soil & Water Conservation Board
Dept. of Natural Resources
3601 C St., Ste. 980
Juneau, AK 99801
Phone: (907) 269-8424
Fax: (907) 269-8918

AMERICAN SAMOA

ARIZONA
Robert E. Yount
Director
Natural Resources Div.
Dept. of State Land
1616 W. Adams
Phoenix, AZ 85007
Phone: (602) 542-4625

ARKANSAS
J. Randy Young
Director
Soil & Water Conservation Comm.
101 E. Capitol Ave., # 350
Little Rock, AR 72201
Phone: (501) 682-1611
Fax: (501) 682-3991

CALIFORNIA
Larry Goldzband
Director
Dept. of Conservation
801 K St.
Sacramento, CA 95814
Phone: (916) 322-1080

COLORADO
Dan Parker
Director
Soil Conservation Board
Dept. of Natural Resources
1313 Sherman St., Rm. 219
Denver, CO 80203
Phone: (303) 866-3351
Fax: (303) 866-8106

CONNECTICUT
Allan Bennett
Executive Director
Council on Soil & Water Conservation
79 Elm St.
Hartford, CT 06106
Phone: (860) 424-3905

DELAWARE
Nicholas A. DiPasquale
Secretary
Dept. of Natural Resources & Environmental Control
P.O. Box 1401
Dover, DE 19903
Phone: (302) 739-4403
Fax: (302) 739-6242
E-mail: ndipasquale@state.de.us

DISTRICT OF COLUMBIA
Magnus Blanchette
Acting Chief
Soil Research Branch
Housing & Environmental Regulation
Consumer & Regulatory Affairs
614 H St., NW, Lower Level
Washington, DC 20001
Phone: (202) 727-7577

FLORIDA
Virginia Wetherell
Secretary
Dept. of Environmental Protection
3900 Commonwealth Blvd., MS-10
Tallahassee, FL 32399-3000
Phone: (850) 488-4805
Fax: (850) 921-4303

GEORGIA
F. Graham Liles
Executive Director
State Soil & Water Conservation Comm.
P.O. Box 8024
Athens, GA 30603
Phone: (404) 542-3065

GUAM
Jesus T. Salas
Administrator
Environmental Protection Agency
15-6101 Mariner Ave., Tiyan
P.O. Box 22439
Barrigada, GU 96921
Phone: (671) 475-1658
Fax: (671) 477-9402

HAWAII
Timothy Johns
Chair
Dept. of Land & Natural Resources
1151 Punchbowl St.
Honolulu, HI 96813
Phone: (808) 587-0400
Fax: (808) 587-0390

IDAHO
Jerry Nicoleson
Acting Administrator
Soil Conservation Comm.
Dept. of Lands
1215 W. State St.
Boise, ID 83720
Phone: (208) 334-0210

ILLINOIS
Brent Manning
Director
Dept. of Natural Resources
Lincoln Towers Plz., Rm. 425
524 S. 2nd St.
Springfield, IL 62706
Phone: (217) 782-6302
Fax: (217) 785-9236

INDIANA
Larry Macklin
Executive Director
Dept. of Natural Resources
IGC-S., Rm. W256
402 W. Washington St.
Indianapolis, IN 46204
Phone: (317) 232-4020
Fax: (317) 233-6811

IOWA
James B. Gulliford
Administrator
Div. of Soil Conservation
Dept. of Agri. & Land
Wallace State Ofc. Bldg.
E. 9th & Grand Aves.
Des Moines, IA 50319
Phone: (515) 281-6146

KANSAS
Tracy Streeter
Director
Conservation Comm.
109 SW 9th St., Ste. 500
Topeka, KS 66612-1299
Phone: (785) 296-3600
Fax: (785) 296-6172

KENTUCKY
William Martin
Commissioner
Div. Natural Areas
Dept. of Natural Resources
Case 105, Eastern KY Univ.
Richmond, KY 40475-3140
Phone: (502) 564-2184
Fax: (502) 564-6193

LOUISIANA
Jack Caldwell
Secretary
Dept. of Natural Resources
P.O. Box 94396
Baton Rouge, LA 70804-9396
Phone: (225) 342-4503
Fax: (225) 342-5861

MAINE
Robert W. Spear
Commissioner
Dept. of Agri., Food & Rural Resources
28 State House Station
Augusta, ME 04333
Phone: (207) 287-3871

MARYLAND
Louise Lawrence
Executive Secretary
Soil Conservation Cmte.
Dept. of Agri.
50 Harry S. Truman Pkwy.
Annapolis, MD 21401
Phone: (410) 841-5863
Fax: (410) 841-5914

MASSACHUSETTS
Lauren A. Liss
Commissioner
Executive Ofc. of Environmental Affairs
Dept. of Environmental Protection
1 Winter St.
Boston, MA 02108
Phone: (617) 292-5856
Fax: (617) 574-6880

MICHIGAN
Russell Harding
Director
Dept. of Environmental Quality
P.O. Box 30473
Lansing, MI 48909-7973
Phone: (517) 373-7917

MINNESOTA
Allen Garber
Commissioner
Dept. of Natural Resources
500 Lafayette Rd.
St. Paul, MN 55155
Phone: (651) 296-2549
Fax: (651) 296-4799

MISSISSIPPI
Gale Martin
Executive Director
Soil & Water Conservation Comm.
Parks & Recreation
680 Monroe St., Ste. B
Jackson, MS 39201
Phone: (601) 354-7645
Fax: (601) 354-6628

MISSOURI
Sarah Fast
Director
Soil & Water Conservation Program
Dept. of Natural Resources
1738 E. Elm
P.O. Box 176
Jefferson City, MO 65102
Phone: (573) 751-4932
Fax: (573) 751-3508
E-mail: nrfasts@mail.dnr.state.mo.us

MONTANA
Ray Peck
Administrator
Conservation & Resources Dev.
Dept. of Natural Resources & Conservation
1625 11th Ave.
Helena, MT 59620
Phone: (406) 444-6667
Fax: (406) 444-2684

NEBRASKA
Dayle E. Williamson
Director
Natural Resources Comm.
301 Centennial Mall, S.
P.O. Box 94876
Lincoln, NE 68509-4876
Phone: (402) 471-2081
Fax: (402) 471-3132

NEVADA
Peter G. Morros
Director
Dept. of Conservation & Natural Resources
123 W. Nye Ln., Rm. 230
Carson City, NV 89706
Phone: (775) 687-4360
Fax: (775) 687-6122

NEW HAMPSHIRE
Stephen Taylor
Commissioner
Agri., Markets & Food
P.O. Box 2042
Concord, NH 03302-2042
Phone: (603) 271-3700
Fax: (603) 271-1109

NEW JERSEY
Samuel R. Race
Executive Secretary
State Soil Conservation Cmte.
Dept. of Agri.
John Fitch Plz.
P.O. Box 330
Trenton, NJ 08625-0330
Phone: (609) 292-5540
Fax: (609) 633-7229

NEW MEXICO
Jeff Lewis
Soil & Water Conservation Specialist 2
Agri. Dept.
P.O. Box 30005
Las Cruces, NM 88003-8005
Phone: (505) 646-3490
Fax: (505) 646-1540

NEW YORK
John Cahill
Commissioner
Dept. of Environmental Conservation
50 Wolf Rd.
Albany, NY 12233-1010
Phone: (518) 457-1162
Fax: (518) 457-7744

NORTH CAROLINA
C. Dewey Botts
Acting Division Director
Soil & Water Conservation
Dept.of Environment & Natural Resources
512 N. Salisbury St.
P.O. Box 27687
Raleigh, NC 27611
Phone: (919) 733-2302
Fax: (919) 715-3559

NORTH DAKOTA

NORTHERN MARIANA ISLANDS
Eugene A. Santos
Secretary
Dept. of Lands & Natural Resources
P.O. Box 10007
Saipan, MP 96950
Phone: (670) 322-9830
Fax: (670) 322-2633

OHIO
Lawrence G. Vance
Chief
Div. of Soil Conservation
Dept. of Natural Resources
Fountain Sq., Bldg. E-2
Columbus, OH 43224
Phone: (614) 265-6614
Fax: (614) 262-2064

OKLAHOMA
Mike Thralls
Executive Director
Conservation Comm.
2800 N. Lincoln Blvd., Ste. 160
Oklahoma City, OK 73105
Phone: (405) 521-2384
Fax: (405) 521-6686

OREGON
Richard Benner
Director
Dept. of Land Conservation & Dev.
1175 Court St., NE
Salem, OR 97310
Phone: (503) 373-0050
Fax: (503) 362-6705

PENNSYLVANIA
James M. Seif
Cabinet Secretary
Dept. of Environmental Protection
Rachel Carson State Ofc. Bldg., 16th Fl.
400 Market St.
Harrisburg, PA 17120
Phone: (717) 787-2814
Fax: (717) 705-4980
E-mail: seif.james@dep.state.pa.us

PUERTO RICO
Daniel Pagan
Secretary
Dept. of Natural Resources
P.O. Box 5887
San Juan, PR 00906
Phone: (787) 723-3090
Fax: (787) 723-4255

RHODE ISLAND
Janet Keller
Chief
Ofc. of Environmental Coordination
Dept. of Environmental Mgmt.
235 Promenade St.
Providence, RI 02908
Phone: (401) 222-3434

SOUTH CAROLINA
Jim O. Stuckey, II
General Counsel
Ofc. of the Governor
P.O. Box 11829
Columbia, SC 29211
Phone: (803) 734-9400

SOUTH DAKOTA
Darrell D. Cruea
Secretary
Dept. of Agri.
Foss Bldg.
523 E. Capitol Ave.
Pierre, SD 57501-3182
Phone: (605) 773-3375
Fax: (605) 773-5926

TENNESSEE
Jim Nance
Director
Agri. Resources
Dept. of Agri.
Ellington Agri. Ctr.
Nashville, TN 37204
Phone: (615) 837-5225
Fax: (615) 837-5025

TEXAS
Robert G. Buckley
Executive Director
State Soil & Water
Conservation Board
P.O. Box 658
Temple, TX 76503
Phone: (254) 773-2250
Fax: (254) 773-3311

U.S. VIRGIN ISLANDS

UTAH
Kyle Jacobson
Soil Conservation
Administrator
Div. of Marketing &
Enhancement
Dept. of Agri. & Food
350 N. Redwood Rd.
Salt Lake City, UT 84116
Phone: (801) 538-7171
Fax: (801) 538-7126
E-mail: jjacobson.agmain
@state.ut.us

VERMONT
John Kassell
Secretary
Agency of Natural
Resources
103 S. Main St.
Waterbury, VT 05671-0301
Phone: (802) 241-3600
Fax: (802) 241-3281

VIRGINIA
David G. Brickley
Director
Dept. of Conservation &
Recreation
203 Governor St., Ste 302
Richmond, VA 23219
Phone: (804) 786-2289
Fax: (804) 786-6141

WASHINGTON
Jennifer Belcher
Commissioner of Public
Lands
Dept. of Natural Resources
P.O. Box 47001
Olympia, WA 98504-7001
Phone: (360) 902-1000
Fax: (360) 902-1775

WEST VIRGINIA
Lance E. Tabor
Executive Director
State Soil Conservation
Cmte.
1900 Kanawha Blvd., E.
Charleston, WV 25305
Phone: (304) 558-2204
Fax: (304) 558-1635

WISCONSIN
Dennis Mack
Chief
Technical Support
Dept. of Natural Resources
P.O. Box 7921
Madison, WI 53707
Phone: (608) 266-0520
Fax: (608) 267-2768

WYOMING
Rick Chancellor
Administrator
Land Quality Div.
Dept. of Environmental
Quality
122 W. 25th St.
Cheyenne, WY 82002
Phone: (307) 777-7756

Solid Waste Management—

Develops and maintains a comprehensive solid waste management program in the state.

ALABAMA
Russell Kelly
Chief
Solid Waste Branch
Dept. of Environmental Mgmt.
1751 Congressman Dickinson Dr.
Montgomery, AL 36130-1463
Phone: (334) 271-7771
Fax: (334) 279-3050

ALASKA
Heather Stockard
Program Manager
Solid Waste Program
Dept. of Environmental Conservation
410 Willoughby Ave., Ste. 105
Juneau, AK 99801-1795
Phone: (907) 465-5150
Fax: (907) 465-5164

AMERICAN SAMOA
Abe U. Malae
Executive Director
Power Authority
AS Govt.
Pago Pago, AS 96799
Phone: (684) 644-5251
Fax: (684) 644-5001

ARIZONA
Jean Calhoun
Director
Ofc. of Waste Programs
Dept. of Environmental Quality
3033 N. Central Ave., 5th Fl.
Phoenix, AZ 85012-2809
Phone: (602) 207-2381

ARKANSAS
Dennis Burks
Chief
Solid Waste Div.
Dept. of Environmental Quality
P.O. Box 8913
Little Rock, AR 72219
Phone: (501) 682-0602
Fax: (501) 682-0611

CALIFORNIA
Dan Pennington
Chair
Integrated Waste Mgmt. Board
8800 California Ctr. Dr.
Sacramento, CA 95826-3268
Phone: (916) 255-2151

COLORADO
Howard Roitman
Director
Hazardous Materials & Waste Mgmt.
Dept. of Public Health & Environment
4300 Cherry Creek Dr., S.
Denver, CO 80246-1530
Phone: (303) 692-3300
Fax: (303) 759-5355

CONNECTICUT
Richard Barlow
Chief
Bur. of Waste Mgmt.
Dept. of Environmental Protection
79 Elm St., 1st Fl.
Hartford, CT 06106
Phone: (860) 424-2051

DELAWARE
N.C. Vasuki
General Manager
Solid Waste Authority
1128 S. Bradford St.
P.O. Box 455
Dover, DE 19903
Phone: (302) 739-5361
Fax: (302) 739-4287

DISTRICT OF COLUMBIA
Leslie Hotaling
Administrator
Solid Waste Mgmt. Administration
Dept. of Public Works
2750 S. Capitol St., SE
Washington, DC 20003
Phone: (202) 767-8512

FLORIDA
William W. Hinkley
Chief
Solid & Hazardous Waste
Dept. of Environmental Protection
2600 Blairstone Rd.
Tallahassee, FL 32399-2400
Phone: (850) 488-0300
Fax: (850) 921-8061

GEORGIA
James Dunbar
Program Manager
Environmental Protection Div.
Dept. of Natural Resources
205 Butler St., Ste. 1152
Atlanta, GA 30334
Phone: (404) 656-2836

GUAM
Jesus T. Salas
Administrator
Environmental Protection Agency
15-6101 Mariner Ave., Tiyan
P.O. Box 22439
Barrigada, GU 96921
Phone: (671) 475-1658
Fax: (671) 477-9402

HAWAII
Steven Chang
Branch Chief
Solid & Hazardous Waste Branch
Dept. of Health
919 Ala Moana Blvd., Ste. 212
Honolulu, HI 96813
Phone: (808) 586-4225
Fax: (808) 586-7509

IDAHO

ILLINOIS
Mitch Beaver
Director
Recycling & Waste Reduction
Dept. of Commerce & Community Affairs
325 W. Adams, Rm. 300
Springfield, IL 62704
Phone: (217) 785-2800

INDIANA
Bruce Palin
Assistant Commissioner
Solid Waste Mgmt. Branch
Dept. of Environmental Mgmt.
P.O. Box 6015
Indianapolis, IN 46206-6015
Phone: (317) 232-3210
Fax: (317) 232-3403

IOWA
Peter Hamlin
Chief
Air Quality & Solid Waste Protection
Dept. of Natural Resources
900 E. Grand Ave.
Des Moines, IA 50319
Phone: (515) 281-8852

KANSAS
William Bider
Director
Bur. of Waste Mgmt., KDHE
Forbes Field Bldg. 740
6700 SW Topeka Blvd.
Topeka, KS 66620-0001
Phone: (785) 296-1600
Fax: (785) 296-1592

KENTUCKY
George Gilbert
Branch Manager
Solid Waste Branch
Div. of Waste Mgmt.
14 Reilly Rd.
Frankfort, KY 40601
Phone: (502) 564-6716
Fax: (502) 564-4049

LOUISIANA
James Brent
Assistant Secretary
Ofc. of Waste Services
Dept. of Environmental Quality
P.O. Box 82178
Baton Rouge, LA 70884-2178
Phone: (225) 765-0355
Fax: (225) 765-0617

MAINE
Paula Clark
Director
Dept. of Environmental Protection
17 State House Station
Augusta, ME 04333
Phone: (207) 287-2812

MARYLAND
Barry Schmidt
Administrator
Solid Waste Program
Dept. of Environment
2500 Broening Hwy.
Baltimore, MD 21224
Phone: (410) 631-3318
Fax: (410) 631-3321

MASSACHUSETTS
Greg Cooper
Director
Div. of Solid Waste Mgmt.
Dept. of Environmental Protection
1 Winter St., 9th Fl.
Boston, MA 02108
Phone: (617) 292-5988
Fax: (617) 292-5778

MICHIGAN
Jim Sygo
Chief
Waste Mgmt. Div.
Dept. of Environmental Quality
P.O. Box 30028
Lansing, MI 48909
Phone: (517) 373-2730

MINNESOTA
Jim Warner
Manager, Metro District
Groundwater & Solid Waste Div.
Pollution Control Agency
520 Lafayette Rd.
St. Paul, MN 55155
Phone: (651) 296-7777
Fax: (651) 296-7782

MISSISSIPPI
Billy Warden
Environmental Scientist
Groundwater Div.
Ofc. of Pollution Control
P.O. Box 10385
Jackson, MS 39289
Phone: (601) 961-5047
Fax: (601) 354-6965

MISSOURI
James Hull
Director
Solid Waste Mgmt. Program
Dept. of Natural Resources
1738 E. Elm
Jefferson City, MO 65102
Phone: (573) 751-5401
Fax: (573) 526-3902
E-mail: nrhullj@mail.dnr.state.mo.us

MONTANA

NEBRASKA
Joe Francis
Associate Director
Customer & Technical Assistance Div.
Dept. of Environmental Quality
P.O. Box 98922
Lincoln, NE 68509-8922
Phone: (402) 471-6974
Fax: (402) 471-2909

NEVADA
Allen Biaggi
Administrator
Air, Mining & Water Section
Div. of Environmental Protection
333 W. Nye Ln., Rm. 138
Carson City, NV 89706
Phone: (775) 687-4670
Fax: (775) 687-5856

NEW HAMPSHIRE
Philip J. O'Brien
Director
Waste Mgmt.
Environmental Services
6 Hazen Dr.
Concord, NH 03301-6509
Phone: (603) 271-2900
Fax: (603) 271-2867

NEW JERSEY
John Castner
Assistant Director
Div. of Solid & Hazardous Waste Mgmt.
Dept. of Environmental Protection
401 E. State St.
P.O. Box 414
Trenton, NJ 08625-0414
Phone: (609) 984-6880
Fax: (609) 633-9839

NEW MEXICO
Jerry Bober
Bureau Chief
Solid Waste Bur.
Dept. of Environment
P.O. Box 26110
Sante Fe, NM 87502
Phone: (505) 827-0197
Fax: (505) 827-2836

NEW YORK
John Cahill
Commissioner
Dept. of Environmental Conservation
50 Wolf Rd.
Albany, NY 12233-1010
Phone: (518) 457-1162
Fax: (518) 457-7744

NORTH CAROLINA
Dexter Matthews
Chief
Div. of Solid Waste Mgmt.
401 Oberlin Rd., Ste. 150
Raleigh, NC 27605-1350
Phone: (919) 733-0692
Fax: (919) 733-4810

NORTH DAKOTA
Neil Knatterud
Director
Waste Mgmt.
Environmental Health Section
P.O. Box 5520
Bismarck, ND 58506-5520
Phone: (701) 328-5166
Fax: (701) 328-5200
E-mail: nknatter@state.nd.us

NORTHERN MARIANA ISLANDS
Edward M. Deleon Guerrero
Secretary
Dept. of Public Works
Lower Base
P.O. Box 2950
Saipan, MP 96950
Phone: (670) 235-5827
Fax: (670) 235-5253

OHIO
Dan Harris
Chief
Solid & Hazardous Waste Mgmt. Div.
Environmental Protection Agency
122 S. Front St.
P.O. Box 1049
Columbus, OH 43228
Phone: (614) 728-5333
Fax: (614) 728-5315

OKLAHOMA
H.A. Caves
Director
Solid Waste Mgmt. Services
Environmental Health Services
P.O. Box 1677
Oklahoma City, OK 73101
Phone: (405) 702-5158

OREGON
Paul Slyman
Manager
Solid Waste Policy & Program Dev.
Dept. of Environmental Quality
811 SW 6th Ave.
Portland, OR 97204
Phone: (503) 229-6165
Fax: (503) 229-6977

PENNSYLVANIA
James P. Snyder
Director
Bur. of Land Recycling & Waste Mgmt.
Dept. of Environmental Protection
Rachel Carson State Ofc. Bldg., 14th Fl.
400 Market St.
Harrisburg, PA 17105
Phone: (717) 787-9870
Fax: (717) 787-1904

PUERTO RICO
Roxanna Longoria
Executive Director
Solid Waste Mgmt. Authority
P.O. Box 40285
San Juan, PR 00940
Phone: (787) 765-7575
Fax: (787) 753-2220

RHODE ISLAND
Jim Fester
Chief
Solid Waste Section
Air & Hazardous Materials Div.
291 Promenade St.
Providence, RI 02908
Phone: (401) 222-2797

SOUTH CAROLINA
Hartsill Truesdale
Chief
Bur. of Solid & Hazardous Waste Mgmt.
Dept. of Health & Environmental Control
2600 Bull St.
Columbia, SC 29201
Phone: (803) 896-4000

SOUTH DAKOTA
Vonni Kallemeyn
Administrator
Div. of Environmental Services
Dept. of Environment & Natural Resources
523 E. Capitol Ave.
Pierre, SD 57501-3181
Phone: (605) 773-3153
Fax: (605) 773-6035

TENNESSEE
Tom Tiesler
Director
Solid Waste Mgmt.
Dept. of Environment & Conservation
L & C Tower, 5th Fl.
401 Church St.
Nashville, TN 37243
Phone: (615) 532-0780
Fax: (615) 532-0886

TEXAS
Leigh Ing
Deputy Director
Ofc. of Waste Mgmt.
Natural Resources Conservation Comm.
P.O. Box 13087
Austin, TX 78711-3087
Phone: (512) 239-2206
Fax: (512) 239-5151

U.S. VIRGIN ISLANDS
Harold G. Thompson
Acting Commissioner
Dept. of Public Works
No. 8 Sub Base
St. Thomas, VI 00802
Phone: (340) 776-4844
Fax: (340) 776-8990

UTAH
Dennis R. Downs
Director
Div. of Solid & Hazardous Waste
Dept. of Environmental Quality
288 N. 1460 W.
Salt Lake City, UT 84116
Phone: (801) 538-6775
Fax: (801) 538-6715
E-mail: ddowns@deq.state.ut.us

VERMONT
Edward Leonard
Director
Div. of Solid Waste Mgmt.
Dept. of Environmental Conservation
103 S. Main St.
Waterbury, VT 05671-0407
Phone: (802) 241-3811
Fax: (802) 241-3273

VIRGINIA
Dennis H. Treacy
Director
Dept. of Environmental Quality
629 E. Main St.
Richmond, VA 23219
Phone: (804) 698-4020
Fax: (804) 698-4019

WASHINGTON
Greg Sorlie
Program Manager
Hazardous Waste & Toxic Reduction
Dept. of Ecology
P.O. Box 47600
Olympia, WA 98504-7600
Phone: (360) 407-7150
Fax: (360) 407-6989

WEST VIRGINIA
Charles Jordan
Director
Solid Waste Mgmt. Board
1615 Washington St., E.
Charleston, WV 25311-2126
Phone: (304) 558-0844
Fax: (304) 558-0899

WISCONSIN
Suzanne Bangert
Director
Bur. of Waste Mgmt.
Dept. of Natural Resources
P.O. Box 7921
Madison, WI 53707
Phone: (608) 266-1327
Fax: (608) 267-2768

WYOMING
David Finley
Administrator
Solid & Hazardous Waste Div.
Dept. of Environmental Quality
Herschler Bldg.
122 W. 25th St.
Cheyenne, WY 82002
Phone: (307) 777-7753

Special Education

Has jurisdiction over the education of exceptional and disabled children.

ALABAMA
Mabrey Whetstone
Director
Special Education Services Div.
Dept. of Education
50 N. Ripley St.
Montgomery, AL 36130
Phone: (334) 242-8114
Fax: (334) 242-9192

ALASKA
Di Ann Brown
Special Education Director
Ofc. for Exceptional Children
Dept. of Education
801 W. 10th St., Ste. 200
Juneau, AK 99801-1894
Phone: (907) 465-2971
Fax: (907) 465-3396

AMERICAN SAMOA
Sapini Siatu'u
Director
Dept. of Human Resources
AS Govt.
Pago Pago, AS 96799
Phone: (684) 633-4485
Fax: (684) 633-1139

Laloulu E. Tagoilelagi
Director
Dept. of Education
AS Govt.
Pago Pago, AS 96799
Phone: (684) 633-5237
Fax: (684) 633-4240

ARIZONA
Lisa Graham Keegan
Superintendent of Public Instruction
Dept. of Education
1535 W. Jefferson
Phoenix, AZ 85007
Phone: (602) 542-6417
Fax: (602) 542-5440

ARKANSAS
Diane Sydoriak
Associate Director
Special Education Section
Dept. of Education
1 Capitol Mall, Bldg. 4
Little Rock, AR 72201
Phone: (501) 682-4221
Fax: (501) 682-4313

CALIFORNIA
Ron Kadish
Director
Special Schools & Services
Dept. of Education
515 L St., Ste.270
Sacramento, CA 95814
Phone: (916) 327-3850

COLORADO
Richard Laughlin
Assistant Commissioner
Ofc. of Special Services
Dept. of Education
201 E. Colfax Ave.
Denver, CO 80203
Phone: (303) 866-6782

CONNECTICUT
Leslie Averna
Acting Chief
Bur. of Special Education & Pupil Services
25 Industrial Park Rd.
Middletown, CT 06457
Phone: (860) 807-2025

DELAWARE
Martha Brooks
Team Leader
Exceptional Children Team
Townsend Bldg.
Federal & Duke of York Sts.
Dover, DE 19901
Phone: (302) 739-5471

DISTRICT OF COLUMBIA
David V. Burkett
Assistant Superintendent
Webster School Special Education
Browne Jr. High School
26th & Benning Rd., NE
Washington, DC 20002
Phone: (202) 724-4018

FLORIDA
Shan Goff
Bureau Chief
Bur. of Institutional Support & Community Services
Dept. of Education
325 W. Gaines St., Ste. 514
Tallahassee, FL 32399-0400
Phone: (850) 488-1570
Fax: (850) 921-8246

GEORGIA
Paulette Bragg
Special Education Director
Dept. of Education
205 Butler St., SW
Atlanta, GA 30334
Phone: (404) 656-3963

GUAM
Michael J. Reidy
Acting Director
Dept. of Education
P.O. Box DE
Hagatna, GU 96932
Phone: (671) 475-0462
Fax: (671) 472-5003

HAWAII
Thelma Yamamoto
Acting Administrator
Educational Specialist
Special Education Section
Dept. of Education
637 18th Ave., Rm. C-102
Honolulu, HI 96816
Phone: (808) 733-4990
Fax: (808) 733-4841

IDAHO
Nolene Weaver
Supervisor
Special Education
Dept. of Education
P.O. Box 83720
Boise, ID 83720-0027
Phone: (208) 334-3940

ILLINOIS
Gordon Riffel
Special Education Contact
State Board of Education
100 N. 1st St., Rm. N-253
Springfield, IL 62777
Phone: (217) 782-9560

INDIANA
Robert A. Marra
Director
Special Education Section
Dept. of Education
State House, Rm. 229
Indianapolis, IN 46204
Phone: (317) 232-0570
Fax: (317) 232-0589

IOWA
Jeananne Hagen
Bureau Chief
Bur. of Special Education
Grimes State Ofc. Bldg.
E. 14th & Grand Aves.
Des Moines, IA 50319
Phone: (515) 281-5735

KANSAS
Carol Dermyer
Team Leader
Student Support Services
State Board of Education
120 E. 10th St.
Topeka, KS 66612
Phone: (785) 296-3869
Fax: (785) 296-1413
E-mail: mremus @ksbe.state.ks.us

KENTUCKY
Mike Armstrong
Director
Exceptional Children Service
Dept. of Education
Capital Plz. Tower
Frankfort, KY 40601
Phone: (502) 564-4970
Fax: (502) 564-6721

Johnnie Grissom
Associate Commissioner
Ofc. of Special Instruction Services
Dept. of Education
Capital Plz. Tower, 8th Fl.
Frankfort, KY 40601
Phone: (502) 564-4970
Fax: (502) 564-6721

LOUISIANA
Virginia C. Berdon
Director
Div. of Special Population
Dept. of Education
P.O. Box 94064
Baton Rouge, LA 70804
Phone: (225) 342-3633
Fax: (225) 342-5880

MAINE
J. Duke Albanese
Commissioner
Dept. of Education
23 State House Station
Augusta, ME 04333-0023
Phone: (207) 287-5802

MARYLAND
Carol Ann Baglin
Assistant State Superintendent
Div. of Special Education
State Dept. of Education
200 W. Baltimore St.
Baltimore, MD 21201
Phone: (410) 767-0238
Fax: (410) 333-3954

MASSACHUSETTS
Michael J. Sentance
Advisor on Education
Executive Ofc. of Education
One Ashburton Pl., Rm. 1401
Boston, MA 02108
Phone: (617) 727-9323
Fax: (617) 727-5570

MICHIGAN
Jacquelyn Thompson
Director
Ofc. of Special Education
Dept. of Education
P.O. Box 30008
Lansing, MI 48909
Phone: (517) 373-9433

MINNESOTA
Christine Jax
Commissioner
Dept. of Children, Families & Learning
550 Cedar St., 7th Fl.
Minneapolis, MN 55101
Phone: (651) 582-8204
Fax: (651) 582-8724

MISSISSIPPI
Carolyn Black
Director
Bur. of Special Education
Dept. of Education
P.O. Box 771
Jackson, MS 39205
Phone: (601) 359-3513
Fax: (601) 359-2198

MISSOURI
Melodie Friedebach
Coordinator of Special Education
Div. of Special Education
Dept. of Elementary & Secondary Education
P.O. Box 480
Jefferson City, MO 65102
Phone: (573) 751-2965
Fax: (573) 526-4404
E-mail: mfriede@dese.mail.state.mo.us

MONTANA
Gail Gray
Assistant Superintendent
Ofc. of Public Instruction
1300 11th Ave.
Helena, MT 59620
Phone: (406) 444-2089
Fax: (406) 444-3924

NEBRASKA
Gary Sherman
Administrator
Special Education Branch
Dept. of Education
P.O. Box 94987
Lincoln, NE 68509
Phone: (402) 471-2471
Fax: (402) 471-0117

NEVADA
Gloria Dopf
Team Leader
Special Education
Dept. of Education
700 E. 5th St.
Carson City, NV 89701
Phone: (775) 687-9171
Fax: (775) 687-9123

NEW HAMPSHIRE
Debra Grabill
Bureau Administrator
Bur. of Special Education
Dept. of Education
101 Pleasant St.
Concord, NH 03301-3890
Phone: (603) 271-6693
Fax: (603) 271-1953

NEW JERSEY
Barbara Gantwerk
Director
Div. of Special Education
Dept. of Education
100 Riverview Plz., 2nd Fl.
P.O. Box 500
Trenton, NJ 08625-0500
Phone: (609) 292-0147
Fax: (609) 984-8422

NEW MEXICO
Robert Pasternack
Director
Special Education Ofc.
Dept. of Education
Education Bldg.
300 Don Gaspar
Santa Fe, NM 87501
Phone: (505) 827-6541
Fax: (505) 827-6696

NEW YORK
Richard P. Mills
Commissioner
State Education Dept.
89 Washington Ave., Rm. 111
Albany, NY 12234
Phone: (518) 474-6569
Fax: (518) 473-4909

NORTH CAROLINA
E. Lowell Harris
Director
Exceptional Children
Dept. of Public Education
301 N. Wilmington St.
Raleigh, NC 27601-2825
Phone: (919) 715-1565
Fax: (919) 715-2825

NORTH DAKOTA
Gary Gronberg
Director
Special Education
Dept. of Public Instruction
600 E. Blvd. Ave., 10th Fl.
Bismarck, ND 58505-0440
Phone: (701) 328-2277
Fax: (701) 328-2461
E-mail: ggronber@mail.dpi.state.nd.us

NORTHERN MARIANA ISLANDS
Barbara Rudy
Special Education Coordinator
Public School System
Lower Base
P.O. Box 1370
Saipan, MP 96950
Phone: (670) 664-3730
Fax: (670) 664-3796
E-mail: pss.ci@saipan.com

OHIO
John Herner
Director
Div. of Special Education
Dept. of Education
933 High St.
Worthington, OH 43085
Phone: (614) 466-2650
Fax: (614) 728-1097

OKLAHOMA
John Corpolongo
Director
Special Education Section
Dept. of Education
2500 N. Lincoln Blvd.
Oklahoma City, OK 73105
Phone: (405) 521-3351
Fax: (405) 522-2066

OREGON
Steve Johnson
Associate Superintendent
Ofc. of Special Education
Div. of Special Student Services
Dept. of Education
255 Capitol St., SE
Salem, OR 97310
Phone: (503) 378-3598
Fax: (503) 373-7968

PENNSYLVANIA
William Penn
Director
Bur. of Special Education
Dept. of Education
333 Market St.
Harrisburg, PA 17126-0333
Phone: (717) 783-6913
Fax: (717) 783-6139

PUERTO RICO
Damaris Cifuentes
Auxiliary Secretary
Special Education Section
Dept. of Education
P.O. Box 759
Hato Rey, PR 00918
Phone: (787) 758-4949

RHODE ISLAND
Robert Pryhoda
Director
Ofc. of Special Needs
Dept. of Elementary & Secondary Education
Shepard Bldg.
255 Westminister St.
Providence, RI 02903
Phone: (401) 222-4600

SOUTH CAROLINA
Luther W. Seabrook
Senior Executive Assistant for Curriculum
State Dept. of Education
1429 Senate St.
Columbia, SC 29201
Phone: (803) 734-8396

SOUTH DAKOTA
Deborah Barnett
Director
Ofc. of Special Education
Div. of Education
Kneip Bldg.
700 Governors Dr.
Pierre, SD 57501
Phone: (605) 773-3678
Fax: (605) 773-6139

TENNESSEE
Joseph Fisher
Executive Director
Special Education
Dept. of Education
Andrew Johnson Tower, 5th Fl.
Nashville, TN 37247
Phone: (615) 741-2851
Fax: (615) 532-9412

TEXAS
Gene Lenz
Director
Special Education
Education Agency
1701 N. Congress Ave.
Austin, TX 78701
Phone: (512) 463-9414

U.S. VIRGIN ISLANDS
Ruby Simmonds
Acting Commissioner
Dept. of Education
44-46 Kongens Gade
St. Thomas, VI 00802
Phone: (340) 774-0100
Fax: (340) 774-4679

UTAH
Mae Taylor-Sweeten
Director, Special Education
Instructional Services
Ofc. of Education
250 E. 500 S.
Salt Lake City, UT 84111
Phone: (801) 538-7711
Fax: (801) 538-7521

VERMONT
Dennis Kane
Director
Special Education Unit
Dept. of Education
120 State St.
Montpelier, VT 05620
Phone: (802) 828-5118
Fax: (802) 828-3140

VIRGINIA
Paul D. Stapleton
Superintendent of Public Instruction
Dept. of Education
Monroe Bldg., 25th Fl.
101 N. 14th St.
Richmond, VA 23219
Phone: (804) 225-2023
Fax: (804) 371-2099

WASHINGTON
Doug Gill
Director of Special Education
P.O. Box 47200
Olympia, WA 98504-7200
Phone: (360) 753-6733
Fax: (360) 586-0247

WEST VIRGINIA
Keith Smith
Director
Div. of Instructional & Student Services
Dept. of Education
1900 Kanawha Blvd., E., Bldg. 6
Charleston, WV 25302-0330
Phone: (304) 558-2691
Fax: (304) 558-0048

WISCONSIN
Juanita S. Pawlisch
Assistant Superintendent
Learning Support Equity & Advocacy Div.
Dept. of Public Instruction
125 S. Webster
P.O. Box 7841
Madison, WI 53703
Phone: (608) 266-1649
Fax: (608) 267-3746

WYOMING
Margie Simineo
Unit Director
Special Education
Dept. of Education
Hathaway Bldg.
2300 Capitol Ave.
Cheyenne, WY 82002
Phone: (307) 777-7221

State Data Center

Center that acts as an information clearinghouse for the Census Bureau and other data sources within the state.

ALABAMA
Annette Watters
Manager
State Data Ctr.
Univ. of AL
P.O. Box 870221
Tuscaloosa, AL 35487
Phone: (205) 348-6191
Fax: (205) 348-2951

ALASKA
Kathryn Lizik
Coordinator
State Data Ctr.
Dept. of Labor
P.O. Box 25504
Juneau, AK 99802-5504
Phone: (907) 465-2437
Fax: (907) 465-2101

AMERICAN SAMOA
John Faumuina, Jr.
Director
Economic Dev. & Planning Ofc.
Dept. of Commerce
Pago Pago, AS 96799
Phone: (684) 633-5155
Fax: (684) 633-4195

ARIZONA
Betty Jeffries
Statistical Analyst
Dept. of Economic Security
1789 W. Jefferson (045Z)
Phoenix, AZ 85007
Phone: (602) 542-5984

ARKANSAS
Sarah Breshears
Division Chief
State Data Ctr.
Univ. of AR at Little Rock
2801 S. Univ.
Little Rock, AR 72204
Phone: (501) 569-8530
Fax: (501) 569-8538

CALIFORNIA
Linda Gage
Chief
Demographic Research
Dept. of Finance
915 L St.
Sacramento, CA 95814
Phone: (916) 322-4651

COLORADO
Rebecca Picaso
Information Officer
Div. of Local Govt.
Demography Section
Dept. of Local Affairs
1313 Sherman St.
Denver, CO 80202
Phone: (303) 866-2156
Fax: (303) 866-4819

Michael Smith
State Demographer
Div. of Local Govt.
Dept. of Local Affairs
1313 Sherman St.
Denver, CO 80202
Phone: (303) 866-2156
Fax: (303) 866-4819

CONNECTICUT
Ann Moore
Undersecretary
Policy Dev. & Planning Div.
Ofc. of Policy & Mgmt.
P.O. Box 341441
Hartford, CT 06134-1441
Phone: (860) 418-6484

DELAWARE
Michael B. Mahaffie
Manager
State Data Ctr.
Dev. Ofc.
99 Kings Hwy.
P.O. Box 1401
Dover, DE 19903
Phone: (302) 739-4271
Fax: (302) 739-5749

DISTRICT OF COLUMBIA
Gan Ahuja
Data Analyst
Ofc. of Planning
415 12th St., NW, Ste. 500
Washington, DC 20004
Phone: (202) 727-6533

FLORIDA
Ed Levine
Policy Coordinator
Systems Design & Dev.
Ofc. of Planning & Budgeting
Executive Ofc. of the Governor
The Capitol, 415 Carlton Bldg.
Tallahassee, FL 32399-0001
Phone: (850) 488-6955
Fax: (850) 921-2353

GEORGIA
Robert Giacomini
Director of Research
State Data & Research Ctr.
250 14th St., NW
Atlanta, GA 30318
Phone: (404) 894-9416
Fax: (404) 894-9372

GUAM
Joseph C. Cruz
Director
Dept. of Commerce
102 M St.
Tiyan, GU 96913
Phone: (671) 475-0321
Fax: (671) 477-9013
E-mail: COMMERCE@ns.gov.gu

HAWAII
Pearl Iboshi
Division Head
Research & Economic Analysis Div.
Business & Economic Dev. & Tourism
250 S. Hotel St., 4th Fl.
Honolulu, HI 96813
Phone: (808) 586-2470
Fax: (808) 586-8449

IDAHO
Karl T. Tueller
Deputy Director
Science & Technology
Dept. of Commerce
P.O. Box 83720
Boise, ID 83720-0093
Phone: (208) 334-2470

ILLINOIS
Suzanne Ebetsch
Coordinator
State Data Ctr.
Bur. of the Budget
605 Stratton Ofc. Bldg.
401 S. Spring
Springfield, IL 62706
Phone: (217) 782-1381
Fax: (217) 524-4876

INDIANA
Sylvia Andrews
Coordinator
State Data Ctr.
State Library
140 N. Senate Ave.
Indianapolis, IN 46204
Phone: (317) 232-3733
Fax: (317) 232-3728

IOWA
Beth Henning
Census Data Center Coordinator
State Library
E. 12th & Grand Aves.
Des Moines, IA 50319
Phone: (515) 281-4350

KANSAS
Marc Galbraith
Director of Reference
State Library
State Capitol Bldg.
300 SW 10th St., Rm. 343-N
Topeka, KS 66612
Phone: (785) 296-3296
Fax: (785) 296-6650

KENTUCKY
Ron Crouch
Director
State Data Ctr.
Urban Research Institute
College of Urban & Public Affairs
Univ. of Louisville
Louisville, KY 40292
Phone: (502) 852-7990
Fax: (502) 852-7386

LOUISIANA
Karen Patterson
State Demographer
Ofc. of Planning & Budget
Div. of Administration
P.O. Box 94095
Baton Rouge, LA 70804
Phone: (225) 342-7410
Fax: (225) 342-7220

Randy Walker
Acting Director
Ofc. of Info. Services
Div. of Administration
P.O. Box 94095
Baton Rouge, LA 70804
Phone: (225) 342-9903
Fax: (225) 342-9902

MAINE
Jean Martin
Manager of Census Data Center
Div. of Economic Analysis & Resources
Dept. of Labor
20 Union St.
Augusta, ME 04330-6826
Phone: (207) 287-2271

MARYLAND
Jane Traynham
Manager
Research & State Data Ctr. Census & Demographic Info.
Ofc. on Planning
301 W. Preston St.
Baltimore, MD 21201
Phone: (410) 767-4450

MASSACHUSETTS
Stephen Colen
Director
Institute for Social & Economic Research
Univ. of MA
128 Thompson Hall
Amherst, MA 01003
Phone: (413) 545-3460
Fax: (413) 545-3686

MICHIGAN
Ching-li Wang
State Demographer
State Info. Ctr.
Dept. of Mgmt. & Budget
P.O. Box 30026
Lansing, MI 48909
Phone: (517) 373-7910

MINNESOTA
Tom Gillaspy
State Demographer
State Planning Agency
300 Centennial Ofc. Bldg.
658 Cedar St.
St. Paul, MN 55155
Phone: (651) 296-2557
Fax: (651) 296-3698
E-mail: tom.gillaspy@mnplan.state.mn.us

MISSISSIPPI
Sue Savtermeister
State Census Director
125 Overlook Point Dr.
Madison, MS 39157
Phone: (601) 853-2753

Max Williams
Director
Ctr. for Population Studies
Univ. of MS
Bondurant Bldg., Rm. 3W
University, MS 38677
Phone: (601) 232-7288
Fax: (601) 232-7736

MISSOURI
Debra Pitts
Coordinator
State Census Data Ctr.
State Library
600 W. Main St.
P.O. Box 387
Jefferson City, MO 65102
Phone: (573) 751-3615
Fax: (573) 526-1142
E-mail: dpitts@mail.sos.state.mo.us

MONTANA
Patricia Roberts
Program Manager
Census & Economic Info. Ctr.
Dept. of Commerce
1424 9th Ave.
Helena, MT 59620
Phone: (406) 444-4393
Fax: (406) 444-1518

NEBRASKA
Jerome Deichert
Manager
State Data Ctr.
Univ. of NE Omaha
Peter Kiewit Ctr., Rm. 232
Omaha, NE 68182
Phone: (402) 595-2311
Fax: (402) 595-2366

NEVADA
Marlene Lockard
Director
Dept. of Info. Technology
Kinkaid Bldg., Rm. 403
505 E. King St.
Carson City, NV 89701
Phone: (775) 684-5801
Fax: (775) 684-5846
E-mail: mlockard@doit.state.nv.us

NEW HAMPSHIRE
Jeffrey Taylor
Director
Ofc. of State Planning, Executive Dept.
Governor's Recycling Program
2 1/2 Beacon St.
Concord, NH 03301-4497
Phone: (603) 271-2155
Fax: (603) 271-1728

NEW JERSEY
Shirly A. Goetz
Director
Div. of Labor Market & Demographic Research
Dept. of Labor
John Fitz Plz.
P.O. Box 388
Trenton, NJ 08625-0388
Phone: (609) 292-0099
Fax: (609) 777-3623

NEW MEXICO
Carol Selleck
Research Program Officer
Economic Dev.
Joseph M. Montoya Bldg.
1100 St. Francis Dr.
Santa Fe, NM 87503
Phone: (505) 827-0278
Fax: (505) 827-0407

NEW YORK
Robert Scardamalia
Chief Demographer
Dept. of Economic Dev.
1 Commerce Plz.
Albany, NY 12245
Phone: (518) 474-1141
Fax: (518) 473-9748

NORTH CAROLINA
Francine Stephenson
Manager
State Data Ctr.
Ofc. of State Planning
116 W. Jones St.
Raleigh, NC 27603-8005
Phone: (919) 733-4131

NORTH DAKOTA
Cole Gustafson
Chair
Agri. Economics
ND State Univ.
P.O. Box 5227 - Univ. Station
Fargo, ND 58105-5227
Phone: (701) 231-7441
Fax: (701) 231-7400

NORTHERN MARIANA ISLANDS
John S. Borja
Director
Statistics Div.
Dept. of Commerce
Caller Box 10007
Saipan, MP 96950
Phone: (670) 664-3033
Fax: (670) 664-3066
E-mail: csd@itecnmi.com

OHIO
Steve Kelley
Office Manager
Ofc. of Strategic Research
Dept. of Dev.
P.O. Box 1001
Columbus, OH 43266-0101
Phone: (614) 466-2116
Fax: (614) 644-5167

OKLAHOMA
Jeff Wallace
Director
State Data Ctr.
Dept. of Commerce
6601 Broadway Extension
P.O. Box 26980
Oklahoma City, OK 73116-8214
Phone: (405) 843-9770

OREGON
David Swanson
Director
Ctr. for Population Research & Census
Portland State Univ.
P.O. Box 751
Portland, OR 97207
Phone: (503) 725-5158
Fax: (503) 725-5162

PENNSYLVANIA
Diane Shoop
Director
Institute of State & Regional Affairs
PA State Univ. at Harrisburg
777 W. Harrisburg Pike
Middletown, PA 17057-4898
Phone: (717) 948-6178
Fax: (717) 948-6306

PUERTO RICO
Norma Burgos Andujar
Secretary of State
Department of State
P.O. Box 3271
San Juan, PR 00902-3271
Phone: (787) 723-4334
Fax: (787) 725-7303

RHODE ISLAND
Richard Dearson
Principal Research Technician
Ofc. of Municipal Affairs
Dept. of Administration
1 Capitol Hill
Providence, RI 02908-5873
Phone: (401) 222-2276

SOUTH CAROLINA
Mike MacFarlane
State Demographer
Div. of Research & Statistics Services
Budget & Control Board
Rembert C. Dennis Bldg., Rm. 425
Columbia, SC 29201
Phone: (803) 734-3788

SOUTH DAKOTA
Nancy Nelson
Director
State Data Ctr.
Business Research Bur.
Univ. of SD School of Business
414 E. Clark
Vermillion, SD 57069
Phone: (605) 677-5539
Fax: (605) 677-5427

TENNESSEE
Bradley Dugger
Chief of Information Systems
State Data Ctr.
Dept. of Finance & Administration
901 5th Ave., N.
Nashville, TN 37243
Phone: (615) 741-2181
Fax: (615) 741-7341

TEXAS
Steve H. Murdock
Professor & Head
Dept. of Rural Sociology
TX A&M Univ.
Special Services Bldg.
College Station, TX 77843-2125
Phone: (409) 845-5332
Fax: (409) 845-8529
E-mail: smurdock@rsocsun.tamu.edu

U.S. VIRGIN ISLANDS

UTAH
Julie Johnsson
Research Analyst
Ofc. of Planning & Budget
Governor's Ofc.
State Capitol, Rm. 116
Salt Lake City, UT 84114
Phone: (801) 538-1554
Fax: (801) 538-1547
E-mail: jjohnsso@gov.state.ut.us

VERMONT

VIRGINIA
Thomas J. Towberman
Commissioner
Employment Comm.
703 E. Main St.
Richmond, VA 23219
Phone: (804) 786-3001
Fax: (804) 225-3923

WASHINGTON
Irv Lefberg
Senior Executive Policy Coordinator
Forecasting Unit
Ofc. of Financial Mgmt.
P.O. Box 43113
Olympia, WA 98504
Phone: (360) 902-0590
Fax: (360) 664-8941

WEST VIRGINIA
Dana Davis
Acting Director
Dev. Ofc.
Bldg. 6, Rm. 525
1900 Kanawha Blvd., E.
Charleston, WV 25305
Phone: (304) 558-2234
Fax: (304) 558-1189

WISCONSIN
Robert Naylor
Census Data Consultant
Demographic Services Ctr.
Dept. of Administration
101 E. Wilson, 6th Fl.
P.O. Box 7868
Madison, WI 53703
Phone: (608) 266-1927
Fax: (608) 267-6931

WYOMING
Buck McVeigh
Administrator
Economic Analysis Div.
Dept. of Administration & Info.
Emerson Bldg.
2001 Capitol Ave.
Cheyenne, WY 82002
Phone: (307) 777-7221

State Fair

Responsible for the annual state fair.

ALABAMA
Tom Drilias
General Manager
State Fair Authority
2331 Bessemer Rd.
Birmingham, AL 35208
Phone: (205) 786-8100
Fax: (205) 786-8222

ALASKA

AMERICAN SAMOA

ARIZONA
Gary Montgomery
Executive Director
Coliseum & Expo Ctr. Board
1826 W. McDowell Rd.
Phoenix, AZ 85005
Phone: (602) 252-6771

ARKANSAS
Jim Pledger
General Manager
Livestock Show Assoc.
2600 Howard St.
Little Rock, AR 72206
Phone: (501) 372-8341
Fax: (501) 372-4197

CALIFORNIA
Norbert Bartosik
Manager
Exposition & State Fair
1600 Exposition Blvd.
Sacramento, CA 95815
Phone: (916) 263-3000

COLORADO
Ed Kruse
Manager
State Fair Authority
1001 Buelah Ave.
Pueblo, CO 81004
Phone: (719) 561-8484
Fax: (719) 561-0283

CONNECTICUT
Charlene Magdich
Correspondence Secretary
Association of CT State Fairs
P.O. Box 563
Somers, CT 06071
Phone: (860) 491-2761

DELAWARE
Dennis Hazzard
General Manager
State Fair
P.O. Box 28
Harrington, DE 19952
Phone: (302) 398-3269

DISTRICT OF COLUMBIA
Betty Jo Gaines
Director
Dept. of Recreation & Parks
3149 16th St., NW, 2nd Fl.
Washington, DC 20010
Phone: (202) 673-7665

FLORIDA
Ann Wainwright
Assistant Commissioner
Ofc. of the Commissioner
Dept. of Agri. & Consumer Services
The Capitol, PL 10
Tallahassee, FL 32399-0810
Phone: (850) 488-3022
Fax: (850) 922-4936

GEORGIA
Michael Froehlich
Executive Director
Agricultural Exposition Authorities
P.O. Box 1367
Perry, GA 31069
Phone: (912) 987-3247

GUAM

HAWAII

IDAHO

ILLINOIS
Bud Ford
State Fair Manager
State Fair
State Fairgrounds
Springfield, IL 62706
Phone: (217) 782-6661
Fax: (217) 782-9115

INDIANA
William H. Stinson
Executive Director
State Fair Comm.
Fairgrounds Administration Bldg.
1202 E. 38th St.
Indianapolis, IN 46205
Phone: (317) 927-7501
Fax: (317) 927-7695

IOWA
Marion Lucas
Secretary
State Fair Authority
State Capitol
1007 E. Grand Ave.
Des Moines, IA 50319
Phone: (515) 262-3111

KANSAS
William Ogg
General Manager
State Fair
2000 N. Poplar
Hutchinson, KS 67502-5598
Phone: (316) 669-3600

KENTUCKY
Harold Workman
President
State Fair Board
Fair & Exposition Ctr.
P.O. Box 37130
Louisville, KY 40233
Phone: (502) 367-5100
Fax: (502) 367-5109

LOUISIANA
Sam Giardano
President/General Manager
State Fair
P.O. Box 38327
Shreveport, LA 71109
Phone: (318) 635-1361
Fax: (318) 631-4409

MAINE
Fred Lunt, Jr.
Fair Coordinator
Dept. of Agri., Food & Rural Resources
28 State House Station
Augusta, ME 04333
Phone: (207) 287-7634
Fax: (207) 287-7548

MARYLAND
Philip Brendel
Chair
Agri. Fair Board
Dept. of Agri.
50 Harry S. Truman Pkwy., Rm. 210
Annapolis, MD 21401
Phone: (410) 841-5770
Fax: (410) 841-5987

MASSACHUSETTS
Wayne McCary
President
Eastern States Exposition
1305 Memorial Ave.
W. Springfield, MA 01089
Phone: (413) 737-2443
Fax: (413) 787-0127

MICHIGAN
John Hertel
Director
State Fair
Dept. of Agri.
1120 W. State Fair Ave.
Detroit, MI 48203
Phone: (313) 256-1442

MINNESOTA
Jerry Hammer
Executive Vice President
State Fair Grounds
1265 Snelling Ave., N.
St. Paul, MN 55108
Phone: (651) 642-2200
Fax: (651) 642-2440
E-mail: fairinfo@statefair.gen.mn.us

MISSISSIPPI
Wayne Smith
Executive Director
Fair & Coliseum Comm.
1207 Mississippi St.
Jackson, MS 39202
Phone: (601) 961-4000
Fax: (601) 354-6545

MISSOURI
Gary Slater
Director
State Fair
Dept. of Agri.
2503 W. 16th St.
Sedalia, MO 65302
Phone: (816) 530-5600
Fax: (816) 530-5609
E-mail: gslater1@mail.state.mo.us

MONTANA

NEBRASKA
John Skold
Manager
State Fair Park
P.O. Box 81223
Lincoln, NE 68501
Phone: (402) 474-5371

NEVADA

NEW HAMPSHIRE
Clifford W. McGinnis
Director/State Veterinarian
Animal Industries Div.
Agri., Markets & Food
P.O. Box 2042
Concord, NH 03302-2042
Phone: (603) 271-2404
Fax: (603) 271-1109

NEW JERSEY
Lynn Mathews
Secretary/Treasurer
Agri. Fair Association
Div. of Markets
Dept. of Agri.
P.O. Box 330
Trenton, NJ 08625-0300
Phone: (609) 292-5566

NEW MEXICO
Rick Murray
Executive Director
State Fair Comm.
P.O. Box 8546
Albuquerque, NM 87198
Phone: (505) 265-1791
Fax: (505) 266-7784

NEW YORK
Donald R. Davidsen
Commissioner
Dept. of Agri. & Markets
One Winners Cir.
Albany, NY 12235
Phone: (518) 457-5496
Fax: (518) 457-3087

NORTH CAROLINA
Wesley Wyatt
Manager
State Fair
Dept. of Agri.
2 W. Edenton St.
Raleigh, NC 27601-1094
Phone: (919) 733-2145
Fax: (919) 733-7059

NORTH DAKOTA
Gerald Iverson
Manager
State Fair Association
P.O. Box 1796
Minot, ND 58702-1796
Phone: (701) 857-7620
Fax: (701) 857-7622

NORTHERN MARIANA ISLANDS
Eugene A. Santos
Secretary
Dept. of Lands & Natural Resources
P.O. Box 10007
Saipan, MP 96950
Phone: (670) 322-9830
Fax: (670) 322-2633

OHIO
Richard Frenette
General Manager
Expositions Ctr.
717 E. 17th Ave.
Columbus, OH 43211-2698
Phone: (614) 644-3247
Fax: (614) 644-4031

OKLAHOMA
Donald J. Hotz
President & General Manager
State Fair
500 Land Rush St.
P.O. Box 74943
Oklahoma City, OK 73107
Phone: (405) 948-6700
Fax: (405) 948-6828
E-mail: oklafair@oklafair.org.

OREGON
Robert Vernon
Director
State Fair & Exposition Ctr.
2330 17th St., NE
Salem, OR 97310
Phone: (503) 378-3247
Fax: (503) 373-1788

PENNSYLVANIA
Warren L. Mathias
Director
Bur. of Markets
Dept. of Agri.
2301 N. Cameron St.
Harrisburg, PA 17110
Phone: (717) 787-6041
Fax: (717) 787-1858

PUERTO RICO

RHODE ISLAND
Larry Mouradjian
Chief
Div. of Parks & Recreation
Dept. of Environmental Mgmt.
2321 Hartford
Johnston, RI 02919
Phone: (401) 222-2632

SOUTH CAROLINA
Gary Goodman
Manager
State Fair
P.O. Box 393
Columbia, SC 29202
Phone: (803) 799-3387

SOUTH DAKOTA
Craig Atkins
Executive Director
State Fair
P.O. Box 1275
Huron, SD 57350
Phone: (605) 353-7340
Fax: (605) 353-7348

TENNESSEE
Tom Womack
Public Affairs
Dept. of Agri.
Ellington Agri. Ctr.
440 Hogan Rd.
Nashville, TN 37220
Phone: (615) 837-5118
Fax: (615) 837-5333

TEXAS
Debbie McAngus
Director
Publications & Special Events Administration
Dept. of Agri.
1700 N. Congress
Austin, TX 78711
Phone: (512) 475-1658
Fax: (512) 463-1104

U.S. VIRGIN ISLANDS
Clement C. Magras
Acting Commissioner of Tourism
Dept. of Tourism
Elainco Bldg.
78-1-2-3 Contant
St. Thomas, VI 00802
Phone: (340) 774-8784
Fax: (340) 777-4390

UTAH
Donna Dahl
Executive Director
Div. of Administration
State Fair Park
155 N. 1000 W.
Salt Lake City, UT 84116
Phone: (801) 538-8449
Fax: (801) 538-8455
E-mail: donna@fiber.net

VERMONT
Louise Calderwood
Deputy Commissioner
Dept. of Agri.
116 State St.
Montpelier, VT 05602
Phone: (802) 828-2416
Fax: (802) 828-2361

VIRGINIA
J. Carlton Courter, III
Commissioner
Dept. of Agri. & Consumer Services
Washington Bldg., Ste. 210
1100 Bank St.
Richmond, VA 23219
Phone: (804) 786-3501
Fax: (804) 371-2945

WASHINGTON
Janet Leister
Director
Intl. Marketing Dev.
Dept. of Agri.
P.O. Box 42560
Olympia, WA 98504-2560
Phone: (360) 902-1931
Fax: (360) 902-2089

WEST VIRGINIA
Ed Rock
Manager
State Fair
P.O. Box 829
Lewisburg, WV 24901
Phone: (304) 645-1090

WISCONSIN
Rick Bjorklund
Director
State Fair Park Board
Agri., Trade & Consumer Protection
State Fair Park
8100 W. Greenfield Ave.
W. Allis, WI 53214
Phone: (414) 266-7000
Fax: (414) 266-7007

WYOMING
Vacant
Director
Div. of State Fair
Dept. of Agri.
State Fairgrounds
400 E. Ctr.
Douglas, WY 82633
Phone: (307) 358-2398

State Library

Serves the information and research needs of state executive and legislative branch officials.

ALABAMA
Lamar Veatch
Director
Public Library Service
6030 Monticello Dr.
Montgomery, AL 36130
Phone: (334) 213-3900
Fax: (334) 213-3993

ALASKA
Karen R. Crane
Director
State Libraries & Archives
Dept. of Education
P.O. Box 110571
Juneau, AK 99811-0571
Phone: (907) 465-2910
Fax: (907) 465-2151

AMERICAN SAMOA
Laloulu E. Tagoilelagi
Director
Dept. of Education
AS Govt.
Pago Pago, AS 96799
Phone: (684) 633-5237
Fax: (684) 633-4240

ARIZONA
Gladys Ann Wells
Director
Library, Archives & Public Records
State Law Library
1700 W. Washington St.
Phoenix, AZ 85007-2812
Phone: (602) 542-4035
Fax: (602) 542-4972

ARKANSAS
John A. Murphy, Jr.
State Librarian
State Library
Dept. of Education
1 Capitol Mall
Little Rock, AR 72201
Phone: (501) 682-1526
Fax: (501) 682-1529

CALIFORNIA
Kevin Starr
State Librarian
Law Serials Unit
State Library
900 N St., Rm. 380
Sacramento, CA 95814-4800
Phone: (916) 654-0174

COLORADO
Nancy Bolt
Assistant Commissioner
State Library & Adult Education Ofc.
Dept. of Education
201 E. Colfax Ave.
Denver, CO 80203
Phone: (303) 866-6900
Fax: (303) 866-6940

CONNECTICUT
E. Frederick Peterson
State Librarian
State Library
231 Capitol Ave.
Hartford, CT 06106
Phone: (860) 566-4301

DELAWARE
Tom W. Sloan
State Librarian
Div. of Libraries
Dept. of Community Affairs
43 S. DuPont Hwy.
Dover, DE 19901
Phone: (302) 739-4748
Fax: (302) 739-6787

DISTRICT OF COLUMBIA
Mary E. Raphael
Director
Public Library
901 G St., NW, Ste. 400
Washington, DC 20001
Phone: (202) 727-1101
Fax: (202) 727-1129

FLORIDA
Debra Sears
Bureau Chief
Bur. of Library & Network Services
Dept. of State
R.A. Gray Bldg.
500 S. Bronough St.
Tallahassee, FL 32399-0250
Phone: (850) 487-2651
Fax: (850) 922-3678

GEORGIA

GUAM
Christine Scott-Smith
Director
Public Library
Nieves M. Flores Library
254 Martyr St.
Hagatna, GU 96910
Phone: (671) 475-4753
Fax: (671) 477-9777
E-mail: csctsmth@kuentos.guam.net

HAWAII
Virginia Lowell
State Librarian
State Public Library System
Dept. of Education
465 S. King St., Rm. B-1
Honolulu, HI 96813
Phone: (808) 586-3704
Fax: (808) 586-3715

IDAHO
Charles A. Bolles
State Librarian
State Library
325 W. State St.
Boise, ID 83702
Phone: (208) 334-5124

ILLINOIS
Jean E. Wilkins
Director
State Library
300 S. 2nd St.
Springfield, IL 62701
Phone: (217) 782-2994

INDIANA
C. Ray Ewick
Director
State Library
140 N. Senate Ave.
Indianapolis, IN 46204
Phone: (317) 232-3692
Fax: (317) 232-0002

IOWA
Sharman B. Smith
State Librarian
State Library Div.
Dept. of Education
E. 12th & Grand Aves.
Des Moines, IA 50319
Phone: (515) 281-4105

KANSAS
Duane F. Johnson
State Librarian
State Library
State Capitol Bldg., 3rd Fl.
300 SW 10th Ave.
Topeka, KS 66612
Phone: (785) 296-3296
Fax: (785) 296-6650

KENTUCKY
James A. Nelson
State Librarian & Commissioner
Education & Humanities Cabinet
Dept. of Library & Archives
300 Coffee Tree Rd.
P.O. Box 537
Frankfort, KY 40602
Phone: (502) 564-8300
Fax: (502) 564-5773

LOUISIANA
Thomas F. Jaques
State Librarian
Ofc. of State Library
Dept. of Culture, Recreation & Tourism
P.O. Box 131
Baton Rouge, LA 70821
Phone: (225) 342-4923
Fax: (225) 342-3547

MAINE
J. Gary Nichols
State Librarian
Bur. of Library Services
64 State House Station
Augusta, ME 04333
Phone: (207) 287-5600

MARYLAND
Lynda C. Davis
Library Division Director
Library Div.
Assembly
90 State Cir., Rm. B-3
Annapolis, MD 21401
Phone: (410) 946-5400

MASSACHUSETTS
Stephen A. Fulchino
State Librarian
State House Library
State House, Rm. 341
24 Beacon St.
Boston, MA 02133
Phone: (617) 727-2592
Fax: (617) 727-5819

MICHIGAN
George Needham
State Librarian
State Library
P.O. Box 30007
Lansing, MI 48909
Phone: (517) 373-1580
Fax: (517) 373-4480

MINNESOTA
Joyce Swonger
Director
Ofc. of Library Dev. & Services
Dept. of Children & Families
1500 Hwy. 36, W.
St. Paul, MN 55113-4266
Phone: (651) 296-2821
Fax: (651) 296-5418
E-mail: joyce.swonger@state.mn.us

MISSISSIPPI

MISSOURI
Sara Ann Parker
State Librarian
State Library
600 W. Main
P.O. Box 387
Jefferson City, MO 65102-0387
Phone: (573) 751-2751
Fax: (573) 751-3612
E-mail: sparker@mail.sos.state.mo.us

MONTANA
Karen Strege
State Librarian
State Library
1515 E. 6th Ave.
Helena, MT 59620
Phone: (406) 444-3115
Fax: (406) 444-5612

NEBRASKA
Marie Wiechman
Librarian
State Library
State Capitol, 3rd Fl.
P.O. Box 98931
Lincoln, NE 68509
Phone: (402) 471-3189
Fax: (402) 471-2197

NEVADA
Dale Erquiaga
Director
Museums, Library & Arts Dept.
100 N. Stewart St.
Carson City, NV 89701
Phone: (775) 687-8315
Fax: (775) 687-8311

NEW HAMPSHIRE
Michael York
State Librarian
State Library
Dept. of Cultural Affairs
20 Park St.
Concord, NH 03301
Phone: (603) 271-2081
Fax: (603) 271-6826

NEW JERSEY
Jack Livingstone
State Librarian
State Library
P.O. Box 520
Trenton, NJ 08625-0520
Phone: (609) 292-6200
Fax: (609) 292-6274

NEW MEXICO
Ben Wakashige
State Librarian
State Library
1209 Camino Carlos Rey
Santa Fe, NM 87505-9860
Phone: (505) 476-9762
Fax: (505) 476-9701

NEW YORK
Janet M. Welch
State Librarian
State Library
Cultural Education Ctr., Rm. 10C34
Empire State Plz.
Albany, NY 12230
Phone: (518) 474-5930
Fax: (518) 486-6880

NORTH CAROLINA
Sandra Cooper
Director
State Library
Dept. of Cultural Resources
109 E. Jones St.
Raleigh, NC 27601-2807
Phone: (919) 733-2570
Fax: (919) 733-8748

NORTH DAKOTA
Mike Jaugstetter
State Librarian
State Library
Liberty Memorial Bldg.
604 E. Blvd. Ave.
Bismarck, ND 58505-0800
Phone: (701) 328-2492
Fax: (701) 328-2040
E-mail: mjaugste@state.nd.us

NORTHERN MARIANA ISLANDS

OHIO
Michael Lucas
State Librarian
State Library
65 S. Front St., Rm. 1206
Columbus, OH 43266-0334
Phone: (614) 644-6843
Fax: (614) 466-3584

OKLAHOMA
Robert L. Clark
Director
Dept. of Libraries
200 NE 18th St.
Oklahoma City, OK 73105
Phone: (405) 521-2502
Fax: (405) 525-7804
E-mail: bclark@ohn.odl.state.ok.us

OREGON
Jim Scheppke
State Librarian
State Library
State Library Bldg.
Salem, OR 97310
Phone: (503) 378-4367
Fax: (503) 588-7119

PENNSYLVANIA
Gary Wolfe
Commissioner of Libraries
State Library
Dept. of Education
P.O. Box 1601
Harrisburg, PA 17105
Phone: (717) 787-2646

PUERTO RICO
Lidia Santiago
Director
Public Library Div.
Dept. of Education
P.O. Box 759
Hato Rey, PR 00919
Phone: (809) 753-9191

RHODE ISLAND
Barbara Weaver
Director
State Library Services
Dept. of Administration
State Library
1 Capitol Hill
Providence, RI 02908
Phone: (401) 222-2726

SOUTH CAROLINA
James B. Johnson
Director
State Library
P.O. Box 11469
Columbia, SC 29211
Phone: (803) 734-8666

SOUTH DAKOTA
Dennis Holub
Acting State Librarian
State Library
State Library Bldg.
800 Governors Dr.
Pierre, SD 57501
Phone: (605) 773-3131
Fax: (605) 773-6962

TENNESSEE
Edwin S. Gleaves
State Librarian & Archivist
State Library & Archives
403 7th Ave., N.
Nashville, TN 37243-0312
Phone: (615) 741-7996
Fax: (615) 741-6471

TEXAS
Robert S. Martin
Director & Librarian
State Library & Archives Comm.
Archives & Library Bldg., Rm. 205
Austin, TX 78701
Phone: (512) 463-5460
Fax: (512) 463-5436

U.S. VIRGIN ISLANDS
E. Marlene Hendricks
Assistant Director
Libraries, Archives & Museums
Dept. of Planning & Natural Resources
23 Dronningens Gade
St. Thomas, VI 00802
Phone: (340) 774-3407
Fax: (340) 775-1887

UTAH
Amy Owen
Director
State Library
Dept. of Community & Economic Dev.
250 N. 1950 W., Ste. A
Salt Lake City, UT 84116-7901
Phone: (801) 715-6770
Fax: (801) 715-6767
E-mail: aowen@library.state.ut.us

VERMONT
Sybil McShane
State Librarian
Dept. of Libraries
109 State St.
Montpelier, VT 05609
Phone: (802) 828-3265
Fax: (802) 828-2199

VIRGINIA
Nolan T. Yelich
State Librarian
State Library
Serials Section
800 E. Broad St.
Richmond, VA 23219
Phone: (804) 692-3535
Fax: (804) 692-3594

WASHINGTON
Nancy L. Zussy
State Librarian
State Library
P.O. Box 42460
Olympia, WA 98504-2460
Phone: (360) 753-2915
Fax: (360) 586-7575

WEST VIRGINIA
David M. Price
Director
Library Comm.
Cultural Ctr.
1900 Kanawha Blvd., E.
Charleston, WV 25305
Phone: (304) 558-2041
Fax: (304) 558-2044

WISCONSIN
Larry Nix
Director
Bur. for Library Dev.
Dept. of Public Instruction
125 S. Webster
P.O. Box 7841
Madison, WI 53707
Phone: (608) 266-2205
Fax: (608) 267-1052

WYOMING
Vacant
State Librarian
State Library
Dept. of Administration & Info.
Supreme Ct. & Library Bldg.
2301 Capitol Ave.
Cheyenne, WY 82002-0600
Phone: (307) 777-7281

State Police

Patrols the state's highways and enforces the motor vehicle laws of the state.

ALABAMA
Cary Sutton
Acting Chief
Hwy. Patrol Div.
Dept. of Public Safety
500 Dexter Ave.
Montgomery, AL 36130
Phone: (334) 424-4393
Fax: (334) 242-4385

ALASKA
Glenn G. Godfrey
Director
Div. of State Troopers
Dept. of Public Safety
5700 E. Tudor Rd.
Anchorage, AK 99507-1225
Phone: (907) 269-5641
Fax: (907) 337-2059

AMERICAN SAMOA
Te'o Fuavai
Commissioner
Dept. of Public Safety
AS Govt.
Pago Pago, AS 96799
Phone: (684) 633-1111
Fax: (684) 633-5111

ARIZONA
Joe Albo
Director
Dept. of Public Safety
2102 W. Encanto Blvd.
Phoenix, AZ 85005-6638
Phone: (602) 223-2359
Fax: (602) 223-2917

ARKANSAS
Tom Mars
Director
State Police
#1 State Police Plz.
Little Rock, AR 72209
Phone: (501) 618-8200
Fax: (501) 618-8222

CALIFORNIA
Dwight Helmick, Jr.
Commissioner
Dept. of Hwy. Patrol
2555 First Ave.
Sacramento, CA 95818
Phone: (916) 657-8152

COLORADO
Lonnie Westphal
Chief
State Patrol
Dept. of Public Safety
700 Kipling
Lakewood, CO 80215
Phone: (303) 239-4403
Fax: (303) 239-4481

CONNECTICUT
Henry Lee
Commissioner
Dept. of Public Safety
P.O. Box 2794
Middletown, CT 06457
Phone: (860) 685-8000

DELAWARE
Alan D. Ellingsworth
Superintendent
State Police
State Police Headquarters
1441 N. DuPont Hwy.
Dover, DE 19901
Phone: (302) 739-5911
Fax: (302) 739-5966

DISTRICT OF COLUMBIA
Charles H. Ramsey
Chief
Metropolitan Police Dept.
300 Indiana Ave., NW, Rm. 5080
Washington, DC 20001
Phone: (202) 727-4218

FLORIDA
Ronald Grimming
Director
Hwy. Patrol
Hwy. Safety & Motor Vehicle Dept.
Neil Kirkman Bldg., Rm. A-437
2900 Apalachee Pkwy.
Tallahassee, FL 32399-0500
Phone: (850) 488-4885
Fax: (850) 922-0148

GEORGIA
Sidney R. Miles
Commissioner
Dept. of Public Safety
P.O. Box 1456
Atlanta, GA 30371
Phone: (404) 624-7710

GUAM
James M. Marques
Chief of Police
Police Dept.
233 Central Ave.
Tiyan, GU 96913
Phone: (671) 475-8508
Fax: (671) 472-4036

HAWAII

IDAHO
E.D. Strickfaden
Superintendent
State Police
P.O. Box 700
Meridian, ID 83680-0700
Phone: (208) 884-7203

ILLINOIS
Sam Nolen
Director
State Police
103 State Armory
Springfield, IL 62706
Phone: (217) 782-7263
Fax: (217) 785-2821

INDIANA
Melvin Carraway
Superintendent
State Police
IGC-N., 3rd Fl.
100 N. Senate Ave.
Indianapolis, IN 46204
Phone: (317) 232-8241
Fax: (317) 232-5682

IOWA
Jon Wilson
Chief
State Patrol
Dept. of Public Safety
Wallace State Ofc. Bldg.
E. 9th & Grand Aves.
Des Moines, IA 50319-0044
Phone: (515) 281-5824

KANSAS
Donald Brownlee
Superintendent
Hwy. Patrol
122 SW 7th St.
Topeka, KS 66603
Phone: (785) 296-6800
Fax: (785) 296-5956

KENTUCKY
Gary Rose
Commissioner
State Police
Justice Cabinet
919 Versailles Rd.
Frankfort, KY 40601
Phone: (502) 695-6300
Fax: (502) 573-1479

LOUISIANA
William Whittington
Deputy Secretary
Dept. of Public Safety Services
P.O. Box 94304
Baton Rouge, LA 70804-9304
Phone: (225) 925-6117
Fax: (225) 925-3742

MAINE
Malcolm T. Dow
Chief
State Police
Dept. of Public Safety
42 State House Station
Augusta, ME 04333
Phone: (207) 287-4478

MARYLAND
David B. Mitchell
Superintendent
Ofc. of the Superintendent
Dept. of State Police
1201 Reisterstown Rd.
Baltimore, MD 21208-3899
Phone: (410) 653-4219
Fax: (410) 653-9651

MASSACHUSETTS
Reed Hillman
Commissioner/Superintendent
Div. of State Police
Dept. of Public Safety
470 Worcester Rd.
Framingham, MA 01701
Phone: (508) 820-2350
Fax: (617) 727-6874

MICHIGAN
Mike Robinson
Director
Dept. of State Police
714 S. Harrison Rd.
E. Lansing, MI 48823
Phone: (517) 336-6157
Fax: (517) 336-6255

MINNESOTA
Anne Beers
Chief
State Patrol Div.
Dept. of Public Safety
444 Cedar St., Ste. 130
St. Paul, MN 55101-5130
Phone: (651) 296-5936
Fax: (651) 296-5937
E-mail: anne.beers@state.mn.us

MISSISSIPPI
Jim Ingram
Commissioner
Dept. of Public Safety
Hwy. Patrol Bldg., I-55 N.
P.O. Box 958
Jackson, MS 39205
Phone: (601) 987-1490
Fax: (601) 987-1498

MISSOURI
Weldon Wilhoit
Superintendent
State Hwy. Patrol
Dept. of Public Safety
1510 E. Elm
P.O. Box 568
Jefferson City, MO 65102
Phone: (573) 751-2901
Fax: (573) 526-1111
E-mail: mshppied@mail.state.mo.us

MONTANA
Craig T. Reap
Chief Administrator
Hwy. Patrol Div.
Dept. of Justice
2550 Prospect Ave.
Helena, MT 59620
Phone: (406) 444-7000
Fax: (406) 444-4169

NEBRASKA
Tom Nesbitt
Superintendent
State Patrol
P.O. Box 94907
Lincoln, NE 68509
Phone: (402) 471-4545
Fax: (402) 479-4002

NEVADA
Mike Hood
Chief
Hwy. Patrol
555 Wright Way
Carson City, NV 89711
Phone: (775) 687-5300
Fax: (775) 684-7879

NEW HAMPSHIRE
John J. Barthelmes
Director
Div. of State Police
Criminal Records Ofc.
Safety Dept.
10 Hazen Dr.
Concord, NH 03305-0002
Phone: (603) 271-3636
Fax: (603) 271-1153

NEW JERSEY
Michael A. Fedorko
Acting Superintendent
Div. of State Police
Dept. of Law & Public Safety
P.O. Box 7068
Trenton, NJ 08625
Phone: (609) 882-2000

NEW MEXICO
Darren White
Secretary
Dept. of Public Safety
P.O. Box 1628
Santa Fe, NM 87504-1628
Phone: (505) 827-3370
Fax: (505) 827-3434

NEW YORK
James McMahon
Superintendent
Div. of State Police
Public Security, Bldg. 22
1220 Washington Ave.
Albany, NY 12226-2252
Phone: (518) 457-6721
Fax: (518) 485-7505

NORTH CAROLINA
Richard W. Holden
Commander
Div. of Hwy. Patrol
Crime Control & Public Safety
P.O. Box 29590
Raleigh, NC 27626-0590
Phone: (919) 733-7952
Fax: (919) 733-1189

NORTH DAKOTA
James M. Hughes
Superintendent
Hwy. Patrol
600 E. Blvd. Ave., Ground Fl. - Judicial Wing
Bismarck, ND 58505-0241
Phone: (701) 328-2455
Fax: (701) 328-1717
E-mail: jhughes@state.nd.us

NORTHERN MARIANA ISLANDS
Jose M. Castro
Director
Dept. of Public Safety
Caller Box 10007
Saipan, MP 96950
Phone: (670) 235-4441
Fax: (670) 234-8531
E-mail: commish@mtccnmi.com

OHIO
Kenneth B. Marshall
Superintendent
State Hwy. Patrol
1970 W. Broad St.
Columbus, OH 43223-1102
Phone: (614) 466-2990
Fax: (614) 752-6409

OKLAHOMA
Bob Ricks
Secretary of Safety & Security
Dept. of Public Safety
3600 N. Martin Luther King, Jr. Dr.
Oklahoma City, OK 73136
Phone: (405) 425-2424
Fax: (405) 425-7709

OREGON
LeRon Howland
Superintendent
State Police
400 Public Services Bldg.
255 Capitol St., NE
Salem, OR 97310
Phone: (503) 378-3720
Fax: (503) 378-8282

PENNSYLVANIA
Paul Evanko
Commissioner
State Police
1800 Elmerton Ave.
Harrisburg, PA 17110
Phone: (717) 783-5558
Fax: (717) 787-2948

PUERTO RICO
Pedro Toledo
Superintendent
State Police Dept.
Dept. of Police
G.P.O. Box 70166
San Juan, PR 00936
Phone: (787) 792-0006
Fax: (787) 781-0080

RHODE ISLAND
Edmund Culhane
Superintendent
Dept. of State Police
311 Danielson Pike
N. Scituate, RI 02857
Phone: (401) 444-1111

SOUTH CAROLINA
R.W. Luther
Deputy Director
Hwy. Patrol
Dept. of Public Safety
5400 Broad River Rd.
Columbia, SC 29212-3540
Phone: (803) 896-7894
Fax: (803) 896-7922

SOUTH DAKOTA
Gene Abdallah
Director
Div. Hwy. Patrol
Dept. of Commerce & Regulation
320 N. Nicollet
Pierre, SD 57501
Phone: (605) 773-3105
Fax: (605) 773-6046

TENNESSEE
Mike Greene
Commissioner
Dept. of Safety
1150 Foster Ave.
Nashville, TN 37249
Phone: (615) 251-5165
Fax: (615) 251-2091

TEXAS
Dudley Thomas
Director
Dept. of Public Safety
5805 N. Lamar Blvd.
Austin, TX 78752
Phone: (512) 424-2000
Fax: (512) 483-5708

U.S. VIRGIN ISLANDS
Franz A. Christian, Sr.
Acting Commissioner
Police Dept.
8172 Sub Base
St. Thomas, VI 00802
Phone: (340) 774-6400
Fax: (340) 776-3317

UTAH
Richard Greenwood
Deputy Commissioner
Hwy. Patrol
Dept. of Public Safety
4501 S. 2700 W.
Salt Lake City, UT 84119
Phone: (801) 965-4062
Fax: (801) 965-4716
E-mail: dgreenwo.psmain@state.ut.us

VERMONT
John Sinclair
Director
State Police
Dept. of Public Safety
103 S. Main St.
Waterbury, VT 05671
Phone: (802) 244-7345

VIRGINIA
M. Wayne Huggins
Superintendent
Dept. of State Police
7700 Midlothian Tpke.
Richmond, VA 23235
Phone: (804) 674-2087
Fax: (804) 674-2132

WASHINGTON
Annette Sandberg
Chief
State Patrol
Administration Bldg.
P.O. Box 42601
Olympia, WA 98504-2601
Phone: (360) 753-6540
Fax: (360) 664-0663

WEST VIRGINIA
Gary L. Edgell
Superintendent
Public Safety Div.
725 Jefferson Rd.
S. Charleston, WV 25309-1698
Phone: (304) 746-2111
Fax: (304) 746-2230

WISCONSIN
Jerry Baumbach
Executive Director
Ofc. of Justice Assistance
Dept. of Administration
131 W. Wilson, Ste. 202
Madison, WI 53702
Phone: (608) 266-3323
Fax: (608) 266-6676

WYOMING
Gene Roccabruna
Director
Hwy. Safety Div.
Dept. of Transportation
5300 Bishop Blvd.
Cheyenne, WY 82002
Phone: (307) 777-4198

Surplus Property

Establishes and promotes ways and means of acquiring and distributing equitable federal personal property to public agencies, etc.

ALABAMA
Shane T. Bailey
Chief
Surplus Property Div.
Economic & Community Affairs Dept.
4401 Northern Bypass
P.O. Box 210487
Montgomery, AL 36121-0487
Phone: (334) 277-5866
Fax: (334) 223-7320

ALASKA
Marsha Hubbard
Director
Div. of Services & Supply
Dept. of Administration
P.O. Box 110210
Juneau, AK 99811
Phone: (907) 465-2250
Fax: (907) 465-2189

AMERICAN SAMOA
Pat Trevola
Director
Ofc. of Procurement
AS Govt.
Pago Pago, AS 96799
Phone: (684) 633-1205

ARIZONA
Steve Perica
Administrator
Surplus Property Div.
Dept. of Administration
1537 W. Jackson
Phoenix, AZ 85007
Phone: (602) 542-5701

ARKANSAS
Roy Wood
Associate Director
Federal Surplus Property
8700 Remount Rd.
N. Little Rock, AR 72118
Phone: (501) 835-3111
Fax: (501) 834-5240

CALIFORNIA
Shirley Oglethorpe
Deputy Director
Procurement
Dept. of Services
4675 Watt Ave.
N. Highlands, CA 95660
Phone: (916) 574-2249

COLORADO
Ron Bachali
Manager
Agency for Surplus Property
Dept. of Corrections
4200 Garfield
Denver, CO 80216
Phone: (303) 321-4012
Fax: (303) 320-1050

CONNECTICUT
Kenn Stephenson
Surplus Property Manager
Bur. of Business Services
Dept. of Administration Services
165 Capitol Ave.
Hartford, CT 06106
Phone: (860) 713-5155

DELAWARE
Normajane Duvall
Administrator
Surplus Property Program
Div. of Purchasing
P.O. Box 299
Delaware City, DE 19706
Phone: (302) 836-7640
Fax: (302) 836-7298

DISTRICT OF COLUMBIA

FLORIDA
Chris Butterworth
Chief
Bur. of Federal Property Assistance
Dept. of Mgmt. Services
813-A Lake Bradford Rd.
Tallahassee, FL 32304
Phone: (850) 488-3524
Fax: (850) 487-3222

GEORGIA
Debra White
Director
Support Services
Dept. of Adm. Services
W. Tower, Floyd Bldg.
200 Piedmont Ave., SE
Atlanta, GA 30334
Phone: (404) 656-5753

GUAM
Fred A. Santiago
Surplus Property Management Officer
Service Administration
Dept. of Administration
P.O. Box FG
Hagatna, GU 96932
Phone: (671) 477-1725
Fax: (671) 472-7538

HAWAII
Craig Kuraoka
Branch Chief
Surplus Property Branch
Dept. of Accounting & Services
729 Kakoi St.
Honolulu, HI 96819
Phone: (808) 831-6757
Fax: (808) 831-6786

IDAHO
Dennis Talbot
Manager
Bur. of Federal Surplus Property
P.O. Box 83720
Boise, ID 83720
Phone: (208) 334-3477

ILLINOIS
Michael S. Schwartz
Director
Dept. of Central Mgmt. Services
715 Stratton Ofc. Bldg.
401 S. Spring
Springfield, IL 62706
Phone: (217) 782-2141
Fax: (217) 524-1880

INDIANA
Earl Morgan
Director
State/Federal Surplus
Dept. of Administration
6400 E. 30th St.
Indianapolis, IN 46219
Phone: (317) 591-5320
Fax: (317) 591-5324

IOWA
Richard Haines
Director
Dept. of Services
Hoover State Ofc. Bldg.
1305 E. Walnut
Des Moines, IA 50319
Phone: (515) 281-3196
Fax: (515) 242-5974

KANSAS
Paul Schwartz
Director of Federal Surplus
Dept. of Corrections
3400 SE 10th St.
Topeka, KS 66607-2513
Phone: (785) 296-2351
Fax: (785) 296-4060

KENTUCKY
Mike Abell
Director
Finance & Administration Cabinet
Div. of Purchases
Capitol Annex, Rm. 367
Frankfort, KY 40601
Phone: (502) 564-4510
Fax: (502) 564-7209

LOUISIANA
Irene Babin
Director
Property Assistance Agency
Div. of Administration
P.O. Box 94095
Baton Rouge, LA 70804-9095
Phone: (225) 342-6890
Fax: (225) 342-6891

MAINE
John Conrad
Director
Federal Surplus Property
Div. of Purchases
9 State House Station
Augusta, ME 04333
Phone: (207) 287-3521

MARYLAND
Anne Mackinnon
Assistant Secretary
State Agency for Surplus Property
Dept. of Services
Brockridge Rd., Box 1039
Jessup, MD 20794
Phone: (410) 799-0440
Fax: (410) 799-2725
E-mail: amackinnon@dgs.state.md.us

MASSACHUSETTS
Ellen Phillips
Director
Surplus Property Div.
Executive Ofc. for Administration & Finance
One Ashburton Pl.
Boston, MA 02108
Phone: (617) 727-7500
Fax: (617) 727-4527

MICHIGAN
Bill Cullimore
Supervisor
State Surplus Property
Ofc. Services Div.
Dept. of Mgmt. & Budget
P.O. Box 30026
Lansing, MI 48909
Phone: (517) 335-8444

MINNESOTA
Kent Allin
Director
Div. of Materials Mgmt.
112 Administration Bldg.
50 Sherburne Ave.
St. Paul, MN 55155
Phone: (651) 296-1442
Fax: (651) 296-3996

MISSISSIPPI
Jim Majure
Director
Ofc. of Surplus Property
P.O. Box 5788
Jackson, MS 39288
Phone: (601) 939-2050
Fax: (601) 939-4505

MISSOURI
Marilyn Steffen
Manager
State Surplus Property
Div. of Purchasing
117 N. Riverside Dr.
P.O. Box 1310
Jefferson City, MO 65102
Phone: (573) 751-3415
Fax: (573) 751-1264
E-mail: steffm@mail.oa.state.mo.us

MONTANA
Mike McMahon
Bureau Chief
Property & Supply Bur.
Dept. of Administration
930 E. Lyndale Ave.
Helena, MT 59620
Phone: (406) 444-4514
Fax: (406) 444-4201

NEBRASKA
Steve Sulek
Manager
DAS Material Div.
P.O. Box 94901
Lincoln, NE 68509
Phone: (402) 479-4890
Fax: (402) 471-2889

NEVADA
William Moell
Administrator
Purchasing Div.
Dept. of Administration
209 E. Musser St., #304
Carson City, NV 89701
Phone: (775) 684-0170
Fax: (775) 684-0188

NEW HAMPSHIRE
Wayne R. Myer
Administrator
Bur. of Purchasing & Property
Adm. Services
25 Capitol St., Rm. 102
Concord, NH 03301-6398
Phone: (603) 271-2201
Fax: (603) 271-2700

NEW JERSEY
Stephen M. Sylvester
Assistant Director
Property Administration
Dept. of Treasury
50 Barrack St.
P.O. Box 240
Trenton, NJ 08646-0240
Phone: (609) 292-8822
Fax: (609) 292-0411

NEW MEXICO
Louis Higgins
Director
Purchasing Div.
Dept. of Services
P.O. Box 26110
Santa Fe, NM 87502
Phone: (505) 827-0472
Fax: (505) 827-2041

NEW YORK
Joseph Seymour
Commissioner
Ofc. of Services
Corning Tower Bldg., 41st Fl.
Empire State Plz.
Albany, NY 12242
Phone: (518) 474-5991
Fax: (518) 486-9179

NORTH CAROLINA
Benny Troutman
Director
Federal Surplus Property
Dept. of Administration
1950 Garner Rd.
Raleigh, NC 27610-3926
Phone: (919) 733-3885
Fax: (919) 733-3883

NORTH DAKOTA
Rod Backman
Director
Surplus Property
Central Services Div.
600 E. Blvd. Ave., 4th Fl.
Bismarck, ND 58505-0400
Phone: (701) 328-9665
Fax: (701) 328-3230
E-mail: rbackman@state.nd.us

NORTHERN MARIANA ISLANDS
Edward B. Palacios
Director
Procurement & Supply Div.
Dept. of Finance
Lower Base
Saipan, MP 96950
Phone: (670) 664-1500
Fax: (670) 664-1515
E-mail: gov.p$s@saipan.com

OHIO
John Thornton, Jr.
Administrator
State Surplus Property
Dept. of Adm. Services
4200 Surface Rd.
Columbus, OH 43228
Phone: (614) 466-6570
Fax: (614) 466-1584

OKLAHOMA
Pam Warren
Secretary of Administration
Dept. of Central Services
2401 N. Lincoln Blvd., Ste. 206
Oklahoma City, OK 73105
Phone: (405) 521-2121
Fax: (405) 425-2713

OREGON
Skip Morton
Manager
State Surplus Property
Dept. of Adm. Services
1655 Salem Industrial Dr., NE
Salem, OR 97310
Phone: (503) 378-2207
Fax: (503) 378-8558

PENNSYLVANIA
Ronald E. Wolf
Director
Bur. of Supply & Surplus Operations
Dept. of Services
22nd & Forster Sts.
Harrisburg, PA 17105
Phone: (717) 787-5940
Fax: (717) 772-2491

PUERTO RICO
Maria T. Mujica
Administrator
Services Administration
P.O. Box 7428
San Juan, PR 00916
Phone: (787) 724-1064
Fax: (787) 722-7965

RHODE ISLAND
Robert L. Carl, Jr.
Director
Dept. of Administration
1 Capitol Hill
Providence, RI 02903
Phone: (401) 222-2280
Fax: (401) 222-6436

SOUTH CAROLINA
Ron Cathey
Program Manager
Agency Mail, Supplies & Surplus Property
Budget & Control Board
1441 Boston Ave.
W. Columbia, SC 29169
Phone: (803) 896-6880

SOUTH DAKOTA
Rich Voorhes
Director
State Property Mgmt. Ofc.
Bur. of Administration
500 E. Capitol Ave.
Pierre, SD 57501
Phone: (605) 773-4935
Fax: (605) 773-3837

TENNESSEE
Larry Haynes
Commissioner
Dept. of Services
Wm. R. Snodgrass TN Towers, 24th Fl.
Nashville, TN 37243-0530
Phone: (615) 741-9263
Fax: (615) 532-8594

TEXAS
Dan Bremer
Director
Services Comm.
State & Federal Surplus Property
Capitol Station
P.O. Box 13047
Austin, TX 78711-3047
Phone: (512) 463-4739

U.S. VIRGIN ISLANDS
Harold G. Thompson
Acting Commissioner
Dept. of Public Works
No. 8 Sub Base
St. Thomas, VI 00802
Phone: (340) 776-4844
Fax: (340) 776-8990

UTAH
Mark Young
Program Manager
Div. of Fleet Operations
Dept. of Adm. Services
477 W. 13800 S.
Draper, UT 84020
Phone: (801) 576-8280
Fax: (801) 576-8279
E-mail: myoung@fo.state.ut.us

VERMONT
Peter E. Noyes
Director
Div. of Purchasing
Dept. of Services
133 State St.
Montpelier, VT 05633-7501
Phone: (802) 828-3394
Fax: (802) 828-2222

VIRGINIA
Donald C. Williams
Director
Dept. of Services
202 N. 9th St., Ste. 209
Richmond, VA 23219
Phone: (804) 786-3311
Fax: (804) 371-8305

WASHINGTON
Linda Bremmer
Assistant Director
Div. of Transportation Services
Dept. of Administration
P.O. Box 41032
Auburn, WA 98504-1032
Phone: (360) 438-8247
Fax: (360) 438-8239

WEST VIRGINIA
Kenneth O. Frye
Director
Surplus Property
Div. of Finance & Administration
2700 Charles Ave.
Dunbar, WV 25064
Phone: (304) 766-2626
Fax: (304) 766-2631

WISCONSIN
Geoffrey Wheeler
Administrator
Div. of State Agency Services
Dept. of Administration
101 E. Wilson, 6th Fl.
P.O. Box 7867
Madison, WI 53707
Phone: (608) 266-1011
Fax: (608) 267-0600

WYOMING
Ellen Stephenson
Warehouse Manager
Procurement Services Div.
Dept. of Administration & Info.
2405 Westland Rd.
Cheyenne, WY 82002
Phone: (307) 777-7901

Telecommunications

Responsible for communications planning and organizing a statewide plan for total communications, especially with local government on emergency matters.

ALABAMA
Julie Robertson
Voice Operation Manager
Telecoms. Div.
Dept. of Finance
64 N. Union, Ste. 204
Montgomery, AL 36130-3053
Phone: (334) 242-3532
Fax: (334) 242-2700

ALASKA
Mark Badger
Director
Div. of Info. Services
Dept. of Administration
P.O. Box 110206
Juneau, AK 99811-0206
Phone: (907) 465-2220
Fax: (907) 465-3450

AMERICAN SAMOA
Aleki Sene
Director
Telecom. Authority
P.O. Box M
Pago Pago, AS 96799
Phone: (684) 633-1121
Fax: (684) 633-9032

ARIZONA
Bill Parker
Assistant Director
Info. Services Div.
Dept. of Administration
1616 W. Adams St.
Phoenix, AZ 85007
Phone: (602) 542-2250
Fax: (602) 542-4272

ARKANSAS
Julie Cullen
Deputy Director
Telecoms. Div.
Dept. of Info. Systems
P.O. Box 3155
Little Rock, AR 72203-3155
Phone: (501) 682-4006
Fax: (501) 682-4310

CALIFORNIA
John Thomas Flynn
Chief Information Officer
801 K St., #2100
Sacramento, CA 95814-3701
Phone: (916) 657-0318

COLORADO
Mike Borrego
Manager
Telecom. Services
Support Services
Dept. of Personnel
2452 W. 2nd Ave., Rm. 19
Denver, CO 80223
Phone: (303) 866-2341
Fax: (303) 922-1811

CONNECTICUT
John Bennett
Executive Director
Ofc. of Info. & Technology
Ofc. of Policy & Mgmt.
450 Capitol Ave., MS# 53OIT
P.O. Box 341441
Hartford, CT 06134-1441
Phone: (860) 418-6273
Fax: (860) 418-6491

DELAWARE
Peter A. LaVenia
Director
Telecom. Mgmt. Ofc.
801 Silver Lake Blvd.
William Penn Bldg.
Dover, DE 19904
Phone: (302) 739-9693

DISTRICT OF COLUMBIA

FLORIDA
Linda L. Nelson
Director
Info. Technology Program
Dept. of Mgmt. Services
Bldg. 4030, Ste. 180
4050 Esplanade Way
Tallahassee, FL 32399-0950
Phone: (904) 488-3595
Fax: (904) 488-9837

GEORGIA
Bob Simpson
Director
Info. Technology
Dept. of Adm. Services
200 Piedmont Ave.
Atlanta, GA 30334
Phone: (404) 656-3992

GUAM
Robert F. Kelley
Director
Civil Defense
Emergency Services Ofc.
P.O. Box 2877
Hagatna, GU 96910
Phone: (671) 475-9600
Fax: (671) 477-3727

HAWAII
Leslie Nakamura
Division Head
Info. & Communication Services
Dept. of Budget & Finance
1151 Punchbowl St., Basement
Honolulu, HI 96813
Phone: (808) 586-1910
Fax: (808) 586-1922

IDAHO
Pamela Ahrens
Director
Dept. of Administration
650 W. State St., Rm. 100
Boise, ID 83720
Phone: (208) 334-3382

ILLINOIS
William M. Vetter
Manager
Communication & Computer Services
120 W. Jefferson St.
Springfield, IL 62702
Phone: (217) 782-4221
Fax: (217) 524-6161

INDIANA
Dawn J. Hahm
Senior Manager
Communication Services
Info. Services Div.
Dept. of Administration
IGC-North, Rm. N551
Indianapolis, IN 46204
Phone: (317) 232-4629
Fax: (317) 232-0748

IOWA
Harold M. Thompson
Director
Telecom. & Technology Comm.
Communications Network
W-4 Railroad Ave., Camp Dodge
P.O. Box 587
Johnston, IA 50131-0587
Phone: (515) 323-4692
Fax: (515) 323-4751

KANSAS
Don Heiman
Director
Info. Systems & Communications
Dept. of Administration
Landon Ofc. Bldg., Rm 751-S
Topeka, KS 66612-1275
Phone: (785) 296-3343
Fax: (785) 296-1168

KENTUCKY
David Ballard
Director
Telecoms. Div.
Dept. of Facilities Mgmt.
Finance & Administration Cabinet
100 Fair Oaks Ln., Ste. 102
Frankfort, KY 40601-1109
Phone: (502) 564-8703
Fax: (502) 564-6856

LOUISIANA
Allen Doescher
Assistant Commissioner
Technical Services & Communications
Div. of Administration
P.O. Box 94095
Baton Rouge, LA 70804-9095
Phone: (225) 342-7085
Fax: (225) 342-1057

MAINE
John W. Libby
Director
Emergency Mgmt. Agency
72 State House Station
Augusta, ME 04333-0072
Phone: (207) 626-4202
Fax: (207) 626-4495

MARYLAND
Preston L. Dillard
Director
Telecoms. Div.
Dept. of Budget & Mgmt.
301 W. Preston St., Rm. 1304
Baltimore, MD 21201
Phone: (410) 767-4647
Fax: (410) 333-7285
E-mail: pdillard@dbm.state.md.us

MASSACHUSETTS
David Lewis
Acting Director
Mgmt. Info. Systems
Executive Ofc. for Administration & Finance
One Ashburton Pl., Rm. 801
Boston, MA 02108
Phone: (617) 973-0975
Fax: (617) 727-3766

MICHIGAN
Richard Boyd
Director
Telecoms. Div.
Dept. of Mgmt. & Budget
P.O. Box 30026
Lansing, MI 48909
Phone: (517) 373-0785

MINNESOTA
Jack Ries
Telecommunications Manager
Telecoms. Div.
Dept. of Administration
658 Cedar St.
St. Paul, MN 55155
Phone: (651) 296-7515
Fax: (651) 297-5368
E-mail: jack.ries@state.mn.us

MISSISSIPPI
Charles Evers
Director
Telecom.
Bur. of Telecom.
301 N. Lamar, Ste. 508
Jackson, MS 39201-1495
Phone: (601) 359-6331
Fax: (601) 359-1500

MISSOURI
James Schutt
Director
Div. of Info. Services
Ofc. of Administration
P.O. Box 809
Jefferson City, MO 65102
Phone: (573) 751-3338
Fax: (573) 526-0132
E-mail: schutj@mail.oa.state.mo.us

MONTANA
Anthony Herbert
Administrator
Info. Services Div.
Dept. of Administration
Mitchell Bldg., Rm. 229
Helena, MT 59620
Phone: (406) 444-2700
Fax: (406) 444-2701

NEBRASKA
Brenda Decker
Director
Div. of Communications
Dept. of Adm. Services
521 S. 14th St., Ste. 300
Lincoln, NE 68508
Phone: (402) 471-2761
Fax: (402) 471-3339

NEVADA
Marlene Lockard
Director
Dept. of Info. Technology
Kinkaid Bldg., Rm. 403
505 E. King St.
Carson City, NV 89701
Phone: (775) 684-5801
Fax: (775) 684-5846
E-mail: mlockard@doit.state.nv.us

NEW HAMPSHIRE
Dennis LeClerc
Supervisor
Telecom. Section
Adm. Services
25 Capitol St., Rm. 405
Concord, NH 03301-6312
Phone: (603) 271-2888
Fax: (603) 271-1115

NEW JERSEY
Adel Ebeid
Chief Technology Officer
Ofc. of Telecoms. & Info. Systems
300 Riverview Plz., 1st Fl.
P.O. Box 212
Trenton, NJ 08625-0212
Phone: (609) 633-8128
Fax: (609) 633-9100

NEW MEXICO
David Ortiz
Deputy Director
Ofc. of Communications
Dept. of Services
P.O. Drawer 26110
Sante Fe, NM 87502
Phone: (505) 827-2000
Fax: (505) 827-2041

NEW YORK
Joseph Seymour
Commissioner
Ofc. of Services
Corning Tower Bldg., 41st Fl.
Empire State Plz.
Albany, NY 12242
Phone: (518) 474-5991
Fax: (518) 486-9179

NORTH CAROLINA
Jim Broadwell
Director
State Telecoms. Services
State Controller's Ofc. - SIPS
3700 Wake Forest Rd.
Raleigh, NC 27609-6880
Phone: (919) 981-5210
Fax: (919) 850-2827

Eric L. Tolbert
Director
Div. of Emergency Mgmt.
Dept. of Crime Control & Public Safety
116 W. Jones St.
Raleigh, NC 27603-1335
Phone: (919) 733-3825
Fax: (919) 733-5406

NORTH DAKOTA
Marvin A. Fettig
Telecommunications Analyst
Info. Services Div.
600 E. Blvd. Ave., Ground Fl. - Judicial Wing
Bismarck, ND 58505-0100
Phone: (701) 328-3190
Fax: (701) 328-3000
E-mail: mfettig@state.nd.us

NORTHERN MARIANA ISLANDS
David Ecret
Special Assistant for Telecommunications
Ofc. of the Governor
P.O. Box 10007
Saipan, MP 96950
Phone: (670) 664-2206
Fax: (670) 644-2211
E-mail: Ecret@aol.com

OHIO
Timothy D. Steiner
Telecommunications Administrator
Div. of Computer Services
Dept. of Adm. Services
30 E. Broad St., 7th Fl.
Columbus, OH 43266
Phone: (614) 466-0747
Fax: (614) 466-8159

OKLAHOMA
Ray Penrod
Chief, Communications Operations
Info. Services Div.
Ofc. of State Finance
State Capitol Bldg., Rm. 4F
2300 N. Lincoln Blvd.
Oklahoma City, OK 73105
Phone: (405) 521-3309
Fax: (405) 521-3089

OREGON
Ralph Cox
Manager
Telecom. Services
Dept. of Adm. Services
955 Ctr. St., NE, 4th Fl.
Salem, OR 97310
Phone: (503) 373-7211
Fax: (503) 378-8333

PENNSYLVANIA
Charles F. Gerhards
Director
Central Mgmt. Ctr.
1 Technology Park
Harrisburg, PA 17110
Phone: (717) 772-8000
Fax: (717) 772-8113

PUERTO RICO
Maria T. Mujica
Administrator
Services Administration
P.O. Box 7428
San Juan, PR 00916
Phone: (787) 724-1064
Fax: (787) 722-7965

RHODE ISLAND
Dennis Lynch
Associate Director
Central Services
Dept. of Administration
1 Capitol Hill
Providence, RI 02903
Phone: (401) 222-6200

SOUTH CAROLINA
Ted Lightle
Director
Div. of Info. Resource Mgmt.
Budget & Control Board
1201 Main St., Ste. 1500
Columbia, SC 29201
Phone: (803) 737-0077

SOUTH DAKOTA
Dennis Nincehelser
Director
Telecom. Services
Bur. of Info. & Telecoms.
700 Governors Dr.
Pierre, SD 57501
Phone: (605) 773-3416
Fax: (605) 773-3741

TENNESSEE
Jack McFadden
Director
Ofc. of Info. Resources
Dept. of Finance & Administration
598 James Robertson Pkwy., 3rd Fl.
Nashville, TN 37243-0560
Phone: (615) 741-5080
Fax: (615) 741-4996

TEXAS
Steve Parker
Director
Telecoms. Services Div.
Services Comm.
1711 San Jacinto
P.O. Box 13047
Austin, TX 78711-3047
Phone: (512) 463-3471

U.S. VIRGIN ISLANDS
Vacant
Coordinator
VITEMA
2-C Contant, AQ Bldg.
St Thomas, VI 00802
Phone: (340) 774-2244
Fax: (340) 774-1491

UTAH
Leon Miller
Director
Div. of Info. Technology Services
Dept. of Adm. Services
6000 State Ofc. Bldg.
Salt Lake City, UT 84114-1172
Phone: (801) 538-3476
Fax: (801) 538-3321
E-mail: lmiller.asitmain@state.ut.us

VERMONT
Thomas W. Torti
Commissioner
Dept. of State Bldgs.
2 Governor Aiken Ave.
Drawer 33
Montpelier, VT 05633-5802
Phone: (802) 828-3314
Fax: (802) 828-3533
E-mail: ttorti@state.vt.us

VIRGINIA
Michael F. Thomas
Director
Dept. of Info. Technology
Richmond Plz. Bldg., 3rd Fl.
110 S. 7th St.
Richmond, VA 23219
Phone: (804) 371-5500
Fax: (804) 371-5273

WASHINGTON
John M. Anderson
Assistant Director
Telecoms. Div.
Dept. of Info. Services
P.O. Box 42445
Olympia, WA 98504-2445
Phone: (360) 902-3333
Fax: (360) 902-3453
E-mail: johna@dis.wa.gov

WEST VIRGINIA
Matthew Brown
Manager
Div. of Telecoms.
Dept. of Administration
Bldg. 6, Rm. B163
1900 Kanawha Blvd., E.
Charleston, WV 25305
Phone: (304) 558-5980

WISCONSIN
Jody McCann
Director
Bur. of Info. & Telecom.
Dept. of Administration
101 E. Wilson, 8th Fl.
P.O. Box 7844
Madison, WI 53703
Phone: (608) 267-0627
Fax: (608) 266-2164

WYOMING
David Bliss
Interim Administrator
Computer Technology Div.
Administration & Fiscal Control Dept.
Emerson Bldg.
2001 Capitol Ave.
Cheyenne, WY 82002
Phone: (307) 777-5000

Textbook Approval

Recommends textbooks for public elementary and secondary schools.

ALABAMA
Anne M. Jones
State Textbook Coordinator
Dept. of Education
50 N. Ripley St.
Montgomery, AL 36130-2101
Phone: (334) 242-9718
Fax: (334) 242-0482

ALASKA

AMERICAN SAMOA
Laloulu E. Tagoilelagi
Director
Dept. of Education
AS Govt.
Pago Pago, AS 96799
Phone: (684) 633-5237
Fax: (684) 633-4240

ARIZONA
Lisa Graham Keegan
Superintendent of Public Instruction
Dept. of Education
1535 W. Jefferson
Phoenix, AZ 85007
Phone: (602) 542-6417
Fax: (602) 542-5440

ARKANSAS
Sue McKenzie
Coordinator
Instructional Materials
Dept. of Education
Education Bldg.
Little Rock, AR 72201
Phone: (501) 682-4593
Fax: (501) 682-4898

CALIFORNIA
Delaine Eastin
State Superintendent of Public Instruction
Dept. of Education
721 Capitol Mall, Rm. 524
Sacramento, CA 95814-4702
Phone: (916) 657-4766

COLORADO
William J. Moloney
Commissioner
Dept. of Education
201 E. Colfax
Denver, CO 80203-1715
Phone: (303) 866-6646
Fax: (303) 830-0793

CONNECTICUT
Abigail Hughes
Bureau Chief
Bur. of Certification & Professional Dev.
Dept. of Education
165 Capitol Ave.
Hartford, CT 06106
Phone: (860) 566-4267

DELAWARE
Carol O. Mayhew
Team Leader
Curriculum, Instruction & Professional Dev.
Dept. of Public Instruction
Townsend Bldg.
Dover, DE 19901
Phone: (302) 739-4647
Fax: (302) 739-4483

DISTRICT OF COLUMBIA

FLORIDA
Don Griesheimer
Administrator
Instructional Materials
Instructional Television
325 W. Gaines St., Ste. 532
Tallahassee, FL 32399
Phone: (850) 487-8791
Fax: (850) 921-9059

GEORGIA
Andrea Gordon
Administrative Specialist
Curriculum & Reading
Dept. of Education
205 Butler St., SW, Rm. 2054
Atlanta, GA 30334
Phone: (404) 651-7272

GUAM
Michael J. Reidy
Acting Director
Dept. of Education
P.O. Box DE
Hagatna, GU 96932
Phone: (671) 475-0462
Fax: (671) 472-5003

HAWAII
Evangeline Barney
Acting Assistant Superintendent
Ofc. Of Accountability & Instructional Support
Dept. of Education
1390 Miller St., Rm. 316
Honolulu, HI 96813
Phone: (808) 586-3446
Fax: (808) 586-3429

IDAHO
Anne C. Fox
Superintendent of Public Instruction
Dept. of Education
650 W. State St.
Boise, ID 83720
Phone: (208) 334-3300

ILLINOIS
Hazel Loucks
Assistant to the Governor for Education
Ofc. of the Governor
2 1/2 State House
Springfield, IL 62706
Phone: (217) 524-1145
Fax: (217) 524-1678

INDIANA
Suellen Reed
Superintendent of Public Instruction
Dept. of Education
State House, Rm. 227
Indianapolis, IN 46204
Phone: (317) 232-6665
Fax: (317) 232-8004

IOWA
Nina Carran
Chief
Bur. of Instructional Services
Dept. Of Education
Grimes State Ofc. Bldg.
E. 14th & Grand Aves.
Des Moines, IA 50319
Phone: (515) 281-3061

KANSAS
Andy Tompkins
Commissioner
State Board of Education
120 E. 10th St.
Topeka, KS 66612-1182
Phone: (785) 296-3201
Fax: (785) 296-7933

KENTUCKY
Wilmer S. Cody
Commissioner
Dept. of Education
Capitol Plz. Tower, 1st Fl.
500 Mero St.
Frankfort, KY 40601
Phone: (502) 564-3141
Fax: (502) 564-5680

LOUISIANA
Cecil Picard
Superintendent
Dept. of Education
P.O. Box 94064
Baton Rouge, LA 70804
Phone: (225) 342-3602
Fax: (225) 342-7316

MAINE

MARYLAND
Margaret Trader
Assistant State Superintendent
Div. of Instruction & Staff Dev.
State Dept. of Education
200 W. Baltimore St.
Baltimore, MD 21201
Phone: (410) 767-0316
Fax: (410) 333-2379

MASSACHUSETTS
David Driscoll
Commissioner
Dept. of Education
350 Main St.
Malden, MA 02148
Phone: (781) 388-3300
Fax: (781) 388-3392

MICHIGAN
Diane Smolen
Director
Ofc. of School Program Services
Dept. of Education
P.O. Box 30008
Lansing, MI 48909
Phone: (517) 373-0048

MINNESOTA
Christine Jax
Commissioner
Dept. of Children, Families & Learning
550 Cedar St., 7th Fl.
Minneapolis, MN 55101
Phone: (651) 582-8204
Fax: (651) 582-8724

MISSISSIPPI
James Easom
Executive Director
Div. of Textbooks
Dept. of Education
P.O. Box 771
636 N. President St.
Jackson, MS 39205
Phone: (601) 359-2791
Fax: (601) 359-1950

MISSOURI
B.J. Stockton
Director
Administration & Accountability Services
Dept. of Elementary & Secondary Education
P.O. Box 480
Jefferson City, MO 65102
Phone: (573) 751-8465
Fax: (573) 526-4261
E-mail: bstockto@mail.dese.state.mo.us

MONTANA

NEBRASKA
Ann Masters
Administrator
Curriculum Instruction Program
Dept. of Education
P.O. Box 94987
Lincoln, NE 68509-4987
Phone: (402) 471-4816
Fax: (402) 471-0117

NEVADA

NEW HAMPSHIRE
David Gebhardt
Education Consultant for Public Schools
Educational Improvement
Education Dept.
101 Pleasant St.
Concord, NH 03301-3860
Phone: (603) 271-3759

NEW JERSEY

NEW MEXICO
Mary Jane Vinella
Bureau Chief
Instructional Materials Div.
Dept. of Education
State Instructional Materials
120 S. Federal Pl., Rm. 206
Santa Fe, NM 87501
Phone: (505) 827-1801
Fax: (505) 827-1826

NEW YORK
Richard P. Mills
Commissioner
State Education Dept.
89 Washington Ave., Rm. 111
Albany, NY 12234
Phone: (518) 474-6569
Fax: (518) 473-4909

NORTH CAROLINA
H. David Bryant
Chair
Textbook Comm.
Dept. of Public Instruction
301 N. Wilmington St.
Raleigh, NC 27601-2825
Phone: (919) 715-1000

NORTH DAKOTA
Wayne G. Sanstead
State Superintendent
Dept. of Public Instruction
600 E. Blvd. Ave., 11th Fl.
Bismarck, ND 58505-0440
Phone: (701) 328-2260
Fax: (701) 328-2461
E-mail: wsanstea@mail.dpi.state.nd.us

NORTHERN MARIANA ISLANDS
Ana C. Larson
Deputy Commissioner of Instruction
Curriculum & Instruction
Public School System
P.O. Box 1370 CK
Saipan, MP 96950
Phone: (670) 664-3721
Fax: (670) 664-3796
E-mail: pss.ci@saipan.com

OHIO
Annie Chapman
Document Mgmt. Services
Dept. of Education
65 S. Front St., 10th Fl.
Columbus, OH 43266-0308
Phone: (614) 466-3151
Fax: (614) 752-3956

Robert L. Moore
Assistant Superintendent
School Results & Accountability
Dept. of Education
65 S. Front St., Rm. 810
Columbus, OH 43266-0308
Phone: (614) 466-5834
Fax: (614) 644-5960

OKLAHOMA
Betty Miller
Director
Dept. of Education
2500 N. Lincoln Blvd.
Oklahoma City, OK 73105
Phone: (405) 521-3456
Fax: (405) 521-6205
E-mail: betty_miller@mail.sde.state.ok.us

OREGON
Joanne Flint
Assistant Superintendent
Ofc. of Curriculum Instruction & Field Services
Dept. of Education
255 Capitol St., NE
Salem, OR 97310
Phone: (503) 378-8004
Fax: (503) 373-7968

PENNSYLVANIA
Michael J. Kozup
Director
Bur. of Curriculum & Academic Service
Dept. of Education
333 Market St., 8th Fl.
Harrisburg, PA 17126-0333
Phone: (717) 787-8913
Fax: (717) 772-3621

PUERTO RICO
Francisco Rodriquez
Director
Textbook Approval
Dept. of Education
P.O. Box 190759
San Juan, PR 00919-0759
Phone: (787) 754-8610
Fax: (787) 753-7926

RHODE ISLAND
Peter McWalters
Commissioner
Dept. of Elementary & Secondary Education
255 Westminster St.
Providence, RI 02903-3400
Phone: (401) 222-2031

SOUTH CAROLINA
Luther W. Seabrook
Senior Executive Assistant for Curriculum
State Dept. of Education
1429 Senate St.
Columbia, SC 29201
Phone: (803) 734-8396

SOUTH DAKOTA
Ray Christensen
Secretary
Dept. of Education & Cultural Affairs
700 Governors Dr.
Pierre, SD 57501
Phone: (605) 773-5669
Fax: (605) 773-6139

TENNESSEE
Larry Gregory
Director
Textbook Services
Dept. of Education
Andrew Johnson Tower, 5th Fl.
Nashville, TN 37247
Phone: (615) 532-6279
Fax: (615) 532-8536

TEXAS
Robert H. Leos
Senior Director
Textbook Div.
Education Agency
1701 N. Congress Ave.
Austin, TX 78701
Phone: (512) 463-9601
Fax: (512) 475-8728
E-mail: rleos@tmail.tea.state.tx.us

U.S. VIRGIN ISLANDS
Rosalia Payne
Superintendent of Schools
Dept. of Education
44-46 Kongens Gade
St. Thomas, VI 00802
Phone: (340) 775-2250
Fax: (340) 775-7381

UTAH
Shawna Stewart
Associate Textbook Adoption Specialist
Instructional Services
Ofc. of Education
250 E. 5th St.
Salt Lake City, UT 84111
Phone: (801) 538-7783
Fax: (801) 538-7521

VERMONT
Marc Hull
Commissioner
Dept. of Education
120 State St.
Montpelier, VT 05620
Phone: (802) 828-3135
Fax: (802) 828-3140

VIRGINIA
Paul D. Stapleton
Superintendent of Public Instruction
Dept. of Education
Monroe Bldg., 25th Fl.
101 N. 14th St.
Richmond, VA 23219
Phone: (804) 225-2023
Fax: (804) 371-2099

WASHINGTON

WEST VIRGINIA
Keith Smith
Director
Div. of Instructional & Student Services
Bldg. 6, Rm. 358
1900 Kanawha Blvd., E.
Charleston, WV 25302-0330
Phone: (304) 558-2691
Fax: (304) 558-0048

WISCONSIN
John Fortier
Assistant Superintendent
Learning Supplies & Instructional Services
Dept. of Public Instruction
125 S. Webster
P.O. Box 7841
Madison, WI 53703
Phone: (608) 266-3361
Fax: (608) 264-9553

WYOMING
Judy Catchpole
Superintendent of Public Instruction
Dept. of Education
Hathaway Bldg., 2nd Fl.
2300 Capitol Ave.
Cheyenne, WY 82002-0050
Phone: (307) 777-7675
Fax: (307) 777-6234

Tourism

Coordinates promotional and advertising programs for the tourism industry in the state.

ALABAMA
Francis Smiley
Director
Dept. of Education & Travel
401 Adams Ave., Ste. 126
Montgomery, AL 36104
Phone: (334) 242-4413
Fax: (334) 242-4554

ALASKA
Tom Garrett
Director
Div. of Tourism
Dept. of Commerce & Economic Dev.
P.O. Box 110801
Juneau, AK 99811-0801
Phone: (907) 465-2012
Fax: (907) 465-2287

AMERICAN SAMOA
John Faumuina, Jr.
Director
Economic Dev. & Planning Ofc.
Dept. of Commerce
Pago Pago, AS 96799
Phone: (684) 633-5155
Fax: (684) 633-4195

ARIZONA
Mark McDermott
Director
Ofc. of Tourism
2702 N. 3rd St., #4015
Phoenix, AZ 85004
Phone: (602) 248-1490
Fax: (602) 248-4600

ARKANSAS
Joe Rice
Director
Tourism Div.
Dept. of Parks & Tourism
1 Capitol Mall
Little Rock, AR 72201
Phone: (501) 682-1088
Fax: (501) 682-1364

CALIFORNIA
John Poimiroo
Director
Ofc. of Tourism
801 K St., Ste. 1600
Sacramento, CA 95814
Phone: (916) 322-5639

COLORADO

CONNECTICUT
Ed Dombroskas
Executive Director
Ofc. of Tourism
Dept. of Economic Dev.
865 Brook St.
Rocky Hill, CT 06067
Phone: (860) 270-8075

DELAWARE
Darrell J. Ninott
Acting Director
Economic Dev. Ofc.
P.O. Box 1401
Dover, DE 19901
Phone: (302) 739-4271
Fax: (302) 739-5749

DISTRICT OF COLUMBIA
Lewis Dawley
General Manager
Washington Convention Ctr.
900 9th St., NW
Washington, DC 20004
Phone: (202) 371-3021
Fax: (202) 789-8365

Daniel Mobley
President
Visitors & Convention Association
1212 New York Ave., NW, Ste. 600
Washington, DC 20005
Phone: (202) 789-7000

Ann Pina
Acting Director
Ofc. of Tourism & Promotions
1212 New York Ave., NW, Ste. 200
Washington, DC 20005

Melanie Suggs
Executive Director
Cmte. to Promote Washington
1212 New York Ave., NW, Ste. 200
Washington, DC 20005-3987
Phone: (202) 724-5644

FLORIDA
Austin Mott, III
Vice President
Visit FL
Div. of Tourism
P.O. Box 1100
Tallahassee, FL 32302
Phone: (850) 488-5607
Fax: (850) 414-9732

GEORGIA
Hanna M. Ledford
Deputy Commissioner
Tourist Div.
Industry, Trade & Tourism
285 Peachtree Ctr. Ave., #1000
Atlanta, GA 30303
Phone: (404) 656-3589

GUAM
James E. Nelson
General Manager
Visitors Bur.
401 Pale San Vitores, Tumon
P.O. Box 3520
Hagatna, GU 96932
Phone: (671) 646-5278
Fax: (671) 646-8861
E-mail: gvbrm@ite.net

HAWAII
Seiji Naya
Director
Dept. of Business, Economic Dev. & Tourism
250 S. Hotel St., 5th Fl.
Honolulu, HI 96813
Phone: (808) 586-2355
Fax: (808) 586-2377

IDAHO
Carl G. Wilgus
Administrator
Tourism Dev.
Dept. of Commerce
700 W. State St.
Boise, ID 83720
Phone: (208) 334-2470

ILLINOIS
Donna Shaw
Dept. of Commerce & Community Affairs
620 E. Adams St., 3rd Fl.
Springfield, IL 62701
Phone: (217) 782-3233
Fax: (217) 524-0864

INDIANA
John Goss
Director
Tourism Dev.
Dept. of Commerce
1 N. Capitol
Indianapolis, IN 46204
Phone: (317) 232-8870
Fax: (317) 233-6887

IOWA
Nancy Landess
Administrator
Div. of Tourism & Visitors
Dept. of Economic Dev.
200 E. Grand Ave.
Des Moines, IA 50309
Phone: (515) 242-4705

KANSAS
Claudia Larkin
Division Director
Travel, Tourism & Film Services
Dept. of Commerce & Housing
700 SW Harrison Ave., Ste. 1300
Topeka, KS 66612
Phone: (785) 296-2009
Fax: (785) 296-6988

KENTUCKY
Ann Latta
Secretary
Tourism Cabinet
Capital Plz. Tower, 24th Fl.
Frankfort, KY 40601
Phone: (502) 564-4270
Fax: (502) 564-1512

LOUISIANA
Barbara Roy
Assistant Secretary
Ofc. of Tourism
Dept. of Culture, Recreation & Tourism
P.O. Box 94291
Baton Rouge, LA 70804
Phone: (225) 342-8125
Fax: (225) 342-1051

MAINE
Dann H. Lewis
Director
Ofc. of Tourism
Dept. of Economic & Community Dev.
59 State House Station
Augusta, ME 04333-0059
Phone: (207) 287-5711

MARYLAND
Susan Smith-Bauk
Assistant Secretary
Div. of Tourism, Film & the Arts
Dept. of Business & Economic Dev.
217 E. Redwood St., 9th Fl.
Baltimore, MD 21202
Phone: (410) 767-6266
Fax: (410) 333-2065

MASSACHUSETTS
Mary Jane McKenna
Executive Director
Travel & Tourism
Dept. of Ecomomic Dev.
10 Park Plz., Ste. 4510
Boston, MA 02116-3933
Phone: (617) 727-3201
Fax: (617) 727-6525

MICHIGAN
Suzy Avery
Director
Travel Michigan
Economic Dev. Corp.
105 W. Allegan St.
Lansing, MI 48909
Phone: (517) 373-0670

MINNESOTA
Steve Markuson
Director
Ofc. of Tourism
500 Metro Sq.
121 E. 7th Pl.
St. Paul, MN 55101-2146
Phone: (651) 296-2755
Fax: (651) 296-7095
E-mail: steve.markuson@state.mn.us

MISSISSIPPI
George Smith
Director
Div. of Tourism
Dept. of Economic & Community Dev.
P.O. Box 849
Jackson, MS 39205-0849
Phone: (601) 359-3297
Fax: (601) 359-5757

MISSOURI
Christopher Jennings
Director
Div. of Tourism
Dept. of Economic Dev.
Truman Bldg., Rm. 290
P.O. Box 1055
Jefferson City, MO 65102
Phone: (573) 526-5900
Fax: (573) 751-5160
E-mail: cjenning@mail.state.mo.us

MONTANA
Matthew T. Cohn
Travel Director
Travel MT
Dept. of Commerce
1424 9th Ave.
Helena, MT 59620
Phone: (406) 444-2654
Fax: (406) 444-1800

NEBRASKA
David Miller
Director
Div. of Travel & Tourism
Dept. of Economic Dev.
P.O. Box 94666
Lincoln, NE 68509-9466
Phone: (402) 471-3795
Fax: (402) 471-3026

NEVADA
Thomas G. Tait
Executive Director
Comm. on Tourism
401 N. Carson St.
Carson City, NV 89701
Phone: (775) 687-4322
Fax: (775) 687-6779
E-mail: ncot@travelnevada.com

NEW HAMPSHIRE
Lauri Ostrander
Director
Travel & Tourism Dev. Div.
Dept. of Resources & Economic Dev.
P.O. Box 1856
Concord, NH 03302-1856
Phone: (603) 271-2665

NEW JERSEY
Donna Blakelaar
Director
Div. of Travel & Tourism
Dept. of Commerce & Economic Dev.
20 W. State St.
P.O. Box 826
Trenton, NJ 08625
Phone: (609) 292-2496

NEW MEXICO
Janet Green
Secretary
Dept. of Tourism
491 Old Santa Fe Trail
Santa Fe, NM 87503
Phone: (505) 827-7400
Fax: (505) 827-2505

NEW YORK
Charles A. Gargano
Commissioner
Dept. of Economic Dev.
One Commerce Plz., 9th Fl.
Albany, NY 12245
Phone: (518) 474-4100
Fax: (518) 473-9374

NORTH CAROLINA
Gordon Clapp
Director
Travel Dev. Div.
Dept. of Commerce
301 N. Wilmington St.
Raleigh, NC 27601
Phone: (919) 733-4171
Fax: (919) 733-8582

NORTH DAKOTA
Bob Martinson
Director
Dept. of Tourism
604 E. Blvd. Ave.
Bismarck, ND 58505-0820
Phone: (701) 328-2525
Fax: (701) 328-4878
E-mail: bmartins@state.nd.us

NORTHERN MARIANA ISLANDS
Anicia A. Tomokane
Managing Director
Marianas Visitors Bur.
P.O. Box 861
Saipan, MP 96950
Phone: (670) 664-3240
Fax: (670) 664-3237

OHIO
Jim Epperson
Deputy Director
Ofc. of Travel & Tourism
Dept. of Dev.
77 S. High St., 29th Fl.
Columbus, OH 43266
Phone: (614) 466-8844
Fax: (614) 466-6744

OKLAHOMA
Jane Jayroe
Executive Director
Dept. of Tourism & Recreation
15 N. Robinson, Ste. 100
Oklahoma City, OK 73102
Phone: (405) 521-2413
Fax: (405) 521-0569
E-mail: jcraven@otrd.state.ok.us

OREGON
Todd Davidson
Manager
Tourism Div.
Dept. of Economic Dev.
775 Summer St.
Salem, OR 97310
Phone: (503) 986-0007
Fax: (503) 986-0001

PENNSYLVANIA
Fritz Smith
Director
Dept. of Community & Economic Dev.
456 Forum Bldg.
Harrisburg, PA 17120
Phone: (717) 720-1304
Fax: (717) 234-4560

PUERTO RICO
Jorge Davila
Director
Tourism Comm.
P.O. Box 4435
San Juan, PR 00903
Phone: (787) 721-2400
Fax: (787) 722-6238

RHODE ISLAND
David C. DePetrillo
Director of Tourism
Economic Dev. Corp.
1 W. Exchange St.
Providence, RI 02903-1058
Phone: (401) 222-2601

SOUTH CAROLINA
William R. Jennings
Director
Dept. of Parks, Recreation & Tourism
1205 Pendleton St.
Columbia, SC 29201
Phone: (803) 734-0166

SOUTH DAKOTA
Patty VanGerpen
Secretary
Dept. of Tourism
Capitol Lake Plz.
711 E. Wells Ave.
Pierre, SD 57501
Phone: (605) 773-3301
Fax: (605) 773-3256

TENNESSEE
John Wade
Commissioner
Dept. of Tourist Dev.
320 6th Ave., N.
Nashville, TN 37243
Phone: (615) 741-9001
Fax: (615) 532-0477

TEXAS
Tracye McDaniel
Deputy Executive Director
Dept. of Economic Dev.
P.O. Box 12728
Austin, TX 78711
Phone: (512) 462-9191
Fax: (512) 936-0088

U.S. VIRGIN ISLANDS
Clement C. Magras
Acting Commissioner of Tourism
Dept. of Tourism
Elainco Bldg.
78-1-2-3 Contant
St. Thomas, VI 00802
Phone: (340) 774-8784
Fax: (340) 777-4390

UTAH
Dean Reeder
Director
Div. of Travel Dev.
Dept. of Community & Economic Dev.
Council Hall/Capitol Hill
Salt Lake City, UT 84114
Phone: (801) 538-1370
Fax: (801) 538-1399
E-mail: dreeder@travel.state.ut.us

VERMONT
Thomas Altemus
Commissioner
Agency of Dev. & Community Affairs
Tourism & Marketing Dept.
6 Baldwin St.
Montpelier, VT 05602
Phone: (802) 828-3649
Fax: (802) 828-3233

VIRGINIA
Mark R. Kilduff
Executive Director
Economic Dev. Partnership
W. Tower, 19th Fl.
901 E. Byrd St.
Richmond, VA 23219
Phone: (804) 371-8108
Fax: (804) 371-8112

WASHINGTON
Robin Pollard
Director
Tourism Dev.
Dept. of Trade & Economic Dev.
P.O. Box 42500
Olympia, WA 98504-2500
Phone: (360) 753-5601
Fax: (360) 753-4470

WEST VIRGINIA
Robert A. Reintsema
Commissioner
Div. of Tourism & Parks
2101 Washington St., E.
Charleston, WV 25305
Phone: (304) 558-2200
Fax: (304) 558-2956

WISCONSIN
Moose Speros
Secretary
Dept. of Tourism
201 W. Washington, 2nd Fl.
P.O. Box 7976
Madison, WI 53707-7976
Phone: (608) 266-2345
Fax: (608) 266-3403

WYOMING
Bill Gentle
Director
Tourism Div.
Dept. of Commerce
I-25 @ College Dr.
Cheyenne, WY 82002
Phone: (307) 777-7777

Training and Development—

Responsible for the training and development of state employees.

ALABAMA
Sharleen Smith
Manager of Training
Training Div.
State Personnel
64 N. Union St., Ste. 300
Montgomery, AL 36130-4100
Phone: (334) 242-3389
Fax: (334) 353-3030

ALASKA
Mike McMullen
Personnel Manager
Div. of Personnel
Dept. of Administration
P.O. Box 110201
Juneau, AK 99811-0201
Phone: (907) 465-4430
Fax: (907) 465-2576

AMERICAN SAMOA
Sapini Siatu'u
Director
Dept. of Human Resources
AS Govt.
Pago Pago, AS 96799
Phone: (684) 633-4485
Fax: (684) 633-1139

ARIZONA
James Matthews
Human Resources Director
Personnel Div.
Dept. of Administration
1831 W. Jefferson
Phoenix, AZ 85007
Phone: (602) 542-5482
Fax: (602) 542-2796

ARKANSAS
Carol H. Philpott
Director
Inter-Agency Training Program
Dept. of Finance & Administration
P.O. Box 3278
Little Rock, AR 72203
Phone: (501) 682-2252
Fax: (501) 682-5094

CALIFORNIA
Mary Fernandez
Division Chief
Training & Dev. Div.
Dept. of Personnel Administration
1515 S St., N. Bldg., Ste. 105
Sacramento, CA 95814-7243
Phone: (916) 445-5121

COLORADO
Rick Garcia
Director
Organizational Dev. & Direct Services
Support Services
Dept. of Personnel
1313 Sherman St., Rm. 115
Denver, CO 80203
Phone: (303) 866-2438
Fax: (303) 866-2334

CONNECTICUT
Christina Lawson
Director
Human Resources
Dept. of Adm. Services
165 Capitol Ave.
Hartford, CT 06106
Phone: (860) 713-5025

DELAWARE
Joe Hickey
Manager
State Personnel Ofc.
Employee Dev.
820 N. French St., 6th Fl.
Wilmington, DE 19801
Phone: (302) 577-3950
Fax: (302) 577-3996

DISTRICT OF COLUMBIA

FLORIDA
Sharon Larson
Director
Human Resource Mgmt.
Dept. of Mgmt. Services
4050 Esplanade Way, Bldg. 4040, Ste. 360
Tallahassee, FL 32399-0950
Phone: (850) 922-5449
Fax: (850) 921-4117

GEORGIA
Diane Schlachter
Director
Training & Organizational Dev.
Merit System
529A Church St.
Decatur, GA 30030-2515
Phone: (404) 371-7371

GUAM
Michael J. Reidy
Director
Dept. of Administration
P.O. Box 884
Hagatna, GU 96932
Phone: (671) 475-1101
Fax: (671) 477-6788

HAWAII
Vacant
Chief
Training & Safety Div.
Dept. of Human Resources Dev.
235 S. Beretania St., #1500
Honolulu, HI 96813-2437
Phone: (808) 587-1058
Fax: (808) 587-1107

IDAHO
Connie Pratt
Training Officer
Personnel Comm.
700 W. State St.
Boise, ID 83720
Phone: (208) 334-3346

ILLINOIS
Diane Hurrelbrink
Manager
Bur. of Personnel Agency Services
Dept. of Central Mgmt. Services
503 Stratton Ofc. Bldg.
401 S. Spring
Springfield, IL 62706
Phone: (217) 782-3379
Fax: (217) 524-0836

INDIANA
David Bryant
Training Director
Training Div.
Dept. of Personnel
402 W. Washington, Rm. W-161
Indianapolis, IN 46204
Phone: (317) 232-3262
Fax: (317) 232-3089

IOWA
Sallie Nostwich
Administrative Assistant
Personnel Dev. Seminars
Dept. of Personnel
Grimes State Ofc. Bldg.
E. 14th & Grand Aves.
Des Moines, IA 50319
Phone: (515) 281-6382

KANSAS
Sandra Lassley
Staff Development Specialist
Personnel & Training Services
Dept. of Human Resources
401 SW Topeka Blvd.
Topeka, KS 66603-3182
Phone: (785) 296-6673
Fax: (785) 296-8177

KENTUCKY
Robert Peters
Executive Director
Governmental Services Ctr.
Kentucky State Univ.
Academic Services Bldg, 4th Fl.
Frankfort, KY 40601
Phone: (502) 564-8170
Fax: (502) 564-2732

LOUISIANA
Sam Breen
Administrator
Comprehensive Public Training Program
Div. of Administration
P.O. Box 94095
Baton Rouge, LA 70804
Phone: (225) 342-7002
Fax: (225) 219-4191

MAINE
Elaine Trubee
Director
State Training & Dev. Program
Dept. of Adm. & Financial Services
4 State House Station
Augusta, ME 04333
Phone: (207) 287-4400

MARYLAND
Joann McCorkle-Smith
Director
Employment Dev. & Training Institute
Dept. of Budget & Mgmt.
300 W. Preston St., Rm. 308
Baltimore, MD 21201
Phone: (410) 767-4028
Fax: (410) 333-5764
E-mail: jmsmitrh @dbm.state.md.us

MASSACHUSETTS
Jack King
Deputy Director
Div. of Employment & Training
19 Staniford St., 3rd Fl.
Boston, MA 02114
Phone: (617) 626-6600
Fax: (617) 727-0315

MICHIGAN

MINNESOTA
Linda Draze
Manager
Training & Dev. Div.
Dept. of Employee Relations
658 Cedar St.
St. Paul, MN 55155
Phone: (651) 296-2380
Fax: (651) 297-8118
E-mail: linda.draze @state.mn.us

MISSISSIPPI
Marianne Gaudin
Division Director
Training Div.
State Personnel Board
301 N. Lamar, Ste. 100
Jackson, MS 39201
Phone: (601) 359-2781
Fax: (601) 359-2729

MISSOURI
Terry McAdams
Section Manager for Employee Development
Div. of Personnel
Ofc. of Administration
Truman Bldg., Rm. 430
P.O. Box 388
Jefferson City, MO 65102
Phone: (573) 751-4514
Fax: (573) 751-8641
E-mail: mcadat @mail.oa.state.mo.us

MONTANA
John Moore
Director
Professional Dev. Ctr.
Dept. of Administration
Mitchell Bldg., Rm. 130
125 Roberts
Helena, MT 59620
Phone: (406) 444-3871
Fax: (406) 444-0544

NEBRASKA
Sherri Wines
Acting Director
Div. of Personnel
Dept. of Adm. Services
P.O. Box 94905
Lincoln, NE 68509
Phone: (402) 471-2075
Fax: (402) 471-3754

NEVADA
John Hastings
Training Manager
Personnel Training
209 E. Musser St., Rm. 101
Carson City, NV 89701
Phone: (775) 687-4120
Fax: (775) 687-1868
E-mail: jhastings @personnel.state.nv.us

NEW HAMPSHIRE
Peter Gamache
Training Coordinator
Div. of Personnel
Adm. Services
25 Capitol St., Rm. 1
Concord, NH 03301-6395
Phone: (603) 271-2833

NEW JERSEY
Gregory J. Smiles
Acting Director
Human Resource Dev. Institute
Dept. of Personnel
P.O. Box 318
Trenton, NJ 08625-0318
Phone: (609) 777-1552
Fax: (609) 777-3810
E-mail: csgsmil @dop.state.nj.us

NEW MEXICO
Alex Valdez
Secretary
Dept. of Human Services
P.O. Box 2348
Santa Fe, NM 87504
Phone: (505) 827-7750
Fax: (505) 827-6286

NEW YORK
George C. Sinnott
Commissioner & President
Dept. of Civil Service
State Campus, Bldg. 1, 2nd Fl.
Albany, NY 12239
Phone: (518) 457-3701
Fax: (518) 457-7547

NORTH CAROLINA
Jack Lemons
Interim Director
Personnel Dev. Ctr.
101 W. Peace St.
Raleigh, NC 27603
Phone: (919) 733-2474
Fax: (919) 733-8359

NORTH DAKOTA
Linda Jensen
Director of Training
Training & Dev. Section
Central Personnel Div.
600 E. Blvd. Ave., 14th Fl.
Bismarck, ND 58505-0120
Phone: (701) 328-3290
Fax: (701) 328-1475
E-mail: lijensen@state.nd.us

NORTHERN MARIANA ISLANDS
Luis S. Camacho
Personnel Officer
Ofc. of Personnel Mgmt.
Ofc. of the Governor
Caller Box 10007
Saipan, MP 96950
Phone: (670) 233-9033
Fax: (670) 234-1013

OHIO
Caryl Rice
Administrator
Training & Education Programs
Dept. of Adm. Services
30 E. Broad St., 29th Fl.
Columbus, OH 43215
Phone: (614) 644-3455
Fax: (614) 466-6061

OKLAHOMA
Larry Fisher
Assistant Administrator
Human Resource Dev. Div.
2101 N. Lincoln Blvd.
Oklahoma City, OK 73105
Phone: (405) 521-3083

OREGON
Vicki Nakashima
Manager
Training, Recruitment & Career Services
155 Cottage St., NE
Salem, OR 97310
Phone: (503) 378-3844
Fax: (503) 373-7684

PENNSYLVANIA
Bette H. Williams
Manager
Employee Training & Dev.
Training & Dev. Div.
512 Finance Bldg.
Harrisburg, PA 17120
Phone: (717) 787-3679
Fax: (717) 783-1875

PUERTO RICO
Maribel Rodriguez
Director
Central Ofc. of Personnel Administration
P.O. Box 8476
San Juan, PR 00910
Phone: (787) 721-4300
Fax: (787) 722-3390

RHODE ISLAND
Robert G. Tetreault
Associate Director
Administration & Personnel
Ofc. of Training
1 Capitol Hill
Providence, RI 02908
Phone: (401) 222-2155

SOUTH CAROLINA
Karen Kuehner
Manager
Staff Dev. & Training
Div. of Human Resources Mgmt.
1201 Main St., Ste. 1000
Columbia, SC 29201
Phone: (803) 737-0930

SOUTH DAKOTA
Ellen Zeller
Director
Classification & Training
Bur. of Personnel
Capitol Bldg.
500 E. Capitol Ave.
Pierre, SD 57501
Phone: (605) 773-3461
Fax: (605) 773-5389

TENNESSEE
Rosie C. Wilson
Director
Employee Dev. & EEOC Ofc.
Dept. of Personnel
James K. Polk Bldg., 2nd Fl.
Nashville, TN 37243
Phone: (615) 741-5546
Fax: (615) 532-0728

TEXAS
Barry Bales
Director
Governor's Ctr. for Mgmt. & Dev.
LBJ School of Public Affairs
Univ. of TX at Austin
3100 Lake Austin Blvd., Ste. 3.306
Austin, TX 78703
Phone: (512) 475-8100
Fax: (512) 475-8111

U.S. VIRGIN ISLANDS
Joanne Barry
Director
Div. of Personnel
GERS Complex, 3rd Fl.
48B-50C Konprindsens Gade
St. Thomas, VI 00802
Phone: (340) 774-8588
Fax: (340) 774-6916

UTAH
James N. West
Director
Compensation, Selection & Dev. Div.
Dept. of Human Resource Mgmt.
2120 State Ofc. Bldg.
Salt Lake City, UT 84114-1531
Phone: (801) 538-3075
Fax: (801) 538-3081
E-mail: jwest.pedhrm@state.ut.us

VERMONT
Nancy Simoes
Director
State Human Resources
Dept. of Personnel
Osgood Bldg.
103 S. Main St.
Waterbury, VT 05671
Phone: (802) 241-1114
Fax: (802) 241-1119

VIRGINIA
Sara Redding Wilson
Director
Dept. of Personnel & Training
Monroe Bldg., 12th Fl.
101 N. 14th St.
Richmond, VA 23219
Phone: (804) 225-2237
Fax: (804) 371-7401

WASHINGTON
Scott Turner
Assistant Director
Div. of Human Resources Dev.
Dept. of Personnel
P.O. Box 47530
Olympia, WA 98504-7530
Phone: (360) 586-1342
Fax: (360) 586-6695

WEST VIRGINIA
Willard Max Farley
Assistant Director
Staffing Services
Div. of Personnel
1900 Kanawha Blvd. E., #B416
Charleston, WV 25305-0002
Phone: (304) 558-5946

WISCONSIN
Greg Jones
Administrator
Div. of Affirmative Action
Dept. of Employment Relations
345 W. Washington, 2nd Fl.
Madison, WI 53702
Phone: (608) 266-5709
Fax: (608) 267-1020

WYOMING
Lorraine Ojeda
Training & Dev.
Dept. of Administration & Info.
2001 Capitol Ave.
Cheyenne, WY 82002
Phone: (307) 777-6723

Transportation

Umbrella agency responsible for planning, designing, constructing and maintaining public transportation services and facilities throughout the state.

ALABAMA
G.M. Roberts
Director
Hwy. Dept.
Dept. of Transportation
1409 Coliseum Blvd.
Montgomery, AL 36130
Phone: (334) 242-6111
Fax: (334) 262-8041

ALASKA
Joseph L. Perkins
Commissioner
Dept. of Transportation & Public Facilities
3132 Channel Dr.
Juneau, AK 99801-7898
Phone: (907) 465-3900
Fax: (907) 586-8365

AMERICAN SAMOA
Fa'aua'a Kataferu
Director
Dept. of Port Admin.
Pago Pago, AS 96799
Phone: (684) 633-4116
Fax: (684) 633-2269

ARIZONA
Mary Peters
Director
Dept. of Transportation
206 S. 17th Ave., # 100A
Phoenix, AZ 85007
Phone: (602) 255-7227
Fax: (602) 255-6941

ARKANSAS
Dan Flowers
Director
Dept. of Hwys. & Transportation
P.O. Box 2261
Little Rock, AR 72203
Phone: (501) 569-2211
Fax: (501) 569-2400

CALIFORNIA
James W. Van Loben Sels
Director
Dept. of Transportation
1120 N St., Ste. 1100
Sacramento, CA 95814
Phone: (916) 654-5267

COLORADO
Tom Norton
Executive Director
Dept. of Transportation
4201 E. Arkansas Ave.
Denver, CO 80222
Phone: (303) 757-9201
Fax: (303) 757-9657

CONNECTICUT
James Sullivan
Commissioner
Dept. of Transportation
2800 Berlin Tpke.
Newington, CT 06111
Phone: (860) 594-3000

DELAWARE
Anne P. Canby
Secretary
Dept. of Transportation
P.O. Box 778
Dover, DE 19903
Phone: (302) 739-4303
Fax: (302) 739-5736
E-mail: acanby@smtp.dot.state.de.us

DISTRICT OF COLUMBIA
Arthuro V. Lawson
Acting Director
Dept. of Public Works
2000 14th St., NW, 6th Fl.
Washington, DC 20009
Phone: (202) 939-8000

Deborah Price
Director
Transportation
Dept. of Public Works
2000 14th St., NW
Washington, DC 20009
Phone: (202) 939-8050

FLORIDA
Ken Moorefield
Assistant Secretary
Transportation Policy
Dept. of Transportation
605 Suwannee St.
Tallahassee, FL 32399-0450
Phone: (850) 414-5220
Fax: (850) 488-5526

GEORGIA
Wayne Shackelford
Commissioner
Dept. of Transportation
2 Capitol Sq.
Atlanta, GA 30334
Phone: (404) 656-5206

GUAM
Daniel Lizama
Acting Director
Dept. of Public Works
542 N. Marine Dr.
Tamuning, GU 96911
Phone: (671) 646-3131
Fax: (671) 649-9178

Tony Martinez
Acting General Manager
Mass Transit Authority
236 E. O'Brien Dr.
P.O. Box 2950
Hagatna, GU 96932
Phone: (671) 475-4682
Fax: (671) 477-4600

HAWAII
Kazu Hayashida
Director
Dept. of Transportation
869 Punchbowl St.
Honolulu, HI 96813
Phone: (808) 587-2150
Fax: (808) 587-2167

IDAHO
Dwight Bower
Director
Dept. of Transportation
P.O. Box 7129
Boise, ID 83707
Phone: (208) 334-8800

ILLINOIS
Kirk Brown
Secretary
Dept. of Transportation
Harry R. Hanley Bldg., Rm. 300
2300 S. Dirksen Pkwy.
Springfield, IL 62764
Phone: (217) 782-5597
Fax: (217) 782-6828

INDIANA
Curtis A. Wiley
Commissioner
Dept. of Transportation
IGC-N., Rm. N755
Indianapolis, IN 46204
Phone: (317) 232-5525
Fax: (317) 232-0238

IOWA
Darrel Rensink
Director
Dept. of Transportation
800 Lincoln Way
Ames, IA 50010
Phone: (515) 239-1111
Fax: (515) 239-1639

KANSAS
E. Dean Carlson
Secretary
Dept. of Transportation
Docking State Ofc. Bldg.
915 Harrison, 7th Fl.
Topeka, KS 66612-1568
Phone: (785) 296-3566
Fax: (785) 296-1095

KENTUCKY
James C. Codell, III
Secretary
Transportation Cabinet
State Ofc. Bldg., 10th Fl.
Frankfort, KY 40601
Phone: (502) 564-4890
Fax: (502) 564-4809

LOUISIANA
Kam Movassaghi
Secretary
Dept. of Transportation & Dev.
P.O. Box 94245
Baton Rouge, LA 70804
Phone: (225) 379-1201
Fax: (225) 379-1851

MAINE
John Melrose
Commissioner
Dept. of Transportation
16 State House Station
Augusta, ME 04333
Phone: (207) 287-2551

MARYLAND
John D. Porcari
Secretary
Ofc. of the Secretary
Dept. of Transportation
P.O. Box 8755
Baltimore, MD 21240
Phone: (410) 865-1000
Fax: (410) 865-1334

MASSACHUSETTS
Kevin Sullivan
Secretary
Executive Ofc. of Transportation & Construction
10 Park Plz., Rm. 3170
Boston, MA 02116
Phone: (617) 973-8080
Fax: (617) 973-8445

MICHIGAN
James R. De Sana
Director
Dept. of Transportation
425 W. Ottawa
Lansing, MI 48909
Phone: (517) 373-2114
Fax: (517) 373-5457

MINNESOTA
Elwyn Tinklenberg
Commissioner
Dept. of Transportation
Transportation Bldg., 4th Fl.
395 John Ireland Blvd.
St. Paul, MN 55155
Phone: (651) 297-2930
Fax: (651) 296-3587

MISSISSIPPI
Kenneth Warren
Executive Director
Dept. of Transportation
401 N. West St.
Jackson, MS 39201
Phone: (601) 359-7001
Fax: (601) 359-7050

MISSOURI
Henry Hungerbeeler
Director
Dept. of Transportation
Support Ctr.
P.O. Box 270
Jefferson City, MO 65102
Phone: (573) 751-4622
Fax: (573) 526-5419
E-mail: hungeh@mail.modot.state.mo.us

MONTANA
Marvin Dye
Director
Dept. of Transportation
2701 Prospect Ave.
Helena, MT 59620
Phone: (406) 444-6201
Fax: (406) 444-7643

NEBRASKA
John Craig
Director
Dept. of Rds.
P.O. Box 94759
Lincoln, NE 68509
Phone: (402) 479-4615
Fax: (402) 479-4325

NEVADA
Tom Stephens
Director
Dept. of Transportation
1263 S. Stewart St., Rm. 201
Carson City, NV 89712
Phone: (775) 888-7440
Fax: (775) 888-7201

NEW HAMPSHIRE
Leon S. Kenison
Commissioner
Dept. of Transportation
P.O. Box 483
Concord, NH 03302-0483
Phone: (603) 271-3734
Fax: (603) 271-3914

NEW JERSEY
James Weinstein
Commissioner of Transportation
Dept. of Transportation
1035 Pkwy. Ave.
P.O. Box 600
Trenton, NJ 08625-0600
Phone: (609) 530-3536
Fax: (609) 530-3894

NEW MEXICO
Pete Rahn
Secretary
Dept. of Hwys. & Transportation
P.O. Box 1149
Santa Fe, NM 87504
Phone: (505) 827-5110
Fax: (505) 827-5469

NEW YORK
Joseph Boardman
Commissioner
Dept. of Transportation
State Ofc. Bldg. Campus, Bldg. 5
Albany, NY 12232
Phone: (518) 457-4422
Fax: (518) 457-5583

NORTH CAROLINA
Norris Tolson
Secretary
Dept. of Transportation
1 S. Wilmington St.
Raleigh, NC 27601-1494
Phone: (919) 733-2520
Fax: (919) 733-9150

NORTH DAKOTA
Marshall W. Moore
Director
Dept. of Transportation
608 E. Blvd. Ave.
Bismarck, ND 58505-0700
Phone: (701) 328-2500
Fax: (701) 328-1420
E-mail: mmoore@state.nd.us

NORTHERN MARIANA ISLANDS
Edward M. Deleon Guerrero
Secretary
Dept. of Public Works
Lower Base
P.O. Box 2950
Saipan, MP 96950
Phone: (670) 235-5827
Fax: (670) 235-5253

OHIO
Gordon Proctor
Director
Dept. of Transportation
1980 W. Broad St.
Columbus, oh 43223
Phone: (614) 466-2335
Fax: (614) 644-0587

OKLAHOMA
Neal McCaleb
Director
Dept. of Transportation
200 NE 21st St.
Oklahoma City, OK 73105
Phone: (405) 521-2631
Fax: (405) 521-2093

OREGON
Grace Crunican
Director
Dept. of Transportation
135 Transportation Bldg.
355 Capitol St.
Salem, OR 97310
Phone: (503) 986-3200
Fax: (503) 986-4264

PENNSYLVANIA
Bradley Mallory
Secretary
Dept. of Transportation
Forum Pl., 9th Fl.
555 Walnut St.
Harrisburg, PA 17105
Phone: (717) 787-5574
Fax: (717) 787-5491

PUERTO RICO
Carlos Pesquera
Secretary
Transportation Dept.
P.O. Box 41269
San Juan, PR 00940-1269
Phone: (787) 722-2929
Fax: (787) 728-8963

RHODE ISLAND
William Ankner
Director
Dept. of Transportation
Two Capitol Hill
Providence, RI 02908
Phone: (401) 222-2481
Fax: (401) 222-6038

SOUTH CAROLINA
Elizabeth S. Mabry
Executive Director
Dept. of Transportation
955 Park St.
P.O. Box 191
Columbia, SC 29202
Phone: (803) 737-1302

SOUTH DAKOTA
Ron Wheeler
Secretary
Dept. of Transportation
700 E. Broadway
Pierre, SD 57501
Phone: (605) 773-3265
Fax: (605) 773-3921

TENNESSEE
Bruce Saltsman
Commissioner
Dept. of Transportation
700 James K. Polk Bldg.
Nashville, TN 37243
Phone: (615) 741-2848
Fax: (615) 741-2508

TEXAS
Charles Heald
Executive Director
Dept. of Transportation
D.C. Greer Bldg., 2nd Fl.
125 E. 11th St.
Austin, TX 78701
Phone: (512) 305-9509
Fax: (512) 305-9567

U.S. VIRGIN ISLANDS
Ian Williams
Director
Div. of Transportation
Dept. of Property & Procurement
Sub Base, Bldg. 1
St. Thomas, VI 00802
Phone: (340) 774-0388
Fax: (340) 774-1163

UTAH
Thomas R. Warne
Executive Director
Administration
Dept. of Transportation
4501 S. 2700 W.
Salt Lake City, UT 84119-5998
Phone: (801) 965-4113
Fax: (801) 965-4338
E-mail: twarne@dot.state.ut.us

VERMONT
Glenn Gershaneck
Secretary
Agency of Transportation
133 State St.
Montpelier, VT 05633-5001
Phone: (802) 828-2657
Fax: (802) 828-3522

VIRGINIA
Shirley J. Ybarra
Secretary of Transportation
Governor's Cabinet
401 E. Broad St., Rm. 414
Richmond, VA 23219
Phone: (804) 786-8032
Fax: (804) 786-6683

WASHINGTON
Sid Morrison
Secretary
Dept. of Transportation
P.O. Box 47316
Olympia, WA 98504-7316
Phone: (360) 705-7000
Fax: (360) 705-6808

WEST VIRGINIA
Samuel G. Bonasso
Acting Secretary
Dept. of Transportation
Bldg. 5, Rm. A109
Charleston, WV 25305
Phone: (304) 558-0444
Fax: (304) 558-1004

WISCONSIN
Charles Thompson
Secretary
Dept. of Transportation
4802 Sheboygan Ave.
P.O. Box 7910
Madison, WI 53707
Phone: (608) 266-1113
Fax: (608) 266-9912

WYOMING
Gene Roccabruna
Director
Hwy. Safety Div.
Dept. of Transportation
5300 Bishop Blvd.
Cheyenne, WY 82002
Phone: (307) 777-4198

Treasurer

The custodian of all state funds and securities belonging to or held in trust by the states.

ALABAMA
Lucy Baxley (D)
State Treasurer
State Capitol, Rm. S106
P.O. Box 302510
Montgomery, AL 36130-2510
Phone: (334) 242-7500
Fax: (334) 242-7592
E-mail: altreas@alaline.com

ALASKA
Ross Kinney (APPT.)
Deputy Commissioner, Treasury
P.O. Box 110405
Juneau, AK 99811
Phone: (907) 465-4880
Fax: (907) 465-2389
E-mail: ross_kinney@revenue.state.ak.us

AMERICAN SAMOA
Tifi Ale
Treasurer
Dept. of the Treasury
AS Govt.
Pago Pago, AS 96799
Phone: (684) 633-4155
Fax: (684) 633-4100

ARIZONA
Carol Springer (R)
State Treasurer
Treasurer's Ofc.
1700 W. Washington, 1st Fl.
Phoenix, AZ 85007
Phone: (602) 542-1463
Fax: (602) 258-6627

ARKANSAS
Jimmie Lou Fisher (D)
State Treasurer
220 State Capitol
Little Rock, AR 72201
Phone: (501) 682-3835
Fax: (501) 682-3842
E-mail: JLFisher@tres.State.AR.US

CALIFORNIA
Phil Angelides (D)
State Treasurer
915 Capitol Mall, Rm. 110
Sacramento, CA 95814
Phone: (916) 653-2995
Fax: (916) 653-3125

COLORADO
Mike Coffman (R)
State Treasurer
Dept. of Treasury
140 State Capitol Bldg.
Denver, CO 80203
Phone: (303) 866-2441
Fax: (303) 866-2123

CONNECTICUT
Denise Nappier (D)
State Treasurer
33 Elm St.
Hartford, CT 06106-1773
Phone: (860) 702-3001
Fax: (203) 566-8820

DELAWARE
Jack Markell (D)
Treasurer
Thomas Collins Bldg.
540 S. DuPont Hwy., Ste. 4
Dover, DE 19901-4516
Phone: (302) 739-3382
Fax: (302) 739-5635

DISTRICT OF COLUMBIA
Thomas F. Huestis (APPT.)
Treasurer
Ofc. of Finance & Treasury
Ofc. of the Chief Financial Officer
1 Judiciary Sq.
441 4th St., NW, Ste. 360
Washington, DC 20001
Phone: (202) 727-6055
Fax: (202) 727-6049

FLORIDA
Bill Nelson (D)
State Treasurer & Insurance Commissioner
Dept. of Insurance
PL-11, The Capitol
Tallahassee, FL 32399-0300
Phone: (850) 922-3100
Fax: (850) 488-6581

GEORGIA
W. Daniel Ebersole (APPT.)
Treasurer
Ofc. of Treasury & Fiscal Services
1202 W. Tower
200 Piedmont Ave., SE
Atlanta, GA 30334
Phone: (404) 656-2168
Fax: (404) 656-9048

GUAM
Y'Asela A. Pereira
Treasurer
Financial Mgmt. Div.
Dept. of Administration
P.O. Box 884
Hagatna, GU 96932
Phone: (671) 475-1122
Fax: (671) 477-6788

HAWAII
Neal Miyahira (APPT.)
Interim Director of Finance
Dept. of Budget & Finance
P.O. Box 150
Honolulu, HI 96810
Phone: (808) 586-1518
Fax: (808) 586-1976

IDAHO
Ron Crane (R)
State Treasurer
102 State Capitol
Boise, ID 83720
Phone: (208) 334-3200
Fax: (208) 334-2543

ILLINOIS
Judy Baar Topinka (R)
State Treasurer
219 State House
Springfield, IL 62706
Phone: (217) 782-2211
Fax: (217) 785-2777

INDIANA
Tim Berry (R)
Treasurer
State House, Rm. 242
200 W. Washington St.
Indianapolis, IN 46204
Phone: (317) 232-6386
Fax: (317) 233-1928

IOWA
Michael L. Fitzgerald (D)
State Treasurer
State Capitol Bldg.
Des Moines, IA 50319
Phone: (515) 281-5366
Fax: (515) 281-6962

KANSAS
Tim Shallenburger
State Treasurer
Landon State Ofc. Bldg.
900 SW Jackson St., Rm. 201-N
Topeka, KS 66612-1235
Phone: (785) 296-3171
Fax: (785) 296-9750

KENTUCKY
John Kennedy Hamilton (D)
State Treasurer
Capitol Annex, Rm. 183
Frankfort, KY 40601
Phone: (502) 564-4722
Fax: (502) 564-6545

LOUISIANA
Ken Duncan (D)
State Treasurer
P.O. Box 44154
Baton Rouge, LA 70804-0154
Phone: (225) 342-0010
Fax: (225) 342-0046
E-mail: kendunc@treasury.state.la.us

MAINE
Dale McCormick (elected by the Legislature)
State Treasurer
State Ofc. Bldg., Rm. 318
39 State House Station
Augusta, ME 04333
Phone: (207) 287-2771
Fax: (207) 287-2367
E-mail: dale.mccormick@state.me.us

MARYLAND
Richard N. Dixon
(elected by the Legislature)
Treasurer
Ofc. of the State Treasurer
State Treasurer's Ofc.
Treasury Bldg., Rm. 109
Annapolis, MD 21401-1991
Phone: (410) 260-7160
Fax: (410) 974-3530
E-mail: rdixon@treasurer.state.md.us

MASSACHUSETTS
Shannon O'Brien (D)
State Treasurer
Rm. 227 - State House
Boston, MA 02133
Phone: (617) 367-6900
Fax: (617) 248-0372

MICHIGAN
Mark Murray (APPT.)
Treasurer
Dept. of Treasury
P.O. Box 11097
Lansing, MI 48901
Phone: (517) 373-3223
Fax: (517) 335-1785

MINNESOTA
Carol Johnson (DFL)
Treasurer
303 Administration Bldg.
50 Sherburne Ave.
St. Paul, MN 55155
Phone: (651) 296-7091
Fax: (651) 296-8615

MISSISSIPPI
Marshall G. Bennett (D)
State Treasurer
Dept. of Treasury
Sillers State Ofc. Bldg., Ste. 404
P.O. Box 138
Jackson, MS 39205
Phone: (601) 359-3600
Fax: (601) 359-2001
E-mail: mbennett@treas.state.ms.us

MISSOURI
Bob Holden (D)
State Treasurer
State Capitol, Rm. 229
P.O. Box 210
Jefferson City, MO 65102
Phone: (573) 751-2411
Fax: (573) 751-9443
E-mail: BOB_HOLDEN@mail.sto.state.mo.us

MONTANA
Lois A. Menzies (APPT.)
Director & Ex Officio State Treasurer
Dept. of Administration
Rm. 155, Mitchell Bldg.
P.O. Box 200101
Helena, MT 59620-0101
Phone: (406) 444-2032
Fax: (406) 444-2812
E-mail: lmenzies@mt.gov

NEBRASKA
David E. Heineman (R)
State Treasurer
State Capitol, Rm. 2003
P.O. Box 94788
Lincoln, NE 68509-4788
Phone: (402) 471-2455
Fax: (402) 471-4390

NEVADA
Brian Krolicki (R)
State Treasurer
101 N. Carson St., Ste. 4
Carson City, NV 89701
Phone: (775) 684-5600
Fax: (775) 684-5623
E-mail: bkkrolicki@treasurer.state.nv.us

NEW HAMPSHIRE
Georgie A. Thomas (R)
(elected by the Legislature)
State Treasurer
121 State House Annex
Concord, NH 03301
Phone: (603) 271-2621
Fax: (603) 271-3922
E-mail: gthomas@tec.nh.us

NEW JERSEY
James A. Di Eleuterio, Jr. (APPT.)
State Treasurer
125 W. State St.
P.O. Box 002
Trenton, NJ 08625-0002
Phone: (609) 292-6748
Fax: (609) 984-3888

NEW MEXICO
Michael A. Montoya (D)
State Treasurer
P.O. Box 608
Santa Fe, NM 87504-0608
Phone: (505) 827-6400
Fax: (505) 827-6395

NEW YORK
George H. Gasser (APPT.)
Treasurer
Dept. of Taxation & Finance
P.O. Box 7002
Albany, NY 12225
Phone: (518) 474-4250
Fax: (518) 473-9163

NORTH CAROLINA
Harlan E. Boyles (D)
State Treasurer
Albemarle Bldg.
325 N. Salisbury St.
Raleigh, NC 27603-1385
Phone: (919) 508-5176
Fax: (919) 508-5167
E-mail: harlan_boyles@treasurer.state.nc.us

NORTH DAKOTA
Kathi Gilmore (D)
Treasurer
Ofc. of State Treasurer
600 E. Blvd. Ave., 3rd Fl.
Bismarck, ND 58505-0600
Phone: (701) 328-2643
Fax: (701) 328-3002
E-mail: kgilmore@pioneer.state.nd.us

NORTHERN MARIANA ISLANDS
Antoinette Calvo
Acting Treasurer
Ofc. of the Governor
Dept. of Finance
P.O. Box 5234, CHRB
Saipan, MP 96950
Phone: (670) 664-1300
Fax: (670) 322-4643

OHIO
Joseph T. Deters (R)
State Treasurer
30 E. Broad St., 9th Fl.
Columbus, OH 43266-0421
Phone: (614) 466-2160
Fax: (614) 644-7313

OKLAHOMA
Robert Butkin (D)
State Treasurer
State Capitol Bldg., Rm. 217
Oklahoma City, OK 73105
Phone: (405) 521-3191
Fax: (405) 521-4994
E-mail: Robert.Butkin@oklaosf.state.ok.us

OREGON
Jim Hill (D)
State Treasurer
159 State Capitol
Salem, OR 97310
Phone: (503) 378-4329
Fax: (503) 373-7051

PENNSYLVANIA
Barbara Hafer (R)
State Treasurer
129 Finance Bldg.
Harrisburg, PA 17120
Phone: (717) 787-2465
Fax: (717) 783-9760
E-mail: bhafer@libertynet.org

PUERTO RICO
Xenia Velez Silva
Secretary of the Treasury
Intendente Ramirez Bldg.
P.O. Box 500
San Juan, PR 00905-4515
Phone: (787) 729-0916
Fax: (787) 723-2838

RHODE ISLAND
Paul J. Tavares (D)
Treasurer
State House, Rm. 102
Providence, RI 02903
Phone: (401) 222-2397

SOUTH CAROLINA
Grady L. Patterson, Jr. (D)
State Treasurer
1200 Senate St.
Wade Hampton Bldg., 1st Fl.
Columbia, SC 29201
Phone: (803) 734-2635
Fax: (803) 734-2039

SOUTH DAKOTA
Richard Butler (D)
State Treasurer
212 State Capitol
500 E. Capitol Ave.
Pierre, SD 57501-5070
Phone: (605) 773-3378
Fax: (605) 773-3115
E-mail: dick.butler@state.sd.us

TENNESSEE
Stephen D. Adams
(elected by the Legislature)
State Treasurer
State Capitol, 1st Fl.
Nashville, TN 37219
Phone: (615) 741-2956
Fax: (615) 253-1591
E-mail: sadam s@mail.state.tn.us

TEXAS
Carole Keeton Rylander (R)
Comptroller
Comptroller of Public Accounts
P.O. Box 13528
Austin, TX 78711-3528
Phone: (512) 463-4000
Fax: (512) 463-4965

U.S. VIRGIN ISLANDS
Bernice Turnbull
Acting Commissioner
Dept. of Finance
76 Kronprindsens Gade
St. Thomas, VI 00802
Phone: (340) 774-4114
Fax: (340) 776-4028

UTAH
Edward T. Alter (R)
State Treasurer
215 State Capitol
Salt Lake City, UT 84114
Phone: (801) 538-1042
Fax: (801) 538-1465
E-mail: ealter.stmain @state.ut.us

VERMONT
James H. Douglas (R)
Treasurer
State Administration Bldg., 2nd Fl.
133 State St.
Montpelier, VT 05633-6200
Phone: (802) 828-2301
Fax: (802) 828-2772
E-mail: jdouglas @tre.state.vt.us

VIRGINIA
Mary G. Morris (APPT.)
State Treasurer
Dept. of the Treasury
Monroe Bldg., 3rd Fl.
101 N. 14th St.
Richmond, VA 23219
Phone: (804) 225-2142
Fax: (804) 225-3187

WASHINGTON
Michael J. Murphy (D)
State Treasurer
Legislative Bldg.
P.O. Box 40200
Olympia, WA 98504-0200
Phone: (360) 902-9000
Fax: (360) 902-9044
E-mail: MichaelJ @TRE.WA.GOV

WEST VIRGINIA
John Perdue (D)
State Treasurer
Bldg. 1, Ste. E145
1900 Kanawha Blvd., E.
Charleston, WV 25305-0860
Phone: (304) 558-5000

WISCONSIN
Jack C. Voight (R)
State Treasurer
1 S. Pinckney St., Ste. 550
P.O. Box 7871
Madison, WI 53707-7871
Phone: (608) 266-3712
Fax: (608) 266-2647
E-mail: jvoight @mail.state.wi.us

WYOMING
Cynthia M. Lummis (R)
State Treasurer
State Capitol Bldg.
Cheyenne, WY 82002
Phone: (307) 777-7408
Fax: (307) 777-5411

Unclaimed Property

Responsible for the marshaling, administration and disposition of unclaimed or abandoned property.

ALABAMA
Ralph Ainsworth
Division Chief
Unclaimed Property Section
Treasurer's Ofc.
RSA Union, Rm. 636
Montgomery, AL 36106
Phone: (334) 242-7500
Fax: (334) 242-7592

ALASKA
Larry E. Meyers
Director
Div. of Income & Excise Audit
Dept. of Revenue
550 W. 7th Ave., Ste. 560
Anchorage, AK 99501-3556
Phone: (907) 269-6620
Fax: (907) 269-6644

AMERICAN SAMOA

ARIZONA
Mark W. Killian
Director
Administration Services Div.
Dept. of Revenue
1600 W. Monroe
Phoenix, AZ 85007
Phone: (602) 542-3572
Fax: (602) 542-4772

ARKANSAS
Gus Wingfield
State Auditor
State Capitol, Rm. 230
1 Capitol Mall
Little Rock, AR 72201
Phone: (501) 682-6030
Fax: (501) 682-2521

CALIFORNIA
Barbara Reagan
Chief
Div. of Unclaimed Property
Ofc. of the Controller
300 Capitol Mall, Ste. 801
Sacramento, CA 95814
Phone: (916) 323-2843

COLORADO
Patty White
Director
Unclaimed Property Div.
Dept. of Treasury
1560 Broadway, Ste. 1225
Denver, CO 80202

CONNECTICUT

DELAWARE
John Carney, Jr.
Secretary
Dept. of Finance
Carvel Bldg.
820 French St.
Wilmington, DE 19801
Phone: (302) 577-2074
Fax: (302) 577-3106
E-mail: jcarney@state.de.us

DISTRICT OF COLUMBIA

FLORIDA
Don Saxon
Director
Div. of Finance
Dept. of Banking & Finance
101 E. Gaines St.
Tallahassee, FL 32399-0350
Phone: (850) 488-9805
Fax: (850) 681-2428

GEORGIA
Kay Powell
Administrative Specialist
Dept. of Revenue
270 Washington St.
Atlanta, GA 30334
Phone: (404) 656-4240

GUAM
Carl J.C. Aguon
Director
Dept. of Land Mgmt.
1 Stop Bldg.
P.O. Box 2950
Anigua-Agana, GU 96932
Phone: (671) 475-5252
Fax: (671) 477-0883

HAWAII
Neal Miyahira
Interim Director of Finance
Dept. of Budget & Finance
P.O. Box 150
Honolulu, HI 96810
Phone: (808) 586-1518
Fax: (808) 586-1976

IDAHO
Dave Bengener
Chief
Unclaimed Property Div.
State Tax Comm.
700 W. State St.
Boise, ID 83722
Phone: (208) 334-7675

ILLINOIS
Sarah D. Vega
Director
Dept. of Financial Institutions
500 Iles Park Pl.
Springfield, IL 62718
Phone: (217) 785-6994
Fax: (217) 785-6999

INDIANA
Priscilla Keith
Director
Div. of Unclaimed Property
Ofc. of Attorney General
402 W. Washington St., 5th Fl.
Indianapolis, IN 46204
Phone: (317) 232-6348
Fax: (317) 232-7979

IOWA
Michael L. Fitzgerald
State Treasurer
State Capitol Bldg.
Des Moines, IA 50319
Phone: (515) 281-5366
Fax: (515) 281-6962

KANSAS

KENTUCKY
John McCarty
Secretary
Finance & Administration Cabinet
Capitol Annex, Rm. 383
Frankfort, KY 40601
Phone: (502) 564-4240
Fax: (502) 564-6785

LOUISIANA
Benjamin Spann
Director
Unclaimed Property Unit
Dept. of Revenue & Taxation
P.O. Box 91010
Baton Rouge, LA 70821
Phone: (225) 925-7407
Fax: (225) 925-3896

MAINE
Dale McCormick
State Treasurer
State Ofc. Bldg., Rm. 318
39 State House Station
Augusta, ME 04333
Phone: (207) 287-2771
Fax: (207) 287-2367
E-mail: dale.mccormick@state.me.us

MARYLAND
Lynn E. Hall
Manager
Unclaimed Property Div.
Comptroller's Ofc.
301 W. Preston St., Rm. 310
Baltimore, MD 21201
Phone: (410) 767-1705
Fax: (410) 333-7150

MASSACHUSETTS
Shannon O'Brien
State Treasurer
Rm. 227 - State House
Boston, MA 02133
Phone: (617) 367-6900
Fax: (617) 248-0372

MICHIGAN
Mark Murray
Treasurer
Dept. of Treasury
P.O. Box 11097
Lansing, MI 48901
Phone: (517) 373-3223
Fax: (517) 335-1785

MINNESOTA
Cheryl Costello
Supervisor
Dept. of Commerce
135 E. 7th St.
St. Paul, MN 55101
Phone: (651) 296-2568
Fax: (651) 296-8591
E-mail: cheryl.costello@state.mn.us

MISSISSIPPI
Jim Majure
Director
Ofc. of Surplus Property
P.O. Box 5788
Jackson, MS 39288
Phone: (601) 939-2050
Fax: (601) 939-4505

MISSOURI
Scott Harper
Director
Unclaimed Property Div.
Ofc. of State Treasurer
Truman Bldg., Rm. 157
P.O. Box 1272
Jefferson City, MO 65102
Phone: (573) 751-0840
Fax: (573) 526-6027
E-mail: scott_harper@sto.state.mo.us

MONTANA
Dot Spurlock
Supervisor
Abandoned Property Section
Dept. of Revenue
2519 Airport Rd.
Helena, MT 59601
Phone: (406) 444-2425
Fax: (406) 444-0750

NEBRASKA
David E. Heineman
State Treasurer
State Capitol, Rm. 2003
P.O. Box 94788
Lincoln, NE 68509-4788
Phone: (402) 471-2455
Fax: (402) 471-4930

NEVADA
Dan Tom
Director
Unclaimed Property Div.
Dept. of Business & Industry
2501 E. Sahara Ave., Ste. 304
Las Vegas, NV 89104
Phone: (702) 486-4140
Fax: (702) 486-4177

NEW HAMPSHIRE
Georgie A. Thomas
State Treasurer
121 State House Annex
Concord, NH 03301
Phone: (603) 271-2621
Fax: (603) 271-3922
E-mail: gthomas@tec.nh.us

NEW JERSEY
Stephen M. Sylvester
Assistant Director
Property Administration
Dept. of Treasury
50 Barrack St.
P.O. Box 240
Trenton, NJ 08646-0240
Phone: (609) 292-8822
Fax: (609) 292-0411

NEW MEXICO
Celia Fernandez
Supervisor
Special Tax Programs
Dept. of Taxation & Revenue
Manuel Lujan Ofc. Bldg.
P.O. Box 25123
Santa Fe, NM 87504-5123
Phone: (505) 827-0767
Fax: (505) 827-1759

NEW YORK
H. Carl McCall
Comptroller
A.E. Smith Ofc. Bldg., 6th Fl.
Albany, NY 12236
Phone: (518) 474-3506
Fax: (518) 473-3004

NORTH CAROLINA
Terry Allen
Administrator, Escheat & Unclaimed Property
Administration Services Div.
State Treasurer's Ofc.
325 N. Salisbury St.
Raleigh, NC 27603-1388
Phone: (919) 508-5979
Fax: (919) 715-0229

NORTH DAKOTA
Steve Brandom
Administrator
Abandoned Property Div.
Land Dept.
P.O. Box 5523
Bismarck, ND 58506-5523
Phone: (701) 328-2805
Fax: (701) 328-3650
E-mail: steve@poldy.land.state.nd.us

NORTHERN MARIANA ISLANDS
Edward B. Palacios
Director
Procurement & Supply Div.
Dept. of Finance
Lower Base
Saipan, MP 96950
Phone: (670) 664-1500
Fax: (670) 664-1515
E-mail: gov.p$s@saipan.com

OHIO
Jessie T. Baker
Chief
Div. of Unclaimed Funds
Dept. of Commerce
77 S. High St., 20th Fl.
Columbus, OH 43266-0545
Phone: (614) 466-4433
Fax: (614) 752-5078

OKLAHOMA
Mark Evans
Director
Account Maintenance/ Unclaimed Property
Tax Comm.
P.O. Box 53545
Oklahoma City, OK 73152-3545
Phone: (405) 521-4275
E-mail: accountmain@oktax.state.ok.us

OREGON
Gary Van Horn
Assistant Director
Finance & Administration
Dept. of State Lands
777 Summer St., NE
Salem, OR 97310
Phone: (503) 378-3805
Fax: (503) 378-4844

PENNSYLVANIA
Barry Drew
Deputy Secretary for Administration
Dept. of Revenue
Strawberry Sq., 11th Fl.
Harrisburg, PA 17127
Phone: (717) 783-3682
Fax: (717) 787-3990

PUERTO RICO

RHODE ISLAND
Paul J. Tavares
Treasurer
State House, Rm. 102
Providence, RI 02903
Phone: (401) 222-2397

SOUTH CAROLINA
Voigt Shealy
State Procurement Officer
Materials Mgmt. Div.
Dept. of Services
1201 Main St., Ste. 600
Columbia, SC 29201
Phone: (803) 737-0600

SOUTH DAKOTA
Richard Butler
State Treasurer
Unclaimed Property Div.
500 E. Capitol Ave.
Pierre, SD 57501-5070
Phone: (605) 773-3378
Fax: (605) 773-3115
E-mail: dick.butler@state.sd.us

TENNESSEE
Stephen D. Adams
State Treasurer
State Capitol
600 Charlotte
Nashville, TN 37243
Phone: (615) 741-2956
Fax: (615) 253-1591
E-mail: sadams@mail.state.tn.us

TEXAS
Carole Keeton Rylander
Comptroller
Comptroller of Public Accounts
P.O. Box 13528
Austin, TX 78711-3528
Phone: (512) 463-4000
Fax: (512) 463-4965

U.S. VIRGIN ISLANDS

UTAH
Douglas E. Johnson
Director
Div. of Unclaimed Property
State Treasurer's Ofc.
341 S. Main St.
Salt Lake City, UT 84101
Phone: (801) 320-5363
Fax: (801) 533-4096
E-mail: djohnson.stupmain@state.ut.us

VERMONT
James H. Douglas
Treasurer
State Administration Bldg., 2nd Fl.
133 State St.
Montpelier, VT 05633-6200
Phone: (802) 828-2301
Fax: (802) 828-2772
E-mail: jdouglas@tre.state.vt.us

Peter E. Noyes
Director
Div. of Purchasing
Dept. of Services
133 State St.
Montpelier, VT 05633-7501
Phone: (802) 828-2211
Fax: (802) 828-2222

VIRGINIA
Mary G. Morris
State Treasurer
Dept. of the Treasury
Monroe Bldg., 3rd Fl.
101 N. 14th St.
Richmond, VA 23219
Phone: (804) 225-2142
Fax: (804) 225-3187

WASHINGTON
Gary O'Neil
Assistant Director
Miscellaneous Tax & Unclaimed Property Section
Dept. of Revenue
P.O. Box 47472
Olympia, WA 98504-7472
Phone: (360) 753-2871
Fax: (360) 664-8438

WEST VIRGINIA
Dwight Smith
Director
Unclaimed Property
Ofc. of the Treasurer
1 Players Club Dr.
Charleston, WV 25311
Phone: (304) 343-4000
Fax: (304) 346-6602

WISCONSIN
Jack C. Voight
State Treasurer
1 S. Pinckney St., Ste. 550
P.O. Box 7871
Madison, WI 53707-7871
Phone: (608) 266-3712
Fax: (608) 266-2647
E-mail: jvoight@mail.state.wi.us

WYOMING
Nancy Sutton
Director
Unclaimed Property Div.
Ofc. of the State Treasurer
State Capitol
200 W. 24th St.
Cheyenne, WY 82002
Phone: (307) 777-7408

Unemployment Insurance —

Administers the unemployment insurance program in the state.

ALABAMA
Bryon Abrams
Director
Unemployment Compensation Div.
649 Monroe St.
Montgomery, AL 36130
Phone: (334) 242-8025
Fax: (334) 242-8258

ALASKA
Rebecca Gamez
Director
Employment Security Div.
Dept. of Labor
P.O. Box 25509
Juneau, AK 99802-1149
Phone: (907) 465-2711
Fax: (907) 465-4537

AMERICAN SAMOA

ARIZONA
John Clayton
Director Designate
Dept. of Economic Security
1717 W. Jefferson
Phoenix, AZ 85007
Phone: (602) 542-5678
Fax: (602) 542-5339

ARKANSAS
Ed Rolle
Director
Employment Security Dept.
#2 Capitol Mall, Rm. 506
Little Rock, AR 72201
Phone: (501) 682-2121
Fax: (501) 682-3713

CALIFORNIA
Ray Remy
Director
Dept. of Employment Dev.
800 Capitol Mall, Rm. 5000
Sacramento, CA 95814
Phone: (916) 654-8210

COLORADO
Donald Peitersen
Director
Ofc. of Unemployment Insurance
Dept. of Labor & Employmnet
1515 Arapahoe St., Tower 2, Ste. 400
Denver, CO 80202
Phone: (303) 620-4712

CONNECTICUT
Alice Carrier
Director
Operational Support
Dept. of Labor
200 Folly Brook Blvd.
Wethersfield, CT 06109
Phone: (860) 263-6575

DELAWARE
W. Thomas MacPherson
Director
Unemployment Insurance Div.
Dept. of Labor
P.O. Box 9950
Wilmington, DE 19809-0950
Phone: (302) 761-8350
Fax: (302) 761-6637

DISTRICT OF COLUMBIA
Bruce Eanet
Associate Director
Unemployment Compensation Ofc.
Dept. of Employment Services
500 C St., NW, Rm. 515
Washington, DC 20001

FLORIDA
Kenneth Holmes
Director
Div. of Unemployment Compensation
Dept. of Labor & Employment Security
107 E. Madison, Rm. 201
Tallahassee, FL 32399
Phone: (850) 921-3889
Fax: (850) 921-3941

GEORGIA
Tom Lowe
Assistant Commissioner
Unemployment Insurance Div.
Dept. of Labor
148 Intl. Blvd., Rm. 718
Atlanta, GA 30303
Phone: (404) 656-3050

GUAM
James Underwood
Acting Director
Dept. of Labor
504 E. Sunset Blvd., Tiyan
P.O. Box 9970
Tamuning, GU 96931
Phone: (671) 475-0101
Fax: (671) 477-2988

HAWAII
Douglas Odo
Administrator
Unemployment Insurance Div.
Dept. of Labor & Industrial Relations
830 Punchbowl St.
Honolulu, HI 96813
Phone: (808) 586-9069
Fax: (808) 586-9077

IDAHO
Dave Wagnon
Administrator
Unemployment Insurance Div.
Dept. of Labor
317 Main St.
Boise, ID 83702
Phone: (208) 334-6280
Fax: (208) 334-6301

ILLINOIS
Linda Renee Baker
Director
Dept. of Employment Security
401 S. State St., 6th Fl.
Chicago, IL 60605
Phone: (312) 793-5700
Fax: (312) 793-9834

INDIANA
Craig E. Hartzer
Commissioner
Dept. of Workforce Dev.
10 N. Senate, Rm. SE-302
Indianapolis, IN 46204
Phone: (317) 233-5661
Fax: (317) 232-1815

IOWA
Renny Dohse
Bureau Chief
Contribution & Benefit Services Div.
Workforce Dev.
1000 E. Grand Ave.
Des Moines, IA 50319
Phone: (515) 281-4986
Fax: (515) 281-6208

KANSAS
Roger Aeschilman
Director of Employment Security
Dept. of Human Resources
401 SW Topeka Blvd.
Topeka, KS 66603
Phone: (785) 296-5075
Fax: (785) 296-2119

KENTUCKY
Ron Holland
Director
Div. of Unemployment Insurance
Cabinet for Human Resources
275 E. Main St.
Frankfort, KY 40621
Phone: (502) 564-2900
Fax: (502) 564-5502

LOUISIANA
Gayle Joseph
Assistant Secretary
Ofc. of Employment Security
Dept. of Labor
P.O. Box 94094
Baton Rouge, LA 70804
Phone: (225) 342-3013
Fax: (225) 342-5208

MAINE
Gail Thayer
Director
Bur. of Employment Security
Dept. of Labor
55 State House Station
Augusta, ME 04333
Phone: (207) 287-3377

MARYLAND
Tom Wendel
Executive Director
Unemployment Insurance Administration
Labor, Licensing & Regulation Dept.
1100 N. Eutaw St., Rm. 501
Baltimore, MD 21201
Phone: (410) 767-2444
Fax: (410) 767-2439

MASSACHUSETTS
John A. King
Deputy Director
Div. of Employment & Training
Dept. of Labor & Workforce Dev.
19 Staniford St., 3rd Fl.
Boston, MA 02114
Phone: (617) 626-6600
Fax: (617) 727-0315

MICHIGAN
Jack F. Wheatley
Acting Director
Unemployment Agency
7310 Woodward Ave., Rm. 510
Detroit, MI 48202
Phone: (313) 876-5901
Fax: (313) 876-5587

MINNESOTA
John Weidenbach
Assistant Commissioner
Job Services & Re-employment Insurance Div.
Dept. of Economic Security
390 N. Robert St.
St. Paul, MN 55101
Phone: (651) 296-1692
Fax: (651) 296-0994

MISSISSIPPI
Tom Lord
Director
Employment Security Comm.
1520 W. Capitol
P.O. Box 1699
Jackson, MS 39215-1699
Phone: (601) 961-7500
Fax: (601) 961-7405

MISSOURI
Marilyn Hutcherson
Deputy Director
Unemployment Insurance Operations
Dept. of Labor & Industrial Relations
P.O. Box 59
Jefferson City, MO 65104
Phone: (573) 751-3643
Fax: (573) 751-4554
E-mail: mhutcherson@central.dolir.state.mo.us

MONTANA
Pat Haffey
Commissioner
Dept. of Labor & Industry
P.O. Box 1728
Helena, MT 59624
Phone: (406) 444-3555
Fax: (406) 444-1394

NEBRASKA
Allan Amsberry
Director
Unemployment Insurance Div.
Dept. of Labor
P.O. Box 94600
Lincoln, NE 68509
Phone: (402) 471-9979
Fax: (402) 471-2318

NEVADA
Stanley Jones
Administrator
Div. of Employment Security
Employment, Training & Rehab. Dept.
500 E. 3rd St.
Carson City, NV 89713
Phone: (775) 684-3909
Fax: (775) 687-3910

NEW HAMPSHIRE
John J. Ratoff
Commissioner
Dept. of Employment Security
32 S. Main St.
Concord, NH 03301-4857
Phone: (603) 224-3311
Fax: (603) 228-4145

NEW JERSEY
Michael P. Malloy
Director
Unemployment Insurance
Dept. of Labor
John Fitch Plz., 10th Fl.
P.O. Box 058
Trenton, NJ 08625-0058
Phone: (609) 292-2460
Fax: (609) 396-1685

NEW MEXICO
Tomey Anaya
Chief
Unemployment Insurance Bur.
Dept. of Labor
P.O. Box 1928
Albuquerque, NM 87103
Phone: (505) 841-8431
Fax: (505) 841-8491

NEW YORK
James J. McGowan
Commissioner
Dept. of Labor
State Ofc. Bldg. Campus, Bldg. 12
Albany, NY 12240
Phone: (518) 457-2741
Fax: (518) 457-6908

NORTH CAROLINA
J. Parker Chesson
Chair
Employment Security Comm.
Dept. of Commerce
700 Wade Ave.
Raleigh, NC 27605
Phone: (919) 733-7546
Fax: (919) 733-1129

NORTH DAKOTA
John Welder
Director
Job Insurance
Job Service
P.O. Box 5507
Bismarck, ND 58506-5507
Phone: (701) 328-2833
Fax: (701) 328-4000
E-mail: jawelder@state.nd.us

NORTHERN MARIANA ISLANDS
Edward H. Manglona
Administrator
Retirement Fund
P.O. Box 1247
Saipan, MP 96950
Phone: (670) 234-7228
Fax: (670) 234-9624
E-mail: nmi.retirement@saipan.com

OHIO
Joe Duda
Director
Unemployment Compensation Benefits
Bur. of Employment Services
145 S. Front St.
Columbus, OH 43215
Phone: (614) 466-9755
Fax: (614) 466-5025

OKLAHOMA
Jon Brock
Executive Director
Employment Security Comm.
2401 N. Lincoln Blvd.
Oklahoma City, OK 73105
Phone: (405) 557-7200
Fax: (405) 557-7256

OREGON
Virlena Crosley
Director
Employment Dept.
875 Union St., NE
Salem, OR 97311
Phone: (503) 947-1477
Fax: (503) 947-1472

PENNSYLVANIA
Alan Williamson
Deputy Secretary
Employment Security & Job Training
Dept. of Labor & Industry
Labor & Industry Bldg., Rm. 1700
Harrisburg, PA 17120
Phone: (717) 787-3907
Fax: (717) 787-8826

PUERTO RICO
Ednidia Padilla
Director
Bur. of Employment Security
Dept. of Labor & Human Resources
505 Munoz Rivera Ave.
Hato Rey, PR 00918
Phone: (787) 754-5375
Fax: (787) 763-2227

RHODE ISLAND
Thomas Morrisey
Associate Director for Benefits
Dept. of Employment & Training
101 Friendship St.
Providence, RI 02903
Phone: (401) 222-3649

SOUTH CAROLINA
Joel T. Cassidy
Executive Director
Employment Security Comm.
P.O. Box 995
Columbia, SC 29202
Phone: (803) 737-2617

SOUTH DAKOTA
Donald Kattke
Director
Div. of Unemployment Insurance
Dept. of Labor
607 N. 4th St.
P.O. Box 1700
Aberdeen, SD 57401
Phone: (605) 626-2452
Fax: (605) 626-2322

TENNESSEE
Hazel Albert
Commissioner
Dept. of Employment Security
Davy Crockett Tower, 12th Fl.
500 James Robertson Pkwy.
Nashville, TN 37245-0001
Phone: (615) 741-2131
Fax: (615) 741-2741

TEXAS
Mike Sheridan
Executive Director
Workforce Comm.
TWC Bldg.
101 E. 15th St.
Austin, TX 78778-0001
Phone: (512) 463-0735
Fax: (512) 475-2321
E-mail: mikesheridian@twc.state.tx.us

U.S. VIRGIN ISLANDS
Eleuteria Roberts
Acting Commissioner
Dept. of Labor
2203 Church St.
Christiansted
St. Croix, VI 00820
Phone: (340) 773-1994
Fax: (340) 773-0094

UTAH
James E. Finch
Director
Div. of Workforce Info. & Payment Services
Dept. of Workforce Services
140 E. 300 S.
Salt Lake City, UT 84111
Phone: (801) 526-9399
Fax: (801) 526-9211
E-mail: jfinch.wsadmpo@state.ut.us

VERMONT
Thomas Douse
Director
Unemployment Insurance Div.
Dept. of Employment & Training Administration
P.O. Box 488
Montpelier, VT 05601
Phone: (802) 828-4100

VIRGINIA
Thomas J. Towberman
Commissioner
Employment Comm.
703 E. Main St.
Richmond, VA 23219
Phone: (804) 786-3001
Fax: (804) 225-3923

WASHINGTON
Carver Gayton
Commissioner
Dept. of Employment Security
212 Maple Park
P.O. Box 49046
Olympia, WA 98507-9046
Phone: (360) 902-9301
Fax: (360) 902-9383

WEST VIRGINIA
William Vieweg
Commissioner
Bur. of Unemployment Programs
Bldg. 4, Rm. 610
112 California Ave.
Charleston, WV 25332
Phone: (304) 558-2630

WISCONSIN

WYOMING
Beth Nelson
Unemployment Insurance Administrator
Unemployment Compensation Div.
Dept. of Employment
P.O. Box 2760
Casper, WY 82602
Phone: (307) 235-3200

Veterans Affairs

Provides services and information to the state's veterans, and their dependents and survivors.

ALABAMA
Frank D. Wilkes
Director
Dept. of Veterans Affairs
770 Washington Ave., Ste. 530
Montgomery, AL 36130-5300
Phone: (334) 242-5077
Fax: (334) 242-5102

ALASKA
Chuck McLeod
Director
Div. of Veterans Affairs
Dept. of Military & Veterans Affairs
P.O. Box 5800
Ft. Richardson, AK 99505-5800
Phone: (907) 428-6068
Fax: (907) 428-6033

AMERICAN SAMOA
Paogofie Fiaigoa
Veterans Affairs Officer
Ofc. of the Governor
AS Govt.
Pago Pago, AS 96799
Phone: (684) 633-4206
Fax: (684) 633-2269

ARIZONA
Pat Chorpenning
Director
Veteran's Service Comm.
3225 N. Central, Ste. 910
Phoenix, AZ 85012
Phone: (602) 255-3373

ARKANSAS
Nick Bacon
Director
Dept. of Veterans Affairs
c/o VA Regional Ofc.
P.O. Box 1280
N. Little Rock, AR 72115
Phone: (501) 370-3820
Fax: (501) 370-3829

CALIFORNIA
Jay R. Vargas
Secretary
Dept. of Veterans Affairs
1227 O St., Ste. 300
Sacramento, CA 95814
Phone: (916) 653-2158

COLORADO
Richard Ceresko
Director
Veterans Affairs Div.
Dept. of Human Services
789 Sherman St., #460
Denver, CO 80203
Phone: (303) 894-7474
Fax: (303) 894-7442

CONNECTICUT
Eugene A. Migliaro, Jr.
Commissioner
Dept. of Veterans Affairs
287 West St.
Rocky Hill, CT 06067
Phone: (860) 721-5891

Sharon R. Wood
Hospital Administrator
Veterans Home & Hospital Comm.
287 West St.
Rocky Hill, CT 06067
Phone: (860) 721-5875

DELAWARE
Antonio Davila
Executive Director
Comm. of Veterans Affairs
25 The Green - Old State House
Dover, DE 19901
Phone: (302) 739-2792
Fax: (302) 739-2794

DISTRICT OF COLUMBIA

FLORIDA
Carlos Rainwater
Executive Director
Dept. of Veterans Affairs
P.O. Box 31003
St. Petersburg, FL 33731
Phone: (813) 898-4443
Fax: (813) 893-2497

GEORGIA
Pete Wheeler
Commissioner
Dept. of Veterans Services
Veterans Memorial Bldg., Ste. E-970
Atlanta, GA 30334
Phone: (404) 656-2300

GUAM
John Blaz
Administrator
Ofc. of Veterans Affairs
107 M St., Tiyan
P.O. Box 3279
Hagatna, GU 96932
Phone: (671) 475-4224
Fax: (671) 477-8858

HAWAII
Walter Ozawa
Director
Ofc. of Veterans Services
Dept. of Defense
919 Ala Moana Blvd., Ste. 100
Honolulu, HI 96814
Phone: (808) 587-3010
Fax: (808) 587-3009

IDAHO
Gary Bermeosolo
Administrator
Div. of Veterans Services
Dept. of Health & Welfare
P.O. Box 7765
Boise, ID 83707
Phone: (208) 334-5000

ILLINOIS
John Johnston
Director
Dept. of Veterans Affairs
833 S. Spring St.
Springfield, IL 62794
Phone: (217) 785-4114
Fax: (217) 524-0344

INDIANA
William D. Jackson
Director
Dept. of Veterans Affairs
302 W. Washington St., Rm. E120
Indianapolis, IN 46204
Phone: (317) 232-3910
Fax: (317) 232-7721

IOWA
Randy Brown
Administrator
Div. of Veterans Affairs
Dept. of Public Defense
7700 NW Beaver Dr.
Johnston, IA 50131
Phone: (515) 242-5333

KANSAS
Don Myer
Executive Director
Comm. on Veterans Affairs
700 SW Jackson St., Rm. 701
Topeka, KS 66603-3743
Phone: (785) 296-3976
Fax: (785) 296-1462

KENTUCKY
John R. Groves, Jr.
Adjutant General
Dept. of Military Affairs
Boone Natl. Guard Ctr.
Frankfort, KY 40601
Phone: (502) 564-8558
Fax: (502) 564-6271

LOUISIANA
Joey Strickland
Executive Director
Veterans Affairs
Ofc. of the Governor
P.O. Box 94095
Baton Rouge, LA 70804-9095
Phone: (225) 922-0500
Fax: (225) 922-0511

MAINE
Earl L. Adams
Commissioner/Adjutant General
Dept. of Defense & Veterans Services
33 State House Station
Augusta, ME 04333-0033
Phone: (207) 626-4225

MARYLAND
Thomas Bratten, Jr.
Director
Ofc. of the State Director
Veteran's Comm.
31 Hopkins Plz., Rm. 110
Baltimore, MD 21201
Phone: (410) 333-4429
Fax: (410) 333-1071

MASSACHUSETTS
Thomas Hudner
Commissioner
Ofc. of Veterans Services
100 Cambridge St., Rm. 1002
Boston, MA 02202
Phone: (617) 727-3570
Fax: (617) 727-5903

MICHIGAN
Mike Rice
Brigadier General
Military Affairs
2500 S. Washington Ave.
Lansing, MI 48913
Phone: (517) 335-3160

MINNESOTA
Bernie Melter
Commissioner
Dept. of Veterans Affairs
Veterans Bldg.
20 W. 12th St.
St. Paul, MN 55155
Phone: (651) 296-2783
Fax: (651) 205-4208
E-mail: bmelter@state.mn.us

MISSISSIPPI
Jack Stephens
Executive Secretary
Veterans Affairs Board
Standard Life Bldg., Ste. 1100
206 W. Pearl
Jackson, MS 39201
Phone: (601) 354-7377
Fax: (601) 354-7386

MISSOURI
Robert Buckner
Executive Director
Veterans Comm.
Dept. of Public Safety
1719 Southridge Dr.
P.O. Drawer 147
Jefferson City, MO 65102
Phone: (573) 751-3779
Fax: (573) 751-6836
E-mail: bucknr@mvc.state.mo.us

MONTANA
James F. Jacobson
Administrator
Veterans Affairs Div.
Dept. of Military Affairs
P.O. Box 4789
Helena, MT 59604
Phone: (406) 841-3741
Fax: (406) 841-3965

NEBRASKA
Keith Fickenscher
Director
Dept. of Veterans Affairs
State Ofc. Bldg., 4th Fl.
P.O. Box 95083
Lincoln, NE 68509-5083
Phone: (402) 471-2458
Fax: (402) 471-2491

NEVADA
Charles G. Abbott
Commissioner for Veterans Affairs
1201 Terminal Way, Rm. 108
Reno, NV 89520
Phone: (775) 688-1653
Fax: (775) 688-1656

NEW HAMPSHIRE
Dennis Viola
Director
Veterans Council
359 Lincoln St.
Manchester, NH 03103-4901
Phone: (603) 624-9230
Fax: (603) 624-9236

NEW JERSEY
Paul J. Glazar
Adjutant General
Dept. of Military & Veterans Affairs
Eggert Crossing Rd.
P.O. Box 340
Trenton, NJ 08625-0340
Phone: (609) 530-6956
Fax: (609) 530-7097

NEW MEXICO
Michael D'Arco
Director
Veterans Service Comm.
P.O. Box 2324
Santa Fe, NM 87504
Phone: (505) 827-6300
Fax: (505) 827-6372

NEW YORK
George Basher
Acting Director
Div. of Veterans Affairs
Corning Tower, 28th Fl.
Empire State Plz.
Albany, NY 12223-1551
Phone: (518) 474-6114
Fax: (518) 474-6924

NORTH CAROLINA
Charles F. Smith
Assistant Secretary
Div. of Veterans Affairs
Dept. of Administration
325 N. Salisbury St., # 1065
Raleigh, NC 27603-1388
Phone: (919) 733-3851
Fax: (919) 733-2834

NORTH DAKOTA
Ray Harkema
Commissioner
Veterans Affairs Dept.
P.O. Box 9003
Fargo, ND 58106-9003
Phone: (701) 239-7165
Fax: (701) 239-7166
E-mail: rharkema@pioneer.state.nd.us

NORTHERN MARIANA ISLANDS
Joseph M. Palacios
Director
Div. of Veterans Affairs
Dept. of Community & Cultural Affairs
Ofc. of the Governor
Saipan, MP 96950
Phone: (670) 288-1150
Fax: (670) 288-1152

OHIO
Dave Alstadt
Administrator
Veterans Affairs
Ofc. of the Governor
77 S. High St.
Columbus, OH 43266
Phone: (614) 644-0898
Fax: (614) 466-9354

OKLAHOMA
Phillip C. Boatner
Executive Director
Dept. of Veterans Affairs
2311 N. Central
P.O. Box 53067
Oklahoma City, OK 73152
Phone: (405) 521-3684
Fax: (405) 521-6533

OREGON
Jon Mangis
Director
Dept. of Veterans Affairs
700 Summer St., NE
Salem, OR 97310
Phone: (503) 373-2388
Fax: (503) 373-2362

PENNSYLVANIA
William B. Lynch
Adjutant General
Dept. of Military & Veterans Affairs
Ft. Indiantown Gap
Annville, PA 17003
Phone: (717) 861-8500
Fax: (717) 861-8481
E-mail: lynchwb@pa.arng.ngb.army

PUERTO RICO
Roberto Gonzalez Vazquez
Director
Ofc. of Veterans Affairs
P.O. Box 11737
San Juan, PR 00910-1737
Phone: (787) 758-5760
Fax: (787) 758-5788

RHODE ISLAND
David Foehr
Chief
Veterans Home
Dept. of Social & Rehabilitative Services
600 New London Ave.
Cranston, RI 02920
Phone: (401) 253-8000

SOUTH CAROLINA
G. Stoney Wages
Director
Div. of Veterans Affairs
Ofc. of the Governor
1205 Pendleton St., Ste. 226
Columbia, SC 29201
Phone: (803) 734-0200
Fax: (803) 734-0197

SOUTH DAKOTA
Dennis Foell
Director
Veterans Div.
Military & Veterans Affairs Dept.
500 E. Capitol Ave.
Pierre, SD 57501
Phone: (605) 773-4981
Fax: (605) 773-5380

TENNESSEE
Fred Tucker
Commissioner
Dept. of Veterans Affairs
215 8th Ave., N.
Nashville, TN 37243-1010
Phone: (615) 741-6663
Fax: (615) 741-4785

TEXAS
James Nier
Executive Director
Veteran Comm.
920 Colorado
Austin, TX 78701
Phone: (512) 463-5538
Fax: (512) 475-2395

U.S. VIRGIN ISLANDS
Gregory Francis
Director
Veterans Affairs
10-13 Est. Richmond
Christiansted
St. Croix, VI 00820
Phone: (340) 773-6663
Fax: (340) 692-9563

UTAH
Lavonne Willis
Director
Veterans' Affairs
Dept. of Community & Economic Dev.
125 S. State St., Rm. 5223
Salt Lake City, UT 84138
Phone: (801) 524-3575
Fax: (801) 524-3575
E-mail: lwillis@dced.state.ut.us

VERMONT
Mae Jennison
Director
Veterans Affairs
118 State St., Drawer 20
Montpelier, VT 05620-4401
Phone: (802) 828-3379

VIRGINIA
Donald W. Duncan
Director
Dept. of Veterans' Affairs
Poff Federal Bldg., Rm. 1012
270 Franklin Rd., SW
Roanoke, VA 24011-2215
Phone: (540) 857-7104
Fax: (540) 857-7573

WASHINGTON
John King
Director
Dept. of Veteran Affairs
505 E. Union
P.O. Box 41150
Olympia, WA 98504
Phone: (360) 709-5230
Fax: (360) 709-5266

WEST VIRGINIA
Gail Harper
Director
Veterans Affairs
1321 Plaza E., # 101
Charleston, WV 25301-1400
Phone: (304) 558-3661
Fax: (304) 558-3662

WISCONSIN
Ray Boland
Secretary
Dept. of Veterans Affairs
30 W. Mifflin
P.O. Box 7843
Madison, WI 53707
Phone: (608) 266-1311
Fax: (608) 267-0403

WYOMING
Stanley Lowe
Chair
Council for Veterans Affairs
Dept. of Employment
1819 Park Ave.
Cheyenne, WY 82007
Phone: (307) 682-8389

Veterinarian

Responsible for the prevention, control and eradication of transmissible diseases of domestic animals and poultry.

ALABAMA
J. Lee Alley
State Veterinarian
Dept. of Agri. & Industry
1445 Federal Dr.
P.O. Box 3336
Montgomery, AL 36193-0336
Phone: (334) 240-7171
Fax: (334) 223-7352

ALASKA
Berton Gore
State Veterinarian
Div. of Environmental Health
Dept. of Environmental Conservation
500 S. Alaska, Ste. A
Palmer, AK 99645-6399
Phone: (907) 745-3236
Fax: (907) 745-8125

AMERICAN SAMOA
Talitua Uele
Veterinarian
Dept. of Agri.
Pago Pago, AS 96799
Phone: (684) 699-1497
Fax: (684) 699-4031

ARIZONA
Sheldon R. Jones
Director
Dept. of Agri.
1688 W. Adams
Phoenix, AZ 85007
Phone: (602) 542-0998
Fax: (602) 542-5420

ARKANSAS
Jack Gibson
Director
Livestock & Poultry Comm.
P.O. Box 5497
Little Rock, AR 72215
Phone: (501) 225-5138
Fax: (501) 225-9727

CALIFORNIA
Kenneth Tomazin
Chief
Bur. of Animal Health
Dept. of Food & Agri.
1220 N St., Rm. A107
Sacramento, CA 95814
Phone: (916) 654-0881

COLORADO
Jerry Bohlender
State Veterinarian
Animal Industry Div.
Dept. of Agri.
710 Kipling St., Rm. 202
Lakewood, CO 80215-5894
Phone: (303) 239-4161
Fax: (303) 239-4164

CONNECTICUT
Bruce Sherman
Acting State Veterinarian
Livestock Div.
Dept. of Agri.
765 Asylum Ave.
Hartford, CT 06105
Phone: (860) 713-2505

DELAWARE
H. Wesley Towers, Jr.
State Veterinarian
Div. of Consumer Protection
Dept. of Agri.
2320 S. DuPont Hwy.
Dover, DE 19901
Phone: (302) 739-4811
Fax: (302) 697-6287

DISTRICT OF COLUMBIA
Richard Levinson
Administrator
Comm. of Public Health
Dept. of Human Services
Vital Records
800 9th St., SW, #100
Washington, DC 20024-2480
Phone: (202) 645-5556

FLORIDA
LeRoy Coffman
Director
Div. of Animal Industry
Dept. of Agri.
Mayo Bldg.
Tallahassee, FL 32399
Phone: (850) 488-7747

GEORGIA
Lee Brooks
State Veterinarian
Animal Industry & Field Inspection
Dept. of Agri.
Agri. Bldg., Rm. 106
Capitol Sq.
Atlanta, GA 30334
Phone: (404) 656-3671

GUAM
Juan Taijito
Acting Director
Dept. of Agri.
192 Dairy Rd.
Mangilao, GU 96923
Phone: (671) 734-3942
Fax: (671) 734-6569

HAWAII
Thomas Sawa
Acting Administrator & State Veterinarian
Animal Industry Div.
Dept. of Agri.
990941 Halawa Valley St.
Aiea, HI 96701
Phone: (808) 483-7111
Fax: (808) 483-7110

IDAHO
Bob Hillman
Administrator
Div. of Animal Industries
Dept. of Agri.
2270 Old Penitentiary Rd.
Boise, ID 83707
Phone: (208) 334-3256

ILLINOIS
Richard Hull
State Veterinarian
Div. of Animal Industries
Dept. of Agri.
P.O. Box 19281
Springfield, IL 62794
Phone: (217) 782-4944

INDIANA
Bret Marsh
State Veterinarian
Animal Health Board
805 Beachway Dr., Ste. 50
Indianapolis, IN 46224
Phone: (317) 227-0300
Fax: (317) 227-0330

IOWA
Walter Felker
Bureau Chief
Div. of Animal Industry
Dept. of Agri.
Wallace State Ofc. Bldg.
E. 9th & Grand Aves.
Des Moines, IA 50319
Phone: (515) 281-5305

KANSAS
George Teagarden
Livestock Commissioner
Animal Health Dept.
712 Kansas Ave., Ste. 4B
Topeka, KS 66603-3808
Phone: (785) 296-2326
Fax: (785) 296-1765

KENTUCKY
Don Notter
State Veterinarian
Dept. of Agri.
100 Fairoaks Ln., Ste. 252
Frankfort, KY 40601
Phone: (502) 564-3956
Fax: (502) 564-7852

LOUISIANA
Terrell Delphin
Assistant Commissioner
Ofc. of Animal Health
Dept. of Agri.
P.O. Box 4048
Baton Rouge, LA 70821
Phone: (225) 925-3962
Fax: (225) 925-4103

MAINE
Shelley F. Falk
Director
Div. of Poultry & Livestock
Dept. of Agri., Food & Rural Resources
28 State House Station
Augusta, ME 04333
Phone: (207) 287-3701

MARYLAND
Clifford Johnson
Chief
Ctr. for Veterinary Public Health
Dept. of Health & Mental Hygiene
201 W. Preston St.
Baltimore, MD 21201
Phone: (410) 767-6703
Fax: (410) 669-4215
E-mail: johnson@dhmh.state.md.us

MASSACHUSETTS
Vacant
State Veterinarian
Dept. of Food & Agri.
100 Cambridge St.
Boston, MA 02202
Phone: (617) 727-3000
Fax: (617) 727-7235

MICHIGAN
Harry Michael Chaddock
State Veterinarian
Dept. of Agri.
P.O. Box 30017
Lansing, MI 48909
Phone: (517) 373-1077

MINNESOTA
Thomas J. Hagerty
Executive Secretary
Board of Animal Health
90 W. Plato Blvd., Rm. 119
St. Paul, MN 55107
Phone: (651) 296-2942
Fax: (651) 296-7417

MISSISSIPPI
Jim Watson
State Veterinarian
Animal Health & Veterinary Diagnostic Laboratory
2531 N. West St.
Jackson, MS 39201
Phone: (601) 359-1170
Fax: (601) 359-1177

MISSOURI
John W. Hunt, Jr.
State Veterinarian
Div. of Animal Health
Dept. of Agri.
1616 Missouri Blvd.
P.O. Box 630
Jefferson City, MO 65102
Phone: (573) 751-3377
Fax: (573) 751-6919
E-mail: jhunt01@mail.state.mo.us

Howard Pue
State Public Health Veterinarian
Section of Communicable Disease Control & Veterinary
Dept. of Health
930 Wildwood
Jefferson City, MO 65102
Phone: (573) 751-6136
Fax: (573) 526-7810
E-mail: pueh@mail.health.state.mo.us

MONTANA
Arnold Gertonson
State Veterinarian
Animal Health Div.
Dept. of Livestock
Scott Hart Bldg.
301 Roberts
Helena, MT 59620
Phone: (406) 444-2043
Fax: (406) 444-1929

NEBRASKA
Larry Williams
State Veterinarian
Dept. of Agri.
P.O. Box 94947
Lincoln, NE 68509
Phone: (402) 471-2351
Fax: (402) 471-2759

NEVADA
David Thain
Acting Veterinarian/Chief
Div. of Animal Industry
Dept. of Agri.
350 Capitol Hill Ave.
Reno, NV 89502
Phone: (775) 688-1182
Fax: (775) 688-1178

NEW HAMPSHIRE
Clifford W. McGinnis
Director/State Veterinarian
Animal Industries Div.
Agri., Markets & Food
P.O. Box 2042
Concord, NH 03302-2042
Phone: (603) 271-2404
Fax: (603) 271-1109

NEW JERSEY
Ernest W. Zirkle
Director
Div. of Animal Health
Dept. of Agri.
John Fitch Plz.
P.O. Box 330
Trenton, NJ 08625-0330
Phone: (609) 292-3965
Fax: (609) 633-2550

NEW MEXICO
Dianne Torrance
Director
Board of Veterinary Medicine
1650 Univ. Blvd, NE, Ste. 400-C
Albuquerque, NM 87102
Phone: (505) 841-9112
Fax: (505) 841-9113

NEW YORK
Donald R. Davidsen
Commissioner
Dept. of Agri. & Markets
One Winners Cir.
Albany, NY 12235
Phone: (518) 457-5496
Fax: (518) 457-3087

NORTH CAROLINA
M.A. Mixson
Director
Veterinary Div.
Dept. of Agri.
2 W. Edenton St.
Raleigh, NC 27601
Phone: (919) 733-7601
Fax: (919) 733-6431

NORTH DAKOTA
Larry Schuler
State Veterinarian
Board of Animal Health
Dept. of Agri.
600 E. Blvd. Ave., 6th Fl.
Bismarck, ND 58505-0020
Phone: (701) 328-2654
Fax: (701) 328-4567
E-mail: lschuler@state.nd.us

NORTHERN MARIANA ISLANDS
Vacant
Director
Div. of Agri. & Quarantine
Dept. of Lands & Natural Resources
Caller Box 10007
Saipan, MP 96950
Phone: (670) 256-3317
Fax: (670) 256-7154

OHIO
R. David Glauer
Chief
Div. of Animal Industry
Dept. of Agri.
8995 E. Main St.
Reynoldsburg, OH 43068
Phone: (614) 728-6220
Fax: (614) 728-6310

OKLAHOMA
Burke Healy
State Veterinarian
Animal Industry Service
Dept. of Agri.
2800 N. Lincoln
Oklahoma City, OK 73105
Phone: (405) 521-3864
Fax: (405) 522-0756
E-mail: bhealy@odagis.oklaosf.state.ok.us

OREGON
Andrew Clark
State Veterinarian
Animal Health Program
Dept. of Agri.
635 Capitol St., NE
Salem, OR 97310
Phone: (503) 986-4680
Fax: (503) 986-4688

PENNSYLVANIA
Phillip Debok
Acting Director
Bur. of Animal Industry
Dept. of Agri.
2301 N. Cameron St., Rm. 408
Harrisburg, PA 17110
Phone: (717) 783-5301
Fax: (717) 787-1868

PUERTO RICO
Carmen Feliciano
Secretary
Dept. of Health
P.O. Box 70184
San Juan, PR 00936-0184
Phone: (787) 274-7600
Fax: (787) 250-6547

Miguel Munoz
Secretary
Dept. of Agri.
P.O. Box 10163
Santurce, PR 00908-0163
Phone: (787) 722-0871
Fax: (787) 723-9747

RHODE ISLAND
Susan Littlefield
Public Health Veterinarian
Agri. & Marketing Div.
Dept. of Environmental Mgmt.
83 Park St.
Providence, RI 02903-1048
Phone: (401) 222-2781

SOUTH CAROLINA
Alana Holmes
Administrator
Board of Veterinary Medical Examiners
Dept. of Labor, Licensing & Regulations
110 Centerview Dr.
Columbia, SC 29210
Phone: (803) 896-4598
Fax: (803) 896-4719

SOUTH DAKOTA
Sam Holland
State Veterinarian
Animal Industry Board
Dept. of Agri.
411 S. Fort St.
Pierre, SD 57501
Phone: (605) 773-3321
Fax: (605) 773-5459

TENNESSEE
Robert Hartin
State Veterinarian
Div. of Animal Industries
Dept. of Agri.
P.O. Box 40627, Melrose Station
Nashville, TN 37204
Phone: (615) 837-5120
Fax: (615) 837-5335

TEXAS
Terry Beals
Executive Director
Animal Health Comm.
P.O. Box 12966
Austin, TX 78758
Phone: (512) 719-0700
Fax: (512) 719-0719

U.S. VIRGIN ISLANDS

UTAH
Michael Marshall
Veterinarian
Div. of Animal Industry
Dept. of Agri.
350 N. Redwood Rd.
Salt Lake City, UT 84116
Phone: (801) 538-7160
Fax: (801) 538-7169
E-mail: mmarshall.agmain@state.ut.us

VERMONT
Samuel Hutchins, III
State Veterinarian
Dept. of Agri.
116 State St.
P.O. Drawer 20
Montpelier, VT 05620
Phone: (802) 828-2421
Fax: (802) 828-2361

VIRGINIA
J. Carlton Courter, III
Commissioner
Dept. of Agri. & Consumer Services
Washington Bldg., Ste. 210
1100 Bank St.
Richmond, VA 23219
Phone: (804) 786-3501
Fax: (804) 371-2945

WASHINGTON
Robert Mead
State Veterinarian
Dept. of Agri.
P.O. Box 42560
Olympia, WA 98504-2560
Phone: (360) 902-1881
Fax: (360) 902-2087

WEST VIRGINIA
Lewis P. Thomas
Director
Animal Health Div.
Dept. of Agri.
State Capitol
1900 Kanawha Blvd., E.
Charleston, WV 25305
Phone: (304) 558-2214
Fax: (304) 558-2231

WISCONSIN
Clarence Siroky
State Veterinarian
Div. of Animal Health
Agri., Trade & Consumer Protection
2811 Agri. Dr.
P.O. Box 8911
Madison, WI 53708
Phone: (608) 224-4873
Fax: (608) 224-4871

WYOMING
Jim Logan
Acting State Veterinarian
Livestock Board
Herschler Bldg., 3rd Fl., E.
122 W. 25th St.
Cheyenne, WY 82002
Phone: (307) 777-7515

Vital Statistics

Maintains a statewide file of birth, death, marriage and divorce records, and issues certified copies of those records.

ALABAMA
Dorothy Harshbarger
State Registrar
Ctr. for Health Statistics
Dept. of Public Health
201 Monroe, Ste. 1168
Montgomery, AL 36104
Phone: (334) 206-5300
Fax: (334) 206-2659

ALASKA
Al Zangri
Chief
Bur. of Vital Statistics
Dept. of Health & Social Services
P.O. Box 110675
Juneau, AK 99811-0675
Phone: (907) 465-3393
Fax: (907) 465-3618

AMERICAN SAMOA

ARIZONA
Renee Gaudino
Assistant State Registrar
Ofc. of Vital Records
Dept. of Health Services
2727 W. Glendale Ave.
Phoenix, AZ 85051
Phone: (602) 255-3260

ARKANSAS
Sharon Leinbach
Director
Vital Records Div.
Dept. of Health
4815 W. Markham St.
Little Rock, AR 72205
Phone: (501) 661-2371
Fax: (501) 661-2601

CALIFORNIA
Michael Davis
Chief
Vital Statistics Branch
Dept. of Health Services
P.O. Box 730241
Sacramento, CA 94244
Phone: (916) 445-1719

COLORADO
Robert O'Doherty
Director
Health & Environmental Info. & Statistics Ctr.
Dept. of Public Health & Environment
4300 Cherry Creek Dr., S.
Denver, CO 80246-1530
Phone: (303) 756-4464

CONNECTICUT
John N. Boccaccio
Registrar of Vital Records
Dept. of Health Services
P.O. Box 340308
Hartford, CT 06134-0308
Phone: (860) 509-7895

DELAWARE
Donald L. Berry
Manager
Health Planning & Resources Mgmt.
Health & Social Services
Jesse Cooper Bldg.
Federal & Water Sts.
Dover, DE 19901
Phone: (302) 739-4776

Michael L. Richards
Director
Vital Statistics Ofc.
Div. of Public Health
P.O. Box 637
Dover, DE 19903
Phone: (302) 739-4721

DISTRICT OF COLUMBIA
Carl W. Wilson
Chief
Paternity & Child Support
800 9th St., SW, #100
Washington, DC 20024-2480
Phone: (202) 727-0682

FLORIDA
Ken Jones
Chief
Ofc. of Vital Statistics
Dept. of Health
P.O. Box 210
Jacksonville, FL 32231
Phone: (904) 359-6955
Fax: (904) 359-6931

GEORGIA
Michael Lavoie
Director
Vital Records Div.
Dept. of Human Resources
47 Trinity Ave., SW, Rm. 217-H
Atlanta, GA 30334
Phone: (404) 656-4750

GUAM
Dennis G. Rodriguez
Director
Dept. of Public Health & Social Services
P.O. Box 2816
Hagatna, GU 96932
Phone: (671) 735-7102
Fax: (671) 734-5910
E-mail: dennis_r_@NS.GOV.GU

HAWAII
Alvin R. Onaka
Acting Chief & State Registrar
Ofc. of Health Status Monitoring
Dept. of Health
1250 Punchbowl St., Rm. 104
Honolulu, HI 96813
Phone: (808) 586-4600
Fax: (808) 586-4606

IDAHO
Jane Smith
State Registrar & Chief
Ctr. for Health Statistics
Dept. of Health & Welfare
450 W. State St.
P.O. Box 83720
Boise, ID 83720-0036
Phone: (208) 334-5976
Fax: (208) 334-0685

ILLINOIS
Steven Perry
Chief
Div. of Vital Records
Dept. of Public Health
605 W. Jefferson
Springfield, IL 62761
Phone: (217) 782-6554

INDIANA
Barbara Stultz
Registrar
Vital Records Section
Dept. of Health
2 N. Meridian St.
Indianapolis, IN 46204
Phone: (317) 233-7523
Fax: (317) 233-5956

IOWA
Jill France
Bureau Chief
Vital Records & Statistics
Dept. of Public Health
Lucas State Ofc. Bldg.
321 E. 12th St.
Des Moines, IA 50319
Phone: (515) 281-6762

KANSAS
Charlene Robuck
Director
Ofc. of Vital Statistics
Dept. of Health & Environment
900 SW Jackson, 1st Fl.
Landon State Ofc. Bldg.
Topeka, KS 66612-1290
Phone: (785) 296-1414
Fax: (785) 296-8075

KENTUCKY
Patrick Rickard
Director
Div. of Vital Records & Health Dev.
Health Services
275 E. Main St.
Frankfort, KY 40621
Phone: (502) 564-4990
Fax: (502) 564-2556

LOUISIANA
William Barlow
Director of Vital Statistics
Ofc. of Public Health
Dept. of Health & Hospitals
P.O. Box 60630
New Orleans, LA 70160
Phone: (504) 568-8353
Fax: (504) 568-5391

MAINE
Donald R. Lemieux
Director
Div. of Vital Records & Statistics
Dept. of Human Services
11 State House Station
Augusta, ME 04333
Phone: (207) 624-5445

MARYLAND
Isabelle L. Horon
Director
Statistics Administration
Dept. of Health & Mental Hygiene
201 W. Preston St.
Baltimore, MD 21201
Phone: (410) 767-5950
Fax: (410) 767-6840
E-Mail: horoni@dhmh.state.md.us

MASSACHUSETTS
Elaine Trudeau
Registrar
Vital Statistics
Dept. of Public Health
470 Atlantic Ave.
Boston, MA 02210-2224
Phone: (617) 753-8600
Fax: (617) 753-8696

MICHIGAN
Carol Getts
State Registrar
Vital & Health Statistics
Dept. of Community Health
P.O. Box 30195
Lansing, MI 48909
Phone: (517) 335-8676

MINNESOTA
Barbara A. Bednarczyk
State Registrar
Vital Records
Dept. of Health
717 Delaware St., SE
Minneapolis, MN 55440
Phone: (651) 623-5771
Fax: (651) 623-5776
E-Mail: barbara.bednarczyk@health.state.mn.us

MISSISSIPPI
David Lohrisch
State Registrar
Vital Records
Dept. of Health
2423 N. State St.
Jackson, MS 39216
Phone: (601) 960-7982
Fax: (601) 354-6123

MISSOURI
Ivra Cross
Vital Records Chief Administrator
Bur. of Vital Records
Dept. of Health
930 Wildwood
P.O. Box 570
Jefferson City, MO 65102
Phone: (573) 751-6381
Fax: (573) 526-3846
E-Mail: crossi@mail.health.state.mo.us

MONTANA
Debra Fulton
Chief
Vital Statistics Bur.
Dept. of Public Health & Human Services
111 Sanders St.
Helena, MT 59604
Phone: (406) 444-4250
Fax: (406) 444-1803

NEBRASKA
Stanley Cooper
Director
Bur. of Vital Statistics
Dept. of Health & Human Services, Finance & Support
P.O. Box 95026
Lincoln, NE 68509-5007
Phone: (402) 471-0915
Fax: (402) 471-0820

NEVADA
Emil DeJan
Chief
State Ofc. of Vital Records
Dept. of Human Resources
505 E. King St., Rm. 102
Carson City, NV 89710
Phone: (775) 684-4242
Fax: (775) 684-4156

NEW HAMPSHIRE
Dianne Luby
Director
Ofc. of Health Mgmt.
Health & Human Services
6 Hazen Dr.
Concord, NH 03301-6527
Phone: (603) 271-4501
Fax: (603) 271-4827

NEW JERSEY
Donald Lipera
Registrar
Vital Statistics
Dept. of Health
S. Warren & Market Sts.
P.O. Box 370
Trenton, NJ 08625-8085
Phone: (609) 292-8085

NEW MEXICO
Betty Hileman
Director
Vital Statistics Bur.
Dept. of Health
1105 S. St. Francis Dr.
Santa Fe, NM 87503
Phone: (505) 827-2342

NEW YORK
Peter Carucci
Director
Vital Records
Empire State Plz.
Albany, NY 12237
Phone: (518) 474-3077
Fax: (518) 474-9168

NORTH CAROLINA
A. Torrey McLean
Head
Vital Records Branch
Dept. of Human Resources
225 N. McDowell St.
Raleigh, NC 27603-5902
Phone: (919) 733-3000
Fax: (919) 829-1359

NORTH DAKOTA
Beverly Wittman
Data Processing Coordinator
Vital Records
Dept. of Health
600 E. Blvd. Ave., 1st Fl. - Judicial Wing
Bismarck, ND 58505-0200
Phone: (701) 328-2360
Fax: (701) 328-1850
E-Mail: bwittman@state.nd.us

NORTHERN MARIANA ISLANDS
Margarita M. Palacios
Court Administrator
Supreme Ct.
P.O. Box 2165
Saipan, MP 96950
Phone: (670) 236-9800
Fax: (670) 236-9701
E-Mail: supreme.court@saipan.com

OHIO
Herman Butler
Chief
Div. of Vital Statistics
Dept. of Health
246 N. High St.
P.O. Box 118
Columbus, OH 43266
Phone: (614) 466-2533
Fax: (614) 644-7740

OKLAHOMA
Roger Pirrong
Director
Vital Records Div.
Dept. of Health
1000 NE 10th St.
Oklahoma City, OK 73152
Phone: (405) 271-4040
Fax: (405) 271-2930

OREGON
Edward J. Johnson, II
State Registrar
Ctr. for Health Statistics
Dept. of Human Resources
800 NE Oregon St.
Portland, OR 97201
Phone: (503) 731-4109
Fax: (503) 731-4084

PENNSYLVANIA
Charles L. Hardester
Director
Div. of Vital Statistics
Dept. of Health
P.O. Box 1528
New Castle, PA 16103
Phone: (412) 656-3100
Fax: (724) 656-3224

PUERTO RICO
Luis Torrado
Director
Demographic Registry
Dept. of Health
Fernandez Juncos Station
San Juan, PR 00910
Phone: (787) 726-1027

RHODE ISLAND
Edward J. Martin
Chief
Vital Statistics
Dept. of Health
75 Davis St.
Providence, RI 02908
Phone: (401) 222-2812

SOUTH CAROLINA
Murray B. Hudson
Director
Vital Records & Public Health
Dept. of Health & Environmental Control
2600 Bull St.
Columbia, SC 29201
Phone: (803) 898-3650

SOUTH DAKOTA
Doneen Hollingsworth
Secretary
Dept. of Health
600 E. Capitol Ave.
Pierre, SD 57501
Phone: (605) 773-3361
Fax: (605) 773-5683

TENNESSEE
Paula Taylor
Director
Div. of Vital Records
Dept. of Health
Cordell Hull Bldg.
Nashville, TN 37247
Phone: (615) 532-2600

TEXAS
Richard Bays
Chief
Bur. of Vital Statistics
Dept. of Health
1100 W. 49th St.
Austin, TX 78756
Phone: (512) 458-7111
Fax: (512) 458-7711

U.S. VIRGIN ISLANDS
Wilbur Callender
Commissioner
Dept. of Health
No. 48 Sugar Estate
St. Thomas, VI 00802
Phone: (340) 774-0117
Fax: (340) 777-4001

UTAH
Barry E. Nangle
Director
Bur. of Vital Records
Dept. of Health
288 N. 1460 W.
P.O. Box 142855
Salt Lake City, UT 84114-2855
Phone: (801) 538-6186
Fax: (801) 538-7012
E-Mail: bnangle@doh.state.ut.us

VERMONT
Linda Davis
Supervisor
Vital Records Div.
Dept. of Health
P.O. Box 70
Burlington, VT 05402
Phone: (802) 863-7275
Fax: (802) 865-7701

VIRGINIA
E. Anne Peterson
Acting Commissioner
Dept. of Health
Main St. Station, Rm. 214
1500 E. Main St.
Richmond, VA 23219
Phone: (804) 786-3561
Fax: (804) 786-4616

WASHINGTON
Teresa Jennings
Director
Ctr. for Health Statistics
Dept. of Health
P.O. Box 47814
Olympia, WA 98504-7814
Phone: (360) 753-5936
Fax: (360) 753-4135

WEST VIRGINIA
Gary Thompson
State Registrar
Vital Registration Ofc.
Bur. of Public Health
Bldg. 3, Rm. 516
Charleston, WV 25305
Phone: (304) 558-2931
Fax: (304) 558-1051

WISCONSIN
Barbara Rudolph
Director
Ctr. for Health Statistics
Dept. of Health & Social Services
1 W. Wilson, 3rd Fl.
Madison, WI 53703
Phone: (608) 266-1939
Fax: (608) 261-6380

WYOMING
Lucinda McCaffrey
Deputy State Registrar
Vital Records
Dept. of Health
Hathaway Bldg.
2300 Capitol Ave.
Cheyenne, WY 82002
Phone: (307) 777-7591

Vocational Education

Administers public vocational education programs that provide individuals with marketable skills.

ALABAMA
Lamona H. Lucas
Commissioner
Dept. of Rehab. Services
2129 E. South Blvd.
Montgomery, AL 36116
Phone: (334) 281-8780
Fax: (334) 281-1973

ALASKA
Duane French
Director
Vocational Rehab.
Dept. of Education
801 W. 10th St., Ste. 200
Juneau, AK 99801-1894
Phone: (907) 465-6933
Fax: (907) 465-2856

AMERICAN SAMOA
Marie F. Mao
Director
Dept. of Human & Social Services
AS Govt.
Pago Pago, AS 96799
Phone: (684) 633-2609
Fax: (684) 633-7449
E-mail: dhss@samoatelco.com

ARIZONA
Bill F. Hernandez
Assistant Director
Employment & Rehab. Services
Dept. of Economic Security
1789 W. Washington St.
Phoenix, AZ 85007
Phone: (602) 542-4910

ARKANSAS
Bobby Simpson
Commissioner
Rehab. Services
Dept. of Education
1616 Brookwood Dr.
Little Rock, AR 72202
Phone: (501) 682-6709
Fax: (501) 682-1509

CALIFORNIA
Brenda Premo
Director
Dept. of Rehab.
2000 Evergreen St.
Sacramento, CA 95815
Phone: (916) 445-3971

COLORADO
Diana Huerta
Director
Vocational Rehab. Div.
Dept. of Human Services
110 16th St., 2nd Fl.
Denver, CO 80202
Phone: (303) 620-4152
Fax: (303) 620-4189

CONNECTICUT
John Halliday
Director
Bur. of Rehabilitative Services
Dept. of Social Services
25 Sigourney St.
Hartford, CT 06106-5001
Phone: (860) 424-4848

DELAWARE
Andrea Guest
Director
Vocational Rehab. Div.
Dept. of Labor
P.O. Box 9969
Wilmington, DE 19809-0969
Phone: (302) 761-8275
Fax: (302) 761-6622

DISTRICT OF COLUMBIA
Ruth Hill
Administrator
Rehab. Services Administration
Dept. of Human Services
800 9th St., SW, 4th Fl.
Washington, DC 20024-2480

FLORIDA
Tamara Bibb Allen
Director
Div. of Vocational Rehab.
Labor & Employment Security
Bldg. A
2002 Old St. Augustine Rd.
Tallahassee, FL 32399-0696
Phone: (850) 488-0059
Fax: (850) 921-7215

GEORGIA
Peggy Rosser
Director
Div. of Rehab. Services
Dept. of Human Resources
2 Peachtree St., Rm. 35-240
Atlanta, GA 30303
Phone: (404) 656-3000

GUAM
Joseph Artero-Cameron
Director
Dept. of Integrated Services for Individuals with Disabilities
1313 Central Ave.
Tiyan, GU 96913
Phone: (671) 475-4646
Fax: (671) 477-2892

HAWAII
Neil Shim
Administrator
Vocational Rehab. & Services for the Blind
Dept. of Human Services
601 Kamokila Blvd., Rm. 515
Kapolei, HI 96707
Phone: (808) 692-7719
Fax: (808) 692-7727

IDAHO
F. Pat Young
Administrator
Vocational Rehab. Div.
State Board of Education
650 W. State St.
Boise, ID 83720-0096
Phone: (208) 334-3390

ILLINOIS

INDIANA
Suellen Jackson-Boner
Executive Director
Governor's Planning Council for People with Disabilities
143 W. Market, Ste. 404
Indianapolis, IN 46204
Phone: (317) 232-7770
Fax: (317) 233-3712
E-mail: gpcpd@in.net

IOWA
Marge Knudsen
Administrator
Vocational Rehabilitative Services
Dept. of Education
510 E. 12th St.
Des Moines, IA 50319
Phone: (515) 281-6731

KANSAS
Joyce Cussimanio
Commissioner
Vocational Rehab. & Blind Services
Social & Rehab. Services
300 SW Oakley, Biddle Bldg.
Topeka, KS 66606-2807
Phone: (785) 296-3911
Fax: (785) 296-0511

KENTUCKY
Sam Serraglio
Commissioner
Dept. of Vocational Rehab.
209 St. Clair
Frankfort, KY 40601
Phone: (502) 564-4440
Fax: (502) 564-6745

LOUISIANA
Madlyn Bagneris
Secretary
Dept. of Social Services
P.O. Box 3776
Baton Rouge, LA 70821
Phone: (225) 342-0286
Fax: (225) 342-8636

MAINE
John G. Shattuck
Director
Bur. of Rehab.
Dept. of Human Services
11 State House Station
Augusta, ME 04333
Phone: (207) 624-5300

MARYLAND
Robert Burns
Assistant State
Superintendent
Div. of Rehab. Services
State Dept. of Education
2301 Argonne Dr.
Baltimore, MD 21218
Phone: (410) 554-9385

MASSACHUSETTS
Elmer C. Bartels
Commissioner
Rehabilitation Comm.
Executive Ofc. of Health &
Human Services
27-43 Wormwood St.,
Ste. 600
Boston, MA 02210
Phone: (617) 204-3600
Fax: (617) 727-1354

MICHIGAN
Robert Davis
Director
Rehab. Services
Economic Div. Corp.
P.O. Box 30010
Lansing, MI 48909
Phone: (517) 335-1343
Fax: (517) 373-0565

MINNESOTA
Michael Coleman
Assistant Commissioner
Rehab. Services Branch
Dept. of Economic Security
390 N. Robert St.
St. Paul, MN 55101
Phone: (651) 296-1822
Fax: (651) 296-0994
E-mail: mick.coleman
@state.mn.us

MISSISSIPPI
Butch McMillian
Executive Director
Dept. of Rehab. Services
P.O. Box 1698
Jackson, MS 39215-1698
Phone: (601) 853-5200
Fax: (601) 853-5205

MISSOURI
Ronald Vessell
Assistant Commissioner
Div. of Vocational Rehab.
Dept. of Elementary &
Secondary Education
3024 W. Truman Blvd.
Jefferson City, MO 65109
Phone: (573) 751-3251
Fax: (573) 751-1441
E-mail: rvessell
@vr.dese.state.mo.us

MONTANA
Joe A. Mathews
Administrator
Disability Services Div.
Dept. of Public Health &
Human Services
111 Sanders St.
Helena, MT 59620
Phone: (406) 444-2591
Fax: (406) 444-3632

NEBRASKA
Frank Lloyd
Director
Rehab. Services Div.
Dept. of Education
P.O. Box 94987
Lincoln, NE 68509
Phone: (402) 471-3649
Fax: (402) 471-0117

NEVADA
Stephen A. Shaw
Administrator
Div. of Child & Family
Services
711 E. 5th St.
Carson City, NV 89701-5092
Phone: (775) 684-4400
Fax: (775) 684-4455
E-mail: sshaw
@govmail.state.nv.us

NEW HAMPSHIRE
Paul K. Leather
Director
Education, Adult Learning
& Rehab.
Dept. of Education
78 Regional Dr., Bldg. 2
Concord, NH 03301-8508
Phone: (603) 271-3471

NEW JERSEY
Richard Herring
Director
Deaf & Hard of Hearing
Div.
Human Services Dept.
P.O. Box 074
Capitol Ctr.
Trenton, NJ 08625
Phone: (609) 984-7281

Jamie C. Hilton
Executive Director
Comm. for the Blind &
Visually Impaired
Human Services Dept.
153 Halsey St.
P.O. Box 47017
Newark, NJ 07107
Phone: (973) 648-2324
Fax: (973) 648-7364

Thomas G. Jennings
Director
Div. of Vocational Rehab.
Services
Dept. of Labor
135 E. State St.
P.O. Box 398
Trenton, NJ 08625-0398
Phone: (609) 292-7318
Fax: (609) 292-5987

NEW MEXICO
Terry Brigance
Director
Div. of Vocational Rehab.
Dept. of Education
435 St. Michaels Dr.,
Bldg. D
Santa Fe, NM 87505
Phone: (505) 954-8511
Fax: (505) 954-8562

NEW YORK
Lawrence Gloeckler
Deputy Commissioner
Ofc. of Vocational &
Educational Services
1 Commerce Plz., Rm. 1606
Albany, NY 12234
Phone: (518) 474-2714
Fax: (518) 474-8802

NORTH CAROLINA
Bob Philbeck
Director
Vocational Rehab.
P.O. Box 26053
Raleigh, NC 27611-6053
Phone: (919) 733-3364
Fax: (919) 733-7968

NORTH DAKOTA
Gene Hysjulien
Director
Developmental Disabilities
Dept. of Human Services
600 S. 2nd St., Ste. 1-B
Bismarck, ND 58504-5729
Phone: (701) 328-8950
Fax: (701) 328-8969
E-mail: sohysg@state.nd.us

NORTHERN MARIANA ISLANDS
Maria T. Persson
Director
Vocational Rehab. Div.
Public Health
Caller Box 10007
Saipan, MP 96950
Phone: (670) 664-6537
Fax: (670) 322-6536

OHIO
Robert Rabe
Administrator
Rehab. Services Comm.
P.O. Box 359001
W. Worthington, OH 43235
Phone: (614) 438-1210
Fax: (614) 438-1257

OKLAHOMA
Linda Parker
Director
Vocational Rehab.
Dept. of Human Services
3535 NW 58th, Ste. 500
Oklahoma City, OK 73112
Phone: (405) 951-3400
Fax: (405) 951-3529

OREGON
Bill Brown
Acting Administrator
Div. of Vocational Rehab.
Dept. of Human Resources
500 Summer St., NE
Salem, OR 97310
Phone: (503) 945-6201
Fax: (503) 947-5025

PENNSYLVANIA
Susan L. Alderte
Executive Director
Ofc. of Rehab.
Dept. of Labor & Industry
1300 Labor & Industry
Bldg.
Harrisburg, PA 17120
Phone: (717) 787-5244
Fax: (717) 783-5221

PUERTO RICO
Jose R. Santana
Administrator
Vocational Rehab.
Dept. of Social Services
P.O. Box 191118
Santurce, PR 00919-1118
Phone: (787) 728-5100
Fax: (787) 728-8070

RHODE ISLAND
Raymond Carroll
Administrator
Vocational Rehab.
Dept. of Human Services
40 Fountain St.
Providence, RI 02903-1898
Phone: (401) 421-7005
Fax: (401) 421-9259

SOUTH CAROLINA
Bob Couch
Director
Ofc. Of Occupational Education
State Dept. of Education
902 Rutledge Bldg.
1429 Senate St.
Columbia, SC 29201
Phone: (803) 734-8410

SOUTH DAKOTA
John Jones
Secretary
Dept. of Human Services
Hillsview Plz.
500 E. Capitol Ave.
Pierre, SD 57501
Phone: (605) 773-5990
Fax: (605) 773-5483

TENNESSEE
Carl Brown
Assistant Commissioner
Div. of Rehab. Services
Dept. of Human Services
Citizen's Plz. Bldg., 15th Fl.
400 Deaderick St.
Nashville, TN 37248-6000
Phone: (615) 313-4714
Fax: (615) 741-4165

TEXAS
Dave Ward
Deputy Commissioner
Rehab. Comm.
Brown-Heatly Bldg.
4900 N. Lamar
Austin, TX 78751-2316
Phone: (512) 424-4773
Fax: (512) 424-4277

U.S. VIRGIN ISLANDS
Sedonie Halbert
Commissioner
Dept. of Human Services
Knud Hansen Complex, Bldg. A
1303 Hospital Grounds
St. Thomas, VI 00802
Phone: (340) 774-0930
Fax: (340) 774-3466

UTAH
William Gibson
Director
Div. of Services for the Blind & Visually Impaired
Ofc. of Rehab.
250 N. 1950 W., Ste. B
Salt Lake City, UT 84116-7902
Phone: (801) 323-4345
Fax: (801) 323-4396
E-mail: bgibson@usor.state.ut.us

VERMONT
Diane Dalmasse
Director
Vocational Rehab. Div.
Dept. of Social & Rehab. Services
103 S. Main, 2nd Fl.
Waterbury, VT 05671
Phone: (802) 241-2186

VIRGINIA
R. David Ross
Acting Commissioner
Dept. of Rehabiliitative Services
8004 Franklin Farms Dr.
Richmond, VA 23229
Phone: (804) 662-7010
Fax: (804) 662-7644

WASHINGTON
Michael Arniss
Program Manager
Vocational Rehab. Section
Dept. of Labor & Industries
P.O. Box 44323
Olympia, WA 98504-4323
Phone: (360) 902-4477
Fax: (360) 902-5035

WEST VIRGINIA
Joseph Jeffers
Director
Rehab. Services
State Capitol
1900 Kanawha Blvd., E.
Charleston, WV 25305
Phone: (304) 776-4671
Fax: (304) 766-4905

WISCONSIN
Tom Dixon
Administrator
Div. of Vocational Rehab.
Dept. of Workforce Dev.
2917 Intl. Ln.
P.O. Box 7852
Madison, WI 53707-7852
Phone: (608) 243-5600
Fax: (608) 243-5680

WYOMING
Gary Child
Administrator
Vocational Rehab. Div.
Dept. of Employment
Herschler Bldg.
Cheyenne, WY 82002
Phone: (307) 777-7341

Vocational Rehabilitation —

Assists and encourages disabled persons to find suitable employment through training programs.

ALABAMA
Lamona H. Lucas
Commissioner
Dept. of Rehab. Services
2129 E. South Blvd.
Montgomery, AL 36116
Phone: (334) 281-8780
Fax: (334) 281-1973

ALASKA
Duane French
Director
Vocational Rehab.
Dept. of Education
801 W. 10th St., Ste. 200
Juneau, AK 99801-1894
Phone: (907) 465-6933
Fax: (907) 465-2856

AMERICAN SAMOA
Marie F. Mao
Director
Dept. of Human & Social Services
AS Govt.
Pago Pago, AS 96799
Phone: (684) 633-2609
Fax: (684) 633-7449
E-mail: dhss@samoatelco.com

ARIZONA
Bill F. Hernandez
Assistant Director
Employment & Rehab. Services
Dept. of Economic Security
1789 W. Washington St.
Phoenix, AZ 85007
Phone: (602) 542-4910

ARKANSAS
Bobby Simpson
Commissioner
Rehab. Services
Dept. of Education
1616 Brookwood Dr.
Little Rock, AR 72202
Phone: (501) 682-6709
Fax: (501) 682-1509

CALIFORNIA
Brenda Premo
Director
Dept. of Rehab.
2000 Evergreen St.
Sacramento, CA 95815
Phone: (916) 445-3971

COLORADO
Diana Huerta
Director
Vocational Rehab. Div.
Dept. of Human Services
110 16th St., 2nd Fl.
Denver, CO 80202
Phone: (303) 620-4152
Fax: (303) 620-4189

CONNECTICUT
John Halliday
Director
Bur. of Rehabilitative Services
Dept. of Social Services
25 Sigourney St.
Hartford, CT 06106-5001
Phone: (860) 424-4848

DELAWARE
Andrea Guest
Director
Vocational Rehab. Div.
Dept. of Labor
P.O. Box 9969
Wilmington, DE 19809-0969
Phone: (302) 761-8275
Fax: (302) 761-6622

DISTRICT OF COLUMBIA
Ruth Hill
Administrator
Rehab. Services Administration
Dept. of Human Services
800 9th St., SW, 4th Fl.
Washington, DC 20024-2480

FLORIDA
Tamara Bibb Allen
Director
Div. of Vocational Rehab.
Labor & Employment Security
Bldg. A
2002 Old St. Augustine Rd.
Tallahassee, FL 32399-0696
Phone: (850) 488-0059
Fax: (850) 921-7215

GEORGIA
Peggy Rosser
Director
Div. of Rehab. Services
Dept. of Human Resources
2 Peachtree St., Rm. 35-240
Atlanta, GA 30303
Phone: (404) 656-3000

GUAM
Joseph Artero-Cameron
Director
Dept. of Integrated Services for Individuals with Disabilities
1313 Central Ave.
Tiyan, GU 96913
Phone: (671) 475-4646
Fax: (671) 477-2892

HAWAII
Neil Shim
Administrator
Vocational Rehab. & Services for the Blind
Dept. of Human Services
601 Kamokila Blvd., Rm. 515
Kapolei, HI 96707
Phone: (808) 692-7719
Fax: (808) 692-7727

IDAHO
F. Pat Young
Administrator
Vocational Rehab. Div.
State Board of Education
650 W. State St.
Boise, ID 83720-0096
Phone: (208) 334-3390

ILLINOIS

INDIANA
Suellen Jackson-Boner
Executive Director
Governor's Planning Council for People with Disabilities
143 W. Market, Ste. 404
Indianapolis, IN 46204
Phone: (317) 232-7770
Fax: (317) 233-3712
E-mail: gpcpd@in.net

IOWA
Marge Knudsen
Administrator
Vocational Rehabilitative Services
Dept. of Education
510 E. 12th St.
Des Moines, IA 50319
Phone: (515) 281-6731

KANSAS
Joyce Cussimanio
Commissioner
Vocational Rehab. & Blind Services
Social & Rehab. Services
300 SW Oakley, Biddle Bldg.
Topeka, KS 66606-2807
Phone: (785) 296-3911
Fax: (785) 296-0511

KENTUCKY
Sam Serraglio
Commissioner
Dept. of Vocational Rehab.
209 St. Clair
Frankfort, KY 40601
Phone: (502) 564-4440
Fax: (502) 564-6745

LOUISIANA
Madlyn Bagneris
Secretary
Dept. of Social Services
P.O. Box 3776
Baton Rouge, LA 70821
Phone: (225) 342-0286
Fax: (225) 342-8636

MAINE
John G. Shattuck
Director
Bur. of Rehab.
Dept. of Human Services
11 State House Station
Augusta, ME 04333
Phone: (207) 624-5300

MARYLAND
Robert Burns
Assistant State Superintendent
Div. of Rehab. Services
State Dept. of Education
2301 Argonne Dr.
Baltimore, MD 21218
Phone: (410) 554-9385

MASSACHUSETTS
Elmer C. Bartels
Commissioner
Rehabilitation Comm.
Executive Ofc. of Health & Human Services
27-43 Wormwood St., Ste. 600
Boston, MA 02210
Phone: (617) 204-3600
Fax: (617) 727-1354

MICHIGAN
Robert Davis
Director
Rehab. Services
Economic Div. Corp.
P.O. Box 30010
Lansing, MI 48909
Phone: (517) 335-1343
Fax: (517) 373-0565

MINNESOTA
Michael Coleman
Assistant Commissioner
Rehab. Services Branch
Dept. of Economic Security
390 N. Robert St.
St. Paul, MN 55101
Phone: (651) 296-1822
Fax: (651) 296-0994
E-mail: mick.coleman@state.mn.us

MISSISSIPPI
Butch McMillian
Executive Director
Dept. of Rehab. Services
P.O. Box 1698
Jackson, MS 39215-1698
Phone: (601) 853-5200
Fax: (601) 853-5205

MISSOURI
Ronald Vessell
Assistant Commissioner
Div. of Vocational Rehab.
Dept. of Elementary & Secondary Education
3024 W. Truman Blvd.
Jefferson City, MO 65109
Phone: (573) 751-3251
Fax: (573) 751-1441
E-mail: rvessell@vr.dese.state.mo.us

MONTANA
Joe A. Mathews
Administrator
Disability Services Div.
Dept. of Public Health & Human Services
111 Sanders St.
Helena, MT 59620
Phone: (406) 444-2591
Fax: (406) 444-3632

NEBRASKA
Frank Lloyd
Director
Rehab. Services Div.
Dept. of Education
P.O. Box 94987
Lincoln, NE 68509
Phone: (402) 471-3649
Fax: (402) 471-0117

NEVADA
Stephen A. Shaw
Administrator
Div. of Child & Family Services
711 E. 5th St.
Carson City, NV 89701-5092
Phone: (775) 684-4400
Fax: (775) 684-4455
E-mail: sshaw@govmail.state.nv.us

NEW HAMPSHIRE
Paul K. Leather
Director
Education, Adult Learning & Rehab.
Dept. of Education
78 Regional Dr., Bldg. 2
Concord, NH 03301-8508
Phone: (603) 271-3471

NEW JERSEY
Richard Herring
Director
Deaf & Hard of Hearing Div.
Human Services Dept.
P.O. Box 074
Capitol Ctr.
Trenton, NJ 08625
Phone: (609) 984-7281

Jamie C. Hilton
Executive Director
Comm. for the Blind & Visually Impaired
Human Services Dept.
153 Halsey St.
P.O. Box 47017
Newark, NJ 07107
Phone: (973) 648-2324
Fax: (973) 648-7364

Thomas G. Jennings
Director
Div. of Vocational Rehab. Services
Dept. of Labor
135 E. State St.
P.O. Box 398
Trenton, NJ 08625-0398
Phone: (609) 292-7318
Fax: (609) 292-5987

NEW MEXICO
Terry Brigance
Director
Div. of Vocational Rehab.
Dept. of Education
435 St. Michaels Dr., Bldg. D
Santa Fe, NM 87505
Phone: (505) 954-8511
Fax: (505) 954-8562

NEW YORK
Lawrence Gloeckler
Deputy Commissioner
Ofc. of Vocational & Educational Services
1 Commerce Plz., Rm. 1606
Albany, NY 12234
Phone: (518) 474-2714
Fax: (518) 474-8802

NORTH CAROLINA
Bob Philbeck
Director
Vocational Rehab.
P.O. Box 26053
Raleigh, NC 27611-6053
Phone: (919) 733-3364
Fax: (919) 733-7968

NORTH DAKOTA
Gene Hysjulien
Director
Developmental Disabilities
Dept. of Human Services
600 S. 2nd St., Ste. 1-B
Bismarck, ND 58504-5729
Phone: (701) 328-8950
Fax: (701) 328-8969
E-mail: sohysg@state.nd.us

NORTHERN MARIANA ISLANDS
Maria T. Persson
Director
Vocational Rehab. Div.
Public Health
Caller Box 10007
Saipan, MP 96950
Phone: (670) 664-6537
Fax: (670) 322-6536

OHIO
Robert Rabe
Administrator
Rehab. Services Comm.
P.O. Box 359001
W. Worthington, OH 43235
Phone: (614) 438-1210
Fax: (614) 438-1257

OKLAHOMA
Linda Parker
Director
Vocational Rehab.
Dept. of Human Services
3535 NW 58th, Ste. 500
Oklahoma City, OK 73112
Phone: (405) 951-3400
Fax: (405) 951-3529

OREGON
Bill Brown
Acting Administrator
Div. of Vocational Rehab.
Dept. of Human Resources
500 Summer St., NE
Salem, OR 97310
Phone: (503) 945-6201
Fax: (503) 947-5025

PENNSYLVANIA
Susan L. Alderte
Executive Director
Ofc. of Rehab.
Dept. of Labor & Industry
1300 Labor & Industry Bldg.
Harrisburg, PA 17120
Phone: (717) 787-5244
Fax: (717) 783-5221

PUERTO RICO
Jose R. Santana
Administrator
Vocational Rehab.
Dept. of Social Services
P.O. Box 191118
Santurce, PR 00919-1118
Phone: (787) 728-5100
Fax: (787) 728-8070

RHODE ISLAND
Raymond Carroll
Administrator
Vocational Rehab.
Dept. of Human Services
40 Fountain St.
Providence, RI 02903-1898
Phone: (401) 421-7005
Fax: (401) 421-9259

SOUTH CAROLINA
Bob Couch
Director
Ofc. Of Occupational Education
State Dept. of Education
902 Rutledge Bldg.
1429 Senate St.
Columbia, SC 29201
Phone: (803) 734-8410

SOUTH DAKOTA
John Jones
Secretary
Dept. of Human Services
Hillsview Plz.
500 E. Capitol Ave.
Pierre, SD 57501
Phone: (605) 773-5990
Fax: (605) 773-5483

TENNESSEE
Carl Brown
Assistant Commissioner
Div. of Rehab. Services
Dept. of Human Services
Citizen's Plz. Bldg., 15th Fl.
400 Deaderick St.
Nashville, TN 37248-6000
Phone: (615) 313-4714
Fax: (615) 741-4165

TEXAS
Dave Ward
Deputy Commissioner
Rehab. Comm.
Brown-Heatly Bldg.
4900 N. Lamar
Austin, TX 78751-2316
Phone: (512) 424-4773
Fax: (512) 424-4277

U.S. VIRGIN ISLANDS
Sedonie Halbert
Commissioner
Dept. of Human Services
Knud Hansen Complex, Bldg. A
1303 Hospital Grounds
St. Thomas, VI 00802
Phone: (340) 774-0930
Fax: (340) 774-3466

UTAH
William Gibson
Director
Div. of Services for the Blind & Visually Impaired
Ofc. of Rehab.
250 N. 1950 W., Ste. B
Salt Lake City, UT 84116-7902
Phone: (801) 323-4345
Fax: (801) 323-4396
E-mail: bgibson@usor.state.ut.us

VERMONT
Diane Dalmasse
Director
Vocational Rehab. Div.
Dept. of Social & Rehab. Services
103 S. Main, 2nd Fl.
Waterbury, VT 05671
Phone: (802) 241-2186

VIRGINIA
R. David Ross
Acting Commissioner
Dept. of Rehabiliitative Services
8004 Franklin Farms Dr.
Richmond, VA 23229
Phone: (804) 662-7010
Fax: (804) 662-7644

WASHINGTON
Michael Arniss
Program Manager
Vocational Rehab. Section
Dept. of Labor & Industries
P.O. Box 44323
Olympia, WA 98504-4323
Phone: (360) 902-4477
Fax: (360) 902-5035

WEST VIRGINIA
Joseph Jeffers
Director
Rehab. Services
State Capitol
1900 Kanawha Blvd., E.
Charleston, WV 25305
Phone: (304) 776-4671
Fax: (304) 766-4905

WISCONSIN
Tom Dixon
Administrator
Div. of Vocational Rehab.
Dept. of Workforce Dev.
2917 Intl. Ln.
P.O. Box 7852
Madison, WI 53707-7852
Phone: (608) 243-5600
Fax: (608) 243-5680

WYOMING
Gary Child
Administrator
Vocational Rehab. Div.
Dept. of Employment
Herschler Bldg.
Cheyenne, WY 82002
Phone: (307) 777-7341

Water Quality

Responsible for water quality protection programs in the state.

ALABAMA
Charles Horn
Chief
Water Quality Branch
Water Div.
Dept. of Environmental Mgmt.
1751 Cong. Dickinson Dr.
Montgomery, AL 36130-1463
Phone: (334) 271-7826
Fax: (334) 279-3051

ALASKA
Mike Conway
Director
Div. of Air & Water Quality
Dept. of Environmental Conservation
410 Willoughby Ave., Ste. 105
Juneau, AK 99801
Phone: (907) 465-5300
Fax: (907) 465-5274

AMERICAN SAMOA
Togipa Tausaga
Director
Environmental Protection Agency
Ofc. of the Governor
Pago Pago, AS 96799
Phone: (684) 633-7691

ARIZONA
Karen L. Smith
Director
Div. of Water Quality
Dept. of Environmental Quality
3033 N. Central Ave.
Phoenix, AZ 85012
Phone: (602) 207-2306

ARKANSAS
Randy Young
Executive Director
Soil & Water Conservation
101 E. Capitol, Ste. 350
Little Rock, AR 72201
Phone: (501) 682-1611
Fax: (501) 682-3991

CALIFORNIA
John Caffrey
Chair
Water Resources Control Board
P.O. Box 944213
Sacramento, CA 94244
Phone: (916) 657-2399

COLORADO
David Holm
Director
Water Quality Control Div.
Dept. of Public Health & Environment
4300 Cherry Creek Dr., S.
Denver, CO 80246-1530
Phone: (303) 692-3500
Fax: (303) 782-0390

CONNECTICUT
Karl J. Wagener
Executive Director
Council on Environmental Quality
Dept. of Environmental Protection
79 Elm St., 3rd Fl.
Hartford, CT 06106
Phone: (860) 424-4000

DELAWARE
Gerald L. Esposito
Director
Div. of Water Resources
Dept. of Natural Resources & Environmental Control
89 Kings Hwy.
Dover, DE 19901
Phone: (302) 739-4860
Fax: (302) 739-3491

DISTRICT OF COLUMBIA
Jerry Johnson
General Manager
Water & Sewer Authority
5000 Overlook Ave., SW
Washington, DC 20032
Phone: (202) 645-6309

FLORIDA
Mimi Drew
Director
Div. of Water Facilities
Dept. of Environmental Protection
2600 Blairstone Rd.
Tallahassee, FL 32399-2400
Phone: (850) 487-1855
Fax: (850) 487-3618

GEORGIA
Alan Hallum
Chief, Water Protection Branch
Environmental Protection Div.
Dept. of Natural Resources
205 Butler St., Ste. 1152
Atlanta, GA 30334
Phone: (404) 656-4905

GUAM
Jesus T. Salas
Administrator
Environmental Protection Agency
15-6101 Mariner Ave., Tiyan
P.O. Box 22439
Barrigada, GU 96921
Phone: (671) 475-1658
Fax: (671) 477-9402

HAWAII
Denis Lau
Chief
Clean Water Branch
Dept. of Health
919 Ala Moana Blvd., Rm. 301
Honolulu, HI 96814
Phone: (808) 586-4309
Fax: (808) 586-4370

IDAHO
Larry L. Koenig
Assistant Administrator
Community Services
Div. of Environmental Quality
1410 N. Hilton St., 2nd Fl.
Boise, ID 83706-1255
Phone: (208) 373-0407

ILLINOIS
Jim Park
Manager
Water Pollution Control Div.
IEPA
P.O. Box 19276
Springfield, IL 62794-9276
Phone: (217) 782-1654

INDIANA
Mary Ellen Gray
Chief
Water Planning Branch
Dept. of Environmental Mgmt.
100 N. Senate
P.O. Box 6015
Indianapolis, IN 46206
Phone: (317) 233-2550
Fax: (317) 232-8406

IOWA
Jack Riessen
Supervisor
Water Resource Section
Wallace State Ofc. Bldg.
E. 4th & Grand Aves.
Des Moines, IA 50319
Phone: (515) 281-8941

KANSAS
Karl Mueldener
Director
Bur. of Water
Dept. of Health & Environment
Forbes Field Bldg. 283
6700 SW Topeka Blvd.
Topeka, KS 66619
Phone: (785) 296-5500
Fax: (785) 296-5509

KENTUCKY

LOUISIANA
Linda Korn Levy
Assistant Secretary
Ofc. of Water Resources
Dept. of Environmental Quality
P.O. Box 82215
Baton Rouge, LA 70884
Phone: (225) 765-0634
Fax: (225) 765-0635

MAINE
Martha Kirkpatrick
Director
Land & Water Quality Control
Dept. of Environmental Protection
17 State House Station
Augusta, ME 04333
Phone: (207) 287-3901

MARYLAND
J.L. Hearn
Director
Water Mgmt. Administration
Dept. of the Environment
2500 Broening Hwy.
Baltimore, MD 21224-6612
Phone: (410) 631-3567
Fax: (410) 631-4894
E-mail: jhearn@mde.state.md.us

MASSACHUSETTS
Yvette DePeiza
Manager
Water Quality Control
Div. of Water Supply
1 Winter St., 6th Fl.
Boston, MA 02108
Phone: (617) 292-5857
Fax: (617) 292-5696

MICHIGAN
Tracy Mehan
Director
Ofc. of the Great Lakes
Dept. of Environmental Quality
P.O. Box 30028
Lansing, MI 48909
Phone: (517) 373-3588

MINNESOTA
Robert Bjork
Manager, North District
Water Quality Div.
Pollution Control Agency
520 Lafayette Rd.
St. Paul, MN 55155
Phone: (651) 296-7202
Fax: (651) 297-2343

Rodney E. Massey
Manager, South District
Water Quality Div.
Pollution Control Agency
520 Lafayette Rd.
St. Paul, MN 55155
Phone: (651) 296-7202
Fax: (651) 297-2343
E-mail: rodney.massey@pca.state.mn.us

MISSISSIPPI
Barry Royals
Chief
Surface Water Branch
Ofc. of Pollution Control
P.O. Box 10385
Jackson, MS 39289-0385
Phone: (601) 961-5102
Fax: (601) 961-5703

MISSOURI
Edwin Knight
Director
Water Pollution Control Program
Div. of Environmental Quality
Dept. of Natural Resources
P.O. Box 176
Jefferson City, MO 65102
Phone: (573) 751-1300
Fax: (573) 751-9396
E-mail: nrknight@mail.dnr.state.mo.us

MONTANA
Tim Fox
Acting Administrator
Planning, Prevention & Assistance
Dept. of Environmental Quality
Metcalf Bldg.
1520 E. 6th Ave.
Helena, MT 59620
Phone: (406) 444-6697
Fax: (406) 444-6836

NEBRASKA
Patrick Rice
Assistant Director
Water Quality Div.
Dept. of Environmental Control
P.O. Box 98922
Lincoln, NE 68509
Phone: (402) 471-3098
Fax: (402) 471-2909

NEVADA
Allen Biaggi
Administrator
Air, Mining & Water Section
Div. of Environmental Protection
333 W. Nye Ln., Rm. 138
Carson City, NV 89706
Phone: (775) 687-4670
Fax: (775) 687-5856

NEW HAMPSHIRE
Harry Stewart
Director
Water Div.
Environmental Services
P.O. Box 95
Concord, NH 03302-0095
Phone: (603) 271-3503
Fax: (603) 271-2867

NEW JERSEY
Dennis Hart
Director
Water Monitoring Mgmt.
Environmental Protection & Energy Dept.
401 E. State St.
P.O. Box 423
Trenton, NJ 08625-0423
Phone: (609) 292-4543
Fax: (609) 777-1330

NEW MEXICO
Greg Lewis
Director
Water & Waste Mgmt. Div.
Dept. of Environment
P.O. Box 26110
Sante Fe, NM 87502
Phone: (505) 827-2855
Fax: (505) 827-2836

NEW YORK
John Cahill
Commissioner
Dept. of Environmental Conservation
50 Wolf Rd.
Albany, NY 12233-1010
Phone: (518) 457-1162
Fax: (518) 457-7744

NORTH CAROLINA
Tommy Stevens
Director of Water Quality
Div. of Water Quality
Dept. of Environment & Natural Resources
P.O. Box 27687
Raleigh, NC 27611
Phone: (919) 733-7015
Fax: (919) 733-2496

NORTH DAKOTA
Dennis Fewless
Director
Water Quality
Environmental Health Section
P.O. Box 5520
Bismarck, ND 58506-5520
Phone: (701) 328-5210
Fax: (701) 328-5200
E-mail: dfewless@state.nd.us

NORTHERN MARIANA ISLANDS
Juan I. Castro
Director
Environmental Quality
Public Works
P.O. Box 1304
Saipan, MP 96950
Phone: (670) 234-1011
Fax: (670) 234-1003
E-mail: john.castro@saipan.com

OHIO
Lisa Morris
Chief
Div. of Surface Water
Environmental Protection Agency
122 S. Front St.
P.O. Box 1049
Columbus, OH 43216
Phone: (614) 644-2856
Fax: (614) 644-2329

OKLAHOMA
Derek Smithee
Chief
Water Quality Control Div.
Water Resources Board
3800 N. Classen Blvd.
Oklahoma City, OK 73118
Phone: (405) 530-8800
Fax: (405) 530-8900

OREGON
Mike Llewelyn
Administrator
Div. of Water Quality
Dept. of Environmental Quality
811 SW 6th Ave..
Portland, OR 97204
Phone: (503) 229-5324
Fax: (503) 229-6124

PENNSYLVANIA
Glenn E. Maurer
Director
Bur. of Water Quality Protection
Dept. of Environmental Resources
400 Market St., 11th Fl.
Harrisburg, PA 17105
Phone: (717) 787-2666
Fax: (717) 772-5156

PUERTO RICO
Hector Russe
President
Environmental Quality Board
P.O. Box 11488
San Juan, PR 00910-1488
Phone: (787) 767-8056
Fax: (787) 754-8294

RHODE ISLAND
Edward Szymanski
Deputy Bureau Chief
Dept. of Environmental Mgmt.
235 Promenade St.
Providence, RI 02908
Phone: (401) 222-2234

SOUTH CAROLINA
Russell W. Sherer
Chief
Div. of Water Pollution Control
Dept. of Health & Environmental Control
2600 Bull St.
Columbia, SC 29201
Phone: (803) 898-4300

SOUTH DAKOTA
Bill Markley
Director
Div. of Environmental Regulation
Dept. of Environment & Natural Resources
523 E. Capitol Ave.
Pierre, SD 57501
Phone: (605) 773-3296
Fax: (605) 773-6035

TENNESSEE
Paul Davis
Director
Technical & Adm. Services Section
Div. of Water Pollution Control
L & C Tower, 6th Fl.
401 Church St.
Nashville, TN 37243
Phone: (615) 532-0625
Fax: (615) 532-0503

TEXAS
Jeffrey Saitas
Executive Director
Natural Resource Conservation Comm.
12100 Park 35 Cir., Bldg. A
P.O. Box 13087, MC 109
Austin, TX 78711-3087
Phone: (512) 239-3900
Fax: (512) 239-3939

U.S. VIRGIN ISLANDS
Leonard Reed
Acting Director
Environmental Protection Div.
Dept. of Planning & Natural Resources
Foster's Plz., 396-1 Anna's Retreat
St. Thomas, VI 00802
Phone: (340) 777-4577
Fax: (340) 774-5416

UTAH
Don A. Ostler
Director
Div. of Water Quality
Dept. of Environmental Quality
288 N. 1460 W.
P.O. Box 144870
Salt Lake City, UT 84116-4870
Phone: (801) 538-6047
Fax: (801) 538-6016
E-mail: dostler@deq.state.ut.us

VERMONT

VIRGINIA
Dennis H. Treacy
Director
Dept. of Environmental Quality
629 E. Main St.
Richmond, VA 23219
Phone: (804) 698-4020
Fax: (804) 698-4019

WASHINGTON
Megan White
Program Manager
Water Quality Program
Dept. of Ecology
P.O. Box 47600
Olympia, WA 98504-7600
Phone: (360) 407-6405
Fax: (360) 407-6426

WEST VIRGINIA
Mark A. Scott
Chief
Ofc. of Water Resources
Dept. of Environmental Protection
1201 Greenbrier St.
Charleston, WV 25311
Phone: (304) 558-2107
Fax: (304) 558-5905

WISCONSIN
Al Shea
Director
Watershed Mgmt.
Dept. of Natural Resources
101 S. Webster, 2nd Fl.
P.O. Box 7921
Madison, WI 53707
Phone: (608) 267-7694
Fax: (608) 267-3579

WYOMING
Gary Beach
Administrator
Water Quality Div.
Dept. of Environmental Quality
122 W. 25th St.
Cheyenne, WY 82002
Phone: (307) 777-7072

Water Resources

Responsible for water conservation, development, use and planning in the state.

ALABAMA
Walter Stevenson
Chief
Ofc. of Water Resources Div.
Economic & Community Affairs
P.O. Box 5690
Montgomery, AL 36103-5690
Phone: (334) 242-5497
Fax: (334) 242-0776

ALASKA
Bob Loeffler
Director
Div. of Mining & Water Mgmt.
Dept. of Natural Resources
3601 C St., Ste. 800
Anchorage, AK 99503
Phone: (907) 269-8624
Fax: (907) 562-1384

AMERICAN SAMOA
Abe U. Malae
Executive Director
Power Authority
AS Govt.
Pago Pago, AS 96799
Phone: (684) 644-5251
Fax: (684) 644-5005

ARIZONA
Rita P. Pearson
Director
Dept. of Water Resources
500 N. 3rd St.
Phoenix, AZ 85004-3903
Phone: (602) 417-2410
Fax: (602) 417-2415

ARKANSAS
Randy Young
Executive Director
Soil & Water Conservation
101 E. Capitol, Ste. 350
Little Rock, AR 72201
Phone: (501) 682-1611
Fax: (501) 682-3991

CALIFORNIA
David Kennedy
Director
Dept. of Water Resources
1416 Ninth St.
Sacramento, CA 95814
Phone: (916) 653-7007

COLORADO
Daries C. Lile
Director
Water Conservation Board
Dept. of Natural Resources
1313 Sherman St., Rm. 721
Denver, CO 80203
Phone: (303) 866-3441
Fax: (303) 866-4474

Hal D. Simpson
State Engineer
Div. of Water Resources
Dept. of Natural Resources
1313 Sherman St., Rm. 818
Denver, CO 80203
Phone: (303) 866-3581
Fax: (303) 866-3589

CONNECTICUT
Robert Smith
Chief
Bur. of Water Mgmt.
Dept. of Environmental Protection
79 Elm St., 1st Fl.
Hartford, CT 06106
Phone: (860) 424-3704

DELAWARE
Gerald L. Esposito
Director
Div. of Water Resources
Dept. of Natural Resources & Environmental Control
89 Kings Hwy.
Dover, DE 19901
Phone: (302) 739-4860
Fax: (302) 739-3491

DISTRICT OF COLUMBIA
Jerry Johnson
General Manager
Water & Sewer Authority
5000 Overlook Ave., SW
Washington, DC 20032
Phone: (202) 645-6309

FLORIDA
Don Berryhill
Bureau Chief
Water Facilities Funding
Dept. of Environmental Protection
2600 Blairstone Rd.
Tallahassee, FL 32399
Phone: (850) 488-8163
Fax: (850) 921-2769

GEORGIA
Nolton G. Johnson
Chief, Water Resources Branch
Environmental Protection Div.
Dept. of Natural Resources
205 Butler St., Rm. 1066
Atlanta, GA 30334
Phone: (404) 656-6328

GUAM
Richard Quintanilla
General Manager
Waterworks Authority
126 Lower E. Sunset Blvd., Tiyan
P.O. Box 3010
Hagatna, GU 96932
Phone: (671) 479-7823
Fax: (671) 649-0158

HAWAII
Edwin Sakoda
Acting Deputy Director
Div. of Water Resource Mgmt.
Land & Natural Resources Dept.
1151 Punchbowl St.
Honolulu, HI 96813
Phone: (808) 587-0214
Fax: (808) 587-0219

IDAHO
Karl Dreher
Director
Dept. of Water Resources
1301 N. Orchard St.
Boise, ID 83720
Phone: (208) 327-7910

ILLINOIS
Donald R. Vonnahme
Director
Ofc. of Water Resources
Dept. of Natural Resources
524 S. Second St.
Springfield, IL 62701-1787
Phone: (217) 782-0690
Fax: (217) 785-5014

INDIANA
Mike Neyer
Director
Div. of Water
Dept. of Natural Resources
402 W. Washington
Indianapolis, IN 46204
Phone: (317) 232-4160
Fax: (317) 233-4579

IOWA
Dennis Alt
Supervisor
Water Supply Section
Surface & Groundwater Protection
Wallace State Ofc. Bldg.
E. 9th & Grand Aves.
Des Moines, IA 50319-0034
Phone: (515) 281-8998

KANSAS
David Pope
Director
Div. of Water Resources
Dept. of Agri.
901 S. Kansas Ave., 2nd Fl.
Topeka, KS 66612-1283
Phone: (785) 296-3717
Fax: (785) 296-1176

KENTUCKY
Pam Wood
Supervisor
Water Quality Mgmt. Section
Dept. for Environmental Protection
Ft. Boone Plz.
14 Reilly Rd.
Frankfort, KY 40601
Phone: (502) 564-3410
Fax: (502) 564-4245

LOUISIANA
Linda Korn Levy
Assistant Secretary
Ofc. of Water Resources
Dept. of Environmental Quality
P.O. Box 82215
Baton Rouge, LA 70884
Phone: (225) 765-0634
Fax: (225) 765-0635

MAINE
Martha Kirkpatrick
Director
Land & Water Quality Control
Dept. of Environmental Protection
17 State House Station
Augusta, ME 04333
Phone: (207) 287-3901

MARYLAND
Michael Nelson
Director
Land & Water Conservation Service
Dept. of Natural Resources
Tawes State Ofc. Bldg., E-4
580 Taylor Ave.
Annapolis, MD 21401
Phone: (410) 260-8401
Fax: (410) 260-8404

MASSACHUSETTS
Mike Rapacz
Program Manager
Groundwater
Div. of Water Supply
20 Riverside Dr.
Lakeville, MA 02347
Phone: (508) 946-2867.
Fax: (508) 947-6557

MICHIGAN
Thomas Rohrer
Chief
Compliance & Enforcement Section
Div. of Surface Water Quality
P.O. Box 30273
Lansing, MI 48909
Phone: (517) 373-1949

MINNESOTA
Kent Lokkesmoe
Director
Div. of Waters
Dept. of Natural Resources
500 Lafayette Rd.
St. Paul, MN 55155
Phone: (651) 296-4810
Fax: (651) 296-0445
E-mail: kent.lokkesmoe@dnr.state.mn.us

MISSISSIPPI
Charles Branch
Office Head
Bur. of Land & Water
Dept. of Environmental Quality
P.O. Box 20305
Jackson, MS 39289-1305
Phone: (601) 961-5200
Fax: (601) 354-6938

MISSOURI
Steve McIntosh
Director
Water Resources Program
Div. of Geology & Land Survey/Dept. of Natural Resources
111 Fairgrounds Rd.
P.O. Box 176
Jefferson City, MO 65102
Phone: (573) 751-2867
Fax: (573) 751-8475
E-mail: nrmcins@mail.dnr.state.mo.us

MONTANA
Jack Stults
Administrator
Water Resources Div.
DNRC
P.O. Box 201601
Helena, MT 59620
Phone: (406) 444-6601
Fax: (406) 444-5918

NEBRASKA
Roger Patterson
Director
Dept. of Water Resources
P.O. Box 94676
Lincoln, NE 68509
Phone: (402) 471-2363
Fax: (402) 471-2900

NEVADA
Michael Turnipseed
State Engineer
Div. of Water Resources
123 W. Nye Ln.
Carson City, NV 89706
Phone: (775) 687-4380
Fax: (775) 687-6972

NEW HAMPSHIRE
Harry Stewart
Director
Water Div.
Environmental Services
P.O. Box 95
Concord, NH 03302-0095
Phone: (603) 271-3503
Fax: (603) 271-2867

NEW JERSEY
Shing-Fu Hseuh
Deputy Director
Water Monitoring Mgmt.
Environmental Protection & Energy Dept.
401 E. State St.
P.O. Box 423
Trenton, NJ 08625-0423
Phone: (609) 292-4543
Fax: (609) 777-1330

NEW MEXICO
Tom C. Turney
State Engineer
101 Bataan Memorial Bldg.
P.O. Box 25102
Santa Fe, NM 87504-5102
Phone: (505) 827-6091
Fax: (505) 827-6188

NEW YORK
Warren Lavery
Director
Bur. of Water Permits
Dept. of Environmental Conservation
50 Wolf Rd., Rm. 302
Albany, NY 12233
Phone: (518) 457-0656
Fax: (518) 485-7786

NORTH CAROLINA
John Morris
Director
Div. of Water Resources
Dept. of Environment & Natural Resources
P.O. Box 27687
Raleigh, NC 27611
Phone: (919) 733-4064
Fax: (919) 733-3558

NORTH DAKOTA
David Sprynczynatyk
State Engineer
Water Comm.
State Ofc. Bldg.
900 E. Blvd. Ave.
Bismarck, ND 58505-0187
Phone: (701) 328-2750
Fax: (701) 328-3696
E-mail: dspry@water.swc.state.nd.us

NORTHERN MARIANA ISLANDS
Timothy P. Villagomez
Executive Director
Commonwealth Utilities Corp.
Ofc. of the Governor
Lower Base
P.O. Box 1220
Saipan, MP 96950
Phone: (670) 322-5088
Fax: (670) 322-4323
E-mail: cuc.edp@mtccnmi.com

OHIO
Lisa Morris
Chief
Div. of Surface Water
Environmental Protection Agency
122 S. Front St.
P.O. Box 1049
Columbus, OH 43216
Phone: (614) 644-2856
Fax: (614) 644-2329

OKLAHOMA
Mike Mathis
Chief
Planning & Dev. Div.
Water Resources Board
3800 N. Classen
Oklahoma City, OK 73118
Phone: (405) 530-8800
Fax: (405) 530-8900

OREGON
Martha Pagel
Director
Dept. of Water Resources
158 12th St., NE
Salem, OR 97310
Phone: (503) 378-2982
Fax: (503) 378-2496

PENNSYLVANIA
Glenn E. Maurer
Director
Bur. of Water Quality Protection
Dept. of Environmental Resources
400 Market St., 11th Fl.
Harrisburg, PA 17105
Phone: (717) 787-2666
Fax: (717) 772-5156

PUERTO RICO
Perfecto Ocasio
Executive Director
Aqueduct & Sewer Authority
Barrio Obrero Station
P.O. Box 7066
Santurce, PR 00916
Phone: (787) 758-5757

RHODE ISLAND
Alicia M. Good
Director
Ofc. of Water Resources
Dept. of Environmental Mgmt.
235 Promenade St.
Providence, RI 02908
Phone: (401) 222-3961

SOUTH CAROLINA
Alfred H. Vang
Deputy Director
Div. of Land, Water & Conservation
Dept. of Natural Resources
1201 Main St., Ste. 1100
Columbia, SC 29201
Phone: (803) 737-0800
Fax: (803) 765-9080

SOUTH DAKOTA
Jim Finney
Natrual Resources Administrator
Watershed Protection Program
Dept.of Environment & Natural Resources
Foss Bldg.
523 E. Capitol Ave.
Pierre, SD 57501
Phone: (605) 773-4216
Fax: (605) 773-4068

TENNESSEE
W. David Draughon, Jr.
Director
Div. of Water Supply
Dept. of Environment & Conservation
L & C Tower, 6th Fl.
401 Church St.
Nashville, TN 37247
Phone: (615) 532-0191
Fax: (615) 532-0503

TEXAS
Craig Pedersen
Executive Administrator
Water Dev. Board
P.O. Box 13231
Austin, TX 78711
Phone: (512) 463-7850
Fax: (512) 475-2053

U.S. VIRGIN ISLANDS
Leonard Reed
Acting Director
Environmental Protection Div.
Dept. of Planning & Natural Resources
Foster's Plz., 396-1 Anna's Retreat
St. Thomas, VI 00802
Phone: (340) 777-4577
Fax: (340) 774-5416

UTAH
D. Larry Anderson
Director
Div. of Water Resources
Dept. of Natural Resources
P.O. Box 146201
Salt Lake City, UT 84114-6201
Phone: (801) 538-7250
Fax: (801) 538-7279
E-mail: landerso.nrwres@state.ut.us

VERMONT
Wallace McLean
Director
Div. of Water Quality
Dept. of Environmental Conservation
103 S. Main St.
Waterbury, VT 05676
Phone: (802) 241-3770
Fax: (802) 241-3287

VIRGINIA
Dennis H. Treacy
Director
Dept. of Environmental Quality
629 E. Main St.
Richmond, VA 23219
Phone: (804) 698-4020
Fax: (804) 698-4019

WASHINGTON
Keith Phillips
Manager
Water Resources Program
Dept. of Ecology
P.O. Box 47600
Olympia, WA 98504-7600
Phone: (360) 407-6602
Fax: (360) 407-7162

WEST VIRGINIA
Mark A. Scott
Chief
Ofc. of Water Resources
Dept. of Environmental Protection
1201 Greenbrier St.
Charleston, WV 25311
Phone: (304) 558-2107
Fax: (304) 558-5905

WISCONSIN
Charles Ledin
Section Chief
Great Lakes & Water Shed Planning
Bur. of Water Resource Mgmt.
101 S. Webster, 2nd Fl.
P.O. Box 7921
Madison, WI 53703
Phone: (608) 267-7610
Fax: (608) 267-2800

WYOMING
Mike Besson
Director
Water Dev. Comm.
Herschler Bldg., 4th Fl., W. Wing
122 W. 25th St.
Cheyenne, WY 82002
Phone: (307) 777-7626

Weights and Measures

Inspects commercially-used measuring and weighing devices.

ALABAMA
Steadman L. Hollis
Director
Div. of Weights & Measures
Agri. & Industries Dept.
P.O. Box 3336
Montgomery, AL 36109
Phone: (334) 240-7133
Fax: (334) 240-7175

ALASKA
Edward Moses
Director
Div. of Measurement Standards
Dept. of Commerce & Economic Dev.
12050 Industry Way
Anchorage, AK 99515-3512
Phone: (907) 345-7750
Fax: (907) 345-6835

AMERICAN SAMOA
Albert Mailo Toetagata
Attorney General
Dept. of Legal Affairs
AS Govt.
Pago Pago, AS 96799
Phone: (684) 633-4163
Fax: (684) 633-1838

ARIZONA
John U. Hays
Director
Dept. of Weights & Measures
9535 E. Doubletree Ranch Rd.
Scottsdale, AZ 85258-5539
Phone: (602) 255-5211
Fax: (602) 255-1950

ARKANSAS
Mike Hile
Director
Bur. of Standards
State Plant Board
4603 W. 61st St.
Little Rock, AR 72209
Phone: (501) 324-9680
Fax: (501) 562-7605

CALIFORNIA
Darrell A. Guensler
Director
Measurement Standards Div.
Dept. of Food & Agri.
8500 Fruitridge Rd.
Sacramento, CA 95826
Phone: (916) 229-3000

COLORADO
David Wallace
Chief
Measurement Standards Section
Dept. of Agri.
3125 Wyandot St.
Denver, CO 80211
Phone: (303) 477-1220

CONNECTICUT
John McGuire
Chief
Weights & Measures Div.
Dept. of Consumer Protection
165 Capitol Ave.
Hartford, CT 06106
Phone: (860) 566-4778

DELAWARE
Bill Lagemann
Supervisor, Weights & Measures
Div. of Consumer Protection
Dept. of Agri.
2320 S. DuPont Hwy.
Dover, DE 19901
Phone: (302) 739-4811
Fax: (302) 697-6287

DISTRICT OF COLUMBIA
Catherine Williams
Administrator
Business Regulation Administration
Consumer & Regulatory Affairs
941 N. Capitol St., NE
Washington, DC 20002
Phone: (202) 442-4400

FLORIDA
Ben Faulk
Director
Div. of Standards
Agri. & Consumer Services Dept.
3125 Conner Blvd.
Tallahassee, FL 32399-1650
Phone: (850) 488-0645
Fax: (850) 922-8971

GEORGIA
Bill Truby
Administrative Assistant to the Commissioner
Fuel & Measure Standards Div.
Dept. of Agri.
321 Agri. Bldg.
Atlanta, GA 30334
Phone: (404) 656-3605

GUAM
Joseph T. Duenas
Director
Dept. of Revenue & Taxation
13-1 Mariner Dr., Tiyan
P.O. Box 23607
GMF, GU 96921
Phone: (671) 475-1817
Fax: (671) 472-2643

HAWAII
Samuel G. Camp
Administrator
Quality Assurance Div.
Dept. of Agri.
725 Ilalo St.
Honolulu, HI 96813
Phone: (808) 586-0870
Fax: (808) 586-0889

IDAHO
James R. Boatman
Chief
Bur. of Weights & Measures
Dept. of Agri.
2216 Kellogg Ln.
Boise, ID 83712
Phone: (208) 334-2345

ILLINOIS
Sidney Coldbrook
Chief
Bur. of Weights & Measures
Dept. of Agri.
P.O. Box 19281
Springfield, IL 62794-9281
Phone: (217) 782-3817
Fax: (217) 524-7801

INDIANA
Lawrence Stump
Director
Div. of Weights & Measures
State Board of Health
1330 W. Michigan St., Rm. 136
Indianapolis, IN 46202
Phone: (317) 233-8134
Fax: (317) 233-8131

IOWA
Darryl Brown
Chief
Weights & Measures Bur.
Dept. of Agri.
Wallace State Ofc. Bldg.
E. 9th & Grand Aves.
Des Moines, IA 50319
Phone: (515) 281-5717

KANSAS
Constantine Cotsoradis
Director
Div. of Weights & Measures
Dept. of Agri.
Bldg. 282, Forbes Field
P.O. Box 19282
Topeka, KS 66619-0282
Phone: (785) 862-2415
Fax: (785) 862-2460

KENTUCKY
Larry Hatfield
Director
Div. of Weights & Measures
Dept. of Agri.
106 W. 2nd St.
Frankfort, KY 40601
Phone: (502) 564-4870
Fax: (502) 564-5669

LOUISIANA
Bob Odom
Commissioner
Dept. of Agri. & Forestry
P.O. Box 631
Baton Rouge, LA 70821-0631
Phone: (225) 922-1234
Fax: (225) 922-1253

MAINE
Robert W. Spear
Commissioner
Dept. of Agri., Food & Rural Resources
28 State House Station
Augusta, ME 04333
Phone: (207) 287-3871

MARYLAND
Louis E. Straub
Chief
Weights & Measures Section
Dept. of Agri.
50 Harry S. Truman Pkwy.
Annapolis, MD 21401
Phone: (410) 841-5790
Fax: (410) 941-2765

MASSACHUSETTS
Donald B. Falvey
Director
Div. of Standards
Executive Ofc. of Consumer Affairs
One Ashburton Pl., Rm. 1115
Boston, MA 02108
Phone: (617) 727-3480
Fax: (617) 727-5705

MICHIGAN
Patrick Mercer
Director
Food Div.
Dept. of Agri.
940 Venture Ln.
Williamston, MI 48955
Phone: (517) 655-8202
Fax: (517) 665-8303

MINNESOTA
Mike Blacik
Director
Weights & Measures Div.
Dept. of Public Service
2277 Hwy. 36
St. Paul, MN 55113
Phone: (651) 639-4010
Fax: (651) 639-4014

MISSISSIPPI
Bill Eldridge
Director
Weights & Measures Div.
Agri. & Commerce Dept.
P.O. Box 1609
Jackson, MS 39215-1609
Phone: (601) 354-7077
Fax: (601) 354-6290

MISSOURI
Roy Humphreys
Director
Div. of Weights & Measures
Dept. of Agri.
1616 Missouri Blvd.
P.O. Box 630
Jefferson City, MO 65102
Phone: (573) 751-4316
Fax: (573) 751-0281

MONTANA
Jack Kane
Bureau Chief
Weights & Measures Bur.
Dept. of Commerce
1424 9th Ave.
Helena, MT 59620
Phone: (406) 444-3164
Fax: (406) 444-4305

NEBRASKA
Steve Malone
Director
Weights & Measures Div.
Dept. of Agri.
P.O. Box 94947
Lincoln, NE 68509-4947
Phone: (402) 471-4292
Fax: (402) 471-2759

NEVADA
Edward Hoganson
Supervisor
Div. of Agri.
Weights & Measures Section
2150 Frazer St.
Sparks, NV 89431
Phone: (775) 688-1166
Fax: (775) 688-2533

NEW HAMPSHIRE
Stephen Taylor
Commissioner
Agri., Markets & Food
P.O. Box 2042
Concord, NH 03302-2042
Phone: (603) 271-3700
Fax: (603) 271-1109

NEW JERSEY
Mark S. Herr
Director
Div. of Consumer Affairs
P.O. Box 45027
Newark, NJ 07102
Phone: (201) 504-6200
Fax: (201) 648-3538

NEW MEXICO
Frank A. DuBois
Secretary
NM State Univ.
Dept. of Agri.
P.O. Box 30005, Dept. 3189
Las Cruces, NM 88003-8005
Phone: (505) 646-3007
Fax: (505) 646-8120

NEW YORK
Donald R. Davidsen
Commissioner
Dept. of Agri. & Markets
One Winners Cir.
Albany, NY 12235
Phone: (518) 457-5496
Fax: (518) 457-3087

NORTH CAROLINA
N. David Smith
Director
Standards Div.
Dept. of Agri.
2 W. Edenton St.
Raleigh, NC 27601-1094
Phone: (919) 733-3313
Fax: (919) 715-0524

NORTH DAKOTA
Alan Moch
Director
Testing & Safety
Public Service Comm.
600 E. Blvd. Ave., 13th Fl.
Bismarck, ND 58505-0480
Phone: (701) 328-2413
Fax: (701) 328-2410
E-mail: msmail.agm@oracle.psc.state.nd.us

NORTHERN MARIANA ISLANDS
Pedro Q. Dela Cruz
Secretary
Ofc. of the Governor
Dept. of Commerce
Caller Box 10007 CK
Saipan, MP 96950
Phone: (670) 664-3000
Fax: (670) 664-3067
E-mail: commerce@mtccnmi.com

OHIO
Leonard Hubert
Chief
Div. of Weights & Measures
Dept. of Agri.
8995 E. Main St.
Reynoldsburg, OH 43068
Phone: (614) 728-6290

OKLAHOMA
Charles Carter
Program Administrator
Weights & Measures Div.
Dept. of Agri.
2800 N. Lincoln Blvd.
Oklahoma City, OK 73105
Phone: (405) 521-3864
Fax: (405) 522-4584

OREGON
Kendrick J. Simila
Administrator
Measurement Standards Div.
Dept. of Agri.
635 Capitol St., NE
Salem, OR 97310
Phone: (503) 986-4669
Fax: (503) 986-4734

PENNSYLVANIA
Charles Bruckner
Director
Bur. of Ride & Measurement Standards
Dept. of Agri.
2301 N. Cameron St., Rm. 206
Harrisburg, PA 17110
Phone: (717) 787-6772
Fax: (717) 783-4158

PUERTO RICO
Jose Antonio Alicea
Secretary
Consumer Affairs Dept.
P.O. Box 41059
San Juan, PR 00940-1059
Phone: (787) 722-7555
Fax: (787) 726-0077

RHODE ISLAND
Lee Arnold
Director
Dept. of Labor & Training
101 Friendship St.
Providence, RI 02903
Phone: (401) 222-3732
Fax: (401) 222-1473

SOUTH CAROLINA
Carol P. Fulmer
Assistant Commissioner
Consumer Service Div.
Dept. of Agri.
P.O. Box 11280
Columbia, SC 29211
Phone: (803) 737-9691

SOUTH DAKOTA
David Volk
Secretary
Div. of Insurance
Dept. of Commerce & Regulation
118 W. Capitol Ave.
Pierre, SD 57501-2017
Phone: (605) 773-3178
Fax: (605) 773-3018

TENNESSEE
Bob Williams
Standards Administrator
Weights & Measures
Dept. of Agri.
P.O. Box 40627, Melrose Station
Nashville, TN 37204
Phone: (615) 837-5144
Fax: (615) 837-5015

TEXAS
Susan Combs
Dept. of Agri.
1700 N. Congress
Austin, TX 78701
Phone: (512) 463-7476
Fax: (512) 463-1104

U.S. VIRGIN ISLANDS
Knolah Nichols
Director
Dept. of Licensing & Consumer Affairs
Property & Project Bldg., #1 Sub Base, Rm. 205
St. Thomas, VI 00802
Phone: (340) 774-3130
Fax: (340) 776-0675

UTAH
Kyle R. Stephens
Director
Div. of Regulatory Services
Dept. of Agri. & Food
350 N. Redwood Rd.
Salt Lake City, UT 84116
Phone: (801) 538-7150
Fax: (801) 538-7126
E-mail: kstephen.agmain@state.ut.us

VERMONT
Henry Marckres
Supervisor of Consumer Assurance
Weights & Measures Ofc.
Dept. of Agri.
116 State St.
Drawer 20
Montpelier, VT 05620-2901
Phone: (802) 828-2436
Fax: (802) 241-3008

VIRGINIA
J. Carlton Courter, III
Commissioner
Dept. of Agri. & Consumer Services
Washington Bldg., Ste. 210
1100 Bank St.
Richmond, VA 23219
Phone: (804) 786-3501
Fax: (804) 371-2945

WASHINGTON
Jerry Buendel
Program Manager
Weights & Measures Section
Dept. of Agri.
1111 Washington St.
P.O. Box 42560
Olympia, WA 98504-2560
Phone: (360) 902-1856
Fax: (360) 902-2086

WEST VIRGINIA
Karl H. Angell
Director
Weights & Measures Section
Div. of Labor
570 W. McCorkle Ave.
St. Albans, WV 25177
Phone: (304) 722-0606
Fax: (304) 722-0605

WISCONSIN
William Oemichen
Administrator
Trade & Consumer Protection Div.
Agri., Trade & Consumer Protection
2811 Agri. Dr.
P.O. Box 8911
Madison, WI 53708
Phone: (608) 224-4970
Fax: (608) 224-4939

WYOMING
Victor Gerber
APSM Compliance Officer
Weights & Measures Div.
Dept. of Agri.
1510 E. Fifth St.
Cheyenne, WY 82002
Phone: (307) 777-6586

Welfare

Administers the delivery of financial and medical benefits to low-income families and individuals.

ALABAMA
Tony Petelos
Commissioner
Dept. of Human Resources
50 N. Ripley St.
Montgomery, AL 36130-4000
Phone: (334) 242-1310
Fax: (334) 242-0198

ALASKA
James Nordlund
Director
Div. of Public Assistance
Dept. of Health & Social Services
P.O. Box 110640
Juneau, AK 99811-0640
Phone: (907) 465-3347
Fax: (907) 465-5154

AMERICAN SAMOA

ARIZONA
Vince Wood
Assistant Director
Div. of Benefits & Medical Eligibility
Dept. of Economic Security
1789 W. Jefferson (939A)
Phoenix, AZ 85005
Phone: (602) 542-3569

ARKANSAS
Kurt Knickrehm
Director
Dept. of Human Services
P.O. Box 1437, Slot 316
Little Rock, AR 72203
Phone: (501) 682-8650
Fax: (501) 682-6836

CALIFORNIA
Eloise Anderson
Director
Dept. of Social Services
744 P St., MS 17-11
Sacramento, CA 95814
Phone: (916) 657-2598

COLORADO
Karen Beye
Managing Director
Dept. of Human Services
1575 Sherman St., 8th Fl.
Denver, CO 80203-1714
Phone: (303) 866-3063
Fax: (303) 866-4214

CONNECTICUT
Pat Wilson-Coker
Commissioner
Dept. of Social Services
25 Sigourney St.
Hartford, CT 06106
Phone: (860) 424-5008

DELAWARE
Elaine Archangelo
Director
Div. of Social Services
P.O. Box 906
New Castle, DE 19720
Phone: (302) 577-4400
Fax: (302) 577-4405

DISTRICT OF COLUMBIA
Kate Jessburg
Administrator
Income Maintenance Administration
Dept. of Human Services
645 H St., NE, 5th Fl.
Washington, DC 20002
Phone: (202) 724-5506

FLORIDA
Linda G. Dilworth
Assistant Secretary
Economic Services Program Ofc.
Dept. of Children & Family Services
Bldg. 3, Rm. 401
1317 Winewood Blvd.
Tallahassee, FL 32399-0700
Phone: (850) 488-3271
Fax: (850) 488-2589

GEORGIA
Peggy Peters
Director
Family & Children Services
Dept. of Human Resources
2 Peachtree St., Rm. 16-200
Atlanta, GA 30303
Phone: (404) 657-7660

GUAM
Dennis G. Rodriguez
Director
Dept. of Public Health & Social Services
P.O. Box 2816
Hagatna, GU 96932
Phone: (671) 735-7102
Fax: (671) 734-5910
E-mail: dennis_r_@NS.GOV.GU

HAWAII
Patricia Murakami
Administrator
Benefit, Employment & Support Services Div.
Dept. of Human Services
820 Mililani St., Ste. 606
Honolulu, HI 96813
Phone: (808) 586-5230
Fax: (808) 586-5229

IDAHO
Joan Silva
Administrator
Div. of Welfare
Dept. of Health & Welfare
P.O. Box 83720
Boise, ID 83720-0036
Phone: (208) 334-6535

ILLINOIS
Ann Patla
Director
Dept. of Public Aid
201 S. Grand Ave., E.
Springfield, IL 62762
Phone: (217) 782-1200
Fax: (217) 524-7979

INDIANA
James Hmurovich
Director
Div. of Families & Children
Family & Social Services Administration
IGC-S., Rm. W392
Indianapolis, IN 46204
Phone: (317) 232-4705
Fax: (317) 232-4490

IOWA
Doug Howard
Chief
Bur. of Economic Assistance
Dept. of Human Services
Hoover State Ofc. Bldg.
1300 E. Walnut
Des Moines, IA 50319
Phone: (515) 281-8629

KANSAS
Ann Koci
Commissioner
Adult & Medical Services
Social & Rehab. Services
Docking Bldg., Rm. 628S
915 Harrison
Topeka, KS 66612-1570
Phone: (785) 296-3981
Fax: (785) 296-4813

KENTUCKY
John Clayton
Commissioner
Cabinet for Families & Children
Dept. for Social Insurance
275 E. Main St.
Frankfort, KY 40621
Phone: (502) 564-3703
Fax: (502) 564-6907

LOUISIANA
Vera Blakes
Assistant Secretary
Ofc. of Family Support
Dept. of Social Services
P.O. Box 94065
Baton Rouge, LA 70804-9065
Phone: (225) 342-3950
Fax: (225) 342-4252

MAINE
Judy Williams
Director
Bur. of Family Independence
Dept. of Human Services
11 State House Station
Augusta, ME 04333
Phone: (207) 287-2826

MARYLAND
Lynda G. Fox
Secretary
Ofc. of the Secretary
Dept. of Human Resources
Saratoga Ctr.
311 W. Saratoga St.
Baltimore, MD 21201
Phone: (410) 767-7109
Fax: (410) 333-0392

MASSACHUSETTS
Claire McIntire
Commissioner
Executive Ofc. of Health & Human Services
Dept. of Transitional Assistance
600 Washington St., 6th Fl.
Boston, MA 02111
Phone: (617) 348-8400
Fax: (617) 348-8575

MICHIGAN
Douglas Howard
Director
Family Independence Agency
P.O. Box 30037
Lansing, MI 48909
Phone: (517) 373-2000
Fax: (517) 373-8471

MINNESOTA
Chuck Johnson
Co-Director
Families With Children
Dept. of Human Services
444 Lafayette Rd., N.
St. Paul, MN 55155-3834
Phone: (651) 297-4727
Fax: (651) 297-5840
E-mail: chuck.johnson@state.mn.us

Ann Sessoms
Co-Director
Families With Children
Dept. of Human Services
444 Lafayette Rd., N.
St. Paul, MN 55155-3834
Phone: (651) 296-0978
Fax: (651) 297-5840
E-mail: ann.sessoms@state.mn.us

MISSISSIPPI
Don Taylor
Executive Director
Dept. of Human Services
P.O. Box 352
Jackson, MS 39205
Phone: (601) 354-4500
Fax: (601) 359-4477

MISSOURI
Denise Cross
Director
Div. of Family Services
Dept. of Social Services
615 Howerton Ct.
P.O. Box 88
Jefferson City, MO 65103
Phone: (573) 751-4247
Fax: (573) 751-0507
E-mail: dcross@mail.state.mo.us

MONTANA
Laurie Ekanger
Director¡
Dept. of Public Health & Human Services
111 Sanders St.
P.O. Box 4210
Helena, MT 59620
Phone: (406) 444-5622
Fax: (406) 444-1970

NEBRASKA
Jeff Elliott
Director
Dept. of Health & Human Services, Finance & Support
P.O. Box 95026
Lincoln, NE 68509
Phone: (402) 471-3121
Fax: (402) 471-9449

NEVADA
Myla Florence
Administrator
Welfare Div.
Dept. of Human Resources
2527 N. Carson St.
Carson City, NV 89706
Phone: (775) 687-4128
Fax: (775) 687-5080

NEW HAMPSHIRE
Richard A. Chevrefils
Assistant Commissioner
Ofc. of Family Services
Health & Human Services
6 Hazen Dr.
Concord, NH 03301-6505
Phone: (603) 271-4321
Fax: (603) 271-4727

NEW JERSEY
David Heins
Director
Div. of Family Dev.
Dept. of Human Services
Quakerbridge Rd.
P.O. Box 716
Trenton, NJ 08625-0716
Phone: (609) 292-2485
Fax: (609) 584-4404

NEW MEXICO
Patsy Barnett
Deputy Director
Dept. of Human Services
P.O. Box 2348
Santa Fe, NM 87504
Phone: (505) 827-7254
Fax: (505) 827-7203

NEW YORK
Brian Wing
Commissioner
Ofc. of Temporary & Disability Assistance
40 N. Pearl St., 16th Fl.
Albany, NY 12243
Phone: (518) 473-8772
Fax: (518) 486-6255

NORTH CAROLINA
Kevin Fitzgerald
Director of Social Services
Dept. of Health & Human Services
325 N. Salisbury St.
Raleigh, NC 27603-5905
Phone: (919) 733-3055
Fax: (919) 715-3581

Paul Perruzzi
Director
Div. of Medical Assistance
Dept. of Health & Human Services
Kirby Bldg.
1985 Umstead Dr.
Raleigh, NC 27603-2001
Phone: (919) 857-4011
Fax: (919) 733-6608

NORTH DAKOTA
Carol K. Olson
Executive Director
Dept. of Human Services
600 E. Blvd. Ave., 3rd Fl. - Judicial Wing
Bismarck, ND 58505-0250
Phone: (701) 328-2310
Fax: (701) 328-2359
E-mail: socols@state.nd.us

NORTHERN MARIANA ISLANDS
Thomas A. Tebuteb
Secretary
Ofc. of the Secretary
Community & Cultural Affairs
P.O. Box 10007
Saipan, MP 96950
Phone: (670) 664-2571
Fax: (670) 664-2570

OHIO
Jon Allen
Director
Dept. of Human Services
30 E. Broad St., 32nd Fl.
Columbus, OH 43266-0423
Phone: (614) 466-6650
Fax: (614) 466-0292

OKLAHOMA
Raymond Haddock
Director
Family Support Services
Dept. of Human Services
P.O. Box 25352
Oklahoma City, OK 73125
Phone: (405) 521-3646
Fax: (405) 521-6458

OREGON
Sandie Hoback
Administrator
Adult & Family Services Div.
Dept. of Human Resources
500 Summer St., NE
Salem, OR 97310
Phone: (503) 945-5600
Fax: (503) 373-7492

PENNSYLVANIA
Feather Houstoun
Secretary
Dept. of Public Welfare
Health & Welfare Bldg., Rm. 333
Harrisburg, PA 17120
Phone: (717) 787-2600
Fax: (717) 772-2062

PUERTO RICO
Angie Varela
Secretary
Dept. of Social Services
P.O. Box 11398
San Juan, PR 00910
Phone: (787) 722-7400
Fax: (787) 723-1223

RHODE ISLAND
John D. Bamford
Associate Director
Social & Economic Services
Dept. of Human Services
600 New London Ave.
Cranston, RI 02920
Phone: (401) 462-1000

SOUTH CAROLINA
Elizabeth G. Patterson
Director
Dept. of Social Services
1535 Confederate Ave., Extension
Columbia, SC 29202
Phone: (803) 898-7360

SOUTH DAKOTA
James Ellenbecker
Secretary
Dept. of Social Services
700 Governors Dr.
Pierre, SD 57501
Phone: (605) 773-3165
Fax: (605) 773-4855

TENNESSEE
Natasha Metcalf
Commissioner
Dept. of Human Services
Citizens Plz., 15th Fl.
400 Deaderick St.
Nashville, TN 37248-0001
Phone: (615) 313-4700
Fax: (615) 741-4165

TEXAS
Eric Bost
Commissioner
Dept. of Human Services
P.O. Box 149030
Austin, TX 78714
Phone: (512) 438-3011

U.S. VIRGIN ISLANDS
Ermine Boschulte
Administrator
Div. of Financial Programs
Dept. of Human Services
Knud Hansen Complex, Bldg. A
1303 Hospital Grounds
St. Thomas, VI 00802
Phone: (340) 774-2399
Fax: (340) 777-5449

UTAH
Robert C. Gross
Executive Director
Ofc. of the Executive Director
Dept. of Workforce Services
140 E. 300 S.
Salt Lake City, UT 84111
Phone: (801) 526-9207
Fax: (801) 526-9211
E-mail: rgross.wsadmpo@state.ut.us

VERMONT
Martha J. Kitchel
Commissioner
Agency of Human Services
Dept. of Social Welfare
103 S. Main St.
Waterbury, VT 05671
Phone: (802) 241-2853
Fax: (802) 241-2830

VIRGINIA
Clarence H. Carter
Commissioner
Dept. of Social Services
Theater Row Bldg.
730 E. Broad St.
Richmond, VA 23219
Phone: (804) 692-1901
Fax: (804) 692-1964

WASHINGTON
Lyle Quasim
Secretary
Dept. of Social & Health Services
P.O. Box 45010
Olympia, WA 98504-5010
Phone: (360) 902-8400
Fax: (360) 902-7848

WEST VIRGINIA
Joan Ohl
Secretary
Dept. of Health & Human Resources
Capitol Complex, Bldg. 3, Rm. 206
1900 Kanawha Blvd., E.
Charleston, WV 25305
Phone: (304) 558-0684
Fax: (304) 558-1130

WISCONSIN
Leonor Rosas DeLeon
Director
Bur. of Welfare Initiatives
Dept. of Workforce Dev.
201 E. Washington, Rm. 171
P.O. Box 7935
Madison, WI 53707
Phone: (608) 267-9022
Fax: (608) 267-3240

WYOMING
Shirley Carson
Director
Dept. of Family Services
Hathaway Bldg., 3rd Fl.
2300 Capitol Ave.
Cheyenne, WY 82002
Phone: (307) 777-6948

Wellness (State Employees)

Administers state employee programs designed to improve employee health; lowers employee health benefit costs, absenteeism and turnover; prevents premature death; and increases employee morale.

ALABAMA
Jim McVay
Director
Health Promotion & Info. Div.
Dept. of Public Health
201 Monroe St., Ste. 960
Montgomery, AL 36104
Phone: (334) 206-5300
Fax: (334) 206-5609

ALASKA

AMERICAN SAMOA

ARIZONA
Mike Schaiberger
Benefits Manager
Div. of Personnel
Dept. of Administration
1624 W. Adams, 4th Fl.
Phoenix, AZ 85007
Phone: (602) 542-5008
Fax: (602) 542-4744

ARKANSAS

CALIFORNIA
Mary Fernandez
Division Chief
Training & Dev. Div.
Dept. of Personnel Administration
1515 S St., N. Bldg., Ste. 105
Sacramento, CA 95814-7243
Phone: (916) 445-5121

COLORADO

CONNECTICUT

DELAWARE
Gregg Sylvester
Secretary
Dept. of Health & Social Services
1901 N. DuPont Hwy.
New Castle, DE 19720
Phone: (302) 577-4500
Fax: (302) 577-4510

DISTRICT OF COLUMBIA

FLORIDA
Jim Howell
Secretary
Dept. of Health
1317 Winewood Blvd.
Tallahassee, FL 32399-0700
Phone: (850) 487-2945
Fax: (850) 487-3729

GEORGIA
Dana R. Russell
Commissioner
State Merit System
W. Tower, Ste. 502
200 Piedmont Ave., SE
Atlanta, GA 30334-5100
Phone: (404) 656-2705

GUAM
Michael J. Reidy
Director
Dept. of Administration
P.O. Box 884
Hagatna, GU 96932
Phone: (671) 475-1101
Fax: (671) 477-6788

HAWAII
Virginia Pressler
Deputy Director
Health Resources Administration
Dept. of Health
1250 Punchbowl St.
Honolulu, HI 96813
Phone: (808) 586-4433
Fax: (808) 586-4444

IDAHO
Patricia L. Johnson
Executive Director
State Board of Accountancy
P.O. Box 83720
Boise, ID 83720-0002
Phone: (208) 334-3389

ILLINOIS
Vicki Alewelt
Employee Health Coordinator
Dept. of Public Health
525 W. Jefferson St.
Springfield, IL 62761
Phone: (217) 524-6580

INDIANA

IOWA
Beverly Allen
Coordinator
Employee Assistance Program & Wellness
Dept. of Personnel
Grimes State Ofc. Bldg.
Des Moines, IA 50319
Phone: (515) 281-6207

Jason Harrington
Benefit Programs Administrator
Health & Dental Insurance
Dept. of Personnel
Grimes State Ofc. Bldg.
Des Moines, IA 50319
Phone: (515) 281-3468

KANSAS

KENTUCKY
Julie True
Director
Div. of Employee Services
Personnel Cabinet
200 Fairoaks, Ste. 529
Frankfort, KY 40601
Phone: (502) 564-7911
Fax: (502) 564-4311

LOUISIANA
Rosemary Haynie
Deputy Commissioner
Personnel Mgmt.
Div. of Administration
P.O. Box 94095
Baton Rouge, LA 70804-9095
Phone: (225) 342-7008
Fax: (225) 342-1057

MAINE
Frank Johnson
Director
State Employee Health
Dept. of Adm. & Financial Services
122 State House Station
Augusta, ME 04333
Phone: (207) 287-4515

MARYLAND
Libby Lewandowski
Director
Wellness Unit
Dept. of Budget & Mgmt.
301 W. Preston St., Rm. 607
Baltimore, MD 21201
Phone: (410) 767-4945
E-mail: llewondo@dbm.state.md.us

MASSACHUSETTS
Howard K. Koh
Commissioner
Dept. of Public Health
250 Washington St.
Boston, MA 02108-4619
Phone: (617) 624-5200
Fax: (617) 624-5206
E-mail: howard.koh@state.ma.us

MICHIGAN
Deborah Foss
Director
Health Awareness Program
Dept. of Civil Service
P.O. Box 30002
Lansing, MI 48909
Phone: (517) 335-5320

MINNESOTA
Kimberley T. Peck
Acting Director
State Employee Assistance Program
Dept. of Administration
200 Univ. Ave., 2nd Fl.
St. Paul, MN 55103
Phone: (651) 296-9722
Fax: (651) 282-2099
E-mail: kim.peck@state.mn.us

MISSISSIPPI

MISSOURI
Naomi Cupp
Executive Director
Governor's Council on Physical Fitness & Health
Truman Bldg., Rm. 760
P.O. Box 809
Jefferson City, MO 65102
Phone: (573) 751-0915
Fax: (573) 751-7819
E-mail: cuppn@mail.oa.state.mo.us

MONTANA
Joyce Brown
Chief
Employee Benefits Bur.
Dept. of Administration
Sam Mitchell Bldg., Rm. 130
125 Roberts
Helena, MT 59620
Phone: (406) 444-2553

NEBRASKA
Michael G. Heyl
Wellness Coordinator
Dept. of Health & Human Services, Regulation & Licensure
P.O. Box 95007
Lincoln, NE 68509
Phone: (402) 471-4419
Fax: (402) 471-0820

NEVADA
Lindley Steere
E.A.P. Counselor
Employee Assistance Program
Dept. of Personnel
675 Fairview Dr., Ste. 221
Carson City, NV 89701
Phone: (775) 687-3869

NEW HAMPSHIRE
Paula Booth
Coordinator
Employee Assistance Program
117 Pleasant St.
Concord, NH 03301
Phone: (603) 271-4336
Fax: (603) 271-6635

NEW JERSEY
John Hennessy
Supervisor
Medical Services Bur.
State Police
P.O. Box 7068
W. Trenton, NJ 08628
Phone: (609) 882-2000

NEW MEXICO
Lydia Pendley
Program Administrator
Health Promotion Section
Dept. of Health
1190 St. Francis
P.O. Box 26110
Santa Fe, NM 87502
Phone: (505) 827-2380
Fax: (505) 827-0021

NEW YORK
Linda Angello
Director
Governor's Ofc. of Employee Relations
Agency Bldg. 2, 12th Fl.
Empire State Plz.
Albany, NY 12223
Phone: (518) 474-6988
Fax: (518) 486-7304

NORTH CAROLINA

NORTH DAKOTA
Kathy Allen
Benefits Planner
Public Employees Retirement System
P.O. Box 1214
Bismarck, ND 58502-1214
Phone: (710) 328-3900
Fax: (701) 328-3920
E-mail: kallen@state.nd.us

NORTHERN MARIANA ISLANDS
Luis S. Camacho
Director of Personnel
Personnel Mgmt. Ofc.
Ofc. of the Governor
Saipan, MP 96950
Phone: (670) 234-6958
Fax: (670) 234-1013

Edward H. Manglona
Administrator
Retirement Fund
P.O. Box 1247
Saipan, MP 96950
Phone: (670) 234-7228
Fax: (670) 234-9624
E-mail: nmi.retirement@saipan.com

OHIO
Sanford Weinberg
Chief
Employee Assistance Program
Dept. of Health
P.O. Box 118
Columbus, OH 43266-0588
Phone: (614) 644-8545

OKLAHOMA
Oscar Jackson
Administrator & Cabinet Secretary of Human Resources
Ofc. of Personnel Mgmt.
2101 N. Lincoln Blvd.
Oklahoma City, OK 73105
Phone: (405) 521-6301
Fax: (405) 524-6942
E-mail: oscar.jackson@oklaosf.state.ok.us

OREGON
Robert J. Cox
Safety & Wellness Manager
Internal Support Div.
Dept. of Adm. Services
1225 Ferry St., SE
Salem, OR 97310
Phone: (503) 378-4202
Fax: (503) 373-6879

PENNSYLVANIA
Jeff Johnston
Program Administrator
State Employee Assistance Program
Bur. of Personnel
513 Finance Bldg.
Harrisburg, PA 17120
Phone: (717) 787-8575
Fax: (717) 772-3153

PUERTO RICO

RHODE ISLAND

SOUTH CAROLINA
Joan McGee
Coordinator
Div. of Insurance Services
Budget & Control Board
1201 Main St.
Columbia, SC 29201
Phone: (803) 734-0578

SOUTH DAKOTA
Sandy Zinter
Commissioner
Bur. of Personnel
500 E. Capitol Ave.
Pierre, SD 57501
Phone: (605) 773-3148
Fax: (605) 773-4344

TENNESSEE
Regina Ranish
State Employee Wellness Manager
Dept. of Finance & Administration
Andrew Jackson Bldg., 14th Fl.
Nashville, TN 37243
Phone: (615) 741-8675
Fax: (615) 741-8196

TEXAS

U.S. VIRGIN ISLANDS

UTAH
Christine Chalkley
Bureau Director
Bur. of Health Education
Dept. of Health-Community & Family Health Services Div.
288 N. 1460 W.
Salt Lake City, UT 84116
Phone: (801) 538-6635
Fax: (801) 538-6629
E-mail: cchalkle@doh.state.ut.us

VERMONT
Kathryn Callaghan
Director
State Employee Wellness
Dept. of Personnel
110 State St.
Montpelier, VT 05602
Phone: (802) 828-3455
Fax: (802) 828-3409

VIRGINIA
Sara Redding Wilson
Director
Dept. of Personnel & Training
Monroe Bldg., 12th Fl.
101 N. 14th St.
Richmond, VA 23219
Phone: (804) 225-2237
Fax: (804) 371-7401

WASHINGTON

WEST VIRGINIA

WISCONSIN
Chet Bradley
Health Education Consultant
Dept. of Public Instruction
125 S. Webster
Madison, WI 53707
Phone: (608) 266-7032
Fax: (608) 267-1052

WYOMING
Ward Gates
Chair
Governor's Council on Physical Therapy
Univ. of WY
Box 3196, Univ. Station
Laramie, WY 82071
Phone: (307) 777-7930

Women

Responsible for reporting on employment practices and social and economic considerations influencing the status of women, and tracking state laws that affect their civil and political rights.

ALABAMA

ALASKA

AMERICAN SAMOA
Fiasili P. Haleck
Director
Dept. of Women & Youth Affairs
AS Govt.
Pago Pago, AS 96799

ARIZONA
Paula Goodson
Director
Div. for Women
Governor's Ofc.
1700 W. Washington, 4th Fl.
Phoenix, AZ 85007
Phone: (602) 542-1755

ARKANSAS

CALIFORNIA
Karmi Speece
Executive Director
Comm. on the Status of Women
1303 J St., Ste. 400
Sacramento, CA 95814-2900
Phone: (916) 445-3173

COLORADO

CONNECTICUT
Leslie Brett
Executive Director
Permanent Comm. on the Status of Women
18-20 Trinity St.
Hartford, CT 06106
Phone: (860) 240-8300
Fax: (860) 240-8314

DELAWARE
Romona S. Fullman
Executive Director
Comm. for Women
4425 N. Market St., 4th Fl.
Wilmington, DE 19802
Phone: (302) 761-8005

DISTRICT OF COLUMBIA
Mary Wolfe
Executive Director
Comm. for Women
2000 14th St., NW, Rm. 354
Washington, DC 20009
Phone: (202) 833-6917

FLORIDA
Nancy Clemons
Executive Director
Comm. on the Status of Women
Dept. of Legal Affairs
Ofc. of the Attorney Gen.
The Capitol
Tallahassee, FL 32399-1050
Phone: (850) 414-3300
Fax: (850) 921-4131

GEORGIA

GUAM
Marie Salas
Executive Director
Bur. of Women's Affairs
103 M St., Tiyan
Hagatna, GU 96932
Phone: (671) 475-9360
Fax: (671) 475-9362

HAWAII
Allicyn Hikida Tasaka
Executive Director
State Comm. on the Status of Women
Ofc. of the Governor
235 S. Beretania St., Rm. 407
Honolulu, HI 96813
Phone: (808) 587-5757
Fax: (808) 586-5756

IDAHO
Linda Hurlbutt
Director
Women's Comm.
450 W. State St., 5th Fl.
Boise, ID 83720
Phone: (208) 334-4673

ILLINOIS
Kevin Wright
Assistant Chief of Staff
Ofc. of the Governor
2 1/2 State House
301 S. 2nd St.
Springfield, IL 62706
Phone: (217) 785-8652
Fax: (217) 524-1678

INDIANA
Yvette Montavon
Executive Director
Comm. for Women
100 N. Senate Ave., Rm. N103
Indianapolis, IN 46204
Phone: (317) 232-6720
Fax: (317) 232-2616

IOWA
Charlotte Nelson
Administrator
Comm. on the Status of Women
Dept. of Human Rights
Lucas State Ofc. Bldg., 1st Fl.
321 E. 12th St.
Des Moines, IA 50319
Phone: (515) 281-4467
Fax: (515) 242-6119

KANSAS

KENTUCKY
Gennie Potter
Executive Director
Comm. on Women
614A Shelby St.
Frankfort, KY 40601
Phone: (502) 564-6643
Fax: (502) 564-2315

LOUISIANA
Vera Clay
Executive Director
Ofc. of Women's Services
Ofc. of the Governor
P.O. Box 94095
Baton Rouge, LA 70804-9095
Phone: (225) 922-0960
Fax: (225) 922-0959

MAINE

MARYLAND
Joanne Saltzberg
Director
Comm. for Women
Dept. of Human Resources
311 W. Saratoga St.
Baltimore, MD 21201
Phone: (410) 767-7556
Fax: (410) 333-0071

MASSACHUSETTS
Joanne Thompson
Chair
Governor's Advisory Comm. on Women's Issues
c/o SOMWBA
10 Park Plz., Rm. 3740
Boston, MA 02116

MICHIGAN
Vacant
Executive Director
Women's Comm.
741 N. Cedar St., Ste. 102
Lansing, MI 48913
Phone: (517) 334-8622
Fax: (517) 334-8641

MINNESOTA
Aviva Breen
Executive Director
Comm. on the Economic Status of Women
100 Constitution Ave.
St. Paul, MN 55155
Phone: (651) 296-8590
Fax: (651) 296-1321
E-mail: abreen@commissions.leg.state.mn.us

MISSISSIPPI

MISSOURI
Sue P. McDaniel
Executive Director
Women's Council
Dept. of Economic Dev.
2023 St. Mary's Blvd.
P.O. Box 1684
Jefferson City, MO 65102
Phone: (573) 751-0810
Fax: (573) 751-8835
E-mail: wcouncil@mail.state.mo.us

MONTANA
Pat Haffey
Commissioner
Dept. of Labor & Industry
P.O. Box 1728
Helena, MT 59624
Phone: (406) 444-3555
Fax: (406) 444-1394

NEBRASKA
Joni Gray
Executive Director
Womens' Comm.
P.O. Box 94985
Lincoln, NE 68509-4985
Phone: (402) 471-2039
Fax: (402) 471-5655

NEVADA

NEW HAMPSHIRE
Kathryn Pedrone
Executive Director
Comm. on the Status of Women
25 Capitol St., Rm. 334
Concord, NH 03301-6312
Phone: (603) 271-2660

NEW JERSEY
Linda B. Bowker
Director
Div. on Women
Dept. of Community Affairs
101 S. Broad St.
P.O. Box 801
Trenton, NJ 08625-0801
Phone: (609) 292-8840
Fax: (609) 633-6821

NEW MEXICO
Rebecca Jo Sakota
Executive Director
Comm. on the Status of Women
2401 12th St., NW
Albuquerque, NM 87104-2304
Phone: (505) 841-8920
Fax: (505) 841-8926

NEW YORK
Elaine W. Conway
Director
Div. for Women
633 3rd Ave.
New York, NY 10017
Phone: (212) 681-4547
Fax: (212) 681-7626

NORTH CAROLINA
Juanita Bryant
Director
Council on Status for Women
Dept. of Administration
526 N. Wilmington St.
Raleigh, NC 27604-1199
Phone: (919) 733-2455
Fax: (919) 733-2464

NORTH DAKOTA
Sheila Auch
Administrative Assistant
Comm. on the Status of Women
Dept. of Economic Dev. & Finance
1833 E. Bismarck Expy.
Bismarck, ND 58504
Phone: (701) 328-5310
Fax: (701) 328-5320
E-mail: sauch@state.nd.us

NORTHERN MARIANA ISLANDS
Remedio R. Sablan
Special Assistant
Women's Affairs
Community & Cultural Affairs
P.O. Box 10007
Saipan, MP 96950
Phone: (670) 288-4102
Fax: (670) 288-0845

OHIO
Susan McKinley
Director
Bur. of Employment Services
Women's Div.
145 S. Front St., 6th Fl.
Columbus, OH 43266-0556
Phone: (614) 466-4496
Fax: (614) 466-7912

OKLAHOMA
Linda J. Maxey
Chair
Comm. on the Status of Women
2300 Lincoln Blvd., Rm. 101
Oklahoma City, OK 73105
Phone: (405) 521-3257

OREGON
Tracy Davies
Executive Director
Comm. for Women
PSU Smith Ctr., Rm. M315
P.O. Box 751
Portland, OR 97207
Phone: (503) 725-5889
Fax: (503) 725-8152

PENNSYLVANIA
Vacant
Executive Director
Comm. for Women
204 Finance Bldg.
Harrisburg, PA 17120
Phone: (717) 787-8128

PUERTO RICO
Enid Gavilan
Executive Director
Women's Affairs Comm.
P.O. Box 11382
San Juan, PR 00910-1382
Phone: (787) 722-2907
Fax: (787) 723-3611

RHODE ISLAND
Jane Anthony
Chair
Comm. on Women
260 W. Exchange St., Ste. 4
Providence, RI 02903
Phone: (401) 222-6105

SOUTH CAROLINA
Rebecca Collier
Executive Director
Comm. on Women
Ofc. of the Governor
1205 Pendleton St., Ste. 368
Columbia, SC 29201
Phone: (803) 734-1609
Fax: (803) 734-0241

SOUTH DAKOTA

TENNESSEE

TEXAS
Ashley Horton
Director
Women's Comm.
Ofc. of the Governor
P.O. Box 12428
Austin, TX 78711
Phone: (512) 475-2615
Fax: (512) 463-1832

U.S. VIRGIN ISLANDS

UTAH
Abbie Vianes
Executive Director
Gov's. Comm. for Women & Families
1160 State Ofc. Bldg.
Salt Lake City, UT 84114
Phone: (801) 538-9550
Fax: (801) 538-3027
E-mail: avianes@gov.state.ut.us

VERMONT
Judith Sutphen
Executive Director
Governor's Comm. on the Status of Women
126 State St.
Montpelier, VT 05633-6801
Phone: (802) 828-2851
Fax: (802) 828-2930

VIRGINIA
John Mills Barr
Commissioner
Dept. of Labor & Industry
Powers-Taylor Bldg.
13 S. 13th St.
Richmond, VA 23219
Phone: (804) 786-2377
Fax: (804) 371-6524

WASHINGTON
Dawn Hitchens
Chair
Interagency Cmte. for State Employed Women
P.O. Box 43430
Olympia, WA 98504-3430
Phone: (360) 753-7831
Fax: (360) 753-7808

WEST VIRGINIA
Joyce M. Stover
Acting Executive Director
Women's Comm.
Bldg. 6, Rm. 637
State Capitol Complex
Charleston, WV 25305
Phone: (304) 558-0070

WISCONSIN
Katie Mnuk
Executive Director
Women's Council
16 N. Carroll St., Ste. 720
Madison, WI 53702
Phone: (608) 266-2219
Fax: (608) 261-2432

WYOMING
Sue Bromley
Chair
Council Women's Issues
Employment Dept.
Herschler Bldg., 2 E.
Cheyenne, WY 82002
Phone: (307) 638-3301
Fax: (307) 778-7194

Workers Compensation

Administers laws providing insurance and compensation for workers for job-related illness, injury or death.

ALABAMA
Scotty Spates
Chief
Workers Compensation Div.
Dept. of Industrial Relations
602 Madison Ave.
Montgomery, AL 36130-3301
Phone: (334) 242-2868
Fax: (334) 261-3143

ALASKA
Paul Grossi
Director
Div. of Workers Compensation
Dept. of Labor
P.O. Box 25512
Juneau, AK 99802
Phone: (907) 465-2790
Fax: (907) 465-2797

AMERICAN SAMOA
Soli Aumocualogo
Chair
Workers Compensation Comm.
Legal Affairs
Pago Pago, AS 96799
Phone: (684) 633-5520
Fax: (684) 633-1841

ARIZONA
Jerry LeCompte
President
State Compensation Fund
3031 N. 2nd St.
Phoenix, AZ 85012
Phone: (602) 631-2050
Fax: (602) 631-2540

ARKANSAS
Eldon Coffman
Chair
Workers Compensation Comm.
P.O. Box 950
Little Rock, AR 72203
Phone: (501) 682-3930
Fax: (501) 682-2777

CALIFORNIA
Casey Young
Administrative Director
Div. of Workers Compensation
Dept. of Industrial Relations
45 Fremont St., #3160
San Francisco, CA 94105
Phone: (415) 975-0700

COLORADO
Mary Ann Whiteside
Director
Div. of Workers Compensation
Dept. of Labor & Employment
Tower 2, Ste. 500
1515 Arapahoe St.
Denver, CO 80202
Phone: (303) 575-8700
Fax: (303) 575-8882

CONNECTICUT
Jesse M. Frankl
Chair
Workers Compensation Comm.
21 Oak St., 4th Fl.
Hartford, CT 06106
Phone: (860) 493-1500
Fax: (860) 247-1361

DELAWARE
Karen Peterson
Director
Div. of Industrial Affairs
Dept. of Labor
4425 N. Market St., 3rd Fl.
Wilmington, DE 19802
Phone: (302) 761-8176
Fax: (302) 761-6601

DISTRICT OF COLUMBIA
Francis Berry
Assistant to the Director
Ofc. of Workers Compensation
Dept. of Employment Services
1200 Upshur St., NW, 3rd Fl.
Washington, DC 20011
Phone: (202) 576-7100

FLORIDA
Jimmy Glisson
Director
Div. of Workers Compensation
Dept. of Labor & Employee Security
303 Forest Bldg.
Tallahassee, FL 32399
Phone: (850) 488-2514
Fax: (850) 922-6779

GEORGIA
Harrill Dawkins
Chair
State Board of Workers Compensation
270 Peachtree St., NW, #518
Atlanta, GA 30303-1205
Phone: (404) 656-2034

GUAM
Juan Taijito
Director
Dept. of Labor
504 E. Sunset Blvd., Tiyan
P.O. Box 9970
Tamuning, GU 96931
Phone: (671) 475-0101
Fax: (671) 477-2988

HAWAII
Gary S. Hamada
Administrator
Disability Compensation Div.
Dept. of Labor & Industrial Relations
830 Punchbowl St.
Honolulu, HI 96813
Phone: (808) 586-9151
Fax: (808) 586-9219

IDAHO
James E. Kerns
Chair
State Industrial Comm.
317 Main
Boise, ID 83720
Phone: (208) 334-6000

ILLINOIS
John W. Hallock, Jr.
Chair
State Industrial Comm.
100 W. Randolph St., Ste. 8-200
Chicago, IL 60601-3219
Phone: (312) 814-6556
Fax: (312) 814-6523

INDIANA
G. Terrence Coriden
Director
Workers Compensation Board
402 W. Washington St., Rm. W196
Indianapolis, IN 46204
Phone: (317) 232-3808
Fax: (317) 233-5493

IOWA
Iris Post
Commissioner
Industrial Services Div.
Dept. of Employment Services
1000 E. Grand Ave.
Des Moines, IA 50319
Phone: (515) 281-5934
Fax: (515) 281-6501

KANSAS
Philip S. Harness
Director
Div. of Workers Compensation
Dept. of Human Resources
800 SW Jackson, Ste. 600
Topeka, KS 66612-1227
Phone: (785) 296-3441
Fax: (785) 296-0839

KENTUCKY
Larry Greathouse
Chairman
Workers Compensation Board
Dept. of Workers Claims
Bush Bldg.
403 Wapping St.
Frankfort, KY 40601
Phone: (502) 564-5550
Fax: (502) 564-5934

LOUISIANA
Dan Boudreaux
Assistant Secretary
Ofc. of Workers Compensation
Dept. of Labor
P.O. Box 94094
Baton Rouge, LA 70804-9094
Phone: (225) 342-7561
Fax: (225) 342-5665

MAINE
Paul R. Dionne
Executive Director
Workers Compensation Board
27 State House Station
Augusta, ME 04333-0027
Phone: (207) 287-3751

MARYLAND
Charles J. Krysiak
Chair
Ofc. of the Chair
Workers Compensation Comm.
6 N. Liberty St., Rm. 940
Baltimore, MD 21201-3785
Phone: (410) 767-0829

MASSACHUSETTS
James Campbell
Commissioner
Industrial Accident Board
Executive Ofc. of Labor
600 Washington St., 7th Fl.
Boston, MA 02111
Phone: (617) 727-4900
Fax: (617) 727-6477

MICHIGAN
Jack F. Wheatley
Director
Bur. of Workers Compensation
Consumer & Industry Services
P.O. Box 30016
Lansing, MI 48909
Phone: (517) 322-1296

MINNESOTA
Gretchen Maglich
Commissioner
Workers Compensation Div.
Dept. of Labor & Industry
443 Lafayette Rd.
St. Paul, MN 55155
Phone: (615) 296-7958
Fax: (651) 282-5405

MISSISSIPPI
Mike Marsh
Chair
Worker's Compensation
1428 Lakeland Dr.
Jackson, MS 39201
Phone: (601) 987-4200
Fax: (601) 987-4233

Ray Minor
Executive Director
Workers Compensation Comm.
1428 Lakeland Dr.
Jackson, MS 39201
Phone: (601) 987-4200
Fax: (601) 987-4233

MISSOURI
JoAnn Karll
Director
Div. of Workers Compensation
Dept. of Labor & Industrial Relations
P.O. Box 58
Jefferson City, MO 65102
Phone: (573) 751-7646
Fax: (573) 526-4960
E-mail: jkarll@dolir.state.mo.us

MONTANA
Carl Swanson
President
State Compensation Insurance Fund
Dept. of Administration
5 S. Last Chance Gulch
Helena, MT 59601
Phone: (406) 444-6501
Fax: (406) 444-7796

NEBRASKA
Ronald Brown
Presiding Judge
Workers Compensation Ct.
P.O. Box 98908
Lincoln, NE 68509
Phone: (402) 471-3923
Fax: (402) 471-2700

NEVADA
Doug Dirks
Chief Executive Officer
Employers Insurance Co.
515 E. Musser St.
Carson City, NV 89714
Phone: (775) 886-1030

NEW HAMPSHIRE
Kathryn J. Barger
Director
Workers Compensation Div.
Labor Dept.
95 Pleasant St.
Concord, NH 03301-3836
Phone: (603) 271-3176
Fax: (603) 271-6149

NEW JERSEY
Paul A. Kapalko
Director
Div. of Workers Compensation
Dept. of Labor
John Fitch Plz.
P.O. Box 381
Trenton, NJ 08625-0381
Phone: (609) 292-2414
Fax: (609) 984-2515

NEW MEXICO
Stephen W. Kennedy
Director
Worker's Compensation Administration
P.O. Box 27198
Albuquerque, NM 87125
Phone: (505) 841-6006
Fax: (505) 841-6866

NEW YORK
Robert R. Snashall
Chair
Executive Ofc.
Workers Compensation Board
20 Park St.
Albany, NY 12207
Phone: (518) 486-3332
Fax: (518) 473-1415

NORTH CAROLINA
J. Howard Bunn, Jr.
Chair
Industrial Comm.
Commerce Dept.
430 N. Salisbury St.
Raleigh, NC 27611
Phone: (919) 733-4820
Fax: (919) 715-0280

NORTH DAKOTA
Pat Traynor
Executive Director
Workers Compensation Bur.
500 E. Front Ave.
Bismarck, ND 58504-5685
Phone: (701) 328-3800
Fax: (701) 328-3820
E-mail: msmail.ptraynor@ranch.state.nd.us

NORTHERN MARIANA ISLANDS
Fred F. Camacho
Acting Administrator
Retirement Fund
P.O. Box 1247
Saipan, MP 96950
Phone: (670) 234-7228
Fax: (670) 234-9624
E-mail: nmi.retirement@saipan.com

OHIO
C. James Conrad
Administrator
Workers Compensation Bur.
30 W. Spring St.
Columbus, OH 43266
Phone: (614) 466-5223
Fax: (614) 728-8428

OKLAHOMA
Johnny Coleman
Administrator
Workers Compensation Div.
4001 Lincoln Blvd.
Oklahoma City, OK 73105
Phone: (405) 528-1500
Fax: (405) 528-5751

OREGON
Mary Neidig
Administrator
Workers Compensation Div.
Dept. of Consumer & Business Services
Labor & Industries Bldg.
350 Winter St., NE
Salem, OR 97310
Phone: (503) 945-7500
Fax: (503) 945-7725

PENNSYLVANIA
Richard Himler
Director
Bur. of Workers Compensation
Dept. of Labor & Industry
1171 S. Cameron St.
Harrisburg, PA 17104-2501
Phone: (717) 783-5421
Fax: (717) 772-0342

PUERTO RICO
Maribel Rodriguez
Director
Central Ofc. of Personnel Administration
P.O. Box 8476
San Juan, PR 00910
Phone: (787) 721-4300
Fax: (787) 722-3390

RHODE ISLAND
Dennis Revens
Administrator
Workers Compensation Comm.
1 Dorrance Plz.
Providence, RI 02903
Phone: (401) 277-3097

SOUTH CAROLINA
Alicia Claussen
Executive Director
Workers Compensation Comm.
P.O. Box 1715
Columbia, SC 29202-1715
Phone: (803) 737-5744
Fax: (803) 737-5764

SOUTH DAKOTA
James E. Marsh
Director
Div. of Labor & Mgmt.
Dept. of Labor
Kneip Bldg.
700 Governors Dr.
Pierre, SD 57501
Phone: (605) 773-3681
Fax: (605) 773-4211

TENNESSEE
James Farmer
Director
Workers Compensation
Dept. of Labor
710 James Robertson Pkwy., 2nd Fl.
Nashville, TN 37243
Phone: (615) 741-2395
Fax: (615) 532-1468

TEXAS
Len Riley
Executive Director
Workers' Compensation Comm.
4000 S. IH 35
Austin, TX 78704
Phone: (512) 448-1950
Fax: (512) 440-3552

U.S. VIRGIN ISLANDS
Eleuteria Roberts
Acting Commissioner
Dept. of Labor
2203 Church St.
Christiansted
St. Croix, VI 00820
Phone: (340) 773-1994
Fax: (340) 773-0094

UTAH
Richard Lee Ellertson
Commissioner
Div. of Administration
Labor Comm.
160 E. 300 S., 3rd Fl.
P.O. Box 146600
Salt Lake City, UT 84114-6600
Phone: (801) 530-6880
Fax: (801) 530-6390
E-mail: rellerts.icmain@state.ut.us

VERMONT
Steve Jansen
Commissioner
Dept. of Labor & Industry
Natl. Life Bldg.
Drawer 20
Montpelier, VT 05620-3401
Phone: (802) 828-2288
Fax: (802) 828-2195

VIRGINIA
Virginia R. Diamond
Chair
Workers' Compensation Comm.
1000 DMV Dr.
Richmond, VA 23220-2036
Phone: (804) 367-8657
Fax: (804) 367-9740

WASHINGTON
Gary Moore
Director
Dept. of Labor & Industries
P.O. Box 44001
Olympia, WA 98504
Phone: (360) 902-5800
Fax: (360) 902-4202

WEST VIRGINIA
William Vieweg
Commissioner
Bur. of Unemployment Programs
Bldg. 4, Rm. 610
112 California Ave.
Charleston, WV 25332
Phone: (304) 558-2630

WISCONSIN

WYOMING
Frank Galeotos
Director
Workers Compensation Div.
Dept. of Employment
122 W. 25th St.
Cheyenne, WY 82002
Phone: (307) 777-6750